ST/ESA/STAT/SER.G/59 (Vol. II)

Department of Economic and Social Affairs
Statistics Division

2010
International Trade Statistics Yearbook

Volume II
Trade by Commodity

United Nations
New York, 2012

DEPARTMENT OF ECONOMIC AND SOCIAL AFFAIRS

The Department of Economic and Social Affairs of the United Nations Secretariat is a vital interface between global policies in the economic, social and environmental spheres and national action. The Department works in three main interlinked areas: (i) it compiles, generates and analyses a wide range of economic, social and environmental data and information on which States Members of the United Nations draw to review common problems and to take stock of policy options; (ii) it facilitates the negotiations of Member States in many intergovernmental bodies on joint courses of action to address ongoing or emerging global challenges; and (iii) it advises interested Governments on the ways and means of translating policy frameworks developed in United Nations conferences and summits into programmes at the country level and, through technical assistance, helps build national capacities.

NOTE

Symbols of United Nations documents are composed of capital letters combined with figures.

The designations employed and the presentation of material in this publication do not imply the expression of any opinion whatsoever on the part of the Secretariat of the United Nations concerning the legal status of any country, territory, city or area, or of its authorities, or concerning the delimitation of its frontiers or boundaries.

Where the designation "country or area" appears in this publication, it covers countries, territories, cities or areas. In previous issues of this publication, where the designation "country" appears in the headings of tables, it should be interpreted to cover countries, territories, cities or areas.

In some tables, the designation "developed" economies is intended for statistical convenience and does not necessarily express a judgement about the stage reached by a particular country or area in the development process.

ST/ESA/STAT/SER.G/59 (Vol. II)

UNITED NATIONS PUBLICATION
Sales No E.12.XVII.3 H

ISBN 978-92-1-161557-9
e-ISBN 978-92-1-055243-1
ISSN 1010-447X

Enquiries should be directed to
Sales and Marketing Section
Outreach Division
Department of Public Information
United Nations
New York 10017
USA

E-mail: publications@un.org
Internet: http://unp.un.org

TABLE OF CONTENTS

TABLE OF CONTENTS (continued)

Part 2 COMMODITY TRADE PROFILES

Full list of included 3-digit SITC groups (SITC, Rev.3)

Food and live animals (SITC Section 0)

Beverages and tobacco (SITC Section 1)

Crude materials, inedible, except fuels (SITC Section 2)

Mineral fuels, lubricants and related materials (SITC Section 3)

Animal and vegetable oils, fats and waxes (SITC Section 4)

Chemicals and related products, n.e.s. (SITC Section 5)

Manufactured goods classified chiefly by material (SITC Section 6)

Miscellaneous manufactured articles (SITC Section 8)

Commodities and transactions not classified elsewhere in SITC (SITC Section 9)

INTRODUCTION

The new yearbook

1. The *2010 International Trade Statistics Yearbook* (2010 ITSY) is being issued in two volumes which were prepared at different points in time during 2011.[1] Volume I has been compiled early in 2011 (in May 2011) to allow for an advanced release of an overview of international merchandise trade in 2010 and for a much earlier publication of the available 2010 country (area) data. Volume II which contains detailed tables showing international trade for individual commodities (3-digit SITC groups) and eleven world trade tables covering trade values and indices has been compiled approximately six months after the submission of Volume I (in November 2011) as the preparation of these tables requires and benefits from the additional country data which, normally, become available later in the year. Volume II contains updated versions of the two world trade tables A and D published in Volume I.

2. Beginning with the 2008 edition, Volume II is published in a redesigned format in respect to the presentation of data for individual commodities (3-digit SITC groups) with the aim to provide a more analytical and condensed view of the exports and imports of a specific commodity (commodity trade profile). Overall, data for a total of 258 commodities are shown in Volume II. The information for 2010 is based on data provided by 141 countries (areas), representing 97.3% of world trade of 2010. All tables of Volume II are made available electronically shortly after the completion of the manuscript.

3. The detailed information about the trade of particular countries by commodity and partner (values and quantities) contained in the tables and graphs for individual countries in Volume I and commodities in Volume II has been taken from the publicly available database UN Comtrade (http://comtrade.un.org/). Users are advised to visit UN Comtrade for any additional and more current information as it is continuously updated.

Concepts and definitions of International Merchandise Trade Statistics

4. The statistics in this Yearbook have been compiled by national statistical authorities largely consistent with the United Nations recommended *International Merchandise Trade Statistics, Concepts and Definitions, Revision 2.*[2] The main elements of the concepts and definitions are:

1. Coverage: As a general guideline, it is recommended that international merchandise trade statistics record all goods which add to or subtract from the stock of material resources of a country by entering (imports) or leaving (exports) its economic territory. Goods simply being transported through a country (goods in transit) or temporarily admitted or withdrawn (except for goods for inward or outward processing) do not add to or subtract from the stock of material resources of a country and are not

[1] The 2010 ITSY is the fifty-ninth edition of this yearbook.

[2] Statistical Papers, Series M No. 52, Rev.2 (United Nations publication, Sales No. E.98.XVII.16).

included in the international merchandise trade statistics. The general guidelines serve as a basis for a set of specific recommendations on the inclusion or exclusion of certain categories of goods.

2. Time of recording: Coherence with the System of National Accounts and the Balance of Payments requires that transactions be recorded at the time when the change of ownership takes place. As a general guideline it is recommended that goods be included at the time when they enter or leave the economic territory of a country.

3. Statistical territory. In international merchandise trade statistics the objective is to record goods entering and leaving the economic territory of a country. In practice, what is recorded is goods that enter or leave the statistical territory, which is the territory with respect to which data are being collected. The statistical territory may coincide with the economic territory of a country or with some part of it. It follows that when the statistical territory of a country and its economic territory differ, international merchandise trade statistics do not provide a complete record of inward and outward flows of goods.

4. The trade systems. There are two trade systems in common use by which international merchandise trade statistics are compiled: the general trade system and the special trade system in its strict definition and relaxed definition.

(a) The general trade system is in use when the statistical territory of a country coincides with its economic territory. Consequently, under the general trade system, imports include all goods entering the economic territory of a compiling country and exports include all goods leaving the economic territory of a compiling country.

(b) *The special trade system* is in use when the statistical territory comprises only a particular part of the economic territory. *The special trade system (strict definition)* is in use when the statistical territory comprises only the free circulation area, that is, the part within which goods "may be disposed of without customs restriction". Consequently, in such a case, imports include all goods entering the free circulation area of a compiling country, which means cleared through customs for home use, and exports include all goods leaving the free circulation area of a compiling country.

(c) *The special trade system (relaxed definition)* is in use when (a) goods that enter a country for or leave it after inward processing and (b) goods that enter or leave an industrial free zone are also recorded and included in international merchandise trade statistics.

5. Classification. It is recommended that countries use the *Harmonized Commodity Description and Coding System* (HS) for the collection, compilation and dissemination of international merchandise trade statistics as suggested by the Statistical Commission at its twenty-seventh session (22 February to 3 March 1993).[3] The Harmonized System was adopted by the Customs Co-operation Council in June 1983,

[3] See Official Records of the Economic and Social Council, 1993, Supplement No. 6 (E/1993/26), para. 162 (d).

and the International Convention on the Harmonized System (HS Convention) entered into force on 1 January 1988 (HS 1988).[4] In accordance with the preamble to the HS Convention, which recognized the importance of ensuring that the HS be kept up to date in the light of changes in technology or in patterns of international trade, the HS is regularly reviewed and revised. The fourth edition, HS 2007 which is a substantial revision from previous versions came into effect 1 January 2007.[5] The *Standard International Trade Classification (SITC)*[6] which was in the past used by countries in data compilation and reporting has been recognized for its continued use in analysis.[7]

6. Valuation. At its fifteenth session, in 1953, the Economic and Social Council, taking the view that trade statistics must reflect economic realities, recommended that the Governments of Member States of the United Nations, wherever possible, use transaction values in the compilation of their national statistics of external trade or, when national practices are based on other values, endeavor to provide supplementary statistical data based on transaction values (Economic and Social Council resolution 469 B (XV)). To promote the comparability of international merchandise trade statistics and taking into account the commercial and data reporting practices of the majority of countries, it is recommended that: (a) The statistical value of imported goods be a CIF-type value; (b) The statistical value of exported goods be an FOB-type value. FOB-type values include the transaction value of the goods and the value of services performed to deliver goods to the border of the exporting country. CIF-type values include the transaction value of the goods, the value of services performed to deliver goods to the border of the exporting country and the value of the services performed to deliver the goods from the border of the exporting country to the border of the importing country.

7. Partner country. It is recommended that in the case of imports, the country of origin be recorded; and that in the case of exports, the country of last known destination be recorded. The country of origin of a good (for imports) is determined by rules of origin established by each country. The country of last known destination is the last country - as far as it is known at the time of exportation - to which goods are to be delivered, irrespective of where they have been initially dispatched to and whether or not, on their way to that last country, they are subject to any commercial transactions or other operations which change their legal status.

5. The commodity trade profiles (part 2 of this publication) are based on the detailed trade data as reported by countries (or areas) and published on UN Comtrade without any adjustments for conceptual differences such as differences in the trade system, valuation and partner attribution. The explanatory notes on UN Comtrade inform about the trade system, valuation and

---

[4] See Customs Co-operation Council, The Harmonized Commodity Description and Coding System, Brussels, 1989.

[5] See World Customs Organization, Harmonized Commodity Description and Coding System, Fourth Edition (2007), Brussels 2005.

[6] Standard International Trade Classification, Original, Statistical Papers, Series M No.10, Second Edition, 1951 (United Nations publication, Sales No. E.51.XVII.1); subsequent editions are published as United Nations publications under Series M No.34.

[7] See Official Records of the Economic and Social Council, 1999, Supplement No. 4 (E/1999/24), para. 24 (c).

partner attribution of individual reporter countries (or areas). For more detailed information on national practices in the compilation and dissemination of international merchandise trade data please go to http://unstats.un.org/unsd/tradereport/introduction_MM.asp.

Sources and Presentation

6. Sources: Figures on the total imports and exports of countries (or areas) presented in world tables A and B are mainly taken from *International Financial Statistics* (IFS) published monthly by the International Monetary Fund (IMF) but also from other sources such as national publications and websites and the *United Nations Monthly Bulletin of Statistics Questionnaire* for the following countries: Andorra, Bermuda, Cayman Islands, Cuba, Gibraltar, Montenegro (beginning 2006), Niue, Occupied Palestinian Territory, Russian Federation (beginning 1994), Serbia and Montenegro (before 2006), Turkmenistan, Turks and Caicos, Tuvalu and Uzbekistan. Table A and B show data as available by end of October 2011.

7. The external trade conversion figures in world table C are derived from *International Financial Statistics* (IFS) published monthly by the International Monetary Fund (IMF). Table C shows data as available by end of October 2011.

8. The data presented in world tables G and H on the volume and unit value indices, and terms of trade for total exports and imports by countries (or areas) and regions are mostly derived from *International Financial Statistics* (IFS) published monthly by the International Monetary Fund (IMF), but also from other sources such as national publications and websites and the *United Nations Monthly Bulletin of Statistics Questionnaire*. Table G and H show data as available by end of October 2011.

9. The data presented in world tables I, J and K on unit value and volume indices and value for manufactured goods exports and fuel imports are obtained from sources such as national publications and websites and the *United Nations Monthly Bulletin of Statistics Questionnaire.* Table I, J and K show data as available by end of October 2011.

10. Figures presented in world tables D, E and F and the commodity tables and graphs in part 2 (commodity trade profiles) are calculated using UN Comtrade data (http://comtrade.un.org/). The data published on UN Comtrade are directly submitted by countries to the United Nations Statistics Division (UNSD) or received via international and regional partner organizations such as the Organization for Economic Co-operation and Development (OECD), the Food and Agriculture Organization of the United Nations (FAO), the International Trade Centre (ITC), the Caribbean Community (CARICOM) Secretariat, the Common Market of Eastern and Southern Africa (COMESA), the Economic Community of West African States (ECOWAS) and the UN regional commissions such as the Economic Commission for Latin America and the Caribbean (ECLAC) and the Economic and Social Commission for Western Asia (ESCWA). Modifications to the received data are only made in the case the provided data is obviously incomplete (in particular in the case of unreported oil exports). Tables D, E and F and the commodity tables and graphs in part 2 use data as available on UN Comtrade by mid of November 2011.

11. The totals of imports and exports presented in table A on the one hand and table D on the other hand are not necessarily identical as IFS and UN Comtrade are based on different data collection systems with different aims, procedures, timetable and sources for update and maintenance. Nevertheless, discrepancies are in general minor and usually do not affect the overall information provided in these tables. A systematic comparison of the figures from both sources (which includes the description of known and relevant conceptual differences) is available at http://unstats.un.org/unsd/trade/imts/annual%20totals.htm. Overall, the discrepancy in the world total (world aggregate) of exports in table A and table D is less than 0.5 percent for all years shown, which is minor, given the differences between the two sources.

12. Estimates: For table A estimates for missing data are made in order to arrive to regional totals but are otherwise not shown. The estimation process is automated using quarterly year-on-year growth rates for the extrapolation of missing quarterly data (unless quarterly data can be estimated using available monthly data within the quarter). Regional totals containing estimated data are printed in bold. For world tables D, E and F and the commodity tables and graphs in part 2 (commodity trade profiles) data for missing reporters are estimated either through the extrapolation of the data of the two adjacent years, or, if this is not possible, through the use of the data reported by the trading partners (so called mirror data). Mirror statistics is also used in case the partner distribution or confidential data make it necessary to adjust the reported data. For tables H, I and J the missing data required for the calculation of regional totals are estimated using a variety of methods and additional data sources. All estimates are reviewed and adjusted where necessary.

13. Currency conversion: For data in this publication, conversion of values from national currencies into United States dollars is done by means of currency conversion factors based on official exchange rates. Values in currencies subject to fluctuation are converted into United States dollars using weighted average exchange rates specially calculated for this purpose. The weighted average exchange rate for a given currency for a given year is the component monthly factors, furnished by the International Monetary Fund in its IFS publication, weighted by the value of the relevant trade in each month; a monthly factor is the exchange rate (or the simple average rate) in effect during that month. These factors are applied to total imports and exports and to the trade in individual commodities with individual countries. The conversion factors applied to the data presented in table A are provided in table C. For data published on UN Comtrade the applied conversion factors are available in a country's metadata on UN Comtrade.

14. Classification: Essentially all countries follow the recommendation to report their detailed merchandise trade data according to the Harmonized Commodity Description and Coding System (HS) (see paragraph 4). In order to provide comparable time series data on UN Comtrade for all countries, the data reported in the latest HS classification is converted into earlier versions of the HS and to corresponding or earlier versions of the Standard International Trade Classification (SITC).[8] Beginning 2007 many countries (or areas) started to compile their

---

[8] Detailed information on the data conversions used for UN Comtrade is available on the website of the United Nations Statistics Division at: http://unstats.un.org/unsd/trade/conversions/HS%20Correlation%20and%20Conversion%20tables.htm.

trade data according to the 2007 edition of the HS classification[9] and following its past practices the United Nations Statistics Division (UNSD) developed and implemented the required conversion tables. - The commodities in this publication are mostly presented according to the three-digit groups of SITC, Rev.3[10] as the SITC groups provide a limited set of economically meaningful commodity categories. In addition, data according to SITC, Rev.3 is available for long time series.

15. Period: Generally, data refer to calendar years; however, for those countries which report according to some other reference year, the data are presented in the year which covers the majority of the reference year used by the country. However, for the latest years (from 2000 onwards) the data for all countries on UN Comtrade is available by calendar year except for Nepal for which the data refers to the fiscal year from mid of July of the previous to mid of July of the current year.

16. Country nomenclature: The naming of countries (or areas) in this publication follows in general the *United Nations Standard Country or Area Codes for Statistical Use.*[11] The names and composition of countries as reporter are changing over time. Also, countries rarely follow the identical nomenclature in the recording of partner information. For example where former geographical entities commonly referred to in national statistics have changed, countries may introduce the corresponding changes in their statistics at different times. In this publication wherever possible parts of the world have been designated by the names they currently bear and the trading partner attribution has been standardized. The following information is relevant for the data presented in this publication:

1. In this publication the data published under the heading China exclude those for Taiwan Province. Figures representing the trade with Taiwan Province, which may have been reported by any reporting country or area, are included in the grouping Other Asia, nes. For statistical purposes, the data for China do not include those for Hong Kong Special Administrative Region and Macao Special Administrative Region.

2. Beginning 1 January 1997, the overseas departments of France were included in the statistical territory of France for the purposes of international trade statistics. Values on this basis have been provided by France for 1996 also, and values are published on that basis in this publication.

3. Beginning 1 January 1999, Belgium and Luxembourg provide their international trade statistics separately.

---

[9] See World Customs Organization, Harmonized Commodity Description and Coding System, Fourth Edition (2007), Brussels 2005.

[10] Standard International Trade Classification, Revision 3, Statistical Papers, Series M No.34/Rev.3, (United Nations publication, Sales No. E.86.XVII.12). SITC, Revision 4 was accepted by the United Nations Statistical Commission at its thirty-seventh session in March 2006 (see Official Records of the Economic and Social Council, 2006, Supplement No. 4, (E/CN.3/2006/32), chapter III, para. 26 (b)). Yet it will require several years until a time series of data according to SITC, Revision 4 will be sufficiently long for publication.

[11] Standard Country or Area Codes for Statistical Use, Series M No. 49, Rev.4, (United Nations publication, Sales No. M.98.XVII.9). The latest information is available online at: http://unstats.un.org/unsd/methods/m49/m49.htm.

4. Beginning 1 January 2000, Botswana, Lesotho, Namibia, South Africa and Swaziland provide their international trade statistics separately. For periods prior to 1 January 2000, unless otherwise indicated, data are shown for the Southern African Customs Union.

5. On 4 February 2003, the official name of the Federal Republic of Yugoslavia has been changed to Serbia and Montenegro. Data provided for Yugoslavia prior to 1 January 1992 refer to the Socialist Federal Republic of Yugoslavia which was composed of six republics. Data referring to the years 1992 and later are attributed to Bosnia and Herzegovina, Croatia, Serbia and Montenegro, Slovenia and the Former Yugoslav Republic of Macedonia.

6. On 3 June 2006, Serbia and Montenegro formally dissolved into two independent countries: Montenegro and Serbia.

17. Regional groupings: This publication uses the regional groupings of the Millennium Development Goal (MDG) Indicator Database which are shown below (for their composition, see world table A and http://unstats.un.org/unsd/mdg/default.aspx - go to Data - Regional Groupings). The category 'Other' applies only to the presentation of data by trading partner and consists of Antarctica, Bunkers, Free Zones, 'Special Categories' (confidential partner) and Areas nes.:

World
Developed Countries
- Asia-Pacific
- Europe
- North America

South-eastern Europe
Commonwealth of Independent States (CIS)
- CIS Europe
- CIS Asia

Northern Africa
Sub-Saharan Africa
Latin America & the Caribbean
- Caribbean
- Latin America

Eastern Asia
Southern Asia
South-eastern Asia
Western Asia
Oceania
Other

18. Regional groupings for World Tables I, J and K: For technical reasons those tables retain the regional breakdown used in the earlier versions of the yearbook, namely:

1) Developed economies
   - Africa (South Africa)
   - America (United States and Canada)
   - Asia (Japan and Israel).

- Europe (Andorra, Austria, Belgium, Denmark, Faeroe Islands, Finland, France, Germany, Gibraltar, Greece, Iceland, Ireland, Italy, Luxembourg, Malta, Netherlands, Norway, Portugal, Spain, Sweden, Switzerland and United Kingdom)
- Oceania (Australia and New Zealand)

2) Developing economies
- Africa (Algeria, Angola, Benin, Botswana, Burkina Faso, Burundi, Cameroon, Cape Verde, Central African Republic, Chad, Comoros, Congo, Côte d'Ivoire, Democratic Republic of the Congo, Djibouti, Egypt, Equatorial Guinea, Eritrea, Ethiopia, Gabon, Gambia, Ghana, Guinea, Guinea Bissau, Kenya, Lesotho, Liberia, Libya, Madagascar, Malawi, Mali, Mauritania, Mauritius, Morocco, Mozambique, Namibia, Niger, Nigeria, Réunion, Rwanda, Saint Helena, Sao Tome and Principe, Senegal, Seychelles, Sierra Leone, Somalia, Sudan, Swaziland, Togo, Tunisia, Uganda, United Republic of Tanzania, Western Sahara, Zambia, and Zimbabwe)
- America (Anguilla, Antigua and Barbuda, Argentina, Aruba, Bahamas, Barbados, Belize, Bermuda, Bolivia, Brazil, British Virgin Islands, Cayman Islands, Chile, Colombia, Costa Rica, Cuba, Dominica, Dominican Republic, Ecuador, El Salvador, Falkland Islands, French Guiana, Greenland, Grenada, Guadeloupe, Guatemala, Guyana, Haiti, Honduras, Jamaica, Martinique, Mexico, Montserrat, Netherlands Antilles, Nicaragua, Panama, Paraguay, Peru, Saint Kitts-Nevis, Saint Lucia, Saint Pierre and Miquelon, Saint Vincent and the Grenadines, Suriname, Trinidad and Tobago, Turks and Caicos, Uruguay, and Venezuela)
- Asia (Afghanistan, Armenia, Azerbaijan, Bahrain, Bangladesh, Bhutan, Brunei Darussalam, Cambodia, China, China Hong Kong SAR, China Macao SAR, Cyprus, Democratic People's Republic of Korea, Georgia, India, Indonesia, Iran, Iraq, Jordan, Kazakhstan, Kuwait, Kyrgyzstan, Lao People's Democratic Republic, Lebanon, Malaysia, Maldives, Mongolia, Myanmar, Nepal, Occupied Palestinian Territory, Oman, Pakistan, Philippines, Qatar, Republic of Korea, Saudi Arabia, Singapore, Sri Lanka, Syrian Arab Republic, Tajikistan, Thailand, Timor-Leste, Turkey, Turkmenistan, United Arab Emirates, Uzbekistan, Viet Nam, and Yemen)
- Europe (Bosnia Herzegovina, Croatia, Slovenia, Serbia and Montenegro, and The former Yugoslav Republic of Macedonia)
- Oceania (American Samoa, Cook Islands, Fiji, Federated States of Micronesia, French Polynesia, Kiribati, Guam, Nauru, New Caledonia, Niue, Norfolk Island, Northern Mariana Islands, Marshall Islands, Palau, Papua New Guinea, Samoa, Solomon Islands, Tokelau, Tonga, Tuvalu, Vanuatu, and Wallis and Futuna Islands)

3) Other
- Eastern Europe (Albania, Bulgaria, Czech Republic, Hungary, Poland, Romania, and Slovakia)
- European countries of the former USSR (Belarus, Estonia, Latvia, Lithuania, Republic of Moldova, Russian Federation and Ukraine)

19. Aggregations: All regional aggregations are calculated as the sum of their components. This also includes the regional and world totals presented in table A (in bold) which in earlier editions (before the 2008 edition) of this yearbook and in the tables currently published in the *United Nations Monthly Bulletin of Statistics* (MBS) are calculated by subtracting re-exports from the imports and exports.

20. Additional country groupings: The composition of the additional country groupings which are used in world table A is as follows:

ANCOM-Andean Common Market
Bolivia (Plurinational State of), Colombia, Ecuador, Peru and Venezuela (Bolivarian Republic of)

APEC-Asian-Pacific Economic Co-operation
Australia, Brunei Darussalam, Canada, Chile, China, Hong Kong Special Administrative Region of China, Indonesia, Japan, Malaysia, Mexico, New Zealand, Papua New Guinea, Peru, Philippines, Republic of Korea, Russian Federation, Singapore, Taiwan Province of China, Thailand, United States of America and Viet Nam

ASEAN-Association of South-East Asian Nations
Brunei Darussalam, Cambodia, Indonesia, Lao People's Democratic Republic, Malaysia, Myanmar, Philippines, Singapore, Thailand and Viet Nam

CACM-Central American Common Market
Costa Rica, El Salvador, Guatemala, Honduras and Nicaragua

CARICOM-Caribbean Community and Common Market
Antigua and Barbuda, Bahamas (member of the Community only), Barbados, Belize, Dominica, Grenada, Guyana, Haiti, Jamaica, Montserrat, Saint Kitts and Nevis, Saint Lucia, Saint Vincent and the Grenadines, Suriname, Trinidad and Tobago

COMESA-Common Market for Eastern and Southern Africa
Burundi, Comoros, Democratic Republic of the Congo, Djibouti, Egypt, Eritrea, Ethiopia, Kenya, Libya, Madagascar, Malawi, Mauritius, Rwanda, Seychelles, Sudan, Swaziland, Uganda, Zambia and Zimbabwe

ECOWAS - Economic Community of West African States
Benin, Burkina Faso, Cape Verde, Cote d'Ivoire, Gambia, Ghana, Guinea, Guinea-Bissau, Liberia, Mali, Niger, Nigeria, Senegal, Sierra Leone and Togo

EFTA - European Free Trade Association
Iceland, Liechtenstein, Norway and Switzerland

EMCCA – Economic and Monetary Community of Central Africa
Cameroon, Central African Republic, Chad, Congo, Equatorial Guinea and Gabon

EU-27 - European Union 27
Austria, Belgium, Cyprus, Czech Republic, Denmark, Estonia, Finland, France, Germany, Greece, Hungary, Ireland, Italy, Latvia, Lithuania, Luxembourg, Malta, Netherlands, Poland, Portugal, Spain, Slovakia, Slovenia, Sweden and United Kingdom (EU25) plus Bulgaria and Romania.

EU-25 - European Union 25
Austria, Belgium, Denmark, Finland, France, Germany, Greece, Ireland, Italy, Luxembourg, Netherlands, Portugal, Spain, Sweden and United Kingdom (EU15) plus Czech Republic, Estonia, Hungary, Latvia, Lithuania, Malta, Poland, Slovakia, Slovenia, and Cyprus

LAIA - Latin American Integration Association (formerly Latin American Free Trade Association)
Argentina, Bolivia (Plurinational State of), Brazil, Chile, Colombia, Cuba, Ecuador, Mexico, Paraguay, Peru, Uruguay and Venezuela (Bolivarian Republic of)

LDC - Least developed countries
Afghanistan, Angola, Bangladesh, Benin, Bhutan, Burkina Faso, Burundi, Cambodia, Cape Verde, Central African Republic, Chad, Comoros, Democratic Republic of the Congo, Djibouti, Equatorial Guinea, Eritrea, Ethiopia, Gambia, Guinea, Guinea-Bissau, Haiti, Kiribati, Lao People's Democratic Republic, Lesotho, Liberia, Madagascar, Malawi, Maldives, Mali, Mauritania, Mozambique, Myanmar, Nepal, Niger, Rwanda, Samoa, Sao Tome and Principe, Senegal, Sierra Leone, Solomon Islands, Somalia, Sudan, Timor-Leste, Togo, Tuvalu, Uganda, United Republic of Tanzania, Vanuatu, Yemen and Zambia

MERCOSUR-Mercado Comun Sud-Americano
Argentina, Brazil, Paraguay and Uruguay

NAFTA-Northern American Free Trade Area
Canada, Mexico and United States of America

OECD-Organization for Economic Cooperation and Development
Australia, Austria, Belgium, Canada, Czech Republic, Denmark, Finland, France, Germany, Greece, Hungary, Iceland, Ireland, Italy, Japan, Luxembourg, Mexico, Netherlands, New Zealand, Norway, Poland, Portugal, Republic of Korea, Slovakia, Spain, Sweden, Switzerland, Turkey, United Kingdom and United States of America

OPEC-Organization of Petroleum Exporting Countries
Algeria, Angola, Ecuador, Indonesia, Iran (Islamic Republic of), Iraq, Kuwait, Libya, Nigeria, Qatar, Saudi Arabia, United Arab Emirates and Venezuela (Bolivarian Republic of).

Description of world trade tables of part 1 (Tables A to K)

21. Total imports and exports by regions and countries or areas in U.S. dollars (Table A): The total value of world trade reached U.S. dollars 15.1 trillion in 2010, measured in terms of exports valued FOB at the border of the exporting country. This is an increase of 21.8 percent compared with the previous year. Table A provides a breakdown of this figure by country (or area) and also shows imports and the trade balance. For example, the biggest exporter in 2010 with exports of U.S dollar 1,578 billion was China, followed by the United States with U.S dollar 1,278 billion and Germany with U.S dollar 1,271 billion. The United States was the biggest importer with imports of U.S. dollar 1,969 billion in 2010 which resulted in a trade deficit of U.S. dollar 691 billion, while Germany and China recorded trade surpluses of U.S. dollar 203 billion and 182 billion respectively.

22. Total imports and exports by countries or areas in national currency (Table B): This table contains totals of imports and exports and the trade balance of individual countries (or areas) in national currency.

23. External trade conversion factors (Table C): The conversion factors for imports and exports shown in table C are used to convert trade data expressed in terms of national currency to U.S. dollars (see paragraph 13 for details).

24. World exports by provenance and destination in U.S. dollars (Table D): This table provides a breakdown of the world exports by regions and countries (or areas) according to their provenance (origin) and destination, both for total of trade and detailed by individual SITC sections and aggregations of sections, groups, subgroups and basic headings of SITC (see below in this paragraph for details). For example, the table shows that in 2010 developed economies of Asia-Pacific, Europe and North America were the destination of 56.0 percent of world exports

(U.S. dollar 8.4 trillion) and the origin of 53.2 percent of world exports (U.S. dollar 8.0 trillion).[12]

Aggregations of SITC, Rev. 3 codes	Description
0-9	Total trade
0 and 1	Food, beverages and tobacco
041-045	Cereals
2 and 4	Crude materials (excluding fuels), oils, fats
22	Oil seeds and, oleaginous fruit
26	Textile fibres
27	Crude fertilizers and minerals
28	Metalliferous ores and metal scrap
4	Animal and vegetable oils, fats and waxes
3	Mineral fuels and related materials
5	Chemicals
7	Machinery and transport equipment
781.2, 784.1, 785.1, 785.2 and 785.31	Passenger road vehicles and their parts
6 and 8	Other manufactured goods
65	Textile yarn and fabrics
67	Iron and steel
68	Non-ferrous metals
691-695, 699 and 812	Other manufactured metal products
84	Clothing

25. Growth of world exports by provenance and destination (Table E): This table shows the growth of world exports in recent years up to the year 2010 by provenance (origin) and destination, for total exports and for a limited set of commodity classes. The table shows that the total exports of developed economies increased on average by 6.8 percent since 2000, which is significantly less than the average growth rate for the world (9.0 percent). The annual average rates of change in percentage terms given in this table have been uniformly calculated by the use of the compound interest formula.

26. Structure of world exports by provenance and destination (Table F): This table shows the distribution (in percent) of exports by provenance (origin) and destination for total exports and a limited set of commodity classes as well as the commodity composition (in percent) of total exports by provenance (origin) and destination. For example, table F shows that the share of total exports of developed economies decreased from 65.1 percent in 2000 to 53.2 percent in 2010. While in 2009 the share of exports of Food, beverages and tobacco (SITC Section 0 and 1) and of Chemicals (SITC Section 5) peaked at 7.0 and 11.4 percent, respectively, they decreased in 2010 to 6.4 and 11.0. The share of Mineral fuels, lubricants and related materials (SITC Section 3) dropped from 17.5 percent in 2008 to 14.8 percent in 2010.

27. Indices of total exports and imports by countries or areas: Quantum and unit value indices and terms of trade in U.S. dollars (2000 = 100) (Table G): This table shows the volume and unit value (or price) indices for total exports and imports as well as the terms of trade and purchasing

[12] These percentages or shares of world trade are measured based on the trade between countries (or areas) which includes the trade of the countries within one region.

power of exports for individual countries or areas in U.S. dollar and with the year 2000 as base year.

28. Indices of total exports and imports by regions: Quantum and unit value indices and terms of trade in U.S. dollars (2000 = 100) (Table H): This table shows the volume and unit value indices for total exports and imports as well as the terms of trade by regions in U.S. dollar and with the year 2000 as base year. For example, the table shows that developed economies experienced a slight decrease in their terms of trade in 2010 as their import unit value index increased by more (from 138 in 2009 to 144) than their export unit value index (from 144 in 2009 to 148). Globally, export volume rose in 2010 after a sharp decrease in 2009.

29. Indices and values of manufactured goods exports: Unit value and volume indices (2000 = 100) and value in thousand million U.S. dollars (Table I): This table presents the unit value and the volume indices and the value of exports of manufactured goods for most developed economies and some developing economies. Manufactured goods are defined here to comprise sections 5 through 8 of the SITC. Unit value indices are presented both in U.S. dollars and in national currency. The table shows that in 2010, the value of manufactured goods exports increased by 1.2 trillion U.S. dollars to 8.2 trillion U.S. dollars (an increase of 17.3 percent). The volume index of manufactured goods exports increased in 2010 by 14.3 percent but remains below its 2008 level.

30. Indices and values of fuel imports – Developed economies: Unit value and volume indices (2000 = 100) and value in thousand million U.S. dollars (Table J): This table presents the unit value and the volume indices and the value of fuels imports for most developed economies. Fuel comprises section 3 of the SITC. Unit value indices are presented both in U.S. dollars and in national currency. The table shows that the value of developed economies' fuel imports amounted to 1.3 trillion in 2010, up from 1.0 trillion in 2009. This increase in value of 26.3 percent is reflecting an increase in volume of 2.5 percent and an increase in average price by 23.7 percent, as indicated in the respective volume and unit value indices.

31. Some indicators on fuel imports - Developed economies (Table K): This table shows fuel imports as a percentage of total imports and exports, and the ratio of unit value indices of manufactured goods exports and fuel imports. The table shows that fuel imports as a share of total imports increased to 15.8 percent in 2010 after falling to 14.7 percent in 2009. At the same time, the ratio of unit value indices of manufactured goods and fuel imports decreased, indicating that the cost of fuel imports in terms of manufactured goods exports has increased. In 2010, the ratio was 60 after 69 in 2009 and suggests that the fuel purchasing power of manufactured goods exports is significantly below its level of 2000.

32. For the general note and footnotes, see the end of the tables. The most recent data for tables B, C, G, I, J and K are published on a monthly or quarterly basis in the *United Nations Monthly Bulletin of Statistics* (MBS).[13] Slightly different versions of Table A containing quarterly and monthly data and table H containing quarterly data are published on a monthly or

[13] The MBS is available as printed publication and its database can be accessed online at: http://unstats.un.org/unsd/mbs/app/DataSearchTable.aspx. In addition the tables are also available online at http://unstats.un.org/unsd/trade/imts/analyticaltradetables.htm.

quarterly basis as table 34 and table 38 in the MBS.[14] Updated, although different versions of Table D, are published as table 40, 41 and 42 in the July, September and November editions of the MBS.

Description of commodity tables and graphs of part 2

33. Part 2 contains detailed data (commodity trade profiles) for 3-digits groups of the *Standard International Trade Classification, Revision 3* (SITC).[15] All SITC groups are covered except the following groups as these were poorly reported and contain many estimates which are not sufficiently explainable: SITC group 286, Ores and concentrates of uranium and thorium; SITC group 345, Coal, water or other producer gases; and SITC group 911, Postal packages not classified according to kind.

34. For certain commodities users will find spikes in growth rates and significant asymmetries between the total values of imports and exports. Reasons for these spikes can often be relatively easy identified (as caused i.e. by changes in the prices or classification changes) but the reasons for the asymmetries between the reported imports and exports are often less apparent.[16] However, it was decided to retain the information on these commodities as the results shown are a reflection of the data provided by countries (the influence of any estimates contained in the data is not significant) and to leave it to the users to assess the usefulness of this information for their specific purposes.

35. The following tables and graphs appear for each SITC commodity group:

36. <u>Imports and exports, 1996–2010, in current prices (Table 1):</u> This table shows the values of imports and exports from 1996 to 2010 for the commodity group and the share of the commodity group on the SITC section to which it belongs and its share on world trade.

37. <u>Top exporting and importing countries or areas in 2010 (Tables 2 and 3)</u>: These tables present the top 15 exporting and importing countries or areas in the order of magnitude based on exports or imports values for the year 2010. For each country (or area), the tables show the value of exports or imports in current U.S. dollar, the average growth rate over the period 2006-2010 (calculated using the compound interest formula), the annual growth rate for 2010, the share of world trade in 2010, and the cumulative share of world trade in 2010. In preparing these tables estimates were made for countries whose data were not yet available; the estimated values of exports and imports are shown in italic.

38. <u>Annual growth rates of exports, 1996–2010 (Graph 1)</u>: This graph presents the annual growth rate of exports of the commodity group, the annual growth rate of exports of the SITC

---

[14] The difference between table A in this publication and table 34 in the MBS relates to the calculation of regional aggregations (see paragraph 19). The volume indices in table H are calculated using the values of table A as input. The volume indices for some regions are therefore slightly different than the ones published in table 39 of the MBS.

[15] Standard International Trade Classification, Revision 3, Statistical Papers, Series M No.34/Rev.3, (United Nations publication, Sales No. E.86.XVII.12).

[16] It should be noted that most countries report their imports valued CIF and their exports valued FOB. Therefore, world trade measured in terms of exports is expected to be lower than world trade measured in terms of imports. This applies to the total of trade as well as all commodities and SITC groups.

section to which the commodity group belongs and the annual growth rate of total exports over the last fifteen years. The annual growth rate of total exports comprises all SITC sections.

39. Trade balance by MDG Regions 2010 (Graph 2): This graph presents, for the year 2010, exports, imports and the trade balance by regions according to the regions used in the Millennium Development Goal (MDG) Indicator Database (for further information on country grouping by MDG regions, see paragraph 17).

Abbreviations and Explanation of symbols

Names of some countries (or areas) or groups of countries (or areas) and of some commodities or groups of commodities have been abbreviated. Exact titles of countries or commodities can be found in various editions of the following publications referred to in the introduction (see paragraphs 14 and 16):

(i) Standard Country or Area Codes for Statistical Use
(ii) Standard International Trade Classification (SITC)
(iii) Harmonized Commodity Description and Coding System (HS)

In addition, the following abbreviations and symbols are used in this publication:

Not available	(na)
Not available	blank
Not available	...
Not applicable	–
Not applicable	.
Magnitude of less than half the unit used	0 or 0.0
More than 100,000 percent	>
Thousand	thsd
Million	mln
Billion	bln
Average	Avg.
Not elsewhere specified	nes
U.S. dollar	US$
Cumulated	Cum.
Imports	Imp
Exports	Exp
Balance	Bal
General trade system	G
Special trade system	S
Cost, insurance and freight	CIF
Free on board	FOB

Disclaimer

The tables, graphs and text contained in part 2 of this publication are provided only for illustration and despite all efforts might contain errors. When using this data users are advised to verify the latest information on UN Comtrade which is the source of this data.

UN Comtrade Subscription information

UN Comtrade is (with the exception of tables A, B, C, G, H, I, J and K) the source of the data in this Volume II of the 2010 ITSY. UN Comtrade is available at http://comtrade.un.org/. All data can be viewed and up to 50,000 records per query can be downloaded for free. The use of additional features requires a subscription – for rates and subscription go to https://unp.un.org/comtrade.aspx.

Contact

This yearbook has been produced by the International Merchandise Trade Statistics Section of the United Nations Statistics Division/ Department of Economic and Social Affairs. For questions or comments please contact us at:

International Merchandise Trade Statistics Section
United Nations Statistics Division
2 United Nations Plaza, DC2-1540
New York, New York 10017
E-mail: comtrade@un.org

http://comtrade.un.org/ or
http://unstats.un.org/unsd/trade/imts/imts_default.htm

2010
INTERNATIONAL TRADE
STATISTICS YEARBOOK

VOLUME II
TRADE BY COMMODITY

PART 1 – WORLD TRADE TABLES

- Total imports and exports by regions and countries or areas in U.S. dollars (Table A)
- Total imports and exports by countries or areas in national currency (Table B)
- External trade conversion factors (Table C)
- World exports by provenance and destination in U.S. dollars (Table D)
- Growth of world exports by provenance and destination (Table E)
- Structure of world exports by provenance and destination (Table F)
- Indices of total exports and imports by countries or areas (Table G)
- Indices of total exports and imports by regions (Table H)
- Indices and values of manufactured goods exports (Table I)
- Indices and values of fuel imports - Developed economies (Table J)
- Some indicators on fuel imports - Developed economies (Table K)

Total imports and exports by regions and countries or areas (Table A)

Imports CIF, exports FOB and balance: million U.S. dollars

Importations et exportations totales par régions et pays ou zones (Tableau A)

Importations CIF, exportations FOB, et balance : en millions de dollars E.-U.

Country or Area - Pays ou Zone	IMP EXP BAL	G/ S	2000	2002	2003	2004	2005	2006	2007	2008	2009	2010
World[1]	IMP		**6530072**	**6526061**	**7609513**	**9291664**	**10581006**	**12158634**	**14032608**	**16224079**	**12471621**	**15085075**
Monde[1]	EXP		**6359030**	**6401990**	**7452551**	**9073690**	**10352507**	**11975864**	**13821604**	**15969709**	**12367464**	**15060481**
	BAL		**-171041**	**-124071**	**-156962**	**-217974**	**-228500**	**-182770**	**-211005**	**-254370**	**-104157**	**-24594**
Developed Countries[2,3]	IMP		**4499489**	**4460073**	**5177791**	**6174475**	**6880610**	**7795107**	**8799519**	**9836335**	**7398802**	**8623069**
Pays Developpés[2,3]	EXP		**4129803**	**4152061**	**4782470**	**5637006**	**6149288**	**6944211**	**7954103**	**8872785**	**6875687**	**7997507**
	BAL		**-369686**	**-308013**	**-395320**	**-537469**	**-731322**	**-850896**	**-845415**	**-963550**	**-523115**	**-625562**
Asia-Pacific	IMP		464934	424949	490733	587170	666504	745319	815912	997567	741599	925898
Asie-Pacifique	EXP		556402	496148	560076	672507	722547	795702	882279	999884	759534	1014493
	BAL		91469	71200	69343	85337	56043	50383	66368	2317	17936	88594
Australia	IMP	G	71537	72693	89089	109383	125283	139279	165364	200564	165470	201640
Australie	EXP	G	63878	65036	71551	86420	105833	123316	141122	187249	153884	212364
	BAL		-7659	-7657	-17539	-22962	-19449	-15963	-24241	-13314	-11587	10724
Japan	IMP	G	379491	337209	383085	454592	514988	579609	619662	762629	550550	692434
Japon	EXP	G	479227	416730	471999	565743	594986	649948	714211	782052	580719	769839
	BAL		99736	79520	88914	111150	79998	70340	94549	19423	30169	77404
New Zealand	IMP	G	13906	15046	18560	23194	26234	26431	30886	34374	25578	31824
Nouvelle-Zélande	EXP	G	13297	14383	16527	20344	21728	22437	26946	30582	24931	32289
	BAL		-608	-664	-2033	-2850	-4506	-3994	-3940	-3792	-647	466
Europe	IMP		2535278	2611707	3143503	3787155	4153887	4780747	5581177	6259579	4729269	5335309
Europe	EXP		2514496	2710029	3224508	3840879	4159689	4720259	5491892	6119024	4744927	5318871
	BAL		-20781	98322	81005	53724	5802	-60487	-89285	-140554	15659	-16438
Andorra	IMP	S	1021	1200	1513	1762	1796	1780	1917	1931	1589	1518
Andorre	EXP	S	45	63	89	123	142	150	127	96	63	54
	BAL		-975	-1136	-1424	-1639	-1654	-1630	-1790	-1835	-1526	-1464
Austria	IMP	S	68986	72796	91595	113344	119950	130945	156760	176174	136081	150326
Autriche	EXP	S	64167	73113	89257	111720	117722	130376	157317	173394	130791	144645
	BAL		-4819	316	-2339	-1623	-2228	-570	557	-2780	-5290	-5681
Belgium	IMP	S	176992	198125	234947	286504	319798	351575	412012	467636	353246	390578
Belgique	EXP	S	187876	215867	255598	307792	335738	366758	431118	473636	370131	410387
	BAL		10884	17742	20650	21288	15941	15184	19106	6000	16885	19809
Croatia	IMP	G	7887	10722	14209	16589	18560	21488	25830	30728	21203	20051
Croatie	EXP	G	4432	4904	6187	8024	8773	10376	12364	14112	10474	11806
	BAL		-3455	-5818	-8022	-8565	-9788	-11112	-13465	-16617	-10729	-8244
Czech Republic	IMP	S	33934	42773	53807	71635	76343	93453	118467	142172	105256	126600
République tchèque	EXP	S	29057	38488	48715	67198	77988	95165	122760	146406	113175	133020
	BAL		-4877	-4285	-5092	-4438	1645	1712	4293	4234	7920	6420
Denmark	IMP	S	44364	48890	56227	66845	74265	85103	97324	109158	81926	84742
Danemark	EXP	S	50390	56308	65280	75568	83569	91703	101954	116069	92843	96773
	BAL		6025	7418	9052	8723	9303	6600	4631	6911	10917	12031
Estonia	IMP	S	4237	4810	6480	8334	10213	13472	15687	16058	10151	12282
Estonie	EXP	S	3166	3448	4539	5934	7676	9705	10948	12468	9058	11607
	BAL		-1070	-1362	-1942	-2400	-2537	-3767	-4739	-3590	-1094	-675
Faeroe Islands	IMP	G	532	494	738	628	743	790	1016	988	783	774
Iles Féroé	EXP	G	472	536	594	616	599	651	746	852	762	817
	BAL		-60	42	-144	-12	-144	-139	-270	-136	-22	44
Finland	IMP	G	33900	33642	41601	50677	58474	69448	81756	92160	60822	68689
Finlande	EXP	G	45482	44671	52514	60916	65238	77287	90091	96890	62859	70022
	BAL		11582	11029	10913	10239	6764	7839	8335	4730	2037	1333

Total imports and exports by regions and countries or areas (Table A)

Imports CIF, exports FOB and balance: million U.S. dollars *[cont.]*

Importations et exportations totales par régions et pays ou zones (Tableau A)

Importations CIF, exportations FOB et balance : en millions de dollars E.-U. *[suite]*

Country or Area - Pays ou Zone	IMP EXP BAL	G/S	2000	2002	2003	2004	2005	2006	2007	2008	2009	2010
France	IMP	S	310831	311860	370056	442568	490611	546505	631447	715669	558628	603700
France	EXP	S	298765	308603	362605	418276	443619	490702	550458	608869	475356	514124
	BAL		-12066	-3257	-7451	-24292	-46992	-55803	-80989	-106800	-83272	-89576
Germany	IMP	S	495450	490230	604742	715903	780514	922376	1055997	1186681	926154	1068054
Allemagne	EXP	S	550222	615695	751829	909513	977970	1122112	1323818	1451390	1120666	1271352
	BAL		54772	125465	147087	193610	197456	199736	267822	264709	194512	203299
Gibraltar	IMP		480	385	468	535	550	676	853	824	750	745
Gibraltar	EXP		126	148	147	199	199	242	304	281	266	259
	BAL		-354	-236	-320	-336	-351	-434	-548	-543	-484	-486
Greece	IMP	S	29221	31570	44852	52760	54436	63619	76247	89681	67775	50694
Grèce	EXP	S	10747	10414	13382	15308	17278	20749	23580	25651	20469	20919
	BAL		-18474	-21156	-31470	-37452	-37158	-42870	-52667	-64031	-47306	-29774
Hungary	IMP	S	31955	37787	47602	59636	65783	77206	94375	106380	78034	87612
Hongrie	EXP	S	28016	34512	42532	54893	62179	74217	93377	107466	84586	94759
	BAL		-3939	-3276	-5070	-4744	-3604	-2989	-997	1085	6552	7147
Iceland	IMP	G	2591	2274	2788	3551	4554	5077	6354	5614	3604	3920
Islande	EXP	G	1891	2227	2385	2896	2944	3241	4509	5191	4057	4605
	BAL		-700	-47	-403	-654	-1610	-1836	-1845	-423	453	685
Ireland	IMP	G	51444	51508	53315	61413	69177	83889	85624	82658	62595	60651
Irlande	EXP	G	77097	87497	92431	104204	109605	104639	122622	126144	117092	118274
	BAL		25653	35990	39117	42791	40428	20750	36998	43485	54498	57623
Italy	IMP	S	238071	246613	297405	355269	384837	440852	509937	563436	414725	486596
Italie	EXP	S	239934	254219	299468	353544	372962	416231	499933	544962	406685	447465
	BAL		1863	7606	2063	-1726	-11875	-24621	-10004	-18474	-8040	-39131
Latvia	IMP	S	3187	4053	5242	7048	8592	11430	15182	15775	9346	11064
Lettonie	EXP	S	1867	2284	2893	3983	5108	5896	7892	9278	7174	8817
	BAL		-1320	-1769	-2350	-3066	-3483	-5535	-7290	-6497	-2173	-2247
Lithuania	IMP	G	5219	7524	9668	12386	15510	19413	24445	31295	18341	23385
Lituanie	EXP	G	3548	5231	6970	9307	11782	14153	17162	23770	16496	20726
	BAL		-1671	-2294	-2698	-3079	-3729	-5259	-7283	-7525	-1845	-2658
Luxembourg	IMP	S	10718	11602	13694	16829	17565	19434	22168	25514	18652	20620
Luxembourg	EXP	S	7950	8499	9980	12181	12699	14172	16021	17590	12786	14155
	BAL		-2768	-3103	-3714	-4648	-4866	-5262	-6147	-7924	-5866	-6465
Malta	IMP	G	3400	2840	3399	3824	3807	4073	4508	5049	3803	4569
Malte	EXP	G	2443	2223	2468	2628	2376	2705	2985	2993	2195	2831
	BAL		-957	-616	-931	-1196	-1432	-1368	-1523	-2056	-1608	-1738
Netherlands	IMP	S	198926	194130	234014	284020	310600	358510	421084	495043	382268	440619
Pays-Bas	EXP	S	213425	219857	264849	318066	349844	399635	476787	541398	431839	492267
	BAL		14499	25727	30835	34046	39244	41125	55703	46355	49571	51647
Norway	IMP	G	34351	34889	39284	48062	55472	64272	80378	90293	69292	77252
Norvège	EXP	G	60063	59576	67103	81709	103738	122112	136371	172621	120880	131395
	BAL		25712	24687	27818	33646	48265	57840	55993	82328	51588	54144
Poland	IMP	S	48970	55141	68153	89096	100759	127260	162437	204873	149723	178149
Pologne	EXP	S	31684	41032	53699	74829	89214	110941	138756	168674	136786	159829
	BAL		-17285	-14108	-14454	-14267	-11545	-16319	-23680	-36200	-12938	-18320
Portugal	IMP	S	38196	38339	40853	49240	53398	65609	76371	94726	71729	75590
Portugal	EXP	S	23280	25543	30719	33035	32129	42894	50241	57565	44343	48742
	BAL		-14916	-12796	-10134	-16205	-21269	-22716	-26129	-37161	-27386	-26848

Total imports and exports by regions and countries or areas (Table A)

Imports CIF, exports FOB and balance: million U.S. dollars *[cont.]*

Importations et exportations totales par régions et pays ou zones (Tableau A)

Importations CIF, exportations FOB et balance : en millions de dollars E.-U. *[suite]*

Country or Area - Pays ou Zone	IMP EXP BAL	G/ S	2000	2002	2003	2004	2005	2006	2007	2008	2009	2010
Slovakia	IMP	S	13413	17460	23760	30469	36168	47250	62102	74034	54807	67719
Slovaquie	EXP	S	11889	14478	21966	27605	31997	41939	57766	70982	55549	64694
	BAL		-1524	-2983	-1794	-2864	-4171	-5311	-4336	-3052	742	-3025
Slovenia	IMP	S	10116	10933	13853	17571	19626	23014	29481	34000	23852	26370
Slovénie	EXP	S	8732	10357	12767	15879	17896	20985	26553	28624	22294	24189
	BAL		-1384	-576	-1086	-1692	-1730	-2029	-2928	-5377	-1558	-2182
Spain	IMP	S	152901	163575	208553	257672	287610	326046	382651	417049	290744	315548
Espagne	EXP	S	113348	123563	156024	182156	191021	213350	246752	277695	220848	246274
	BAL		-39553	-40012	-52529	-75516	-96589	-112697	-135899	-139353	-69897	-69274
Sweden	IMP	G	73331	67667	84197	100791	111324	126609	153463	168993	120256	148473
Suède	EXP	G	87759	82965	102405	123307	130205	147236	168979	183907	131043	158114
	BAL		14428	15298	18208	22516	18881	20627	15516	14914	10787	9642
Switzerland	IMP	S	76104	82387	95600	110324	119784	132030	153181	173683	147894	166910
Suisse	EXP	S	74867	87370	100744	117820	126099	141679	164809	191810	166847	185774
	BAL		-1237	4983	5144	7496	6314	9649	11627	18127	18953	18865
United Kingdom	IMP	G	334550	335490	380889	451870	483066	547543	622125	641303	485238	561511
Royaume-Uni	EXP	G	281754	276340	304372	341652	371381	428261	434790	468244	356516	410176
	BAL		-52797	-59150	-76517	-110219	-111685	-119282	-187335	-173060	-128722	-151335
North America	IMP		**1499277**	**1423418**	**1543554**	**1800150**	**2060219**	**2269041**	**2402430**	**2579189**	**1927935**	**2361862**
Amérique du Nord	EXP		**1058904**	**945884**	**997886**	**1123620**	**1267052**	**1428250**	**1579932**	**1753877**	**1371225**	**1664143**
	BAL		**-440373**	**-477534**	**-545668**	**-676530**	**-793167**	**-840791**	**-822498**	**-825312**	**-556710**	**-697719**
Bermuda	IMP	G	720	747	833	988	985	1094	1167	1160	1067	1050
Bermudes	EXP	G	...	56	52	73	49	27	27	24	29	32
	BAL		...	-691	-781	-915	-936	-1067	-1140	-1136	-1038	-1018
Canada[4]	IMP	G	238811	221962	239085	273084	323365	348958	379794	407165	320287	390527
Canada[4]	EXP	G	276641	252407	272699	304623	359411	389513	416432	452170	313981	386011
	BAL		37830	30445	33614	31538	36046	40555	36638	45005	-6306	-4515
Greenland	IMP	G	363	391	465	546	593	618	678	871	680	779
Groenland	EXP	G	272	307	349	382	402	396	431	489	360	383
	BAL		-92	-84	-117	-164	-190	-222	-247	-383	-320	-396
United States[5]	IMP	G	1259300	1200230	1303050	1525370	1735060	1918080	2020400	2169490	1605300	1968760
Etats-Unis[5]	EXP	G	781918	693103	724771	818520	907158	1038270	1162980	1301110	1056750	1277580
	BAL		-477382	-507127	-578279	-706850	-827902	-879810	-857420	-868380	-548550	-691180
South-Eastern Europe	IMP		29538	39735	51865	69728	**82986**	103593	140430	170949	114542	125184
Europe du Sud-est	EXP		19549	24365	31032	41415	**49008**	61183	76807	94028	73459	89815
	BAL		-9989	-15370	-20833	-28314	**-33979**	-42410	-63624	-76920	-41083	-35368
Albania	IMP	G	1091	1504	1864	2309	2618	3058	4188	5251	4550	4601
Albanie	EXP	G	261	330	448	605	658	798	1078	1355	1091	1550
	BAL		-829	-1173	-1416	-1704	-1960	-2261	-3110	-3896	-3459	-3051
Bosnia and Herzegovina	IMP	S	3083	4068	4853	5991	7072	7345	9772	12282	8794	9204
Bosnie-Herzégovine	EXP	S	1067	1020	1409	1916	2400	3323	4166	5066	3939	4802
	BAL		-2017	-3048	-3445	-4075	-4672	-4023	-5606	-7217	-4856	-4402
Bulgaria	IMP	S	6505	7987	10887	14467	18162	23270	30086	37018	23552	25361
Bulgarie	EXP	S	4809	5749	7540	9931	11739	15101	18575	22485	16378	20608
	BAL		-1696	-2238	-3346	-4536	-6423	-8168	-11511	-14532	-7175	-4753
Montenegro[6]	IMP	S	.	.	.	.	.	1874	3206	3644	2310	2182
Monténégro[6]	EXP	S	.	.	.	.	.	791	827	659	403	437
	BAL		.	.	.	.	.	-1082	-2378	-2985	-1908	-1745

Total imports and exports by regions and countries or areas (Table A)

Imports CIF, exports FOB and balance: million U.S. dollars *[cont.]*

Importations et exportations totales par régions et pays ou zones (Tableau A)

Importations CIF, exportations FOB et balance : en millions de dollars E.-U. *[suite]*

Country or Area - Pays ou Zone	IMP EXP BAL	G/S	2000	2002	2003	2004	2005	2006	2007	2008	2009	2010
Romania	IMP	S	13055	17862	24003	32664	40463	51106	69602	82965	54256	61885
Roumanie	EXP	S	10367	13876	17619	23485	27730	32336	40042	49539	40621	49357
	BAL		-2688	-3986	-6384	-9179	-12733	-18770	-29560	-33426	-13635	-12528
Serbia[6]	IMP	S	.	.	.	.	.	13188	18400	22945	16047	16502
Serbie[6]	EXP	S	.	.	.	.	.	6437	8817	11004	8338	9772
	BAL		.	.	.	.	.	-6752	-9584	-11941	-7709	-6731
Serbia and Montenegro[6]	IMP	S	3711	6320	7952	11366	...	.	.	.	.	.
Serbie et Monténégro[6]	EXP	S	1723	2275	2650	3801	...	.	.	.	.	.
	BAL		-1988	-4045	-5302	-7565	...	.	.	.	.	.
TFYR Macedonia	IMP	S	2094	1995	2306	2932	3228	3752	5177	6844	5032	5449
L'ex-Ry de Macédoine	EXP	S	1323	1116	1367	1676	2041	2398	3302	3920	2691	3291
	BAL		-771	-880	-939	-1256	-1187	-1355	-1875	-2923	-2341	-2159
CIS	IMP		**70777**	90627	114705	**151075**	**188633**	**253241**	**352232**	**468958**	**303961**	**387723**
CEI	EXP		**143256**	152972	191629	**263552**	**336579**	**418435**	**497491**	**707334**	**440219**	**575850**
	BAL		**72479**	62345	76924	**112477**	**147945**	**165195**	**145259**	**238376**	**136258**	**188127**
Asia	IMP		**13519**	17343	21377	**28245**	**34788**	**45334**	**59477**	**72860**	**59216**	**58417**
Asie	EXP		**17793**	19638	24171	**34469**	**43806**	**58030**	**70649**	**138894**	**76194**	**99879**
	BAL		**4274**	2296	2794	**6224**	**9018**	**12696**	**11172**	**66034**	**16978**	**41462**
Armenia	IMP	S	882	987	1280	1351	1768	2194	3282	4427	3303	3783
Arménie	EXP	S	294	505	686	715	950	1004	1219	1057	698	1011
	BAL		-588	-482	-594	-636	-818	-1190	-2063	-3370	-2605	-2771
Azerbaijan	IMP	G	1172	1666	2626	3516	4211	5267	5714	7170	6123	6599
Azerbaïdjan	EXP	G	1745	2167	2590	3616	4347	6372	6058	47756	14701	21325
	BAL		573	502	-36	100	136	1106	345	40586	8578	14726
Georgia	IMP	G	709	796	1141	1846	2490	3678	5217	6066	4386	5097
Géorgie	EXP	G	323	346	461	647	865	993	1240	1507	1140	1581
	BAL		-387	-450	-680	-1199	-1624	-2685	-3977	-4559	-3246	-3516
Kazakhstan	IMP	G	5040	8040	9554	13818	17979	24120	33260	38452	28409	24024
Kazakhstan	EXP	G	8812	10027	13233	20603	28301	38762	48351	71971	43196	57244
	BAL		3772	1987	3679	6785	10322	14642	15091	33519	14787	33220
Kyrgyzstan	IMP	S	558	590	722	947	1101	1718	2412	4072	3040	3228
Kirghizistan	EXP	S	511	487	583	721	672	794	1134	1618	1442	1489
	BAL		-47	-102	-139	-226	-429	-924	-1278	-2455	-1599	-1739
Tajikistan	IMP	G	675	721	881	1191	1354	1723	2455	3270	2569	4900
Tadjikistan	EXP	G	784	737	797	915	891	1399	1468	1406	1010	2306
	BAL		109	16	-84	-276	-464	-324	-987	-1864	-1559	-2594
Turkmenistan	IMP	G	...	2119	2512	...	...	...	...	...	...	...
Turkménistan	EXP	G	...	2856	2632	...	...	...	...	...	...	...
	BAL		...	736	120	...	...	...	...	...	...	...
Uzbekistan	IMP	G	2697	2425	2662	3392	3666	4380	4848	7076	9023	8386
Ouzbékistan	EXP	G	2817	2513	3189	4280	4749	5617	8029	10369	10735	11587
	BAL		120	88	527	888	1083	1237	3181	3293	1712	3201
Europe	IMP		57259	73285	93328	122830	153845	207907	292755	396098	244745	329306
Europe	EXP		125463	133334	167458	229083	292772	360406	426842	568440	364025	475971
	BAL		68205	60049	74130	106253	138927	152499	134087	172342	119280	146665
Belarus	IMP	G	8646	9092	11558	16491	16708	22351	28693	39381	28569	34884
Bélarus	EXP	G	7326	8021	9946	13774	15979	19734	24275	32571	21304	25284
	BAL		-1320	-1071	-1612	-2717	-729	-2618	-4418	-6811	-7265	-9601

Total imports and exports by regions and countries or areas (Table A)

Imports CIF, exports FOB and balance: million U.S. dollars *[cont.]*

Importations et exportations totales par régions et pays ou zones (Tableau A)

Importations CIF, exportations FOB et balance : en millions de dollars E.-U. *[suite]*

Country or Area - Pays ou Zone	IMP EXP BAL	G/S	2000	2002	2003	2004	2005	2006	2007	2008	2009	2010
Republic of Moldova	IMP	G	776	1039	1403	1773	2293	2710	3690	4081	3278	3855
République de Moldova	EXP	G	472	644	789	980	1091	1060	1340	1335	1283	1542
	BAL		-305	-395	-614	-793	-1202	-1650	-2350	-2746	-1995	-2314
Russian Federation	IMP	G	33880	46177	57347	75569	98708	137807	199754	267101	167411	229655
Fédération de Russie	EXP	G	103093	106712	133656	181663	241473	301244	351930	467581	301656	397668
	BAL		69213	60535	76309	106093	142766	163437	152176	200480	134245	168013
Ukraine	IMP	G	13956	16977	23020	28997	36136	45039	60618	85535	45487	60911
Ukraine	EXP	G	14573	17957	23067	32666	34228	38368	49296	66954	39782	51478
	BAL		617	980	47	3669	-1908	-6671	-11322	-18581	-5705	-9433
Northern Africa	IMP		**46953**	**50284**	**52760**	**67990**	**80214**	**86800**	**112469**	**164473**	**146452**	**161411**
Afrique du nord	EXP		**49876**	**48053**	**60740**	**79004**	**109622**	**131233**	**153521**	**207537**	**134078**	**164232**
	BAL		**2923**	**-2231**	**7980**	**11014**	**29408**	**44433**	**41051**	**43064**	**-12374**	**2821**
Algeria	IMP	S	9169	11969	12392	18166	20356	20985	27525	39578	39333	40228
Algérie	EXP	S	22030	18801	23206	31300	46000	52760	59761	79587	45240	57786
	BAL		12861	6832	10814	13133	25644	31775	32236	40010	5907	17558
Egypt[7,8]	IMP	G	13963	12496	10878	12831	19816	20722	27063	48775	44946	52923
Egypte[7,8]	EXP	G	4675	4687	6163	7683	10652	13694	16200	26246	23062	26438
	BAL		-9288	-7809	-4715	-5149	-9163	-7028	-10863	-22528	-21884	-26485
Libya	IMP	G	3703	4412	4312	6333	6058	6053	6753	9116	10037	10506
Libye	EXP	G	10137	9837	14557	20403	31278	40333	47048	62031	37265	46016
	BAL		6434	5425	10245	14069	25220	34280	40295	52915	27228	35510
Morocco	IMP	S	11534	11864	14250	17822	20790	23980	32010	42366	32881	35522
Maroc	EXP	S	7175	7849	8778	9925	11190	12744	15340	20345	14054	17559
	BAL		-4359	-4014	-5472	-7897	-9601	-11236	-16670	-22021	-18827	-17963
Tunisia	IMP	G	8567	9526	10910	12818	13177	15043	19101	24622	19241	22218
Tunisie	EXP	G	5850	6871	8027	9685	10494	11694	15163	19319	14449	16427
	BAL		-2717	-2655	-2883	-3133	-2683	-3349	-3938	-5303	-4791	-5791
Sub-Saharan Africa[1]	IMP		**78693**	**82226**	**105025**	**135405**	**165901**	**197707**	**244987**	**300662**	**251573**	**282906**
Afrique subsaharienne[1]	EXP		**93240**	**92676**	**112815**	**150244**	**203289**	**232645**	**277429**	**362176**	**254792**	**328788**
	BAL		**14547**	**10449**	**7790**	**14839**	**37388**	**34937**	**32442**	**61514**	**3218**	**45882**
Angola[4]	IMP	S	3040	3760	5480	5832	8353	8778	13661	20982	22660	16574
Angola[4]	EXP	S	7703	7516	9237	12975	23670	31084	43452	72179	40080	46437
	BAL		4663	3756	3757	7143	15317	22306	29791	51197	17420	29864
Benin	IMP	S	567	729	898	896	1018	1228	2037	2290	2110	2354
Bénin	EXP	S	392	451	541	564	574	741	1052	1285	1109	1240
	BAL		-174	-278	-357	-332	-445	-487	-984	-1005	-1001	-1113
Botswana	IMP	G	2079	1865	2467	3237	3172	3076	4077	5232	4771	5668
Botswana	EXP	G	2661	2445	2809	3516	4455	4509	5170	5077	3514	4700
	BAL		581	580	342	279	1283	1434	1093	-155	-1257	-967
Burkina Faso	IMP	G	608	746	932	1273	1255	1323	1685	2008	1882	2157
Burkina Faso	EXP	G	213	248	320	480	467	588	623	693	893	1203
	BAL		-395	-498	-612	-793	-788	-735	-1062	-1315	-989	-954
Burundi	IMP	S	148	129	157	176	267	431	319	402	402	509
Burundi	EXP	S	50	30	38	47	56	58	62	54	62	100
	BAL		-98	-99	-119	-129	-211	-372	-257	-348	-340	-409
Cameroon	IMP	S	1483	1876	2176	2411	2725	3161	4218	5376	4322	4847
Cameroun	EXP	S	1823	1814	2297	2481	2849	3587	3622	4279	3391	3896
	BAL		341	-62	122	70	123	427	-596	-1097	-931	-952

Total imports and exports by regions and countries or areas (Table A)

Imports CIF, exports FOB and balance: million U.S. dollars *[cont.]*

Importations et exportations totales par régions et pays ou zones (Tableau A)

Importations CIF, exportations FOB et balance : en millions de dollars E.-U. *[suite]*

Country or Area - Pays ou Zone	IMP EXP BAL	G/ S	2000	2002	2003	2004	2005	2006	2007	2008	2009	2010
Cape Verde	IMP	G	237	276	352	432	438	543	753	819	709	743
Cap-Vert	EXP	G	11	11	13	15	18	21	19	32	35	45
	BAL		-227	-266	-339	-417	-420	-522	-734	-788	-674	-698
Cent. Afr. Rep.	IMP	S	118	122	119	152	175	203	251	298	300	341
Rép. centrafricaine	EXP	S	163	150	128	134	127	158	181	150	121	139
	BAL		45	27	9	-18	-48	-44	-70	-149	-179	-202
Chad	IMP	S	483	1638	788	953	954	1346	1794	1906	2289	2507
Tchad	EXP	S	236	184	599	2192	3095	3342	3653	4345	2636	3411
	BAL		-248	-1454	-189	1239	2141	1995	1859	2439	347	903
Comoros	IMP	S	43	53	70	86	98	116	139	174	171	190
Comores	EXP	S	14	19	27	19	12	10	14	9	16	18
	BAL		-29	-34	-43	-67	-86	-106	-125	-165	-155	-172
Congo	IMP	S	480	695	856	999	1344	2072	2605	3145	2984	2990
Congo	EXP	S	2482	2290	2686	3435	4733	6092	5649	8288	6123	8192
	BAL		2003	1596	1830	2437	3389	4020	3045	5144	3139	5202
Cote d'Ivoire	IMP	S	2485	2605	3285	4724	5860	5825	6694	7863	6973	7844
Côte d'Ivoire	EXP	S	3611	5279	5803	6955	7693	8477	8692	10301	10518	10532
	BAL		1127	2674	2518	2231	1834	2652	1998	2438	3545	2688
Dem. Rep. of the Congo	IMP	S	697	1081	1495	2051	2690	2892	3400	4300	3800	4500
Rép. dém. du Congo	EXP	S	824	1132	1378	1917	2403	2705	3100	4400	3500	5400
	BAL		126	52	-117	-134	-288	-187	-300	100	-300	900
Djibouti	IMP	G	...	197	238	261	277	336	473	574	451	420
Djibouti	EXP	G	...	36	37	38	40	55	58	69	77	100
	BAL		...	-161	-201	-223	-238	-281	-415	-505	-373	-320
Equatorial Guinea	IMP	G	451	508	909	1089	1310	2023	2369	3933	5205	5680
Guinée équatoriale	EXP	G	1097	2121	2803	4588	7062	8218	10205	15995	9108	9964
	BAL		646	1613	1895	3498	5753	6195	7836	12062	3903	4285
Ethiopia	IMP	G	1261	1593	2686	2874	4095	5207	5805	8268	7644	...
Ethiopie	EXP	G	486	480	496	678	903	1043	1279	1606	1635	...
	BAL		-775	-1113	-2190	-2195	-3191	-4164	-4526	-6663	-6009	...
Gabon	IMP	S	996	1136	1206	1344	1472	1726	2155	2607	2199	2492
Gabon	EXP	S	2605	2411	3063	3719	5068	5454	6302	9566	5499	8374
	BAL		1610	1275	1857	2375	3596	3728	4147	6959	3299	5882
Gambia	IMP	G	187	159	156	229	260	259	323	324	304	301
Gambie	EXP	G	15	12	8	10	8	11	13	14	15	15
	BAL		-172	-147	-148	-219	-252	-248	-310	-310	-289	-286
Ghana	IMP	G	2974	2710	3208	4072	5344	6748	8057	10243	8038	11038
Ghana	EXP	G	1317	...	...	...	2801	3725	4322	5625	...	...
	BAL		-1657	...	...	...	-2543	-3023	-3735	-4618	...	...
Guinea	IMP	S	612	667	640	780	820	956	1218	1366	1060	1100
Guinée	EXP	S	666	709	609	744	853	1033	1203	1342	1050	1450
	BAL		54	42	-31	-36	33	77	-15	-24	-10	350
Guinea-Bissau	IMP	G	59	59	66	96	119	111	111	159	...	...
Guinée-Bissau	EXP	G	62	54	65	75	90	74	106	131	119	118
	BAL		4	-5	-1	-21	-29	-37	-5	-28	...	...
Kenya	IMP	G	3105	3245	3725	4553	6149	7311	8989	11074	10207	12076
Kenya	EXP	G	1734	2116	2411	2684	3293	3437	4080	4972	4463	5145
	BAL		-1372	-1129	-1314	-1869	-2856	-3874	-4910	-6102	-5743	-6931

Total imports and exports by regions and countries or areas (Table A)

Imports CIF, exports FOB and balance: million U.S. dollars *[cont.]*

Importations et exportations totales par régions et pays ou zones (Tableau A)

Importations CIF, exportations FOB et balance : en millions de dollars E.-U. *[suite]*

Country or Area - Pays ou Zone	IMP EXP BAL	G/ S	2000	2002	2003	2004	2005	2006	2007	2008	2009	2010
Lesotho	IMP	G	809	822	1129	1450	1410	1496	1741	1995	1973	2206
Lesotho	EXP	G	221	361	481	714	650	689	770	883	723	801
	BAL		-589	-461	-649	-736	-760	-807	-971	-1113	-1250	-1404
Liberia	IMP	S	...	178	170	337	310	467	499	813	552	650
Libéria	EXP	S	...	176	109	104	131	158	200	242	150	200
	BAL		...	-2	-61	-233	-179	-309	-299	-571	-402	-450
Madagascar	IMP	S	999	629	1311	1616	1685	1810	2671	3800	3197	2507
Madagascar	EXP	S	828	490	863	946	835	993	1262	1304	1050	1087
	BAL		-171	-139	-449	-670	-850	-817	-1408	-2496	-2147	-1420
Malawi	IMP	G	533	691	785	932	1163	1206	1380	1700	2096	...
Malawi	EXP	G	379	405	520	483	508	541	709	860	1080	1130
	BAL		-153	-286	-265	-449	-655	-665	-671	-840	-1015	...
Mali	IMP	S	807	927	1270	1365	1544	1819	2183	3343	2646	2855
Mali	EXP	S	552	873	926	979	1092	1559	1567	2082	2055	2248
	BAL		-255	-54	-345	-386	-453	-260	-616	-1261	-590	-607
Mauritania	IMP	S	354	357	387	1346	1344	1089	1417	1669	1337	1708
Mauritanie	EXP	S	343	320	321	435	556	1268	1410	1651	1322	1711
	BAL		-11	-37	-66	-911	-787	180	-8	-18	-14	3
Mauritius	IMP	G	2091	2159	2364	2771	3157	3627	3894	4655	3729	4403
Maurice	EXP	G	1551	1801	1899	1993	2138	2329	2238	2386	1942	2240
	BAL		-540	-358	-465	-778	-1018	-1298	-1656	-2269	-1787	-2163
Mozambique	IMP	S	1158	1543	1753	2035	2408	2869	3050	4008	3764	4550
Mozambique	EXP	S	364	810	1045	1504	1783	2381	2412	2653	2147	3200
	BAL		-794	-733	-708	-531	-625	-488	-638	-1355	-1617	-1350
Namibia	IMP	G	1539	1484	1999	2408	2567	2868	3528	4314	5066	5372
Namibie	EXP	G	1317	1077	1269	1833	2067	2638	2924	3113	3379	4096
	BAL		-222	-407	-730	-575	-500	-230	-604	-1201	-1687	-1276
Niger	IMP	S	390	474	630	757	934	955	1163	1659	1926	2212
Niger	EXP	S	284	278	353	439	490	507	664	902	888	907
	BAL		-107	-196	-277	-318	-444	-448	-499	-757	-1038	-1305
Nigeria	IMP	G	8721	7547	10853	14164	21314	26760	37576	42378	33906	37000
Nigéria	EXP	G	20975	15107	19887	31148	55145	57444	65133	80615	53000	79000
	BAL		12254	7560	9034	16984	33831	30684	27557	38237	19094	42000
Rwanda	IMP	G	211	248	258	285	432	547	736	1131	1227	1401
Rwanda	EXP	G	52	65	63	99	125	147	176	267	193	255
	BAL		-159	-182	-195	-187	-307	-400	-559	-865	-1035	-1146
Sao Tome and Principe	IMP	S	30	31	41	41	50	71	79	114	103	125
Sao Tomé-et-Principe	EXP	S	3	5	7	5	7	8	7	11	8	11
	BAL		-27	-26	-34	-36	-43	-63	-72	-103	-95	-114
Senegal	IMP	G	1513	2044	2394	2853	3190	3444	4271	5706	4549	4442
Sénégal	EXP	G	921	1070	1263	1510	1576	1556	1652	2007	1906	2059
	BAL		-592	-975	-1131	-1344	-1614	-1888	-2618	-3699	-2643	-2383
Seychelles	IMP	G	343	421	412	497	675	758	861	1106	821	989
Seychelles	EXP	G	193	228	273	291	340	380	356	437	402	400
	BAL		-150	-194	-139	-206	-335	-378	-506	-668	-419	-588
Sierra Leone	IMP	S	149	264	305	286	345	389	445	535	518	...
Sierra Leone	EXP	S	13	49	92	139	159	231	245	216	232	...
	BAL		-136	-215	-214	-147	-186	-158	-199	-319	-285	...

Total imports and exports by regions and countries or areas (Table A)

Imports CIF, exports FOB and balance: million U.S. dollars *[cont.]*

Importations et exportations totales par régions et pays ou zones (Tableau A)

Importations CIF, exportations FOB et balance : en millions de dollars E.-U. *[suite]*

Country or Area - Pays ou Zone	IMP EXP BAL	G/S	2000	2002	2003	2004	2005	2006	2007	2008	2009	2010
South Africa[4,9]	IMP	G	26795	25990	34204	47421	54848	67644	79873	94901	64439	80131
Afrique du Sud[4,9]	EXP	G	29987	29733	36503	46148	51640	58197	69787	84488	62627	81822
	BAL		3192	3743	2299	-1272	-3208	-9447	-10086	-10413	-1812	1691
Sudan	IMP	G	1553	2446	2882	4075	6757	8074	8775	9352	9691	9960
Soudan	EXP	G	1807	1949	2542	3778	4824	5657	8879	11671	7834	10500
	BAL		254	-497	-340	-297	-1933	-2417	104	2319	-1857	540
Swaziland	IMP	G	1039	962	1534	1937	1897	1918	1853	...	1617	1710
Swaziland	EXP	G	903	1038	1656	1962	1761	1779	1885	...	1479	1557
	BAL		-137	76	122	25	-136	-139	33	...	-138	-153
Togo	IMP	S	562	595	775	883	1054	1088	1243	1499	1409	1502
Togo	EXP	S	362	430	600	601	659	631	700	901	801	850
	BAL		-200	-165	-176	-281	-396	-457	-543	-598	-607	-652
Uganda	IMP	G	1512	1053	1375	1731	2049	2555	3497	4559	3787	4264
Ouganda	EXP	G	469	480	564	758	1017	1188	2003	2717	2327	2164
	BAL		-1043	-573	-811	-974	-1033	-1367	-1494	-1841	-1461	-2100
United Rep. of Tanzania	IMP	G	1523	1661	2125	2515	2661	4254	5337	7081	6296	7714
Rép.-Unie de Tanzanie	EXP	G	663	902	1129	1336	1479	1655	2022	2674	2367	3524
	BAL		-860	-758	-996	-1179	-1182	-2598	-3315	-4407	-3929	-4190
Zambia	IMP	S	997	1284	1576	2018	2567	2931	4014	5023	3791	...
Zambie	EXP	S	681	988	980	1576	1780	3828	4641	5186	4389	7207
	BAL		-316	-295	-595	-442	-786	896	628	163	599	...
Zimbabwe	IMP	G	1861	1751	1710	2204	2350	2300	2550	2950	2900	3700
Zimbabwe	EXP	G	1923	2012	1670	1887	1850	2000	2400	2200	2269	2500
	BAL		62	261	-40	-317	-500	-300	-150	-750	-631	-1200
Latin America & The Caribbean	IMP		**376134**	**344178**	**356535**	**434703**	**515070**	**614231**	**733210**	**896644**	**674948**	**851829**
Amérique latine et les Caraïbes	EXP		**354602**	**345205**	**378111**	**466904**	**563004**	**675050**	**757718**	**886929**	**683191**	**869369**
	BAL		**-21532**	**1027**	**21575**	**32201**	**47934**	**60819**	**24509**	**-9715**	**8243**	**17540**
The Caribbean	IMP		**26914**	**26808**	**27725**	**29935**	**37615**	**44022**	**50407**	**61307**	**48643**	**51130**
Les Caraïbes	EXP		**11412**	**10281**	**11676**	**13475**	**17534**	**23739**	**24782**	**30511**	**22412**	**32102**
	BAL		**-15503**	**-16528**	**-16048**	**-16460**	**-20081**	**-20283**	**-25626**	**-30796**	**-26231**	**-19028**
Anguilla	IMP	S	99	74	80	105	133	143	248	272	169	157
Anguilla	EXP	S	4	4	4	6	7	13	9	11	23	12
	BAL		-95	-69	-76	-100	-126	-130	-239	-260	-146	-145
Antigua and Barbuda	IMP	G	338	336	391	454	550	623	727	742	650	520
Antigua-et-Barbuda	EXP	G	23	12	46	57	124	153	174	198	181	48
	BAL		-316	-325	-346	-397	-426	-470	-553	-544	-469	-472
Aruba	IMP	S	835	841	848	875	1028	1041	1114	1134	1090	1003
Aruba	EXP	S	173	128	83	80	102	109	98	100	136	124
	BAL		-662	-713	-764	-796	-927	-932	-1016	-1034	-955	-878
Bahamas[10]	IMP	G	2074	1728	1762	1905	2230	2401	2449	2354	2699	2863
Bahamas[10]	EXP	G	576	446	425	477	562	674	485	560	585	620
	BAL		-1498	-1282	-1337	-1428	-1668	-1726	-1965	-1794	-2114	-2243
Barbados	IMP	G	1156	1071	1195	1413	1604	1586	1709	1879	1471	1562
Barbade	EXP	G	272	242	250	278	359	385	419	445	369	429
	BAL		-884	-829	-946	-1135	-1245	-1201	-1291	-1433	-1102	-1133
Cayman Islands	IMP	G	693	605	666	877	1191	1042	1032	1055	883	826
Îles Caïmanes	EXP	G	4	3	24	25	60	26	27	17	19	13
	BAL		-689	-602	-642	-852	-1130	-1017	-1005	-1039	-864	-813

Total imports and exports by regions and countries or areas (Table A)

Imports CIF, exports FOB and balance: million U.S. dollars *[cont.]*

Importations et exportations totales par régions et pays ou zones (Tableau A)

Importations CIF, exportations FOB et balance : en millions de dollars E.-U. *[suite]*

Country or Area - Pays ou Zone	IMP EXP BAL	G/S	2000	2002	2003	2004	2005	2006	2007	2008	2009	2010
Cuba	IMP	S	3363	4151	4613	5562	8130	10174	10889	14249	...	...
Cuba	EXP	S	1219	1504	1672	2188	2159	2980	3998	3680	...	...
	BAL		-2144	-2647	-2941	-3374	-5972	-7194	-6892	-10570	...	...
Dominica	IMP	S	148	116	128	145	165	167	196	247	233	224
Dominique	EXP	S	54	46	41	41	41	42	38	40	36	34
	BAL		-95	-70	-87	-104	-124	-124	-158	-207	-197	-189
Dominican Republic[4,11]	IMP	G	6416	6037	5266	5368	7207	8745	11289	14020	9946	12885
République dominicaine[4,11]	EXP	G	966	834	1041	1251	1398	1933	2635	2394	1690	2518
	BAL		-5450	-5204	-4225	-4117	-5809	-6812	-8654	-11626	-8256	-10367
Grenada	IMP	S	246	202	254	253	334	331	365	377	293	317
Grenade	EXP	S	78	39	42	32	28	25	33	30	29	24
	BAL		-168	-163	-213	-220	-306	-305	-332	-347	-264	-293
Haiti	IMP	G	1040	1122	1187	1317	1449	1880	1681	2310	2122	3147
Haïti	EXP	G	313	279	346	394	470	480	522	475	576	579
	BAL		-727	-842	-841	-923	-979	-1401	-1159	-1835	-1546	-2568
Jamaica	IMP	G	3302	3533	3633	3772	4458	5314	6394	7734	4860	5201
Jamaïque	EXP	G	1295	1114	1177	1390	1499	1874	2070	2542	1319	1331
	BAL		-2007	-2419	-2457	-2382	-2959	-3440	-4324	-5192	-3540	-3870
Montserrat	IMP	S	...	25	28	29	30	30	30	38	30	30
Montserrat	EXP	S	...	1	2	4	1	1	3	4	3	1
	BAL		...	-24	-27	-24	-28	-29	-27	-34	-26	-29
Neth. Antilles	IMP	S	2862	2268	2606	1723	1950	2209	2549	3079	2607	2800
Antilles néer.	EXP	S	2009	1609	1161	521	608	695	676	1088	810	800
	BAL		-853	-659	-1445	-1202	-1342	-1515	-1872	-1991	-1797	-2000
Saint Kitts-Nevis	IMP	S	196	202	200	182	210	250	272	325	302	228
Saint-Kitts-et-Nevis	EXP	S	29	35	51	37	30	35	32	43	43	45
	BAL		-167	-167	-149	-145	-180	-214	-241	-282	-260	-183
Saint Lucia	IMP	S	355	309	403	437	479	592	635	657	539	581
Sainte-Lucie	EXP	S	47	49	85	125	89	98	107	145	163	165
	BAL		-308	-260	-318	-312	-390	-494	-528	-512	-376	-416
Saint Vincent-Grenadines	IMP	S	148	179	200	225	241	269	327	373	334	345
St.Vincent-Grenadines	EXP	S	50	39	38	37	40	38	48	52	50	44
	BAL		-97	-139	-162	-189	-201	-231	-279	-321	-284	-301
Trinidad and Tobago	IMP	S	3308	3644	3892	4858	5694	6484	7662	9596	6953	6390
Trinité-et-Tobago	EXP	S	4274	3883	5177	6518	9941	14159	13393	18663	9140	11156
	BAL		966	239	1285	1660	4247	7675	5731	9067	2187	4766
Turks and Caicos Islands	IMP	G	149	177	171	220	304	498	581	591	...	...
Îles Turques et Caïques	EXP	G	9	9	10	12	15	18	16	25	...	...
	BAL		-140	-169	-161	-208	-289	-480	-564	-566	...	...
Latin America	IMP		**349220**	**317369**	**328811**	**404767**	**477455**	**570209**	**682802**	**835336**	**626305**	**800699**
Amérique latine	EXP		**343191**	**334924**	**366435**	**453429**	**545470**	**651311**	**732937**	**856418**	**660779**	**837267**
	BAL		**-6030**	**17555**	**37624**	**48661**	**68015**	**81102**	**50135**	**21081**	**34474**	**36568**
Argentina	IMP	S	25154	8990	13833	22445	28693	34158	44707	57413	39105	42981
Argentine	EXP	S	26341	25650	29566	34576	40351	46568	55779	70588	56065	62240
	BAL		1187	16660	15732	12131	11658	12410	11072	13174	16961	19259
Belize	IMP	G	524	525	552	514	593	676	684	837	668	699
Belize	EXP	G	218	169	205	213	208	266	254	271	250	...
	BAL		-306	-356	-347	-301	-385	-410	-430	-566	-418	...

Total imports and exports by regions and countries or areas (Table A)

Imports CIF, exports FOB and balance: million U.S. dollars *[cont.]*

Importations et exportations totales par régions et pays ou zones (Tableau A)

Importations CIF, exportations FOB et balance : en millions de dollars E.-U. *[suite]*

Country or Area - Pays ou Zone	IMP EXP BAL	G/S	2000	2002	2003	2004	2005	2006	2007	2008	2009	2010
Bolivia (Plurinational State of)	IMP	G	1830	1770	1616	1844	2341	2814	3457	5081	4434	5182
Bolivie (État plurinational de)	EXP	G	1230	1299	1598	2146	2791	3875	4458	7058	4918	6179
	BAL		-600	-471	-18	302	450	1060	1001	1977	483	998
Brazil	IMP	G	58643	49723	50881	66433	77628	95838	126645	182377	133673	191464
Brésil	EXP	G	55119	60439	73203	96678	118529	137807	160649	197942	152995	201915
	BAL		-3524	10716	22322	30244	40901	41969	34004	15565	19322	10451
Chile	IMP	S	18507	17092	19322	24794	32735	38406	47164	61903	42571	58956
Chili	EXP	S	19210	18180	21664	32520	41267	58680	67666	66456	54004	71028
	BAL		703	1088	2342	7727	8532	20274	20502	4553	11434	12073
Colombia	IMP	G	11539	12711	13889	16746	21204	26046	33164	39320	32898	40683
Colombie	EXP	G	13043	11911	13080	16224	21146	24388	29786	38265	32784	39710
	BAL		1505	-800	-809	-522	-59	-1658	-3378	-1055	-114	-973
Costa Rica	IMP	S	6389	7188	7663	8268	9812	11520	12952	15366	11460	13557
Costa Rica	EXP	S	5850	5264	6102	6301	7026	8216	9340	9575	8711	9343
	BAL		-539	-1924	-1561	-1967	-2786	-3305	-3613	-5791	-2750	-4214
Ecuador	IMP	G	3721	6431	6703	8226	10287	12114	13565	18852	15090	20591
Equateur	EXP	G	4927	5042	6223	7753	10100	12728	13852	18818	13863	17415
	BAL		1206	-1390	-480	-473	-187	615	287	-34	-1227	-3176
El Salvador	IMP	S	4948	5184	5754	6329	6834	7628	8677	9754	7255	8548
El Salvador	EXP	S	2941	2995	3128	3305	3387	3513	3977	4579	3797	4472
	BAL		-2006	-2189	-2626	-3024	-3448	-4115	-4700	-5175	-3457	-4077
Guatemala	IMP	S	5171	6304	6722	7812	8810	10157	11861	12835	10066	12051
Guatemala	EXP	S	2711	2473	2632	2939	3477	3665	4468	5412	3835	5907
	BAL		-2460	-3831	-4090	-4873	-5333	-6492	-7393	-7423	-6232	-6145
Guyana	IMP	S	582	576	576	652	788	889	1059	1312	1161	1400
Guyana	EXP	S	502	496	513	593	553	588	679	795	763	877
	BAL		-80	-81	-63	-59	-235	-301	-381	-518	-398	-523
Honduras	IMP	S	2980	3082	3448	4212	4853	5695	6762	8831	6133	7079
Honduras	EXP	S	1297	1240	1359	1640	1892	2054	2120	2883	2304	2712
	BAL		-1682	-1842	-2089	-2572	-2960	-3641	-4642	-5948	-3829	-4367
Mexico[4,12]	IMP	G	174500	168679	170490	197347	221414	256130	283264	310561	234385	301482
Mexique[4,12]	EXP	G	166367	160682	165396	189084	213891	250441	272055	291827	229683	298138
	BAL		-8133	-7997	-5094	-8263	-7523	-5689	-11209	-18734	-4702	-3344
Nicaragua	IMP	G	1805	1754	1879	2212	2595	3000	3579	4300	3438	4229
Nicaragua	EXP	G	643	561	605	756	858	1027	1194	1473	1393	1845
	BAL		-1163	-1193	-1275	-1457	-1737	-1973	-2385	-2827	-2045	-2384
Panama[13]	IMP	S	3379	2982	3086	3594	4180	4831	6872	9050	7801	9145
Panama[13]	EXP	S	859	846	864	944	1018	1093	1164	1247	948	832
	BAL		-2519	-2136	-2222	-2651	-3162	-3738	-5709	-7803	-6853	-8313
Paraguay	IMP	S	2193	1672	2228	3097	3790	6090	5859	9033	6940	10040
Paraguay	EXP	S	869	951	1242	1627	1688	1906	2817	4463	3167	4534
	BAL		-1324	-721	-986	-1470	-2102	-4184	-3042	-4570	-3773	-5507
Peru[4]	IMP	S	7407	7440	8244	9812	12084	14897	19580	28373	21006	28818
Pérou[4]	EXP	S	6955	7714	9091	12809	17368	23830	27882	31529	26885	35565
	BAL		-452	274	846	2997	5284	8933	8301	3157	5879	6747
Suriname	IMP	G	243	311	444	597	861	894	1111	1521	1356	1310
Suriname	EXP	G	395	363	519	713	789	1123	1287	1668	1393	1851
	BAL		152	52	75	116	-72	229	177	146	37	541

Total imports and exports by regions and countries or areas (Table A)

Imports CIF, exports FOB and balance: million U.S. dollars *[cont.]*

Importations et exportations totales par régions et pays ou zones (Tableau A)

Importations CIF, exportations FOB et balance : en millions de dollars E.-U. *[suite]*

Country or Area - Pays ou Zone	IMP EXP BAL	G/ S	2000	2002	2003	2004	2005	2006	2007	2008	2009	2010
Uruguay	IMP	G	3466	1964	2190	3114	3879	4757	5667	8943	6209	8619
Uruguay	EXP	G	2295	1861	2206	2931	3405	3953	4490	6421	5417	6707
	BAL		-1171	-103	16	-183	-474	-804	-1178	-2523	-792	-1912
Venezuela (Bolivarian Rep.	IMP	G	16213	12963	9256	16679	24027	33615	46097	49602	40597	33815
Venezuela (Rép. bolivarienne	EXP	G	31413	26781	27230	39668	55716	65578	69010	95138	57595	65786
	BAL		15200	13818	17974	22989	31689	31963	22913	45536	16998	31971
Eastern Asia	IMP		**743016**	**772157**	**955806**	**1231411**	**1410160**	**1646432**	**1909526**	**2206817**	**1857507**	**2516851**
Asie Orientale	EXP		**779060**	**822233**	**1003758**	**1293254**	**1538470**	**1840228**	**2185632**	**2473784**	**2089331**	**2714120**
	BAL		**36043**	**50076**	**47952**	**61843**	**128311**	**193795**	**276106**	**266968**	**231824**	**197269**
China	IMP	S	225024	295170	412760	561229	660206	791797	956233	1131620	1004170	1396200
Chine	EXP	S	249203	325596	438228	593326	761953	969380	1217815	1428660	1201790	1578270
	BAL		24179	30426	25468	32097	101747	177583	261582	297040	197620	182070
China, Hong Kong SAR	IMP	G	212805	207644	231896	271074	299533	334681	367864	388505	347311	433193
Chine, Hong Kong RAS	EXP	G	201860	200092	223762	259260	289337	316816	344629	362675	318510	390174
	BAL		-10945	-7552	-8134	-11814	-10196	-17865	-23235	-25830	-28801	-43019
China, Macao SAR	IMP	G	2255	2530	2755	3478	3913	4565	5366	5365	4622	5513
Chine, Macao RAS	EXP	G	2539	2356	2581	2812	2476	2557	2543	1997	961	870
	BAL		284	-174	-174	-666	-1438	-2008	-2823	-3368	-3661	-4643
Korea, Republic of	IMP	G	160481	152126	178827	224463	261238	309383	356648	435275	322843	425212
Corée, République de	EXP	G	172267	162471	193817	253845	284419	325465	371554	422007	361614	466384
	BAL		11786	10345	14990	29382	23181	16082	14906	-13268	38771	41172
Mongolia	IMP	G	615	691	801	1021	1184	1486	2117	3616	2131	3278
Mongolie	EXP	G	536	524	616	870	1065	1543	1889	2539	1903	2899
	BAL		-79	-167	-185	-151	-119	57	-228	-1077	-229	-379
Southern Asia	IMP		94680	106816	131158	175434	**235690**	**280572**	**342773**	**465386**	**378756**	**479484**
Asie Méridionale	EXP		90988	94836	116083	145486	**187124**	**233641**	**277006**	**351133**	**283242**	**370511**
	BAL		-3693	-11980	-15075	-29948	**-48566**	**-46931**	**-65768**	**-114253**	**-95515**	**-108973**
Afghanistan	IMP	G	1176	2452	2101	2177	...	...	...	...	...	...
Afghanistan	EXP	G	137	100	144	314	...	...	...	...	...	...
	BAL		-1039	-2352	-1957	-1863	...	...	...	...	...	...
Bangladesh	IMP	G	8358	7913	9516	12611	12881	14964	17263	22473	20631	26071
Bangladesh	EXP	G	4787	4566	5263	6615	7233	9103	10233	11777	12443	14195
	BAL		-3572	-3348	-4253	-5996	-5648	-5861	-7030	-10695	-8188	-11877
Bhutan	IMP	G	175	196	249	411	387	419	526	546	529	759
Bhoutan	EXP	G	103	113	133	183	258	414	675	522	496	540
	BAL		-72	-84	-116	-228	-129	-5	149	-24	-33	-219
India[14]	IMP	G	51563	56496	72559	99757	142865	178485	229349	321026	257200	329065
Inde[14]	EXP	G	42378	50353	58964	76647	99618	121812	150160	194816	164912	222794
	BAL		-9185	-6143	-13595	-23110	-43247	-56674	-79189	-126210	-92288	-106271
Iran (Islamic Rep. of)[15,16]	IMP	S	14347	20617	24798	31976	40041	40772	44942	57401	50469	62670
Iran (Rép. islamique d')[15,16]	EXP	S	28345	24440	33750	41697	56252	77012	88733	113668	78830	100900
	BAL		13998	3823	8952	9721	16211	36240	43791	56267	28361	38230
Maldives	IMP	G	389	392	471	642	745	927	1096	1388	967	1095
Maldives	EXP	G	76	90	113	122	103	135	108	126	76	74
	BAL		-313	-301	-358	-519	-641	-791	-989	-1262	-891	-1021
Nepal	IMP	G	1526	1418	1755	1939	2282	2489	3139	3562	4398	5502
Népal	EXP	G	700	568	662	772	863	838	870	937	823	951
	BAL		-826	-850	-1093	-1167	-1419	-1651	-2269	-2625	-3574	-4551

Total imports and exports by regions and countries or areas (Table A)

Imports CIF, exports FOB and balance: million U.S. dollars *[cont.]*

Importations et exportations totales par régions et pays ou zones (Tableau A)

Importations CIF, exportations FOB et balance : en millions de dollars E.-U. *[suite]*

Country or Area - Pays ou Zone	IMP EXP BAL	G/S	2000	2002	2003	2004	2005	2006	2007	2008	2009	2010
Pakistan	IMP	G	10864	11227	13038	17949	25356	29828	32590	42326	31648	37783
Pakistan	EXP	G	9028	9908	11930	13379	16050	16932	17837	20323	17523	21409
	BAL		-1836	-1319	-1107	-4570	-9306	-12896	-14753	-22003	-14125	-16373
Sri Lanka	IMP	G	6281	6105	6672	7973	8833	10259	11301	13953	10049	13512
Sri Lanka	EXP	G	5433	4699	5125	5757	6347	6886	7740	8137	7085	8307
	BAL		-848	-1406	-1547	-2216	-2487	-3373	-3560	-5816	-2965	-5205
South-eastern Asia	IMP		379501	355119	**398695**	**500673**	**600478**	**688640**	**776921**	**946880**	**728484**	**952113**
Asie du Sud-est	EXP		431651	407511	**453754**	**568191**	**653858**	**770881**	**865370**	**998342**	**813677**	**1051666**
	BAL		52149	52392	**55059**	**67518**	**53380**	**82241**	**88449**	**51462**	**85193**	**99553**
Brunei Darussalam	IMP	S	1107	1556	1327	1422	1447	1679	2101	2572	2449	3359
Brunéi Darussalam	EXP	S	3907	3701	4423	5060	6242	7634	7693	10319	7200	9160
	BAL		2801	2145	3096	3638	4794	5956	5592	7747	4751	5801
Cambodia	IMP	S	1424	2318	2560	3193	3927	4749	5300	6508	5876	7500
Cambodge	EXP	S	1123	1923	2118	2798	3200	3800	4400	4708	4302	5030
	BAL		-302	-395	-442	-395	-727	-949	-900	-1800	-1574	-2470
Indonesia	IMP	S	43075	30540	41568	55009	75631	80659	93101	127454	93802	132099
Indonésie	EXP	S	65404	58774	64109	70767	86995	103528	118014	139605	119646	157823
	BAL		22329	28233	22541	15758	11365	22869	24913	12151	25844	25724
Lao P.Dem.R.	IMP	S	535	447	462	713	882	1060	1067	1405	1461	2060
Rép. dém. populaire lao	EXP	S	330	301	335	363	553	882	923	1085	1053	1746
	BAL		-205	-146	-127	-349	-329	-177	-144	-320	-408	-314
Malaysia	IMP	G	81963	79869	81948	105298	114410	131085	146767	164410	123693	164734
Malaisie	EXP	G	98230	93265	99369	125745	140870	160571	176028	209668	157483	198800
	BAL		16266	13396	17421	20446	26459	29486	29261	45258	33790	34067
Myanmar	IMP	G	2401	2348	2092	2196	1927	2564	3277	4299	4393	4807
Myanmar	EXP	G	1647	3046	2485	2380	3813	4585	6313	6950	6731	8749
	BAL		-755	698	392	184	1887	2021	3036	2651	2338	3941
Philippines	IMP	G	36887	37202	39502	42345	46963	54077	57708	60492	45743	58229
Philippines	EXP	G	39794	36510	36231	39680	39879	47413	50270	49205	38308	51432
	BAL		2907	-692	-3271	-2664	-7084	-6665	-7438	-11287	-7435	-6797
Singapore	IMP	G	134546	116448	127935	163851	200050	238711	263155	319781	245785	310791
Singapour	EXP	G	137806	125177	144183	198633	229652	271809	299270	338176	269832	351867
	BAL		3259	8729	16248	34782	29602	33098	36115	18396	24048	41076
Thailand	IMP	S	61923	64645	75824	94410	118158	128654	141294	178680	134827	184591
Thaïlande	EXP	S	68963	68108	80324	96248	110178	130795	153858	175897	151986	195376
	BAL		7039	3463	4499	1838	-7980	2142	12563	-2783	17159	10785
Viet Nam	IMP	G	15638	19746	25256	31969	36761	45015	62682	80714	69949	83779
Viet Nam	EXP	G	14447	16706	20149	26485	32442	39826	48561	62685	57096	71658
	BAL		-1191	-3040	-5107	-5484	-4319	-5188	-14121	-18029	-12853	-12121
Western Asia[1]	IMP		**204345**	**217003**	**255723**	**340513**	**410204**	**479804**	**605894**	**750082**	**600769**	**685967**
Asie Occidentale[1]	EXP		**261901**	**257450**	**316405**	**422164**	**555013**	**659803**	**766522**	**1004954**	**710996**	**888602**
	BAL		**57556**	**40447**	**60682**	**81651**	**144809**	**179998**	**160628**	**254872**	**110226**	**202635**
Bahrain	IMP	G	4634	5013	5657	7385	9393	10515	11488	10800	7300	9800
Bahreïn	EXP	G	6195	5794	6632	7558	10242	12200	13634	17316	11874	15400
	BAL		1561	781	974	173	849	1685	2146	6516	4574	5600
Cyprus	IMP	G	3846	3863	4288	5659	6282	6951	8687	10873	7882	8568
Chypre	EXP	G	951	770	834	1081	1303	1153	1254	1755	1342	1514
	BAL		-2895	-3094	-3455	-4577	-4979	-5798	-7433	-9118	-6540	-7054

Total imports and exports by regions and countries or areas (Table A)

Imports CIF, exports FOB and balance: million U.S. dollars *[cont.]*

Importations et exportations totales par régions et pays ou zones (Tableau A)

Importations CIF, exportations FOB et balance : en millions de dollars E.-U. *[suite]*

Country or Area - Pays ou Zone	IMP EXP BAL	G/S	2000	2002	2003	2004	2005	2006	2007	2008	2009	2010
Israel[17]	IMP	S	37686	35517	36303	42864	47142	50334	59039	67656	49278	61209
Israël[17]	EXP	S	31404	29347	31784	38618	42770	46789	54065	60825	47934	58392
	BAL		-6282	-6170	-4519	-4245	-4371	-3544	-4973	-6831	-1344	-2817
Jordan	IMP	G	4597	5076	5743	8128	10506	11447	13511	16764	14534	15085
Jordanie	EXP	G	1899	2770	3082	3922	4302	5175	5725	7788	6531	7023
	BAL		-2698	-2306	-2662	-4206	-6204	-6272	-7786	-8976	-8002	-8062
Kuwait	IMP	S	7156	9007	10992	12630	15534	17252	21388	24836	20340	21996
Koweït	EXP	S	19434	15378	20678	28599	45189	56022	62871	87648	51979	66042
	BAL		12278	6372	9685	15968	29655	38769	41483	62812	31638	44046
Lebanon	IMP	G	6230	6560	7315	9609	9633	9647	12251	16754	16574	18460
Liban	EXP	G	715	1238	1813	2199	2337	2814	3574	4454	4187	5021
	BAL		-5515	-5322	-5502	-7410	-7296	-6833	-8677	-12300	-12387	-13439
Occupied Palestinian Territory	IMP	S	2383	1516	1800	2373	2668	2759	3141	3466	3593	...
Territoire palestinien occupé	EXP	S	401	241	280	313	335	367	513	558	506	...
	BAL		-1982	-1275	-1521	-2061	-2332	-2392	-2628	-2908	-3087	...
Oman	IMP	G	5040	6005	6572	8865	8827	10915	15978	22925	17865	19775
Oman	EXP	G	11319	11172	11669	13341	18692	21585	24136	37719	28053	36601
	BAL		6279	5166	5096	4476	9865	10670	8158	14795	10188	16827
Qatar	IMP	S	3252	4052	4898	6005	10061	16440	23429	27900	24922	22000
Qatar	EXP	S	11594	10978	13382	18684	25762	34052	42019	56593	41000	61500
	BAL		8342	6926	8485	12680	15701	17611	18590	28693	16078	39500
Saudi Arabia	IMP	S	30197	32293	36915	44744	59458	69800	90215	115133	95544	97078
Arabie saoudite	EXP	S	77480	72453	93245	125997	180736	211306	233300	313427	192296	251149
	BAL		47283	40160	56331	81253	121278	141506	143086	198294	96752	154071
Syrian Arab Rep.	IMP	S	4055	5097	5119	8411	10862	11488	14655	18150	15443	...
République arabe syrienne	EXP	S	4674	6520	5731	7485	9174	10919	11546	15304	10559	...
	BAL		620	1423	611	-926	-1688	-569	-3109	-2846	-4884	...
Turkey	IMP	S	54503	51554	69340	97540	116774	139576	170063	201964	140928	185544
Turquie	EXP	S	27775	36059	47253	63167	73476	85535	107272	132027	102143	113883
	BAL		-26728	-15495	-22087	-34373	-43298	-54041	-62791	-69937	-38785	-71661
United Arab Emirates	IMP	G	35009	42652	52074	72082	84654	100057	132500	177000	150000	170000
Emirats arabes unis	EXP	G	49835	52163	67135	90997	117287	145587	178630	239213	185000	235000
	BAL		14827	9511	15061	18915	32633	45530	46130	62213	35000	65000
Yemen	IMP	S	2327	2927	3680	3988	5401	6081	8513	10548	9206	9746
Yémen	EXP	S	3795	3335	3732	4072	5604	6653	6299	7584	6256	8497
	BAL		1469	408	52	85	204	572	-2215	-2964	-2949	-1249
Oceania	IMP		**6945**	**7841**	**9449**	**10258**	**11059**	**12506**	**14649**	**16895**	**15826**	**18539**
Océanie	EXP		**5106**	**4628**	**5754**	**6471**	**7251**	**8555**	**10007**	**10707**	**8794**	**10021**
	BAL		**-1840**	**-3213**	**-3695**	**-3788**	**-3808**	**-3951**	**-4642**	**-6187**	**-7032**	**-8518**
American Samoa[18]	IMP	S	506	499	624	604	520	579	650	680	600	550
Samoa américaines[18]	EXP	S	346	388	460	446	374	439	450	570	470	480
	BAL		-160	-111	-164	-158	-146	-141	-200	-110	-130	-70
Cook Islands	IMP	G	50	47	71	76	81	100	99	140	185	...
Iles Cook	EXP	G	9	5	9	7	5	3	5	4	3	...
	BAL		-41	-42	-62	-69	-76	-96	-94	-136	-182	...
Fiji	IMP	G	857	906	1208	1444	1607	1802	1801	2245	1440	...
Fidji	EXP	G	538	518	675	694	700	694	758	921	630	724
	BAL		-319	-387	-533	-750	-907	-1107	-1043	-1324	-809	...

Total imports and exports by regions and countries or areas (Table A)

Imports CIF, exports FOB and balance: million U.S. dollars *[cont.]*

Importations et exportations totales par régions et pays ou zones (Tableau A)

Importations CIF, exportations FOB et balance : en millions de dollars E.-U. *[suite]*

Country or Area - Pays ou Zone	IMP EXP BAL	G/S	2000	2002	2003	2004	2005	2006	2007	2008	2009	2010
French Polynesia	IMP	S	905	1336	1585	1500	1723	1656	1863	2187	1732	1740
Polynésie française	EXP	S	200	183	156	199	217	235	197	273	167	175
	BAL		-705	-1153	-1429	-1301	-1506	-1420	-1667	-1914	-1565	-1565
Guam	IMP	G	...	...	...	...	...	501	688	649	635	698
Guam	EXP	G	...	50	43	53	52	53	91	105	51	46
	BAL		...	...	...	...	...	-448	-596	-544	-584	-652
Kiribati	IMP	G	39	50	52	59	74	63	70	70	68	100
Kiribati	EXP	G	4	3	3	2	4	6	10	15	20	15
	BAL		-36	-46	-49	-57	-70	-57	-60	-55	-48	-85
Marshall Islands	IMP	G	55	...	...	68	68	...	...	...	...	...
Iles Marshall	EXP	G	9	...	...	...	...	...	...	...	...	...
	BAL		-46	...	...	...	...	...	...	...	...	...
New Caledonia	IMP	S	922	1008	1541	1636	1774	2117	2809	3233	2574	3313
Nouvelle-Calédonie	EXP	S	606	492	785	1033	1093	1352	2104	1300	1029	1272
	BAL		-317	-516	-756	-603	-681	-766	-705	-1933	-1546	-2041
Niue	IMP	G	2	2	2	8	...	4	7	8	...	...
Nioué	EXP	G	0	0	0	0	0	1	3	0	...	...
	BAL		-2	-2	-2	-8	...	-2	-4	-8	...	...
Palau	IMP	S	123	97	...	...	...	...	...	...	...	...
Palaos	EXP	S	...	...	...	...	...	...	...	...	...	...
	BAL		...	...	...	...	...	...	...	...	...	...
Papua New Guinea	IMP	G	1151	1235	1368	1681	1728	2287	2945	3550	...	...
Papouasie-Nouvelle-Guinée	EXP	G	2068	1642	2212	2555	3276	4167	4685	5719	4635	5414
	BAL		917	407	844	874	1548	1880	1740	2169	...	...
Samoa	IMP	S	106	127	128	155	187	219	227	249	204	278
Samoa	EXP	S	14	14	15	11	12	11	15	11	12	13
	BAL		-92	-114	-113	-145	-175	-208	-212	-238	-193	-265
Solomon Islands	IMP	S	98	67	94	121	185	217	287	329	270	300
Iles Salomon	EXP	S	65	58	74	97	103	121	165	210	163	221
	BAL		-33	-9	-20	-24	-82	-95	-123	-119	-107	-79
Tonga	IMP	G	69	89	94	105	120	116	143	168	145	159
Tonga	EXP	G	9	14	18	15	10	10	9	9	8	8
	BAL		-60	-75	-76	-90	-110	-107	-134	-158	-137	-151
Tuvalu	IMP	G	5	11	8	11	13	13	16	...	...	...
Tuvalu	EXP	G	0	0	0	0	0	0	0	...	...	...
	BAL		-5	-11	-8	-11	-13	-13	-16	...	...	...
Vanuatu	IMP	G	87	90	106	128	149	217	231	314	300	324
Vanuatu	EXP	G	26	20	27	37	38	49	50	57	57	61
	BAL		-61	-70	-79	-91	-111	-168	-180	-258	-242	-263
Non Petrol. Export[19]	IMP		...	...	...	...	...	...	...	...	...	...
Pétrole N. Compris[19]	EXP		**102397**	**92853**	**86061**	**79766**	**73931**	**68523**	**63510**	**58864**	**54558**	**50567**
	BAL		...	...	...	...	...	...	...	...	...	...
Additional Country Groupings												
ANCOM	IMP		40709	41315	39708	53308	69944	89486	115863	141228	114025	129088
ANCOM	EXP		57567	52746	57221	78600	107121	130399	144988	190809	136044	164655
	BAL		16859	11431	17513	25292	37177	40913	29125	49581	22020	35567

Total imports and exports by regions and countries or areas (Table A)

Imports CIF, exports FOB and balance: million U.S. dollars *[cont.]*

Importations et exportations totales par régions et pays ou zones (Tableau A)

Importations CIF, exportations FOB et balance : en millions de dollars E.-U. *[suite]*

Country or Area - Pays ou Zone	IMP EXP BAL	G/S	2000	2002	2003	2004	2005	2006	2007	2008	2009	2010
APEC	IMP		3312672	3205467	3633938	4414654	5088610	5780588	6436015	7375902	**5701991**	**7352937**
CEAP	EXP		3116485	2957445	3338160	4065700	4686790	5458744	6219978	7070235	5634286	7231483
	BAL		-196187	-248021	-295779	-348954	-401820	-321844	-216037	-305667	**-67706**	**-121454**
ASEAN	IMP		379501	355119	398474	500406	600157	688251	776452	946314	727977	951949
ANASE	EXP		431651	407511	453725	568159	653824	770844	865330	998299	813638	1051642
	BAL		52149	52392	55251	67754	53668	82592	88878	51984	85660	99693
CACM	IMP		21293	23512	25466	28833	32904	37999	43831	51085	38353	45464
MCAC	EXP		13442	12532	13825	14941	16640	18475	21098	23921	20040	24279
	BAL		-7850	-10980	-11641	-13892	-16264	-19524	-22732	-27164	-18313	-21186
CARICOM	IMP		**13681**	13878	14847	16753	19686	22386	25302	30301	23669	24816
CARICOM	EXP		**8127**	7212	8917	10911	14735	19942	19543	25930	14898	**17407**
	BAL		**-5555**	-6665	-5929	-5842	-4951	-2443	-5760	-4372	-8771	**-7409**
COMESA	IMP		**34638**	**35194**	**38165**	**47704**	**62685**	**69391**	**83882**	**119466**	**111513**	**127883**
COMESA	EXP		**26753**	**27805**	**36149**	**47253**	**63826**	**80188**	**96403**	**128107**	**93059**	**114558**
	BAL		**-7885**	**-7389**	**-2016**	**-451**	**1141**	**10797**	**12522**	**8641**	**-18454**	**-13325**
ECOWAS	IMP		**20021**	19982	25934	33147	43803	51915	68257	81005	**66812**	**75022**
CEDEA	EXP		**29437**	**26955**	**32681**	**45701**	71753	76755	86193	106389	**78300**	**105545**
	BAL		**9417**	**6973**	**6747**	**12554**	27950	24840	17936	25383	**11488**	**30523**
EMCCA	IMP		4011	5975	6053	6948	7980	10531	13391	17266	17299	18858
CEMAC	EXP		8407	8970	11576	16549	22935	26851	29613	42623	26877	33976
	BAL		4396	2995	5523	9601	14955	16320	16222	25357	9578	15119
LAIA	IMP		326534	293585	303265	376100	446213	535039	640059	785708	**589381**	**753550**
ALAI	EXP		328987	322013	352169	438203	528410	632735	712441	832185	**644569**	**823277**
	BAL		2452	28428	48904	62103	82196	97696	72382	46476	**55188**	**69727**
LDCs	IMP		**42133**	**49365**	**59336**	**72141**	**85677**	**100021**	**123001**	**159626**	**152809**	**167236**
PMA	EXP		**33264**	**37518**	**43955**	**58422**	**80109**	**100162**	**126050**	**174320**	**124534**	**152602**
	BAL		**-8869**	**-11847**	**-15381**	**-13719**	**-5567**	**142**	**3049**	**14694**	**-28275**	**-14635**
MERCOSUR	IMP		89456	62348	69132	95089	113990	140843	182879	257767	185926	253104
MERCOSUR	EXP		84624	88900	106217	135811	163973	190235	223735	279414	217644	275396
	BAL		-4832	26552	37084	40722	49983	49392	40856	21647	31718	22292
NAFTA	IMP		1672611	1590871	1712625	1995801	2279839	2523168	2683458	2887216	2159972	2660769
ALENA	EXP		1224926	1106192	1162866	1312227	1480460	1678224	1851467	2045107	1600414	1961729
	BAL		-447685	-484679	-549759	-683575	-799379	-844944	-831991	-842109	-559558	-699039
OECD	IMP		4851728	4788247	5539458	6623452	7398844	8402057	9488341	10644953	8004791	9431974
OCDE	EXP		4471035	4481706	5151866	6095934	6666042	7540322	8625383	9625576	7499851	8794254
	BAL		-380693	-306541	-387592	-527518	-732802	-861735	-862957	-1019378	-504940	-637720
OPEC[20]	IMP		**137959**	**161572**	**183699**	**247069**	**313153**	**369168**	**478686**	**608092**	**530258**	**562031**
OPEP[20]	EXP		**298303**	**267727**	**337688**	**465350**	**664936**	**803551**	**925493**	**1241660**	**817484**	**1047047**
	BAL		**160344**	**106155**	**153989**	**218281**	**351783**	**434383**	**446807**	**633568**	**287226**	**485016**
EU27	IMP		2435718	2509069	3028080	3658493	4017334	4635961	5420024	6086373	4569844	5159954
UE27	EXP		2388726	2575599	3073251	3663990	3957968	4490399	5232533	5807841	4499920	5055639
	BAL		-46992	66530	45171	5497	-59366	-145562	-187491	-278532	-69924	-104315
Extra-EU27[21]	IMP		913310	884624	1057673	1277865	1465103	1699468	1966873	2306624	1671715	1989022
Extra-UE27[21]	EXP		781270	843095	984116	1185169	1307303	1458219	1702746	1930284	1527713	1785453
	BAL		-132040	-41529	-73557	-92696	-157800	-241250	-264127	-376340	-144003	-203568
EU25	IMP		2416159	2483220	2993191	3611363	3958708	4561585	5320336	5966390	4492035	5072708
UE25	EXP		2373550	2555975	3048092	3630574	3918499	4442961	5173916	5735817	4442921	4985674
	BAL		-42609	72754	54902	19211	-40209	-118624	-146420	-230574	-49114	-87034

Total imports and exports by regions and countries or areas (Table A)

Imports CIF, exports FOB and balance: million U.S. dollars *[cont.]*

Importations et exportations totales par régions et pays ou zones (Tableau A)

Importations CIF, exportations FOB et balance : en millions de dollars E.-U. *[suite]*

Country or Area - Pays ou Zone	IMP EXP BAL	G/S	2000	2002	2003	2004	2005	2006	2007	2008	2009	2010
Extra-EU25[21]	IMP		916360	889542	1063891	1283846	1456866	1702321	1967370	...	...	...
Extra-UE25[21]	EXP		788642	854112	999614	1205511	1330464	1489696	1742459	...	...	...
	BAL		-127718	-35430	-64277	-78335	-126402	-212625	-224911	...	...	...
Memorandum Items												
World excluding intra-EU27 trade	IMP		**5007664**	**4901616**	**5639105**	**6911036**	**8028775**	**9222142**	**10579457**	**12444330**	**9573492**	**11914143**
Monde excl. le intra-UE27 com.	EXP		**4751575**	**4669486**	**5363416**	**6594869**	**7701842**	**8943684**	**10291816**	**12092152**	**9395257**	**11790296**
	BAL		**-256089**	**-232130**	**-275690**	**-316167**	**-326934**	**-278458**	**-287641**	**-352178**	**-178235**	**-123847**
World excluding intra-EU27 trade	IMP		**77**	**75**	**74**	**74**	**76**	**76**	**75**	**77**	**77**	**79**
Monde excl. le intra-UE27	EXP		**75**	**73**	**72**	**73**	**74**	**75**	**74**	**76**	**76**	**78**

Total imports and exports by regions and countries or areas (Table A)

Imports CIF, exports FOB and balance: million U.S. dollars *[cont.]*

Importations et exportations totales par régions et pays ou zones (Tableau A)

Importations CIF, exportations FOB, et balance: en millions de dollars E.-U. *[suite]*

General note:

Table A is based on data as available at the end of October 2011. An earlier version of this table has been published in Volume I of the 2010 ITSY which has been produced earlier this year. The totals of imports and exports presented in world trade table A and D are not necessarily identical as table A is mainly based on data of the IMF's International Financial Statistics (IFS) which is a different data collection system with different aims, procedures, timetable and sources for update and maintenance than UN Comtrade on which table D is based (see the introduction for details). Nevertheless, discrepancies between both tables are in general minor and usually do not affect the overall information provided. A systematic comparison of the figures from both sources (which includes the description of known and relevant conceptual differences) is available at http://unstats.un.org/unsd/trade/imts/annual%20totals.htm. Overall, the discrepancies in the world total or world aggregate of exports in table A and table D is less than 0.5 percent for all years shown, which is minor, given the differences between the two sources.
Column "G/S" indicates the trade system: G = General Trade System; S = Special Trade System. For further information on sources and presentation of table A as well as for a brief table description please see the introduction, paragraphs 6 - 20 and paragraph 21.

1 In June 2011, the estimates for exports (and also imports) of some major oil exporting countries of the Western Asia and the Sub-Saharan Africa region were revised upwards significantly.

2 This classification is intended for statistical convenience and does not, necessarily, express a judgement about the stage reached by a particular country in the development process.

3 Developed Economies of America, Europe, and the Asia-Pacific region.

4 Imports FOB.

5 Including the trade of the U.S. Virgin Islands and Puerto Rico but excluding shipments of merchandise between the United States and its other possessions (Guam and American Samoa). Data include imports and exports of non-monetary gold.

6 Beginning 2006, data for Serbia and Montenegro is reported separately.

7 Prior to 2008, special trade.

8 Imports exclude petroleum imported without stated value. Exports cover domestic exports.

9 Exports include gold.

10 Trade statistics exclude certain oil and chemical products.

11 Export and import values exclude trade in the processing zone.

12 Trade data include maquiladoras and exclude goods from customs-bonded warehouses. Total exports include revaluation and exports of silver.

13 Exports include petroleum products.

Remarque générale

Tableau A est basé sur les données telles que disponible fin octobre 2011. Une version antérieure de ce tableau est publiée dans le volume I de l'annuaire 2010 ITSY qui a été produit plus tôt cette année. Les importations et exportations totales présentées dans les tableaux A et D ne sont pas nécessairement identiques du fait que le tableau A est basé principalement sur les données des Statistiques Financières Internationales (IFS) du FMI qui est un différent système de collecte des données avec des objectifs, des procédures, un calendrier et des sources de mise à jour et de maintenance différents de ceux de UN Comtrade sur lequel le tableau D est basé (voir l'introduction pour les détails). Toutefois, les écarts entre les deux tableaux sont en général mineurs et n'affectent pas substantiellement l'information fournie. Une comparaison systématique des données de ces deux sources (incluant une description des différences conceptuelles pertinentes connues) est disponible à http://unstats.un.org/unsd/trade/imts/annual%20totals.htm. En général, la différence entre les totaux des exportations mondiales présentés dans les tableaux A et D est inférieure à 0.5 pour cent pour chacune des années publiées, ce qui est mineur étant donné les différences entre les deux sources.
La colonne "G/S" indique le système commercial : G=Système du Commerce Général ; S= Système du Commerce Spécial. Pour plus d'information sur les sources et la présentation du tableau A ainsi qu'une brève description, veuillez vous référer aux paragraphes 6-20 et 21 de l'introduction.

1 En juin 2011, les estimations des données d'exportations (et d'importations) pour certains pays de l'Asie Occidentale et de l'Afrique Sub-saharienne, exportateurs majeurs du pétrole, ont étés significativement révisées à la hausse.

2 Cette classification est utilisée pour plus de commodité dans la présentation des statistiques et n'implique pas nécessairement un jugement quant au stade de développement auquel est parvenu un pays donné.

3 Économies développées de l'Amérique, de l'Europe, et de la région Asie-Pacifique.

4 Importations FOB.

5 Y compris le commerce des Iles Vierges américaines et de Porto Rico mais non compris les échanges de marchandise, entre les Etats-Unis et leurs autres possessions (Guam et Samoa américaines). Les données comprennent les importations et exportations d'or non-monétaire.

6 Depuis début 2006, les données relatives à la Serbie et au Monténégro sont déclarées séparément.

7 Avant 2008, commerce special.

8 Non compris le pétrole brute dont la valeur des importations ne sont pas stipulée. Les exportations sont les exportations d'intérieur.

9 Les exportations comprennent l'or.

10 Les statistiques commerciales font exclusion de certains produits pétroliers et chimiques.

11 Les valeurs à l'exportation et à l'importation excluent le commerce de la zone de transformation.

12 Les statistiques du commerce extérieur comprennent maquiladoras et ne comprennent pas les marchandises provenant des entrepôts en douane. Les exportations comprennent la réévaluation et les données sur les exportations d'argent.

13 Exportations comprennent produits pétroliers.

Total imports and exports by regions and countries or areas (Table A)

Imports CIF, exports FOB and balance: million U.S. dollars *[cont.]*

Importations et exportations totales par régions et pays ou zones (Tableau A)

Importations CIF, exportations FOB, et balance: en millions de dollars E.-U. *[suite]*

14 Excluding military goods, fissionable materials, bunkers, ships, and aircraft.

15 Year ending 20 March of the year stated.

16 Data include oil and gas.The value of oil exports and total exports are rough estimates based on information published in various petroleum industry journals.

17 Imports and exports net of returned goods. The figures also exclude Judea and Samaria and the Gaza area.

18 Year ending 30 September of the years stated.

19 Data refer to total exports less petroleum exports of Asia Middle East countries where petroleum, in this case, is the sum of SITC groups 333, 334 and 335.

20 The figures for the grouping OPEC always reflect the membership of OPEC of the latest year published.

21 Excluding intra-EU trade.

14 À l'exclusion des marchandises militaires, des matières fissibles, des soutes, des bateaux, et de l'avion.

15 Année finissant le 20 mars de l'année indiquée.

16 Les données comprennent le pétrole et le gaz. La valeur des exportations de pétrole et des exportations totales sont des évaluations grossières basées sur l'information publiée à divers journaux d'industrie de pétrole.

17 Importations et exportations nets, ne comprennant pas les marchandises retournées. Sont également exclues les données de la Judée et de Samaria et ainsi que la zone de Gaza.

18 Année finissant le 30 septembre de l'année indiquée.

19 Les données se rapportent aux exportations totales moins les exportations pétrolières de Moyen-Orient d'Asie. Dans ce cas, le pétrole est la somme des groupes CTCI 333, 334 et 335.

20 Les données pour le groupe OPEP reflètent toujours sa composition telle que lors la dernière année publiée.

21 Non compris le commerce d'intra-UE.

Total imports and exports by countries or areas (Table B)

Imports CIF, exports FOB and balance: million of national currency

Importations et exportations totales par pays ou zone (Tableau B)

Importations CIF, exportations FOB et balance : en millions de monnaie nationale

Country or Area - Pays ou Zone	IMP EXP BAL	G/ S	2000	2002	2003	2004	2005	2006	2007	2008	2009	2010
Albania	IMP	G	157218	210436	225982	236073	262080	299134	376194	439894	431107	478708
Albanie	EXP	G	37547	46193	54485	62101	65766	78122	97171	112572	103244	161505
leks	BAL		-119671	-164243	-171497	-173972	-196314	-221012	-279023	-327322	-327863	-317203
Algeria	IMP	S	690208	953737	958181	1309270	1491690	1525940	1903390	2549100	2857890	2991940
Algérie	EXP	S	1658050	1497940	1792700	2255790	3370810	3837340	4128640	5108650	3286510	4297730
dinars	BAL		967842	544203	834519	946520	1879120	2311400	2225250	2559550	428620	1305790
Andorra	IMP	S	1111	1269	1336	1411	1442	1417	1396	1314	1138	1143
Andorre	EXP	S	49	67	79	98	114	120	93	65	46	41
euros	BAL		-1062	-1202	-1257	-1313	-1328	-1297	-1304	-1248	-1093	-1102
Anguilla[1]	IMP	S	269	199	217	285	360	386	669	734	456	425
Anguilla[1]	EXP	S	12	12	11	16	20	36	25	31	62	34
EC dollars	BAL		-257	-187	-206	-269	-340	-350	-645	-703	-394	-391
Australia	IMP	G	123461	133424	136577	148744	164137	184750	196756	236528	208834	219177
Australie	EXP	G	110464	119483	109811	117577	138716	163551	168067	222364	196091	230820
dollars	BAL		-12997	-13941	-26766	-31167	-25421	-21199	-28689	-14164	-12743	11643
Austria	IMP	S	74935	77104	80993	91094	96499	104201	114255	119568	97573	113452
Autriche	EXP	S	69692	77400	78903	89848	94705	103742	114680	117525	93739	109193
euros	BAL		-5243	296	-2091	-1247	-1794	-459	425	-2043	-3834	-4259
Bahamas[2]	IMP	G	2074	1728	1762	1905	2230	2401	2449	2354	2699	2863
Bahamas[2]	EXP	G	576	446	425	477	562	674	485	560	585	620
dollars	BAL		-1498	-1282	-1337	-1428	-1668	-1726	-1965	-1794	-2114	-2243
Bahrain	IMP	G	1742	1885	2127	2777	3532	3954	4319	4061	2745	3685
Bahreïn	EXP	G	2329	2179	2494	2842	3851	4587	5126	6511	4464	5790
dinars	BAL		587	294	366	65	319	634	807	2450	1720	2106
Bangladesh	IMP	G	436450	458119	553235	750513	828667	1032510	1188832	1541410	1424360	1817430
Bangladesh	EXP	G	249860	264295	306090	393862	465466	627999	704728	807824	859045	989345
taka	BAL		-186590	-193824	-247145	-356651	-363201	-404511	-484104	-733586	-565315	-828085
Barbados	IMP	G	2312	2142	2391	2826	3209	3172	3419	3757	2941	3124
Barbade	EXP	G	545	483	500	557	719	770	837	891	737	858
dollars	BAL		-1767	-1659	-1891	-2269	-2490	-2402	-2582	-2866	-2204	-2266
Belgium	IMP	S	192180	209730	207690	230330	257000	280060	300300	317030	253340	294520
Belgique	EXP	S	203940	228570	225950	247470	269740	292090	314450	320820	265350	309520
euros	BAL		11760	18840	18260	17140	12740	12030	14150	3790	12010	15000
Belize	IMP	G	1049	1049	1104	1028	1186	1352	1369	1674	1336	1399
Belize	EXP	G	436	338	410	426	416	532	508	541	499	...
dollars	BAL		-613	-711	-694	-602	-770	-819	-861	-1133	-837	...
Benin[3]	IMP	S	400636	505167	518312	472168	536963	642109	976266	1025190	996313	1163900
Bénin[3]	EXP	S	279400	312251	314429	300366	305000	384847	501725	574200	519405	619096
CFA francs	BAL		-121236	-192916	-203883	-171802	-231963	-257262	-474541	-450990	-476908	-544804
Bhutan	IMP	G	7874	9554	11599	18625	17036	19012	21745	23635	25626	34752
Bhoutan	EXP	G	4629	5479	6190	8293	11387	18772	27891	22684	24002	24692
ngultrum	BAL		-3245	-4075	-5408	-10332	-5649	-240	6145	-951	-1625	-10060
Bosnia and Herzegovina	IMP	S	6583	8368	8365	9423	11181	11389	13898	16287	12324	13611
Bosnie-Herzégovine	EXP	S	2265	2099	2428	3013	3783	5164	5937	6714	5510	7097
marka	BAL		-4318	-6269	-5937	-6410	-7398	-6225	-7961	-9573	-6815	-6514
Botswana	IMP	G	10617	11675	12117	15165	16154	18011	24965	35575	33830	38430
Botswana	EXP	G	13647	15345	13909	16487	22615	26434	31765	33799	24726	31884
pula	BAL		3031	3670	1792	1322	6461	8424	6800	-1777	-9104	-6546

Total imports and exports by countries or areas (Table B)

Imports CIF, exports FOB and balance: million of national currency *[cont.]*

Importations et exportations totales par pays ou zone (Tableau B)

Importations CIF, exportations FOB et balance : en millions de monnaie nationale *[suite]*

Country or Area - Pays ou Zone	IMP EXP BAL	G/ S	2000	2002	2003	2004	2005	2006	2007	2008	2009	2010
Brunei Darussalam	IMP	S	1908	2786	2312	2404	2410	2663	3166	3647	3570	4582
Brunéi Darussalam	EXP	S	6734	6629	7702	8547	10397	12133	11556	14593	10477	12477
dollars	BAL		4826	3843	5390	6144	7987	9470	8390	10945	6908	7896
Bulgaria	IMP	S	13857	16451	18797	22726	28688	36142	42757	49079	33006	37477
Bulgarie	EXP	S	10247	11858	13042	15617	18515	23493	26427	29736	22882	30488
leva	BAL		-3610	-4593	-5755	-7109	-10173	-12649	-16330	-19343	-10124	-6988
Burkina Faso[3]	IMP	G	435018	515074	537610	670922	664610	689692	804264	903555	883121	1067480
Burkina Faso[3]	EXP	G	148803	171976	186300	253200	246855	307459	298583	310400	420246	594332
CFA francs	BAL		-286215	-343098	-351310	-417722	-417755	-382233	-505681	-593155	-462875	-473148
Burundi	IMP	S	106059	121050	169742	194054	286960	442512	346099	477345	494828	626742
Burundi	EXP	S	35223	28867	40698	51706	61489	60536	67364	64301	76330	123698
francs	BAL		-70836	-92183	-129044	-142348	-225472	-381976	-278735	-413044	-418498	-503044
Cameroon[3]	IMP	S	1060100	1300580	1257370	1271210	1442630	1647350	2012920	2418150	2030400	2402090
Cameroun[3]	EXP	S	1305100	1255970	1326620	1308440	1509220	1868450	1727470	1925560	1591270	1931580
CFA francs	BAL		245000	-44610	69250	37230	66590	221100	-285450	-492590	-439130	-470510
Canada[4]	IMP	G	354728	348198	334331	354859	391658	395550	406360	432271	364268	402069
Canada[4]	EXP	G	410994	396020	381655	395897	434874	441764	446418	478983	357373	397358
dollars	BAL		56266	47822	47324	41038	43216	46214	40058	46712	-6895	-4711
Cape Verde	IMP	G	27517	32338	34294	38304	38856	47654	60416	62128	56296	61810
Cap-Vert	EXP	G	1271	1235	1245	1340	1562	1815	1548	2408	2796	3708
escudos	BAL		-26245	-31103	-33049	-36964	-37294	-45839	-58867	-59720	-53499	-58102
Cayman Islands	IMP	G	575	496	546	719	976	869	860	879	736	688
Îles Caïmanes	EXP	G	3	2	20	20	49	22	22	14	16	11
dollars	BAL		-572	-494	-527	-699	-927	-847	-838	-866	-720	-677
Cent. Afr. Rep.[3]	IMP	S	83301	83639	68582	79900	92307	105900	119817	134342	141656	168394
Rép. centrafricaine[3]	EXP	S	114628	102457	74394	70700	67516	82400	86268	67171	56662	69339
CFA francs	BAL		31327	18818	5812	-9200	-24791	-23500	-33549	-67171	-84994	-99055
Chad[3]	IMP	S	342260	1147240	459148	503455	501095	705902	862680	850830	1086030	1238190
Tchad[3]	EXP	S	166725	128943	349301	1157470	1625100	1752700	1757100	1939000	1251290	1683940
CFA francs	BAL		-175535	-1018297	-109847	654015	1124005	1046798	894420	1088170	165260	445750
Comoros	IMP	S	22961	27705	30513	33917	39041	45189	49716	58775	60204	70577
Comores	EXP	S	7476	9932	11639	7382	4757	3893	4965	3023	5666	6686
francs	BAL		-15485	-17773	-18875	-26535	-34284	-41296	-44751	-55752	-54538	-63891
Congo	IMP	S	341001	484581	497467	527257	708228	1084080	1248920	1406780	1410420	1479390
Congo	EXP	S	1772110	1589130	1555870	1813600	2502840	3177900	2700670	3716780	2880340	4061270
CFA francs	BAL		1431109	1104549	1058403	1286343	1794612	2093820	1451750	2310000	1469920	2581880
Cote d'Ivoire[3]	IMP	S	1770500	1811480	1905760	2490720	3093580	3043440	3203000	3530350	3286390	3878020
Côte d'Ivoire[3]	EXP	S	2573000	3676610	3363990	3655200	4060100	4432540	4154700	4652700	4959500	5185550
CFA francs	BAL		802500	1865130	1458230	1164480	966520	1389100	951700	1122350	1673110	1307530
Cuba	IMP	S	3363	4151	4613	5562	7528	9420	10083	13194	...	...
Cuba	EXP	S	1219	1504	1672	2188	1999	2759	3701	3407	...	...
pesos	BAL		-2144	-2647	-2941	-3374	-5529	-6661	-6381	-9787	...	...
Cyprus[5]	IMP	G	2402	2353	2212	2646	2920	3185	3688	7367	5654	6459
Chypre[5]	EXP	G	590	470	430	506	606	530	535	1190	963	1142
euros	BAL		-1812	-1883	-1782	-2140	-2314	-2655	-3154	-6176	-4691	-5318
Czech Republic	IMP	S	1309570	1392000	1512760	1836550	1829960	2104810	2391320	2406490	1989040	2411560
République tchèque	EXP	S	1121100	1254390	1370930	1722660	1868590	2144570	2479230	2473740	2138620	2532800
koruny	BAL		-188470	-137610	-141830	-113890	38630	39760	87910	67250	149580	121240

Total imports and exports by countries or areas (Table B)

Imports CIF, exports FOB and balance: million of national currency *[cont.]*

Importations et exportations totales par pays ou zone (Tableau B)

Importations CIF, exportations FOB et balance : en millions de monnaie nationale *[suite]*

Country or Area - Pays ou Zone	IMP EXP BAL	G/ S	2000	2002	2003	2004	2005	2006	2007	2008	2009	2010
Denmark	IMP	S	358871	384710	369701	400124	445797	505379	528719	553294	437999	476366
Danemark	EXP	S	408239	442754	429272	452400	501552	544628	553587	587602	495577	544022
kroner	BAL		49368	58044	59571	52276	55755	39249	24868	34308	57578	67656
Djibouti	IMP	G	...	35022	42339	46449	49285	59664	84103	101940	80101	74643
Djibouti	EXP	G	...	6331	6620	6750	7020	9805	10320	12219	13750	17772
francs	BAL		...	-28691	-35719	-39699	-42265	-49859	-73783	-89722	-66351	-56871
Dominica	IMP	S	401	313	345	392	446	451	528	667	630	604
Dominique	EXP	S	145	125	112	112	112	115	102	108	98	93
EC dollars	BAL		-256	-188	-234	-280	-335	-336	-426	-559	-533	-511
Equatorial Guinea[3]	IMP	G	321101	353373	527730	576887	690983	1056240	1135860	1750920	2455370	2823080
Guinée équatoriale[3]	EXP	G	781038	1475520	1627940	2429500	3726030	4291360	4893310	7120100	4296900	4952770
CFA francs	BAL		459937	1122147	1100210	1852613	3035047	3235120	3757450	5369180	1841530	2129690
Estonia	IMP	S	72230	79465	89426	104882	128766	167598	178991	170488	113780	144994
Estonie	EXP	S	53900	56991	62628	74614	96747	120775	124860	132483	101412	136915
krooni	BAL		-18330	-22474	-26798	-30268	-32019	-46823	-54131	-38005	-12368	-8079
Ethiopia	IMP	G	10369	13653	23098	24817	35487	45297	52080	79453	90310	...
Ethiopie	EXP	G	3991	4115	4269	5858	7826	9072	11451	15377	19058	...
birr	BAL		-6378	-9538	-18830	-18959	-27661	-36224	-40629	-64076	-71252	...
Extra-EU25[6]	IMP		995980	942207	940757	1032359	1173500	1355091	1433825	...	...	...
Extra-UE25[6]	EXP		857782	903549	882887	969293	1071375	1185070	1269384	...	...	...
euros	BAL		-138198	-38658	-57870	-63066	-102125	-170021	-164442	...	...	...
Extra-EU27[6]	IMP		992695	936967	935265	1027522	1179569	1352787	1433402	1564946	1199288	1501568
Extra-UE27[6]	EXP		849740	891899	869237	952955	1052720	1160101	1240541	1309818	1094229	1348629
euros	BAL		-142956	-45068	-66028	-74567	-126849	-192686	-192861	-255128	-105059	-152938
Fiji	IMP	G	1822	1970	2285	2502	2723	3120	2890	3571	2808	...
Fidji	EXP	G	1152	1126	1266	1201	1185	1202	1215	1470	1231	1381
dollars	BAL		-671	-844	-1018	-1301	-1537	-1918	-1675	-2101	-1577	...
Finland	IMP	G	36837	35611	36775	40729	47028	55253	59615	62402	43622	51835
Finlande	EXP	G	49485	47245	46378	48915	52453	61489	65688	65581	45055	52834
euros	BAL		12647	11634	9604	8186	5425	6236	6073	3179	1433	999
France	IMP	S	337489	330485	327214	355779	394287	435307	460263	485529	400763	455457
France	EXP	S	324256	326881	320403	336383	356543	390910	401458	412901	341065	387865
euros	BAL		-13233	-3604	-6811	-19396	-37744	-44397	-58805	-72628	-59698	-67592
Gabon[3]	IMP	S	708000	791120	700830	711790	775920	901909	1033780	1160260	1038810	1238190
Gabon[3]	EXP	S	1852560	1679250	1779690	1969250	2671630	2849750	3023690	4256840	2597020	4160330
CFA francs	BAL		1144560	888130	1078860	1257460	1895710	1947841	1989910	3096580	1558210	2922140
Gambia	IMP	G	2391	3199	4273	6873	7418	7277	7984	7151	8098	8404
Gambie	EXP	G	192	239	218	300	229	322	311	303	400	420
dalasis	BAL		-2199	-2960	-4054	-6573	-7189	-6955	-7672	-6847	-7699	-7983
Germany	IMP	S	538311	518532	534534	575448	628087	733990	769887	805842	664615	806163
Allemagne	EXP	S	597440	651320	664453	731544	786265	893041	965236	984139	803312	959499
euros	BAL		59129	132788	129919	156096	158178	159051	195349	178297	138697	153336
Ghana[7]	IMP	G	1617	2155	2782	3664	4846	6189	7539	10863	11336	15799
Ghana[7]	EXP	G	732	...	...	...	2540	3415	4041	5947	...	...
cedis	BAL		-885	...	...	...	-2307	-2774	-3498	-4916	...	...
Gibraltar	IMP		318	256	286	292	303	366	426	450	479	483
Gibraltar	EXP		84	99	90	108	110	131	152	154	170	167
pounds	BAL		-234	-158	-196	-184	-193	-236	-274	-296	-310	-315

Total imports and exports by countries or areas (Table B)

Imports CIF, exports FOB and balance: million of national currency *[cont.]*

Importations et exportations totales par pays ou zone (Tableau B)

Importations CIF, exportations FOB et balance : en millions de monnaie nationale *[suite]*

Country or Area - Pays ou Zone	IMP EXP BAL	G/S	2000	2002	2003	2004	2005	2006	2007	2008	2009	2010
Grenada[1]	IMP	S	664	545	687	682	902	893	986	1019	790	855
Grenade[1]	EXP	S	211	105	113	86	75	69	90	82	79	65
EC dollars	BAL		-453	-440	-574	-595	-827	-825	-896	-937	-712	-790
Guinea-Bissau[3]	IMP	G	42400	40400	37800	50700	63300	57518	52719	72270	...	...
Guinée-Bissau[3]	EXP	G	44300	37637	37778	40150	47200	38694	51299	57400	56662	59433
CFA francs	BAL		1900	-2763	-22	-10550	-16100	-18824	-1421	-14870	...	...
Guyana	IMP	S	106113	109865	111693	129268	157564	178065	214469	267225	236700	285120
Guyana	EXP	S	91521	94479	99592	117706	110536	117710	137419	161819	155511	178592
dollars	BAL		-14593	-15386	-12101	-11562	-47028	-60355	-77050	-105406	-81189	-106528
Haiti	IMP	G	21936	33061	50324	50088	58802	75779	61983	90553	87498	125207
Haïti	EXP	G	6725	8203	14682	15007	19017	19226	19232	18626	23741	23045
gourdes	BAL		-15211	-24858	-35642	-35081	-39785	-56553	-42750	-71927	-63756	-102162
Hungary	IMP	S	9064020	9704100	10662800	12063700	13145500	16224700	17280840	18102100	15634900	18205700
Hongrie	EXP	S	7942780	8873970	9528610	11093900	12425500	15591100	17095740	18301700	16946100	19688600
forint	BAL		-1121240	-830130	-1134190	-969800	-720000	-633600	-185100	199600	1311200	1482900
Iceland	IMP	G	203847	207632	213590	249063	287257	357965	404979	468598	446128	477222
Islande	EXP	G	148516	204078	182960	202824	185286	227785	287648	452428	500855	561032
kronur	BAL		-55331	-3554	-30630	-46239	-101971	-130180	-117332	-16170	54727	83810
India[8]	IMP	G	2316550	2746720	3374760	4521180	6300170	8091050	9435340	13939400	12398400	15045300
Inde[8]	EXP	G	1906530	2448390	2743190	3472670	4393450	5521660	6190170	8412350	7967180	10180700
rupees	BAL		-410020	-298330	-631570	-1048510	-1906720	-2569390	-3245170	-5527050	-4431220	-4864600
Ireland	IMP	G	55909	54805	47107	49347	55586	66623	62443	56008	45061	45738
Irlande	EXP	G	83889	92893	81639	83807	88091	83481	89512	85736	84239	89203
euros	BAL		27980	38088	34532	34460	32505	16858	27069	29729	39178	43465
Italy	IMP	S	258507	261226	262997	285633	309292	351034	371936	382049	297608	367120
Italie	EXP	S	260414	269064	264615	284412	299923	331206	364528	369015	291732	337810
euros	BAL		1907	7838	1618	-1221	-9369	-19828	-7408	-13034	-5876	-29310
Jamaica	IMP	G	141987	171201	209852	230964	277869	349303	442859	559908	426608	452907
Jamaïque	EXP	G	55621	53897	67931	85017	93441	123220	142858	183976	115838	116061
dollars	BAL		-86366	-117304	-141921	-145947	-184428	-226083	-300001	-375932	-310770	-336846
Japan	IMP	G	40915000	42177000	44319300	49146800	56852400	67407600	72854000	78959000	51365900	60622700
Japon	EXP	G	51649000	52109000	54548500	61170200	65661500	75621200	83931400	81018100	54170600	67405300
yen	BAL		10734000	9932000	10229200	12023400	8809100	8213600	11077400	2059100	2804700	6782600
Jordan	IMP	G	3259	3599	4072	5763	7449	8116	9579	11897	10319	10710
Jordanie	EXP	G	1347	1964	2185	2781	3050	3669	4059	5527	4637	4986
dinars	BAL		-1913	-1635	-1887	-2982	-4399	-4447	-5520	-6370	-5682	-5724
Kenya	IMP	G	236613	255569	282616	360812	464495	526870	605121	766743	788097	957949
Kenya	EXP	G	132183	166635	183121	212602	248929	247900	274596	342954	344949	408103
shillings	BAL		-104430	-88934	-99495	-148210	-215566	-278970	-330525	-423789	-443148	-549846
Kuwait	IMP	S	2195	2736	3274	3722	4536	5003	6072	6678	5854	6305
Koweït	EXP	S	5963	4671	6162	8428	13195	16255	17818	23511	14947	18902
dinars	BAL		3767	1935	2888	4706	8659	11251	11746	16833	9093	12596
Latvia	IMP	S	1934	2497	2989	3805	4867	6378	7780	7528	4710	5870
Lettonie	EXP	S	1131	1409	1651	2150	2888	3295	4040	4429	3602	4677
lati	BAL		-803	-1089	-1339	-1655	-1979	-3083	-3740	-3099	-1108	-1193
Lesotho	IMP	G	5614	8591	8480	9302	8967	10157	12245	16564	16524	16107
Lesotho	EXP	G	1527	3773	3598	4573	4137	4697	5421	7289	6066	5857
maloti	BAL		-4088	-4818	-4883	-4729	-4830	-5460	-6824	-9274	-10458	-10250

Total imports and exports by countries or areas (Table B)

Imports CIF, exports FOB and balance: million of national currency *[cont.]*

Importations et exportations totales par pays ou zone (Tableau B)

Importations CIF, exportations FOB et balance : en millions de monnaie nationale *[suite]*

Country or Area - Pays ou Zone	IMP EXP BAL	G/ S	2000	2002	2003	2004	2005	2006	2007	2008	2009	2010
Libya	IMP	G	1911	5586	5598	8255	7954	7935	8501	11195	12535	13301
Libye	EXP	G	5222	12457	18938	26634	41028	52885	59306	75959	46583	58336
dinars	BAL		3310	6871	13339	18379	33075	44950	50805	64764	34048	45034
Lithuania	IMP	G	20877	27479	29438	34384	43152	53275	61504	73006	45311	60953
Lituanie	EXP	G	14193	19117	21263	25819	32767	38888	43192	55511	40732	54039
litai	BAL		-6684	-8362	-8175	-8564	-10385	-14386	-18311	-17495	-4579	-6914
Luxembourg	IMP	S	11647	12276	12109	13533	14124	15475	16174	17290	13371	15568
Luxembourg	EXP	S	8619	9005	8834	9794	10201	11287	11697	11890	9163	10684
euros	BAL		-3028	-3271	-3275	-3739	-3923	-4188	-4477	-5400	-4208	-4884
Madagascar	IMP	S	1349440	856321	1615290	3139690	3417820	3863970	4937980	6458850	6260890	5224870
Madagascar	EXP	S	1115280	664066	1060010	1853180	1711870	2110720	2319270	2237530	2057900	2257150
ariary	BAL		-234160	-192255	-555280	-1286510	-1705950	-1753250	-2618710	-4221320	-4202990	-2967720
Malawi	IMP	G	32283	53302	76568	101549	137982	164463	193141	238898	295947	...
Malawi	EXP	G	23625	31221	51178	52621	60251	73800	99259	120850	152460	170050
kwacha	BAL		-8658	-22080	-25391	-48928	-77731	-90663	-93882	-118048	-143487	...
Malaysia	IMP	G	311459	303502	311402	400133	433196	480506	504094	546593	434452	529195
Malaisie	EXP	G	373270	354407	377602	477829	533372	588588	604514	697274	553474	639427
ringgit	BAL		61811	50905	66200	77696	100176	108082	100420	150681	119022	110232
Mali[3]	IMP	S	573900	646805	738706	720580	814199	951536	1047120	1495190	1248520	1411540
Mali[3]	EXP	S	392300	609168	539354	515835	580700	810480	745860	939101	958538	1114370
CFA francs	BAL		-181600	-37637	-199352	-204745	-233499	-141056	-301260	-556089	-289982	-297170
Malta[9]	IMP	G	1492	1228	1280	1315	1318	1387	1400	3419	2734	3448
Malte[9]	EXP	G	1072	961	929	905	822	920	928	2032	1572	2136
euros	BAL		-420	-266	-351	-410	-496	-467	-472	-1388	-1162	-1312
Mauritania	IMP	S	84529	96872	101840	346266	356730	292386	367023	395103	350657	474100
Mauritanie	EXP	S	81881	86950	84370	111935	147717	340634	363641	392204	346826	473827
ouguiyas	BAL		-2647	-9921	-17471	-234331	-209013	48248	-3382	-2899	-3831	-273
Mauritius	IMP	G	54928	64608	65942	76387	93282	115502	121037	132165	118303	135394
Maurice	EXP	G	40882	53893	53022	54905	63219	74037	69708	67970	61784	68866
rupees	BAL		-14046	-10715	-12920	-21482	-30063	-41465	-51329	-64195	-56519	-66528
Montenegro[10]	IMP	S	.	.	.	.	.	1483	2318	2471	1652	1654
Monténégro[10]	EXP	S	.	.	.	.	.	627	601	445	288	330
euros	BAL		.	.	.	.	.	-855	-1717	-2026	-1364	-1324
Morocco	IMP	S	122527	130409	136070	157921	184380	210554	261287	326042	263982	299124
Maroc	EXP	S	76242	86389	83887	87897	99264	111979	125517	155740	113020	147850
dirhams	BAL		-46286	-44020	-52183	-70025	-85116	-98575	-135770	-170302	-150962	-151274
Myanmar	IMP	G	15426	15373	12721	12637	11104	14773	18210	23244	24299	26910
Myanmar	EXP	G	10601	19980	15123	13687	21887	26487	35159	37664	37102	48817
kyats	BAL		-4826	4607	2402	1050	10783	11714	16948	14420	12802	21907
Namibia	IMP	G	10755	15495	14978	15475	16391	19530	24800	35854	42199	39242
Namibie	EXP	G	9164	11296	9547	11802	13164	17922	20584	25745	28373	29944
dollars	BAL		-1591	-4199	-5431	-3673	-3227	-1608	-4216	-10109	-13826	-9298
Nepal	IMP	G	108505	110507	133552	142747	162951	181293	207316	250448	339990	402351
Népal	EXP	G	49823	44234	50406	56861	61608	60959	57675	65490	63788	69497
rupees	BAL		-58682	-66273	-83146	-85886	-101343	-120334	-149641	-184958	-276202	-332854
Netherlands	IMP	S	216056	205575	206867	228247	249845	285370	306821	335920	274019	332350
Pays-Bas	EXP	S	231854	232704	234166	255660	281300	318094	347316	367435	309472	371154
euros	BAL		15798	27129	27299	27413	31455	32724	40495	31515	35453	38804

Total imports and exports by countries or areas (Table B)

Imports CIF, exports FOB and balance: million of national currency *[cont.]*

Importations et exportations totales par pays ou zone (Tableau B)

Importations CIF, exportations FOB et balance : en millions de monnaie nationale *[suite]*

Country or Area - Pays ou Zone	IMP EXP BAL	G/S	2000	2002	2003	2004	2005	2006	2007	2008	2009	2010
New Zealand	IMP	G	30736	32337	31782	34915	37279	40716	41869	48514	40221	44024
Nouvelle-Zélande	EXP	G	29257	31034	28397	30712	30817	34634	36557	42900	39672	44764
dollars	BAL		-1479	-1303	-3385	-4203	-6462	-6082	-5312	-5614	-549	740
Niger[3]	IMP	S	281400	326190	361507	396214	497402	496223	550541	759672	897154	1089610
Niger[3]	EXP	S	201500	194460	204583	230860	257932	265600	317891	407503	420246	445749
CFA francs	BAL		-79900	-131730	-156924	-165354	-239470	-230623	-232650	-352169	-476908	-643861
Niue	IMP	G	4	4	4	12	...	6	9	11	...	...
Nioué	EXP	G	1	0	0	0	0	2	4	0	...	...
NZ dollars	BAL		-4	-4	-3	-12	...	-4	-5	-11	...	...
Norway	IMP	G	302852	276563	279240	323081	357657	411755	468918	504481	432378	466810
Norvège	EXP	G	529814	473265	476981	549672	668760	782943	795366	959002	756811	792575
kroner	BAL		226962	196702	197741	226591	311103	371188	326448	454521	324433	325765
Oman	IMP	G	1938	2309	2527	3409	3394	4197	6143	8815	6869	7603
Oman	EXP	G	4352	4296	4487	5130	7187	8300	9280	14503	10787	14073
rials Omani	BAL		2414	1986	1960	1721	3793	4103	3137	5689	3917	6470
Pakistan	IMP	G	582681	670575	752788	1045980	1509810	1797830	1979320	2949020	2587860	3218900
Pakistan	EXP	G	484476	591714	688882	779286	955464	1020480	1083390	1423450	1433550	1824380
rupees	BAL		-98205	-78861	-63906	-266694	-554346	-777350	-895930	-1525570	-1154310	-1394520
Panama[11]	IMP	S	3379	2982	3086	3594	4180	4831	6872	9050	7801	9145
Panama[11]	EXP	S	859	846	864	944	1018	1093	1164	1247	948	832
balboas	BAL		-2519	-2136	-2222	-2651	-3162	-3738	-5709	-7803	-6853	-8313
Papua New Guinea	IMP	G	3196	4826	4866	5414	5363	6997	8748	9611	...	...
Papouasie-Nouvelle-Guinée	EXP	G	5742	6392	7864	8224	10154	12734	13881	15426	12107	14140
kina	BAL		2546	1566	2998	2810	4792	5737	5134	5815	...	...
Philippines	IMP	G	1636810	1919160	2141230	2373190	2587380	2773800	2652970	2668510	2180040	2623800
Philippines	EXP	G	1773140	1884320	1965590	2224270	2196760	2432040	2317440	2171350	1825690	2318110
pesos	BAL		136330	-34840	-175640	-148920	-390620	-341760	-335530	-497160	-354350	-305690
Poland	IMP	S	213072	224816	265134	324663	326120	394030	446895	485833	463383	536221
Pologne	EXP	S	137909	167338	208944	272106	288682	343779	382199	399353	423241	481058
zlotys	BAL		-75163	-57478	-56190	-52557	-37438	-50251	-64696	-86480	-40142	-55163
Portugal	IMP	S	41425	40656	36146	39597	42939	52232	55627	64194	51368	57053
Portugal	EXP	S	25241	27090	27102	26586	25874	34137	36655	38950	31768	36762
euros	BAL		-16184	-13566	-9044	-13011	-17066	-18095	-18972	-25244	-19600	-20291
Qatar	IMP	S	11838	14749	17827	21857	36622	59842	85282	101556	90716	80080
Qatar	EXP	S	42203	39960	48711	68010	93774	123946	152951	205997	149240	223860
riyals	BAL		30365	25211	30884	46153	57152	64104	67669	104441	58524	143780
Rwanda	IMP	G	82586	117891	139253	163844	240070	302370	403210	621619	697270	816383
Rwanda	EXP	G	20521	30899	33872	56682	69516	81267	96685	146375	109491	148698
francs	BAL		-62065	-86992	-105381	-107162	-170554	-221103	-306525	-475244	-587779	-667685
Saint Kitts-Nevis[1]	IMP	S	529	545	539	493	568	674	735	877	816	616
Saint-Kitts-et-Nevis[1]	EXP	S	79	95	138	101	81	96	86	116	115	122
EC dollars	BAL		-450	-450	-401	-391	-487	-578	-649	-761	-701	-494
Saint Lucia[1]	IMP	S	959	834	1088	1180	1293	1598	1715	1775	1454	1568
Sainte-Lucie[1]	EXP	S	127	133	230	338	239	265	288	392	439	444
EC dollars	BAL		-832	-702	-858	-842	-1054	-1334	-1427	-1383	-1015	-1124
Saint Vincent-Grenadines[1]	IMP	S	399	482	541	609	649	727	882	1007	901	933
St.Vincent-Grenadines[1]	EXP	S	136	106	103	99	108	103	129	141	135	119
EC dollars	BAL		-263	-376	-438	-510	-542	-624	-754	-866	-766	-814

Total imports and exports by countries or areas (Table B)

Imports CIF, exports FOB and balance: million of national currency *[cont.]*

Importations et exportations totales par pays ou zone (Tableau B)

Importations CIF, exportations FOB et balance : en millions de monnaie nationale *[suite]*

Country or Area - Pays ou Zone	IMP EXP BAL	G/S	2000	2002	2003	2004	2005	2006	2007	2008	2009	2010
Samoa	IMP	S	349	430	382	432	508	608	594	659	550	690
Samoa	EXP	S	47	46	44	30	32	30	40	30	31	34
talas	BAL		-302	-384	-337	-402	-475	-578	-553	-630	-519	-657
Saudi Arabia	IMP	S	113240	121100	138430	167790	222790	261400	338090	431750	358290	364040
Arabie saoudite	EXP	S	290550	271700	349670	472490	677140	791340	874400	1175350	721110	941800
riyals	BAL		177310	150600	211240	304700	454350	529940	536310	743600	362820	577760
Senegal[3]	IMP	G	1081500	1415600	1389600	1505000	1686340	1795600	2036880	2534380	2141970	2202040
Sénégal[3]	EXP	G	655000	743400	730600	797182	832400	813600	790790	895210	895780	1020270
CFA francs	BAL		-426500	-672200	-659000	-707818	-853940	-982000	-1246090	-1639170	-1246190	-1181770
Serbia[10]	IMP	S	.	.	.	.	.	878227	1069410	1260290	1080965	1286900
Serbie[10]	EXP	S	.	.	.	.	.	428051	513222	603512	559851	763500
dinars	BAL		.	.	.	.	.	-450176	-556188	-656778	-521114	-523400
Seychelles	IMP	G	1955	2304	2227	2731	3712	4181	5757	9959	10979	11956
Seychelles	EXP	G	1106	1249	1479	1599	1868	2097	2413	4070	5381	4828
rupees	BAL		-849	-1055	-748	-1132	-1843	-2084	-3344	-5890	-5598	-7127
Sierra Leone	IMP	S	314639	554741	712375	773824	996003	1152180	1327420	1592540	1761570	...
Sierra Leone	EXP	S	26771	102157	216600	374373	457994	684311	732081	643014	780941	...
leones	BAL		-287868	-452584	-495775	-399451	-538009	-467869	-595339	-949526	-980629	...
Singapore	IMP	G	232176	208324	222811	276894	333191	378924	395980	450893	356299	423222
Singapour	EXP	G	237826	223901	251096	335615	382532	431559	450587	476762	391118	478841
dollars	BAL		5650	15577	28285	58721	49341	52635	54607	25869	34819	55619
Slovakia[12]	IMP	S	619789	785374	868982	981075	1124440	1397535	1525560	1573010	39220	51086
Slovaquie[12]	EXP	S	548527	652018	803238	889705	994571	1239359	1419850	1509110	39716	48791
euros	BAL		-71262	-133356	-65744	-91370	-129869	-158176	-105710	-63900	496	-2295
Solomon Islands	IMP	S	499	452	704	909	1393	1650	2197	2549	2175	2419
Iles Salomon	EXP	S	331	391	555	728	779	924	1259	1631	1316	1786
dollars	BAL		-168	-61	-149	-181	-614	-725	-938	-918	-859	-633
South Africa[4,13,14]	IMP	G	186382	272682	256833	304432	349181	461042	561678	777808	541038	585573
Afrique du Sud[4,13,14]	EXP	G	208476	311679	274505	296080	328760	396584	490643	692359	523013	596879
rands	BAL		22094	38997	17672	-8352	-20421	-64458	-71035	-85449	-18025	11306
Spain	IMP	S	166138	172789	184095	207126	231345	259559	278783	282251	208437	238082
Espagne	EXP	S	123100	130814	137815	146452	153576	169872	179918	188184	158254	185799
euros	BAL		-43038	-41975	-46280	-60674	-77769	-89687	-98865	-94067	-50183	-52283
Sri Lanka	IMP	G	485084	584491	643749	808364	888358	1066620	1251140	1510730	1154390	1526600
Sri Lanka	EXP	G	420114	449850	494648	583968	638275	716579	856806	881320	813911	937737
rupees	BAL		-64970	-134641	-149101	-224396	-250083	-350041	-394334	-629410	-340479	-588863
Suriname	IMP	G	324	738	1156	1632	2352	2453	3049	4176	3723	3597
Suriname	EXP	G	533	852	1354	1950	2156	3082	3534	4578	3823	5082
dollars	BAL		209	114	197	318	-196	629	485	402	100	1485
Swaziland	IMP	G	7261	10066	11490	12434	12083	13001	12999	...	13558	12446
Swaziland	EXP	G	6312	10846	12389	12590	11256	12121	13245	...	12287	11348
emalangeni	BAL		-949	780	899	156	-827	-880	247	...	-1271	-1098
Sweden	IMP	G	672400	656700	679300	738900	831100	931900	1034700	1097900	912900	1067100
Suède	EXP	G	804200	805800	825800	904500	971900	1084200	1139600	1194400	996700	1136000
kronor	BAL		131800	149100	146500	165600	140800	152300	104900	96500	83800	68900
Switzerland	IMP	S	128615	128207	128595	136987	149094	165410	183578	186883	160187	173685
Suisse	EXP	S	126549	135741	135472	146312	156977	177475	197533	206330	180534	193253
francs	BAL		-2066	7534	6877	9325	7883	12065	13955	19447	20347	19568

Total imports and exports by countries or areas (Table B)

Imports CIF, exports FOB and balance: million of national currency *[cont.]*

Importations et exportations totales par pays ou zone (Tableau B)

Importations CIF, exportations FOB et balance : en millions de monnaie nationale *[suite]*

Country or Area - Pays ou Zone	IMP EXP BAL	G/S	2000	2002	2003	2004	2005	2006	2007	2008	2009	2010
Syrian Arab Rep.	IMP	S	187530	235754	236768	389006	502369	531324	677787	839419	714216	...
République arabe syrienne	EXP	S	216190	301553	265038	346166	424300	505012	533979	707798	488330	...
pounds	BAL		28660	65799	28270	-42840	-78069	-26312	-143807	-131621	-225886	...
Thailand	IMP	S	2494140	2774840	3138780	3801170	4754640	4871630	4870190	5946310	4605170	5839390
Thaïlande	EXP	S	2773830	2923940	3325630	3874820	4439310	4946450	5302120	5851370	5197120	6176420
baht	BAL		279690	149100	186850	73650	-315330	74820	431930	-94940	591950	337030
Togo[3]	IMP	S	400131	411920	450430	464891	559229	567154	592909	675911	661061	742916
Togo[3]	EXP	S	258447	297614	347558	317499	348200	329600	335487	403025	377749	420985
CFA francs	BAL		-141684	-114306	-102872	-147392	-211029	-237554	-257422	-272886	-283312	-321931
Tonga	IMP	G	123	195	201	207	235	236	281	324	292	302
Tonga	EXP	G	16	32	38	30	20	20	18	18	16	16
pa'anga	BAL		-107	-163	-163	-177	-215	-216	-263	-306	-276	-286
Trinidad and Tobago	IMP	S	20840	22764	24501	30601	35869	40932	48491	60325	43993	40741
Trinité-et-Tobago	EXP	S	26925	24245	32594	41052	62628	89349	84772	117301	57721	71127
dollars	BAL		6086	1481	8093	10451	26759	48417	36281	56977	13728	30386
Tunisia	IMP	G	11738	13511	14039	15960	17102	20004	24437	30241	25878	31817
Tunisie	EXP	G	8005	9749	10343	12055	13608	15558	19410	23637	19469	23519
dinars	BAL		-3733	-3762	-3696	-3905	-3494	-4446	-5028	-6604	-6408	-8298
Tuvalu	IMP	G	9	21	12	16	17	17	18	...	...	...
Tuvalu	EXP	G	0	0	0	0	0	0	0	...	...	...
Aust. dollars	BAL		-9	-20	-11	-15	-17	-17	-18	...	...	...
Uganda	IMP	G	2486270	1892820	2700120	3124590	3657730	4683590	6020770	7786490	7678215	9310965
Ouganda	EXP	G	759273	864622	1105570	1374240	1810950	2175110	3445310	4651150	4712362	4702027
shillings	BAL		-1726997	-1028198	-1594550	-1750350	-1846780	-2508480	-2575460	-3135340	-2965853	-4608938
United Kingdom	IMP	G	221027	223433	232868	246625	265696	297135	310641	345202	310010	363106
Royaume-Uni	EXP	G	186171	184161	186175	186418	204402	232761	217112	252086	227645	265329
pounds	BAL		-34856	-39272	-46693	-60207	-61294	-64374	-93529	-93116	-82365	-97777
United Rep. of Tanzania	IMP	G	1219380	1604950	2210260	2732320	3011910	5344830	6621420	8470080	8309960	10877900
Rép.-Unie de Tanzanie	EXP	G	531058	873819	1174790	1448590	1676090	2075610	2510570	3201860	3124060	4988840
shillings	BAL		-688322	-731131	-1035470	-1283730	-1335820	-3269220	-4110850	-5268220	-5185900	-5889060
United States[15]	IMP	G	1259300	1200230	1303050	1525370	1735060	1918080	2020400	2169490	1605300	1968760
Etats-Unis[15]	EXP	G	781918	693103	724771	818520	907158	1038270	1162980	1301110	1056750	1277580
dollars	BAL		-477382	-507127	-578279	-706850	-827902	-879810	-857420	-868380	-548550	-691180
Vanuatu	IMP	G	11975	12484	12830	14306	16295	24039	23503	31776	31393	31010
Vanuatu	EXP	G	3579	2784	3299	4167	4124	5397	5106	5747	6140	5814
vatu	BAL		-8396	-9700	-9531	-10139	-12171	-18643	-18398	-26028	-25253	-25196
Yemen	IMP	S	375833	513001	674173	736532	1029880	1196810	1693230	2106740	1863120	2130020
Yémen	EXP	S	613937	585946	684786	752497	1073920	1311180	1253200	1514970	1269610	1866510
rials	BAL		238104	72945	10613	15965	44040	114370	-440030	-591770	-593510	-263510
Zambia	IMP	S	3089070	5509980	7448280	9639690	11493500	10521000	16085792	18859111	18941257	...
Zambie	EXP	S	2071820	4206590	4640710	7529730	8077880	13584900	18481500	19098000	21759100	34540700
kwacha	BAL		-1017250	-1303390	-2807570	-2109960	-3415620	3063900	2395708	238889	2817843	...

Total imports and exports by countries or areas (Table B)

Imports CIF, exports FOB and balance: millions of national currency *[cont.]*

Importations et exportations totales par pays ou zone (Tableau B)

Importations CIF, exportations FOB, et balance : en millions de monnaie nationale *[suite]*

General note:

This table contains totals of imports and exports of countries or areas which report data in national currency. Countries that are not included in this table may report their trade in US dollars and are shown in Table A. Export and import values are as compiled by the International Monetary Fund (IMF) except for Andorra, Bermuda, Cayman Is., Cuba, Gibraltar, Montenegro, Niue, Occupied Palestinian Territory, Russian Federation (beginning 1994), Serbia and Montenegro, Turkmenistan, Turks and Caicos, Tuvalu and Uzbekistan.
Column "G/S" indicates the trade system: G = General Trade System; S = Special Trade System. For further information on sources and presentation as well as for a brief table description please see the introduction, paragraphs 6-20 and 22.

1 East Caribbean dollar.
2 Trade statistics exclude certain oil and chemical products.
3 Comptoirs Francais du Afrique franc pegged to the euro at CFAF 655.957 per euro.
4 Imports FOB.
5 Prior to January 2008, data for Cyprus are in pounds.
6 Excluding intra-EU trade.
7 In July 2007 the Ghanaian cedi (GHC) was redenominated and our time series were adjusted accordingly. The new Ghana cedi (GHS) is equal to 10,000 old Ghanaian cedis (1 GHS = 10,000 GHC).
8 Excluding military goods, fissionable materials, bunkers, ships, and aircraft.
9 Prior to January 2008, data for Malta are in liri.
10 Beginning 2006, data for Serbia and Montenegro is reported separately.
11 Exports include petroleum products.
12 Prior to January 2009, data for Slovakia are in koruny.
13 Foreign trade data refer to South Africa only, excluding intra-trade of the Southern African Common Customs Area.
14 Exports include gold.
15 Including the trade of the U.S. Virgin Islands and Puerto Rico but excluding shipments of merchandise between the United States and its other possessions (Guam and American Samoa). Data include imports and exports of non-monetary gold.

Note générale :

Cette table contient des totaux d'd'importations et d'd'exportations les pays ou les secteurs qui rapportent des données dans la monnaie nationale.Les pays qui ne sont pas inclus dans cette table peuvent rapporter leurs échanges des dollars d'USA et sont montrés dans le Tableau A. Export et les valeurs d'importation sont comme compilé par le Fonds monétaire international (FMI) excepté Andorre, les Bermudes, Iles Caïmanes, le Cuba, la Fédération Russe (commençant 1994), Gibraltar, Montenegro, Nioué, Serbie et Monténégro, Territoire Palestinien Occupé, Turkmenistan, Iles Turque Caicos, Tuvalu et Ouzbékistan.
La colonne "G/S" indique le système commercial : G=Système du Commerce Général ; S= Système du Commerce Spécial. Pour plus d'information sur les sources et la présentation ainsi qu'une brève description du tableau, veuillez vous référer aux paragraphes 6-20 et 22 de l'introduction.

1 Dollar des caraïbes orientales.
2 Les statistiques commerciales font exclusion de certains produits pétroliers et chimiques.
3 Comptoirs Français du Afrique franc est chevillé à l'euro à CFAF 655,957 par euro.
4 Importations FOB.
5 Avant janvier 2008, les données de Chypre étaient en livres.
6 Non compris le commerce d'intra-UE.
7 Le 1er juillet 2007 le cedi ghanéen (GHC) a été redenominé et nos séries temporelles ont été réajustées afin d'en tenir compte. Le nouveau cedi ghanéen (GHS) vaut 10.000 ancien cedis (1 GHS=10.000 GHC).
8 À l'exclusion des marchandises militaires, des matières fissibles, des soutes, des bateaux, et de l'avion.
9 Avant janvier 2008, les données de Malte étaient en lire.
10 Depuis début 2006, les données relatives à la Serbie et au Monténégro sont déclarées séparément.
11 Exportations comprennent produits pétroliers.
12 Avant janvier 2009, les données de Slovaquie étaient en couronnes.
13 Les données de commerce extérieur se rapportent à l'Afrique du Sud seulement, à l'exclusion de intra-commercent de la région commune africaine méridionale de douane.
14 Les exportations comprennent l'or.
15 Y compris le commerce des Iles Vierges américaines et de Porto Rico mais non compris les échanges de marchandise, entre les Etats-Unis et leurs autres possessions (Guam et Samoa américaines). Les données comprennent les importations et exportations d'or non-monétaire.

External trade conversion factors (Table C)

Imports, exports: US dollars per national currency

Facteurs de conversion pour le commerce extérieur (Tableau C)

Importations, exportations : monnaie nationale en dollars É.-U.

Country or Area	Unit	2000	2002	2003	2004	2005	2006	2007	2008	2009	2010
						Imports - Importations					
Albania	lek	0.00694	0.00715	0.00825	0.00978	0.00999	0.01022	0.01113	0.01194	0.01055	0.00961
Algeria	dinar	0.01328	0.01255	0.01293	0.01388	0.01365	0.01375	0.01446	0.01553	0.01376	0.01345
Andorra	euro	0.91856	0.94517	1.13234	1.24840	1.24575	1.25635	1.37289	1.46993	1.39638	1.32850
Anguilla	EC dollar	0.37037	0.37037	0.37037	0.37037	0.37037	0.37037	0.37037	0.37037	0.37037	0.37037
Australia	dollar	0.57943	0.54483	0.65230	0.73538	0.76328	0.75388	0.84045	0.84795	0.79235	0.91999
Austria	euro[1]	0.92061	0.94412	1.13090	1.24425	1.24302	1.25666	1.37202	1.47342	1.39466	1.32502
Bahamas	dollar	1.00000	1.00000	1.00000	1.00000	1.00000	1.00000	1.00000	1.00000	1.00000	1.00000
Bahrain	dinar	2.65957	2.65957	2.65957	2.65957	2.65957	2.65957	2.65957	2.65957	2.65957	2.65957
Bangladesh	taka	0.01915	0.01727	0.01720	0.01680	0.01554	0.01449	0.01452	0.01458	0.01448	0.01435
Barbados	dollar	0.50000	0.50000	0.50000	0.50000	0.50000	0.50000	0.50000	0.50000	0.50000	0.50000
Belgium	euro	0.92097	0.94467	1.13124	1.24389	1.24435	1.25535	1.37200	1.47505	1.39436	1.32615
Belize	dollar	0.50000	0.50000	0.50000	0.50000	0.50000	0.50000	0.50000	0.50000	0.50000	0.50000
Benin	CFA franc[2,3]	0.00142	0.00144	0.00173	0.00190	0.00190	0.00191	0.00209	0.00223	0.00212	0.00202
Bhutan	ngultrum	0.02228	0.02055	0.02146	0.02206	0.02272	0.02203	0.02420	0.02311	0.02064	0.02184
Bosnia and Herzegovina	marka	0.46840	0.48610	0.58019	0.63577	0.63248	0.64496	0.70309	0.75413	0.71357	0.67617
Botswana	pula	0.19586	0.15974	0.20357	0.21344	0.19636	0.17078	0.16330	0.14708	0.14102	0.14748
Brunei Darussalam	dollar	0.58002	0.55834	0.57393	0.59163	0.60052	0.63034	0.66365	0.70514	0.68607	0.73301
Bulgaria	lev	0.46942	0.48551	0.57918	0.63659	0.63311	0.64383	0.70366	0.75425	0.71358	0.67672
Burkina Faso	CFA franc[3]	0.00140	0.00145	0.00173	0.00190	0.00189	0.00192	0.00209	0.00222	0.00213	0.00202
Burundi	franc	0.00139	0.00107	0.00092	0.00091	0.00093	0.00097	0.00092	0.00084	0.00081	0.00081
Cameroon	CFA franc[3]	0.00140	0.00144	0.00173	0.00190	0.00189	0.00192	0.00210	0.00222	0.00213	0.00202
Canada	dollar	0.67322	0.63746	0.71511	0.76956	0.82563	0.88221	0.93462	0.94192	0.87926	0.97129
Cape Verde	escudo	0.00863	0.00854	0.01025	0.01128	0.01127	0.01139	0.01247	0.01319	0.01259	0.01201
Cent. Afr. Rep.	CFA franc[2,3]	0.00142	0.00146	0.00173	0.00190	0.00190	0.00191	0.00209	0.00222	0.00212	0.00202
Chad	CFA franc[2,3]	0.00141	0.00143	0.00172	0.00189	0.00190	0.00191	0.00208	0.00224	0.00211	0.00202
Comoros	franc	0.00187	0.00192	0.00230	0.00253	0.00252	0.00256	0.00279	0.00296	0.00284	0.00270
Congo	CFA franc[2]	0.00141	0.00143	0.00172	0.00189	0.00190	0.00191	0.00209	0.00224	0.00212	0.00202
Cote d'Ivoire	CFA franc[3]	0.00140	0.00144	0.00172	0.00190	0.00189	0.00191	0.00209	0.00223	0.00212	0.00202
Cyprus	euro[4]	1.60134	1.64212	1.93856	2.13884	2.15118	2.18248	2.35531	1.47595	1.39396	1.32644
Czech Republic	koruna	0.02591	0.03073	0.03557	0.03901	0.04172	0.04440	0.04954	0.05908	0.05292	0.05250
Denmark	krone	0.12362	0.12708	0.15209	0.16706	0.16659	0.16839	0.18407	0.19729	0.18705	0.17789
Djibouti	franc	...	0.00563	0.00563	0.00563	0.00563	0.00563	0.00563	0.00563	0.00563	0.00563
Dominica	EC dollar[5]	0.37037	0.37037	0.37037	0.37037	0.37037	0.37037	0.37037	0.37037	0.37037	0.37037
Equatorial Guinea	CFA franc[3]	0.00140	0.00144	0.00172	0.00189	0.00190	0.00191	0.00209	0.00225	0.00212	0.00201
Estonia	kroon	0.05866	0.06053	0.07247	0.07946	0.07931	0.08038	0.08764	0.09419	0.08922	0.08471
Ethiopia	birr	0.12160	0.11671	0.11628	0.11580	0.11538	0.11495	0.11147	0.10406	0.08464	...
Extra-EU25	euro	0.92006	0.94411	1.13089	1.24360	1.24147	1.25624	1.37211	...	...	...
Extra-EU27	euro	0.92003	0.94414	1.13088	1.24364	1.24207	1.25627	1.37217	1.47393	1.39392	1.32463
Fiji	dollar	0.47029	0.45967	0.52852	0.57720	0.59029	0.57749	0.62298	0.62873	0.51273	...
Finland	euro[1]	0.92026	0.94471	1.13123	1.24425	1.24339	1.25692	1.37140	1.47687	1.39430	1.32514
France	euro[1]	0.92101	0.94364	1.13093	1.24394	1.24430	1.25545	1.37193	1.47400	1.39391	1.32548
French Guiana	franc	.	.	.	1.24330	.	.	.	.	.	.
Gabon	CFA franc[2,3]	0.00141	0.00144	0.00172	0.00189	0.00190	0.00191	0.00208	0.00225	0.00212	0.00201
Gambia	dalasi	0.07831	0.04967	0.03650	0.03332	0.03500	0.03563	0.04040	0.04531	0.03755	0.03577
Germany	euro[1]	0.92038	0.94542	1.13134	1.24408	1.24269	1.25666	1.37163	1.47260	1.39352	1.32486
Ghana	cedi[6]	1.83930	1.25748	1.15289	1.11116	1.10265	1.09025	1.06865	0.94292	0.70912	0.69865
Gibraltar	pound	1.51023	1.50141	1.63511	1.83102	1.81623	1.84441	2.00293	1.83115	1.56517	1.54366
Grenada	EC dollar[5]	0.37037	0.37037	0.37037	0.37037	0.37037	0.37037	0.37037	0.37037	0.37037	0.37037
Guinea-Bissau	CFA franc[3]	0.00139	0.00145	0.00174	0.00190	0.00188	0.00193	0.00211	0.00220	...	...
Guyana	dollar	0.00548	0.00525	0.00516	0.00504	0.00500	0.00499	0.00494	0.00491	0.00490	0.00491

2000	2002	2003	2004	2005	2006	2007	2008	2009	2010	Unité	Pays ou Zone
				Exports - Exportations							
0.00696	0.00715	0.00822	0.00975	0.01001	0.01021	0.01109	0.01204	0.01056	0.00960	lek	Albanie
0.01329	0.01255	0.01294	0.01388	0.01365	0.01375	0.01447	0.01558	0.01377	0.01345	dinar	Algérie
0.91870	0.94504	1.13220	1.24825	1.24575	1.24932	1.37288	1.47712	1.39441	1.32073	euro	Andorre
0.37037	0.37037	0.37037	0.37037	0.37037	0.37037	0.37037	0.37037	0.37037	0.37037	dollar C.O.	Anguilla
0.57827	0.54431	0.65158	0.73501	0.76295	0.75399	0.83968	0.84208	0.78476	0.92004	dollar	Australie
0.92072	0.94460	1.13123	1.24344	1.24303	1.25673	1.37179	1.47538	1.39527	1.32468	euro[1]	Autriche
1.00000	1.00000	1.00000	1.00000	1.00000	1.00000	1.00000	1.00000	1.00000	1.00000	dollar	Bahamas
2.65957	2.65957	2.65957	2.65957	2.65957	2.65957	2.65957	2.65957	2.65957	2.65957	dinar	Bahreïn
0.01916	0.01727	0.01719	0.01679	0.01554	0.01449	0.01452	0.01458	0.01448	0.01435	taka	Bangladesh
0.50000	0.50000	0.50000	0.50000	0.50000	0.50000	0.50000	0.50000	0.50000	0.50000	dollar	Barbade
0.92123	0.94442	1.13121	1.24376	1.24467	1.25563	1.37102	1.47633	1.39488	1.32588	euro	Belgique
0.50000	0.50000	0.50000	0.50000	0.50000	0.50000	0.50000	0.50000	0.50000	...	dollar	Belize
0.00140	0.00144	0.00172	0.00188	0.00188	0.00192	0.00210	0.00224	0.00213	0.00200	franc CFA[2,3]	Bénin
0.02225	0.02056	0.02147	0.02206	0.02269	0.02205	0.02421	0.02301	0.02066	0.02185	ngultrum	Bhoutan
0.47100	0.48587	0.58009	0.63600	0.63434	0.64339	0.70175	0.75446	0.71484	0.67656	marka	Bosnie-Herzégovine
0.19495	0.15931	0.20192	0.21324	0.19700	0.17059	0.16276	0.15022	0.14212	0.14742	pula	Botswana
0.58029	0.55833	0.57421	0.59200	0.60031	0.62922	0.66572	0.70715	0.68722	0.73413	dollar	Brunéi Darussalam
0.46931	0.48481	0.57815	0.63591	0.63406	0.64280	0.70289	0.75617	0.71575	0.67594	lev	Bulgarie
0.00143	0.00144	0.00172	0.00189	0.00189	0.00191	0.00209	0.00223	0.00213	0.00202	franc CFA[3]	Burkina Faso
0.00142	0.00105	0.00093	0.00091	0.00091	0.00096	0.00092	0.00084	0.00081	0.00081	franc	Burundi
0.00140	0.00144	0.00173	0.00190	0.00189	0.00192	0.00210	0.00222	0.00213	0.00202	franc CFA[3]	Cameroun
0.67310	0.63736	0.71452	0.76945	0.82647	0.88172	0.93283	0.94402	0.87858	0.97145	dollar	Canada
0.00859	0.00853	0.01025	0.01128	0.01122	0.01135	0.01242	0.01321	0.01252	0.01206	escudo	Cap-Vert
0.00142	0.00146	0.00171	0.00190	0.00188	0.00192	0.00210	0.00223	0.00214	0.00201	franc CFA[2,3]	Rép. centrafricaine
0.00141	0.00143	0.00172	0.00189	0.00190	0.00191	0.00208	0.00224	0.00211	0.00203	franc CFA[2,3]	Tchad
0.00187	0.00192	0.00230	0.00253	0.00252	0.00256	0.00279	0.00296	0.00284	0.00269	franc	Comores
0.00140	0.00144	0.00173	0.00189	0.00189	0.00192	0.00209	0.00223	0.00213	0.00202	franc CFA[2]	Congo
0.00140	0.00144	0.00172	0.00190	0.00189	0.00191	0.00209	0.00221	0.00212	0.00203	franc CFA[3]	Côte d'Ivoire
1.61099	1.63747	1.93631	2.13771	2.15054	2.17544	2.34513	1.47432	1.39317	1.32568	euro[4]	Chypre
0.02592	0.03068	0.03553	0.03901	0.04174	0.04437	0.04952	0.05918	0.05292	0.05252	couronne	République tchèque
0.12343	0.12718	0.15207	0.16704	0.16662	0.16838	0.18417	0.19753	0.18734	0.17788	couronne	Danemark
...	0.00563	0.00563	0.00563	0.00563	0.00563	0.00563	0.00563	0.00563	0.00563	franc	Djibouti
0.37037	0.37037	0.37037	0.37037	0.37037	0.37037	0.37037	0.37037	0.37037	0.37037	dollar C.O.[5]	Dominique
0.00140	0.00144	0.00172	0.00189	0.00190	0.00191	0.00209	0.00225	0.00212	0.00201	franc CFA[3]	Guinée équatoriale
0.05874	0.06050	0.07247	0.07953	0.07934	0.08036	0.08768	0.09411	0.08932	0.08477	kroon	Estonie
0.12182	0.11672	0.11628	0.11581	0.11539	0.11498	0.11170	0.10442	0.08581	...	birr	Ethiopie
0.91940	0.94529	1.13221	1.24370	1.24183	1.25705	1.37268	...	...	...	euro	Extra-UE25
0.91942	0.94528	1.13216	1.24368	1.24183	1.25698	1.37258	1.47370	1.39615	1.32390	euro	Extra-UE27
0.46700	0.46030	0.53265	0.57753	0.59080	0.57772	0.62371	0.62674	0.51213	0.52394	dollar	Fidji
0.91911	0.94552	1.13229	1.24534	1.24375	1.25693	1.37151	1.47740	1.39517	1.32532	euro[1]	Finlande
0.92139	0.94408	1.13171	1.24345	1.24422	1.25528	1.37115	1.47461	1.39374	1.32552	euro[1]	France
.	.	.	1.24330	.	.	.	.	.	.	franc	Guyane française
0.00141	0.00144	0.00172	0.00189	0.00190	0.00191	0.00208	0.00225	0.00212	0.00201	franc CFA[2,3]	Gabon
0.07833	0.05035	0.03671	0.03330	0.03497	0.03563	0.04016	0.04548	0.03756	0.03578	dalasi	Gambie
0.92097	0.94530	1.13150	1.24328	1.24382	1.25651	1.37150	1.47478	1.39506	1.32502	euro[1]	Allemagne
1.79936	...	...	...	1.10275	1.09065	1.06940	0.94582	...	...	cedi[6]	Ghana
1.50704	1.50555	1.63601	1.83204	1.81242	1.84738	2.00487	1.82327	1.56954	1.54645	livre	Gibraltar
0.37037	0.37037	0.37037	0.37037	0.37037	0.37037	0.37037	0.37037	0.37037	0.37037	dollar C.O.[5]	Grenade
0.00141	0.00143	0.00172	0.00187	0.00190	0.00192	0.00208	0.00229	0.00211	0.00199	franc CFA[3]	Guinée-Bissau
0.00548	0.00524	0.00515	0.00504	0.00500	0.00499	0.00494	0.00491	0.00490	0.00491	dollar	Guyana

External trade conversion factors (Table C)

Imports, exports: US dollars per national currency *[cont.]*

Facteurs de conversion pour le commerce extérieur (Tableau C)

Importations, exportations : monnaie nationale en dollars É.-U. *[suite]*

Country or Area	Unit	2000	2002	2003	2004	2005	2006	2007	2008	2009	2010
						Imports - Importations *[cont.]*					
Haiti	gourde	0.04740	0.03392	0.02360	0.02630	0.02464	0.02481	0.02712	0.02550	0.02425	0.02513
Hungary	forint	0.00353	0.00389	0.00446	0.00494	0.00500	0.00476	0.00546	0.00588	0.00499	0.00481
Iceland	krona	0.01271	0.01095	0.01305	0.01426	0.01585	0.01418	0.01569	0.01198	0.00808	0.00821
India	rupee	0.02226	0.02057	0.02150	0.02206	0.02268	0.02206	0.02431	0.02303	0.02074	0.02187
Ireland	euro[1]	0.92013	0.93984	1.13177	1.24452	1.24450	1.25916	1.37124	1.47584	1.38911	1.32606
Italy	euro[1]	0.92095	0.94406	1.13083	1.24380	1.24425	1.25587	1.37103	1.47477	1.39353	1.32544
Jamaica	dollar	0.02325	0.02064	0.01731	0.01633	0.01604	0.01521	0.01444	0.01381	0.01139	0.01148
Japan	yen	0.00928	0.00800	0.00864	0.00925	0.00906	0.00860	0.00851	0.00966	0.01072	0.01142
Jordan	dinar	1.41044	1.41044	1.41044	1.41044	1.41044	1.41044	1.41044	1.40908	1.40845	1.40845
Kenya	shilling	0.01312	0.01270	0.01318	0.01262	0.01324	0.01388	0.01486	0.01444	0.01295	0.01261
Kuwait	dinar	3.25974	3.29243	3.35720	3.39329	3.42469	3.44816	3.52271	3.71925	3.47464	3.48851
Latvia	lat	1.64778	1.62275	1.75376	1.85225	1.76533	1.79203	1.95139	2.09557	1.98447	1.88500
Lesotho	loti	0.14414	0.09564	0.13319	0.15589	0.15726	0.14728	0.14216	0.12047	0.11943	0.13694
Libya	dinar	1.93754	0.78984	0.77018	0.76720	0.76161	0.76288	0.79436	0.81428	0.80068	0.78987
Lithuania	lita	0.25000	0.27382	0.32843	0.36022	0.35944	0.36439	0.39746	0.42866	0.40478	0.38365
Luxembourg	euro[1]	0.92029	0.94506	1.13089	1.24349	1.24361	1.25583	1.37065	1.47564	1.39501	1.32451
Madagascar	ariary	0.00074	0.00073	0.00081	0.00051	0.00049	0.00047	0.00054	0.00059	0.00051	0.00048
Malawi	kwacha	0.01650	0.01296	0.01025	0.00918	0.00843	0.00733	0.00714	0.00712	0.00708	...
Malaysia	ringgit	0.26316	0.26316	0.26316	0.26316	0.26411	0.27281	0.29115	0.30079	0.28471	0.31129
Mali	CFA franc[2,3]	0.00141	0.00143	0.00172	0.00189	0.00190	0.00191	0.00209	0.00224	0.00212	0.00202
Malta	euro[7]	2.27827	2.31322	2.65557	2.90685	2.88838	2.93558	3.21953	1.47660	1.39110	1.32509
Mauritania	ouguiya	0.00419	0.00368	0.00380	0.00389	0.00377	0.00372	0.00386	0.00422	0.00381	0.00360
Mauritius	rupee	0.03807	0.03342	0.03585	0.03628	0.03384	0.03140	0.03217	0.03522	0.03152	0.03252
Montenegro	euro	.	.	.	.	.	1.26362	1.38311	1.47495	1.39837	1.31874
Morocco	dirham	0.09413	0.09097	0.10473	0.11286	0.11276	0.11389	0.12251	0.12994	0.12456	0.11875
Myanmar	kyat	0.15567	0.15276	0.16447	0.17381	0.17353	0.17357	0.17995	0.18496	0.18077	0.17865
Namibia	dollar	0.14310	0.09578	0.13345	0.15560	0.15662	0.14687	0.14226	0.12032	0.12004	0.13690
Nepal	rupee	0.01407	0.01283	0.01314	0.01359	0.01400	0.01373	0.01514	0.01422	0.01293	0.01367
Netherlands	euro[1]	0.92071	0.94433	1.13123	1.24435	1.24317	1.25630	1.37241	1.47369	1.39504	1.32577
New Zealand	dollar	0.45242	0.46530	0.58397	0.66431	0.70372	0.64916	0.73768	0.70854	0.63595	0.72287
Niger	CFA franc[3]	0.00139	0.00145	0.00174	0.00191	0.00188	0.00192	0.00211	0.00218	0.00215	0.00203
Niue	NZ dollar	0.45360	0.46488	0.58317	0.66470	...	0.65005	0.73592	0.70944	...	...
Norway	krone	0.11343	0.12615	0.14068	0.14876	0.15510	0.15609	0.17141	0.17898	0.16026	0.16549
Oman	rial Omani	2.60078	2.60077	2.60078	2.60078	2.60078	2.60078	2.60078	2.60078	2.60078	2.60079
Pakistan	rupee	0.01865	0.01674	0.01732	0.01716	0.01679	0.01659	0.01647	0.01435	0.01223	0.01174
Panama	balboa	1.00000	1.00000	1.00000	1.00000	1.00000	1.00000	1.00000	1.00000	1.00000	1.00000
Papua New Guinea	kina	0.36017	0.25593	0.28119	0.31054	0.32221	0.32685	0.33668	...	...	...
Philippines	peso	0.02254	0.01938	0.01845	0.01784	0.01815	0.01950	0.02175	0.02267	0.02098	0.02219
Poland	zloty	0.22983	0.24527	0.25705	0.27443	0.30896	0.32297	0.36348	0.42169	0.32311	0.33223
Portugal	euro[1]	0.92205	0.94301	1.13021	1.24353	1.24357	1.25612	1.37292	1.47562	1.39638	1.32491
Qatar	riyal	0.27473	0.27473	0.27473	0.27473	0.27473	0.27473	0.27473	0.27473	0.27473	0.27473
Rwanda	franc	0.00255	0.00210	0.00186	0.00174	0.00180	0.00181	0.00182	0.00182	0.00176	0.00172
Saint Kitts-Nevis	EC dollar[5]	0.37037	0.37037	0.37037	0.37037	0.37037	0.37037	0.37037	0.37037	0.37037	0.37037
Saint Lucia	EC dollar[5]	0.37037	0.37037	0.37037	0.37037	0.37037	0.37037	0.37037	0.37037	0.37037	0.37037
Saint Vincent-Grenadines	EC dollar[5]	0.37037	0.37037	0.37037	0.37037	0.37037	0.37037	0.37037	0.37037	0.37037	0.37037
Samoa	tala	0.30374	0.29614	0.33414	0.35986	0.36869	0.35986	0.38259	0.37763	0.37144	0.40300
Saudi Arabia	riyal	0.26667	0.26667	0.26667	0.26667	0.26688	0.26702	0.26684	0.26667	0.26667	0.26667
Senegal	CFA franc[3]	0.00140	0.00144	0.00172	0.00190	0.00189	0.00192	0.00210	0.00225	0.00212	0.00202
Serbia	dinar	.	0.01657	0.01799	0.01707	0.01468	0.01502	0.01721	0.01821	0.01484	0.01282
Seychelles	rupee	0.17549	0.18286	0.18502	0.18180	0.18180	0.18120	0.14962	0.11101	0.07475	0.08270

2000	2002	2003	2004	2005	2006	2007	2008	2009	2010	Unité	Pays ou Zone
					Exports - Exportations *[suite]*						
0.04649	0.03406	0.02357	0.02628	0.02470	0.02494	0.02715	0.02548	0.02424	0.02513	gourde	Haïti
0.00353	0.00389	0.00446	0.00495	0.00500	0.00476	0.00546	0.00587	0.00499	0.00481	forint	Hongrie
0.01273	0.01091	0.01304	0.01428	0.01589	0.01423	0.01568	0.01147	0.00810	0.00821	couronne	Islande
0.02223	0.02057	0.02149	0.02207	0.02267	0.02206	0.02426	0.02316	0.02070	0.02188	roupie	Inde
0.91904	0.94192	1.13219	1.24338	1.24422	1.25345	1.36990	1.47130	1.39000	1.32589	euro[1]	Irlande
0.92136	0.94483	1.13171	1.24307	1.24353	1.25671	1.37145	1.47680	1.39403	1.32461	euro[1]	Italie
0.02328	0.02066	0.01732	0.01635	0.01604	0.01521	0.01449	0.01382	0.01139	0.01147	dollar	Jamaïque
0.00928	0.00800	0.00865	0.00925	0.00906	0.00859	0.00851	0.00965	0.01072	0.01142	yen	Japon
1.41044	1.41044	1.41044	1.41044	1.41044	1.41044	1.41044	1.40903	1.40845	1.40845	dinar	Jordanie
0.01312	0.01270	0.01317	0.01262	0.01323	0.01386	0.01486	0.01450	0.01294	0.01261	shilling	Kenya
3.25932	3.29239	3.35551	3.39329	3.42469	3.44654	3.52857	3.72796	3.47761	3.49399	dinar	Koweït
1.65011	1.62104	1.75252	1.85233	1.76872	1.78931	1.95344	2.09491	1.99146	1.88523	lat	Lettonie
0.14443	0.09571	0.13368	0.15618	0.15722	0.14671	0.14201	0.12109	0.11918	0.13680	loti	Lesotho
1.94149	0.78967	0.76869	0.76603	0.76235	0.76266	0.79331	0.81664	0.79997	0.78882	dinar	Libye
0.25000	0.27361	0.32782	0.36046	0.35956	0.36395	0.39735	0.42820	0.40500	0.38355	lita	Lituanie
0.92240	0.94373	1.12978	1.24368	1.24483	1.25558	1.36972	1.47934	1.39552	1.32488	euro[1]	Luxembourg
0.00074	0.00074	0.00081	0.00051	0.00049	0.00047	0.00054	0.00058	0.00051	0.00048	ariary	Madagascar
0.01605	0.01297	0.01017	0.00918	0.00843	0.00733	0.00714	0.00712	0.00708	0.00664	kwacha	Malawi
0.26316	0.26316	0.26316	0.26316	0.26411	0.27281	0.29119	0.30070	0.28454	0.31090	ringgit	Malaisie
0.00141	0.00143	0.00172	0.00190	0.00188	0.00192	0.00210	0.00222	0.00214	0.00202	franc CFA[2,3]	Mali
2.27775	2.31298	2.65754	2.90238	2.89004	2.93896	3.21645	1.47295	1.39612	1.32526	euro[7]	Malte
0.00419	0.00368	0.00380	0.00389	0.00377	0.00372	0.00388	0.00421	0.00381	0.00361	ouguiya	Mauritanie
0.03794	0.03343	0.03581	0.03630	0.03383	0.03146	0.03211	0.03510	0.03144	0.03252	rupee	Maurice
.	.	.	.	.	1.26143	1.37725	1.48166	1.39902	1.32172	euro	Monténégro
0.09411	0.09086	0.10464	0.11292	0.11273	0.11380	0.12222	0.13063	0.12435	0.11876	dirham	Maroc
0.15536	0.15247	0.16429	0.17389	0.17423	0.17312	0.17955	0.18453	0.18142	0.17921	kyat	Myanmar
0.14370	0.09533	0.13288	0.15530	0.15702	0.14720	0.14205	0.12093	0.11909	0.13679	dollar	Namibie
0.01405	0.01284	0.01313	0.01358	0.01401	0.01375	0.01508	0.01431	0.01291	0.01368	rupee	Népal
0.92051	0.94479	1.13103	1.24410	1.24367	1.25634	1.37278	1.47345	1.39541	1.32631	euro[1]	Pays-Bas
0.45450	0.46345	0.58199	0.66242	0.70508	0.64784	0.73710	0.71287	0.62844	0.72133	dollar	Nouvelle-Zélande
0.00141	0.00143	0.00172	0.00190	0.00190	0.00191	0.00209	0.00221	0.00211	0.00203	franc CFA[3]	Niger
0.45625	0.46297	0.58071	0.66319	0.70409	0.64899	0.73408	0.71697	...	...	dollar NZ	Nioué
0.11337	0.12588	0.14068	0.14865	0.15512	0.15596	0.17146	0.18000	0.15972	0.16578	couronne	Norvège
2.60078	2.60077	2.60078	2.60078	2.60078	2.60078	2.60078	2.60078	2.60078	2.60079	rial omani	Oman
0.01864	0.01674	0.01732	0.01717	0.01680	0.01659	0.01646	0.01428	0.01222	0.01174	rupee	Pakistan
1.00000	1.00000	1.00000	1.00000	1.00000	1.00000	1.00000	1.00000	1.00000	1.00000	balboa	Panama
0.36016	0.25692	0.28134	0.31073	0.32260	0.32721	0.33749	...	...	...	kina	Papouasie-Nouvelle-Guinée
0.02244	0.01938	0.01843	0.01784	0.01815	0.01950	0.02169	0.02266	0.02098	0.02219	peso	Philippines
0.22975	0.24521	0.25700	0.27500	0.30904	0.32271	0.36305	0.42237	0.32319	0.33224	zloty	Pologne
0.92232	0.94289	1.13346	1.24256	1.24175	1.25653	1.37066	1.47791	1.39582	1.32587	euro[1]	Portugal
0.27473	0.27473	0.27473	0.27473	0.27473	0.27473	0.27473	0.27473	0.27473	0.27473	riyal	Qatar
0.00255	0.00212	0.00187	0.00174	0.00180	0.00181	0.00182	0.00182	0.00176	0.00171	franc	Rwanda
0.37037	0.37037	0.37037	0.37037	0.37037	0.37037	0.37037	0.37037	0.37037	0.37037	dollar C.O.[5]	Saint-Kitts-et-Nevis
0.37037	0.37037	0.37037	0.37037	0.37037	0.37037	0.37037	0.37037	0.37037	0.37037	dollar C.O.[5]	Sainte-Lucie
0.37037	0.37037	0.37037	0.37037	0.37037	0.37037	0.37037	0.37037	0.37037	0.37037	dollar C.O.[5]	St.Vincent-Grenadines
0.30446	0.29732	0.33443	0.35911	0.36885	0.35979	0.38398	0.37987	0.37169	0.40232	tala	Samoa
0.26667	0.26667	0.26667	0.26667	0.26691	0.26702	0.26681	0.26667	0.26667	0.26667	riyal	Arabie saoudite
0.00141	0.00144	0.00173	0.00189	0.00189	0.00191	0.00209	0.00224	0.00213	0.00202	franc CFA.[3]	Sénégal
.	0.01657	0.01799	0.01707	0.01473	0.01504	0.01718	0.01823	0.01489	0.01280	dinar	Serbie
0.17468	0.18215	0.18461	0.18180	0.18180	0.18108	0.14746	0.10742	0.07472	0.08289	rupee	Seychelles

External trade conversion factors (Table C)

Imports, exports: US dollars per national currency *[cont.]*

Facteurs de conversion pour le commerce extérieur (Tableau C)

Importations, exportations : monnaie nationale en dollars É.-U. *[suite]*

Country or Area	Unit	2000	2002	2003	2004	2005	2006	2007	2008	2009	2010
		Imports - Importations *[cont.]*									
Sierra Leone	leone	0.00047	0.00048	0.00043	0.00037	0.00035	0.00034	0.00033	0.00034	0.00029	...
Singapore	dollar	0.57950	0.55897	0.57419	0.59175	0.60041	0.62997	0.66457	0.70922	0.68983	0.73435
Slovakia	euro[8]	0.02164	0.02223	0.02734	0.03106	0.03217	0.03381	0.04071	0.04707	1.39742	1.32559
Solomon Islands	dollar	0.19652	0.14791	0.13319	0.13361	0.13276	0.13144	0.13068	0.12919	0.12415	0.12400
South Africa	rand	0.14376	0.09531	0.13318	0.15577	0.15708	0.14672	0.14220	0.12201	0.11910	0.13684
Spain	euro[1]	0.92032	0.94667	1.13285	1.24403	1.24321	1.25615	1.37258	1.47758	1.39488	1.32537
Sri Lanka	rupee	0.01295	0.01044	0.01036	0.00986	0.00994	0.00962	0.00903	0.00924	0.00871	0.00885
Suriname	dollar	0.75087	0.42111	0.38403	0.36584	0.36591	0.36446	0.36430	0.36430	0.36430	0.36424
Swaziland	lilangeni	0.14311	0.09556	0.13353	0.15577	0.15699	0.14749	0.14252	...	0.11926	0.13741
Sweden	krona	0.10906	0.10304	0.12395	0.13641	0.13395	0.13586	0.14832	0.15392	0.13173	0.13914
Switzerland	franc	0.59172	0.64261	0.74342	0.80536	0.80342	0.79820	0.83442	0.92937	0.92326	0.96099
Syrian Arab Rep.	pound	0.02162	0.02162	0.02162	0.02162	0.02162	...	...	...	...	...
Thailand	baht	0.02483	0.02330	0.02416	0.02484	0.02485	0.02641	0.02901	0.03005	0.02928	0.03161
Togo	CFA franc[2,3]	0.00141	0.00144	0.00172	0.00190	0.00189	0.00192	0.00210	0.00222	0.00213	0.00202
Tonga	pa'anga	0.56409	0.45619	0.46692	0.50756	0.51366	0.49387	0.50805	0.51710	0.49573	0.52617
Trinidad and Tobago	dollar	0.15874	0.16006	0.15884	0.15876	0.15874	0.15841	0.15801	0.15907	0.15805	0.15685
Tunisia	dinar	0.72984	0.70506	0.77712	0.80309	0.77051	0.75204	0.78163	0.81420	0.74352	0.69829
Tuvalu	Aust. dollar	0.58059	0.54583	0.67564	0.73892	0.76341	0.76129	0.85025	...	...	...
Uganda	shilling	0.00061	0.00056	0.00051	0.00055	0.00056	0.00055	0.00058	0.00059	0.00049	0.00046
United Kingdom	pound	1.51362	1.50152	1.63564	1.83222	1.81812	1.84274	2.00272	1.85776	1.56523	1.54641
United Rep. of Tanzania	shilling	0.00125	0.00103	0.00096	0.00092	0.00088	0.00080	0.00081	0.00084	0.00076	0.00071
Vanuatu	vatu	0.00725	0.00721	0.00825	0.00897	0.00914	0.00902	0.00981	0.00989	0.00955	0.01044
Yemen	rial	0.00619	0.00571	0.00546	0.00541	0.00524	0.00508	0.00503	0.00501	0.00494	0.00458
Zambia	kwacha	0.00032	0.00023	0.00021	0.00021	0.00022	0.00028	0.00025	0.00027	0.00020	...

2000	2002	2003	2004	2005	2006	2007	2008	2009	2010	Unité	Pays ou Zone
				Exports - Exportations *[suite]*							
0.00049	0.00048	0.00042	0.00037	0.00035	0.00034	0.00033	0.00034	0.00030	...	leone	Sierra Leone
0.57944	0.55907	0.57421	0.59185	0.60035	0.62983	0.66418	0.70932	0.68990	0.73483	dollar	Singapour
0.02167	0.02220	0.02735	0.03103	0.03217	0.03384	0.04068	0.04704	1.39866	1.32595	euro[8]	Slovaquie
0.19654	0.14717	0.13323	0.13362	0.13276	0.13143	0.13067	0.12903	0.12415	0.12400	dollar	Iles Salomon
0.14384	0.09540	0.13298	0.15586	0.15707	0.14675	0.14224	0.12203	0.11974	0.13708	rand	Afrique du Sud
0.92078	0.94457	1.13213	1.24379	1.24382	1.25594	1.37147	1.47566	1.39553	1.32548	euro[1]	Espagne
0.01293	0.01045	0.01036	0.00986	0.00994	0.00961	0.00903	0.00923	0.00870	0.00886	rupee	Sri Lanka
0.74176	0.42562	0.38368	0.36586	0.36602	0.36444	0.36430	0.36430	0.36430	0.36425	dollar	Suriname
0.14300	0.09574	0.13369	0.15584	0.15648	0.14673	0.14234	...	0.12040	0.13721	lilangeni	Swaziland
0.10913	0.10296	0.12401	0.13633	0.13397	0.13580	0.14828	0.15397	0.13148	0.13919	couronne	Suède
0.59161	0.64365	0.74365	0.80527	0.80329	0.79830	0.83433	0.92963	0.92418	0.96130	franc	Suisse
0.02162	0.02162	0.02162	0.02162	0.02162	...	...	...	...	...	livre	République arabe syrienne
0.02486	0.02329	0.02415	0.02484	0.02482	0.02644	0.02902	0.03006	0.02924	0.03163	baht	Thaïlande
0.00140	0.00144	0.00172	0.00189	0.00189	0.00191	0.00209	0.00224	0.00212	0.00202	franc CFA[2,3]	Togo
0.55465	0.45248	0.46993	0.50806	0.50972	0.49525	0.50918	0.51311	0.50336	0.52832	pa'anga	Tonga
0.15873	0.16014	0.15884	0.15877	0.15874	0.15847	0.15799	0.15910	0.15834	0.15685	dollar	Trinité-et-Tobago
0.73083	0.70485	0.77609	0.80339	0.77115	0.75167	0.78120	0.81733	0.74217	0.69844	dinar	Tunisie
0.57480	0.54547	0.65557	0.73574	0.76222	0.75492	0.84252	...	...	...	dollar aust.	Tuvalu
0.00062	0.00056	0.00051	0.00055	0.00056	0.00055	0.00058	0.00058	0.00049	0.00046	shilling	Ouganda
1.51341	1.50054	1.63487	1.83272	1.81691	1.83992	2.00261	1.85748	1.56610	1.54591	livre	Royaume-Uni
0.00125	0.00103	0.00096	0.00092	0.00088	0.00080	0.00081	0.00084	0.00076	0.00071	shilling	Rép.-Unie de Tanzanie
0.00726	0.00725	0.00827	0.00895	0.00915	0.00900	0.00984	0.00987	0.00936	0.01050	vatu	Vanuatu
0.00618	0.00569	0.00545	0.00541	0.00522	0.00507	0.00503	0.00501	0.00493	0.00455	rial	Yémen
0.00033	0.00023	0.00021	0.00021	0.00022	0.00028	0.00025	0.00027	0.00020	0.00021	kwacha	Zambie

External trade conversion factors (Table C)

Imports, exports: US dollars per national currency *[cont.]*

Facteurs de conversion pour le commerce extérieur (Tableau C)

Importations, exportations : monnaie nationale en dollars É.-U. *[suite]*

General note:

Trade conversion factors are weighted averages of monthly or quarterly exchange rates, the weights being the corresponding monthly or quarterly values of imports and exports. The exchange rates are as compiled by the IMF or provided by the country concerned. The conversion factors shown in this table are used to obtain trade data in terms of US dollars.
For further information on sources and presentation as well as for a brief table description please see the introduction, paragraphs 6-20 and 23.

1 The conversion factors are calculated for each country of euro zone separately and may vary due to differences in relative weights of monthly or quarterly values of imports and exports.

2 The conversion factors are not trade weighted.

3 Comptoirs Francais du Afrique franc pegged to the euro at CFAF 655.957 per euro.

4 Prior to January 2008, data for Cyprus are in pounds.

5 East Caribbean dollar.

6 In July 2007 the Ghanaian cedi (GHC) was redenominated and our time series were adjusted accordingly. The new Ghana cedi (GHS) is equal to 10,000 old Ghanaian cedis (1 GHS = 10,000 GHC).

7 Prior to January 2008, data for Malta are in liri.

8 Prior to January 2009, data for Slovakia are in koruny.

Remarque générale:

Les facteurs de conversion pour le commerce extérieur sont les moyennes pondérées des taux de change mensuelles ou trimestrielles. Les coefficients de pondération sont les valeurs mensuelles ou trimestrielles correspondantes des importations ou des exportations. Les taux de change sont les taux calculés par le secrétariat du FMI ou fournis par le pays. Les facteurs de conversion montrés dans cette table sont employés pour obtenir les données commerciales en termes de dollars de E.U.
Pour plus d'information sur les sources et la présentation ainsi qu'une brève description du tableau, veuillez vous référer aux paragraphes 6-20 et 23 de l'introduction.

1 Les facteurs de conversion sont calculés pour chaque pays d'euro zone séparément et peuvent varier en raison des différences dans les ponderation relatifs de valeurs mensuelles ou trimestrielles des importations et des exportations.

2 Les facteurs de conversion ne sont pas pondérés.

3 Comptoirs Français du Afrique franc est chevillé à l'euro à CFAF 655,957 par euro.

4 Avant janvier 2008, les données de Chypre étaient en livres.

5 Dollar des caraïbes orientales.

6 Le 1er juillet 2007 le cedi ghanéen (GHC) a été redenominé et nos séries temporelles ont été réajustées afin d'en tenir compte. Le nouveau cedi ghanéen (GHS) vaut 10.000 ancien cedis (1 GHS=10.000 GHC).

7 Avant janvier 2008, les données de Malte étaient en lire.

8 Avant janvier 2009, les données de Slovaquie étaient en couronnes.

World exports by provenance and destination (Table D)

In million U.S. dollars f.o.b.

Exports to ⟶ / ↓ Exports from	Year	World 1/ Monde 1/	Developed economies 2/ Economies développées 2/ Total	Asia-Pacific Asie-Pacifique Total	Asia-Pacific Japan Japon	Europe Total	Europe Germany Allemagne	North America Amérique du Nord Total	North America U.S.A. É.-U.	Commonwealth of Independent States Communauté d'Etats Indépendants Total	CIS Europe
					Total trade (SITC, Rev. 3, 0-9) 3/						
World 1/	2000	6337847	4375773	413799	337705	2549417	475000	1412557	1176815	77403	65291
	2007	13828914	8674094	790630	618686	5614828	970672	2268636	1894247	403992	336000
	2008	15946668	9622077	837650	633083	6361484	1118295	2422943	1968844	518022	427806
	2009	12395701	7210284	608319	441858	4794079	861283	1807886	1452008	313406	243959
	2010	15025812	8408909	753407	550392	5442202	1001159	2213301	1779843	399490	324420
Developed Economies - Asia-Pacific 2/	2000	556339	283778	30765	14422	93424	21063	159589	150831	1004	824
	2007	880380	359183	59224	28866	130269	24305	169690	157213	13349	12634
	2008	998843	383873	80118	45307	139257	26140	164498	152014	20845	20007
	2009	759418	268557	57392	31762	96682	18166	114483	105249	4848	4332
	2010	1007411	331697	73639	41538	115968	22128	142089	131244	10412	9621
Japan	2000	479276	243818	9835	.	83786	19997	150197	142480	793	624
	2007	714327	281892	16698	.	108971	22636	156223	145624	12518	11896
	2008	781412	284386	19818	.	115044	23955	149524	138705	19335	18629
	2009	580719	196115	13675	.	79347	16653	103092	95303	4120	3700
	2010	769774	243061	17798	.	95563	20290	129700	120338	9161	8543
Developed Economies - Europe 2/	2000	2511802	2110333	63263	45917	1790576	343436	256494	231910	31171	28093
	2007	5507401	4419839	104143	66872	3886811	705777	428886	384699	176437	161858
	2008	6127335	4843718	114178	70354	4284717	803237	444823	396943	220238	203103
	2009	4734391	3718254	93458	57749	3277510	620926	347286	310349	135610	120770
	2010	5324424	4119323	107355	65765	3617007	707325	394961	351939	164075	148684
France	2000	295345	239365	6445	4983	204528	44461	28392	25937	2392	1952
	2007	539731	416375	11459	7916	367014	77915	37902	34097	10391	9288
	2008	594505	447724	13701	8255	394488	86842	39534	35110	13803	12437
	2009	464113	342892	10405	6649	301736	68985	30751	27347	9372	8087
	2010	511651	371697	12364	7793	326578	82989	32755	29231	10476	9481
Germany	2000	549607	458641	15684	12137	382583	.	60374	56393	8923	8069
	2007	1328841	1049227	26923	17913	912493	.	109811	100561	53859	49394
	2008	1466137	1134421	29702	18848	990263	.	114455	105211	65207	60585
	2009	1127840	865255	24702	15068	758245	.	82308	75017	40011	36127
	2010	1271096	946837	28739	17374	821272	.	96826	86847	48260	43828
Developed Economies - North America 2/	2000	1057790	699131	86693	71335	193929	31336	418509	241624	3504	2715
	2007	1582828	981833	95288	71267	305734	53204	580811	331608	12086	10058
	2008	1756128	1061625	104488	77038	341455	58895	615683	353789	15814	13047
	2009	1372482	795812	82057	58478	271616	46480	442139	236475	9350	7321
	2010	1664371	937706	96157	69519	303149	51731	538400	289460	10700	8799
United States	2000	780332	436300	79685	65252	179776	29242	176839	.	3325	2563
	2007	1162538	601905	84682	62664	268149	49611	249073	.	10641	8861
	2008	1299899	655762	91571	66573	302443	54672	261747	.	13823	11404
	2009	1056712	520933	72935	51178	242463	43221	205536	.	8200	6437
	2010	1277109	599501	85165	60543	265503	48041	248832	.	9164	7484
South-Eastern Europe	2000	19514	13491	50	37	12585	2634	857	764	994	854
	2007	76877	52657	200	155	50830	10697	1628	1483	4032	3376
	2008	93910	61376	228	148	59576	12661	1572	1431	5537	4791
	2009	73589	49989	193	138	48860	11465	935	849	3575	3001
	2010	89896	59319	263	216	57746	13489	1310	1135	4959	4263
Commonwealth of Independent States	2000	143026	80471	2958	2943	70243	11069	7269	5779	29063	24135
	2007	497116	275074	8299	8206	255837	21898	10938	9961	106646	79714
	2008	710866	408805	12206	11919	371291	37872	25307	23021	135588	102416
	2009	439954	236729	8029	7816	213640	22285	15060	12359	86825	62810
	2010	578066	311873	14067	13836	277184	29259	20621	16487	107697	80866
Russian Federation	2000	103093	65496	2771	2764	57875	9232	4850	4648	13824	10807
	2007	352266	215164	7543	7491	199977	18605	7644	7312	59756	41378
	2008	467994	294155	10516	10429	268946	33187	14693	13753	69921	48410
	2009	301796	179803	7427	7263	162602	18708	9775	9286	46941	31192
	2010	400100	238827	12965	12833	212262	25103	13600	12467	59867	42283

For general note and footnotes see end of table

Exportations mondiales par provenance et destination (Tableau D)

En millions de dollars E.-U. f.o.b.

South-Eastern Europe Europe du Sud-est	Northern Africa Afrique du Nord	Sub-Saharan Africa Afrique subsahari-enne	Latin America and the Caribbean Amérique latine et Caraïbes	Eastern Asia Asie orientale	Southern Asia Asie méridionale	South-eastern Asia Asie du Sud-est	Western Asia Asie occidentale	Oceania Océanie	Others 4/ Autre 4/	Année	← Exportations vers / Exportations en provenance de ↓
			Commerce total (CTCI, Rev. 3, 0-9) 3/								
27378	54315	74386	363393	699309	80536	355077	190992	6348	32936	2000	Monde 1/
125004	141444	231466	704859	1825879	318090	722963	558775	16699	105648	2007	
150343	183844	288056	883505	2185740	389873	849199	697701	23038	155268	2008	
103040	161237	245569	678153	1894658	353236	697619	567613	25625	145261	2009	
115713	178366	289269	883732	2564456	440238	911998	651035	25938	156667	2010	
153	1694	4909	22054	140231	6988	78409	13637	2260	1223	2000	Economies Développées - Asie-Pacifique 2/
583	3568	12064	36306	289254	19381	105037	35231	4527	1899	2007	
825	4754	13332	43350	327332	25887	126114	45169	4612	2750	2008	
370	3469	9377	34207	282693	23696	98367	27597	4508	1729	2009	
422	4118	12141	46359	393669	31535	135540	32799	6490	2228	2010	
108	1196	3721	20779	124536	4751	68494	10619	460	0	2000	Japon
428	2844	8649	33266	247799	10203	87168	28345	1209	5	2007	
637	3867	9447	39201	271282	12612	103462	35785	1397	...	2008	
321	2671	6777	31349	225619	10138	80399	21776	1435	...	2009	
384	3160	8849	42346	306983	14261	112867	25991	2710	0	2010	
19331	29933	31303	57248	77496	21606	40227	83203	1256	8695	2000	Economies Développées - Europe 2/
80075	66335	77751	111980	195135	65898	79823	201198	3515	29416	2007	
98566	86605	91350	131857	220390	76360	88128	236713	4730	28680	2008	
70334	77081	75569	99577	203316	64557	74916	188110	2577	24490	2009	
76054	82498	85563	127721	264931	74238	87823	216573	3182	22444	2010	
1282	9180	7741	7237	9366	2416	4752	10136	822	658	2000	France
4792	17278	13495	12698	22156	7536	10656	22085	1606	661	2007	
5737	21731	15742	16170	23413	8453	13395	25340	1889	1109	2008	
4228	19013	13613	10903	19415	6204	12036	24120	1579	738	2009	
4676	20396	15016	13984	26338	7000	13568	25906	1610	983	2010	
4185	4001	5607	13858	21330	4087	9799	17506	132	1537	2000	Allemagne
17481	9064	15095	28369	66106	17101	21295	48513	535	2195	2007	
21876	11916	17094	35613	77169	20088	22928	56766	332	2728	2008	
15782	10938	13115	26344	73359	18415	19196	43364	185	1876	2009	
16420	11127	15445	35536	100250	19628	23476	53170	532	415	2010	
562	5660	6348	174597	88921	5584	48918	23864	393	308	2000	Economies Développées - Amérique du Nord 2/
1437	10564	16245	253791	161311	23949	64150	56481	553	429	2007	
2304	11934	20722	301454	170313	26749	72629	71695	703	187	2008	
1349	10670	16563	247110	153244	24137	57509	55752	751	235	2009	
1408	12628	18984	312665	203287	28003	74626	63154	834	377	2010	
509	5028	5928	170376	83248	4635	47368	22928	378	307	2000	Etats-Unis
1229	9257	14402	242990	146672	20998	60570	52957	490	428	2007	
1929	10017	18613	287831	153590	22629	68156	66749	619	183	2008	
1153	9141	15135	237538	138015	20596	53844	51250	674	234	2009	
1137	11215	17076	300493	183656	24298	70437	59046	709	376	2010	
2212	358	156	159	218	139	76	1700	1	9	2000	Europe du Sud-est
9241	814	274	657	545	847	458	6968	61	322	2007	
13096	1112	911	821	769	994	565	8320	84	326	2008	
10086	1176	596	449	913	701	520	5356	21	207	2009	
12160	1293	881	487	1382	837	565	7654	16	343	2010	
2635	1375	555	5984	9137	2996	1716	9070	4	19	2000	Communauté d'Etats Indépendants
17584	5798	1678	6902	31379	12869	4340	34655	9	182	2007	
15979	8815	2649	11779	44395	19252	7670	55819	8	108	2008	
7113	6516	1975	5286	35043	18335	6186	32216	77	3654	2009	
10189	7144	1902	7024	52281	18886	10638	42557	4	7871	2010	
1822	746	344	4307	6980	1896	1120	6556	2	0	2000	Fédération de Russie
14001	3502	663	4533	23152	6538	2563	22324	8	62	2007	
10644	5103	1182	6669	31533	9403	4371	34987	7	20	2008	
4272	4295	969	3357	24551	9487	3608	20986	76	3451	2009	
6106	4407	695	4164	34400	10722	6729	26992	2	7187	2010	

Voir la fin du tableau pour la remarque générale et les notes.

World exports by provenance and destination (Table D)

In million U.S. dollars f.o.b.

Exports to → / ↓ Exports from	Year	World 1/ Monde 1/	Developed economies 2/ Economies développées 2/ Total	Asia-Pacific Asie-Pacifique Total	Japan Japon	Europe Total	Germany Allemagne	North America Amérique du Nord Total	U.S.A. É.-U.	Commonwealth of Independent States Communauté d'Etats Indépendants Total	Europe
Total trade (SITC, Rev. 3, 0-9) 3/ *[cont.]*											
Northern Africa	2000	50201	41077	490	424	35543	3933	5043	4216	101	81
	2007	153150	120058	1152	932	90956	7926	27949	23160	393	325
	2008	206917	161155	2732	2104	127243	10718	31180	25653	707	589
	2009	135155	97435	723	546	79566	6339	17146	14541	489	460
	2010	163590	118380	994	521	95703	6740	21684	18474	592	525
Sub-Saharan Africa	2000	94739	57005	2651	2078	32080	3098	22275	21302	194	191
	2007	258223	148304	11820	9702	72384	8367	64100	59983	630	561
	2008	344271	193027	13277	11169	91700	9792	88051	82563	950	885
	2009	240888	118392	6899	5919	64570	6102	46923	41920	686	614
	2010	322693	162825	10485	8218	81304	8338	71037	63838	896	806
South Africa	2000	26298	13520	1866	1355	9026	1900	2629	2409	33	32
	2007	64027	39457	8421	7039	22637	5106	8399	7529	224	189
	2008	73966	43419	9737	8120	25229	5749	8453	7987	391	378
	2009	53864	26845	4889	4096	16742	3513	5214	4860	243	215
	2010	71484	36166	7461	6425	21196	5529	7508	7061	385	354
Latin America and the Caribbean	2000	353079	266101	8563	7720	43766	6931	213771	207458	1330	1280
	2007	771254	497431	20127	18096	116042	18133	361262	344683	6906	6578
	2008	886493	536564	21552	18378	133780	21702	381231	364254	8925	8473
	2009	697599	412381	16614	14473	102087	14920	293680	262243	6110	5733
	2010	886754	507978	24107	21242	120220	17919	363652	328276	8120	7747
Brazil	2000	55119	33696	2852	2481	16229	2520	14615	14049	522	487
	2007	160649	75857	5015	4332	42515	7136	28326	25946	4344	4145
	2008	197942	87554	7466	6134	49277	8843	30811	28938	5526	5239
	2009	152995	60563	4812	4281	37178	6250	18573	16678	3332	3137
	2010	197356	74437	7750	7123	45134	8080	21553	19240	4747	4510
Eastern Asia	2000	776206	410959	101772	90093	125356	27229	183831	173168	4995	3848
	2007	2192507	966982	194025	159726	383422	76058	389535	359564	61798	46648
	2008	2483374	1066515	218059	177602	438765	87717	409692	377313	81155	55328
	2009	2101812	887826	184914	148327	356661	73770	346250	319800	47263	27767
	2010	2724543	1119064	230348	183810	447130	95596	441585	408251	68075	47625
China	2000	249203	142806	45499	41654	41976	9278	55331	52156	3183	2411
	2007	1220060	624235	122221	102062	249400	48744	252613	233169	48129	34728
	2008	1430693	712184	140889	116132	296563	59209	274732	252844	64719	41075
	2009	1201647	598610	120642	97911	238921	49920	239047	221295	38973	21471
	2010	1577764	771088	151029	121044	313723	68047	306336	283780	53821	36052
Southern Asia	2000	91744	55121	8446	7710	29168	3860	17507	16426	1851	1206
	2007	275575	132995	26457	24921	74996	8578	31542	29562	4012	2263
	2008	337887	156136	33165	31254	90590	9867	32382	30241	4972	2717
	2009	294576	103008	6159	4090	67577	9223	29271	27368	3748	2078
	2010	349813	121223	8347	5894	77375	10199	35501	33321	5160	3343
South-Eastern Asia	2000	426829	219005	69566	58134	65493	12053	83945	80934	606	556
	2007	860458	348291	123810	88555	112121	19842	112360	106366	3795	3562
	2008	984324	382171	149223	105222	121388	21685	111560	104976	5633	5261
	2009	811581	303084	113142	78514	101189	17953	88752	82367	3821	3332
	2010	1052184	378514	146389	103946	125471	23137	106654	100346	4799	4337
Western Asia	2000	251580	136309	36750	35955	56346	8169	43214	42153	2575	1496
	2007	764213	366047	142369	140074	134038	15614	89640	85681	13903	8419
	2008	1006064	360809	84403	81336	159762	17669	116643	56356	17655	11186
	2009	725003	213298	35302	33112	112339	13376	65657	38194	11075	5734
	2010	852632	235522	37408	34694	122559	15030	75554	36822	13996	7796
Oceania	2000	4996	2993	1832	937	908	190	252	249	15	11
	2007	8931	5398	3718	1316	1387	272	293	287	4	4
	2008	10254	6303	4021	1251	1962	338	321	291	4	4
	2009	9253	5521	3437	934	1780	279	304	295	6	5
	2010	9434	5486	3848	1194	1386	268	252	249	8	8

For general note and footnotes see end of table

Exportations mondiales par provenance et destination (Tableau D)

En millions de dollars E.-U. f.o.b.

South-Eastern Europe Europe du Sud-est	Northern Africa Afrique septentrio-nale	Sub-Saharan Africa Afrique du Nord	Latin America and the Caribbean Amérique latine et Caraïbes	Eastern Asia Asie orientale	Southern Asia Asie méridionale	South-eastern Asia Asie du Sud-est	Western Asia Asie occidentale	Oceania Océanie	Others 4/ Autre 4/	Année	← Exportations vers Exportations en provence de ↓
			Commerce total (CTCI, Rev. 3, 0-9) 3/ *[suite]*								
92	1179	336	2058	315	793	277	3122	1	849	2000	Afrique du Nord
235	4187	1986	4718	4415	5532	1484	5913	57	4173	2007	
636	7113	2990	6596	6471	6869	1680	10497	3	2201	2008	
488	6065	2429	3380	7393	4142	1114	10519	5	1698	2009	
526	6398	3415	4318	8899	5691	1439	12320	11	1600	2010	
64	418	12180	2545	8634	5259	1952	2094	40	4354	2000	Afrique subsaharienne
223	1347	35372	9220	40978	9114	3433	5867	44	3690	2007	
326	1710	47338	14256	56449	15216	4540	6705	75	3678	2008	
434	1734	43132	8920	41100	13889	4327	6485	439	1349	2009	
198	2168	50566	11991	56929	19094	7023	9228	188	1587	2010	
27	91	3903	572	1797	524	731	971	6	4122	2000	Afrique du sud
129	444	9029	1363	7034	1852	1518	2423	28	527	2007	
153	532	12006	1446	7754	2735	1995	2806	39	690	2008	
39	435	10092	782	8451	2588	1643	2134	71	540	2009	
53	445	11882	1559	12118	3522	2236	2629	36	454	2010	
324	1359	1674	61584	8836	2276	2799	2808	17	3972	2000	Amérique latine et Caraïbes
1617	5296	9977	165972	51910	9182	9383	9543	81	3954	2007	
1859	7243	11099	215688	63700	9019	14917	13487	66	3927	2008	
1480	5681	8375	156249	68912	10827	14637	11763	66	1118	2009	
1633	7757	8235	186818	102524	13728	18492	14678	49	16741	2010	
129	506	888	13886	2603	621	926	1338	4	...	2000	Brésil
658	2584	6810	42330	14991	3210	4351	5493	16	4	2007	
801	3145	7743	51912	23011	2865	6825	8538	22	0	2008	
573	3038	5938	35880	25752	5616	5305	6972	26	...	2009	
603	4182	5053	47682	37983	6603	6597	9440	28	...	2010	
688	3065	8359	25177	220132	13063	68295	18703	1258	1513	2000	Asie orientale
5196	14532	38383	86270	679114	64529	191157	77424	3890	3232	2007	
6629	19168	50439	116740	725750	81869	226831	97675	6721	3883	2008	
4656	19474	45451	91116	635236	76484	197847	81682	12724	2054	2009	
5655	22720	57288	138418	838936	104798	258981	98264	9288	3057	2010	
356	1410	3602	7125	62121	4510	17341	6683	65	2	2000	Chine
3556	10766	26625	51268	269050	42572	94727	48178	954	...	2007	
4934	14320	36784	71240	296081	52553	114326	62430	1121	...	2008	
3658	14135	33512	56558	245199	49778	106320	52703	2201	...	2009	
4371	15588	44235	91249	322611	68699	138203	64868	3032	...	2010	
48	2666	2172	1906	13214	3400	3789	7538	32	8	2000	Asie méridionale
430	6750	11672	5342	44107	17043	15364	37022	65	774	2007	
572	9034	14053	8008	53847	21392	21229	47027	178	1440	2008	
712	5456	12110	5941	64742	18071	20290	53181	74	7243	2009	
638	6268	16331	11227	78350	23076	25676	60654	172	1038	2010	
156	1009	4130	6783	75962	11334	97884	8580	996	386	2000	Asie Sud-est
503	3675	11567	17530	191644	37237	217398	24571	3483	765	2007	
713	5450	16439	24453	214576	45767	251536	31959	4423	1205	2008	
497	4665	14546	19600	195519	40098	199729	25511	3555	956	2009	
715	6036	18660	27118	263448	52432	264966	29478	4823	1195	2010	
1112	5600	2222	2988	55697	7083	10449	16672	9	10864	2000	Asie occidentale
7882	18577	14416	6145	134821	52303	30438	63895	238	55548	2007	
8838	20907	16667	8483	300428	60220	32751	72631	1181	105496	2008	
5514	19249	15411	6291	205277	58218	21379	69430	666	99195	2009	
6115	19338	15264	9563	298307	67797	25505	63670	728	96828	2010	
2	0	41	310	514	15	287	2	80	736	2000	Océanie
0	0	82	27	1267	205	500	8	176	1264	2007	
0	0	66	22	1321	280	609	6	255	1387	2008	
7	1	35	27	1268	83	797	11	163	1334	2009	
0	0	39	23	1511	124	725	6	155	1358	2010	

Voir la fin du tableau pour la remarque générale et les notes.

World exports by provenance and destination (Table D)

In million U.S. dollars f.o.b.

Exports to → / ↓ Exports from	Year	World 1/ Monde 1/	Developed economies 2/ Economies développées 2/ Total	Asia-Pacific Asie-Pacifique Total	Asia-Pacific Japan Japon	Europe Total	Europe Germany Allemagne	North America Amérique du Nord Total	North America U.S.A. É.-U.	Commonwealth of Independent States Communauté d'Etats Indépendants Total	Commonwealth of Independent States Europe
Food, beverages and tobacco (SITC, Rev. 3, 0 and 1)											
World 1/	2000	386429	270929	40623	36977	174954	32426	55351	43871	9865	8662
	2007	800754	536655	51092	42285	386633	63915	98931	76381	35983	30310
	2008	952036	610453	59195	48767	444121	74262	107137	81738	47065	39501
	2009	870836	553156	53041	43292	399781	67204	100334	75590	36220	30063
	2010	968395	590318	60435	48930	417634	70585	112250	84394	44470	37734
Developed Economies - Asia-Pacific 2/	2000	19827	9705	4296	3299	2443	277	2967	2615	52	44
	2007	34025	16374	6894	4424	4407	496	5074	4378	364	291
	2008	39723	17657	8124	5303	4637	589	4896	4258	700	605
	2009	35858	15294	6743	4194	4032	456	4518	3952	347	282
	2010	41755	16131	7646	4517	3938	434	4548	3953	698	597
Japan	2000	2088	612	72	.	107	14	432	395	9	9
	2007	3531	814	67	.	140	23	607	567	36	36
	2008	3867	920	76	.	163	29	681	634	50	50
	2009	3895	938	78	.	170	31	691	650	51	51
	2010	4615	957	81	.	193	34	683	640	81	80
Developed Economies - Europe 2/	2000	177876	151306	5141	4316	135733	26322	10432	8968	3783	3518
	2007	385877	329758	7575	5595	302977	51787	19206	16275	12950	12280
	2008	446238	375830	8749	6402	347846	60333	19235	15969	16094	15284
	2009	399827	338756	7705	5587	313991	54992	17060	14122	12405	11751
	2010	423989	351428	8306	5953	324062	56861	19060	15798	15669	14790
France	2000	31410	26548	981	902	23387	4572	2180	1853	351	335
	2007	56734	47737	1499	1290	42706	6754	3532	2890	899	860
	2008	65387	53274	1635	1379	48358	7641	3280	2569	1088	1046
	2009	55320	45343	1343	1148	41033	6763	2966	2370	759	726
	2010	58758	45877	1426	1190	41011	6755	3441	2776	902	852
Germany	2000	21712	18446	290	250	17384	.	772	696	643	595
	2007	55112	48798	789	611	46369	.	1640	1430	2159	1967
	2008	66524	57796	962	741	55159	.	1676	1429	2817	2584
	2009	60755	52998	797	566	50644	.	1558	1330	2190	1997
	2010	62920	53953	774	524	51373	.	1806	1554	2757	2530
Developed Economies - North America 2/	2000	63390	38861	13367	12830	6717	914	18777	10624	986	886
	2007	101187	55233	13093	11955	10314	1321	31826	16548	1962	1847
	2008	123560	63317	16301	14956	11148	1337	35869	18333	2803	2614
	2009	104074	55669	13883	12502	9019	1096	32767	15561	1932	1781
	2010	118065	61081	14885	13367	9979	1297	36218	17305	1883	1679
United States	2000	47084	25762	11994	11534	5619	835	8149	.	955	858
	2007	73623	34560	11078	10177	8216	1186	15266	.	1688	1597
	2008	91269	40311	13951	12842	8837	1178	17523	.	2303	2154
	2009	76576	36104	11936	10806	6975	941	17193	.	1685	1562
	2010	88113	39643	12717	11457	8054	1158	18872	.	1475	1306
South-Eastern Europe	2000	1232	650	17	12	588	125	45	39	87	69
	2007	4813	2692	20	5	2569	354	104	90	239	222
	2008	7155	3425	27	11	3278	382	120	101	285	262
	2009	7176	3971	19	5	3829	396	123	102	210	196
	2010	8679	4413	21	6	4278	450	113	91	328	296
Commonwealth of Independent States	2000	3276	710	150	145	524	90	35	32	2130	1733
	2007	17448	2267	192	190	1966	346	109	94	9269	5629
	2008	23397	2910	147	146	2654	344	108	94	12482	7575
	2009	21207	2249	298	293	1852	285	99	88	9634	5783
	2010	21793	2059	256	249	1687	260	116	104	11518	7624
Russian Federation	2000	1016	394	140	137	231	34	23	21	379	91
	2007	7624	1023	130	129	829	112	63	53	2769	786
	2008	7426	854	125	124	676	123	53	45	3255	880
	2009	8340	807	228	224	531	126	48	43	2709	610
	2010	7304	895	215	211	615	97	65	59	2044	658

For general note and footnotes see end of table

Exportations mondiales par provenance et destination (Tableau D)

En millions de dollars E.-U. f.o.b.

← Exportations vers

South-Eastern Europe Europe du Sud-est	Northern Africa Afrique septentrio-nale	Sub-Saharan Africa Afrique du Nord	Latin America and the Caribbean Amérique latine et Caraïbes	Eastern Asia Asie orientale	Southern Asia Asie méridionale	South-eastern Asia Asie du Sud-est	Western Asia Asie occidentale	Oceania Océanie	Others 4/ Autre 4/	Année	Exportations en provence de ↓
			Produits alimentaires, boisson et tabac (CTCI, Rev. 3, 0 et 1)								
2493	7282	8372	22170	23740	5204	16064	17788	783	1739	2000	Monde 1/
8556	16104	22708	44156	43493	13246	35057	40368	1505	2924	2007	
12051	21156	29503	57793	52280	18524	44554	54021	1868	2768	2008	
11164	17075	28238	49229	54383	20033	42930	53009	1804	3593	2009	
11644	21689	31183	56508	71081	22634	55189	58474	1991	3214	2010	
5	396	398	490	3385	864	3024	963	446	98	2000	Economies Développées - Asie-Pacifique 2/
7	484	618	1144	6250	786	5051	1936	720	290	2007	
12	658	858	1315	7137	848	6663	2995	776	106	2008	
9	587	681	762	7216	1058	5419	2601	705	1179	2009	
14	827	870	988	9453	1560	7013	2978	824	399	2010	
0	0	18	23	1135	6	205	26	56	0	2000	Japon
0	16	33	25	2070	7	416	52	62	...	2007	
0	21	54	29	2103	11	562	71	45	...	2008	
0	28	28	29	2219	8	474	76	43	...	2009	
0	39	29	37	2728	14	593	103	33	...	2010	
1688	2958	3092	3113	2850	484	2052	5475	135	940	2000	Economies Développées - Europe 2/
5475	4912	6637	4582	5588	953	3877	9526	269	1350	2007	
7953	7439	8477	5298	6464	1453	4305	11179	318	1429	2008	
7123	5794	7708	4334	6578	1283	4017	10440	295	1094	2009	
7104	7013	8798	5148	8846	1369	4980	12874	316	443	2010	
79	984	883	429	542	106	406	968	112	2	2000	France
187	1751	1717	412	1315	122	1044	1322	223	6	2007	
269	3190	2224	494	1481	203	1241	1641	260	22	2008	
212	2371	1842	403	1547	105	1034	1451	240	12	2009	
243	3103	2206	611	2247	131	1345	1825	255	14	2010	
193	367	112	203	255	126	188	974	1	204	2000	Allemagne
686	401	302	244	447	131	303	1426	2	211	2007	
1106	632	546	301	604	392	377	1709	3	241	2008	
1076	442	658	251	564	430	376	1747	2	19	2009	
1026	507	746	333	733	300	426	2110	2	25	2010	
73	1936	805	9298	5475	785	2248	2770	78	74	2000	Economies Développées - Amérique du Nord 2/
137	3294	2287	18670	9122	1665	4163	4236	110	309	2007	
200	3378	2899	24253	12361	2881	5823	5376	169	99	2008	
133	1926	2187	19393	11231	2169	4700	4434	228	72	2009	
121	2936	2584	21626	14633	2072	5678	5048	231	171	2010	
71	1499	658	8266	4943	268	1952	2558	77	74	2000	Etats-Unis
101	2783	1790	16688	8047	700	3268	3584	105	309	2007	
157	2308	2314	21936	11154	1231	4825	4480	153	99	2008	
101	1323	1774	17355	9997	710	4034	3205	216	72	2009	
94	2355	2081	19367	12760	828	4981	4145	214	171	2010	
284	44	6	3	4	34	5	114	1	1	2000	Europe du Sud-est
1472	75	14	7	12	7	15	275	0	6	2007	
2059	157	162	7	41	247	24	720	0	27	2008	
2149	85	97	12	83	36	33	476	0	24	2009	
2597	126	52	6	182	91	122	749	0	14	2010	
27	17	15	7	160	31	2	163	...	14	2000	Communauté d'Etats Indépendants
153	1900	240	12	417	783	37	2260	...	110	2007	
138	1885	232	102	578	1672	64	3269	0	65	2008	
110	1804	378	92	1872	1711	350	2964	0	43	2009	
112	1887	297	91	2047	839	155	2656	0	132	2010	
6	6	0	1	155	7	1	67	...	0	2000	Fédération de Russie
105	1428	185	4	336	520	24	1213	...	17	2007	
51	897	150	23	391	567	24	1204	0	9	2008	
63	1062	127	43	1566	408	94	1454	0	7	2009	
62	985	132	39	1914	124	51	985	...	73	2010	

Voir la fin du tableau pour la remarque générale et les notes.

World exports by provenance and destination (Table D)

In million U.S. dollars f.o.b.

Exports to → / ↓ Exports from	Year	World 1/ Monde 1/	Developed economies 2/ Economies développées 2/								Commonwealth of Independent States Communauté d'Etats Indépendants	
				Asia-Pacific Asie-Pacifique		Europe		North America Amérique du Nord			
			Total	Total	Japan Japon	Total	Germany Allemagne	Total	U.S.A. É.-U.	Total	Europe
			Food, beverages and tobacco (SITC, Rev. 3, 0 and 1) *[cont.]*								
Northern Africa	2000	2277	1661	281	279	1299	71	81	58	63	63
	2007	4864	2912	150	145	2652	134	110	61	262	260
	2008	7097	3864	211	203	3462	178	190	139	445	439
	2009	7906	3700	155	148	3326	211	219	163	418	405
	2010	8496	3653	129	121	3295	222	229	171	459	451
Sub-Saharan Africa	2000	10624	6488	527	454	5340	619	620	545	113	112
	2007	19745	11703	582	442	10063	898	1058	878	273	240
	2008	22626	12924	561	432	11063	1042	1300	1127	345	306
	2009	25506	13409	609	476	11301	1043	1499	1311	328	288
	2010	28154	14978	847	554	12070	1228	2061	1579	381	333
South Africa	2000	2168	1261	176	144	923	69	161	110	8	7
	2007	4165	2552	259	178	2028	191	265	174	105	99
	2008	5202	2710	243	165	2193	221	274	168	133	131
	2009	5266	2543	226	152	2052	223	265	172	132	127
	2010	5977	2920	297	199	2294	247	329	203	186	181
Latin America and the Caribbean	2000	46822	31099	2604	2313	13570	2246	14925	14245	1095	1082
	2007	104336	61590	4229	3723	30726	4599	26635	24863	5418	5223
	2008	126059	69601	5173	4536	35957	5373	28471	26652	7215	6959
	2009	119513	63632	4579	3977	31285	4705	27768	25903	5398	5164
	2010	139727	71364	5761	5137	34435	5194	31169	28800	6803	6560
Brazil	2000	10142	6609	710	514	4599	667	1300	1179	471	460
	2007	33445	16700	1329	1135	12417	1917	2954	2536	3682	3507
	2008	40330	18317	1949	1719	13386	2203	2982	2554	4654	4430
	2009	38904	15749	1333	1195	11532	1978	2885	2365	3109	2949
	2010	48051	18169	1823	1701	13047	2210	3299	2678	4258	4052
Eastern Asia	2000	21096	11205	7902	7705	1449	309	1854	1614	297	255
	2007	41204	20335	10167	9431	4686	1057	5481	4831	1820	1567
	2008	45487	21304	9774	8906	5275	1216	6255	5505	2148	1817
	2009	45815	20586	9766	8906	4892	1153	5928	5154	1764	1440
	2010	56795	24746	11706	10688	5903	1345	7137	6212	2222	1843
China	2000	13027	7217	4960	4877	1214	296	1044	910	189	162
	2007	32140	17095	8159	7665	4379	1032	4556	4031	1491	1281
	2008	34291	17718	7507	6888	4961	1188	5251	4637	1775	1492
	2009	34244	17055	7535	6950	4595	1126	4925	4298	1490	1209
	2010	43054	20634	9041	8313	5554	1309	6039	5282	1923	1585
Southern Asia	2000	8369	3495	830	756	1720	289	945	858	584	435
	2007	21166	5599	845	640	3452	495	1302	1140	1195	864
	2008	28369	6532	1060	834	4068	609	1403	1207	1459	1018
	2009	23697	5567	816	604	3434	425	1317	1140	1323	901
	2010	28170	6155	1081	861	3677	512	1397	1198	1532	1020
South-Eastern Asia	2000	23696	12542	5245	4705	3057	465	4241	3874	168	159
	2007	45926	21183	6909	5517	7166	1145	7108	6389	847	776
	2008	59039	25679	8473	6676	8908	1406	8297	7480	1365	1258
	2009	55806	23559	7975	6345	7510	1173	8074	7240	881	789
	2010	65765	27046	9266	7210	8570	1382	9210	8335	1071	968
Western Asia	2000	7466	2827	152	105	2319	625	356	328	508	307
	2007	19257	6364	266	146	5388	1210	711	632	1379	1108
	2008	22145	6641	392	259	5495	1327	755	661	1718	1360
	2009	23437	6127	306	167	5032	1173	789	685	1577	1277
	2010	25970	6583	310	159	5451	1291	822	679	1898	1566
Oceania	2000	478	382	113	58	196	76	73	72	0	0
	2007	908	645	170	72	268	75	208	203	4	4
	2008	1141	770	202	104	330	124	237	212	4	4
	2009	1013	635	186	89	277	96	173	170	5	5
	2010	1037	681	220	109	290	107	171	169	7	7

For general note and footnotes see end of table

Exportations mondiales par provenance et destination (Tableau D)

En millions de dollars E.-U. f.o.b.

South-Eastern Europe Europe du Sud-est	Northern Africa Afrique septentrio-nale	Sub-Saharan Africa Afrique du Nord	Latin America and the Caribbean Amérique latine et Caraïbes	Eastern Asia Asie orientale	Southern Asia Asie méridionale	South-eastern Asia Asie du Sud-est	Western Asia Asie occidentale	Oceania Océanie	Others 4/ Autre 4/	Année	← Exportations vers Exportations en provence de ↓
Produits alimentaires, boisson et tabac (CTCI, Rev. 3, 0 et 1) *[suite]*											
10	169	84	5	11	2	10	238	1	24	2000	Afrique du Nord
31	430	397	40	31	12	40	625	1	80	2007	
47	648	508	51	31	53	34	1312	2	101	2008	
56	704	647	42	20	77	66	1952	2	224	2009	
44	854	984	55	34	116	76	2121	2	98	2010	
23	204	2077	82	237	458	190	714	6	32	2000	Afrique subsaharienne
29	364	4302	165	467	702	558	1098	7	78	2007	
67	479	5205	315	433	929	672	1156	21	81	2008	
93	532	5648	1503	453	1173	678	1517	95	77	2009	
91	647	5998	616	823	1032	1071	1886	104	528	2010	
4	8	536	11	103	65	36	130	0	7	2000	Afrique du sud
6	14	803	29	220	38	127	231	2	39	2007	
7	22	1590	24	199	63	134	275	5	39	2008	
2	53	1643	22	198	97	202	325	9	41	2009	
5	44	1602	37	396	60	203	482	13	29	2010	
167	810	562	8676	1541	396	736	1499	11	229	2000	Amérique latine et Caraïbes
529	2614	3101	17784	4095	1552	2944	4474	40	195	2007	
631	3918	3842	23884	5256	2097	3349	6012	34	220	2008	
572	3218	3773	21041	6562	3815	4450	6821	27	203	2009	
633	4580	3917	25078	8516	4909	5692	8005	18	211	2010	
85	185	264	1061	372	139	250	705	0	...	2000	Brésil
368	1369	1748	2503	1624	1296	1138	3011	7	...	2007	
431	1667	2203	4171	2235	1055	1502	4087	9	...	2008	
339	1761	2533	3190	2733	3049	1824	4610	6	...	2009	
371	2837	2732	4412	3258	3737	2703	5569	5	...	2010	
26	146	346	185	6268	196	2055	310	34	28	2000	Asie orientale
95	321	763	771	10244	598	4981	1147	120	9	2007	
114	444	1042	1194	11448	571	5630	1369	201	21	2008	
89	488	1055	976	11597	906	6831	1356	151	15	2009	
87	545	1182	1527	14003	1042	9490	1778	160	13	2010	
26	142	295	145	3365	152	1242	247	5	...	2000	Chine
89	313	710	696	6815	473	3502	890	65	...	2007	
110	416	973	1094	6715	460	3928	1028	74	...	2008	
85	464	990	898	6680	779	4746	1005	52	...	2009	
84	512	1108	1415	8372	937	6700	1298	72	...	2010	
11	217	182	104	414	821	623	1915	2	1	2000	Asie méridionale
48	338	1468	152	1177	3301	2210	5660	5	13	2007	
67	508	1439	229	1660	4644	3417	8373	23	18	2008	
51	412	1053	167	1250	3706	2566	7511	4	87	2009	
42	627	1432	221	1793	4637	3181	8514	7	30	2010	
36	127	650	150	3276	655	5001	976	46	70	2000	Asie Sud-est
92	459	1938	658	5838	1860	10758	1893	154	247	2007	
147	851	3811	1010	6602	1753	13951	3360	223	286	2008	
141	750	3865	782	7252	2345	13141	2645	218	227	2009	
153	816	3917	979	8950	2572	16924	2802	257	278	2010	
143	257	145	58	99	478	84	2651	0	217	2000	Asie occidentale
487	913	941	168	213	1027	291	7240	2	231	2007	
617	791	1020	126	229	1374	413	8902	2	312	2008	
638	776	1144	119	220	1754	450	10292	2	341	2009	
644	829	1151	165	1757	2394	594	9062	3	892	2010	
0	...	8	0	21	0	33	0	22	10	2000	Océanie
0	0	1	3	39	1	133	0	77	5	2007	
0	0	7	8	41	2	207	0	100	1	2008	
0	0	2	7	47	1	229	0	79	6	2009	
0	0	1	8	45	1	215	1	72	7	2010	

Voir la fin du tableau pour la remarque générale et les notes.

World exports by provenance and destination (Table D)

In million U.S. dollars f.o.b.

Exports to → / ↓ Exports from	Year	World 1/ Monde 1/	Developed economies 2/ Economies développées 2/ — Total	Asia-Pacific Asie-Pacifique — Total	Japan Japon	Europe — Total	Germany Allemagne	North America Amérique du Nord — Total	U.S.A. É.-U.	Commonwealth of Independent States Communauté d'Etats Indépendants — Total	Europe
					Cereals (SITC, Rev. 3, 041-045)						
World 1/	2000	33037	11119	3019	2935	6955	794	1146	848	618	517
	2007	72306	24954	5209	4992	17330	2147	2414	1654	1367	578
	2008	104239	33980	7848	7508	22435	2903	3697	2738	1678	712
	2009	77781	24593	5614	5338	16176	2368	2804	2076	1025	333
	2010	83613	24822	5969	5680	16257	2299	2596	1921	1209	423
Developed Economies - Asia-Pacific 2/	2000	2868	509	440	401	69	0	1	0	0	0
	2007	2224	442	435	347	6	1	1	1	0	0
	2008	4414	899	855	716	43	7	1	1	1	1
	2009	4442	528	443	381	84	0	1	0	0	0
	2010	4635	566	514	425	50	0	2	1	0	0
Japan	2000	14	0	0	.	0	.	0	0	0	0
	2007	10	1	0	.	0	0	1	1	0	0
	2008	20	1	0	.	0	0	1	1	0	0
	2009	14	1	0	.	1	0	0	0	0	0
	2010	28	2	0	.	1	0	0	0	0	0
Developed Economies - Europe 2/	2000	8350	5722	32	30	5623	747	67	63	229	210
	2007	16215	12314	32	25	12253	1884	29	25	165	164
	2008	22993	16145	26	17	16053	2528	66	57	193	192
	2009	17418	12526	24	16	12441	2207	62	57	75	75
	2010	18442	12531	37	30	12445	2096	49	45	159	148
France	2000	3913	2939	2	2	2928	409	9	9	11	10
	2007	6357	4588	4	4	4577	556	6	5	35	35
	2008	9639	6271	7	6	6248	788	16	13	60	60
	2009	6798	4468	4	3	4459	615	5	4	21	21
	2010	7678	4389	7	6	4378	628	4	4	22	20
Germany	2000	1594	700	28	28	672	.	0	0	45	37
	2007	2258	1603	19	18	1584	.	0	0	7	7
	2008	3514	2279	9	9	2253	.	16	16	25	25
	2009	2819	1570	6	6	1554	.	9	9	12	12
	2010	2673	1602	10	10	1590	.	2	2	8	8
Developed Economies - North America 2/	2000	12694	3716	2350	2343	603	26	763	508	130	109
	2007	26638	7622	4170	4140	1704	32	1749	1069	15	11
	2008	37226	11082	6561	6529	1736	65	2785	1957	20	20
	2009	23643	7378	4534	4494	982	44	1862	1249	15	15
	2010	25664	7143	4568	4538	988	39	1587	1047	12	12
United States	2000	9733	2775	2096	2094	424	26	255	.	130	109
	2007	21120	5608	3793	3770	1136	28	680	.	14	10
	2008	28949	7827	5918	5893	1081	40	828	.	19	19
	2009	17419	5125	4207	4169	305	10	613	.	10	10
	2010	20084	5245	4224	4196	481	36	540	.	10	9
South-Eastern Europe	2000	149	20	NULL	.	20	3	0	0	24	18
	2007	531	206	0	.	206	39	0	0	10	10
	2008	1731	335	4	4	331	19	0	0	20	17
	2009	1686	811	NULL	.	811	16	0	0	11	11
	2010	2344	973	0	0	973	52	0	0	47	35
Commonwealth of Independent States	2000	281	34	NULL	.	31	0	3	3	118	81
	2007	6179	616	11	11	603	54	2	2	1036	290
	2008	8657	1237	2	2	1235	57	0	0	1221	309
	2009	7789	709	78	78	623	20	8	8	710	77
	2010	5994	340	45	45	292	17	3	3	771	57
Russian Federation	2000	96	5	NULL	.	5	0	0	0	35	5
	2007	4084	370	11	11	359	12	0	0	402	100
	2008	3255	129	1	1	128	8	0	0	369	24
	2009	3444	52	10	10	41	2	0	0	359	5
	2010	2404	33	8	8	25	0	0	0	178	6

For general note and footnotes see end of table

Exportations mondiales par provenance et destination (Tableau D)

En millions de dollars E.-U. f.o.b.

South-Eastern Europe Europe du Sud-est	Northern Africa Afrique septentrionale	Sub-Saharan Africa Afrique du Nord	Latin America and the Caribbean Amérique latine et Caraïbes	Eastern Asia Asie orientale	Southern Asia Asie méridionale	South-eastern Asia Asie du Sud-est	Western Asia Asie occidentale	Oceania Océanie	Others 4/ Autre 4/	Année	← Exportations vers Exportations en provence de ↓
											Céréales (CTCI, Rev. 3, 041-045)
176	3111	2002	5106	2826	1786	2542	3550	105	97	2000	Monde 1/
782	7102	5793	10410	4464	3217	5063	8436	176	541	2007	
1031	9793	8979	15253	6130	6612	7343	13015	303	122	2008	
796	6051	7971	10406	4935	4576	5574	10268	279	1308	2009	
986	8019	7919	11740	6016	3833	7328	10935	317	489	2010	
...	117	230	8	434	500	696	274	90	11	2000	Economies Développées - Asie-Pacifique 2/
0	54	100	0	297	172	596	268	91	203	2007	
0	87	254	24	709	48	1350	931	111	0	2008	
...	67	211	2	506	210	1059	716	80	1064	2009	
...	165	275	6	672	318	1606	649	108	269	2010	
...	...	7	...	4	0	0	2	0	...	2000	Japon
...	0	3	...	3	1	3	0	0	...	2007	
...	0	10	1	4	3	1	0	0	...	2008	
...	0	8	0	4	0	1	0	0	...	2009	
...	0	9	0	10	6	2	0	0	...	2010	
91	822	224	136	108	172	8	831	0	6	2000	Economies Développées - Europe 2/
473	1570	490	8	22	41	0	1131	0	1	2007	
672	3417	806	130	57	342	9	1220	0	3	2008	
360	2181	905	66	86	279	12	927	0	0	2009	
419	2637	1017	168	133	47	94	1235	0	1	2010	
11	463	171	84	54	70	0	110	0	...	2000	France
16	986	443	3	4	13	0	268	0	...	2007	
31	2269	547	33	23	112	6	284	0	2	2008	
22	1538	425	22	74	18	3	206	0	0	2009	
31	2150	595	109	71	1	14	295	0	0	2010	
1	193	14	0	26	85	1	529	...	0	2000	Allemagne
3	174	28	1	0	0	...	442	...	...	2007	
4	309	197	46	1	219	0	434	...	...	2008	
3	184	331	29	1	250	6	434	...	0	2009	
5	184	332	23	16	39	0	463	...	0	2010	
15	1603	528	3224	1224	502	734	940	4	74	2000	Economies Développées - Amérique du Nord 2/
10	2774	1551	7315	2488	691	1588	2269	6	309	2007	
9	2569	2000	10741	4108	1868	2162	2531	38	99	2008	
6	1213	1463	6989	2799	754	1144	1708	102	72	2009	
4	1902	1704	7391	3488	602	1162	1991	96	171	2010	
15	1231	411	2641	1042	95	501	816	4	74	2000	Etats-Unis
10	2357	1176	6336	2364	229	885	1826	6	309	2007	
7	1661	1563	9455	3988	765	1441	2086	38	99	2008	
6	746	1186	5826	2586	129	760	871	102	72	2009	
3	1487	1362	6197	3106	65	819	1528	92	171	2010	
28	14	2	0	0	22	...	41	...	0	2000	Europe du Sud-est
148	38	0	0	0	0	1	127	0	1	2007	
270	114	147	1	26	230	4	584	0	0	2008	
359	54	85	0	67	20	7	271	0	0	2009	
501	91	43	0	161	75	98	354	0	0	2010	
2	8	...	3	2	12	...	103	...	0	2000	Communauté d'Etats Indépendants
80	1727	219	1	10	611	16	1862	...	...	2007	
51	1774	198	25	176	1112	44	2819	0	...	2008	
35	1719	356	44	291	1118	313	2494	0	...	2009	
43	1785	280	38	106	409	114	2106	0	0	2010	
0	4	...	...	1	7	...	45	...	...	2000	Fédération de Russie
77	1399	183	...	5	509	16	1122	...	...	2007	
22	879	143	21	55	531	14	1091	...	...	2008	
29	1043	124	36	31	332	84	1354	...	...	2009	
26	974	130	36	39	104	39	844	...	0	2010	

Voir la fin du tableau pour la remarque générale et les notes.

World exports by provenance and destination (Table D)

In million U.S. dollars f.o.b.

Exports to ⟶			Developed economies 2/ Economies développées 2/							Commonwealth of Independent States Communauté d'Etats Indépendants	
				Asia-Pacific Asie-Pacifique		Europe		North America Amérique du Nord			
↓ Exports from	Year	World 1/ Monde 1/	Total	Total	Japan Japon	Total	Germany Allemagne	Total	U.S.A. É.-U.	Total	Europe
					Cereals (SITC, Rev. 3, 041-045) ***[cont.]***						
Northern Africa	2000	111	2	0	0	1	0	0	0	0	0
	2007	407	42	0	0	34	3	8	8	9	8
	2008	202	24	0	.	22	3	2	2	12	9
	2009	504	58	0	.	36	1	22	22	16	10
	2010	398	27	0	0	27	1	0	0	3	3
Sub-Saharan Africa	2000	152	31	26	26	5	0	0	0	...	...
	2007	371	11	0	0	6	0	4	4	6	6
	2008	893	5	0	0	4	0	1	0	...	...
	2009	699	4	0	0	3	0	0	0	0	...
	2010	620	48	23	23	25	0	0	0	...	...
South Africa	2000	92	25	25	25	1	.	0	0	...	...
	2007	52	1	0	0	1	0	0	0	0	...
	2008	678	1	0	0	1	0	0	0	...	...
	2009	497	3	0	0	3	0	0	0	...	...
	2010	331	42	23	23	19	0	0	0	...	...
Latin America and the Caribbean	2000	2906	427	48	46	279	3	100	100	2	0
	2007	7983	2293	126	124	1969	102	199	197	13	11
	2008	10774	2432	37	35	2112	173	283	279	13	13
	2009	6928	870	119	118	498	36	253	249	14	14
	2010	9470	1347	360	358	699	44	288	281	10	10
Brazil	2000	17	1	1	0	0	0	0	0	...	...
	2007	2043	1291	11	10	1274	86	5	5	...	...
	2008	1931	849	3	1	835	126	12	12	1	1
	2009	1635	143	44	44	73	1	26	25	6	6
	2010	2601	501	116	116	333	0	52	52	0	0
Eastern Asia	2000	1666	63	56	56	5	1	2	1	63	59
	2007	1975	342	266	264	13	1	62	55	24	7
	2008	725	116	85	78	15	1	16	13	26	13
	2009	639	129	111	106	12	1	5	4	40	19
	2010	560	117	101	97	13	1	4	3	24	13
China	2000	1643	61	56	55	5	0	1	1	63	59
	2007	1967	338	266	264	13	1	59	53	24	7
	2008	673	111	84	78	14	1	13	12	26	13
	2009	618	118	106	106	11	1	1	1	40	19
	2010	539	109	97	97	12	1	1	0	24	13
Southern Asia	2000	1181	174	7	1	120	6	46	36	8	8
	2007	4043	355	36	1	231	14	88	67	21	18
	2008	6450	566	58	21	378	26	130	88	13	11
	2009	4969	361	36	2	219	15	106	80	31	15
	2010	5356	371	35	2	250	14	87	58	58	38
South-Eastern Asia	2000	2357	370	60	33	149	6	161	135	20	19
	2007	5209	660	132	79	259	17	268	223	68	54
	2008	9427	1103	218	105	477	23	408	336	155	128
	2009	8222	1157	268	144	414	22	475	398	110	96
	2010	9115	1270	286	161	428	25	556	464	121	106
Western Asia	2000	321	50	0	0	49	3	1	1	23	13
	2007	530	50	0	0	46	0	3	3	1	0
	2008	744	36	0	0	30	1	6	5	4	1
	2009	842	62	1	0	52	6	10	9	2	1
	2010	1014	88	1	0	68	9	19	19	2	1
Oceania	2000	0	0	0	.	.	.	.	.	...	...
	2007	0	0	0	.	.	.	0	0	...	...
	2008	2	0	0	.	.	.	0	0	...	...
	2009	1	0	0	.	.	.	0	0	0	0
	2010	1	0	0	.	0	.	0	0	0	0

For general note and footnotes see end of table

Exportations mondiales par provenance et destination (Tableau D)

En millions de dollars E.-U. f.o.b.

South-Eastern Europe Europe du Sud-est	Northern Africa Afrique septentrio-nale	Sub-Saharan Africa Afrique du Nord	Latin America and the Caribbean Amérique latine et Caraïbes	Eastern Asia Asie orientale	Southern Asia Asie méridionale	South-eastern Asia Asie du Sud-est	Western Asia Asie occidentale	Oceania Océanie	Others 4/ Autre 4/	Année	← Exportations vers Exportations en provence de ↓
											Céréales (CTCI, Rev. 3, 041-045) *[suite]*
9	30	12	...	...	0	...	57	...	0	2000	Afrique du Nord
17	78	38	0	6	0	10	207	...	0	2007	
7	41	18	...	1	1	0	99	...	...	2008	
21	34	25	...	0	0	...	269	...	80	2009	
7	183	30	...	1	2	...	144	0	0	2010	
0	2	95	0	4	7	1	12	0	0	2000	Afrique subsaharienne
2	0	316	13	3	6	9	2	0	2	2007	
3	1	781	1	3	36	30	32	0	2	2008	
0	0	663	1	0	9	18	2	0	2	2009	
0	1	406	3	87	15	44	15	0	1	2010	
...	0	49	0	4	6	0	7	0	0	2000	Afrique du sud
2	0	34	7	0	0	5	0	...	2	2007	
3	0	609	1	1	34	19	8	0	2	2008	
...	0	469	1	0	8	14	1	0	1	2009	
0	0	144	1	86	9	38	11	0	1	2010	
0	313	118	1660	5	137	31	207	...	5	2000	Amérique latine et Caraïbes
49	673	592	2851	159	560	313	466	0	14	2007	
6	1632	840	3856	105	996	197	695	...	1	2008	
4	687	462	3101	256	575	357	600	0	2	2009	
2	1127	354	3880	410	730	886	723	0	1	2010	
...	...	1	14	...	...	...	0	...	...	2000	Brésil
45	19	34	57	114	446	...	37	...	...	2007	
...	134	178	264	101	200	93	110	...	...	2008	
0	134	226	242	227	293	194	169	...	...	2009	
...	379	176	369	280	288	382	225	...	...	2010	
12	21	184	41	685	43	504	51	0	0	2000	Asie orientale
2	0	133	24	908	35	441	23	42	...	2007	
2	10	198	3	207	22	59	13	71	...	2008	
0	1	128	2	259	18	37	11	15	...	2009	
1	2	63	2	271	24	37	5	13	0	2010	
12	21	166	41	682	42	504	51	0	...	2000	Chine
2	0	133	24	904	35	441	23	42	...	2007	
2	1	198	2	200	22	58	9	44	...	2008	
0	1	127	2	252	18	36	11	14	...	2009	
1	2	62	1	263	24	36	5	13	...	2010	
0	72	96	0	2	154	36	639	0	0	2000	Asie méridionale
1	52	950	3	31	735	301	1591	0	3	2007	
4	19	668	14	228	1357	548	3027	1	6	2008	
3	11	563	2	43	1089	378	2429	0	58	2009	
2	15	711	1	21	1001	493	2669	0	13	2010	
3	18	504	34	362	164	533	338	11	0	2000	Asie Sud-est
0	20	1386	193	532	221	1786	298	36	8	2007	
6	116	3047	458	511	123	2933	884	82	9	2008	
5	49	3088	197	624	29	2230	636	82	15	2009	
5	57	3020	249	660	108	2744	763	98	19	2010	
15	90	10	0	0	75	0	57	...	1	2000	Asie occidentale
0	117	18	0	8	145	1	191	...	1	2007	
2	12	24	0	1	477	7	179	...	2	2008	
2	36	23	1	3	475	20	204	...	14	2009	
3	54	17	1	5	500	51	281	0	12	2010	
...	...	...	...	...	...	...	...	0	0	2000	Océanie
...	...	...	0	...	...	0	0	0	...	2007	
...	...	0	...	0	...	...	...	2	...	2008	
...	...	0	...	...	...	...	...	1	...	2009	
...	...	0	...	...	...	...	...	0	...	2010	

Voir la fin du tableau pour la remarque générale et les notes.

World exports by provenance and destination (Table D)

In million U.S. dollars f.o.b.

Exports to → / ↓ Exports from	Year	World 1/ Monde 1/	Developed economies 2/ Economies développées 2/ Total	Asia-Pacific Asie-Pacifique Total	Asia-Pacific Asie-Pacifique Japan Japon	Europe Total	Europe Germany Allemagne	North America Amérique du Nord Total	North America Amérique du Nord U.S.A. É.-U.	Commonwealth of Independent States Communauté d'Etats Indépendants Total	Commonwealth of Independent States Communauté d'Etats Indépendants Europe
Crude materials (excluding fuels), oils, fats (SITC, Rev. 3, 2 and 4)											
World 1/	2000	212912	134977	21281	19734	83821	15204	29875	23141	3298	2947
	2007	547820	287195	43663	40757	197944	35296	45587	33976	11006	8974
	2008	653267	323993	48174	44471	224513	40545	51306	38680	15153	12752
	2009	495232	217272	33355	30943	150343	27667	33574	24760	9483	7787
	2010	694124	298622	50830	47646	202804	37837	44988	33204	12236	10326
Developed Economies - Asia-Pacific 2/	2000	17277	6994	3049	2577	2422	328	1523	1155	175	174
	2007	46296	12483	7446	6820	3522	429	1514	1075	486	483
	2008	60327	16078	9882	9206	3961	501	2234	1827	704	700
	2009	51381	10501	6738	6259	1910	414	1853	1446	351	342
	2010	81493	15595	11186	10549	2872	637	1538	1136	575	541
Japan	2000	3369	747	30	.	437	96	280	268	5	4
	2007	9038	1283	38	.	772	277	474	452	14	12
	2008	10337	1553	48	.	961	247	544	524	36	33
	2009	9005	1069	42	.	543	129	484	469	31	25
	2010	10992	1554	44	.	824	162	686	667	57	49
Developed Economies - Europe 2/	2000	60995	51423	1528	1331	47527	9912	2368	2049	810	783
	2007	152471	123807	2362	1892	116692	23640	4754	4015	2569	2388
	2008	169709	135317	2384	1931	127967	26100	4966	4255	3401	3203
	2009	122048	93542	1943	1551	88294	18263	3306	2869	2380	2244
	2010	158303	120523	2355	1862	114064	23648	4105	3470	2784	2636
France	2000	6036	5195	62	54	4960	957	173	159	43	39
	2007	13533	11825	67	48	11498	2221	260	236	112	106
	2008	15360	13401	69	53	13051	2480	280	256	197	184
	2009	10118	8362	55	41	8108	1690	199	178	125	120
	2010	13471	11107	66	50	10818	2019	223	201	157	150
Germany	2000	9272	7481	98	75	7114	.	269	236	175	169
	2007	25787	21232	175	118	19874	.	1184	1025	525	501
	2008	29058	23534	215	143	21997	.	1323	1171	816	776
	2009	19413	15106	157	104	14291	.	658	601	582	556
	2010	25909	20697	205	138	19539	.	953	860	637	610
Developed Economies - North America 2/	2000	53039	35036	6987	6666	10335	1651	17714	12780	60	49
	2007	100496	50730	8262	7794	20602	2855	21866	14131	194	182
	2008	119056	55160	9528	8868	22106	3810	23527	14655	337	328
	2009	91167	36028	5971	5630	14911	2146	15146	9275	240	230
	2010	121241	49483	7876	7391	21808	2972	19799	12178	332	298
United States	2000	30471	15489	4053	3903	6505	965	4931	.	55	43
	2007	65401	24155	4561	4356	11896	1879	7698	.	158	147
	2008	81110	28350	5142	4936	14390	2448	8818	.	274	266
	2009	65183	19652	3270	3099	10550	1459	5832	.	209	201
	2010	85505	26687	4215	3947	14854	1878	7618	.	296	264
South-Eastern Europe	2000	1742	850	9	8	826	121	15	5	108	108
	2007	5055	2497	93	93	2257	365	148	104	53	51
	2008	6244	2989	76	76	2819	361	93	76	66	62
	2009	4796	2364	92	92	2260	323	12	11	35	32
	2010	6901	3350	163	162	3172	459	15	15	51	43
Commonwealth of Independent States	2000	9303	4919	598	597	4233	461	88	79	1650	1383
	2007	26521	9815	812	812	8907	608	96	87	5397	3846
	2008	33337	12022	543	541	11365	699	115	97	7154	5358
	2009	21609	6532	377	375	6034	426	121	95	4228	2939
	2010	28513	9411	384	382	8769	644	259	246	4761	3388
Russian Federation	2000	4752	2850	588	587	2214	173	48	40	338	229
	2007	14930	6341	806	805	5463	306	72	66	1439	507
	2008	17537	6966	542	540	6329	310	95	81	1895	573
	2009	10009	3562	372	370	3110	219	80	69	1197	284
	2010	13274	5253	364	363	4687	352	202	191	1248	381

For general note and footnotes see end of table

Exportations mondiales par provenance et destination (Tableau D)

En millions de dollars E.-U. f.o.b.

South-Eastern Europe Europe du Sud-est	Northern Africa Afrique septentrionale	Sub-Saharan Africa Afrique du Nord	Latin America and the Caribbean Amérique latine et Caraïbes	Eastern Asia Asie orientale	Southern Asia Asie méridionale	South-eastern Asia Asie du Sud-est	Western Asia Asie occidentale	Oceania Océanie	Others 4/ Autre 4/	Année	← Exportations vers / Exportations en provenance de ↓
Matières brutes (sauf combustibles), huiles et graisses (CTCI, Rev. 3, 2 et 4)											
1141	2689	3045	10281	32745	6987	9124	6391	83	2152	2000	Monde 1/
4618	7500	8468	22479	135888	26150	21770	20160	178	2408	2007	
5848	11874	10300	30115	168460	29928	28137	28091	203	1164	2008	
3735	8104	7932	19248	160435	26843	22250	18679	210	1040	2009	
5442	11106	10785	27660	232224	35405	31517	28097	220	809	2010	
56	116	351	117	6158	678	1505	377	29	721	2000	Economies Développées - Asie-Pacifique 2/
66	63	748	105	25362	1807	2329	1440	68	1338	2007	
58	30	701	236	35943	1776	2752	1605	65	381	2008	
13	23	548	183	34633	1444	2219	1309	69	89	2009	
11	47	731	252	56614	2523	3332	1657	92	63	2010	
1	3	41	33	1879	111	525	22	1	...	2000	Japon
0	5	117	28	6472	199	858	60	1	...	2007	
0	10	138	43	7169	214	1100	73	1	...	2008	
2	9	136	41	6510	183	953	70	1	...	2009	
6	11	170	53	7490	230	1329	90	2	...	2010	
397	1136	626	613	2814	636	633	1535	11	360	2000	Economies Développées - Europe 2/
1522	2617	1125	1349	10545	2356	1436	4436	23	687	2007	
2086	3705	1363	1608	11287	2743	1850	5890	27	433	2008	
1517	2874	1106	1328	10766	2597	1556	4099	22	262	2009	
2198	3636	1449	1540	14311	3316	1901	6377	24	243	2010	
16	118	62	61	280	115	29	109	7	0	2000	France
68	234	82	108	736	118	81	158	11	0	2007	
87	310	102	122	715	134	94	181	17	1	2008	
64	272	86	85	746	130	69	166	12	0	2009	
72	300	102	107	1032	171	129	281	10	3	2010	
95	91	101	110	601	125	140	206	1	146	2000	Allemagne
251	137	185	220	1751	438	256	544	2	245	2007	
275	265	286	290	1838	489	349	746	1	168	2008	
197	317	202	271	1572	348	306	511	2	0	2009	
270	247	297	287	1980	421	330	735	7	0	2010	
26	190	314	5427	8312	522	1923	975	21	232	2000	Economies Développées - Amérique du Nord 2/
84	900	544	9357	28595	2271	4097	3574	31	120	2007	
101	1669	971	13152	34826	2034	5409	5272	41	84	2008	
81	1360	557	8843	33532	2472	4459	3411	23	162	2009	
138	1848	640	11512	43868	2792	5546	4843	35	205	2010	
21	165	250	5057	6440	360	1472	911	19	232	2000	Etats-Unis
26	782	364	8484	23188	1526	3518	3052	26	120	2007	
76	1436	663	11475	28138	1560	4662	4367	25	84	2008	
44	1176	409	8068	26915	1912	3730	2888	18	162	2009	
35	1519	481	10328	35122	2024	4717	4070	20	205	2010	
231	122	2	8	102	6	3	310	0	0	2000	Europe du Sud-est
882	149	27	32	192	84	5	1131	0	2	2007	
1210	183	59	23	181	25	5	1500	0	3	2008	
712	159	112	8	255	93	7	1048	0	2	2009	
1100	177	141	12	381	81	6	1594	0	8	2010	
129	270	6	49	1264	180	65	771	0	0	2000	Communauté d'Etats Indépendants
555	934	19	72	5900	1396	278	2149	1	5	2007	
702	1959	58	207	6856	1660	228	2490	1	0	2008	
369	797	29	30	5661	2312	112	1537	0	0	2009	
642	1021	71	80	8378	1429	150	2564	1	6	2010	
23	190	1	12	973	45	21	300	0	0	2000	Fédération de Russie
156	626	9	28	4521	354	222	1228	1	5	2007	
164	1410	39	117	4979	358	183	1426	1	0	2008	
61	417	14	22	3703	384	85	565	0	0	2009	
65	508	27	50	4572	456	91	996	1	6	2010	

Voir la fin du tableau pour la remarque générale et les notes.

World exports by provenance and destination (Table D)

In million U.S. dollars f.o.b.

Exports to → / ↓ Exports from	Year	World 1/ Monde 1/	Developed economies 2/ Economies développées 2/ Total	Asia-Pacific Asie-Pacifique Total	Asia-Pacific Asie-Pacifique Japan Japon	Europe Total	Europe Germany Allemagne	North America Amérique du Nord Total	North America Amérique du Nord U.S.A. É.-U.	Commonwealth of Independent States Communauté d'Etats Indépendants Total	Commonwealth of Independent States Communauté d'Etats Indépendants Europe
		Crude materials (excluding fuels), oils, fats (SITC, Rev. 3, 2 and 4) *[cont.]*									
Northern Africa	2000	1414	946	61	24	773	42	111	102	12	12
	2007	3198	1897	102	27	1543	62	253	235	16	16
	2008	6036	3526	422	45	2503	103	601	587	42	39
	2009	3715	1615	70	18	1203	72	342	329	9	9
	2010	4435	2083	132	25	1508	90	442	423	21	20
Sub-Saharan Africa	2000	7468	4489	522	506	3430	537	537	477	15	15
	2007	21303	10578	1045	986	8184	1481	1350	864	180	177
	2008	27766	12695	1750	1671	9439	1529	1506	1060	407	397
	2009	22717	8754	959	921	6627	923	1168	790	212	203
	2010	31206	11781	1608	1524	8298	1339	1875	1266	374	359
South Africa	2000	2693	1932	411	400	1205	338	315	306	8	8
	2007	7173	3808	851	806	2448	923	509	363	13	13
	2008	10737	5176	1419	1356	3321	991	436	404	110	110
	2009	8538	2970	724	705	1877	568	369	313	17	15
	2010	13231	4630	1209	1145	3018	825	404	385	94	94
Latin America and the Caribbean	2000	25139	15209	2677	2602	7713	1255	4819	3999	149	149
	2007	87721	39653	10566	10299	20053	3387	9033	7466	436	393
	2008	103443	44727	9858	9547	25279	4498	9590	8159	555	514
	2009	80802	30267	7241	7019	16212	3056	6814	5580	377	338
	2010	121451	44697	12404	12016	23343	4858	8951	7230	747	693
Brazil	2000	9140	6169	900	881	4222	771	1047	980	12	12
	2007	29110	14323	1758	1717	10235	1457	2330	1827	108	104
	2008	42307	19543	2880	2740	14020	2414	2643	2031	219	181
	2009	35272	13204	1777	1730	9536	1314	1891	1264	99	75
	2010	54257	19555	3922	3790	13083	2666	2550	1810	321	295
Eastern Asia	2000	11347	4318	1979	1894	1470	229	869	814	91	88
	2007	21300	8143	2700	2524	3442	548	2002	1771	305	275
	2008	25680	10189	3385	3122	4331	846	2474	2180	394	351
	2009	19019	6871	2529	2345	2736	578	1606	1401	225	193
	2010	25959	9488	3318	3121	3923	790	2246	1933	350	321
China	2000	4575	2767	1241	1205	1051	169	475	454	56	53
	2007	9428	5358	1490	1400	2529	420	1340	1182	168	143
	2008	11914	6610	1941	1784	3015	549	1655	1476	229	191
	2009	8495	4472	1455	1356	1907	450	1111	974	133	107
	2010	11994	6162	1885	1773	2767	590	1510	1316	203	177
Southern Asia	2000	2592	1254	296	277	665	105	292	279	92	72
	2007	14074	2512	698	613	1354	237	460	433	182	56
	2008	15961	2789	638	585	1531	299	621	590	278	82
	2009	13865	2245	606	520	1207	211	433	401	105	37
	2010	19731	2767	471	416	1603	307	693	658	581	497
South-Eastern Asia	2000	18178	7769	3106	2833	3214	376	1448	1324	71	69
	2007	58676	21109	8475	7922	8708	1274	3926	3643	953	918
	2008	72215	24098	8662	8007	10009	1389	5427	5074	1364	1326
	2009	54326	15748	6062	5571	7056	994	2631	2440	1093	1063
	2010	81738	25590	9845	9259	10829	1701	4916	4524	1370	1312
Western Asia	2000	2648	1083	115	110	884	115	83	73	61	47
	2007	7824	2277	125	108	1976	214	176	142	238	190
	2008	10111	2371	218	165	2011	199	143	110	451	392
	2009	7547	1553	132	94	1283	152	138	117	228	157
	2010	10063	2143	125	94	1876	235	142	120	290	218
Oceania	2000	1769	688	353	308	329	71	7	6	3	0
	2007	2884	1693	978	868	704	196	11	10	0	0
	2008	3381	2031	828	707	1193	211	11	10	0	0
	2009	2239	1250	634	549	610	108	6	5	0	0
	2010	3091	1711	964	844	740	158	6	6	1	1

For general note and footnotes see end of table

Exportations mondiales par provenance et destination (Tableau D)

En millions de dollars E.-U. f.o.b.

South-Eastern Europe Europe du Sud-est	Northern Africa Afrique septentrio-nale	Sub-Saharan Africa Afrique du Nord	Latin America and the Caribbean Amérique latine et Caraïbes	Eastern Asia Asie orientale	Southern Asia Asie méridionale	South-eastern Asia Asie du Sud-est	Western Asia Asie occidentale	Oceania Océanie	Others 4/ Autre 4/	← Exportations vers Année	Exportations en provence de ↓
											Matières brutes (sauf combustibles), huiles et graisses (CTCI, Rev. 3, 2 et 4) ***[suite]***
35	45	13	89	63	63	32	106	0	9	2000	Afrique du Nord
54	193	77	175	213	241	56	266	0	11	2007	
121	302	147	393	301	422	123	641	...	18	2008	
27	274	195	144	397	341	94	483	...	135	2009	
38	327	225	261	369	443	125	515	0	28	2010	
18	109	1007	116	755	329	374	228	1	27	2000	Afrique subsaharienne
59	241	2974	175	4749	784	898	626	2	38	2007	
64	224	3373	243	7317	1284	1393	737	10	19	2008	
48	161	2614	214	7812	945	1255	661	34	7	2009	
58	193	3544	621	10467	1225	1656	1199	6	82	2010	
10	6	112	23	358	62	154	29	0	0	2000	Afrique du sud
24	10	212	90	2313	254	392	46	1	9	2007	
38	9	364	117	3732	496	559	127	7	2	2008	
3	10	228	72	4390	291	459	95	1	2	2009	
13	15	323	84	6606	577	770	114	2	1	2010	
145	361	222	3372	3244	1370	669	389	1	7	2000	Amérique latine et Caraïbes
954	1344	895	9620	25710	5256	2523	1260	1	69	2007	
1023	2196	830	12073	31973	4208	3344	2441	2	72	2008	
677	1177	548	7117	33754	3204	2111	1354	1	216	2009	
827	1821	764	10737	50720	4932	3260	2911	2	32	2010	
41	196	50	682	1211	328	210	241	1	...	2000	Brésil
233	543	286	1565	9088	1207	1058	699	0	...	2007	
270	912	375	2197	14329	1013	1803	1645	2	0	2008	
105	691	141	1052	17163	756	1132	929	0	...	2009	
143	859	182	2229	26216	824	1628	2297	1	...	2010	
7	33	46	97	5248	440	948	116	1	1	2000	Asie orientale
66	98	197	422	8672	1079	1634	682	3	0	2007	
112	115	301	560	9546	1299	2383	773	6	0	2008	
53	100	234	443	7382	1042	2097	564	9	0	2009	
82	145	308	628	9311	1694	3160	788	4	0	2010	
6	18	23	42	1000	251	360	52	0	...	2000	Chine
61	71	86	208	1910	525	602	437	2	...	2007	
102	85	136	300	2302	625	1014	505	4	...	2008	
48	70	111	235	1693	500	871	355	7	...	2009	
74	109	150	346	2324	851	1277	496	2	...	2010	
6	31	40	56	495	216	223	179	0	0	2000	Asie méridionale
77	62	85	88	7920	1575	711	841	3	20	2007	
24	94	117	144	8637	1951	926	987	1	14	2008	
62	76	134	89	8268	1380	718	738	2	49	2009	
23	82	159	137	11516	2149	1150	1140	3	24	2010	
41	202	375	281	4017	2230	2379	794	15	4	2000	Asie Sud-est
109	739	1629	1027	16080	7703	7440	1840	41	7	2007	
170	1207	2257	1366	18922	10854	9153	2771	42	9	2008	
69	985	1661	784	15696	9655	7090	1492	44	8	2009	
142	1677	2614	1813	22901	12955	10563	2051	50	13	2010	
49	73	34	55	161	306	140	612	0	75	2000	Asie occidentale
190	159	148	52	1137	1409	188	1915	0	111	2007	
178	190	122	104	1832	1416	331	2984	1	132	2008	
108	118	194	60	1652	1292	247	1984	0	110	2009	
182	133	138	62	2482	1754	315	2459	0	104	2010	
1	...	8	1	112	10	229	...	4	714	2000	Océanie
0	...	1	4	814	189	177	0	6	0	2007	
0	0	2	6	838	257	240	0	7	0	2008	
0	...	1	4	628	67	284	0	5	0	2009	
0	...	1	5	906	112	352	0	4	0	2010	

Voir la fin du tableau pour la remarque générale et les notes.

World exports by provenance and destination (Table D)

In million U.S. dollars f.o.b.

Exports from ↓ / Exports to →	Year	World 1/ Monde 1/	Developed economies 2/ Economies développées 2/							Commonwealth of Independent States Communauté d'Etats Indépendants	
				Asia-Pacific Asie-Pacifique		Europe		North America Amérique du Nord			
			Total	Total	Japan Japon	Total	Germany Allemagne	Total	U.S.A. É.-U.	Total	Europe
Oil seeds and, oleaginous fruit (SITC, Rev. 3, 22)											
World 1/	2000	14376	7300	1663	1637	5059	978	579	313	96	80
	2007	34290	13267	2651	2576	9719	2277	897	626	407	356
	2008	53137	21083	3711	3623	15843	4093	1529	1069	554	505
	2009	47984	16243	2811	2780	12264	3235	1168	759	393	329
	2010	56207	16910	3063	3028	12709	3001	1137	771	656	604
Developed Economies - Asia-Pacific 2/	2000	419	154	110	106	7	1	38	36	...	...
	2007	138	87	74	69	7	0	7	6	0	0
	2008	338	222	79	72	133	32	10	7	0	0
	2009	604	418	83	77	321	21	14	12	0	0
	2010	536	282	119	114	158	2	5	3	0	0
Japan	2000	1	0	NULL	.	0	0	0	0	...	...
	2007	7	2	0	.	1	0	1	1	0	0
	2008	3	2	0	.	1	0	2	1	0	0
	2009	3	2	0	.	1	0	1	1	0	0
	2010	2	2	0	.	1	0	1	1	0	0
Developed Economies - Europe 2/	2000	1529	1329	2	1	1315	564	12	11	13	13
	2007	4102	3783	5	2	3768	1646	10	9	135	134
	2008	6286	5822	4	2	5804	2388	14	12	235	233
	2009	4665	4391	3	2	4380	2039	8	6	103	101
	2010	5312	4924	2	1	4909	1930	12	10	138	134
France	2000	558	429	0	0	428	178	1	1	5	5
	2007	944	870	1	0	868	456	1	1	24	24
	2008	1601	1502	1	0	1498	783	2	2	56	55
	2009	886	823	0	0	822	481	1	1	33	33
	2010	1034	941	0	0	939	366	1	1	45	45
Germany	2000	159	125	0	0	125	.	0	0	0	0
	2007	283	237	1	0	235	.	1	1	28	28
	2008	468	401	0	0	400	.	1	0	55	53
	2009	291	264	0	0	263	.	1	0	17	15
	2010	347	304	0	0	303	.	1	1	25	23
Developed Economies - North America 2/	2000	6985	3005	1250	1239	1411	146	345	141	2	1
	2007	14339	4493	2134	2116	1635	378	723	480	38	38
	2008	22165	6708	2967	2962	2472	847	1269	851	25	24
	2009	22098	4598	2216	2212	1476	513	906	545	70	68
	2010	24910	5533	2423	2420	2220	609	891	575	74	74
United States	2000	5818	2338	823	813	1311	137	204	.	2	1
	2007	11119	2624	1181	1166	1199	345	244	.	38	38
	2008	16933	3710	1487	1486	1805	780	418	.	24	23
	2009	17628	2506	1179	1177	966	464	361	.	55	53
	2010	19752	2849	1220	1220	1312	538	316	.	51	51
South-Eastern Europe	2000	60	34	NULL	.	34	6	0	0	0	0
	2007	465	149	0	0	146	8	3	3	4	4
	2008	1119	679	0	0	677	58	3	3	16	16
	2009	1016	698	0	0	696	79	1	1	12	11
	2010	1373	893	0	0	891	106	1	1	18	18
Commonwealth of Independent States	2000	414	231	0	.	228	18	3	3	49	35
	2007	793	360	0	0	359	10	1	1	95	50
	2008	1596	1286	0	0	1285	96	0	0	93	56
	2009	1312	933	0	0	930	37	4	4	115	61
	2010	1289	831	0	0	816	60	16	16	118	88
Russian Federation	2000	191	105	NULL	.	105	14	0	0	6	1
	2007	78	45	NULL	.	45	3	0	0	23	1
	2008	89	51	0	0	51	8	0	0	25	1
	2009	111	76	NULL	.	76	8	0	0	17	0
	2010	84	66	NULL	.	66	13	0	0	5	0

For general note and footnotes see end of table

Exportations mondiales par provenance et destination (Tableau D)

En millions de dollars E.-U. f.o.b.

← Exportations vers

South-Eastern Europe Europe du Sud-est	Northern Africa Afrique septentrionale	Sub-Saharan Africa Afrique du Nord	Latin America and the Caribbean Amérique latine et Caraïbes	Eastern Asia Asie orientale	Southern Asia Asie méridionale	South-eastern Asia Asie du Sud-est	Western Asia Asie occidentale	Oceania Océanie	Others 4/ Autre 4/	Année	Exportations en provenance de ↓
											Graines et fruits oléagineux (CTCI, Rev. 3, 22)
33	167	107	1676	3233	264	793	464	4	240	2000	Monde 1/
214	649	208	3299	11832	893	1745	1650	5	123	2007	
357	960	154	5112	19494	829	2267	2216	12	99	2008	
273	979	214	3524	20751	1172	2253	1994	17	171	2009	
487	1146	196	4449	25578	1140	2796	2619	9	222	2010	
...	0	1	13	193	41	8	7	1	...	2000	Economies Développées - Asie-Pacifique 2/
0	1	2	1	10	34	2	0	1	...	2007	
0	...	4	0	4	76	2	28	1	...	2008	
0	...	8	1	26	118	3	29	2	...	2009	
0	...	0	1	25	205	4	15	2	...	2010	
...	...	0	0	0	...	0	0	...	...	2000	Japon
...	...	...	0	5	0	0	...	0	...	2007	
...	...	...	0	1	0	0	...	...	...	2008	
...	...	0	0	0	...	0	...	0	...	2009	
...	...	0	0	0	...	0	0	...	...	2010	
9	12	2	7	47	90	0	19	0	0	2000	Economies Développées - Europe 2/
98	12	8	25	3	15	0	23	0	0	2007	
149	12	5	6	2	3	1	50	0	0	2008	
121	10	4	4	2	1	1	27	0	0	2009	
183	9	21	4	4	1	1	27	0	1	2010	
2	10	0	5	31	73	0	3	0	...	2000	France
24	0	2	1	0	15	0	7	0	0	2007	
29	1	1	1	0	2	0	10	0	0	2008	
23	1	1	1	1	1	0	2	0	0	2009	
35	2	1	1	2	0	0	6	0	0	2010	
0	0	0	1	15	17	0	0	...	0	2000	Allemagne
3	2	0	12	0	0	0	0	...	...	2007	
8	1	0	2	1	0	0	1	...	...	2008	
7	0	0	1	0	0	0	0	0	0	2009	
15	0	0	1	0	0	0	1	...	0	2010	
3	51	3	1098	1927	32	457	173	2	232	2000	Economies Développées - Amérique du Nord 2/
22	272	3	2219	5461	337	868	504	3	120	2007	
35	494	8	3345	9352	131	1075	901	7	84	2008	
29	602	5	2413	11653	364	1354	842	6	162	2009	
17	630	9	2829	12698	486	1452	970	7	205	2010	
3	43	3	923	1674	0	428	171	2	232	2000	Etats-Unis
13	264	1	1782	5092	0	805	377	3	120	2007	
34	445	6	2553	8493	2	991	585	7	84	2008	
29	601	2	1982	10261	107	1276	641	6	162	2009	
17	594	6	2148	11854	79	1363	580	6	205	2010	
4	...	0	5	6	0	0	10	...	0	2000	Europe du Sud-est
48	0	0	4	0	32	0	227	...	...	2007	
115	6	...	3	0	4	0	294	...	...	2008	
73	0	7	1	0	57	0	169	...	...	2009	
219	3	24	3	0	33	0	180	...	0	2010	
10	11	...	1	9	5	...	98	...	0	2000	Communauté d'Etats Indépendants
15	5	...	8	3	139	0	169	...	0	2007	
7	10	0	9	10	66	0	114	...	0	2008	
12	4	9	4	5	80	0	150	...	0	2009	
14	16	1	1	2	27	2	278	0	...	2010	
...	1	...	...	9	3	...	68	...	...	2000	Fédération de Russie
0	1	...	...	1	0	...	7	...	0	2007	
0	5	...	...	2	0	0	6	...	...	2008	
0	1	9	...	3	4	...	1	...	...	2009	
...	...	...	...	0	2	...	10	...	...	2010	

Voir la fin du tableau pour la remarque générale et les notes.

World exports by provenance and destination (Table D)

In million U.S. dollars f.o.b.

Exports to → / ↓ Exports from	Year	World 1/ Monde 1/	Developed economies 2/ Economies développées 2/							Commonwealth of Independent States Communauté d'Etats Indépendants	
				Asia-Pacific Asie-Pacifique		Europe		North America Amérique du Nord			
			Total	Total	Japan Japon	Total	Germany Allemagne	Total	U.S.A. É.-U.	Total	Europe
Oil seeds and, oleaginous fruit (SITC, Rev. 3, 22) *[cont.]*											
Northern Africa	2000	12	4	0	.	4	1	0	0	0	0
	2007	13	5	0	0	5	1	0	0	...	...
	2008	40	9	1	0	9	1	0	0	0	0
	2009	104	29	0	0	27	1	1	1	0	0
	2010	94	24	1	0	23	1	1	1	0	0
Sub-Saharan Africa	2000	329	104	38	37	58	2	9	8	1	0
	2007	838	201	66	65	112	8	24	21	2	2
	2008	991	318	116	115	169	4	33	31	5	5
	2009	1177	182	68	67	76	3	39	35	2	2
	2010	1563	288	121	115	133	8	34	31	1	1
South Africa	2000	26	17	7	6	9	1	1	1	0	...
	2007	17	10	6	6	4	1	0	0	...	...
	2008	114	62	13	12	48	0	0	0	0	0
	2009	111	12	6	5	6	0	0	0	0	...
	2010	110	26	9	8	17	1	0	0	...	...
Latin America and the Caribbean	2000	3743	2029	120	116	1786	218	123	70	0	0
	2007	11776	3563	185	170	3328	144	49	46	59	59
	2008	18181	5236	382	329	4790	555	64	53	94	93
	2009	15186	4470	327	322	4036	473	106	81	45	45
	2010	18940	3578	271	265	3211	226	95	74	226	216
Brazil	2000	2190	1612	103	103	1508	201	1	1	...	...
	2007	6741	2993	112	110	2881	118	0	0	37	37
	2008	11009	4468	269	220	4197	477	2	2	60	60
	2009	11493	3954	247	247	3705	456	2	1	4	4
	2010	11096	2667	193	193	2474	135	0	0	175	164
Eastern Asia	2000	428	251	119	113	128	11	5	2	20	20
	2007	720	335	108	105	191	49	36	24	38	36
	2008	1013	437	115	109	263	74	60	47	46	43
	2009	751	271	67	62	159	44	45	36	19	17
	2010	719	254	77	72	152	29	25	15	21	17
China	2000	417	251	118	113	128	11	5	2	20	20
	2007	710	335	108	105	191	49	36	23	38	36
	2008	1001	436	114	108	263	74	59	46	46	43
	2009	735	270	66	62	159	44	45	36	19	17
	2010	707	253	77	72	152	29	24	15	21	17
Southern Asia	2000	244	85	8	8	47	7	30	29	7	7
	2007	661	157	32	5	87	17	39	34	14	13
	2008	884	238	15	4	152	23	71	62	15	14
	2009	619	146	16	7	89	15	42	35	7	7
	2010	974	177	12	3	113	20	52	42	23	23
South-Eastern Asia	2000	131	27	13	13	2	1	11	11	0	0
	2007	240	57	38	37	18	4	1	1	3	3
	2008	262	46	27	27	18	3	1	1	4	4
	2009	196	35	22	22	11	1	1	1	1	0
	2010	233	42	31	31	10	1	1	1	1	1
Western Asia	2000	65	39	2	2	36	4	1	1	3	3
	2007	178	72	8	8	62	10	3	2	19	16
	2008	212	79	4	4	71	12	4	3	20	17
	2009	219	72	8	8	62	9	2	2	18	16
	2010	235	83	6	6	74	9	3	3	36	33
Oceania	2000	17	8	1	1	6	1	0	0	...	...
	2007	27	4	1	.	3	1	0	0	...	...
	2008	52	2	2	.	0	.	0	.	...	...
	2009	37	2	2	.	0	.	.	.	...	...
	2010	29	0	0	.	.	.	.	.	...	...

For general note and footnotes see end of table

Exportations mondiales par provenance et destination (Tableau D)

En millions de dollars E.-U. f.o.b.

South-Eastern Europe Europe du Sud-est	Northern Africa Afrique septentrionale	Sub-Saharan Africa Afrique du Nord	Latin America and the Caribbean Amérique latine et Caraïbes	Eastern Asia Asie orientale	Southern Asia Asie méridionale	South-eastern Asia Asie du Sud-est	Western Asia Asie occidentale	Oceania Océanie	Others 4/ Autre 4/	Année	← Exportations vers Exportations en provenance de ↓
				Graines et fruits oléagineux (CTCI, Rev. 3, 22) *[suite]*							
0	6	0	...	...	...	...	1	...	0	2000	Afrique du Nord
0	3	0	0	0	0	0	5	...	...	2007	
0	8	0	0	0	...	...	21	...	0	2008	
2	22	0	0	0	0	0	49	...	2	2009	
0	10	1	0	0	1	0	58	...	0	2010	
1	35	81	7	22	0	1	71	...	6	2000	Afrique subsaharienne
0	70	155	16	136	23	34	198	...	2	2007	
0	83	116	19	106	38	46	253	2	5	2008	
3	61	168	39	315	39	55	302	9	1	2009	
0	73	130	41	327	31	142	523	0	8	2010	
0	...	8	1	0	0	0	0	...	0	2000	Afrique du sud
...	...	5	0	0	...	0	0	...	1	2007	
...	...	35	1	0	3	2	12	0	1	2008	
...	...	32	1	0	0	23	43	...	0	2009	
0	0	27	1	1	0	54	0	...	0	2010	
0	24	15	528	920	62	142	24	...	0	2000	Amérique latine et Caraïbes
7	237	33	992	5861	220	446	358	0	0	2007	
11	284	7	1668	9453	356	712	350	1	9	2008	
15	244	6	1033	8345	320	446	262	0	0	2009	
31	338	3	1537	12106	162	601	359	0	0	2010	
...	19	0	87	379	62	20	10	...	...	2000	Brésil
...	84	1	45	3061	111	292	116	...	...	2007	
9	97	1	55	5635	40	542	99	1	...	2008	
13	134	3	44	6767	101	363	110	...	...	2009	
24	16	2	33	7548	40	447	145	...	...	2010	
3	11	2	4	73	1	43	20	0	0	2000	Asie orientale
15	24	2	17	194	3	48	44	1	...	2007	
29	20	5	19	345	11	53	47	1	...	2008	
12	18	2	11	259	16	81	63	0	...	2009	
15	42	2	14	174	26	85	86	0	...	2010	
3	11	2	4	65	1	41	20	0	...	2000	Chine
15	24	2	17	185	3	47	44	1	...	2007	
29	20	5	19	335	11	52	47	1	...	2008	
12	18	2	10	249	16	76	63	0	...	2009	
15	42	2	14	166	26	82	86	0	...	2010	
0	15	2	12	12	15	67	27	0	0	2000	Asie méridionale
3	12	4	11	115	36	225	84	0	0	2007	
5	19	4	37	121	71	257	117	0	0	2008	
2	7	4	14	72	76	214	73	0	4	2009	
3	14	3	15	152	76	405	102	0	3	2010	
0	0	1	1	22	5	74	0	0	...	2000	Asie Sud-est
0	13	1	3	48	3	99	12	0	0	2007	
0	16	3	3	98	6	72	13	0	0	2008	
0	5	2	1	73	6	66	9	0	0	2009	
0	6	3	1	87	6	76	11	0	0	2010	
2	1	0	0	0	6	1	14	...	0	2000	Asie occidentale
5	1	0	2	1	51	0	25	...	0	2007	
6	8	1	3	1	67	0	27	...	0	2008	
5	7	0	2	0	94	0	19	...	1	2009	
3	5	1	3	1	87	1	10	...	5	2010	
...	...	...	0	...	8	0	...	0	0	2000	Océanie
...	...	0	0	...	0	23	...	0	...	2007	
...	...	0	0	0	0	49	0	0	...	2008	
...	...	...	...	0	0	34	...	0	...	2009	
...	...	...	...	0	0	29	...	0	...	2010	

Voir la fin du tableau pour la remarque générale et les notes.

World exports by provenance and destination (Table D)

In million U.S. dollars f.o.b.

Exports to → / ↓ Exports from	Year	World 1/ Monde 1/	Developed economies 2/ Economies développées 2/ Total	Asia-Pacific Asie-Pacifique Total	Japan Japon	Europe Total	Germany Allemagne	North America Amérique du Nord Total	U.S.A. É.-U.	Commonwealth of Independent States Communauté d'Etats Indépendants Total	Europe
Textile fibres (SITC, Rev. 3, 26)											
World 1/	2000	21838	9006	931	834	7027	944	1047	675	645	631
	2007	33883	9972	752	603	7672	1122	1548	1237	1014	892
	2008	33979	9745	833	670	7429	1136	1482	1190	1036	966
	2009	28189	6634	528	372	5057	799	1048	823	826	780
	2010	38944	8529	648	504	6587	1104	1294	1029	1091	1032
Developed Economies - Asia-Pacific 2/	2000	4239	1397	272	234	1018	140	108	100	6	4
	2007	4493	921	119	84	655	80	147	143	11	9
	2008	3983	840	104	71	595	70	141	136	29	26
	2009	3361	493	68	39	313	42	112	106	29	24
	2010	4855	704	92	64	482	59	130	123	53	46
Japan	2000	1008	169	9	.	117	27	43	40	2	1
	2007	1239	293	11	.	161	51	121	119	7	5
	2008	1209	291	11	.	161	44	119	117	27	24
	2009	1115	223	14	.	112	26	97	91	28	22
	2010	1417	274	10	.	153	33	111	107	51	44
Developed Economies - Europe 2/	2000	4646	3224	66	49	3045	390	112	101	94	90
	2007	6912	4113	49	27	3783	485	281	246	284	258
	2008	7019	4106	66	38	3763	551	277	244	276	250
	2009	5229	2751	35	20	2571	406	145	125	273	254
	2010	6261	3285	46	28	3084	495	156	135	337	314
France	2000	594	455	16	16	427	40	11	10	5	4
	2007	565	334	7	7	316	37	10	10	2	2
	2008	473	274	7	7	251	35	16	15	2	1
	2009	382	187	5	5	174	28	7	6	2	2
	2010	475	224	5	5	210	34	9	9	1	0
Germany	2000	1394	967	12	6	915	.	40	37	42	40
	2007	2171	1271	10	4	1151	.	110	95	101	94
	2008	2205	1236	10	4	1118	.	109	94	109	97
	2009	1296	650	4	2	596	.	50	45	107	98
	2010	1420	750	5	2	694	.	51	45	81	71
Developed Economies - North America 2/	2000	3431	954	201	192	383	76	370	44	8	7
	2007	6703	829	174	164	386	54	268	43	27	27
	2008	7097	781	204	194	336	30	241	37	67	66
	2009	5471	524	94	84	236	18	194	33	80	79
	2010	8214	634	131	117	285	31	218	30	98	98
United States	2000	3248	902	199	192	378	76	325	.	6	5
	2007	6477	773	173	163	375	53	225	.	27	27
	2008	6867	733	203	193	327	28	203	.	67	66
	2009	5278	484	93	83	230	17	161	.	80	79
	2010	8006	596	129	116	279	30	188	.	98	97
South-Eastern Europe	2000	43	18	0	0	17	5	1	0	2	2
	2007	165	110	0	0	109	21	0	0	3	3
	2008	157	116	0	0	116	34	0	0	4	3
	2009	111	77	0	0	77	28	1	0	3	3
	2010	155	113	0	0	112	39	0	0	5	4
Commonwealth of Independent States	2000	1785	774	7	7	759	74	7	7	509	504
	2007	2399	276	1	1	273	36	2	2	568	488
	2008	2507	217	2	0	213	33	2	2	537	514
	2009	2418	112	2	0	108	19	3	2	359	346
	2010	2762	198	1	1	194	41	3	2	462	443
Russian Federation	2000	37	9	0	0	9	4	0	0	3	1
	2007	78	15	0	.	15	6	0	0	15	5
	2008	40	5	1	0	4	2	0	0	16	6
	2009	27	7	1	.	6	1	0	.	11	2
	2010	37	11	1	.	11	5	.	.	8	2

For general note and footnotes see end of table

Exportations mondiales par provenance et destination (Tableau D)

En millions de dollars E.-U. f.o.b.

South-Eastern Europe Europe du Sud-est	Northern Africa Afrique septentrionale	Sub-Saharan Africa Afrique du Nord	Latin America and the Caribbean Amérique latine et Caraïbes	Eastern Asia Asie orientale	Southern Asia Asie méridionale	South-eastern Asia Asie du Sud-est	Western Asia Asie occidentale	Oceania Océanie	Others 4/ Autre 4/	Année	← Exportations vers Exportations en provence de ↓
				Fibres textiles (CTCI, Rev. 3, 26)							
173	286	754	1634	4598	1372	2140	1181	11	39	2000	Monde 1/
455	559	1262	2091	8682	3930	3010	2543	29	335	2007	
459	668	1446	2126	7990	4461	3566	2196	19	265	2008	
315	577	1453	1682	7233	4034	3303	2053	25	54	2009	
366	689	1662	2645	12514	3842	4396	3160	20	30	2010	
3	8	49	41	1595	348	718	63	10	2	2000	Economies Développées - Asie-Pacifique 2/
10	10	128	17	2276	330	464	47	13	266	2007	
5	14	147	22	1895	280	481	52	14	205	2008	
1	15	145	18	1835	231	507	50	12	24	2009	
0	17	177	14	2707	379	716	70	17	0	2010	
1	1	35	9	498	51	227	13	0	...	2000	Japon
0	3	108	5	473	123	204	21	0	...	2007	
0	9	125	8	372	100	254	25	0	...	2008	
0	7	128	10	358	65	263	34	0	...	2009	
0	9	158	6	498	74	305	40	0	...	2010	
116	147	280	87	233	77	36	350	0	2	2000	Economies Développées - Europe 2/
348	269	481	136	381	244	72	581	2	1	2007	
354	361	586	141	309	238	54	595	1	0	2008	
252	315	565	82	325	138	55	472	0	0	2009	
293	304	598	95	502	166	95	586	0	0	2010	
2	10	22	2	74	8	1	15	0	...	2000	France
2	19	22	4	156	7	0	19	0	...	2007	
2	26	26	4	114	8	1	17	1	...	2008	
3	19	28	2	119	7	0	15	0	0	2009	
1	20	27	2	171	8	0	21	0	...	2010	
59	36	59	41	33	28	23	105	0	2	2000	Allemagne
120	54	86	68	53	144	27	246	0	...	2007	
126	69	109	73	68	134	27	253	0	...	2008	
71	76	113	38	82	40	23	96	0	0	2009	
62	54	122	29	137	44	38	104	...	0	2010	
3	16	108	993	600	133	359	257	0	...	2000	Economies Développées - Amérique du Nord 2/
2	34	208	1246	2217	503	779	845	12	...	2007	
3	46	256	1292	2425	489	1112	623	4	0	2008	
2	44	231	1040	1660	553	794	544	0	...	2009	
2	99	266	1538	3132	502	1007	935	0	...	2010	
3	16	83	987	520	129	347	256	0	...	2000	Etats-Unis
1	32	102	1233	2214	473	775	836	12	...	2007	
2	42	138	1273	2419	468	1108	615	4	...	2008	
1	40	130	1025	1658	532	789	538	0	...	2009	
1	94	154	1523	3130	479	1003	928	0	...	2010	
9	1	0	0	0	1	0	11	...	0	2000	Europe du Sud-est
11	2	3	0	1	1	0	35	0	...	2007	
8	1	3	0	0	0	0	23	...	...	2008	
5	1	6	0	3	1	0	15	0	0	2009	
7	1	9	0	2	2	0	17	...	0	2010	
29	4	4	30	157	92	36	150	...	0	2000	Communauté d'Etats Indépendants
18	22	0	5	550	766	50	145	...	0	2007	
21	30	0	0	490	1082	34	96	0	0	2008	
8	18	0	0	375	1341	16	189	0	...	2009	
6	52	0	3	1319	262	44	416	0	0	2010	
1	0	0	0	2	2	0	20	...	...	2000	Fédération de Russie
2	...	0	1	11	7	0	27	...	0	2007	
1	...	0	0	5	4	0	9	...	...	2008	
0	0	0	...	2	4	...	3	...	...	2009	
1	0	0	0	7	7	0	3	0	0	2010	

Voir la fin du tableau pour la remarque générale et les notes.

World exports by provenance and destination (Table D)

In million U.S. dollars f.o.b.

Exports from ↓ / Exports to →	Year	World 1/ Monde 1/	Developed economies 2/ Economies développées 2/ Total	Asia-Pacific Asie-Pacifique Total	Japan Japon	Europe Total	Germany Allemagne	North America Amérique du Nord Total	U.S.A. É.-U.	Commonwealth of Independent States Communauté d'Etats Indépendants Total	Europe
Textile fibres (SITC, Rev. 3, 26) *[cont.]*											
Northern Africa	2000	223	117	10	10	91	6	16	15	0	0
	2007	228	57	6	6	49	4	2	2	1	1
	2008	282	55	3	3	51	5	1	0	1	1
	2009	186	40	2	2	37	3	1	0	1	1
	2010	399	57	3	3	50	8	4	1	1	0
Sub-Saharan Africa	2000	1459	608	22	21	562	78	23	18	0	0
	2007	1940	661	14	12	604	72	43	42	0	0
	2008	1861	586	22	18	550	51	14	12	1	1
	2009	1988	393	21	11	367	23	5	4	0	0
	2010	2263	513	17	10	489	28	7	7	0	0
South Africa	2000	190	119	10	10	100	13	9	4	0	0
	2007	276	149	6	5	140	27	3	3	0	0
	2008	261	125	6	4	116	20	3	3	0	...
	2009	264	81	4	3	76	8	1	1	...	...
	2010	298	125	6	4	117	9	2	2	...	...
Latin America and the Caribbean	2000	1003	428	21	20	240	58	167	165	1	1
	2007	1612	469	50	49	304	114	114	112	0	0
	2008	1750	486	62	61	322	105	102	99	0	0
	2009	1513	291	31	29	190	52	71	69	0	0
	2010	2010	419	40	40	264	83	115	113	0	0
Brazil	2000	92	35	0	0	32	15	2	2	...	...
	2007	690	112	36	36	58	12	17	17	0	0
	2008	870	146	43	43	92	10	10	10	0	0
	2009	809	72	20	19	50	8	2	2	0	0
	2010	1025	109	29	29	63	10	16	16	0	0
Eastern Asia	2000	3414	1010	263	244	550	60	197	182	5	5
	2007	4888	1725	228	171	967	167	531	495	98	97
	2008	4710	1664	236	175	911	169	517	479	94	93
	2009	3921	1242	183	117	695	127	363	337	61	55
	2010	5217	1699	212	154	1016	211	470	435	113	109
China	2000	1085	495	159	158	320	27	16	16	2	1
	2007	2040	838	115	100	541	87	182	172	31	30
	2008	2037	825	108	92	473	81	244	230	27	26
	2009	1544	582	74	57	332	58	175	166	20	16
	2010	2368	901	96	83	573	118	232	219	47	44
Southern Asia	2000	463	148	19	16	111	17	19	16	16	16
	2007	2571	226	14	11	175	35	38	35	16	6
	2008	2681	278	24	21	209	37	44	40	21	7
	2009	2213	248	17	13	181	34	50	44	9	8
	2010	4407	331	21	17	243	47	67	63	8	6
South-Eastern Asia	2000	589	91	38	28	34	7	19	17	0	0
	2007	1251	296	64	48	130	24	101	98	0	0
	2008	1378	341	86	69	134	26	121	120	1	1
	2009	1352	277	61	44	127	22	89	86	3	3
	2010	1883	349	74	62	171	25	105	102	5	4
Western Asia	2000	543	237	12	12	215	33	10	9	3	2
	2007	721	290	34	31	237	30	20	18	5	3
	2008	553	276	24	20	229	27	22	21	7	5
	2009	426	185	14	13	156	24	15	14	7	6
	2010	518	228	10	10	198	37	19	19	10	8
Oceania	2000	1	0	0	.	0	.	0	0	...	...
	2007	1	0	0	.	0	.	0	0	...	...
	2008	0	0	0	.	0	.	0	0	...	...
	2009	0	0	0	0	0	.	0	0	...	...
	2010	0	0	0	0	0	.	0	0	0	0

For general note and footnotes see end of table

Exportations mondiales par provenance et destination (Tableau D)

En millions de dollars E.-U. f.o.b.

South-Eastern Europe Europe du Sud-est	Northern Africa Afrique septentrio-nale	Sub-Saharan Africa Afrique du Nord	Latin America and the Caribbean Amérique latine et Caraïbes	Eastern Asia Asie orientale	Southern Asia Asie méridionale	South-eastern Asia Asie du Sud-est	Western Asia Asie occidentale	Oceania Océanie	Others 4/ Autre 4/	Année	← Exportations vers / Exportations en provenance de ↓
											Fibres textiles (CTCI, Rev. 3, 26) *[suite]*
1	1	5	6	29	29	13	23	0	0	2000	Afrique du Nord
0	10	9	7	32	86	4	21	...	1	2007	
1	5	13	4	23	136	2	41	...	1	2008	
2	7	16	5	38	46	3	29	...	0	2009	
2	8	21	6	82	169	11	42	...	0	2010	
0	40	263	63	117	151	175	24	0	16	2000	Afrique subsaharienne
12	82	255	35	348	199	304	36	0	6	2007	
6	60	225	26	334	200	389	27	0	6	2008	
18	46	248	23	582	178	466	22	11	1	2009	
4	45	294	315	401	181	471	37	0	2	2010	
0	4	19	1	33	7	2	4	0	0	2000	Afrique du sud
11	0	13	1	80	18	2	0	0	1	2007	
5	0	11	2	93	21	2	1	0	0	2008	
2	1	8	1	139	22	9	2	0	0	2009	
2	2	12	0	111	35	8	3	0	0	2010	
0	2	1	345	156	22	17	30	0	0	2000	Amérique latine et Caraïbes
15	10	5	384	382	120	165	62	0	1	2007	
8	6	6	368	421	176	219	57	0	1	2008	
3	7	5	273	497	90	290	54	...	1	2009	
4	20	5	357	637	123	320	124	...	0	2010	
0	0	1	39	2	3	3	9	...	...	2000	Brésil
...	8	3	123	173	96	143	32	0	...	2007	
...	5	4	121	218	157	191	29	...	...	2008	
...	5	2	100	278	74	249	29	...	...	2009	
0	8	1	105	346	100	277	80	...	...	2010	
1	16	15	50	1452	310	493	60	0	1	2000	Asie orientale
29	52	114	215	1103	635	518	398	0	0	2007	
41	46	163	226	964	612	557	341	0	0	2008	
14	49	126	197	830	550	581	271	0	0	2009	
35	62	160	255	982	761	781	370	0	0	2010	
0	1	2	12	224	171	163	15	0	...	2000	Chine
24	30	21	94	247	380	120	255	0	...	2007	
35	22	37	106	238	380	153	216	0	...	2008	
10	24	21	95	205	307	121	161	0	...	2009	
28	33	30	121	266	484	226	232	0	...	2010	
2	8	19	8	63	67	86	46	0	0	2000	Asie méridionale
1	24	19	23	1092	700	278	191	0	1	2007	
2	31	30	28	878	964	337	110	0	2	2008	
4	24	76	21	801	625	224	169	0	10	2009	
5	28	92	35	2322	920	431	222	0	13	2010	
0	4	5	8	183	88	179	31	0	...	2000	Asie Sud-est
1	14	12	21	245	184	361	116	1	1	2007	
2	17	11	17	197	231	368	192	1	0	2008	
1	13	15	16	232	239	358	197	1	0	2009	
2	19	18	23	351	322	509	286	1	0	2010	
8	39	3	4	13	53	28	135	0	18	2000	Asie occidentale
7	31	29	2	55	161	16	66	0	59	2007	
7	49	6	3	53	53	13	38	0	49	2008	
5	38	21	7	53	42	9	41	0	17	2009	
6	34	22	3	78	56	12	55	0	15	2010	
0	...	1	...	...	0	0	...	0	0	2000	Océanie
0	...	0	0	0	0	0	0	0	...	2007	
...	...	0	0	0	0	0	...	0	...	2008	
...	...	0	0	...	0	0	...	0	...	2009	
...	...	0	0	0	...	0	...	0	...	2010	

Voir la fin du tableau pour la remarque générale et les notes.

World exports by provenance and destination (Table D)

In million U.S. dollars f.o.b.

Exports to → / ↓ Exports from	Year	World 1/ Monde 1/	Developed economies 2/ Economies développées 2/							Commonwealth of Independent States Communauté d'Etats Indépendants	
				Asia-Pacific Asie-Pacifique		Europe		North America Amérique du Nord			
			Total	Total	Japan Japon	Total	Germany Allemagne	Total	U.S.A. É.-U.	Total	Europe
Crude fertilizers and minerals (SITC, Rev. 3, 27)											
World 1/	2000	13330	8866	1119	967	6064	841	1683	1242	269	234
	2007	24952	14763	1350	1097	11026	1505	2387	1763	1027	870
	2008	37499	19660	2269	1483	13818	1794	3573	2850	1594	1396
	2009	24527	12834	1128	901	9510	1371	2196	1615	944	779
	2010	30068	16061	1606	1269	11396	1561	3059	2396	1127	964
Developed Economies - Asia-Pacific 2/	2000	463	201	110	93	48	6	42	40	1	1
	2007	851	271	147	120	84	12	39	36	1	1
	2008	990	242	85	55	113	12	44	43	3	3
	2009	577	163	68	39	60	10	36	35	0	0
	2010	813	240	85	51	102	30	54	52	1	0
Japan	2000	184	46	6	.	19	4	21	21	1	1
	2007	369	45	9	.	12	5	23	23	0	0
	2008	619	49	10	.	16	7	23	22	0	0
	2009	330	46	11	.	16	6	20	19	0	0
	2010	466	57	13	.	23	9	22	21	0	0
Developed Economies - Europe 2/	2000	5194	4298	76	64	4006	722	216	191	61	59
	2007	9772	7816	77	57	7459	1296	280	239	215	207
	2008	11453	8804	78	53	8440	1528	287	251	244	234
	2009	8756	6715	55	36	6466	1179	194	165	174	168
	2010	10103	7586	79	62	7273	1263	235	195	210	201
France	2000	508	445	6	6	426	99	12	11	5	4
	2007	872	742	6	4	716	128	20	16	8	8
	2008	1015	802	6	5	767	142	29	24	13	13
	2009	753	630	5	4	599	117	25	16	10	10
	2010	865	691	5	4	660	132	26	17	13	13
Germany	2000	836	730	9	7	712	.	9	8	6	5
	2007	1772	1510	12	10	1484	.	15	13	29	27
	2008	2176	1787	14	11	1753	.	20	17	35	33
	2009	1694	1496	8	6	1476	.	11	10	24	23
	2010	1829	1551	11	8	1523	.	18	16	26	25
Developed Economies - North America 2/	2000	2525	1652	375	324	508	64	768	397	4	3
	2007	3252	2003	367	294	571	85	1065	588	20	17
	2008	5133	2696	502	290	605	98	1589	1008	28	27
	2009	2749	1606	199	149	402	78	1005	540	10	8
	2010	3636	2148	346	245	581	121	1220	689	11	10
United States	2000	1790	1187	330	297	487	60	371	.	4	3
	2007	2105	1306	313	290	517	75	476	.	15	12
	2008	2467	1437	310	285	546	85	581	.	16	15
	2009	1845	990	164	145	362	71	464	.	9	8
	2010	2459	1325	265	240	530	104	530	.	11	9
South-Eastern Europe	2000	61	33	0	0	32	3	1	1	4	4
	2007	159	86	0	0	85	1	1	1	6	5
	2008	197	107	0	0	106	1	1	1	6	5
	2009	149	84	0	0	84	1	0	0	4	3
	2010	184	104	0	0	104	5	0	0	3	2
Commonwealth of Independent States	2000	461	219	2	2	210	2	7	0	122	98
	2007	1406	483	2	2	474	17	8	7	593	486
	2008	3867	875	16	16	853	23	6	6	951	822
	2009	1446	552	12	12	530	6	9	9	537	427
	2010	1715	508	4	4	477	16	27	27	610	499
Russian Federation	2000	298	155	2	2	146	1	7	0	46	35
	2007	613	271	1	1	263	10	6	6	114	72
	2008	2256	612	16	16	591	10	6	6	122	84
	2009	742	419	12	12	397	4	9	9	85	46
	2010	824	336	4	4	310	10	22	22	101	64

For general note and footnotes see end of table

Exportations mondiales par provenance et destination (Tableau D)

En millions de dollars E.-U. f.o.b.

← Exportations vers

South-Eastern Europe Europe du Sud-est	Northern Africa Afrique septentrionale	Sub-Saharan Africa Afrique du Nord	Latin America and the Caribbean Amérique latine et Caraïbes	Eastern Asia Asie orientale	Southern Asia Asie méridionale	South-eastern Asia Asie du Sud-est	Western Asia Asie occidentale	Oceania Océanie	Others 4/ Autre 4/	Année	Exportations en provenance de ↓
				Engrais et minéraux bruts (CTCI, Rev. 3, 27)							
107	211	229	685	1244	334	683	587	9	106	2000	Monde 1/
246	397	468	1126	3164	897	1088	1622	17	137	2007	
375	2036	901	2114	4799	1559	1829	2426	28	178	2008	
223	409	563	1172	3551	1482	1560	1498	24	269	2009	
238	594	705	1587	4658	1497	1756	1644	33	166	2010	
0	0	2	2	170	8	72	3	3	0	2000	Economies Développées - Asie-Pacifique 2/
0	0	3	5	412	14	126	13	6	0	2007	
0	0	5	4	539	43	92	20	8	34	2008	
0	1	10	3	297	14	67	13	7	0	2009	
0	1	20	5	413	19	91	10	10	2	2010	
...	0	1	0	100	7	28	1	0	...	2000	Japon
...	0	1	1	257	10	50	3	1	...	2007	
...	0	2	1	458	35	65	8	1	...	2008	
...	1	1	1	222	10	44	4	1	...	2009	
...	1	2	2	315	17	66	4	1	...	2010	
40	114	45	81	197	38	87	140	2	93	2000	Economies Développées - Europe 2/
96	258	95	148	456	129	148	311	3	97	2007	
108	609	145	169	531	180	181	386	3	93	2008	
81	246	109	132	484	216	212	292	2	92	2009	
94	300	156	196	663	226	236	326	2	108	2010	
2	15	12	7	6	2	5	9	1	...	2000	France
4	39	18	10	20	4	11	15	1	...	2007	
5	110	23	11	19	4	10	16	2	0	2008	
4	37	19	9	19	3	8	13	2	0	2009	
5	59	21	15	28	4	11	15	1	1	2010	
6	11	6	10	7	5	32	13	1	10	2000	Allemagne
16	20	18	23	15	17	52	38	1	33	2007	
15	79	53	27	29	14	67	50	0	18	2008	
11	13	9	24	31	12	40	33	0	0	2009	
13	13	12	32	59	21	65	37	0	0	2010	
0	19	37	328	296	38	118	34	0	0	2000	Economies Développées - Amérique du Nord 2/
2	11	46	422	540	63	94	50	1	...	2007	
2	10	181	906	980	91	130	99	10	...	2008	
1	13	41	440	406	84	86	61	4	...	2009	
1	15	42	568	572	82	117	71	10	...	2010	
0	8	14	233	227	11	80	26	0	...	2000	États-Unis
1	11	16	327	286	20	74	47	1	...	2007	
1	10	20	498	318	31	83	53	1	...	2008	
1	12	24	388	275	30	64	52	1	...	2009	
1	14	18	537	384	32	90	45	0	...	2010	
21	0	0	0	0	0	0	2	0	0	2000	Europe du Sud-est
49	6	0	0	1	0	0	13	...	0	2007	
56	12	0	0	1	0	0	15	...	0	2008	
47	2	0	0	1	0	0	11	...	0	2009	
50	5	0	0	1	1	0	14	...	4	2010	
11	52	0	3	14	12	15	14	...	0	2000	Communauté d'Etats Indépendants
30	48	1	18	128	54	22	28	0	0	2007	
43	1230	30	100	320	115	21	184	...	0	2008	
35	33	2	12	119	83	41	33	0	0	2009	
23	115	4	33	171	144	36	70	0	0	2010	
8	50	0	3	13	8	12	5	...	...	2000	Fédération de Russie
4	42	0	18	95	39	21	9	0	0	2007	
5	967	29	99	163	78	19	161	...	...	2008	
15	14	1	10	83	62	40	14	...	0	2009	
7	87	1	17	89	115	35	35	...	0	2010	

Voir la fin du tableau pour la remarque générale et les notes.

World exports by provenance and destination (Table D)

In million U.S. dollars f.o.b.

Exports to → / ↓ Exports from	Year	World 1/ Monde 1/	Developed economies 2/ Economies développées 2/								Commonwealth of Independent States Communauté d'Etats Indépendants	
				Asia-Pacific Asie-Pacifique		Europe		North America Amérique du Nord			
			Total	Total	Japan Japon	Total	Germany Allemagne	Total	U.S.A. É.-U.	Total	Europe
			Crude fertilizers and minerals (SITC, Rev. 3, 27) *[cont.]*									
Northern Africa	2000	540	331	43	6	218	4	70	64	5	5
	2007	1155	600	81	8	373	9	145	133	4	4
	2008	3369	2049	404	28	1202	33	443	442	31	28
	2009	1640	606	59	8	356	6	191	190	1	1
	2010	1786	947	113	8	549	4	284	276	10	10
Sub-Saharan Africa	2000	508	245	23	21	185	5	37	34	0	0
	2007	1010	497	22	16	419	10	56	50	1	1
	2008	1270	627	22	15	538	9	67	58	1	1
	2009	768	423	14	11	363	5	46	41	1	1
	2010	1699	887	22	18	590	6	275	272	2	2
South Africa	2000	208	154	13	12	111	1	30	28	0	...
	2007	458	275	19	15	217	6	39	33	1	1
	2008	650	332	18	14	263	5	51	42	1	1
	2009	318	219	12	10	170	1	37	32	1	1
	2010	449	315	21	17	257	3	37	35	2	2
Latin America and the Caribbean	2000	724	537	49	48	194	6	293	282	0	0
	2007	1377	863	136	132	343	17	385	330	2	2
	2008	1813	1152	162	157	426	21	564	499	3	3
	2009	1532	897	143	138	298	21	456	400	2	2
	2010	1791	1043	143	138	397	37	502	450	5	5
Brazil	2000	281	212	31	31	148	1	33	33	0	0
	2007	641	417	51	50	277	10	89	53	0	0
	2008	712	488	44	44	334	10	110	65	0	0
	2009	579	345	25	25	209	11	111	72	0	0
	2010	709	405	21	21	270	23	114	75	...	...
Eastern Asia	2000	1379	820	361	338	255	12	204	192	47	47
	2007	2076	1131	398	379	413	12	320	303	76	69
	2008	3529	1829	799	729	553	18	476	458	109	97
	2009	1950	901	426	400	278	17	197	182	79	68
	2010	3118	1667	664	633	619	19	383	365	118	110
China	2000	1103	704	296	275	215	11	192	180	27	27
	2007	1682	991	317	299	371	11	303	287	42	35
	2008	2863	1647	668	598	521	15	457	439	63	51
	2009	1635	801	359	333	257	14	184	169	44	34
	2010	2606	1484	546	515	576	15	362	345	57	49
Southern Asia	2000	400	188	26	22	133	6	29	27	9	7
	2007	1413	526	38	26	422	18	65	56	14	3
	2008	1623	440	42	29	329	17	69	62	20	5
	2009	1545	392	41	28	304	15	47	40	11	5
	2010	1583	348	54	41	244	17	50	43	15	9
South-Eastern Asia	2000	492	83	40	37	39	2	4	3	0	0
	2007	673	96	66	50	24	3	6	5	1	1
	2008	1126	108	80	58	18	2	10	10	1	1
	2009	1176	82	64	53	12	2	6	6	1	1
	2010	1134	88	71	60	10	3	8	7	2	2
Western Asia	2000	582	260	14	11	234	9	12	11	15	10
	2007	1807	392	14	13	360	25	18	14	93	75
	2008	3130	733	80	52	637	32	16	12	197	170
	2009	2237	412	47	27	358	29	7	6	123	96
	2010	2505	495	25	9	449	40	21	19	139	114
Oceania	2000	2	0	0	0	0	.	0	0	...	...
	2007	2	0	0	0	0	.	0	0	...	...
	2008	1	0	0	0	0	0	0	0	...	...
	2009	1	0	0	0	0	.	0	0	...	...
	2010	1	0	0	0	0	0	0	0	...	...

For general note and footnotes see end of table

Exportations mondiales par provenance et destination (Tableau D)

En millions de dollars E.-U. f.o.b.

South-Eastern Europe Europe du Sud-est	Northern Africa Afrique septentrio-nale	Sub-Saharan Africa Afrique du Nord	Latin America and the Caribbean Amérique latine et Caraïbes	Eastern Asia Asie orientale	Southern Asia Asie méridionale	South-eastern Asia Asie du Sud-est	Western Asia Asie occidentale	Oceania Océanie	Others 4/ Autre 4/	← Exportations vers Année	Exportations en provenance de ↓
			Engrais et minéraux bruts (CTCI, Rev. 3, 27) *[suite]*								
19	5	7	79	24	26	18	26	0	0	2000	Afrique du Nord
30	28	38	163	79	90	47	72	0	4	2007	
98	88	58	381	141	228	113	178	...	4	2008	
12	47	52	127	279	215	88	98	...	116	2009	
31	82	60	235	72	162	102	76	...	8	2010	
2	1	105	21	20	47	33	34	0	2	2000	Afrique subsaharienne
1	5	207	36	45	38	32	139	0	8	2007	
2	9	370	13	76	53	31	83	2	3	2008	
1	9	197	4	41	24	17	49	1	2	2009	
0	4	307	64	118	32	15	265	3	2	2010	
0	0	24	2	18	3	4	2	0	0	2000	Afrique du sud
1	4	54	34	43	7	29	5	0	3	2007	
2	8	199	10	46	12	28	11	2	0	2008	
1	8	43	2	25	5	8	6	1	0	2009	
0	4	65	3	34	9	8	8	2	0	2010	
0	1	9	127	26	12	11	2	0	1	2000	Amérique latine et Caraïbes
0	2	15	275	145	40	21	11	0	4	2007	
0	4	12	407	142	42	31	15	0	5	2008	
0	4	16	378	148	43	30	10	0	5	2009	
0	5	23	369	247	50	42	6	1	1	2010	
...	...	7	19	23	10	8	2	...	...	2000	Brésil
0	0	13	34	116	35	17	10	0	...	2007	
0	0	8	42	102	34	24	13	0	...	2008	
...	0	15	44	107	37	23	8	0	...	2009	
0	1	21	50	165	38	26	4	0	...	2010	
3	5	10	14	313	72	83	13	1	0	2000	Asie orientale
3	5	18	35	519	64	158	67	1	0	2007	
4	17	27	49	890	149	367	87	1	0	2008	
2	10	28	36	543	79	202	68	2	0	2009	
3	13	46	63	744	125	265	73	1	0	2010	
2	5	9	14	201	65	64	11	0	...	2000	Chine
3	5	15	34	349	50	134	60	0	...	2007	
3	17	24	49	542	111	324	83	1	...	2008	
2	10	24	35	407	67	178	66	1	...	2009	
3	13	39	62	532	111	234	70	1	...	2010	
0	3	4	2	96	27	26	44	0	0	2000	Asie méridionale
1	14	20	16	414	158	57	191	0	1	2007	
1	11	40	37	516	186	71	298	1	2	2008	
1	12	19	20	544	181	88	269	2	7	2009	
0	14	21	31	662	168	90	227	2	4	2010	
0	0	2	0	56	13	179	157	2	0	2000	Asie Sud-est
1	0	5	1	164	36	350	14	5	1	2007	
0	1	13	2	195	95	680	27	4	1	2008	
0	0	9	1	190	234	600	54	5	0	2009	
0	0	6	0	235	107	643	48	4	0	2010	
11	12	8	28	34	43	43	117	...	11	2000	Asie occidentale
33	20	20	7	260	211	33	713	...	23	2007	
62	44	21	44	469	378	112	1034	...	36	2008	
44	33	80	19	499	309	130	543	0	46	2009	
36	40	20	25	759	380	118	459	0	35	2010	
...	...	0	...	...	...	0	...	1	0	2000	Océanie
...	...	0	...	0	...	0	...	1	0	2007	
0	...	...	...	...	...	0	0	0	...	2008	
...	...	0	...	0	...	0	0	0	...	2009	
...	...	0	0	0	0	0	...	0	...	2010	

Voir la fin du tableau pour la remarque générale et les notes.

World exports by provenance and destination (Table D)

In million U.S. dollars f.o.b.

Exports from ↓ / Exports to →	Year	World 1/ Monde 1/	Developed economies 2/ Economies développées 2/ Total	Asia-Pacific Asie-Pacifique Total	Asia-Pacific Japan Japon	Europe Total	Europe Germany Allemagne	North America Amérique du Nord Total	North America U.S.A. É.-U.	Commonwealth of Independent States Communauté d'Etats Indépendants Total	Commonwealth of Independent States Europe
Metalliferous ores and metal scrap (SITC, Rev. 3, 28)											
World 1/	2000	48942	31400	6542	6263	18844	3723	6013	3507	1217	1079
	2007	221080	113388	25393	24683	74584	14469	13411	7304	3763	3166
	2008	257464	123535	26346	25669	80849	15924	16340	9827	5348	4793
	2009	188212	73451	18293	17817	45320	8968	9838	5973	2473	2279
	2010	299555	121434	31581	30748	76277	15622	13576	7728	3593	3236
Developed Economies - Asia-Pacific 2/	2000	8135	3562	1686	1556	968	111	908	567	163	163
	2007	33444	8723	5724	5501	2218	247	781	374	442	441
	2008	46657	12066	8073	7838	2476	294	1517	1136	633	633
	2009	39862	7480	5436	5308	770	278	1274	889	308	305
	2010	65656	11879	9519	9310	1526	436	834	463	490	464
Japan	2000	879	105	1	.	78	10	26	24	...	...
	2007	4635	347	2	.	254	148	90	86	2	1
	2008	5234	542	2	.	397	122	143	138	2	2
	2009	4667	339	1	.	174	52	165	163	1	1
	2010	4974	541	1	.	286	31	254	254	3	3
Developed Economies - Europe 2/	2000	10878	9161	185	182	8511	1818	465	357	90	89
	2007	50463	39721	448	404	38015	8021	1258	898	136	81
	2008	53828	41412	405	371	39468	8476	1538	1230	139	110
	2009	31721	21647	315	302	20579	4472	753	657	56	50
	2010	52005	37230	484	452	35437	7770	1309	1079	95	90
France	2000	1300	1258	7	6	1203	262	48	46	1	0
	2007	5496	5069	14	12	4989	847	66	61	1	1
	2008	5989	5551	16	14	5458	711	78	73	13	8
	2009	3131	2672	10	9	2611	402	51	47	1	1
	2010	5265	4547	17	16	4467	672	63	58	3	3
Germany	2000	2336	2053	12	12	1948	.	93	72	2	2
	2007	10896	9360	32	24	8848	.	480	363	12	11
	2008	11730	9951	39	35	9175	.	738	638	10	10
	2009	6405	5055	17	16	4705	.	333	310	8	8
	2010	10895	9042	41	38	8442	.	559	516	16	15
Developed Economies - North America 2/	2000	7430	5402	638	600	2356	334	2408	1141	8	6
	2007	35794	20515	2516	2404	12131	1475	5868	2414	21	20
	2008	42761	23186	2684	2534	13054	1883	7448	3277	95	93
	2009	28722	13886	1142	1077	8778	903	3966	1974	2	2
	2010	40535	21473	1987	1858	13560	1470	5926	2716	68	43
United States	2000	4357	2588	382	368	940	197	1266	.	8	6
	2007	23291	10259	1363	1325	5474	749	3421	.	13	12
	2008	29751	13008	1542	1507	7343	742	4122	.	76	74
	2009	20178	8323	614	584	5752	353	1956	.	2	2
	2010	28621	13032	1106	991	8716	567	3210	.	68	43
South-Eastern Europe	2000	589	252	7	7	235	45	9	1	88	88
	2007	2437	1134	8	8	990	221	136	92	28	28
	2008	2798	1022	2	2	938	154	82	65	22	22
	2009	1910	638	0	0	637	126	1	1	6	6
	2010	3001	1002	0	0	998	188	4	4	12	8
Commonwealth of Independent States	2000	2716	1225	29	29	1163	203	33	33	686	558
	2007	8521	2809	14	14	2768	222	26	26	2603	2152
	2008	11774	4030	19	18	3980	229	32	30	3530	3136
	2009	6285	1450	11	10	1409	122	30	25	1762	1638
	2010	9928	3142	26	26	3015	168	100	98	1859	1631
Russian Federation	2000	985	495	27	27	457	46	11	11	170	155
	2007	3640	1590	10	10	1563	32	17	17	347	235
	2008	4647	2044	18	18	2005	56	21	21	475	265
	2009	1729	548	6	6	529	27	12	10	145	133
	2010	3330	1370	8	8	1288	46	74	72	231	152

For general note and footnotes see end of table

Exportations mondiales par provenance et destination (Tableau D)

En millions de dollars E.-U. f.o.b.

South-Eastern Europe Europe du Sud-est	Northern Africa Afrique septentrio-nale	Sub-Saharan Africa Afrique du Nord	Latin America and the Caribbean Amérique latine et Caraïbes	Eastern Asia Asie orientale	Southern Asia Asie méridionale	South-eastern Asia Asie du Sud-est	Western Asia Asie occidentale	Oceania Océanie	Others 4/ Autre 4/	Année	← Exportations vers Exportations en provence de ↓
Minerais métallifères et déchets de métaux (CTCI, Rev. 3, 28)											
463	340	589	1396	8569	1150	1385	1319	1	1114	2000	Monde 1/
2432	1399	2414	5790	69805	8888	5238	7042	5	915	2007	
2804	2248	2618	6955	87367	8363	6847	11191	16	171	2008	
1567	1098	1891	3504	86300	6784	4627	6399	15	101	2009	
2639	2231	2927	6138	131293	10434	6432	12323	33	79	2010	
51	100	271	14	2906	177	266	248	1	375	2000	Economies Développées - Asie-Pacifique 2/
54	44	575	36	19308	1255	862	1252	1	891	2007	
50	8	497	131	29511	1183	1090	1354	1	132	2008	
7	3	344	105	28798	849	764	1131	9	64	2009	
2	22	477	153	48337	1572	1194	1448	21	61	2010	
...	0	1	0	723	8	42	1	...	...	2000	Japon
0	0	0	0	4164	17	102	3	...	...	2007	
...	0	2	0	4543	15	123	7	...	...	2008	
...	0	0	1	4202	9	113	2	...	...	2009	
0	0	1	1	4322	7	97	2	...	...	2010	
50	65	30	62	743	243	158	259	0	18	2000	Economies Développées - Europe 2/
314	446	87	211	5875	1376	410	1884	1	2	2007	
397	746	72	214	5668	1610	598	2971	1	0	2008	
224	307	28	172	5421	1585	498	1779	2	0	2009	
596	891	38	150	6807	2142	575	3474	7	1	2010	
2	1	1	4	15	10	1	7	0	...	2000	France
10	23	4	6	312	43	10	19	0	...	2007	
13	7	4	8	283	67	11	32	0	...	2008	
2	34	4	4	294	73	7	40	...	...	2009	
2	51	4	8	411	104	10	124	0	1	2010	
1	0	8	5	160	40	20	33	0	13	2000	Allemagne
30	2	22	9	1160	187	26	87	1	2	2007	
4	24	19	29	1212	250	61	171	0	...	2008	
4	2	10	19	924	194	68	118	1	...	2009	
42	2	16	26	1150	249	64	282	6	...	2010	
4	1	18	351	1442	71	109	23	0	0	2000	Economies Développées - Amérique du Nord 2/
50	238	24	976	11134	724	950	1163	1	0	2007	
47	566	65	1768	12408	681	1543	2394	9	...	2008	
36	239	61	838	10801	712	985	1158	4	...	2009	
104	481	48	1280	13477	699	1160	1741	5	...	2010	
0	1	18	345	1249	57	75	16	0	...	2000	Etats-Unis
4	170	24	869	9529	565	887	970	1	...	2007	
26	427	61	1555	10493	601	1427	2071	6	...	2008	
2	91	44	705	8739	643	688	939	3	...	2009	
6	229	44	1048	11071	600	956	1563	5	...	2010	
75	0	0	2	52	4	3	112	0	0	2000	Europe du Sud-est
512	11	23	28	156	45	1	498	...	...	2007	
669	32	54	20	145	17	2	816	...	...	2008	
330	11	97	7	218	27	4	572	...	...	2009	
510	9	107	7	313	33	1	1008	...	...	2010	
56	38	0	5	340	31	8	328	0	0	2000	Communauté d'Etats Indépendants
328	123	0	30	1451	62	55	1060	0	...	2007	
510	143	0	23	2290	57	65	1126	...	...	2008	
220	31	0	1	2281	67	11	462	...	...	2009	
464	5	0	9	3485	59	14	892	...	...	2010	
1	7	0	2	211	3	4	92	...	...	2000	Fédération de Russie
117	75	0	1	673	35	52	750	0	...	2007	
127	62	...	2	1094	32	64	746	...	...	2008	
23	11	...	1	774	31	10	185	...	...	2009	
22	5	0	0	1149	27	9	516	...	...	2010	

Voir la fin du tableau pour la remarque générale et les notes.

World exports by provenance and destination (Table D)

In million U.S. dollars f.o.b.

Exports to → / ↓ Exports from	Year	World 1/ Monde 1/	Developed economies 2/ Economies développées 2/ — Total	Asia-Pacific Asie-Pacifique — Total	Asia-Pacific Asie-Pacifique — Japan Japon	Europe — Total	Europe — Germany Allemagne	North America Amérique du Nord — Total	North America Amérique du Nord — U.S.A. É.-U.	Commonwealth of Independent States Communauté d'Etats Indépendants — Total	Commonwealth of Independent States Communauté d'Etats Indépendants — Europe
Metalliferous ores and metal scrap (SITC, Rev. 3, 28) *[cont.]*											
Northern Africa	2000	174	136	0	0	132	13	3	1	6	6
	2007	705	403	0	0	402	26	1	1	5	5
	2008	812	414	0	0	413	32	2	2	3	3
	2009	417	219	1	1	219	23	0	0	...	...
	2010	658	303	1	1	302	25	0	0	0	0
Sub-Saharan Africa	2000	2440	1949	223	217	1386	314	340	291	13	13
	2007	11469	5599	628	595	4022	1112	950	504	158	156
	2008	16640	7176	1199	1166	4844	1141	1132	720	375	366
	2009	13146	4821	619	609	3318	676	884	533	192	183
	2010	18406	6551	1181	1138	4181	956	1189	664	340	325
South Africa	2000	1383	1094	194	188	702	264	199	196	8	8
	2007	5305	2735	533	501	1787	829	415	276	12	12
	2008	8253	3798	1037	1004	2439	897	323	301	109	109
	2009	6807	2210	504	496	1411	515	295	245	16	14
	2010	10892	3613	943	903	2349	759	321	306	91	91
Latin America and the Caribbean	2000	10210	6699	1794	1760	3155	739	1750	1046	92	92
	2007	50140	24191	9288	9178	10585	2805	4317	2928	183	144
	2008	53586	24943	8071	8027	12419	3340	4453	3245	194	160
	2009	42544	16583	5991	5871	7731	2143	2861	1836	80	46
	2010	74192	28927	10987	10741	13878	4074	4062	2578	199	170
Brazil	2000	3536	2135	465	461	1396	435	273	221	12	12
	2007	13627	6295	1293	1275	4120	1219	882	439	15	15
	2008	20525	9197	2177	2156	5934	1768	1086	543	42	8
	2009	15937	5697	1296	1269	3612	692	789	221	28	7
	2010	33014	11815	3407	3294	7433	2316	975	300	67	52
Eastern Asia	2000	897	269	170	157	72	8	28	24	11	10
	2007	4875	1351	634	607	684	15	33	31	16	5
	2008	5626	1733	603	573	1054	165	76	71	17	5
	2009	3379	698	412	399	257	25	29	23	6	3
	2010	4899	1344	709	693	544	70	91	70	2	2
China	2000	114	61	32	30	23	2	7	6	2	1
	2007	1023	586	126	115	453	1	6	6	10	1
	2008	1084	646	123	109	517	11	6	6	9	0
	2009	221	115	43	40	68	8	5	5	0	0
	2010	836	374	160	155	181	18	34	30	2	2
Southern Asia	2000	556	217	157	153	37	1	22	21	30	27
	2007	7041	563	447	424	109	8	7	7	46	17
	2008	7912	541	425	425	106	20	10	9	105	34
	2009	7392	538	417	378	110	14	11	9	15	2
	2010	10011	593	257	254	326	54	9	9	456	430
South-Eastern Asia	2000	2774	1838	1277	1257	533	67	28	12	0	0
	2007	11150	6298	4752	4708	1523	101	22	21	45	45
	2008	9092	4911	4041	3999	836	26	34	33	66	66
	2009	8850	4331	3336	3324	974	113	21	21	32	32
	2010	13590	7007	5460	5419	1509	276	38	38	48	48
Western Asia	2000	682	228	74	74	140	16	14	11	26	26
	2007	3273	830	40	37	780	92	11	8	81	72
	2008	3976	722	72	60	632	58	18	9	169	167
	2009	2677	356	29	21	319	28	7	4	13	12
	2010	4787	734	48	40	672	77	14	8	26	25
Oceania	2000	1460	462	302	270	157	54	3	3	3	...
	2007	1768	1250	893	803	358	124	0	0	0	0
	2008	2000	1380	753	655	628	107	0	0	0	0
	2009	1307	804	585	518	219	45	0	0	0	0
	2010	1887	1249	921	816	327	59	0	0	0	0

For general note and footnotes see end of table

Exportations mondiales par provenance et destination (Tableau D)

En millions de dollars E.-U. f.o.b.

South-Eastern Europe Europe du Sud-est	Northern Africa Afrique septentrio-nale	Sub-Saharan Africa Afrique du Nord	Latin America and the Caribbean Amérique latine et Caraïbes	Eastern Asia Asie orientale	Southern Asia Asie méridionale	South-eastern Asia Asie du Sud-est	Western Asia Asie occidentale	Oceania Océanie	Others 4/ Autre 4/	Année	← Exportations vers / Exportations en provence de ↓
Minerais métallifères et déchets de métaux (CTCI, Rev. 3, 28) *[suite]*											
16	0	0	...	9	2	0	6	...	0	2000	Afrique du Nord
23	11	11	2	94	40	4	112	...	1	2007	
17	21	5	3	128	36	5	176	...	4	2008	
10	2	6	7	74	26	1	68	...	3	2009	
2	0	4	15	204	49	4	71	...	5	2010	
13	0	146	13	235	24	36	11	...	0	2000	Afrique subsaharienne
32	8	1486	52	3483	296	285	63	0	6	2007	
32	1	1713	104	5894	742	473	123	5	1	2008	
4	1	1226	64	6021	456	311	50	0	0	2009	
46	10	1926	71	8304	601	441	114	0	2	2010	
9	0	6	13	206	13	29	4	...	0	2000	Afrique du sud
11	2	63	46	2083	161	170	19	...	3	2007	
31	0	24	96	3427	386	306	70	5	0	2008	
0	0	19	59	4062	235	177	29	0	0	2009	
10	9	33	66	6205	472	304	90	0	0	2010	
144	125	83	916	1416	262	238	233	...	0	2000	Amérique latine et Caraïbes
923	451	195	4407	15010	3069	1242	468	...	0	2007	
988	662	172	4609	16777	2130	1731	1380	...	1	2008	
649	479	108	2292	19372	1385	903	694	0	0	2009	
784	805	301	4425	32898	2305	1554	1994	...	0	2010	
41	111	30	335	556	34	78	205	...	...	2000	Brésil
230	360	92	914	4532	356	383	450	...	...	2007	
254	584	101	1400	6389	357	828	1373	...	...	2008	
87	433	29	460	7968	206	344	685	...	...	2009	
115	722	82	1520	15593	438	712	1950	...	...	2010	
0	0	10	1	576	7	24	1	0	0	2000	Asie orientale
0	0	5	16	3261	121	100	4	0	...	2007	
0	0	23	40	3541	144	121	7	0	0	2008	
0	0	10	9	2498	40	108	9	0	...	2009	
0	0	17	16	3093	132	292	2	0	...	2010	
0	0	5	0	36	2	7	0	0	...	2000	Chine
0	0	0	6	370	45	5	0	...	...	2007	
0	0	1	22	367	20	15	3	...	...	2008	
...	0	8	3	72	8	10	5	0	...	2009	
0	0	12	2	355	37	53	0	0	...	2010	
2	0	2	18	238	28	4	18	...	0	2000	Asie méridionale
67	0	2	3	6066	139	34	107	2	10	2007	
10	13	13	0	6790	251	45	138	...	6	2008	
48	19	4	0	6504	142	59	42	...	20	2009	
7	1	6	1	7939	565	43	399	...	0	2010	
28	0	19	16	457	151	264	1	0	...	2000	Asie Sud-est
...	...	3	7	2915	792	1088	3	0	0	2007	
0	0	2	13	2646	526	926	2	0	0	2008	
0	0	5	0	3009	765	704	3	0	...	2009	
...	0	1	2	4585	1171	768	8	0	...	2010	
24	10	4	0	93	150	59	80	...	8	2000	Asie occidentale
129	66	2	22	789	809	114	425	0	6	2007	
84	56	3	30	1269	772	139	703	0	28	2008	
39	6	2	10	1042	694	72	430	0	14	2009	
123	5	2	9	1540	1030	135	1173	0	11	2010	
1	...	5	...	62	...	215	...	0	713	2000	Océanie
...	...	0	...	263	159	95	0	0	...	2007	
...	...	0	...	298	214	107	...	0	...	2008	
0	...	0	0	261	37	204	...	0	...	2009	
...	...	0	...	312	75	252	...	0	...	2010	

Voir la fin du tableau pour la remarque générale et les notes.

World exports by provenance and destination (Table D)

In million U.S. dollars f.o.b.

Exports to → / ↓ Exports from	Year	World 1/ Monde 1/	Developed economies 2/ Economies développées 2/ Total	Asia-Pacific Asie-Pacifique Total	Japan Japon	Europe Total	Germany Allemagne	North America Amérique du Nord Total	U.S.A. É.-U.	Commonwealth of Independent States Communauté d'Etats Indépendants Total	Europe
					Animal and vegetable oils, fats and waxes (SITC, Rev. 3, 4)						
World 1/	2000	19159	9124	727	528	6715	801	1681	1403	539	455
	2007	60573	27160	1662	1112	21191	3713	4308	3595	1967	1644
	2008	88235	39779	2247	1599	31133	4601	6399	5470	3023	2515
	2009	64118	27327	1604	1094	21321	3041	4402	3547	2209	1832
	2010	79506	31311	1952	1355	23980	3468	5378	4442	2719	2226
Developed Economies - Asia-Pacific 2/	2000	326	115	59	48	26	3	30	29	0	0
	2007	533	117	51	17	28	6	38	35	0	0
	2008	787	166	72	23	41	7	53	49	0	0
	2009	588	158	62	25	43	7	52	49	0	0
	2010	736	155	61	24	43	6	50	45	0	0
Japan	2000	81	37	1	.	11	2	25	24	0	0
	2007	85	46	1	.	17	4	28	25	0	0
	2008	110	67	1	.	28	5	38	34	0	0
	2009	111	53	1	.	17	5	35	32	0	0
	2010	137	64	1	.	22	5	40	36	0	0
Developed Economies - Europe 2/	2000	6462	5131	188	105	4450	624	493	438	268	257
	2007	16508	14637	400	189	13218	3044	1019	896	504	475
	2008	23866	20972	394	249	19419	3655	1158	1027	827	779
	2009	17469	15154	359	204	13874	2377	921	812	560	540
	2010	18776	16125	400	228	14665	2652	1059	929	594	570
France	2000	436	332	3	3	324	34	6	5	10	10
	2007	1235	1151	5	5	1131	175	15	12	22	22
	2008	1757	1601	7	7	1582	211	11	9	45	44
	2009	1341	1235	6	5	1216	153	12	11	31	31
	2010	1421	1317	8	7	1294	149	15	13	27	26
Germany	2000	1012	827	8	3	811	.	8	8	58	57
	2007	1839	1649	19	10	1606	.	24	22	104	102
	2008	2987	2609	21	10	2559	.	29	26	227	223
	2009	2194	1804	19	8	1762	.	24	22	180	178
	2010	2443	2005	24	16	1959	.	22	20	189	187
Developed Economies - North America 2/	2000	1871	754	79	74	159	10	515	314	26	19
	2007	4383	1817	168	150	342	40	1307	812	16	12
	2008	6832	2803	214	191	376	46	2213	1551	21	20
	2009	5019	2099	156	137	255	9	1688	1049	9	8
	2010	6980	2446	157	139	376	31	1913	1214	6	5
United States	2000	1439	404	59	55	143	9	202	.	26	18
	2007	2968	871	92	79	284	20	495	.	5	1
	2008	4567	1112	93	77	358	43	661	.	2	1
	2009	3340	958	84	69	236	8	638	.	1	1
	2010	4459	1096	74	62	324	16	698	.	2	1
South-Eastern Europe	2000	50	18	NULL	.	17	2	1	0	5	5
	2007	261	149	0	0	149	24	0	0	1	1
	2008	439	242	0	0	242	25	0	0	2	0
	2009	385	237	0	.	237	14	0	0	0	0
	2010	516	346	0	.	345	16	0	0	0	0
Commonwealth of Independent States	2000	338	102	0	0	98	3	3	3	127	80
	2007	2379	978	0	0	977	5	1	1	599	391
	2008	2938	1132	0	.	1130	38	1	1	892	542
	2009	2804	847	0	.	836	14	12	1	591	304
	2010	3486	955	0	0	953	14	1	1	856	491
Russian Federation	2000	79	3	0	0	3	0	0	0	29	1
	2007	502	173	0	0	172	2	1	1	102	1
	2008	809	407	0	.	406	26	1	1	209	3
	2009	781	302	0	.	301	1	1	0	161	3
	2010	626	264	0	0	264	8	0	0	157	4

For general note and footnotes see end of table

Exportations mondiales par provenance et destination (Tableau D)

En millions de dollars E.-U. f.o.b.

← Exportations vers

South-Eastern Europe Europe du Sud-est	Northern Africa Afrique septentrio-nale	Sub-Saharan Africa Afrique du Nord	Latin America and the Caribbean Amérique latine et Caraïbes	Eastern Asia Asie orientale	Southern Asia Asie méridionale	South-eastern Asia Asie du Sud-est	Western Asia Asie occidentale	Oceania Océanie	Others 4/ Autre 4/	Année	Exportations en provenance de ↓
											Huiles et graisses d'origine animale ou végétale (CTCI, Rev. 3, 4)
118	753	744	1495	1622	2773	873	1045	20	54	2000	Monde 1/
421	2034	2743	3716	8677	7760	3198	2723	39	134	2007	
721	3249	3654	6036	11356	10593	4611	5038	54	122	2008	
472	2493	2625	3850	9384	9241	3496	2888	43	91	2009	
604	3343	3945	5092	11007	12674	5577	3051	47	139	2010	
...	0	14	0	126	36	32	0	2	0	2000	Economies Développées - Asie-Pacifique 2/
0	0	14	2	315	30	43	4	6	...	2007	
0	0	16	11	487	37	56	7	6	0	2008	
0	0	13	5	323	30	50	4	6	...	2009	
0	0	20	4	425	59	59	5	7	0	2010	
...	0	0	0	27	1	16	0	0	...	2000	Japon
0	...	...	1	25	0	12	0	0	...	2007	
0	...	0	1	27	1	15	0	0	...	2008	
0	...	...	1	44	0	12	0	0	...	2009	
0	...	...	1	57	1	15	0	0	...	2010	
80	274	164	146	91	55	27	189	6	31	2000	Economies Développées - Europe 2/
189	120	161	315	190	42	67	185	15	83	2007	
400	270	240	424	238	47	91	283	19	53	2008	
285	311	166	346	215	52	75	240	14	50	2009	
358	145	375	412	261	62	102	247	11	85	2010	
3	34	12	2	2	6	2	28	5	...	2000	France
2	8	10	6	14	1	2	14	7	0	2007	
4	12	21	7	30	2	3	20	11	0	2008	
2	13	10	6	17	2	3	15	8	...	2009	
2	8	11	7	19	2	6	16	6	0	2010	
13	26	10	5	33	19	4	16	0	1	2000	Allemagne
19	13	4	7	14	5	11	12	0	...	2007	
33	40	5	11	17	5	14	26	...	...	2008	
23	129	5	14	14	5	7	14	0	0	2009	
31	64	85	15	14	7	12	19	...	0	2010	
9	41	78	534	200	42	25	161	0	0	2000	Economies Développées - Amérique du Nord 2/
0	193	171	1102	652	64	47	321	0	...	2007	
0	377	330	1881	754	61	93	511	1	0	2008	
2	293	146	1254	670	152	114	279	1	...	2009	
1	391	182	1630	1632	221	98	372	1	...	2010	
9	40	77	526	139	38	20	161	0	...	2000	Etats-Unis
0	193	134	1045	314	62	28	316	0	...	2007	
0	377	315	1793	369	56	35	506	0	...	2008	
2	293	139	1209	212	148	101	276	1	...	2009	
1	391	168	1579	574	219	76	354	1	...	2010	
16	1	...	0	...	...	...	10	...	0	2000	Europe du Sud-est
93	...	0	0	0	0	0	18	0	0	2007	
162	0	0	0	0	...	0	33	0	0	2008	
130	4	0	0	0	2	0	11	0	0	2009	
163	0	...	...	0	0	0	7	0	0	2010	
5	69	...	3	1	10	0	21	...	0	2000	Communauté d'Etats Indépendants
86	330	9	2	10	156	0	209	0	0	2007	
61	179	19	58	3	123	7	464	1	0	2008	
34	411	15	1	13	511	8	371	0	0	2009	
56	465	56	1	45	663	6	381	1	2	2010	
2	36	...	0	1	0	0	8	...	...	2000	Fédération de Russie
16	104	0	...	9	59	...	39	0	0	2007	
17	10	1	...	2	32	0	129	1	0	2008	
5	93	1	0	12	59	0	148	0	...	2009	
5	52	16	1	13	40	...	76	1	2	2010	

Voir la fin du tableau pour la remarque générale et les notes.

World exports by provenance and destination (Table D)

In million U.S. dollars f.o.b.

Exports to → / ↓ Exports from	Year	World 1/ Monde 1/	Developed economies 2/ Economies développées 2/ Total	Asia-Pacific Asie-Pacifique Total	Asia-Pacific Asie-Pacifique Japan Japon	Europe Total	Europe Germany Allemagne	North America Amérique du Nord Total	North America Amérique du Nord U.S.A. É.-U.	Commonwealth of Independent States Communauté d'Etats Indépendants Total	Commonwealth of Independent States Communauté d'Etats Indépendants Europe
			Animal and vegetable oils, fats and waxes (SITC, Rev. 3, 4) *[cont.]*								
Northern Africa	2000	245	188	0	0	178	0	10	10	...	...
	2007	757	599	1	1	510	2	88	84	3	3
	2008	1074	718	1	1	590	4	127	118	3	3
	2009	742	425	0	0	311	3	114	107	2	2
	2010	725	418	1	0	304	3	113	107	3	3
Sub-Saharan Africa	2000	226	105	2	2	101	6	2	2	0	0
	2007	439	116	2	2	111	7	2	2	0	0
	2008	559	143	8	5	132	20	3	2	0	0
	2009	503	111	4	4	103	15	4	3	0	0
	2010	721	148	10	10	131	49	6	5	0	0
South Africa	2000	38	5	0	.	5	0	1	0	...	...
	2007	33	8	0	0	7	2	1	1	0	...
	2008	112	41	4	0	37	1	1	1	0	0
	2009	90	6	0	0	5	1	1	0	...	...
	2010	152	8	1	1	5	1	2	2	0	0
Latin America and the Caribbean	2000	2611	341	44	32	206	25	90	84	40	40
	2007	9098	1639	106	54	1265	96	268	244	22	19
	2008	12782	3201	194	100	2656	177	351	302	49	45
	2009	7668	1217	83	38	875	100	258	217	3	2
	2010	8652	1275	134	64	873	88	268	225	9	2
Brazil	2000	476	83	24	20	41	5	18	18	1	1
	2007	1939	529	30	21	467	16	33	32	10	7
	2008	2965	848	65	29	748	13	34	34	44	42
	2009	1454	295	26	15	241	15	28	28	0	0
	2010	1630	241	45	35	149	21	47	46	0	0
Eastern Asia	2000	304	54	21	17	19	4	14	12	2	2
	2007	468	149	57	47	53	8	39	35	7	5
	2008	809	200	91	80	58	10	51	44	27	20
	2009	496	169	57	47	49	9	63	53	9	6
	2010	592	201	56	45	56	17	89	77	10	8
China	2000	116	33	12	10	15	3	7	6	0	0
	2007	311	118	41	34	50	8	28	25	2	1
	2008	595	159	67	60	53	10	38	33	9	2
	2009	339	134	41	35	46	8	47	39	4	2
	2010	391	157	36	28	52	16	69	60	5	3
Southern Asia	2000	284	164	21	20	107	5	36	36	25	12
	2007	901	263	38	34	183	8	42	42	44	6
	2008	1036	398	53	49	281	17	64	63	54	6
	2009	785	283	43	40	190	10	51	50	30	3
	2010	974	389	43	39	274	9	72	71	34	6
South-Eastern Asia	2000	6010	1948	307	229	1173	103	468	459	38	36
	2007	23443	6056	817	608	3817	406	1422	1385	762	729
	2008	35129	9100	1189	883	5576	500	2335	2285	1131	1096
	2009	26155	6099	816	586	4098	415	1184	1163	991	961
	2010	35920	8303	1064	788	5468	479	1771	1742	1193	1137
Western Asia	2000	271	41	1	0	21	2	18	16	9	3
	2007	1016	307	18	9	210	3	79	58	9	4
	2008	1392	150	24	18	85	5	41	26	15	4
	2009	1105	143	20	14	68	7	55	43	12	4
	2010	994	141	23	17	84	6	35	26	11	3
Oceania	2000	163	162	3	.	159	14	0	0	...	...
	2007	387	332	4	0	328	64	1	1	...	...
	2008	592	553	4	0	548	97	1	1	...	...
	2009	401	386	4	0	382	61	0	0	0	0
	2010	438	408	3	0	404	97	1	1	1	1

For general note and footnotes see end of table

Exportations mondiales par provenance et destination (Tableau D)

En millions de dollars E.-U. f.o.b.

← Exportations vers

South-Eastern Europe Europe du Sud-est	Northern Africa Afrique septentrionale	Sub-Saharan Africa Afrique du Nord	Latin America and the Caribbean Amérique latine et Caraïbes	Eastern Asia Asie orientale	Southern Asia Asie méridionale	South-eastern Asia Asie du Sud-est	Western Asia Asie occidentale	Oceania Océanie	Others 4/ Autre 4/	Année	Exportations en provenance de ↓
											Huiles et graisses d'origine animale ou végétale (CTCI, Rev. 3, 4) *[suite]*
...	15	1	3	0	0	...	30	...	7	2000	Afrique du Nord
0	115	16	2	2	0	0	15	...	5	2007	
3	144	49	1	2	2	1	140	...	10	2008	
1	138	42	0	1	0	0	121	...	11	2009	
1	140	47	1	2	3	0	97	...	12	2010	
0	0	112	0	5	0	2	1	0	0	2000	Afrique subsaharienne
...	0	311	0	3	1	4	2	0	2	2007	
0	0	364	3	3	4	22	19	0	1	2008	
0	1	348	1	17	4	3	16	0	2	2009	
...	1	506	1	12	2	6	40	0	7	2010	
0	0	26	0	5	0	1	0	...	0	2000	Afrique du sud
...	0	22	0	2	0	0	0	0	0	2007	
...	0	39	0	2	2	9	18	0	1	2008	
...	0	81	0	1	0	0	0	0	1	2009	
...	0	138	0	5	0	1	0	0	0	2010	
0	175	89	732	114	995	78	43	1	4	2000	Amérique latine et Caraïbes
4	606	575	1999	2165	1745	216	95	0	31	2007	
4	1173	548	3205	2563	1437	222	336	0	46	2008	
0	417	350	1903	2219	1256	121	166	0	17	2009	
0	623	329	2351	1411	2184	266	191	1	12	2010	
...	48	7	47	47	213	24	5	1	...	2000	Brésil
...	63	160	142	371	590	40	34	...	...	2007	
0	197	239	270	864	413	45	44	...	...	2008	
0	104	72	176	438	298	37	32	0	...	2009	
...	104	39	185	815	190	16	39	0	...	2010	
0	0	0	1	215	2	28	1	0	0	2000	Asie orientale
1	1	2	5	190	5	67	41	0	0	2007	
1	7	3	7	279	39	138	106	0	0	2008	
1	2	4	6	214	8	70	12	0	0	2009	
1	2	5	8	242	12	97	13	0	...	2010	
0	0	0	1	74	1	7	0	0	...	2000	Chine
1	0	1	5	103	3	36	40	0	...	2007	
1	7	2	6	167	37	104	104	0	...	2008	
1	2	3	5	131	5	43	11	0	...	2009	
1	1	4	8	138	9	59	10	0	...	2010	
0	1	3	1	29	34	19	7	0	0	2000	Asie méridionale
0	1	5	9	88	344	35	112	0	1	2007	
0	2	7	7	106	251	72	139	0	1	2008	
0	2	7	13	202	155	45	44	0	4	2009	
1	2	8	17	273	145	49	52	0	2	2010	
5	175	270	68	839	1569	663	421	10	4	2000	Asie Sud-est
44	644	1409	276	5010	5301	2702	1219	15	4	2007	
83	1077	2010	437	6899	8531	3856	1978	23	4	2008	
16	903	1488	317	5489	7016	2977	835	20	4	2009	
21	1544	2367	661	6671	9237	4847	1039	26	10	2010	
1	2	13	5	1	30	1	161	0	8	2000	Asie occidentale
4	25	71	3	9	72	8	502	0	8	2007	
5	20	68	3	13	62	27	1023	0	6	2008	
3	10	46	4	20	54	22	789	0	3	2009	
3	32	49	6	33	86	18	606	0	9	2010	
0	...	...	...	...	0	0	...	0	0	2000	Océanie
...	...	0	...	45	0	8	...	2	0	2007	
...	0	0	...	8	0	27	...	3	...	2008	
...	...	0	0	2	0	11	...	2	...	2009	
...	...	0	0	1	0	27	0	1	...	2010	

Voir la fin du tableau pour la remarque générale et les notes.

World exports by provenance and destination (Table D)

In million U.S. dollars f.o.b.

Exports to → / ↓ Exports from	Year	World 1/ Monde 1/	Developed economies 2/ Economies développées 2/ — Total	Asia-Pacific Asie-Pacifique — Total	Asia-Pacific — Japan Japon	Europe — Total	Europe — Germany Allemagne	North America Amérique du Nord — Total	North America — U.S.A. É.-U.	Commonwealth of Independent States Communauté d'Etats Indépendants — Total	CIS — Europe
Mineral fuels and related materials (SITC, Rev. 3, 3)											
World 1/	2000	655526	441637	71935	66959	221467	29183	148236	137527	11180	9725
	2007	1957856	1257649	233820	212866	643033	65991	380797	351313	30355	23458
	2008	2789977	1666916	220588	190708	949576	92635	496752	402232	50308	40847
	2009	1737616	946656	101184	82815	569124	53041	276349	213238	31865	25999
	2010	2226190	1181892	127994	103735	702721	66404	351176	274301	38359	32639
Developed Economies - Asia-Pacific 2/	2000	15224	7843	5798	5119	901	85	1144	1143	7	7
	2007	42105	20517	15281	12934	3241	234	1995	1961	51	50
	2008	80747	39343	31068	26325	6366	502	1909	1908	100	97
	2009	57092	24541	21285	18609	2691	123	564	543	40	39
	2010	74265	30482	25200	22064	4180	237	1102	1030	55	53
Japan	2000	1520	518	83	.	40	4	395	394	7	7
	2007	9280	3115	618	.	716	10	1781	1747	51	50
	2008	18776	4211	2349	.	1131	7	731	731	73	71
	2009	10530	2320	1285	.	649	9	386	365	40	39
	2010	13048	2884	1467	.	568	3	849	778	54	53
Developed Economies - Europe 2/	2000	130040	117996	136	102	100926	20418	16933	13145	384	367
	2007	343092	295587	572	509	258001	42383	37014	30544	1639	1482
	2008	473759	406659	972	833	361394	60170	44294	37350	2498	2283
	2009	291419	251792	430	381	225206	34782	26156	21747	1671	1518
	2010	367618	314133	518	468	284398	45456	29217	24484	2154	1938
France	2000	8183	7258	28	13	6660	1009	570	561	16	15
	2007	20741	17766	46	41	16131	2326	1589	1499	21	20
	2008	30139	24863	56	50	21753	2959	3054	2863	8	8
	2009	16389	12901	39	35	11701	1629	1161	1098	17	16
	2010	18717	14723	42	39	13341	1826	1340	1227	10	10
Germany	2000	7757	5384	13	9	4961	.	410	406	35	33
	2007	30311	23115	24	15	21243	.	1848	1845	161	139
	2008	37526	27977	30	20	26347	.	1601	1564	204	173
	2009	23147	21626	26	18	21060	.	539	536	190	161
	2010	23907	22558	37	24	22297	.	225	213	320	279
Developed Economies - North America 2/	2000	49685	41512	1485	1328	2019	97	38009	35232	8	8
	2007	129183	103487	1735	1464	7683	412	94069	83659	128	125
	2008	202339	158240	3918	3511	20920	941	133401	116912	201	196
	2009	126736	92722	2809	2500	14219	526	75694	66022	121	111
	2010	172787	118224	3964	3677	16628	1188	97633	85141	492	446
United States	2000	13340	5570	1001	845	1793	80	2776	.	8	7
	2007	41957	17860	802	534	6649	236	10409	.	120	117
	2008	76533	35577	1722	1319	17367	635	16488	.	189	185
	2009	54720	23616	1189	884	12755	357	9672	.	117	108
	2010	80728	29744	2097	1815	15156	931	12491	.	483	439
South-Eastern Europe	2000	1442	243	NULL	.	231	6	12	12	243	170
	2007	6573	2098	0	0	1934	56	163	162	962	678
	2008	9342	2570	0	0	2440	118	130	130	1483	1145
	2009	5550	1875	0	0	1798	85	77	77	787	526
	2010	6943	2476	0	0	2405	120	71	71	1042	716
Commonwealth of Independent States	2000	62943	41876	302	302	40040	3736	1534	215	10354	9064
	2007	268503	190197	4445	4443	182121	12569	3631	3004	26846	20663
	2008	426100	305836	6687	6684	286148	15714	13002	11384	44852	36407
	2009	250975	179772	5793	5687	165672	10037	8307	6005	28675	23400
	2010	334817	235588	11685	11579	212718	12205	11185	8119	33748	28872
Russian Federation	2000	52166	36681	302	302	36076	3554	303	189	6979	6287
	2007	216515	156583	4443	4443	149633	12187	2507	2298	19641	14870
	2008	307371	225989	6538	6538	213437	14285	6014	5267	29946	23365
	2009	190171	141687	5791	5687	131599	8743	4296	3903	18741	15121
	2010	257616	186383	11654	11579	168154	11096	6575	5989	26177	23117

For general note and footnotes see end of table

Exportations mondiales par provenance et destination (Tableau D)

En millions de dollars E.-U. f.o.b.

South-Eastern Europe Europe du Sud-est	Northern Africa Afrique septentrio-nale	Sub-Saharan Africa Afrique du Nord	Latin America and the Caribbean Amérique latine et Caraïbes	Eastern Asia Asie orientale	Southern Asia Asie méridionale	South-eastern Asia Asie du Sud-est	Western Asia Asie occidentale	Oceania Océanie	Others 4/ Autre 4/	← Exportations vers Année	Exportations en provenance de ↓
				Combustibles minéraux et produits assimiles (CTCI, Rev. 3, 3)							
3229	7443	5879	34003	89672	11368	25378	12343	1115	12278	2000	Monde 1/
18369	22312	29094	90915	258815	54426	101285	48932	2638	43064	2007	
26108	27544	42487	140638	483046	71079	138472	62598	3260	77521	2008	
11503	18485	32726	89370	355356	61038	99589	41243	2798	46988	2009	
15480	22548	41095	115907	492014	67675	138548	51539	3317	57817	2010	
0	8	65	320	3610	499	1633	112	421	706	2000	Economies Développées - Asie-Pacifique 2/
35	88	201	1041	9860	2480	5223	164	589	1856	2007	
83	74	471	2782	19001	5589	9475	835	401	2594	2008	
17	62	123	1429	18152	4473	7112	229	508	406	2009	
0	11	353	2427	23608	7195	8695	289	551	601	2010	
...	0	2	42	701	27	220	4	0	...	2000	Japon
4	0	42	340	3550	253	1805	39	80	...	2007	
1	1	12	1349	7588	595	4781	160	5	...	2008	
17	1	15	395	3604	148	3956	35	0	...	2009	
0	1	14	1068	4577	186	4232	32	0	...	2010	
784	1350	1171	767	506	436	286	1983	6	4373	2000	Economies Développées - Europe 2/
2642	4827	6660	5934	597	342	1204	5391	17	18251	2007	
3546	6729	9764	6562	1319	564	1828	8154	20	26114	2008	
2293	4611	7969	4263	1161	732	1373	6263	18	9273	2009	
3083	6602	11568	6383	1473	441	1844	7450	47	12441	2010	
8	212	257	130	23	21	19	204	3	34	2000	France
28	680	775	319	58	24	109	814	5	142	2007	
30	1296	691	922	111	121	123	1707	4	262	2008	
28	684	705	273	141	83	117	1273	4	163	2009	
21	716	1329	260	49	93	157	875	4	478	2010	
22	10	35	117	35	12	13	38	0	2056	2000	Allemagne
58	65	96	64	81	49	38	95	0	6488	2007	
83	34	140	89	120	31	50	262	0	8535	2008	
59	49	172	113	132	33	55	191	0	527	2009	
73	58	203	109	179	44	94	215	0	54	2010	
73	105	134	6228	821	95	419	287	2	0	2000	Economies Développées - Amérique du Nord 2/
180	620	600	18790	2016	416	1900	1047	1	...	2007	
470	833	1450	31317	3534	926	2715	2652	1	0	2008	
56	919	1108	22825	3716	1047	2724	1497	2	0	2009	
159	1135	1425	38875	5495	1125	4068	1789	2	0	2010	
61	96	125	6142	582	85	418	251	2	...	2000	États-Unis
179	608	596	18268	1206	404	1798	917	1	...	2007	
329	819	1441	30361	1844	887	2674	2411	1	...	2008	
52	866	1095	22238	1836	980	2600	1319	1	...	2009	
159	1133	1411	38100	3025	1101	3965	1606	2	...	2010	
661	13	65	17	0	1	12	186	...	1	2000	Europe du Sud-est
1466	95	3	28	2	18	277	1480	0	145	2007	
2411	112	238	75	1	13	277	2161	1	0	2008	
1447	147	101	12	2	44	304	823	2	7	2009	
2018	45	165	12	3	69	234	840	5	35	2010	
1626	28	22	4633	697	251	464	2990	1	2	2000	Communauté d'Etats Indépendants
13565	331	86	1938	15262	2732	1753	15781	5	9	2007	
18787	719	355	3264	23494	4461	2772	21553	3	4	2008	
7209	826	287	1461	16083	3189	2661	10591	76	146	2009	
9818	1131	74	1897	27852	3639	6021	15018	0	31	2010	
1407	24	15	3416	590	15	428	2611	0	0	2000	Fédération de Russie
12232	304	79	1515	12174	349	1222	12405	5	6	2007	
16667	567	244	1693	17453	286	1208	13313	3	0	2008	
5759	603	273	1070	12516	700	1540	7206	76	0	2009	
7775	756	24	1188	20135	886	3753	10515	0	24	2010	

Voir la fin du tableau pour la remarque générale et les notes.

World exports by provenance and destination (Table D)

In million U.S. dollars f.o.b.

Exports to → / ↓ Exports from	Year	World 1/ Monde 1/	Developed economies 2/ Economies développées 2/ Total	Asia-Pacific Asie-Pacifique Total	Asia-Pacific Asie-Pacifique Japan Japon	Europe Total	Europe Germany Allemagne	North America Amérique du Nord Total	North America Amérique du Nord U.S.A. É.-U.	Commonwealth of Independent States Communauté d'Etats Indépendants Total	Commonwealth of Independent States Communauté d'Etats Indépendants Europe
		Mineral fuels and related materials (SITC, Rev. 3, 3) *[cont.]*									
Northern Africa	2000	34262	28468	95	95	24088	2706	4285	3508	10	0
	2007	115887	95207	827	736	67374	6206	27006	22302	71	15
	2008	153414	128371	1882	1786	97267	8440	29222	23800	112	19
	2009	89372	71345	417	331	55737	4271	15191	12718	6	6
	2010	110338	88384	615	291	68499	4280	19269	16301	35	0
Sub-Saharan Africa	2000	45329	27709	229	193	9432	279	18048	17393	3	3
	2007	137052	76657	2801	2161	21792	1602	52065	49399	8	8
	2008	203551	117531	2770	2364	39099	2468	75662	71180	19	19
	2009	124109	62346	1277	1193	23221	1250	37849	34467	29	27
	2010	170425	88683	1836	882	29770	1197	57077	52241	1	1
South Africa	2000	2664	1005	72	36	902	32	31	29	0	0
	2007	6759	2696	47	40	2288	48	360	288	8	8
	2008	7120	3035	24	14	2953	100	58	58	19	19
	2009	6023	2134	43	33	2058	78	32	32	17	14
	2010	7198	1443	43	32	1343	121	58	58	0	0
Latin America and the Caribbean	2000	62277	44109	434	371	3996	406	39679	38841	2	1
	2007	161027	109993	132	130	15555	1108	94307	92655	3	3
	2008	205328	123686	145	145	18342	1547	105199	103460	14	14
	2009	140153	80599	160	160	13701	242	66738	51685	3	3
	2010	178619	94933	423	414	14398	330	80111	67965	0	0
Brazil	2000	908	600	0	0	66	6	533	529	...	...
	2007	13297	5675	0	0	1996	205	3678	3674	0	0
	2008	18689	7527	0	0	2552	150	4974	4971	3	3
	2009	13657	4377	0	0	1780	112	2597	2590	0	0
	2010	19843	7330	72	72	2788	247	4470	4136	...	...
Eastern Asia	2000	19504	7958	5952	5704	452	46	1553	1477	97	78
	2007	60516	17460	8178	6900	3068	194	6214	6071	329	271
	2008	90364	23417	11187	8985	7127	439	5103	4794	467	366
	2009	56624	13681	5992	4091	4518	206	3171	3077	217	178
	2010	75587	17384	7724	5760	4576	276	5085	4867	442	357
China	2000	7855	3226	2080	1973	436	46	711	689	70	51
	2007	20878	6003	3075	2920	1509	193	1420	1292	251	199
	2008	31773	10213	5012	4760	2597	435	2605	2361	367	273
	2009	20383	3511	1945	1617	808	202	758	696	121	90
	2010	26673	4607	2240	2032	1317	273	1050	868	294	222
Southern Asia	2000	26843	16072	5330	5318	10595	184	147	147	11	3
	2007	98977	51581	21863	21859	29038	158	680	680	61	15
	2008	129198	65806	27742	27738	37816	229	248	247	74	15
	2009	80957	22430	1393	1236	20754	31	283	278	65	6
	2010	98609	26751	2468	2358	23644	6	640	639	70	8
South-Eastern Asia	2000	45384	18836	16791	13818	423	19	1622	1616	2	2
	2007	124407	42277	37695	23148	1745	27	2837	2826	10	9
	2008	177763	61602	53430	33901	4818	51	3354	3347	16	15
	2009	124204	36635	31499	20019	3056	30	2081	2075	12	11
	2010	169270	48270	42690	27068	2762	35	2818	2672	25	24
Western Asia	2000	161895	88421	34788	34609	28363	1199	25270	24800	58	22
	2007	469025	251312	139015	138478	51479	1040	60818	58050	248	139
	2008	636420	232575	79509	78197	67839	2015	85228	27720	472	268
	2009	389465	108217	29428	28516	38550	1457	40238	14544	241	173
	2010	465957	116029	30316	29129	38743	1074	46969	10770	297	226
Oceania	2000	699	595	595	0	0	.	0	0	...	...
	2007	1509	1279	1277	104	2	.	0	0	...	...
	2008	1653	1280	1279	239	1	0	0	0	...	...
	2009	959	702	700	91	1	.	0	0	...	...
	2010	955	555	554	44	1	.	0	0	...	...

For general note and footnotes see end of table

Exportations mondiales par provenance et destination (Tableau D)

En millions de dollars E.-U. f.o.b.

South-Eastern Europe Europe du Sud-est	Northern Africa Afrique septentrio-nale	Sub-Saharan Africa Afrique du Nord	Latin America and the Caribbean Amérique latine et Caraïbes	Eastern Asia Asie orientale	Southern Asia Asie méridionale	South-eastern Asia Asie du Sud-est	Western Asia Asie occidentale	Oceania Océanie	Others 4/ Autre 4/	Année	← Exportations vers / Exportations en provenance de ↓
											Combustibles minéraux et produits assimiles (CTCI, Rev. 3, 3) ***[suite]***
35	472	59	1830	167	173	173	2219	...	656	2000	Afrique du Nord
33	1929	835	3890	4009	4318	1312	3069	55	1161	2007	
203	3239	856	4860	5825	3416	971	3969	...	1591	2008	
188	2055	130	2681	6350	2147	551	3151	...	769	2009	
219	2019	138	3014	7915	3061	691	3895	0	968	2010	
9	37	3593	1794	6333	4023	787	294	28	720	2000	Afrique subsaharienne
39	212	10008	7854	31562	6161	658	856	21	3016	2007	
41	119	14845	12460	43234	10871	978	862	19	2571	2008	
138	447	13509	6322	27387	10375	1297	1202	130	927	2009	
12	804	15131	8950	37155	14373	3091	1471	17	737	2010	
2	35	580	45	129	83	42	168	1	573	2000	Afrique du sud
36	196	917	302	1312	528	115	326	15	309	2007	
28	110	1257	414	218	718	262	464	18	579	2008	
13	22	921	115	396	1287	164	476	43	436	2009	
12	74	1044	371	956	1890	405	613	0	388	2010	
3	1	92	15535	438	209	179	106	0	1602	2000	Amérique latine et Caraïbes
6	182	1398	42698	4112	1044	580	816	2	193	2007	
4	110	1370	65577	8399	941	3773	961	5	488	2008	
9	281	423	42744	8359	2185	4633	709	1	207	2009	
18	291	702	41744	17465	2306	5681	597	0	14882	2010	
...	...	25	238	36	1	8	0	...	...	2000	Brésil
...	0	983	5043	956	1	427	212	...	...	2007	
...	5	901	7711	1703	20	677	143	...	...	2008	
...	0	315	6183	1365	873	496	49	0	...	2009	
...	0	55	6590	4054	1255	530	29	...	...	2010	
10	7	77	363	6606	489	2581	66	133	1116	2000	Asie orientale
2	66	473	3840	16573	1461	16625	886	146	2655	2007	
4	30	955	7082	27259	3487	22383	1536	334	3410	2008	
8	81	465	3286	16890	1442	17644	661	455	1794	2009	
0	294	791	4630	22269	1908	23426	1270	650	2523	2010	
10	6	59	209	2528	334	1360	53	0	...	2000	Chine
1	13	160	1653	6913	552	4814	493	24	...	2007	
4	27	469	3826	10574	1202	4393	632	66	...	2008	
8	6	300	1655	7722	350	6149	495	66	...	2009	
0	10	507	2761	8912	645	8081	735	122	...	2010	
0	2008	8	679	7173	177	502	212	0	0	2000	Asie méridionale
2	4513	3171	1278	22532	3701	4117	7738	1	283	2007	
3	6133	4072	2305	29703	4306	5820	10345	26	604	2008	
8	2502	2591	1149	38144	2417	3862	6960	0	829	2009	
7	2895	3874	3654	40431	2783	7870	9866	0	407	2010	
3	9	28	78	13205	1669	10917	110	523	3	2000	Asie Sud-est
12	87	293	422	30006	6097	42814	345	1785	259	2007	
23	145	970	343	41211	9909	59852	1149	2087	455	2008	
4	82	884	312	33786	7168	42766	597	1351	607	2009	
7	175	1644	544	46116	9387	59698	775	1868	760	2010	
25	3405	564	1760	50014	3347	7425	3777	...	3100	2000	Asie occidentale
388	9363	5368	3199	122273	25657	24660	11357	2	15197	2007	
531	9301	7141	4011	279995	26594	27498	8422	309	39570	2008	
126	6472	5136	2881	185254	25821	14507	8560	250	32000	2009	
140	7146	5230	3773	261994	21388	17105	8279	169	24407	2010	
0	...	0	...	101	...	2	...	1	0	2000	Océanie
...	...	...	2	12	...	163	0	14	40	2007	
...	...	0	0	70	0	130	...	52	120	2008	
...	...	0	4	70	0	155	0	5	23	2009	
0	...	1	5	238	0	125	0	5	26	2010	

Voir la fin du tableau pour la remarque générale et les notes.

World exports by provenance and destination (Table D)

In million U.S. dollars f.o.b.

Exports to ⟶ / ↓ Exports from	Year	World 1/ Monde 1/	Developed economies 2/ Economies développées 2/: Total	Asia-Pacific Asie-Pacifique: Total	Asia-Pacific Asie-Pacifique: Japan Japon	Europe: Total	Europe: Germany Allemagne	North America Amérique du Nord: Total	North America Amérique du Nord: U.S.A. É.-U.	Commonwealth of Independent States Communauté d'Etats Indépendants: Total	Commonwealth of Independent States Communauté d'Etats Indépendants: Europe
Chemicals (SITC, Rev. 3, 5)											
World 1/	2000	565958	375639	29219	21276	261082	42954	85339	65979	7364	6175
	2007	1446176	935421	58131	40112	691198	123244	186093	148653	37937	32906
	2008	1647892	1041575	68031	46862	768101	137979	205443	164598	46797	40560
	2009	1416270	895996	60110	41681	655439	118558	180447	143563	35196	29459
	2010	1658840	998759	74009	52224	720677	127188	204073	162704	44685	38503
Developed Economies - Asia-Pacific 2/	2000	39061	14664	1393	353	6096	976	7176	6972	23	19
	2007	73256	20221	2305	421	8940	1882	8975	8732	107	102
	2008	77974	21756	2637	565	9534	1953	9584	9315	154	149
	2009	69110	18517	2215	417	7842	1502	8460	8259	114	109
	2010	86979	21370	2502	524	9026	1715	9841	9586	159	151
Japan	2000	35160	12405	386	.	5500	899	6520	6354	22	18
	2007	65191	16460	572	.	7769	1700	8119	7974	103	100
	2008	69137	17455	630	.	8410	1769	8414	8261	148	144
	2009	61416	14830	539	.	6794	1342	7497	7379	110	106
	2010	78419	17469	559	.	8145	1570	8765	8594	153	147
Developed Economies - Europe 2/	2000	317507	260855	11752	8614	212637	36874	36465	33723	4371	4039
	2007	836913	683477	22051	14624	571809	105868	89617	80740	25075	23304
	2008	927546	747735	24427	16312	629848	116824	93460	84677	30273	28182
	2009	808334	656225	25594	17693	539825	99894	90806	82389	23575	21641
	2010	887575	707354	28049	19055	583204	105892	96101	87122	29756	27470
France	2000	40440	32870	1270	908	27982	5990	3618	3362	530	469
	2007	87850	68422	2495	1693	58169	11831	7758	6985	2602	2395
	2008	99984	76738	2974	2112	65035	13925	8729	7781	3406	3167
	2009	86490	65083	2897	1947	54520	11108	7667	6751	2501	2297
	2010	91304	67228	3399	2446	56267	11793	7562	6703	3168	2931
Germany	2000	69666	53574	3003	2398	43607	.	6964	6328	1211	1124
	2007	183977	140207	4520	3260	120992	.	14695	13366	7015	6566
	2008	214293	162544	5129	3695	138517	.	18898	17462	8361	7868
	2009	172088	135754	5056	3735	115023	.	15675	14495	6237	5769
	2010	187400	144104	5597	4143	124276	.	14232	12961	7641	7099
Developed Economies - North America 2/	2000	94865	61283	8502	6582	24815	2845	27966	12116	312	267
	2007	188980	119119	12435	9423	56513	8904	50171	25126	807	732
	2008	216802	131273	14855	10962	61423	10524	54995	27884	1077	993
	2009	187318	115266	12756	9184	57086	10625	45424	20992	795	701
	2010	221888	129968	15938	12064	60942	11032	53087	24580	1208	1123
United States	2000	80057	48161	8179	6371	24133	2719	15849	.	302	260
	2007	154266	88689	12007	9157	51644	8545	25038	.	754	686
	2008	178881	99536	14255	10621	58176	10199	27104	.	1009	937
	2009	159408	90885	12283	8911	54177	10425	24425	.	755	669
	2010	188730	101947	15415	11738	58031	10638	28500	.	1158	1077
South-Eastern Europe	2000	1338	541	2	2	513	46	26	26	204	195
	2007	4916	2280	24	18	2080	295	176	174	508	460
	2008	6308	2898	44	21	2701	326	153	146	645	577
	2009	4288	1752	13	11	1683	286	56	53	571	510
	2010	5731	2540	14	13	2387	469	138	136	809	733
Commonwealth of Independent States	2000	8547	4568	35	33	3214	282	1319	1286	1364	840
	2007	23984	9203	114	77	7736	621	1354	1267	5065	3461
	2008	37374	14350	267	103	10768	1107	3315	3016	6908	4902
	2009	21210	7203	92	52	6091	473	1020	886	4752	2978
	2010	28234	9672	129	66	7807	570	1736	1298	5545	4005
Russian Federation	2000	6181	3740	23	21	2535	218	1183	1165	607	189
	2007	14684	5856	92	63	5175	319	589	568	2433	1259
	2008	22359	8559	143	91	6531	755	1885	1816	3677	2297
	2009	12482	4172	73	47	3589	278	511	483	2490	1288
	2010	16451	6445	84	55	5512	362	850	749	2609	1689

For general note and footnotes see end of table

Exportations mondiales par provenance et destination (Tableau D)

En millions de dollars E.-U. f.o.b.

South-Eastern Europe Europe du Sud-est	Northern Africa Afrique septentrio-nale	Sub-Saharan Africa Afrique du Nord	Latin America and the Caribbean Amérique latine et Caraïbes	Eastern Asia Asie orientale	Southern Asia Asie méridionale	South-eastern Asia Asie du Sud-est	Western Asia Asie occidentale	Oceania Océanie	Others 4/ Autre 4/	← Exportations vers Année	Exportations en provence de ↓
				Produits chimiques (CTCI, Rev. 3, 5)							
2698	4514	7669	38981	68063	8957	27526	16985	324	7238	2000	Monde 1/
12568	12711	22057	86484	178041	33156	64887	50025	737	12152	2007	
16105	15844	27056	110360	192523	46847	75503	58218	1452	15613	2008	
13522	14988	23551	90647	179696	40167	63736	52629	1118	5024	2009	
14536	16693	27248	113555	238627	50602	84125	60807	1291	7913	2010	
2	52	161	1390	16114	491	5662	301	95	107	2000	Economies Développées - Asie-Pacifique 2/
19	114	932	1010	39981	1064	8814	706	183	105	2007	
28	104	815	1176	41654	1477	9692	899	205	13	2008	
31	101	433	1059	38611	1229	7978	825	190	21	2009	
36	73	560	1272	50079	1513	10795	868	226	29	2010	
2	45	105	1298	15458	446	5143	230	6	...	2000	Japon
14	99	186	767	38419	825	7710	602	6	...	2007	
22	92	207	927	40047	971	8496	766	7	...	2008	
16	87	190	791	37025	914	6771	676	6	...	2009	
29	65	249	1038	48084	1155	9441	730	5	...	2010	
2195	3333	3874	9258	8747	2823	4879	10675	146	6351	2000	Economies Développées - Europe 2/
9940	8114	9212	20071	24924	7377	10089	27416	342	10877	2007	
12495	10001	10368	24135	28356	8740	11984	31209	401	11852	2008	
10783	9376	9075	20971	28549	8459	10793	28592	357	1582	2009	
11450	10215	10492	25884	34151	9709	13508	32765	363	1928	2010	
193	1065	1052	1207	1065	286	690	1358	122	2	2000	France
778	2392	2391	2325	2577	772	1803	3435	285	69	2007	
1047	2975	2640	2735	3046	850	2016	4192	324	15	2008	
927	2839	2649	2499	2881	832	1847	4129	293	12	2009	
871	2945	2928	2988	3331	941	2292	4306	301	5	2010	
423	372	616	2378	2718	681	1316	2344	6	4026	2000	Allemagne
1976	1024	1606	4967	7861	1944	2444	5851	9	9073	2007	
2443	1351	1981	6454	8922	2397	2920	6773	12	10138	2008	
2062	1134	1477	5340	8958	2364	2714	5961	11	77	2009	
2113	1328	1894	6547	10814	2770	3257	6813	6	111	2010	
19	215	666	17202	9182	676	3844	1453	13	0	2000	Economies Développées - Amérique du Nord 2/
68	618	1359	33546	21603	1941	6388	3514	19	0	2007	
115	675	1593	41553	22705	5809	8057	3905	41	0	2008	
103	743	1437	33906	20747	4142	6643	3501	36	0	2009	
94	851	1595	42784	27389	4646	8856	4441	56	0	2010	
17	207	648	16767	8305	619	3605	1413	12	...	2000	États-Unis
61	601	1268	32591	19356	1698	5888	3343	17	...	2007	
109	657	1446	40003	20292	5045	7019	3732	34	...	2008	
61	700	1372	33091	19540	3645	5997	3333	31	...	2009	
58	792	1500	41074	25789	4206	7927	4230	50	...	2010	
223	21	21	18	9	19	19	262	0	1	2000	Europe du Sud-est
1143	47	24	111	27	67	11	673	0	25	2007	
1498	85	84	218	38	116	14	677	0	35	2008	
1209	76	39	51	71	76	18	414	0	12	2009	
1385	73	58	62	88	84	50	577	0	6	2010	
65	78	40	548	1031	246	118	488	1	1	2000	Communauté d'Etats Indépendants
344	211	177	2901	3237	1092	305	1431	0	18	2007	
507	259	651	5021	4421	2477	740	2018	1	21	2008	
244	117	365	2101	3004	1888	453	1068	0	14	2009	
255	124	450	2987	4789	2125	855	1392	0	39	2010	
38	48	16	378	889	159	62	243	1	0	2000	Fédération de Russie
149	130	70	1970	2466	642	187	779	0	2	2007	
287	88	279	3051	2988	1644	650	1134	0	1	2008	
152	82	249	1349	1935	1071	286	696	0	1	2009	
132	45	199	1713	2414	1526	531	819	0	18	2010	

Voir la fin du tableau pour la remarque générale et les notes.

World exports by provenance and destination (Table D)

In million U.S. dollars f.o.b.

Exports to → / ↓ Exports from	Year	World 1/ Monde 1/	Developed economies 2/ Economies développées 2/								Commonwealth of Independent States Communauté d'Etats Indépendants	
				Asia-Pacific Asie-Pacifique		Europe		North America Amérique du Nord			
			Total	Total	Japan Japon	Total	Germany Allemagne	Total	U.S.A. É.-U.	Total	Europe
						Chemicals (SITC, Rev. 3, 5) *[cont.]*					
Northern Africa	2000	2350	1095	25	2	1015	49	55	54	3	3
	2007	5436	2467	43	7	2246	69	178	177	6	2
	2008	12174	4694	149	22	4208	165	337	333	16	7
	2009	7562	2647	23	5	2464	112	160	131	10	2
	2010	9926	3792	26	10	3455	159	311	276	24	10
Sub-Saharan Africa	2000	2848	948	141	79	446	64	361	331	38	38
	2007	7090	2553	336	245	1244	194	972	910	19	17
	2008	10097	3089	266	161	1737	191	1087	1040	10	8
	2009	7330	1838	208	115	1008	118	622	610	8	7
	2010	8534	2224	222	117	987	130	1015	996	9	9
South Africa	2000	2055	874	137	79	382	57	355	324	1	0
	2007	4340	1873	335	244	906	155	632	606	6	5
	2008	5724	2182	264	160	1130	172	788	761	3	2
	2009	4100	1411	202	113	698	108	510	499	3	2
	2010	5077	1808	219	115	846	118	743	726	3	3
Latin America and the Caribbean	2000	16493	7456	325	259	2074	315	5056	4937	12	11
	2007	38995	16646	678	541	5728	868	10241	9732	66	60
	2008	47532	20517	821	607	6600	780	13096	12465	76	68
	2009	40871	16834	1081	957	5977	686	9776	9394	52	46
	2010	47471	19070	906	729	7367	742	10796	10356	80	74
Brazil	2000	3565	1471	157	141	649	152	665	641	3	3
	2007	10682	4422	345	300	2375	351	1703	1651	27	27
	2008	12627	5655	359	312	2970	403	2326	2234	32	30
	2009	10486	4173	357	319	2438	374	1378	1318	16	16
	2010	12235	5080	417	358	2849	377	1814	1744	21	21
Eastern Asia	2000	45640	11728	4104	3441	4184	868	3439	3221	444	368
	2007	143597	37259	12728	10067	13778	2621	10752	9966	3527	2909
	2008	170774	48668	16418	12931	17729	3905	14521	13419	4307	3483
	2009	140356	36847	11748	9023	13943	3203	11155	10397	2832	2070
	2010	190692	51071	16890	13333	18989	4198	15192	14164	3972	3073
China	2000	12098	6060	1714	1493	2570	645	1775	1661	131	93
	2007	60341	24891	7242	6100	10351	2131	7298	6759	2226	1765
	2008	79313	33571	9410	7566	13599	3282	10562	9740	2891	2271
	2009	62008	25146	6266	4984	10663	2543	8217	7650	1954	1384
	2010	87519	35343	9397	7605	14940	3352	11006	10218	2698	2094
Southern Asia	2000	5012	1853	170	101	1149	223	534	482	233	152
	2007	20022	7128	460	319	4144	857	2525	2288	844	503
	2008	25101	9365	640	401	5427	1001	3298	2962	1036	621
	2009	26289	8576	553	334	4856	785	3167	2928	864	497
	2010	31844	10674	734	436	5827	965	4112	3875	999	606
South-Eastern Asia	2000	21083	6188	2395	1681	2424	199	1369	1309	43	41
	2007	64835	22157	5776	3969	9952	486	6429	5141	206	201
	2008	66899	20018	6693	4532	8452	445	4873	3726	273	263
	2009	60217	17185	5339	3682	7539	285	4308	2620	155	146
	2010	80765	22669	8027	5687	10166	591	4475	4053	215	197
Western Asia	2000	11197	4458	374	128	2512	213	1571	1522	315	201
	2007	38122	12902	1178	399	7023	579	4701	4397	1706	1155
	2008	49272	17198	806	245	9670	757	6722	5613	2022	1307
	2009	43351	13095	483	208	7120	591	5491	4901	1470	752
	2010	59161	18343	563	190	10515	725	7266	6261	1908	1051
Oceania	2000	18	3	1	0	2	0	0	0	...	...
	2007	32	10	5	0	4	0	1	1	0	0
	2008	39	14	8	1	5	0	1	1	0	0
	2009	34	11	5	0	4	0	1	1	0	0
	2010	41	14	7	0	5	0	1	1	0	...

For general note and footnotes see end of table

Exportations mondiales par provenance et destination (Tableau D)

En millions de dollars E.-U. f.o.b.

South-Eastern Europe Europe du Sud-est	Northern Africa Afrique septentrionale	Sub-Saharan Africa Afrique du Nord	Latin America and the Caribbean Amérique latine et Caraïbes	Eastern Asia Asie orientale	Southern Asia Asie méridionale	South-eastern Asia Asie du Sud-est	Western Asia Asie occidentale	Oceania Océanie	Others 4/ Autre 4/	Année	← Exportations vers Exportations en provence de ↓
			Produits chimiques (CTCI, Rev. 3, 5) *[suite]*								
9	172	44	118	32	545	42	255	...	34	2000	Afrique du Nord
81	442	123	577	61	917	40	632	0	91	2007	
174	691	370	1233	214	2885	263	1412	0	222	2008	
144	642	383	456	324	1433	152	1176	0	195	2009	
111	750	497	879	204	1885	160	1432	0	190	2010	
5	9	1247	105	116	233	72	66	0	6	2000	Afrique subsaharienne
2	22	3126	174	301	440	160	256	3	33	2007	
5	30	4609	233	344	1177	249	316	5	31	2008	
20	26	3822	229	317	635	182	208	10	35	2009	
6	36	3999	293	470	961	257	256	5	18	2010	
5	9	658	101	114	160	70	62	0	1	2000	Afrique du sud
2	16	1317	169	276	286	130	241	1	22	2007	
2	23	1724	210	305	820	172	263	2	20	2008	
2	19	1481	178	282	373	151	170	3	28	2009	
4	30	1783	239	415	354	208	222	3	8	2010	
2	19	147	8159	362	66	163	83	0	24	2000	Amérique latine et Caraïbes
27	80	507	19311	1270	216	301	364	2	204	2007	
23	85	564	23643	1174	573	384	281	0	211	2008	
20	80	459	20426	1615	469	480	242	0	194	2009	
13	90	455	24547	1720	427	473	381	3	212	2010	
1	10	88	1693	156	21	80	40	0	...	2000	Brésil
8	51	407	4956	386	110	105	208	0	...	2007	
10	54	405	5688	351	171	143	119	0	...	2008	
6	45	335	4594	746	246	220	104	0	...	2009	
2	38	309	5570	657	206	186	164	3	...	2010	
42	205	628	1317	23683	1634	5179	759	17	3	2000	Asie orientale
275	1077	2699	6295	64117	9110	14704	4476	55	3	2007	
341	1377	3608	9194	67936	11110	18630	5520	81	2	2008	
231	1195	3027	6475	58715	10506	15951	4494	81	2	2009	
278	1505	3787	9120	77624	15857	21378	6008	88	5	2010	
23	91	219	511	2632	779	1356	290	6	...	2000	Chine
144	580	1481	4303	11015	6282	6964	2426	29	...	2007	
205	759	2188	6426	12917	7899	9278	3135	44	...	2008	
154	699	1988	4527	10186	6913	7846	2539	56	...	2009	
191	841	2557	6309	14455	10910	10730	3429	55	...	2010	
8	65	352	280	647	492	517	560	4	0	2000	Asie méridionale
77	317	1419	1047	2323	2273	2039	2530	11	15	2007	
94	349	2002	1428	2409	2794	2448	3137	15	22	2008	
79	393	2092	1332	4047	3090	2355	3395	16	51	2009	
102	443	2523	1754	4908	3282	3027	4060	17	53	2010	
14	55	275	232	6051	1229	6583	369	43	1	2000	Asie Sud-est
55	205	946	548	15990	4132	18930	1553	105	7	2007	
46	259	1126	1019	15833	4677	21604	1896	138	11	2008	
20	214	1025	2719	15365	4415	17385	1611	115	7	2009	
33	257	1183	2532	22265	6260	23339	1849	152	11	2010	
113	291	206	354	2089	502	445	1712	0	711	2000	Asie occidentale
538	1465	1534	891	4206	4526	3105	6473	1	774	2007	
780	1929	1265	1505	7439	5011	1436	6946	546	3194	2008	
638	2026	1389	923	8330	3826	1345	7101	297	2912	2009	
772	2275	1643	1442	14940	3850	1427	6775	363	5422	2010	
0	0	8	0	0	0	3	...	4	0	2000	Océanie
0	0	2	1	0	0	2	0	16	0	2007	
0	...	1	1	0	0	3	0	19	0	2008	
0	...	4	0	1	0	1	1	16	0	2009	
0	...	5	0	1	2	1	1	17	0	2010	

Voir la fin du tableau pour la remarque générale et les notes.

World exports by provenance and destination (Table D)

In million U.S. dollars f.o.b.

Exports from ↓ / Exports to →	Year	World 1/ Monde 1/	Developed economies 2/ Economies développées 2/ Total	Asia-Pacific Asie-Pacifique Total	Japan Japon	Europe Total	Germany Allemagne	North America Amérique du Nord Total	U.S.A. É.-U.	Commonwealth of Independent States Communauté d'Etats Indépendants Total	Europe
						Machinery and transport equipment (SITC, Rev. 3, 7)					
World 1/	2000	2615774	1795953	137027	102480	982564	187837	676363	554583	19765	15868
	2007	5038120	3019464	218406	145959	1891370	363753	909688	744274	153806	131755
	2008	5407201	3127363	235293	153269	1988504	393005	903566	737789	198618	172324
	2009	4206351	2348064	181562	117514	1472384	305585	694118	571001	96372	76024
	2010	5136997	2747915	228508	147048	1651341	354806	868066	712665	131599	110750
Developed Economies - Asia-Pacific 2/	2000	338298	189906	9501	291	63126	14800	117279	110881	536	422
	2007	466111	213808	15465	204	77872	14940	120471	111474	11383	10995
	2008	500095	211100	16621	188	79525	15646	114954	105806	17773	17253
	2009	349333	135291	12098	136	48724	10247	74469	68107	3238	2943
	2010	471514	170048	15894	217	59112	13145	95042	87425	7623	7150
Japan	2000	329680	185109	7675	.	61931	14533	115503	109214	526	414
	2007	451952	206671	12221	.	76217	14606	118233	109394	11334	10955
	2008	484399	203082	13444	.	77853	15303	111784	102868	17692	17185
	2009	337758	129686	9567	.	47399	10003	72720	66504	3164	2882
	2010	458036	163744	12958	.	57669	12865	93117	85702	7565	7106
Developed Economies - Europe 2/	2000	1015546	832162	24275	16823	693925	126654	113962	104674	11246	9770
	2007	2073002	1569763	39944	22714	1363045	245220	166774	151687	83939	76360
	2008	2219172	1629853	43911	22559	1417318	262387	168624	151679	106933	97773
	2009	1661669	1215032	31962	15882	1060073	208937	122998	110767	56777	49159
	2010	1868584	1331008	38541	19314	1148465	234287	144003	128483	69449	62151
France	2000	132952	103387	1699	1089	86545	19223	15143	14101	962	653
	2007	214875	152030	3840	2192	132579	30873	15611	14447	4330	3694
	2008	227846	155196	5227	1765	134883	34606	15086	13741	6456	5616
	2009	174992	116559	2989	1075	101804	29124	11766	10929	4199	3378
	2010	199558	131919	4132	1539	115433	39671	12354	11472	4181	3746
Germany	2000	272345	223326	8768	6855	175308	.	39250	37072	4105	3664
	2007	629551	467359	14677	9296	385677	.	67005	61416	30072	27313
	2008	677257	487045	15994	9414	403963	.	67088	61746	35889	33203
	2009	501949	356833	13115	7231	297393	.	46324	42001	19743	17654
	2010	584810	396711	15509	8546	322673	.	58529	51928	23995	21368
Developed Economies - North America 2/	2000	523666	335332	36795	28250	99405	18363	199133	101693	1535	1086
	2007	664329	385309	36610	23939	121693	28032	227006	106167	7269	5897
	2008	670612	371896	36734	22670	125968	29719	209195	91697	9335	7357
	2009	450950	236497	21213	12055	67746	16799	147538	64549	4209	2980
	2010	550265	283607	24424	13069	72712	17575	186471	80781	4813	3714
United States	2000	412200	227821	35994	27866	94397	17580	97431	.	1458	1018
	2007	536840	268868	34920	23181	113128	26762	120820	.	6433	5235
	2008	556909	270105	35140	22130	117486	28349	117478	.	8244	6520
	2009	366966	163117	19830	11498	60316	15422	82971	.	3497	2473
	2010	449130	193263	22926	12499	64670	16374	105667	.	3945	2992
South-Eastern Europe	2000	2785	2115	3	0	2009	521	103	93	111	100
	2007	18309	13899	39	26	13553	4521	307	285	1357	1160
	2008	23900	17814	45	26	17404	5812	366	336	1928	1753
	2009	22342	17423	28	15	17057	5767	337	311	1204	1052
	2010	26538	20246	31	17	19801	6422	413	375	1710	1517
Commonwealth of Independent States	2000	10414	3201	38	34	2870	479	293	271	4452	3318
	2007	29165	5111	49	33	4657	774	405	370	19299	13558
	2008	36938	6537	103	84	5994	960	440	383	23565	16717
	2009	22862	4911	132	101	4435	864	345	315	11867	7391
	2010	28039	5430	250	228	4661	997	519	442	15976	12045
Russian Federation	2000	6422	2634	35	34	2410	387	189	179	1573	749
	2007	13254	2572	36	31	2308	435	229	213	7158	3116
	2008	17292	3577	92	83	3208	447	277	238	8338	3723
	2009	11605	2759	103	89	2395	463	261	240	4380	1390
	2010	12407	3065	236	227	2467	562	362	292	4512	2368

For general note and footnotes see end of table

Exportations mondiales par provenance et destination (Tableau D)

En millions de dollars E.-U. f.o.b.

South-Eastern Europe Europe du Sud-est	Northern Africa Afrique septentrionale	Sub-Saharan Africa Afrique du Nord	Latin America and the Caribbean Amérique latine et Caraïbes	Eastern Asia Asie orientale	Southern Asia Asie méridionale	South-eastern Asia Asie du Sud-est	Western Asia Asie occidentale	Oceania Océanie	Others 4/ Autre 4/	Année	← Exportations vers / Exportations en provenance de ↓
											Machines et matériel de transport (CTCI, Rev. 3, 7)
7388	17501	28874	158685	287541	22816	198687	71409	2011	5144	2000	Monde 1/
38688	44146	85108	281867	768939	95256	325336	210603	8124	6785	2007	
47788	57237	103390	333216	804518	109862	353806	249891	12113	9401	2008	
30119	53962	83644	256866	725785	97603	295457	194878	16043	7561	2009	
32491	56316	97264	348659	983615	120178	375574	223476	14481	5430	2010	
76	919	3093	17123	67403	2899	46357	8977	622	389	2000	Economies Développées - Asie-Pacifique 2/
360	2311	7530	28197	119900	6429	49743	24439	1851	161	2007	
544	3355	8324	32640	128767	7957	56318	31115	2120	82	2008	
238	2093	5730	26439	105979	5854	44300	17939	2189	42	2009	
269	2588	7615	34989	150972	8665	62994	21921	3778	51	2010	
74	909	2942	16949	66606	2790	45359	8114	304	0	2000	Japon
350	2287	7091	27871	118475	6149	48422	22311	986	5	2007	
538	3331	7761	32130	127282	7656	54720	28949	1257	...	2008	
229	2060	5361	26133	104880	5631	42759	16565	1290	...	2009	
264	2566	7166	34611	149507	8405	61397	20237	2574	...	2010	
6112	11738	15229	29107	38550	8210	22907	36121	550	3612	2000	Economies Développées - Europe 2/
31121	26063	36720	53645	97636	30750	42980	94252	2119	4015	2007	
37856	33435	40683	63014	110381	35075	47447	106222	3137	5135	2008	
22893	31386	32742	45190	101512	29377	39777	83422	1232	2329	2009	
24505	31837	34103	59114	140366	32135	44958	96794	1763	2552	2010	
536	4200	4160	4149	5250	1384	2817	5172	337	600	2000	France
2391	7602	5640	7354	12626	4906	5914	11140	624	318	2007	
2674	8814	6608	9386	12551	5467	7941	11332	746	674	2008	
1821	8115	5680	5712	9232	3468	7269	11884	588	466	2009	
2141	8564	5485	7480	13680	4041	7781	13296	603	388	2010	
1738	1857	3307	7626	12322	1917	5981	9509	102	555	2000	Allemagne
8554	4862	9554	15902	40203	9582	13505	28200	457	1303	2007	
10854	6311	10054	20110	47750	10946	13969	32596	257	1475	2008	
6368	5926	7441	13949	46408	9981	11387	23676	121	116	2009	
6638	6061	8708	19992	67556	10367	13717	30565	476	26	2010	
266	2440	3056	84864	48817	2259	32401	12523	171	1	2000	Economies Développées - Amérique du Nord 2/
714	3676	8725	108633	70440	11892	37850	29569	251	0	2007	
1079	3906	10612	120974	66129	8907	40170	37324	279	0	2008	
588	3400	7315	95602	48129	6312	25444	23247	205	1	2009	
581	2795	8120	120595	64712	7204	31984	25589	266	1	2010	
244	2348	2934	83422	47397	2166	32085	12159	164	1	2000	Etats-Unis
636	3193	7954	104606	68298	11388	36893	28361	211	...	2007	
961	3566	9887	116675	64018	8320	39075	35808	250	...	2008	
532	2924	6758	92065	46017	5818	24395	21663	180	...	2009	
520	2537	7211	116778	62627	6723	30927	24399	198	...	2010	
193	70	20	25	35	42	17	154	0	2	2000	Europe du Sud-est
980	248	154	389	165	253	83	722	59	2	2007	
1536	382	258	410	224	293	144	828	82	0	2008	
1335	414	159	303	308	175	100	902	19	0	2009	
1202	480	376	273	409	274	95	1465	8	1	2010	
197	155	103	138	842	677	146	496	1	6	2000	Communauté d'Etats Indépendants
419	290	194	345	1351	1307	276	552	3	19	2007	
615	316	989	475	1426	2010	350	650	2	3	2008	
498	395	138	652	1579	2115	239	464	0	3	2009	
550	502	166	684	1925	1627	412	726	1	40	2010	
165	100	84	117	765	568	115	294	1	6	2000	Fédération de Russie
229	195	137	283	1139	1012	212	295	3	18	2007	
265	243	902	380	1193	1722	293	375	2	2	2008	
252	259	64	432	1311	1667	163	315	0	2	2009	
303	366	84	434	1647	1118	299	540	1	39	2010	

Voir la fin du tableau pour la remarque générale et les notes.

World exports by provenance and destination (Table D)

In million U.S. dollars f.o.b.

Exports to → / ↓ Exports from	Year	World 1/ Monde 1/	Developed economies 2/ Economies développées 2/ Total	Asia-Pacific Asie-Pacifique Total	Japan Japon	Europe Total	Germany Allemagne	North America Amérique du Nord Total	U.S.A. É.-U.	Commonwealth of Independent States Communauté d'Etats Indépendants Total	Europe
		Machinery and transport equipment (SITC, Rev. 3, 7) *[cont.]*									
Northern Africa	2000	1754	1566	1	1	1559	277	6	5	1	1
	2007	5448	4841	3	1	4807	492	31	26	4	2
	2008	8347	6356	25	24	6200	769	131	129	17	16
	2009	7288	5295	29	28	5144	733	121	119	13	7
	2010	9237	6901	52	51	6674	953	175	173	10	5
Sub-Saharan Africa	2000	5318	3400	403	155	2351	969	647	613	15	14
	2007	16669	10163	1980	1062	6424	1831	1759	1344	49	26
	2008	21748	12016	1959	896	7008	2270	3048	2882	85	75
	2009	14878	7836	834	405	4675	1505	2326	2161	62	47
	2010	18475	9829	1052	505	5848	2494	2929	2697	71	48
South Africa	2000	4570	3150	390	143	2156	950	604	577	14	14
	2007	13412	8945	1944	1043	5345	1789	1656	1254	45	24
	2008	16229	10636	1928	869	6075	2213	2633	2486	79	72
	2009	10787	6375	789	371	3428	1462	2158	2019	53	38
	2010	13451	8582	1027	487	4934	2459	2621	2406	69	46
Latin America and the Caribbean	2000	122218	108761	764	615	6613	1779	101384	98502	19	18
	2007	195580	149247	1396	736	12379	5390	135472	130482	618	596
	2008	218784	163246	2069	825	15813	6773	145364	140345	756	720
	2009	168039	129519	1375	773	11356	4598	116788	110079	74	56
	2010	221088	167695	1740	1023	13065	5167	152890	144882	327	313
Brazil	2000	15416	8675	358	290	3065	497	5252	5157	3	3
	2007	36286	13886	346	94	5952	2007	7589	6538	317	300
	2008	41823	15257	819	133	6261	2481	8177	7738	468	448
	2009	26322	9524	450	229	4892	1807	4182	3748	38	29
	2010	33109	9903	436	230	5688	1797	3779	3561	76	74
Eastern Asia	2000	347614	188126	37112	32789	64658	14462	86355	82182	1052	698
	2007	1105298	479123	81762	66965	204980	44905	192381	179501	23518	19345
	2008	1230382	517062	88789	72837	227040	49480	201233	186977	30140	25142
	2009	1080409	435966	77390	62097	181468	40411	177108	164963	14876	10327
	2010	1415679	565947	99469	79006	237675	54723	228802	213489	25972	20493
China	2000	82600	46255	10601	9716	16464	3921	19191	18323	325	217
	2007	577819	298318	48586	40004	127639	27654	122093	115227	13615	10710
	2008	674065	333933	55029	45253	149129	32539	129774	121382	18119	14715
	2009	591128	285849	48130	38596	121034	26248	116685	109669	9675	6532
	2010	781074	376271	63827	50927	161483	37055	150961	142241	16412	12828
Southern Asia	2000	3625	1641	151	104	958	204	532	511	71	33
	2007	19162	7889	473	241	4661	1047	2755	2629	408	291
	2008	27297	11407	644	258	7517	1628	3246	3112	512	351
	2009	29480	10941	675	304	7190	1529	3075	2958	325	219
	2010	34595	12614	735	250	7962	1530	3918	3782	594	507
South-Eastern Asia	2000	225602	118448	27613	23210	38204	7472	52631	51247	145	131
	2007	375375	147165	39940	29733	50219	11244	57006	55173	1105	1036
	2008	369909	141683	42014	31016	48815	11626	50853	48934	1553	1445
	2009	325338	116692	35009	25354	40553	10184	41130	39314	799	705
	2010	414753	141927	45555	33029	49741	12729	46631	44493	1123	1008
Western Asia	2000	18775	11183	341	203	6822	1826	4021	3894	570	265
	2007	69476	33014	642	305	27057	5357	5316	5131	4858	2489
	2008	79823	38245	2292	1884	29852	5935	6101	5499	6022	3721
	2009	72706	31884	618	283	23454	3948	7813	7292	2926	1137
	2010	78041	32519	698	340	25552	4783	6269	5638	3930	1799
Oceania	2000	160	110	30	4	63	31	18	17	11	11
	2007	197	132	103	1	24	0	5	4	0	0
	2008	194	146	85	2	50	1	11	9	0	0
	2009	1058	778	199	80	509	62	69	64	0	0
	2010	187	144	66	1	73	1	5	5	0	0

For general note and footnotes see end of table

Exportations mondiales par provenance et destination (Tableau D)

En millions de dollars E.-U. f.o.b.

South-Eastern Europe Europe du Sud-est	Northern Africa Afrique septentrio-nale	Sub-Saharan Africa Afrique du Nord	Latin America and the Caribbean Amérique latine et Caraïbes	Eastern Asia Asie orientale	Southern Asia Asie méridionale	South-eastern Asia Asie du Sud-est	Western Asia Asie occidentale	Oceania Océanie	Others 4/ Autre 4/	Année	← Exportations vers / Exportations en provenance de ↓
											Machines et matériel de transport (CTCI, Rev. 3, 7) *[suite]*
0	62	28	0	1	3	1	66	0	26	2000	Afrique du Nord
5	234	153	5	26	17	3	59	0	100	2007	
28	516	314	11	13	11	262	661	0	158	2008	
56	661	293	9	22	11	215	561	2	149	2009	
86	706	351	12	38	14	347	623	9	142	2010	
4	25	1373	92	140	40	118	98	3	9	2000	Afrique subsaharienne
8	181	4506	252	252	247	150	796	5	59	2007	
96	373	7016	412	277	149	306	936	7	76	2008	
76	350	4812	310	286	249	178	580	112	28	2009	
16	321	6321	516	406	261	172	498	16	47	2010	
4	21	967	88	136	25	96	65	2	2	2000	Afrique du sud
3	156	2864	223	209	233	138	549	3	44	2007	
61	320	3643	249	232	110	225	651	2	20	2008	
8	285	2939	181	167	208	138	413	7	12	2009	
16	221	3407	264	329	169	125	242	13	15	2010	
3	47	290	11636	632	99	526	174	1	30	2000	Amérique latine et Caraïbes
44	477	1823	37544	2945	501	1334	943	20	83	2007	
105	383	2410	45085	3150	578	1710	1268	12	82	2008	
132	439	1613	31057	2540	526	972	1008	31	125	2009	
106	390	1422	44964	3182	521	1241	1183	20	37	2010	
1	41	254	6013	131	70	97	130	1	...	2000	Brésil
28	391	1610	17695	560	357	674	765	4	...	2007	
65	345	2097	20345	914	349	1047	931	7	...	2008	
78	360	1440	12887	740	277	348	615	16	...	2009	
62	313	1166	19351	829	232	360	803	16	...	2010	
234	1157	3450	11493	92416	4160	37353	7457	528	189	2000	Asie orientale
2669	6532	17728	43760	376087	26046	93517	32808	3126	382	2007	
3479	9422	24654	58733	396454	35502	106660	42467	5566	243	2008	
2571	9529	22372	48448	367126	34343	95520	38192	11437	27	2009	
3235	10920	28470	73740	490618	44738	118922	45384	7707	27	2010	
39	283	1034	2120	21483	1303	7934	1814	10	...	2000	Chine
1411	4033	10203	22357	147299	18193	45117	16623	651	...	2007	
2246	6195	15449	30983	163421	24439	55681	22970	629	...	2008	
1878	5830	13781	26763	146984	24609	52527	21595	1637	...	2009	
2372	6061	19157	42795	196975	30524	62648	25503	2355	...	2010	
3	69	318	125	154	337	457	448	1	1	2000	Asie méridionale
44	529	1871	868	788	1354	1669	3709	12	22	2007	
77	846	2384	1239	957	1785	3429	4501	31	129	2008	
377	985	2651	1014	1408	1568	5373	4668	17	151	2009	
196	1122	4018	1522	1299	2518	5449	5129	17	118	2010	
31	254	1347	3706	37740	3156	57970	2659	114	32	2000	Asie Sud-est
120	1271	2780	7069	98245	10774	96918	9400	440	87	2007	
175	1860	2796	8644	93969	11679	95746	10978	574	253	2008	
154	1464	2346	6362	94297	10611	81826	10040	685	61	2009	
264	1925	3113	9503	124525	13528	106760	11261	751	72	2010	
268	564	568	375	809	935	420	2236	7	839	2000	Asie occidentale
2204	2334	2923	1157	1079	5684	793	13352	223	1856	2007	
2199	2442	2943	1578	2767	5912	1254	12940	284	3238	2008	
1194	2845	3471	1470	2433	6458	1436	13851	98	4641	2009	
1481	2732	3187	2746	5154	8692	2226	12903	128	2342	2010	
0	...	1	1	2	0	13	0	13	10	2000	Océanie
0	0	1	1	26	2	19	1	15	0	2007	
0	0	6	1	4	4	9	2	20	2	2008	
6	0	1	7	165	2	77	4	15	2	2009	
0	0	1	2	8	0	14	1	17	0	2010	

Voir la fin du tableau pour la remarque générale et les notes.

World exports by provenance and destination (Table D)

In million U.S. dollars f.o.b.

Exports to → / ↓ Exports from	Year	World 1/ Monde 1/	Developed economies 2/ Economies développées 2/							Commonwealth of Independent States Communauté d'Etats Indépendants	
				Asia-Pacific Asie-Pacifique		Europe		North America Amérique du Nord			
			Total	Total	Japan Japon	Total	Germany Allemagne	Total	U.S.A. É.-U.	Total	Europe
Passenger road vehicles and their parts (SITC, Rev. 3, 781.2, 784.1, 785.1, 785.2 and 785.31)											
World 1/	2000	318748	280299	12905	6829	143720	24145	123673	108428	1654	1446
	2007	650305	506282	23802	8785	314307	51606	168173	142216	31479	28771
	2008	668055	489878	24131	8064	307879	53996	157869	131822	42966	40450
	2009	459497	354903	17831	6034	234094	46618	102978	85753	9570	8436
	2010	582934	413428	25530	7955	244852	41092	143045	121384	19291	17570
Developed Economies - Asia-Pacific 2/	2000	63560	52590	3693	30	12486	2479	36412	33920	154	148
	2007	117302	80213	6863	8	21512	2895	51838	47258	8733	8545
	2008	124814	76649	7544	7	20477	2490	48628	43891	13605	13322
	2009	67204	45858	5582	5	11774	1789	28503	25361	1565	1449
	2010	95933	58677	7739	5	13965	2017	36972	33189	5401	5095
Japan	2000	62192	52147	3482	.	12472	2478	36193	33701	154	148
	2007	114842	79658	6459	.	21477	2893	51722	47143	8733	8545
	2008	121632	75346	7231	.	20441	2488	47674	43006	13604	13322
	2009	65877	45610	5380	.	11751	1786	28480	25338	1565	1449
	2010	94231	58370	7474	.	13936	2015	36961	33178	5401	5094
Developed Economies - Europe 2/	2000	162277	148795	6302	5066	122246	18640	20248	19425	1177	1102
	2007	349108	303588	9381	5826	256725	34901	37482	34575	12368	11443
	2008	348021	293179	8848	4936	250409	35742	33923	30810	16441	15776
	2009	259230	224612	6615	3850	196938	34198	21059	18419	5424	4951
	2010	298161	242641	9477	5219	203925	28878	29240	25901	8224	7690
France	2000	19406	17382	163	131	17193	2757	26	15	28	28
	2007	31760	28131	435	157	27521	4446	176	100	553	541
	2008	28500	24686	381	168	24213	4425	92	45	660	648
	2009	20496	18225	150	82	18024	4170	51	15	213	211
	2010	21614	19076	378	222	18655	3273	44	19	220	219
Germany	2000	61492	55191	4192	3688	37221	.	13778	13357	786	726
	2007	140585	119290	5223	3572	88681	.	25386	23371	4754	4277
	2008	142424	117319	5410	3380	87999	.	23911	21689	5535	5213
	2009	104284	86038	4474	2820	66846	.	14719	12778	2046	1823
	2010	130646	99157	6311	3709	72233	.	20613	18066	3400	3116
Developed Economies - North America 2/	2000	53034	48252	1254	948	2618	1281	44380	34581	21	17
	2007	83595	67943	1556	687	13573	7295	52815	36856	1195	929
	2008	84644	63841	1671	739	14942	8632	47228	31770	1674	1262
	2009	52746	39814	980	466	7272	4774	31562	22663	245	80
	2010	77290	56878	1340	523	7454	4119	48084	36168	461	237
United States	2000	18078	13450	1150	845	2503	1265	9798	.	18	15
	2007	45960	30874	1541	681	13375	7258	15958	.	1154	893
	2008	52095	31867	1654	733	14757	8592	15456	.	1657	1249
	2009	29382	17021	959	453	7166	4748	8896	.	241	78
	2010	40379	20577	1318	510	7346	4099	11913	.	456	233
South-Eastern Europe	2000	62	19	NULL	.	19	0	0	0	1	1
	2007	1191	844	0	0	843	209	1	1	95	94
	2008	1593	1035	0	0	1035	245	0	0	160	160
	2009	2516	2146	0	.	2145	848	1	1	30	29
	2010	2985	2439	0	0	2438	490	1	1	68	66
Commonwealth of Independent States	2000	482	135	0	0	134	7	1	1	251	140
	2007	2352	61	0	0	57	1	4	3	2239	1812
	2008	2749	123	2	1	116	2	5	4	2572	2168
	2009	847	66	1	1	63	4	2	2	739	551
	2010	1549	76	1	0	71	3	4	4	1431	1123
Russian Federation	2000	360	132	0	0	131	6	1	1	142	34
	2007	821	56	0	0	52	1	4	3	726	412
	2008	922	71	2	1	64	1	5	4	811	538
	2009	240	50	1	1	47	2	2	2	163	65
	2010	279	53	1	0	49	2	3	3	208	113

For general note and footnotes see end of table

Exportations mondiales par provenance et destination (Tableau D)

En millions de dollars E.-U. f.o.b.

← Exportations vers

South-Eastern Europe Europe du Sud-est	Northern Africa Afrique septentrionale	Sub-Saharan Africa Afrique du Nord	Latin America and the Caribbean Amérique latine et Caraïbes	Eastern Asia Asie orientale	Southern Asia Asie méridionale	South-eastern Asia Asie du Sud-est	Western Asia Asie occidentale	Oceania Océanie	Others 4/ Autre 4/	Année	Exportations en provence de ↓
Véhicules routiers et pièces détachées pour transports passagères (CTCI, Rev. 3, 781.2, 784.1, 785.1, 785.2 et 785.31)											
650	1378	2307	11641	3870	859	4287	11464	194	145	2000	Monde 1/
6239	5917	10329	29149	15902	3766	7328	33322	426	165	2007	
6896	7281	10372	32022	20111	4269	9425	43392	443	1000	2008	
2538	5961	7862	20290	19646	2895	7831	26759	313	929	2009	
2763	6557	10507	34630	37802	4051	11917	40976	382	631	2010	
21	95	453	2729	1350	381	1826	3888	73	...	2000	Economies Développées - Asie-Pacifique 2/
91	807	2055	5562	4353	828	2343	12145	172	0	2007	
241	1218	1974	5592	5709	998	2906	15726	195	...	2008	
17	398	1279	2616	4884	695	2014	7745	133	...	2009	
46	459	1786	4868	8322	1189	2871	12148	167	...	2010	
21	94	451	2696	1346	380	1712	3123	67	...	2000	Japon
91	807	2026	5547	4345	793	2330	10353	161	...	2007	
241	1218	1970	5572	5652	967	2882	14002	178	...	2008	
17	398	1271	2615	4864	690	1973	6761	113	...	2009	
46	459	1780	4859	8315	1188	2840	10834	139	...	2010	
495	953	1337	1610	1198	180	793	5576	101	61	2000	Economies Développées - Europe 2/
5073	2320	3743	3185	7479	768	1112	9334	132	6	2007	
5670	2823	3120	3677	9488	1106	1438	10939	136	4	2008	
2211	2525	2602	2361	10226	788	1293	7101	85	1	2009	
2395	2625	3200	4123	20906	644	2037	11260	102	3	2010	
52	490	275	347	30	101	44	591	67	0	2000	France
388	701	387	263	137	412	30	685	68	5	2007	
348	784	237	231	74	661	22	728	66	3	2008	
109	682	119	111	91	466	14	430	36	1	2009	
134	660	189	255	148	159	46	682	43	1	2010	
224	175	520	601	871	53	425	2578	17	51	2000	Allemagne
1528	818	1557	1676	5428	236	658	4609	30	0	2007	
1847	958	1237	1934	6942	353	873	5396	30	0	2008	
732	907	1114	1350	7604	194	632	3637	29	0	2009	
829	1009	1494	2361	15591	213	867	5686	39	0	2010	
13	22	76	3539	299	2	86	721	4	0	2000	Economies Développées - Amérique du Nord 2/
60	103	1266	5725	1460	125	401	5301	17	...	2007	
138	157	1772	6124	1852	97	492	8480	18	0	2008	
39	252	1270	3543	1635	211	507	5218	11	...	2009	
24	245	1664	5297	4602	138	496	7476	8	...	2010	
12	22	73	3448	278	2	85	685	4	...	2000	États-Unis
52	93	1200	5363	1446	123	399	5239	17	...	2007	
130	140	1692	5790	1840	91	488	8381	18	...	2008	
34	211	1201	3273	1617	195	505	5072	11	...	2009	
21	212	1586	4974	4582	120	492	7351	8	...	2010	
9	4	0	3	17	0	0	8	...	0	2000	Europe du Sud-est
81	65	11	0	0	0	0	91	3	0	2007	
155	121	13	0	0	3	0	100	4	...	2008	
98	126	8	0	0	0	0	104	4	...	2009	
100	140	16	0	0	0	0	215	7	0	2010	
9	3	1	15	14	1	9	45	...	0	2000	Communauté d'Etats Indépendants
9	15	1	1	3	0	0	22	...	0	2007	
6	13	1	1	10	0	3	19	...	...	2008	
1	12	4	2	13	0	0	11	...	...	2009	
1	5	0	2	9	0	1	23	...	2	2010	
8	2	1	15	14	1	1	44	...	...	2000	Fédération de Russie
9	15	0	1	3	0	0	10	...	0	2007	
6	12	0	1	10	...	3	8	...	...	2008	
0	12	0	1	10	...	0	3	...	...	2009	
0	5	0	0	8	0	1	2	...	2	2010	

Voir la fin du tableau pour la remarque générale et les notes.

World exports by provenance and destination (Table D)

In million U.S. dollars f.o.b.

Exports to → / ↓ Exports from	Year	World 1/ Monde 1/	Developed economies 2/ Economies développées 2/ Total	Asia-Pacific Asie-Pacifique Total	Asia-Pacific Japan Japon	Europe Total	Europe Germany Allemagne	North America Amérique du Nord Total	North America U.S.A. É.-U.	Commonwealth of Independent States Communauté d'Etats Indépendants Total	CIS Europe
Passenger road vehicles and their parts (SITC, Rev. 3, 781.2, 784.1, 785.1, 785.2 and 785.31) *[cont.]*											
Northern Africa	2000	6	4	0	0	4	0	0	0	...	...
	2007	118	114	1	1	112	2	0	0	0	0
	2008	152	133	2	2	132	7	0	0	0	0
	2009	130	59	0	0	59	22	0	0	...	...
	2010	148	73	0	0	73	40	1	0	0	0
Sub-Saharan Africa	2000	1113	895	269	136	533	395	93	93	0	0
	2007	2981	2397	1649	960	185	8	563	544	0	0
	2008	4796	3817	1597	803	447	104	1773	1772	9	9
	2009	3346	2754	576	308	591	435	1586	1586	0	0
	2010	4620	3824	776	425	1201	1039	1847	1816	0	0
South Africa	2000	1048	874	262	130	520	394	92	92	0	0
	2007	2645	2351	1643	955	147	5	561	542	...	...
	2008	4549	3776	1593	799	412	102	1772	1771	9	9
	2009	3076	2710	573	304	553	433	1584	1584	0	0
	2010	4139	3806	773	422	1188	1038	1845	1814	0	...
Latin America and the Caribbean	2000	19792	16933	185	165	947	715	15801	14262	0	0
	2007	27619	18267	338	218	3666	3357	14263	13282	131	131
	2008	31524	20673	260	193	4992	4414	15421	14298	62	62
	2009	22147	14252	223	144	2836	2730	11194	10358	2	2
	2010	32955	19706	317	143	2858	2750	16531	15606	196	196
Brazil	2000	2025	526	1	0	224	7	302	301	...	...
	2007	5555	1016	28	2	773	728	215	96	3	3
	2008	5930	1280	31	5	1103	1086	147	34	4	4
	2009	3838	847	51	2	698	693	98	3	1	1
	2010	5197	615	68	1	538	526	9	7	0	0
Eastern Asia	2000	16141	11584	1081	456	3790	407	6713	6129	25	23
	2007	46280	24618	2492	984	11068	2220	11057	9590	5330	5019
	2008	45690	21184	2429	1149	8073	1412	10682	9116	6506	6052
	2009	32910	16012	2729	1089	4855	1028	8428	6795	1285	1117
	2010	45289	19238	3548	1028	5786	958	9904	8330	2867	2549
China	2000	1855	772	232	197	62	6	478	467	3	3
	2007	8513	3203	758	641	1292	259	1152	1092	1191	1132
	2008	10391	3956	921	800	1590	358	1444	1356	1334	1283
	2009	6776	3021	869	757	1109	324	1042	955	205	191
	2010	9390	3422	929	758	1201	259	1292	1214	435	417
Southern Asia	2000	265	104	3	1	99	5	2	2	3	0
	2007	2002	621	5	2	613	50	3	2	97	87
	2008	3342	1200	7	5	1185	204	8	4	138	124
	2009	4086	2123	20	4	2097	350	6	4	32	28
	2010	5976	2013	168	3	1836	139	9	7	89	85
South-Eastern Asia	2000	849	375	118	25	237	40	20	11	0	0
	2007	6285	2160	1478	82	544	80	138	100	77	77
	2008	8474	2552	1702	167	659	83	191	149	139	138
	2009	6279	1766	1051	117	524	96	192	149	18	18
	2010	9967	2926	2120	573	673	82	132	89	121	119
Western Asia	2000	1166	612	1	1	609	176	3	3	21	15
	2007	11467	5451	39	16	5404	587	8	4	1212	633
	2008	12254	5490	69	63	5411	660	10	8	1658	1376
	2009	7871	5331	28	26	4866	325	436	406	228	210
	2010	8059	4933	42	36	4571	576	320	273	432	410
Oceania	2000	1	1	0	0	0	.	0	0	...	...
	2007	6	5	0	0	5	.	0	0	0	...
	2008	2	2	1	0	1	0	0	0	0	0
	2009	185	110	26	24	75	19	10	10	0	...
	2010	3	2	1	0	1	0	0	.	...	...

For general note and footnotes see end of table

Exportations mondiales par provenance et destination (Tableau D)

En millions de dollars E.-U. f.o.b.

South-Eastern Europe Europe du Sud-est	Northern Africa Afrique septentrionale	Sub-Saharan Africa Afrique du Nord	Latin America and the Caribbean Amérique latine et Caraïbes	Eastern Asia Asie orientale	Southern Asia Asie méridionale	South-eastern Asia Asie du Sud-est	Western Asia Asie occidentale	Oceania Océanie	Others 4/ Autre 4/	← Exportations vers Année	Exportations en provence de ↓
Véhicules routiers et pièces détachées pour transports passagères (CTCI, Rev. 3, 781.2, 784.1, 785.1, 785.2 et 785.31) [suite]											
...	1	0	...	...	...	0	0	...	0	2000	Afrique du Nord
0	2	0	0	0	...	0	1	...	...	2007	
0	3	6	0	0	0	0	9	...	1	2008	
0	54	5	0	2	...	0	10	0	0	2009	
0	61	5	0	2	0	0	7	...	0	2010	
0	1	126	0	57	0	31	3	0	0	2000	Afrique subsaharienne
0	19	342	3	64	1	53	92	0	10	2007	
41	79	431	3	65	1	70	279	0	1	2008	
3	62	376	1	69	1	30	51	0	0	2009	
6	29	584	1	131	2	39	5	0	0	2010	
0	0	86	0	56	0	30	0	0	0	2000	Afrique du sud
0	18	60	1	63	1	52	88	0	10	2007	
28	78	248	0	64	0	69	276	0	1	2008	
3	58	159	0	68	0	30	48	0	0	2009	
6	28	128	0	131	2	37	1	0	0	2010	
0	10	52	2758	10	19	5	5	0	0	2000	Amérique latine et Caraïbes
0	115	122	8718	130	55	41	36	0	1	2007	
0	79	148	10283	102	56	46	73	1	1	2008	
0	64	132	7419	135	34	62	43	2	2	2009	
0	76	66	11977	595	16	139	182	0	1	2010	
...	10	51	1409	2	19	3	4	0	...	2000	Brésil
0	71	118	4237	1	55	31	22	0	...	2007	
0	74	135	4321	6	56	37	15	1	...	2008	
...	50	128	2712	0	32	56	11	2	...	2009	
0	63	60	4343	0	9	102	4	0	...	2010	
61	211	220	913	884	182	1183	811	14	54	2000	Asie orientale
364	1398	1671	5176	2152	541	1395	3442	68	124	2007	
224	1719	1856	5146	2658	692	1500	4104	62	40	2008	
40	1703	1504	3668	2509	615	1622	3887	46	18	2009	
46	1687	2081	6824	2856	1141	2275	6198	57	19	2010	
4	12	62	80	180	31	651	60	1	...	2000	Chine
35	305	916	1451	275	193	619	318	8	...	2007	
54	448	1211	1778	266	268	675	394	6	...	2008	
20	290	843	894	289	282	525	403	5	...	2009	
13	358	1151	1817	324	587	746	529	8	...	2010	
0	8	22	21	0	80	11	15	0	0	2000	Asie méridionale
1	255	252	243	5	279	51	197	1	0	2007	
31	388	384	348	26	360	95	368	3	1	2008	
27	229	449	216	14	331	89	529	1	45	2009	
9	556	799	592	26	664	524	682	2	19	2010	
0	6	7	52	26	7	337	37	2	1	2000	Asie Sud-est
1	145	231	471	56	149	1881	1078	31	5	2007	
1	130	188	784	95	177	2801	1571	24	12	2008	
1	95	167	448	86	149	2173	1337	31	8	2009	
1	118	234	904	143	166	3528	1778	37	11	2010	
41	66	12	1	13	7	7	356	0	29	2000	Asie occidentale
559	673	634	67	199	1020	51	1582	0	19	2007	
387	552	478	63	107	778	74	1724	1	942	2008	
95	442	67	14	37	71	9	723	0	854	2009	
137	556	73	42	209	91	8	1003	0	575	2010	
...	...	0	...	...	...	...	...	0	0	2000	Océanie
0	...	0	0	0	0	0	...	0	...	2007	
...	...	0	0	0	0	...	0	0	0	2008	
5	...	0	1	37	1	32	0	0	0	2009	
...	0	0	0	0	...	0	...	0	...	2010	

Voir la fin du tableau pour la remarque générale et les notes.

World exports by provenance and destination (Table D)

In million U.S. dollars f.o.b.

Exports from ↓ / Exports to →	Year	World 1/ Monde 1/	Developed economies 2/ Economies développées 2/ Total	Asia-Pacific Asie-Pacifique Total	Japan Japon	Europe Total	Germany Allemagne	North America Amérique du Nord Total	U.S.A. É.-U.	Commonwealth of Independent States Communauté d'Etats Indépendants Total	Europe
Other manufactured goods (SITC, Rev. 3, 6 and 8)											
World 1/	2000	1640866	1158864	104845	84886	681143	138054	372876	314397	20369	16901
	2007	3475800	2258521	170294	129411	1510714	272195	577513	486540	111437	86299
	2008	3801600	2393549	187603	140121	1620707	296690	585239	488297	138911	101559
	2009	2979455	1834924	153718	112128	1227740	227974	453466	375814	87097	58885
	2010	3573917	2138449	184212	135264	1401232	267104	553005	459630	104744	77909
Developed Economies - Asia-Pacific 2/	2000	102599	42203	5327	1932	13659	3644	23218	22050	218	166
	2007	160127	51828	8795	2958	19869	5168	23165	21732	845	692
	2008	176879	53701	9324	3063	21023	5658	23354	21777	1211	1066
	2009	137454	39634	6567	1483	15605	4361	17462	16171	687	583
	2010	180417	48864	8658	2578	18325	4602	21880	20362	1193	1073
Japan	2000	89968	35395	1375	.	12381	3478	21639	20559	215	164
	2007	136120	39671	2032	.	17038	4924	20601	19337	825	677
	2008	152817	41498	2420	.	18378	5380	20700	19296	1178	1039
	2009	119370	31252	1851	.	13715	4098	15687	14550	668	567
	2010	158209	37908	2275	.	16136	4341	19497	18145	1170	1053
Developed Economies - Europe 2/	2000	676465	569906	17806	13219	485853	100678	66247	61012	9400	8645
	2007	1450871	1175839	28238	19337	1049288	196891	98313	89966	46024	42210
	2008	1566724	1248927	29685	19850	1123654	213419	95588	86669	54878	50734
	2009	1185069	939736	22714	14887	846922	159257	70100	63465	34756	30887
	2010	1333651	1051410	26049	17080	941130	184389	84231	75986	39930	35797
France	2000	69667	58683	2212	1860	50245	11675	6226	5461	431	384
	2007	133185	108327	3191	2398	96545	21506	8591	7554	2166	1966
	2008	141421	112786	3326	2576	100973	22548	8487	7371	2416	2198
	2009	108572	85187	2723	2127	76010	16517	6454	5539	1588	1385
	2010	115937	89980	2840	2158	79945	18313	7194	6270	1865	1616
Germany	2000	127887	107652	3018	2157	93679	.	10955	10095	2264	2096
	2007	314084	254093	5649	3806	227889	.	20555	18897	11620	10778
	2008	341374	272488	5945	3830	245625	.	20919	19150	14035	13107
	2009	263504	211770	4677	2957	191759	.	15334	13997	8910	8093
	2010	294261	233565	5534	3540	209229	.	18802	17236	10230	9440
Developed Economies - North America 2/	2000	222921	151023	16851	14088	39474	6253	94699	51858	395	318
	2007	324976	214621	19971	15090	65838	9897	128812	68682	1474	1185
	2008	342258	221351	19954	14616	70707	10512	130689	66095	1828	1498
	2009	271998	171193	16046	11066	56685	8362	98462	46145	1009	812
	2010	322714	197829	18905	13682	62760	10025	116164	54492	1205	1020
United States	2000	165174	95373	15874	13228	36670	5947	42829	.	349	279
	2007	239245	136233	18277	13731	57872	9371	60084	.	1243	994
	2008	258913	145752	18334	13357	62873	9964	64546	.	1580	1289
	2009	214377	119200	15202	10494	51727	7983	52270	.	897	724
	2010	253278	135531	17789	12912	56103	9621	61640	.	1050	896
South-Eastern Europe	2000	10591	8970	17	13	8304	1808	648	582	193	166
	2007	36116	28345	24	12	27607	4939	714	653	911	804
	2008	39374	30575	36	14	29857	5418	682	615	1116	990
	2009	27241	21291	38	12	20959	4382	294	258	754	676
	2010	32378	24757	29	15	24194	5312	534	423	997	940
Commonwealth of Independent States	2000	31254	16356	1250	1246	12213	2078	2892	2794	5115	3966
	2007	100221	49153	2490	2457	41654	4947	5008	4873	22414	14540
	2008	113385	49360	3642	3545	39647	5164	6071	5910	26555	17378
	2009	69177	27675	1656	1628	22697	3165	3322	3258	15955	9039
	2010	88025	38119	1806	1774	31897	4769	4416	4319	18235	13072
Russian Federation	2000	20412	12932	1181	1179	9588	1460	2163	2115	1350	486
	2007	56786	35123	2030	2014	29152	3230	3941	3872	8708	3422
	2008	59199	32484	2667	2643	25581	3392	4237	4192	9654	4158
	2009	39419	20245	1363	1350	15967	1878	2915	2871	6346	1636
	2010	48382	27115	1147	1133	22583	2858	3385	3328	5816	2607

For general note and footnotes see end of table

Exportations mondiales par provenance et destination (Tableau D)

En millions de dollars E.-U. f.o.b.

South-Eastern Europe Europe du Sud-est	Northern Africa Afrique septentrio-nale	Sub-Saharan Africa Afrique du Nord	Latin America and the Caribbean Amérique latine et Caraïbes	Eastern Asia Asie orientale	Southern Asia Asie méridionale	South-eastern Asia Asie du Sud-est	Western Asia Asie occidentale	Oceania Océanie	Others 4/ Autre 4/	← Exportations vers Année	Exportations en provence de ↓
			Articles manufacturés divers (CTCI, Rev. 3, 6 et 8)								
9854	13599	17985	87019	180685	22577	66688	56731	1638	4856	2000	Monde 1/
37995	35975	54234	155679	401537	81672	154067	170953	2445	11284	2007	
45602	45914	62991	184708	430228	96745	181139	208047	2680	11086	2008	
30675	43801	57081	143671	368307	84447	148070	172271	2441	6670	2009	
33726	44955	66329	188397	481344	118044	193803	193464	2821	7842	2010	
20	205	720	2343	37318	1498	15120	2101	435	418	2000	Economies Développées - Asie-Pacifique 2/
77	486	1369	3678	67340	3047	25226	5420	742	69	2007	
74	453	1460	4549	74129	3404	31092	5973	765	68	2008	
53	520	1160	3727	60937	3459	22143	4414	669	51	2009	
60	537	1409	5395	80658	4370	32242	4812	789	86	2010	
18	201	563	2211	34439	1304	13567	1972	83	...	2000	Japon
52	411	1088	3462	61908	2550	21330	4760	64	...	2007	
63	378	1126	4332	69303	2948	26691	5230	70	...	2008	
48	461	890	3584	56238	2984	19173	3988	83	...	2009	
56	447	1070	5100	75492	3867	28614	4402	84	...	2010	
7705	8474	6121	12103	19815	7927	7761	23558	367	3329	2000	Economies Développées - Europe 2/
25843	18017	15180	23116	48550	21465	15699	53355	659	7123	2007	
30389	23220	17513	26889	54096	24406	17525	61730	743	6408	2008	
21920	21096	14710	19753	47835	19114	14642	48097	616	2794	2009	
23653	21382	16395	25351	58238	23509	17089	52814	604	3277	2010	
431	2476	1193	1051	1971	424	652	2111	235	8	2000	France
1291	4316	2639	1938	4291	1430	1433	4814	446	94	2007	
1554	4796	3164	2185	4868	1485	1722	5817	526	102	2008	
1092	4413	2404	1591	4286	1398	1436	4694	429	54	2009	
1256	4412	2727	2157	5337	1410	1585	4723	427	59	2010	
1524	1044	1070	2787	3817	904	1667	3434	15	1709	2000	Allemagne
4569	2089	2762	5820	12448	4028	3702	9472	36	3445	2007	
5345	2502	3098	6893	13833	4823	4305	11476	31	2544	2008	
4147	2269	2570	5126	12347	3928	3582	8803	44	8	2009	
4677	2296	2844	6843	15304	4146	4275	10048	26	7	2010	
60	697	1043	43277	13811	979	6732	4841	63	0	2000	Economies Développées - Amérique du Nord 2/
204	1229	2105	53309	27186	4254	8070	12445	77	1	2007	
272	1274	2341	58527	28164	5208	8493	14706	93	1	2008	
199	1267	2202	48645	24287	4503	7285	11334	74	0	2009	
193	1332	2435	57903	32258	6825	9143	13477	113	0	2010	
53	641	1002	42513	13143	880	6514	4643	61	...	2000	Etats-Unis
179	1079	1851	51119	24348	3788	7567	11767	69	...	2007	
236	1037	2097	55914	25821	4675	7985	13731	84	...	2008	
176	1111	2017	47014	22212	4135	6875	10676	64	...	2009	
155	1162	2248	55711	29736	6200	8681	12699	104	...	2010	
587	85	31	84	67	31	17	523	0	3	2000	Europe du Sud-est
3259	200	49	90	147	407	63	2641	1	3	2007	
4271	191	106	85	283	294	77	2371	0	6	2008	
2701	290	80	60	180	228	53	1598	1	6	2009	
3185	386	70	116	302	153	50	2355	1	5	2010	
568	688	262	560	3652	1051	876	2125	1	1	2000	Communauté d'Etats Indépendants
2061	1806	892	1403	4904	5136	1608	10824	0	20	2007	
2908	2648	951	2000	6404	5616	3219	13711	0	14	2008	
967	1215	692	856	6222	4974	2313	8298	0	10	2009	
1439	1251	641	1296	6661	6072	2499	11745	2	63	2010	
171	319	145	381	2710	817	484	1103	0	0	2000	Fédération de Russie
642	529	172	507	2280	3390	627	4795	0	14	2007	
897	903	231	699	3329	3713	1755	5527	0	7	2008	
274	554	227	367	2935	3467	1404	3595	0	5	2009	
403	539	142	752	3111	3980	1477	4988	1	58	2010	

Voir la fin du tableau pour la remarque générale et les notes.

World exports by provenance and destination (Table D)

In million U.S. dollars f.o.b.

Exports to → / ↓ Exports from	Year	World 1/ Monde 1/	Developed economies 2/ Economies développées 2/								Commonwealth of Independent States Communauté d'Etats Indépendants	
				Asia-Pacific Asie-Pacifique		Europe		North America Amérique du Nord				
			Total	Total	Japan Japon	Total	Germany Allemagne	Total	U.S.A. É.-U.		Total	Europe
			Other manufactured goods (SITC, Rev. 3, 6 and 8) *[cont.]*									
Northern Africa	2000	8011	7227	27	23	6791	787	409	394		9	1
	2007	14729	12145	28	15	11791	849	326	313		33	31
	2008	19332	14115	42	25	13460	1056	612	577		74	70
	2009	17502	11973	28	16	10869	933	1076	1043		34	31
	2010	18862	13014	39	23	11809	1031	1166	1125		43	37
Sub-Saharan Africa	2000	17944	12667	827	690	9804	619	2036	1920		8	8
	2007	49474	33602	5067	4804	22371	2341	6165	6016		85	79
	2008	51528	32824	5958	5644	21486	2271	5379	5207		63	59
	2009	36015	19667	2992	2793	14058	1239	2617	2542		28	24
	2010	53916	30700	4891	4610	20816	1932	4993	4903		41	39
South Africa	2000	8588	5284	678	552	3444	452	1162	1062		2	2
	2007	27736	19446	4977	4728	9504	1988	4965	4839		46	40
	2008	28723	19601	5853	5555	9490	2040	4258	4106		47	45
	2009	18943	11377	2904	2722	6593	1068	1880	1825		22	19
	2010	26284	16753	4667	4446	8733	1757	3352	3281		32	30
Latin America and the Caribbean	2000	73611	55268	1737	1539	7961	870	45571	44772		21	19
	2007	153010	96523	2981	2566	24431	2707	69111	67030		248	187
	2008	160960	95621	3454	2687	23274	2679	68892	66791		305	195
	2009	121137	67450	2064	1485	13331	1260	52055	50530		191	111
	2010	148517	82262	2855	1907	17380	1540	62027	60050		162	106
Brazil	2000	14499	8863	718	645	3358	408	4787	4533		8	8
	2007	32753	17944	1220	1068	8401	1197	8323	7975		124	121
	2008	36306	17826	1437	1206	8475	1191	7914	7623		147	144
	2009	24153	10507	882	794	5089	583	4536	4317		67	66
	2010	28042	12730	1080	972	6271	783	5379	5094		71	69
Eastern Asia	2000	327649	186361	44289	38459	52386	11301	89686	83791		3013	2361
	2007	810729	400466	77442	62972	151053	26663	171971	156934		32290	22275
	2008	907087	441388	87087	69664	174998	31696	179304	163907		43689	24164
	2009	740202	363680	75738	60507	141470	28132	146473	134204		27330	13546
	2010	940483	444683	89768	70637	172561	34161	182355	167057		35099	21526
China	2000	128535	77216	24867	22355	20229	4200	32120	30105		2412	1835
	2007	517274	271695	52984	43288	102939	17304	115771	104547		30373	20628
	2008	597627	309061	61158	49049	123207	21204	124697	113072		41331	22130
	2009	483761	261497	54474	43573	99863	19343	107160	97827		25586	12140
	2010	625981	327004	63780	49539	127609	25454	135615	123705		32280	19139
Southern Asia	2000	44205	30085	1630	1131	13773	2805	14682	13790		844	507
	2007	100034	57779	2085	1228	32082	5744	23612	22194		1318	531
	2008	108710	59181	2347	1390	33768	6027	23066	21647		1603	623
	2009	108986	52383	2003	1005	29675	6165	20705	19383		1040	400
	2010	128692	59912	2708	1501	33591	6565	23613	22049		1266	604
South-Eastern Asia	2000	84362	51806	13529	11297	16385	3164	21892	20868		149	129
	2007	164984	83702	21910	17257	27785	5132	34007	32356		619	573
	2008	182689	90112	24732	18913	30165	5518	35215	33322		896	794
	2009	161112	79521	22843	16785	26673	4805	30006	28395		853	593
	2010	200104	98188	27197	20842	33156	5942	37836	35791		949	786
Western Asia	2000	39469	25850	855	696	14221	4035	10774	10441		1005	615
	2007	108271	53736	907	446	36574	6917	16254	15737		5178	3193
	2008	130523	55718	1056	513	38334	7269	16329	15725		6693	3990
	2009	101518	40156	816	337	28491	5903	10849	10374		4459	2181
	2010	124136	48128	1000	422	33403	6834	13725	13006		5623	2908
Oceania	2000	1784	1141	701	554	317	11	124	123		0	0
	2007	2258	781	357	269	370	1	55	54		0	0
	2008	2148	677	287	198	334	2	56	55		0	0
	2009	2044	564	211	124	305	8	47	46		0	0
	2010	2021	582	306	194	209	2	67	66		0	0

For general note and footnotes see end of table

Exportations mondiales par provenance et destination (Tableau D)

En millions de dollars E.-U. f.o.b.

← Exportations vers

South-Eastern Europe Europe du Sud-est	Northern Africa Afrique septentrio-nale	Sub-Saharan Africa Afrique du Nord	Latin America and the Caribbean Amérique latine et Caraïbes	Eastern Asia Asie orientale	Southern Asia Asie méridionale	South-eastern Asia Asie du Sud-est	Western Asia Asie occidentale	Oceania Océanie	Others 4/ Autre 4/	Année	Exportations en provence de ↓
				Articles manufacturés divers (CTCI, Rev. 3, 6 et 8) *[suite]*							
3	260	107	17	41	7	19	220	0	101	2000	Afrique du Nord
32	953	400	28	75	28	32	917	1	86	2007	
63	1708	791	48	85	79	26	2234	0	110	2008	
18	1717	774	47	278	130	35	2268	1	226	2009	
27	1722	857	70	337	167	39	2412	0	174	2010	
4	27	2575	356	1038	165	407	673	2	21	2000	Afrique subsaharienne
85	324	7630	593	3365	770	996	1819	6	198	2007	
53	477	8751	584	4705	803	938	2151	12	168	2008	
57	212	8367	318	4590	506	736	1375	58	103	2009	
13	159	10334	975	7360	1195	769	2270	36	65	2010	
3	13	1049	305	958	119	333	516	2	3	2000	Afrique du sud
59	52	2902	550	2434	508	604	1026	5	103	2007	
16	48	3418	432	2935	526	642	1024	5	30	2008	
11	46	2879	213	2848	332	529	655	9	22	2009	
3	60	3719	564	3182	471	525	955	6	13	2010	
3	120	280	14082	2616	131	503	509	3	73	2000	Amérique latine et Caraïbes
53	596	1252	36760	13484	569	1563	1556	13	392	2007	
70	551	1322	44494	13724	574	2136	1793	12	358	2008	
36	484	1237	32453	15723	539	1692	1156	5	171	2009	
35	585	965	39654	20899	630	2125	1061	7	131	2010	
2	74	154	4157	696	61	275	209	1	...	2000	Brésil
19	230	894	9455	2374	220	919	571	4	...	2007	
22	163	1007	10992	3478	210	1450	1008	4	...	2008	
26	180	876	7569	3004	342	1048	529	3	...	2009	
25	135	610	9528	2969	349	1190	430	4	...	2010	
368	1508	3791	11708	84943	5973	19780	9557	543	105	2000	Asie orientale
2087	6341	16316	31090	200207	25212	58903	37351	437	30	2007	
2557	7771	19855	39925	206983	29340	69309	45726	532	13	2008	
1701	8074	18267	31414	166856	27664	58520	36088	589	19	2009	
1960	9306	22719	48714	214861	39078	80496	42879	675	12	2010	
252	860	1960	4095	31066	1530	5081	4019	44	...	2000	Chine
1850	5662	13796	21994	94754	16078	33601	27288	183	...	2007	
2265	6834	17558	28591	99864	17709	39953	34158	304	...	2008	
1485	7063	16330	22455	71728	16507	34100	26625	384	...	2009	
1649	8052	20740	37600	91341	24777	48711	33401	426	...	2010	
19	274	1257	648	4311	1174	1429	4135	24	4	2000	Asie méridionale
180	984	3375	1874	9322	4768	4093	16063	34	245	2007	
305	1091	3979	2606	9878	5835	4719	19049	38	427	2008	
126	1072	3564	2109	11512	5642	4403	26649	34	452	2009	
178	1098	4208	3078	18331	7075	4794	28439	39	274	2010	
27	349	1149	1281	10611	2213	13244	3350	176	8	2000	Asie Sud-est
113	875	2440	3236	21914	6192	36663	8743	420	66	2007	
144	1077	2722	3947	24492	6291	42003	10531	397	78	2008	
107	1041	2812	3492	24416	5548	34488	8450	338	46	2009	
114	1103	2928	4524	31949	7255	42712	9863	457	61	2010	
488	911	632	252	2185	1424	796	5136	0	790	2000	Asie occidentale
4002	4165	3148	487	4669	9810	1143	19814	8	2111	2007	
4498	5453	3150	1050	6916	14879	1597	28069	32	2467	2008	
2790	6812	3191	794	5115	12129	1725	22538	15	1795	2009	
2869	6094	3337	1317	9176	21706	1829	21331	59	2668	2010	
1	0	17	309	277	5	5	2	24	2	2000	Océanie
0	0	76	15	374	13	6	6	47	939	2007	
0	0	50	6	367	17	6	3	56	967	2008	
1	0	26	4	355	12	36	6	42	998	2009	
0	0	30	2	313	9	16	4	38	1027	2010	

Voir la fin du tableau pour la remarque générale et les notes.

World exports by provenance and destination (Table D)

In million U.S. dollars f.o.b.

Exports from ↓ / Exports to →	Year	World 1/ Monde 1/	Developed economies 2/ Economies développées 2/ Total	Asia-Pacific Asie-Pacifique Total	Japan Japon	Europe Total	Germany Allemagne	North America Amérique du Nord Total	U.S.A. É.-U.	Commonwealth of Independent States Communauté d'Etats Indépendants Total	Europe
Textile yarn and fabrics (SITC, Rev. 3, 65)											
World 1/	2000	165948	81572	6533	4738	55526	10726	19513	15342	2415	2078
	2007	247467	116029	8568	6109	81237	14650	26224	21816	8310	6429
	2008	257756	116961	9379	6743	82046	15218	25536	21132	10667	7537
	2009	217575	95448	8681	6362	64998	12435	21769	18089	7777	5054
	2010	258841	109119	9603	6935	72748	14319	26769	22401	9719	6784
Developed Economies - Asia-Pacific 2/	2000	7516	1628	247	9	697	153	685	637	10	10
	2007	7759	1667	352	5	670	152	645	612	12	11
	2008	7947	1675	332	5	721	159	622	591	15	15
	2009	6574	1201	275	4	488	106	438	413	10	9
	2010	7590	1506	313	5	629	132	563	533	15	14
Japan	2000	7023	1334	56	.	656	151	621	582	10	10
	2007	7108	1231	29	.	638	149	564	538	12	11
	2008	7340	1265	28	.	691	157	546	521	15	15
	2009	6109	879	26	.	465	102	388	367	10	9
	2010	7086	1137	32	.	601	127	504	480	15	14
Developed Economies - Europe 2/	2000	57190	45319	1016	712	41070	7964	3233	2908	928	909
	2007	80555	60699	1169	736	55833	10177	3698	3306	2497	2431
	2008	80111	59460	1175	752	55063	10231	3223	2841	2679	2603
	2009	61432	45516	922	577	42279	8168	2314	2022	1811	1747
	2010	66279	48793	942	589	45150	9045	2700	2341	2050	1975
France	2000	6607	4840	95	69	4436	911	309	284	43	42
	2007	7560	5118	87	51	4774	822	257	236	128	125
	2008	7367	4810	84	47	4500	781	226	209	141	138
	2009	5608	3613	60	35	3384	588	169	154	86	77
	2010	5684	3649	61	39	3382	645	206	188	77	70
Germany	2000	11037	8356	127	72	7783	.	446	409	308	302
	2007	15487	11668	221	134	10851	.	596	537	545	525
	2008	15901	11870	226	142	11110	.	534	486	571	549
	2009	12089	9016	182	109	8419	.	415	381	429	411
	2010	13245	9705	195	121	9015	.	494	448	498	477
Developed Economies - North America 2/	2000	13157	6733	440	284	1449	194	4844	2013	27	23
	2007	14702	6532	427	251	1385	251	4720	2013	59	56
	2008	14463	6219	453	253	1411	269	4354	1715	60	55
	2009	11559	5048	362	195	1090	227	3597	1430	28	25
	2010	14064	5871	426	228	1347	265	4099	1668	36	34
United States	2000	10952	4618	424	279	1362	184	2832	.	24	21
	2007	12386	4402	406	248	1291	237	2705	.	46	43
	2008	12470	4399	431	248	1329	254	2639	.	53	48
	2009	9915	3541	345	191	1030	215	2166	.	27	24
	2010	12157	4110	407	225	1273	252	2430	.	34	32
South-Eastern Europe	2000	410	299	3	2	270	57	27	23	29	29
	2007	1597	1296	1	0	1274	214	21	20	93	83
	2008	1717	1367	2	1	1345	232	20	19	105	94
	2009	1437	1186	1	0	1169	190	16	14	67	60
	2010	1585	1294	2	0	1274	209	18	16	84	81
Commonwealth of Independent States	2000	1292	504	16	16	424	68	64	63	546	503
	2007	1791	538	9	8	495	122	34	32	901	769
	2008	1809	479	13	8	446	114	20	19	1056	912
	2009	1708	454	6	3	421	111	28	27	858	718
	2010	2325	532	4	3	491	121	37	36	1094	973
Russian Federation	2000	394	237	0	0	208	21	29	28	97	65
	2007	369	132	3	2	123	32	7	7	191	93
	2008	318	91	2	1	83	25	7	7	186	82
	2009	260	81	2	1	74	24	5	5	142	48
	2010	260	85	1	1	80	24	4	3	121	67

For general note and footnotes see end of table

Exportations mondiales par provenance et destination (Tableau D)

En millions de dollars E.-U. f.o.b.

South-Eastern Europe Europe du Sud-est	Northern Africa Afrique septentrio-nale	Sub-Saharan Africa Afrique du Nord	Latin America and the Caribbean Amérique latine et Caraïbes	Eastern Asia Asie orientale	Southern Asia Asie méridionale	South-eastern Asia Asie du Sud-est	Western Asia Asie occidentale	Oceania Océanie	Others 4/ Autre 4/	← Exportations vers Année	Exportations en provence de ↓
			Fils et tissus de matières textiles (CTCI, Rev. 3, 65)								
2509	3580	3444	11582	35008	5149	10714	8719	473	782	2000	Monde 1/
5323	6924	7381	17832	40653	10764	17603	15219	232	1197	2007	
5567	8243	8514	19552	38529	12278	19652	16505	184	1105	2008	
4426	7218	7671	15900	33164	12222	18281	14640	155	673	2009	
4744	7792	8854	20844	40093	15844	24044	16997	174	616	2010	
1	5	32	64	4333	137	933	291	81	0	2000	Economies Développées - Asie-Pacifique 2/
2	9	43	54	4399	137	1006	375	55	0	2007	
3	14	48	61	4366	140	1111	463	49	1	2008	
2	8	33	50	3699	134	972	428	38	0	2009	
5	13	45	55	4137	161	1230	380	43	0	2010	
1	4	27	60	4271	122	877	287	31	...	2000	Japon
2	8	33	50	4323	121	953	369	8	...	2007	
3	14	41	57	4303	124	1056	458	4	...	2008	
2	8	27	45	3652	123	936	424	3	...	2009	
4	13	40	51	4100	154	1196	376	2	...	2010	
2154	2673	552	766	1601	278	590	1922	20	388	2000	Economies Développées - Europe 2/
3968	3990	816	1105	2787	547	784	2803	26	533	2007	
4111	4221	975	1158	2729	599	800	2868	25	486	2008	
3312	3401	885	867	2066	489	611	2291	24	160	2009	
3562	3584	916	1035	2489	545	686	2480	20	120	2010	
169	943	98	69	148	19	56	214	8	0	2000	France
315	1196	123	72	202	42	101	250	13	0	2007	
348	1260	135	82	212	42	90	233	14	0	2008	
294	1033	103	54	148	25	61	178	12	0	2009	
290	1000	118	72	169	43	67	185	13	0	2010	
800	355	69	100	180	58	132	386	3	290	2000	Allemagne
1048	335	142	177	412	99	178	572	1	310	2007	
1094	347	175	209	441	110	191	636	1	257	2008	
865	270	166	164	377	97	177	526	2	0	2009	
930	309	171	211	504	120	203	592	1	0	2010	
8	18	57	5245	627	65	181	194	4	0	2000	Economies Développées - Amérique du Nord 2/
8	22	54	6501	979	98	270	176	2	0	2007	
5	47	65	6415	1046	115	284	206	3	0	2008	
3	21	49	5072	796	129	220	191	1	0	2009	
3	15	63	6291	1150	142	255	234	4	0	2010	
6	16	49	5209	607	64	173	183	4	...	2000	Etats-Unis
4	20	50	6425	919	93	257	168	2	...	2007	
3	40	61	6361	978	106	269	198	2	...	2008	
2	19	46	5031	739	125	211	172	1	...	2009	
3	13	59	6243	1093	136	245	220	1	...	2010	
49	3	3	2	4	2	0	19	...	0	2000	Europe du Sud-est
121	10	0	2	4	11	2	56	0	1	2007	
145	11	1	2	14	9	7	54	0	3	2008	
97	12	1	2	9	5	4	49	0	4	2009	
110	12	1	2	10	5	3	62	0	2	2010	
10	1	3	4	79	33	4	107	0	0	2000	Communauté d'Etats Indépendants
18	4	3	4	37	26	2	257	0	1	2007	
16	9	4	10	35	17	2	181	0	0	2008	
13	9	5	6	52	32	1	279	0	1	2009	
18	5	3	8	185	42	1	435	0	1	2010	
3	1	3	3	30	10	1	8	...	...	2000	Fédération de Russie
3	0	1	3	14	4	1	18	0	1	2007	
3	1	1	6	11	6	1	11	...	0	2008	
3	0	3	2	7	12	0	9	0	1	2009	
4	0	2	5	14	12	1	14	0	1	2010	

Voir la fin du tableau pour la remarque générale et les notes.

World exports by provenance and destination (Table D)

In million U.S. dollars f.o.b.

Exports to → / ↓ Exports from	Year	World 1/ Monde 1/	Developed economies 2/ Economies développées 2/ — Total	Asia-Pacific Asie-Pacifique — Total	Asia-Pacific Asie-Pacifique — Japan Japon	Europe — Total	Europe — Germany Allemagne	North America Amérique du Nord — Total	North America Amérique du Nord — U.S.A. É.-U.	Commonwealth of Independent States Communauté d'Etats Indépendants — Total	Commonwealth of Independent States Communauté d'Etats Indépendants — Europe
Textile yarn and fabrics (SITC, Rev. 3, 65) *[cont.]*											
Northern Africa	2000	688	592	2	0	502	41	87	84	0	0
	2007	1111	972	3	1	929	43	40	37	1	1
	2008	1570	1235	9	6	1099	52	127	117	6	5
	2009	1723	1280	13	6	1031	70	237	221	10	10
	2010	2075	1545	16	8	1239	88	290	267	12	12
Sub-Saharan Africa	2000	676	313	18	3	238	31	58	54	1	1
	2007	864	277	27	6	207	25	43	39	24	24
	2008	913	234	25	7	173	19	36	33	2	2
	2009	831	172	19	3	129	13	24	22	1	1
	2010	970	200	24	4	136	12	39	36	2	2
South Africa	2000	237	122	15	1	71	10	36	33	1	1
	2007	332	175	24	4	114	17	37	35	1	1
	2008	301	152	24	6	98	13	30	28	1	1
	2009	226	107	17	2	73	10	17	15	0	0
	2010	231	111	23	3	69	9	19	17	2	2
Latin America and the Caribbean	2000	4614	2834	69	52	233	52	2532	2423	1	1
	2007	6085	2817	34	18	255	36	2528	2423	4	4
	2008	6560	2523	33	21	238	29	2253	2165	4	4
	2009	5172	1966	23	15	162	27	1782	1721	2	2
	2010	5737	2200	26	19	192	29	1982	1913	3	3
Brazil	2000	895	373	46	41	122	26	205	182	0	0
	2007	1436	528	19	13	112	21	397	381	2	2
	2008	1361	457	20	17	96	17	341	334	2	2
	2009	953	306	14	11	58	13	234	230	1	1
	2010	1094	295	18	16	64	14	213	209	2	2
Eastern Asia	2000	54516	10743	3254	2639	3564	615	3925	3460	429	318
	2007	89772	22100	4901	3925	8612	1590	8587	7813	3040	1819
	2008	97372	24847	5508	4375	10158	1904	9181	8314	4720	2291
	2009	86921	22731	5516	4467	8809	1605	8406	7625	3662	1491
	2010	108931	28006	5934	4707	11139	2029	10933	9928	4584	2259
China	2000	16135	5077	2059	1786	1618	349	1400	1233	208	115
	2007	56032	17776	3938	3150	7122	1325	6716	6092	2782	1640
	2008	65367	20724	4525	3581	8708	1645	7490	6764	4424	2104
	2009	59824	19470	4728	3843	7665	1406	7077	6409	3453	1377
	2010	76871	24106	4987	3939	9780	1787	9338	8473	4303	2079
Southern Asia	2000	11718	6655	580	351	3507	844	2568	2307	167	112
	2007	19634	10347	520	263	5577	929	4250	3963	312	170
	2008	20389	10069	562	287	5504	1031	4003	3734	395	216
	2009	17967	8400	439	193	4537	862	3424	3196	217	135
	2010	23093	10277	529	231	5480	1116	4269	3989	284	197
South-Eastern Asia	2000	8255	2841	843	650	1157	142	841	759	8	7
	2007	10941	3201	1039	861	1350	197	811	754	27	24
	2008	11103	3136	1160	974	1201	194	776	715	36	33
	2009	10455	2647	1022	867	952	155	673	627	19	18
	2010	13120	3417	1284	1096	1292	232	841	773	44	41
Western Asia	2000	5834	3096	33	20	2415	565	647	610	268	166
	2007	12629	5577	81	35	4649	915	847	802	1341	1037
	2008	13787	5713	103	55	4688	985	922	869	1589	1308
	2009	11786	4842	81	33	3932	900	829	771	1094	839
	2010	13064	5474	98	46	4377	1042	998	900	1511	1191
Oceania	2000	83	15	13	0	1	0	1	1	...	...
	2007	26	6	6	0	0	0	0	0	...	...
	2008	15	5	5	0	0	0	0	0	...	...
	2009	9	4	4	0	0	0	0	0	0	...
	2010	9	5	4	0	1	0	0	0	0	...

For general note and footnotes see end of table

Exportations mondiales par provenance et destination (Tableau D)

En millions de dollars E.-U. f.o.b.

← Exportations vers

South-Eastern Europe Europe du Sud-est	Northern Africa Afrique septentrionale	Sub-Saharan Africa Afrique du Nord	Latin America and the Caribbean Amérique latine et Caraïbes	Eastern Asia Asie orientale	Southern Asia Asie méridionale	South-eastern Asia Asie du Sud-est	Western Asia Asie occidentale	Oceania Océanie	Others 4/ Autre 4/	Année	Exportations en provenance de ↓
				Fils et tissus de matières textiles (CTCI, Rev. 3, 65) ***[suite]***							
2	9	7	3	10	1	1	35	0	28	2000	Afrique du Nord
2	24	16	5	5	5	1	57	0	23	2007	
4	70	30	21	4	18	5	148	0	29	2008	
2	100	41	17	12	17	6	218	0	22	2009	
3	72	53	29	15	24	5	288	0	30	2010	
0	1	277	24	19	7	12	15	0	7	2000	Afrique subsaharienne
1	4	441	22	16	22	19	24	0	15	2007	
1	3	538	17	17	17	21	34	0	31	2008	
1	4	497	16	18	15	14	32	3	56	2009	
0	6	480	184	13	14	21	38	1	11	2010	
0	0	61	22	11	4	8	9	0	0	2000	Afrique du sud
0	1	75	20	9	16	16	16	0	2	2007	
0	1	84	10	9	5	16	21	0	2	2008	
0	1	81	4	2	6	5	16	0	2	2009	
0	1	92	5	1	4	1	13	0	1	2010	
0	5	8	1539	188	4	10	16	0	9	2000	Amérique latine et Caraïbes
1	11	17	3099	53	9	29	15	0	30	2007	
2	11	28	3841	50	11	24	12	0	55	2008	
3	7	18	3088	31	11	20	8	0	18	2009	
4	7	20	3385	65	10	19	10	1	13	2010	
0	2	5	497	7	1	1	8	0	...	2000	Brésil
1	9	13	849	10	3	13	7	0	...	2007	
1	8	18	847	10	3	10	5	0	...	2008	
3	3	14	603	6	4	9	3	0	...	2009	
4	4	15	746	11	2	11	3	0	...	2010	
69	396	1406	3284	24870	3212	6889	2826	309	80	2000	Asie orientale
212	1251	4188	5255	29002	6436	12415	5747	103	21	2007	
265	1629	5107	6054	26888	7147	14108	6544	59	4	2008	
222	1712	4495	5069	22780	7063	13484	5662	41	1	2009	
241	1972	5344	7350	26754	9640	18079	6907	54	1	2010	
30	152	702	739	6310	865	1228	807	17	...	2000	Chine
192	1108	3669	3868	11711	4802	5849	4250	27	...	2007	
244	1485	4600	4813	11249	5592	7237	4966	33	...	2008	
201	1539	4137	3974	9600	5720	7386	4312	30	...	2009	
208	1793	4995	6040	11418	8059	10539	5372	38	...	2010	
9	188	649	303	1483	538	361	1356	7	1	2000	Asie méridionale
40	464	1091	938	1470	1727	442	2709	10	84	2007	
52	505	1088	1169	1378	2267	509	2868	11	79	2008	
43	397	1001	850	1622	2425	520	2396	8	87	2009	
53	594	1216	1438	2445	2939	826	2986	10	24	2010	
3	62	323	298	1675	576	1695	724	48	0	2000	Asie Sud-est
11	183	320	780	1723	786	2518	1351	31	13	2007	
13	208	334	716	1788	814	2679	1339	30	10	2008	
14	259	341	739	1900	841	2367	1281	38	11	2009	
13	251	411	878	2526	1115	2841	1573	36	15	2010	
203	219	127	49	56	296	38	1214	0	269	2000	Asie occidentale
939	952	390	67	159	959	115	1651	3	476	2007	
951	1516	296	88	208	1124	102	1787	4	408	2008	
712	1288	307	124	179	1062	61	1804	0	313	2009	
732	1260	301	190	305	1208	75	1603	4	400	2010	
1	...	0	1	63	0	0	...	3	0	2000	Océanie
0	0	0	0	18	0	0	0	2	0	2007	
...	...	0	0	6	0	0	0	3	0	2008	
0	...	0	0	2	0	1	0	2	0	2009	
0	...	0	0	0	0	1	0	2	0	2010	

Voir la fin du tableau pour la remarque générale et les notes.

World exports by provenance and destination (Table D)

In million U.S. dollars f.o.b.

Exports to → / ↓ Exports from	Year	World 1/ / Monde 1/	Developed economies 2/ / Economies développées 2/ — Total	Asia-Pacific / Asie-Pacifique — Total	Asia-Pacific — Japan / Japon	Europe — Total	Europe — Germany / Allemagne	North America / Amérique du Nord — Total	North America — U.S.A. / É.-U.	Commonwealth of Independent States / Communauté d'Etats Indépendants — Total	CIS — Europe
Iron and steel (SITC, Rev. 3, 67)											
World 1/	2000	139976	88227	4441	3393	61238	12119	22548	17413	2282	1688
	2007	473029	269438	11795	7892	211229	41650	46415	36108	15984	10998
	2008	580084	311351	16358	10788	235808	46484	59185	46739	20253	13028
	2009	318363	150286	7982	4783	116473	22720	25831	18636	11492	5441
	2010	415384	205386	12329	8391	152774	31578	40284	29452	13385	9846
Developed Economies - Asia-Pacific 2/	2000	15647	2932	406	32	693	64	1833	1594	46	28
	2007	35744	4912	945	22	1443	160	2524	2158	210	136
	2008	45933	6051	1240	13	1601	176	3210	2802	292	218
	2009	32099	4074	703	25	1315	182	2056	1699	108	62
	2010	43548	5018	879	36	1387	155	2751	2425	369	332
Japan	2000	14833	2510	259	.	609	63	1642	1415	46	28
	2007	34395	4197	587	.	1341	160	2269	1924	209	136
	2008	44106	5058	824	.	1524	174	2710	2315	291	218
	2009	31145	3598	468	.	1230	180	1900	1556	108	62
	2010	41974	4247	577	.	1281	153	2389	2087	369	332
Developed Economies - Europe 2/	2000	65450	57519	426	200	51765	11056	5328	4606	512	433
	2007	208215	172827	1041	405	162759	35979	9027	7956	3026	2499
	2008	234694	190782	1230	443	179519	40516	10032	8878	3485	2935
	2009	131032	100475	674	234	94628	20046	5173	4632	2228	1762
	2010	160313	127969	792	305	119699	26920	7478	6532	3383	3073
France	2000	8850	7853	52	22	6883	1841	919	756	12	7
	2007	21671	18153	121	55	17162	4847	871	739	144	118
	2008	23075	18971	131	77	18011	5270	830	693	81	50
	2009	14209	10959	83	50	10421	2841	456	404	141	130
	2010	16198	13051	71	51	12373	3661	607	543	219	213
Germany	2000	13445	11343	64	32	10039	.	1240	1071	122	109
	2007	41397	33121	132	46	30960	.	2029	1775	812	678
	2008	45999	36456	191	70	33766	.	2500	2175	886	766
	2009	28143	21549	126	53	20206	.	1216	1062	608	539
	2010	31731	25394	117	40	23567	.	1710	1444	910	838
Developed Economies - North America 2/	2000	9535	7205	206	169	749	146	6250	3071	30	21
	2007	22246	15822	257	142	2118	329	13448	6199	54	42
	2008	29476	19495	292	140	2493	360	16709	7918	84	66
	2009	18021	10936	180	86	1333	188	9423	4036	76	61
	2010	24250	16177	261	146	1763	312	14153	6150	61	51
United States	2000	6319	4075	195	161	701	142	3179	.	29	21
	2007	15137	9332	220	129	1866	314	7246	.	44	36
	2008	20142	11131	242	122	2103	340	8786	.	76	60
	2009	13236	6712	150	77	1177	180	5385	.	73	60
	2010	17198	9803	220	132	1580	306	8002	.	57	50
South-Eastern Europe	2000	1634	1069	0	0	864	148	205	174	26	18
	2007	7302	4279	2	1	4086	689	191	187	54	30
	2008	8391	5135	4	0	4868	853	263	244	90	49
	2009	3230	1549	3	0	1514	294	32	30	51	36
	2010	4794	2466	2	1	2226	494	238	160	95	90
Commonwealth of Independent States	2000	11627	3308	60	58	2128	356	1120	1045	1615	1176
	2007	44790	14963	592	584	12186	1644	2185	2145	10020	6459
	2008	61867	22268	1213	1163	17987	1905	3068	2973	12260	7736
	2009	32031	8615	363	354	7585	1011	667	648	6259	2819
	2010	40205	14225	748	733	11823	2108	1654	1624	6765	4729
Russian Federation	2000	6146	2251	40	40	1537	288	674	639	379	91
	2007	20648	8959	214	212	7330	1075	1415	1403	3445	1344
	2008	28423	12934	350	343	11071	1368	1514	1507	4357	2028
	2009	16518	6105	119	118	5446	513	540	526	2692	462
	2010	19072	8473	193	191	7377	1143	904	894	2202	1003

For general note and footnotes see end of table

Exportations mondiales par provenance et destination (Tableau D)

En millions de dollars E.-U. f.o.b.

South-Eastern Europe Europe du Sud-est	Northern Africa Afrique septentrio-nale	Sub-Saharan Africa Afrique du Nord	Latin America and the Caribbean Amérique latine et Caraïbes	Eastern Asia Asie orientale	Southern Asia Asie méridionale	South-eastern Asia Asie du Sud-est	Western Asia Asie occidentale	Oceania Océanie	Others 4/ Autre 4/	Année	← Exportations vers / Exportations en provenance de ↓
				Fer et acier (CTCI, Rev. 3, 67)							
994	1777	1606	6626	20606	2614	9021	5865	107	250	2000	Monde 1/
6723	7847	8162	19283	55720	19789	33526	35652	281	622	2007	
8765	12407	10171	28803	71165	20411	44785	51076	373	522	2008	
3707	11147	8012	16753	46743	16855	27903	24870	257	339	2009	
4932	9134	8555	25489	56985	21308	37554	31182	353	1122	2010	
1	57	172	704	7099	468	3634	479	54	0	2000	Economies Développées - Asie-Pacifique 2/
8	210	307	1224	17494	1212	8177	1861	129	1	2007	
13	140	481	1654	22165	1387	11782	1838	124	5	2008	
12	238	388	1281	16177	1466	7036	1234	85	0	2009	
11	127	492	2085	20638	1985	11160	1533	102	29	2010	
1	57	159	651	6971	456	3517	460	6	...	2000	Japon
7	207	292	1173	17358	1201	7918	1830	2	...	2007	
13	138	453	1627	22047	1378	11312	1779	9	...	2008	
12	238	367	1267	16058	1453	6865	1177	3	...	2009	
11	126	470	1978	20469	1972	10871	1452	7	...	2010	
341	777	525	1186	1287	686	652	1761	20	185	2000	Economies Développées - Europe 2/
3071	3140	2022	3537	5714	3707	2163	8530	34	443	2007	
3753	5746	2294	4552	6391	4457	2686	10340	47	162	2008	
1997	4922	1754	2735	4976	3360	1984	6412	29	159	2009	
2543	4238	1887	3772	4417	3109	1627	6742	33	592	2010	
11	180	92	150	146	82	80	230	13	0	2000	France
105	361	351	278	541	492	202	1026	17	0	2007	
133	382	370	334	757	478	308	1235	25	0	2008	
84	498	236	179	455	440	207	996	14	0	2009	
102	406	299	289	467	351	123	877	13	1	2010	
50	111	101	317	441	233	141	422	0	163	2000	Allemagne
338	332	334	796	1842	1407	424	1687	0	304	2007	
362	402	367	903	2177	1677	603	2165	1	0	2008	
255	499	281	651	1717	1063	475	1044	1	0	2009	
273	326	280	835	1408	848	333	1123	0	0	2010	
1	23	40	1681	254	80	139	82	2	0	2000	Economies Développées - Amérique du Nord 2/
14	154	231	3789	984	365	364	467	3	...	2007	
22	187	274	6130	1708	416	495	663	3	0	2008	
13	200	320	3907	1231	433	471	433	2	0	2009	
16	97	227	4931	1092	477	666	492	15	...	2010	
1	22	39	1642	239	62	132	77	2	...	2000	Etats-Unis
13	142	216	3431	922	257	349	427	3	...	2007	
18	146	252	5527	1626	334	433	596	3	...	2008	
10	194	298	3699	1168	308	388	385	1	...	2009	
8	86	211	4575	1030	341	625	448	15	...	2010	
101	19	1	58	47	19	12	279	0	1	2000	Europe du Sud-est
958	124	4	44	45	287	24	1485	0	0	2007	
1434	93	69	38	84	154	30	1264	0	0	2008	
649	123	38	26	31	163	16	584	...	0	2009	
893	172	23	28	13	76	11	1016	0	0	2010	
472	586	207	428	2221	553	787	1448	1	0	2000	Communauté d'Etats Indépendants
1319	1638	805	976	2153	4311	1409	7194	...	3	2007	
1936	2288	828	1472	3422	4328	2972	10094	0	0	2008	
512	984	619	592	3553	3715	2031	5149	0	0	2009	
875	1019	555	893	3078	4488	2128	6161	1	16	2010	
122	235	103	271	1360	377	403	644	...	0	2000	Fédération de Russie
255	376	135	186	1405	2756	474	2655	...	3	2007	
376	576	148	286	2245	2622	1555	3323	...	...	2008	
68	362	176	158	1848	2401	1171	1537	0	...	2009	
105	337	81	474	1857	2632	1194	1701	1	16	2010	

Voir la fin du tableau pour la remarque générale et les notes.

World exports by provenance and destination (Table D)

In million U.S. dollars f.o.b.

Exports to → / ↓ Exports from	Year	World 1/ Monde 1/	Developed economies 2/ Economies développées 2/							Commonwealth of Independent States Communauté d'Etats Indépendants	
				Asia-Pacific Asie-Pacifique		Europe		North America Amérique du Nord			
			Total	Total	Japan Japon	Total	Germany Allemagne	Total	U.S.A. É.-U.	Total	Europe
Iron and steel (SITC, Rev. 3, 67) *[cont.]*											
Northern Africa	2000	331	201	8	8	185	5	8	5	7	0
	2007	1699	887	9	4	855	12	23	22	24	23
	2008	2252	1097	0	.	1095	14	1	1	46	46
	2009	1045	249	NULL	.	247	3	2	2	13	13
	2010	1559	505	3	3	500	3	2	2	16	16
Sub-Saharan Africa	2000	3026	1814	315	284	942	101	557	487	1	1
	2007	8272	3652	586	532	2259	468	807	756	31	30
	2008	9565	5251	916	807	3102	658	1233	1124	35	35
	2009	5649	1972	279	231	1343	309	350	327	12	12
	2010	8537	3811	591	515	2371	523	850	813	18	17
South Africa	2000	2758	1709	275	245	877	81	557	486	1	1
	2007	7460	3631	584	532	2242	468	805	754	31	30
	2008	8860	5189	915	807	3042	657	1232	1124	33	33
	2009	5116	1928	279	231	1301	308	348	326	11	10
	2010	7735	3650	582	506	2242	504	825	788	18	17
Latin America and the Caribbean	2000	8037	4930	169	155	1306	109	3455	3166	3	1
	2007	23786	12672	550	479	5067	889	7055	6801	121	74
	2008	28027	13256	784	628	4329	804	8143	7823	99	50
	2009	15319	5303	323	307	1799	182	3181	3028	104	39
	2010	19191	7777	443	423	2260	215	5075	4731	66	16
Brazil	2000	3633	2261	145	137	716	89	1400	1273	0	0
	2007	10145	5262	246	212	2187	536	2829	2732	33	32
	2008	13659	6019	538	418	2153	282	3329	3257	32	32
	2009	7438	2335	279	277	954	67	1102	1035	13	13
	2010	8893	3367	336	334	1340	125	1690	1570	7	7
Eastern Asia	2000	17591	6217	2503	2249	1136	38	2577	2213	29	6
	2007	85214	28410	6411	5083	13250	886	8750	7610	1877	1352
	2008	111221	34886	8715	6790	13316	575	12855	11490	3235	1665
	2009	51175	11458	4113	3167	3762	258	3583	2991	2133	530
	2010	77139	19092	7032	5437	6421	460	5640	4817	2046	1310
China	2000	4391	1673	627	597	385	12	661	566	17	3
	2007	51531	17544	2688	2116	9658	736	5198	4459	1623	1142
	2008	70951	22108	4009	3106	9703	393	8397	7443	2897	1391
	2009	23660	5101	1373	975	1808	169	1920	1562	1936	392
	2010	39565	8944	2747	1959	3889	307	2307	1801	1639	1000
Southern Asia	2000	1591	787	51	44	308	25	428	361	3	0
	2007	10129	4307	192	147	2868	240	1248	1204	123	78
	2008	13596	5851	363	314	3483	219	2005	1941	134	86
	2009	7513	1962	143	113	1117	105	702	677	95	48
	2010	11722	3762	426	389	2071	199	1266	1209	117	75
South-Eastern Asia	2000	2653	947	227	127	284	22	435	385	1	1
	2007	12547	2591	983	272	897	86	711	672	20	14
	2008	14627	3041	1405	299	941	93	695	648	31	27
	2009	8661	1745	1096	172	374	28	274	240	177	8
	2010	9945	1926	966	231	570	41	390	334	143	56
Western Asia	2000	2482	1072	6	3	748	49	319	275	9	3
	2007	12133	3530	18	11	3105	268	407	358	426	261
	2008	19622	3755	26	21	2802	310	928	855	463	116
	2009	12034	1678	17	7	1299	115	361	301	236	51
	2010	13493	2257	23	11	1501	149	734	600	306	80
Oceania	2000	371	227	65	63	130	1	32	32	...	...
	2007	951	585	210	209	335	.	41	41	...	...
	2008	812	484	171	168	272	0	42	42	...	...
	2009	556	270	88	87	157	.	26	26	0	0
	2010	688	400	163	162	183	.	54	54	...	...

For general note and footnotes see end of table

Exportations mondiales par provenance et destination (Tableau D)

En millions de dollars E.-U. f.o.b.

South-Eastern Europe Europe du Sud-est	Northern Africa Afrique septentrionale	Sub-Saharan Africa Afrique du Nord	Latin America and the Caribbean Amérique latine et Caraïbes	Eastern Asia Asie orientale	Southern Asia Asie méridionale	South-eastern Asia Asie du Sud-est	Western Asia Asie occidentale	Oceania Océanie	Others 4/ Autre 4/	Année	← Exportations vers / Exportations en provenance de ↓
				Fer et acier (CTCI, Rev. 3, 67) *[suite]*							
0	72	12	0	5	0	5	28	...	1	2000	Afrique du Nord
22	248	50	2	1	1	22	437	...	4	2007	
34	396	116	3	0	7	11	539	...	4	2008	
3	255	96	2	1	25	9	388	0	4	2009	
1	318	83	2	24	37	2	567	0	4	2010	
0	2	299	164	424	75	131	116	0	2	2000	Afrique subsaharienne
65	31	1652	330	1515	238	413	316	3	26	2007	
16	15	1592	299	1592	269	254	227	2	12	2008	
9	22	1269	130	1606	161	289	165	5	9	2009	
1	23	1741	319	1859	286	207	267	1	3	2010	
0	2	190	164	408	74	131	79	0	1	2000	Afrique du sud
56	30	891	330	1512	227	411	313	3	25	2007	
14	13	986	298	1591	251	252	223	2	9	2008	
9	22	808	120	1602	155	288	164	5	5	2009	
1	23	1167	300	1829	277	204	264	1	3	2010	
0	65	94	1930	618	50	199	147	0	1	2000	Amérique latine et Caraïbes
29	452	453	6038	2303	345	716	649	3	4	2007	
40	374	371	8187	3234	290	1174	982	0	20	2008	
5	327	556	4840	2634	278	817	447	0	6	2009	
2	408	340	6277	2738	325	913	339	0	6	2010	
...	39	21	666	383	21	160	81	0	...	2000	Brésil
0	114	239	2579	1066	101	576	176	0	...	2007	
0	34	206	3250	2478	65	1044	531	0	...	2008	
0	55	298	1813	1904	215	676	129	0	...	2009	
0	26	117	2503	1776	232	773	91	0	...	2010	
51	40	81	340	7803	343	2191	481	14	0	2000	Asie orientale
255	739	1301	2998	23491	6413	13322	6347	61	0	2007	
285	1410	2572	5378	30047	6359	16780	10147	122	0	2008	
107	1110	1728	2526	14657	4554	9344	3454	100	2	2009	
194	953	1733	6171	19682	7156	14634	5379	96	2	2010	
15	12	35	62	1717	81	581	196	0	...	2000	Chine
179	559	1114	1877	12280	4343	7972	4019	20	...	2007	
187	1110	2319	3568	18556	3803	9046	7298	60	...	2008	
48	900	1478	1273	5408	1958	3587	1917	54	...	2009	
95	688	1506	3623	8988	4076	6671	3271	63	...	2010	
1	6	114	27	136	136	167	213	0	0	2000	Asie méridionale
66	79	660	191	717	1053	698	2217	1	17	2007	
163	122	740	483	853	1250	944	3021	2	32	2008	
36	328	568	389	697	1236	734	1430	1	37	2009	
48	101	736	433	1379	1642	482	2936	1	85	2010	
0	14	10	30	423	126	1022	68	14	0	2000	Asie Sud-est
3	120	251	75	944	1400	6143	956	45	1	2007	
18	202	243	132	1130	1025	7326	1408	64	8	2008	
1	101	136	57	675	606	4636	495	32	1	2009	
2	86	212	68	968	654	5294	490	99	2	2010	
26	118	49	78	151	73	83	763	...	59	2000	Asie occidentale
913	912	350	79	83	449	74	5193	0	124	2007	
1050	1434	542	474	280	456	331	10554	5	278	2008	
365	2537	518	269	253	846	535	4677	0	119	2009	
347	1592	498	510	847	1065	428	5260	1	382	2010	
0	0	0	...	138	5	0	...	1	0	2000	Océanie
0	...	76	1	277	9	0	0	2	...	2007	
...	...	49	0	261	14	0	0	3	0	2008	
...	...	21	0	252	10	0	0	2	...	2009	
...	0	30	0	250	6	0	0	3	...	2010	

Voir la fin du tableau pour la remarque générale et les notes.

World exports by provenance and destination (Table D)

In million U.S. dollars f.o.b.

Exports from ↓ / Exports to →	Year	World 1/ Monde 1/	Developed economies 2/ Economies développées 2/ Total	Asia-Pacific Asie-Pacifique Total	Japan Japon	Europe Total	Germany Allemagne	North America Amérique du Nord Total	U.S.A. É.-U.	Commonwealth of Independent States Communauté d'Etats Indépendants Total	Europe
Non-ferrous metals (SITC, Rev. 3, 68)											
World 1/	2000	112671	79430	8867	8230	49974	9548	20589	17563	807	717
	2007	353076	229124	21529	19897	158447	29340	49149	43436	3309	2755
	2008	344971	216186	23296	21349	147157	28156	45734	39822	3648	3050
	2009	231599	132052	12061	10398	91490	17408	28501	24924	2004	1598
	2010	328464	189987	19343	16635	129751	26346	40893	35441	2473	2085
Developed Economies - Asia-Pacific 2/	2000	10460	3587	1687	1490	869	175	1032	986	18	3
	2007	24675	6104	2873	2488	1988	158	1244	1212	61	26
	2008	24503	5924	2968	2604	1827	142	1129	1088	54	51
	2009	18217	3158	1364	1044	1277	163	518	504	7	5
	2010	24571	4890	2498	2084	1309	213	1084	1049	11	6
Japan	2000	4854	990	31	.	348	105	612	588	18	3
	2007	12297	1572	54	.	836	141	682	670	61	26
	2008	13017	1714	43	.	924	119	747	727	54	51
	2009	10278	1268	35	.	787	117	445	439	6	5
	2010	14365	1385	26	.	631	191	728	718	8	4
Developed Economies - Europe 2/	2000	45144	40130	1546	1395	34114	8186	4470	4288	307	296
	2007	124404	107550	2658	2289	96840	23625	8052	7727	1373	1320
	2008	124108	104548	3175	2780	93764	22335	7610	7168	1468	1372
	2009	78489	64078	1230	976	58818	13869	4030	3794	804	704
	2010	109165	91901	1886	1570	83201	21080	6815	6118	898	832
France	2000	3859	3505	50	43	3256	922	198	183	7	6
	2007	9178	7880	127	105	7392	2338	362	329	48	48
	2008	8485	7225	125	100	6726	1948	374	344	44	43
	2009	5253	4279	56	41	4030	1143	194	178	30	25
	2010	6573	5297	62	37	4901	1532	334	314	27	25
Germany	2000	10368	8668	319	266	7379	.	969	912	122	119
	2007	30959	25306	524	437	22152	.	2630	2516	576	552
	2008	31385	25124	545	461	22125	.	2454	2346	650	613
	2009	19571	15782	280	211	14265	.	1237	1164	318	294
	2010	26283	21234	381	283	18842	.	2012	1912	373	332
Developed Economies - North America 2/	2000	16445	12861	1067	1006	2325	298	9469	6794	8	8
	2007	39700	29696	2769	2658	6359	954	20568	16452	43	36
	2008	37285	27587	2407	2278	5752	1087	19428	15247	58	47
	2009	22988	15774	1017	890	3253	639	11504	8919	30	29
	2010	32403	22422	1439	1294	4742	996	16241	12508	12	10
United States	2000	8272	5132	729	685	1728	289	2675	.	8	8
	2007	16834	9525	1745	1682	3664	873	4116	.	43	35
	2008	17203	9499	1440	1351	3877	1033	4182	.	57	46
	2009	11398	5773	689	579	2500	615	2584	.	28	28
	2010	15918	8025	977	845	3316	979	3733	.	11	10
South-Eastern Europe	2000	1376	1092	3	3	1069	73	21	13	12	12
	2007	5110	3942	1	0	3886	305	54	52	20	19
	2008	5457	4259	1	0	4216	315	42	36	33	33
	2009	3243	2293	1	0	2269	352	22	17	35	34
	2010	4526	3074	1	0	3042	548	31	26	77	77
Commonwealth of Independent States	2000	9325	7843	1129	1128	5568	412	1146	1142	426	374
	2007	31980	25516	1793	1787	21638	1813	2085	2045	1236	969
	2008	25989	19053	2333	2324	14275	1733	2445	2429	1232	984
	2009	17840	12682	1213	1210	9373	957	2095	2090	668	520
	2010	24643	16187	948	943	13121	1467	2118	2106	937	759
Russian Federation	2000	8137	7079	1096	1095	4927	283	1056	1053	76	32
	2007	24409	21430	1738	1733	17733	1459	1959	1937	616	371
	2008	18639	15168	2270	2263	10600	1302	2297	2285	567	348
	2009	13396	10627	1182	1178	7502	831	1943	1941	278	145
	2010	17778	13885	857	852	11082	1179	1947	1943	365	217

For general note and footnotes see end of table

Exportations mondiales par provenance et destination (Tableau D)

En millions de dollars E.-U. f.o.b.

South-Eastern Europe Europe du Sud-est	Northern Africa Afrique septentrio-nale	Sub-Saharan Africa Afrique du Nord	Latin America and the Caribbean Amérique latine et Caraïbes	Eastern Asia Asie orientale	Southern Asia Asie méridionale	South-eastern Asia Asie du Sud-est	Western Asia Asie occidentale	Oceania Océanie	Others 4/ Autre 4/	← Exportations vers / Année	Exportations en provence de ↓
				Metaux non ferreux (CTCI, Rev. 3, 68)							
318	428	760	4410	16507	1305	5748	2523	19	417	2000	Monde 1/
2262	2305	2262	12378	60018	7611	20403	11766	50	1588	2007	
2472	2845	2219	12910	57706	10232	21801	13249	51	1652	2008	
1588	2210	1779	8311	52888	4389	15070	10835	44	429	2009	
2373	2815	2585	12911	72812	6516	21982	13357	47	607	2010	
0	2	82	51	4512	135	1964	99	8	0	2000	Economies Développées - Asie-Pacifique 2/
6	69	70	59	11617	427	5484	758	20	0	2007	
3	71	61	59	11371	324	5920	694	21	0	2008	
1	48	48	49	10206	391	4048	247	14	0	2009	
1	74	66	95	12945	431	5809	228	21	0	2010	
0	2	14	32	2576	49	1118	53	0	...	2000	Japon
6	6	20	33	7411	98	2759	333	0	...	2007	
3	10	11	40	7833	72	2982	297	0	...	2008	
1	4	7	34	6637	88	2144	89	0	...	2009	
1	7	9	58	9063	138	3580	115	0	...	2010	
186	297	223	563	1498	423	395	759	6	356	2000	Economies Développées - Europe 2/
1209	1208	455	1197	5661	977	1097	2262	19	1396	2007	
1373	1433	456	1287	6445	2227	867	2627	16	1360	2008	
963	1338	321	866	5932	917	735	2179	11	346	2009	
1509	1666	410	1219	6070	1470	1220	2417	11	374	2010	
3	74	32	24	88	9	35	77	3	3	2000	France
23	239	79	79	356	58	43	363	7	3	2007	
21	249	89	82	281	56	49	377	7	5	2008	
13	198	62	41	269	29	34	287	7	2	2009	
31	230	81	62	327	45	111	356	7	1	2010	
35	55	73	308	433	56	152	208	0	259	2000	Allemagne
314	266	143	543	1447	262	428	712	1	960	2007	
386	334	130	700	1460	327	445	853	2	973	2008	
266	209	104	478	1281	284	361	486	2	0	2009	
383	261	133	696	1436	339	695	732	1	0	2010	
2	6	186	1752	1153	21	258	198	1	0	2000	Economies Développées - Amérique du Nord 2/
8	18	133	4195	4197	315	593	502	0	0	2007	
6	20	39	4461	3706	210	524	673	1	0	2008	
3	19	28	3206	3001	134	365	427	1	0	2009	
6	10	41	4699	4158	196	478	379	1	...	2010	
2	5	185	1692	870	17	176	185	1	...	2000	Etats-Unis
8	16	72	3949	2215	244	353	408	0	...	2007	
6	18	35	4212	2310	142	368	556	1	...	2008	
3	18	24	3028	1783	79	274	386	1	...	2009	
6	9	40	4359	2651	141	340	335	1	...	2010	
94	19	2	20	7	4	2	125	...	0	2000	Europe du Sud-est
424	18	3	4	66	46	6	582	0	0	2007	
438	16	3	4	134	54	13	501	0	1	2008	
335	72	2	2	72	2	11	421	...	0	2009	
445	75	5	3	163	1	19	663	0	0	2010	
11	0	6	79	696	25	19	219	...	0	2000	Communauté d'Etats Indépendants
306	1	2	253	1939	116	70	2542	...	...	2007	
343	50	9	299	2074	202	92	2635	0	...	2008	
114	7	6	85	1802	176	85	2214	0	0	2009	
176	5	3	129	2775	160	114	4157	0	0	2010	
4	0	6	73	678	21	18	181	...	...	2000	Fédération de Russie
238	1	1	248	366	41	46	1422	...	...	2007	
221	47	9	297	660	107	73	1490	...	...	2008	
76	1	6	82	673	78	70	1505	0	...	2009	
150	1	2	104	738	36	63	2434	...	0	2010	

Voir la fin du tableau pour la remarque générale et les notes.

World exports by provenance and destination (Table D)

In million U.S. dollars f.o.b.

Exports from ↓ / Exports to →	Year	World 1/ Monde 1/	Developed economies 2/ Economies développées 2/ Total	Asia-Pacific Asie-Pacifique Total	Asia-Pacific Asie-Pacifique Japan Japon	Europe Total	Europe Germany Allemagne	North America Amérique du Nord Total	North America Amérique du Nord U.S.A. É.-U.	Commonwealth of Independent States Communauté d'Etats Indépendants Total	Commonwealth of Independent States Communauté d'Etats Indépendants Europe
						Non-ferrous metals (SITC, Rev. 3, 68) ***[cont.]***					
Northern Africa	2000	266	214	8	8	202	4	4	4	0	0
	2007	702	577	5	5	558	18	14	14	0	...
	2008	1590	872	4	4	834	63	33	33	1	1
	2009	1245	505	1	1	488	34	16	16	...	...
	2010	1639	814	5	4	788	83	21	21	0	...
Sub-Saharan Africa	2000	2282	1367	315	311	913	32	139	130	0	0
	2007	20117	16322	4193	4144	8535	1082	3593	3570	9	9
	2008	19782	15064	4742	4700	7882	920	2439	2435	9	9
	2009	13370	9313	2499	2480	5625	406	1189	1182	3	3
	2010	22355	15617	4037	4016	9332	742	2248	2234	14	14
South Africa	2000	1209	526	246	242	169	7	110	102	0	0
	2007	13019	11509	4149	4100	3820	905	3539	3517	6	6
	2008	12578	10596	4701	4659	3461	881	2433	2430	5	5
	2009	8614	6980	2467	2448	3332	363	1181	1174	3	3
	2010	11973	10077	3912	3896	4049	713	2116	2105	9	9
Latin America and the Caribbean	2000	11189	7834	1142	1135	3436	170	3256	3235	2	2
	2007	40921	24538	1876	1781	12269	678	10394	9610	9	2
	2008	38721	22963	2013	1711	11587	718	9363	8619	55	1
	2009	29411	13318	1201	862	5672	222	6445	5916	11	0
	2010	41370	18484	1824	1185	8281	207	8380	7829	0	0
Brazil	2000	1757	1477	391	388	735	11	350	348	1	1
	2007	4618	3363	751	737	2057	53	556	545	2	2
	2008	4093	3040	651	648	1962	233	427	423	1	1
	2009	2486	1450	429	428	647	33	374	372	0	0
	2010	2668	1784	538	536	904	26	341	338	0	0
Eastern Asia	2000	9406	2290	965	854	672	75	653	593	9	8
	2007	38281	8799	3147	2767	3269	331	2383	2027	394	277
	2008	38027	9982	3604	3096	3821	419	2558	2116	545	441
	2009	26900	6892	1925	1509	2759	351	2208	2058	299	218
	2010	38324	10108	4010	3125	3082	419	3016	2659	383	317
China	2000	3363	1340	563	498	500	29	278	252	6	5
	2007	19231	6256	1765	1506	2576	251	1916	1615	378	267
	2008	19540	6851	1969	1581	2808	280	2074	1704	528	428
	2009	12089	4275	997	652	1434	154	1844	1738	289	210
	2010	17945	6939	2296	1543	2235	332	2408	2178	369	308
Southern Asia	2000	499	100	4	2	64	18	32	29	4	3
	2007	5557	913	40	29	781	42	93	84	6	4
	2008	5408	848	95	78	686	43	68	56	5	3
	2009	5120	847	63	40	622	126	162	141	34	33
	2010	8357	421	81	63	276	22	64	55	6	5
South-Eastern Asia	2000	3876	1079	770	683	160	9	150	140	3	2
	2007	14575	3077	2063	1869	588	33	426	407	15	12
	2008	14903	2980	1867	1711	711	44	402	385	15	14
	2009	10561	1955	1480	1353	299	39	176	157	6	6
	2010	15099	3867	2466	2318	751	158	651	621	8	7
Western Asia	2000	2400	1032	232	215	584	96	216	209	18	9
	2007	7049	2090	111	80	1734	299	244	238	141	83
	2008	9197	2104	87	62	1801	336	216	209	174	94
	2009	4214	1237	65	33	1036	250	136	132	109	47
	2010	5978	2168	116	32	1826	411	225	215	128	57
Oceania	2000	1	1	0	.	0	.	0	0	...	...
	2007	5	2	1	.	2	.	0	0	...	...
	2008	1	1	1	.	0	.	0	0	...	...
	2009	2	1	1	.	0	0	0	0	...	...
	2010	33	33	33	.	0	0	0	0	...	...

For general note and footnotes see end of table

Exportations mondiales par provenance et destination (Tableau D)

En millions de dollars E.-U. f.o.b.

South-Eastern Europe Europe du Sud-est	Northern Africa Afrique septentrio-nale	Sub-Saharan Africa Afrique du Nord	Latin America and the Caribbean Amérique latine et Caraïbes	Eastern Asia Asie orientale	Southern Asia Asie méridionale	South-eastern Asia Asie du Sud-est	Western Asia Asie occidentale	Oceania Océanie	Others 4/ Autre 4/	Année	← Exportations vers Exportations en provenance de ↓
				Metaux non ferreux (CTCI, Rev. 3, 68) ***[suite]***							
0	18	2	0	2	0	11	19	...	0	2000	Afrique du Nord
...	70	5	2	23	5	4	15	...	3	2007	
3	144	37	1	27	12	2	490	...	2	2008	
1	154	51	1	48	18	3	461	...	1	2009	
9	166	135	2	48	15	7	442	...	1	2010	
0	1	174	82	425	10	145	78	0	0	2000	Afrique subsaharienne
9	235	818	66	1445	321	480	378	0	34	2007	
5	399	717	118	2308	272	536	352	2	0	2008	
0	117	585	36	2420	172	302	415	7	0	2009	
0	60	880	209	4410	238	378	545	3	0	2010	
0	0	40	48	394	9	143	49	0	0	2000	Afrique du sud
0	3	234	64	746	174	132	117	0	34	2007	
0	12	210	36	1108	141	302	168	0	0	2008	
0	9	100	22	1126	90	184	101	...	0	2009	
...	9	114	154	1188	98	255	68	0	0	2010	
0	7	17	1782	1242	14	58	210	...	23	2000	Amérique latine et Caraïbes
2	30	76	6131	9392	13	224	500	1	5	2007	
2	36	39	6088	8938	26	224	344	0	5	2008	
2	16	28	3599	11781	29	295	327	0	5	2009	
3	67	44	5624	16268	46	481	347	...	6	2010	
...	3	10	207	17	6	13	23	...	...	2000	Brésil
2	16	60	762	281	4	42	87	0	...	2007	
2	20	25	772	91	3	14	125	0	...	2008	
2	8	23	405	428	9	45	117	0	...	2009	
1	16	34	497	244	5	15	72	...	...	2010	
2	6	25	68	5432	289	1123	160	1	0	2000	Asie orientale
59	174	423	376	20741	1307	4874	1131	5	0	2007	
50	211	539	475	18351	1275	5191	1403	5	0	2008	
21	147	448	376	13215	1165	3408	923	5	0	2009	
29	218	651	821	17551	1921	5495	1142	6	0	2010	
2	2	15	21	1541	32	352	52	0	...	2000	Chine
55	124	362	319	8099	699	2156	780	4	...	2007	
48	167	485	412	7281	702	2062	997	4	...	2008	
20	114	393	328	4240	517	1264	646	4	...	2009	
28	169	589	753	5320	738	2145	891	5	...	2010	
0	3	10	1	97	55	126	104	0	0	2000	Asie méridionale
7	193	148	11	901	635	1134	1610	0	0	2007	
2	139	165	21	553	627	1346	1696	0	4	2008	
0	28	119	31	1095	319	804	1839	2	3	2009	
0	7	157	29	4635	453	1220	1427	0	2	2010	
1	5	17	5	1015	259	1430	61	1	0	2000	Asie Sud-est
0	61	51	68	3878	828	6297	294	4	1	2007	
0	57	89	89	3667	747	6991	264	5	0	2008	
0	43	65	39	3033	589	4652	175	3	1	2009	
0	55	84	63	3233	959	6447	378	4	1	2010	
20	65	16	6	428	71	217	491	0	36	2000	Asie occidentale
232	229	80	15	158	2621	140	1194	0	148	2007	
246	267	64	10	132	4256	95	1570	0	279	2008	
147	221	79	22	282	477	362	1206	0	73	2009	
193	412	108	17	556	627	315	1232	0	222	2010	
...	...	0	...	0	...	...	...	0	0	2000	Océanie
...	...	...	0	0	...	2	0	0	...	2007	
...	...	0	0	0	0	0	0	0	...	2008	
...	...	0	...	0	0	0	...	0	...	2009	
...	...	...	...	0	0	0	...	0	...	2010	

Voir la fin du tableau pour la remarque générale et les notes.

World exports by provenance and destination (Table D)

In million U.S. dollars f.o.b.

Exports to → / ↓ Exports from	Year	World 1/ Monde 1/	Developed economies 2/ Economies développées 2/ Total	Asia-Pacific Asie-Pacifique Total	Asia-Pacific Asie-Pacifique Japan Japon	Europe Total	Europe Germany Allemagne	North America Amérique du Nord Total	North America Amérique du Nord U.S.A. É.-U.	Commonwealth of Independent States Communauté d'Etats Indépendants Total	Commonwealth of Independent States Communauté d'Etats Indépendants Europe
Other manufactured metal products (SITC, Rev. 3, 691-695, 699 and 812)											
World 1/	2000	117489	88447	4456	3152	56983	12688	27008	19427	1312	997
	2007	286814	201169	12009	8291	143600	29214	45560	35702	10413	8492
	2008	327802	220461	13817	9164	160321	33789	46323	35945	13717	11000
	2009	248176	159335	11480	6915	114440	23344	33416	25251	8358	5958
	2010	280205	179435	13046	8303	126905	26643	39484	29689	10167	7804
Developed Economies - Asia-Pacific 2/	2000	6630	2982	252	23	861	168	1870	1762	8	6
	2007	11031	4120	461	30	1490	364	2169	2046	80	73
	2008	12387	4278	442	38	1688	412	2147	1960	109	93
	2009	9676	2900	385	31	1073	194	1441	1343	69	63
	2010	12506	3652	489	36	1276	251	1888	1748	47	38
Japan	2000	6114	2675	70	.	820	162	1785	1692	8	5
	2007	9873	3542	129	.	1388	349	2025	1909	77	71
	2008	11126	3662	89	.	1577	397	1996	1818	104	91
	2009	8601	2387	74	.	982	182	1332	1255	63	58
	2010	11289	3086	105	.	1186	236	1795	1666	44	36
Developed Economies - Europe 2/	2000	59863	52018	904	549	47030	10395	4083	3632	743	637
	2007	154603	126859	1949	1061	117328	24135	7582	6721	5532	5080
	2008	173778	140018	2179	1179	130076	27830	7762	6811	6760	6237
	2009	126513	100639	1631	841	93385	19224	5622	4884	4012	3449
	2010	137840	109015	1854	945	100677	21266	6485	5715	4745	4231
France	2000	6147	5280	64	44	4751	1283	464	384	32	25
	2007	12419	9817	238	78	8981	2326	598	511	127	107
	2008	13879	10568	215	123	9717	2630	637	536	152	126
	2009	9916	7271	184	123	6503	1661	584	429	96	72
	2010	10508	7413	189	83	6696	1674	528	451	149	77
Germany	2000	15167	13206	266	161	11808	.	1132	1036	217	190
	2007	41842	34070	582	323	31043	.	2445	2187	1771	1633
	2008	46652	37194	640	304	34155	.	2399	2145	2324	2140
	2009	34503	27555	494	236	25268	.	1792	1602	1371	1184
	2010	38471	30307	606	316	27513	.	2188	1974	1576	1454
Developed Economies - North America 2/	2000	20273	13612	580	410	2211	425	10821	4367	32	24
	2007	28111	18377	1195	855	4077	698	13105	5849	146	113
	2008	29949	19035	1285	882	4502	779	13247	5695	243	199
	2009	23078	13941	909	568	3273	564	9759	3712	163	125
	2010	27138	16146	1112	686	3742	738	11292	4129	212	167
United States	2000	15573	9038	550	392	2037	402	6451	.	25	18
	2007	21383	12146	1113	817	3785	654	7248	.	110	84
	2008	23207	12880	1205	849	4135	705	7541	.	201	163
	2009	18568	9881	847	542	3001	526	6033	.	144	112
	2010	22051	11606	1031	653	3417	663	7157	.	171	137
South-Eastern Europe	2000	356	269	0	0	254	58	14	14	12	9
	2007	2364	1759	2	1	1725	334	33	24	175	151
	2008	2777	2064	2	1	2023	419	39	33	179	162
	2009	1959	1484	1	0	1456	335	26	24	94	87
	2010	2348	1781	2	1	1749	428	30	26	118	107
Commonwealth of Independent States	2000	2116	1624	24	24	1505	639	95	92	360	244
	2007	3456	1252	51	48	866	258	335	323	1831	1201
	2008	4065	1073	20	15	859	307	194	191	2372	1484
	2009	2757	817	17	14	576	172	224	219	1430	828
	2010	2845	708	7	4	500	127	201	196	1686	1093
Russian Federation	2000	1780	1527	24	24	1416	626	87	85	147	52
	2007	1962	822	45	41	461	174	316	308	874	371
	2008	2076	646	11	7	453	202	181	181	933	364
	2009	1489	511	11	9	285	107	215	212	561	151
	2010	1427	428	4	2	229	57	194	192	655	241

For general note and footnotes see end of table

Exportations mondiales par provenance et destination (Tableau D)

En millions de dollars E.-U. f.o.b.

South-Eastern Europe Europe du Sud-est	Northern Africa Afrique septentrio-nale	Sub-Saharan Africa Afrique du Nord	Latin America and the Caribbean Amérique latine et Caraïbes	Eastern Asia Asie orientale	Southern Asia Asie méridionale	South-eastern Asia Asie du Sud-est	Western Asia Asie occidentale	Oceania Océanie	Others 4/ Autre 4/	← Exportations vers Année	Exportations en provence de ↓
Autres produits en métal manufacturés (CTCI, Rev. 3, 691-695, 699 et 812)											
671	933	1608	8305	6605	1035	5186	3067	159	160	2000	Monde 1/
4409	2847	6226	13980	17290	4574	12330	12197	404	973	2007	
5490	4166	8279	16980	20106	5589	15893	15484	447	1190	2008	
3755	4483	7489	13263	17508	5621	12890	14171	457	846	2009	
3742	4598	7877	16750	21916	6366	15981	11737	515	1122	2010	
1	14	51	222	1615	165	1420	83	68	0	2000	Economies Développées - Asie-Pacifique 2/
27	23	122	368	3527	225	2160	213	158	9	2007	
13	33	151	461	4013	305	2576	285	155	8	2008	
7	25	127	330	3467	334	2045	224	145	4	2009	
15	31	148	434	4525	414	2828	218	177	18	2010	
1	13	45	218	1585	158	1336	71	5	...	2000	Japon
9	21	72	355	3457	203	1952	181	5	...	2007	
10	30	57	438	3922	281	2373	246	4	...	2008	
6	22	41	313	3422	314	1835	193	6	...	2009	
13	27	43	413	4471	390	2608	187	7	...	2010	
554	663	751	1376	983	321	733	1571	48	101	2000	Economies Développées - Europe 2/
3366	1629	2424	2769	3184	1264	1652	5134	122	666	2007	
4180	2265	3062	3562	3689	1506	2040	5817	139	740	2008	
2911	2374	2345	2629	3631	1478	1677	4393	112	311	2009	
2923	2219	2767	3338	4230	1441	2073	4519	108	461	2010	
15	165	161	120	79	47	52	157	37	0	2000	France
217	459	610	185	282	164	110	356	92	1	2007	
284	572	914	224	319	184	149	409	104	1	2008	
177	464	538	205	301	212	175	398	76	2	2009	
221	485	732	276	388	163	206	394	79	2	2010	
99	77	126	425	362	76	186	378	1	15	2000	Allemagne
658	151	391	941	1470	353	435	1244	4	354	2007	
847	241	415	1116	1684	415	461	1544	2	407	2008	
654	211	376	777	1617	412	402	1117	9	1	2009	
663	192	399	1063	2052	455	512	1248	2	1	2010	
8	52	87	5140	616	52	407	259	9	0	2000	Economies Développées - Amérique du Nord 2/
25	88	229	6367	1356	160	710	643	8	1	2007	
35	112	343	6662	1595	215	832	870	7	1	2008	
31	130	382	5387	1396	200	721	721	6	0	2009	
27	151	374	6705	1639	226	877	764	15	0	2010	
7	50	82	5084	590	51	394	244	8	...	2000	Etats-Unis
18	79	190	6129	1278	148	672	609	5	...	2007	
23	96	291	6419	1512	199	778	802	6	...	2008	
24	117	334	5226	1301	182	684	669	5	...	2009	
19	137	341	6483	1544	209	824	704	14	...	2010	
51	4	1	0	1	1	0	17	...	0	2000	Europe du Sud-est
292	12	13	12	8	25	3	64	1	0	2007	
384	31	8	11	9	26	4	60	0	0	2008	
240	37	13	11	9	13	4	54	0	0	2009	
233	48	16	27	15	18	4	87	0	0	2010	
9	4	3	10	47	40	2	17	0	0	2000	Communauté d'Etats Indépendants
68	11	15	19	68	125	19	45	0	2	2007	
55	91	30	35	77	222	32	77	0	0	2008	
36	14	9	35	78	233	36	69	0	0	2009	
36	13	14	43	112	152	19	52	0	9	2010	
3	1	1	8	46	37	2	8	...	0	2000	Fédération de Russie
11	10	8	10	65	102	18	40	0	2	2007	
10	84	22	16	72	197	22	73	...	0	2008	
10	13	6	16	71	222	22	57	0	0	2009	
8	10	8	33	97	128	16	36	0	9	2010	

Voir la fin du tableau pour la remarque générale et les notes.

World exports by provenance and destination (Table D)

In million U.S. dollars f.o.b.

Exports to → / ↓ Exports from	Year	World 1/ Monde 1/	Developed economies 2/ Economies développées 2/ Total	Asia-Pacific Asie-Pacifique Total	Japan Japon	Europe Total	Germany Allemagne	North America Amérique du Nord Total	U.S.A. É.-U.	Commonwealth of Independent States Communauté d'Etats Indépendants Total	Europe
Other manufactured metal products (SITC, Rev. 3, 691-695, 699 and 812) *[cont.]*											
Northern Africa	2000	465	411	1	1	408	4	2	1	0	0
	2007	631	346	0	0	337	12	8	7	1	1
	2008	1176	487	6	6	476	24	5	5	3	3
	2009	1177	316	0	0	313	8	3	3	2	1
	2010	1009	342	0	0	338	9	4	3	4	2
Sub-Saharan Africa	2000	638	265	49	31	173	14	42	33	0	0
	2007	1590	520	126	90	321	34	74	59	4	1
	2008	1917	660	153	113	428	29	78	64	2	1
	2009	1423	342	62	32	219	22	62	52	2	2
	2010	1900	467	70	33	289	29	108	98	0	0
South Africa	2000	442	172	30	12	104	13	38	29	0	0
	2007	1091	315	106	71	164	31	45	31	4	1
	2008	1267	306	112	73	143	28	51	37	2	1
	2009	939	214	60	31	108	17	46	36	2	1
	2010	1222	300	68	32	132	27	100	90	0	0
Latin America and the Caribbean	2000	4852	3809	17	7	156	23	3636	3581	0	0
	2007	9298	6771	39	19	543	114	6189	6047	4	3
	2008	10378	6826	63	41	730	118	6033	5891	7	5
	2009	8216	5549	35	24	911	102	4603	4498	1	1
	2010	9011	5948	44	30	1150	127	4753	4617	2	2
Brazil	2000	531	200	12	4	63	9	126	120	0	0
	2007	1542	694	26	14	300	69	368	346	3	3
	2008	2076	896	49	37	457	70	390	369	6	4
	2009	1951	1069	25	20	756	73	289	277	1	0
	2010	2168	1246	32	25	938	82	276	266	1	1
Eastern Asia	2000	16396	10611	1974	1604	3084	668	5553	5130	62	44
	2007	55368	32530	6086	4628	12509	2282	13934	12647	1872	1482
	2008	64822	35386	6977	5128	14289	2625	14120	12760	2952	2260
	2009	50231	24773	5372	3980	9377	1804	10024	8987	1818	1143
	2010	60498	31280	6694	4774	11966	2433	12620	11225	2466	1853
China	2000	5952	3677	780	653	1193	248	1704	1585	33	18
	2007	36947	22296	3894	2878	9112	1554	9290	8407	1657	1291
	2008	44955	24395	4535	3176	10584	1825	9275	8308	2682	2017
	2009	33479	16719	3422	2413	6751	1244	6545	5826	1607	992
	2010	41329	21137	4224	2786	8486	1640	8428	7430	2116	1553
Southern Asia	2000	894	515	34	9	236	40	245	233	14	3
	2007	3115	1737	96	29	986	227	656	599	73	21
	2008	4313	2134	116	35	1258	309	760	686	101	33
	2009	3162	1431	93	22	840	239	499	448	58	19
	2010	3874	1930	102	28	1170	302	657	595	58	18
South-Eastern Asia	2000	3198	1309	578	468	382	96	349	317	6	2
	2007	9631	3850	1889	1473	1038	213	923	843	31	27
	2008	12602	4644	2422	1669	1213	242	1009	942	69	41
	2009	11280	4569	2886	1370	985	212	698	644	65	24
	2010	12426	5053	2527	1689	1649	313	877	791	42	27
Western Asia	2000	1801	1016	43	27	677	156	296	263	73	27
	2007	7599	3037	106	57	2378	543	553	537	663	340
	2008	9623	3849	145	57	2776	695	929	908	919	481
	2009	8668	2550	80	33	2016	467	454	437	642	215
	2010	8796	3104	136	77	2399	621	569	546	787	266
Oceania	2000	9	7	2	0	3	2	2	2	...	...
	2007	16	10	9	0	1	.	0	0	0	0
	2008	14	8	6	0	2	0	0	0	0	0
	2009	35	25	9	0	15	1	1	0	0	0
	2010	15	8	8	0	1	0	0	0	0	0

For general note and footnotes see end of table

Exportations mondiales par provenance et destination (Tableau D)

En millions de dollars E.-U. f.o.b.

South-Eastern Europe Europe du Sud-est	Northern Africa Afrique septentrio-nale	Sub-Saharan Africa Afrique du Nord	Latin America and the Caribbean Amérique latine et Caraïbes	Eastern Asia Asie orientale	Southern Asia Asie méridionale	South-eastern Asia Asie du Sud-est	Western Asia Asie occidentale	Oceania Océanie	Others 4/ Autre 4/	⟵ Exportations vers Année	Exportations en provence de ↓
											Autres produits en métal manufacturés (CTCI, Rev. 3, 691-695, 699 et 812) *[suite]*
0	18	11	7	1	0	0	13	0	3	2000	Afrique du Nord
0	158	65	1	2	1	1	48	0	8	2007	
3	298	146	2	1	3	1	225	0	9	2008	
2	421	144	2	2	3	4	267	0	14	2009	
3	329	140	1	4	2	1	176	0	6	2010	
0	1	306	17	14	5	13	15	0	1	2000	Afrique subsaharienne
0	6	791	86	51	7	25	81	0	19	2007	
2	8	1054	43	46	9	44	32	1	17	2008	
26	13	848	37	64	11	32	34	1	14	2009	
1	8	1136	68	120	18	29	36	2	14	2010	
0	1	211	16	11	5	12	11	0	1	2000	Afrique du sud
0	4	596	85	20	5	22	24	0	15	2007	
0	5	825	32	12	8	42	28	1	6	2008	
0	4	623	30	11	9	14	25	0	7	2009	
0	4	801	43	11	9	23	23	2	4	2010	
0	4	18	977	7	10	12	12	1	2	2000	Amérique latine et Caraïbes
1	13	84	2193	63	38	60	32	2	37	2007	
2	27	192	3035	70	49	82	56	1	30	2008	
6	14	110	2345	60	22	69	25	1	15	2009	
3	8	78	2709	142	29	46	35	1	10	2010	
0	2	14	294	4	2	4	10	1	...	2000	Brésil
1	10	73	660	26	21	31	22	1	...	2007	
1	11	172	829	34	30	51	46	1	...	2008	
4	8	95	691	23	11	33	14	1	...	2009	
1	6	65	755	34	13	31	14	1	...	2010	
11	89	244	482	2910	269	1232	468	18	1	2000	Asie orientale
193	458	1698	1904	7892	1935	3916	2929	41	1	2007	
282	661	2116	2717	9067	2210	5067	4282	83	1	2008	
149	761	2059	2154	7541	2355	4320	4163	136	1	2009	
176	1017	2196	2950	9003	2679	5515	3089	126	0	2010	
7	57	146	195	1095	108	387	242	4	...	2000	Chine
163	376	1203	1354	4254	1342	2314	1961	26	...	2007	
251	520	1929	2054	5181	1603	3258	3015	68	...	2008	
119	543	1856	1604	4157	1671	2748	2333	123	...	2009	
137	678	2023	2284	4813	1934	3664	2438	105	...	2010	
1	17	51	20	27	41	58	150	0	0	2000	Asie méridionale
16	73	280	53	50	159	153	517	1	3	2007	
17	102	473	96	195	203	193	791	2	6	2008	
7	89	383	61	64	193	169	629	1	76	2009	
8	92	406	110	73	256	191	684	1	65	2010	
2	13	37	26	345	81	1298	68	13	0	2000	Asie Sud-est
5	41	175	144	988	312	3578	440	66	1	2007	
9	57	261	247	1201	465	4965	625	55	2	2008	
14	61	675	197	1110	333	3745	460	50	2	2009	
23	96	231	235	1466	480	4320	402	76	2	2010	
34	54	48	28	41	51	11	395	...	50	2000	Asie occidentale
414	336	330	66	99	323	53	2051	0	226	2007	
507	482	442	110	144	375	55	2362	0	376	2008	
327	545	393	73	84	446	68	3132	0	408	2009	
295	587	370	129	584	650	77	1675	3	536	2010	
...	...	0	0	0	0	0	...	2	0	2000	Océanie
0	...	0	0	0	0	1	0	5	0	2007	
0	0	0	0	0	0	0	0	5	0	2008	
0	0	0	1	3	0	1	0	4	1	2009	
0	0	0	0	0	0	0	0	4	1	2010	

Voir la fin du tableau pour la remarque générale et les notes.

World exports by provenance and destination (Table D)

In million U.S. dollars f.o.b.

Exports to → / ↓ Exports from	Year	World 1/ Monde 1/	Developed economies 2/ Economies développées 2/								Commonwealth of Independent States Communauté d'Etats Indépendants	
				Asia-Pacific Asie-Pacifique		Europe		North America Amérique du Nord				
			Total	Total	Japan Japon	Total	Germany Allemagne	Total	U.S.A. É.-U.		Total	Europe
Clothing (SITC, Rev. 3, 84)												
World 1/	2000	202021	162106	20995	18604	83163	19915	57949	54390		3159	2790
	2007	362857	273588	26635	22311	163643	30389	83309	74909		20890	16185
	2008	379630	289145	28505	23667	179977	33070	80663	72763		24544	14617
	2009	332366	260454	27724	23316	160553	31042	72178	65353		14545	9024
	2010	370111	285868	30201	24881	172452	34469	83215	75521		17578	11534
Developed Economies - Asia-Pacific 2/	2000	846	450	169	7	138	26	142	136		1	1
	2007	931	578	275	6	171	22	132	124		1	1
	2008	994	567	276	5	179	19	111	103		3	3
	2009	823	465	249	5	143	21	73	66		2	2
	2010	934	530	294	5	151	22	86	76		3	3
Japan	2000	534	222	5	.	119	21	98	92		1	0
	2007	523	236	7	.	132	18	97	93		1	1
	2008	591	237	11	.	147	16	79	75		2	2
	2009	484	179	7	.	118	18	55	52		2	1
	2010	531	191	8	.	121	19	62	58		3	3
Developed Economies - Europe 2/	2000	52826	46908	1561	1442	42208	9553	3139	2881		993	955
	2007	100025	84697	2097	1830	78736	11712	3864	3315		5550	5246
	2008	109970	91537	2141	1826	85617	12696	3779	3205		6845	6470
	2009	94518	80074	1756	1521	75625	11946	2694	2266		4524	4218
	2010	97034	82510	1747	1483	77885	12707	2877	2426		4540	4208
France	2000	5303	4353	329	318	3698	610	325	291		66	63
	2007	10795	8891	356	324	8057	938	478	406		445	420
	2008	11635	9455	370	335	8608	1071	477	408		540	508
	2009	10042	8265	305	278	7584	1087	376	322		347	319
	2010	9996	8145	355	322	7326	1029	464	395		336	297
Germany	2000	6852	6348	96	80	6043	.	209	166		165	156
	2007	16011	14084	125	67	13615	.	344	221		1231	1163
	2008	18138	15882	142	73	15389	.	351	224		1428	1355
	2009	16490	14813	128	72	14462	.	223	138		942	891
	2010	16971	15413	115	54	15108	.	189	113		838	785
Developed Economies - North America 2/	2000	10706	3691	509	477	429	55	2754	1997		7	5
	2007	5885	3725	341	271	730	119	2653	1382		19	16
	2008	5730	3739	374	281	792	132	2573	1070		24	21
	2009	5187	3298	366	278	737	117	2195	832		16	14
	2010	5850	3688	405	301	804	105	2479	951		25	20
United States	2000	8629	1635	495	465	383	50	757	.		5	3
	2007	4297	2193	320	258	604	78	1270	.		14	11
	2008	4457	2527	354	268	672	98	1501	.		17	14
	2009	4180	2342	348	265	634	89	1361	.		12	10
	2010	4674	2574	379	289	671	79	1525	.		20	16
South-Eastern Europe	2000	3689	3635	1	1	3393	1091	240	233		7	7
	2007	7870	7666	1	1	7570	1962	95	78		23	22
	2008	7905	7602	2	2	7535	2041	65	52		26	25
	2009	6224	5903	3	3	5866	1603	33	25		22	21
	2010	6129	5910	3	2	5875	1646	33	25		28	26
Commonwealth of Independent States	2000	1070	888	0	0	700	318	188	184		132	124
	2007	1745	1229	0	0	1193	350	35	32		429	382
	2008	1877	1095	0	0	1074	314	21	18		662	618
	2009	1508	923	0	0	889	279	34	32		479	441
	2010	1789	911	0	0	894	273	17	16		778	753
Russian Federation	2000	234	208	0	0	140	53	68	68		10	4
	2007	144	94	0	0	93	8	1	1		44	14
	2008	116	67	0	0	66	9	1	1		43	13
	2009	99	53	0	0	52	6	0	0		36	10
	2010	98	68	0	0	67	15	1	0		24	11

For general note and footnotes see end of table

Exportations mondiales par provenance et destination (Tableau D)

En millions de dollars E.-U. f.o.b.

South-Eastern Europe Europe du Sud-est	Northern Africa Afrique septentrio-nale	Sub-Saharan Africa Afrique du Nord	Latin America and the Caribbean Amérique latine et Caraïbes	Eastern Asia Asie orientale	Southern Asia Asie méridionale	South-eastern Asia Asie du Sud-est	Western Asia Asie occidentale	Oceania Océanie	Others 4/ Autre 4/	← Exportations vers Année	Exportations en provenance de ↓
				Vêtements (CTCI, Rev. 3, 84)							
1087	1488	1280	11357	13962	310	2243	4726	105	198	2000	Monde 1/
2788	3080	4421	12868	20399	1246	7466	14286	137	1690	2007	
3102	2684	3939	13068	19164	1432	6641	14071	143	1696	2008	
2490	2764	3745	10077	15794	1468	5824	13638	124	1442	2009	
2524	2857	4294	13542	18032	1964	6977	14923	150	1402	2010	
0	1	2	2	336	2	35	6	12	0	2000	Economies Développées - Asie-Pacifique 2/
0	0	6	2	269	2	40	13	17	0	2007	
0	0	6	4	327	1	46	17	21	0	2008	
0	0	6	3	273	1	43	14	16	1	2009	
0	0	6	3	298	2	58	12	21	0	2010	
0	1	1	2	280	1	23	4	0	...	2000	Japon
0	0	2	1	252	1	23	6	0	...	2007	
0	0	2	3	308	0	32	7	0	...	2008	
0	0	2	2	261	0	31	6	0	...	2009	
0	0	1	2	284	1	43	6	0	...	2010	
924	841	127	436	1049	45	143	1296	32	33	2000	Economies Développées - Europe 2/
1703	904	249	858	2334	102	375	3146	41	67	2007	
2051	963	320	971	2695	156	423	3884	46	79	2008	
1689	925	271	794	2193	118	369	3489	37	35	2009	
1647	850	283	820	2594	133	400	3189	43	24	2010	
101	194	41	48	235	2	29	214	21	0	2000	France
72	306	85	49	395	8	47	455	34	8	2007	
83	318	94	56	426	11	59	538	40	16	2008	
63	288	92	43	380	10	56	464	33	2	2009	
70	266	101	43	479	12	74	429	38	2	2010	
64	35	9	20	83	4	15	96	0	12	2000	Allemagne
140	38	26	45	210	11	31	194	0	0	2007	
185	38	26	48	235	13	37	247	0	0	2008	
177	37	23	39	203	11	33	210	1	0	2009	
161	48	22	39	181	14	29	225	0	0	2010	
2	6	10	6778	89	6	46	66	3	0	2000	Economies Développées - Amérique du Nord 2/
2	4	24	1689	205	14	42	155	5	0	2007	
3	7	25	1413	230	12	55	216	6	0	2008	
3	6	28	1368	207	13	54	188	6	0	2009	
2	7	30	1539	250	30	62	210	6	...	2010	
2	6	10	6772	85	5	46	59	3	...	2000	Etats-Unis
2	3	22	1676	190	13	39	139	5	...	2007	
3	5	22	1402	216	11	50	199	5	...	2008	
3	5	27	1358	193	12	51	171	6	...	2009	
2	5	28	1527	231	29	58	194	6	...	2010	
33	0	0	1	1	...	0	13	...	0	2000	Europe du Sud-est
130	0	1	0	5	1	0	42	0	0	2007	
181	2	1	0	5	1	0	86	0	0	2008	
137	1	1	0	7	1	1	150	0	0	2009	
139	1	1	0	10	1	1	38	0	0	2010	
1	0	0	5	14	0	1	29	0	0	2000	Communauté d'Etats Indépendants
36	1	1	0	2	1	0	45	0	1	2007	
65	1	0	0	2	1	1	48	0	2	2008	
38	3	0	2	5	5	0	52	0	1	2009	
35	1	0	2	2	2	1	54	0	2	2010	
0	0	0	0	14	0	1	1	...	0	2000	Fédération de Russie
0	0	0	0	1	1	0	2	0	1	2007	
0	1	0	0	1	1	0	2	...	1	2008	
0	1	0	0	2	5	0	2	0	1	2009	
0	0	0	0	1	0	1	1	0	1	2010	

Voir la fin du tableau pour la remarque générale et les notes.

World exports by provenance and destination (Table D)

In million U.S. dollars f.o.b.

Exports to →			Developed economies 2/ Economies développées 2/							Commonwealth of Independent States Communauté d'Etats Indépendants	
				Asia-Pacific Asie-Pacifique		Europe		North America Amérique du Nord			
↓ Exports from	Year	World 1/ Monde 1/	Total	Total	Japan Japon	Total	Germany Allemagne	Total	U.S.A. É.-U.	Total	Europe
					Clothing (SITC, Rev. 3, 84) ***[cont.]***						
Northern Africa	2000	4942	4857	4	4	4579	640	274	268	0	0
	2007	7268	7197	4	2	7048	601	146	141	2	2
	2008	7960	7824	4	2	7476	678	344	337	1	1
	2009	7527	7322	6	3	6603	599	713	704	1	1
	2010	7374	7205	5	3	6457	591	742	730	1	1
Sub-Saharan Africa	2000	1994	1786	6	4	938	73	841	829	0	0
	2007	2268	1908	5	2	1202	125	702	690	1	1
	2008	2593	2077	7	1	1341	129	729	716	1	1
	2009	1840	1373	6	1	854	82	513	504	1	1
	2010	1710	1327	9	1	742	85	576	568	1	1
South Africa	2000	218	181	2	1	62	2	117	117	0	0
	2007	119	61	2	0	30	3	30	28	0	0
	2008	119	45	2	0	23	1	20	19	0	0
	2009	100	34	2	0	20	1	11	11	0	0
	2010	101	28	3	0	17	1	9	8	0	0
Latin America and the Caribbean	2000	11700	10845	50	12	206	57	10590	10529	1	1
	2007	14458	10770	37	23	405	87	10328	10213	4	4
	2008	15063	10729	38	24	401	90	10290	10186	3	3
	2009	11760	8695	88	73	340	57	8268	8168	1	1
	2010	12743	9272	38	22	310	50	8924	8797	2	1
Brazil	2000	282	140	4	4	35	12	101	99	...	...
	2007	281	148	10	9	65	7	73	70	1	1
	2008	252	108	12	10	55	4	42	38	1	1
	2009	173	66	9	7	35	2	22	20	0	0
	2010	157	51	7	6	27	2	17	15	0	0
Eastern Asia	2000	70341	50636	16462	14772	13827	2997	20347	18846	1325	1171
	2007	149027	93331	21922	18596	34580	7126	36829	31902	13900	9820
	2008	152369	101152	23377	19689	43292	8775	34483	30444	15912	6692
	2009	132759	93803	22800	19436	38583	8287	32419	29023	8736	3774
	2010	156742	108239	24481	20435	45153	10352	38605	34865	11076	5684
China	2000	36071	22838	12571	11513	4943	923	5324	4780	1230	1087
	2007	115520	65387	19022	16498	23712	4770	22652	18795	13774	9702
	2008	120405	74346	20545	17686	32276	6318	21526	18566	15751	6542
	2009	107264	72117	20068	17441	29576	6212	22473	19941	8609	3656
	2010	129820	85789	21737	18450	35988	8208	28065	25208	10897	5517
Southern Asia	2000	15434	13611	265	167	6116	1370	7230	6784	417	283
	2007	26676	24003	254	153	13694	3247	10054	9262	268	106
	2008	27064	23822	305	170	13960	3253	9557	8799	270	87
	2009	27730	24446	331	188	14925	3701	9189	8424	163	63
	2010	30501	26384	526	302	16081	3721	9777	8880	266	163
South-Eastern Asia	2000	18844	16506	1455	1311	5098	1191	9954	9528	63	60
	2007	28056	24657	1611	1409	6636	1570	16409	15792	200	198
	2008	30275	26015	1891	1652	7023	1603	17101	16302	284	275
	2009	27025	23295	2045	1789	6393	1501	14857	14178	201	196
	2010	32555	28003	2612	2307	7619	1825	17772	16926	252	242
Western Asia	2000	8580	7574	14	9	5378	2544	2182	2109	212	184
	2007	17607	13745	25	14	11660	3468	2059	1975	492	387
	2008	16741	12879	27	14	11243	3340	1609	1531	512	421
	2009	14407	10808	33	18	9586	2849	1189	1130	399	294
	2010	15666	11837	33	19	10478	3090	1326	1260	607	430
Oceania	2000	1049	720	500	397	153	2	68	68	0	0
	2007	1044	83	63	6	18	0	2	2	0	0
	2008	1088	106	62	2	43	2	1	1	0	0
	2009	1060	51	42	0	9	2	1	0	0	0
	2010	1085	51	48	0	2	1	1	1	0	0

For general note and footnotes see end of table

Exportations mondiales par provenance et destination (Tableau D)

En millions de dollars E.-U. f.o.b.

South-Eastern Europe Europe du Sud-est	Northern Africa Afrique septentrio-nale	Sub-Saharan Africa Afrique du Nord	Latin America and the Caribbean Amérique latine et Caraïbes	Eastern Asia Asie orientale	Southern Asia Asie méridionale	South-eastern Asia Asie du Sud-est	Western Asia Asie occidentale	Oceania Océanie	Others 4/ Autre 4/	Année	← Exportations vers / Exportations en provenance de ↓
				Vêtements (CTCI, Rev. 3, 84) *[suite]*							
0	10	19	1	1	0	0	13	0	40	2000	Afrique du Nord
0	10	21	4	5	1	1	20	0	6	2007	
2	24	21	4	8	2	1	66	0	7	2008	
1	37	53	4	6	1	1	84	0	16	2009	
1	15	34	5	11	1	1	75	0	25	2010	
0	0	161	6	4	1	1	33	0	3	2000	Afrique subsaharienne
0	0	323	6	8	1	2	16	0	2	2007	
0	0	466	7	19	3	1	16	0	4	2008	
0	0	434	5	11	2	1	12	0	1	2009	
1	1	341	6	9	5	1	18	0	1	2010	
0	0	26	3	1	0	0	7	0	0	2000	Afrique du sud
0	0	39	1	2	0	1	14	0	1	2007	
0	0	56	1	2	1	0	13	0	0	2008	
0	0	54	0	2	1	0	9	0	1	2009	
0	0	58	1	1	1	0	10	0	0	2010	
0	0	2	821	6	0	1	8	0	17	2000	Amérique latine et Caraïbes
0	0	12	3599	23	0	4	12	0	33	2007	
1	0	20	4231	21	1	6	15	0	36	2008	
0	0	15	2999	17	1	7	13	0	13	2009	
0	0	11	3410	20	0	6	10	0	12	2010	
0	0	1	139	0	0	0	1	0	...	2000	Brésil
0	0	10	112	1	0	1	8	0	...	2007	
0	0	18	114	0	0	1	9	0	...	2008	
0	0	14	84	1	0	0	7	0	...	2009	
0	0	10	90	1	0	0	5	0	...	2010	
83	388	530	2581	11820	126	1385	1431	27	8	2000	Asie orientale
478	1542	3036	5693	16791	745	5973	7500	38	0	2007	
317	1030	2322	5158	14794	796	4945	5909	34	0	2008	
254	1157	2180	3743	12032	766	4346	5709	34	0	2009	
234	1441	2859	6302	13263	1205	5293	6788	41	0	2010	
81	277	287	1316	8384	52	611	991	5	...	2000	Chine
467	1528	2715	5172	13784	639	5052	6983	20	...	2007	
303	1014	1999	4692	12239	680	3996	5364	20	...	2008	
242	1135	1958	3419	10294	666	3526	5277	20	...	2009	
227	1415	2670	5928	11189	1086	4268	6329	22	...	2010	
3	9	129	157	85	48	85	882	6	1	2000	Asie méridionale
15	34	291	280	103	124	131	1412	7	8	2007	
22	34	301	335	131	163	150	1818	8	11	2008	
15	29	330	342	137	146	186	1907	6	22	2009	
33	33	331	501	209	192	203	2331	8	8	2010	
8	51	241	262	515	45	536	592	22	4	2000	Asie Sud-est
24	37	252	692	608	80	885	584	24	14	2007	
29	46	259	902	854	89	1000	759	24	14	2008	
20	56	221	800	859	93	801	650	23	7	2009	
21	67	240	934	1273	113	940	673	27	12	2010	
33	183	59	8	19	37	7	357	0	92	2000	Asie occidentale
400	548	205	31	42	176	12	1338	0	618	2007	
432	576	197	37	76	207	14	1234	0	576	2008	
333	549	205	17	46	321	14	1367	0	348	2009	
409	441	157	19	90	280	11	1524	0	290	2010	
...	...	0	298	24	0	3	0	3	1	2000	Océanie
0	...	0	13	3	0	0	1	3	939	2007	
0	...	0	5	4	0	0	3	4	967	2008	
...	...	3	0	1	0	2	4	2	996	2009	
0	...	0	0	3	0	0	2	2	1026	2010	

Voir la fin du tableau pour la remarque générale et les notes.

World exports by provenance and destination (Table D)

General Note

Table D is based on data of UN Comtrade as of mid November 2011. An earlier version of this table has been published in Volume I of the 2010 ITSY which has been produced earlier this year. The totals of imports and exports presented in table A and D are not necessarily identical as table A is mainly based on the data of the IMF's International Financial Statistics (IFS) which is a different data collection system with different aims, procedures, timetable and sources for update and maintenance than UN Comtrade (see the introduction for details). Nevertheless, discrepancies between both tables are in general minor and usually do not affect the overall information provided. A systematic comparison of the figures from both sources (which includes the description of known and relevant conceptual differences) is available at http://unstats.un.org/unsd/trade/imts/annual%20totals.htm.

Overall, the discrepancies in the world total or world aggregate of exports in table A and table D is less than 0.5 percent for all years shown, which is minor, given the differences between the two sources. For further information on sources and presentation of table D as well as for a brief table description please see the introduction, paragraphs 6 - 20 and paragraph 24.

1/ Exports for which country of destination is not available are included in the totals for the 'World' and in region "Others" (see footnote number 4 for further explanation).
2/ This classification is intended for statistical convenience and does not, necessarily, express a judgment about the stage reached by a particular country in the development process.
3/ Section 9 of the SITC, which comprises commodities and transactions not classified elsewhere, is included in the total trade but is not shown.
4/ The region "Others" as destination for exports contains the following trading partners: Antarctica, bunkers, free zones, confidential and not elsewhere specified countries

Exportations mondiales par provenance et destination (Tableau D)

Remarque générale

Tableau D est basée sur les données de UN Comtrade telles que disponible mi-novembre 2011. Une version antérieure de cette table est publiée dans le volume I de l'annuaire 2010 ITSY qui a été produit plus tôt cette année. Les importations et exportations totales présentées dans les tableaux A et D ne sont pas nécessairement identiques du fait que le tableau A est basé principalement sur les données des Statistiques Financières Internationales (IFS) du FMI qui est un différent système de collecte des données avec des objectifs, des procédures, un calendrier et des sources de mise à jour et de maintenance différents de ceux de UN Comtrade sur lequel le tableau D est basé (voir l'introduction pour les détails). Toutefois, les écarts entre les deux tableaux sont en général mineurs et n'affectent pas substantiellement l'information fournie. Une comparaison systématique des données de ces deux sources (incluant une description des différences conceptuelles pertinentes connues) est disponible à
http://unstats.un.org/unsd/trade/imts/annual%20totals.htm.

En général, la différence entre les totaux des exportations mondiales présentés dans les tableaux A et D est inférieure à 0.5 pour cent pur chacune des années publiées, ce qui est mineur étant donné les différences entre les deux sources. Pour plus d'information sur les sources et la présentation du tableau
D ainsi qu'une brève description, veuillez vous référer aux paragraphes 6-20 et 24 de l'introduction.

1/ Pour la composition des régions géographiques, se référer à http://unstats.un.org/unsd/mdg/default.aspx
2/ Cette classification est utilisée pour plus de commodité dans la présentation des statistiques et n'implique pas nécessairement un jugement quant au stade de développement auquel est parvenu un pays donné.
3/ Section 9 de la CTCI, qui représente les articles et transactions non classes ailleurs est comprise dans le commerce total mais n'est pas présentée séparément dans ce tableau.
4/ La région "Autres" comme destination des exportations comprend les partenaires commerciaux suivants: Antarctique, combustibles de soute, zones franches, partenaires confidentiels ou non spécifiés ailleurs

Growth of world exports by provenance and destination (Table E)

Annual average rate: in per cent

Exports to ⟶ / ↓ Exports from	Year	World 1/ Monde 1/	Developed economies 2/ Economies développées 2/ Total	Asia-Pacific Asie-Pacifique Total	Japan Japon	Europe Total	Germany Allemagne	North America Amérique du Nord Total	U.S.A. É.-U.	Commonwealth of Independent States Communauté d'Etats Indépendants Total	Europe
Origin of exports of major commodity classes											
0-9 All commodities 3/	2000/2010	9.0	6.8	6.1	4.9	7.8	8.7	4.6	5.0	15.0	14.3
	2006/2007	15.3	14.5	11.1	10.5	16.1	18.4	11.0	12.1	19.0	18.5
	2007/2008	15.3	11.4	13.5	9.4	11.3	10.3	10.9	11.8	43.0	34.1
	2008/2009	-22.3	-22.7	-24.0	-25.7	-22.7	-23.1	-21.8	-18.7	-38.1	-36.4
	2009/2010	21.2	16.5	32.7	32.6	12.5	12.7	21.3	20.9	31.4	31.4
0&1 Food, live animals, beverages and tobacco	2000/2010	9.6	8.4	7.7	8.3	9.1	11.2	6.4	6.5	20.9	20.5
	2006/2007	19.4	18.9	8.6	15.4	19.2	17.2	21.2	24.1	45.8	42.9
	2007/2008	18.9	17.0	16.7	9.5	15.6	20.7	22.1	24.0	34.1	37.5
	2008/2009	-8.5	-11.4	-9.7	0.7	-10.4	-8.7	-15.8	-16.1	-9.4	-5.7
	2009/2010	11.2	8.2	16.4	18.5	6.0	3.6	13.4	15.1	2.8	-2.0
2&4 Crude materials, oils and fats, (fuels excluded)	2000/2010	12.5	10.6	16.8	12.6	10.0	10.8	8.6	10.9	11.9	11.8
	2006/2007	22.3	20.0	17.0	14.6	20.2	20.8	21.1	25.2	27.1	29.4
	2007/2008	19.2	16.7	30.3	14.4	11.3	12.7	18.5	24.0	25.7	24.2
	2008/2009	-24.2	-24.2	-14.8	-12.9	-28.1	-33.2	-23.4	-19.6	-35.2	-37.6
	2009/2010	40.2	36.4	58.6	22.1	29.7	33.5	33.0	31.2	32.0	35.8
3 Mineral fuels, lubricants and related material	2000/2010	13.0	12.2	17.2	24.0	11.0	11.9	13.3	19.7	18.2	17.3
	2006/2007	15.1	9.8	16.5	57.4	7.3	7.0	15.0	20.3	39.6	45.1
	2007/2008	42.5	47.1	91.8	102.3	38.1	23.8	56.6	82.4	58.7	42.6
	2008/2009	-37.7	-37.2	-29.3	-43.9	-38.5	-38.3	-37.4	-28.5	-41.1	-38.3
	2009/2010	28.1	29.3	30.1	23.9	26.1	3.3	36.3	47.5	33.4	34.0
5 Chemicals	2000/2010	11.4	10.2	8.3	8.4	10.8	10.4	8.9	9.0	12.7	11.0
	2006/2007	17.9	17.0	14.0	12.7	17.8	17.1	14.6	13.9	27.3	25.7
	2007/2008	13.9	11.2	6.4	6.1	10.8	16.5	14.7	16.0	55.8	56.4
	2008/2009	-14.1	-12.9	-11.4	-11.2	-12.9	-19.7	-13.6	-10.9	-43.2	-46.6
	2009/2010	17.1	12.4	25.9	27.7	9.8	8.9	18.5	18.4	33.1	31.9
7 Machinery and transport equipment	2000/2010	7.0	4.4	3.4	3.3	6.3	7.9	0.5	0.9	10.4	10.0
	2006/2007	12.8	11.7	9.8	9.7	13.5	14.3	7.5	8.6	30.5	29.9
	2007/2008	7.3	5.8	7.3	7.2	7.1	7.6	0.9	3.7	26.7	27.5
	2008/2009	-22.2	-27.4	-30.1	-30.3	-25.1	-25.9	-32.8	-34.1	-38.1	-37.0
	2009/2010	22.1	17.4	35.0	35.6	12.5	16.5	22.0	22.4	22.6	20.5
6&8 Other manufactured goods	2000/2010	8.1	6.2	5.8	5.8	7.0	8.7	3.8	4.4	10.9	9.6
	2006/2007	16.1	14.8	8.7	7.4	17.3	15.9	7.8	9.0	22.6	21.3
	2007/2008	9.4	7.7	10.5	12.3	8.0	8.7	5.3	8.2	13.1	12.1
	2008/2009	-21.6	-23.6	-22.3	-21.9	-24.4	-22.8	-20.5	-17.2	-39.0	-38.8
	2009/2010	20.0	15.2	31.3	32.5	12.5	11.7	18.6	18.1	27.2	25.4
Destination of exports of major commodity classes											
0-9 All commodities 3/	2000/2010	9.0	6.8	6.2	5.0	7.9	7.7	4.6	4.2	17.8	17.4
	2006/2007	15.3	13.2	13.7	13.2	16.3	14.3	6.0	5.5	39.2	39.3
	2007/2008	15.3	10.9	5.9	2.3	13.3	15.2	6.8	3.9	28.2	27.3
	2008/2009	-22.3	-25.1	-27.4	-30.2	-24.6	-23.0	-25.4	-26.3	-39.5	-43.0
	2009/2010	21.2	16.6	23.9	24.6	13.5	16.2	22.4	22.6	27.5	33.0
0&1 Food, live animals, beverages and tobacco	2000/2010	9.6	8.1	4.1	2.8	9.1	8.1	7.3	6.8	16.3	15.9
	2006/2007	19.4	16.6	7.9	5.3	19.7	18.3	9.9	7.9	25.5	22.2
	2007/2008	18.9	13.8	15.9	15.3	14.9	16.2	8.3	7.0	30.8	30.3
	2008/2009	-8.5	-9.4	-10.4	-11.2	-10.0	-9.5	-6.4	-7.5	-23.0	-23.9
	2009/2010	11.2	6.7	13.9	13.0	4.5	5.0	11.9	11.6	22.8	25.5
2&4 Crude materials, oils and fats, (fuels excluded)	2000/2010	12.5	8.3	9.1	9.2	9.2	9.5	4.2	3.7	14.0	13.4
	2006/2007	22.3	17.6	15.2	15.0	21.2	21.1	5.9	3.5	34.1	31.8
	2007/2008	19.2	12.8	10.3	9.1	13.4	14.9	12.5	13.8	37.7	42.1
	2008/2009	-24.2	-32.9	-30.8	-30.4	-33.0	-31.8	-34.6	-36.0	-37.4	-38.9
	2009/2010	40.2	37.4	52.4	54.0	34.9	36.8	34.0	34.1	29.0	32.6
3 Mineral fuels, lubricants and related material	2000/2010	13.0	10.3	5.9	4.5	12.2	8.6	9.0	7.1	13.1	12.9
	2006/2007	15.1	14.5	26.4	27.5	12.8	0.2	10.9	11.1	75.7	83.6
	2007/2008	42.5	32.5	-5.7	-10.4	47.7	40.4	30.5	14.5	65.7	74.1
	2008/2009	-37.7	-43.2	-54.1	-56.6	-40.1	-42.7	-44.4	-47.0	-36.7	-36.3
	2009/2010	28.1	24.8	26.5	25.3	23.5	25.2	27.1	28.6	20.4	25.5
5 Chemicals	2000/2010	11.4	10.3	9.7	9.4	10.7	11.5	9.1	9.4	19.8	20.1
	2006/2007	17.9	16.3	12.2	9.6	18.8	23.0	8.8	8.7	28.1	27.2
	2007/2008	13.9	11.3	17.0	16.8	11.1	12.0	10.4	10.7	23.4	23.3
	2008/2009	-14.1	-14.0	-11.6	-11.1	-14.7	-14.1	-12.2	-12.8	-24.8	-27.4
	2009/2010	17.1	11.5	23.1	25.3	10.0	7.3	13.1	13.3	27.0	30.7
7 Machinery and transport equipment	2000/2010	7.0	4.3	5.2	3.7	5.3	6.6	2.5	2.5	20.9	21.4
	2006/2007	12.8	9.8	9.1	6.6	13.5	13.8	3.0	2.3	43.8	45.6
	2007/2008	7.3	3.6	7.7	5.0	5.1	8.0	-0.7	-0.9	29.1	30.8
	2008/2009	-22.2	-24.9	-22.8	-23.3	-26.0	-22.2	-23.2	-22.6	-51.5	-55.9
	2009/2010	22.1	17.0	25.9	25.1	12.2	16.1	25.1	24.8	36.6	45.7
6&8 Other manufactured goods	2000/2010	8.1	6.3	5.8	4.8	7.5	6.8	4.0	3.9	17.8	16.5
	2006/2007	16.1	13.9	7.5	4.7	18.8	18.2	4.4	4.0	41.3	40.7
	2007/2008	9.4	6.0	10.2	8.3	7.3	9.0	1.3	0.4	24.7	17.7
	2008/2009	-21.6	-23.3	-18.1	-20.0	-24.2	-23.2	-22.5	-23.0	-37.3	-42.0
	2009/2010	20.0	16.5	19.8	20.6	14.1	17.2	22.0	22.3	20.3	32.3

For general note and footnotes see end of Special Table F.

Croissance des exportations mondiales par provenance et destination (Tableau E)

Taux annuel moyen: en pourcentage

← Exportations vers

South-Eastern Europe Europe du Sud-est	Northern Africa Afrique du Nord	Sub-Sahara Africa Afrique subsahari-enne	Latin America and the Caribbean Amérique latine et Caraïbes	Eastern Asia Asie orientale	Southern Asia Asie méridionale	outh-easter Asia Asie du Sud-est	Western Asia Asie occidentale	Oceania Océanie	Others 4/ Autre 4/	xportations Année ↓		
Provenance des exportations de grandes catégories de marchandises												
16.5	12.5	13.0	9.6	13.4	14.3	9.4	13.0	6.6	0.0	2000/2010	0-9	Tous produits 3/
25.9	15.2	11.3	13.4	18.8	24.3	12.1	14.1	15.3	0.0	2006/2007		
22.2	35.1	33.3	14.9	13.3	22.6	14.4	31.6	14.8	0.0	2007/2008		
-21.6	-34.7	-30.0	-21.3	-15.4	-12.8	-17.5	-27.9	-9.8	0.0	2008/2009		
22.2	21.0	34.0	27.1	29.6	18.8	29.6	17.6	2.0	0.0	2009/2010		
21.6	14.1	10.2	11.6	10.4	12.9	10.7	13.3	8.1	0.0	2000/2010	0&1	Produits alimentaires, boissons et tabacs
31.4	26.0	10.3	18.4	18.3	26.5	20.5	20.1	9.6	0.0	2006/2007		
48.6	45.9	14.6	20.8	10.4	34.0	28.6	15.0	25.7	0.0	2007/2008		
0.3	11.4	12.7	-5.2	0.7	-16.5	-5.5	5.8	-11.2	0.0	2008/2009		
20.9	7.5	10.4	16.9	24.0	18.9	17.8	10.8	2.4	0.0	2009/2010		
14.8	12.1	15.4	17.1	8.6	22.5	16.2	14.3	5.7	0.0	2000/2010	2&4	Matières premières huiles & graisses (combust. exclu.)
18.7	4.2	24.0	27.5	16.2	31.6	27.9	11.6	23.8	0.0	2006/2007		
23.5	88.7	30.3	17.9	20.6	13.4	23.1	29.2	17.2	0.0	2007/2008		
-23.2	-38.5	-18.2	-21.9	-25.9	-13.1	-24.8	-25.4	-33.8	0.0	2008/2009		
43.9	19.4	37.4	50.3	36.5	42.3	50.5	33.3	38.1	0.0	2009/2010		
17.0	12.4	14.2	11.1	14.5	13.9	14.1	11.2	3.2	0.0	2000/2010	3	Combustibles minéraux et produits
9.3	13.9	5.6	9.2	19.4	38.0	10.8	11.7	6.4	0.0	2006/2007		
42.1	32.4	48.5	27.5	49.3	30.5	42.9	35.7	9.5	0.0	2007/2008		
-40.6	-41.7	-39.0	-31.7	-37.3	-37.3	-30.1	-38.8	-42.0	0.0	2008/2009		
25.1	23.5	37.3	27.4	33.5	21.8	36.3	19.6	-0.3	0.0	2009/2010		
15.7	15.5	11.6	11.2	15.4	20.3	14.4	18.1	8.5	0.0	2000/2010	5	Produits chimiques
33.3	18.9	12.1	15.7	25.5	18.4	14.3	21.7	18.8	0.0	2006/2007		
28.3	124.0	42.4	21.9	18.9	25.4	3.2	29.2	24.3	0.0	2007/2008		
-32.0	-37.9	-27.4	-14.0	-17.8	4.7	-10.0	-12.0	-13.3	0.0	2008/2009		
33.6	31.3	16.4	16.1	35.9	21.1	34.1	36.5	18.5	0.0	2009/2010		
25.3	18.1	13.3	6.1	15.1	25.3	6.3	15.3	1.6	0.0	2000/2010	7	Machines et matériels de transports
39.8	16.1	15.6	6.0	18.0	28.9	6.9	28.2	33.3	0.0	2006/2007		
30.5	53.2	30.5	11.9	11.3	42.5	-1.5	14.9	-1.7	0.0	2007/2008		
-6.5	-12.7	-31.6	-23.2	-12.2	8.0	-12.0	-8.9	446.2	0.0	2008/2009		
18.8	26.8	24.2	31.6	31.0	17.4	27.5	7.3	-82.3	0.0	2009/2010		
11.8	8.9	11.6	7.3	11.1	11.3	9.0	12.1	1.3	0.0	2000/2010	6&8	Articles manufacturés divers
21.0	17.5	19.4	9.0	19.2	12.1	14.5	22.8	17.3	0.0	2006/2007		
9.0	31.3	4.2	5.2	11.9	8.7	10.7	20.6	-4.8	0.0	2007/2008		
-30.8	-9.5	-30.1	-24.7	-18.4	0.3	-11.8	-22.2	-4.9	0.0	2008/2009		
18.9	7.8	49.7	22.6	27.1	18.1	24.2	22.3	-1.1	0.0	2009/2010		
Destination des exportations de grandes catégories de marchandises												
15.5	12.6	14.5	9.3	13.9	18.5	9.9	13.0	15.1	16.9	2000/2010	0-9	Tous produits 3/
26.8	29.6	15.9	17.6	16.4	22.4	13.4	19.6	29.0	15.4	2006/2007		
20.3	30.0	24.4	25.3	19.7	22.6	17.5	24.9	38.0	47.0	2007/2008		
-31.5	-12.3	-14.7	-23.2	-13.3	-9.4	-17.8	-18.6	11.2	-6.4	2008/2009		
12.3	10.6	17.8	30.3	35.4	24.6	30.7	14.7	1.2	7.9	2009/2010		
16.7	11.5	14.1	9.8	11.6	15.8	13.1	12.6	9.8	6.3	2000/2010	0&1	Produits alimentaires, boissons et tabacs
34.0	43.0	21.2	27.4	20.1	12.9	28.4	28.1	15.5	27.3	2006/2007		
40.9	31.4	29.9	30.9	20.2	39.8	27.1	33.8	24.2	-5.3	2007/2008		
-7.4	-19.3	-4.3	-14.8	4.0	8.1	-3.6	-1.9	-3.4	29.8	2008/2009		
4.3	27.0	10.4	14.8	30.7	13.0	28.6	10.3	10.4	-10.6	2009/2010		
16.9	15.2	13.5	10.4	21.6	17.6	13.2	16.0	10.2	-9.3	2000/2010	2&4	Matières premières huiles & graisses (combust. exclu.)
30.0	29.5	40.0	20.6	26.5	39.3	27.7	26.1	13.7	21.9	2006/2007		
26.6	58.3	21.6	34.0	24.0	14.5	29.2	39.3	14.0	-51.6	2007/2008		
-36.1	-31.8	-23.0	-36.1	-4.8	-10.3	-20.9	-33.5	3.4	-10.7	2008/2009		
45.7	37.1	36.0	43.7	44.7	31.9	41.6	50.4	5.0	-22.2	2009/2010		
17.0	11.7	21.5	13.0	18.6	19.5	18.5	15.4	11.5	16.8	2000/2010	3	Combustibles minéraux et produits
103.9	43.2	-15.0	17.9	23.8	-6.5	-1.7	-3.4	-0.5	62.6	2006/2007		
42.1	23.4	46.0	54.7	86.6	30.6	36.7	27.9	23.6	80.0	2007/2008		
-55.9	-32.9	-23.0	-36.5	-26.4	-14.1	-28.1	-34.1	-14.2	-39.4	2008/2009		
34.6	22.0	25.6	29.7	38.5	10.9	39.1	25.0	18.5	23.0	2009/2010		
18.3	14.0	13.5	11.3	13.4	18.9	11.8	13.6	14.8	0.9	2000/2010	5	Produits chimiques
25.7	28.7	20.1	21.8	18.5	31.8	17.8	23.2	11.7	9.5	2006/2007		
28.1	24.6	22.7	27.6	8.1	41.3	16.4	16.4	96.9	28.5	2007/2008		
-16.0	-5.4	-13.0	-17.9	-6.7	-14.3	-15.6	-9.6	-23.0	-67.8	2008/2009		
7.5	11.4	15.7	25.3	32.8	26.0	32.0	15.5	15.5	57.5	2009/2010		
16.0	12.4	12.9	8.2	13.1	18.1	6.6	12.1	21.8	0.5	2000/2010	7	Machines et matériels de transports
29.3	28.2	19.0	14.1	13.7	30.3	12.0	20.7	58.5	34.8	2006/2007		
23.5	29.7	21.5	18.2	4.6	15.3	8.8	18.7	49.1	38.6	2007/2008		
-37.0	-5.7	-19.1	-22.9	-9.8	-11.2	-16.5	-22.0	32.4	-19.6	2008/2009		
7.9	4.4	16.3	35.7	35.5	23.1	27.1	14.7	-9.7	-28.2	2009/2010		
13.1	12.7	13.9	8.0	10.3	18.0	11.3	13.1	5.6	4.9	2000/2010	6&8	Articles manufacturés divers
4.8	24.4	26.7	17.0	12.9	34.9	21.2	26.6	11.3	1.8	2006/2007		
20.0	27.6	16.1	18.6	7.1	18.5	17.6	21.7	9.6	-1.8	2007/2008		
-32.7	-4.6	-9.4	-22.2	-14.4	-12.7	-18.3	-17.2	-8.9	-39.8	2008/2009		
9.9	2.6	16.2	31.1	30.7	39.8	30.9	12.3	15.6	17.6	2009/2010		

Voir la fin du Tableau Spécial F pour la remarque générale et les notes.

Structure of world exports by provenance and destination (Table F)

in per cent

SITC Commodity classes ↓ / Origin or destination →		Year	World 1/ Monde 1/	Developed economies 2/ Economies développées 2/ Total	Asia-Pacific Asie-Pacifique Total	Asia-Pacific Asie-Pacifique Japan Japon	Europe Total	Europe Germany Allemagne	North America Amérique du Nord Total	North America Amérique du Nord U.S.A. É.-U.	Commonwealth of Independent States Communauté d'Etats Indépendants Total	Commonwealth of Independent States Communauté d'Etats Indépendants Europe
						Origin of exports of major commodity classes						
0-9	All commodities 3/	2000	100.0	65.1	8.8	7.6	39.6	8.7	16.7	12.3	2.3	2.0
		2007	100.0	57.6	6.4	5.2	39.8	9.6	11.4	8.4	3.6	3.1
		2008	100.0	55.7	6.3	4.9	38.4	9.2	11.0	8.2	4.5	3.6
		2009	100.0	55.4	6.1	4.7	38.2	9.1	11.1	8.5	3.5	2.9
		2010	100.0	53.2	6.7	5.1	35.4	8.5	11.1	8.5	3.8	3.2
0&1	Food, live animals, beverages and tobacco	2000	100.0	67.6	5.1	0.5	46.0	5.6	16.4	12.2	0.8	0.7
		2007	100.0	65.1	4.2	0.4	48.2	6.9	12.6	9.2	2.2	1.7
		2008	100.0	64.0	4.2	0.4	46.9	7.0	13.0	9.6	2.5	2.0
		2009	100.0	62.0	4.1	0.4	45.9	7.0	12.0	8.8	2.4	2.0
		2010	100.0	60.3	4.3	0.5	43.8	6.5	12.2	9.1	2.3	1.8
2&4	Crude materials, oils and fats, (fuels excluded)	2000	100.0	61.7	8.1	1.6	28.6	4.4	24.9	14.3	4.4	3.4
		2007	100.0	54.6	8.5	1.6	27.8	4.7	18.3	11.9	4.8	3.8
		2008	100.0	53.4	9.2	1.6	26.0	4.4	18.2	12.4	5.1	4.0
		2009	100.0	53.4	10.4	1.8	24.6	3.9	18.4	13.2	4.4	3.3
		2010	100.0	52.0	11.7	1.6	22.8	3.7	17.5	12.3	4.1	3.2
3	Mineral fuels, lubricants and related material	2000	100.0	29.7	2.3	0.2	19.8	1.2	7.6	2.0	9.6	8.3
		2007	100.0	26.3	2.2	0.5	17.5	1.5	6.6	2.1	13.7	11.6
		2008	100.0	27.1	2.9	0.7	17.0	1.3	7.3	2.7	15.3	11.6
		2009	100.0	27.4	3.3	0.6	16.8	1.3	7.3	3.1	14.4	11.5
		2010	100.0	27.6	3.3	0.6	16.5	1.1	7.8	3.6	15.0	12.1
5	Chemicals	2000	100.0	79.8	6.9	6.2	56.1	12.3	16.8	14.1	1.5	1.5
		2007	100.0	76.0	5.1	4.5	57.9	12.7	13.1	10.7	1.7	1.5
		2008	100.0	74.2	4.7	4.2	56.3	13.0	13.2	10.9	2.3	2.0
		2009	100.0	75.2	4.9	4.3	57.1	12.2	13.2	11.3	1.5	1.3
		2010	100.0	72.1	5.2	4.7	53.5	11.3	13.4	11.4	1.7	1.4
7	Machinery and transport equipment	2000	100.0	71.8	12.9	12.6	38.8	10.4	20.0	15.8	0.4	0.4
		2007	100.0	63.6	9.3	9.0	41.1	12.5	13.2	10.7	0.6	0.5
		2008	100.0	62.7	9.2	9.0	41.0	12.5	12.4	10.3	0.7	0.6
		2009	100.0	58.5	8.3	8.0	39.5	11.9	10.7	8.7	0.5	0.5
		2010	100.0	56.3	9.2	8.9	36.4	11.4	10.7	8.7	0.5	0.5
6&8	Other manufactured goods	2000	100.0	61.1	6.3	5.5	41.2	7.8	13.6	10.1	1.9	1.8
		2007	100.0	55.7	4.6	3.9	41.7	9.0	9.3	6.9	2.9	2.5
		2008	100.0	54.9	4.7	4.0	41.2	9.0	9.0	6.8	3.0	2.6
		2009	100.0	53.5	4.6	4.0	39.8	8.8	9.1	7.2	2.3	2.0
		2010	100.0	51.4	5.0	4.4	37.3	8.2	9.0	7.1	2.5	2.1
						Destination of exports of major commodity classes						
0-9	All commodities 3/	2000	100.0	69.0	6.5	5.3	40.2	7.5	22.3	18.6	1.2	1.0
		2007	100.0	62.7	5.7	4.5	40.6	7.0	16.4	13.7	2.9	2.4
		2008	100.0	60.3	5.3	4.0	39.9	7.0	15.2	12.3	3.2	2.7
		2009	100.0	58.2	4.9	3.6	38.7	6.9	14.6	11.7	2.5	2.0
		2010	100.0	56.0	5.0	3.7	36.2	6.7	14.7	11.8	2.7	2.2
0&1	Food, live animals, beverages and tobacco	2000	100.0	70.1	10.5	9.6	45.3	8.4	14.3	11.4	2.6	2.2
		2007	100.0	67.0	6.4	5.3	48.3	8.0	12.4	9.5	4.5	3.8
		2008	100.0	64.1	6.2	5.1	46.6	7.8	11.3	8.6	4.9	4.1
		2009	100.0	63.5	6.1	5.0	45.9	7.7	11.5	8.7	4.2	3.5
		2010	100.0	61.0	6.2	5.1	43.1	7.3	11.6	8.7	4.6	3.9
2&4	Crude materials, oils and fats, (fuels excluded)	2000	100.0	63.4	10.0	9.3	39.4	7.1	14.0	10.9	1.5	1.4
		2007	100.0	52.4	8.0	7.4	36.1	6.4	8.3	6.2	2.0	1.6
		2008	100.0	49.6	7.4	6.8	34.4	6.2	7.9	5.9	2.3	2.0
		2009	100.0	43.9	6.7	6.2	30.4	5.6	6.8	5.0	1.9	1.6
		2010	100.0	43.0	7.3	6.9	29.2	5.5	6.5	4.8	1.8	1.5
3	Mineral fuels, lubricants and related material	2000	100.0	67.4	11.0	10.2	33.8	4.5	22.6	21.0	1.7	1.5
		2007	100.0	64.2	11.9	10.9	32.8	3.4	19.4	17.9	1.6	1.2
		2008	100.0	59.7	7.9	6.8	34.0	3.3	17.8	14.4	1.8	1.5
		2009	100.0	54.5	5.8	4.8	32.8	3.1	15.9	12.3	1.8	1.5
		2010	100.0	53.1	5.7	4.7	31.6	3.0	15.8	12.3	1.7	1.5
5	Chemicals	2000	100.0	66.4	5.2	3.8	46.1	7.6	15.1	11.7	1.3	1.1
		2007	100.0	64.7	4.0	2.8	47.8	8.5	12.9	10.3	2.6	2.3
		2008	100.0	63.2	4.1	2.8	46.6	8.4	12.5	10.0	2.8	2.5
		2009	100.0	63.3	4.2	2.9	46.3	8.4	12.7	10.1	2.5	2.1
		2010	100.0	60.2	4.5	3.1	43.4	7.7	12.3	9.8	2.7	2.3
7	Machinery and transport equipment	2000	100.0	68.7	5.2	3.9	37.6	7.2	25.9	21.2	0.8	0.6
		2007	100.0	59.9	4.3	2.9	37.5	7.2	18.1	14.8	3.1	2.6
		2008	100.0	57.8	4.4	2.8	36.8	7.3	16.7	13.6	3.7	3.2
		2009	100.0	55.8	4.3	2.8	35.0	7.3	16.5	13.6	2.3	1.8
		2010	100.0	53.5	4.4	2.9	32.1	6.9	16.9	13.9	2.6	2.2
6&8	Other manufactured goods	2000	100.0	70.6	6.4	5.2	41.5	8.4	22.7	19.2	1.2	1.0
		2007	100.0	65.0	4.9	3.7	43.5	7.8	16.6	14.0	3.2	2.5
		2008	100.0	63.0	4.9	3.7	42.6	7.8	15.4	12.8	3.7	2.7
		2009	100.0	61.6	5.2	3.8	41.2	7.7	15.2	12.6	2.9	2.0
		2010	100.0	59.8	5.2	3.8	39.2	7.5	15.5	12.9	2.9	2.2

For general note and footnotes see end of Special Table F.

Structure des exportations mondiales par provenance et destination (Tableau F)

en pourcentage

South-Eastern Europe Europe du Sud-est	Northern Africa Afrique du Nord	Sub-Saharan Africa Afrique subsahari-enne	Latin America and the Caribbean Amérique latine et Caraïbes	Eastern Asia Asie orientale	Southern Asia Asie méridionale	South-eastern Asia Asie du Sud-est	Western Asia Asie occidentale	Oceania Océanie	Others 4/ Autre 4/	← En provenance ou vers Année		CTCI: Classes de marchandises ↓
Provenance des exportations de grandes catégories de marchandises												
0.3	0.8	1.5	5.6	12.2	1.4	6.7	4.0	0.1	0.0	2000	0-9	Tous produits 3/
0.6	1.1	1.9	5.6	15.9	2.0	6.2	5.5	0.1	0.0	2006		
0.6	1.3	2.2	5.6	15.6	2.1	6.2	6.3	0.1	0.0	2007		
0.6	1.1	1.9	5.6	17.0	2.4	6.5	5.8	0.1	0.0	2008		
0.6	1.1	2.1	5.9	18.1	2.3	7.0	5.7	0.1	0.0	2009		
0.3	0.6	2.7	12.1	5.5	2.2	6.1	1.9	0.1	0.0	2000	0&1	Produits alimentaires, boissons et tabacs
0.6	0.6	2.5	13.0	5.1	2.6	5.7	2.4	0.1	0.0	2006		
0.8	0.7	2.4	13.2	4.8	3.0	6.2	2.3	0.1	0.0	2007		
0.8	0.9	2.9	13.7	5.3	2.7	6.4	2.7	0.1	0.0	2008		
0.9	0.9	2.9	14.4	5.9	2.9	6.8	2.7	0.1	0.0	2009		
0.8	0.7	3.5	11.8	5.3	1.2	8.5	1.2	0.8	0.0	2000	2&4	Matières premières huiles & graisses (combust. exclu.)
0.9	0.6	3.9	16.0	3.9	2.6	10.7	1.4	0.5	0.0	2006		
1.0	0.9	4.3	15.8	3.9	2.4	11.1	1.5	0.5	0.0	2007		
1.0	0.8	4.6	16.3	3.8	2.8	11.0	1.5	0.5	0.0	2008		
1.0	0.6	4.5	17.5	3.7	2.8	11.8	1.4	0.4	0.0	2009		
0.2	5.2	6.9	9.5	3.0	4.1	6.9	24.7	0.1	0.0	2000	3	Combustibles minéraux et produits
0.3	5.9	7.0	8.2	3.1	5.1	6.4	24.0	0.1	0.0	2006		
0.3	5.5	7.3	7.4	3.2	4.6	6.4	22.8	0.1	0.0	2007		
0.3	5.1	7.1	8.1	3.3	4.7	7.1	22.4	0.1	0.0	2008		
0.3	5.0	7.7	8.0	3.4	4.4	7.6	20.9	0.0	0.0	2009		
0.2	0.4	0.5	2.9	8.1	0.9	3.7	2.0	0.0	0.0	2000	5	Produits chimiques
0.3	0.4	0.5	2.7	9.9	1.4	4.5	2.6	0.0	0.0	2006		
0.4	0.7	0.6	2.9	10.4	1.5	4.1	3.0	0.0	0.0	2007		
0.3	0.5	0.5	2.9	9.9	1.9	4.3	3.1	0.0	0.0	2008		
0.3	0.6	0.5	2.9	11.5	1.9	4.9	3.6	0.0	0.0	2009		
0.1	0.1	0.2	4.7	13.3	0.1	8.6	0.7	0.0	0.0	2000	7	Machines et matériels de transports
0.4	0.1	0.3	3.9	21.9	0.4	7.5	1.4	0.0	0.0	2006		
0.4	0.2	0.4	4.0	22.8	0.5	6.8	1.5	0.0	0.0	2007		
0.5	0.2	0.4	4.0	25.7	0.7	7.7	1.7	0.0	0.0	2008		
0.5	0.2	0.4	4.3	27.6	0.7	8.1	1.5	0.0	0.0	2009		
0.6	0.5	1.1	4.5	20.0	2.7	5.1	2.4	0.1	0.0	2000	6&8	Articles manufacturés divers
1.0	0.4	1.4	4.4	23.3	2.9	4.7	3.1	0.1	0.0	2006		
1.0	0.5	1.4	4.2	23.9	2.9	4.8	3.4	0.1	0.0	2007		
0.9	0.6	1.2	4.1	24.8	3.7	5.4	3.4	0.1	0.0	2008		
0.9	0.5	1.5	4.2	26.3	3.6	5.6	3.5	0.1	0.0	2009		
Destination des exportations de grandes catégories de marchandises												
0.4	0.9	1.2	5.7	11.0	1.3	5.6	3.0	0.1	0.5	2000	0-9	Tous produits 3/
0.9	1.0	1.7	5.1	13.2	2.3	5.2	4.0	0.1	0.8	2006		
0.9	1.2	1.8	5.5	13.7	2.4	5.3	4.4	0.1	1.0	2007		
0.8	1.3	2.0	5.5	15.3	2.8	5.6	4.6	0.2	1.2	2008		
0.8	1.2	1.9	5.9	17.1	2.9	6.1	4.3	0.2	1.0	2009		
0.6	1.9	2.2	5.7	6.1	1.3	4.2	4.6	0.2	0.5	2000	0&1	Produits alimentaires, boissons et tabacs
1.1	2.0	2.8	5.5	5.4	1.7	4.4	5.0	0.2	0.4	2006		
1.3	2.2	3.1	6.1	5.5	1.9	4.7	5.7	0.2	0.3	2007		
1.3	2.0	3.2	5.7	6.2	2.3	4.9	6.1	0.2	0.4	2008		
1.2	2.2	3.2	5.8	7.3	2.3	5.7	6.0	0.2	0.3	2009		
0.5	1.3	1.4	4.8	15.4	3.3	4.3	3.0	0.0	1.0	2000	2&4	Matières premières huiles & graisses (combust. exclu.)
0.8	1.4	1.5	4.1	24.8	4.8	4.0	3.7	0.0	0.4	2006		
0.9	1.8	1.6	4.6	25.8	4.6	4.3	4.3	0.0	0.2	2007		
0.8	1.6	1.6	3.9	32.4	5.4	4.5	3.8	0.0	0.2	2008		
0.8	1.6	1.6	4.0	33.5	5.1	4.5	4.0	0.0	0.1	2009		
0.5	1.1	0.9	5.2	13.7	1.7	3.9	1.9	0.2	1.9	2000	3	Combustibles minéraux et produits
0.9	1.1	1.5	4.6	13.2	2.8	5.2	2.5	0.1	2.2	2006		
0.9	1.0	1.5	5.0	17.3	2.5	5.0	2.2	0.1	2.8	2007		
0.7	1.1	1.9	5.1	20.5	3.5	5.7	2.4	0.2	2.7	2008		
0.7	1.0	1.8	5.2	22.1	3.0	6.2	2.3	0.1	2.6	2009		
0.5	0.8	1.4	6.9	12.0	1.6	4.9	3.0	0.1	1.3	2000	5	Produits chimiques
0.9	0.9	1.5	6.0	12.3	2.3	4.5	3.5	0.1	0.8	2006		
1.0	1.0	1.6	6.7	11.7	2.8	4.6	3.5	0.1	0.9	2007		
1.0	1.1	1.7	6.4	12.7	2.8	4.5	3.7	0.1	0.4	2008		
0.9	1.0	1.6	6.8	14.4	3.1	5.1	3.7	0.1	0.5	2009		
0.3	0.7	1.1	6.1	11.0	0.9	7.6	2.7	0.1	0.2	2000	7	Machines et matériels de transports
0.8	0.9	1.7	5.6	15.3	1.9	6.5	4.2	0.2	0.1	2006		
0.9	1.1	1.9	6.2	14.9	2.0	6.5	4.6	0.2	0.2	2007		
0.7	1.3	2.0	6.1	17.3	2.3	7.0	4.6	0.4	0.2	2008		
0.6	1.1	1.9	6.8	19.1	2.3	7.3	4.4	0.3	0.1	2009		
0.6	0.8	1.1	5.3	11.0	1.4	4.1	3.5	0.1	0.3	2000	6&8	Articles manufacturés divers
1.1	1.0	1.6	4.5	11.6	2.3	4.4	4.9	0.1	0.3	2006		
1.2	1.2	1.7	4.9	11.3	2.5	4.8	5.5	0.1	0.3	2007		
1.0	1.5	1.9	4.8	12.4	2.8	5.0	5.8	0.1	0.2	2008		
0.9	1.3	1.9	5.3	13.5	3.3	5.4	5.4	0.1	0.2	2009		

Voir la fin du Tableau Spécial F pour la remarque générale et les notes.

Structure of world exports by provenance and destination (Table F)

in per cent

Origin or destination → / SITC Commodity classes		Year	World 1/ Monde 1/	Developed economies 2/ Economies développées 2/ Total	Asia-Pacific Asie-Pacifique Total	Japan Japon	Europe Total	Germany Allemagne	North America Amérique du Nord Total	U.S.A. É.-U.	Commonwealth of Independent States Communauté d'Etats Indépendants Total	Europe
Commodity composition of the total exports of selected regions												
0-9	All commodities 3/	2000	100.0	100.0	100.0	100.0	100.0	100.0	100.0	100.0	100.0	100.0
		2007	100.0	100.0	100.0	100.0	100.0	100.0	100.0	100.0	100.0	100.0
		2008	100.0	100.0	100.0	100.0	100.0	100.0	100.0	100.0	100.0	100.0
		2009	100.0	100.0	100.0	100.0	100.0	100.0	100.0	100.0	100.0	100.0
		2010	100.0	100.0	100.0	100.0	100.0	100.0	100.0	100.0	100.0	100.0
0&1	Food, live animals, beverages and tobacco	2000	6.1	6.3	3.6	0.4	7.1	4.0	6.0	6.0	2.3	2.1
		2007	5.8	6.5	3.9	0.5	7.0	4.1	6.4	6.3	3.5	3.2
		2008	6.0	6.9	4.0	0.5	7.3	4.5	7.0	7.0	3.3	3.3
		2009	7.0	7.9	4.7	0.7	8.4	5.4	7.6	7.2	4.8	4.9
		2010	6.4	7.3	4.1	0.6	8.0	5.0	7.1	6.9	3.8	3.6
2&4	Crude materials, oils and fats, (fuels excluded)	2000	3.4	3.2	3.1	0.7	2.4	1.7	5.0	3.9	6.5	5.7
		2007	4.0	3.8	5.3	1.3	2.8	1.9	6.3	5.6	5.3	4.9
		2008	4.1	3.9	6.0	1.3	2.8	2.0	6.8	6.2	4.7	4.5
		2009	4.0	3.9	6.8	1.6	2.6	1.7	6.6	6.2	4.9	4.5
		2010	4.6	4.5	8.1	1.4	3.0	2.0	7.3	6.7	4.9	4.6
3	Mineral fuels, lubricants and related material	2000	10.3	4.7	2.7	0.3	5.2	1.4	4.7	1.7	44.0	43.4
		2007	14.2	6.5	4.8	1.3	6.2	2.3	8.2	3.6	54.0	53.3
		2008	17.5	8.5	8.1	2.4	7.7	2.6	11.5	5.9	59.9	56.7
		2009	14.0	6.9	7.5	1.8	6.2	2.1	9.2	5.2	57.0	55.0
		2010	14.8	7.7	7.4	1.7	6.9	1.9	10.4	6.3	57.9	56.1
5	Chemicals	2000	8.9	10.9	7.0	7.3	12.6	12.7	9.0	10.3	6.0	6.7
		2007	10.5	13.8	8.3	9.1	15.2	13.8	11.9	13.3	4.8	5.0
		2008	10.3	13.8	7.8	8.8	15.1	14.6	12.3	13.8	5.3	5.9
		2009	11.4	15.5	9.1	10.6	17.1	15.3	13.6	15.1	4.8	4.9
		2010	11.0	15.0	8.6	10.2	16.7	14.7	13.3	14.8	4.9	5.0
7	Machinery and transport equipment	2000	41.3	45.5	60.8	68.8	40.4	49.6	49.5	52.8	7.3	8.0
		2007	36.4	40.2	52.9	63.3	37.6	47.4	42.0	46.2	5.9	6.2
		2008	33.9	38.2	50.1	62.0	36.2	46.2	38.2	42.8	5.2	5.9
		2009	33.9	35.9	46.0	58.2	35.1	44.5	32.9	34.7	5.2	5.9
		2010	34.2	36.1	46.8	59.5	35.1	46.0	33.1	35.2	4.9	5.4
6&8	Other manufactured goods	2000	25.9	24.3	18.4	18.8	26.9	23.3	21.1	21.2	21.9	23.9
		2007	25.1	24.3	18.2	19.1	26.3	23.6	20.5	20.6	20.2	20.5
		2008	23.8	23.5	17.7	19.6	25.6	23.3	19.5	19.9	16.0	17.1
		2009	24.0	23.2	18.1	20.6	25.0	23.4	19.8	20.3	15.7	16.5
		2010	23.8	23.0	17.9	20.6	25.0	23.2	19.4	19.8	15.2	15.7
Commodity composition of the world exports to selected regions												
0-9	All commodities 3/	2000	100.0	100.0	100.0	100.0	100.0	100.0	100.0	100.0	100.0	100.0
		2007	100.0	100.0	100.0	100.0	100.0	100.0	100.0	100.0	100.0	100.0
		2008	100.0	100.0	100.0	100.0	100.0	100.0	100.0	100.0	100.0	100.0
		2009	100.0	100.0	100.0	100.0	100.0	100.0	100.0	100.0	100.0	100.0
		2010	100.0	100.0	100.0	100.0	100.0	100.0	100.0	100.0	100.0	100.0
0&1	Food, live animals, beverages and tobacco	2000	6.1	6.2	9.8	10.9	6.9	6.8	3.9	3.7	12.7	13.3
		2007	5.8	6.2	6.5	6.8	6.9	6.6	4.4	4.0	8.9	9.0
		2008	6.0	6.3	7.1	7.7	7.0	6.6	4.4	4.2	9.1	9.2
		2009	7.0	7.7	8.7	9.8	8.3	7.8	5.5	5.2	11.6	12.3
		2010	6.4	7.0	8.0	8.9	7.7	7.1	5.1	4.7	11.1	11.6
2&4	Crude materials, oils and fats, (fuels excluded)	2000	3.4	3.1	5.1	5.8	3.3	3.2	2.1	2.0	4.3	4.5
		2007	4.0	3.3	5.5	6.6	3.5	3.6	2.0	1.8	2.7	2.7
		2008	4.1	3.4	5.8	7.0	3.5	3.6	2.1	2.0	2.9	3.0
		2009	4.0	3.0	5.5	7.0	3.1	3.2	1.9	1.7	3.0	3.2
		2010	4.6	3.6	6.7	8.7	3.7	3.8	2.0	1.9	3.1	3.2
3	Mineral fuels, lubricants and related material	2000	10.3	10.1	17.4	19.8	8.7	6.1	10.5	11.7	14.4	14.9
		2007	14.2	14.5	29.6	34.4	11.5	6.8	16.8	18.5	7.5	7.0
		2008	17.5	17.3	26.3	30.1	14.9	8.3	20.5	20.4	9.7	9.5
		2009	14.0	13.1	16.6	18.7	11.9	6.2	15.3	14.7	10.2	10.7
		2010	14.8	14.1	17.0	18.8	12.9	6.6	15.9	15.4	9.6	10.1
5	Chemicals	2000	8.9	8.6	7.1	6.3	10.2	9.0	6.0	5.6	9.5	9.5
		2007	10.5	10.8	7.4	6.5	12.3	12.7	8.2	7.8	9.4	9.8
		2008	10.3	10.8	8.1	7.4	12.1	12.3	8.5	8.4	9.0	9.5
		2009	11.4	12.4	9.9	9.4	13.7	13.8	10.0	9.9	11.2	12.1
		2010	11.0	11.9	9.8	9.5	13.2	12.7	9.2	9.1	11.2	11.9
7	Machinery and transport equipment	2000	41.3	41.0	33.1	30.3	38.5	39.5	47.9	47.1	25.5	24.3
		2007	36.4	34.8	27.6	23.6	33.7	37.5	40.1	39.3	38.1	39.2
		2008	33.9	32.5	28.1	24.2	31.3	35.1	37.3	37.5	38.3	40.3
		2009	33.9	32.6	29.8	26.6	30.7	35.5	38.4	39.3	30.7	31.2
		2010	34.2	32.7	30.3	26.7	30.3	35.4	39.2	40.0	32.9	34.1
6&8	Other manufactured goods	2000	25.9	26.5	25.3	25.1	26.7	29.1	26.4	26.7	26.3	25.9
		2007	25.1	26.0	21.5	20.9	26.9	28.0	25.5	25.7	27.6	25.7
		2008	23.8	24.9	22.4	22.1	25.5	26.5	24.2	24.8	26.8	23.7
		2009	24.0	25.4	25.3	25.4	25.6	26.5	25.1	25.9	27.8	24.1
		2010	23.8	25.4	24.5	24.6	25.7	26.7	25.0	25.8	26.2	24.0

For general note and footnotes see end of Special Table F.

Structure des exportations mondiales par provenance et destination (Tableau F)

en pourcentage

South-Eastern Europe Europe du Sud-est	Northern Africa Afrique du Nord	Sub-Saharan Africa Afrique subsahari-enne	Latin America and the Caribbean Amérique latine et Caraïbes	Eastern Asia Asie orientale	Southern Asia Asie méridionale	South-eastern Asia Asie du Sud-est	Western Asia Asie occidentale	Oceania Océanie	Others 4/ Autre 4/	Année	← En provenance ou vers	CTCI: Classes de marchandises ↓
Composition par marchandises des exportations mondiales des régions sélectionnées												
100.0	100.0	100.0	100.0	100.0	100.0	100.0	100.0	100.0	0.0	2000	0-9	Tous produits 3/
100.0	100.0	100.0	100.0	100.0	100.0	100.0	100.0	100.0	0.0	2006		
100.0	100.0	100.0	100.0	100.0	100.0	100.0	100.0	100.0	0.0	2007		
100.0	100.0	100.0	100.0	100.0	100.0	100.0	100.0	100.0	0.0	2008		
100.0	100.0	100.0	100.0	100.0	100.0	100.0	100.0	100.0	0.0	2009		
6.3	4.5	11.2	13.3	2.7	9.1	5.6	3.0	9.6	0.0	2000	0&1	Produits alimentaires, boissons et tabacs
6.3	3.2	7.6	13.5	1.9	7.7	5.3	2.5	10.2	0.0	2006		
7.6	3.4	6.6	14.2	1.8	8.4	6.0	2.2	11.1	0.0	2007		
9.8	5.8	10.6	17.1	2.2	8.0	6.9	3.2	10.9	0.0	2008		
9.7	5.2	8.7	15.8	2.1	8.1	6.3	3.0	11.0	0.0	2009		
8.9	2.8	7.9	7.1	1.5	2.8	4.3	1.1	35.4	0.0	2000	2&4	Matières premières huiles & graisses (combust. exclu.)
6.6	2.1	8.3	11.4	1.0	5.1	6.8	1.0	32.3	0.0	2006		
6.6	2.9	8.1	11.7	1.0	4.7	7.3	1.0	33.0	0.0	2007		
6.5	2.7	9.4	11.6	0.9	4.7	6.7	1.0	24.2	0.0	2008		
7.7	2.7	9.7	13.7	1.0	5.6	7.8	1.2	32.8	0.0	2009		
7.4	68.2	47.8	17.6	2.5	29.3	10.6	64.4	14.0	0.0	2000	3	Combustibles minéraux et produits
8.6	75.7	53.1	20.9	2.8	35.9	14.5	61.4	16.9	0.0	2006		
9.9	74.1	59.1	23.2	3.6	38.2	18.1	63.3	16.1	0.0	2007		
7.5	66.1	51.5	20.1	2.7	27.5	15.3	53.7	10.4	0.0	2008		
7.7	67.4	52.8	20.1	2.8	28.2	16.1	54.6	10.1	0.0	2009		
6.9	4.7	3.0	4.7	5.9	5.5	4.9	4.5	0.4	0.0	2000	5	Produits chimiques
6.4	3.5	2.7	5.1	6.5	7.3	7.5	5.0	0.4	0.0	2006		
6.7	5.9	2.9	5.4	6.9	7.4	6.8	4.9	0.4	0.0	2007		
5.8	5.6	3.0	5.9	6.7	8.9	7.4	6.0	0.4	0.0	2008		
6.4	6.1	2.6	5.4	7.0	9.1	7.7	6.9	0.4	0.0	2009		
14.3	3.5	5.6	34.6	44.8	4.0	52.9	7.5	3.2	0.0	2000	7	Machines et matériels de transports
23.8	3.6	6.5	25.4	50.4	7.0	43.6	9.1	2.2	0.0	2006		
25.4	4.0	6.3	24.7	49.5	8.1	37.6	7.9	1.9	0.0	2007		
30.4	5.4	6.2	24.1	51.4	10.0	40.1	10.0	11.4	0.0	2008		
29.5	5.6	5.7	24.9	52.0	9.9	39.4	9.2	2.0	0.0	2009		
54.3	16.0	18.9	20.8	42.2	48.2	19.8	15.7	35.7	0.0	2000	6&8	Articles manufacturés divers
47.0	9.6	19.2	19.8	37.0	36.3	19.2	14.2	25.3	0.0	2006		
41.9	9.3	15.0	18.2	36.5	32.2	18.6	13.0	21.0	0.0	2007		
37.0	12.9	15.0	17.4	35.2	37.0	19.9	14.0	22.1	0.0	2008		
36.0	11.5	16.7	16.7	34.5	36.8	19.0	14.6	21.4	0.0	2009		
Composition par marchandises des exportations mondiales vers régions sélectionnées												
100.0	100.0	100.0	100.0	100.0	100.0	100.0	100.0	100.0	100.0	2000	0-9	Tous produits 3/
100.0	100.0	100.0	100.0	100.0	100.0	100.0	100.0	100.0	100.0	2006		
100.0	100.0	100.0	100.0	100.0	100.0	100.0	100.0	100.0	100.0	2007		
100.0	100.0	100.0	100.0	100.0	100.0	100.0	100.0	100.0	100.0	2008		
100.0	100.0	100.0	100.0	100.0	100.0	100.0	100.0	100.0	100.0	2009		
9.1	13.4	11.3	6.1	3.4	6.5	4.5	9.3	12.3	5.3	2000	0&1	Produits alimentaires, boissons et tabacs
6.8	11.4	9.8	6.3	2.4	4.2	4.8	7.2	9.0	2.8	2006		
8.0	11.5	10.2	6.5	2.4	4.8	5.2	7.7	8.1	1.8	2007		
10.8	10.6	11.5	7.3	2.9	5.7	6.2	9.3	7.0	2.5	2008		
10.1	12.2	10.8	6.4	2.8	5.1	6.1	9.0	7.7	2.1	2009		
4.2	5.0	4.1	2.8	4.7	8.7	2.6	3.3	1.3	6.5	2000	2&4	Matières premières huiles & graisses (combust. exclu.)
3.7	5.3	3.7	3.2	7.4	8.2	3.0	3.6	1.1	2.3	2006		
3.9	6.5	3.6	3.4	7.7	7.7	3.3	4.0	0.9	0.7	2007		
3.6	5.0	3.2	2.8	8.5	7.6	3.2	3.3	0.8	0.7	2008		
4.7	6.2	3.7	3.1	9.1	8.0	3.5	4.3	0.8	0.5	2009		
11.8	13.7	7.9	9.4	12.8	14.1	7.1	6.5	17.6	37.3	2000	3	Combustibles minéraux et produits
14.7	15.8	12.6	12.9	14.2	17.1	14.0	8.8	15.8	40.8	2006		
17.4	15.0	14.7	15.9	22.1	18.2	16.3	9.0	14.1	49.9	2007		
11.2	11.5	13.3	13.2	18.8	17.3	14.3	7.3	10.9	32.3	2008		
13.4	12.6	14.2	13.1	19.2	15.4	15.2	7.9	12.8	36.9	2009		
9.9	8.3	10.3	10.7	9.7	11.1	7.8	8.9	5.1	22.0	2000	5	Produits chimiques
10.1	9.0	9.5	12.3	9.8	10.4	9.0	9.0	4.4	11.5	2006		
10.7	8.6	9.4	12.5	8.8	12.0	8.9	8.3	6.3	10.1	2007		
13.1	9.3	9.6	13.4	9.5	11.4	9.1	9.3	4.4	3.5	2008		
12.6	9.4	9.4	12.8	9.3	11.5	9.2	9.3	5.0	5.1	2009		
27.0	32.2	38.8	43.7	41.1	28.3	56.0	37.4	31.7	15.6	2000	7	Machines et matériels de transports
30.9	31.2	36.8	40.0	42.1	29.9	45.0	37.7	48.6	6.4	2006		
31.8	31.1	35.9	37.7	36.8	28.2	41.7	35.8	52.6	6.1	2007		
29.2	33.5	34.1	37.9	38.3	27.6	42.4	34.3	62.6	5.2	2008		
28.1	31.6	33.6	39.5	38.4	27.3	41.2	34.3	55.8	3.5	2009		
36.0	25.0	24.2	23.9	25.8	28.0	18.8	29.7	25.8	14.7	2000	6&8	Articles manufacturés divers
30.4	25.4	23.4	22.1	22.0	25.7	21.3	30.6	14.6	10.7	2006		
30.3	25.0	21.9	20.9	19.7	24.8	21.3	29.8	11.6	7.1	2007		
29.8	27.2	23.2	21.2	19.4	23.9	21.2	30.4	9.5	4.6	2008		
29.1	25.2	22.9	21.3	18.8	26.8	21.3	29.7	10.9	5.0	2009		

Voir la fin du Tableau Spécial F pour la remarque générale et les notes.

Growth and structure of world exports by provenance and destination (Tables E and F)
Croissance et structure des exportations mondiales par provenance et destination (Tableaux E et F)

General note

The figures in tables E and F are derived from the data in Special Table D.
The commodity classification is in accordance with the United Nations' Standard International Trade Classification (SITC), Revision 3, except for countries which report trade data only in terms of the SITC, Revision 2, or the SITC, Revised.
The data approximate total exports of all countries and areas of the world. They are based on official export figures converted, where necessary, to U.S. dollars according to conversion factors published in Table C for each country in this volume. Where official figures are not available estimates based on the imports reported by partner countries and on other subsidiary data are used. Some official national data have been adjusted
(a) to approximate the commodity groupings of the SITC and
(b) to approximate calendar years.
The data include special category (confidential) exports, ships' stores and bunkers and exports of minor importance, the destination of which cannot be determined. These data are included in the world totals for each commodity group and in total exports, and are available separately in region "Others"

1/ For the country composition of geographical regions, please refer to http://mdgs.un.org/unsd/mdg/Host.aspx?Content=Data/RegionalGroupings.htm
2/ This classification is intended for statistical convenience and does not, necessarily, express a judgment about the stage reached by a particular country in the development process.
3/ Section 9 of the SITC, which comprises commodities and transactions not classified elsewhere, is included in the total trade but is not shown separately in this table.
4/ The region "Others" as destination for exports contains the following trading partners: Antarctica, bunkers, free zones, confidential and not elsewhere specified countries

Remarque générale

Les données des tables E et F sont dérivées de celles publiées dans le Tableau Spécial D.
La classification par marchandise utilisée est la Classification Type pour le Commerce International (CTCI), Revision 3,) en dehors des pays qui rapportent exclusivement les données du commerce en accord avec la CTCI, Revision 2, ou la CTCI, Revisée.
Les données sont une estimation des exportations totales de tous les pays et régions du monde. Elles sont basées sur les chiffres des exportations officielles nationales convertis en dollars E.-U. selon les facteurs de conversion pour chaque pays publiés dans le Tableau C de ce volume. Quand les chiffres officiels ne sont pas disponibles, des estimations basées sur les importations rapportées par les pays partenaires ou sur d'autres données subsidiaires sont utilisées. Quelques données officielles nationales ont été ajustées afin
(a) qu'elles correspondent aux groupes des marchandises de la CTCI et
(b) qu'elles correspondent aux années civiles.
Les données comprennent les exportations de 'special category' (confidentielles), les approvisionnments des navires et combustible de soute et autres exportations de moindre importance dont la destination n'a pu être déterminée. Ces données sont comprises dans le total pour chaque groupe de marchandise et dans les exportations totales, et sont disponibles séparément dans la région "Autres".

1/ Pour la composition des régions géographiques, se référer à http://mdgs.un.org/unsd/mdg/Host.aspx?Content=Data/RegionalGroupings.htm
2/ Cette classification est utilisée pour plus de commodité dans la présentation des statistiques et n'implique pas nécessairement un jugement quant au stade de développement auquel est parvenu un pays donné.
3/ Section 9 de la CTCI, qui représente les articles et transactions non ailleurs est comprise dans le commerce total mais n'est pas présentée séparément dans ce tableau.
4/ La région "Autres" comme destination des exportations comprend les partenaires commerciaux suivants: Antarctique, combustibles de soute, zones franches, partenaires confidentiels ou non specifiés ailleurs.

Indices of total exports and imports by countries or areas (Table G)

Quantum and unit value indices and terms of trade in US dollars (2000 = 100)

Indices des exportations et importations totales par pays ou zones (Tableau G)

Indices du quantum et de la valeur unitaire et termes de l'échange en dollars É.-U. (2000 = 100)

Countries	1995	2002	2003	2004	2005	2006	2007	2008	2009	2010	Pays
Argentina											Argentine
Imp: Quantum	61	38	58	87	108	125	150	177	137	188	Imp: quantum
Imp: Unit Value	124	94	94	102	105	108	115	128	...	...	Imp: valeur unitaire
Exp: Quantum	94	105	110	118	135	143	154	156	142	165	Exp: quantum
Exp: Unit Value	120	93	102	111	113	122	137	213	178	178	Exp: valeur unitaire
Terms of Trade	*97*	*99*	*108*	*110*	*107*	*113*	*119*	*167*	...	...	*Termes de l'échange*
Purchasing Power of Exports	*92*	*104*	*120*	*129*	*145*	*163*	*183*	*260*	...	...	*Pouvoir d'achat des export.*
Australia											Australie
Imp: Quantum	63	108	120	137	129	145	155	186	164	172	Imp: quantum
Imp: Unit Value[1]	117	95	104	111	117	120	128	141	132	145	Imp: valeur unitaire[1]
Exp: Quantum	69	104	102	106	119	141	144	191	168	198	Exp: quantum
Exp: Unit Value[1]	117	100	111	129	153	175	196	246	214	260	Exp: valeur unitaire[1]
Terms of Trade	*100*	*106*	*106*	*116*	*131*	*146*	*153*	*174*	*162*	*179*	*Termes de l'échange*
Purchasing Power of Exports	*68*	*110*	*108*	*123*	*156*	*205*	*220*	*331*	*272*	*354*	*Pouvoir d'achat des export.*
Austria											Autriche
Imp: Quantum	80	107	111	118	125	131	143	142	120	131	Imp: quantum
Imp: Unit Value	181	100	114	125	123	130	144	162	147	147	Imp: valeur unitaire
Exp: Quantum	74	112	117	127	132	142	156	156	127	142	Exp: quantum
Exp: Unit Value	182	101	114	126	126	132	146	164	152	150	Exp: valeur unitaire
Terms of Trade	*101*	*101*	*100*	*101*	*102*	*102*	*101*	*102*	*104*	*102*	*Termes de l'échange*
Purchasing Power of Exports	*74*	*114*	*117*	*128*	*135*	*144*	*158*	*158*	*132*	*145*	*Pouvoir d'achat des export.*
Belgium											Belgique
Imp: Quantum	78	109	111	118	126	131	137	138	121	128	Imp: quantum
Imp: Unit Value	121	103	120	136	143	151	169	191	164	172	Imp: valeur unitaire
Exp: Quantum	77	111	113	121	126	131	135	133	117	126	Exp: quantum
Exp: Unit Value	126	104	121	135	142	150	170	190	169	174	Exp: valeur unitaire
Terms of Trade	*104*	*101*	*100*	*99*	*99*	*99*	*101*	*100*	*103*	*101*	*Termes de l'échange*
Purchasing Power of Exports	*79*	*112*	*113*	*120*	*125*	*129*	*136*	*132*	*120*	*127*	*Pouvoir d'achat des export.*
Bolivia (Plurinational State of)											Bolivie (État plurinational de)
Imp: Quantum	...	...	...	...	...	...	...	...	...	...	Imp: quantum
Imp: Unit Value	...	...	...	...	...	...	...	...	...	...	Imp: valeur unitaire
Exp: Quantum	94	129	145	173	126	142	153	238	257	403	Exp: quantum
Exp: Unit Value	128	81	91	122	169	252	292	402	316	384	Exp: valeur unitaire
Terms of Trade	...	...	...	...	...	...	...	...	...	...	*Termes de l'échange*
Purchasing Power of Exports	...	...	...	...	...	...	...	...	...	...	*Pouvoir d'achat des export.*
Brazil											Brésil
Imp: Quantum	95	99	136	111	101	110	128	134	112	149	Imp: quantum
Imp: Unit Value	95	86	64	102	131	148	168	231	204	218	Imp: valeur unitaire
Exp: Quantum	82	121	131	154	162	173	189	192	186	213	Exp: quantum
Exp: Unit Value	103	91	101	114	133	144	154	187	149	172	Exp: valeur unitaire
Terms of Trade	*108*	*106*	*158*	*112*	*101*	*97*	*92*	*81*	*73*	*79*	*Termes de l'échange*
Purchasing Power of Exports	*89*	*128*	*208*	*173*	*165*	*168*	*173*	*156*	*136*	*168*	*Pouvoir d'achat des export.*
Bulgaria											Bulgarie
Imp: Quantum	...	...	...	...	...	...	...	...	...	...	Imp: quantum
Imp: Unit Value[1]	...	98	112	130	140	156	182	208	178	177	Imp: valeur unitaire[1]
Exp: Quantum	...	...	...	...	...	...	...	...	...	...	Exp: quantum
Exp: Unit Value[1]	...	95	114	133	142	162	194	227	188	197	Exp: valeur unitaire[1]
Terms of Trade	...	*98*	*102*	*102*	*102*	*104*	*107*	*109*	*106*	*112*	*Termes de l'échange*
Purchasing Power of Exports	...	...	...	...	...	...	...	...	...	...	*Pouvoir d'achat des export.*

Indices of total exports and imports by countries or areas (Table G)

Quantum and unit value indices and terms of trade in US dollars (2000 = 100)

Indices des exportations et importations totales par pays ou zones (Tableau G)

Indices du quantum et de la valeur unitaire et termes de l'échange en dollars É.-U. (2000 = 100)

Countries	1995	2002	2003	2004	2005	2006	2007	2008	2009	2010	Pays
Canada											Canada
Imp: Quantum	63	96	100	108	116	123	130	131	109	126	Imp: quantum
Imp: Unit Value	99	95	100	106	114	122	128	137	128	137	Imp: valeur unitaire
Exp: Quantum	66	97	95	100	102	103	105	97	81	87	Exp: quantum
Exp: Unit Value	102	96	106	117	130	140	150	166	140	156	Exp: valeur unitaire
Terms of Trade	*103*	*101*	*106*	*110*	*114*	*114*	*118*	*121*	*110*	*115*	*Termes de l'échange*
Purchasing Power of Exports	*68*	*97*	*101*	*111*	*117*	*118*	*123*	*117*	*88*	*100*	*Pouvoir d'achat des export.*
China, Hong Kong SAR[2]											Chine, Hong Kong RAS[2]
Imp: Quantum	81	106	119	136	148	162	179	184	167	198	Imp: quantum
Imp: Unit Value	111	93	93	96	98	101	102	107	107	114	Imp: valeur unitaire
Exp: Quantum	77	105	120	138	154	169	183	189	166	196	Exp: quantum
Exp: Unit Value	110	95	94	95	96	97	99	103	105	109	Exp: valeur unitaire
Terms of Trade	*99*	*102*	*101*	*99*	*98*	*97*	*97*	*96*	*98*	*96*	*Termes de l'échange*
Purchasing Power of Exports	*76*	*107*	*121*	*137*	*151*	*164*	*177*	*182*	*162*	*188*	*Pouvoir d'achat des export.*
Colombia											Colombie
Imp: Quantum	...	...	...	...	...	...	...	...	...	...	Imp: quantum
Imp: Unit Value[1]	121	95	95	103	114	114	117	125	116	...	Imp: valeur unitaire[1]
Exp: Quantum	...	...	...	...	...	...	...	...	...	...	Exp: quantum
Exp: Unit Value[1]	111	84	87	96	111	119	130	159	151	...	Exp: valeur unitaire[1]
Terms of Trade	*92*	*89*	*92*	*93*	*97*	*104*	*111*	*128*	*130*	...	*Termes de l'échange*
Purchasing Power of Exports	...	...	...	...	...	...	...	...	...	...	*Pouvoir d'achat des export.*
Czech Republic											République tchèque
Imp: Quantum	...	...	...	...	...	...	...	...	...	...	Imp: quantum
Imp: Unit Value	123	107	123	137	148	158	175	201	173	175	Imp: valeur unitaire
Exp: Quantum	...	...	...	...	...	...	...	...	...	...	Exp: quantum
Exp: Unit Value	125	111	130	147	155	164	185	210	189	185	Exp: valeur unitaire
Terms of Trade	*101*	*104*	*105*	*107*	*105*	*104*	*106*	*105*	*109*	*106*	*Termes de l'échange*
Purchasing Power of Exports	...	...	...	...	...	...	...	...	...	...	*Pouvoir d'achat des export.*
Denmark											Danemark
Imp: Quantum	81	108	106	113	122	135	147	141	117	128	Imp: quantum
Imp: Unit Value	128	102	119	133	138	143	160	173	154	149	Imp: valeur unitaire
Exp: Quantum	78	109	107	110	116	123	131	130	116	122	Exp: quantum
Exp: Unit Value	131	103	122	136	143	148	160	178	159	159	Exp: valeur unitaire
Terms of Trade	*102*	*101*	*102*	*102*	*104*	*103*	*100*	*103*	*103*	*107*	*Termes de l'échange*
Purchasing Power of Exports	*80*	*110*	*109*	*113*	*121*	*128*	*132*	*133*	*120*	*130*	*Pouvoir d'achat des export.*
Dominica											Dominique
Imp: Quantum	...	82	...	...	...	...	...	...	...	...	Imp: quantum
Imp: Unit Value	...	91	...	...	...	...	...	...	...	...	Imp: valeur unitaire
Exp: Quantum	79	72	...	...	...	...	...	...	...	...	Exp: quantum
Exp: Unit Value	113	101	...	...	...	...	...	...	...	...	Exp: valeur unitaire
Terms of Trade	...	*111*	...	...	...	...	...	...	...	...	*Termes de l'échange*
Purchasing Power of Exports	...	*80*	...	...	...	...	...	...	...	...	*Pouvoir d'achat des export.*
Ecuador											Equateur
Imp: Quantum	100	148	161	168	204	229	262	280	274	331	Imp: quantum
Imp: Unit Value	...	...	...	...	...	...	...	...	...	...	Imp: valeur unitaire
Exp: Quantum	100	99	107	133	117	143	139	141	137	133	Exp: quantum
Exp: Unit Value	76	94	107	118	150	182	209	284	201	264	Exp: valeur unitaire
Terms of Trade	...	...	...	...	...	...	...	...	...	...	*Termes de l'échange*
Purchasing Power of Exports	...	...	...	...	...	...	...	...	...	...	*Pouvoir d'achat des export.*

Indices of total exports and imports by countries or areas (Table G)

Quantum and unit value indices and terms of trade in US dollars (2000 = 100)

Indices des exportations et importations totales par pays ou zones (Tableau G)

Indices du quantum et de la valeur unitaire et termes de l'échange en dollars É.-U. (2000 = 100)

Countries	1995	2002	2003	2004	2005	2006	2007	2008	2009	2010	Pays
Estonia											Estonie
Imp: Quantum	...	...	...	...	...	...	...	...	...	...	Imp: quantum
Imp: Unit Value	...	103	121	135	140	148	166	189	170	176	Imp: valeur unitaire
Exp: Quantum	...	...	...	...	...	...	...	...	...	...	Exp: quantum
Exp: Unit Value	113	136	173	194	199	210	247	276	252	254	Exp: valeur unitaire
Terms of Trade	...	*132*	*143*	*144*	*143*	*142*	*148*	*146*	*149*	*144*	*Termes de l'échange*
Purchasing Power of Exports	...	...	...	...	...	...	...	...	...	...	*Pouvoir d'achat des export.*
Finland											Finlande
Imp: Quantum	75	104	103	108	114	127	128	130	100	109	Imp: quantum
Imp: Unit Value[1]	119	97	115	131	146	151	167	186	161	163	Imp: valeur unitaire[1]
Exp: Quantum	71	104	106	112	111	124	120	121	88	94	Exp: quantum
Exp: Unit Value[1]	124	94	107	117	127	124	136	147	127	126	Exp: valeur unitaire[1]
Terms of Trade	*104*	*97*	*93*	*89*	*87*	*82*	*81*	*79*	*79*	*77*	*Termes de l'échange*
Purchasing Power of Exports	*74*	*101*	*98*	*99*	*96*	*102*	*97*	*96*	*70*	*73*	*Pouvoir d'achat des export.*
France											France
Imp: Quantum	59	112	112	125	136	147	154	162	149	162	Imp: quantum
Imp: Unit Value[1]	149	95	114	123	122	128	142	160	141	141	Imp: valeur unitaire[1]
Exp: Quantum	59	112	110	118	125	137	140	145	130	146	Exp: quantum
Exp: Unit Value[1]	159	97	118	127	127	129	143	158	143	139	Exp: valeur unitaire[1]
Terms of Trade	*106*	*103*	*104*	*104*	*104*	*101*	*101*	*99*	*102*	*99*	*Termes de l'échange*
Purchasing Power of Exports	*63*	*115*	*114*	*123*	*130*	*138*	*141*	*143*	*132*	*145*	*Pouvoir d'achat des export.*
Germany											Allemagne
Imp: Quantum	67	100	110	121	126	142	146	148	133	153	Imp: quantum
Imp: Unit Value	139	98	111	121	123	129	144	159	139	139	Imp: valeur unitaire
Exp: Quantum	64	104	115	129	136	153	162	164	137	160	Exp: quantum
Exp: Unit Value	149	102	119	129	130	132	147	160	147	144	Exp: valeur unitaire
Terms of Trade	*107*	*104*	*107*	*107*	*105*	*102*	*103*	*100*	*106*	*103*	*Termes de l'échange*
Purchasing Power of Exports	*69*	*109*	*123*	*139*	*143*	*157*	*166*	*165*	*146*	*165*	*Pouvoir d'achat des export.*
Greece											Grèce
Imp: Quantum	63	...	...	...	...	...	...	...	...	...	Imp: quantum
Imp: Unit Value[1]	134	106	127	144	158	165	185	213	198	201	Imp: valeur unitaire[1]
Exp: Quantum	67	...	...	...	...	...	...	...	...	...	Exp: quantum
Exp: Unit Value[1]	124	104	124	143	149	158	177	202	180	187	Exp: valeur unitaire[1]
Terms of Trade	*93*	*98*	*98*	*99*	*95*	*95*	*96*	*95*	*91*	*93*	*Termes de l'échange*
Purchasing Power of Exports	*62*	...	...	...	...	...	...	...	...	...	*Pouvoir d'achat des export.*
Honduras											Honduras
Imp: Quantum	...	...	...	...	...	...	...	...	...	...	Imp: quantum
Imp: Unit Value	...	...	...	...	...	...	...	...	...	...	Imp: valeur unitaire
Exp: Quantum	70	100	93	112	96	103	114	117	109	113	Exp: quantum
Exp: Unit Value[1]	126	96	83	102	125	128	135	161	149	181	Exp: valeur unitaire[1]
Terms of Trade	...	...	...	...	...	...	...	...	...	...	*Termes de l'échange*
Purchasing Power of Exports	...	...	...	...	...	...	...	...	...	...	*Pouvoir d'achat des export.*
Hungary											Hongrie
Imp: Quantum	43	109	120	139	147	168	189	197	164	185	Imp: quantum
Imp: Unit Value[1]	124	107	123	135	138	142	156	171	147	144	Imp: valeur unitaire[1]
Exp: Quantum	43	114	125	147	164	194	225	234	206	235	Exp: quantum
Exp: Unit Value[1]	128	107	122	134	134	136	149	160	140	138	Exp: valeur unitaire[1]
Terms of Trade	*104*	*100*	*100*	*99*	*97*	*95*	*95*	*94*	*96*	*95*	*Termes de l'échange*
Purchasing Power of Exports	*44*	*114*	*124*	*146*	*159*	*185*	*214*	*219*	*197*	*224*	*Pouvoir d'achat des export.*

Indices of total exports and imports by countries or areas (Table G)

Quantum and unit value indices and terms of trade in US dollars (2000 = 100)

Indices des exportations et importations totales par pays ou zones (Tableau G)

Indices du quantum et de la valeur unitaire et termes de l'échange en dollars É.-U. (2000 = 100)

Countries	1995	2002	2003	2004	2005	2006	2007	2008	2009	2010	Pays
Iceland											Islande
Imp: Quantum	60	...	...	...	...	...	...	...	...	...	Imp: quantum
Imp: Unit Value	113	...	...	...	...	...	...	...	...	...	Imp: valeur unitaire
Exp: Quantum	86	...	...	...	...	...	...	...	...	...	Exp: quantum
Exp: Unit Value	110	...	...	...	...	...	...	...	...	...	Exp: valeur unitaire
Terms of Trade	*98*	...	...	...	...	...	...	...	...	...	*Termes de l'échange*
Purchasing Power of Exports	*84*	...	...	...	...	...	...	...	...	...	*Pouvoir d'achat des export.*
India											Inde
Imp: Quantum	74	115	139	155	197	239	290	241	233	...	Imp: quantum
Imp: Unit Value	100	104	113	134	143	135	179	173	152	...	Imp: valeur unitaire
Exp: Quantum	67	126	134	152	185	193	212	206	206	...	Exp: quantum
Exp: Unit Value	107	92	107	122	130	148	161	152	160	...	Exp: valeur unitaire
Terms of Trade	*108*	*89*	*95*	*91*	*91*	*109*	*90*	*88*	*105*	...	*Termes de l'échange*
Purchasing Power of Exports	*72*	*112*	*127*	*138*	*169*	*212*	*191*	*181*	*216*	...	*Pouvoir d'achat des export.*
Indonesia											Indonésie
Imp: Quantum	...	...	...	...	...	...	...	...	...	...	Imp: quantum
Imp: Unit Value	...	...	...	...	...	...	...	...	...	...	Imp: valeur unitaire
Exp: Quantum	81	100	97	101	64	...	...	...	...	...	Exp: quantum
Exp: Unit Value	103	96	103	120	81	...	...	...	...	...	Exp: valeur unitaire
Terms of Trade	...	...	...	...	...	...	...	...	...	...	*Termes de l'échange*
Purchasing Power of Exports	...	...	...	...	...	...	...	...	...	...	*Pouvoir d'achat des export.*
Ireland											Irlande
Imp: Quantum	53	97	90	98	112	115	118	106	88	86	Imp: quantum
Imp: Unit Value	121	101	112	120	121	126	137	149	134	133	Imp: valeur unitaire
Exp: Quantum	46	104	99	110	113	113	119	119	114	120	Exp: quantum
Exp: Unit Value	120	104	115	116	119	120	128	133	126	123	Exp: valeur unitaire
Terms of Trade	*99*	*102*	*103*	*97*	*99*	*95*	*93*	*89*	*94*	*93*	*Termes de l'échange*
Purchasing Power of Exports	*45*	*107*	*103*	*107*	*111*	*108*	*111*	*106*	*107*	*111*	*Pouvoir d'achat des export.*
Israel											Israël
Imp: Quantum	71	93	92	103	105	105	114	116	99	115	Imp: quantum
Imp: Unit Value	111	99	104	112	120	127	138	157	134	144	Imp: valeur unitaire
Exp: Quantum	59	97	101	116	119	124	137	134	111	132	Exp: quantum
Exp: Unit Value	103	96	100	106	114	119	127	147	136	141	Exp: valeur unitaire
Terms of Trade	*92*	*98*	*96*	*95*	*95*	*94*	*92*	*93*	*102*	*98*	*Termes de l'échange*
Purchasing Power of Exports	*54*	*95*	*97*	*110*	*113*	*116*	*126*	*124*	*113*	*130*	*Pouvoir d'achat des export.*
Italy											Italie
Imp: Quantum	80	101	102	108	108	113	116	109	94	105	Imp: quantum
Imp: Unit Value	109	102	122	138	149	165	185	217	185	194	Imp: valeur unitaire
Exp: Quantum	94	101	99	104	104	110	115	110	89	97	Exp: quantum
Exp: Unit Value	105	106	126	142	149	158	181	206	191	192	Exp: valeur unitaire
Terms of Trade	*96*	*103*	*104*	*103*	*100*	*96*	*98*	*95*	*103*	*99*	*Termes de l'échange*
Purchasing Power of Exports	*90*	*104*	*103*	*106*	*104*	*105*	*112*	*104*	*92*	*96*	*Pouvoir d'achat des export.*
Japan											Japon
Imp: Quantum	81	100	107	115	118	123	119	119	102	116	Imp: quantum
Imp: Unit Value	109	86	91	101	112	120	133	164	139	153	Imp: valeur unitaire
Exp: Quantum	80	97	102	113	114	123	130	128	94	117	Exp: quantum
Exp: Unit Value	115	89	96	104	109	110	115	127	129	138	Exp: valeur unitaire
Terms of Trade	*106*	*104*	*105*	*103*	*98*	*92*	*86*	*77*	*93*	*90*	*Termes de l'échange*
Purchasing Power of Exports	*85*	*101*	*108*	*116*	*111*	*113*	*112*	*99*	*87*	*105*	*Pouvoir d'achat des export.*

Indices of total exports and imports by countries or areas (Table G)

Quantum and unit value indices and terms of trade in US dollars (2000 = 100)

Indices des exportations et importations totales par pays ou zones (Tableau G)

Indices du quantum et de la valeur unitaire et termes de l'échange en dollars É.-U. (2000 = 100)

Countries	1995	2002	2003	2004	2005	2006	2007	2008	2009	2010	Pays
Jordan											Jordanie
Imp: Quantum	85	104	109	136	155	154	162	166	155	138	Imp: quantum
Imp: Unit Value	96	105	115	130	148	162	184	221	197	243	Imp: valeur unitaire
Exp: Quantum	84	142	152	190	182	188	173	158	142	188	Exp: quantum
Exp: Unit Value	111	102	102	114	131	143	170	261	237	207	Exp: valeur unitaire
Terms of Trade	*116*	*97*	*88*	*87*	*88*	*88*	*92*	*118*	*120*	*85*	*Termes de l'échange*
Purchasing Power of Exports	*98*	*137*	*135*	*166*	*161*	*166*	*160*	*186*	*171*	*160*	*Pouvoir d'achat des export.*
Kenya											Kenya
Imp: Quantum	90	...	...	...	...	...	...	...	...	...	Imp: quantum
Imp: Unit Value	102	...	...	...	...	...	...	...	...	...	Imp: valeur unitaire
Exp: Quantum	...	...	...	...	...	...	...	...	...	...	Exp: quantum
Exp: Unit Value	117	...	...	...	...	...	...	...	...	...	Exp: valeur unitaire
Terms of Trade	*114*	...	...	...	...	...	...	...	...	...	*Termes de l'échange*
Purchasing Power of Exports	...	...	...	...	...	...	...	...	...	...	*Pouvoir d'achat des export.*
Korea, Republic of											Corée, République de
Imp: Quantum	74	110	118	132	140	155	169	170	166	195	Imp: quantum
Imp: Unit Value	117	88	96	107	117	126	134	165	124	138	Imp: valeur unitaire
Exp: Quantum	46	114	134	163	178	202	223	237	239	277	Exp: quantum
Exp: Unit Value	162	83	85	92	93	93	96	102	84	94	Exp: valeur unitaire
Terms of Trade	*139*	*95*	*89*	*85*	*79*	*74*	*72*	*62*	*68*	*68*	*Termes de l'échange*
Purchasing Power of Exports	*64*	*108*	*119*	*140*	*141*	*149*	*160*	*147*	*163*	*188*	*Pouvoir d'achat des export.*
Latvia											Lettonie
Imp: Quantum	...	...	...	...	...	...	...	...	...	...	Imp: quantum
Imp: Unit Value	...	106	122	140	150	166	191	224	198	201	Imp: valeur unitaire
Exp: Quantum	...	...	...	...	...	...	...	...	...	...	Exp: quantum
Exp: Unit Value	112	104	121	145	153	169	209	242	207	212	Exp: valeur unitaire
Terms of Trade	...	*98*	*99*	*104*	*102*	*102*	*109*	*108*	*104*	*106*	*Termes de l'échange*
Purchasing Power of Exports	...	...	...	...	...	...	...	...	...	...	*Pouvoir d'achat des export.*
Libya											Libye
Imp: Quantum	171	214	...	...	...	...	...	...	...	...	Imp: quantum
Imp: Unit Value	120	48	...	...	...	...	...	...	...	...	Imp: valeur unitaire
Exp: Quantum	132	95	...	...	...	...	...	...	...	...	Exp: quantum
Exp: Unit Value	78	88	...	...	...	...	...	...	...	...	Exp: valeur unitaire
Terms of Trade	*65*	*185*	...	...	...	...	...	...	...	...	*Termes de l'échange*
Purchasing Power of Exports	*86*	*175*	...	...	...	...	...	...	...	...	*Pouvoir d'achat des export.*
Lithuania											Lituanie
Imp: Quantum	...	143	155	182	209	233	257	280	197	239	Imp: quantum
Imp: Unit Value	...	101	117	127	138	151	174	211	169	178	Imp: valeur unitaire
Exp: Quantum	...	145	161	185	214	234	250	284	251	296	Exp: quantum
Exp: Unit Value	...	101	120	137	151	160	185	216	179	191	Exp: valeur unitaire
Terms of Trade	...	*100*	*102*	*108*	*109*	*106*	*106*	*102*	*106*	*107*	*Termes de l'échange*
Purchasing Power of Exports	...	*146*	*164*	*199*	*233*	*247*	*266*	*289*	*265*	*316*	*Pouvoir d'achat des export.*
Malaysia											Malaisie
Imp: Quantum	...	97	...	...	...	...	...	...	...	...	Imp: quantum
Imp: Unit Value	...	99	...	...	...	...	...	...	...	...	Imp: valeur unitaire
Exp: Quantum	75	102	...	...	...	...	...	...	...	...	Exp: quantum
Exp: Unit Value	...	93	...	...	...	...	...	...	...	...	Exp: valeur unitaire
Terms of Trade	...	*94*	...	...	...	...	...	...	...	...	*Termes de l'échange*
Purchasing Power of Exports	...	*96*	...	...	...	...	...	...	...	...	*Pouvoir d'achat des export.*

Indices of total exports and imports by countries or areas (Table G)

Quantum and unit value indices and terms of trade in US dollars (2000 = 100)

Indices des exportations et importations totales par pays ou zones (Tableau G)

Indices du quantum et de la valeur unitaire et termes de l'échange en dollars É.-U. (2000 = 100)

Countries	1995	2002	2003	2004	2005	2006	2007	2008	2009	2010	Pays
Mauritius											Maurice
Imp: Quantum	...	103	96	102	107	111	114	114	108	115	Imp: quantum
Imp: Unit Value[1]	118	99	80	90	98	102	111	133	112	124	Imp: valeur unitaire[1]
Exp: Quantum	...	121	92	89	96	106	95	96	87	101	Exp: quantum
Exp: Unit Value[1]	118	98	84	92	90	89	96	102	91	91	Exp: valeur unitaire[1]
Terms of Trade	*100*	*98*	*105*	*101*	*92*	*87*	*87*	*77*	*81*	*73*	*Termes de l'échange*
Purchasing Power of Exports	...	*119*	*96*	*90*	*89*	*93*	*82*	*73*	*71*	*74*	*Pouvoir d'achat des export.*
Mexico											Mexique
Imp: Quantum	...	...	...	...	...	...	...	...	...	...	Imp: quantum
Imp: Unit Value[1]	98	100	103	108	114	119	125	136	131	136	Imp: valeur unitaire[1]
Exp: Quantum	...	...	...	...	...	...	...	...	...	...	Exp: quantum
Exp: Unit Value[1]	95	100	105	117	127	137	144	158	135	151	Exp: valeur unitaire[1]
Terms of Trade	*97*	*100*	*102*	*108*	*112*	*115*	*114*	*116*	*103*	*111*	*Termes de l'échange*
Purchasing Power of Exports	...	...	...	...	...	...	...	...	...	...	*Pouvoir d'achat des export.*
Morocco											Maroc
Imp: Quantum	...	105	113	127	140	155	176	...	...	...	Imp: quantum
Imp: Unit Value	138	98	110	122	129	134	152	...	...	...	Imp: valeur unitaire
Exp: Quantum	...	107	104	103	118	127	131	...	...	...	Exp: quantum
Exp: Unit Value	124	99	116	127	128	135	150	...	...	...	Exp: valeur unitaire
Terms of Trade	*90*	*101*	*105*	*105*	*99*	*100*	*98*	...	...	...	*Termes de l'échange*
Purchasing Power of Exports	...	*108*	*110*	*108*	*117*	*128*	*129*	...	...	...	*Pouvoir d'achat des export.*
Netherlands											Pays-Bas
Imp: Quantum	73	95	98	106	121	133	141	146	129	145	Imp: quantum
Imp: Unit Value	128	101	118	131	129	135	150	169	148	151	Imp: valeur unitaire
Exp: Quantum	72	103	106	116	122	134	144	147	134	150	Exp: quantum
Exp: Unit Value	130	100	116	127	134	140	155	174	151	154	Exp: valeur unitaire
Terms of Trade	*102*	*98*	*99*	*96*	*104*	*104*	*103*	*103*	*103*	*102*	*Termes de l'échange*
Purchasing Power of Exports	*73*	*101*	*104*	*112*	*127*	*139*	*149*	*152*	*137*	*153*	*Pouvoir d'achat des export.*
New Zealand											Nouvelle-Zélande
Imp: Quantum	83	111	124	142	151	152	166	164	148	164	Imp: quantum
Imp: Unit Value[1]	122	98	109	118	125	126	167	147	122	138	Imp: valeur unitaire[1]
Exp: Quantum	84	109	112	119	118	121	129	124	135	137	Exp: quantum
Exp: Unit Value[1]	123	99	111	129	138	138	182	184	137	176	Exp: valeur unitaire[1]
Terms of Trade	*101*	*102*	*102*	*109*	*111*	*110*	*109*	*126*	*113*	*128*	*Termes de l'échange*
Purchasing Power of Exports	*84*	*111*	*115*	*130*	*130*	*133*	*141*	*156*	*152*	*175*	*Pouvoir d'achat des export.*
Norway											Norvège
Imp: Quantum[3]	69	103	106	118	129	142	156	157	138	148	Imp: quantum[3]
Imp: Unit Value[3]	145	104	116	127	133	139	159	173	154	157	Imp: valeur unitaire[3]
Exp: Quantum[3]	78	107	107	108	108	106	107	107	104	101	Exp: quantum[3]
Exp: Unit Value[3]	88	94	104	127	161	194	213	268	185	219	Exp: valeur unitaire[3]
Terms of Trade	*60*	*91*	*90*	*100*	*122*	*139*	*134*	*155*	*120*	*139*	*Termes de l'échange*
Purchasing Power of Exports	*47*	*97*	*97*	*109*	*131*	*147*	*143*	*166*	*125*	*140*	*Pouvoir d'achat des export.*
Pakistan											Pakistan
Imp: Quantum	94	123	123	142	165	153	169	184	178	173	Imp: quantum
Imp: Unit Value	99	95	109	122	138	151	167	216	178	203	Imp: valeur unitaire
Exp: Quantum	73	109	110	103	126	127	124	133	126	131	Exp: quantum
Exp: Unit Value	118	90	96	103	103	106	110	124	115	131	Exp: valeur unitaire
Terms of Trade	*120*	*95*	*89*	*85*	*75*	*70*	*66*	*57*	*65*	*65*	*Termes de l'échange*
Purchasing Power of Exports	*88*	*104*	*98*	*87*	*95*	*89*	*81*	*76*	*82*	*85*	*Pouvoir d'achat des export.*

Indices of total exports and imports by countries or areas (Table G)

Quantum and unit value indices and terms of trade in US dollars (2000 = 100)

Indices des exportations et importations totales par pays ou zones (Tableau G)

Indices du quantum et de la valeur unitaire et termes de l'échange en dollars É.-U. (2000 = 100)

Countries	1995	2002	2003	2004	2005	2006	2007	2008	2009	2010	Pays
Panama											Panama
Imp: Quantum	...	...	...	...	...	...	...	...	...	...	Imp: quantum
Imp: Unit Value	...	...	...	...	...	...	...	...	...	...	Imp: valeur unitaire
Exp: Quantum	...	81	84	83	98	100	105	82	68	66	Exp: quantum
Exp: Unit Value	...	...	...	...	...	...	...	...	...	...	Exp: valeur unitaire
Terms of Trade	...	...	...	...	...	...	...	...	...	...	*Termes de l'échange*
Purchasing Power of Exports	...	...	...	...	...	...	...	...	...	...	*Pouvoir d'achat des export.*
Papua New Guinea											Papouasie-Nouvelle-Guinée
Imp: Quantum	...	...	...	...	...	...	...	...	...	...	Imp: quantum
Imp: Unit Value	...	...	...	...	...	...	...	...	...	...	Imp: valeur unitaire
Exp: Quantum	...	88	105	99	106	92	94	100	102	100	Exp: quantum
Exp: Unit Value	99	85	101	126	157	247	271	329	234	303	Exp: valeur unitaire
Terms of Trade	...	...	...	...	...	...	...	...	...	...	*Termes de l'échange*
Purchasing Power of Exports	...	...	...	...	...	...	...	...	...	...	*Pouvoir d'achat des export.*
Peru											Pérou
Imp: Quantum	...	...	...	...	...	...	...	...	...	...	Imp: quantum
Imp: Unit Value	...	...	...	...	...	...	...	...	...	...	Imp: valeur unitaire
Exp: Quantum	79	126	122	135	134	126	138	154	156	152	Exp: quantum
Exp: Unit Value	88	87	97	128	170	280	307	251	236	346	Exp: valeur unitaire
Terms of Trade	...	...	...	...	...	...	...	...	...	...	*Termes de l'échange*
Purchasing Power of Exports	...	...	...	...	...	...	...	...	...	...	*Pouvoir d'achat des export.*
Philippines											Philippines
Imp: Quantum	...	116	118	137	123	126	...	...	...	...	Imp: quantum
Imp: Unit Value[1]	174	83	82	81	97	113	...	...	...	...	Imp: valeur unitaire[1]
Exp: Quantum	...	104	98	110	104	124	...	...	...	...	Exp: quantum
Exp: Unit Value[1]	141	77	79	75	84	88	...	...	...	...	Exp: valeur unitaire[1]
Terms of Trade	*81*	*93*	*96*	*93*	*87*	*78*	...	...	...	...	*Termes de l'échange*
Purchasing Power of Exports	...	*97*	*94*	*102*	*90*	*97*	...	...	...	...	*Pouvoir d'achat des export.*
Poland											Pologne
Imp: Quantum	48	111	119	140	148	173	199	217	185	210	Imp: quantum
Imp: Unit Value[1]	123	101	116	131	141	151	171	198	172	...	Imp: valeur unitaire[1]
Exp: Quantum	57	122	143	170	189	219	240	257	235	267	Exp: quantum
Exp: Unit Value[1]	126	107	118	139	150	160	186	213	185	...	Exp: valeur unitaire[1]
Terms of Trade	*102*	*105*	*102*	*107*	*107*	*107*	*109*	*107*	*107*	...	*Termes de l'échange*
Purchasing Power of Exports	*59*	*129*	*146*	*182*	*201*	*234*	*261*	*276*	*252*	...	*Pouvoir d'achat des export.*
Portugal											Portugal
Imp: Quantum	...	94	94	104	111	112	123	114	98	118	Imp: quantum
Imp: Unit Value[1]	138	91	110	118	117	119	125	140	114	126	Imp: valeur unitaire[1]
Exp: Quantum	...	95	97	95	93	101	99	93	81	92	Exp: quantum
Exp: Unit Value[1]	144	96	112	122	121	125	134	144	127	134	Exp: valeur unitaire[1]
Terms of Trade	*105*	*106*	*102*	*104*	*104*	*106*	*107*	*103*	*112*	*106*	*Termes de l'échange*
Purchasing Power of Exports	...	*101*	*99*	*98*	*96*	*106*	*105*	*96*	*90*	*97*	*Pouvoir d'achat des export.*
Republic of Moldova											République de Moldova
Imp: Quantum	...	139	180	205	248	267	330	379	284	327	Imp: quantum
Imp: Unit Value	...	92	95	119	124	130	156	213	180	165	Imp: valeur unitaire
Exp: Quantum	...	142	170	199	215	197	232	254	236	276	Exp: quantum
Exp: Unit Value	...	87	88	107	107	107	127	164	135	125	Exp: valeur unitaire
Terms of Trade	...	*95*	*93*	*90*	*86*	*83*	*82*	*77*	*75*	*76*	*Termes de l'échange*
Purchasing Power of Exports	...	*134*	*158*	*178*	*186*	*163*	*190*	*196*	*176*	*208*	*Pouvoir d'achat des export.*

Indices of total exports and imports by countries or areas (Table G)

Quantum and unit value indices and terms of trade in US dollars (2000 = 100)

Indices des exportations et importations totales par pays ou zones (Tableau G)

Indices du quantum et de la valeur unitaire et termes de l'échange en dollars É.-U. (2000 = 100)

Countries	1995	2002	2003	2004	2005	2006	2007	2008	2009	2010	Pays
Romania											Roumanie
Imp: Quantum	...	143	169	207	244	293	369	394	299	345	Imp: quantum
Imp: Unit Value	...	96	106	106	112	116	100	103	92	96	Imp: valeur unitaire
Exp: Quantum	...	132	144	166	179	191	204	225	216	259	Exp: quantum
Exp: Unit Value	...	102	119	125	137	148	107	111	100	107	Exp: valeur unitaire
Terms of Trade	...	*106*	*112*	*118*	*122*	*127*	*108*	*108*	*109*	*112*	*Termes de l'échange*
Purchasing Power of Exports	...	*139*	*161*	*195*	*218*	*244*	*221*	*243*	*235*	*289*	*Pouvoir d'achat des export.*
Russian Federation											Fédération de Russie
Imp: Quantum	...	136	168	222	288	398	...	470	492	672	Imp: quantum
Imp: Unit Value	...	...	...	...	...	...	...	...	...	...	Imp: valeur unitaire
Exp: Quantum	...	105	133	180	240	303	...	261	291	387	Exp: quantum
Exp: Unit Value	...	...	...	...	...	...	...	...	...	...	Exp: valeur unitaire
Terms of Trade	...	...	...	...	...	...	...	...	...	...	*Termes de l'échange*
Purchasing Power of Exports	...	...	...	...	...	...	...	...	...	...	*Pouvoir d'achat des export.*
Serbia											Serbie
Imp: Quantum	.	.	.	.	.	...	129	109	85	108	Imp: quantum
Imp: Unit Value	.	.	.	.	.	...	106	113	79	96	Imp: valeur unitaire
Exp: Quantum	.	.	.	.	.	...	126	112	90	122	Exp: quantum
Exp: Unit Value	.	.	.	.	.	...	110	110	83	97	Exp: valeur unitaire
Terms of Trade	.	.	.	.	.	...	*104*	*97*	*104*	*102*	*Termes de l'échange*
Purchasing Power of Exports	.	.	.	.	.	...	*131*	*109*	*94*	*125*	*Pouvoir d'achat des export.*
Seychelles											Seychelles
Imp: Quantum	46	...	...	...	...	...	...	...	...	...	Imp: quantum
Imp: Unit Value	148	...	...	...	...	...	...	...	...	...	Imp: valeur unitaire
Exp: Quantum	21	...	...	...	...	...	...	...	...	...	Exp: quantum
Exp: Unit Value	94	...	...	...	...	...	...	...	...	...	Exp: valeur unitaire
Terms of Trade	*63*	...	...	...	...	...	...	...	...	...	*Termes de l'échange*
Purchasing Power of Exports	*13*	...	...	...	...	...	...	...	...	...	*Pouvoir d'achat des export.*
Singapore											Singapour
Imp: Quantum	80	90	96	117	134	148	158	174	150	177	Imp: quantum
Imp: Unit Value[1]	115	96	99	104	111	119	124	136	122	130	Imp: valeur unitaire[1]
Exp: Quantum	71	100	116	155	173	192	208	217	195	235	Exp: quantum
Exp: Unit Value[1]	120	91	90	93	96	103	104	113	101	109	Exp: valeur unitaire[1]
Terms of Trade	*104*	*94*	*91*	*89*	*87*	*86*	*84*	*83*	*83*	*83*	*Termes de l'échange*
Purchasing Power of Exports	*75*	*95*	*106*	*139*	*151*	*165*	*176*	*180*	*161*	*196*	*Pouvoir d'achat des export.*
Slovakia											Slovaquie
Imp: Quantum	...	...	...	...	...	...	...	...	...	...	Imp: quantum
Imp: Unit Value[1]	...	106	129	147	157	177	196	235	210	207	Imp: valeur unitaire[1]
Exp: Quantum	...	...	...	...	...	...	...	...	...	...	Exp: quantum
Exp: Unit Value[1]	...	105	139	174	191	204	221	248	235	258	Exp: valeur unitaire[1]
Terms of Trade	...	*99*	*108*	*118*	*121*	*116*	*112*	*106*	*112*	*125*	*Termes de l'échange*
Purchasing Power of Exports	...	...	...	...	...	...	...	...	...	...	*Pouvoir d'achat des export.*
Slovenia											Slovénie
Imp: Quantum	...	105	111	...	...	...	...	...	...	...	Imp: quantum
Imp: Unit Value	...	104	124	141	152	164	175	183	166	179	Imp: valeur unitaire
Exp: Quantum	...	110	115	...	...	...	...	...	...	...	Exp: quantum
Exp: Unit Value	...	106	126	142	149	159	168	171	163	172	Exp: valeur unitaire
Terms of Trade	...	*102*	*102*	*101*	*98*	*97*	*96*	*94*	*98*	*96*	*Termes de l'échange*
Purchasing Power of Exports	...	*112*	*117*	...	...	...	...	...	...	...	*Pouvoir d'achat des export.*

Indices of total exports and imports by countries or areas (Table G)

Quantum and unit value indices and terms of trade in US dollars (2000 = 100)

Indices des exportations et importations totales par pays ou zones (Tableau G)

Indices du quantum et de la valeur unitaire et termes de l'échange en dollars É.-U. (2000 = 100)

Countries	1995	2002	2003	2004	2005	2006	2007	2008	2009	2010	Pays
South Africa											Afrique du Sud
Imp: Quantum	87	105	115	131	144	...	...	...	...	...	Imp: quantum
Imp: Unit Value	117	93	115	136	144	...	...	...	...	...	Imp: valeur unitaire
Exp: Quantum	76	102	103	105	112	...	...	...	...	...	Exp: quantum
Exp: Unit Value	123	96	123	148	156	...	...	...	...	...	Exp: valeur unitaire
Terms of Trade	*106*	*104*	*107*	*108*	*109*	...	...	...	...	...	*Termes de l'échange*
Purchasing Power of Exports	*80*	*106*	*110*	*114*	*122*	...	...	...	...	...	*Pouvoir d'achat des export.*
Spain											Espagne
Imp: Quantum	...	109	117	129	137	149	159	154	...	...	Imp: quantum
Imp: Unit Value	127	99	116	131	138	143	158	177	149	149	Imp: valeur unitaire
Exp: Quantum	...	107	114	120	121	127	133	135	...	...	Exp: quantum
Exp: Unit Value	132	102	121	134	140	148	166	182	160	156	Exp: valeur unitaire
Terms of Trade	*104*	*103*	*104*	*102*	*102*	*103*	*105*	*103*	*107*	*104*	*Termes de l'échange*
Purchasing Power of Exports	...	*111*	*118*	*123*	*123*	*132*	*139*	*139*	...	...	*Pouvoir d'achat des export.*
Sri Lanka											Sri Lanka
Imp: Quantum	73	101	111	122	126	135	140	147	131	149	Imp: quantum
Imp: Unit Value	...	90	...	...	...	...	...	...	...	...	Imp: valeur unitaire
Exp: Quantum	71	93	98	106	113	97	126	126	133	130	Exp: quantum
Exp: Unit Value	99	91	97	101	104	109	113	119	118	132	Exp: valeur unitaire
Terms of Trade	...	*101*	...	...	...	...	...	...	...	...	*Termes de l'échange*
Purchasing Power of Exports	...	*94*	...	...	...	...	...	...	...	...	*Pouvoir d'achat des export.*
Sweden											Suède
Imp: Quantum	69	94	100	108	116	126	139	141	119	140	Imp: quantum
Imp: Unit Value[1]	120	99	117	132	139	149	166	183	155	164	Imp: valeur unitaire[1]
Exp: Quantum	67	101	106	117	122	131	135	137	114	131	Exp: quantum
Exp: Unit Value[1]	131	94	111	121	124	131	148	158	139	145	Exp: valeur unitaire[1]
Terms of Trade	*109*	*95*	*95*	*92*	*90*	*88*	*89*	*87*	*89*	*89*	*Termes de l'échange*
Purchasing Power of Exports	*73*	*96*	*101*	*108*	*109*	*116*	*121*	*119*	*102*	*116*	*Pouvoir d'achat des export.*
Switzerland											Suisse
Imp: Quantum	75	99	100	104	106	117	119	121	108	117	Imp: quantum
Imp: Unit Value	136	105	121	135	143	149	162	181	173	180	Imp: valeur unitaire
Exp: Quantum	80	105	105	111	115	132	132	136	116	124	Exp: quantum
Exp: Unit Value	131	107	124	137	141	143	158	182	186	193	Exp: valeur unitaire
Terms of Trade	*96*	*102*	*102*	*102*	*99*	*96*	*97*	*100*	*108*	*107*	*Termes de l'échange*
Purchasing Power of Exports	*77*	*106*	*107*	*113*	*114*	*127*	*128*	*136*	*125*	*133*	*Pouvoir d'achat des export.*
Thailand											Thaïlande
Imp: Quantum	113	100	112	137	162	164	171	192	148	187	Imp: quantum
Imp: Unit Value	100	102	107	110	117	124	131	147	144	155	Imp: valeur unitaire
Exp: Quantum	70	101	109	119	143	159	178	187	160	188	Exp: quantum
Exp: Unit Value	117	97	105	118	113	119	126	139	139	152	Exp: valeur unitaire
Terms of Trade	*116*	*95*	*99*	*108*	*97*	*96*	*96*	*94*	*97*	*98*	*Termes de l'échange*
Purchasing Power of Exports	*82*	*96*	*108*	*128*	*138*	*152*	*171*	*176*	*155*	*184*	*Pouvoir d'achat des export.*
Turkey											Turquie
Imp: Quantum	49	91	113	137	153	166	187	185	161	195	Imp: quantum
Imp: Unit Value	123	98	111	129	138	150	164	197	159	172	Imp: valeur unitaire
Exp: Quantum	64	142	169	192	212	238	265	283	261	278	Exp: quantum
Exp: Unit Value	128	96	108	126	133	138	155	180	151	158	Exp: valeur unitaire
Terms of Trade	*104*	*97*	*97*	*98*	*97*	*92*	*95*	*91*	*95*	*92*	*Termes de l'échange*
Purchasing Power of Exports	*67*	*137*	*164*	*188*	*205*	*220*	*251*	*258*	*248*	*255*	*Pouvoir d'achat des export.*

Indices of total exports and imports by countries or areas (Table G)

Quantum and unit value indices and terms of trade in US dollars (2000 = 100)

Indices des exportations et importations totales par pays ou zones (Tableau G)

Indices du quantum et de la valeur unitaire et termes de l'échange en dollars É.-U. (2000 = 100)

Countries	1995	2002	2003	2004	2005	2006	2007	2008	2009	2010	Pays
United Kingdom											Royaume-Uni
Imp: Quantum	66	110	112	120	128	141	138	135	118	131	Imp: quantum
Imp: Unit Value[1]	116	96	104	116	120	125	137	144	125	132	Imp: valeur unitaire[1]
Exp: Quantum	73	101	101	102	111	124	111	113	99	109	Exp: quantum
Exp: Unit Value[1]	116	97	108	121	126	130	142	150	130	136	Exp: valeur unitaire[1]
Terms of Trade	*100*	*102*	*104*	*105*	*105*	*104*	*104*	*105*	*104*	*103*	*Termes de l'échange*
Purchasing Power of Exports	*73*	*103*	*105*	*107*	*117*	*129*	*115*	*118*	*103*	*113*	*Pouvoir d'achat des export.*
United States											Etats-Unis
Imp: Quantum	61	101	107	118	125	132	133	128	107	123	Imp: quantum
Imp: Unit Value[1]	101	94	97	102	110	115	120	134	119	127	Imp: valeur unitaire[1]
Exp: Quantum[4]	72	90	93	101	109	120	128	135	115	133	Exp: quantum[4]
Exp: Unit Value[1,4]	104	98	100	104	107	111	116	123	117	123	Exp: valeur unitaire[1,4]
Terms of Trade	*103*	*104*	*103*	*101*	*97*	*96*	*97*	*92*	*99*	*97*	*Termes de l'échange*
Purchasing Power of Exports	*74*	*94*	*96*	*102*	*105*	*115*	*124*	*124*	*114*	*129*	*Pouvoir d'achat des export.*
Uruguay											Uruguay
Imp: Quantum	...	...	...	...	...	...	...	...	...	...	Imp: quantum
Imp: Unit Value	112	87	...	...	...	...	...	...	...	...	Imp: valeur unitaire
Exp: Quantum	...	...	...	...	...	...	...	...	...	...	Exp: quantum
Exp: Unit Value	125	93	...	...	...	...	...	...	...	...	Exp: valeur unitaire
Terms of Trade	*112*	*106*	...	...	...	...	...	...	...	...	*Termes de l'échange*
Purchasing Power of Exports	...	...	...	...	...	...	...	...	...	...	*Pouvoir d'achat des export.*
Venezuela (Bolivarian Rep. of)											Venezuela (Rép. bolivarienne du)
Imp: Quantum	...	...	...	...	...	...	...	...	...	...	Imp: quantum
Imp: Unit Value[1]	105	105	112	123	126	132	150	179	227	236	Imp: valeur unitaire[1]
Exp: Quantum	...	...	...	...	...	...	...	...	...	...	Exp: quantum
Exp: Unit Value	...	...	...	...	...	...	...	...	...	...	Exp: valeur unitaire
Terms of Trade	...	...	...	...	...	...	...	...	...	...	*Termes de l'échange*
Purchasing Power of Exports	...	...	...	...	...	...	...	...	...	...	*Pouvoir d'achat des export.*

General Note:
The volume and unit value/price indices are as compiled by countries. They show the changes in the volume (volume index) and the average price (unit value/price index) of total imports and exports. Using these indices UNSD calculates the terms of trade indices (export unit value/price indices divided by the corresponding import unit value/price indices), and the index of the purchasing power of exports (the terms of trade multiplied by the volume index of exports). Country footnotes which appear in Special Table B of this volume also apply to the country indices published in this table.
For further information on sources and presentation as well as for a brief table description please see the introduction, paragraphs 6-20 and 27.

Remarque générale:
Les indices du volume et les indices de la valeur unitaire/prix sont comme compilées par les pays. Ils indiquent les variations des quantités (indice du volume) et des prix moyens (indice de la valeur unitaire/prix) des importations ou exportations totales. Utilisant ces indices la Division de Statistique des Nations Unies calcule les indices des termes de l'échange (sont obtenus en divisant les indices de la valeur unitaire à l'exportation par ceux à l'importation), et l'indice du pouvoir d'achat des exportations (sont obtenu en multipliant l'indice des termes de l'échange du volume des exportations). Les notes se rapportant aux pays qui apparaissent dans le Tableau Spécial B de ce tome s'appliquent aussi aux indices de ce tableau.
Pour plus d'information sur les sources et la présentation ainsi qu'une brève description du tableau, veuillez vous référer aux paragraphes 6-20 et 27 de l'introduction.

1 Price indices.
2 See explanatory notes pertaining to China, Hong Kong SAR and China, Macao SAR on page viii.
3 Index numbers exclude ships.
4 Excluding military goods.

1 Les indices des prix.
2 Voir les notes explicatives concernant Chine, Hong Kong RAS et Chine, Macao RAS à la page viii.
3 Les indices ne comprennent pas de navires.
4 Hors matériel militaire.

Indices of total exports and imports by regions (Table H)

Quantum and unit value indices and terms of trade in US dollars (2000 = 100)

Indices des exportations et importations totales par région (Tableau H)

Indices du quantum et de la valeur unitaire et termes de l'échange en dollars É.-U. (2000 = 100)

Regions - Régions	1995	1999	2001	2002	2003	2004	2005	2006	2007	2008	2009	2010
Exports - Unit value index / Exportations - Indice de la valeur unitaire[1]												
Total - Totaux	119	102	97	97	107	116	121	126	136	148	135	141
Developed economies - Economies développées[2]	122	103	98	99	111	121	126	131	144	158	144	148
North America - Amérique du Nord	103	98	100	98	101	107	113	117	124	132	122	130
Europe	131	107	98	101	117	130	134	139	155	171	153	154
Asia-Pacific - Asie-Pacifique	115	96	94	91	98	108	115	117	124	142	141	154
Africa - Afrique	110	95	94	95	109	122	123	123	127	122	119	126
Northern Africa - Afrique du Nord	93	86	90	93	95	99	100	102	110	116	114	111
Sub-Saharan Africa - Afrique subsaharienne	122	101	95	97	119	141	149	148	146	128	124	140
Latin America & The Caribbean - Amérique latine et les Caraïbes	87	92	94	95	101	109	117	126	134	149	134	145
Latin America - Amérique latine	87	92	94	95	101	109	117	126	134	150	135	145
Western Asia - Asie Occidentale[3]	115	102	97	96	105	117	126	131	145	170	148	154
Other Asia - Autres Pays d'Asie	118	99	94	90	93	99	101	105	109	116	106	116
Eastern Asia - Asie Orientale	117	97	93	90	92	98	100	101	103	109	97	106
Southern Asia - Asie Méridionale	110	103	94	92	105	119	126	141	153	149	154	172
South-eastern Asia - Asie du Sud-est	121	102	94	90	92	96	99	105	110	120	111	120
Imports - Unit value index / Importations - Indice de la valeur unitaire[1]												
Total - Totaux	115	99	96	96	104	114	120	127	139	157	142	146
Developed economies - Economies développées[2]	118	100	96	96	106	116	122	129	141	158	138	144
North America - Amérique du Nord	100	94	96	94	97	103	111	116	121	135	120	128
Europe	129	104	97	99	114	127	131	138	153	170	148	152
Asia-Pacific - Asie-Pacifique	110	93	88	88	94	104	113	120	133	159	137	151
Africa - Afrique	118	100	94	94	113	131	137	...	...	...	...	...
Northern Africa - Afrique du Nord	131	109	93	76	83	87	95	101	117	123	111	108
Sub-Saharan Africa - Afrique subsaharienne	115	99	...	...	...	...	...	...	...	...	...	...
Latin America & The Caribbean - Amérique latine et les Caraïbes	98	98	99	91	90	101	121	134	148	184	175	184
Western Asia - Asie Occidentale[3]	116	96	99	99	109	123	133	144	158	187	154	167
Other Asia - Autres Pays d'Asie	105	94	95	93	96	105	110	116	124	...	...	139
Eastern Asia - Asie Orientale	111	92	94	91	95	104	109	115	120	136	117	129
Southern Asia - Asie Méridionale	100	96	96	102	113	132	142	137	177	177	155	188
South-eastern Asia - Asie du Sud-est	115	97	97	95	98	101	110	120	125	138	127	137
Terms of trade / Termes de l'échange[4]												
Developed economies - Economies développées[2]	103	104	102	103	104	104	104	102	102	100	104	103
North America - Amérique du Nord	103	105	103	104	104	104	102	101	102	98	101	101
Europe	101	103	100	102	103	102	103	101	101	100	104	102
Asia-Pacific - Asie-Pacifique	104	103	107	103	105	104	101	98	93	89	103	102
Africa - Afrique	94	96	99	101	97	93	90	...	...	...	...	...
Northern Africa - Afrique du Nord	71	79	97	122	114	114	105	101	94	94	103	104
Sub-Saharan Africa - Afrique subsaharienne	106	102	...	...	...	...	...	...	...	...	...	...
Latin America & The Caribbean - Amérique latine et les Caraïbes	89	94	95	104	113	108	96	94	90	81	77	79
Western Asia - Asie Occidentale[3]	99	106	98	97	96	95	95	91	92	91	96	92
Other Asia - Autres Pays d'Asie	112	105	98	97	97	94	92	90	88	...	...	83
Eastern Asia - Asie Orientale	106	105	99	99	97	94	91	87	86	80	83	82
Southern Asia - Asie Méridionale	110	107	98	90	94	90	88	103	87	84	100	92
South-eastern Asia - Asie du Sud-est	105	104	96	94	94	95	89	88	88	87	87	88

Indices of total exports and imports by regions (Table H)

Quantum and unit value indices and terms of trade in US dollars (2000 = 100)

Indices des exportations et importations totales par région (Tableau H)

Indices du quantum et de la valeur unitaire et termes de l'échange en dollars É.-U. (2000 = 100)

Regions - Régions	1995	1999	2001	2002	2003	2004	2005	2006	2007	2008	2009	2010
			Exports - Volume index / Exportations - Indice du volume[5]									
Total - Totaux	68	88	99	103	109	122	133	148	157	165	142	165
Developed economies - Economies développées[2]	71	90	99	102	104	112	118	128	134	136	115	131
North America - Amérique du Nord	71	90	94	92	93	99	106	115	121	126	106	121
Europe	69	90	103	107	109	118	124	135	141	142	123	137
Asia-Pacific - Asie-Pacifique	79	91	91	98	102	112	113	122	127	127	97	118
Africa - Afrique	68	85	101	103	111	132	177	206	237	327	228	272
Northern Africa - Afrique du Nord	77	86	102	104	128	160	220	257	280	360	236	295
Sub-Saharan Africa - Afrique subsaharienne	63	84	100	103	102	114	147	168	204	303	221	252
Latin America & The Caribbean - Amérique latine et les Caraïbes	73	90	102	102	106	121	136	152	160	168	144	170
Latin America - Amérique latine	73	91	102	103	106	121	136	151	159	166	143	168
Western Asia - Asie Occidentale[3]	52	76	96	102	115	137	168	192	201	226	183	221
Other Asia - Autres Pays d'Asie	62	84	99	113	130	156	181	208	235	254	231	275
Eastern Asia - Asie Orientale	62	85	101	117	140	170	198	234	272	292	275	329
Southern Asia - Asie Méridionale	65	80	104	114	121	135	163	182	199	259	202	236
South-eastern Asia - Asie du Sud-est	62	83	96	105	114	137	153	170	182	193	170	203
			Imports - Volume index / Importations - Indice du volume[5]									
Total - Totaux	69	89	100	104	111	124	133	144	152	154	132	155
Developed economies - Economies développées[2]	67	91	100	103	108	118	125	135	139	139	119	133
North America - Amérique du Nord	62	91	97	101	106	117	124	130	132	128	107	123
Europe	67	91	102	104	108	118	126	137	144	145	126	139
Asia-Pacific - Asie-Pacifique	80	91	104	104	112	122	127	134	132	135	117	132
Africa - Afrique	79	100	111	112	112	123	143	...	...	...	...	...
Northern Africa - Afrique du Nord	74	94	109	140	135	166	180	182	206	285	282	319
Sub-Saharan Africa - Afrique subsaharienne	79	99	...	...	...	...	...	...	...	...	...	...
Latin America & The Caribbean - Amérique latine et les Caraïbes	67	88	99	101	106	114	113	122	132	130	103	124
Western Asia - Asie Occidentale[3]	65	89	98	107	115	135	151	163	188	196	191	201
Other Asia - Autres Pays d'Asie	78	85	98	109	127	150	167	185	200	...	...	233
Eastern Asia - Asie Orientale	69	85	99	114	136	160	173	192	214	218	213	262
Southern Asia - Asie Méridionale	78	94	105	111	123	140	175	216	204	277	259	270
South-eastern Asia - Asie du Sud-est	81	84	94	98	107	130	143	151	164	181	151	184

Indices of total exports and imports by regions (Table H)

Quantum and unit value indices and terms of trade in US dollars (2000 = 100)

Indices des exportations et importations totales par région (Tableau H)

Indices du quantum et de la valeur unitaire et termes de l'échange en dollars É.-U. (2000 = 100)

Source:
Compiled by the United Nations Statistics Division from international and national publications. For the composition of the regions, see Table A of this issue.
For further information on sources and presentation as well as for brief table description, please see the introduction, paragraphs 6-20 and 28.

1 Regional aggregates are current period weighted.

2 This classification is intended for statistical convenience and does not, necessarily, express a judgement about the stage reached by a particular country in the development process.

3 Index does not include data of the major oil producing countries.

4 Unit value index of exports divided by unit value index of imports.

5 Volume indices are derived from value data and unit value indices. They are base period weighted.

Source:
Compilé par la Division de statistique des Nations Unies à partir de publications internationales et nationales. Pour la composition des régions, voir tableau A du présent volume.
Pour plus d'informaton sur les sources et présentation ainsi qu'une brève description de la table, veuillez vois référer aux paragraphes 6-20 et 28 de l'introduction.

1 Les totaux régionaux sont à coéfficients de pondération correspondant à la période en cours.

2 Cette classification est utilisée pour plus de commodité dans la présentation des statistiques et n'implique pas nécessairement un jugement quant au stade de développement auquel est parvenu un pays donné.

3 L'index n'inclut pas de données des pays producteurs de pétrole importants.

4 Indice de la valeur unitaire des exportations divisé par l'indice de la valeur unitaire des importations.

5 Les indices du volume sont calculés à partir de chiffres de la valeur et des indices de la valeur unitaire. Ils sont à coéfficients de pondération correspondant à la période en base.

Indices and values of manufactured goods exports (Table I)

Unit value and volume indices (2000=100) and value in thousand million U.S. dollars

Indices et valeurs des exportations des produits manufacturés (Tableau I)

Indices de valeur unitaire et de volume (2000=100), et valeur en milliards de dollars E.-U.

Region, country or area	1995	1999	2001	2002	2003	2004	2005	2006	2007	2008	2009	2010
	Unit value indices in U.S. dollars - Indices de valeur unitaire en dollars des E.-U. 2000 = 100											
Total 1/	**122**	**103**	**98**	**98**	**104**	**110**	**111**	**114**	**125**	**131**	**121**	**124**
Developed economies	**123**	**105**	**98**	**99**	**108**	**117**	**120**	**123**	**133**	**139**	**132**	**134**
America	100	99	99	100	103	106	108	111	115	118	112	118
Canada	104	99	98	96	103	112	119	128	135	...	...	...
United States 2/	98	99	100	102	103	104	104	107	110	116	113	117
Europe	135	110	99	100	112	122	125	130	142	149	139	139
Austria 3/	205	118	94	100	...	...	...	...	...	...	...	...
Belgium	132	108	99	106	125	141	148	156	178	186	172	173
Denmark	134	112	100	103	122	136	138	141	145	157	144	148
Finland	128	104	95	100	117	120	131	141	166	177	158	163
France	139	113	98	84	101	111	111	109	118	124	...	...
Germany 4/	150	111	99	104	118	128	128	132	143	155	145	140
Greece	149	107	...	...	...	...	...	...	...	...	...	...
Iceland 5/	128	...	...	...	...	...	...	...	...	...	...	...
Ireland 5/	125	...	...	...	...	...	...	...	...	...	...	...
Italy 5/	120	113	100	...	104	...	118	125	136	139	136	142
Netherlands 6/	141	109	104	104	120	130	139	144	175	...	...	...
Norway	135	106	97	100	110	126	131	145	169	177	148	155
Portugal 5/	138	110	99	...	...	...	...	...	...	...	...	...
Spain 5/	132	...	...	...	...	...	...	...	...	...	...	...
Sweden	131	106	...	...	...	...	...	...	...	...	...	...
Switzerland 5/	128	109	104	109	...	...	...	...	...	...	...	...
United Kingdom	116	108	95	98	108	120	120	123	133	135	124	125
Other developed economies	118	98	93	91	97	107	113	114	119	128	129	138
Australia	121	97	93	92	101	133	151	203	245	223	155	205
Israel	77	83	98	95	95	99	109	118	124	126	120	121
Japan	119	98	94	92	97	107	112	112	117	129	133	141
New Zealand	134	96	98	99	112	125	136	140	155	163	131	152
South Africa	190	...	...	...	...	...	...	...	...	...	...	...
Developing economies	**120**	**97**	**98**	**96**	**97**	**99**	**98**	**102**	**110**	**117**	**103**	**108**
China, Hong Kong SAR	111	102	95	93	93	94	96	93	94	99	100	105
India	117	121	92	99	...	...	...	...	...	...	...	...
Korea, Republic of	136	96	92	82	83	92	96	101	106	99	84	90
Pakistan	113	106	100	96	101	108	106	108	108	108	101	118
Singapore	127	101	98	100	99	98	78	81	109	109	105	109
Turkey 7/	139	105	99	96	108	124	130	127	137	171	...	153
	Unit value indices in 'SDR' - Indices de valeur unitaire en 'DTS' 2000 = 100											
Total	106	99	102	99	99	97	99	102	107	109	103	107
Developed economies	**107**	**101**	**102**	**100**	**102**	**103**	**107**	**110**	**114**	**116**	**112**	**116**
Developing economies	**104**	**93**	**102**	**98**	**92**	**87**	**87**	**91**	**94**	**97**	**88**	**93**

For general note and footnotes see end of Table K.

Indices and values of manufactured goods exports (Table I)

Unit value and volume indices (2000=100) and value in thousand million U.S. dollars

Indices et valeurs des exportations des produits manufacturés (Tableau I)

Indices de valeur unitaire et de volume (2000=100), et valeur en milliards de dollars E.-U.

Unit value indices in national currency - Indices de valeur unitaire en monnaie nationale

2000 = 100

1995	1999	2001	2002	2003	2004	2005	2006	2007	2008	2009	2010	Région, pays ou zones
...	...	...	...	...	...	...	...	...	...	...	...	**Totaux 1/**
...	...	...	...	...	...	...	...	...	...	...	...	**Economies développées**
...	...	...	...	...	...	...	...	...	...	...	...	Amérique
96	99	102	102	98	98	97	98	97	...	...	...	Canada
98	99	100	102	103	104	104	107	110	116	113	117	Etats-Unis 2/
...	...	...	...	...	...	...	...	...	...	...	...	Europe
138	102	98	98	...	...	...	...	...	...	...	...	Autriche 3/
89	94	102	103	103	105	110	115	120	116	114	121	Belgique
93	97	102	100	101	101	102	103	97	98	95	103	Danemark
87	90	98	98	96	89	97	104	112	111	105	114	Finlande
97	98	101	83	83	82	82	81	80	78	...	...	France
101	97	102	102	96	95	95	97	97	97	96	97	Allemagne 4/
95	90	...	...	...	...	...	...	...	...	...	...	Grèce
...	...	...	...	...	...	...	...	...	...	...	...	Islande
...	...	...	...	...	...	...	...	...	...	...	...	Irlande
...	...	...	...	...	...	...	...	...	...	...	...	Italie
94	95	107	102	98	97	103	106	118	...	...	...	Pays-Bas 6/
97	94	99	91	89	96	96	106	112	111	105	106	Norvège
...	...	...	...	...	...	...	...	...	...	...	...	Portugal
...	...	...	...	...	...	...	...	...	...	...	...	Espagne
102	96	...	...	...	...	...	...	...	...	...	...	Suède
...	...	...	...	...	...	...	...	...	...	...	...	Suisse
111	101	99	99	100	99	100	101	101	111	120	122	Royaume-Uni
...	...	...	...	...	...	...	...	...	...	...	...	Autres économies développées
94	87	104	97	89	104	114	156	169	153	114	129	Australie
...	...	...	...	...	...	...	...	...	...	...	...	Israël
103	104	110	106	105	107	114	121	127	124	115	115	Japon
93	83	105	97	88	86	88	98	96	104	95	95	Nouvelle-Zélande
99	...	...	...	...	...	...	...	...	...	...	...	Afrique du Sud
...	...	...	...	...	...	...	...	...	...	...	...	**Economies en voie de développement**
110	101	96	93	93	94	96	93	94	99	99	104	Chine, Hong-Kong RAS
84	116	95	107	...	...	...	...	...	...	...	...	Inde
93	101	105	91	87	93	87	85	87	94	95	92	Corée, République de
68	100	117	108	111	119	119	123	124	143	156	191	Pakistan
...	...	...	...	...	...	76	75	95	89	88	86	Singapour
...	...	...	...	...	...	...	...	...	...	...	...	Turquie

Voir à la fin du Tableau K pour la remarque générale et les notes.

Indices and values of manufactured goods exports (Table I)

Unit value and volume indices (2000=100) and value in thousand million U.S. dollars

Indices et valeurs des exportations des produits manufacturés (Tableau I)

Indices de valeur unitaire et de volume (2000=100), et valeur en milliards de dollars E.-U.

Region, country or area	1995	1999	2001	2002	2003	2004	2005	2006	2007	2008	2009	2010
					Volume indices - Indices de volume 2000 = 100							
Total	66	88	100	103	111	128	139	153	145	146	126	144
Developed economies	70	89	102	101	105	115	120	130	136	136	112	127
America	72	91	101	88	88	97	104	113	119	120	99	110
Canada	67	90	94	94	92	97	100	99	100	...	...	...
United States	73	91	103	86	87	97	105	118	126	126	104	117
Europe	68	89	106	108	113	124	128	139	145	146	123	138
Austria	50	86	124	118	...	...	...	...	...	...	...	...
Belgium	76	92	100	100	100	106	107	107	109	112	84	93
Denmark	69	95	105	114	119	119	129	137	148	152	135	187
Finland	68	89	103	98	98	109	108	116	116	115	84	85
France	64	86	119	120	118	127	132	148	152	159	...	...
Germany	63	86	105	107	114	128	138	152	166	153	138	163
Greece	66	86	...	...	...	...	...	...	...	...	...	...
Iceland	52	...	...	...	...	...	...	...	...	...	...	...
Ireland	38	...	...	...	...	...	...	...	...	...	...	...
Italy	82	86	105	...	119	...	128	135	148	156	118	125
Netherlands	64	88	115	117	122	135	136	147	148	...	...	...
Norway	65	96	92	110	110	112	119	129	141	148	134	139
Portugal	67	93	103	...	...	...	...	...	...	...	...	...
Spain	60	...	...	...	...	...	...	...	...	...	...	...
Sweden	77	100	...	...	...	...	...	...	...	...	...	...
Switzerland	78	94	97	99	...	...	...	...	...	...	...	...
United Kingdom	75	90	96	102	103	104	111	124	113	114	96	107
Other developed economies	77	90	91	96	103	112	112	120	127	128	94	115
Australia	61	91	99	104	103	88	88	73	73	85	93	86
Israel	75	98	95	98	105	124	125	123	134	135	123	145
Japan	79	89	89	94	100	110	109	117	123	121	86	108
New Zealand	70	99	108	105	109	116	115	117	119	113	112	113
South Africa	46	...	...	...	...	...	...	...	...	...	...	...
Developing economies	57	86	96	107	124	157	184	208	167	169	156	182
China, Hong Kong SAR	113	93	88	93	70	71	75	77	60	45	27	31
India	57	69	105	115	...	...	...	...	...	...	...	...
Korea, Republic of	54	87	95	97	118	145	175	188	203	241	249	297
Pakistan	77	90	101	114	140	137	155	160	163	176	163	165
Singapore	67	82	89	90	104	129	188	225	180	184	162	200
Turkey	51	88	114	138	162	189	204	240	279	269	...	259

For general note and footnotes see end of Table K.

Indices and values of manufactured goods exports (Table I)

Unit value and volume indices (2000=100) and value in thousand million U.S. dollars

Indices et valeurs des exportations des produits manufacturés (Tableau I)

Indices de valeur unitaire et de volume (2000=100), et valeur en milliards de dollars E.-U.

n thousand million U.S. dollars — En milliards de dollars E.-U.

1995	2000	2001	2002	2003	2004	2005	2006	2007	2008	2009	2010	Région, pays ou zones
					Value - Valeur In thousand million U.S. dollars - En milliards de dollars E.-U.							
3744.7	4620.8	4548.3	4648.6	5356.1	6495.7	7135.9	8104.2	8379.3	8881.5	7029.9	8247.0	**Totaux**
2775.1	3209.4	3215.6	3196.4	3653.2	4312.7	4590.7	5128.2	5792.7	6098.9	4746.1	5492.0	**Economies développées**
557.0	780.3	781.7	685.3	704.0	803.2	872.2	983.2	1070.3	1105.3	869.6	1017.5	Amérique
128.2	184.0	169.1	166.6	173.6	200.2	219.2	234.6	247.8	235.2	169.8	203.4	Canada
428.8	596.3	612.6	518.8	530.4	603.0	653.1	748.6	822.5	870.2	699.8	814.1	Etats-Unis
1741.8	1903.5	1986.4	2051.3	2426.2	2877.4	3055.3	3426.3	3926.7	4135.5	3242.2	3638.0	Europe
51.4	49.8	58.3	59.0	76.8	96.7	100.2	114.0	133.6	150.0	112.0	121.4	Autriche
133.6	132.5	131.6	139.5	166.3	198.7	209.9	222.3	258.2	274.5	191.1	212.8	Belgique
29.4	31.8	33.5	37.2	46.4	51.4	56.6	61.1	68.3	76.1	61.9	88.2	Danemark
34.7	39.7	38.9	38.9	45.4	51.8	56.1	65.1	76.8	81.3	52.6	55.4	Finlande
222.9	249.2	290.2	251.9	298.5	351.8	365.3	404.9	449.2	489.7	383.7	419.0	France
455.8	481.0	499.2	534.8	644.3	790.3	849.0	970.0	1143.7	1142.6	961.9	1094.8	Allemagne
6.0	6.1	6.0	5.7	8.7	8.5	10.7	12.0	14.0	15.4	11.7	...	Grèce
0.4	0.6	0.7	0.7	0.8	1.0	1.1	1.3	1.9	2.9	2.0	2.6	Islande
31.2	65.6	75.1	77.7	79.4	88.7	94.0	96.5	101.9	107.7	98.2	98.6	Irlande
209.0	212.6	223.2	226.1	262.5	309.7	320.2	357.9	426.3	460.0	341.6	375.1	Italie
113.9	127.5	152.8	154.6	186.1	224.7	240.4	271.0	331.4	350.9	285.7	324.3	Pays-Bas
14.5	16.6	14.8	18.3	20.3	23.5	25.9	31.1	39.5	43.6	33.1	35.6	Norvège
19.5	21.0	21.4	22.4	27.5	30.5	28.8	32.1	32.9	39.7	30.3	35.1	Portugal
71.4	89.4	91.4	99.0	124.0	142.8	150.1	166.8	196.8	209.2	...	...	Espagne
67.4	67.2	58.7	66.9	82.4	101.0	111.0	124.1	143.1	150.9	107.3	127.6	Suède
77.8	78.2	78.8	84.5	96.8	113.7	123.3	138.2	157.8	182.0	...	...	Suisse
201.3	232.5	210.2	232.6	258.1	290.2	310.5	355.4	348.4	356.3	277.8	310.9	Royaume-Uni
476.2	525.6	447.5	459.8	523.1	632.1	663.2	718.6	795.7	858.1	634.3	836.5	Autres économies développées
15.6	21.2	19.5	20.2	22.0	25.0	28.2	31.6	38.1	40.3	30.6	37.2	Australie
17.1	29.7	27.6	27.5	29.5	36.5	40.5	43.3	49.4	50.7	44.1	52.1	Israël
425.8	454.8	378.0	391.8	443.3	534.1	553.7	597.3	654.1	707.8	518.9	695.3	Japon
4.4	4.7	5.0	4.9	5.7	6.8	7.3	7.7	8.6	8.7	6.9	8.0	Nouvelle-Zélande
13.4	15.2	17.5	15.3	22.5	29.7	33.5	38.7	45.5	50.7	33.8	...	Afrique du Sud
969.6	1411.4	1332.7	1452.2	1702.8	2183.0	2545.1	2976.0	2586.6	2782.5	2283.8	2754.9	**Economies en voie de développement**
28.2	22.4	18.9	19.4	14.7	15.1	16.3	16.0	12.5	10.0	6.1	7.2	Chine, Hong-Kong RAS
23.3	35.0	33.5	39.9	48.8	59.1	74.1	86.1	96.9	116.7	...	...	Inde
115.5	156.9	137.3	125.4	153.0	207.9	262.8	297.5	338.6	373.2	328.8	420.3	Corée, République de
6.7	7.7	7.8	8.4	10.9	11.4	12.7	13.4	13.6	14.7	12.7	15.1	Pakistan
101.0	119.3	103.7	106.7	122.8	151.7	175.7	217.4	233.8	240.3	203.0	259.4	Singapour
16.3	23.1	26.1	30.8	40.3	54.2	61.1	70.9	88.7	106.3	80.3	91.7	Turquie

Voir à la fin du Tableau K pour la remarque générale et les notes.

Indices and values of fuel imports - Developed economies (Table J)

Unit value and volume indices (2000=100) and value in thousand million U.S. dollars

Indices et valeurs des importations de produits énergétiques - Pays à économies développées (Tableau J)

Indices de valeur unitaire et de volume (2000=100), et valeur en milliards de dollars E.-U.

Region, country or area	1995	1999	2001	2002	2003	2004	2005	2006	2007	2008	2009	2010
Unit Value Indices in U.S. dollars - Indices de valeur unitaire en dollars des E.-U. 2000 = 100												
Developed economies	68	64	90	90	103	128	171	184	197	277	190	235
America	60	61	87	85	102	129	187	220	243	329	206	263
Canada	81	73	112	109	133	161	215	255	279	...	...	...
United States 2/...............	59	60	86	83	100	127	185	217	240	328	204	259
Europe	72	66	92	94	107	131	166	187	196	266	182	216
Austria 3/........................	79	84	92	92	111	141	190	227	244	347	231	268
Belgium.............................	73	68	92	90	108	135	185	210	217	316	194	248
Denmark	77	69	93	99	117	147	188	220	241	333	210	249
Finland	69	71	91	91	107	121	167	205	224	316	211	261
France	82	73	98	100	104	128	198	240	263	370	...	...
Germany 4/......................	74	64	97	102	116	141	189	227	234	342	227	255
Greece	75	63	...	...	...	...	...	...	...	...	...	...
Iceland 5/........................	71	...	...	...	...	...	...	...	...	...	...	...
Ireland 5/.........................	74	...	...	...	...	...	...	...	...	...	...	...
Italy 5/.............................	70	...	...	...	...	...	...	...	...	...	...	...
Netherlands 5/	75	...	...	...	...	...	...	...	...	...	...	...
Norway	85	80	95	99	120	137	183	221	241	333	220	276
Portugal 5/	67	61	93	...	...	...	...	...	...	...	...	...
Spain 5/..........................	54	50	75	73	88	107	135	161	174	231	150	...
Sweden	68	65	...	...	...	...	...	...	...	...	...	...
Switzerland 5/.................	70	62	95	88	107	138	...	...	...	...	...	...
United Kingdom	72	70	89	100	119	157	222	275	300	399	267	338
Other developed economies ..	72	65	88	88	96	120	159	138	149	242	190	253
Australia	66	65	87	86	121	153	214	265	284	405	248	327
Israel	66	65	89	90	90	117	190	205	228	349	227	285
Japan	71	64	89	89	95	116	154	128	138	234	186	249
New Zealand	70	64	89	92	110	144	196	244	265	363	211	277
South Africa	...	...	...	...	...	...	...	...	...	...	...	...

For general note and footnotes see end of Table K.

Indices and values of fuel imports - Developed economies (Table J)

Unit value and volume indices (2000=100) and value in thousand million U.S. dollars

Indices et valeurs des importations de produits énergétiques - Pays à économies développées (Tableau J)

Indices de valeur unitaire et de volume (2000=100), et valeur en milliards de dollars E.-U.

thousand million U.S. dollars — En milliards de dollars E.-U.

1995	1999	2001	2002	2003	2004	2005	2006	2007	2008	2009	2010	Région, pays ou zones
Unit value indices in national currency - Indices de valeur unitaire en monnaie nationale												
2000 = 100												
...	...	...	...	...	...	...	...	...	...	...	...	**Economies développées**
...	...	...	...	...	...	...	...	...	...	...	...	Amérique
75	73	116	115	126	141	176	195	201	...	...	...	Canada
59	60	86	83	100	127	185	217	240	328	204	259	Etats-Unis 2/
...	...	...	...	...	...	...	...	...	...	...	...	Europe
53	73	95	90	91	105	141	167	165	218	153	187	Autriche 3/
49	59	95	88	88	100	139	154	146	198	129	173	Belgique
53	60	94	97	97	109	139	161	162	209	139	173	Danemark
47	61	94	89	88	90	124	151	151	198	140	182	Finlande
58	64	101	98	85	95	147	176	177	232	...	...	France
50	55	100	100	95	105	140	167	158	214	151	178	Allemagne 4/
47	53	...	...	...	...	...	...	...	...	...	...	Grèce
...	...	...	...	...	...	...	...	...	...	...	...	Islande 5/
...	...	...	...	...	...	...	...	...	...	...	...	Irlande 5/
...	...	...	...	...	...	...	...	...	...	...	...	Italie 5/
...	...	...	...	...	...	...	...	...	...	...	...	Pays-Bas 5/
61	71	97	89	97	105	133	161	160	210	156	189	Norvège
...	...	...	...	...	...	...	...	...	...	...	...	Portugal 5/
37	44	77	72	72	79	100	119	117	145	100	...	Espagne 5/
53	58	...	...	...	...	...	...	...	...	...	...	Suède
49	55	95	81	86	101	...	...	...	...	...	...	Suisse 5/
69	65	93	101	110	130	185	226	227	327	258	331	Royaume-Uni
...	...	...	...	...	...	...	...	...	...	...	...	Autres économies développées
52	58	98	91	108	121	163	204	197	277	183	207	Australie
...	...	...	...	...	...	...	...	...	...	...	...	Israël
62	68	104	104	102	116	157	138	151	225	161	202	Japon
48	54	96	89	85	98	126	170	163	232	150	173	Nouvelle-Zélande
...	...	...	...	...	...	...	...	...	...	...	...	Afrique du Sud

Voir à la fin du Tableau K pour la remarque générale et les notes.

Indices and values of fuel imports - Developed economies (Table J)

Unit value and volume indices (2000=100) and value in thousand million U.S. dollars

Indices et valeurs des importations de produits énergétiques - Pays à économies développées (Tableau J)

Indices de valeur unitaire et de volume (2000=100), et valeur en milliards de dollars E.-U.

Region, country or area	1995	1999	2001	2002	2003	2004	2005	2006	2007	2008	2009	2010
						Volume indices - indices de volume 2000 = 100						
Developed economies	84	94	106	102	112	118	124	140	140	141	122	125
America	75	94	106	103	110	115	111	109	107	107	96	98
Canada	59	78	83	80	91	96	107	100	102	...	...	...
United States	76	95	108	105	112	117	111	110	108	107	95	98
Europe	86	93	108	101	114	124	140	154	155	162	146	152
Austria	102	74	138	138	175	194	205	218	172	163	166	160
Belgium	83	89	107	110	123	132	135	132	131	145	126	128
Denmark	74	81	78	78	87	95	106	100	89	104	111	107
Finland	94	95	106	106	118	126	118	129	126	127	120	120
France	74	84	113	91	115	124	109	110	106	108	108	...
Germany	89	96	101	90	103	108	110	114	111	111	107	111
Greece	63	60	...	...	...	...	...	...	...	...	...	...
Iceland	79	...	...	...	...	...	...	...	...	...	...	...
Ireland	70	...	...	...	...	...	...	...	...	...	...	...
Italy	94	...	...	...	...	...	...	...	...	...	...	...
Netherlands	81	...	...	...	...	...	...	...	...	...	...	...
Norway	81	93	103	90	112	115	91	97	106	96	117	139
Portugal	99	107	100	...	...	...	...	...	...	...	...	...
Spain	94	113	125	132	133	147	163	173	181	189	170	...
Sweden	98	105	...	...	...	...	...	...	...	...	...	...
Switzerland	87	104	106	104	103	100	...	...	...	...	...	...
United Kingdom	87	87	112	97	105	129	130	133	134	140	126	127
Other developed economies ..	93	98	103	102	110	111	111	159	162	151	113	109
Australia	76	102	101	102	100	113	113	120	130	135	146	143
Israel	70	78	99	96	116	107	99	90	105	100	85	96
Japan	98	100	102	102	111	110	110	162	162	147	106	103
New Zealand	70	91	105	101	104	107	105	105	111	110	120	110
South Africa	...	...	...	...	...	...	...	...	...	...	...	...

For general note and footnotes see end of Table K.

Indices and values of fuel imports - Developed economies (Table J)

Unit value and volume indices (2000=100) and value in thousand million U.S. dollars

Indices et valeurs des importations de produits énergétiques - Pays à économies développées (Tableau J)

Indices de valeur unitaire et de volume (2000=100), et valeur en milliards de dollars E.-U.

thousand million U.S. dollars — En milliards de dollars E.-U.

1995	2000	2001	2002	2003	2004	2005	2006	2007	2008	2009	2010	Région, pays ou zones
												Value - Valeur In thousand million U.S. dollars - En milliards de dollars E.-U.
252.5	441.6	420.2	404.0	509.8	668.6	937.4	1137.4	1217.9	1723.2	1024.6	1294.2	**Economies développées**
68.9	152.1	140.6	132.8	170.7	225.3	315.2	365.4	396.3	538.4	300.4	392.6	Amérique
5.9	12.5	11.6	10.9	15.1	19.4	28.9	31.9	35.4	50.5	30.1	39.1	Canada
63.0	139.6	129.0	121.9	155.6	205.9	286.4	333.5	360.9	487.9	270.3	353.5	Etats-Unis
122.1	197.3	196.0	188.0	241.4	321.0	459.1	570.0	599.2	848.5	526.4	646.9	Europe
3.0	3.7	4.7	4.7	7.2	10.2	14.4	18.3	15.6	21.1	14.3	15.9	Autriche
9.4	15.4	15.2	15.2	20.3	27.4	38.2	42.6	43.8	70.5	37.6	49.0	Belgique
1.4	2.5	1.8	2.0	2.6	3.5	5.0	5.6	5.4	8.8	5.9	6.7	Danemark
2.6	4.0	3.8	3.9	5.1	6.1	7.9	10.5	11.2	16.1	10.1	12.5	Finlande
18.6	30.5	33.6	27.8	36.3	48.4	65.9	80.3	84.8	121.7	76.1	88.5	France
28.3	43.1	42.0	39.8	52.0	65.9	89.6	112.0	111.7	164.1	105.3	122.3	Allemagne
1.9	4.0	4.3	4.4	6.2	6.7	9.8	12.2	11.5	7.6	3.1	...	Grèce
0.1	0.2	0.2	0.2	0.2	0.4	0.5	0.5	0.6	0.7	0.4	0.5	Islande
1.1	2.1	2.1	1.7	2.0	3.1	4.8	5.6	6.5	10.2	6.4	7.4	Irlande
15.0	22.9	22.5	22.0	26.5	33.5	60.6	77.4	83.1	112.8	72.3	92.3	Italie
12.1	20.0	19.8	19.5	24.4	33.3	45.3	59.0	66.3	90.4	59.9	80.1	Pays-Bas
1.0	1.4	1.3	1.2	1.8	2.2	2.3	3.0	3.5	4.4	3.5	5.3	Norvège
2.7	4.1	3.8	3.9	4.8	6.2	9.0	10.0	9.2	15.0	9.0	11.0	Portugal
9.4	18.6	17.4	18.0	21.6	29.1	40.8	51.8	58.4	81.3	47.4	...	Espagne
4.0	6.1	4.7	5.9	7.7	9.8	13.0	15.7	16.9	24.4	14.0	20.0	Suède
2.3	3.8	3.9	3.5	4.2	5.3	9.1	11.2	11.2	16.2	11.2	...	Suisse
9.3	14.7	14.7	14.3	18.3	29.7	42.6	53.9	59.1	82.4	49.5	63.3	Royaume-Uni
61.4	92.1	83.7	83.2	97.8	122.4	163.1	202.0	222.5	336.3	197.9	254.7	Autres économies développées
2.9	5.8	5.1	5.1	7.0	10.0	13.9	18.5	21.4	31.6	20.9	27.1	Australie
1.7	3.6	3.2	3.1	3.8	4.5	6.8	6.6	8.6	12.5	6.9	9.8	Israël
53.9	77.4	70.2	70.4	81.2	98.7	131.4	160.4	173.2	266.2	152.4	198.0	Japon
0.7	1.5	1.4	1.4	1.7	2.3	3.1	3.9	4.5	6.1	3.8	4.6	Nouvelle-Zélande
2.2	3.8	3.7	3.3	4.1	6.9	7.9	12.7	14.9	20.0	13.8	...	Afrique du Sud

Voir à la fin du Tableau K pour la remarque générale et les notes.

Some indicators on fuel imports - Developed economies (Table K)

Fuel imports as a percentage of total imports and exports, and ratio of unit value indices of manufactured goods exports and fuel imports

Quelques indicateurs sur les importations de produits énergétiques - Pays à économies développées (Tableau K)

Importation des produits énergétiques en pourcentage des importations et des exportations totales,
et quotient des indices de la valeur unitaire des exportations des produits manufacturés et des importations des produits énergétiques

Region, country or area	1995	2000	2001	2002	2003	2004	2005	2006	2007	2008	2009	2010
Fuel Imports as percent of total imports / Importation des produits énergétiques en pourcentage des importations totales												
Developed economies	7.3	10.1	9.9	9.4	10.3	11.3	14.4	15.3	14.6	18.6	14.7	15.8
America	7.4	10.2	10.0	9.3	11.1	12.5	15.8	16.1	16.6	20.9	15.6	16.6
Canada	3.6	5.2	5.2	4.9	6.3	7.1	8.9	9.1	9.3	12.4	9.4	10.0
United States	8.2	11.1	10.9	10.1	11.9	13.5	17.1	17.4	18.0	22.5	16.9	18.0
Europe	6.0	8.4	8.3	7.8	8.5	9.3	12.2	13.3	12.0	15.3	12.6	13.6
Austria	4.5	5.8	7.1	6.9	7.9	9.4	12.2	13.7	10.2	12.0	10.5	10.6
Belgium	5.9	8.7	8.5	7.7	8.6	9.6	11.9	12.0	10.5	15.0	10.7	12.6
Denmark	3.3	5.7	4.1	4.0	4.6	5.3	6.6	6.5	5.5	7.9	7.2	8.0
Finland	8.8	11.8	11.5	11.5	12.2	12.2	13.5	15.3	13.8	17.4	16.9	18.4
France	6.8	9.8	9.5	9.2	10.1	10.9	13.8	15.0	13.8	17.5	15.1	14.8
Germany	6.1	8.4	8.5	8.1	8.6	9.2	11.5	12.2	10.5	13.6	11.2	11.5
Greece	7.2	13.4	15.3	13.4	13.9	13.0	19.7	20.6	15.3	9.8	5.2	...
Iceland	7.2	9.4	8.9	8.6	7.7	10.0	10.5	9.7	8.7	12.7	11.7	13.1
Ireland	3.3	4.1	3.9	3.2	3.7	5.1	6.9	7.4	7.6	12.4	10.3	12.3
Italy	7.3	9.7	9.3	8.9	9.1	9.4	15.7	17.6	16.3	20.2	17.5	19.0
Netherlands	7.7	11.5	12.1	10.1	10.5	11.7	14.6	16.5	15.8	18.5	15.6	18.2
Norway	2.9	4.0	4.1	3.5	4.7	4.6	4.2	4.7	4.4	5.0	5.2	6.9
Portugal	8.1	10.3	9.7	10.0	11.7	12.5	16.8	15.2	12.0	16.7	13.4	14.6
Spain	8.2	12.1	11.3	11.0	10.4	11.3	14.2	15.9	15.3	19.5	16.3	...
Sweden	6.5	8.9	8.0	8.8	9.4	9.7	12.1	12.4	11.3	14.8	11.8	13.5
Switzerland	2.9	4.6	4.6	4.4	4.6	4.9	7.9	8.5	7.3	9.3	7.5	...
United Kingdom	3.5	4.5	4.3	4.1	4.8	6.6	8.8	9.9	9.5	13.0	10.2	11.3
Other developed economies	13.3	17.4	17.2	17.0	17.3	18.1	21.1	23.3	23.3	29.2	23.1	23.9
Australia	5.0	8.1	8.5	7.0	7.8	9.1	11.1	13.2	12.9	15.7	12.6	13.4
Israel	5.7	10.0	9.5	8.8	11.0	11.0	15.1	13.9	14.7	18.5	14.0	16.0
Japan	16.0	20.4	20.1	20.8	21.2	21.9	25.5	27.7	27.9	34.9	27.7	28.6
New Zealand	5.3	10.4	8.5	9.3	9.4	10.1	11.9	14.6	14.4	21.6	15.0	15.6
South Africa	8.3	12.9	13.2	11.2	10.0	13.2	12.6	17.5	18.6	22.0	21.5	...
Fuel imports as percent of total exports / Importations des produits énergétiques en pourcentage des exportations totales												
Developed economies	7.3	10.9	10.6	10.0	11.1	12.3	15.9	17.1	16.1	20.5	15.8	17.1
America	9.3	14.4	14.2	14.0	17.1	20.1	24.9	25.6	25.1	30.6	21.9	23.6
Canada	3.1	4.5	4.5	4.3	5.6	6.4	8.0	8.2	8.5	11.1	9.6	10.1
United States	11.5	17.8	17.6	17.6	21.5	25.2	31.7	32.1	31.0	37.5	25.6	27.7
Europe	5.7	8.3	8.0	7.4	8.1	9.0	12.0	13.2	12.0	15.4	12.4	13.6
Austria	5.2	6.3	7.6	6.9	8.1	9.4	12.4	13.7	10.1	12.2	10.9	11.0
Belgium	5.3	8.2	8.0	7.0	7.9	8.9	11.4	11.5	10.1	14.8	10.2	11.9
Denmark	2.9	5.1	3.6	3.5	3.9	4.6	5.9	6.1	5.2	7.6	6.4	7.0
Finland	6.4	8.8	8.6	8.7	9.6	10.0	12.1	13.7	12.5	16.6	16.2	18.1
France	6.5	10.1	9.6	9.1	10.2	11.4	15.1	16.7	15.4	20.2	17.3	17.3
Germany	5.4	7.7	7.4	6.5	6.9	7.2	9.2	9.9	8.4	11.2	9.3	9.6
Greece	17.1	36.5	42.0	40.4	46.7	44.6	63.3	60.5	49.0	30.2	15.4	...
Iceland	7.0	11.8	9.2	8.0	9.0	12.3	16.2	15.6	11.7	13.8	10.4	11.2
Ireland	2.4	2.7	2.4	1.9	2.2	3.0	4.4	5.0	5.3	8.1	5.5	6.2
Italy	6.5	9.6	9.0	8.6	9.1	9.5	16.2	18.6	16.6	20.9	17.7	20.6
Netherlands	6.8	9.6	9.2	8.8	9.4	10.5	13.0	14.8	13.9	16.7	13.9	16.3
Norway	2.3	2.3	2.3	2.0	2.7	2.7	2.3	2.5	2.5	2.7	2.9	4.1
Portugal	11.7	16.9	15.6	15.1	15.5	18.6	27.9	23.2	18.2	26.3	21.1	22.6
Spain	10.3	15.8	15.1	14.5	13.9	16.0	21.3	24.3	23.7	29.3	21.4	...
Sweden	5.2	7.8	6.2	7.2	7.7	7.9	10.1	10.7	10.1	13.3	10.7	12.6
Switzerland	2.8	4.7	4.7	4.2	4.3	4.6	7.4	7.9	6.8	8.4	6.7	...
United Kingdom	3.9	5.3	5.7	5.0	6.1	8.7	11.4	12.6	13.6	17.9	13.9	15.4
Other developed economies	11.1	14.8	15.5	15.0	15.6	16.3	20.0	22.4	22.2	29.4	22.7	22.1
Australia	5.7	8.6	8.1	7.8	9.9	11.5	13.2	15.0	15.2	16.9	13.6	12.7
Israel	8.8	11.4	10.9	10.6	11.8	11.7	15.9	14.3	15.9	20.5	14.4	16.8
Japan	12.2	16.2	17.4	16.9	17.2	17.6	22.1	24.7	24.4	33.8	26.2	25.7
New Zealand	5.6	10.9	9.2	9.8	10.5	11.5	14.4	17.2	16.5	22.1	15.4	15.3
South Africa	7.9	12.8	12.8	11.0	11.2	14.9	15.2	21.8	21.3	24.7	22.1	...

For general note and footnotes see end of table.

Some indicators on fuel imports - Developed economies (Table K)

Fuel imports as a percentage of total imports and exports, and ratio of unit value indices of manufactured goods exports and fuel imports

Quelques indicateurs sur les importations de produits énergétiques - Pays à économies développées (Tableau K)

Importation des produits énergétiques en pourcentage des importations et des exportations totales,
et quotient des indices de la valeur unitaire des exportations des produits manufacturés et des importations des produits énergétiques

1995	1999	2001	2002	2003	2004	2005	2006	2007	2008	2009	2010	Région, pays ou zones
Ratio of unit value indices of manufactured goods exports and fuel imports Quotient des indices de la valeur unitaire des exportations des produits manufacturés et des importations des produits énergétiques 2000 = 100												
180	165	109	110	105	91	70	67	67	50	69	60	**Economies développées**
165	164	114	118	101	82	58	50	47	36	55	45	Amérique
129	136	88	89	77	69	55	50	49	...	...	...	Canada
167	167	116	122	103	82	57	49	46	35	55	45	Etats-Unis
188	167	107	106	105	93	75	69	72	56	76	70	Europe
260	141	103	109	...	...	...	...	...	...	...	...	Autriche
181	160	107	117	116	104	80	75	82	59	89	70	Belgique
175	162	108	103	105	93	74	64	60	47	69	59	Danemark
186	147	105	109	109	99	78	69	74	56	75	63	Finlande
169	155	100	84	98	87	56	46	45	33	...	...	France
204	175	103	102	101	91	68	58	61	45	64	55	Allemagne
200	168	...	...	...	...	...	...	...	...	...	...	Grèce
180	...	...	...	...	...	...	...	...	...	...	...	Islande
170	...	...	...	...	...	...	...	...	...	...	...	Irlande
173	...	...	...	...	...	...	...	...	...	...	...	Italie
188	...	...	...	...	...	...	...	...	...	...	...	Pays-Bas
159	131	103	102	92	92	72	66	70	53	67	56	Norvège
205	178	106	...	...	...	...	...	...	...	...	...	Portugal
245	...	...	...	...	...	...	...	...	...	...	...	Espagne
194	165	...	...	...	...	...	...	...	...	...	...	Suède
184	174	110	124	...	...	...	...	...	...	...	...	Suisse
162	155	106	98	91	76	54	45	44	34	47	37	Royaume-Uni
164	150	106	103	101	90	71	83	80	53	68	55	Autres économies développées
183	150	107	107	84	87	71	77	86	55	62	63	Australie
116	127	109	105	105	84	57	58	54	36	53	42	Israël
167	153	106	103	103	92	72	88	84	55	71	57	Japon
191	152	110	108	102	86	69	58	59	45	62	55	Nouvelle-Zélande
...	...	...	...	...	...	...	...	...	...	...	...	Afrique du Sud

Tables I, J and K

General note: Manufactured goods are here defined to comprise sections 5 through 8 of the Standard International Trade Classification (SITC). These sections are: chemicals and related products, manufactured goods classified chiefly by material, machinery and transport equipment and miscellaneous manufactured articles. Fuels are here defined to comprise all the products in section 3 of the SITC. These products are: coal, coke and briquettes, petroleum, petroleum products and related materials gas and electric current.

In 1990 the exports of manufactured goods by all Developed' and Developing' economies accounted for approximately 96 per cent of world exports of manufactured goods. The unit value indices are obtained from national sources, except those of a few countries which the United Nations Statistics Division compiles using their quantity and value figures. For countries that do not compile indices for manufactured goods exports and fuel imports conforming to the above definition, sub-indices are aggregated to approximate an index of SITC sections 5-8 and SITC section 3 respectively. Unit value indices obtained from national indices are rebased, where necessary, so that 2000=100. Indices in national currency are converted into U.S. dollars using conversion factors obtained by dividing the weighted average exchange rate of a given currency in the current period by the weighted average exchange rate in the base period. All aggregate unit value indices are current period weighted. The indices in SDRs are calculated by multiplying the equivalent aggregate indices in U.S. dollars by conversion factors obtained by dividing the SDR/$US exchange rate in the current period by the rate in the base period. The quantum indices are derived from the value data and the unit value indices. All aggregate quantum indices are base period weighted. The figures in Table K are calculated from those prepared for Tables I and J.

Total imports and exports used in the calculations are, in general, those published in Table A.

1/ Excludes trade of the countries of Eastern Europe and the former USSR.

2/ Beginning 1989, derived from price indices; national unit value index is discontinued.

3/ Series linked at 1988 and 1995 by factors calculated by the United Nations Statistics Division.

4/ Data prior to January 1991, pertain to the territorial boundaries of the Federal Republic of Germany and the former German Democratic Republic prior to 3 October, 1990 (see explanatory notes on data pertaining to Germany in the introduction).

5/ For the years beginning 1981, indices are calculated by the United Nations Statistics Division; for Netherlands beginning 1988, for Belgium 1988-1992, and for Switzerland 1988 to 1995.

6/ Derived from sub-indices using current weights; for Netherlands from 1989 to 1996.

7/ Industrial product.

Tableaux I, J et K

Remarque générale: Les produits manufacturés comprennent les sections 5 à 8 de la Classification type pour le commerce international (CTCI). Ces sections sont produits chimiques et produits connexes, articles manufacturés classés principalement d'après la matière primière, machines et matériel de transport et articles manufacturés divers. Les produits énergétiques comprennent tous les produits appartenant à la section 3 de la CTCI. Ces produits sont huiles, cokes et briquettes, pétrole, produits dérives du pétrole et produits connexes, gaz et énergie électrique. En 1990, les exportations des produits manufacturés par tous les Economies développées' et les 'Economies en voie de développement' représentaient approximativement 96 pourcent de l'ensemble des exportations mondiales des produits manufacturés. Les indices de la valeur unitaire sont obtenus de sources nationales, á l'exception de quelque pays pour lesquels la Division de Statistique des Nations Unies calcule ces indices en utilisant le chiffres de la valeur et du volume fournis par ces pays. Pour les pays ne calculant pas leurs indices des exportations des produits manufacturés et importations des produits énergétiques selon la définition décrite ci-dessus les sous-indices sont agrégés en un indice qui se rapproche les sections 5 à 8 de la CTCI et la section 3 de la CTCI respectivement. Les indices en monnaie nationale son convertis en dollars des E.-U. en les multipliant par un facteur de conversion obtenu en divisant le taux de change courant, moyenne pondérés, d'une monnaie donnée par celui de la période de base. Tous les agrégés des indices de la valeur unitaire, sont à coéfficients de pondération correspondant à la période indiquée. Les indices indices en DTS son calculés en multipliant les indices totaux équivalents en dollars E.-U. par un facteur de conversion obtenu en divisant le taux de change cournat du DTS/$E-U d'une monnaie donnée par celui de la période de base. Les indices du quantum sont calculés à partir de chiffres de la valeur et lés indices de la valeur unitaire. Tous les agrégés des indices du quantum sont à coéfficients de pondération correspondant à la période en base. Les chiffres dans le tableau K sont calculés selon des données préparées pour les tableaux I et J.
Les totaux des importations et exportations utilisées dans les calculs sont, en général, celles publiées dans le Tableau A.

1/ Non compris le commerce des pays de l'Europe de l'Est et l'ancienne URSS.

2/ A partir de 1989, calculés à partir des indices des prix; l'indice de valeur unitaire national est discontinué.

3/ Les séries sont enchainées à 1988 et à 1995 par facteurs calculé par la Division de Statistique des Nations Unies.

4/ Les données relatives à la période précédent janvier 1991 correspondent aux limites territoriales de la République Fédérale d'Allemagne antérieur au 3 octobre 1990 (Aussi voir les notes explicatives sur les données concernant l'Allemagne dans l'introduction).

5/ Pour les années à partir 1981, les indices sont calculés par la Division de Statistique des Nations Unies; pour les Pays-Bas à partir de 1988, pour la Belgique 1988-1992, et pour la Suisse 1988-1995.

6/ Calculés à partir de sous-indices à coéfficients de pondération correspondant à la période en cours; pour les Pays-Bas de 1989 à 1996.

7/ Produit industriel.

2010
INTERNATIONAL TRADE STATISTICS YEARBOOK

VOLUME II
TRADE BY COMMODITY

PART 2 – COMMODITY TRADE PROFILES

- Food and live animals (SITC Section 0)
- Beverages and tobacco (SITC Section 1)
- Crude materials, inedible, except fuels (SITC Section 2)
- Mineral fuels, lubricants and related materials (SITC Section 3)
- Animal and vegetable oils, fats and waxes (SITC Section 4)
- Chemicals and related products, n.e.s. (SITC Section 5)
- Manufactured goods classified chiefly by material (SITC Section 6)
- Machinery and transport equipment (SITC Section 7)
- Miscellaneous manufactured articles (SITC Section 8)
- Commodities and transactions not classified elsewhere in SITC (SITC Section 9)

Food and live animals

(SITC Section 0)

001 Live animals other than animals of division 03

During the recent five years, the value (in current prices) of exports of live animals (SITC group 001) increased on average by 5.8 percent and amounted to 18.1 bln US$ in 2010 (see table 2). Imports, displaying a similar development, increased on average by 6.4 percent to reach 18.4 bln US$ (see table 3). Graph 1 shows that the increase in exports for 2010 in this product group was exceeded by increases of 11.2 percent in world exports of food and live animals (SITC section 0) and of 21.2 percent in total world exports. Exports of live animals (SITC group 001) accounted for 1.9 percent of world exports of SITC section 0 and 0.1 percent of total world exports in 2010 (see table 1).

France, the top exporting country, accounted for 12.6 percent of world exports in 2010 (see table 2). Other major exporting countries were Netherlands and Canada, respectively with 11.6 and 9.0 percent of world exports. USA, Italy and Germany were the top importing countries (see table 3). By MDG regions (see graph 2), Developed Europe accounted for the majority of trade in live animals (SITC group 001). In 2010, its exports and imports were valued respectively at 10.2 bln US$ and 8.8 bln US$, resulting in a trade surplus of 1.4 bln US$. Sub-Saharan Africa and Developed Asia-Pacific recorded a trade surplus amounting to 0.9 and 0.8 bln US$. Top trade deficits were recorded by Western Asia (-1.7 bln US$), South-eastern Asia (-0.5 bln US$) and Northern Africa (-0.4 bln US$).

Table 1: Imports (Imp.) and exports (Exp.), 1996-2010, in current prices

		1996	1997	1998	1999	2000	2001	2002	2003	2004	2005	2006	2007	2008	2009	2010
Values in Bln US$	Imp.	10.1	9.5	9.3	9.3	9.4	8.8	9.5	9.5	10.5	12.7	14.4	15.5	17.0	16.3	18.4
	Exp.	10.0	9.3	9.1	8.8	9.0	8.9	9.8	10.1	11.1	13.0	14.4	15.8	17.3	17.2	18.1
As a percentage of SITC section (%)	Imp.	2.3	2.2	2.2	2.2	2.3	2.1	2.1	1.9	1.8	2.0	2.1	1.9	1.7	1.8	1.9
	Exp.	2.3	2.2	2.2	2.2	2.3	2.2	2.3	2.1	2.0	2.2	2.2	2.0	1.8	2.0	1.9
As a percentage of world trade (%)	Imp.	0.2	0.2	0.2	0.2	0.1	0.1	0.1	0.1	0.1	0.1	0.1	0.1	0.1	0.1	0.1
	Exp.	0.2	0.2	0.2	0.2	0.1	0.1	0.2	0.1	0.1	0.1	0.1	0.1	0.1	0.1	0.1

Graph 1: Annual growth rates of exports, 1996–2010

(In percentage by year)

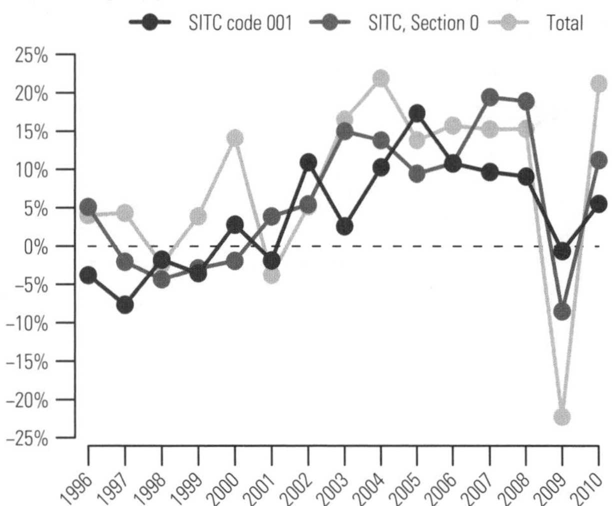

Table 2: Top exporting countries or areas in 2010

Country or area	Value (million US$)	Avg. Growth (%) 06-10	Growth (%) 09-10	World share %	Cum.
World	18117.0	5.8	5.5	100.0	
France	2286.6	0.9	0.1	12.6	12.6
Netherlands	2092.8	10.7	-1.6	11.6	24.2
Canada	1626.4	-2.1	13.5	9.0	33.1
Germany	1270.5	6.4	5.9	7.0	40.2
Australia	1022.7	11.3	13.2	5.6	45.8
Denmark	834.2	16.5	-5.5	4.6	50.4
USA	813.6	1.9	2.1	4.5	54.9
Brazil	697.2	67.4	48.0	3.8	58.8
United Kingdom	574.3	-3.9	-15.4	3.2	61.9
Mexico	542.4	-4.8	35.7	3.0	64.9
Belgium	506.6	8.4	-5.6	2.8	67.7
China	454.0	8.1	2.7	2.5	70.2
Spain	453.4	5.5	13.4	2.5	72.7
Ireland	448.7	0.5	9.0	2.5	75.2
Somalia	*370.0*	24.5	34.8	2.0	77.2

Graph 2: Trade Balance by MDG regions 2010

(Bln US$)

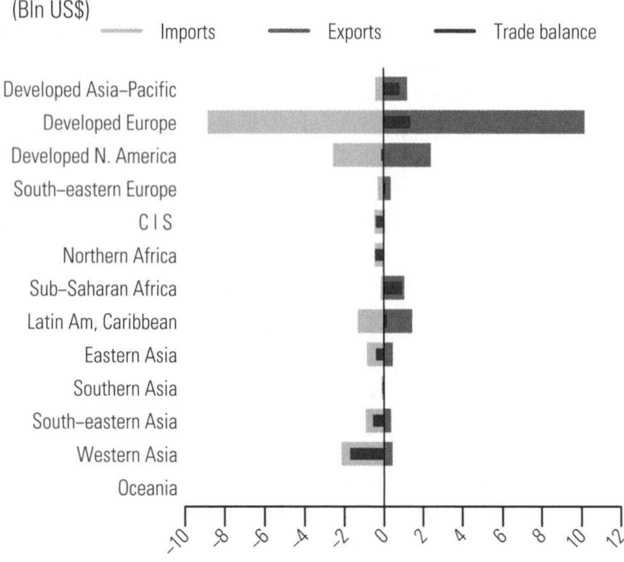

Table 3: Top importing countries or areas in 2010

Country or area	Value (million US$)	Avg. Growth (%) 06-10	Growth (%) 09-10	World share %	Cum.
World	18375.7	6.4	12.6	100.0	
USA	2384.4	-2.5	17.3	13.0	13.0
Italy	1889.6	-1.2	8.4	10.3	23.3
Germany	1689.7	7.2	1.0	9.2	32.5
Venezuela	1011.5	63.9	61.7	5.5	38.0
Netherlands	905.5	11.3	1.0	4.9	42.9
Belgium	738.0	12.1	0.0	4.0	46.9
United Kingdom	696.7	-7.3	1.8	3.8	50.7
Spain	655.9	5.4	52.5	3.6	54.3
Saudi Arabia	596.0	-0.9	9.7	3.2	57.5
China, Hong Kong SAR	479.6	11.6	3.2	2.6	60.1
Indonesia	450.6	40.0	2.8	2.5	62.6
France	337.4	-1.2	-4.1	1.8	64.4
Turkey	333.3	115.2	890.1	1.8	66.2
Lebanon	324.9	20.1	26.1	1.8	68.0
Russian Federation	319.7	6.5	-32.0	1.7	69.7

After a 11.4 percent drop in 2009, the value (in current prices) of exports of meat of bovine animals, fresh, chilled or frozen (SITC group 011) bounced back by 12.7 percent in 2010 to reach 32.5 bln US$ (see table 2). Imports, after a 7.0 percent drop in 2009, increased by 7.7 percent in 2010 and totaled 30.3 bln US$ (see table 3). Graph 1 shows that the increase in exports for 2010 in this product group exceeded the increase in world exports of food and live animals (SITC section 0) of 11.2 percent but was below the increase in total world exports of 21.2 percent. Exports of bovine meat, fresh, chilled or frozen (SITC group 011) accounted for 3.4 percent of world exports of SITC section 0 and 0.2 percent of total world exports in 2010 (see table 1).

In 2010, Australia, Brazil and USA were the top exporting countries (see table 2). They accounted respectively for 12.1, 11.9 and 10.5 percent of world exports. Italy, USA and Japan were the top destinations (see table 3). By MDG regions (see graph 2), Developed Europe accounted for a large share of trade in fresh, chilled or frozen bovine meat (SITC group 011). In 2010, its exports and imports were valued respectively at 11.9 bln US$ and 12.8 bln US$, resulting in a trade deficit of 0.9 bln US$. Top trade deficits were also recorded by Eastern Asia (-2.0 bln US$), Commonwealth of Independent States (-1.7 bln US$) and Western Asia (-1.7 bln US$). Latin America and the Caribbean and Developed Asia-Pacific recorded trade surpluses amounting respectively to 5.4 bln US$ and 3.0 bln US$.

Table 1: Imports (Imp.) and exports (Exp.), 1996-2010, in current prices

		1996	1997	1998	1999	2000	2001	2002	2003	2004	2005	2006	2007	2008	2009	2010
Values in Bln US$	Imp.	13.5	13.9	13.6	14.4	14.4	12.8	14.1	16.5	18.1	20.5	23.2	26.1	30.3	28.1	30.3
	Exp.	13.2	13.7	13.3	14.3	14.3	12.7	14.3	16.6	18.7	21.5	24.2	26.6	32.5	28.8	32.5
As a percentage of SITC section (%)	Imp.	3.0	3.2	3.2	3.4	3.5	3.0	3.2	3.2	3.1	3.2	3.3	3.1	3.1	3.2	3.1
	Exp.	3.0	3.2	3.3	3.6	3.7	3.2	3.4	3.4	3.4	3.5	3.6	3.3	3.4	3.3	3.4
As a percentage of world trade (%)	Imp.	0.3	0.2	0.2	0.3	0.2	0.2	0.2	0.2	0.2	0.2	0.2	0.2	0.2	0.2	0.2
	Exp.	0.3	0.2	0.2	0.3	0.2	0.2	0.2	0.2	0.2	0.2	0.2	0.2	0.2	0.2	0.2

Graph 1: Annual growth rates of exports, 1996–2010

(In percentage by year)

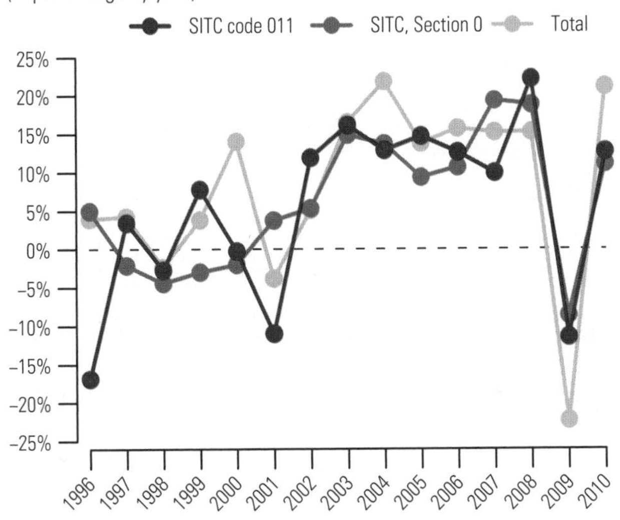

Graph 2: Trade Balance by MDG regions 2010

(Bln US$)

Imports — Exports — Trade balance

Developed Asia-Pacific
Developed Europe
Developed N. America
South-eastern Europe
C I S
Northern Africa
Sub-Saharan Africa
Latin Am, Caribbean
Eastern Asia
Southern Asia
South-eastern Asia
Western Asia
Oceania

-14 -12 -10 -8 -6 -4 -2 0 2 4 6 8 10 12

Table 2: Top exporting countries or areas in 2010

Country or area	Value (million US$)	Avg. Growth (%) 06-10	Growth (%) 09-10	World share %	Cum.
World	32 502.5	7.7	12.7	100.0	
Australia	3 925.1	1.7	16.2	12.1	12.1
Brazil	3 861.1	5.3	27.7	11.9	24.0
USA	3 397.1	24.2	36.7	10.5	34.4
Netherlands	2 385.9	2.9	-8.7	7.3	41.7
Germany	1 935.4	2.3	-1.3	6.0	47.7
Ireland	1 733.1	1.1	-0.3	5.3	53.0
India	1 696.5	25.9	72.4	5.2	58.3
New Zealand	1 374.8	4.2	21.9	4.2	62.5
France	1 310.9	3.8	-2.7	4.0	66.5
Canada	1 273.9	3.6	26.8	3.9	70.4
Uruguay	*1 186.1*	6.1	24.5	3.6	74.1
Argentina	1 049.0	-1.5	-31.4	3.2	77.3
Poland	983.1	20.1	23.6	3.0	80.3
Paraguay	880.1	21.5	59.1	2.7	83.0
Belgium	719.3	5.9	4.6	2.2	85.3

Table 3: Top importing countries or areas in 2010

Country or area	Value (million US$)	Avg. Growth (%) 06-10	Growth (%) 09-10	World share %	Cum.
World	30 302.9	6.9	7.7	100.0	
Italy	2 763.0	1.9	-2.5	9.1	9.1
USA	2 704.9	-1.9	9.5	8.9	18.0
Japan	2 288.1	4.2	14.6	7.6	25.6
Russian Federation	2 174.3	8.0	-6.1	7.2	32.8
Germany	1 710.3	8.5	9.0	5.6	38.4
France	1 589.3	2.2	-2.7	5.2	43.7
Netherlands	1 418.8	6.9	-1.2	4.7	48.3
United Kingdom	1 190.9	1.1	6.2	3.9	52.3
Rep. of Korea	1 080.4	8.1	35.5	3.6	55.8
Mexico	874.7	-2.6	4.2	2.9	58.7
Iran	780.8	197.3	8.4	2.6	61.3
Spain	751.3	0.0	0.4	2.5	63.8
Chile	730.4	24.0	56.4	2.4	66.2
Egypt	729.9	15.5	79.0	2.4	68.6
Canada	722.5	12.2	9.2	2.4	71.0

Source: UN Comtrade

012 Other meat, meat offal, fresh, chilled, frozen (for human)

After several years of continuous growth marked by a peak of 59.8 bln US$ in 2008, the value (in current prices) of exports of other meat, meat offal, fresh, chilled or frozen (SITC group 012) dropped by 9.9 percent in 2009, but bounced back by 9.0 percent and amounted to 58.7 bln US$ in 2010 (see table 2). Similarly, imports dropped by 8.7 percent in 2009 but increased by 7.7 percent to reach 57.0 bln US$ in 2010 (see table 3). Graph 1 shows that the increase in exports for 2010 in this product group was exceeded by increases of 11.2 percent in world exports of food and live animals (SITC section 0) and of 21.1 percent in total world exports. Exports of other meat, meat offal, fresh, chilled or frozen (SITC group 012) accounted for 6.1 percent of world exports of SITC section 0 and 0.4 percent of total world exports in 2010 (see table 1).

Exports of the USA, the top exporting country, increased by 6.0 percent and represented 14.2 percent of world exports in 2010 (see table 2). Other major exporting countries were Brazil and Germany, respectively with 12.7 and 9.7 percent of world exports. Japan, Germany and China, Hong Kong SAR were the top importing countries or areas (see table 3). By MDG regions (see graph 2), top surpluses were recorded by Developed North America (+8.3 bln US$), Latin America and the Caribbean (+5.7 bln US$) and Developed Europe (+5.4 bln US$). Major deficits were recorded by Eastern Asia (-4.5 bln US$), Commonwealth of Independent States (-4.0 bln US$) and Western Asia (-3.2 bln US$).

Table 1: Imports (Imp.) and exports (Exp.), 1996-2010, in current prices

		1996	1997	1998	1999	2000	2001	2002	2003	2004	2005	2006	2007	2008	2009	2010
Values in Bln US$	Imp.	26.2	24.7	22.7	22.6	23.6	25.9	26.1	29.5	34.5	38.9	39.7	46.3	58.0	52.9	57.0
	Exp.	27.1	25.3	22.6	22.0	23.0	26.1	24.7	28.6	34.1	39.2	39.9	47.3	59.8	53.9	58.7
As a percentage of SITC section (%)	Imp.	5.9	5.7	5.4	5.4	5.8	6.1	5.8	5.8	5.9	6.1	5.7	5.6	5.9	5.9	5.8
	Exp.	6.3	6.0	5.6	5.6	6.0	6.5	5.9	5.9	6.2	6.5	6.0	5.9	6.3	6.2	6.1
As a percentage of world trade (%)	Imp.	0.5	0.4	0.4	0.4	0.4	0.4	0.4	0.4	0.4	0.4	0.3	0.3	0.4	0.4	0.4
	Exp.	0.5	0.5	0.4	0.4	0.4	0.4	0.4	0.4	0.4	0.4	0.3	0.3	0.4	0.4	0.4

Graph 1: Annual growth rates of exports, 1996–2010

(In percentage by year)

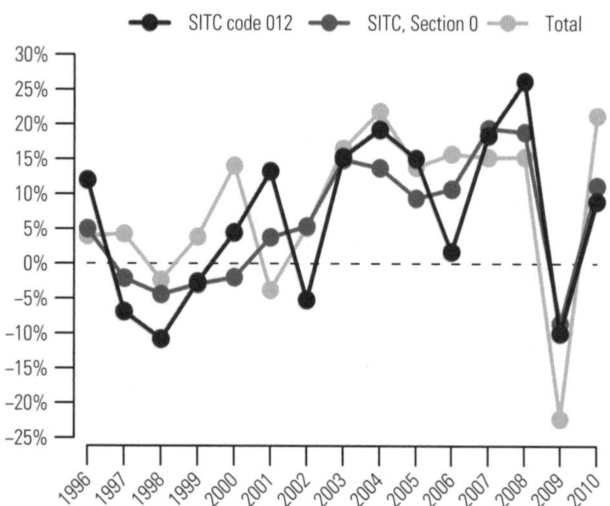

Graph 2: Trade Balance by MDG regions 2010

(Bln US$)

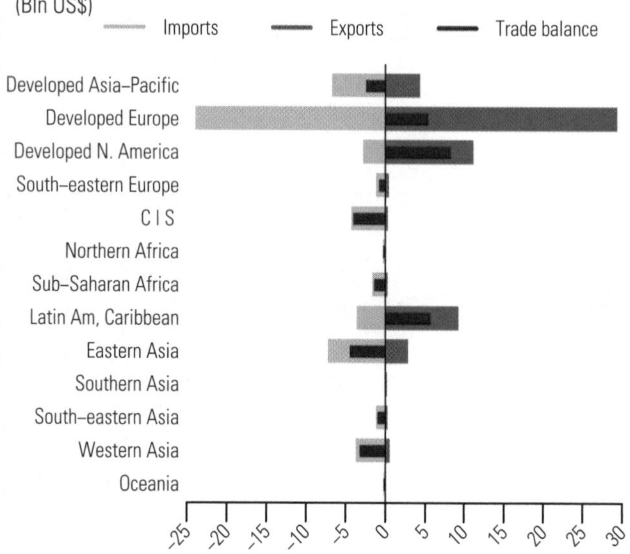

Table 2: Top exporting countries or areas in 2010

Country or area	Value (million US$)	Avg. Growth (%) 06-10	Growth (%) 09-10	World share %	Cum.
World	58 710.7	10.1	9.0	100.0	
USA	8 321.3	13.7	6.0	14.2	14.2
Brazil	7 447.9	15.5	17.6	12.7	26.9
Germany	5 682.3	13.3	2.0	9.7	36.5
Netherlands	4 339.9	6.7	5.2	7.4	43.9
Denmark	3 637.7	-0.4	-0.1	6.2	50.1
Belgium	2 960.6	4.9	0.1	5.0	55.2
Spain	2 896.7	11.5	3.5	4.9	60.1
Canada	2 839.9	6.5	17.6	4.8	64.9
France	2 659.2	4.0	0.8	4.5	69.5
New Zealand	2 243.2	5.0	6.7	3.8	73.3
Australia	2 028.4	6.1	15.4	3.5	76.7
China, Hong Kong SAR	1 846.9	38.8	14.9	3.1	79.9
Poland	1 697.0	12.2	31.0	2.9	82.8
United Kingdom	1 238.0	7.5	12.0	2.1	84.9
Hungary	984.9	13.0	20.7	1.7	86.6

Table 3: Top importing countries or areas in 2010

Country or area	Value (million US$)	Avg. Growth (%) 06-10	Growth (%) 09-10	World share %	Cum.
World	57 038.6	9.5	7.7	100.0	
Japan	6 196.3	8.2	16.6	10.9	10.9
Germany	3 882.5	1.2	-3.8	6.8	17.7
China, Hong Kong SAR	3 698.8	28.2	12.9	6.5	24.2
Russian Federation	3 319.6	5.0	-6.4	5.8	30.0
France	3 181.0	6.9	1.6	5.6	35.6
United Kingdom	3 163.3	0.4	5.1	5.5	41.1
Italy	2 854.0	1.9	6.1	5.0	46.1
Mexico	2 223.6	10.2	25.0	3.9	50.0
China	2 183.1	32.3	29.1	3.8	53.8
USA	1 861.5	4.0	22.1	3.3	57.1
Saudi Arabia	1 601.0	21.6	22.0	2.8	59.9
Netherlands	1 460.1	6.5	4.1	2.6	62.5
Poland	1 377.2	32.1	-2.8	2.4	64.9
Belgium	1 169.1	3.9	-0.9	2.0	66.9
Rep. of Korea	982.1	1.2	12.3	1.7	68.6

After a 12.4 percent drop in 2009, the value (in current prices) of exports of meat, edible offal, salted, in brine, dried, etc; flours, meals (SITC group 016) increased by 4.2 percent in 2010 to reach 4.2 bln US$ (see table 2). Imports, on the other hand, continued the decrease by 2.4 percent to 3.9 bln US$ in 2010 (see table 3). Graph 1 shows that the increase in exports for 2010 in this product group was exceeded by increases of 11.2 percent in world exports of food and live animals (SITC section 0) and of 21.2 percent in total world exports. Exports of meat, edible offal, salted, in brine, dried, etc; flours, meals (SITC group 016) accounted for 0.4 percent of world exports of SITC section 0 and less than 0.1 percent of total world exports in 2010 (see table 1).

Italy, Netherlands and Brazil were the top exporting countries in 2010 (see table 2). They accounted respectively for 18.6, 14.8 and 13.3 percent of world exports. The United Kingdom accounted for 32.0 percent of world imports and was the top importing country. Other major importing countries were France and Germany (see table 3). By MDG regions (see graph 2), Developed Europe accounted for a large share of trade in meat, edible offal, salted, in brine, dried, etc; flours, meals (SITC group 016). In 2010, its exports and imports amounted respectively to 3.1 bln US$ and 3.3 bln US$, resulting in a trade deficit of 0.2 bln US$. Latin America and the Caribbean recorded a surplus amounting to 0.5 bln US$.

Table 1: Imports (Imp.) and exports (Exp.), 1996-2010, in current prices

		1996	1997	1998	1999	2000	2001	2002	2003	2004	2005	2006	2007	2008	2009	2010
Values in Bln US$	Imp.	1.9	1.8	1.6	1.6	1.8	2.3	2.2	2.6	2.5	2.5	2.8	3.7	4.1	4.0	3.9
	Exp.	2.0	1.9	1.6	1.6	1.7	1.9	1.9	2.4	2.7	2.6	3.0	3.9	4.6	4.1	4.2
As a percentage of SITC section (%)	Imp.	0.4	0.4	0.4	0.4	0.4	0.5	0.5	0.5	0.4	0.4	0.4	0.4	0.4	0.4	0.4
	Exp.	0.5	0.4	0.4	0.4	0.4	0.5	0.5	0.5	0.5	0.4	0.4	0.5	0.5	0.5	0.4
As a percentage of world trade (%)	Imp.	0.0	0.0	0.0	0.0	0.0	0.0	0.0	0.0	0.0	0.0	0.0	0.0	0.0	0.0	0.0
	Exp.	0.0	0.0	0.0	0.0	0.0	0.0	0.0	0.0	0.0	0.0	0.0	0.0	0.0	0.0	0.0

Graph 1: Annual growth rates of exports, 1996–2010
(In percentage by year)

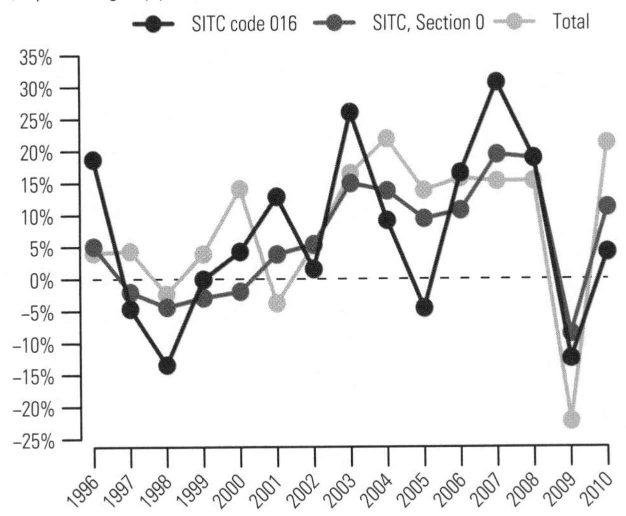

Table 2: Top exporting countries or areas in 2010

Country or area	Value (million US$)	Avg. Growth (%) 06-10	Growth (%) 09-10	World share %	Cum.
World	4229.3	9.2	4.2	100.0	
Italy	784.8	6.8	7.5	18.6	18.6
Netherlands	626.7	3.7	-4.4	14.8	33.4
Brazil	564.0	127.9	6.2	13.3	46.7
Germany	367.2	2.1	0.9	8.7	55.4
Denmark	359.7	-2.7	-8.2	8.5	63.9
Spain	325.1	4.6	6.8	7.7	71.6
USA	318.0	14.8	51.9	7.5	79.1
Belgium	147.4	1.5	-5.6	3.5	82.6
Canada	120.7	0.7	8.6	2.9	85.4
France	112.4	-1.1	-14.2	2.7	88.1
Poland	110.4	82.6	4.5	2.6	90.7
United Kingdom	89.0	17.7	-8.0	2.1	92.8
Austria	52.7	8.2	1.2	1.2	94.1
Switzerland	49.7	20.7	20.9	1.2	95.2
Chile	31.5	25.4	17.9	0.7	96.0

Graph 2: Trade Balance by MDG regions 2010
(Bln US$)

Imports — Exports — Trade balance

Developed Asia-Pacific
Developed Europe
Developed N. America
South-eastern Europe
C I S
Northern Africa
Sub-Saharan Africa
Latin Am, Caribbean
Eastern Asia
Southern Asia
South-eastern Asia
Western Asia
Oceania

-4 -3 -2 -1 0 1 2 3 4

Table 3: Top importing countries or areas in 2010

Country or area	Value (million US$)	Avg. Growth (%) 06-10	Growth (%) 09-10	World share %	Cum.
World	3865.9	8.1	-2.4	100.0	
United Kingdom	1238.3	4.6	-7.4	32.0	32.0
France	395.9	5.8	-4.4	10.2	42.3
Germany	392.7	7.9	-8.4	10.2	52.4
Netherlands	372.6	29.6	3.9	9.6	62.1
Belgium	167.9	8.9	-11.2	4.3	66.4
USA	150.4	-0.5	3.0	3.9	70.3
Denmark	122.5	8.7	-2.0	3.2	73.5
Italy	107.3	4.8	-3.1	2.8	76.2
Mexico	80.4	9.1	26.6	2.1	78.3
Canada	58.8	1.7	13.0	1.5	79.8
Austria	56.7	22.4	20.8	1.5	81.3
Switzerland	53.6	10.9	-1.4	1.4	82.7
Portugal	49.9	8.5	15.1	1.3	84.0
Sweden	48.7	8.5	4.0	1.3	85.2
Ireland	43.4	11.5	-1.7	1.1	86.4

017 Meat and edible meat offal, prepared or preserved, nes

After several years of continuous growth marked by a peak of 16.8 bln US$ in 2008, the value (in current prices) of exports of prepared or preserved meat and edible meat offal, nes (SITC group 017) decreased by 7.4 percent in 2009 but increased again by 4.8 percent in 2010 and amounted to 16.3 bln US$ (see table 2). Imports, with a similar development, increased by 2.7 percent in 2010 to reach 15.5 bln US$ (see table 3). Graph 1 shows that the increase in exports for 2010 in this product group was exceeded by increases of 11.2 percent in world exports of food and live animals (SITC section 0) and of 21.2 percent in total world exports. Exports of prepared or preserved meat and edible meat offal, nes (SITC group 017) accounted for 1.7 percent of world exports of SITC section 0 and 0.1 percent of total world exports in 2010 (see table 1).

In 2010, Germany, Thailand and China were the top exporting countries (see table 2). They accounted respectively for 12.8, 11.4 and 9.0 percent of world exports. Japan, United Kingdom and Germany were the top importing countries (see table 3). By MDG regions (graph 2), Developed Europe accounted for a large share of trade in prepared or preserved meat and edible meat offal, nes (SITC group 017). In 2010, its exports and imports amounted respectively to 8.7 bln US$ and 9.1 bln US$, resulting in a trade deficit of 0.4 bln US$. Top surpluses were recorded in South-eastern Asia (+1.8 bln US$) and Latin America and the Caribbean (+1.2 bln US$). A deficit of more than 2.4 bln US$ was recorded by Developed Asia-Pacific.

Table 1: Imports (Imp.) and exports (Exp.), 1996-2010, in current prices

		1996	1997	1998	1999	2000	2001	2002	2003	2004	2005	2006	2007	2008	2009	2010
Values in Bln US$	Imp.	5.6	5.5	5.4	5.4	5.4	5.9	6.3	7.4	8.7	10.4	11.4	13.4	15.9	15.1	15.5
	Exp.	6.2	6.4	6.0	5.4	5.5	6.0	6.5	7.5	8.9	10.7	11.7	13.9	16.8	15.6	16.3
As a percentage of SITC section (%)	Imp.	1.3	1.3	1.3	1.3	1.3	1.4	1.4	1.4	1.5	1.6	1.6	1.6	1.6	1.7	1.6
	Exp.	1.4	1.5	1.5	1.4	1.4	1.5	1.5	1.6	1.6	1.8	1.8	1.7	1.8	1.8	1.7
As a percentage of world trade (%)	Imp.	0.1	0.1	0.1	0.1	0.1	0.1	0.1	0.1	0.1	0.1	0.1	0.1	0.1	0.1	0.1
	Exp.	0.1	0.1	0.1	0.1	0.1	0.1	0.1	0.1	0.1	0.1	0.1	0.1	0.1	0.1	0.1

Graph 1: Annual growth rates of exports, 1996–2010
(In percentage by year)

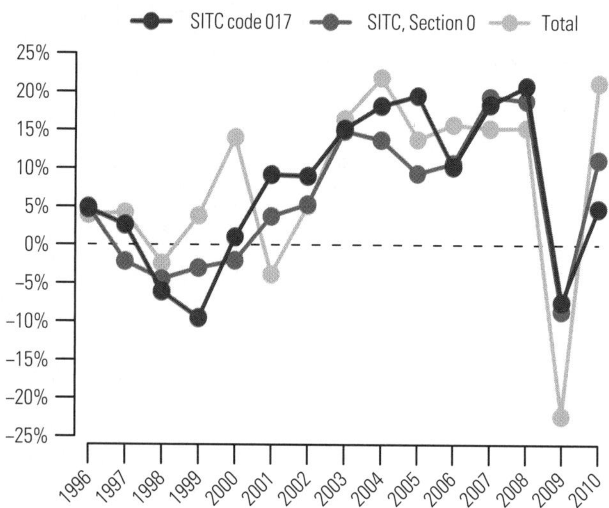

Graph 2: Trade Balance by MDG regions 2010
(Bln US$)

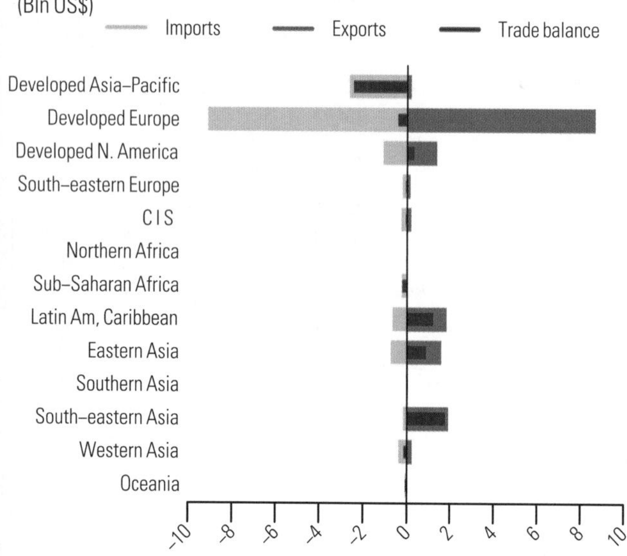

Table 2: Top exporting countries or areas in 2010

Country or area	Value (million US$)	Avg. Growth (%) 06-10	Growth (%) 09-10	World share %	Cum.
World	16309.5	8.6	4.8	100.0	
Germany	2080.9	8.9	-0.8	12.8	12.8
Thailand	1864.5	17.0	11.7	11.4	24.2
China	1461.6	3.5	26.4	9.0	33.2
Brazil	1448.4	5.1	-10.4	8.9	42.0
USA	1206.5	13.4	16.0	7.4	49.4
Belgium	824.6	5.0	-0.7	5.1	54.5
France	736.8	5.2	-2.2	4.5	59.0
Netherlands	688.1	7.1	-6.4	4.2	63.2
Italy	659.2	10.4	7.9	4.0	67.3
Denmark	624.9	4.6	1.2	3.8	71.1
Ireland	578.2	-2.2	-4.4	3.5	74.6
Poland	510.9	23.2	21.9	3.1	77.8
Spain	432.1	9.6	7.6	2.6	80.4
Austria	374.7	13.3	5.9	2.3	82.7
United Kingdom	325.5	8.3	0.8	2.0	84.7

Table 3: Top importing countries or areas in 2010

Country or area	Value (million US$)	Avg. Growth (%) 06-10	Growth (%) 09-10	World share %	Cum.
World	15492.4	7.9	2.7	100.0	
Japan	2525.4	7.0	12.7	16.3	16.3
United Kingdom	2263.3	4.7	-0.8	14.6	30.9
Germany	1543.2	6.9	-2.8	10.0	40.9
Netherlands	880.9	10.1	3.5	5.7	46.6
France	698.8	8.7	-4.5	4.5	51.1
China, Hong Kong SAR	590.5	23.5	12.8	3.8	54.9
Belgium	578.2	4.4	-1.8	3.7	58.6
Canada	556.2	9.7	15.3	3.6	62.2
USA	497.5	-10.1	-19.9	3.2	65.4
Denmark	358.3	9.8	14.9	2.3	67.7
Italy	334.5	11.3	2.6	2.2	69.9
Ireland	316.9	4.3	3.8	2.0	71.9
Spain	304.0	8.7	0.6	2.0	73.9
Sweden	280.9	9.8	9.1	1.8	75.7
Austria	226.3	10.0	-0.6	1.5	77.2

Source: UN Comtrade

After several years of continuous growth marked by a peak of 36.4 bln US$ in 2008, the value (in current prices) of exports of milk and cream and milk products other than butter or cheese (SITC group 022) decreased by 22.9 percent in 2009, but bounced back by 21.2 percent and amounted to 34.0 bln US$ in 2010 (see table 2). Imports showed a similar development with a decline of 20.3 percent in 2009 but an increase of 19.0 percent to reach 33.4 bln US$ in 2010(see table 3). Graph 1 shows that increase in exports for 2010 in this product group exceeded the increase in world exports of food and live animals (SITC section 0) of 11.2 percent and was similar to the increase in total world exports of 21.2 percent. Exports of milk and cream and milk products other than butter or cheese (SITC group 022) accounted for 3.5 percent of world exports of SITC section 0 and 0.2 percent of total world exports in 2010 (see table 1).

In 2010, New Zealand, Germany and France were the top exporting countries (see table 2). They accounted respectively for 14.1, 13.6 and 9.6 percent of world exports. Italy, Germany and Netherlands were the top destinations (see table 3). By MDG regions (see graph 2), Developed Europe accounted for the majority of trade in milk and cream and milk products other than butter or cheese (SITC group 022). In 2010, its exports and imports amounted respectively to 20.4 bln US$ and 15.6 bln US$, resulting in a trade surplus of 4.8 bln US$. Another major surplus was recorded by Developed Asia-Pacific (+5.4 bln US$). Large deficits were by recorded by Eastern Asia (-2.7 bln US$) and South-eastern Asia (-2.7 bln US$).

Table 1: Imports (Imp.) and exports (Exp.), 1996-2010, in current prices

		1996	1997	1998	1999	2000	2001	2002	2003	2004	2005	2006	2007	2008	2009	2010
Values in Bln US$	Imp.	14.7	14.1	14.3	14.2	14.2	15.0	14.5	17.1	20.2	22.0	23.8	31.9	35.2	28.1	33.4
	Exp.	14.8	14.3	14.2	13.9	14.0	15.2	14.2	17.0	20.4	22.3	23.8	32.1	36.4	28.0	34.0
As a percentage of SITC section (%)	Imp.	3.3	3.2	3.4	3.4	3.5	3.6	3.2	3.3	3.5	3.5	3.4	3.8	3.6	3.2	3.4
	Exp.	3.4	3.4	3.5	3.5	3.6	3.8	3.4	3.5	3.7	3.7	3.5	4.0	3.8	3.2	3.5
As a percentage of world trade (%)	Imp.	0.3	0.3	0.3	0.2	0.2	0.2	0.2	0.2	0.2	0.2	0.2	0.2	0.2	0.2	0.2
	Exp.	0.3	0.3	0.3	0.2	0.2	0.2	0.2	0.2	0.2	0.2	0.2	0.2	0.2	0.2	0.2

Graph 1: Annual growth rates of exports, 1996–2010
(In percentage by year)

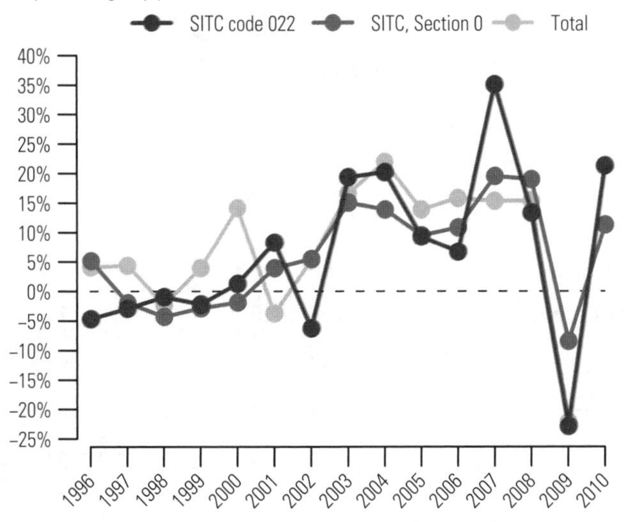

Graph 2: Trade Balance by MDG regions 2010
(Bln US$)

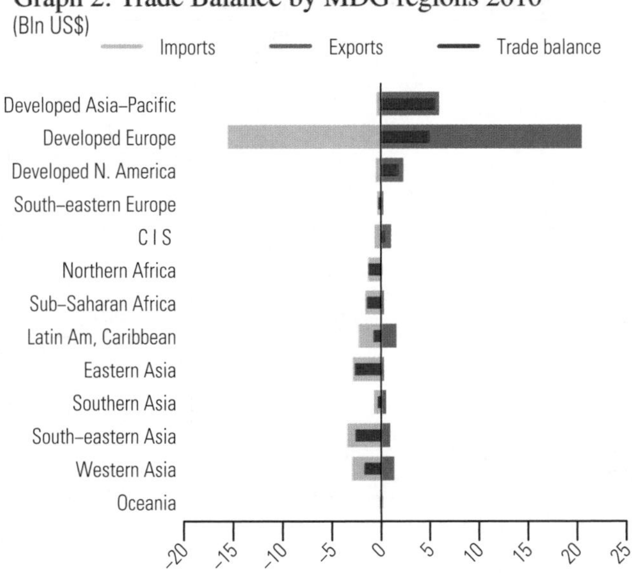

Table 2: Top exporting countries or areas in 2010

Country or area	Value (million US$)	Avg. Growth (%) 06-10	Growth (%) 09-10	World share %	Cum.
World	34000.7	9.3	21.2	100.0	
New Zealand	4789.0	17.1	47.0	14.1	14.1
Germany	4610.8	5.7	12.5	13.6	27.6
France	3271.0	7.2	13.6	9.6	37.3
Netherlands	2604.2	10.6	18.0	7.7	44.9
Belgium	2269.0	9.3	15.0	6.7	51.6
USA	2032.7	17.0	77.0	6.0	57.6
Australia	1052.0	0.1	11.0	3.1	60.7
United Kingdom	878.5	3.8	26.4	2.6	63.3
Poland	869.5	6.2	22.9	2.6	65.8
Denmark	784.8	12.1	22.2	2.3	68.1
Belarus	684.7	24.4	79.7	2.0	70.1
Austria	681.0	4.1	2.3	2.0	72.1
Argentina	643.4	2.7	40.2	1.9	74.0
Spain	614.6	3.8	-6.9	1.8	75.8
Ireland	589.1	3.2	30.3	1.7	77.6

Table 3: Top importing countries or areas in 2010

Country or area	Value (million US$)	Avg. Growth (%) 06-10	Growth (%) 09-10	World share %	Cum.
World	33402.1	8.8	19.0	100.0	
Italy	2313.8	6.8	17.1	6.9	6.9
Germany	2115.2	5.9	14.1	6.3	13.3
Netherlands	1956.8	0.8	17.7	5.9	19.1
China	1795.4	37.7	97.6	5.4	24.5
Belgium	1519.6	4.9	16.3	4.5	29.0
France	1458.6	6.1	5.1	4.4	33.4
United Kingdom	1272.0	6.2	6.5	3.8	37.2
Spain	1136.0	1.9	-7.9	3.4	40.6
Algeria	908.1	9.1	13.1	2.7	43.3
Saudi Arabia	789.6	6.5	12.5	2.4	45.7
Indonesia	789.4	11.7	55.1	2.4	48.1
Mexico	773.3	3.9	18.3	2.3	50.4
Singapore	678.4	13.2	40.2	2.0	52.4
United Arab Emirates	636.4	18.1	10.9	1.9	54.3
China, Hong Kong SAR	635.4	21.9	27.3	1.9	56.2

023 Butter and other fats and oils derived from milk

From 2006 to 2010, the value (in current prices) of exports of butter and other fats and oils derived from milk (SITC group 023) increased on average by 14.0 percent and amounted to 6.8 bln US$ (see table 2). During the same period, imports increased on average by 9.0 percent to 6.3 bln US$ (see table 3). Graph 1 shows that the increase in exports for 2010 in this product group was well above the increases in world exports of food and live animals (SITC section 0) of 11.2 percent and in total world exports of 21.2 percent. Exports of butter and other fats and oils derived from milk (SITC group 023) accounted for 0.7 percent of world exports of SITC section 0 and less than 0.1 percent of total world exports in 2010 (see table 1).

New Zealand was the top exporting country in 2010. It accounted for 22.7 percent of world exports (see table 2). Other major exporting countries were Netherlands and Belgium. France, Germany and Belgium were the top destinations (see table 3). By MDG regions (see graph 2), Developed Europe accounted for the majority of trade in butter and other fats and oils derived from milk (SITC group 023). In 2010, its exports and imports amounted respectively to 4.2 bln US$ and 3.6 bln US$, resulting in a trade surplus of 0.6 bln US$. A trade surplus was also recorded by Developed Asia-Pacific (+1.7 bln US$). Top trade deficits were recorded by Western Asia (-443 mln US$), South-eastern Asia (-374 mln US$) and Northern Africa and (-281 mln US$).

Table 1: Imports (Imp.) and exports (Exp.), 1996-2010, in current prices

		1996	1997	1998	1999	2000	2001	2002	2003	2004	2005	2006	2007	2008	2009	2010
Values in Bln US$	Imp.	3.4	3.4	3.4	3.0	2.8	2.9	3.0	3.7	4.3	4.4	4.5	5.4	5.6	4.7	6.3
	Exp.	3.8	3.6	3.5	3.0	2.7	2.7	2.6	3.4	4.2	4.2	4.0	5.3	6.1	4.7	6.8
As a percentage of SITC section (%)	Imp.	0.8	0.8	0.8	0.7	0.7	0.7	0.7	0.7	0.7	0.7	0.6	0.6	0.6	0.5	0.6
	Exp.	0.9	0.8	0.9	0.8	0.7	0.7	0.6	0.7	0.8	0.7	0.6	0.7	0.6	0.5	0.7
As a percentage of world trade (%)	Imp.	0.1	0.1	0.1	0.1	0.0	0.0	0.0	0.0	0.0	0.0	0.0	0.0	0.0	0.0	0.0
	Exp.	0.1	0.1	0.1	0.1	0.0	0.0	0.0	0.0	0.0	0.0	0.0	0.0	0.0	0.0	0.0

Graph 1: Annual growth rates of exports, 1996–2010

(In percentage by year)

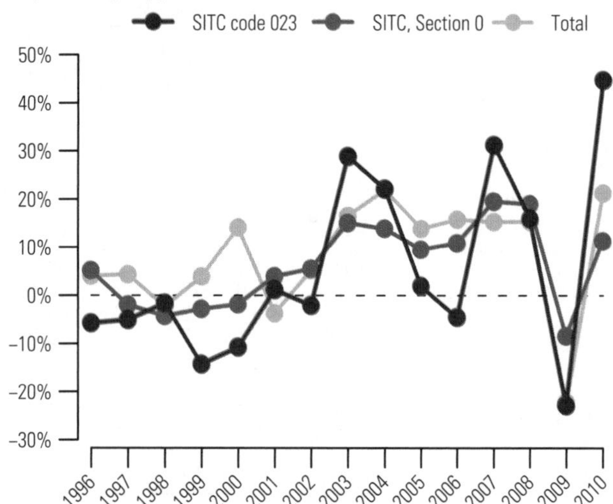

Graph 2: Trade Balance by MDG regions 2010

(Bln US$)

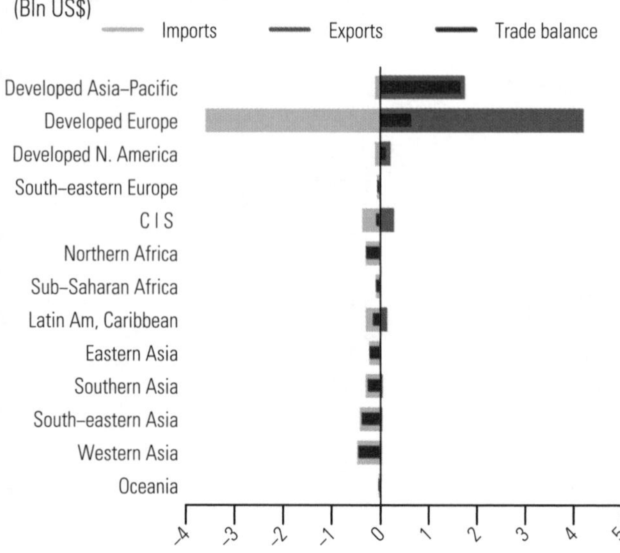

Table 2: Top exporting countries or areas in 2010

Country or area	Value (million US$)	Avg. Growth (%) 06-10	Growth (%) 09-10	World share %	Cum.
World	6808.5	14.0	44.6	100.0	
New Zealand	1545.3	21.9	62.7	22.7	22.7
Netherlands	820.6	10.9	31.3	12.1	34.7
Belgium	661.7	9.7	25.0	9.7	44.5
Ireland	557.9	6.5	44.0	8.2	52.7
Germany	514.4	17.7	51.2	7.6	60.2
France	392.5	14.3	35.6	5.8	66.0
Denmark	298.6	3.9	11.1	4.4	70.4
Belarus	268.1	26.6	15.5	3.9	74.3
Australia	221.3	10.3	25.0	3.3	77.6
USA	205.6	77.0	149.0	3.0	80.6
Spain	175.8	12.4	258.4	2.6	83.2
Finland	135.2	7.6	13.6	2.0	85.1
United Kingdom	124.4	3.1	39.9	1.8	87.0
Italy	121.3	35.8	274.5	1.8	88.8
Poland	113.8	19.8	102.1	1.7	90.4

Table 3: Top importing countries or areas in 2010

Country or area	Value (million US$)	Avg. Growth (%) 06-10	Growth (%) 09-10	World share %	Cum.
World	6318.7	9.0	35.5	100.0	
France	693.0	8.2	38.0	11.0	11.0
Germany	619.1	-1.9	54.3	9.8	20.8
Belgium	509.3	5.7	37.5	8.1	28.8
United Kingdom	441.9	-7.5	18.7	7.0	35.8
Italy	349.8	17.8	74.6	5.5	41.4
Russian Federation	257.6	6.9	58.6	4.1	45.4
Iran	223.6	44.5	8.4	3.5	49.0
Netherlands	195.7	-1.5	-17.3	3.1	52.1
Saudi Arabia	179.5	14.8	66.2	2.8	54.9
Mexico	171.5	11.5	13.0	2.7	57.6
Denmark	169.3	13.2	176.4	2.7	60.3
Egypt	156.5	44.5	9.5	2.5	62.8
Singapore	103.9	14.6	77.3	1.6	64.4
Morocco	94.7	8.0	39.2	1.5	65.9
Philippines	93.7	49.7	115.8	1.5	67.4

After a 15.3 percent drop in 2009, the value (in current prices) of exports of cheese and curd (SITC group 024) increased by 11.3 percent and amounted to 25.5 bln US$ in 2010 (see table 2). Imports, after a 13.0 percent drop in 2009, increased by 9.1 percent to reach 24.3 bln US$ (see table 3). Graph 1 shows that the increase in exports for 2010 in this product group was similar to the increase in world exports of food and live animals (SITC section 0) of 11.2 percent but was well below the increase in total world exports of 21.2 percent. Exports of cheese and curd (SITC group 024) accounted for 2.6 percent of world exports of SITC section 0 and 0.2 percent of total world exports in 2010 (see table 1).

Germany, France and Netherlands were the top exporting countries in 2010 (see table 2). They accounted respectively for 15.6, 13.8 and 12.7 percent of world exports. Germany was also the top destination accounting for 14.2 percent of world imports (see table 3). Other major importing countries were Italy and United Kingdom. By MDG regions (see graph 2), Developed Europe accounted for a majority of trade in cheese and curd (SITC group 024). In 2010, its exports and imports amounted respectively to 20.0 bln US$ and 16.2 bln US$, resulting in a trade surplus of 3.8 bln US$. Top trade deficits were recorded by Western Asia (-742 mln US$), Eastern Asia (-528 mln US$) and Developed North America (-510 mln US$).

Table 1: Imports (Imp.) and exports (Exp.), 1996-2010, in current prices

		1996	1997	1998	1999	2000	2001	2002	2003	2004	2005	2006	2007	2008	2009	2010
Values in Bln US$	Imp.	11.0	10.3	10.4	10.5	9.6	10.4	11.2	13.3	15.6	16.5	17.7	21.3	25.6	22.3	24.3
	Exp.	11.7	10.7	10.9	10.4	9.9	11.0	11.2	13.7	16.1	17.2	18.5	22.2	27.1	22.9	25.5
As a percentage of SITC section (%)	Imp.	2.5	2.4	2.5	2.5	2.3	2.5	2.5	2.6	2.7	2.6	2.6	2.6	2.6	2.5	2.5
	Exp.	2.7	2.5	2.7	2.6	2.6	2.7	2.6	2.8	2.9	2.8	2.8	2.8	2.8	2.6	2.6
As a percentage of world trade (%)	Imp.	0.2	0.2	0.2	0.2	0.1	0.2	0.2	0.2	0.2	0.2	0.1	0.2	0.2	0.2	0.2
	Exp.	0.2	0.2	0.2	0.2	0.2	0.2	0.2	0.2	0.2	0.2	0.2	0.2	0.2	0.2	0.2

Graph 1: Annual growth rates of exports, 1996–2010

(In percentage by year)

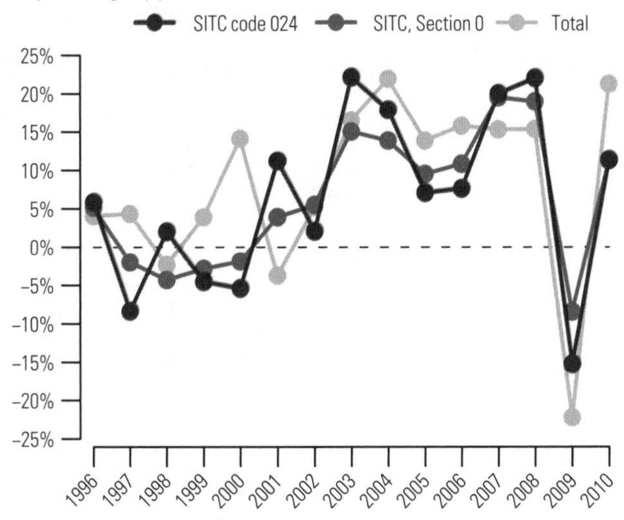

Graph 2: Trade Balance by MDG regions 2010

(Bln US$)

Imports | Exports | Trade balance

Developed Asia-Pacific
Developed Europe
Developed N. America
South-eastern Europe
CIS
Northern Africa
Sub-Saharan Africa
Latin Am, Caribbean
Eastern Asia
Southern Asia
South-eastern Asia
Western Asia
Oceania

-20 -15 -10 -5 0 5 10 15 20 25

Table 2: Top exporting countries or areas in 2010

Country or area	Value (million US$)	Avg. Growth (%) 06-10	Growth (%) 09-10	World share %	Cum.
World	25512.1	8.4	11.3	100.0	
Germany	3989.3	7.2	10.7	15.6	15.6
France	3524.5	5.3	1.3	13.8	29.5
Netherlands	3236.6	5.9	18.2	12.7	42.1
Italy	2198.7	9.1	9.4	8.6	50.8
Denmark	1343.5	3.0	-1.5	5.3	56.0
New Zealand	1023.5	6.3	19.6	4.0	60.0
Belgium	799.9	6.7	11.1	3.1	63.2
Ireland	743.4	8.4	7.0	2.9	66.1
USA	701.9	29.5	60.6	2.8	68.8
Australia	666.7	1.4	21.3	2.6	71.4
Poland	582.9	10.2	14.9	2.3	73.7
Switzerland	537.4	7.3	2.9	2.1	75.8
United Kingdom	526.7	6.5	19.3	2.1	77.9
Belarus	524.5	24.9	32.9	2.1	80.0
Austria	514.8	6.4	4.0	2.0	82.0

Table 3: Top importing countries or areas in 2010

Country or area	Value (million US$)	Avg. Growth (%) 06-10	Growth (%) 09-10	World share %	Cum.
World	24289.3	8.2	9.1	100.0	
Germany	3446.0	4.1	1.5	14.2	14.2
Italy	1985.1	4.7	7.4	8.2	22.4
United Kingdom	1892.1	4.0	2.3	7.8	30.2
France	1394.8	8.0	-0.6	5.7	35.9
Russian Federation	1319.9	22.1	48.0	5.4	41.3
Belgium	1311.4	4.5	1.0	5.4	46.7
Spain	1122.5	9.4	6.1	4.6	51.3
USA	1003.1	-1.6	-4.3	4.1	55.5
Japan	936.5	6.7	14.9	3.9	59.3
Netherlands	862.7	9.2	11.7	3.6	62.9
Greece	515.3	6.1	2.3	2.1	65.0
Sweden	487.5	11.8	8.7	2.0	67.0
Saudi Arabia	485.6	9.9	6.1	2.0	69.0
Austria	419.4	7.8	1.6	1.7	70.7
Australia	366.2	12.4	39.4	1.5	72.2

Source: UN Comtrade

025 Eggs, birds', egg yolks, fresh, dried or preserved; egg albumin

During the recent five years, the value (in current prices) of exports of eggs, birds', egg yolks, fresh, dried or preserved; egg albumin (SITC group 025) displayed a continuous increase on average of 16.3 percent each year to reach 4.4 bln US$ in 2010 (see table 2). During the same period, imports increased similarly on average by 13.1 percent and totaled 4.1 bln US$ (see table 3). Graph 1 shows that the increase of 3.7 percent in exports for 2010 in this product group was exceeded by the increases in world exports of food and live animals (SITC section 0) of 11.2 percent and in total world exports of 21.2 percent. Exports of eggs, birds', egg yolks, fresh, dried or preserved; egg albumin (SITC group 025) accounted for 0.5 percent of world exports of SITC section 0 and less than 0.1 percent of total world exports in 2010 (see table 1).

Netherlands was the top exporting country in 2010: it accounted for 25.5 percent of world exports (see table 2). Other major exporting countries were USA and Germany, respectively with 8.2 and 7.0 percent of world exports. Germany is the top importing country accounting for 25.0 percent of world imports. Other major importing countries were Netherlands and United Kingdom (see table 3). By MDG regions (see graph 2), Developed Europe accounted for a majority of trade in eggs, birds', egg yolks, fresh, dried or preserved; egg albumin (SITC group 025). In 2010, its exports and imports amounted respectively to 2.9 bln US$ and 2.6 bln US$, resulting in a trade surplus of 0.3 bln US$. Developed North America recorded a surplus of 0.3 bln US$ and Developed Asia-Pacific, a deficit of 0.1 bln US$.

Table 1: Imports (Imp.) and exports (Exp.), 1996-2010, in current prices

		1996	1997	1998	1999	2000	2001	2002	2003	2004	2005	2006	2007	2008	2009	2010
Values in Bln US$	Imp.	1.7	1.7	1.6	1.4	1.4	1.5	1.6	1.9	2.2	2.4	2.5	3.1	3.8	4.0	4.1
	Exp.	1.8	1.7	1.6	1.4	1.4	1.5	1.5	2.0	2.1	2.2	2.4	3.2	4.1	4.2	4.4
As a percentage of SITC section (%)	Imp.	0.4	0.4	0.4	0.3	0.3	0.4	0.4	0.4	0.4	0.4	0.4	0.4	0.4	0.4	0.4
	Exp.	0.4	0.4	0.4	0.4	0.4	0.4	0.4	0.4	0.4	0.4	0.4	0.4	0.4	0.5	0.5
As a percentage of world trade (%)	Imp.	0.0	0.0	0.0	0.0	0.0	0.0	0.0	0.0	0.0	0.0	0.0	0.0	0.0	0.0	0.0
	Exp.	0.0	0.0	0.0	0.0	0.0	0.0	0.0	0.0	0.0	0.0	0.0	0.0	0.0	0.0	0.0

Graph 1: Annual growth rates of exports, 1996–2010

(In percentage by year)

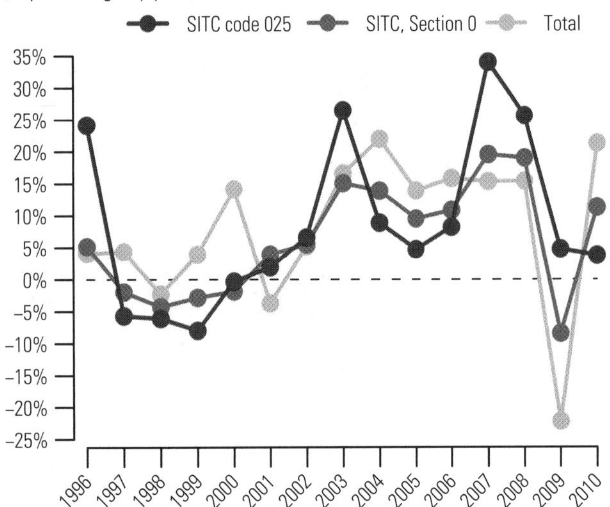

Graph 2: Trade Balance by MDG regions 2010

(Bln US$)

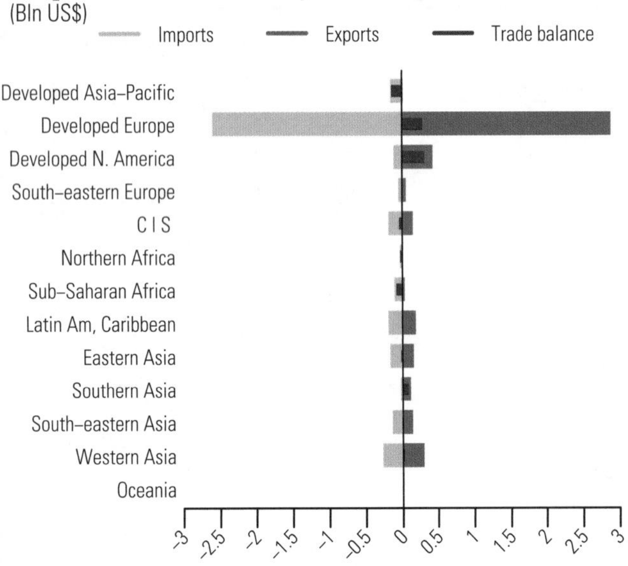

Table 2: Top exporting countries or areas in 2010

Country or area	Value (million US$)	Avg. Growth (%) 06-10	Growth (%) 09-10	World share %	Cum.
World	4401.4	16.3	3.7	100.0	
Netherlands	1120.4	17.4	2.8	25.5	25.5
USA	360.9	11.3	4.0	8.2	33.7
Germany	310.0	8.1	0.0	7.0	40.7
France	309.6	8.3	1.5	7.0	47.7
Poland	232.7	31.4	-4.3	5.3	53.0
Spain	196.7	7.4	-20.5	4.5	57.5
Belgium	173.4	8.8	3.5	3.9	61.4
Italy	158.0	21.8	7.9	3.6	65.0
Turkey	156.2	70.8	23.4	3.5	68.6
China	142.9	16.3	17.0	3.2	71.8
Brazil	114.8	39.8	33.0	2.6	74.4
Malaysia	104.1	18.6	16.4	2.4	76.8
Ukraine	97.2	141.8	34.8	2.2	79.0
India	74.0	7.0	-4.7	1.7	80.7
United Kingdom	72.0	12.5	2.5	1.6	82.3

Table 3: Top importing countries or areas in 2010

Country or area	Value (million US$)	Avg. Growth (%) 06-10	Growth (%) 09-10	World share %	Cum.
World	4074.0	13.1	2.9	100.0	
Germany	1020.0	14.4	3.1	25.0	25.0
Netherlands	274.0	19.9	17.1	6.7	31.8
United Kingdom	215.4	6.8	-7.9	5.3	37.1
France	171.9	6.5	-11.5	4.2	41.3
Belgium	151.5	11.6	-0.4	3.7	45.0
Japan	143.5	6.5	3.1	3.5	48.5
China, Hong Kong SAR	134.4	14.3	6.9	3.3	51.8
Russian Federation	115.1	23.1	44.7	2.8	54.6
Singapore	105.3	16.6	12.6	2.6	57.2
Switzerland	100.7	11.3	-4.6	2.5	59.7
Austria	84.1	11.6	-4.9	2.1	61.8
Italy	83.4	22.2	3.9	2.0	63.8
United Arab Emirates	79.4	17.5	8.1	1.9	65.8
Spain	73.0	12.5	-7.8	1.8	67.5
Canada	70.6	11.0	0.2	1.7	69.3

After a slight drop of 1.5 percent in 2009, the value (in current prices) of exports of fresh, chilled or frozen fish (SITC group 034) went up in 2010 by 17.2 percent and amounted to nearly 50.6 bln US$ (see table 2). Imports, displaying a similar but less sharp change, increased by 11.1 percent and totaled 53.3 bln US$ in 2010. Graph 1 shows that the increase in exports for 2010 in this product group exceeded the increase in world exports of food and live animals (SITC section 0) of 11.2 percent but was slightly below the increase in total world exports of 21.2 percent. Exports of fresh, chilled or frozen fish (SITC group 034) accounted for 5.2 percent of world exports of SITC section 0 and 0.3 percent of total world exports in 2010 (see table 1).

In 2010, Norway was the top exporting country with 14.9 percent of world exports (see table 2). Other major exporting countries were China and USA, respectively with 11.4 and 5.6 percent of world exports. Japan, USA and China were the top destinations (see table 3). By MDG regions (see graph 2), Developed Europe accounted for a significant share of trade in fresh, chilled or frozen fish (SITC group 034). In 2010, its exports and imports amounted respectively to 21.7 bln US$ and 21.3 bln US$ resulting in a trade surplus of 0.4 bln US$. Top trade surpluses were recorded by Latin America and the Caribbean (+2.4 bln US$), Eastern Asia (+2.0 bln US$) and South-eastern Asia (+1.3 bln US$). Developed Asia-Pacific and Developed North America recorded trade deficits amounting respectively to 6.1 bln US$ and 2.4 bln US$.

Table 1: Imports (Imp.) and exports (Exp.), 1996-2010, in current prices

		1996	1997	1998	1999	2000	2001	2002	2003	2004	2005	2006	2007	2008	2009	2010
Values in Bln US$	Imp.	24.0	23.8	23.5	25.1	25.1	26.3	27.1	29.7	33.4	38.0	42.5	47.1	51.0	47.9	53.3
	Exp.	19.3	19.9	19.4	20.8	21.1	22.4	23.2	25.9	29.7	33.9	37.3	40.2	43.8	43.2	50.6
As a percentage of SITC section (%)	Imp.	5.4	5.5	5.5	6.0	6.1	6.2	6.1	5.8	5.7	6.0	6.1	5.7	5.2	5.4	5.5
	Exp.	4.5	4.7	4.8	5.3	5.5	5.6	5.5	5.3	5.4	5.6	5.6	5.0	4.6	5.0	5.2
As a percentage of world trade (%)	Imp.	0.4	0.4	0.4	0.4	0.4	0.4	0.4	0.4	0.4	0.4	0.3	0.3	0.3	0.4	0.4
	Exp.	0.4	0.4	0.4	0.4	0.3	0.4	0.4	0.3	0.3	0.3	0.3	0.3	0.3	0.3	0.3

Graph 1: Annual growth rates of exports, 1996–2010

(In percentage by year)

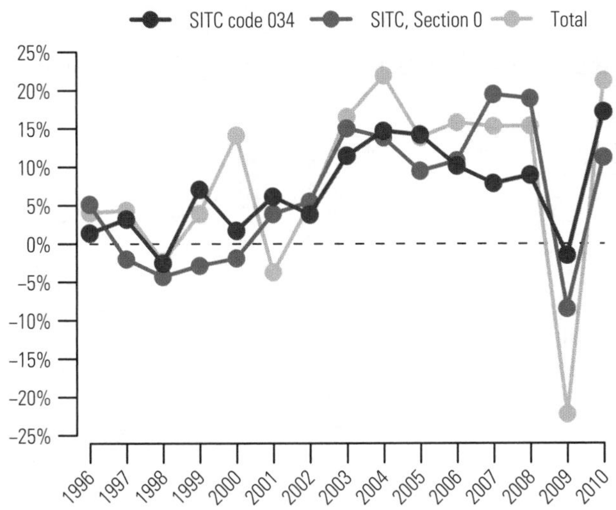

Table 2: Top exporting countries or areas in 2010

Country or area	Value (million US$)	Avg. Growth (%) 06-10	Growth (%) 09-10	World share %	Cum.
World	50581.0	7.9	17.2	100.0	
Norway	7527.9	14.6	26.9	14.9	14.9
China	5743.8	13.4	28.0	11.4	26.2
USA	2838.9	-0.2	13.2	5.6	31.9
Chile	2306.5	-1.8	-3.7	4.6	36.4
Viet Nam	*2229.3*	19.7	25.6	4.4	40.8
Sweden	2111.9	16.0	32.0	4.2	45.0
Russian Federation	1869.6	41.7	29.1	3.7	48.7
Spain	1611.8	2.9	4.1	3.2	51.9
Netherlands	1513.3	2.2	9.3	3.0	54.9
Canada	1324.8	1.3	19.9	2.6	57.5
Denmark	1318.5	-2.1	7.1	2.6	60.1
Other Asia, nes	1258.8	4.6	26.4	2.5	62.6
United Kingdom	1201.9	9.2	20.7	2.4	65.0
Iceland	1128.3	-0.3	12.2	2.2	67.2
Rep. of Korea	1039.9	17.2	19.7	2.1	69.2

Graph 2: Trade Balance by MDG regions 2010

(Bln US$)

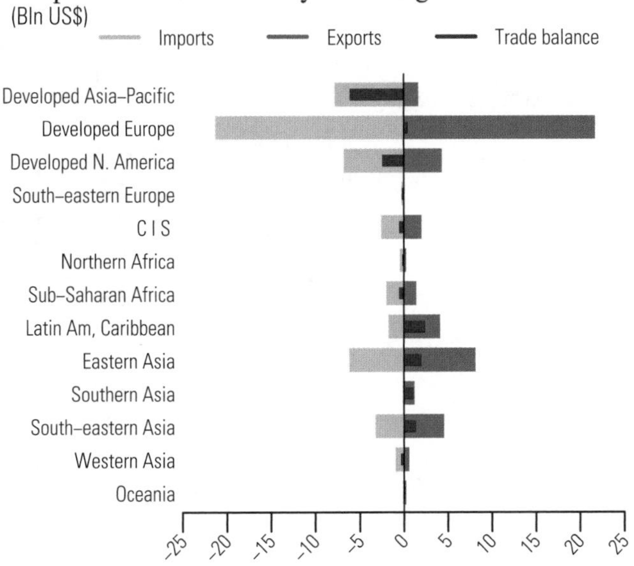

Table 3: Top importing countries or areas in 2010

Country or area	Value (million US$)	Avg. Growth (%) 06-10	Growth (%) 09-10	World share %	Cum.
World	53253.7	5.8	11.1	100.0	
Japan	7436.4	3.1	11.5	14.0	14.0
USA	5928.8	3.9	9.7	11.1	25.1
China	3324.1	7.4	16.5	6.2	31.3
France	2841.7	4.3	7.5	5.3	36.7
Spain	2610.3	-0.3	0.6	4.9	41.6
Sweden	2460.3	15.5	28.3	4.6	46.2
Germany	2425.1	2.5	2.9	4.6	50.8
Italy	1933.3	4.3	7.4	3.6	54.4
Rep. of Korea	1820.3	4.6	18.9	3.4	57.8
Thailand	1805.1	8.8	8.8	3.4	61.2
United Kingdom	1717.7	-3.6	1.3	3.2	64.4
Russian Federation	1704.7	14.3	17.3	3.2	67.6
Poland	1317.5	16.3	30.0	2.5	70.1
Netherlands	1269.2	6.8	5.3	2.4	72.5
Denmark	1065.6	-0.4	12.1	2.0	74.5

035 Fish, dried, salted or in brine; smoked fish; flours, meals, etc

After several years of continuous growth marked by a peak of 4.8 bln US$ in 2008, the value (in current prices) of exports of fish, dried, salted or in brine; smoked fish; flour, meals, etc (SITC group 035) declined by 10.7 percent in 2009 but bounced back by 12.5 percent increase to reach 4.8 bln US$ in 2010 (see table 2). During the same period, imports showed a similar development with an increase of 9.9 percent to reach 5.1 bln US$ in 2010 (see table 3). Graph 1 shows that the increase in exports for 2010 in this product group slightly exceeded the increase in world exports of food and live animals (SITC section 0) of 11.2 percent but was below the increase in total world exports of 21.2 percent. Exports of fish, dried, salted or in brine; smoked fish; flour, meals, etc (SITC group 035) accounted for 0.5 percent of world exports of SITC section 0 and less than 0.1 percent of total world exports in 2010 (see table 1).

Norway was the top exporting country with 19.0 percent of world exports in 2010 (see table 2). Other major exporting countries were Poland and Iceland respectively with 11.1 and 7.7 percent of world exports. Top destinations were Germany, China, Hong Kong SAR and Italy (see table 3). By MDG regions (see graph 2), Developed Europe accounted for a majority of trade in fish, dried, salted or in brine; smoked fish; flour, meals, etc (SITC group 035). In 2010, its exports and imports amounted respectively to 3.3 bln US$ and 2.8 bln US$ resulting in a trade surplus of 0.5 bln US$. South-eastern Asia recorded a surplus of 0.2 bln US$ while Latin-America and the Caribbean recorded a deficit of 0.3 bln US$.

Table 1: Imports (Imp.) and exports (Exp.), 1996-2010, in current prices

		1996	1997	1998	1999	2000	2001	2002	2003	2004	2005	2006	2007	2008	2009	2010
Values in Bln US$	Imp.	2.9	2.7	2.7	2.8	2.8	2.8	2.7	2.9	3.3	3.6	3.9	4.6	4.9	4.6	5.1
	Exp.	2.8	2.7	2.8	2.7	2.7	2.8	2.8	3.0	3.5	3.7	3.9	4.5	4.8	4.3	4.8
As a percentage of SITC section (%)	Imp.	0.7	0.6	0.6	0.7	0.7	0.7	0.6	0.6	0.6	0.6	0.6	0.6	0.5	0.5	0.5
	Exp.	0.7	0.6	0.7	0.7	0.7	0.7	0.7	0.6	0.6	0.6	0.6	0.6	0.5	0.5	0.5
As a percentage of world trade (%)	Imp.	0.1	0.0	0.0	0.0	0.0	0.0	0.0	0.0	0.0	0.0	0.0	0.0	0.0	0.0	0.0
	Exp.	0.1	0.0	0.1	0.0	0.0	0.0	0.0	0.0	0.0	0.0	0.0	0.0	0.0	0.0	0.0

Graph 1: Annual growth rates of exports, 1996–2010
(In percentage by year)

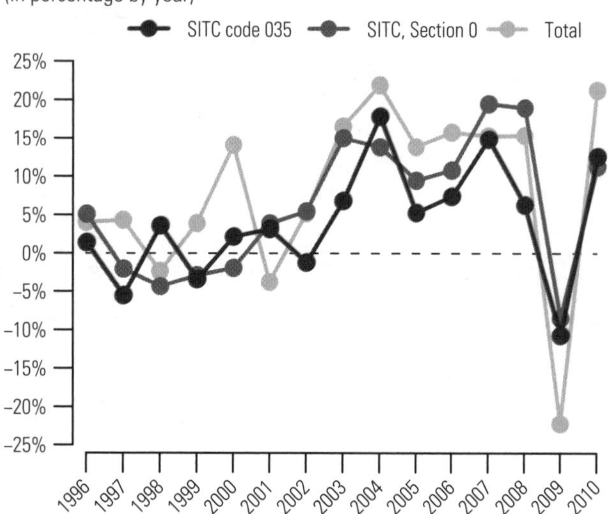

Table 2: Top exporting countries or areas in 2010

Country or area	Value (million US$)	Avg. Growth (%) 06-10	Growth (%) 09-10	World share %	Cum.
World	4823.9	5.2	12.5	100.0	
Norway	914.7	3.4	16.1	19.0	19.0
Poland	533.6	13.5	30.6	11.1	30.0
Iceland	371.8	2.4	-1.2	7.7	37.7
China	352.4	12.1	23.5	7.3	45.0
Sweden	335.7	7.3	32.0	7.0	52.0
Denmark	277.8	0.1	-1.8	5.8	57.8
Germany	194.9	10.6	1.1	4.0	61.8
Canada	152.3	-2.5	-1.4	3.2	65.0
China, Hong Kong SAR	120.5	-5.0	-5.5	2.5	67.5
United Kingdom	111.3	3.8	32.5	2.3	69.8
Spain	105.5	1.8	0.9	2.2	71.9
Portugal	89.8	0.2	16.4	1.9	73.8
Faeroe Isds	*88.0*	-2.1	7.3	1.8	75.6
France	83.6	7.7	-1.8	1.7	77.4
Thailand	80.2	4.1	20.0	1.7	79.0

Graph 2: Trade Balance by MDG regions 2010
(Bln US$)

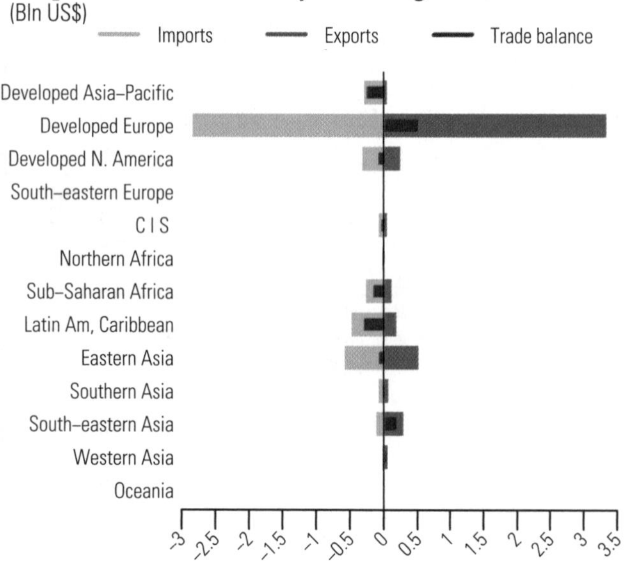

Table 3: Top importing countries or areas in 2010

Country or area	Value (million US$)	Avg. Growth (%) 06-10	Growth (%) 09-10	World share %	Cum.
World	5070.3	6.8	9.9	100.0	
Germany	601.1	15.6	-1.2	11.9	11.9
China, Hong Kong SAR	470.7	5.9	17.2	9.3	21.1
Italy	441.6	4.6	10.9	8.7	29.8
Portugal	369.7	4.0	18.6	7.3	37.1
Sweden	337.9	4.9	28.0	6.7	43.8
Brazil	305.9	13.5	42.7	6.0	49.8
Spain	283.5	-3.1	2.8	5.6	55.4
Japan	252.6	2.0	-2.4	5.0	60.4
USA	246.4	5.0	-1.4	4.9	65.3
France	184.3	7.7	19.9	3.6	68.9
Nigeria	165.0	36.8	-4.3	3.3	72.2
Netherlands	146.5	5.9	-7.4	2.9	75.1
Belgium	95.8	5.6	5.0	1.9	76.9
Denmark	94.7	4.5	25.8	1.9	78.8
Sri Lanka	67.4	6.1	-1.7	1.3	80.1

After a 2.3 percent drop in 2009, the value (in current prices) of exports of crustaceans, molluscs, aquatic invertebrates; flours and pellets (SITC group 036) increased by 18.6 percent and amounted to 26.2 bln US$ in 2010 (see table 2). Imports showed a similar development with an increase of 14.9 percent to 26.1 bln US$ (see table 3). Graph 1 shows that the increase in exports for 2010 in this product group exceeded the increase in world exports of food and live animals (SITC section 0) of 11.2 percent but was below the increase in total world exports of 21.2 percent. Exports of crustaceans, molluscs, aquatic invertebrates; flours and pellets (SITC group 036) accounted for 2.7 percent of world exports of SITC section 0 and 0.2 percent of total world exports in 2010 (see table 1).

China, Viet Nam and Thailand were the top exporting countries in 2010 (see table 2). They accounted respectively for 10.3, 8.5 and 8.2 percent of world exports. USA, Japan and Spain were the top destination (see table 3). By MDG regions (see graph 2), South-eastern Asia was the origin, and Developed Europe the destination, of a large share of trade in crustaceans, molluscs, aquatic invertebrates; flours and pellets (SITC group 036). In 2010, South-eastern Asia's exports amounted to 6.3 bln US$ resulting in a trade surplus of 5.4 bln US$ while Developed Europe's imports reached 9.6 bln US$ resulting in a trade deficit of 5.2 bln US$. Latin America and the Caribbean recorded a surplus of 3.3 bln US$. Major trade deficits were recorded by Developed North America (-3.2 bln US$) and Developed Asia-Pacific (-3.0 bln US$).

Table 1: Imports (Imp.) and exports (Exp.), 1996-2010, in current prices

		1996	1997	1998	1999	2000	2001	2002	2003	2004	2005	2006	2007	2008	2009	2010
Values in Bln US$	Imp.	17.6	17.3	17.1	17.6	19.2	18.2	18.3	20.2	21.3	21.9	23.5	24.6	25.3	22.7	26.1
	Exp.	16.2	16.0	15.3	15.5	17.3	16.3	16.6	18.2	18.9	19.4	20.8	21.9	22.6	22.0	26.2
As a percentage of SITC section (%)	Imp.	3.9	4.0	4.1	4.2	4.7	4.3	4.1	3.9	3.7	3.4	3.4	3.0	2.6	2.6	2.7
	Exp.	3.7	3.8	3.8	3.9	4.5	4.1	3.9	3.7	3.4	3.2	3.1	2.7	2.4	2.5	2.7
As a percentage of world trade (%)	Imp.	0.3	0.3	0.3	0.3	0.3	0.3	0.3	0.3	0.2	0.2	0.2	0.2	0.2	0.2	0.2
	Exp.	0.3	0.3	0.3	0.3	0.3	0.3	0.3	0.2	0.2	0.2	0.2	0.2	0.1	0.2	0.2

Graph 1: Annual growth rates of exports, 1996–2010

(In percentage by year)

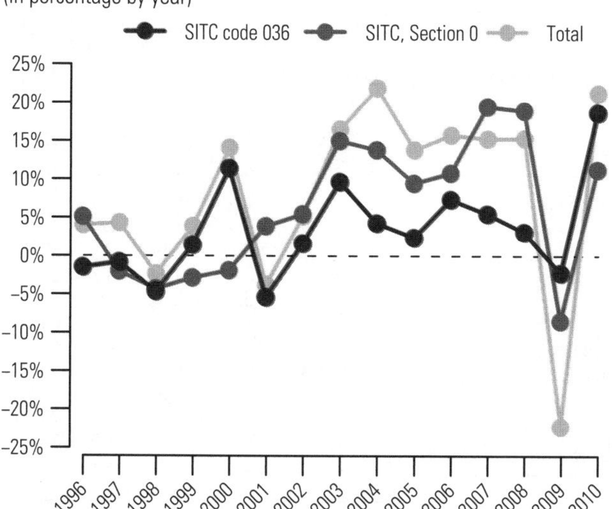

Graph 2: Trade Balance by MDG regions 2010

(Bln US$)

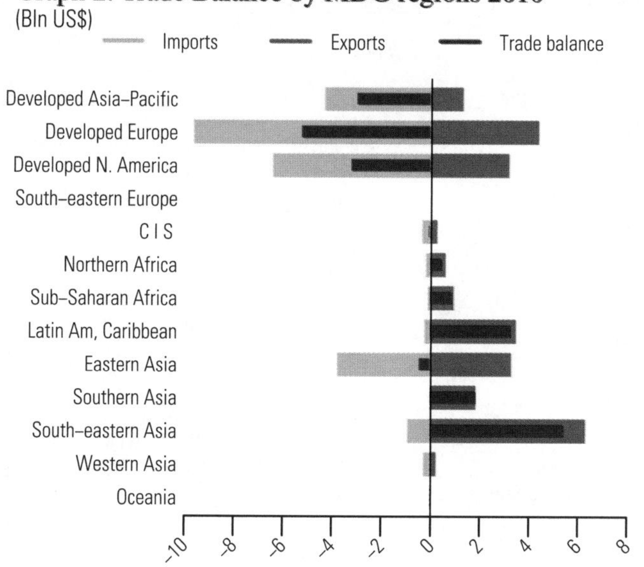

Table 2: Top exporting countries or areas in 2010

Country or area	Value (million US$)	Avg. Growth (%) 06-10	Growth (%) 09-10	World share %	Cum.
World	26153.2	5.9	18.6	100.0	
China	2699.6	27.0	33.0	10.3	10.3
Viet Nam	*2231.9*	5.6	25.6	8.5	18.9
Thailand	2139.7	7.1	19.7	8.2	27.0
Canada	1919.0	2.8	17.4	7.3	34.4
India	1409.4	5.0	40.1	5.4	39.8
USA	1127.7	5.3	17.2	4.3	44.1
Indonesia	1058.9	-1.4	13.7	4.0	48.1
Ecuador	852.5	9.5	27.9	3.3	51.4
Spain	841.3	4.7	8.4	3.2	54.6
Argentina	657.9	1.3	53.0	2.5	57.1
Netherlands	629.1	5.2	3.2	2.4	59.5
United Kingdom	610.3	-0.7	12.1	2.3	61.9
Australia	596.4	-1.7	13.0	2.3	64.1
Morocco	536.1	3.6	-1.1	2.0	66.2
Malaysia	498.9	6.9	36.7	1.9	68.1

Table 3: Top importing countries or areas in 2010

Country or area	Value (million US$)	Avg. Growth (%) 06-10	Growth (%) 09-10	World share %	Cum.
World	26106.5	2.6	14.9	100.0	
USA	5648.8	0.4	13.3	21.6	21.6
Japan	3971.6	-0.4	10.5	15.2	36.9
Spain	2777.8	-0.8	21.0	10.6	47.5
Italy	1780.2	1.7	12.3	6.8	54.3
France	1642.8	2.8	15.2	6.3	60.6
China, Hong Kong SAR	1565.4	11.8	19.0	6.0	66.6
China	980.5	13.4	40.8	3.8	70.4
Rep. of Korea	887.5	2.8	15.5	3.4	73.8
Canada	725.6	2.8	20.5	2.8	76.5
Belgium	694.9	-1.1	7.0	2.7	79.2
United Kingdom	475.3	1.1	7.9	1.8	81.0
Portugal	462.2	9.9	18.1	1.8	82.8
Germany	422.6	7.5	9.6	1.6	84.4
Netherlands	364.2	2.1	-2.8	1.4	85.8
Other Asia, nes	285.5	17.9	14.9	1.1	86.9

037 Fish, crustaceans, molluscs, aquatic invertebrates, prepared, nes

During the recent five years, the value (in current prices) of exports of prepared or preserved fish, crustaceans, molluscs, aquatic invertebrates, nes (SITC group 037) increased on average by 4.5 percent and amounted to 20.4 bln US$ in 2010 (see table 2). Imports, displaying a similar development, increased on average by 5.2 percent to reach 19.2 bln US$. Graph 1 shows that the increase in exports for 2010 in this product group was exceeded by the increases in world exports of food and live animals (SITC section 0) of 11.2 percent and in total world exports of 21.2 percent. Exports of prepared or preserved fish, crustaceans, molluscs, aquatic invertebrates, nes (SITC group 037) accounted for 2.1 percent of world exports of SITC section 0 and 0.1 percent of total world exports in 2010 (see table 1).

In 2010, China, Thailand and Viet Nam were the top exporting countries (see table 2). They accounted respectively for 21.6, 20.2 and 3.9 percent of world exports. Top destinations were USA, Japan and United Kingdom (see table 3). By MDG regions (see graph 2), top surpluses were recorded by South-eastern Asia (+5.5 bln US$) and Eastern Asia (+3.9 bln US$). With imports amounting to 8.3 bln US$, Developed Europe was the major destination of trade in prepared or preserved fish, crustaceans, molluscs, aquatic invertebrates, nes (SITC group 037) and recorded the top deficit of 3.4 bln US$. Developed North America and Developed Asia-Pacific also recorded deficits amounting respectively to 3.1 bln US$ and 2.5 bln US$.

Table 1: Imports (Imp.) and exports (Exp.), 1996-2010, in current prices

		1996	1997	1998	1999	2000	2001	2002	2003	2004	2005	2006	2007	2008	2009	2010
Values in Bln US$	Imp.	9.5	9.4	9.5	9.5	9.8	9.8	10.5	11.6	13.1	14.1	15.6	17.2	19.8	18.1	19.2
	Exp.	9.4	9.5	9.1	9.0	9.4	9.6	10.1	11.5	13.1	14.6	17.1	18.8	21.6	18.6	20.4
As a percentage of SITC section (%)	Imp.	2.1	2.2	2.2	2.3	2.4	2.3	2.4	2.3	2.2	2.2	2.2	2.1	2.0	2.0	2.0
	Exp.	2.2	2.2	2.2	2.3	2.4	2.4	2.4	2.4	2.4	2.4	2.6	2.4	2.3	2.1	2.1
As a percentage of world trade (%)	Imp.	0.2	0.2	0.2	0.2	0.1	0.2	0.2	0.2	0.1	0.1	0.1	0.1	0.1	0.1	0.1
	Exp.	0.2	0.2	0.2	0.2	0.1	0.2	0.2	0.2	0.1	0.1	0.1	0.1	0.1	0.1	0.1

Graph 1: Annual growth rates of exports, 1996–2010

(In percentage by year)

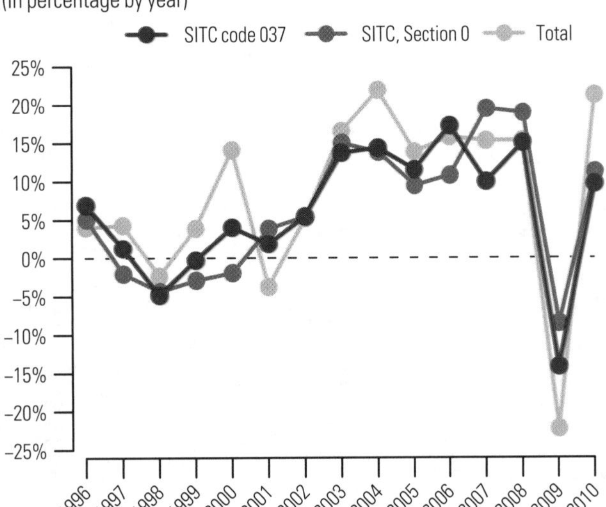

Table 2: Top exporting countries or areas in 2010

Country or area	Value (million US$)	Avg. Growth (%) 06-10	Growth (%) 09-10	World share %	Cum.
World	20373.3	4.5	9.7	100.0	
China	4402.3	1.1	28.7	21.6	21.6
Thailand	4119.4	8.3	10.8	20.2	41.8
Viet Nam	*797.4*	19.1	25.6	3.9	45.7
Denmark	681.8	-0.6	-6.9	3.3	49.1
Spain	678.0	4.0	1.0	3.3	52.4
Germany	677.7	3.1	-9.9	3.3	55.7
Japan	647.0	12.9	31.1	3.2	58.9
Morocco	612.1	6.1	-3.3	3.0	61.9
Ecuador	603.7	1.6	-4.6	3.0	64.9
Indonesia	543.7	14.5	0.8	2.7	67.6
Netherlands	519.4	6.1	-5.6	2.5	70.1
USA	449.4	1.3	-6.4	2.2	72.3
Canada	406.8	-4.1	28.7	2.0	74.3
Poland	382.7	14.1	6.4	1.9	76.2
Philippines	295.7	23.3	-1.1	1.5	77.6

Graph 2: Trade Balance by MDG regions 2010

(Bln US$)

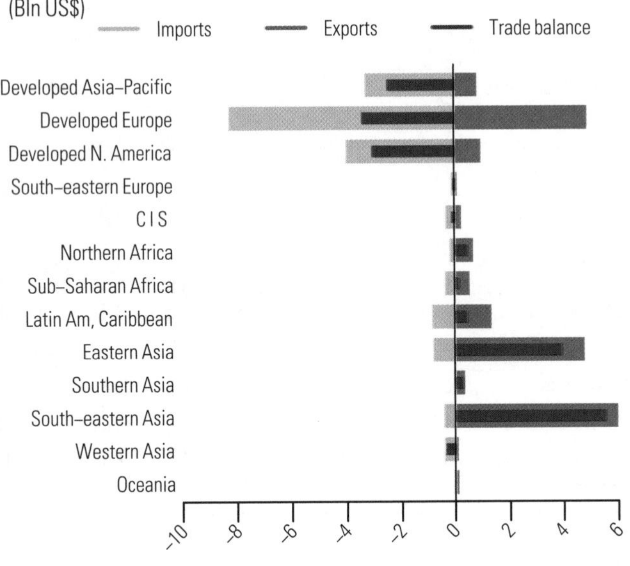

Table 3: Top importing countries or areas in 2010

Country or area	Value (million US$)	Avg. Growth (%) 06-10	Growth (%) 09-10	World share %	Cum.
World	19155.8	5.2	5.6	100.0	
USA	3515.0	3.2	13.5	18.3	18.3
Japan	2733.2	0.6	13.0	14.3	32.6
United Kingdom	1232.4	3.8	0.6	6.4	39.1
France	1162.4	4.3	-7.2	6.1	45.1
Italy	1119.5	2.9	-8.5	5.8	51.0
Germany	927.2	2.2	2.8	4.8	55.8
Spain	748.5	6.1	4.0	3.9	59.7
Netherlands	548.4	21.1	15.3	2.9	62.6
Australia	516.2	14.4	12.3	2.7	65.3
Canada	476.7	5.4	1.3	2.5	67.8
Belgium	447.4	4.3	-3.3	2.3	70.1
Denmark	421.7	4.3	11.0	2.2	72.3
Sweden	318.5	7.6	11.1	1.7	74.0
Rep. of Korea	315.3	1.0	17.1	1.6	75.6
China, Hong Kong SAR	298.5	13.5	23.2	1.6	77.2

After a sharp decline of 28.4 percent in 2009, the value (in current prices) of exports of unmilled wheat, meslin (SITC group 041) increased by 1.8 percent and totaled 32.6 bln US$ in 2010 (see table 2). During the same period, imports displayed a similar development and increased 3.6 percent to 34.7 bln US$ (see table 3). Graph 1 shows that the increase in exports for 2010 in this product group was well below the increases in world exports of food and live animals (SITC section 0) of 11.2 percent and in total world exports of 21.2 percent. Exports of unmilled wheat, meslin (SITC group 041) accounted for 3.4 percent of world exports of SITC section 0 and 0.2 percent of total world exports in 2010 (see table 1).

USA, the top exporting country, accounted for 20.7 percent of world exports in 2010 (see table 2). Other major exporting countries include France and Canada, respectively with 14.3 and 13.9 percent. Top importing countries were Egypt, Italy and Japan (see table 3). By MDG regions (see graph 2), Developed Europe accounted for a large share of trade in unmilled wheat, meslin (SITC group 041). In 2010, its exports and imports were valued respectively at 10.3 bln US$ and 7.6 bln US$, resulting in a trade surplus of 2.7 bln US$. Larger trade surpluses were recorded by Developed North America (+10.7 bln US$) and Commonwealth of Independent States (+3.2 bln US$). Top trade deficits were recorded by Northern Africa (-5.0 bln US$) and Sub-Saharan Africa (-3.8 bln US$).

Table 1: Imports (Imp.) and exports (Exp.), 1996-2010, in current prices

		1996	1997	1998	1999	2000	2001	2002	2003	2004	2005	2006	2007	2008	2009	2010
Values in Bln US$	Imp.	22.6	19.2	16.4	15.4	15.2	15.7	16.6	17.4	21.1	20.1	22.2	33.4	48.2	33.5	34.7
	Exp.	20.5	18.3	15.3	14.3	13.6	14.6	15.4	15.8	19.4	17.7	20.6	30.4	44.7	32.0	32.6
As a percentage of SITC section (%)	Imp.	5.1	4.4	3.9	3.7	3.7	3.7	3.7	3.4	3.6	3.2	3.2	4.0	4.9	3.8	3.6
	Exp.	4.7	4.3	3.8	3.6	3.5	3.6	3.7	3.2	3.5	2.9	3.1	3.8	4.7	3.7	3.4
As a percentage of world trade (%)	Imp.	0.4	0.3	0.3	0.3	0.2	0.2	0.3	0.2	0.2	0.2	0.2	0.2	0.3	0.3	0.2
	Exp.	0.4	0.3	0.3	0.3	0.2	0.2	0.2	0.2	0.2	0.2	0.2	0.2	0.3	0.3	0.2

Graph 1: Annual growth rates of exports, 1996–2010

(In percentage by year)

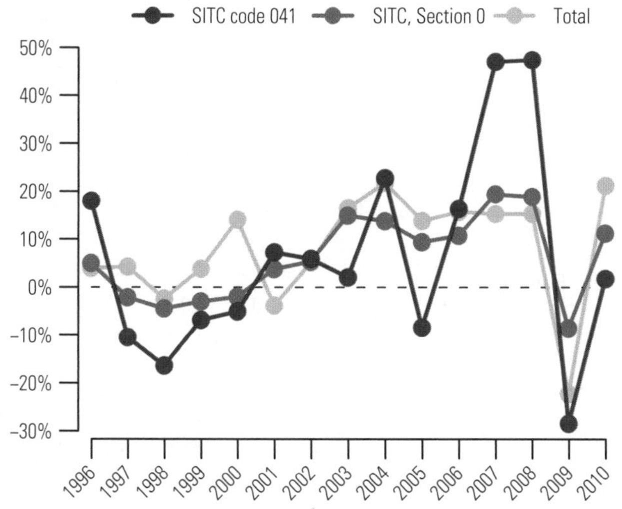

Table 2: Top exporting countries or areas in 2010

Country or area	Value (million US$)	Avg. Growth (%) 06-10	Growth (%) 09-10	World share %	Cum.
World	32586.2	12.1	1.8	100.0	
USA	6751.0	12.4	25.5	20.7	20.7
France	4655.1	14.6	23.9	14.3	35.0
Canada	4537.8	8.9	-14.2	13.9	48.9
Australia	3754.5	10.2	0.6	11.5	60.5
Russian Federation	2069.1	10.9	-24.8	6.3	66.8
Germany	1964.7	17.2	-10.6	6.0	72.8
Kazakhstan	911.5	14.9	44.0	2.8	75.6
Ukraine	906.4	11.1	-49.0	2.8	78.4
Argentina	901.8	-11.5	-10.0	2.8	81.2
United Kingdom	702.6	18.9	47.3	2.2	83.3
Romania	500.1	43.2	19.9	1.5	84.9
Bulgaria	451.9	28.8	49.4	1.4	86.3
Hungary	435.0	8.0	28.7	1.3	87.6
Denmark	324.5	25.3	17.2	1.0	88.6
Uruguay	*324.4*	110.6	24.5	1.0	89.6

Graph 2: Trade Balance by MDG regions 2010

(Bln US$)

Imports — Exports — Trade balance

Developed Asia-Pacific
Developed Europe
Developed N. America
South-eastern Europe
CIS
Northern Africa
Sub-Saharan Africa
Latin Am, Caribbean
Eastern Asia
Southern Asia
South-eastern Asia
Western Asia
Oceania

-8 -6 -4 -2 0 2 4 6 8 10 12

Table 3: Top importing countries or areas in 2010

Country or area	Value (million US$)	Avg. Growth (%) 06-10	Growth (%) 09-10	World share %	Cum.
World	34662.2	11.8	3.6	100.0	
Egypt	2181.9	22.6	38.4	6.3	6.3
Italy	1874.4	7.8	8.0	5.4	11.7
Japan	1667.6	6.8	15.2	4.8	16.5
Brazil	1528.3	11.5	26.4	4.4	20.9
Indonesia	1424.3	14.9	8.2	4.1	25.0
Algeria	1251.6	5.8	-31.6	3.6	28.6
Netherlands	1076.2	12.2	11.8	3.1	31.7
Rep. of Korea	1066.8	12.9	12.4	3.1	34.8
Spain	1053.3	4.7	-23.6	3.0	37.9
Germany	894.8	25.3	5.5	2.6	40.4
Morocco	878.5	25.7	28.6	2.5	43.0
Mexico	847.2	5.2	16.4	2.4	45.4
Nigeria	839.7	-11.4	-24.2	2.4	47.8
Belgium	807.5	8.8	0.4	2.3	50.2
Yemen	*780.5*	18.9	6.1	2.3	52.4

Source: UN Comtrade

042 Rice

During the recent five years, the value (in current prices) of exports of rice (SITC group 042) increased on average by 18.0 percent each year and amounted to 20.5 bln US$ in 2010 (see table 2). During the same period, imports increased on average by 17.2 percent each year to reach 19.8 bln US$ in 2010 (see table 3). Graph 1 shows that the increase in exports for 2010 in this product group was exceeded by the increases in world exports of food and live animals (SITC section 0) of 11.2 percent and in total world exports of 21.2 percent. Exports of rice (SITC group 042) accounted for 2.1 percent of world exports of SITC section 0 and 0.1 percent of total world exports in 2010 (see table 1).

Thailand, the top exporting country, accounted for 26.1 percent of world exports in 2010 (see table 2). Other major exporting countries were Viet Nam and USA, respectively with 16.4 and 11.5 percent. Top importing countries were Philippines, United Arab Emirates and Saudi Arabia (see table 3). By MDG regions (see graph 2), top trade surpluses were recorded by South-eastern Asia (+6.0 bln US$), Southern Asia (+3.3 bln US$) and Developed North America (+1.4 bln US$). Top trade deficits were recorded by Western Asia (-3.8 bln US$), Sub-Saharan Africa (-3.4 bln US$) and Developed Europe (-0.9 bln US$).

Table 1: Imports (Imp.) and exports (Exp.), 1996-2010, in current prices

		1996	1997	1998	1999	2000	2001	2002	2003	2004	2005	2006	2007	2008	2009	2010
Values in Bln US$	Imp.	8.4	7.7	8.9	8.4	6.6	6.4	6.5	7.4	8.9	9.9	10.5	13.4	21.1	19.8	19.8
	Exp.	7.6	7.8	9.6	7.9	6.5	6.9	6.7	7.3	8.7	10.1	10.5	13.2	21.1	19.1	20.5
As a percentage of SITC section (%)	Imp.	1.9	1.8	2.1	2.0	1.6	1.5	1.5	1.5	1.5	1.6	1.5	1.6	2.2	2.2	2.0
	Exp.	1.7	1.8	2.4	2.0	1.7	1.7	1.6	1.5	1.6	1.7	1.6	1.6	2.2	2.2	2.1
As a percentage of world trade (%)	Imp.	0.2	0.1	0.2	0.1	0.1	0.1	0.1	0.1	0.1	0.1	0.1	0.1	0.1	0.2	0.1
	Exp.	0.1	0.1	0.2	0.1	0.1	0.1	0.1	0.1	0.1	0.1	0.1	0.1	0.1	0.2	0.1

Graph 1: Annual growth rates of exports, 1996–2010

(In percentage by year)

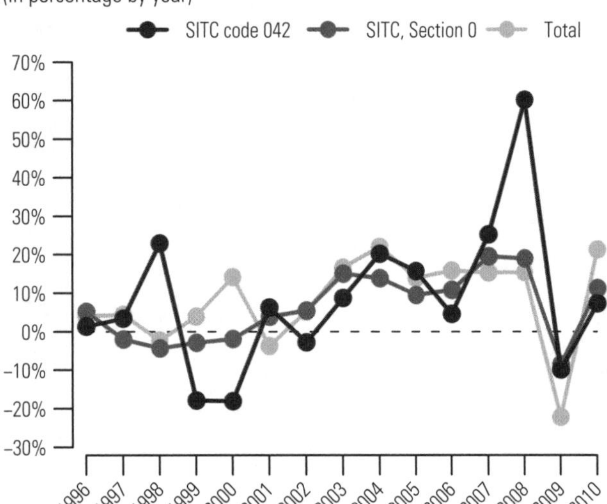

Table 2: Top exporting countries or areas in 2010

Country or area	Value (million US$)	Avg. Growth (%) 06-10	Growth (%) 09-10	World share %	Cum.
World	20457.3	18.0	7.4	100.0	
Thailand	5341.1	20.0	5.8	26.1	26.1
Viet Nam	*3349.6*	27.3	25.6	16.4	42.5
USA	2354.1	16.3	7.7	11.5	54.0
India	2295.8	12.1	-4.3	11.2	65.2
Pakistan	2277.1	18.6	28.3	11.1	76.3
Italy	648.2	10.3	-12.7	3.2	79.5
Uruguay	*574.4*	27.3	24.5	2.8	82.3
United Arab Emirates	521.5	43.9	0.6	2.5	84.9
China	416.1	0.4	-20.5	2.0	86.9
Egypt	365.5	4.9	-23.2	1.8	88.7
Belgium	236.4	11.7	-17.2	1.2	89.8
Argentina	233.7	14.5	-14.2	1.1	91.0
Spain	188.2	7.3	46.3	0.9	91.9
Guyana	173.3	36.4	52.8	0.8	92.8
Brazil	157.6	27.4	-41.1	0.8	93.5

Graph 2: Trade Balance by MDG regions 2010

(Bln US$)

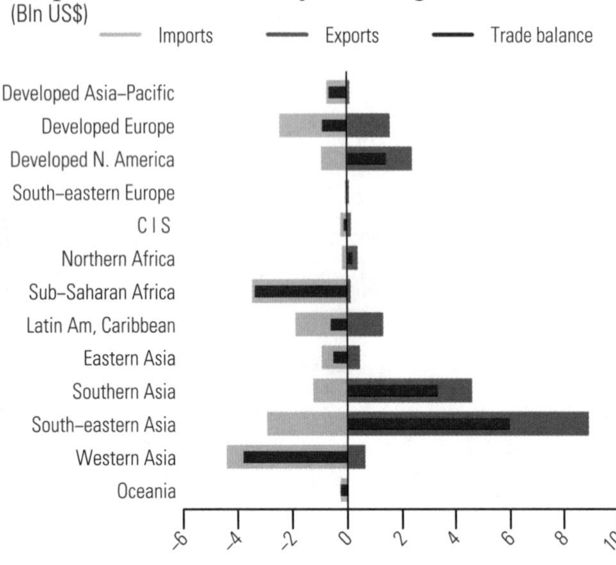

Table 3: Top importing countries or areas in 2010

Country or area	Value (million US$)	Avg. Growth (%) 06-10	Growth (%) 09-10	World share %	Cum.
World	19835.0	17.2	0.2	100.0	
Philippines	1652.6	34.0	57.6	8.3	8.3
United Arab Emirates	1337.7	36.9	7.2	6.7	15.1
Saudi Arabia	1310.5	25.4	-5.4	6.6	21.7
Iran	942.0	58.4	8.4	4.7	26.4
USA	628.6	14.3	-0.9	3.2	29.6
United Kingdom	529.3	13.9	-5.3	2.7	32.3
Japan	517.3	14.3	-17.8	2.6	34.9
Malaysia	501.2	15.0	-9.2	2.5	37.4
Nigeria	494.8	4.0	4.9	2.5	39.9
Cuba	*467.0*	27.5	0.0	2.4	42.3
Côte d'Ivoire	460.2	12.1	-23.0	2.3	44.6
France	430.1	11.2	-14.0	2.2	46.7
South Africa	414.5	13.8	-6.8	2.1	48.8
Brazil	376.6	21.2	38.2	1.9	50.7
Indonesia	360.8	28.4	233.6	1.8	52.5

After a sharp decline of 41.0 percent in 2009, the value (in current prices) of exports of unmilled barley (SITC group 043) rose in 2010 by 8.9 percent and amounted to 4.9 bln US$ (see table 2). Similarly, imports, after a 40.0 percent decline in 2009, went up by 10.7 percent in 2010 and totaled 5.8 bln US$ (see table 3). Graph 1 shows that the increase in exports for 2010 in this product group was below the increases in world exports of food and live animals (SITC section 0) of 11.2 percent and in total world exports of 21.2 percent. Exports of unmilled barley (SITC group 043) accounted for 0.5 percent of world exports of SITC section 0 and less than 0.1 percent of total world exports in 2010 (see table 1).

In 2010, France, Ukraine and Australia were the top exporting countries (see table 2). They accounted respectively for 20.9, 15.0 and 14.6 percent of world exports. With 33.2 percent of world imports, Saudi Arabia was the top importing country (see table 3). Other major destinations were China and Netherlands. By MDG regions (see graph 2), Commonwealth of Independent States and Developed Europe recorded trade surpluses amounting respectively to 1.0 bln US$ and 0.8 bln US$ while Western Asia recorded a deficit of 2.4 bln US$ in 2010.

Table 1: Imports (Imp.) and exports (Exp.), 1996-2010, in current prices

		1996	1997	1998	1999	2000	2001	2002	2003	2004	2005	2006	2007	2008	2009	2010
Values in Bln US$	Imp.	3.9	3.4	2.4	2.5	3.0	2.7	2.6	2.8	3.5	4.0	3.9	6.0	8.7	5.2	5.8
	Exp.	3.8	3.3	2.1	2.4	2.8	2.4	2.5	2.9	3.3	3.6	3.5	5.4	7.7	4.5	4.9
As a percentage of SITC section (%)	Imp.	0.9	0.8	0.6	0.6	0.7	0.6	0.6	0.6	0.6	0.6	0.6	0.7	0.9	0.6	0.6
	Exp.	0.9	0.8	0.5	0.6	0.7	0.6	0.6	0.6	0.6	0.6	0.5	0.7	0.8	0.5	0.5
As a percentage of world trade (%)	Imp.	0.1	0.1	0.0	0.0	0.0	0.0	0.0	0.0	0.0	0.0	0.0	0.0	0.1	0.0	0.0
	Exp.	0.1	0.1	0.0	0.0	0.0	0.0	0.0	0.0	0.0	0.0	0.0	0.0	0.0	0.0	0.0

Graph 1: Annual growth rates of exports, 1996–2010

(In percentage by year)

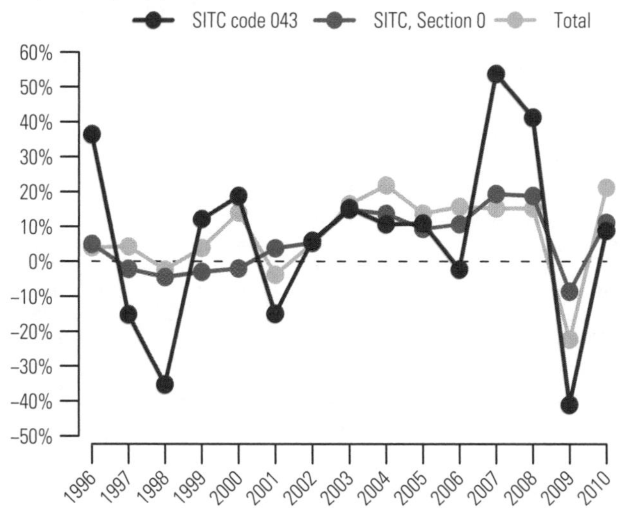

Table 2: Top exporting countries or areas in 2010

Country or area	Value (million US$)	Avg. Growth (%) 06-10	Growth (%) 09-10	World share %	Cum.
World	4939.6	8.7	8.9	100.0	
France	1030.4	11.9	-1.7	20.9	20.9
Ukraine	740.0	6.9	1.4	15.0	35.8
Australia	723.2	0.8	20.4	14.6	50.5
Germany	333.7	1.7	59.8	6.8	57.2
Canada	316.6	7.5	-18.3	6.4	63.6
United Kingdom	198.3	19.1	17.0	4.0	67.7
Denmark	197.3	14.9	140.2	4.0	71.7
Russian Federation	197.1	5.7	-55.1	4.0	75.6
Romania	122.4	69.3	44.2	2.5	78.1
Argentina	107.5	17.7	-43.2	2.2	80.3
Sweden	102.2	23.9	92.8	2.1	82.4
Spain	92.0	82.2	1097.9	1.9	84.2
Bulgaria	79.4	37.3	27.8	1.6	85.8
Turkey	74.9	4.9	77.7	1.5	87.4
Belgium	63.7	14.0	80.7	1.3	88.6

Graph 2: Trade Balance by MDG regions 2010

(Bln US$)

Imports — Exports — Trade balance

Developed Asia-Pacific, Developed Europe, Developed N. America, South-eastern Europe, C I S, Northern Africa, Sub-Saharan Africa, Latin Am, Caribbean, Eastern Asia, Southern Asia, South-eastern Asia, Western Asia, Oceania

-3, -2.5, -2, -1.5, -1, -0.5, 0, 0.5, 1, 1.5, 2, 2.5

Table 3: Top importing countries or areas in 2010

Country or area	Value (million US$)	Avg. Growth (%) 06-10	Growth (%) 09-10	World share %	Cum.
World	5782.1	10.0	10.7	100.0	
Saudi Arabia	1917.2	12.1	49.3	33.2	33.2
China	536.1	7.2	23.4	9.3	42.4
Netherlands	348.5	10.4	23.1	6.0	48.5
Belgium	341.3	11.9	-6.4	5.9	54.4
Japan	336.8	6.6	14.1	5.8	60.2
Germany	248.4	9.2	-23.9	4.3	64.5
Syria	*245.7*	45.2	-15.7	4.2	68.7
Spain	170.8	-5.9	-41.9	3.0	71.7
Italy	157.7	7.3	32.0	2.7	74.4
Iran	103.5	55.8	8.4	1.8	76.2
Kuwait	*100.0*	32.6	8.1	1.7	77.9
Tunisia	88.8	3.0	651.6	1.5	79.5
Israel	80.6	16.6	25.4	1.4	80.9
Portugal	79.5	11.7	-0.8	1.4	82.2
Colombia	65.4	12.1	0.8	1.1	83.4

044 Maize (not including sweet corn), unmilled

After several years of continuous growth marked by a peak of 27.2 bln US$ in 2008, the value (in current prices) of exports of unmilled maize (SITC group 044) dropped by 26.9 percent in 2009 but increased again by 16.0 percent in 2010 and amounted to 23.0 bln US$ (see table 2). During the same period, imports showed a similar development and increased by 13.5 percent to 25.7 bln US$ in 2010 (see table 3). Graph 1 shows that the increase in exports for 2010 in this product group was above the increase in world exports of food and live animals (SITC section 0) of 11.2 percent but below the increase in total world exports of 21.2 percent. Exports of unmilled maize (SITC group 044) accounted for 2.4 percent of world exports of SITC section 0 and 0.2 percent of total world exports in 2010 (see table 1).

USA was the top exporting country in 2010: it accounted for 43.9 percent of exports (see table 2). Other major exporting countries were Argentina and Brazil, respectively at 13.7 and 9.6 percent of world exports. Top destinations were Japan, Republic of Korea and Mexico (see table 3). By MDG regions (see graph 2), Developed North America recorded a trade surplus amounting to 9.7 bln US$ in 2010. Top trade deficits were recorded by Developed Asia-Pacific (-4.0 bln US$), Eastern Asia (-3.6 bln US$) and Northern Africa (-2.6 bln US$).

Table 1: Imports (Imp.) and exports (Exp.), 1996-2010, in current prices

		1996	1997	1998	1999	2000	2001	2002	2003	2004	2005	2006	2007	2008	2009	2010
Values in Bln US$	Imp.	14.1	11.6	10.3	9.9	10.2	10.1	11.1	12.6	14.5	13.7	15.1	23.9	31.0	22.6	25.7
	Exp.	12.9	10.2	9.2	8.7	8.8	8.9	9.9	11.1	11.7	11.2	13.2	20.6	27.2	19.8	23.0
As a percentage of SITC section (%)	Imp.	3.2	2.7	2.4	2.4	2.5	2.4	2.5	2.5	2.5	2.1	2.2	2.9	3.2	2.5	2.6
	Exp.	3.0	2.4	2.3	2.2	2.3	2.2	2.3	2.3	2.1	1.8	2.0	2.6	2.9	2.3	2.4
As a percentage of world trade (%)	Imp.	0.3	0.2	0.2	0.2	0.2	0.2	0.2	0.2	0.2	0.1	0.1	0.2	0.2	0.2	0.2
	Exp.	0.2	0.2	0.2	0.2	0.1	0.1	0.2	0.1	0.1	0.1	0.1	0.1	0.2	0.2	0.2

Graph 1: Annual growth rates of exports, 1996–2010
(In percentage by year)

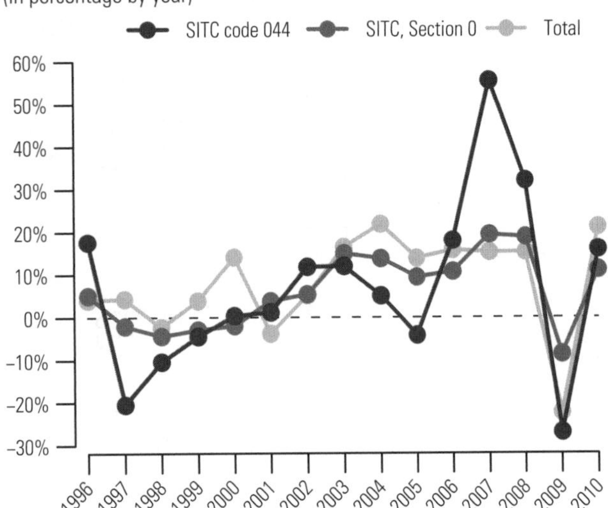

Graph 2: Trade Balance by MDG regions 2010
(Bln US$)

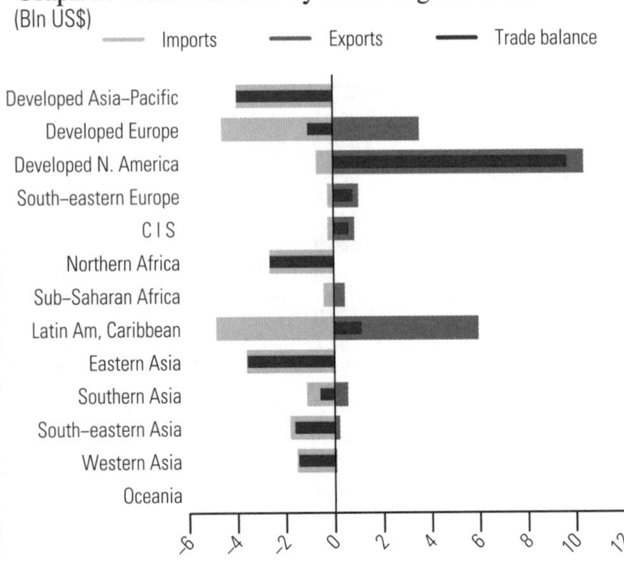

Table 2: Top exporting countries or areas in 2010

Country or area	Value (million US$)	Avg. Growth (%) 06-10	Growth (%) 09-10	World share %	Cum.
World	23 020.6	14.9	16.0	100.0	
USA	10 110.5	8.5	11.3	43.9	43.9
Argentina	3 145.3	25.6	95.0	13.7	57.6
Brazil	2 215.0	46.4	70.1	9.6	67.2
France	1 840.3	8.6	-0.6	8.0	75.2
Hungary	887.0	22.0	6.8	3.9	79.1
Ukraine	785.9	45.1	-22.4	3.4	82.5
India	533.8	50.4	0.2	2.3	84.8
Romania	519.8	81.9	50.8	2.3	87.0
Serbia	334.9	16.8	16.2	1.5	88.5
South Africa	305.5	21.2	-32.1	1.3	89.8
Canada	249.3	50.0	157.9	1.1	90.9
Paraguay	239.4	10.3	2.3	1.0	91.9
Germany	193.1	0.0	-3.6	0.8	92.8
Chile	166.1	13.3	-15.7	0.7	93.5
Bulgaria	158.7	48.0	59.8	0.7	94.2

Table 3: Top importing countries or areas in 2010

Country or area	Value (million US$)	Avg. Growth (%) 06-10	Growth (%) 09-10	World share %	Cum.
World	25 680.1	14.1	13.5	100.0	
Japan	3 956.3	11.2	4.9	15.4	15.4
Rep. of Korea	1 989.9	12.0	21.5	7.7	23.2
Mexico	1 583.3	8.6	10.2	6.2	29.3
Egypt	1 270.6	23.6	52.4	4.9	34.3
Other Asia, nes	1 225.5	12.8	27.9	4.8	39.0
Spain	967.0	6.9	3.3	3.8	42.8
Iran	919.6	122.3	8.4	3.6	46.4
Colombia	805.8	14.7	20.1	3.1	49.5
Malaysia	767.8	17.9	35.1	3.0	52.5
Netherlands	656.7	8.9	-7.4	2.6	55.1
Algeria	637.7	17.2	56.5	2.5	57.6
Germany	587.8	7.6	-4.0	2.3	59.8
Viet Nam	*545.8*	54.6	66.9	2.1	62.0
Italy	501.8	11.7	-0.5	2.0	63.9
Saudi Arabia	471.5	21.9	23.0	1.8	65.8

After a significant 33.8 percent drop in 2009, the value (in current prices) of exports of unmilled cereals, other than wheat, rice, barley and maize (SITC group 045) rose by 12.4 percent to reach 2.6 bln US$ in 2010 (see table 2). During the same period, imports showed a similar development with an increase of 6.6 percent to 2.8 bln US$ (see table 3). Graph 1 shows that the increase in exports for 2010 in this product group was slightly above the increase in world exports of food and live animals (SITC section 0) of 11.2 percent but below the increase in total world exports of 21.2 percent. Exports of unmilled cereals, other than wheat, rice, barley and maize (SITC group 045) accounted for 0.3 percent of world exports of SITC section 0 and less than 0.1 percent of total world exports in 2010 (see table 1).

Top exporting countries were USA, Canada and Argentina in 2010 (see table 2). They accounted respectively for 31.8, 18.0 and 8.9 percent of world exports. Japan was the top destination: it accounted for 17.0 percent of world imports (see table 3). Other major destinations included Mexico and USA, respectively with 16.7 and 13.2 percent of world imports. By MDG regions (see graph 2), Developed North America recorded a surplus amounting to 0.9 bln US$. Top deficits were recorded by Developed Asia-Pacific and Latin America and the Caribbean at 0.4 bln US$ each.

Table 1: Imports (Imp.) and exports (Exp.), 1996-2010, in current prices

		1996	1997	1998	1999	2000	2001	2002	2003	2004	2005	2006	2007	2008	2009	2010
Values in Bln US$	Imp.	2.5	1.8	1.5	1.5	1.6	1.6	1.7	1.8	1.9	1.8	2.0	3.0	4.3	2.6	2.8
	Exp.	2.2	1.5	1.4	1.3	1.4	1.4	1.5	1.5	1.6	1.6	1.8	2.8	3.5	2.3	2.6
As a percentage of	Imp.	0.6	0.4	0.4	0.4	0.4	0.4	0.4	0.3	0.3	0.3	0.3	0.4	0.4	0.3	0.3
SITC section (%)	Exp.	0.5	0.4	0.3	0.3	0.4	0.4	0.3	0.3	0.3	0.3	0.3	0.3	0.4	0.3	0.3
As a percentage of	Imp.	0.0	0.0	0.0	0.0	0.0	0.0	0.0	0.0	0.0	0.0	0.0	0.0	0.0	0.0	0.0
world trade (%)	Exp.	0.0	0.0	0.0	0.0	0.0	0.0	0.0	0.0	0.0	0.0	0.0	0.0	0.0	0.0	0.0

Graph 1: Annual growth rates of exports, 1996–2010
(In percentage by year)

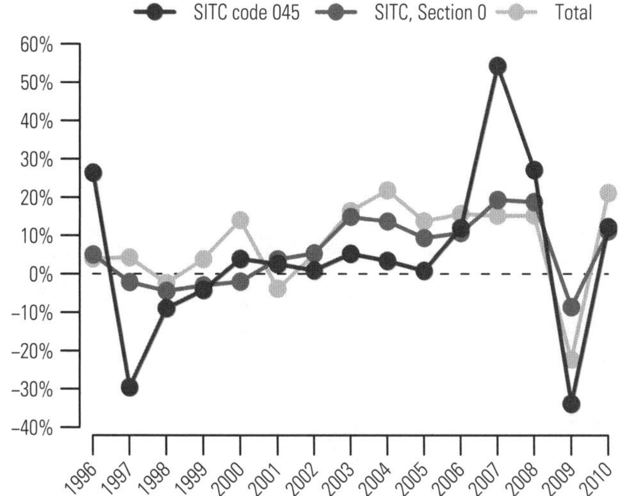

Table 2: Top exporting countries or areas in 2010

Country or area	Value (million US$)	Avg. Growth (%) 06-10	Growth (%) 09-10	World share %	Cum.
World	2608.8	9.9	12.4	100.0	
USA	829.6	6.1	13.5	31.8	31.8
Canada	469.1	5.6	6.3	18.0	49.8
Argentina	233.1	71.9	69.2	8.9	58.7
Poland	116.5	47.1	-4.9	4.5	63.2
Germany	107.8	-16.8	-14.4	4.1	67.3
China	86.0	11.9	52.0	3.3	70.6
India	85.8	45.5	76.6	3.3	73.9
France	75.4	2.5	16.0	2.9	76.8
Australia	62.8	7.8	5.5	2.4	79.2
Finland	56.2	3.9	-16.4	2.2	81.4
Bolivia	48.9	47.6	6.9	1.9	83.2
Sweden	34.8	12.2	-19.0	1.3	84.6
Netherlands	34.1	10.6	-44.7	1.3	85.9
Ukraine	32.4	23.0	-4.5	1.2	87.1
Hungary	23.5	15.6	65.7	0.9	88.0

Graph 2: Trade Balance by MDG regions 2010
(Bln US$)

Imports — Exports — Trade balance

Developed Asia-Pacific
Developed Europe
Developed N. America
South-eastern Europe
CIS
Northern Africa
Sub-Saharan Africa
Latin Am, Caribbean
Eastern Asia
Southern Asia
South-eastern Asia
Western Asia
Oceania

-0.8 -0.6 -0.4 -0.2 0 0.2 0.4 0.6 0.8 1 1.2 1.4

Table 3: Top importing countries or areas in 2010

Country or area	Value (million US$)	Avg. Growth (%) 06-10	Growth (%) 09-10	World share %	Cum.
World	2793.8	9.0	6.6	100.0	
Japan	474.3	12.4	7.9	17.0	17.0
Mexico	467.5	5.6	-3.2	16.7	33.7
USA	369.9	3.9	-0.4	13.2	47.0
Germany	174.7	24.5	8.5	6.3	53.2
Spain	140.1	-6.6	12.1	5.0	58.2
Chile	114.6	84.7	37.3	4.1	62.3
Netherlands	105.0	5.4	-15.9	3.8	66.1
Belgium	75.9	15.6	11.8	2.7	68.8
Italy	54.0	11.5	13.1	1.9	70.7
Ethiopia	40.8	129.3	54.6	1.5	72.2
Eritrea	*40.6*	41.2	267.5	1.5	73.6
Colombia	38.9	38.2	-10.8	1.4	75.0
China	35.5	53.7	135.7	1.3	76.3
Morocco	34.5	53.8	325.7	1.2	77.5
France	30.5	12.7	-6.3	1.1	78.6

046 Meal and flour of wheat and flour of meslin

After several years of continuous growth marked by a peak of 5.7 bln US$ in 2008, the value (in current prices) of exports of meal, flour of wheat and flour of meslin (SITC group 046) contracted in 2009 by 23.9 percent then continued to drop by 1.1 percent to 4.3 bln US$ in 2010 (see table 2). During the same period, imports showed a similar development with a decrease of 4.2 percent and totaled 4.1 bln US$ (see table 3). Graph 1 shows the decrease in exports for 2010 in this product group, compared to the increases in world exports of food and live animals (SITC section 0) of 11.2 percent and in total world exports of 21.2 percent. Exports of meal, flour of wheat and flour of meslin (SITC group 046) accounted for 0.4 percent of world exports of SITC section 0 and less than 0.1 percent of total world exports in 2010 (see table 1).

The top exporting countries in 2010 were Turkey, Kazakhstan and Argentina (see table 2). They accounted respectively for 14.4, 12.6 and 6.7 percent of world exports. Indonesia, Afghanistan and Uzbekistan were the top destinations (see table 3). By MDG regions (see graph 2), top surpluses were recorded by Western Asia (+508 mln US$), Developed Europe (+503 mln US$) and Commonwealth of Independent States (+209 mln US$). Top deficits were recorded by Sub-Saharan Africa (-545 mln US$) and South-eastern Asia (-410 mln US$).

Table 1: Imports (Imp.) and exports (Exp.), 1996-2010, in current prices

		1996	1997	1998	1999	2000	2001	2002	2003	2004	2005	2006	2007	2008	2009	2010
Values in Bln US$	Imp.	3.3	2.7	2.1	1.7	1.8	1.7	1.7	1.8	2.2	2.4	2.4	3.5	5.0	4.3	4.1
	Exp.	3.2	2.9	2.2	1.9	1.8	1.8	1.9	2.1	2.3	2.5	2.5	3.8	5.7	4.4	4.3
As a percentage of SITC section (%)	Imp.	0.7	0.6	0.5	0.4	0.4	0.4	0.4	0.4	0.4	0.4	0.3	0.4	0.5	0.5	0.4
	Exp.	0.7	0.7	0.5	0.5	0.5	0.4	0.4	0.4	0.4	0.4	0.4	0.5	0.6	0.5	0.4
As a percentage of world trade (%)	Imp.	0.1	0.0	0.0	0.0	0.0	0.0	0.0	0.0	0.0	0.0	0.0	0.0	0.0	0.0	0.0
	Exp.	0.1	0.1	0.0	0.0	0.0	0.0	0.0	0.0	0.0	0.0	0.0	0.0	0.0	0.0	0.0

Graph 1: Annual growth rates of exports, 1996–2010

(In percentage by year)

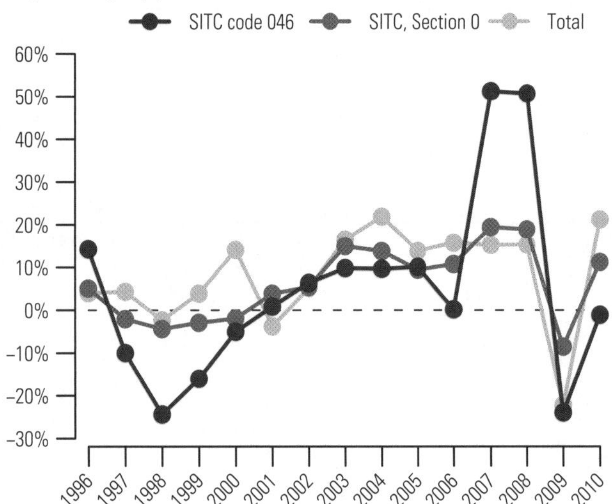

Table 2: Top exporting countries or areas in 2010

Country or area	Value (million US$)	Avg. Growth (%) 06-10	Growth (%) 09-10	World share %	Cum.
World	4305.9	14.4	-1.1	100.0	
Turkey	621.0	22.0	4.1	14.4	14.4
Kazakhstan	543.0	33.2	-5.5	12.6	27.0
Argentina	290.4	65.4	-3.7	6.7	33.8
France	278.6	4.9	-13.9	6.5	40.2
Belgium	240.1	5.3	-7.2	5.6	45.8
Germany	233.8	7.2	-4.0	5.4	51.2
USA	150.3	23.8	5.3	3.5	54.7
China	117.7	4.9	22.6	2.7	57.5
Canada	110.4	3.8	-2.6	2.6	60.0
United Kingdom	109.9	23.6	2.8	2.6	62.6
Sri Lanka	104.6	28.0	164.2	2.4	65.0
Italy	82.8	-4.7	-2.4	1.9	66.9
Japan	66.9	-0.3	14.6	1.6	68.5
Dominican Rep.	53.2	43.1	147.5	1.2	69.7
Australia	48.1	-8.9	-6.4	1.1	70.8

Graph 2: Trade Balance by MDG regions 2010

(Bln US$)

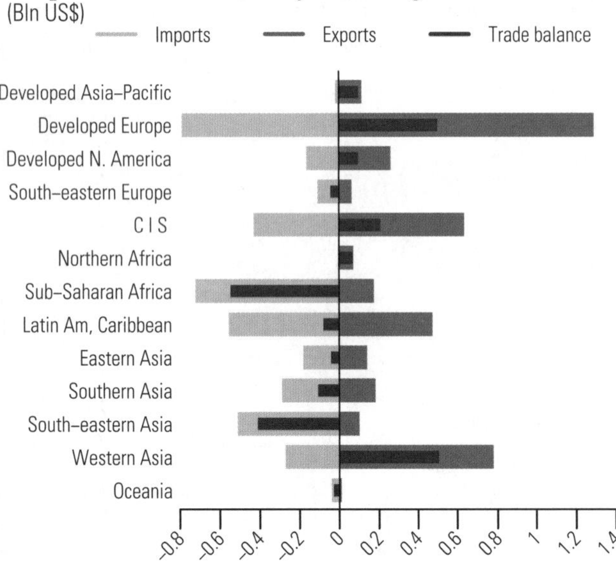

Table 3: Top importing countries or areas in 2010

Country or area	Value (million US$)	Avg. Growth (%) 06-10	Growth (%) 09-10	World share %	Cum.
World	4069.9	14.2	-4.2	100.0	
Indonesia	261.7	16.3	17.2	6.4	6.4
Afghanistan	229.6	15.1	-36.2	5.6	12.1
Uzbekistan	*229.2*	31.9	-7.5	5.6	17.7
Brazil	226.3	59.4	11.7	5.6	23.3
Angola	*154.6*	19.3	-14.1	3.8	27.1
Netherlands	146.7	11.3	-0.4	3.6	30.7
Tajikistan	*143.9*	24.6	54.6	3.5	34.2
USA	119.6	6.9	2.2	2.9	37.1
France	106.4	9.4	-14.7	2.6	39.8
Iraq	*102.5*	20.8	-2.9	2.5	42.3
China, Hong Kong SAR	89.5	8.3	-4.2	2.2	44.5
Belgium	78.9	6.7	-24.0	1.9	46.4
Zimbabwe	74.5	156.1	93.3	1.8	48.2
Dem.Rep. of the Congo	*73.3*	26.5	41.1	1.8	50.0
Bolivia	73.1	21.8	-29.7	1.8	51.8

After a 11.0 percent drop in 2009, the value (in current prices) of exports of other cereal meals and flours (SITC group 047) continued to decrease by 3.0 percent and amounted to 1.0 bln US$ in 2010 (see table 2). During the same period, imports showed a similar development with a decline of 10.9 percent and totaled 1.2 bln US$ (see table 3). Graph 1 shows that the decline in exports for 2010 in this product group, compared with increases in world exports of food and live animals (SITC section 0) of 11.2 percent and in total world exports of 21.2 percent. Exports of other cereal meals and flours (SITC group 047) accounted for 0.1 percent of world exports of SITC section 0 and less than 0.1 percent of total world exports in 2010 (see table 1).

USA was the top exporting country in 2010: it accounted for 15.1 percent of world exports (see table 2). Other major exporting countries were Thailand and Italy, respectively with 10.6 and 8.3 percent of exports. USA was also the top destination, together with Spain and Angola (see table 3). By MDG regions (see graph 2), Developed North America and South-eastern Asia recorded trade surpluses amounting respectively to 68 mln US$ and 52 mln US$. Sub-Saharan Africa and Western Asia recorded trade deficits amounting respectively to 180 mln US$ and 48 mln US$.

Table 1: Imports (Imp.) and exports (Exp.), 1996-2010, in current prices

		1996	1997	1998	1999	2000	2001	2002	2003	2004	2005	2006	2007	2008	2009	2010
Values in Bln US$	Imp.	0.5	0.5	0.5	0.5	0.5	0.5	0.6	0.6	0.7	0.7	0.7	1.0	1.4	1.4	1.2
	Exp.	0.6	0.5	0.5	0.4	0.4	0.5	0.5	0.5	0.6	0.7	0.7	0.9	1.2	1.1	1.0
As a percentage of SITC section (%)	Imp.	0.1	0.1	0.1	0.1	0.1	0.1	0.1	0.1	0.1	0.1	0.1	0.1	0.1	0.2	0.1
	Exp.	0.1	0.1	0.1	0.1	0.1	0.1	0.1	0.1	0.1	0.1	0.1	0.1	0.1	0.1	0.1
As a percentage of world trade (%)	Imp.	0.0	0.0	0.0	0.0	0.0	0.0	0.0	0.0	0.0	0.0	0.0	0.0	0.0	0.0	0.0
	Exp.	0.0	0.0	0.0	0.0	0.0	0.0	0.0	0.0	0.0	0.0	0.0	0.0	0.0	0.0	0.0

Graph 1: Annual growth rates of exports, 1996–2010

(In percentage by year)

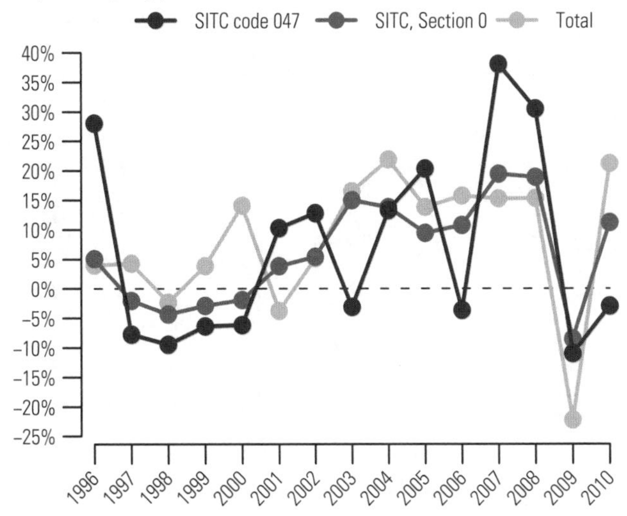

Table 2: Top exporting countries or areas in 2010

Country or area	Value (million US$)	Avg. Growth (%) 06-10	Growth (%) 09-10	World share %	Cum.
World	1 039.0	11.7	-3.0	100.0	
USA	157.0	4.8	-13.2	15.1	15.1
Thailand	110.1	15.9	20.2	10.6	25.7
Italy	85.9	8.3	-10.4	8.3	34.0
Canada	84.2	12.5	-8.3	8.1	42.1
France	72.7	3.8	-13.9	7.0	49.1
South Africa	52.0	49.1	-20.4	5.0	54.1
Germany	39.6	7.3	9.1	3.8	57.9
El Salvador	32.6	9.7	-4.7	3.1	61.0
Mexico	31.4	12.6	-10.0	3.0	64.1
Brazil	28.2	19.3	-22.3	2.7	66.8
Turkey	26.1	45.3	58.2	2.5	69.3
Netherlands	21.4	24.3	4.0	2.1	71.3
India	17.8	31.0	11.8	1.7	73.1
Belarus	15.0	44.0	262.2	1.4	74.5
Ukraine	14.1	9.9	6.6	1.4	75.9

Graph 2: Trade Balance by MDG regions 2010

(Mln US$)

Imports — Exports — Trade balance

Developed Asia-Pacific
Developed Europe
Developed N. America
South-eastern Europe
C I S
Northern Africa
Sub-Saharan Africa
Latin Am, Caribbean
Eastern Asia
Southern Asia
South-eastern Asia
Western Asia
Oceania

-400 -300 -200 -100 0 100 200 300 400

Table 3: Top importing countries or areas in 2010

Country or area	Value (million US$)	Avg. Growth (%) 06-10	Growth (%) 09-10	World share %	Cum.
World	1 208.3	13.2	-10.9	100.0	
USA	127.9	12.4	-4.4	10.6	10.6
Spain	78.4	20.6	11.0	6.5	17.1
Angola	*52.4*	13.7	-35.1	4.3	21.4
Canada	45.0	13.1	-14.1	3.7	25.1
Malaysia	41.9	16.5	13.7	3.5	28.6
Israel	40.7	25.2	74.4	3.4	32.0
Lesotho	*40.6*	10.2	11.8	3.4	35.3
Germany	33.7	12.9	-17.8	2.8	38.1
Netherlands	31.8	15.6	36.1	2.6	40.8
Zimbabwe	30.4	42.9	-42.4	2.5	43.3
France	28.1	11.3	-9.4	2.3	45.6
Mexico	25.9	7.8	3.1	2.1	47.7
Guatemala	24.3	11.8	26.2	2.0	49.7
China, Hong Kong SAR	23.5	8.2	28.6	1.9	51.7
Belgium	23.4	20.1	-4.2	1.9	53.6

048 Cereal, flour or starch preparations of fruits or vegetables

During the recent five years, the value (in current prices) of exports of cereal, flour or starch preparations of fruit or vegetables (SITC group 048) increased on average by 8.4 percent and reached 38.1 bln US$ in 2010 (see table 2). Imports, displaying a similar development, increased on average by 9.0 percent and amounted to 38.5 bln US$ (see table 3). Graph 1 shows that the increase in exports for 2010 in this product group was well below the increases in world exports of food and live animals (SITC section 0) of 11.2 percent and in total world exports of 21.2 percent. Exports of cereal, flour or starch preparations of fruit or vegetables (SITC group 048) accounted for 3.9 percent of world exports of SITC section 0 and 0.3 percent of total world exports in 2010 (see table 1).

In 2010, top exporting countries were Germany, Italy and France (see table 2). They accounted respectively for 12.1, 9.5 and 7.9 percent of world exports. Top importing countries were USA, France and Germany (see table 3). By MDG regions (see graph 2), Developed Europe accounted for the majority of trade in cereal, flour or starch preparations of fruit or vegetables (SITC group 048). In 2010, its exports and imports amounted respectively to 23.2 bln US$ and 19.3 bln US$, resulting in a trade surplus of 3.9 bln US$. Both Sub-Saharan Africa and Developed North America recorded a trade deficit exceeding 1.0 bln US$. Major trade deficit was also recorded by Developed Asia-Pacific(-0.8 bln US$).

Table 1: Imports (Imp.) and exports (Exp.), 1996-2010, in current prices

		1996	1997	1998	1999	2000	2001	2002	2003	2004	2005	2006	2007	2008	2009	2010
Values in Bln US$	Imp.	14.1	13.5	13.8	14.0	13.5	14.8	16.7	19.9	23.1	25.0	27.3	33.1	39.5	37.6	38.5
	Exp.	14.3	14.3	14.1	13.9	13.5	14.6	16.6	19.9	23.1	25.0	27.6	32.7	39.6	37.1	38.1
As a percentage of SITC section (%)	Imp.	3.2	3.1	3.3	3.3	3.3	3.5	3.7	3.9	4.0	3.9	3.9	4.0	4.0	4.2	3.9
	Exp.	3.3	3.4	3.5	3.5	3.5	3.6	3.9	4.1	4.2	4.1	4.1	4.1	4.2	4.3	3.9
As a percentage of world trade (%)	Imp.	0.3	0.2	0.3	0.2	0.2	0.2	0.3	0.3	0.2	0.2	0.2	0.2	0.2	0.3	0.3
	Exp.	0.3	0.3	0.3	0.3	0.2	0.2	0.3	0.3	0.3	0.2	0.2	0.2	0.2	0.3	0.3

Graph 1: Annual growth rates of exports, 1996–2010
(In percentage by year)

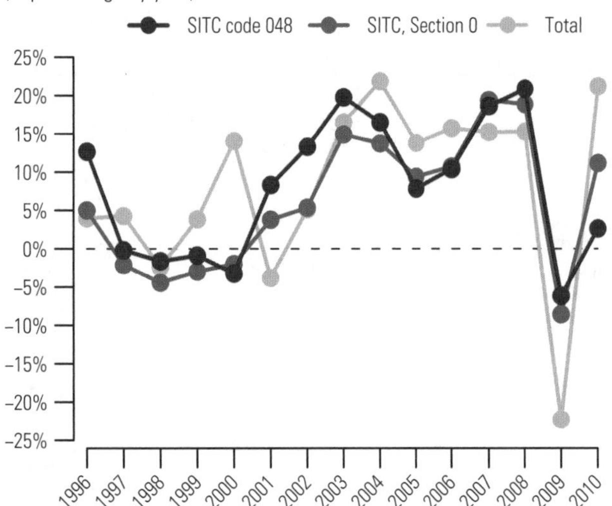

Table 2: Top exporting countries or areas in 2010

Country or area	Value (million US$)	Avg. Growth (%) 06-10	Growth (%) 09-10	World share %	Cum.
World	38128.1	8.4	2.7	100.0	
Germany	4620.6	7.8	1.0	12.1	12.1
Italy	3628.3	6.8	-1.7	9.5	21.6
France	3021.6	5.6	-1.5	7.9	29.6
USA	2750.2	6.2	3.6	7.2	36.8
Belgium	2693.8	4.7	-8.3	7.1	43.8
Canada	2563.4	6.7	5.5	6.7	50.6
United Kingdom	1889.4	2.7	-1.8	5.0	55.5
Netherlands	1478.6	6.3	0.1	3.9	59.4
Poland	935.2	12.0	7.8	2.5	61.8
Spain	875.1	5.8	0.6	2.3	64.1
Mexico	816.9	14.4	13.5	2.1	66.3
Turkey	788.6	19.3	18.7	2.1	68.4
Austria	777.8	13.8	4.8	2.0	70.4
China	667.2	14.6	15.1	1.8	72.1
Australia	622.0	12.3	1.9	1.6	73.8

Graph 2: Trade Balance by MDG regions 2010
(Bln US$)

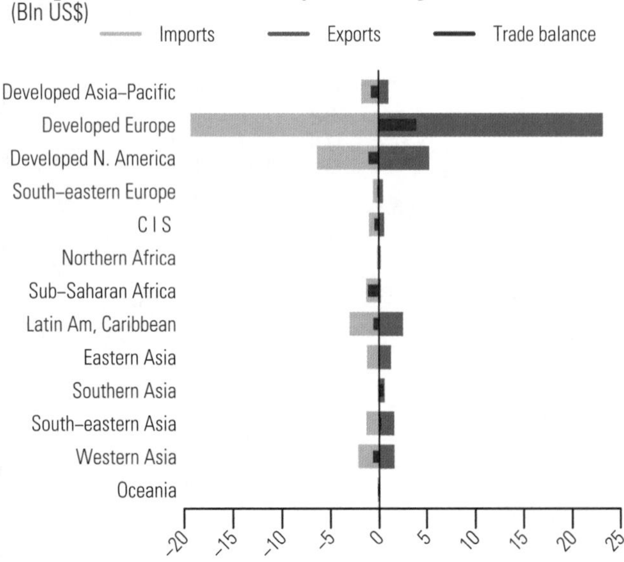

Table 3: Top importing countries or areas in 2010

Country or area	Value (million US$)	Avg. Growth (%) 06-10	Growth (%) 09-10	World share %	Cum.
World	38520.1	9.0	2.5	100.0	
USA	4466.5	7.3	9.4	11.6	11.6
France	2626.4	6.6	-5.2	6.8	18.4
Germany	2557.3	4.4	-2.6	6.6	25.1
United Kingdom	2437.5	6.0	-3.4	6.3	31.4
Canada	1845.1	10.1	6.3	4.8	36.2
Belgium	1527.2	5.8	-11.4	4.0	40.1
Italy	1293.6	6.0	7.1	3.4	43.5
Netherlands	1211.8	10.1	-8.3	3.1	46.6
Japan	1055.2	6.9	-2.6	2.7	49.4
Spain	997.2	3.6	-4.5	2.6	52.0
Austria	772.5	7.5	-7.0	2.0	54.0
Ireland	699.0	4.3	-2.7	1.8	55.8
Switzerland	600.6	11.5	1.1	1.6	57.3
Mexico	554.7	-8.3	-6.1	1.4	58.8
Brazil	520.4	16.3	-11.4	1.4	60.1

After several years of continuous growth marked by a peak of 48.7 bln US$ in 2008, the value (in current prices) of exports of vegetables, fresh, chilled, frozen, simply preserved; roots (SITC group 054) dropped slightly by 1.4 percent in 2009, but bounced back by 13.2 percent and amounted to 54.4 bln US$ in 2010 (see table 2). Similarly, imports dropped by 4.7 percent in 2009 but increased by 13.6 percent to reach 54.2 bln US$ (see table 3). Graph 1 shows that the increase in exports for 2010 in this product group was above the increase in world exports of food and live animals (SITC section 0) of 11.2 percent but below the increase in total world exports of 21.2 percent. Exports of vegetables, fresh, chilled, frozen, simply preserved; roots (SITC group 054) accounted for 5.6 percent of world exports of SITC section 0 and 0.4 percent of total world exports in 2010 (see table 1).

The top exporting countries in 2010 were Netherlands, China and Spain (see table 2). They accounted respectively for 12.4, 11.1 and 9.7 percent of world exports. USA, Germany and United Kingdom were the top destinations (see table 3). By MDG regions (see graph 2), Developed Europe was the origin and destination of a majority of trade in vegetables, fresh, chilled, frozen, simply preserved; roots (SITC group 054). In 2010, its exports and imports amounted respectively to 22.6 bln US$ and 25.5 bln US$, resulting in a trade deficit of 2.9 bln US$. Latin America and the Caribbean and Eastern Asia recorded trade surpluses amounting respectively to 4.1 bln US$ and 3.7 bln US$.

Table 1: Imports (Imp.) and exports (Exp.), 1996-2010, in current prices

		1996	1997	1998	1999	2000	2001	2002	2003	2004	2005	2006	2007	2008	2009	2010
Values in Bln US$	Imp.	22.7	21.5	22.7	22.2	21.4	23.1	24.6	28.1	31.2	34.1	38.4	45.6	50.1	47.7	54.2
	Exp.	20.6	19.6	20.4	20.6	19.5	21.6	22.8	27.1	29.6	32.3	37.3	44.0	48.7	48.1	54.4
As a percentage of SITC section (%)	Imp.	5.1	5.0	5.4	5.3	5.2	5.5	5.5	5.5	5.4	5.4	5.5	5.5	5.1	5.4	5.6
	Exp.	4.7	4.6	5.0	5.2	5.1	5.4	5.4	5.6	5.3	5.3	5.6	5.5	5.1	5.5	5.6
As a percentage of world trade (%)	Imp.	0.4	0.4	0.4	0.4	0.3	0.4	0.4	0.4	0.3	0.3	0.3	0.3	0.3	0.4	0.4
	Exp.	0.4	0.4	0.4	0.4	0.3	0.4	0.4	0.4	0.3	0.3	0.3	0.3	0.3	0.4	0.4

Graph 1: Annual growth rates of exports, 1996–2010

(In percentage by year)

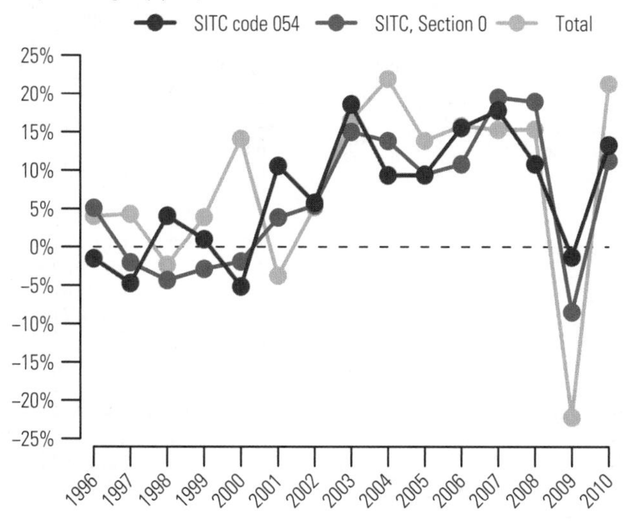

Table 2: Top exporting countries or areas in 2010

Country or area	Value (million US$)	Avg. Growth (%) 06-10	Growth (%) 09-10	World share %	Cum.
World	54411.1	9.9	13.2	100.0	
Netherlands	6737.4	7.5	14.2	12.4	12.4
China	6031.3	18.2	43.6	11.1	23.5
Spain	5288.1	4.7	-4.2	9.7	33.2
Mexico	4320.6	5.6	17.1	7.9	41.1
USA	3663.4	9.2	11.4	6.7	47.9
Canada	3362.6	15.2	11.3	6.2	54.0
France	2319.2	4.7	10.0	4.3	58.3
Belgium	2298.0	4.1	1.1	4.2	62.5
Italy	1666.9	10.7	23.8	3.1	65.6
Myanmar	*1112.9*	17.9	-3.0	2.0	67.6
Germany	1082.6	4.9	3.1	2.0	69.6
Thailand	1069.3	12.3	25.2	2.0	71.6
Turkey	1065.4	12.3	8.9	2.0	73.5
Poland	962.5	10.8	19.7	1.8	75.3
India	886.3	11.7	15.2	1.6	76.9

Graph 2: Trade Balance by MDG regions 2010

(Bln US$)

Imports — Exports — Trade balance

Developed Asia-Pacific
Developed Europe
Developed N. America
South-eastern Europe
C I S
Northern Africa
Sub-Saharan Africa
Latin Am, Caribbean
Eastern Asia
Southern Asia
South-eastern Asia
Western Asia
Oceania

-30 -25 -20 -15 -10 -5 0 5 10 15 20 25

Table 3: Top importing countries or areas in 2010

Country or area	Value (million US$)	Avg. Growth (%) 06-10	Growth (%) 09-10	World share %	Cum.
World	54207.9	9.0	13.6	100.0	
USA	6857.0	7.5	19.7	12.6	12.6
Germany	5634.8	4.3	10.3	10.4	23.0
United Kingdom	3832.4	1.4	6.9	7.1	30.1
France	3032.0	6.5	7.5	5.6	35.7
Canada	2342.9	7.9	12.5	4.3	40.0
Russian Federation	2255.4	24.4	36.2	4.2	44.2
Netherlands	2021.5	5.6	14.5	3.7	47.9
Japan	1929.5	3.0	25.0	3.6	51.5
Italy	1682.1	7.8	5.8	3.1	54.6
Belgium	1586.1	4.1	-0.6	2.9	57.5
China	1557.7	19.4	44.6	2.9	60.4
India	1357.6	11.6	-34.4	2.5	62.9
Spain	1215.2	1.9	5.5	2.2	65.1
United Arab Emirates	878.0	18.0	18.1	1.6	66.7
Malaysia	691.8	12.5	35.9	1.3	68.0

056 Vegetables, roots and tubers, prepared or preserved, nes

During the recent five years, the value (in current prices) of exports of prepared or preserved vegetables, roots and tubers, nes (SITC group 056) increased on average by 8.6 percent and amounted to 24.8 bln US$ in 2010 (see table 2). Imports increased on average by 7.9 percent and totaled 23.0 bln US$ (see table 3). Graph 1 shows that the increase in exports for 2010 in this product group was exceeded by the increases in world exports of food and live animals (SITC section 0) of 11.2 percent and in total world exports of 21.2 percent. Exports of prepared or preserved vegetables, roots and tubers, nes (SITC group 056) accounted for 2.6 percent of world exports of SITC section 0 and 0.2 percent of total world exports in 2010 (see table 1).

China, Netherlands and Italy were the top exporting countries in 2010 (see table 2). They accounted respectively for 18.1, 9.6 and 9.2 percent of world exports. Top destinations were USA, Germany and Japan (see table 3). By MDG regions (see graph 2), Developed Europe accounted for a majority of trade in prepared or preserved vegetables, roots and tubers, nes (SITC group 056). In 2010, its exports and imports amounted respectively to 12.8 bln US$ and 11.1 bln US$, resulting in a trade surplus of 1.7 bln US$. Trade balance showed a surplus amounting to 3.8 bln US$ for Eastern Asia and a deficit of 2.3 bln US$ for Developed Asia-Pacific.

Table 1: Imports (Imp.) and exports (Exp.), 1996-2010, in current prices

		1996	1997	1998	1999	2000	2001	2002	2003	2004	2005	2006	2007	2008	2009	2010
Values in Bln US$	Imp.	10.2	9.9	10.2	10.8	9.9	10.1	11.0	12.7	14.5	15.4	16.9	20.2	22.4	22.0	23.0
	Exp.	10.4	10.0	10.2	10.7	9.8	10.2	11.3	13.2	15.1	15.9	17.8	21.5	24.0	23.2	24.8
As a percentage of SITC section (%)	Imp.	2.3	2.3	2.4	2.6	2.4	2.4	2.5	2.5	2.5	2.4	2.4	2.4	2.3	2.5	2.4
	Exp.	2.4	2.4	2.5	2.7	2.5	2.5	2.7	2.7	2.7	2.6	2.7	2.7	2.5	2.7	2.6
As a percentage of world trade (%)	Imp.	0.2	0.2	0.2	0.2	0.2	0.2	0.2	0.2	0.2	0.1	0.1	0.1	0.1	0.2	0.2
	Exp.	0.2	0.2	0.2	0.2	0.2	0.2	0.2	0.2	0.2	0.2	0.1	0.2	0.2	0.2	0.2

Graph 1: Annual growth rates of exports, 1996–2010

(In percentage by year)

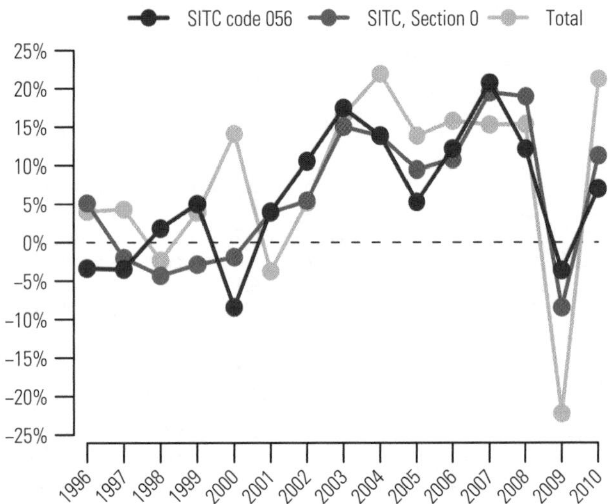

Graph 2: Trade Balance by MDG regions 2010

(Bln US$)

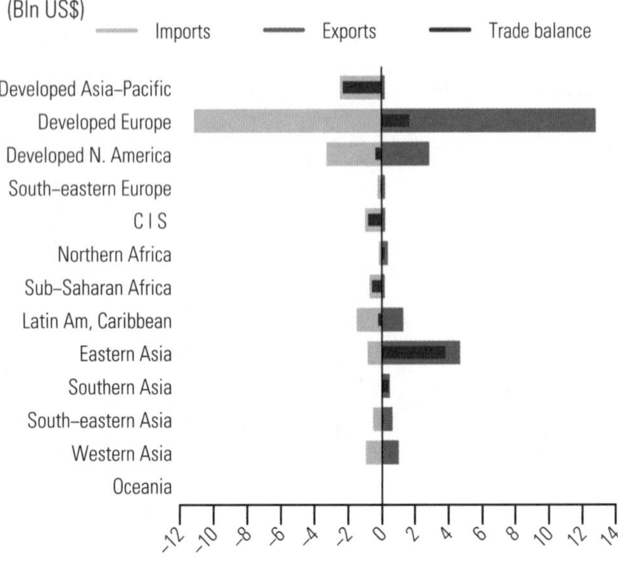

Table 2: Top exporting countries or areas in 2010

Country or area	Value (million US$)	Avg. Growth (%) 06-10	Growth (%) 09-10	World share %	Cum.
World	24775.6	8.6	7.0	100.0	
China	4478.5	14.2	36.2	18.1	18.1
Netherlands	2390.0	6.9	-3.2	9.6	27.7
Italy	2271.7	9.7	-5.6	9.2	36.9
USA	1933.8	9.2	5.0	7.8	44.7
Belgium	1900.1	11.9	4.8	7.7	52.4
Spain	1629.5	5.3	2.3	6.6	58.9
France	1170.6	4.2	7.4	4.7	63.7
Germany	1057.0	3.7	-4.1	4.3	67.9
Canada	962.0	2.7	-3.6	3.9	71.8
Turkey	658.3	8.9	-3.5	2.7	74.5
Greece	527.6	7.5	14.7	2.1	76.6
Peru	410.8	10.6	15.0	1.7	78.3
Poland	402.8	9.0	13.1	1.6	79.9
Thailand	361.4	3.3	11.4	1.5	81.3
Hungary	333.3	1.8	0.5	1.3	82.7

Table 3: Top importing countries or areas in 2010

Country or area	Value (million US$)	Avg. Growth (%) 06-10	Growth (%) 09-10	World share %	Cum.
World	22951.7	7.9	4.2	100.0	
USA	2558.2	4.6	5.4	11.1	11.1
Germany	2082.3	4.2	-6.8	9.1	20.2
Japan	1994.1	4.9	13.4	8.7	28.9
France	1811.8	6.9	-1.7	7.9	36.8
United Kingdom	1576.8	5.7	3.3	6.9	43.7
Italy	855.0	5.8	-7.4	3.7	47.4
Netherlands	779.7	12.5	-4.4	3.4	50.8
Russian Federation	703.1	9.3	9.8	3.1	53.9
Belgium	695.9	10.8	6.7	3.0	56.9
Canada	680.2	10.0	12.0	3.0	59.9
Spain	564.3	5.1	-3.7	2.5	62.3
Brazil	459.6	28.2	52.5	2.0	64.3
Rep. of Korea	396.1	8.3	28.8	1.7	66.0
Australia	375.9	15.7	4.2	1.6	67.7
Sweden	343.8	5.3	-5.5	1.5	69.2

After a 3.9 percent decline in 2009, the value (in current prices) of exports of fresh or dried fruit and nuts, excluding oil nuts (SITC group 057) bounced back by 10.4 percent in 2010 to reach 72.5 bln US$ (see table 2). Imports, after a 4.5 percent drop in 2009, increased by 9.1 percent and totaled 78.5 bln US$ (see table 3). Graph 1 shows that the increase in exports for 2010 in this product group was similar to the increase in world exports of food and live animals (SITC section 0) of 11.2 percent but below the increase in total world exports of 21.2 percent. Exports of fresh or dried fruit and nuts, excluding oil nuts (SITC group 057) accounted for 7.5 percent of world exports of SITC section 0 and 0.5 percent of total world exports in 2010 (see table 1).

In 2010, top exporting countries were USA, Spain and Chile (see table 2). They accounted respectively for 13.7, 9.8 and 5.5 percent of world exports. USA was also the top destination, together with Germany and Russian Federation (see table 3). By MDG regions (see graph 2), Developed Europe accounted for a large share of trade in fresh or dried fruit and nuts, excluding oil nuts (SITC group 057). In 2010, its exports and imports amounted respectively to 23.7 bln US$ and 37.2 bln US$, resulting in a trade deficit of 13.5 bln US$. Latin America and the Caribbean recorded a surplus amounting to 12.3 bln US$ while Commonwealth of Independent States recorded a deficit of 5.4 bln US$.

Table 1: Imports (Imp.) and exports (Exp.), 1996-2010, in current prices

		1996	1997	1998	1999	2000	2001	2002	2003	2004	2005	2006	2007	2008	2009	2010
Values in Bln US$	Imp.	33.5	33.5	32.8	33.1	31.4	32.0	34.7	41.2	46.7	52.6	57.0	65.6	75.3	71.9	78.5
	Exp.	28.1	29.2	28.9	28.5	27.2	27.8	29.8	35.8	40.4	46.9	50.5	59.1	68.3	65.6	72.5
As a percentage of SITC section (%)	Imp.	7.5	7.7	7.8	7.9	7.7	7.6	7.8	8.0	8.0	8.3	8.2	7.9	7.7	8.1	8.0
	Exp.	6.5	6.9	7.1	7.2	7.0	6.9	7.0	7.4	7.3	7.8	7.5	7.4	7.2	7.5	7.5
As a percentage of world trade (%)	Imp.	0.6	0.6	0.6	0.6	0.5	0.5	0.5	0.5	0.5	0.5	0.5	0.5	0.5	0.6	0.5
	Exp.	0.5	0.5	0.5	0.5	0.4	0.5	0.5	0.5	0.4	0.5	0.4	0.4	0.4	0.5	0.5

Graph 1: Annual growth rates of exports, 1996–2010

(In percentage by year)

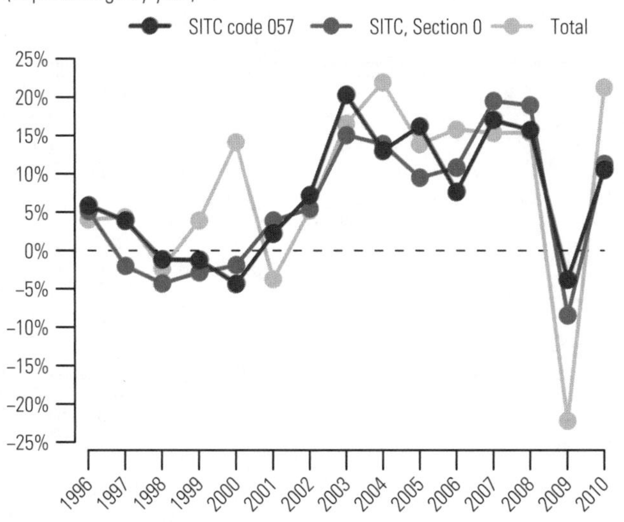

Table 2: Top exporting countries or areas in 2010

Country or area	Value (million US$)	Avg. Growth (%) 06-10	Growth (%) 09-10	World share %	Cum.
World	72 483.0	9.5	10.4	100.0	
USA	9 951.9	10.4	16.5	13.7	13.7
Spain	7 086.2	5.4	4.9	9.8	23.5
Chile	4 013.0	11.4	22.4	5.5	29.0
Italy	3 639.4	6.1	13.7	5.0	34.1
Netherlands	3 625.0	8.8	3.9	5.0	39.1
Turkey	3 445.1	10.1	16.2	4.8	43.8
Belgium	2 809.8	0.7	-9.6	3.9	47.7
China	2 411.0	21.7	11.5	3.3	51.0
Iran	2 308.9	11.5	6.3	3.2	54.2
Mexico	2 212.1	9.9	5.7	3.1	57.3
South Africa	2 110.4	16.4	30.8	2.9	60.2
Ecuador	2 101.0	13.2	1.5	2.9	63.1
France	1 900.5	1.0	5.9	2.6	65.7
Costa Rica	1 476.4	5.6	48.9	2.0	67.7
Germany	1 413.4	2.7	6.6	1.9	69.7

Graph 2: Trade Balance by MDG regions 2010

(Bln US$)

Imports — Exports — Trade balance

Developed Asia-Pacific
Developed Europe
Developed N. America
South-eastern Europe
CIS
Northern Africa
Sub-Saharan Africa
Latin Am, Caribbean
Eastern Asia
Southern Asia
South-eastern Asia
Western Asia
Oceania

-40 -35 -30 -25 -20 -15 -10 -5 0 5 10 15 20 25

Table 3: Top importing countries or areas in 2010

Country or area	Value (million US$)	Avg. Growth (%) 06-10	Growth (%) 09-10	World share %	Cum.
World	78 489.1	8.3	9.1	100.0	
USA	9 585.3	8.5	12.1	12.2	12.2
Germany	7 086.0	2.6	0.9	9.0	21.2
Russian Federation	5 423.2	16.5	24.7	6.9	28.1
United Kingdom	4 746.4	1.1	4.6	6.0	34.2
Netherlands	4 279.3	6.6	2.8	5.5	39.6
France	4 058.3	4.9	3.8	5.2	44.8
Canada	3 421.0	8.5	13.2	4.4	49.2
Belgium	3 300.2	1.2	-6.5	4.2	53.4
Italy	2 590.8	3.9	-0.8	3.3	56.7
Japan	2 544.3	6.1	4.3	3.2	59.9
China, Hong Kong SAR	2 490.8	23.9	25.2	3.2	63.1
China	2 061.9	31.9	25.0	2.6	65.7
Spain	1 924.8	4.7	4.6	2.5	68.2
United Arab Emirates	1 293.0	19.8	22.5	1.6	69.8
Poland	1 193.7	8.1	12.9	1.5	71.3

058 Fruits, preserved, and fruit preparations (excluding fruit juices)

After a 14.1 percent drop in 2009, the value of (in current prices) of exports of preserved fruits and fruit preparations, excluding fruit juices (SITC group 058) increased by 9.3 percent and amounted to 15.2 bln US$ in 2010 (see table 2). Imports, after a decline of 11.4 percent in 2009, increased by 7.3 percent and totaled 14.9 bln US$ (see table 3). Graph 1 shows that the increase in exports for 2010 in this product group was exceeded by increases in world exports of food and live animals (SITC section 0) of 11.2 percent and in total world exports of 21.2 percent. Exports of preserved fruits and fruit preparations, excluding fruit juices (SITC group 058) accounted for 1.6 percent of world exports of SITC section 0 and 0.1 percent of total world exports in 2010 (see table 1).

China was the top exporting country in 2010 with 14.6 percent of world exports (see table 2). Other major exporting countries were USA and Thailand, respectively with 7.5 and 6.2 percent of world exports. USA was the top importing country, together with Germany and France (see table 3). By MDG regions (see graph 2), top deficits were recorded in Developed Europe (-1.8 bln US$), Developed North America (-1.5 bln US$) and Developed Asia-Pacific (-1.1 bln US$). Significant surpluses were recorded by Eastern Asia (+1.6 bln US$), South-eastern Asia (+1.2 bln US$) and Latin America and the Caribbean (+1.1 bln US$) .

Table 1: Imports (Imp.) and exports (Exp.), 1996-2010, in current prices

		1996	1997	1998	1999	2000	2001	2002	2003	2004	2005	2006	2007	2008	2009	2010
Values in Bln US$	Imp.	6.5	6.5	6.5	6.7	6.3	6.3	6.8	8.3	9.5	10.6	11.7	13.6	15.7	13.9	14.9
	Exp.	6.4	6.1	6.1	6.1	5.7	6.0	6.6	7.9	9.0	10.0	11.3	13.7	16.2	13.9	15.2
As a percentage of SITC section (%)	Imp.	1.5	1.5	1.5	1.6	1.5	1.5	1.5	1.6	1.6	1.7	1.7	1.6	1.6	1.6	1.5
	Exp.	1.5	1.4	1.5	1.5	1.5	1.5	1.6	1.6	1.6	1.7	1.7	1.7	1.7	1.6	1.6
As a percentage of world trade (%)	Imp.	0.1	0.1	0.1	0.1	0.1	0.1	0.1	0.1	0.1	0.1	0.1	0.1	0.1	0.1	0.1
	Exp.	0.1	0.1	0.1	0.1	0.1	0.1	0.1	0.1	0.1	0.1	0.1	0.1	0.1	0.1	0.1

Graph 1: Annual growth rates of exports, 1996–2010

(In percentage by year)

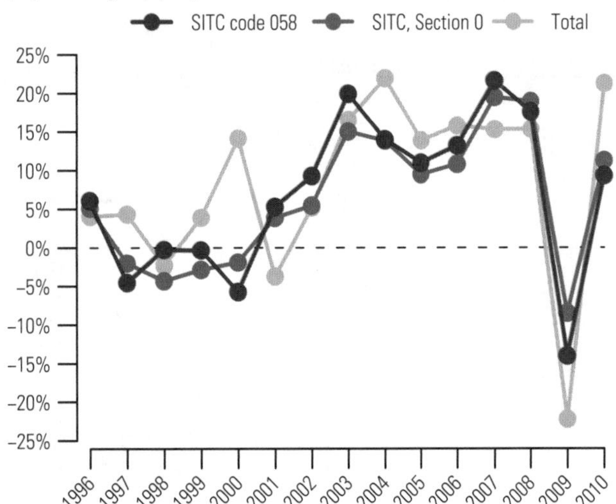

Table 2: Top exporting countries or areas in 2010

Country or area	Value (million US$)	Avg. Growth (%) 06-10	Growth (%) 09-10	World share %	Cum.
World	15177.1	7.6	9.3	100.0	
China	2211.7	12.6	19.7	14.6	14.6
USA	1145.3	9.9	9.8	7.5	22.1
Thailand	940.8	6.3	11.2	6.2	28.3
Turkey	812.3	4.8	30.6	5.4	33.7
Germany	803.2	2.1	-8.0	5.3	39.0
Netherlands	731.4	11.0	-4.4	4.8	43.8
Poland	580.9	5.7	8.7	3.8	47.6
Italy	532.6	5.2	10.4	3.5	51.1
France	506.6	7.1	2.5	3.3	54.5
Belgium	473.7	5.7	-3.9	3.1	57.6
Spain	466.6	2.6	-5.5	3.1	60.7
Chile	447.9	10.6	5.5	3.0	63.6
Greece	440.2	4.4	8.0	2.9	66.5
Canada	413.9	0.3	4.7	2.7	69.2
Mexico	411.3	20.2	32.5	2.7	71.9

Graph 2: Trade Balance by MDG regions 2010

(Bln US$)

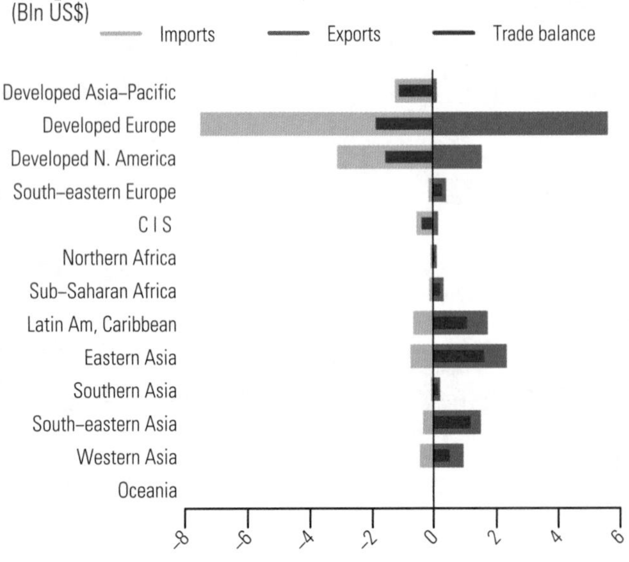

Table 3: Top importing countries or areas in 2010

Country or area	Value (million US$)	Avg. Growth (%) 06-10	Growth (%) 09-10	World share %	Cum.
World	14889.0	6.1	7.3	100.0	
USA	2450.6	6.3	8.8	16.5	16.5
Germany	1746.5	-0.4	-1.4	11.7	28.2
France	1209.6	6.2	0.2	8.1	36.3
Japan	917.9	0.7	14.1	6.2	42.5
United Kingdom	732.2	3.0	6.6	4.9	47.4
Netherlands	652.9	8.2	-4.5	4.4	51.8
Canada	645.0	9.7	6.0	4.3	56.1
Belgium	443.4	3.9	-0.7	3.0	59.1
Italy	387.9	5.5	21.2	2.6	61.7
Russian Federation	375.7	14.4	29.1	2.5	64.2
Austria	324.3	7.1	7.2	2.2	66.4
Poland	277.7	7.7	20.5	1.9	68.3
China	267.3	26.4	33.6	1.8	70.1
Spain	264.1	4.6	-1.8	1.8	71.8
Rep. of Korea	244.6	7.0	29.0	1.6	73.5

After several years of continuous growth marked by a peak of 15.3 bln US$ in 2008, the value (in current prices) of exports of fruit and vegetable juices, unfermented and without added spirit (SITC group 059) decreased by 16.7 percent in 2009 but increased again by 6.5 percent in 2010 to reach 13.6 bln US$ (see table 2). Imports, with a similar development, declined by 18.7 percent in 2009 then increased by 2.7 percent in 2010 to 13.6 bln US$ (see table 3). Graph 1 shows that the increase in exports for 2010 in this product group was exceeded by the increases in world exports of food and live animals (SITC section 0) of 11.2 percent and in total world exports of 21.2 percent. Exports of fruit and vegetable juices, unfermented and without added spirit (SITC group 059) accounted for 1.4 percent of world exports of SITC section 0 and 0.1 percent of total world exports in 2010 (see table 1).

Brazil, Netherlands and USA were the top exporting countries in 2010 (see table 2). They accounted respectively for 14.2, 8.5 and 8.4 percent of world exports. Major destinations were USA, Germany and Netherlands (see table 3). By MDG regions (see graph 2), Developed Europe accounted for a large share of trade. In 2010, its exports and imports amounted respectively to 5.8 bln US$ and 7.6 bln US$, resulting in a trade deficit of 1.8 bln US$. Major deficits were also recorded by Developed North America (-1.0 bln US$) and Developed Asia-Pacific (-0.7 bln US$). Latin America and the Caribbean recorded a surplus of 2.9 bln US$.

Table 1: Imports (Imp.) and exports (Exp.), 1996-2010, in current prices

		1996	1997	1998	1999	2000	2001	2002	2003	2004	2005	2006	2007	2008	2009	2010
Values in Bln US$	Imp.	7.0	6.2	6.4	7.0	6.7	6.2	6.9	8.1	8.5	9.4	11.1	14.4	16.2	13.2	13.6
	Exp.	6.6	5.9	6.3	6.6	6.3	5.9	6.4	7.7	7.9	8.9	10.9	14.3	15.3	12.8	13.6
As a percentage of SITC section (%)	Imp.	1.6	1.4	1.5	1.7	1.6	1.5	1.5	1.6	1.5	1.5	1.6	1.7	1.7	1.5	1.4
	Exp.	1.5	1.4	1.6	1.7	1.6	1.5	1.5	1.6	1.4	1.5	1.6	1.8	1.6	1.5	1.4
As a percentage of world trade (%)	Imp.	0.1	0.1	0.1	0.1	0.1	0.1	0.1	0.1	0.1	0.1	0.1	0.1	0.1	0.1	0.1
	Exp.	0.1	0.1	0.1	0.1	0.1	0.1	0.1	0.1	0.1	0.1	0.1	0.1	0.1	0.1	0.1

Graph 1: Annual growth rates of exports, 1996–2010

(In percentage by year)

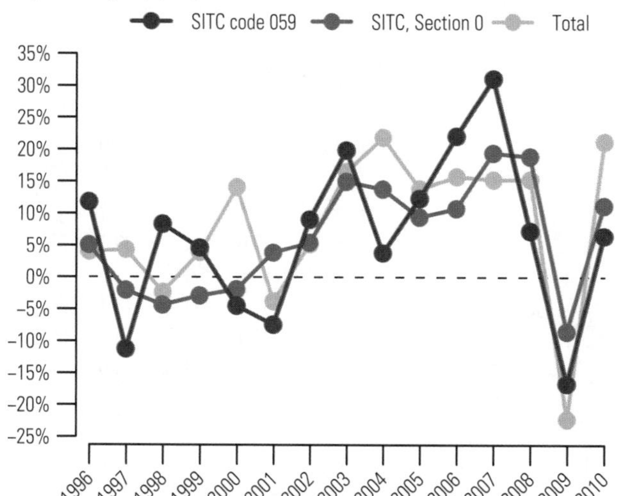

Graph 2: Trade Balance by MDG regions 2010

(Bln US$)

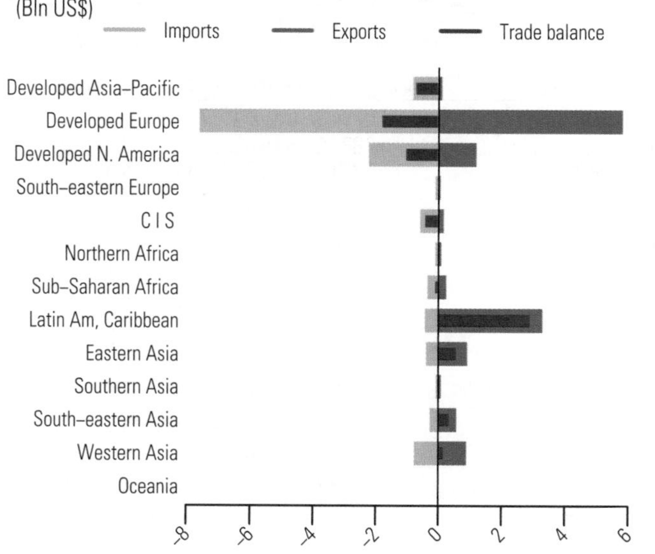

Table 2: Top exporting countries or areas in 2010

Country or area	Value (million US$)	Avg. Growth (%) 06-10	Growth (%) 09-10	World share %	Cum.
World	13585.5	5.7	6.5	100.0	
Brazil	1924.7	5.2	9.9	14.2	14.2
Netherlands	1160.1	8.5	0.1	8.5	22.7
USA	1139.1	6.2	11.2	8.4	31.1
Belgium	1108.6	-0.3	3.6	8.2	39.3
Germany	864.8	0.7	-10.2	6.4	45.6
China	864.1	6.5	13.3	6.4	52.0
Spain	639.9	5.5	-3.3	4.7	56.7
Italy	609.3	7.6	8.8	4.5	61.2
Poland	440.4	-2.8	1.3	3.2	64.4
Thailand	379.3	12.8	17.4	2.8	67.2
Argentina	317.0	5.4	-2.4	2.3	69.5
Mexico	316.1	17.9	18.4	2.3	71.9
Austria	289.8	0.2	-3.5	2.1	74.0
Saudi Arabia	273.5	16.9	5.4	2.0	76.0
France	233.2	4.0	0.5	1.7	77.7

Table 3: Top importing countries or areas in 2010

Country or area	Value (million US$)	Avg. Growth (%) 06-10	Growth (%) 09-10	World share %	Cum.
World	13554.6	5.2	2.7	100.0	
USA	1582.0	6.5	1.3	11.7	11.7
Germany	1352.9	-0.3	6.9	10.0	21.7
Netherlands	1231.4	11.7	4.3	9.1	30.7
France	1105.7	7.5	-3.8	8.2	38.9
United Kingdom	902.6	0.5	0.4	6.7	45.6
Belgium	821.4	5.9	-17.3	6.1	51.6
Canada	622.2	1.6	1.0	4.6	56.2
Japan	611.0	-0.8	-0.2	4.5	60.7
Russian Federation	393.4	6.5	25.1	2.9	63.6
Austria	297.0	1.4	14.0	2.2	65.8
Spain	285.1	4.8	3.3	2.1	67.9
Italy	248.1	0.5	6.6	1.8	69.7
Saudi Arabia	230.4	12.7	2.4	1.7	71.4
Poland	209.5	11.7	60.7	1.5	73.0
Ireland	180.3	2.9	3.7	1.3	74.3

Source: UN Comtrade

061 Sugars, molasses and honey

Since 2006, the value (in current prices) of exports of sugars, molasses and honey (SITC group 061) increased on average by 13.3 percent each year and reached 37.2 bln US$ in 2010 (see table 2). During the same period, imports increased on average by 10.0 percent to 35.3 bln US$. Graph 1 shows that the increase in exports for 2010 in this product group was well above the increases in world exports of food and live animals (SITC section 0) of 11.2 percent and in total world exports of 21.2 percent. Exports of sugars, molasses and honey (SITC group 061) accounted for 3.8 percent of world exports of SITC section 0 and 0.2 percent of total world exports in 2010 (see table 1).

In 2010, Brazil was the top exporting country: it accounted for 34.5 percent of world exports (see table 2). Other major exporting countries were Thailand and Cuba, respectively with 6.0 and 4.6 percent of world exports. USA, Russian Federation and United Kingdom were the top destinations (see table 3). By MDG regions (see graph 2), Latin America and the Caribbean recorded a surplus of 16.0 bln US$. Top deficits were recorded by Southern Asia (-2.1 bln US$), Commonwealth of Independent States(-1.9 bln US$) and Developed North America (-1.8 bln US$).

Table 1: Imports (Imp.) and exports (Exp.), 1996-2010, in current prices

		1996	1997	1998	1999	2000	2001	2002	2003	2004	2005	2006	2007	2008	2009	2010
Values in Bln US$	Imp.	17.6	15.8	14.5	13.0	11.4	14.1	13.6	14.9	16.1	20.0	24.1	24.6	26.8	28.0	35.3
	Exp.	16.0	14.6	13.3	11.0	9.7	12.1	12.0	13.2	14.1	17.4	22.6	22.1	24.1	27.4	37.2
As a percentage of SITC section (%)	Imp.	3.9	3.6	3.4	3.1	2.8	3.3	3.0	2.9	2.8	3.1	3.5	3.0	2.7	3.1	3.6
	Exp.	3.7	3.4	3.3	2.8	2.5	3.0	2.8	2.7	2.6	2.9	3.4	2.8	2.5	3.1	3.8
As a percentage of world trade (%)	Imp.	0.3	0.3	0.3	0.2	0.2	0.2	0.2	0.2	0.2	0.2	0.2	0.2	0.2	0.2	0.2
	Exp.	0.3	0.3	0.2	0.2	0.2	0.2	0.2	0.2	0.2	0.2	0.2	0.2	0.2	0.2	0.2

Graph 1: Annual growth rates of exports, 1996–2010

(In percentage by year)

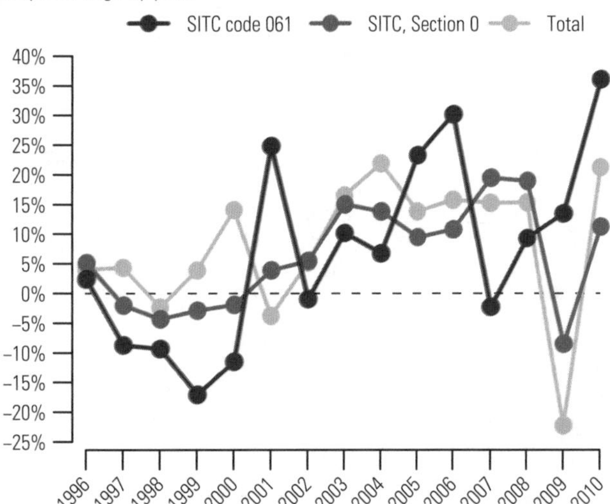

Graph 2: Trade Balance by MDG regions 2010

(Bln US$)

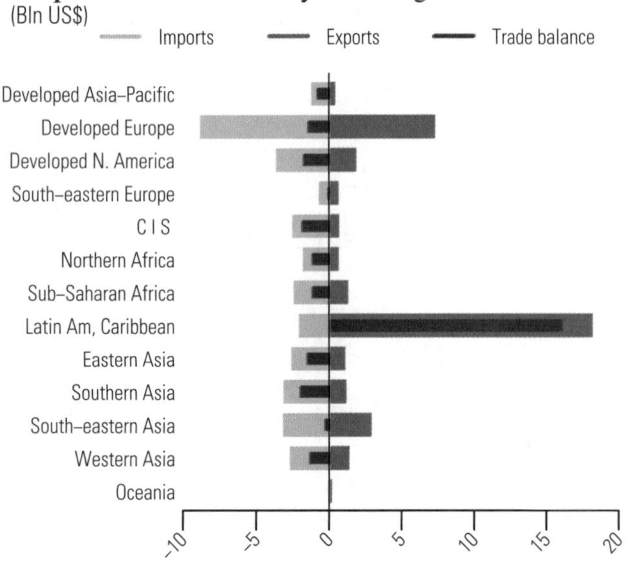

Table 2: Top exporting countries or areas in 2010

Country or area	Value (million US$)	Avg. Growth (%) 06-10	Growth (%) 09-10	World share %	Cum.
World	37 240.0	13.3	36.0	100.0	
Brazil	12 830.3	19.9	51.6	34.5	34.5
Thailand	2 236.9	29.2	18.2	6.0	40.5
Cuba	*1 720.1*	307.6	85.8	4.6	45.1
France	1 592.2	-1.3	-5.6	4.3	49.4
USA	1 382.7	16.1	63.5	3.7	53.1
Germany	1 223.1	3.6	2.0	3.3	56.4
India	1 052.5	11.5	1190.7	2.8	59.2
Mexico	853.1	15.6	28.0	2.3	61.5
United Arab Emirates	827.4	21.7	47.3	2.2	63.7
Guatemala	775.7	23.2	35.5	2.1	65.8
Belgium	754.0	-7.2	24.8	2.0	67.8
China	731.6	24.9	48.0	2.0	69.8
Netherlands	621.9	2.0	0.8	1.7	71.4
Colombia	455.6	5.4	16.1	1.2	72.7
United Kingdom	452.1	-1.2	-6.0	1.2	73.9

Table 3: Top importing countries or areas in 2010

Country or area	Value (million US$)	Avg. Growth (%) 06-10	Growth (%) 09-10	World share %	Cum.
World	35 294.3	10.0	26.0	100.0	
USA	2 887.0	9.0	41.5	8.2	8.2
Russian Federation	1 328.2	3.6	115.4	3.8	11.9
United Kingdom	1 279.0	-0.5	-5.9	3.6	15.6
Indonesia	1 255.5	19.4	78.7	3.6	19.1
Germany	1 192.6	3.2	-5.6	3.4	22.5
Rep. of Korea	1 104.1	12.2	34.3	3.1	25.6
Italy	1 007.6	10.8	-3.5	2.9	28.5
China	985.8	13.8	125.3	2.8	31.3
Japan	983.9	8.7	34.5	2.8	34.1
Saudi Arabia	970.0	20.4	59.0	2.7	36.8
Mexico	905.2	21.4	44.3	2.6	39.4
Malaysia	867.2	19.3	31.9	2.5	41.8
Pakistan	832.3	3.9	318.5	2.4	44.2
Iran	784.4	188.9	8.4	2.2	46.4
Canada	759.7	7.9	23.3	2.2	48.6

During the recent five years, the value (in current prices) of exports of sugar confectionery (SITC group 062) increased on average by 7.0 percent and amounted to 9.2 bln US$ in 2010 (see table 2). Imports, showing a similar development, increased on average by 5.8 percent to 8.5 bln US$ (see table 3). Graph 1 shows that the increase in exports for 2010 in this product group was exceeded by the increases in world exports of food and live animals (SITC section 0) of 11.2 percent and in total world exports of 21.2 percent. Exports of sugar confectionery (SITC group 062) accounted for 0.9 percent of world exports of SITC section 0 and 0.1 percent of total world exports in 2010 (see table 1).

Germany, China and Belgium were the top exporting countries in 2010 (see table 2). They accounted respectively for 9.0, 7.4 and 6.2 percent of world exports. Major destinations were USA, Germany and United Kingdom (see table 3). By MDG regions (see graph 2), top surpluses were recorded by Eastern Asia (+523 mln US$), Latin America and the Caribbean (+517 mln US$) and Developed Europe (+461 mln US$). Large deficits were recorded by Developed North America (-889 mln US$), Sub-Saharan Africa (-172 mln US$) and Developed Asia-Pacific (-166 mln US$).

Table 1: Imports (Imp.) and exports (Exp.), 1996-2010, in current prices

		1996	1997	1998	1999	2000	2001	2002	2003	2004	2005	2006	2007	2008	2009	2010
Values in Bln US$	Imp.	4.1	4.0	3.8	4.0	4.1	4.2	4.6	5.4	6.0	6.5	6.8	7.7	8.4	8.0	8.5
	Exp.	4.6	4.6	4.3	4.2	4.3	4.4	4.6	5.5	6.2	6.5	7.0	8.2	9.1	8.7	9.2
As a percentage of SITC section (%)	Imp.	0.9	0.9	0.9	1.0	1.0	1.0	1.0	1.1	1.0	1.0	1.0	0.9	0.9	0.9	0.9
	Exp.	1.1	1.1	1.1	1.1	1.1	1.1	1.1	1.1	1.1	1.1	1.0	1.0	1.0	1.0	0.9
As a percentage of world trade (%)	Imp.	0.1	0.1	0.1	0.1	0.1	0.1	0.1	0.1	0.1	0.1	0.1	0.1	0.1	0.1	0.1
	Exp.	0.1	0.1	0.1	0.1	0.1	0.1	0.1	0.1	0.1	0.1	0.1	0.1	0.1	0.1	0.1

Graph 1: Annual growth rates of exports, 1996–2010

(In percentage by year)

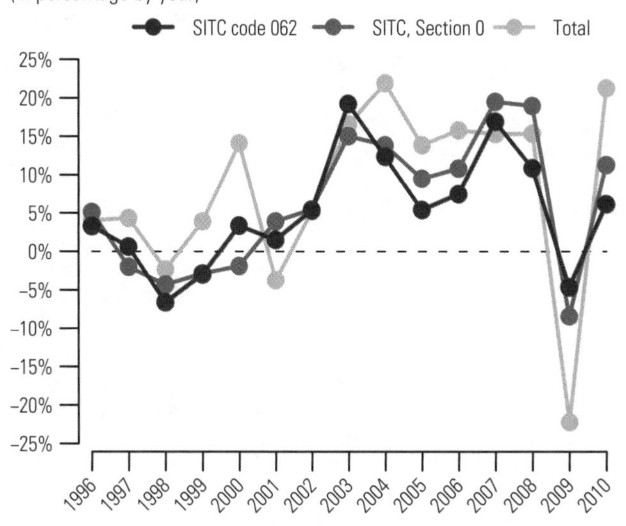

Table 2: Top exporting countries or areas in 2010

Country or area	Value (million US$)	Avg. Growth (%) 06-10	Growth (%) 09-10	World share %	Cum.
World	9180.6	7.0	6.1	100.0	
Germany	830.8	6.8	2.3	9.0	9.0
China	680.7	13.3	26.0	7.4	16.5
Belgium	572.6	5.1	-0.1	6.2	22.7
Mexico	512.5	3.8	2.4	5.6	28.3
Canada	435.6	1.3	12.7	4.7	33.0
Netherlands	423.1	9.3	6.0	4.6	37.6
Spain	408.9	1.4	-5.4	4.5	42.1
USA	391.1	7.1	-0.4	4.3	46.4
Thailand	308.0	17.4	25.1	3.4	49.7
Turkey	281.3	9.4	8.6	3.1	52.8
United Kingdom	228.2	2.2	3.7	2.5	55.3
France	227.0	0.3	5.9	2.5	57.7
Colombia	218.3	2.2	-6.6	2.4	60.1
Poland	216.8	8.5	-6.8	2.4	62.5
Ukraine	180.5	22.7	40.7	2.0	64.4

Graph 2: Trade Balance by MDG regions 2010

(Bln US$)

Imports — Exports — Trade balance

Developed Asia-Pacific
Developed Europe
Developed N. America
South-eastern Europe
C I S
Northern Africa
Sub-Saharan Africa
Latin Am, Caribbean
Eastern Asia
Southern Asia
South-eastern Asia
Western Asia
Oceania

-4 -3 -2 -1 0 1 2 3 4 5

Table 3: Top importing countries or areas in 2010

Country or area	Value (million US$)	Avg. Growth (%) 06-10	Growth (%) 09-10	World share %	Cum.
World	8456.9	5.8	6.3	100.0	
USA	1387.3	2.3	10.4	16.4	16.4
Germany	605.3	3.0	1.7	7.2	23.6
United Kingdom	528.4	3.9	3.3	6.2	29.8
France	377.3	4.8	2.1	4.5	34.3
Canada	319.8	5.8	9.5	3.8	38.1
Belgium	244.7	6.4	-3.2	2.9	40.9
Netherlands	236.9	3.7	-7.5	2.8	43.7
Russian Federation	204.7	12.2	18.4	2.4	46.2
Sweden	180.3	2.8	-3.2	2.1	48.3
China, Hong Kong SAR	179.1	3.8	12.6	2.1	50.4
Italy	167.6	1.7	4.2	2.0	52.4
Australia	159.7	10.4	15.5	1.9	54.3
Poland	144.5	14.9	10.9	1.7	56.0
Spain	139.8	4.5	13.8	1.7	57.7
Austria	121.8	2.3	-6.8	1.4	59.1

071 Coffee and coffee substitutes

After a 9.9 percent drop in 2009, the value (in current prices) of exports of coffee and coffee substitutes (SITC group 071) bounced back by 22.2 percent and amounted to 29.6 bln US$ in 2010 (see table 2). Imports, after a 7.5 percent drop in 2009, bounced back by 17.2 percent to reach 29.3 bln US$ (see table 3). Graph 1 shows that the increase in exports for 2010 in this product group was more than the increase in world exports of food and live animals (SITC section 0) of 11.2 percent but close to that of total world exports of 21.2 percent. Exports of coffee and coffee substitutes (SITC group 071) accounted for 3.1 percent of world exports of SITC section 0 and 0.2 percent of total world exports in 2010 (see table 1).

Brazil, the top exporting country in 2010, accounted for 19.5 percent of world exports (see table 2). Other major exporting countries were Germany and Viet Nam, respectively with 9.4 and 7.5 percent of world exports. Top destinations were USA, Germany and France (see table 3). By MDG regions (see graph 2), Latin America and the Caribbean, South-eastern Asia and Sub-Saharan Africa recorded trade surpluses amounting respectively to 11.0 bln US$, 3.1 bln US$ and 1.7 bln US$. On the other hand, Developed Europe, Developed North America and Developed Asia-Pacific recorded trade deficits amounting to 6.2 bln US$, 5.0 bln US$ and 1.9 bln US$ in 2010, respectively.

Table 1: Imports (Imp.) and exports (Exp.), 1996-2010, in current prices

		1996	1997	1998	1999	2000	2001	2002	2003	2004	2005	2006	2007	2008	2009	2010
Values in Bln US$	Imp.	14.7	17.9	16.7	13.6	12.3	9.6	9.1	10.9	12.6	16.5	18.5	22.1	27.1	25.0	29.3
	Exp.	14.2	17.0	15.8	13.2	11.4	8.7	8.5	9.9	11.7	15.5	18.3	22.1	26.9	24.2	29.6
As a percentage of SITC section (%)	Imp.	3.3	4.1	4.0	3.2	3.0	2.3	2.0	2.1	2.2	2.6	2.7	2.7	2.8	2.8	3.0
	Exp.	3.3	4.0	3.9	3.4	3.0	2.2	2.0	2.0	2.1	2.6	2.7	2.8	2.8	2.8	3.1
As a percentage of world trade (%)	Imp.	0.3	0.3	0.3	0.2	0.2	0.2	0.1	0.1	0.1	0.2	0.2	0.2	0.2	0.2	0.2
	Exp.	0.3	0.3	0.3	0.2	0.2	0.1	0.1	0.1	0.1	0.1	0.2	0.2	0.2	0.2	0.2

Graph 1: Annual growth rates of exports, 1996–2010
(In percentage by year)

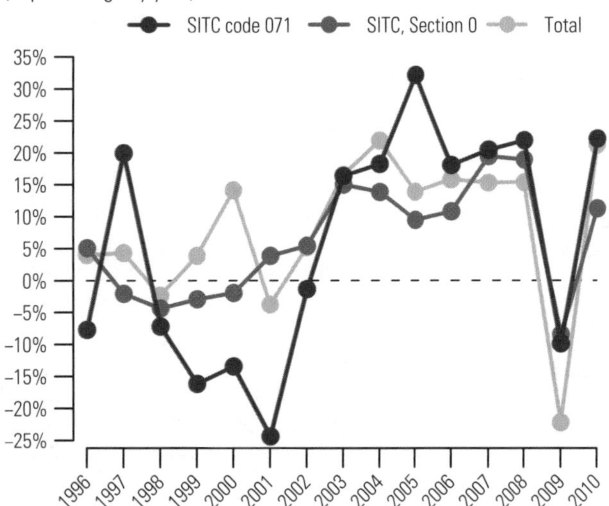

Table 2: Top exporting countries or areas in 2010

Country or area	Value (million US$)	Avg. Growth (%) 06-10	Growth (%) 09-10	World share %	Cum.
World	29593.2	12.7	22.2	100.0	
Brazil	5762.8	14.4	34.7	19.5	19.5
Germany	2774.9	9.5	10.2	9.4	28.9
Viet Nam	*2215.0*	15.8	25.6	7.5	36.3
Colombia	2156.9	7.2	20.2	7.3	43.6
Switzerland	1453.0	50.3	29.7	4.9	48.5
Belgium	1129.6	16.8	10.1	3.8	52.4
Italy	991.7	9.0	3.3	3.4	55.7
Indonesia	983.0	12.2	7.0	3.3	59.0
Peru	889.1	14.6	51.9	3.0	62.0
USA	883.9	9.8	19.1	3.0	65.0
Guatemala	720.5	11.3	21.5	2.4	67.4
Ethiopia	699.1	13.2	89.1	2.4	69.8
India	558.3	6.8	36.2	1.9	71.7
France	532.5	19.7	12.5	1.8	73.5
Honduras	*532.3*	8.1	3.2	1.8	75.3

Graph 2: Trade Balance by MDG regions 2010
(Bln US$)

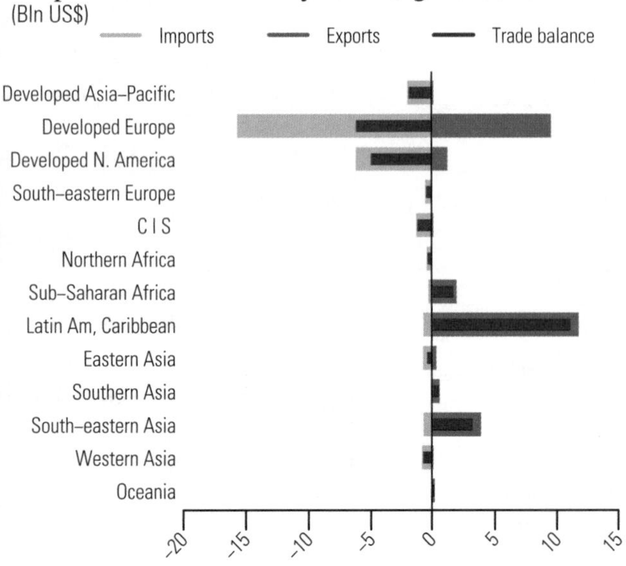

Table 3: Top importing countries or areas in 2010

Country or area	Value (million US$)	Avg. Growth (%) 06-10	Growth (%) 09-10	World share %	Cum.
World	29329.2	12.2	17.2	100.0	
USA	5100.3	10.2	21.2	17.4	17.4
Germany	3977.5	10.9	21.4	13.6	31.0
France	1911.3	14.4	15.1	6.5	37.5
Japan	1534.0	7.6	19.3	5.2	42.7
Italy	1371.3	10.4	5.4	4.7	47.4
Belgium	1195.9	15.6	11.1	4.1	51.5
Canada	1112.2	11.8	22.0	3.8	55.2
United Kingdom	1029.8	13.2	15.4	3.5	58.8
Spain	1002.5	15.9	17.3	3.4	62.2
Russian Federation	781.6	15.8	29.5	2.7	64.8
Netherlands	696.3	6.2	15.9	2.4	67.2
Poland	594.8	12.8	8.1	2.0	69.2
Switzerland	593.4	21.2	32.4	2.0	71.3
Sweden	505.0	11.4	36.0	1.7	73.0
Austria	430.9	10.3	7.5	1.5	74.5

During the recent five years, the value (in current prices) of exports of cocoa (SITC group 072) steadily increased, averaging 18.9 percent and amounted to 17.9 bln US$ in 2010 (see table 2). Similarly for the same period, imports also increased on average by 17.5 percent to reach 19.1 bln US$ (see table 3). Graph 1 shows that the increase in exports for 2010 in this product group slightly exceeded the increase in world exports of food and live animals (SITC section 0) of 11.2 percent but was below that of total world exports of 21.2 percent. Exports of cocoa (SITC group 072) accounted for 1.9 percent of world exports of SITC section 0 and 0.1 percent of total world exports in 2010 (see table 1).

Cote d'Ivoire, Netherlands and Indonesia were the top exporting countries in 2010, respectively with 20.6, 18.8 and 8.9 percent of world exports (see table 2). Top destinations were USA, Netherlands and Germany (see table 3). By MDG regions (see graph 2), Developed Europe accounted for a large share of imports of cocoa (SITC group 072). In 2010, its imports amounted to 10.5 bln US$ while exports were 6.1 bln US$, resulting in a trade deficit of 4.4 bln US$. Major deficits were also recorded by Developed North America (-2.7 bln US$) and Commonwealth of Independent States (-1.0 bln US$). Sub-Saharan Africa and South-eastern Asia recorded surpluses amounting to 6.6 bln US$ and 1.4 bln US$, respectively.

Table 1: Imports (Imp.) and exports (Exp.), 1996-2010, in current prices

		1996	1997	1998	1999	2000	2001	2002	2003	2004	2005	2006	2007	2008	2009	2010
Values in Bln US$	Imp.	6.2	5.8	6.5	6.0	4.6	4.9	6.8	9.7	9.2	9.8	10.0	12.2	15.2	16.0	19.1
	Exp.	5.8	5.4	5.6	5.0	3.8	4.3	6.6	8.0	8.5	8.4	9.0	10.5	13.1	15.8	17.9
As a percentage of SITC section (%)	Imp.	1.4	1.3	1.5	1.4	1.1	1.2	1.5	1.9	1.6	1.5	1.4	1.5	1.6	1.8	2.0
	Exp.	1.3	1.3	1.4	1.3	1.0	1.1	1.6	1.7	1.5	1.4	1.3	1.3	1.4	1.8	1.9
As a percentage of world trade (%)	Imp.	0.1	0.1	0.1	0.1	0.1	0.1	0.1	0.1	0.1	0.1	0.1	0.1	0.1	0.1	0.1
	Exp.	0.1	0.1	0.1	0.1	0.1	0.1	0.1	0.1	0.1	0.1	0.1	0.1	0.1	0.1	0.1

Graph 1: Annual growth rates of exports, 1996–2010

(In percentage by year)

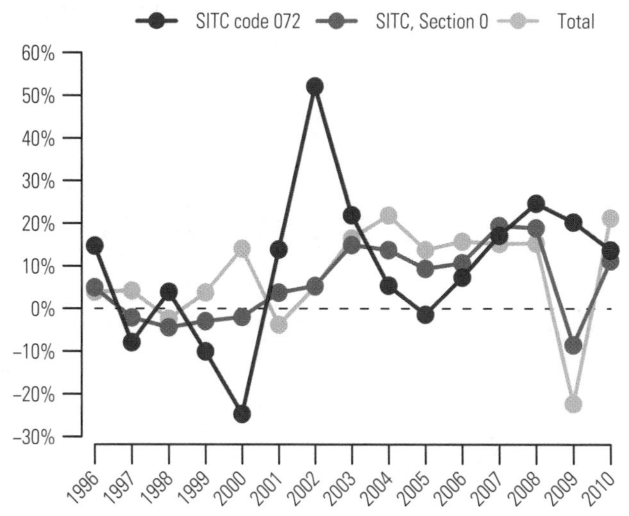

Table 2: Top exporting countries or areas in 2010

Country or area	Value (million US$)	Avg. Growth (%) 06-10	Growth (%) 09-10	World share %	Cum.
World	17946.7	18.9	13.7	100.0	
Côte d'Ivoire	3699.1	17.4	2.6	20.6	20.6
Netherlands	3365.7	20.8	31.0	18.8	39.4
Indonesia	1597.6	17.5	15.5	8.9	48.3
Nigeria	1277.5	197.3	-10.5	7.1	55.4
Malaysia	1191.1	24.4	42.5	6.6	62.0
Ghana	970.2	-5.9	-16.0	5.4	67.4
Germany	808.2	38.6	56.2	4.5	71.9
Cameroon	707.4	28.4	15.7	3.9	75.9
France	701.8	10.4	4.6	3.9	79.8
Ecuador	418.9	26.1	5.6	2.3	82.1
Belgium	382.3	10.3	2.2	2.1	84.2
USA	351.7	13.0	55.1	2.0	86.2
Singapore	327.3	23.4	22.5	1.8	88.0
Brazil	298.8	7.7	26.6	1.7	89.7
Spain	295.3	36.6	81.3	1.6	91.3

Graph 2: Trade Balance by MDG regions 2010

(Bln US$)

Imports — Exports — Trade balance

Developed Asia-Pacific
Developed Europe
Developed N. America
South-eastern Europe
C I S
Northern Africa
Sub-Saharan Africa
Latin Am, Caribbean
Eastern Asia
Southern Asia
South-eastern Asia
Western Asia
Oceania

-12 -10 -8 -6 -4 -2 0 2 4 6 8

Table 3: Top importing countries or areas in 2010

Country or area	Value (million US$)	Avg. Growth (%) 06-10	Growth (%) 09-10	World share %	Cum.
World	19054.8	17.5	18.8	100.0	
USA	2673.6	15.9	22.4	14.0	14.0
Netherlands	2455.7	22.6	3.0	12.9	26.9
Germany	2288.1	22.7	20.1	12.0	38.9
France	1255.1	12.3	5.5	6.6	45.5
Belgium	1205.8	11.6	9.9	6.3	51.8
Malaysia	1052.4	11.5	32.0	5.5	57.4
Russian Federation	668.0	20.9	27.1	3.5	60.9
United Kingdom	647.3	8.8	-10.5	3.4	64.3
Italy	560.2	20.1	20.8	2.9	67.2
Spain	495.1	24.9	48.0	2.6	69.8
Canada	443.5	8.1	18.0	2.3	72.1
Japan	397.4	8.5	9.2	2.1	74.2
Poland	390.4	17.5	44.5	2.0	76.3
Singapore	386.9	26.8	40.0	2.0	78.3
Switzerland	362.9	15.6	14.2	1.9	80.2

073 Chocolate and other food preparations containing cocoa, nes

After a 5.6 percent drop in 2009, the value (in current prices) of exports of chocolate and other food preparations containing cocoa, nes (SITC group 073) bounced back by 9.7 percent in 2010 and amounted to 20.0 bln US$ (see table 2). Imports, after a 6.1 percent drop in 2009, also increased by 9.7 percent in 2010 and totaled 19.2 bln US$ (see table 3). Graph 1 shows that the increase in exports for 2010 in this product group was less than the increases in world exports of food and live animals (SITC section 0) of 11.2 percent and in total world exports of 21.2 percent. Exports of chocolate and other food preparations containing cocoa, nes (SITC group 073) accounted for 2.1 percent of world exports of SITC section 0 and 0.1 percent of total world exports in 2010 (see table 1).

The top exporting countries in 2010 were Germany, Belgium and France (see table 2). Their exports represented respectively 16.6, 11.4 and 6.6 percent of world exports. Top destinations were USA, France and Germany (see table 3). By MDG regions (see graph 2), Developed Europe accounted for a majority of trade in chocolate and other food preparations containing cocoa, nes (SITC group 073). In 2010, its exports and imports amounted respectively to 13.9 bln US$ and 10.6 bln US$, resulting in a trade surplus of 3.3 bln US$. Top deficits were recorded by Developed Asia-Pacific (-666 mln US$) and Developed North America (-584 mln US$).

Table 1: Imports (Imp.) and exports (Exp.), 1996-2010, in current prices

		1996	1997	1998	1999	2000	2001	2002	2003	2004	2005	2006	2007	2008	2009	2010
Values in Bln US$	Imp.	7.2	7.0	7.0	6.9	6.7	7.2	8.0	9.7	11.3	12.3	13.6	16.3	18.6	17.5	19.2
	Exp.	8.6	7.8	7.4	7.1	6.9	7.6	8.2	10.0	11.7	12.5	14.1	16.9	19.3	18.3	20.0
As a percentage of SITC section (%)	Imp.	1.6	1.6	1.7	1.7	1.6	1.7	1.8	1.9	1.9	1.9	2.0	2.0	1.9	2.0	2.0
	Exp.	2.0	1.8	1.8	1.8	1.8	1.9	1.9	2.1	2.1	2.1	2.1	2.1	2.0	2.1	2.1
As a percentage of world trade (%)	Imp.	0.1	0.1	0.1	0.1	0.1	0.1	0.1	0.1	0.1	0.1	0.1	0.1	0.1	0.1	0.1
	Exp.	0.2	0.1	0.1	0.1	0.1	0.1	0.1	0.1	0.1	0.1	0.1	0.1	0.1	0.1	0.1

Graph 1: Annual growth rates of exports, 1996–2010

(In percentage by year)

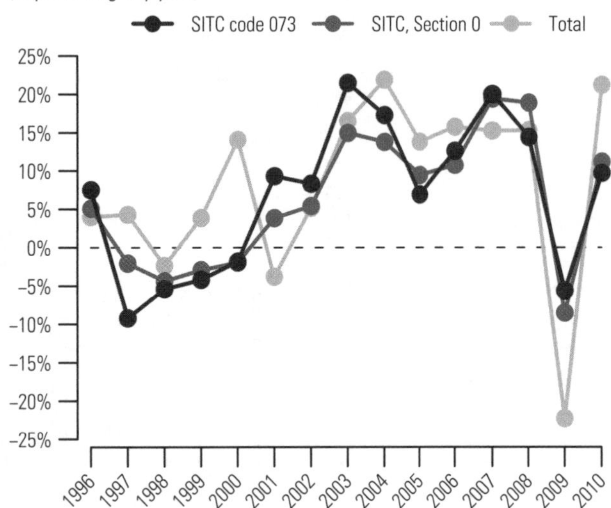

Table 2: Top exporting countries or areas in 2010

Country or area	Value (million US$)	Avg. Growth (%) 06-10	Growth (%) 09-10	World share %	Cum.
World	20034.1	9.2	9.7	100.0	
Germany	3328.1	10.5	6.3	16.6	16.6
Belgium	2292.2	4.9	2.3	11.4	28.1
France	1327.8	7.7	4.6	6.6	34.7
Italy	1290.0	14.1	8.4	6.4	41.1
Netherlands	1184.4	4.4	-7.1	5.9	47.0
USA	1034.9	11.1	10.7	5.2	52.2
Poland	896.7	20.7	33.8	4.5	56.7
Canada	889.6	5.4	33.6	4.4	61.1
Switzerland	743.5	8.6	8.7	3.7	64.8
United Kingdom	584.1	0.8	2.2	2.9	67.7
Ukraine	576.4	23.4	33.8	2.9	70.6
Mexico	505.1	37.3	28.4	2.5	73.1
Austria	442.0	5.4	5.1	2.2	75.3
Turkey	364.5	10.8	10.9	1.8	77.2
Spain	363.5	15.5	12.7	1.8	79.0

Graph 2: Trade Balance by MDG regions 2010

(Bln US$)

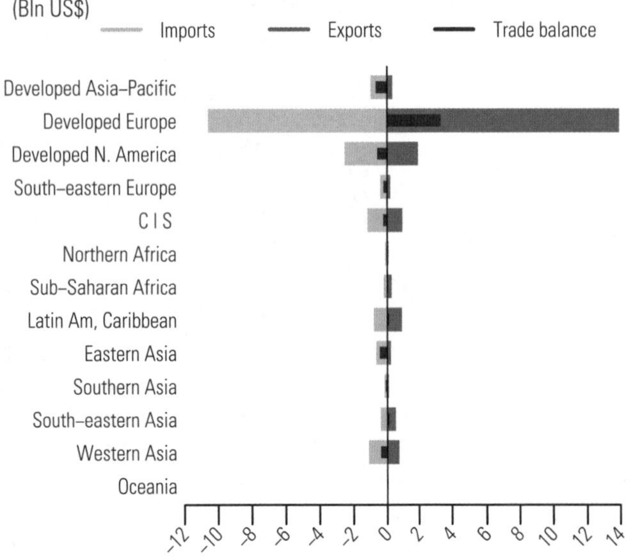

Table 3: Top importing countries or areas in 2010

Country or area	Value (million US$)	Avg. Growth (%) 06-10	Growth (%) 09-10	World share %	Cum.
World	19164.3	8.9	9.7	100.0	
USA	1741.5	7.1	23.7	9.1	9.1
France	1656.0	8.3	4.1	8.6	17.7
Germany	1550.9	8.1	4.9	8.1	25.8
United Kingdom	1530.8	7.9	7.1	8.0	33.8
Canada	756.9	9.0	10.6	3.9	37.8
Netherlands	747.5	6.3	0.8	3.9	41.7
Russian Federation	614.4	19.9	34.0	3.2	44.9
Spain	567.8	10.6	1.9	3.0	47.8
Belgium	529.7	2.9	-0.4	2.8	50.6
Italy	521.0	5.6	7.6	2.7	53.3
Japan	511.9	6.3	12.8	2.7	56.0
Austria	419.0	3.9	-0.8	2.2	58.2
Poland	400.3	13.8	27.1	2.1	60.3
Australia	321.5	18.7	6.3	1.7	61.9
Mexico	320.8	6.0	13.9	1.7	63.6

The value (in current prices) of exports of tea and mate (SITC group 074) dropped slightly in 2009 but bounced back by 16.0 percent in 2010 and amounted to 7.3 bln US$ (see table 2). Similarly, after a small drop in 2009, imports increased by 15.9 percent to reach 6.7 bln US$ (see table 3). Graph 1 shows that the increase in exports for 2010 in this product group was higher than the increase in world exports of food and live animals (SITC section 0) of 11.2 percent but less than the increase in total world exports of 21.2 percent. Exports of tea and mate (SITC group 074) accounted for 0.8 percent of world exports of SITC section 0 and less than 0.1 percent of total world exports in 2010 (see table 1).

Sri Lanka, Kenya and China were the top exporting countries in 2010 (see table 2). They accounted respectively for 18.9, 16.0 and 11.4 percent of world exports. Top destinations were Russian Federation, USA and United Arab Emirates (see table 3). By MDG regions (see graph 2), top surpluses were recorded by Southern Asia (+1.6 bln US$), Sub-Saharan Africa (+1.2 bln US$) and Eastern Asia (+680 mln US$). Western Asia, Commonwealth of Independent States and Developed North America recorded deficits of 925 mln US$, 884 mln US$ and 412 mln US$, respectively.

Table 1: Imports (Imp.) and exports (Exp.), 1996-2010, in current prices

		1996	1997	1998	1999	2000	2001	2002	2003	2004	2005	2006	2007	2008	2009	2010
Values in Bln US$	Imp.	2.7	3.1	3.3	3.1	3.0	3.1	3.1	3.3	3.6	3.9	4.4	4.8	5.9	5.8	6.7
	Exp.	2.5	3.2	3.6	3.1	3.2	3.2	2.8	3.4	3.8	4.2	4.7	5.3	6.4	6.3	7.3
As a percentage of SITC section (%)	Imp.	0.6	0.7	0.8	0.7	0.7	0.7	0.7	0.6	0.6	0.6	0.6	0.6	0.6	0.6	0.7
	Exp.	0.6	0.8	0.9	0.8	0.8	0.8	0.7	0.7	0.7	0.7	0.7	0.7	0.7	0.7	0.8
As a percentage of world trade (%)	Imp.	0.1	0.1	0.1	0.1	0.0	0.0	0.0	0.0	0.0	0.0	0.0	0.0	0.0	0.0	0.0
	Exp.	0.0	0.1	0.1	0.1	0.1	0.1	0.0	0.0	0.0	0.0	0.0	0.0	0.0	0.1	0.0

Graph 1: Annual growth rates of exports, 1996–2010
(In percentage by year)

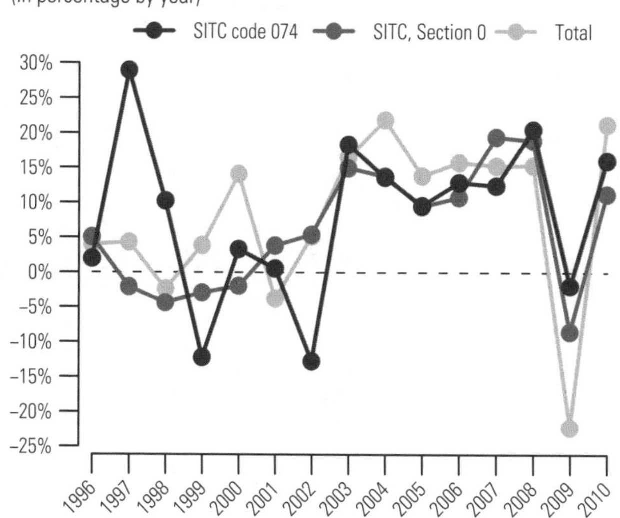

Table 2: Top exporting countries or areas in 2010

Country or area	Value (million US$)	Avg. Growth (%) 06-10	Growth (%) 09-10	World share %	Cum.
World	7270.5	11.4	16.0	100.0	
Sri Lanka	1377.6	11.8	16.2	18.9	18.9
Kenya	1163.8	15.2	30.2	16.0	35.0
China	825.2	9.5	11.5	11.4	46.3
India	720.0	12.9	23.8	9.9	56.2
United Kingdom	337.0	3.8	16.6	4.6	60.8
Netherlands	277.1	31.3	15.6	3.8	64.7
Germany	247.4	4.6	-1.5	3.4	68.1
USA	234.9	18.6	21.0	3.2	71.3
Viet Nam	*226.7*	19.1	25.6	3.1	74.4
Indonesia	182.3	7.9	4.5	2.5	76.9
Argentina	138.2	15.8	23.8	1.9	78.8
Ireland	117.3	20.5	109.7	1.6	80.4
Canada	109.8	7.8	11.3	1.5	81.9
Belgium	84.9	6.2	13.4	1.2	83.1
Poland	83.0	24.2	26.6	1.1	84.2

Graph 2: Trade Balance by MDG regions 2010
(Bln US$)

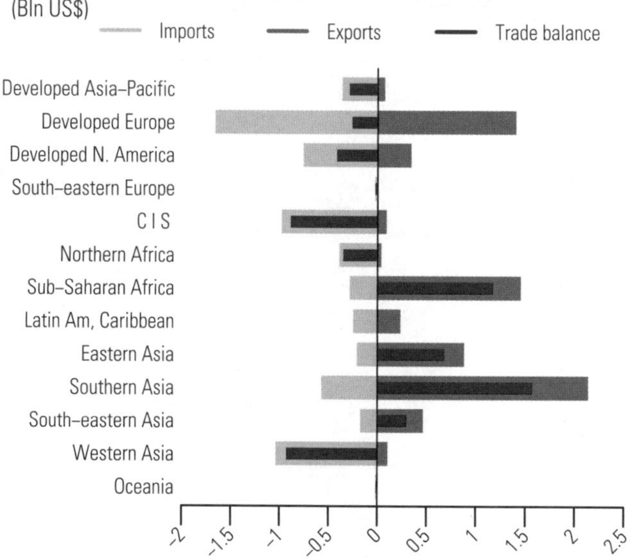

Table 3: Top importing countries or areas in 2010

Country or area	Value (million US$)	Avg. Growth (%) 06-10	Growth (%) 09-10	World share %	Cum.
World	6688.3	11.3	15.9	100.0	
Russian Federation	607.2	12.5	13.8	9.1	9.1
USA	546.8	7.9	18.1	8.2	17.3
United Arab Emirates	519.0	17.4	43.4	7.8	25.0
United Kingdom	433.0	6.0	14.5	6.5	31.5
Pakistan	303.1	8.0	35.2	4.5	36.0
Japan	228.2	3.1	15.9	3.4	39.4
Saudi Arabia	223.0	12.9	19.5	3.3	42.8
Egypt	221.6	118.2	-2.8	3.3	46.1
Canada	208.6	8.9	8.7	3.1	49.2
Germany	189.5	-1.8	-4.0	2.8	52.0
France	187.7	6.2	12.5	2.8	54.8
Iran	154.5	59.8	8.4	2.3	57.1
Poland	143.9	21.2	12.9	2.2	59.3
Netherlands	141.2	16.8	18.2	2.1	61.4
Ukraine	131.9	14.2	20.6	2.0	63.4

Source: UN Comtrade

075 Spices

During the recent five years, the value (in current prices) of exports of spices (SITC group 075) increased on average by 15.2 percent and amounted to 6.0 bln US$ in 2010 (see table 2). Similarly, imports increased on average by 14.9 percent to 5.8 bln US$ (see table 3). Graph 1 shows that the increase in exports for 2010 in this product group was more than the increase in world exports of food and live animals (SITC section 0) of 11.2 percent but less than the increase in total world exports of 21.2 percent. Exports of spices (SITC group 075) accounted for 0.6 percent of world exports of SITC section 0 and less than 0.1 percent of total world exports in 2010 (see table 1).

India, China and Viet Nam were the top exporting countries in 2010 (see table 2). They accounted respectively for 15.5, 12.9 and 8.2 percent of world exports. USA accounted for 14.6 percent of world imports and was the top importing country (see table 3). Other major destinations were Germany and Japan. By MDG regions (see graph 2), top surpluses were recorded by Southern Asia (+1.1 bln US$), Eastern Asia (+664 mln US$) and South-eastern Asia (+658 mln US$). Significant deficits were recorded by Developed North America (-835 mln US$) and Developed Europe (-805 mln US$) among others.

Table 1: Imports (Imp.) and exports (Exp.), 1996-2010, in current prices

		1996	1997	1998	1999	2000	2001	2002	2003	2004	2005	2006	2007	2008	2009	2010
Values in Bln US$	Imp.	2.2	2.6	2.6	2.8	2.9	2.7	2.7	3.0	3.3	3.1	3.3	4.1	4.9	4.7	5.8
	Exp.	2.0	2.4	2.5	2.6	2.7	2.5	2.6	2.8	3.1	3.0	3.4	4.4	5.2	5.1	6.0
As a percentage of SITC section (%)	Imp.	0.5	0.6	0.6	0.7	0.7	0.6	0.6	0.6	0.6	0.5	0.5	0.5	0.5	0.5	0.6
	Exp.	0.5	0.6	0.6	0.7	0.7	0.6	0.6	0.6	0.6	0.5	0.5	0.6	0.5	0.6	0.6
As a percentage of world trade (%)	Imp.	0.0	0.0	0.0	0.0	0.0	0.0	0.0	0.0	0.0	0.0	0.0	0.0	0.0	0.0	0.0
	Exp.	0.0	0.0	0.0	0.0	0.0	0.0	0.0	0.0	0.0	0.0	0.0	0.0	0.0	0.0	0.0

Graph 1: Annual growth rates of exports, 1996–2010

(In percentage by year)

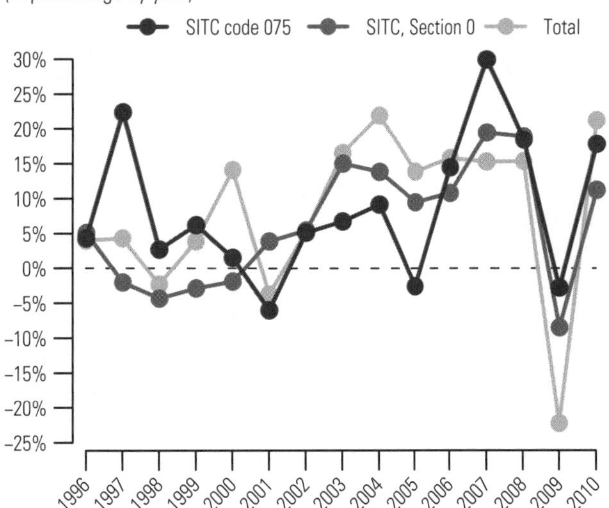

Graph 2: Trade Balance by MDG regions 2010

(Bln US$)

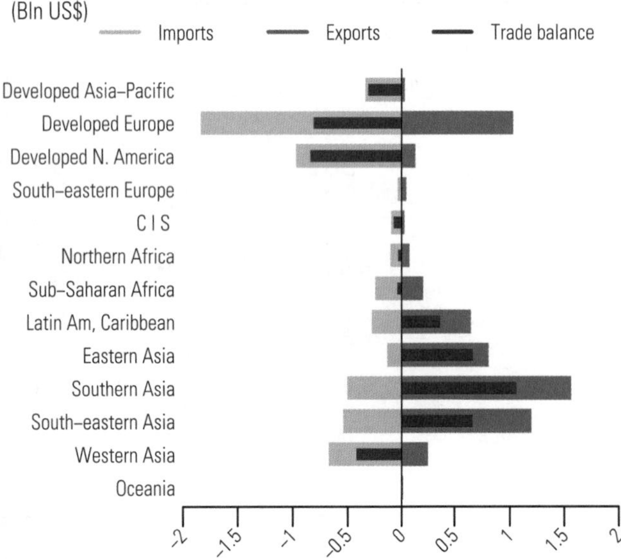

Table 2: Top exporting countries or areas in 2010

Country or area	Value (million US$)	Avg. Growth (%) 06-10	Growth (%) 09-10	World share %	Cum.
World	5994.2	15.2	17.8	100.0	
India	926.9	23.9	31.7	15.5	15.5
China	771.1	17.8	25.0	12.9	28.3
Viet Nam	*492.4*	22.8	25.6	8.2	36.5
Indonesia	435.9	21.9	69.5	7.3	43.8
Iran	341.8	34.3	6.3	5.7	49.5
Guatemala	310.9	38.5	1.6	5.2	54.7
Netherlands	241.7	14.2	7.8	4.0	58.7
Spain	194.7	13.4	-9.5	3.2	62.0
Germany	185.6	6.2	4.0	3.1	65.1
Sri Lanka	182.2	15.0	54.3	3.0	68.1
Brazil	134.9	0.3	-3.4	2.3	70.4
Singapore	116.9	1.4	-2.6	2.0	72.3
France	107.9	-0.1	1.3	1.8	74.1
Peru	104.3	8.6	-1.2	1.7	75.9
USA	100.1	9.0	10.8	1.7	77.5

Table 3: Top importing countries or areas in 2010

Country or area	Value (million US$)	Avg. Growth (%) 06-10	Growth (%) 09-10	World share %	Cum.
World	5770.2	14.9	22.5	100.0	
USA	843.1	11.7	23.0	14.6	14.6
Germany	377.2	13.0	27.3	6.5	21.1
Japan	275.8	9.7	21.3	4.8	25.9
Saudi Arabia	270.4	25.5	54.3	4.7	30.6
United Arab Emirates	244.7	24.6	55.2	4.2	34.9
Malaysia	243.9	17.7	35.6	4.2	39.1
Netherlands	235.4	18.8	34.9	4.1	43.2
United Kingdom	228.5	16.8	25.4	4.0	47.1
Spain	184.6	14.9	-6.8	3.2	50.3
France	175.5	13.3	13.2	3.0	53.4
India	150.8	4.9	-11.4	2.6	56.0
Singapore	145.5	3.5	-4.2	2.5	58.5
Bangladesh	*142.4*	30.3	81.8	2.5	61.0
Nigeria	123.5	105.7	969.9	2.1	63.1
Mexico	121.2	9.5	-0.6	2.1	65.2

After a 3.6 percent drop in 2009, the value (in current prices) of exports of feeding stuff for animals, not including unmilled cereals (SITC group 081) bounced back by 8.9 percent in 2010 and amounted to 57.3 bln US$ (see table 2). Imports showed a similar development with a decline of 7.5 percent in 2009 but increased by 11.6 percent in 2010 to reach 62.5 bln US$ (see table 3). Graph 1 shows that the increase in exports for 2010 in this product group was exceeded by the increases in world exports of food and live animals (SITC section 0) of 11.2 percent and in total world exports of 21.2 percent. Exports of feeding stuff for animals, not including unmilled cereals (SITC group 081) accounted for 5.9 percent of world exports of SITC section 0 and 0.4 percent of total world exports in 2010 (see table 1).

In 2010, USA, Argentina and Brazil were the top exporting countries (see table 2). They accounted respectively for 16.2, 15.3 and 8.8 percent of world exports. Japan, Germany and Netherlands were the top destinations (see table 3). By MDG regions (see graph 2), Developed Europe accounted for a large share of trade in feeding stuff for animals (SITC group 081). In 2010, its exports and imports amounted respectively to 19.8 bln US$ and 26.6 bln US$, resulting in a trade deficit of 6.8 bln US$. Major deficits were also recorded by South-eastern Asia (-6.1 bln US$) and Developed Asia-Pacific (-3.7 bln US$). Latin America and the Caribbean and Developed North America recorded trade surpluses amounting respectively to 12.0 bln US$ and 7.6 bln US$.

Table 1: Imports (Imp.) and exports (Exp.), 1996-2010, in current prices

		1996	1997	1998	1999	2000	2001	2002	2003	2004	2005	2006	2007	2008	2009	2010
Values in Bln US$	Imp.	26.2	26.0	23.1	20.6	22.4	23.8	25.0	27.9	33.2	33.5	36.2	45.2	60.5	56.0	62.5
	Exp.	24.2	24.6	20.6	18.9	20.2	21.9	23.0	25.5	29.5	30.0	33.0	41.4	54.6	52.6	57.3
As a percentage of SITC section (%)	Imp.	5.9	6.0	5.5	4.9	5.5	5.6	5.6	5.4	5.7	5.3	5.2	5.4	6.2	6.3	6.4
	Exp.	5.6	5.8	5.1	4.8	5.2	5.5	5.4	5.2	5.3	5.0	4.9	5.2	5.7	6.0	5.9
As a percentage of world trade (%)	Imp.	0.5	0.5	0.4	0.4	0.3	0.4	0.4	0.4	0.4	0.3	0.3	0.3	0.4	0.4	0.4
	Exp.	0.5	0.4	0.4	0.3	0.3	0.4	0.4	0.3	0.3	0.3	0.3	0.3	0.3	0.4	0.4

Graph 1: Annual growth rates of exports, 1996–2010
(In percentage by year)

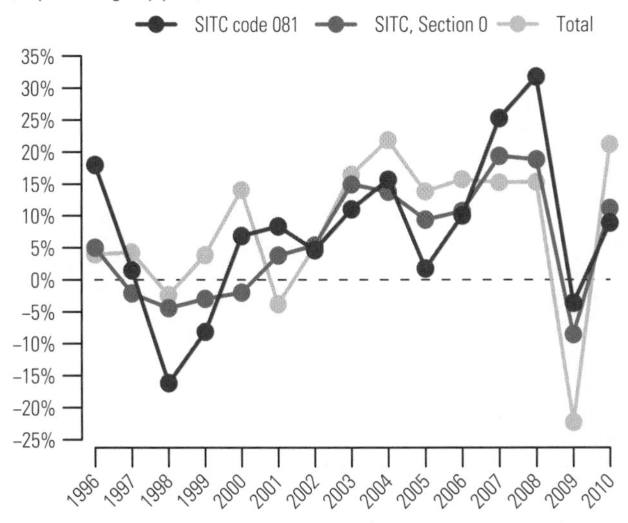

Table 2: Top exporting countries or areas in 2010

Country or area	Value (million US$)	Avg. Growth (%) 06-10	Growth (%) 09-10	World share %	Cum.
World	57 323.9	14.8	8.9	100.0	
USA	9 307.5	18.6	15.8	16.2	16.2
Argentina	8 784.6	17.2	1.9	15.3	31.6
Brazil	5 038.0	18.1	3.2	8.8	40.3
Netherlands	4 712.8	10.7	9.1	8.2	48.6
Germany	3 370.2	11.2	0.5	5.9	54.5
France	2 792.1	7.7	-0.3	4.9	59.3
India	2 066.7	13.0	21.0	3.6	62.9
China	1 979.2	38.7	10.9	3.5	66.4
Belgium	1 880.9	14.9	18.3	3.3	69.7
Peru	1 712.0	9.5	13.0	3.0	72.6
Canada	1 261.1	14.2	32.7	2.2	74.8
Denmark	1 035.8	3.4	6.5	1.8	76.7
Thailand	1 017.5	14.0	31.2	1.8	78.4
United Kingdom	1 000.0	10.6	10.4	1.7	80.2
Spain	962.4	15.6	16.4	1.7	81.9

Graph 2: Trade Balance by MDG regions 2010
(Bln US$)

Imports | Exports | Trade balance

Developed Asia-Pacific
Developed Europe
Developed N. America
South-eastern Europe
C I S
Northern Africa
Sub-Saharan Africa
Latin Am, Caribbean
Eastern Asia
Southern Asia
South-eastern Asia
Western Asia
Oceania

-30 -25 -20 -15 -10 -5 0 5 10 15 20

Table 3: Top importing countries or areas in 2010

Country or area	Value (million US$)	Avg. Growth (%) 06-10	Growth (%) 09-10	World share %	Cum.
World	62 502.4	14.6	11.6	100.0	
Japan	3 895.6	8.9	10.8	6.2	6.2
Germany	3 536.1	8.9	-0.2	5.7	11.9
Netherlands	3 416.5	17.1	9.7	5.5	17.4
China	3 301.0	26.3	77.5	5.3	22.6
Viet Nam	*2 946.9*	42.8	66.9	4.7	27.4
France	2 873.9	11.0	-1.3	4.6	32.0
United Kingdom	2 640.7	9.1	9.6	4.2	36.2
Italy	2 109.4	8.5	0.0	3.4	39.6
Rep. of Korea	1 895.2	16.5	11.5	3.0	42.6
Indonesia	1 871.0	20.7	11.4	3.0	45.6
Belgium	1 744.1	8.1	-2.5	2.8	48.4
Spain	1 736.5	4.4	-8.6	2.8	51.1
Thailand	1 623.9	18.6	17.2	2.6	53.7
USA	1 534.4	12.5	14.0	2.5	56.2
Canada	1 424.2	11.4	3.9	2.3	58.5

Source: UN Comtrade

091 Margarine and shortening

After a 19.6 percent drop in 2009, the value (in current prices) of exports of margarine and shortening (SITC group 091) increased by 2.2 percent in 2010 and amounted to 4.9 bln US$ (see table 2). Imports showed a similar development with an increase of 7.1 percent to 4.3 bln US$ (see table 3). Graph 1 shows that the increase in exports for 2010 in this product group was exceeded by the increases in world exports of food and live animals (SITC section 0) of 11.2 percent and in total world exports of 21.2 percent. Exports of margarine and shortening (SITC group 091) accounted for 0.5 percent of world exports of SITC section 0 and less than 0.1 percent of total world exports in 2010 (see table 1).

The top exporting countries in 2010 were Belgium, Netherlands and USA (see table 2). They accounted respectively for 12.5, 11.2 and 7.8 percent of world exports. Top destinations were France, Chile and Germany (see table 3). By MDG regions (see graph 2), Developed Europe's exports amounted to 2.6 bln US$ while imports reached 1.9 bln US$, resulting in a trade surplus of 0.7 bln US$. South-eastern Asia and Developed North America also recorded surpluses of 615 mln US$ and 208 mln US$ respectively. Significant deficits were recorded by Sub-Saharan Africa (-274 mln US$), Commonwealth of Independent States (-192 mln US$) and Eastern Asia (-146 mln US$) among others.

Table 1: Imports (Imp.) and exports (Exp.), 1996-2010, in current prices

		1996	1997	1998	1999	2000	2001	2002	2003	2004	2005	2006	2007	2008	2009	2010
Values in Bln US$	Imp.	1.3	1.4	1.4	1.4	1.3	1.4	1.5	1.7	2.1	2.3	2.6	3.4	4.8	4.0	4.3
	Exp.	1.7	2.0	1.9	1.6	1.4	1.4	1.6	2.0	2.4	2.6	3.0	4.0	6.0	4.8	4.9
As a percentage of	Imp.	0.3	0.3	0.3	0.3	0.3	0.3	0.3	0.3	0.4	0.4	0.4	0.4	0.5	0.4	0.4
SITC section (%)	Exp.	0.4	0.5	0.5	0.4	0.4	0.3	0.4	0.4	0.4	0.4	0.4	0.5	0.6	0.6	0.5
As a percentage of	Imp.	0.0	0.0	0.0	0.0	0.0	0.0	0.0	0.0	0.0	0.0	0.0	0.0	0.0	0.0	0.0
world trade (%)	Exp.	0.0	0.0	0.0	0.0	0.0	0.0	0.0	0.0	0.0	0.0	0.0	0.0	0.0	0.0	0.0

Graph 1: Annual growth rates of exports, 1996–2010

(In percentage by year)

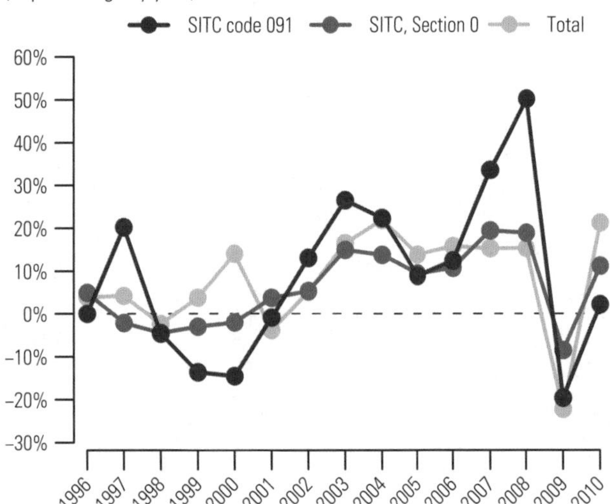

Table 2: Top exporting countries or areas in 2010

Country or area	Value (million US$)	Avg. Growth (%) 06-10	Growth (%) 09-10	World share %	Cum.
World	4908.0	13.3	2.2	100.0	
Belgium	615.6	13.3	-0.1	12.5	12.5
Netherlands	547.9	12.7	-16.1	11.2	23.7
USA	381.3	29.3	22.9	7.8	31.5
Indonesia	346.6	26.4	31.1	7.1	38.5
Malaysia	321.7	8.7	-22.3	6.6	45.1
Germany	298.4	9.7	-2.1	6.1	51.2
Sweden	221.1	11.7	9.3	4.5	55.7
Argentina	199.7	8.6	32.6	4.1	59.7
Denmark	179.1	0.6	-9.1	3.6	63.4
Poland	148.0	35.8	20.7	3.0	66.4
Turkey	124.4	11.9	33.7	2.5	68.9
Russian Federation	116.6	21.7	-1.3	2.4	71.3
United Kingdom	106.7	1.7	-5.5	2.2	73.5
Australia	89.0	14.2	28.3	1.8	75.3
Singapore	79.5	20.2	33.3	1.6	76.9

Graph 2: Trade Balance by MDG regions 2010

(Bln US$)

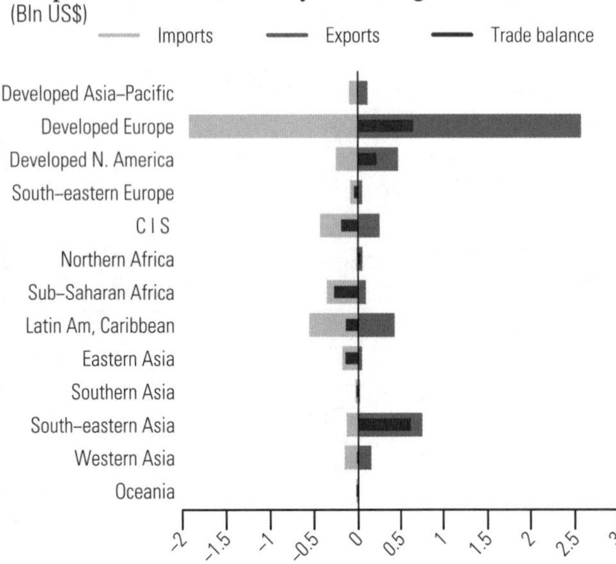

Table 3: Top importing countries or areas in 2010

Country or area	Value (million US$)	Avg. Growth (%) 06-10	Growth (%) 09-10	World share %	Cum.
World	4276.9	13.5	7.1	100.0	
France	396.5	14.4	0.1	9.3	9.3
Chile	278.1	12.5	23.4	6.5	15.8
Germany	229.0	1.5	-3.7	5.4	21.1
Russian Federation	153.8	20.2	72.4	3.6	24.7
Netherlands	153.6	17.5	6.1	3.6	28.3
USA	131.7	17.4	-18.2	3.1	31.4
Nigeria	128.8	98.9	109.8	3.0	34.4
Canada	117.5	23.1	5.0	2.7	37.2
United Kingdom	115.0	12.8	0.9	2.7	39.8
Belgium	105.5	10.8	-10.9	2.5	42.3
Poland	98.2	36.2	36.2	2.3	44.6
Ukraine	91.9	14.5	3.6	2.1	46.8
Spain	87.8	8.6	0.6	2.1	48.8
Italy	80.7	9.5	6.1	1.9	50.7
Czech Rep.	78.3	25.7	31.8	1.8	52.5

During the recent five years, the value (in current prices) of exports of edible products and preparations, nes (SITC group 098) increased on average by 10.0 percent and amounted to 52.2 bln US$ in 2010 (see table 2). Imports, displaying a similar development, increased on average by 9.8 percent to reach 54.6 bln US$ (see table 3). Graph 1 shows that the increase in exports for 2010 in this product group was exceeded by the increases in world exports of food and live animals (SITC section 0) of 11.2 percent and in total world exports of 21.2 percent. Exports of edible products and preparations, nes (SITC group 098) accounted for 5.4 percent of world exports of SITC section 0 and 0.3 percent of total world exports in 2010 (see table 1).

USA, Germany and Netherlands were the top exporting countries in 2010 (see table 2). They accounted respectively for 11.1, 8.5 and 8.4 percent of world exports. Top destinations were USA, United Kingdom and Germany (see table 3). By MDG regions (see graph 2), Developed Europe accounted for a large share of trade in edible products and preparations, nes (SITC group 098). In 2010, its exports and imports amounted respectively to 27.9 bln US$ and 21.9 bln US$, resulting in a trade surplus of 6.0 bln US$. A major trade surplus was also recorded by Developed North America (+1.4 bln US$). Top trade deficits were recorded by Western Asia (-2.1 bln US$), Commonwealth of Independent States (-1.7 bln US$) and Latin America and the Caribbean (-1.5 bln US$).

Table 1: Imports (Imp.) and exports (Exp.), 1996-2010, in current prices

		1996	1997	1998	1999	2000	2001	2002	2003	2004	2005	2006	2007	2008	2009	2010
Values in Bln US$	Imp.	17.7	18.0	18.3	18.9	18.4	20.0	22.1	26.2	30.9	34.1	37.6	44.3	51.9	51.0	54.6
	Exp.	18.0	17.9	17.5	17.5	17.6	19.1	20.8	24.7	29.2	32.6	35.7	41.9	49.3	47.5	52.2
As a percentage of SITC section (%)	Imp.	4.0	4.2	4.3	4.5	4.5	4.7	4.9	5.1	5.3	5.4	5.4	5.3	5.3	5.7	5.6
	Exp.	4.1	4.2	4.3	4.4	4.6	4.8	4.9	5.1	5.3	5.4	5.3	5.2	5.2	5.5	5.4
As a percentage of world trade (%)	Imp.	0.3	0.3	0.3	0.3	0.3	0.3	0.3	0.3	0.3	0.3	0.3	0.3	0.3	0.4	0.4
	Exp.	0.3	0.3	0.3	0.3	0.3	0.3	0.3	0.3	0.3	0.3	0.3	0.3	0.3	0.4	0.3

Graph 1: Annual growth rates of exports, 1996–2010

(In percentage by year)

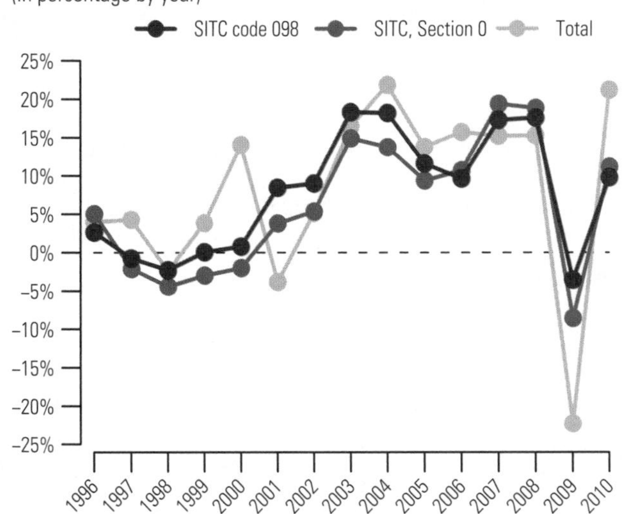

Graph 2: Trade Balance by MDG regions 2010

(Bln US$)

Imports — Exports — Trade balance

Developed Asia-Pacific
Developed Europe
Developed N. America
South-eastern Europe
C I S
Northern Africa
Sub-Saharan Africa
Latin Am, Caribbean
Eastern Asia
Southern Asia
South-eastern Asia
Western Asia
Oceania

-25 -20 -15 -10 -5 0 5 10 15 20 25 30

Table 2: Top exporting countries or areas in 2010

Country or area	Value (million US$)	Avg. Growth (%) 06-10	Growth (%) 09-10	World share %	Cum.
World	52217.3	10.0	9.8	100.0	
USA	5788.2	6.2	10.0	11.1	11.1
Germany	4413.5	7.8	-0.1	8.5	19.5
Netherlands	4408.6	11.7	3.8	8.4	28.0
France	3063.3	9.9	9.0	5.9	33.8
Italy	2290.9	7.9	4.6	4.4	38.2
China	2145.0	11.9	17.6	4.1	42.3
Ireland	1901.2	-1.8	2.9	3.6	46.0
Belgium	1612.4	6.0	7.1	3.1	49.1
United Kingdom	1582.5	4.8	9.9	3.0	52.1
Thailand	1534.0	15.6	17.2	2.9	55.0
Denmark	1515.3	4.5	-2.8	2.9	57.9
Canada	1416.9	2.6	10.9	2.7	60.7
Singapore	1388.3	20.1	22.0	2.7	63.3
Spain	1263.9	9.5	-3.1	2.4	65.7
Poland	1146.3	20.4	19.2	2.2	67.9

Table 3: Top importing countries or areas in 2010

Country or area	Value (million US$)	Avg. Growth (%) 06-10	Growth (%) 09-10	World share %	Cum.
World	54601.9	9.8	7.1	100.0	
USA	3501.8	5.0	13.6	6.4	6.4
United Kingdom	3198.8	9.7	-3.0	5.9	12.3
Germany	3094.6	4.8	-9.7	5.7	17.9
France	2218.9	8.2	0.8	4.1	22.0
Canada	2215.1	8.6	11.5	4.1	26.1
Japan	1852.4	3.6	10.9	3.4	29.5
Spain	1707.4	4.8	-2.7	3.1	32.6
China	1648.2	28.4	24.6	3.0	35.6
Netherlands	1440.2	9.6	-0.6	2.6	38.2
Australia	1432.2	11.8	15.5	2.6	40.9
Saudi Arabia	1300.8	14.4	20.9	2.4	43.2
Russian Federation	1268.0	19.0	24.5	2.3	45.6
Belgium	1228.7	7.3	-0.9	2.3	47.8
China, Hong Kong SAR	1163.7	12.4	19.6	2.1	49.9
Italy	1094.9	8.3	-0.2	2.0	52.0

Beverages and tobacco

(SITC Section 1)

111 Non-alcoholic beverages, nes

After a 9.6 percent drop in 2009, the value (in current prices) of exports of non-alcoholic beverages, nes (SITC group 111) increased by 2.5 percent in 2010 and amounted to 16.4 bln US$ (see table 2). Imports, after an 8.2 percent drop in 2009, also increased by 2.6 percent to reach 15.5 bln US$ in 2010 (see table 3). Graph 1 shows that the increase in exports for 2010 in this product group was well below the increases in world exports of beverages and tobacco (SITC section 1) of 11.2 percent and in total world exports of 21.2 percent. Exports of non-alcoholic beverages, nes (SITC group 111) accounted for 1.7 percent of world exports of SITC section 1 and 0.1 percent of world exports in 2010 (see table 1).

The top exporting countries in 2010 were Austria, Germany and France (see table 2). They accounted respectively for 10.8, 9.3 and 9.2 percent of world exports. Top destinations were USA, United Kingdom and Germany (see table 3). By MDG regions (see graph 2), Developed Europe accounted for a majority of trade in non-alcoholic beverages, nes (SITC group 111). In 2010, its exports and imports amounted respectively to 10.9 bln US$ and 7.5 bln US$, resulting in a trade surplus of 3.4 bln US$. Developed North America, Developed Asia-Pacific and Sub-Saharan Africa recorded trade deficits amounting respectively to 1.6 bln US$, 0.5 bln US$ and 0.3 bln US$.

Table 1: Imports (Imp.) and exports (Exp.), 1996-2010, in current prices

		1996	1997	1998	1999	2000	2001	2002	2003	2004	2005	2006	2007	2008	2009	2010
Values in Bln US$	Imp.	4.1	4.2	4.4	5.0	5.2	5.7	6.6	7.9	9.1	10.4	12.0	14.8	16.5	15.1	15.5
	Exp.	4.5	4.6	4.4	5.1	5.2	5.8	6.6	8.3	9.8	10.8	12.7	15.0	17.7	16.0	16.4
As a percentage of SITC section (%)	Imp.	0.9	1.0	1.1	1.2	1.3	1.3	1.5	1.5	1.6	1.6	1.7	1.8	1.7	1.7	1.6
	Exp.	1.0	1.1	1.1	1.3	1.3	1.4	1.6	1.7	1.8	1.8	1.9	1.9	1.9	1.8	1.7
As a percentage of world trade (%)	Imp.	0.1	0.1	0.1	0.1	0.1	0.1	0.1	0.1	0.1	0.1	0.1	0.1	0.1	0.1	0.1
	Exp.	0.1	0.1	0.1	0.1	0.1	0.1	0.1	0.1	0.1	0.1	0.1	0.1	0.1	0.1	0.1

Graph 1: Annual growth rates of exports, 1996–2010

(In percentage by year)

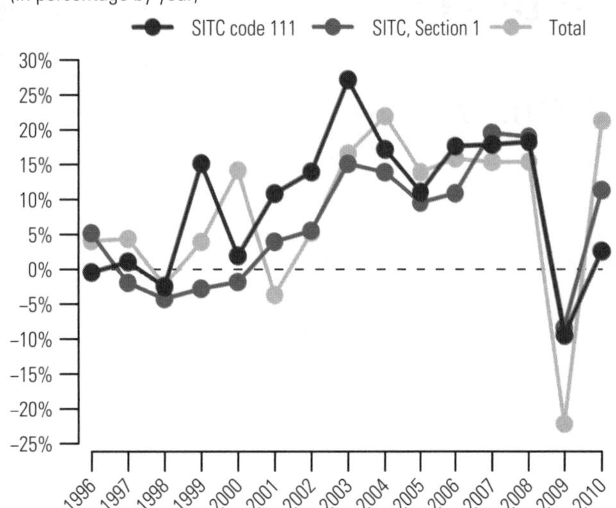

Table 2: Top exporting countries or areas in 2010

Country or area	Value (million US$)	Avg. Growth (%) 06-10	Growth (%) 09-10	World share %	Cum.
World	16405.4	6.6	2.5	100.0	
Austria	1763.6	-1.1	9.5	10.8	10.8
Germany	1527.4	2.5	-4.2	9.3	20.1
France	1515.7	-2.1	-1.5	9.2	29.3
Switzerland	1353.7	28.0	6.7	8.3	37.6
Netherlands	1253.1	7.5	-2.5	7.6	45.2
USA	896.4	12.6	0.0	5.5	50.7
Belgium	776.1	-2.3	-11.5	4.7	55.4
Italy	626.6	6.8	3.0	3.8	59.2
Syria	*623.5*	76.4	-26.2	3.8	63.0
United Kingdom	544.1	6.4	10.2	3.3	66.3
China	458.7	5.7	4.8	2.8	69.1
Thailand	388.2	32.2	43.8	2.4	71.5
Mexico	282.2	0.1	0.5	1.7	73.2
Poland	233.8	7.6	-3.6	1.4	74.6
Spain	212.1	-3.0	-6.9	1.3	75.9

Graph 2: Trade Balance by MDG regions 2010

(Bln US$)

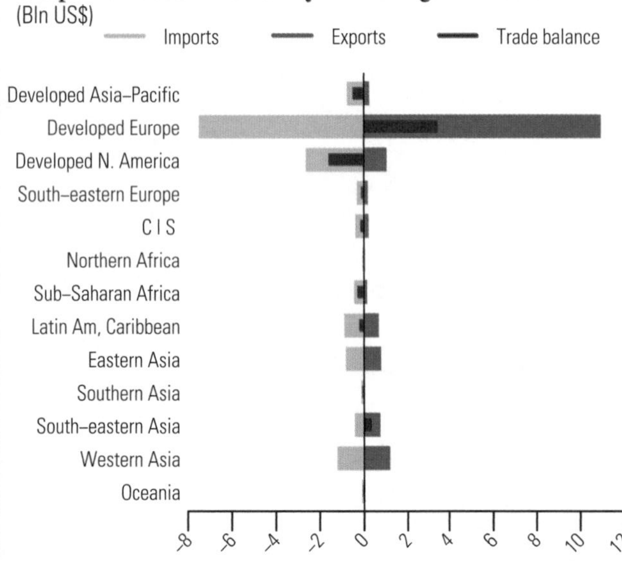

Table 3: Top importing countries or areas in 2010

Country or area	Value (million US$)	Avg. Growth (%) 06-10	Growth (%) 09-10	World share %	Cum.
World	15506.0	6.6	2.6	100.0	
USA	1945.7	0.0	10.5	12.5	12.5
United Kingdom	1089.4	0.8	-2.7	7.0	19.6
Germany	1066.4	5.5	23.0	6.9	26.5
Belgium	865.2	4.2	2.1	5.6	32.0
France	785.9	5.5	-9.8	5.1	37.1
Netherlands	723.1	1.4	-13.3	4.7	41.8
Canada	657.5	18.1	1.5	4.2	46.0
China, Hong Kong SAR	594.4	10.5	6.3	3.8	49.8
Japan	489.2	-2.8	-4.0	3.2	53.0
Spain	354.6	10.1	1.1	2.3	55.3
Ireland	301.7	3.6	-7.7	1.9	57.2
Italy	274.8	5.9	-2.2	1.8	59.0
Switzerland	249.0	4.8	8.0	1.6	60.6
Iraq	*196.0*	28.7	-27.4	1.3	61.9
Australia	188.6	12.8	6.6	1.2	63.1

Alcoholic beverages 112

After a 11.8 percent drop in 2009, the value (in current prices) of exports of alcoholic beverages (SITC group 112) increased by 11.0 percent in 2010 and amounted to 64.2 bln US$ (see table 2). Imports, showing a similar development, declined by 12.1 percent in 2009 and increased by 8.8 percent in 2010 to reach 63.7 bln US$ (see able 3). Graph 1 shows that the increase in exports for 2010 in this product group was similar to the increase in world exports of beverages and tobacco (SITC section 1) of 11.2 percent but below the increase in total world exports of 21.2 percent. Exports of alcoholic beverages (SITC group 112) accounted for 6.6 percent of world exports of SITC section 1 and 0.4 percent of world exports in 2010 (see table 1).

In 2010, France was the top exporting country: it accounted for 19.8 percent of world exports (see table 2). Other major exporting countries were United Kingdom and Italy, respectively with 12.6 and 9.8 percent of world exports. USA, United Kingdom and Germany were the top destinations (see table 3). By MDG regions (see graph 2), Developed Europe accounted for a large share of exports and imports of alcoholic beverages, nes (SITC group 112). In 2010, its exports and imports amounted respectively to 44.1 bln US$ and 28.3 bln US$, resulting in a trade surplus of 15.8 bln US$. Developed North America recorded a deficit of 13.6 bln US$ and Latin America and the Caribbean recorded a surplus amounting to 4.2 bln US$.

Table 1: Imports (Imp.) and exports (Exp.), 1996-2010, in current prices

		1996	1997	1998	1999	2000	2001	2002	2003	2004	2005	2006	2007	2008	2009	2010
Values in Bln US$	Imp.	27.6	28.7	29.6	30.5	29.6	30.7	33.5	38.6	43.9	47.3	52.0	61.4	66.6	58.5	63.7
	Exp.	28.9	29.2	29.1	30.0	28.9	29.7	32.9	38.8	43.5	45.8	50.9	60.9	65.7	57.9	64.2
As a percentage of SITC section (%)	Imp.	6.2	6.6	7.0	7.3	7.2	7.3	7.5	7.6	7.5	7.4	7.5	7.4	6.8	6.6	6.5
	Exp.	6.7	6.9	7.2	7.6	7.5	7.4	7.8	8.0	7.9	7.6	7.6	7.6	6.9	6.6	6.6
As a percentage of world trade (%)	Imp.	0.5	0.5	0.5	0.5	0.5	0.5	0.5	0.5	0.5	0.4	0.4	0.4	0.4	0.5	0.4
	Exp.	0.6	0.5	0.5	0.5	0.5	0.5	0.5	0.5	0.5	0.4	0.4	0.4	0.4	0.5	0.4

Graph 1: Annual growth rates of exports, 1996–2010

(In percentage by year)

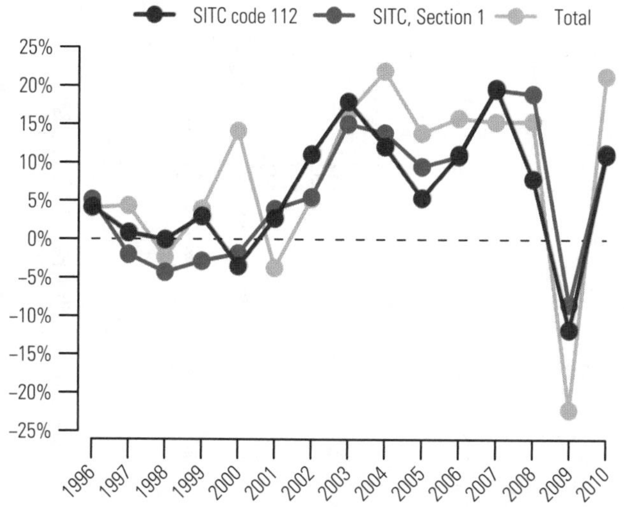

Table 2: Top exporting countries or areas in 2010

Country or area	Value (million US$)	Avg. Growth (%) 06-10	Growth (%) 09-10	World share %	Cum.
World	64237.5	6.0	11.0	100.0	
France	12714.5	2.8	13.1	19.8	19.8
United Kingdom	8112.5	6.0	13.1	12.6	32.4
Italy	6287.5	6.1	7.0	9.8	42.2
Germany	3801.3	7.5	8.7	5.9	48.1
Spain	3190.8	6.1	-1.6	5.0	53.1
USA	2890.7	9.4	20.1	4.5	57.6
Mexico	2753.8	1.8	9.7	4.3	61.9
Netherlands	2521.7	1.3	0.5	3.9	65.8
Australia	2009.7	-1.7	5.9	3.1	68.9
Singapore	1735.6	16.6	26.2	2.7	71.6
Chile	1580.5	12.8	12.4	2.5	74.1
Ireland	1343.5	-2.3	4.3	2.1	76.2
Belgium	1251.2	6.8	-8.8	1.9	78.1
Portugal	1080.3	6.1	5.8	1.7	79.8
South Africa	932.2	12.5	11.1	1.5	81.3

Graph 2: Trade Balance by MDG regions 2010

(Bln US$)

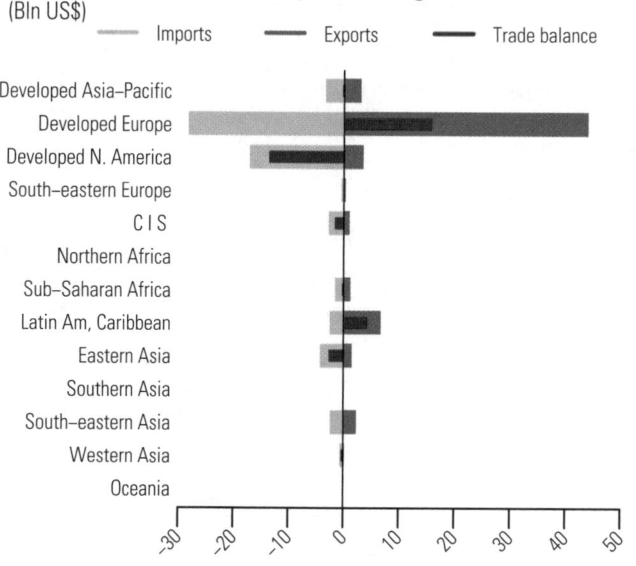

Table 3: Top importing countries or areas in 2010

Country or area	Value (million US$)	Avg. Growth (%) 06-10	Growth (%) 09-10	World share %	Cum.
World	63678.2	5.2	8.8	100.0	
USA	14072.8	1.2	8.2	22.1	22.1
United Kingdom	6188.1	1.2	6.7	9.7	31.8
Germany	4765.0	3.4	2.0	7.5	39.3
Canada	3022.6	7.6	15.8	4.7	44.0
France	2532.2	6.2	2.0	4.0	48.0
Russian Federation	2093.8	10.5	28.0	3.3	51.3
Japan	2006.1	1.2	10.8	3.2	54.5
Netherlands	1831.6	5.8	2.4	2.9	57.3
Spain	1783.5	-0.7	4.1	2.8	60.1
Belgium	1664.9	2.4	-7.2	2.6	62.8
China	1565.6	30.0	48.9	2.5	65.2
Singapore	1548.9	12.2	22.7	2.4	67.6
Italy	1407.6	2.8	4.9	2.2	69.9
China, Hong Kong SAR	1400.0	32.6	51.1	2.2	72.1
Switzerland	1348.5	6.8	3.9	2.1	74.2

Source: UN Comtrade

121 Tobacco, unmanufactured; tobacco refuse

After several years of continuous growth marked by a peak of 11.4 bln US$ in 2009, the value (in current prices) of exports of unmanufactured tobacco; tobacco refuse (SITC group 121) took a slight 4.0 percent drop in 2010 and totaled 10.9 bln US$ (see table 2). During the same period, imports have been increasing on average by 11.8 percent to reach 12.2 bln US$. Graph 1 shows the decrease in exports for 2010 in this product group in contrast to the increases in world exports of beverages and tobacco (SITC section 1) of 11.2 percent and in total world exports of 21.2 percent. Exports of unmanufactured tobacco; tobacco refuse (SITC group 121) accounted for 1.1 percent of world exports of SITC section 1 and 0.1 percent of total world exports in 2010 (see table 1).

In 2010, Brazil, the top exporting country accounted for 24.7 percent of world exports (see table 2). Other major exporting countries were USA and India, respectively with 10.7 and 6.5 percent of world exports. Russian Federation, Germany and Netherlands were the top destinations (see table 3). By MDG regions (see graph 2), Latin America and the Caribbean recorded a surplus amounting to 2.7 bln US$. Significant deficits were recorded by Developed Europe (-2.2 bln US$), Commonwealth of Independent States (-1.4 bln US$) and South-eastern Asia (-0.7 bln USD).

Table 1: Imports (Imp.) and exports (Exp.), 1996-2010, in current prices

		1996	1997	1998	1999	2000	2001	2002	2003	2004	2005	2006	2007	2008	2009	2010
Values in Bln US$	Imp.	7.4	8.2	7.6	7.6	6.9	7.0	7.3	7.4	7.7	7.7	7.8	9.2	10.5	11.8	12.2
	Exp.	6.6	7.0	6.4	6.3	5.5	5.8	5.3	5.7	6.8	7.0	7.5	8.7	10.3	11.4	10.9
As a percentage of SITC section (%)	Imp.	1.7	1.9	1.8	1.8	1.7	1.7	1.6	1.4	1.3	1.2	1.1	1.1	1.1	1.3	1.3
	Exp.	1.5	1.6	1.6	1.6	1.4	1.5	1.3	1.2	1.2	1.2	1.1	1.1	1.1	1.3	1.1
As a percentage of world trade (%)	Imp.	0.1	0.1	0.1	0.1	0.1	0.1	0.1	0.1	0.1	0.1	0.1	0.1	0.1	0.1	0.1
	Exp.	0.1	0.1	0.1	0.1	0.1	0.1	0.1	0.1	0.1	0.1	0.1	0.1	0.1	0.1	0.1

Graph 1: Annual growth rates of exports, 1996–2010

(In percentage by year)

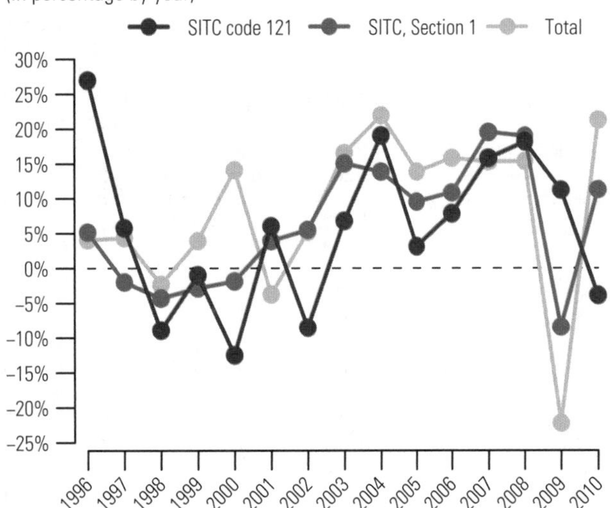

Table 2: Top exporting countries or areas in 2010

Country or area	Value (million US$)	Avg. Growth (%) 06-10	Growth (%) 09-10	World share %	Cum.
World	10941.6	9.9	-4.0	100.0	
Brazil	2706.7	12.4	-9.5	24.7	24.7
USA	1175.1	0.7	1.0	10.7	35.5
India	713.3	26.7	-3.5	6.5	42.0
China	615.9	20.9	15.5	5.6	47.6
Malawi	585.2	9.3	-23.0	5.3	53.0
Zimbabwe	420.0	12.3	73.7	3.8	56.8
Turkey	401.3	-5.5	-18.3	3.7	60.5
Belgium	381.6	21.9	-5.0	3.5	64.0
Germany	352.9	7.6	5.8	3.2	67.2
Argentina	291.5	5.1	-18.9	2.7	69.9
Italy	289.1	7.2	1.5	2.6	72.5
Greece	278.8	-2.0	-26.7	2.5	75.0
Indonesia	195.6	17.5	13.3	1.8	76.8
France	194.3	3.4	-5.3	1.8	78.6
Bulgaria	191.2	19.6	-34.0	1.7	80.4

Graph 2: Trade Balance by MDG regions 2010

(Bln US$)

Imports — Exports — Trade balance

Developed Asia-Pacific
Developed Europe
Developed N. America
South-eastern Europe
C I S
Northern Africa
Sub-Saharan Africa
Latin Am, Caribbean
Eastern Asia
Southern Asia
South-eastern Asia
Western Asia
Oceania

-5 -4 -3 -2 -1 0 1 2 3 4

Table 3: Top importing countries or areas in 2010

Country or area	Value (million US$)	Avg. Growth (%) 06-10	Growth (%) 09-10	World share %	Cum.
World	12201.1	11.8	3.5	100.0	
Russian Federation	1032.6	11.0	-0.8	8.5	8.5
Germany	985.0	5.0	0.5	8.1	16.5
Netherlands	768.0	11.4	0.4	6.3	22.8
USA	721.8	-1.0	-21.9	5.9	28.7
China	707.6	14.7	-4.6	5.8	34.5
Zimbabwe	541.3	88.9	1545.1	4.4	39.0
Belgium	519.7	19.5	-12.8	4.3	43.2
Japan	427.6	19.1	4.9	3.5	46.7
Poland	398.6	17.5	22.0	3.3	50.0
Indonesia	378.7	26.0	30.5	3.1	53.1
Viet Nam	*359.1*	41.9	66.9	2.9	56.1
Ukraine	314.3	7.4	15.4	2.6	58.6
United Kingdom	299.3	8.3	-17.4	2.5	61.1
Turkey	275.5	12.5	-5.0	2.3	63.3
Switzerland	259.9	12.3	-2.5	2.1	65.5

Tobacco, manufactured (whether or not containing tobacco substitutes) 122

During the recent five years, the value (in current prices) of exports of manufactured tobacco, whether or not containing tobacco substitutes (SITC group 122) increased on average by 7.2 percent and amounted to 25.1 bln US$ in 2010 (see table 2). Imports, displaying a similar development, increased on average by 5.4 percent to 25.8 bln US$ (see table 3). Graph 1 shows that the increase in exports for 2010 in this product group was below the increases in world exports of beverages and tobacco (SITC section 1) of 11.2 percent and in total world exports of 21.2 percent. Exports of manufactured tobacco, whether or not containing tobacco substitutes (SITC group 122) accounted for 2.6 percent of world exports of SITC section 1 and 0.2 percent of world exports in 2010 (see table 1).

Germany, Netherlands and Poland were the top major exporting countries in 2010 (see table 2). They accounted respectively for 16.9, 16.0 and 6.1 percent of world exports. Japan, Italy and France were the top destinations (see table 3). By MDG regions (see graph 2), Developed Europe accounted for a majority of trade in manufactured tobacco (SITC group 122). In 2010, its exports and imports amounted respectively to 14.7 bln US$ and 13.1 bln US$, resulting in a trade surplus of 1.6 bln US$. Latin America and the Caribbean recorded a surplus of 1.8 bln US$. Top deficits were recorded by Developed Asia-Pacific (-3.3 bln US$) and Western Asia (-1.1 bln US$).

Table 1: Imports (Imp.) and exports (Exp.), 1996-2010, in current prices

		1996	1997	1998	1999	2000	2001	2002	2003	2004	2005	2006	2007	2008	2009	2010
Values in Bln US$	Imp.	14.8	15.0	14.2	13.9	13.9	14.6	15.2	16.7	19.3	21.1	20.9	22.8	24.3	24.4	25.8
	Exp.	20.5	19.7	18.2	16.2	16.1	15.2	15.8	16.0	16.9	18.2	19.0	21.3	23.7	23.6	25.1
As a percentage of SITC section (%)	Imp.	3.3	3.5	3.4	3.3	3.4	3.4	3.4	3.3	3.3	3.3	3.0	2.7	2.5	2.7	2.6
	Exp.	4.7	4.6	4.5	4.1	4.2	3.8	3.7	3.3	3.1	3.0	2.8	2.7	2.5	2.7	2.6
As a percentage of world trade (%)	Imp.	0.3	0.3	0.3	0.2	0.2	0.2	0.2	0.2	0.2	0.2	0.2	0.2	0.2	0.2	0.2
	Exp.	0.4	0.4	0.3	0.3	0.3	0.2	0.2	0.2	0.2	0.2	0.2	0.2	0.1	0.2	0.2

Graph 1: Annual growth rates of exports, 1996–2010

(In percentage by year)

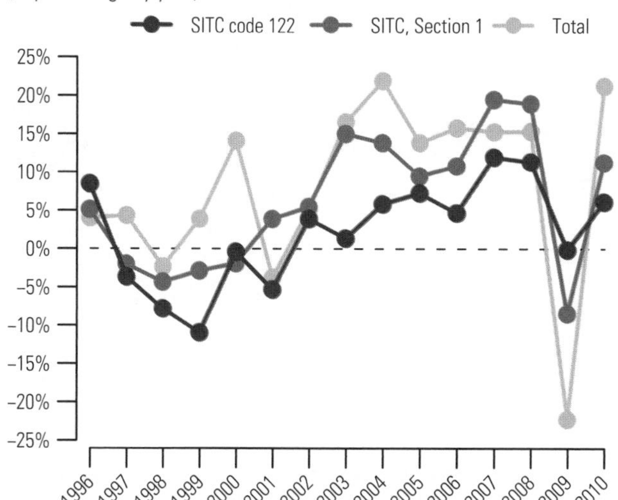

Table 2: Top exporting countries or areas in 2010

Country or area	Value (million US$)	Avg. Growth (%) 06-10	Growth (%) 09-10	World share %	Cum.
World	25061.0	7.2	6.1	100.0	
Germany	4225.4	5.8	0.1	16.9	16.9
Netherlands	4018.6	0.4	0.7	16.0	32.9
Poland	1517.0	36.8	6.8	6.1	38.9
Cuba	*1195.6*	53.4	72.3	4.8	43.7
China, Hong Kong SAR	797.5	7.4	11.4	3.2	46.9
Belgium	767.0	14.2	5.5	3.1	50.0
Switzerland	649.6	12.9	-0.1	2.6	52.6
France	573.2	3.3	0.2	2.3	54.8
Singapore	563.0	9.2	15.4	2.2	57.1
United Arab Emirates	556.1	18.2	15.5	2.2	59.3
Rep. of Korea	538.6	12.5	14.4	2.1	61.5
United Kingdom	516.4	-13.3	-15.8	2.1	63.5
Romania	503.7	161.0	-1.0	2.0	65.5
USA	494.9	-22.4	-7.3	2.0	67.5
Indonesia	477.0	19.1	12.8	1.9	69.4

Graph 2: Trade Balance by MDG regions 2010

(Bln US$)

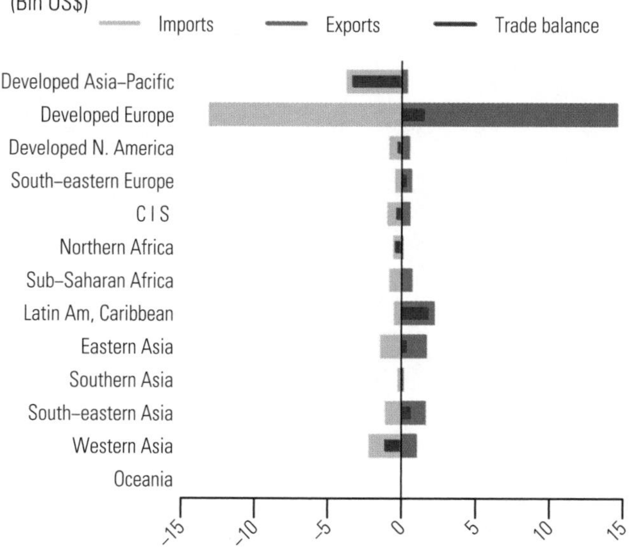

Table 3: Top importing countries or areas in 2010

Country or area	Value (million US$)	Avg. Growth (%) 06-10	Growth (%) 09-10	World share %	Cum.
World	25764.0	5.4	5.7	100.0	
Japan	3540.7	2.4	0.4	13.7	13.7
Italy	2880.8	4.6	-4.4	11.2	24.9
France	2069.4	-1.1	-2.7	8.0	33.0
Spain	1777.8	6.1	-3.2	6.9	39.9
United Kingdom	1176.2	26.6	240.7	4.6	44.4
Germany	1073.4	1.7	-21.4	4.2	48.6
USA	733.7	4.5	6.3	2.8	51.4
Belgium	712.0	5.2	17.7	2.8	54.2
Saudi Arabia	692.0	10.7	23.8	2.7	56.9
Netherlands	664.0	1.0	3.1	2.6	59.5
China, Hong Kong SAR	546.0	5.4	6.4	2.1	61.6
Austria	504.2	34.7	61.7	2.0	63.5
Other Asia, nes	500.3	-4.6	12.1	1.9	65.5
Singapore	488.0	10.7	16.4	1.9	67.4
Greece	268.8	1.6	-22.8	1.0	68.4

Source: UN Comtrade

Crude materials, inedible, except fuels
(SITC Section 2)

211 Hides and skins (except furskins), raw

The value (in current prices) of exports of raw hides and skins, except furskins (SITC group 211) decreased during the recent two consecutive years but bounced back by 55.6 percent in 2010 amounting to 6.4 bln US$ (see table 2). Imports showed a similar development with an increase of 49.5 percent and reached 6.3 bln US$ in 2010 (see table 3). Graph 1 shows that the increase in exports for 2010 in this product group was well above the increases in world exports of inedible crude materials, except fuels (SITC section 2) of 40.2 percent and in total world exports of 21.2 percent. Exports of raw hides and skins, except furskins (SITC group 211) accounted for 0.9 percent of world exports of SITC section 2 and less than 0.1 percent of total world exports in 2010 (see table 1).

USA was the top exporting country in 2010: it accounted for 31.7 percent of world exports (see table 2). Other major exporting countries were Australia and France, respectively with 10.1 and 5.9 percent of world exports. China was the top destination with a share of 32.5 percent of world imports. Other major destinations were Italy and China, Hong Kong SAR (see table 3). By MDG regions (see graph 2), Developed North America recorded a trade surplus of 2.3 bln US$. Major trade surpluses were also recorded by Developed Asia-Pacific (+0.8 bln US$) and Developed Europe (+0.4 bln US$). Eastern Asia recorded a trade deficit amounting to 2.8 bln US$.

Table 1: Imports (Imp.) and exports (Exp.), 1996-2010, in current prices

		1996	1997	1998	1999	2000	2001	2002	2003	2004	2005	2006	2007	2008	2009	2010
Values in Bln US$	Imp.	6.3	6.1	4.9	4.1	5.2	5.8	5.5	5.5	5.6	5.6	5.9	6.3	6.2	4.2	6.3
	Exp.	5.9	5.8	4.6	3.9	5.1	5.7	5.4	5.6	5.7	5.7	6.0	6.3	5.9	4.1	6.4
As a percentage of SITC section (%)	Imp.	2.5	2.4	2.1	1.8	2.1	2.5	2.3	1.9	1.5	1.3	1.2	1.0	0.8	0.8	0.8
	Exp.	2.6	2.5	2.2	2.0	2.4	2.8	2.5	2.2	1.8	1.6	1.3	1.1	0.9	0.8	0.9
As a percentage of world trade (%)	Imp.	0.1	0.1	0.1	0.1	0.1	0.1	0.1	0.1	0.1	0.1	0.0	0.0	0.0	0.0	0.0
	Exp.	0.1	0.1	0.1	0.1	0.1	0.1	0.1	0.1	0.1	0.1	0.1	0.0	0.0	0.0	0.0

Graph 1: Annual growth rates of exports, 1996–2010
(In percentage by year)

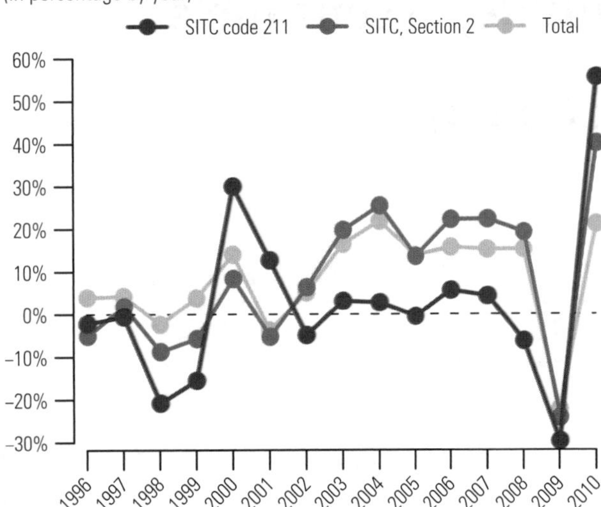

Table 2: Top exporting countries or areas in 2010

Country or area	Value (million US$)	Avg. Growth (%) 06-10	Growth (%) 09-10	World share %	Cum.
World	6433.6	1.7	55.6	100.0	
USA	2042.1	2.7	56.8	31.7	31.7
Australia	647.3	6.7	58.0	10.1	41.8
France	379.6	-0.8	64.6	5.9	47.7
Germany	325.8	1.9	98.3	5.1	52.8
Canada	284.6	0.1	77.1	4.4	57.2
Spain	269.3	2.0	51.9	4.2	61.4
United Kingdom	248.5	2.7	72.5	3.9	65.2
China, Hong Kong SAR	229.9	0.5	33.9	3.6	68.8
Netherlands	229.8	3.6	32.9	3.6	72.4
Italy	226.8	6.2	59.6	3.5	75.9
New Zealand	137.6	1.9	32.2	2.1	78.0
Ireland	122.8	2.3	70.0	1.9	80.0
South Africa	97.4	5.8	48.0	1.5	81.5
Japan	93.6	3.4	9.1	1.5	82.9
Austria	86.2	8.6	60.3	1.3	84.3

Graph 2: Trade Balance by MDG regions 2010
(Bln US$)

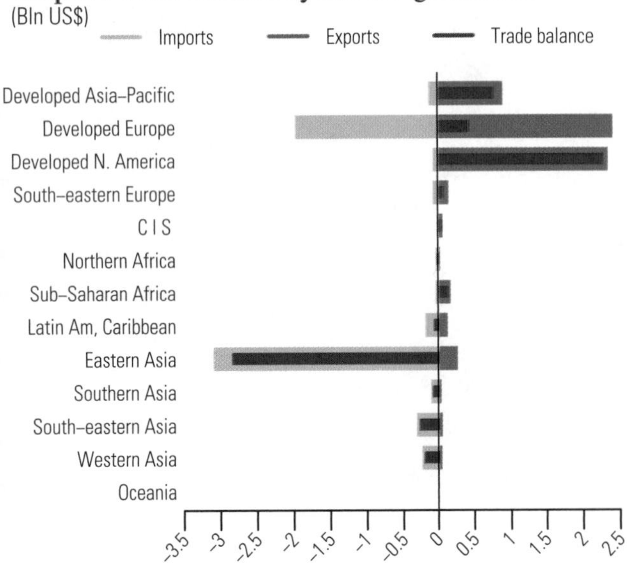

Table 3: Top importing countries or areas in 2010

Country or area	Value (million US$)	Avg. Growth (%) 06-10	Growth (%) 09-10	World share %	Cum.
World	6263.1	1.5	49.5	100.0	
China	2033.0	9.0	41.0	32.5	32.5
Italy	1013.8	-3.1	69.6	16.2	48.6
China, Hong Kong SAR	414.1	7.3	37.6	6.6	55.3
Rep. of Korea	407.3	1.3	41.4	6.5	61.8
Other Asia, nes	244.0	-2.7	51.6	3.9	65.7
Turkey	225.3	-9.5	84.3	3.6	69.3
Germany	184.2	0.0	92.3	2.9	72.2
Thailand	182.3	5.9	53.3	2.9	75.1
Austria	163.8	3.6	166.0	2.6	77.7
Mexico	152.0	-1.2	42.9	2.4	80.1
Netherlands	126.6	4.4	66.3	2.0	82.2
Japan	122.5	-5.8	26.4	2.0	84.1
France	100.4	-1.9	31.7	1.6	85.7
Viet Nam	*77.5*	-0.1	66.9	1.2	87.0
India	74.7	4.6	-3.1	1.2	88.2

After a 20.7 percent drop in 2009, the value (in current prices) of exports of raw furskins, including heads, tails, paws, etc (SITC group 212) bounced back by 57.8 percent in 2010 to reach 3.8 bln US$ (see table 2). Similarly, imports decreased by 18.7 percent in 2009 but increased by 51.8 percent in 2010 and totaled 2.5 bln US$ (see table 3). Graph 1 shows that the increase in exports for 2010 in this product group was well above the increases in world exports of inedible crude materials, except fuels (SITC section 2) of 40.2 percent and in total world exports of 21.2 percent. Exports of raw furskins, including heads, tails, paws, etc (SITC group 212) accounted for 0.6 percent of world exports of SITC section 2 and less than 0.1 percent of total world exports in 2010 (see table 1).

Denmark, China, Hong Kong SAR and Finland were the top exporting countries or areas in 2010, respectively with 34.3, 17.7 and 17.1 percent of world exports (see table 2). China, Hong Kong SAR was the top destination with 38.0 percent of world imports (see table 3). Other major importing countries were China and Denmark. By MDG regions (see graph 2), Developed Europe was the origin of a majority of exports of raw furskins (SITC group 212). It recorded exports of 2.4 bln US$ and imports of 0.8 bln US$ resulting in a trade surplus of 1.6 bln US$. Eastern Asia recorded a trade deficit of 791 mln US$.

Table 1: Imports (Imp.) and exports (Exp.), 1996-2010, in current prices

		1996	1997	1998	1999	2000	2001	2002	2003	2004	2005	2006	2007	2008	2009	2010
Values in Bln US$	Imp.	1.6	1.4	1.2	0.9	1.0	1.1	1.2	1.3	1.6	1.7	2.1	1.9	2.1	1.7	2.5
	Exp.	1.7	1.5	1.4	1.1	1.4	1.5	1.6	1.8	2.2	2.3	3.1	2.5	3.1	2.4	3.8
As a percentage of SITC section (%)	Imp.	0.6	0.5	0.5	0.4	0.4	0.5	0.5	0.5	0.4	0.4	0.4	0.3	0.3	0.3	0.3
	Exp.	0.8	0.7	0.7	0.6	0.7	0.7	0.7	0.7	0.7	0.6	0.7	0.5	0.5	0.5	0.6
As a percentage of world trade (%)	Imp.	0.0	0.0	0.0	0.0	0.0	0.0	0.0	0.0	0.0	0.0	0.0	0.0	0.0	0.0	0.0
	Exp.	0.0	0.0	0.0	0.0	0.0	0.0	0.0	0.0	0.0	0.0	0.0	0.0	0.0	0.0	0.0

Graph 1: Annual growth rates of exports, 1996–2010

(In percentage by year)

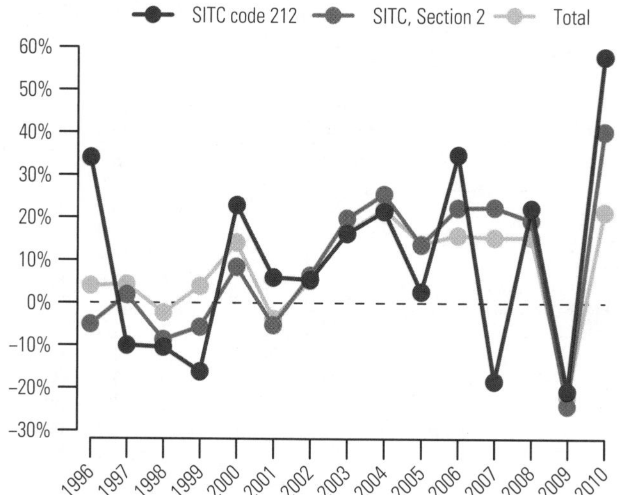

Graph 2: Trade Balance by MDG regions 2010

(Bln US$)

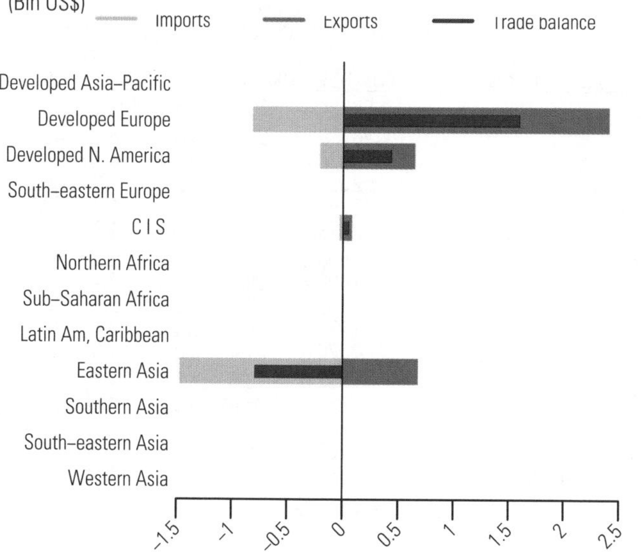

Table 2: Top exporting countries or areas in 2010

Country or area	Value (million US$)	Avg. Growth (%) 06-10	Growth (%) 09-10	World share %	Cum.
World	3830.1	5.7	57.8	100.0	
Denmark	1312.6	6.2	69.8	34.3	34.3
China, Hong Kong SAR	677.4	7.1	33.2	17.7	52.0
Finland	653.1	7.1	108.0	17.1	69.0
Canada	399.5	6.5	55.2	10.4	79.4
USA	246.4	2.6	45.5	6.4	85.9
Poland	128.2	50.8	68.9	3.3	89.2
Netherlands	61.2	-8.6	-34.9	1.6	90.8
Russian Federation	53.2	-15.6	4.8	1.4	92.2
Norway	49.0	-1.0	37.4	1.3	93.5
France	34.1	40.7	215.5	0.9	94.4
Belarus	26.3	7.0	48.5	0.7	95.1
Sweden	24.3	-5.2	30.8	0.6	95.7
Spain	22.5	20.3	244.5	0.6	96.3
Germany	20.8	-15.8	17.9	0.5	96.8
Greece	17.2	31.4	231.7	0.5	97.3

Table 3: Top importing countries or areas in 2010

Country or area	Value (million US$)	Avg. Growth (%) 06-10	Growth (%) 09-10	World share %	Cum.
World	2536.5	5.0	51.8	100.0	
China, Hong Kong SAR	964.6	4.9	56.3	38.0	38.0
China	382.6	23.1	46.8	15.1	53.1
Denmark	296.3	17.3	81.3	11.7	64.8
Finland	183.0	-0.1	3.2	7.2	72.0
Rep. of Korea	122.6	5.0	73.9	4.8	76.8
USA	119.9	8.2	39.7	4.7	81.6
Greece	98.9	-3.7	78.1	3.9	85.5
Italy	93.4	-9.6	53.6	3.7	89.1
Canada	88.4	-5.0	-1.2	3.5	92.6
Poland	52.7	-7.4	181.1	2.1	94.7
Germany	21.2	-6.5	156.4	0.8	95.5
Russian Federation	20.3	122.3	363.2	0.8	96.3
Estonia	17.2	-7.1	48.7	0.7	97.0
Lithuania	14.7	26.8	355.1	0.6	97.6
France	13.7	-19.5	50.3	0.5	98.1

Source: UN Comtrade

222 Oil-seeds and oleaginous fruits used for extraction of 'soft' fixed oils

After a 9.0 percent drop in 2009, the value (in current prices) of exports of oil-seeds and oleaginous fruits used for extraction of soft fixed oils (SITC group 222) bounced back by 18.0 percent in 2010 and amounted to 54.0 bln US$ (see table 2). Imports, after a 16.2 percent drop in 2009, increased by 16.2 percent and totaled 58.6 bln US$ in 2010, still below its 2008 peak value (see table 3). Graph 1 shows that the increase in exports for 2010 in this product group was below the increases in world exports of inedible crude materials, except fuels (SITC section 2) of 40.2 percent and in total world exports of 21.2 percent. Exports of oil-seeds and oleaginous fruits used for extraction of soft fixed oils (SITC group 222) accounted for 7.8 percent of world exports of SITC section 2 and 0.4 percent of total world exports in 2010 (see table 1).

USA, Brazil and Argentina were the three major exporting countries in 2010, accounting jointly for more than half (66.0 percent) of world exports (see table 2). China was the top destination. It accounted for 45.1 percent of world imports (see table 3). By MDG regions (see graph 2), top surpluses were recorded by Developed North America (+23.1 bln US$) and Latin America and the Caribbean (+15.7 bln US$). A deficit amounting to 27.8 bln US$ was recorded by Eastern Asia.

Table 1: Imports (Imp.) and exports (Exp.), 1996-2010, in current prices

		1996	1997	1998	1999	2000	2001	2002	2003	2004	2005	2006	2007	2008	2009	2010
Values in Bln US$	Imp.	16.0	17.0	15.3	14.3	15.4	16.6	16.7	22.4	26.3	25.4	24.9	35.8	60.2	50.4	58.6
	Exp.	14.7	16.0	14.2	12.5	13.6	14.6	14.8	20.4	21.4	21.4	22.7	32.3	50.4	45.8	54.0
As a percentage of SITC section (%)	Imp.	6.3	6.6	6.5	6.3	6.2	7.1	6.9	7.8	7.0	6.1	5.0	5.8	7.9	9.3	7.8
	Exp.	6.6	7.0	6.8	6.3	6.4	7.2	6.9	7.9	6.6	5.8	5.1	5.9	7.7	9.2	7.8
As a percentage of world trade (%)	Imp.	0.3	0.3	0.3	0.3	0.2	0.3	0.3	0.3	0.3	0.2	0.2	0.3	0.4	0.4	0.4
	Exp.	0.3	0.3	0.3	0.2	0.2	0.2	0.2	0.3	0.2	0.2	0.2	0.2	0.3	0.4	0.4

Graph 1: Annual growth rates of exports, 1996–2010

(In percentage by year)

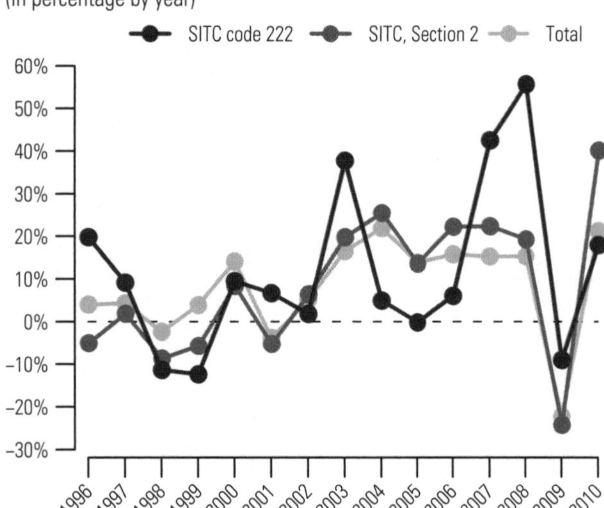

Table 2: Top exporting countries or areas in 2010

Country or area	Value (million US$)	Avg. Growth (%) 06-10	Growth (%) 09-10	World share %	Cum.
World	54042.0	24.2	18.0	100.0	
USA	19279.0	27.1	12.8	35.7	35.7
Brazil	11095.8	18.2	-3.5	20.5	56.2
Argentina	5293.2	28.5	171.8	9.8	66.0
Canada	4807.8	23.7	14.7	8.9	74.9
Paraguay	1660.6	37.7	84.6	3.1	78.0
Ukraine	1019.4	39.3	4.0	1.9	79.9
France	1005.6	7.6	16.0	1.9	81.7
India	877.3	26.0	75.7	1.6	83.3
Netherlands	877.0	18.0	3.0	1.6	85.0
Romania	744.0	35.8	41.5	1.4	86.3
Nigeria	641.9	295.5	229.7	1.2	87.5
China	621.7	3.9	-6.1	1.2	88.7
Hungary	577.8	27.3	-1.6	1.1	89.7
Uruguay	*571.6*	39.7	24.5	1.1	90.8
Bulgaria	562.1	37.8	25.4	1.0	91.8

Graph 2: Trade Balance by MDG regions 2010

(Bln US$)

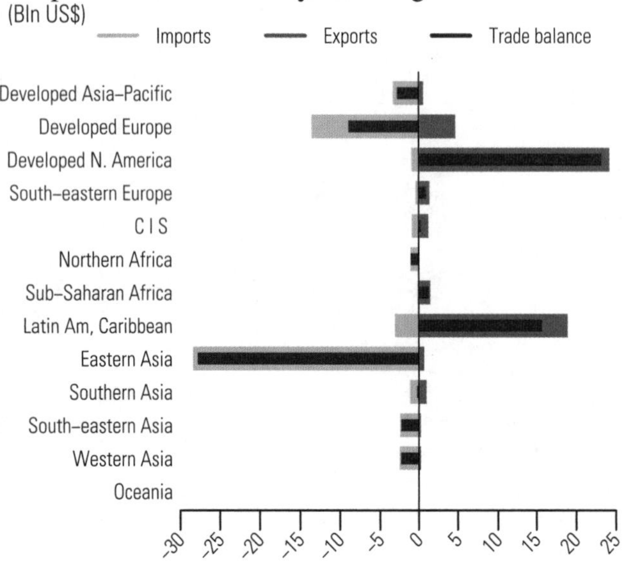

Table 3: Top importing countries or areas in 2010

Country or area	Value (million US$)	Avg. Growth (%) 06-10	Growth (%) 09-10	World share %	Cum.
World	58584.4	23.9	16.2	100.0	
China	26436.8	35.1	28.4	45.1	45.1
Japan	3328.2	10.5	11.9	5.7	50.8
Germany	2959.8	14.0	-10.5	5.1	55.9
Netherlands	2790.3	18.3	6.3	4.8	60.6
Mexico	2473.5	14.4	17.6	4.2	64.8
Spain	1658.3	17.3	2.2	2.8	67.7
Turkey	1400.2	28.0	60.8	2.4	70.1
Belgium	1330.9	16.5	16.3	2.3	72.3
Other Asia, nes	1239.1	17.1	14.3	2.1	74.5
Indonesia	1070.6	31.4	33.4	1.8	76.3
Italy	932.0	13.8	5.2	1.6	77.9
France	885.1	35.9	5.7	1.5	79.4
Thailand	873.2	22.0	20.9	1.5	80.9
Egypt	780.2	45.2	9.9	1.3	82.2
Russian Federation	744.6	56.0	13.6	1.3	83.5

After a 21.9 percent drop in 2009, the value (in current prices) of exports of oil seeds and oleaginous fruits used for the extraction of other fixed oils (SITC group 223) decreased further by 0.5 percent and amounted to 2.2 bln US$ in 2010 (see table 2). However, imports increased by 9.5 percent to reach 2.3 bln US$ in 2010 (see table 3). Graph 1 shows the decline in exports for 2010 in this product group compared with increases in world exports of inedible crude materials, except fuels (SITC section 2) of 40.2 percent and in total world exports of 21.2 percent. Exports of oil seeds and oleaginous fruits used for the extraction of other fixed oils (SITC group 223) accounted for 0.3 percent of world exports of SITC section 2 and less than 0.1 percent of total world exports in 2010 (see table 1).

USA, Canada and Netherlands were the major exporting countries in 2010. They accounted respectively for 21.9, 16.1 and 11.5 percent of world exports (see table 2). Belgium, Mexico and Germany were the major destinations (see table 3). By MDG regions (see graph 2), Developed North America was the origin of a large share of exports of oil seeds and oleaginous fruits used for the extraction of other fixed oils (SITC group 223). In 2010, its exports were valued at 822 mln US$, resulting in a trade surplus of 622 mln US$. Developed Europe was the destination of a majority of goods. Its imports exceeded 1.0 bln US$ and it recorded a trade deficit of 348 mln US$. A deficit amounting to 364 mln US$ was recorded by Latin America and the Caribbean.

Table 1: Imports (Imp.) and exports (Exp.), 1996-2010, in current prices

		1996	1997	1998	1999	2000	2001	2002	2003	2004	2005	2006	2007	2008	2009	2010
Values in Bln US$	Imp.	0.9	1.0	0.9	0.8	0.7	0.8	0.9	1.0	1.2	1.3	1.4	1.8	2.6	2.1	2.3
	Exp.	0.7	0.8	0.9	0.7	0.7	0.7	0.8	0.9	1.2	1.5	1.4	1.9	2.8	2.2	2.2
As a percentage of SITC section (%)	Imp.	0.4	0.4	0.4	0.4	0.3	0.3	0.4	0.4	0.3	0.3	0.3	0.3	0.3	0.4	0.3
	Exp.	0.3	0.4	0.4	0.4	0.3	0.4	0.4	0.3	0.4	0.4	0.3	0.4	0.4	0.4	0.3
As a percentage of world trade (%)	Imp.	0.0	0.0	0.0	0.0	0.0	0.0	0.0	0.0	0.0	0.0	0.0	0.0	0.0	0.0	0.0
	Exp.	0.0	0.0	0.0	0.0	0.0	0.0	0.0	0.0	0.0	0.0	0.0	0.0	0.0	0.0	0.0

Graph 1: Annual growth rates of exports, 1996–2010

(In percentage by year)

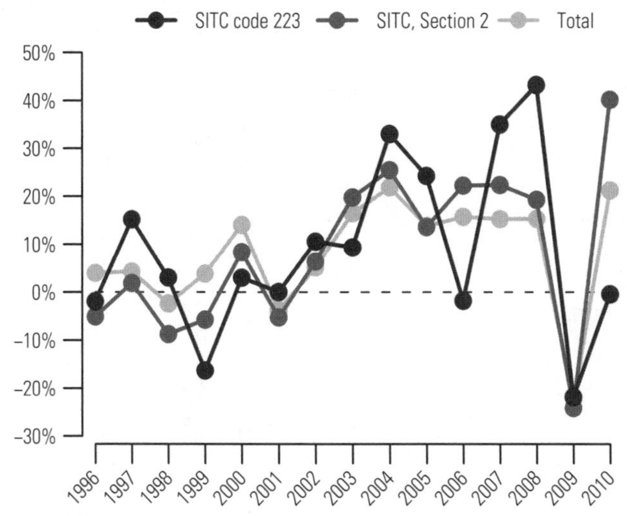

Graph 2: Trade Balance by MDG regions 2010

(Bln US$)

Imports — Exports — Trade balance

Developed Asia-Pacific
Developed Europe
Developed N. America
South-eastern Europe
CIS
Northern Africa
Sub-Saharan Africa
Latin Am, Caribbean
Eastern Asia
Southern Asia
South-eastern Asia
Western Asia
Oceania

-1.2 -1 -0.8 -0.6 -0.4 -0.2 0 0.2 0.4 0.6 0.8 1

Table 2: Top exporting countries or areas in 2010

Country or area	Value (million US$)	Avg. Growth (%) 06-10	Growth (%) 09-10	World share %	Cum.
World	2165.5	10.7	-0.5	100.0	
USA	473.4	4.0	-11.3	21.9	21.9
Canada	349.1	14.6	25.7	16.1	38.0
Netherlands	248.4	23.7	5.2	11.5	49.5
Belgium	100.5	7.2	-46.1	4.6	54.1
China	85.5	19.7	16.5	3.9	58.0
Austria	60.2	24.8	13.3	2.8	60.8
Turkey	52.7	5.9	10.5	2.4	63.3
Russian Federation	49.6	40.8	32.4	2.3	65.5
Czech Rep.	44.6	-0.9	4.7	2.1	67.6
Bolivia	37.8	16.3	10.7	1.7	69.3
Ethiopia	37.1	46.2	-20.2	1.7	71.1
United Kingdom	36.1	19.7	22.7	1.7	72.7
Egypt	35.1	139.6	120.9	1.6	74.4
India	33.8	11.3	-38.9	1.6	75.9
Germany	28.2	21.5	11.1	1.3	77.2

Table 3: Top importing countries or areas in 2010

Country or area	Value (million US$)	Avg. Growth (%) 06-10	Growth (%) 09-10	World share %	Cum.
World	2273.1	13.8	9.5	100.0	
Belgium	320.1	16.8	20.6	14.1	14.1
Mexico	205.3	13.6	0.1	9.0	23.1
Germany	171.2	10.4	-1.7	7.5	30.6
USA	169.3	13.5	0.5	7.4	38.1
Dominican Rep.	169.1	15.4	5.4	7.4	45.5
China	104.2	49.6	11.7	4.6	50.1
United Kingdom	84.9	22.6	56.4	3.7	53.8
Nigeria	79.5	151.6	5590.9	3.5	57.3
Netherlands	72.5	15.3	9.2	3.2	60.5
Austria	62.1	23.5	13.2	2.7	63.3
Spain	57.1	20.6	44.3	2.5	65.8
Philippines	56.3	50.9	37.5	2.5	68.3
Rep. of Korea	52.9	16.4	4.6	2.3	70.6
France	43.0	9.3	2.1	1.9	72.5
Peru	40.4	16.7	3.5	1.8	74.3

231 Natural rubber, balata, gutta-percha, chicle, etc, in primary forms

After several years of continuous growth marked by a peak of 19.7 bln US$ in 2008, the value (in current prices) of exports of natural rubber, balata, gutta-percha, chicle, etc, in primary forms (SITC group 231) decreased by 40.3 percent in 2009, but bounced back by a huge 102.6 percent reaching 23.9 bln US$ in 2010 (see table 2). Similarly, imports dropped by 40.7 percent in 2009 but increased by 101.4 percent to 23.8 bln US$ (see table 3). Graph 1 shows the increase in exports for 2010 in this product group was well above the increases in world exports of inedible crude materials, except fuels (SITC section 2) of 40.2 percent and in total world exports of 21.2 percent. Exports of natural rubber, balata, gutta-percha, chicle, etc, in primary forms (SITC group 231) accounted for 3.4 percent of world exports of SITC section 2 and 0.2 percent of total world exports in 2009 (see table 1).

Thailand and Indonesia were the two major exporting countries in 2010. They accounted respectively for 33.1 and 30.7 percent of world exports (see table 2). China, USA and Japan were the top destinations (see table 3). By MDG regions (graph 2), South-eastern Asia recorded a surplus amounting to 17.8 bln US$ and top deficits were recorded by Eastern Asia (-7.1 bln US$), Developed Europe (-3.4 bln US$) and Developed North America (-3.3 bln US$) .

Table 1: Imports (Imp.) and exports (Exp.), 1996-2010, in current prices

		1996	1997	1998	1999	2000	2001	2002	2003	2004	2005	2006	2007	2008	2009	2010
Values in Bln US$	Imp.	7.6	6.4	4.8	3.9	4.8	4.1	4.7	6.8	9.0	9.9	14.5	15.9	19.9	11.8	23.8
	Exp.	7.5	5.7	4.1	3.4	3.9	3.3	4.3	6.5	8.6	9.8	15.0	16.3	19.7	11.8	23.9
As a percentage of SITC section (%)	Imp.	3.0	2.5	2.1	1.7	1.9	1.7	1.9	2.4	2.4	2.4	2.9	2.6	2.6	2.2	3.2
	Exp.	3.3	2.5	1.9	1.7	1.8	1.6	2.0	2.5	2.7	2.7	3.3	3.0	3.0	2.4	3.4
As a percentage of world trade (%)	Imp.	0.1	0.1	0.1	0.1	0.1	0.1	0.1	0.1	0.1	0.1	0.1	0.1	0.1	0.1	0.2
	Exp.	0.1	0.1	0.1	0.1	0.1	0.1	0.1	0.1	0.1	0.1	0.1	0.1	0.1	0.1	0.2

Graph 1: Annual growth rates of exports, 1996–2010
(In percentage by year)

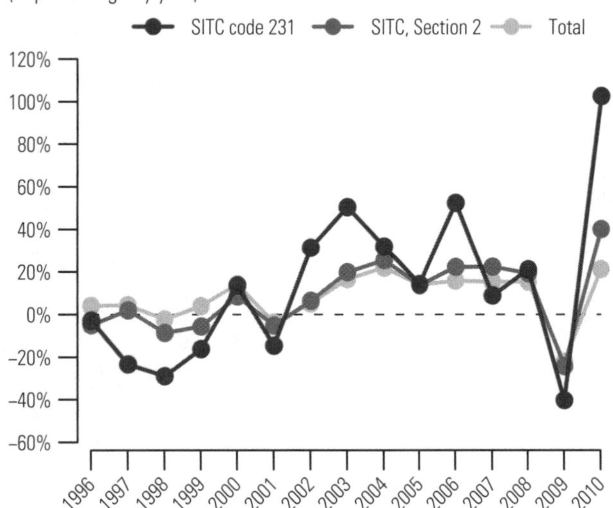

Graph 2: Trade Balance by MDG regions 2010
(Bln US$)

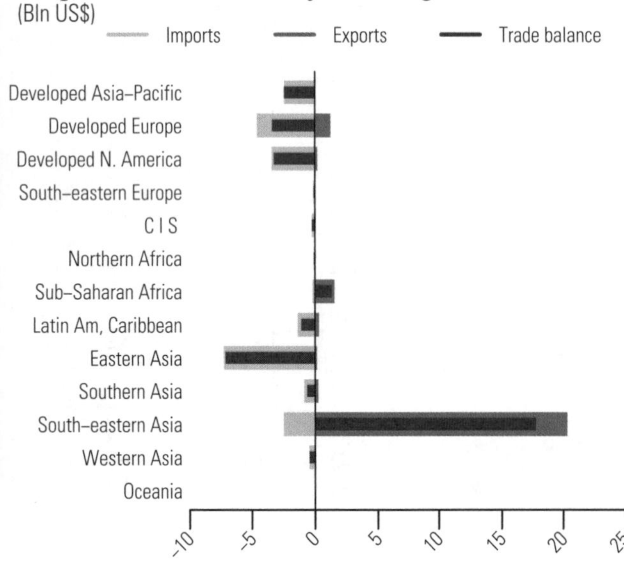

Table 2: Top exporting countries or areas in 2010

Country or area	Value (million US$)	Avg. Growth (%) 06-10	Growth (%) 09-10	World share %	Cum.
World	23875.5	12.4	102.6	100.0	
Thailand	7896.0	9.8	83.3	33.1	33.1
Indonesia	7329.1	14.1	125.9	30.7	63.8
Malaysia	2863.6	6.3	126.0	12.0	75.8
Viet Nam	*1392.9*	5.2	25.6	5.8	81.6
Côte d'Ivoire	680.4	21.2	97.4	2.8	84.4
Nigeria	555.3	138.8	225.9	2.3	86.8
Singapore	396.4	0.1	121.3	1.7	88.4
Germany	309.3	51.7	163.9	1.3	89.7
Luxembourg	279.2	292.7	804.2	1.2	90.9
Netherlands	273.9	131.2	1577.9	1.1	92.0
Myanmar	*252.2*	61.3	232.7	1.1	93.1
Guatemala	236.8	26.1	73.8	1.0	94.1
Sri Lanka	170.5	16.7	73.0	0.7	94.8
USA	149.6	20.9	66.8	0.6	95.4
France	127.8	30.6	102.6	0.5	96.0

Table 3: Top importing countries or areas in 2010

Country or area	Value (million US$)	Avg. Growth (%) 06-10	Growth (%) 09-10	World share %	Cum.
World	23774.4	13.1	101.4	100.0	
China	5666.7	16.9	101.4	23.8	23.8
USA	2987.2	9.2	119.9	12.6	36.4
Japan	2423.3	7.2	106.1	10.2	46.6
Malaysia	1798.1	33.8	41.8	7.6	54.2
Germany	1261.4	16.8	166.4	5.3	59.5
Rep. of Korea	1194.8	13.0	99.0	5.0	64.5
Brazil	790.5	19.7	179.3	3.3	67.8
France	578.0	3.5	119.1	2.4	70.2
Spain	573.4	8.3	132.9	2.4	72.7
India	547.2	53.1	103.0	2.3	75.0
Canada	444.6	9.9	114.1	1.9	76.8
Turkey	432.2	10.7	113.5	1.8	78.6
Italy	411.9	3.0	110.4	1.7	80.4
Singapore	380.1	1.4	105.8	1.6	82.0
Other Asia, nes	378.2	15.4	122.9	1.6	83.6

After several years of continuous growth marked by a peak of 18.7 bln US$ in 2008 , the value (in current prices) of exports of synthetic and reclaimed rubber; waste, scrap of unhardened rubber (SITC group 232) decreased by 26.5 percent in 2009 but bounced back by 47.9 percent in 2010 amounting to 20.4 bln US$ (see table 2). Imports showed a similar development with an increase of 46.5 percent to 22.3 bln US$ (see table 3). Graph 1 shows that the increase in exports for 2010 in this product group exceeded the increases in world exports of inedible crude materials, except fuels (SITC section 2) of 40.2 percent and in total world exports of 21.2 percent. Exports of synthetic and reclaimed rubber; waste, scrap of unhardened rubber (SITC group 232) accounted for 2.9 percent of world exports of SITC section 2 and 0.1 percent of total world exports in 2010 (see table 1).

USA, Rep. of Korea and Japan were the top exporting countries in 2010 (see table 2). They accounted respectively for 16.0, 12.0 and 11.7 percent of world exports. China, USA and Germany were the three main destinations (see table 3). By MDG regions (see graph 2), top surpluses were recorded by Developed Asia-Pacific (+1.7 bln US$), Commonwealth of Independent States (+1.5 bln US$) and Developed North America (+1.5 bln US$). Top trade deficits were recorded by South-eastern Asia (-1.9 bln US$), Eastern Asia (-1.2 bln US$) and Developed Europe (-1.1 bln US$).

Table 1: Imports (Imp.) and exports (Exp.), 1996-2010, in current prices

		1996	1997	1998	1999	2000	2001	2002	2003	2004	2005	2006	2007	2008	2009	2010
Values in Bln US$	Imp.	7.5	7.2	7.1	7.1	7.8	7.5	7.8	9.1	11.0	13.3	15.3	17.5	21.4	15.2	22.3
	Exp.	6.1	5.8	5.5	5.5	6.2	6.2	6.5	7.5	9.4	11.7	13.7	15.8	18.7	13.8	20.4
As a percentage of SITC section (%)	Imp.	3.0	2.8	3.0	3.1	3.2	3.2	3.3	3.2	2.9	3.2	3.1	2.8	2.8	2.8	3.0
	Exp.	2.7	2.5	2.6	2.8	2.9	3.1	3.0	2.9	2.9	3.2	3.1	2.9	2.9	2.8	2.9
As a percentage of world trade (%)	Imp.	0.1	0.1	0.1	0.1	0.1	0.1	0.1	0.1	0.1	0.1	0.1	0.1	0.1	0.1	0.1
	Exp.	0.1	0.1	0.1	0.1	0.1	0.1	0.1	0.1	0.1	0.1	0.1	0.1	0.1	0.1	0.1

Graph 1: Annual growth rates of exports, 1996–2010
(In percentage by year)

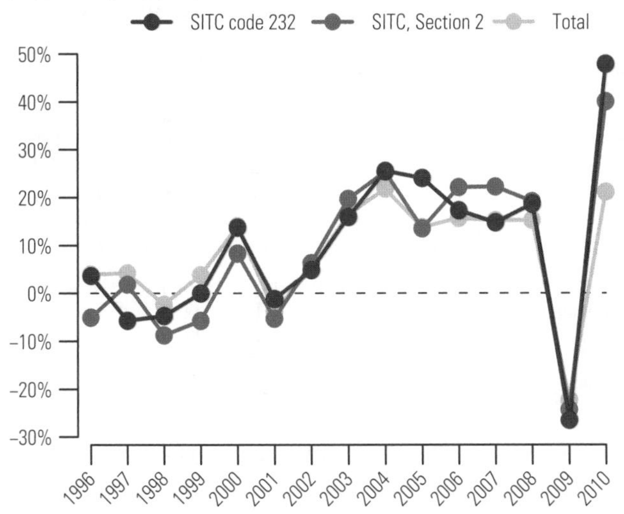

Table 2: Top exporting countries or areas in 2010

Country or area	Value (million US$)	Avg. Growth (%) 06-10	Growth (%) 09-10	World share %	Cum.
World	20373.2	10.4	47.9	100.0	
USA	3252.8	5.1	41.7	16.0	16.0
Rep. of Korea	2442.9	25.3	55.6	12.0	28.0
Japan	2381.8	14.9	46.9	11.7	39.6
Russian Federation	2004.6	14.6	75.9	9.8	49.5
Germany	1575.6	12.9	42.2	7.7	57.2
Belgium	1526.9	8.0	42.8	7.5	64.7
Other Asia, nes	1094.8	8.5	38.6	5.4	70.1
France	833.2	-0.9	21.9	4.1	74.2
China	656.8	39.5	155.5	3.2	77.4
Italy	412.4	9.5	26.1	2.0	79.4
Mexico	392.8	11.9	62.8	1.9	81.4
Netherlands	381.7	-7.4	0.4	1.9	83.2
Canada	379.6	0.6	29.7	1.9	85.1
Poland	360.8	20.7	95.7	1.8	86.9
Thailand	320.6	5.2	43.3	1.6	88.4

Graph 2: Trade Balance by MDG regions 2010
(Bln US$)

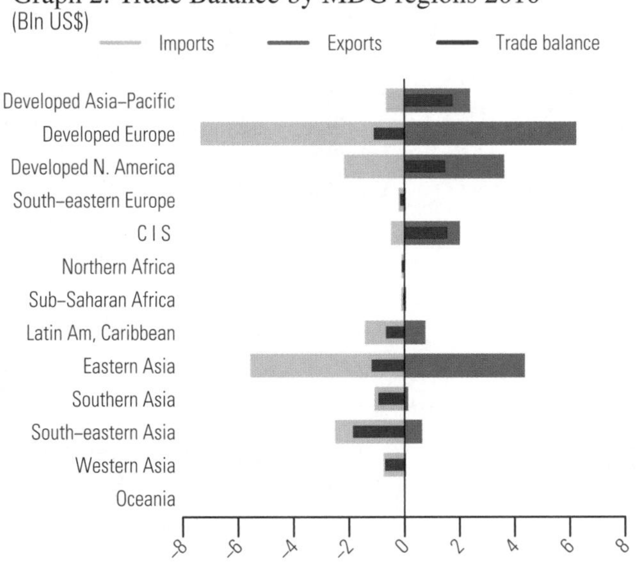

Table 3: Top importing countries or areas in 2010

Country or area	Value (million US$)	Avg. Growth (%) 06-10	Growth (%) 09-10	World share %	Cum.
World	22341.3	10.0	46.5	100.0	
China	4289.3	15.8	42.4	19.2	19.2
USA	1569.9	5.2	57.1	7.0	26.2
Germany	1467.3	7.8	54.3	6.6	32.8
Belgium	933.2	6.5	36.8	4.2	37.0
Thailand	816.3	17.6	67.5	3.7	40.6
India	815.5	16.8	45.4	3.7	44.3
France	762.1	3.1	35.8	3.4	47.7
Italy	748.6	2.3	37.5	3.4	51.0
Brazil	611.6	15.2	40.6	2.7	53.8
Spain	597.1	3.8	42.2	2.7	56.4
Canada	594.1	1.0	39.5	2.7	59.1
Malaysia	591.3	18.6	62.2	2.6	61.8
Indonesia	588.8	27.0	58.4	2.6	64.4
Turkey	584.0	15.6	59.6	2.6	67.0
Rep. of Korea	578.8	11.3	42.8	2.6	69.6

244 Cork, natural, raw, and waste (including natural cork in blocks or sheets)

The value (in current prices) of exports of natural, raw and waste cork, including natural cork in blocks or sheets (SITC group 244) experienced a decrease over two consecutive years resulting in its lowest value of 143 mln US$ in 2009. However, in 2010 the value increased by 2.3 percent and totaled 146 mln US$ (see table 2). Imports declined by 34.4 percent in 2009 but increased by 16.4 percent and totaled 198 mln US$ (see table 3). Graph 1 shows that the increase in exports for 2010 in this product group was well below the increases in world exports of inedible crude materials, except fuels (SITC section 2) of 40.2 percent and in total world exports of 21.2 percent. Exports of natural, raw and waste cork, including natural cork in blocks or sheets (SITC group 244) accounted for less than 0.1 percent of both world exports of SITC section 2 and total world exports in 2010 (see table 1).

Spain and Portugal were the origin of a majority of exports in 2010 (see table 2): they accounted respectively for 51.8 and 33.4 percent of world exports, jointly for more than 85.0 percent. They also accounted respectively for 8.7 and 47.9 percent of world imports (see table 3). As a consequence, Developed Europe was the origin and the destination of a majority of trade in natural, raw and waste cork (SITC group 244) (see graph 2). In 2010, its exports amounted to 131 mln US$ and imports to 148 mln US$, resulting in a trade deficit of 17 mln US$. Top trade deficits were also recorded by Developed North America (-10 mln US$) and Eastern Asia (-9 mln US$). Northern Africa recorded a surplus of 5 mln US$.

Table 1: Imports (Imp.) and exports (Exp.), 1996-2010, in current prices

		1996	1997	1998	1999	2000	2001	2002	2003	2004	2005	2006	2007	2008	2009	2010
Values in Mln US$	Imp.	136.5	159.2	169.4	198.1	255.8	216.8	203.4	264.3	244.0	232.0	225.7	255.7	258.7	169.7	197.6
	Exp.	129.7	142.7	161.8	178.5	245.8	202.9	191.0	254.4	234.6	230.4	234.8	247.2	244.7	142.7	146.0
As a percentage of SITC section (%)	Imp.	0.1	0.1	0.1	0.1	0.1	0.1	0.1	0.1	0.1	0.1	0.0	0.0	0.0	0.0	0.0
	Exp.	0.1	0.1	0.1	0.1	0.1	0.1	0.1	0.1	0.1	0.1	0.1	0.0	0.0	0.0	0.0
As a percentage of world trade (%)	Imp.	0.0	0.0	0.0	0.0	0.0	0.0	0.0	0.0	0.0	0.0	0.0	0.0	0.0	0.0	0.0
	Exp.	0.0	0.0	0.0	0.0	0.0	0.0	0.0	0.0	0.0	0.0	0.0	0.0	0.0	0.0	0.0

Graph 1: Annual growth rates of exports, 1996–2010
(In percentage by year)

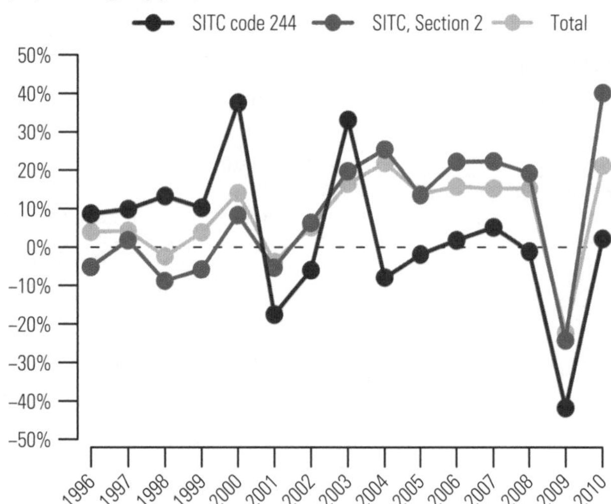

Graph 2: Trade Balance by MDG regions 2010
(Mln US$)

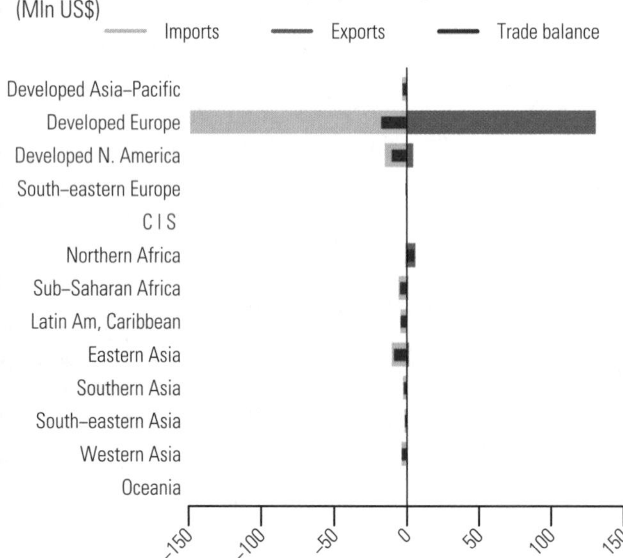

Table 2: Top exporting countries or areas in 2010

Country or area	Value (million US$)	Avg. Growth (%) 06-10	Growth (%) 09-10	World share %	Cum.
World	146.0	-11.2	2.3	100.0	
Spain	75.6	-10.6	6.9	51.8	51.8
Portugal	48.7	-12.9	-4.9	33.4	85.1
USA	4.4	0.3	13.2	3.0	88.1
Morocco	3.8	-18.2	17.4	2.6	90.8
Italy	3.2	11.9	-0.1	2.2	93.0
Tunisia	2.1	-19.2	0.6	1.4	94.4
France	1.1	-22.0	-5.2	0.7	95.1
South Africa	1.0	187.7	5659.5	0.7	95.8
United Kingdom	1.0	16.5	190.1	0.7	96.5
China	0.7	-20.3	-64.3	0.5	97.0
India	0.6	3.1	131.3	0.4	97.4
China, Hong Kong SAR	0.5	-29.7	-34.8	0.4	97.8
Algeria	0.4	151.3	-5.2	0.3	98.1
Canada	0.4	2.3	1.1	0.3	98.4
Other Asia, nes	0.3	36.7	229.3	0.2	98.6

Table 3: Top importing countries or areas in 2010

Country or area	Value (million US$)	Avg. Growth (%) 06-10	Growth (%) 09-10	World share %	Cum.
World	197.6	-3.3	16.4	100.0	
Portugal	94.7	-3.9	31.9	47.9	47.9
Spain	17.2	-17.9	-12.4	8.7	56.6
USA	14.6	65.5	84.2	7.4	64.0
Italy	10.5	-16.4	-34.2	5.3	69.4
China	8.3	-0.9	-5.2	4.2	73.5
France	6.6	-4.4	-29.1	3.4	76.9
Nigeria	5.4	...	500.7	2.7	79.6
Germany	4.9	14.9	24.7	2.5	82.1
Netherlands	3.1	4.3	0.6	1.6	83.7
Japan	2.9	-2.3	37.9	1.5	85.1
Belgium	2.8	-3.2	11.2	1.4	86.6
Slovakia	2.5	86.0	18.3	1.3	87.8
India	2.4	5.1	-7.3	1.2	89.0
United Kingdom	2.3	-1.7	4.7	1.2	90.2
Brazil	1.9	-4.3	7.9	0.9	91.2

Source: UN Comtrade

During the recent five years, the value (in current prices) of exports of fuel wood (excluding wood waste) and wood charcoal (SITC group 245) has been increasing smoothly on average by 13.7 percent each year to reach 1.1 bln US$ in 2010 (see table 2). Imports showed a similar development with an average increase of 10.4 percent each year to amount to 1.2 bln US$ (see table 3). Graph 1 shows that the increase in exports for 2010 in this product group was well below the increases in world exports of inedible crude materials, except fuels (SITC section 2) of 40.2 percent and in total world exports of 21.2 percent. Exports of fuel wood (excluding wood waste) and wood charcoal (SITC group 245) accounted for 0.2 percent of world exports of SITC section 2 and less than 0.1 percent of total world exports in 2010 (see table 1).

The top exporting countries in 2010 were Latvia, Poland and Ukraine (see table 2). They accounted respectively for 6.8, 6.6 and 6.4 percent of world exports. Top destinations were Germany, Japan and Italy (see table 3). By MDG regions (see graph 2), Developed Europe's exports amounted to 434 mln US$ while imports to 710 mln US$, resulting in a trade deficit of 276 mln US$. Developed Asia-Pacific also recorded a deficit of 111 mln US$. Top trade surpluses were recorded by Latin America & the Caribbean (+129 mln US$), South-eastern Asia (+127 mln US$) and Sub-Saharan Africa (+85 mln US$).

Table 1: Imports (Imp.) and exports (Exp.), 1996-2010, in current prices

		1996	1997	1998	1999	2000	2001	2002	2003	2004	2005	2006	2007	2008	2009	2010
Values in Bln US$	Imp.	0.3	0.3	0.3	0.3	0.4	0.4	0.4	0.5	0.6	0.7	0.8	0.9	1.0	1.1	1.2
	Exp.	0.3	0.3	0.3	0.3	0.3	0.3	0.3	0.5	0.5	0.6	0.6	0.8	0.9	1.0	1.1
As a percentage of SITC section (%)	Imp.	0.1	0.1	0.1	0.1	0.2	0.2	0.2	0.2	0.2	0.2	0.2	0.1	0.1	0.2	0.2
	Exp.	0.1	0.1	0.2	0.1	0.2	0.2	0.2	0.2	0.2	0.2	0.1	0.1	0.1	0.2	0.2
As a percentage of world trade (%)	Imp.	0.0	0.0	0.0	0.0	0.0	0.0	0.0	0.0	0.0	0.0	0.0	0.0	0.0	0.0	0.0
	Exp.	0.0	0.0	0.0	0.0	0.0	0.0	0.0	0.0	0.0	0.0	0.0	0.0	0.0	0.0	0.0

Graph 1: Annual growth rates of exports, 1996–2010
(In percentage by year)

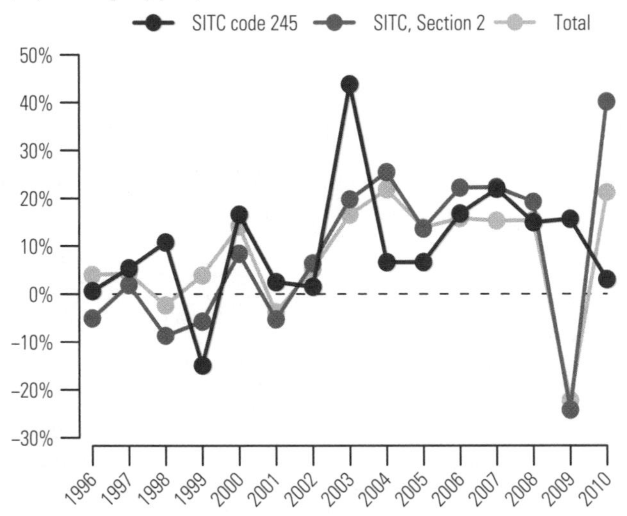

Table 2: Top exporting countries or areas in 2010

Country or area	Value (million US$)	Avg. Growth (%) 06-10	Growth (%) 09-10	World share %	Cum.
World	1 075.1	13.7	3.1	100.0	
Latvia	72.9	37.6	50.0	6.8	6.8
Poland	71.4	14.9	21.0	6.6	13.4
Ukraine	68.6	20.3	19.1	6.4	19.8
Indonesia	65.4	20.8	-0.5	6.1	25.9
Somalia	*62.4*	20.8	-23.4	5.8	31.7
Cuba	*52.2*	144.9	117.3	4.9	36.6
Belgium	45.9	14.4	8.2	4.3	40.8
Argentina	44.8	11.6	-15.9	4.2	45.0
France	41.1	13.8	25.3	3.8	48.8
Bosnia Herzegovina	36.8	6.5	-3.5	3.4	52.2
Paraguay	36.2	29.8	-4.4	3.4	55.6
China	35.8	7.8	37.0	3.3	58.9
USA	30.8	20.0	30.9	2.9	61.8
Myanmar	*30.5*	27.1	38.4	2.8	64.6
Slovenia	24.8	17.8	15.1	2.3	66.9

Graph 2: Trade Balance by MDG regions 2010
(Mln US$)

Imports — Exports — Trade balance

Developed Asia-Pacific
Developed Europe
Developed N. America
South-eastern Europe
C I S
Northern Africa
Sub-Saharan Africa
Latin Am, Caribbean
Eastern Asia
Southern Asia
South-eastern Asia
Western Asia
Oceania

-800 -700 -600 -500 -400 -300 -200 -100 0 100 200 300 400 500

Table 3: Top importing countries or areas in 2010

Country or area	Value (million US$)	Avg. Growth (%) 06-10	Growth (%) 09-10	World share %	Cum.
World	1 166.8	10.4	4.0	100.0	
Germany	114.3	7.7	5.2	9.8	9.8
Japan	112.6	8.5	1.1	9.7	19.4
Italy	103.3	2.5	-1.0	8.9	28.3
Rep. of Korea	70.3	9.1	5.4	6.0	34.3
France	60.7	22.6	31.5	5.2	39.5
Austria	59.5	17.7	2.0	5.1	44.6
United Kingdom	43.3	8.6	25.4	3.7	48.3
Greece	41.3	12.7	-5.6	3.5	51.9
Norway	40.4	8.9	47.0	3.5	55.3
Belgium	38.3	9.0	-22.0	3.3	58.6
USA	37.2	3.3	0.3	3.2	61.8
Sweden	31.6	14.0	-14.7	2.7	64.5
Denmark	31.3	3.2	2.5	2.7	67.2
Netherlands	23.6	3.8	-11.4	2.0	69.2
China	23.2	38.2	29.6	2.0	71.2

Source: UN Comtrade

246 Wood in chips or particles and wood waste

After a 14.3 percent drop in 2009, the value (in current prices) of exports of wood in chips or particles and wood waste (SITC group 246) bounced back by 24.4 percent in 2010 to reach 5.1 bln US$ (see table 2). Imports, with a similar development, increased by 29.2 percent to 6.5 bln US$ (see table 3). Graph 1 shows that the increase in exports for 2010 in this product group was exceeded by the increase in world exports of inedible crude materials, except fuels (SITC section 2) of 40.2 percent but was greater than the increase in total world exports of 21.2 percent. Exports of wood in chips or particles and wood waste (SITC group 246) accounted for 0.7 percent of world exports of SITC section 2 and less than 0.1 percent of total world exports in 2010 (see table 1).

Australia was the top exporting country in 2010: it accounted for 16.3 percent of world exports (see table 2). Other major exporting countries were Canada and Chile, respectively with 7.1 and 6.7 percent of world exports. Japan was the destination of more than one-third of goods (38.9 percent of world imports). Other major importing countries were China and Denmark (see table 3). By MDG regions (see graph 2), top surpluses were recorded by South-eastern Asia (+601 mln US$), Latin America & the Caribbean (+547 mln US$) and Developed North America (+459 mln US$). Developed Asia-Pacific recorded a deficit of 1.7 bln US$.

Table 1: Imports (Imp.) and exports (Exp.), 1996-2010, in current prices

		1996	1997	1998	1999	2000	2001	2002	2003	2004	2005	2006	2007	2008	2009	2010
Values in Bln US$	Imp.	2.9	2.8	2.7	2.6	2.6	2.5	2.4	2.8	3.3	3.7	4.2	5.0	5.9	5.0	6.5
	Exp.	2.0	1.9	1.8	1.8	1.8	1.8	1.8	2.1	2.5	2.9	3.3	3.9	4.8	4.1	5.1
As a percentage of SITC section (%)	Imp.	1.1	1.1	1.1	1.2	1.1	1.0	1.0	1.0	0.9	0.9	0.8	0.8	0.8	0.9	0.9
	Exp.	0.9	0.8	0.9	0.9	0.9	0.9	0.8	0.8	0.8	0.8	0.7	0.7	0.7	0.8	0.7
As a percentage of world trade (%)	Imp.	0.1	0.1	0.0	0.0	0.0	0.0	0.0	0.0	0.0	0.0	0.0	0.0	0.0	0.0	0.0
	Exp.	0.0	0.0	0.0	0.0	0.0	0.0	0.0	0.0	0.0	0.0	0.0	0.0	0.0	0.0	0.0

Graph 1: Annual growth rates of exports, 1996–2010

(In percentage by year)

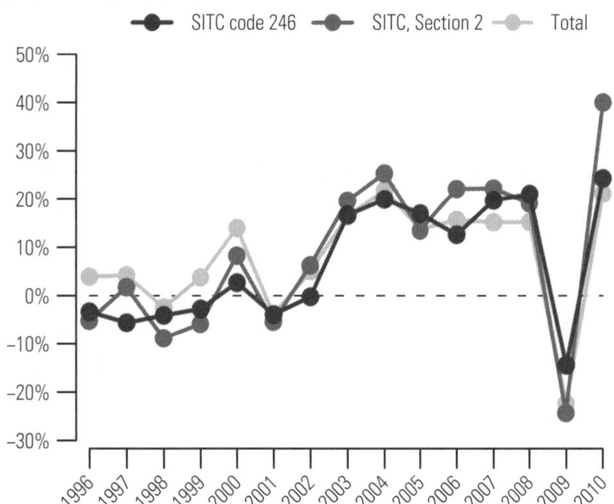

Table 2: Top exporting countries or areas in 2010

Country or area	Value (million US$)	Avg. Growth (%) 06-10	Growth (%) 09-10	World share %	Cum.
World	5068.1	11.5	24.4	100.0	
Australia	825.8	5.0	22.3	16.3	16.3
Canada	361.5	10.1	32.1	7.1	23.4
Chile	339.0	15.3	23.2	6.7	30.1
USA	328.8	13.0	13.1	6.5	36.6
Germany	321.5	14.8	5.5	6.3	42.9
Viet Nam	*299.4*	23.7	25.6	5.9	48.9
South Africa	243.9	-4.8	30.4	4.8	53.7
Thailand	204.2	78.2	108.8	4.0	57.7
Latvia	197.7	10.4	26.5	3.9	61.6
Russian Federation	185.5	26.9	15.4	3.7	65.3
Austria	172.2	9.3	28.3	3.4	68.7
Brazil	110.8	0.1	21.4	2.2	70.8
Uruguay	*99.1*	9.4	24.5	2.0	72.8
France	99.0	8.9	23.3	2.0	74.7
Estonia	98.1	3.2	22.9	1.9	76.7

Graph 2: Trade Balance by MDG regions 2010

(Bln US$)

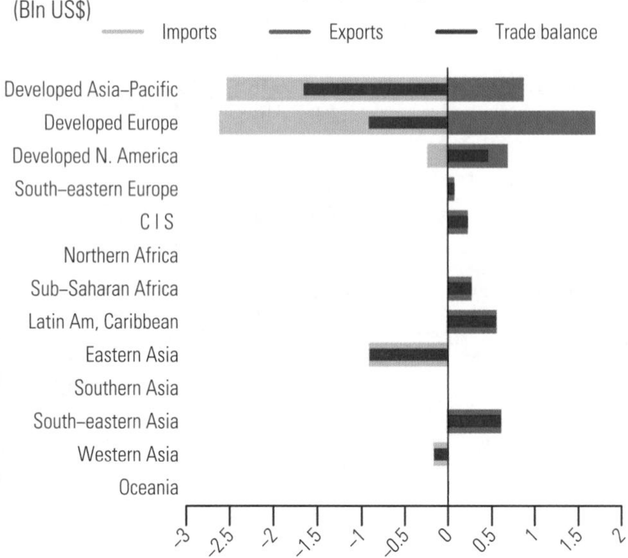

Table 3: Top importing countries or areas in 2010

Country or area	Value (million US$)	Avg. Growth (%) 06-10	Growth (%) 09-10	World share %	Cum.
World	6483.6	11.7	29.2	100.0	
Japan	2523.3	4.5	18.1	38.9	38.9
China	675.4	53.7	90.1	10.4	49.3
Denmark	331.8	21.3	85.3	5.1	54.5
Italy	303.8	15.4	44.0	4.7	59.1
Sweden	267.6	11.7	15.0	4.1	63.3
Finland	225.1	16.4	23.2	3.5	66.7
Netherlands	207.9	22.6	4.7	3.2	69.9
Belgium	205.1	14.8	-28.1	3.2	73.1
Austria	177.4	10.2	12.7	2.7	75.8
Germany	171.0	20.4	44.3	2.6	78.5
Turkey	147.4	6.7	17.2	2.3	80.8
Other Asia, nes	127.8	11.3	75.3	2.0	82.7
United Kingdom	125.0	39.6	171.8	1.9	84.7
USA	121.0	-8.2	4.4	1.9	86.5
Spain	118.2	18.7	102.3	1.8	88.3

During the recent five years, the value (in current prices) of exports of wood in the rough or roughly squared (SITC group 247) experienced a decrease over two consecutive years resulting in its lowest value of 9.8 bln US$ in 2009. However, in 2010 it increased by 32.0 percent and amounted to 12.9 bln US$ (see table 2). Imports, showing a similar development, with the lowest value of 11.4 bln US$ in 2009, increased by 29.2 percent in 2010 to 14.7 bln US$ (see table 3). Graph 1 shows that the increase in exports for 2010 in this product group was exceeded by the increase in world exports of inedible crude materials, except fuels (SITC section 2) of 40.2 percent but was greater than the increase in total world exports of 21.2 percent. Exports of wood in the rough or roughly squared (SITC group 247) accounted for 1.9 percent of world exports of SITC section 2 and 0.1 percent of total world exports in 2010 (see table 1).

USA, Russian Federation and New Zealand were the top exporting countries in 2010 (see table 2). They accounted respectively for 14.5, 14.3 and 7.5 percent of world exports. Top destinations were China, Japan and India (see table 3). By MDG regions (see graph 2), top surpluses were recorded by Commonwealth of Independent States (+2.1 bln US$), Developed North America (+1.9 bln US$) and Sub-Saharan Africa (+1.2 bln US$). Top trade deficits were recorded by Eastern Asia (-7.0 bln US$) and Southern Asia (-1.0 bln US$).

Table 1: Imports (Imp.) and exports (Exp.), 1996-2010, in current prices

		1996	1997	1998	1999	2000	2001	2002	2003	2004	2005	2006	2007	2008	2009	2010
Values in Bln US$	Imp.	11.2	10.8	8.6	9.5	10.4	9.5	9.5	10.6	12.4	13.2	14.2	17.6	16.6	11.4	14.7
	Exp.	8.0	7.9	6.7	7.3	7.7	6.9	7.5	7.7	9.2	10.6	11.5	14.6	13.7	9.8	12.9
As a percentage of SITC section (%)	Imp.	4.4	4.2	3.6	4.2	4.2	4.0	4.0	3.7	3.3	3.2	2.9	2.9	2.2	2.1	2.0
	Exp.	3.6	3.5	3.2	3.7	3.6	3.4	3.5	3.0	2.8	2.9	2.6	2.7	2.1	2.0	1.9
As a percentage of world trade (%)	Imp.	0.2	0.2	0.2	0.2	0.2	0.2	0.1	0.1	0.1	0.1	0.1	0.1	0.1	0.1	0.1
	Exp.	0.2	0.1	0.1	0.1	0.1	0.1	0.1	0.1	0.1	0.1	0.1	0.1	0.1	0.1	0.1

Graph 1: Annual growth rates of exports, 1996–2010

(In percentage by year)

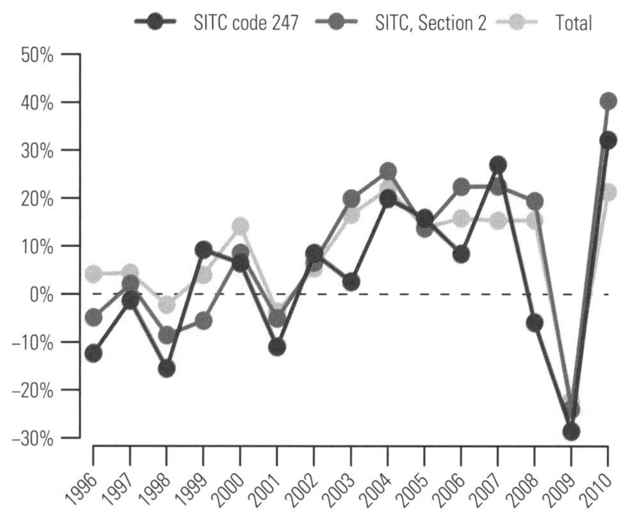

Table 2: Top exporting countries or areas in 2010

Country or area	Value (million US$)	Avg. Growth (%) 06-10	Growth (%) 09-10	World share %	Cum.
World	12892.6	2.9	32.0	100.0	
USA	1873.8	5.4	34.8	14.5	14.5
Russian Federation	1849.7	-13.2	1.0	14.3	28.9
New Zealand	962.3	27.4	60.7	7.5	36.3
Myanmar	*865.5*	10.7	28.4	6.7	43.1
Malaysia	666.1	1.9	15.4	5.2	48.2
Gabon	*589.8*	18.0	56.4	4.6	52.8
Papua New Guinea	*487.6*	4.0	56.6	3.8	56.6
Canada	450.9	-4.9	53.9	3.5	60.1
France	394.4	8.1	30.7	3.1	63.1
Germany	351.0	-13.1	1.0	2.7	65.9
Czech Rep.	327.1	11.0	26.7	2.5	68.4
Latvia	264.3	14.8	87.9	2.0	70.4
Uruguay	*244.6*	34.8	24.5	1.9	72.3
Slovakia	242.7	26.6	17.1	1.9	74.2
Congo	*202.0*	10.6	48.5	1.6	75.8

Graph 2: Trade Balance by MDG regions 2010

(Bln US$)

Imports — Exports — Trade balance

Developed Asia-Pacific
Developed Europe
Developed N. America
South-eastern Europe
C I S
Northern Africa
Sub-Saharan Africa
Latin Am, Caribbean
Eastern Asia
Southern Asia
South-eastern Asia
Western Asia
Oceania

-8 -7 -6 -5 -4 -3 -2 -1 0 1 2 3 4

Table 3: Top importing countries or areas in 2010

Country or area	Value (million US$)	Avg. Growth (%) 06-10	Growth (%) 09-10	World share %	Cum.
World	14742.4	0.9	29.2	100.0	
China	6073.0	11.5	48.6	41.2	41.2
Japan	1005.5	-14.0	23.1	6.8	48.0
India	981.4	4.6	-13.7	6.7	54.7
Austria	738.9	1.0	10.4	5.0	59.7
Rep. of Korea	725.7	-1.0	16.3	4.9	64.6
Germany	562.4	10.4	68.6	3.8	68.4
Sweden	452.4	2.6	50.5	3.1	71.5
Finland	439.7	-12.6	68.5	3.0	74.5
Viet Nam	*418.1*	19.5	66.9	2.8	77.3
Italy	368.1	-8.6	11.8	2.5	79.8
Canada	310.4	-7.0	2.9	2.1	81.9
Belgium	260.1	11.2	33.2	1.8	83.7
France	211.8	-9.4	2.9	1.4	85.1
Other Asia, nes	189.9	0.2	34.2	1.3	86.4
Czech Rep.	148.7	20.8	31.4	1.0	87.4

248 Wood, simply worked, and railway sleepers of wood

During the recent five years, the value (in current prices) of exports of wood, simply worked, and railway sleepers of wood (SITC group 248) experienced a decrease over two consecutive years resulting in its lowest value of 28.1 bln US$ in 2009. However, in 2010 it increased by 20.5 percent to reach 33.8 bln US$ (see table 2). Similarly, imports recorded its lowest value of 28.9 bln US$ in 2009 but increased by 21.9 percent to amount to 35.2 bln US$ in 2010 (see table 3). Graph 1 shows that the increase in exports for 2010 in this product group was exceeded by the increase in world exports of inedible crude materials, except fuels (SITC section 2) of 40.2 percent but near the same level as the increase in total world exports of 21.2 percent. Exports of wood, simply worked, and railway sleepers of wood (SITC group 248) accounted for 4.9 percent of world exports of SITC section 2 and 0.2 percent of total world exports in 2010 (see table 1).

The top exporting countries in 2010 were Canada and Sweden (see table 2). They accounted respectively for 14.9 and 10.1 percent of world exports. USA and China were the top destinations (see table 3). A large share of trade in wood, simply worked, and railway sleepers of wood (SITC group 248) took place in Developed Europe (see graph 2) . In 2010, both its exports and imports amounted close to 13.8 bln US$ resulting in a trade deficit of 61 mln US$. Top trade deficits were recorded by Eastern Asia (-3.8 bln US$) and Developed Asia-Pacific (-2.4 bln US$). Commonwealth of Independent States and Developed North America recorded trade surpluses amounting respectively to 2.8 and 2.2 bln US$.

Table 1: Imports (Imp.) and exports (Exp.), 1996-2010, in current prices

		1996	1997	1998	1999	2000	2001	2002	2003	2004	2005	2006	2007	2008	2009	2010
Values in Bln US$	Imp.	28.9	30.6	26.6	29.3	29.1	26.8	27.7	30.0	36.6	38.4	40.4	43.7	38.0	28.9	35.2
	Exp.	26.6	27.8	24.4	25.2	26.4	24.4	25.4	27.5	33.6	35.1	38.3	41.8	36.5	28.1	33.8
As a percentage of SITC section (%)	Imp.	11.4	11.9	11.3	12.9	11.8	11.4	11.5	10.4	9.8	9.2	8.2	7.1	5.0	5.3	4.7
	Exp.	11.9	12.2	11.7	12.8	12.4	12.1	11.8	10.7	10.4	9.6	8.6	7.6	5.6	5.7	4.9
As a percentage of world trade (%)	Imp.	0.5	0.6	0.5	0.5	0.4	0.4	0.4	0.4	0.4	0.4	0.3	0.3	0.2	0.2	0.2
	Exp.	0.5	0.5	0.5	0.5	0.4	0.4	0.4	0.4	0.4	0.3	0.3	0.3	0.2	0.2	0.2

Graph 1: Annual growth rates of exports, 1996–2010

(In percentage by year)

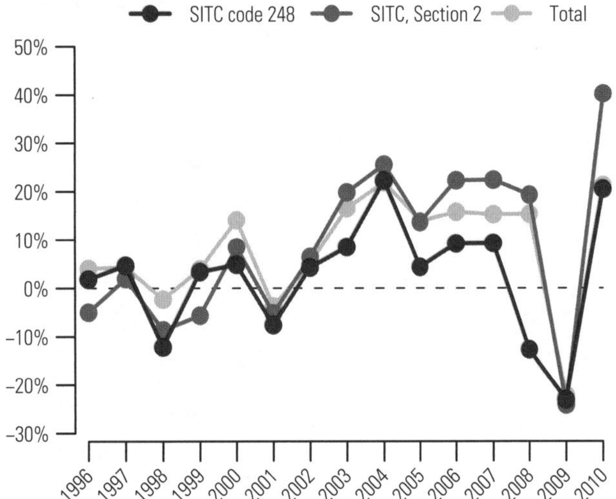

Table 2: Top exporting countries or areas in 2010

Country or area	Value (million US$)	Avg. Growth (%) 06-10	Growth (%) 09-10	World share %	Cum.
World	33 800.9	-3.1	20.5	100.0	
Canada	5 019.7	-12.4	40.0	14.9	14.9
Sweden	3 399.3	-0.2	11.2	10.1	24.9
Russian Federation	3 086.5	6.8	15.8	9.1	34.0
USA	2 601.3	-0.5	39.2	7.7	41.7
Germany	2 133.7	-2.5	11.7	6.3	48.0
Austria	1 690.7	-1.1	11.6	5.0	53.0
Finland	1 601.0	-4.1	24.2	4.7	57.8
Malaysia	1 008.8	-3.9	14.2	3.0	60.8
China	996.9	-2.1	5.8	2.9	63.7
Brazil	923.0	-10.7	16.9	2.7	66.5
Romania	745.2	6.2	26.7	2.2	68.7
Chile	727.9	-9.4	27.6	2.2	70.8
New Zealand	689.8	3.4	32.5	2.0	72.8
Thailand	573.9	13.5	48.3	1.7	74.5
Latvia	562.8	-0.5	48.9	1.7	76.2

Graph 2: Trade Balance by MDG regions 2010

(Bln US$)

Imports — Exports — Trade balance

Developed Asia-Pacific
Developed Europe
Developed N. America
South-eastern Europe
C I S
Northern Africa
Sub-Saharan Africa
Latin Am, Caribbean
Eastern Asia
Southern Asia
South-eastern Asia
Western Asia
Oceania

-15 -10 -5 0 5 10 15

Table 3: Top importing countries or areas in 2010

Country or area	Value (million US$)	Avg. Growth (%) 06-10	Growth (%) 09-10	World share %	Cum.
World	35 200.3	-3.4	21.9	100.0	
USA	4 485.0	-19.8	24.7	12.7	12.7
China	3 898.3	22.6	66.3	11.1	23.8
Japan	2 598.7	-4.1	21.9	7.4	31.2
United Kingdom	2 132.6	-4.7	22.6	6.1	37.3
Italy	1 993.0	-6.1	10.9	5.7	42.9
Germany	1 566.0	-2.7	16.1	4.4	47.4
France	1 556.1	1.4	11.5	4.4	51.8
Netherlands	1 100.0	-4.3	8.5	3.1	54.9
Canada	963.0	-2.4	32.5	2.7	57.6
Egypt	893.5	12.6	10.2	2.5	60.2
Belgium	840.9	-3.3	7.3	2.4	62.6
Austria	638.0	2.7	10.3	1.8	64.4
Viet Nam	*618.9*	13.9	66.9	1.8	66.1
Saudi Arabia	602.7	33.3	82.2	1.7	67.9
Australia	597.5	9.8	34.1	1.7	69.6

After a 24.3 percent decrease in 2009, the value (in current prices) of exports of pulp and waste paper (SITC group 251) bounced back by 42.0 percent and amounted to 43.7 bln US$ in 2010 (see table 2). Imports, showing a similar development, after a drop of 26.8 percent in 2009, increased by 44.0 percent to reach 48.9 bln US$ (see table 3). Graph 1 shows that the increase in exports for 2010 in this product group was above the increases in world exports of inedible crude materials, except fuels (SITC section 2) of 40.2 percent and in total world exports of 21.2 percent. Exports of pulp and waste paper (SITC group 251) accounted for 6.3 percent of world exports of SITC section 2 and 0.3 percent of total world exports in 2010 (see table 1).

USA, Canada and Brazil were the top exporting countries in 2010 (see table 2). They accounted respectively for 20.2, 16.2 and 10.9 percent of world exports. China was the top destination with 29.0 percent of world imports (see table 3). Other major destinations were Germany and USA. By MDG regions (see graph 2), top trade surpluses were recorded by Developed North America (+11.5 bln US$) and Latin America and the Caribbean (+5.3 bln US$) and top deficits were recorded by Eastern Asia (-16.8 bln US$) and Developed Europe (-3.8 bln US$).

Table 1: Imports (Imp.) and exports (Exp.), 1996-2010, in current prices

		1996	1997	1998	1999	2000	2001	2002	2003	2004	2005	2006	2007	2008	2009	2010
Values in Bln US$	Imp.	20.7	19.7	18.6	19.8	27.1	21.6	21.1	24.0	28.3	30.0	33.1	40.2	46.4	34.0	48.9
	Exp.	18.0	17.8	16.8	16.8	24.3	19.0	18.8	21.9	24.7	25.9	29.7	36.7	40.7	30.8	43.7
As a percentage of	Imp.	8.2	7.7	7.9	8.7	11.0	9.2	8.8	8.3	7.6	7.2	6.7	6.5	6.1	6.3	6.5
SITC section (%)	Exp.	8.0	7.8	8.1	8.6	11.4	9.4	8.8	8.5	7.7	7.1	6.6	6.7	6.2	6.2	6.3
As a percentage of	Imp.	0.4	0.4	0.3	0.3	0.4	0.3	0.3	0.3	0.3	0.3	0.3	0.3	0.3	0.3	0.3
world trade (%)	Exp.	0.3	0.3	0.3	0.3	0.4	0.3	0.3	0.3	0.3	0.2	0.2	0.3	0.3	0.2	0.3

Graph 1: Annual growth rates of exports, 1996–2010

(In percentage by year)

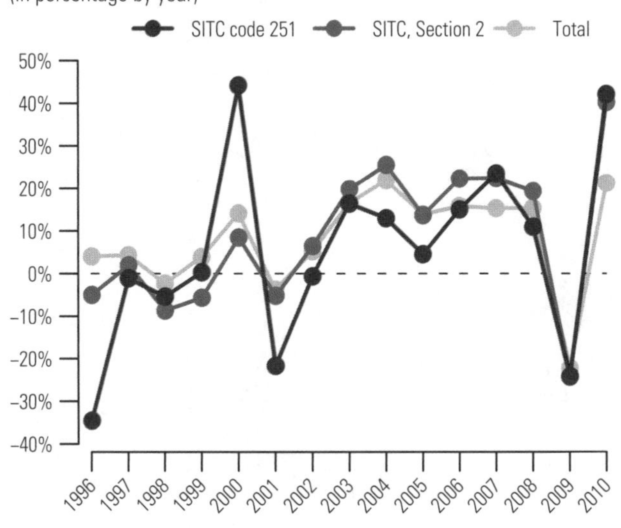

Graph 2: Trade Balance by MDG regions 2010

(Bln US$)

Imports — Exports — Trade balance

Developed Asia-Pacific
Developed Europe
Developed N. America
South-eastern Europe
CIS
Northern Africa
Sub-Saharan Africa
Latin Am, Caribbean
Eastern Asia
Southern Asia
South-eastern Asia
Western Asia
Oceania

-20 -15 -10 -5 0 5 10 15 20

Table 2: Top exporting countries or areas in 2010

Country or area	Value (million US$)	Avg. Growth (%) 06-10	Growth (%) 09-10	World share %	Cum.
World	43720.8	10.1	42.0	100.0	
USA	8849.9	10.9	30.1	20.2	20.2
Canada	7078.7	4.8	52.5	16.2	36.4
Brazil	4761.6	17.7	43.6	10.9	47.3
Sweden	2704.8	8.2	35.2	6.2	53.5
Chile	2428.5	15.5	20.5	5.6	59.1
Finland	1649.7	1.2	105.2	3.8	62.8
Indonesia	1468.9	6.9	69.1	3.4	66.2
Netherlands	1301.6	16.2	46.1	3.0	69.2
Germany	1296.3	5.7	22.4	3.0	72.1
Belgium	1163.6	5.4	37.5	2.7	74.8
Russian Federation	1149.5	7.8	61.3	2.6	77.4
Japan	1149.3	18.8	48.6	2.6	80.1
Spain	973.1	9.7	51.7	2.2	82.3
France	894.7	12.6	44.4	2.0	84.3
United Kingdom	838.6	7.9	52.5	1.9	86.2

Table 3: Top importing countries or areas in 2010

Country or area	Value (million US$)	Avg. Growth (%) 06-10	Growth (%) 09-10	World share %	Cum.
World	48908.5	10.3	44.0	100.0	
China	14178.2	18.7	33.3	29.0	29.0
Germany	4865.6	7.7	55.5	9.9	38.9
USA	4027.5	4.8	57.5	8.2	47.2
Italy	2676.6	4.8	49.4	5.5	52.6
Rep. of Korea	2239.3	9.7	53.6	4.6	57.2
France	1837.1	7.7	53.0	3.8	61.0
Indonesia	1596.4	17.0	67.9	3.3	64.2
Japan	1499.2	0.8	43.2	3.1	67.3
Netherlands	1416.8	7.7	56.4	2.9	70.2
Mexico	1166.4	9.8	43.5	2.4	72.6
Belgium	1084.0	3.8	30.1	2.2	74.8
United Kingdom	945.7	-1.9	27.5	1.9	76.7
Spain	896.3	7.5	35.5	1.8	78.6
India	863.7	9.4	12.3	1.8	80.3
Other Asia, nes	848.1	4.2	52.2	1.7	82.1

261 Silk

During the recent five years, the value (in current prices) of exports of silk (SITC group 261) increased on average by 8.9 percent and amounted to 479 mln US$ in 2010 (see table 2). During the same period, imports showed an average 4.4 percent decrease and totaled 408 mln US$ (see table 3). Graph 1 shows that the 50.4 percent increase in exports for 2010 in this product group was above the increases in world exports of inedible crude materials, except fuels (SITC section 2) of 40.2 percent and in total world exports of 21.2 percent. Exports of silk (SITC group 261) accounted for 0.1 percent of world exports of SITC section 2 and less than 0.1 percent of total world exports in 2010 (see table 1).

China was the origin of a majority of exports of silk (SITC group 261) in 2010: it accounted for 76.9 percent of world exports (see table 2). Other major exporting countries were Mozambique and Uzbekistan. India was the top destination with 37.0 percent of world imports (see table 3). Other major importing countries were Italy and Viet Nam. By MDG regions (see graph 2), Eastern Asia and Southern Asia accounted for a large share of the trade in silk (SITC group 261). Eastern Asia's exports amounted to 370 mln US$ with a trade surplus of 326 mln US$ while Southern Asia's imports amounted to 165 mln US$ with a trade deficit of 155 mln US$.

Table 1: Imports (Imp.) and exports (Exp.), 1996-2010, in current prices

		1996	1997	1998	1999	2000	2001	2002	2003	2004	2005	2006	2007	2008	2009	2010
Values in Mln US$	Imp.	661.0	694.8	504.9	522.8	503.2	420.3	398.5	359.3	370.6	454.8	489.8	461.0	479.5	376.6	408.5
	Exp.	510.8	550.2	397.9	384.5	434.1	360.2	338.5	303.2	317.3	350.5	340.5	454.0	438.1	318.3	478.7
As a percentage of	Imp.	0.3	0.3	0.2	0.2	0.2	0.2	0.2	0.1	0.1	0.1	0.1	0.1	0.1	0.1	0.1
SITC section (%)	Exp.	0.2	0.2	0.2	0.2	0.2	0.2	0.2	0.1	0.1	0.1	0.1	0.1	0.1	0.1	0.1
As a percentage of	Imp.	0.0	0.0	0.0	0.0	0.0	0.0	0.0	0.0	0.0	0.0	0.0	0.0	0.0	0.0	0.0
world trade (%)	Exp.	0.0	0.0	0.0	0.0	0.0	0.0	0.0	0.0	0.0	0.0	0.0	0.0	0.0	0.0	0.0

Graph 1: Annual growth rates of exports, 1996–2010

(In percentage by year)

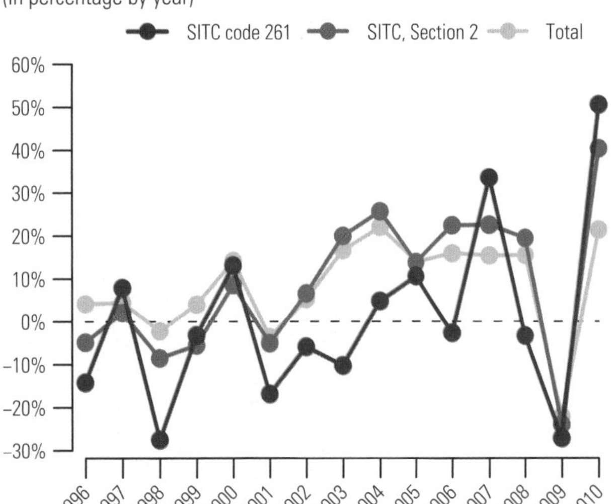

Graph 2: Trade Balance by MDG regions 2010

(Mln US$)

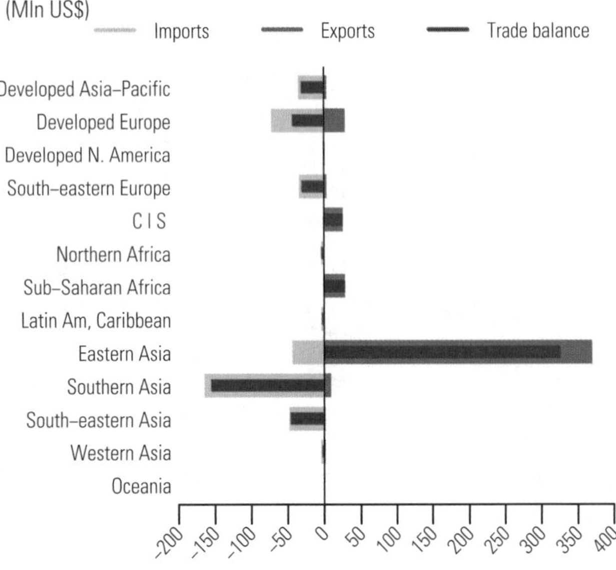

Table 2: Top exporting countries or areas in 2010

Country or area	Value (million US$)	Avg. Growth (%) 06-10	Growth (%) 09-10	World share %	Cum.
World	478.7	8.9	50.4	100.0	
China	368.0	11.8	39.8	76.9	76.9
Mozambique	29.1	5091.6		6.1	82.9
Uzbekistan	*21.9*	32.1	60.4	4.6	87.5
Italy	16.1	-20.3	83.3	3.4	90.9
Germany	11.0	-2.0	45.7	2.3	93.2
India	9.4	3.9	86.1	2.0	95.2
Romania	4.0	-17.1	31.6	0.8	96.0
Tajikistan	*2.7*	-2.6	91.0	0.6	96.5
Japan	2.3	2.9	225.4	0.5	97.0
Australia	1.9	93.4		0.4	97.4
United Kingdom	1.7	-7.9	-10.6	0.4	97.8
United Arab Emirates	1.7	-23.0	46.7	0.3	98.1
USA	1.5	0.3	-25.1	0.3	98.4
China, Hong Kong SAR	1.2	14.4	155.0	0.3	98.7
Viet Nam	*1.1*	-14.2	25.6	0.2	98.9

Table 3: Top importing countries or areas in 2010

Country or area	Value (million US$)	Avg. Growth (%) 06-10	Growth (%) 09-10	World share %	Cum.
World	408.5	-4.4	8.5	100.0	
India	151.0	-1.7	-23.9	37.0	37.0
Italy	47.9	-14.3	66.1	11.7	48.7
Viet Nam	*43.1*	11.1	66.9	10.5	59.3
Japan	34.5	-9.6	37.7	8.4	67.7
Romania	32.7	-5.4	78.3	8.0	75.7
Rep. of Korea	27.2	-7.1	21.2	6.6	82.4
China	14.2	10.0	188.9	3.5	85.8
Germany	13.3	0.1	72.6	3.2	89.1
Bangladesh	*6.4*	9.6	-4.8	1.6	90.6
France	5.2	-9.1	0.5	1.3	91.9
Pakistan	5.2	-2.4	-4.3	1.3	93.2
Tunisia	2.9	14.1	69.7	0.7	93.9
Turkey	2.4	-2.2	56.7	0.6	94.5
Thailand	2.2	-27.8	27.7	0.5	95.0
Iran	2.1	24.4	8.4	0.5	95.5

After a 14.3 percent decline in 2009, the value (in current prices) of exports of cotton (SITC group 263) bounced back by 53.5 percent and amounted to 17.0 bln US$ in 2010 (see table 2). Imports, displaying a similar development, after a drop of 29.3 percent in 2009, increased by 62.6 percent in 2010 to 16.1 bln US$ (see table 3). Graph 1 shows that the increase in exports for 2010 in this product group exceeded both the increases in world exports of inedible crude materials, except fuels (SITC section 2) of 40.2 percent and in total world exports of 21.2 percent. Exports of cotton (SITC group 263) accounted for 2.5 percent of world exports of SITC section 2 and 0.1 percent of total world exports in 2010 (see table 1).

USA, the top exporting country in 2010, accounted for 35.2 percent of world exports (see table 2). Other major exporting countries were India and Uzbekistan, respectively with 18.0 and 9.7 percent of world exports. China was the top destination with 36.4 percent of world imports (see table 3). Other major importing countries were Turkey and Indonesia. By MDG regions (see graph 2), top surpluses were recorded by Developed North America (+5.9 bln US$), Commonwealth of Independent States (+2.2 bln US$) and Southern Asia (+1.6 bln US$). Eastern Asia and South-eastern Asia recorded trade deficits amounting respectively to 6.7 bln US$ and 2.6 bln US$.

Table 1: Imports (Imp.) and exports (Exp.), 1996-2010, in current prices

		1996	1997	1998	1999	2000	2001	2002	2003	2004	2005	2006	2007	2008	2009	2010
Values in Bln US$	Imp.	11.9	11.3	9.5	7.8	8.1	8.2	6.9	8.8	12.0	10.8	12.6	12.5	14.0	9.9	16.1
	Exp.	11.7	10.5	8.8	7.2	7.6	7.4	6.8	9.7	11.9	10.5	11.8	12.4	12.9	11.1	17.0
As a percentage of SITC section (%)	Imp.	4.7	4.4	4.1	3.4	3.3	3.5	2.9	3.0	3.2	2.6	2.5	2.0	1.8	1.8	2.1
	Exp.	5.2	4.6	4.2	3.7	3.6	3.7	3.2	3.8	3.7	2.9	2.6	2.3	2.0	2.2	2.5
As a percentage of world trade (%)	Imp.	0.2	0.2	0.2	0.1	0.1	0.1	0.1	0.1	0.1	0.1	0.1	0.1	0.1	0.1	0.1
	Exp.	0.2	0.2	0.2	0.1	0.1	0.1	0.1	0.1	0.1	0.1	0.1	0.1	0.1	0.1	0.1

Graph 1: Annual growth rates of exports, 1996–2010

(In percentage by year)

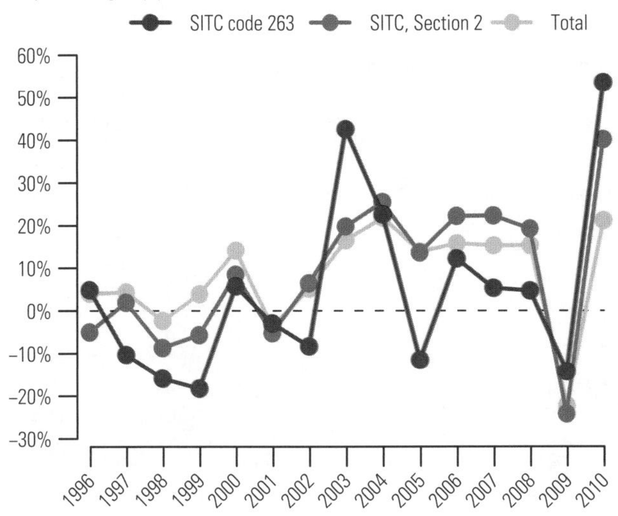

Table 2: Top exporting countries or areas in 2010

Country or area	Value (million US$)	Avg. Growth (%) 06-10	Growth (%) 09-10	World share %	Cum.
World	17025.8	9.7	53.5	100.0	
USA	5985.2	6.5	69.6	35.2	35.2
India	3065.8	32.4	195.7	18.0	53.2
Uzbekistan	*1657.7*	6.9	-1.9	9.7	62.9
Australia	935.3	5.1	121.8	5.5	68.4
Brazil	835.1	24.1	19.8	4.9	73.3
Greece	519.0	5.8	22.0	3.0	76.3
Nigeria	336.6	426.7	438.9	2.0	78.3
Turkmenistan	*335.8*	47.2	36.1	2.0	80.3
Pakistan	288.6	25.3	31.2	1.7	82.0
Tajikistan	*274.0*	4.7	181.4	1.6	83.6
Egypt	267.7	19.2	189.3	1.6	85.2
Burkina Faso	224.0	-13.1	-10.2	1.3	86.5
Mali	167.8	-9.9	-22.9	1.0	87.5
Zimbabwe	158.2	15.2	53.9	0.9	88.4
Turkey	156.8	1.4	28.8	0.9	89.3

Graph 2: Trade Balance by MDG regions 2010

(Bln US$)

Imports — Exports — Trade balance

Developed Asia-Pacific
Developed Europe
Developed N. America
South-eastern Europe
C I S
Northern Africa
Sub-Saharan Africa
Latin Am, Caribbean
Eastern Asia
Southern Asia
South-eastern Asia
Western Asia
Oceania

-8 -6 -4 -2 0 2 4 6

Table 3: Top importing countries or areas in 2010

Country or area	Value (million US$)	Avg. Growth (%) 06-10	Growth (%) 09-10	World share %	Cum.
World	16076.8	6.3	62.6	100.0	
China	5846.4	4.1	164.4	36.4	36.4
Turkey	1726.4	15.4	71.2	10.7	47.1
Indonesia	1151.3	16.6	46.9	7.2	54.3
Bangladesh	*793.2*	-1.6	-35.8	4.9	59.2
Pakistan	763.2	17.5	58.6	4.7	63.9
Thailand	742.7	6.6	51.1	4.6	68.6
Viet Nam	*659.0*	31.3	66.9	4.1	72.7
Mexico	641.5	6.6	53.4	4.0	76.7
Other Asia, nes	427.8	4.8	61.1	2.7	79.3
Rep. of Korea	408.1	7.8	39.5	2.5	81.9
Russian Federation	184.2	-9.8	0.7	1.1	83.0
China, Hong Kong SAR	180.3	1.7	41.6	1.1	84.1
Italy	178.8	-10.5	36.8	1.1	85.2
Japan	178.5	-4.6	42.0	1.1	86.3
Egypt	163.8	22.1	20.3	1.0	87.4

264 Jute, other textile bast fibres, nes, not spun; tow and waste

Since 2006, the value (in current prices) of exports of jute, other textile bast fibres, nes, not spun; tow and waste (SITC group 264) increased on average by 10.1 percent each year with a 0.2 percent decrease in 2010 amounting to 230 mln US$ (see table 2). During the same period, imports showed a different development. After a 1.3 percent drop in 2009, it bounced back by 40.4 percent to reach 292 mln US$. Graph 1 shows that the decrease in exports for 2010 in this product group was contrary to the increases in world exports of inedible crude materials, except fuels (SITC section 2) of 40.2 percent and in total world exports of 21.2 percent. Exports of jute, other textile bast fibres, nes, not spun; tow and waste (SITC group 264) accounted for less than 0.1 percent of both world exports of SITC section 2 and total world exports in 2010 (see table 1).

Bangladesh, the top exporting country accounted for 68.0 percent of world exports in 2010 (see table 2). Other major exporting countries were India and Kenya respectively with 14.6 and 8.7 percent of world exports. China, Pakistan and India were the major destinations respectively with 27.4, 23.2 and 14.8 percent of world imports (see table 3). By MDG regions (see graph 2), Southern Asia accounted for a large share of trade in jute, other textile bast fibres, nes, not spun; tow and waste (SITC group 264). In 2010, its exports amounted to 190 mln US$ and imports to 140 mln US$, resulting in a trade surplus of 50 mln US$. Sub-Saharan Africa recorded a trade surplus of 11 mln US$. Eastern Asia recorded a deficit of 87 mln US$.

Table 1: Imports (Imp.) and exports (Exp.), 1996-2010, in current prices

		1996	1997	1998	1999	2000	2001	2002	2003	2004	2005	2006	2007	2008	2009	2010
Values in Mln US$	Imp.	121.9	137.3	100.8	87.3	95.2	89.1	115.1	101.8	101.1	120.8	160.5	187.7	211.0	208.2	292.3
	Exp.	87.6	115.4	98.4	74.6	79.6	55.6	62.5	59.5	103.4	139.3	155.9	228.4	221.8	229.9	229.5
As a percentage of SITC section (%)	Imp.	0.0	0.1	0.0	0.0	0.0	0.0	0.0	0.0	0.0	0.0	0.0	0.0	0.0	0.0	0.0
	Exp.	0.0	0.1	0.0	0.0	0.0	0.0	0.0	0.0	0.0	0.0	0.0	0.0	0.0	0.0	0.0
As a percentage of world trade (%)	Imp.	0.0	0.0	0.0	0.0	0.0	0.0	0.0	0.0	0.0	0.0	0.0	0.0	0.0	0.0	0.0
	Exp.	0.0	0.0	0.0	0.0	0.0	0.0	0.0	0.0	0.0	0.0	0.0	0.0	0.0	0.0	0.0

Graph 1: Annual growth rates of exports, 1996–2010

(In percentage by year)

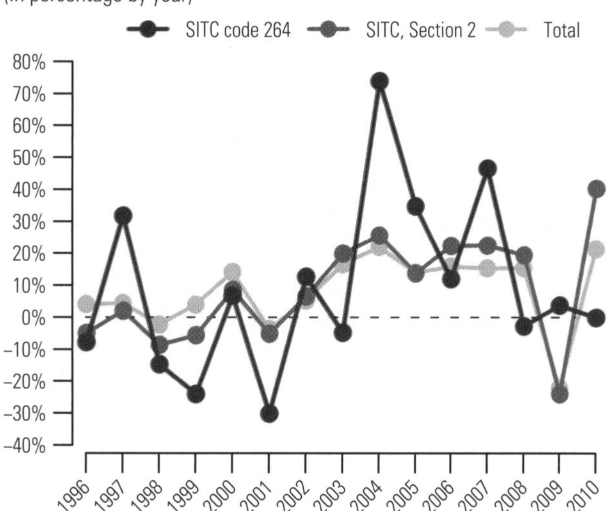

Graph 2: Trade Balance by MDG regions 2010

(Mln US$)

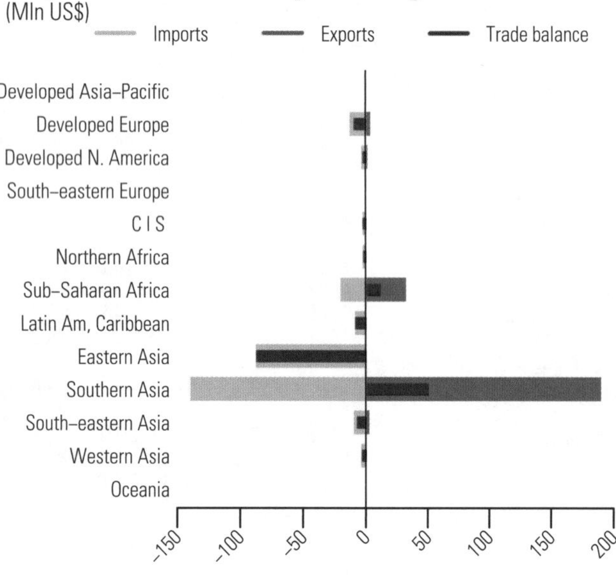

Table 2: Top exporting countries or areas in 2010

Country or area	Value (million US$)	Avg. Growth (%) 06-10	Growth (%) 09-10	World share %	Cum.
World	229.5	10.1	-0.2	100.0	
Bangladesh	*156.1*	2.5	-16.2	68.0	68.0
India	33.5	128.9	374.7	14.6	82.6
Kenya	20.0	1462.9	20.0	8.7	91.3
United Rep. of Tanzania	8.2	211.2	-4.3	3.6	94.9
Mozambique	2.5	16.9	122.5	1.1	96.0
Belgium	1.6	-4.2	20.7	0.7	96.7
Viet Nam	*1.3*	-7.4	25.6	0.6	97.2
USA	0.9	13.6	-3.3	0.4	97.6
Madagascar	0.9	...	-21.3	0.4	98.0
Myanmar	*0.6*	-27.9	-66.0	0.3	98.3
France	0.5	-7.9	9.9	0.2	98.5
United Arab Emirates	0.3	14.2	-24.8	0.1	98.7
Egypt	0.3	...	57.6	0.1	98.8
Israel	0.3	...	555.0	0.1	98.9
Italy	0.3	-11.4	-12.8	0.1	99.0

Table 3: Top importing countries or areas in 2010

Country or area	Value (million US$)	Avg. Growth (%) 06-10	Growth (%) 09-10	World share %	Cum.
World	292.3	16.2	40.4	100.0	
China	80.2	25.5	73.0	27.4	27.4
Pakistan	67.8	10.1	26.0	23.2	50.6
India	43.3	3.9	13.2	14.8	65.4
Nepal	27.8	100.1	69.3	9.5	75.0
Côte d'Ivoire	15.6	24.7	199.0	5.3	80.3
Brazil	7.2	66.4	496.8	2.5	82.8
Rep. of Korea	7.1	28.6	154.1	2.4	85.2
Malaysia	4.8	42.6	134.8	1.6	86.8
Viet Nam	*3.9*	8.1	66.9	1.3	88.2
United Kingdom	3.5	18.5	-35.3	1.2	89.4
USA	3.1	22.6	54.5	1.0	90.4
Ethiopia	3.0	5.0	5.7	1.0	91.4
Russian Federation	2.5	12.4	50.9	0.9	92.3
Saudi Arabia	2.4	39.2	56.2	0.8	93.1
Germany	1.9	25.3	49.1	0.7	93.8

Source: UN Comtrade

During the recent five years, the value (in current prices) of exports of vegetable textile fibres (other than cotton or jute) not spun; waste (SITC group 265) increased on average by 1.3 percent to reach 775 mln US$ in 2010 (see table 2). During the same period, imports increased on average by 2.1 percent to 774 mln US$ (see table 3). Graph 1 shows that the increase in exports for 2010 in this product group was below the increase in world exports of inedible crude materials, except fuels (SITC section 2) of 40.2 percent but was greater than the increase in total world exports of 21.2 percent. Exports of vegetable textile fibres (other than cotton or jute) not spun; waste (SITC group 265) accounted for 0.1 percent of world exports of SITC section 2 and less than 0.1 percent of total world exports in 2010 (see table 1).

France was the top exporting country in 2010 and accounted for nearly a third (32.1 percent) of world exports (see table 2). Other major exporting countries were Belgium and Sri Lanka, respectively with 18.5 and 12.5 percent of world exports. China, the top destination accounted for 50.0 percent of imports (see table 3). Other destinations were Belgium and USA. By MDG regions (see graph 2), Developed Europe's exports amounted to 438 mln US$ compared to 245 mln US$ for imports, resulting in a trade surplus of 193 mln US$. Eastern Asia recorded a trade deficit of 379 mln US$.

Table 1: Imports (Imp.) and exports (Exp.), 1996-2010, in current prices

		1996	1997	1998	1999	2000	2001	2002	2003	2004	2005	2006	2007	2008	2009	2010
Values in Mln US$	Imp.	425.1	456.5	456.1	510.6	615.7	553.0	546.5	722.8	820.8	722.8	713.9	775.4	677.3	583.4	774.3
	Exp.	386.6	413.6	432.7	499.1	602.9	512.0	536.6	713.8	783.5	693.8	735.1	713.8	638.4	579.2	775.2
As a percentage of SITC section (%)	Imp.	0.2	0.2	0.2	0.2	0.2	0.2	0.2	0.3	0.2	0.2	0.1	0.1	0.1	0.1	0.1
	Exp.	0.2	0.2	0.2	0.3	0.3	0.3	0.3	0.3	0.2	0.2	0.2	0.1	0.1	0.1	0.1
As a percentage of world trade (%)	Imp.	0.0	0.0	0.0	0.0	0.0	0.0	0.0	0.0	0.0	0.0	0.0	0.0	0.0	0.0	0.0
	Exp.	0.0	0.0	0.0	0.0	0.0	0.0	0.0	0.0	0.0	0.0	0.0	0.0	0.0	0.0	0.0

Graph 1: Annual growth rates of exports, 1996–2010
(In percentage by year)

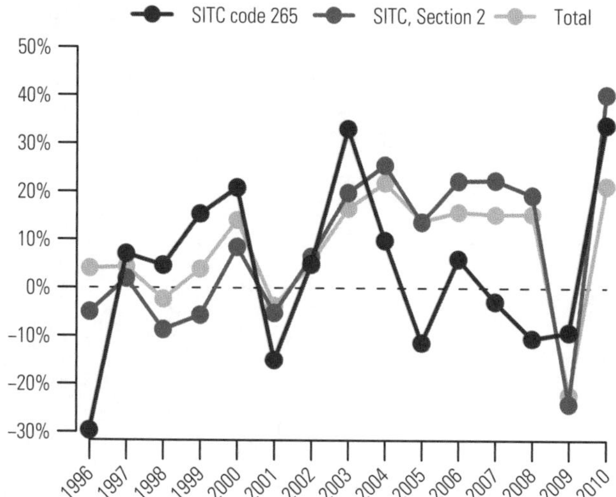

Graph 2: Trade Balance by MDG regions 2010
(Mln US$)

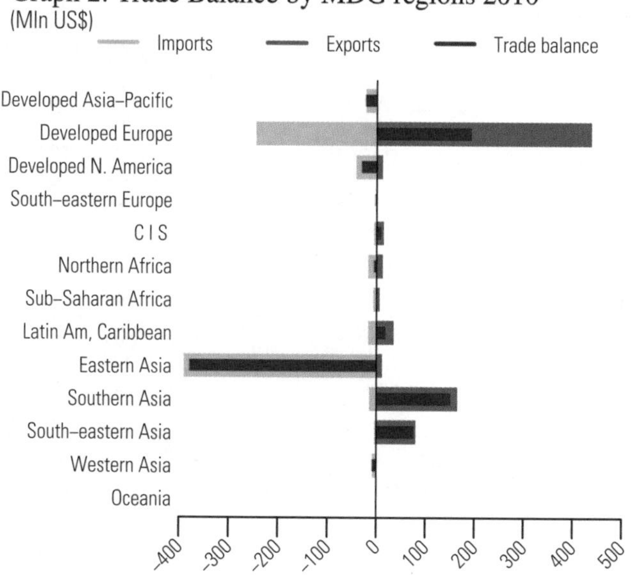

Table 2: Top exporting countries or areas in 2010

Country or area	Value (million US$)	Avg. Growth (%) 06-10	Growth (%) 09-10	World share %	Cum.
World	775.2	1.3	33.8	100.0	
France	248.8	-0.2	42.9	32.1	32.1
Belgium	143.3	-1.1	49.1	18.5	50.6
Sri Lanka	96.6	16.8	25.2	12.5	63.0
India	67.2	40.8	47.9	8.7	71.7
Viet Nam	*32.6*	8.8	25.6	4.2	75.9
Brazil	21.0	-10.1	13.7	2.7	78.6
Philippines	16.8	2.1	45.1	2.2	80.8
Netherlands	16.6	-8.7	2.6	2.1	82.9
Thailand	16.1	35.4	38.8	2.1	85.0
Ecuador	13.1	13.4	1.9	1.7	86.7
Belarus	12.7	1.8	115.6	1.6	88.4
Egypt	12.3	-3.6	7.7	1.6	89.9
Lithuania	10.6	-8.6	69.8	1.4	91.3
China	9.9	4.5	39.7	1.3	92.6
Canada	9.9	-17.5	-37.0	1.3	93.9

Table 3: Top importing countries or areas in 2010

Country or area	Value (million US$)	Avg. Growth (%) 06-10	Growth (%) 09-10	World share %	Cum.
World	774.3	2.1	32.7	100.0	
China	386.8	7.9	48.3	50.0	50.0
Belgium	82.3	-2.0	28.1	10.6	60.6
USA	37.8	10.0	8.9	4.9	65.5
Netherlands	22.1	0.2	-11.5	2.9	68.3
Spain	21.6	-6.5	-7.4	2.8	71.1
Japan	20.4	0.1	40.0	2.6	73.7
United Kingdom	20.2	1.8	17.5	2.6	76.3
France	18.8	-5.3	25.6	2.4	78.8
Poland	14.5	-8.8	80.8	1.9	80.6
Lithuania	14.3	-10.0	87.9	1.8	82.5
Italy	11.3	-24.0	42.4	1.5	83.9
Germany	11.2	-4.2	27.8	1.5	85.4
India	10.0	2.7	0.6	1.3	86.7
Mexico	9.8	12.6	88.8	1.3	87.9
Tunisia	9.5	13.4	86.6	1.2	89.2

Source: UN Comtrade

266 Synthetic fibres suitable for spinning

After a 23.1 percent decrease in 2009, the value (in current prices) of exports of synthetic fibres suitable for spinning (SITC group 266) bounced back by 37.7 percent and amounted to 7.2 bln US$ (see table 2). Imports, with a similar development, after a 20.0 percent drop in 2009, increased by 31.4 percent and amounted to 8.7 bln US$ (see table 3). Graph 1 shows that the increase in exports for 2010 in this product group was close to the increase in world exports of inedible crude materials, except fuels (SITC section 2) of 40.2 percent and above the increase in total world exports of 21.2 percent. Exports of synthetic fibres suitable for spinning (SITC group 266) accounted for 1.0 percent of world exports of SITC section 2 and less than 0.1 percent of total world exports in 2010 (see table 1).

The top exporting countries in 2010 were Rep. of Korea and China (see table 2). They accounted respectively for 14.8 and 12.6 percent of world exports. China, USA and Germany were the top destinations (see table 3). By MDG regions (see graph 2), Eastern Asia's exports amounted to 2.9 bln US$ compared to 1.1 bln US$ for imports, resulting in a trade surplus of 1.8 bln US$. A large trade surplus was also recorded by Developed Asia-Pacific (+0.6 bln US$). Top trade deficits were recorded by Developed Europe (-1.4 bln US$), Western Asia (-0.7 bln US$) and Southern Asia (-0.6 bln US$).

Table 1: Imports (Imp.) and exports (Exp.), 1996-2010, in current prices

		1996	1997	1998	1999	2000	2001	2002	2003	2004	2005	2006	2007	2008	2009	2010
Values in Bln US$	Imp.	6.7	6.6	5.8	5.1	5.8	5.3	5.5	6.3	7.2	7.7	7.4	8.1	8.3	6.6	8.7
	Exp.	5.2	5.4	4.7	4.2	4.7	4.0	4.3	4.8	5.5	5.9	5.9	6.8	6.8	5.2	7.2
As a percentage of SITC section (%)	Imp.	2.6	2.6	2.4	2.2	2.3	2.3	2.3	2.2	1.9	1.9	1.5	1.3	1.1	1.2	1.2
	Exp.	2.3	2.4	2.2	2.2	2.2	2.0	2.0	1.9	1.7	1.6	1.3	1.2	1.0	1.1	1.0
As a percentage of world trade (%)	Imp.	0.1	0.1	0.1	0.1	0.1	0.1	0.1	0.1	0.1	0.1	0.1	0.1	0.1	0.1	0.1
	Exp.	0.1	0.1	0.1	0.1	0.1	0.1	0.1	0.1	0.1	0.1	0.0	0.0	0.0	0.0	0.0

Graph 1: Annual growth rates of exports, 1996–2010

(In percentage by year)

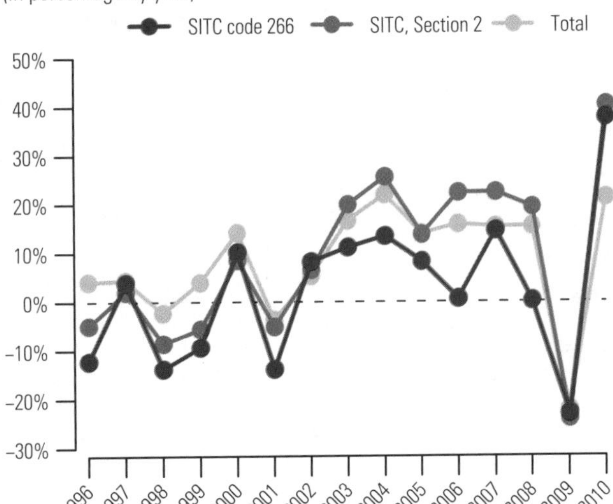

Table 2: Top exporting countries or areas in 2010

Country or area	Value (million US$)	Avg. Growth (%) 06-10	Growth (%) 09-10	World share %	Cum.
World	7 209.4	5.0	37.7	100.0	
Rep. of Korea	1 064.7	5.8	35.1	14.8	14.8
China	911.0	20.6	66.9	12.6	27.4
Other Asia, nes	908.6	-0.3	26.0	12.6	40.0
Japan	822.0	1.3	33.8	11.4	51.4
Thailand	530.2	8.8	39.9	7.4	58.8
USA	434.4	-2.9	53.1	6.0	64.8
Belgium	301.9	8.3	42.6	4.2	69.0
India	293.2	23.2	65.8	4.1	73.0
Belarus	233.5	10.6	43.7	3.2	76.3
Portugal	135.9	3.2	20.2	1.9	78.2
Malaysia	117.7	10.3	46.0	1.6	79.8
Ireland	115.4	3.2	14.7	1.6	81.4
Germany	111.3	-8.2	-5.1	1.5	82.9
Nigeria	95.9	101.0	89.3	1.3	84.3
Indonesia	93.1	-1.6	15.6	1.3	85.6

Graph 2: Trade Balance by MDG regions 2010

(Bln US$)

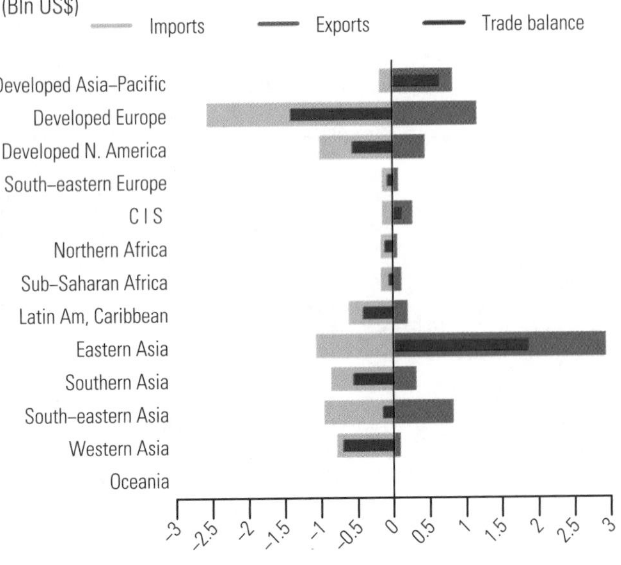

Table 3: Top importing countries or areas in 2010

Country or area	Value (million US$)	Avg. Growth (%) 06-10	Growth (%) 09-10	World share %	Cum.
World	8 707.8	4.1	31.4	100.0	
China	944.7	-4.3	35.0	10.8	10.8
USA	839.2	0.8	40.5	9.6	20.5
Germany	688.7	5.8	36.0	7.9	28.4
Italy	484.2	-0.9	32.7	5.6	34.0
Turkey	411.2	3.5	38.3	4.7	38.7
Iran	400.2	45.0	8.4	4.6	43.3
Viet Nam	*392.1*	21.1	66.9	4.5	47.8
Indonesia	334.7	22.4	62.1	3.8	51.6
Pakistan	259.9	19.6	38.6	3.0	54.6
United Kingdom	240.6	1.0	19.9	2.8	57.4
France	238.8	-0.9	27.5	2.7	60.1
Mexico	217.0	-4.0	28.5	2.5	62.6
Canada	165.1	-0.7	36.2	1.9	64.5
Belgium	157.8	2.7	25.4	1.8	66.3
Syria	*157.5*	14.7	-15.7	1.8	68.1

During the recent five years , the value (in current prices) of exports of other man-made fiber suitable for spinning; waste of man-made fibres (SITC group 267) increased on average by 5.7 percent and amounted to 4.3 bln US$ in 2010 (see table 2). Imports showed a similar development with an average increase of 12.7 percent to amount to 5.1 bln US$ (see table 3). Graph 1 shows that the increase in exports for 2010 in this product group was exceeded by the increases in world exports of inedible crude materials, except fuels (SITC section 2) of 40.2 percent and in total world exports of 21.2 percent. Exports of other man-made fiber suitable for spinning; waste of man-made fibres (SITC group 267) accounted for 0.6 percent of world exports of SITC section 2 and less than 0.1 percent of total world exports in 2010 (see table 1).

The top exporting countries in 2010 were USA, Germany and Japan (see table 2). They accounted respectively for 22.7, 13.5 and 11.3 percent of world exports. China, Turkey and USA were the three major destinations (see table 3). By MDG regions (see graph 2), a large share of trade in other man-made fiber suitable for spinning; waste of man-made fibres (SITC group 267) occurred in Developed Europe. In 2010, its exports amounted to 1.2 bln US$ while imports were valued at 1.1 bln US$ resulting in a trade surplus of 0.1 bln US$. Developed North America also recorded a surplus of 0.7 bln US$ while significant deficits were recorded by Western Asia (-0.7 bln US$), Eastern Asia (-0.7 bln US$) among others.

Table 1: Imports (Imp.) and exports (Exp.), 1996-2010, in current prices

		1996	1997	1998	1999	2000	2001	2002	2003	2004	2005	2006	2007	2008	2009	2010
Values in Bln US$	Imp.	2.3	2.3	2.2	2.1	2.2	2.2	2.3	2.5	3.0	3.0	3.1	4.1	4.6	4.3	5.1
	Exp.	2.9	2.7	2.4	2.1	2.3	2.2	2.6	2.7	3.3	3.2	3.5	4.4	4.4	3.6	4.3
As a percentage of SITC section (%)	Imp.	0.9	0.9	1.0	0.9	0.9	0.9	1.0	0.9	0.8	0.7	0.6	0.7	0.6	0.8	0.7
	Exp.	1.3	1.2	1.1	1.1	1.1	1.1	1.2	1.1	1.0	0.9	0.8	0.8	0.7	0.7	0.6
As a percentage of world trade (%)	Imp.	0.0	0.0	0.0	0.0	0.0	0.0	0.0	0.0	0.0	0.0	0.0	0.0	0.0	0.0	0.0
	Exp.	0.1	0.0	0.0	0.0	0.0	0.0	0.0	0.0	0.0	0.0	0.0	0.0	0.0	0.0	0.0

Graph 1: Annual growth rates of exports, 1996–2010

(In percentage by year)

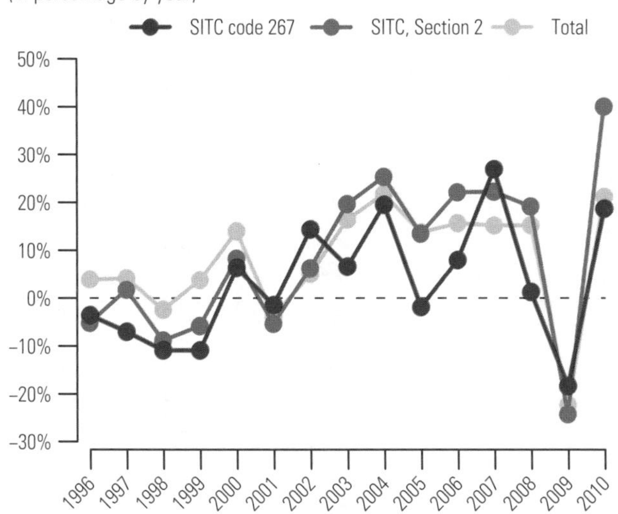

Graph 2: Trade Balance by MDG regions 2010

(Bln US$)

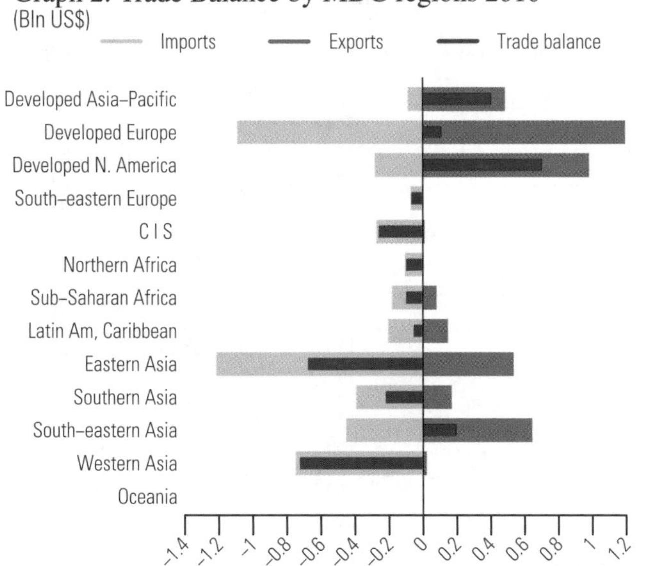

Table 2: Top exporting countries or areas in 2010

Country or area	Value (million US$)	Avg. Growth (%) 06-10	Growth (%) 09-10	World share %	Cum.
World	4317.6	5.7	18.7	100.0	
USA	981.3	11.9	2.1	22.7	22.7
Germany	582.9	-17.5	4.3	13.5	36.2
Japan	489.7	20.1	20.7	11.3	47.6
Indonesia	410.9	29.0	55.5	9.5	57.1
Belgium	318.4	10.6	8.7	7.4	64.5
China	267.0	27.2	16.2	6.2	70.6
Thailand	210.8	30.4	62.8	4.9	75.5
United Kingdom	201.1	14.3	20.8	4.7	80.2
Other Asia, nes	196.7	0.6	7.0	4.6	84.7
India	169.1	46.7	39.4	3.9	88.7
Mexico	84.7	5.5	25.7	2.0	90.6
Chad	*79.7*	...		1.8	92.5
Brazil	59.5	11.7	12.8	1.4	93.8
Rep. of Korea	46.0	8.9	786.9	1.1	94.9
China, Hong Kong SAR	29.9	5.6	-25.7	0.7	95.6

Table 3: Top importing countries or areas in 2010

Country or area	Value (million US$)	Avg. Growth (%) 06-10	Growth (%) 09-10	World share %	Cum.
World	5066.6	12.7	16.9	100.0	
China	881.1	23.1	21.2	17.4	17.4
Turkey	648.2	19.0	36.0	12.8	30.2
USA	246.1	13.5	8.2	4.9	35.0
Germany	224.4	6.7	18.0	4.4	39.5
Rep. of Korea	211.5	12.5	17.8	4.2	43.6
Pakistan	195.8	11.1	45.1	3.9	47.5
Indonesia	191.9	36.4	7.6	3.8	51.3
Russian Federation	170.3	18.8	4.0	3.4	54.7
Italy	130.6	-3.4	9.7	2.6	57.2
Nigeria	122.1	47.3	203.7	2.4	59.6
Viet Nam	*116.3*	48.5	66.9	2.3	61.9
Belgium	103.7	19.5	-17.1	2.0	64.0
France	96.6	4.1	14.0	1.9	65.9
Spain	86.1	0.7	13.2	1.7	67.6
Poland	74.6	3.4	8.6	1.5	69.1

268 Wool and other animal hair (including wool tops)

After a 25.2 percent drop in 2009, the value (in current prices) of exports of wool and other animal hair, including wool tops (SITC group 268) bounced back by 35.1 percent in 2010 and amounted to 5.5 bln US$ (see table 2). During the same period, imports showed a similar development and increased by 39.0 percent to 5.5 bln US$ in 2010 (see table 3). Graph 1 shows that the increase in exports for 2010 in this product group was below the increase in world exports of inedible crude materials, except fuels (SITC section 2) of 40.2 percent but above the increase in total world exports of 21.2 percent. Exports of wool and other animal hair, including wool tops (SITC group 268) accounted for 0.8 percent of world exports of SITC section 2 and less than 0.1 percent of total world exports in 2010 (see table 1).

Exports of Australia, the top exporting country in 2010, accounted for 36.7 percent of world exports (see table 2). Other major exporting countries were China and New Zealand, respectively with 14.5 and 8.3 percent of world exports. China, the top destination in 2010, accounted for 39.2 percent of world imports (see table 3). Other major destinations were Italy and Germany. By MDG regions (see graph 2), Eastern Asia and Developed Europe accounted for a large share of imports in wool and other animal hair (SITC group 268) in 2010. They also recorded trade deficits amounting respectively to 1.5 bln US$ and 1.0 bln US$. Developed Asia-Pacific's exports amounted to 2.5 bln US$, resulting in a trade surplus of 2.3 bln US$.

Table 1: Imports (Imp.) and exports (Exp.), 1996-2010, in current prices

		1996	1997	1998	1999	2000	2001	2002	2003	2004	2005	2006	2007	2008	2009	2010
Values in Bln US$	Imp.	6.8	6.7	5.1	4.4	5.1	4.7	4.7	5.0	5.3	5.1	5.2	6.0	5.7	4.0	5.5
	Exp.	6.9	6.8	4.7	4.2	4.7	4.3	4.7	4.7	5.0	4.9	5.2	6.1	5.4	4.0	5.5
As a percentage of SITC section (%)	Imp.	2.7	2.6	2.2	1.9	2.1	2.0	2.0	1.7	1.4	1.2	1.1	1.0	0.7	0.7	0.7
	Exp.	3.1	3.0	2.2	2.1	2.2	2.1	2.2	1.8	1.6	1.3	1.2	1.1	0.8	0.8	0.8
As a percentage of world trade (%)	Imp.	0.1	0.1	0.1	0.1	0.1	0.1	0.1	0.1	0.1	0.0	0.0	0.0	0.0	0.0	0.0
	Exp.	0.1	0.1	0.1	0.1	0.1	0.1	0.1	0.1	0.1	0.0	0.0	0.0	0.0	0.0	0.0

Graph 1: Annual growth rates of exports, 1996–2010

(In percentage by year)

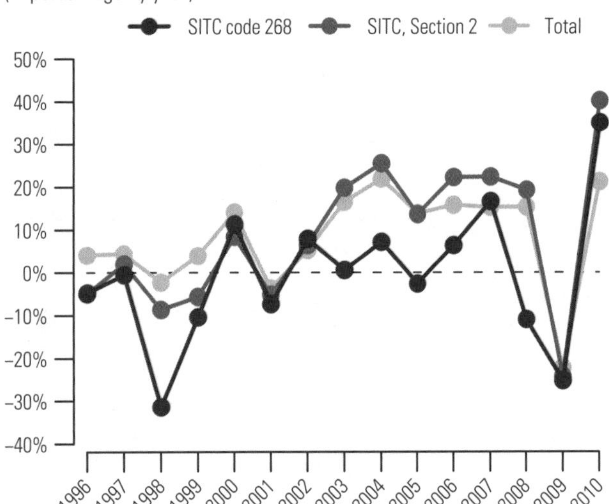

Table 2: Top exporting countries or areas in 2010

Country or area	Value (million US$)	Avg. Growth (%) 06-10	Growth (%) 09-10	World share %	Cum.
World	5453.3	1.2	35.1	100.0	
Australia	1999.1	2.9	38.5	36.7	36.7
China	788.1	6.0	67.5	14.5	51.1
New Zealand	449.9	-0.5	33.1	8.3	59.4
Germany	295.4	1.1	52.6	5.4	64.8
South Africa	266.9	7.4	15.0	4.9	69.7
Argentina	229.6	6.7	57.3	4.2	73.9
Uruguay	*194.9*	3.7	24.5	3.6	77.5
Italy	191.0	2.2	19.6	3.5	81.0
Czech Rep.	166.8	4.5	57.9	3.1	84.0
United Kingdom	100.5	-16.7	36.5	1.8	85.9
Mongolia	*99.6*	-10.8	-48.6	1.8	87.7
Other Asia, nes	53.5	-8.9	30.3	1.0	88.7
Peru	53.2	11.0	35.2	1.0	89.6
India	48.9	16.6	33.5	0.9	90.5
Spain	42.9	-2.9	19.5	0.8	91.3

Graph 2: Trade Balance by MDG regions 2010

(Bln US$)

Imports — Exports — Trade balance

Developed Asia-Pacific
Developed Europe
Developed N. America
South-eastern Europe
CIS
Northern Africa
Sub-Saharan Africa
Latin Am, Caribbean
Eastern Asia
Southern Asia
South-eastern Asia
Western Asia
Oceania

-2.5 -2 -1.5 -1 -0.5 0 0.5 1 1.5 2 2.5

Table 3: Top importing countries or areas in 2010

Country or area	Value (million US$)	Avg. Growth (%) 06-10	Growth (%) 09-10	World share %	Cum.
World	5514.8	1.5	39.0	100.0	
China	2159.7	11.0	33.7	39.2	39.2
Italy	862.4	-3.2	47.6	15.6	54.8
Germany	373.3	0.1	88.0	6.8	61.6
India	253.1	2.2	31.2	4.6	66.2
Rep. of Korea	233.5	5.9	36.1	4.2	70.4
Czech Rep.	205.1	4.9	73.3	3.7	74.1
Turkey	148.8	-3.2	40.6	2.7	76.8
Poland	132.8	9.6	54.5	2.4	79.2
Japan	118.0	-10.6	38.9	2.1	81.4
United Kingdom	107.0	-15.4	59.4	1.9	83.3
Romania	84.3	7.5	17.1	1.5	84.8
Other Asia, nes	72.3	-2.9	51.0	1.3	86.1
Bulgaria	69.7	-8.5	48.8	1.3	87.4
Mexico	55.8	-2.6	17.9	1.0	88.4
Belgium	54.2	-13.4	2.3	1.0	89.4

After several years of continuous growth marked by a peak of 3.1 bln US$ in 2008, the value (in current prices) of exports of worn clothing and other worn textile articles; rags (SITC group 269) had a slight decrease of 0.6 percent in 2009 but increased by 13.0 percent in 2010 to reach 3.5 bln US$ (see table 2). During the same period, imports increased on average by 10.9 percent to 2.9 bln US$ (see table 3). Graph 1 shows that the increase of exports for 2010 in this product group was exceeded by both increases in world exports of inedible crude materials, except fuels (SITC section 2) of 40.2 percent and in total world exports of 21.2 percent. Exports of worn clothing and other worn textile articles; rags (SITC group 269) accounted for 0.5 percent of world exports of SITC section 2 and less than 0.1 percent of total world exports in 2010 (see table 1).

USA, United Kingdom and Germany were the top exporting countries in 2010 (see table 2). They accounted respectively for 16.2, 12.6 and 10.3 percent of world exports. Major destinations in 2010 were Russian Federation, Poland and Pakistan (see table 3). By MDG regions (see graph 2), Developed Europe was the origin of a majority of exports of worn clothing and other worn textile articles; rags (SITC group 269). In 2010, its exports were valued at 1.7 bln US$ compared to 0.6 bln US$ for imports, resulting in a trade surplus of 1.1 bln US$. The top trade deficit was recorded by Sub-Saharan Africa at 0.7 bln US$.

Table 1: Imports (Imp.) and exports (Exp.), 1996-2010, in current prices

		1996	1997	1998	1999	2000	2001	2002	2003	2004	2005	2006	2007	2008	2009	2010
Values in Bln US$	Imp.	1.5	1.5	1.4	1.4	1.4	1.4	1.6	1.6	1.7	1.9	1.9	2.3	2.7	2.8	2.9
	Exp.	1.7	1.7	1.6	1.5	1.5	1.5	1.7	1.7	1.9	2.1	2.4	2.9	3.1	3.1	3.5
As a percentage of SITC section (%)	Imp.	0.6	0.6	0.6	0.6	0.6	0.6	0.7	0.5	0.5	0.4	0.4	0.4	0.4	0.5	0.4
	Exp.	0.7	0.8	0.8	0.8	0.7	0.8	0.8	0.7	0.6	0.6	0.5	0.5	0.5	0.6	0.5
As a percentage of world trade (%)	Imp.	0.0	0.0	0.0	0.0	0.0	0.0	0.0	0.0	0.0	0.0	0.0	0.0	0.0	0.0	0.0
	Exp.	0.0	0.0	0.0	0.0	0.0	0.0	0.0	0.0	0.0	0.0	0.0	0.0	0.0	0.0	0.0

Graph 1: Annual growth rates of exports, 1996–2010

(In percentage by year)

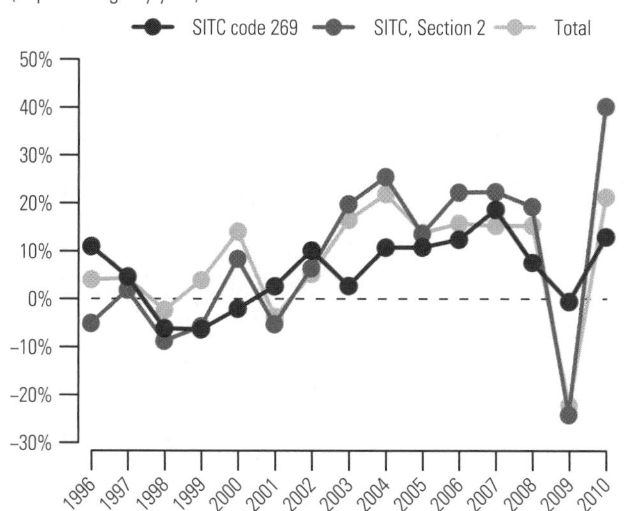

Table 2: Top exporting countries or areas in 2010

Country or area	Value (million US$)	Avg. Growth (%) 06-10	Growth (%) 09-10	World share %	Cum.
World	3455.1	9.4	13.0	100.0	
USA	560.0	13.6	21.0	16.2	16.2
United Kingdom	433.9	10.3	15.6	12.6	28.8
Germany	357.3	7.7	-3.7	10.3	39.1
Rep. of Korea	237.4	13.1	-1.8	6.9	46.0
Canada	184.2	1.9	10.3	5.3	51.3
Netherlands	167.8	4.1	7.1	4.9	56.2
Italy	136.5	12.9	18.0	4.0	60.1
Belgium	125.2	8.6	-3.2	3.6	63.7
Japan	96.6	17.0	10.0	2.8	66.5
Poland	80.0	17.9	18.0	2.3	68.8
France	63.4	9.8	6.6	1.8	70.7
Malaysia	62.8	17.9	42.3	1.8	72.5
India	57.5	101.1	-29.3	1.7	74.2
Lithuania	49.6	30.5	52.7	1.4	75.6
Switzerland	46.8	8.2	3.2	1.4	77.0

Graph 2: Trade Balance by MDG regions 2010

(Bln US$)

Imports — Exports — Trade balance

Developed Asia-Pacific
Developed Europe
Developed N. America
South-eastern Europe
C I S
Northern Africa
Sub-Saharan Africa
Latin Am, Caribbean
Eastern Asia
Southern Asia
South-eastern Asia
Western Asia
Oceania

-0.8 -0.6 -0.4 -0.2 0 0.2 0.4 0.6 0.8 1 1.2 1.4 1.6 1.8

Table 3: Top importing countries or areas in 2010

Country or area	Value (million US$)	Avg. Growth (%) 06-10	Growth (%) 09-10	World share %	Cum.
World	2938.2	10.9	5.1	100.0	
Russian Federation	133.2	31.5	49.9	4.5	4.5
Poland	122.3	23.6	25.4	4.2	8.7
Pakistan	108.9	20.6	16.8	3.7	12.4
Ukraine	100.6	20.3	75.6	3.4	15.8
Malaysia	89.0	12.7	-6.9	3.0	18.9
USA	85.6	-4.7	14.6	2.9	21.8
Angola	*83.6*	20.5	-20.8	2.8	24.6
Kenya	82.4	20.4	40.4	2.8	27.4
Tunisia	79.3	11.4	5.0	2.7	30.1
India	74.6	11.3	-39.7	2.5	32.7
Canada	70.0	4.6	6.7	2.4	35.0
Netherlands	69.0	7.3	12.7	2.3	37.4
Cameroon	67.5	11.2	-4.9	2.3	39.7
Cambodia	66.5	9.4	9.3	2.3	41.9
Ghana	65.6	9.7	11.3	2.2	44.2

Source: UN Comtrade

272 Fertilizers crude, other than those of division 56

The values (in current prices) of trade in crude fertilizer, other than those of division 56 (SITC group 272) underwent a big change during the recent five years. Exports increased by 197.8 percent in 2008 then contracted sharply by 49.9 percent in 2009 and increased by 19.3 percent in 2010 to 3.4 bln US$ (see table 2). Imports had a similar development and increased by 15.0 percent in 2010 totaling 3.6 bln US$ (see table 3). Graph 1 shows that the increase in exports for 2010 in this product group was well below the increases in world exports of inedible crude materials, except fuels (SITC section 2) of 40.2 percent and in total world exports of 21.2 percent. Exports of crude fertilizer, other than those of division 56 (SITC group 272) accounted for 0.5 percent of world exports of SITC section 2 and less than 0.1 percent of total world exports in 2010 (see table 1).

The top exporting countries in 2010 were Morocco, Jordan and Russian Federation (see table 2). They accounted respectively for 31.5, 11.0 and 6.6 percent of world exports. Major destinations were India, USA and Belgium (see table 3). By MDG regions (see graph 2), Southern Asia and Developed Europe accounted for a large share of imports. They both recorded trade deficit amounting to 0.6 bln US$. Northern Africa recorded a trade surplus of 1.3 bln US$.

Table 1: Imports (Imp.) and exports (Exp.), 1996-2010, in current prices

		1996	1997	1998	1999	2000	2001	2002	2003	2004	2005	2006	2007	2008	2009	2010
Values in Bln US$	Imp.	1.9	2.0	2.0	1.9	1.7	1.6	1.6	1.6	1.9	2.2	2.2	2.7	7.2	3.1	3.6
	Exp.	1.4	1.6	1.6	1.6	1.2	1.3	1.4	1.4	1.7	1.8	1.8	1.9	5.7	2.8	3.4
As a percentage of SITC section (%)	Imp.	0.7	0.8	0.9	0.8	0.7	0.7	0.6	0.6	0.5	0.5	0.4	0.4	0.9	0.6	0.5
	Exp.	0.6	0.7	0.8	0.8	0.5	0.7	0.6	0.5	0.5	0.5	0.4	0.3	0.9	0.6	0.5
As a percentage of world trade (%)	Imp.	0.0	0.0	0.0	0.0	0.0	0.0	0.0	0.0	0.0	0.0	0.0	0.0	0.0	0.0	0.0
	Exp.	0.0	0.0	0.0	0.0	0.0	0.0	0.0	0.0	0.0	0.0	0.0	0.0	0.0	0.0	0.0

Graph 1: Annual growth rates of exports, 1996–2010

(In percentage by year)

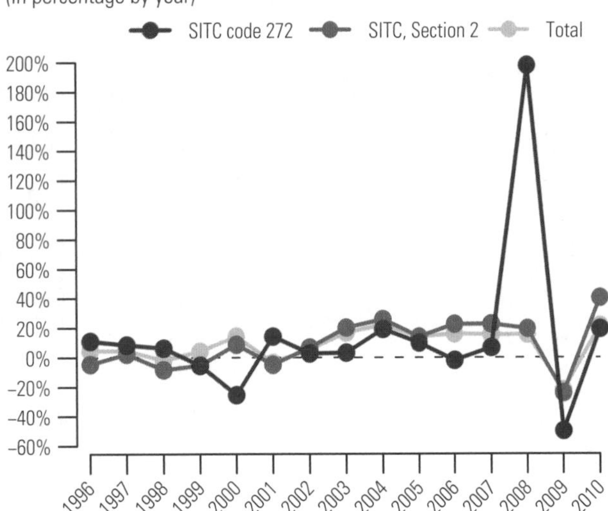

Table 2: Top exporting countries or areas in 2010

Country or area	Value (million US$)	Avg. Growth (%) 06-10	Growth (%) 09-10	World share %	Cum.
World	3386.2	17.3	19.3	100.0	
Morocco	1067.0	18.3	92.4	31.5	31.5
Jordan	372.5	-2.7	0.2	11.0	42.5
Russian Federation	225.1	8.1	-38.6	6.6	49.2
Syria	*210.8*	34.3	-26.2	6.2	55.4
Italy	167.8	35.8	21.7	5.0	60.3
China	153.4	11.7	43.7	4.5	64.9
Egypt	133.4	51.6	-46.5	3.9	68.8
Belgium	125.6	26.4	46.2	3.7	72.5
Netherlands	121.7	16.5	26.1	3.6	76.1
Chile	100.0	30.1	45.4	3.0	79.1
Israel	82.0	35.7	9.9	2.4	81.5
Peru	61.8	168.4	797.7	1.8	83.3
Tunisia	56.9	20.8	39.6	1.7	85.0
Germany	52.9	21.1	53.9	1.6	86.5
USA	44.9	...	75.2	1.3	87.9

Graph 2: Trade Balance by MDG regions 2010

(Bln US$)

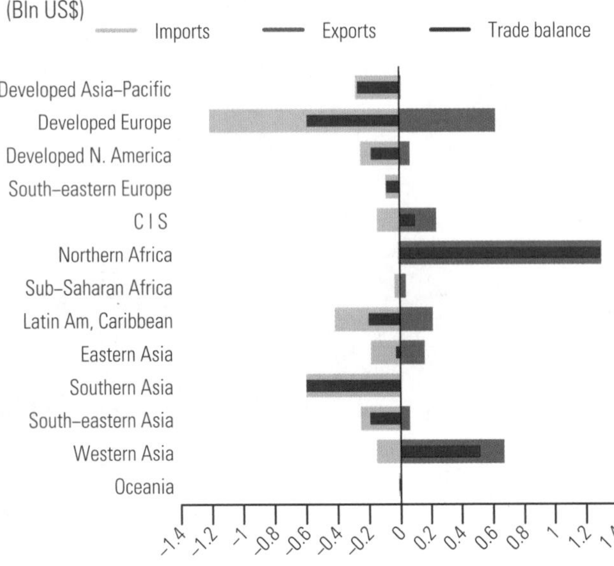

Table 3: Top importing countries or areas in 2010

Country or area	Value (million US$)	Avg. Growth (%) 06-10	Growth (%) 09-10	World share %	Cum.
World	3622.9	13.0	15.0	100.0	
India	512.3	10.7	-26.9	14.1	14.1
USA	227.4	17.0	48.0	6.3	20.4
Belgium	188.4	9.9	29.3	5.2	25.6
Lithuania	186.9	18.3	10.9	5.2	30.8
Brazil	148.6	19.8	54.4	4.1	34.9
New Zealand	142.9	27.6	158.8	3.9	38.8
Poland	140.6	8.9	147.1	3.9	42.7
Rep. of Korea	136.7	7.4	36.7	3.8	46.5
Spain	131.2	6.6	66.1	3.6	50.1
Mexico	128.1	24.8	526.2	3.5	53.6
Indonesia	121.9	13.3	-28.1	3.4	57.0
Netherlands	121.8	14.2	61.7	3.4	60.4
Belarus	95.0	27.3	28.8	2.6	63.0
Japan	91.0	-5.5	-62.6	2.5	65.5
France	77.6	15.3	30.2	2.1	67.6

After a 15.1 percent drop in 2009, the value (in current prices) of exports of stone, sand and gravel (SITC group 273) increased by 4.6 percent in 2010 and amounted to 8.5 bln US$ (see table 2). During the same period, imports showed a similar development and increased by 2.8 percent totaling 10.8 bln US$ (see table 3). Graph 1 shows that the increase in exports for 2010 in this product group was well below the increases in world exports of inedible crude materials, except fuels (SITC section 2) of 40.2 percent and in total world exports of 21.2 percent. Exports of stone, sand and gravel (SITC group 273) accounted for 1.2 percent of world exports of SITC section 2 and 0.1 percent of total world exports in 2010 (see table 1).

Turkey, Germany and India were the top exporting countries in 2010 (see table 2). They accounted respectively for 10.0, 7.4 and 7.0 percent of world exports. China, Netherlands and Germany were the three major destinations (see table 3). By MDG regions (see graph 2), Developed Europe accounted for a large share of trade in stone, sand and gravel (SITC group 273). In 2010, its exports amounted to 3.8 bln US$ compared to 4.0 bln US$ for imports, resulting in a trade deficit of 0.2 bln US$. Eastern Asia recorded a larger deficit of 2.8 bln US$. Western Asia recorded a surplus of 0.6 bln US$.

Table 1: Imports (Imp.) and exports (Exp.), 1996-2010, in current prices

		1996	1997	1998	1999	2000	2001	2002	2003	2004	2005	2006	2007	2008	2009	2010
Values in Bln US$	Imp.	4.9	5.0	4.7	4.8	5.2	4.8	5.1	6.0	7.0	7.8	8.9	10.7	12.4	10.5	10.8
	Exp.	3.8	3.8	3.6	3.7	3.7	3.8	4.1	4.7	5.5	5.9	7.4	8.4	9.6	8.2	8.5
As a percentage of SITC section (%)	Imp.	1.9	2.0	2.0	2.1	2.1	2.1	2.1	2.1	1.9	1.9	1.8	1.7	1.6	1.9	1.4
	Exp.	1.7	1.7	1.7	1.9	1.8	1.9	1.9	1.8	1.7	1.6	1.7	1.5	1.5	1.6	1.2
As a percentage of world trade (%)	Imp.	0.1	0.1	0.1	0.1	0.1	0.1	0.1	0.1	0.1	0.1	0.1	0.1	0.1	0.1	0.1
	Exp.	0.1	0.1	0.1	0.1	0.1	0.1	0.1	0.1	0.1	0.1	0.1	0.1	0.1	0.1	0.1

Graph 1: Annual growth rates of exports, 1996–2010
(In percentage by year)

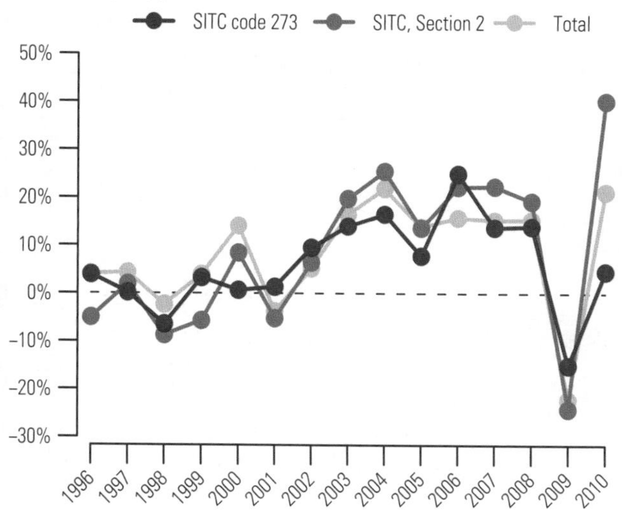

Graph 2: Trade Balance by MDG regions 2010
(Bln US$)

Imports
Exports
Trade balance

Developed Asia-Pacific
Developed Europe
Developed N. America
South-eastern Europe
CIS
Northern Africa
Sub-Saharan Africa
Latin Am, Caribbean
Eastern Asia
Southern Asia
South-eastern Asia
Western Asia
Oceania

-5 -4 -3 -2 -1 0 1 2 3 4

Table 2: Top exporting countries or areas in 2010

Country or area	Value (million US$)	Avg. Growth (%) 06-10	Growth (%) 09-10	World share %	Cum.
World	8541.8	3.6	4.6	100.0	
Turkey	850.5	26.2	45.2	10.0	10.0
Germany	631.5	1.9	-10.0	7.4	17.3
India	595.6	1.8	3.1	7.0	24.3
Italy	501.0	6.3	16.0	5.9	30.2
USA	491.8	7.7	45.4	5.8	35.9
Spain	450.4	-2.2	21.4	5.3	41.2
Belgium	424.5	3.6	7.3	5.0	46.2
Norway	305.7	2.7	24.2	3.6	49.8
France	263.1	-0.4	5.1	3.1	52.8
United Arab Emirates	252.3	-21.1	-26.2	3.0	55.8
Brazil	224.1	1.9	60.3	2.6	58.4
Ukraine	209.5	15.3	-6.1	2.5	60.9
Iran	187.8	26.2	6.3	2.2	63.1
Egypt	185.6	15.6	-60.2	2.2	65.2
Netherlands	170.5	4.8	-0.1	2.0	67.2

Table 3: Top importing countries or areas in 2010

Country or area	Value (million US$)	Avg. Growth (%) 06-10	Growth (%) 09-10	World share %	Cum.
World	10770.6	4.8	2.8	100.0	
China	2331.7	22.0	58.2	21.6	21.6
Netherlands	592.7	3.5	1.4	5.5	27.2
Germany	544.1	2.6	1.0	5.1	32.2
Italy	523.5	-8.9	6.0	4.9	37.1
Singapore	484.8	37.0	-54.6	4.5	41.6
Other Asia, nes	447.5	-2.5	2.0	4.2	45.7
Belgium	409.0	3.1	-3.5	3.8	49.5
USA	366.3	-10.8	13.9	3.4	52.9
France	314.9	2.3	-6.5	2.9	55.8
United Kingdom	281.8	-4.5	4.1	2.6	58.5
India	281.7	23.3	-0.9	2.6	61.1
Russian Federation	278.0	14.8	58.8	2.6	63.7
Japan	238.0	-2.6	20.7	2.2	65.9
Switzerland	237.6	7.9	10.3	2.2	68.1
Qatar	189.2	4.6	-39.9	1.8	69.8

Source: UN Comtrade

274 Sulphur and unroasted iron pyrites

The value (in current prices) of trade in sulphur and unroasted iron pyrites (SITC group 274) underwent a high change during the recent five years. Exports increased 358.7 percent in 2008 then contracted sharply by 85.2 percent in 2009 and increased by 88.6 percent in 2010 totaling 1.8 bln US$ (see table 2). Imports showed a similar development with 75.7 percent increase in 2010 to 3.4 bln US$ (see table 3). Graph 1 shows that the increase in exports for 2010 in this product group was well above the increases in world exports of inedible crude materials, except fuels (SITC section 2) of 40.2 percent and in total world exports of 21.2 percent. Exports of sulphur and unroasted iron pyrites (SITC group 274) accounted for 0.3 percent of world exports of SITC section 2 and less than 0.1 percent of total world exports in 2010 (see table 1).

Canada was the top exporting country in 2010: it accounted for 25.5 percent of world exports (see table 2). Other major exporting countries were USA and Kazakhstan, respectively with 9.4 and 8.8 percent of world exports. China, the top destination, accounted for 39.4 percent of world imports (see table 3). Other major destinations were Morocco and Brazil. By MDG regions (see graph 2), top surpluses were recorded by Developed North America (+0.4 bln US$) and Commonwealth of Independent States (+0.3 bln US$). Top trade deficits were recorded by Eastern Asia (-1.3 bln US$), Northern Africa (-0.5 bln US$) and Latin America and the Caribbean (-0.3 bln US$).

Table 1: Imports (Imp.) and exports (Exp.), 1996-2010, in current prices

		1996	1997	1998	1999	2000	2001	2002	2003	2004	2005	2006	2007	2008	2009	2010
Values in Bln US$	Imp.	1.0	0.9	0.8	0.9	1.0	0.8	0.9	1.5	2.0	2.2	2.0	3.0	12.5	1.9	3.4
	Exp.	0.7	0.6	0.5	0.5	0.6	0.4	0.5	0.7	0.9	1.1	1.1	1.4	6.3	0.9	1.8
As a percentage of SITC section (%)	Imp.	0.4	0.4	0.4	0.4	0.4	0.3	0.4	0.5	0.5	0.5	0.4	0.5	1.6	0.4	0.5
	Exp.	0.3	0.3	0.2	0.2	0.3	0.2	0.2	0.3	0.3	0.3	0.2	0.3	1.0	0.2	0.3
As a percentage of world trade (%)	Imp.	0.0	0.0	0.0	0.0	0.0	0.0	0.0	0.0	0.0	0.0	0.0	0.0	0.1	0.0	0.0
	Exp.	0.0	0.0	0.0	0.0	0.0	0.0	0.0	0.0	0.0	0.0	0.0	0.0	0.0	0.0	0.0

Graph 1: Annual growth rates of exports, 1996–2010

(In percentage by year)

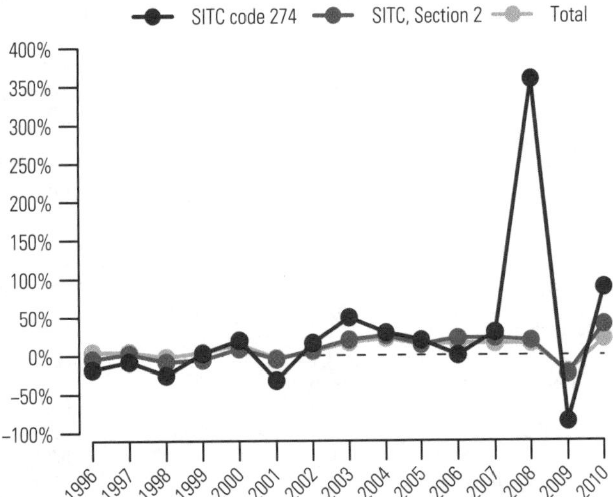

Graph 2: Trade Balance by MDG regions 2010

(Bln US$)

Imports — Exports — Trade balance

Developed Asia-Pacific
Developed Europe
Developed N. America
South-eastern Europe
CIS
Northern Africa
Sub-Saharan Africa
Latin Am, Caribbean
Eastern Asia
Southern Asia
South-eastern Asia
Western Asia
Oceania

-1.4 -1.2 -1 -0.8 -0.6 -0.4 -0.2 0 0.2 0.4 0.6 0.8

Table 2: Top exporting countries or areas in 2010

Country or area	Value (million US$)	Avg. Growth (%) 06-10	Growth (%) 09-10	World share %	Cum.
World	1769.9	13.6	88.6	100.0	
Canada	451.9	6.2	75.1	25.5	25.5
USA	165.8	43.2	110.2	9.4	34.9
Kazakhstan	156.1	40.0	148.6	8.8	43.7
Germany	138.0	11.7	60.5	7.8	51.5
Russian Federation	132.2	22.0	330.4	7.5	59.0
Japan	92.6	11.0	94.3	5.2	64.2
Malaysia	77.4	14.7	18.1	4.4	68.6
France	68.2	8.7	124.9	3.9	72.4
Qatar	*60.1*	34.2	24.3	3.4	75.8
Rep. of Korea	43.2	16.7	133.4	2.4	78.3
Poland	39.1	8.7	235.8	2.2	80.5
Netherlands	37.8	15.6	62.8	2.1	82.6
Other Asia, nes	37.3	17.3	84.6	2.1	84.7
Italy	35.6	13.8	141.1	2.0	86.8
Mexico	30.8	10.4	5640.1	1.7	88.5

Table 3: Top importing countries or areas in 2010

Country or area	Value (million US$)	Avg. Growth (%) 06-10	Growth (%) 09-10	World share %	Cum.
World	3400.7	14.8	75.7	100.0	
China	1338.3	17.2	87.4	39.4	39.4
Morocco	365.8	10.9	95.3	10.8	50.1
Brazil	247.0	24.3	25.3	7.3	57.4
USA	234.7	24.7	276.0	6.9	64.3
India	167.9	11.2	50.4	4.9	69.2
Tunisia	144.9	4.8	19.0	4.3	73.5
Israel	79.7	10.5	134.1	2.3	75.8
Belgium	61.7	14.5	142.6	1.8	77.6
Indonesia	54.6	27.5	55.0	1.6	79.2
Australia	52.6	11.0	56.4	1.5	80.8
Senegal	51.8	83.1	439.2	1.5	82.3
South Africa	51.8	4.4	24.0	1.5	83.8
Mexico	38.8	52.6	125.2	1.1	85.0
Argentina	25.6	13.5	41.0	0.8	85.7
Germany	24.1	14.1	62.2	0.7	86.4

During the recent five years, the value (in current prices) of exports of natural abrasives, nes (SITC group 277) increased on average by 8.8 percent and amounted to 1.5 bln US$ in 2010 (see table 2). Imports, showing a different development, had a three-year continuous decline with its lowest value at 1.0 bln US$ in 2009, but bounced back by 35.3 percent in 2010 totaling 1.4 bln US$ (see table 3). Graph 1 shows that the increase in exports for 2010 in this product group was below the increase in world exports of inedible crude materials, except fuels (SITC section 2) of 40.2 percent and in the increase in total world exports of 21.2 percent. Exports of natural abrasives, nes (SITC group 277) accounted for 0.2 percent of world exports of SITC section 2 and less than 0.1 percent of total world exports in 2010 (see table 1).

The top exporting countries in 2010 were Zimbabwe, Singapore and China (see table 2). They accounted respectively for 14.3, 10.0 and 9.0 percent of world exports. Zimbabwe, USA and Singapore were the top destinations (see table 3). By MDG regions (see graph 2), Sub-Saharan Africa and Southern Asia recorded trade surpluses amounting respectively to 228 mln US$ and 89 mln US$ and Developed Europe recorded a deficit of 115 mln US$.

Table 1: Imports (Imp.) and exports (Exp.), 1996-2010, in current prices

		1996	1997	1998	1999	2000	2001	2002	2003	2004	2005	2006	2007	2008	2009	2010
Values in Bln US$	Imp.	1.1	1.2	1.2	1.7	1.2	1.0	1.0	1.2	1.2	1.2	1.4	1.3	1.3	1.0	1.4
	Exp.	0.9	0.8	1.0	1.0	1.0	0.9	1.0	1.2	1.1	1.2	1.1	1.2	1.3	1.3	1.5
As a percentage of SITC section (%)	Imp.	0.4	0.5	0.5	0.8	0.5	0.4	0.4	0.4	0.3	0.3	0.3	0.2	0.2	0.2	0.2
	Exp.	0.4	0.4	0.5	0.5	0.5	0.5	0.5	0.5	0.3	0.3	0.2	0.2	0.2	0.3	0.2
As a percentage of world trade (%)	Imp.	0.0	0.0	0.0	0.0	0.0	0.0	0.0	0.0	0.0	0.0	0.0	0.0	0.0	0.0	0.0
	Exp.	0.0	0.0	0.0	0.0	0.0	0.0	0.0	0.0	0.0	0.0	0.0	0.0	0.0	0.0	0.0

Graph 1: Annual growth rates of exports, 1996–2010

(In percentage by year)

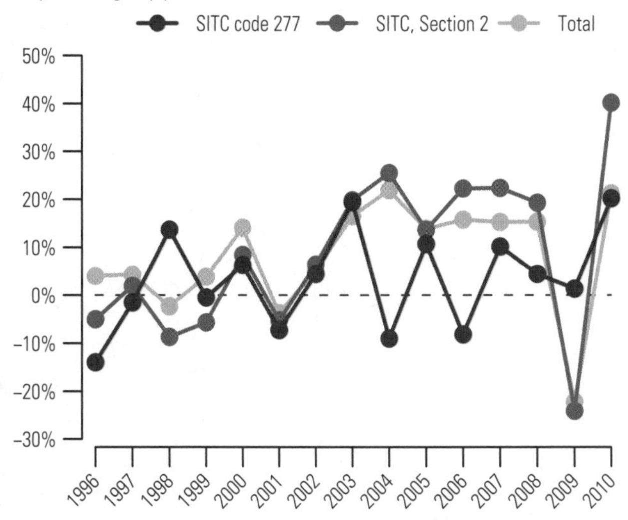

Graph 2: Trade Balance by MDG regions 2010

(Mln US$)

Imports — Exports — Trade balance

Developed Asia-Pacific
Developed Europe
Developed N. America
South-eastern Europe
C I S
Northern Africa
Sub-Saharan Africa
Latin Am, Caribbean
Eastern Asia
Southern Asia
South-eastern Asia
Western Asia
Oceania

-400 -300 -200 -100 0 100 200 300 400 500

Table 2: Top exporting countries or areas in 2010

Country or area	Value (million US$)	Avg. Growth (%) 06-10	Growth (%) 09-10	World share %	Cum.
World	1 528.2	8.8	20.2	100.0	
Zimbabwe	218.4	712.5	2211.7	14.3	14.3
Singapore	152.2	18.2	-47.3	10.0	24.2
China	137.9	18.1	89.9	9.0	33.3
USA	121.2	-1.2	33.1	7.9	41.2
India	110.0	24.2	-51.4	7.2	48.4
Namibia	*104.7*	7.6	21.2	6.9	55.3
Central African Rep.	*85.9*	49.4	73.0	5.6	60.9
Russian Federation	69.5	48.2	118.2	4.5	65.4
United Kingdom	62.4	2.3	65.8	4.1	69.5
Belgium	51.6	-4.4	46.5	3.4	72.9
China, Hong Kong SAR	48.3	13.0	111.7	3.2	76.0
South Africa	46.8	-0.3	311.6	3.1	79.1
Israel	35.8	25.2	514.4	2.3	81.4
Rep. of Korea	33.2	5.3	45.2	2.2	83.6
Japan	29.3	10.0	51.0	1.9	85.5

Table 3: Top importing countries or areas in 2010

Country or area	Value (million US$)	Avg. Growth (%) 06-10	Growth (%) 09-10	World share %	Cum.
World	1 362.4	-0.7	35.3	100.0	
Zimbabwe	218.4	847.6	>	16.0	16.0
USA	170.2	-0.1	75.0	12.5	28.5
Singapore	140.7	11.5	-50.1	10.3	38.8
United Kingdom	69.3	-18.4	145.1	5.1	43.9
Belgium	64.6	-9.8	15.3	4.7	48.7
Japan	63.9	-3.9	65.5	4.7	53.4
Italy	52.5	-7.8	51.5	3.9	57.2
China, Hong Kong SAR	47.8	5.5	38.5	3.5	60.7
Rep. of Korea	44.6	3.2	33.3	3.3	64.0
Israel	37.6	-0.4	137.2	2.8	66.8
South Africa	35.7	23.2	158.6	2.6	69.4
China	30.6	-4.3	53.1	2.2	71.6
India	29.8	16.9	-8.5	2.2	73.8
Germany	24.5	-10.9	37.4	1.8	75.6
Qatar	22.9	17.6	74.6	1.7	77.3

278 Other crude minerals

After several years of continuous growth marked by a peak of 14.6 bln US$ in 2008, the value (in current prices) of exports of other crude minerals (SITC group 278) contracted sharply in 2009 (by 22.6 percent) but bounced back in 2010 by 31.2 percent to amount to 14.8 bln US$ (see table 2). Imports showed a similar development with an increase of 24.3 percent to 19.3 bln US$ in 2010 (see table 3). Graph 1 shows that the increase in exports for 2010 in this product group was below the increase in world exports of inedible crude materials, except fuels (SITC section 2) of 40.2 percent but well above the increase in total world exports of 21.2 percent. Exports of other crude minerals (SITC group 278) accounted for 2.1 percent of world exports of SITC section 2 and 0.1 percent of total world exports in 2010 (see table 1).

China was the top exporting country in 2010 (see table 2). Its exports increased by 71.6 percent to represent 14.4 percent of world exports. Other major exporting countries were USA and Germany, respectively with 11.0 and 6.7 percent of world exports. Japan, USA and Germany were the top destinations (see table 3). By MDG regions (see graph 2), Developed Europe accounted for a large share of trade in other crude minerals (SITC group 278). In 2010, its exports and imports were valued respectively at 5.1 bln US$ and 7.2 bln US$. This resulted in a trade deficit of 2.1 bln US$. Major trade deficits were also recorded by Developed Asia-Pacific (-1.5 bln US$) and South-eastern Asia (-1.2 bln US$).

Table 1: Imports (Imp.) and exports (Exp.), 1996-2010, in current prices

		1996	1997	1998	1999	2000	2001	2002	2003	2004	2005	2006	2007	2008	2009	2010
Values in Bln US$	Imp.	9.8	10.0	9.3	9.0	9.3	9.3	9.5	10.4	13.2	13.7	14.9	16.3	20.4	15.6	19.3
	Exp.	7.4	7.4	7.0	6.9	6.8	7.0	7.1	8.2	9.6	10.1	11.3	12.0	14.6	11.3	14.8
As a percentage of	Imp.	3.9	3.9	4.0	3.9	3.8	4.0	3.9	3.6	3.5	3.3	3.0	2.7	2.7	2.9	2.6
SITC section (%)	Exp.	3.3	3.2	3.4	3.5	3.2	3.5	3.3	3.2	3.0	2.8	2.5	2.2	2.2	2.3	2.1
As a percentage of	Imp.	0.2	0.2	0.2	0.2	0.1	0.1	0.1	0.1	0.1	0.1	0.1	0.1	0.1	0.1	0.1
world trade (%)	Exp.	0.1	0.1	0.1	0.1	0.1	0.1	0.1	0.1	0.1	0.1	0.1	0.1	0.1	0.1	0.1

Graph 1: Annual growth rates of exports, 1996–2010

(In percentage by year)

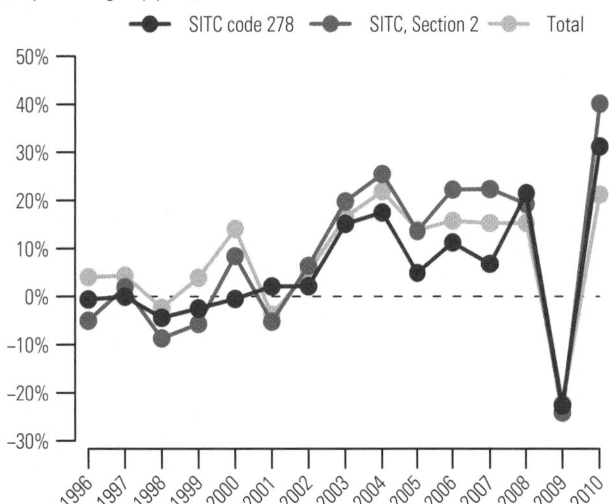

Table 2: Top exporting countries or areas in 2010

Country or area	Value (million US$)	Avg. Growth (%) 06-10	Growth (%) 09-10	World share %	Cum.
World	14841.7	7.2	31.2	100.0	
China	2143.8	17.2	71.6	14.4	14.4
USA	1635.2	2.4	24.8	11.0	25.5
Germany	992.0	2.1	15.9	6.7	32.1
Belgium	652.9	5.9	19.1	4.4	36.5
Netherlands	608.2	0.9	4.8	4.1	40.6
Canada	549.9	7.2	20.7	3.7	44.3
Nigeria	517.4	3139.2	62612.6	3.5	47.8
Spain	513.5	9.9	27.4	3.5	51.3
France	512.1	5.3	13.3	3.5	54.7
Brazil	480.0	5.6	9.8	3.2	58.0
United Kingdom	479.7	-5.0	-9.4	3.2	61.2
India	429.5	23.4	38.1	2.9	64.1
Russian Federation	381.9	15.3	28.5	2.6	66.7
Turkey	344.5	7.2	32.6	2.3	69.0
Mexico	332.1	13.5	13.2	2.2	71.2

Graph 2: Trade Balance by MDG regions 2010

(Bln US$)

Imports — Exports — Trade balance

Developed Asia-Pacific
Developed Europe
Developed N. America
South-eastern Europe
C I S
Northern Africa
Sub-Saharan Africa
Latin Am, Caribbean
Eastern Asia
Southern Asia
South-eastern Asia
Western Asia
Oceania

-8 -7 -6 -5 -4 -3 -2 -1 0 1 2 3 4 5 6

Table 3: Top importing countries or areas in 2010

Country or area	Value (million US$)	Avg. Growth (%) 06-10	Growth (%) 09-10	World share %	Cum.
World	19334.9	6.8	24.3	100.0	
Japan	1854.7	8.0	34.7	9.6	9.6
USA	1675.7	6.4	18.9	8.7	18.3
Germany	1343.3	4.7	34.1	6.9	25.2
China	1154.4	16.1	77.2	6.0	31.2
Italy	789.4	0.2	29.4	4.1	35.3
Belgium	703.0	5.9	16.3	3.6	38.9
France	692.1	5.3	18.0	3.6	42.5
Rep. of Korea	675.9	14.0	27.3	3.5	46.0
Netherlands	583.2	2.8	49.3	3.0	49.0
Other Asia, nes	491.3	6.7	19.1	2.5	51.5
United Kingdom	488.7	5.2	25.9	2.5	54.1
Canada	430.6	-0.8	4.9	2.2	56.3
Indonesia	406.9	16.4	40.4	2.1	58.4
Spain	351.1	-2.4	28.7	1.8	60.2
Viet Nam	*342.3*	29.3	66.9	1.8	62.0

After several years of continuous growth marked by a peak of 66.1 bln US$ in 2008, the value (in current prices) of exports of iron ore and concentrates (SITC group 281) contracted sharply in 2009 (by 14.1 percent) but bounced back in 2010 by 82.4 percent to amount to 103.5 bln US$ (see table 2). Imports showed a similar development with an increase of 71.1 percent to 132.4 bln US$ (see table 3). Graph 1 shows that the increase in exports for 2010 in this product group exceeded the increases in world exports of inedible crude materials, except fuels (SITC section 2) of 40.2 percent and of 21.2 percent in total world exports. Exports of iron ore and concentrates (SITC group 281) accounted for 14.9 percent of world exports of SITC section 2 and 0.7 percent of total world exports in 2010 (see table 1).

Australia was the top exporting country in 2010 (see table 2). Its exports increased by 87.9 percent to represent 42.8 percent of world exports (see table 2). Other major exporting countries were Brazil and India, respectively with 27.9 and 5.9 percent of world exports. China was the destination of a majority of exports (60.2 percent). Other major destinations were Japan and Rep. of Korea (see table 3). By MDG regions (see graph 2), Latin America and the Caribbean and Developed Asia-Pacific recorded trade surpluses amounting respectively to 30.6 bln US$ and 28.5 bln US$ while Eastern Asia recorded a deficit of 88.7 bln US$.

Table 1: Imports (Imp.) and exports (Exp.), 1996-2010, in current prices

		1996	1997	1998	1999	2000	2001	2002	2003	2004	2005	2006	2007	2008	2009	2010
Values in Bln US$	Imp.	12.4	13.3	12.9	11.3	13.1	12.7	13.0	16.8	29.5	40.6	47.6	65.8	108.5	77.4	132.4
	Exp.	8.9	9.7	9.8	8.2	9.1	9.1	9.9	11.3	16.5	28.0	32.9	40.0	66.1	56.7	103.5
As a percentage of SITC section (%)	Imp.	4.9	5.2	5.5	4.9	5.3	5.4	5.4	5.8	7.9	9.8	9.6	10.7	14.2	14.2	17.6
	Exp.	4.0	4.3	4.7	4.2	4.3	4.5	4.6	4.4	5.1	7.7	7.3	7.3	10.1	11.5	14.9
As a percentage of world trade (%)	Imp.	0.2	0.2	0.2	0.2	0.2	0.2	0.2	0.2	0.3	0.4	0.4	0.5	0.7	0.6	0.9
	Exp.	0.2	0.2	0.2	0.1	0.1	0.1	0.2	0.2	0.2	0.3	0.3	0.3	0.4	0.5	0.7

Graph 1: Annual growth rates of exports, 1996–2010
(In percentage by year)

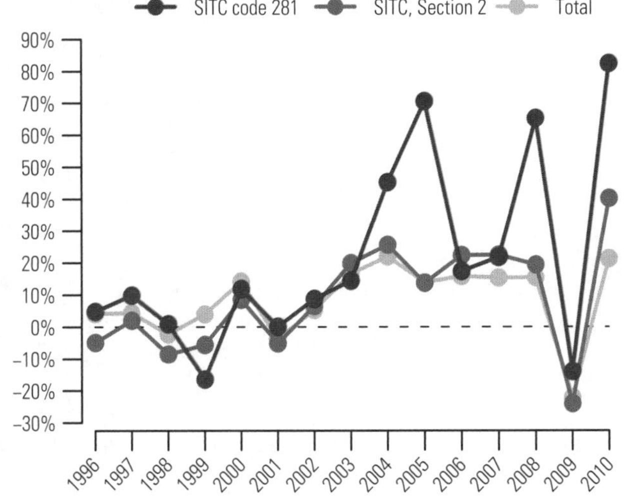

Graph 2: Trade Balance by MDG regions 2010
(Bln US$)

Imports — Exports — Trade balance

Developed Asia-Pacific
Developed Europe
Developed N. America
South-eastern Europe
C I S
Northern Africa
Sub-Saharan Africa
Latin Am, Caribbean
Eastern Asia
Southern Asia
South-eastern Asia
Western Asia
Oceania

-100 -80 -60 -40 -20 0 20 40 60

Table 2: Top exporting countries or areas in 2010

Country or area	Value (million US$)	Avg. Growth (%) 06-10	Growth (%) 09-10	World share %	Cum.
World	103468.7	33.2	82.4	100.0	
Australia	44290.2	42.0	87.9	42.8	42.8
Brazil	28911.9	34.1	118.3	27.9	70.7
India	6146.9	13.0	16.0	5.9	76.7
South Africa	5408.4	46.8	72.5	5.2	81.9
Canada	3099.4	16.5	4.7	3.0	84.9
Sweden	2565.6	17.4	95.3	2.5	87.4
Ukraine	2456.2	32.2	97.6	2.4	89.8
Russian Federation	1854.7	20.4	103.4	1.8	91.6
Kazakhstan	1189.7	15.2	27.1	1.1	92.7
Bahrain	1187.3	69.8	355.6	1.1	93.9
Iran	1124.3	83.2	6.3	1.1	94.9
Chile	1110.4	35.6	107.8	1.1	96.0
USA	1091.8	14.5	206.4	1.1	97.1
Venezuela	682.9	...	296.2	0.7	97.7
Peru	523.3	19.6	75.8	0.5	98.2

Table 3: Top importing countries or areas in 2010

Country or area	Value (million US$)	Avg. Growth (%) 06-10	Growth (%) 09-10	World share %	Cum.
World	132424.0	29.1	71.1	100.0	
China	79722.4	39.7	59.0	60.2	60.2
Japan	15494.9	21.2	78.3	11.7	71.9
Rep. of Korea	6600.9	29.1	86.6	5.0	76.9
Germany	5325.3	18.1	87.5	4.0	80.9
Other Asia, nes	2516.7	24.0	136.6	1.9	82.8
France	1893.8	14.0	122.8	1.4	84.2
Bahrain	1784.6	98.6	733.6	1.3	85.6
Italy	1564.2	7.6	105.0	1.2	86.8
United Kingdom	1411.9	9.2	93.2	1.1	87.8
Saudi Arabia	1359.0	26.7	93.7	1.0	88.9
Austria	1325.3	20.0	109.9	1.0	89.9
Netherlands	1141.4	14.3	121.4	0.9	90.7
Belgium	958.4	11.1	213.8	0.7	91.4
Turkey	923.7	14.5	2.4	0.7	92.1
Canada	890.3	11.0	238.1	0.7	92.8

Source: UN Comtrade

282 Ferrous waste and scrap; remelting scrap ingots of iron or steel

After several years of continuous growth marked by a peak of 51.4 bln US$ in 2008, the value (in current prices) of exports of ferrous waste and scrap; remelting scrap ingots of iron or steel (SITC group 282) contracted sharply in 2009 (by 41.1 percent) but bounced back in 2010 by 45.3 percent and to amount to 44.0 bln US$ (see table 2). Imports showed a similar development with an increase of 43.2 percent to 44.9 bln US$ (see table 3). Graph 1 shows that the increase in exports for 2010 in this product group was similar to the increase in world exports of inedible crude materials, except fuels (SITC section 2) of 40.2 percent but exceeded the increase in total world exports of 21.2 percent. Exports of ferrous waste and scrap; remelting scrap ingots of iron or steel (SITC group 282) accounted for 6.3 percent of world exports of SITC section 2 and 0.3 percent of total world exports in 2010 (see table 1).

USA, Germany and Netherlands were the top exporting countries in 2010 (see table 2). They accounted respectively for 19.1, 10.9 and 8.8 percent of world exports. Top destinations were Turkey, Rep. of Korea and China (see table 3). By MDG regions (see graph 2), Developed Europe was the origin and the destination of a large share of trade in ferrous waste and scrap; remelting scrap ingots of iron or steel (SITC group 282). Its exports amounted to 21.8 bln US$ while imports were valued at 17.7 bln US$ resulting in a trade surplus of 4.1 bln US$. Developed North America also recorded a surplus of 8.0 bln US$. A deficit of 8.3 bln US$ was recorded by Eastern Asia.

Table 1: Imports (Imp.) and exports (Exp.), 1996-2010, in current prices

		1996	1997	1998	1999	2000	2001	2002	2003	2004	2005	2006	2007	2008	2009	2010
Values in Bln US$	Imp.	8.3	8.9	7.6	6.9	9.0	8.4	9.8	14.9	27.1	27.0	32.9	44.8	58.3	31.4	44.9
	Exp.	6.8	7.8	6.7	6.0	7.5	7.4	8.7	12.8	23.1	23.9	30.9	41.6	51.4	30.3	44.0
As a percentage of SITC section (%)	Imp.	3.3	3.5	3.2	3.0	3.6	3.6	4.1	5.2	7.2	6.5	6.6	7.3	7.6	5.8	6.0
	Exp.	3.0	3.4	3.2	3.1	3.5	3.7	4.1	5.0	7.1	6.5	6.9	7.6	7.9	6.1	6.3
As a percentage of world trade (%)	Imp.	0.2	0.2	0.1	0.1	0.1	0.1	0.1	0.2	0.3	0.3	0.3	0.3	0.4	0.3	0.3
	Exp.	0.1	0.1	0.1	0.1	0.1	0.1	0.1	0.2	0.3	0.2	0.3	0.3	0.3	0.2	0.3

Graph 1: Annual growth rates of exports, 1996–2010

(In percentage by year)

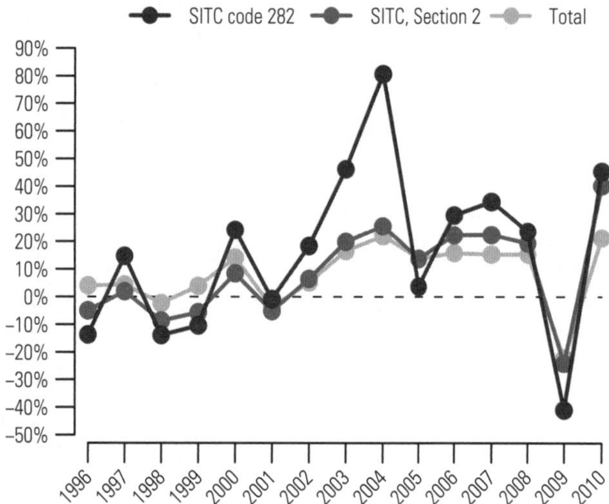

Graph 2: Trade Balance by MDG regions 2010

(Bln US$)

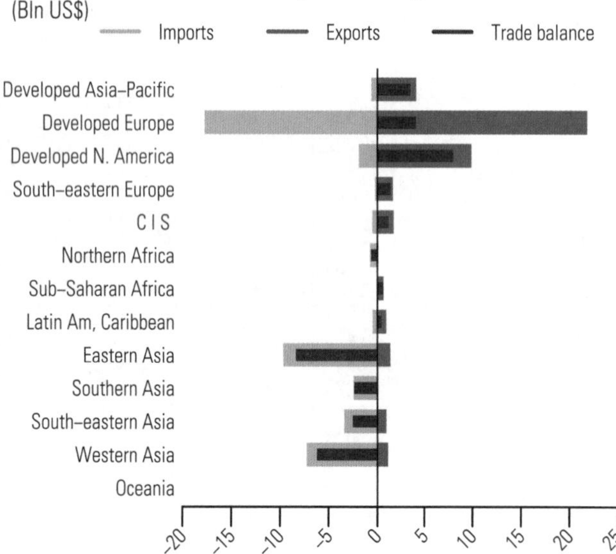

Table 2: Top exporting countries or areas in 2010

Country or area	Value (million US$)	Avg. Growth (%) 06-10	Growth (%) 09-10	World share %	Cum.
World	43 962.5	9.2	45.3	100.0	
USA	8 385.5	18.5	17.7	19.1	19.1
Germany	4 794.2	8.0	81.0	10.9	30.0
Netherlands	3 855.4	7.6	81.3	8.8	38.7
Japan	3 295.7	5.2	-0.3	7.5	46.2
United Kingdom	3 009.8	8.3	62.8	6.8	53.1
France	2 742.8	6.4	75.0	6.2	59.3
Canada	1 512.5	6.7	42.2	3.4	62.8
Belgium	1 427.8	12.2	55.6	3.2	66.0
Russian Federation	1 118.5	-13.9	93.8	2.5	68.6
Romania	958.7	17.0	39.4	2.2	70.7
Denmark	701.2	10.3	50.9	1.6	72.3
Czech Rep.	678.0	12.0	81.1	1.5	73.9
Poland	663.0	10.8	87.9	1.5	75.4
Australia	650.6	11.6	20.1	1.5	76.9
Rep. of Korea	645.3	22.3	57.0	1.5	78.3

Table 3: Top importing countries or areas in 2010

Country or area	Value (million US$)	Avg. Growth (%) 06-10	Growth (%) 09-10	World share %	Cum.
World	44 939.1	8.1	43.2	100.0	
Turkey	7 120.5	16.2	68.0	15.8	15.8
Rep. of Korea	3 814.0	14.8	45.7	8.5	24.3
China	3 006.1	12.7	-41.0	6.7	31.0
Belgium	2 853.5	3.6	82.8	6.3	37.4
Other Asia, nes	2 710.8	12.8	76.0	6.0	43.4
Germany	2 524.7	4.2	102.7	5.6	49.0
Spain	2 381.4	-1.2	57.2	5.3	54.3
Netherlands	2 088.1	5.0	78.6	4.6	59.0
Italy	1 857.5	2.7	110.6	4.1	63.1
India	1 745.5	7.6	-6.4	3.9	67.0
USA	1 470.0	3.0	72.4	3.3	70.3
Finland	1 463.1	-2.3	110.6	3.3	73.5
Viet Nam	*1 138.2*	69.4	66.9	2.5	76.0
Malaysia	964.8	3.7	62.4	2.1	78.2
France	930.9	0.2	49.9	2.1	80.3

After a drop of 11.0 percent in 2009, the value (in current prices) of exports of copper ores and concentrates; copper mattes and cement copper (SITC group 283) increased in 2010 by 43.2 percent to amount to 45.1 bln US$ (see table 2). Imports showed a similar development with an increase of 47.0 percent to 45.3 bln US$ (see table 3). Graph 1 shows that the increase in exports for 2010 in this product group was similar to the increase in world exports of inedible crude materials, except fuels (SITC section 2) of 40.2 percent but exceeded the increase in total world exports of 21.2 percent. Exports of copper ores and concentrates; copper mattes and cement copper (SITC group 283) accounted for 6.5 percent of world exports of SITC section 2 and 0.3 percent of total world exports in 2010 (see table 1).

Chile, the top exporting country in 2010, accounted for 30.7 percent of world exports (see table 2). Other major exporting countries were Indonesia and Peru. Top destinations were China, Japan and Rep. of Korea (see table 3). By MDG regions (see graph 2), Latin America and the Caribbean was the origin of a majority of exports of copper ores and concentrates; copper mattes and cement copper (SITC group 283). In 2010, its exports amounted to 23.5 bln US$ and it recorded a trade surplus of 22.0 bln US$. Major destinations were Eastern Asia and Developed Asia-Pacific: their imports were valued respectively at 18.0 bln US$ and 12.1 bln US$, resulting in a trade deficit of 17.1 bln US$ and 7.6 bln US$.

Table 1: Imports (Imp.) and exports (Exp.), 1996-2010, in current prices

		1996	1997	1998	1999	2000	2001	2002	2003	2004	2005	2006	2007	2008	2009	2010
Values in Bln US$	Imp.	5.9	5.8	4.9	5.4	6.5	6.4	6.0	7.3	12.2	16.4	32.8	37.8	38.2	30.8	45.3
	Exp.	6.0	5.9	4.9	5.0	6.5	6.3	6.2	8.1	13.1	18.9	32.8	37.1	35.4	31.5	45.1
As a percentage of SITC section (%)	Imp.	2.3	2.3	2.1	2.4	2.6	2.7	2.5	2.5	3.3	3.9	6.6	6.1	5.0	5.7	6.0
	Exp.	2.7	2.6	2.3	2.5	3.1	3.1	2.9	3.2	4.1	5.2	7.3	6.8	5.4	6.4	6.5
As a percentage of world trade (%)	Imp.	0.1	0.1	0.1	0.1	0.1	0.1	0.1	0.1	0.1	0.2	0.3	0.3	0.2	0.2	0.3
	Exp.	0.1	0.1	0.1	0.1	0.1	0.1	0.1	0.1	0.1	0.2	0.3	0.3	0.2	0.3	0.3

Graph 1: Annual growth rates of exports, 1996–2010

(In percentage by year)

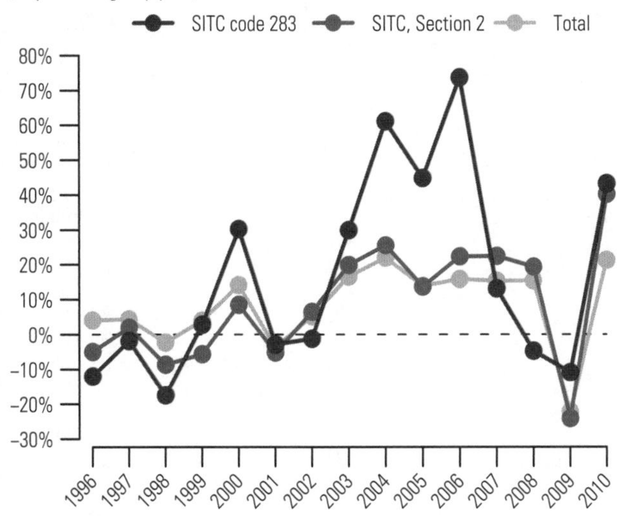

Table 2: Top exporting countries or areas in 2010

Country or area	Value (million US$)	Avg. Growth (%) 06-10	Growth (%) 09-10	World share %	Cum.
World	45086.1	8.2	43.2	100.0	
Chile	13832.1	2.4	46.4	30.7	30.7
Indonesia	6882.2	10.3	34.9	15.3	45.9
Peru	6154.0	21.0	56.9	13.6	59.6
Australia	4469.3	9.2	50.2	9.9	69.5
Canada	2089.6	5.2	59.9	4.6	74.1
Argentina	1504.8	3.0	33.6	3.3	77.5
Papua New Guinea	*1240.1*	5.4	36.3	2.8	80.2
Brazil	1238.9	22.8	54.3	2.7	83.0
USA	1229.3	8.3	17.2	2.7	85.7
Mongolia	*845.7*	7.4	3.3	1.9	87.6
Mexico	723.8	41.2	144.0	1.6	89.2
Dem.Rep. of the Congo	*621.9*	22.4	23.9	1.4	90.6
Kazakhstan	546.5	44.6	19.5	1.2	91.8
Portugal	505.6	1.9	28.9	1.1	92.9
Turkey	483.7	27.2	69.2	1.1	94.0

Graph 2: Trade Balance by MDG regions 2010

(Bln US$)

Table 3: Top importing countries or areas in 2010

Country or area	Value (million US$)	Avg. Growth (%) 06-10	Growth (%) 09-10	World share %	Cum.
World	45291.4	8.4	47.0	100.0	
China	13358.5	20.8	54.1	29.5	29.5
Japan	12087.8	7.1	46.8	26.7	56.2
Rep. of Korea	4587.1	8.2	38.9	10.1	66.3
India	3321.1	-6.9	9.7	7.3	73.6
Germany	2538.5	5.6	51.0	5.6	79.2
Spain	2407.6	12.5	92.5	5.3	84.6
Philippines	1326.8	36.4	45.8	2.9	87.5
Bulgaria	1099.3	4.9	46.6	2.4	89.9
Brazil	965.4	-2.3	54.6	2.1	92.1
Finland	871.2	-1.3	100.8	1.9	94.0
Sweden	657.4	4.0	30.0	1.5	95.4
Zambia	620.5	118.5	142.8	1.4	96.8
Canada	534.2	-8.2	21.5	1.2	98.0
Chile	399.4	15.8	303.7	0.9	98.9
Belgium	163.0	11.7	-21.8	0.4	99.2

284 Nickel ores and concentrates; nickel mattes, nickel oxide sinters

After a sharp decline of 39.3 percent in 2009, the value (in current prices) of exports of nickel ores and concentrates; nickel mattes, nickel oxide sinters (SITC group 284) rose significantly in 2010 by 85.9 percent to amount to 10.6 bln US$ (see table 2). Imports showed a similar development with an increase of 82.0 percent to 12.1 bln US$ (see table 3). Graph 1 shows that the increase in exports for 2010 in this product group by far exceeded the increases in world exports of inedible crude materials, except fuels (SITC section 2) of 40.2 percent and in total world exports of 21.2 percent. Exports of nickel ores and concentrates; nickel mattes, nickel oxide sinters (SITC group 284) accounted for 1.5 percent of world exports of SITC section 2 and 0.1 percent of total world exports in 2010 (see table 1).

Canada, Cuba and Indonesia were the top exporting countries in 2010 (see table 2). They accounted respectively for 25.5, 22.5 and 18.5 percent of world exports. Top destinations were China, Norway and Japan (see table 3). By MDG regions (see graph 2), Eastern Asia, Developed Europe and Developed Asia-Pacific were the destination of a majority of trade in nickel ores and concentrates; nickel mattes, nickel oxide sinters (SITC group 284): their imports were valued respectively at 4.3 bln US$, 4.1 bln US$ and 2.2 bln US$ with trade deficits of 4.3 bln US$, 3.9 bln US$ and 1.4 bln US$. Major exporting regions were Developed North America and Latin America and the Caribbean: their exports amounted respectively to 2.8 bln US$ and 2.6 bln US$, with trade surpluses of 2.3 bln US$ and 2.6 bln US$.

Table 1: Imports (Imp.) and exports (Exp.), 1996-2010, in current prices

		1996	1997	1998	1999	2000	2001	2002	2003	2004	2005	2006	2007	2008	2009	2010
Values in Bln US$	Imp.	2.5	2.5	1.9	1.7	2.7	2.2	2.2	3.2	5.1	6.0	8.9	18.5	13.3	6.7	12.1
	Exp.	2.2	2.1	1.9	1.6	2.4	2.0	2.0	2.7	5.0	5.4	5.9	12.1	9.4	5.7	10.6
As a percentage of SITC section (%)	Imp.	1.0	1.0	0.8	0.7	1.1	0.9	0.9	1.1	1.4	1.4	1.8	3.0	1.7	1.2	1.6
	Exp.	1.0	0.9	0.9	0.8	1.1	1.0	0.9	1.1	1.6	1.5	1.3	2.2	1.4	1.2	1.5
As a percentage of world trade (%)	Imp.	0.0	0.0	0.0	0.0	0.0	0.0	0.0	0.0	0.1	0.1	0.1	0.1	0.1	0.1	0.1
	Exp.	0.0	0.0	0.0	0.0	0.0	0.0	0.0	0.0	0.1	0.1	0.0	0.1	0.1	0.0	0.1

Graph 1: Annual growth rates of exports, 1996–2010

(In percentage by year)

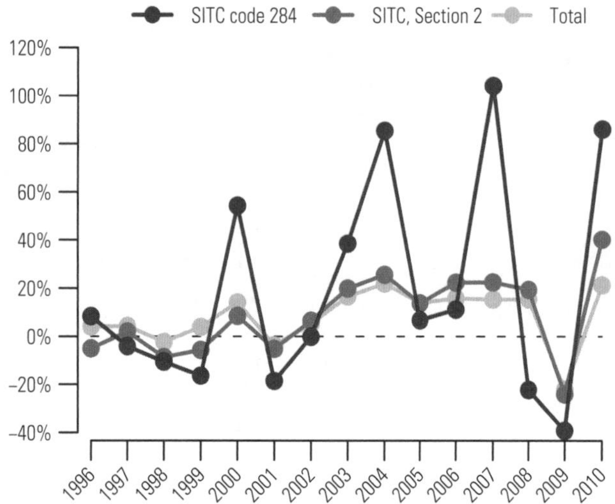

Table 2: Top exporting countries or areas in 2010

Country or area	Value (million US$)	Avg. Growth (%) 06-10	Growth (%) 09-10	World share %	Cum.
World	10622.9	15.6	85.9	100.0	
Canada	2713.7	6.2	105.2	25.5	25.5
Cuba	*2386.1*	...	123.4	22.5	48.0
Indonesia	1962.1	8.0	128.6	18.5	66.5
Australia	793.4	-6.3	29.7	7.5	73.9
Zimbabwe	710.5	25.0	68.2	6.7	80.6
Botswana	578.2	1661.3	32.9	5.4	86.1
New Caledonia	510.7	6.4	48.0	4.8	90.9
Philippines	276.4	17.3	97.5	2.6	93.5
Brazil	193.8	19.7	203.0	1.8	95.3
South Africa	126.7	7.1	-28.9	1.2	96.5
Spain	104.2	2.2	19.3	1.0	97.5
Russian Federation	56.6	1327.6	1.9	0.5	98.0
Germany	50.5	1.1	144.0	0.5	98.5
USA	47.8	22.0	129.4	0.5	98.9
Zambia	35.0	...	246.6	0.3	99.3

Graph 2: Trade Balance by MDG regions 2010

(Bln US$)

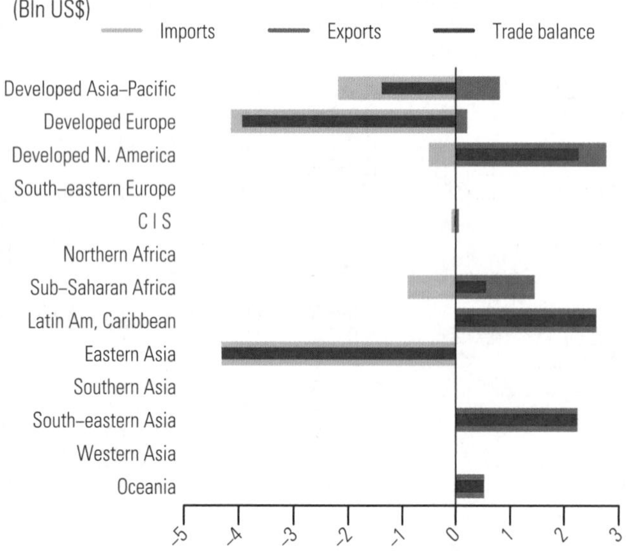

Table 3: Top importing countries or areas in 2010

Country or area	Value (million US$)	Avg. Growth (%) 06-10	Growth (%) 09-10	World share %	Cum.
World	12129.8	8.1	82.0	100.0	
China	3364.2	27.1	65.8	27.7	27.7
Norway	2213.7	4.8	57.2	18.3	46.0
Japan	2184.6	2.2	74.0	18.0	64.0
Zimbabwe	860.7	246.9	501.5	7.1	71.1
United Kingdom	787.9	3.7	182.0	6.5	77.6
Finland	726.5	-3.5	115.4	6.0	83.6
Rep. of Korea	596.7	-3.4	68.7	4.9	88.5
Canada	495.3	28.8	103.4	4.1	92.6
Other Asia, nes	351.6	-0.1	86.4	2.9	95.5
France	233.2	1.3	11.8	1.9	97.4
Netherlands	101.7	537.5	4443.4	0.8	98.2
Ukraine	77.2	8.4	29.0	0.6	98.9
Botswana	43.7	-8.0	-28.8	0.4	99.2
Poland	22.6	312.0	-15.6	0.2	99.4
Sweden	21.4	-28.4	12.4	0.2	99.6

After several years of continuous growth marked by a peak of 14.9 bln US$ in 2008, the value (in current prices) of exports of aluminum ores and concentrates (SITC group 285) contracted sharply in 2009 (by 36.0 percent) but bounced back in 2010 by 42.0 percent to amount to 13.6 bln US$ (see table 2). Imports showed a similar development with an increase of 26.8 percent to 14.7 bln US$ in 2010 (see table 3). Graph 1 shows that the increase in exports for 2010 in this product group was similar to the increase in world exports of inedible crude materials, except fuels (SITC section 2) of 40.2 percent and well-above the increase in total world exports of 21.2 percent. Exports of aluminum ores and concentrates (SITC group 285) accounted for 2.0 percent of world exports of SITC section 2 and 0.1 percent of total world exports in 2010 (see table 1).

Australia, the top exporting country in 2010, accounted for more than a third (35.0 percent) of exports (see table 2). Other major exporting countries were Brazil and India. Top destinations were China, Canada and Russian Federation (see table 3). By MDG regions (see graph 2), top surpluses were recorded by Developed Asia-Pacific (+4.5 bln US$) and Latin America and the Caribbean (+2.5 bln US$) while top deficits were recorded by Eastern Asia (-3.0 bln US$), Developed Europe (-2.1 bln US$) and Developed North America (-1.8 bln US$).

Table 1: Imports (Imp.) and exports (Exp.), 1996-2010, in current prices

		1996	1997	1998	1999	2000	2001	2002	2003	2004	2005	2006	2007	2008	2009	2010
Values in Bln US$	Imp.	7.0	6.7	6.5	5.9	7.3	7.0	6.6	7.6	9.8	12.4	15.0	16.6	18.9	11.6	14.7
	Exp.	5.5	5.7	5.2	5.0	5.9	5.7	5.3	6.3	8.0	9.9	12.5	13.9	14.9	9.5	13.6
As a percentage of SITC section (%)	Imp.	2.8	2.6	2.8	2.6	3.0	3.0	2.8	2.6	2.6	3.0	3.0	2.7	2.5	2.1	1.9
	Exp.	2.4	2.5	2.5	2.6	2.8	2.8	2.4	2.4	2.5	2.7	2.8	2.5	2.3	1.9	2.0
As a percentage of world trade (%)	Imp.	0.1	0.1	0.1	0.1	0.1	0.1	0.1	0.1	0.1	0.1	0.1	0.1	0.1	0.1	0.1
	Exp.	0.1	0.1	0.1	0.1	0.1	0.1	0.1	0.1	0.1	0.1	0.1	0.1	0.1	0.1	0.1

Graph 1: Annual growth rates of exports, 1996–2010
(In percentage by year)

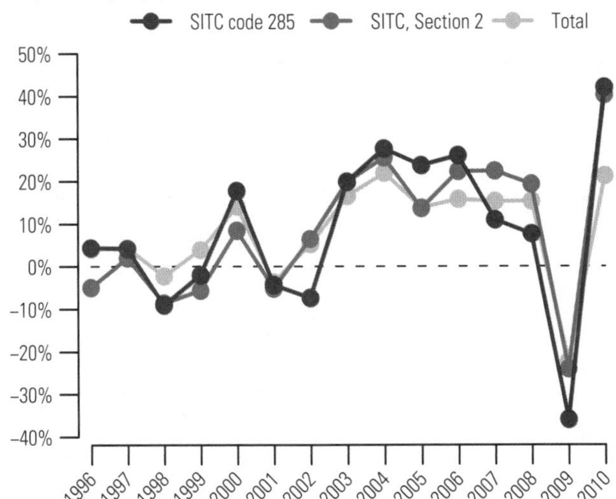

Graph 2: Trade Balance by MDG regions 2010
(Bln US$)

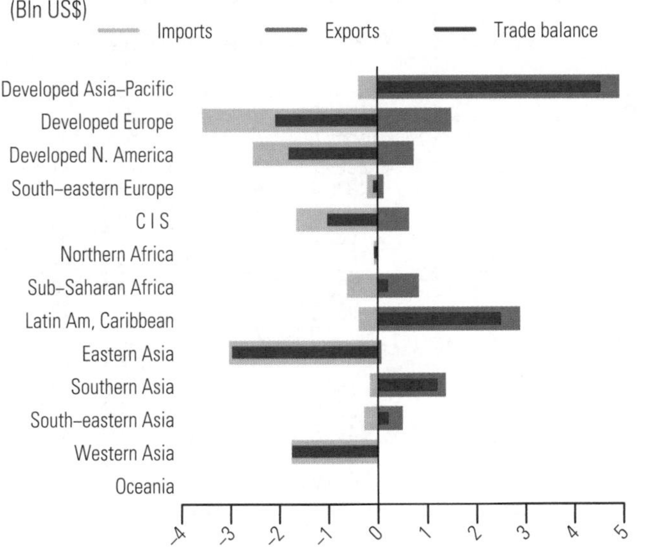

Table 2: Top exporting countries or areas in 2010

Country or area	Value (million US$)	Avg. Growth (%) 06-10	Growth (%) 09-10	World share %	Cum.
World	13551.4	2.0	42.0	100.0	
Australia	4742.5	0.9	26.0	35.0	35.0
Brazil	1986.3	11.6	36.4	14.7	49.7
India	1352.8	23.6	613.4	10.0	59.6
Guinea	*744.5*	14.7	38.1	5.5	65.1
USA	712.8	-3.9	59.3	5.3	70.4
Jamaica	531.5	-17.6	18.3	3.9	74.3
Indonesia	479.0	69.4	91.8	3.5	77.8
Ireland	425.8	-3.9	106.2	3.1	81.0
Ukraine	406.6	5.8	24.0	3.0	84.0
Germany	347.4	4.2	24.9	2.6	86.6
France	268.4	10.0	35.7	2.0	88.5
Kazakhstan	225.6	-18.9	-25.1	1.7	90.2
Venezuela	195.0	1.5	263.0	1.4	91.6
Japan	185.0	7.2	42.6	1.4	93.0
Guyana	169.2	52.7	113.0	1.2	94.3

Table 3: Top importing countries or areas in 2010

Country or area	Value (million US$)	Avg. Growth (%) 06-10	Growth (%) 09-10	World share %	Cum.
World	14684.9	-0.5	26.8	100.0	
China	2808.6	-4.3	39.8	19.1	19.1
Canada	1445.3	-1.9	16.9	9.8	29.0
Russian Federation	1398.6	-3.1	21.0	9.5	38.5
USA	1087.2	-1.3	17.3	7.4	45.9
United Arab Emirates	954.5	17.2	43.2	6.5	52.4
Norway	679.7	-6.8	18.8	4.6	57.0
South Africa	541.3	-2.8	45.1	3.7	60.7
Iceland	515.5	23.0	21.3	3.5	64.2
Germany	434.4	-2.1	16.1	3.0	67.2
Bahrain	433.7	10.1	-2.5	3.0	70.1
France	335.6	-1.4	4.7	2.3	72.4
Netherlands	315.8	12.9	56.7	2.2	74.6
Argentina	266.0	8.9	20.2	1.8	76.4
Spain	210.3	1.5	-16.5	1.4	77.8
New Zealand	202.5	-2.8	64.9	1.4	79.2

287 Ores and concentrates of base metals, nes

After a drop of 39.3 percent in 2009, the value (in current prices) of exports of ores and concentrates of base metals, nes (SITC group 287) increased in 2010 by 54.4 percent to amount to 27.8 bln US$ (see table 2). Imports showed a similar development with an increase of 51.3 percent to 31.8 bln US$ in 2010 (see table 3). Graph 1 shows that the increase in exports for 2010 in this product group exceeded the increase in world exports of inedible crude materials, except fuels (SITC section 2) of 40.2 percent and more than doubled the increase in total world exports of 21.2 percent. Exports of ores and concentrates of base metals, nes (SITC group 287) accounted for 4.0 percent of world exports of SITC section 2 and 0.2 percent of total world exports in 2010 (see table 1).

Australia, South Africa and Peru were the top exporting countries in 2010 (see table 2). They accounted respectively for 14.2, 13.0 and 11.7 percent of world exports. China was the top destination with 41.1 percent of world imports (see table 3). Other top destinations were Rep. of Korea and Japan. By MDG regions (see graph 2), top surpluses were recorded by Latin America and the Caribbean (+6.3 bln US$) and Sub-Saharan Africa (+5.4 bln US$) while top deficits were recorded by Eastern Asia (-14.3 bln US$) and Developed Europe (-4.6 bln US$).

Table 1: Imports (Imp.) and exports (Exp.), 1996-2010, in current prices

		1996	1997	1998	1999	2000	2001	2002	2003	2004	2005	2006	2007	2008	2009	2010
Values in Bln US$	Imp.	6.5	7.1	6.1	5.8	6.3	6.4	6.1	7.4	13.3	20.7	25.0	33.6	36.8	21.0	31.8
	Exp.	5.5	6.2	5.5	5.2	5.3	5.2	5.0	5.7	10.8	17.8	23.0	29.6	29.7	18.0	27.8
As a percentage of SITC section (%)	Imp.	2.6	2.8	2.6	2.5	2.6	2.7	2.5	2.6	3.5	5.0	5.0	5.4	4.8	3.9	4.2
	Exp.	2.5	2.7	2.6	2.6	2.5	2.6	2.3	2.2	3.3	4.9	5.1	5.4	4.5	3.6	4.0
As a percentage of world trade (%)	Imp.	0.1	0.1	0.1	0.1	0.1	0.1	0.1	0.1	0.1	0.2	0.2	0.2	0.2	0.2	0.2
	Exp.	0.1	0.1	0.1	0.1	0.1	0.1	0.1	0.1	0.1	0.2	0.2	0.2	0.2	0.1	0.2

Graph 1: Annual growth rates of exports, 1996–2010
(In percentage by year)

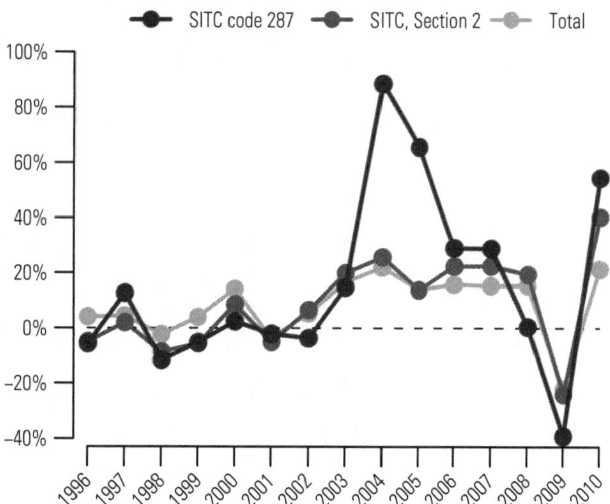

Graph 2: Trade Balance by MDG regions 2010
(Bln US$)

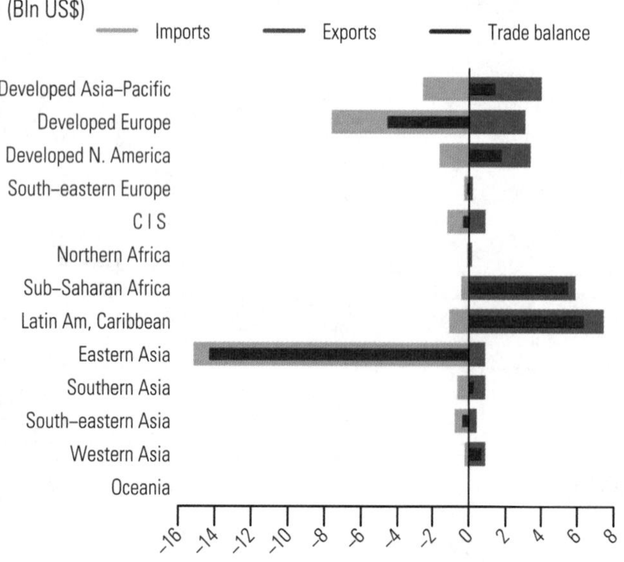

Table 2: Top exporting countries or areas in 2010

Country or area	Value (million US$)	Avg. Growth (%) 06-10	Growth (%) 09-10	World share %	Cum.
World	27 809.9	4.9	54.4	100.0	
Australia	3 943.5	8.5	68.4	14.2	14.2
South Africa	3 605.0	26.5	80.6	13.0	27.1
Peru	3 255.5	1.6	40.1	11.7	38.8
USA	2 765.0	-2.6	58.5	9.9	48.8
Chile	1 276.5	-14.3	9.1	4.6	53.4
Bolivia	1 139.5	16.4	29.4	4.1	57.5
Belgium	1 086.6	-6.6	35.4	3.9	61.4
Mexico	939.4	6.3	66.6	3.4	64.8
Dem.Rep. of the Congo	*925.7*	16.9	27.8	3.3	68.1
Turkey	749.4	28.2	88.8	2.7	70.8
India	624.5	0.0	85.9	2.2	73.0
Canada	578.7	-6.2	17.7	2.1	75.1
China	514.7	-12.9	259.7	1.9	77.0
Netherlands	504.1	-10.9	70.8	1.8	78.8
Ireland	451.5	-5.0	28.1	1.6	80.4

Table 3: Top importing countries or areas in 2010

Country or area	Value (million US$)	Avg. Growth (%) 06-10	Growth (%) 09-10	World share %	Cum.
World	31 756.5	6.2	51.3	100.0	
China	12 368.6	31.0	41.1	38.9	38.9
Rep. of Korea	2 608.2	2.3	49.3	8.2	47.2
Japan	2 375.4	-5.5	44.0	7.5	54.6
Belgium	1 898.2	-2.2	151.3	6.0	60.6
Spain	1 008.2	-10.7	59.7	3.2	63.8
Netherlands	992.2	-9.6	54.8	3.1	66.9
Germany	970.7	-6.0	25.1	3.1	70.0
USA	909.5	-2.9	42.7	2.9	72.8
Canada	733.0	-2.7	41.5	2.3	75.1
Ukraine	674.1	38.8	75.2	2.1	77.3
India	583.2	15.1	108.4	1.8	79.1
Finland	572.5	-8.2	69.8	1.8	80.9
Italy	493.8	-6.1	60.6	1.6	82.5
Norway	467.1	6.2	64.9	1.5	83.9
Chile	410.6	-7.8	7.7	1.3	85.2

Source: UN Comtrade

After a drop of 31.8 percent in 2009, the value (in current prices) of exports of non-ferrous base metal waste and scrap, nes (SITC group 288) increased in 2010 by 58.5 percent to amount to 37.5 bln US$ (see table 2). Imports showed a similar development with an increase of 75.6 percent to 46.1 bln US$ in 2010 (see table 3). Graph 1 shows that the increase in exports for 2010 in this product group exceeded the increase in world exports of inedible crude materials, except fuels (SITC section 2) of 40.2 percent and the increase in total world exports of 21.2 percent. Exports of non-ferrous base metal waste and scrap, nes (SITC group 288) accounted for 5.4 percent of world exports of SITC section 2 and 0.2 percent of total world exports in 2010 (see table 1).

USA, Germany and United Kingdom were the top exporting countries in 2010 (see table 2). They accounted respectively for 18.7, 11.1 and 7.7 percent of world exports. Top destinations were China, Germany and Japan (see table 3). By MDG regions (see graph 2), Developed Europe was the origin and the destination of a large share of trade in non-ferrous base metal waste and scrap, nes (SITC group 288). In 2010, its exports and imports amounted respectively to 18.5 bln US$ and 17.2 bln US$ resulting in a trade surplus of 1.3 bln US$. Eastern Asia was another major destination: its imports were valued at 20.3 bln US$ and it recorded a trade deficit of 19.3 bln US$. Significant trade surpluses were recorded by Developed North America (+6.3 bln US$) and Latin America and the Caribbean (+2.3 bln US$).

Table 1: Imports (Imp.) and exports (Exp.), 1996-2010, in current prices

		1996	1997	1998	1999	2000	2001	2002	2003	2004	2005	2006	2007	2008	2009	2010
Values in Bln US$	Imp.	9.5	10.6	9.2	9.1	10.9	10.4	9.6	11.0	16.2	19.1	32.0	40.4	38.5	26.3	46.1
	Exp.	7.7	9.1	7.8	7.3	8.3	7.7	8.0	9.4	12.9	16.9	29.9	35.8	34.7	23.6	37.5
As a percentage of SITC section (%)	Imp.	3.7	4.2	3.9	4.0	4.4	4.4	4.0	3.8	4.3	4.6	6.5	6.5	5.0	4.8	6.1
	Exp.	3.4	4.0	3.8	3.7	3.9	3.8	3.7	3.7	4.0	4.6	6.7	6.5	5.3	4.8	5.4
As a percentage of world trade (%)	Imp.	0.2	0.2	0.2	0.2	0.2	0.2	0.1	0.1	0.2	0.2	0.3	0.3	0.2	0.2	0.3
	Exp.	0.1	0.2	0.1	0.1	0.1	0.1	0.1	0.1	0.1	0.2	0.2	0.3	0.2	0.2	0.2

Graph 1: Annual growth rates of exports, 1996–2010
(In percentage by year)

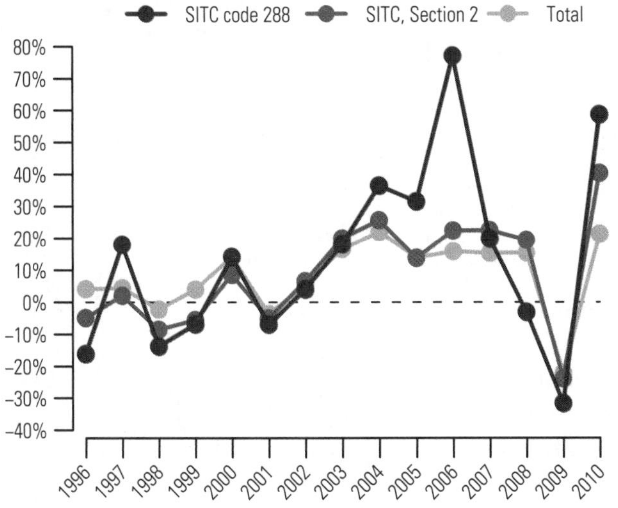

Graph 2: Trade Balance by MDG regions 2010
(Bln US$)

Imports
Exports
Trade balance

Developed Asia-Pacific
Developed Europe
Developed N. America
South-eastern Europe
CIS
Northern Africa
Sub-Saharan Africa
Latin Am, Caribbean
Eastern Asia
Southern Asia
South-eastern Asia
Western Asia
Oceania

-25 -20 -15 -10 -5 0 5 10 15 20

Table 2: Top exporting countries or areas in 2010

Country or area	Value (million US$)	Avg. Growth (%) 06-10	Growth (%) 09-10	World share %	Cum.
World	37 464.3	5.8	58.5	100.0	
USA	7 007.9	6.9	59.4	18.7	18.7
Germany	4 156.1	5.5	69.5	11.1	29.8
United Kingdom	2 897.9	9.8	58.9	7.7	37.5
France	2 056.0	0.7	73.6	5.5	43.0
Canada	1 638.6	1.8	46.3	4.4	47.4
Netherlands	1 623.3	2.0	39.2	4.3	51.7
Chile	1 108.7	21.2	119.3	3.0	54.7
Spain	1 063.3	11.0	53.1	2.8	57.5
Japan	1 037.0	4.3	11.2	2.8	60.3
Belgium	1 013.5	1.2	61.7	2.7	63.0
Mexico	975.3	2.6	50.4	2.6	65.6
Italy	924.7	11.7	50.0	2.5	68.1
Czech Rep.	822.7	21.3	55.4	2.2	70.3
Australia	756.0	8.5	54.8	2.0	72.3
Poland	627.0	8.8	83.5	1.7	74.0

Table 3: Top importing countries or areas in 2010

Country or area	Value (million US$)	Avg. Growth (%) 06-10	Growth (%) 09-10	World share %	Cum.
World	46 111.1	9.6	75.6	100.0	
China	16 621.9	28.5	86.8	36.0	36.0
Germany	4 539.8	1.3	80.0	9.8	45.9
Japan	2 779.3	10.0	71.6	6.0	51.9
Belgium	2 401.8	2.8	77.3	5.2	57.1
Rep. of Korea	2 291.6	4.8	74.5	5.0	62.1
USA	1 676.8	-4.9	52.2	3.6	65.7
Italy	1 519.3	-5.9	102.9	3.3	69.0
United Kingdom	1 518.6	1.0	56.8	3.3	72.3
Austria	1 408.1	16.7	82.7	3.1	75.4
India	1 276.2	7.4	51.7	2.8	78.1
Netherlands	1 055.3	2.9	46.5	2.3	80.4
France	904.1	-1.9	65.6	2.0	82.4
Other Asia, nes	863.9	-5.9	86.2	1.9	84.3
Sweden	761.9	14.1	47.6	1.7	85.9
Spain	730.9	-1.5	80.6	1.6	87.5

289 Ores, concentrates of precious metals; waste, scrap and sweepings (no gold)

After a drop of 20.5 percent in 2009, the value (in current prices) of exports of ores, concentrates of precious metals; waste, scrap and sweepings (SITC group 289) increased in 2010 by 45.2 percent to amount to 16.6 bln US$ (see table 2). Imports showed a similar development with an increase of 32.2 percent to 11.0 bln US$ in 2010 (see table 3). Graph 1 shows that the increase in exports for 2010 in this product group exceeded the increase in world exports of inedible crude materials, except fuels (SITC section 2) of 40.2 percent and the increase in total world exports of 21.2 percent. Exports of ores, concentrates of precious metals; waste, scrap and sweepings (SITC group 289) accounted for 2.4 percent of world exports of SITC section 2 and 0.1 percent of total world exports in 2010 (see table 1).

Exports of the USA, the top exporting country in 2010, increased by 46.5 percent and accounted for 44.5 percent of world exports (see table 2). Other major exporting countries were Germany and Australia, respectively with 8.4 and 4.6 percent of world exports. Top destinations were Germany, United Kingdom and Italy (see table 3). By MDG regions (see graph 2), Developed Europe accounted for a large share of trade: its imports were valued at 6.6 bln US$ compared to 3.1 bln US$ for exports, resulting in a trade deficit of 3.5 bln US$. Top trade surpluses were recorded by Developed North America (+6.1 bln US$), Latin America and the Caribbean (+2.0 bln US$) and Sub-Saharan Africa (+0.8 bln US$).

Table 1: Imports (Imp.) and exports (Exp.), 1996-2010, in current prices

		1996	1997	1998	1999	2000	2001	2002	2003	2004	2005	2006	2007	2008	2009	2010
Values in Bln US$	Imp.	2.5	2.6	2.9	2.9	3.9	4.0	3.4	3.5	3.5	4.6	7.2	10.0	13.1	8.3	11.0
	Exp.	2.2	2.2	2.5	2.7	3.5	2.9	2.7	2.9	3.2	3.8	6.3	9.6	14.4	11.4	16.6
As a percentage of SITC section (%)	Imp.	1.0	1.0	1.2	1.3	1.6	1.7	1.4	1.2	0.9	1.1	1.5	1.6	1.7	1.5	1.5
	Exp.	1.0	1.0	1.2	1.4	1.7	1.4	1.2	1.1	1.0	1.0	1.4	1.8	2.2	2.3	2.4
As a percentage of world trade (%)	Imp.	0.0	0.0	0.1	0.1	0.1	0.1	0.1	0.0	0.0	0.0	0.1	0.1	0.1	0.1	0.1
	Exp.	0.0	0.0	0.0	0.0	0.1	0.0	0.0	0.0	0.0	0.0	0.1	0.1	0.1	0.1	0.1

Graph 1: Annual growth rates of exports, 1996–2010

(In percentage by year)

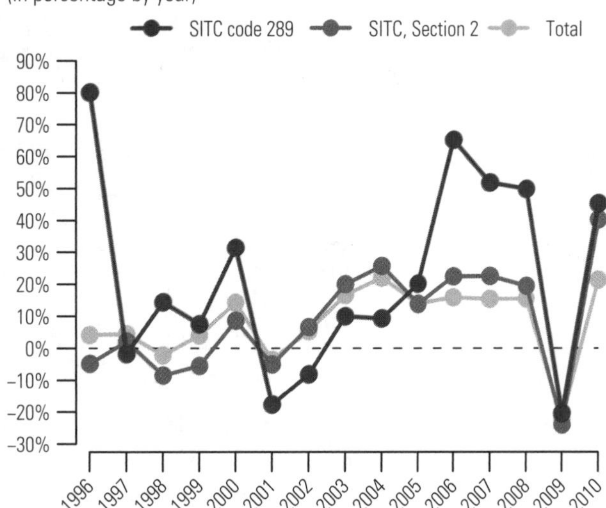

Table 2: Top exporting countries or areas in 2010

Country or area	Value (million US$)	Avg. Growth (%) 06-10	Growth (%) 09-10	World share %	Cum.
World	16 568.4	27.2	45.2	100.0	
USA	7 380.9	42.2	46.5	44.5	44.5
Germany	1 392.2	12.0	50.0	8.4	53.0
Australia	764.2	125.3	355.9	4.6	57.6
Bolivia	684.9	43.0	14.9	4.1	61.7
Switzerland	505.5	27.4	80.8	3.1	64.7
Guatemala	500.6	...	48.9	3.0	67.8
United Rep. of Tanzania	461.5	26.9	-7.3	2.8	70.6
Japan	444.9	8.0	55.4	2.7	73.2
South Africa	331.3	-9.7	-26.8	2.0	75.2
Peru	319.8	29.4	46.5	1.9	77.2
India	304.0	26.1	207.3	1.8	79.0
United Kingdom	303.4	14.7	76.4	1.8	80.8
Argentina	279.2	70.4	116.0	1.7	82.5
Canada	263.1	4.8	38.1	1.6	84.1
China, Hong Kong SAR	242.4	20.6	78.4	1.5	85.6

Graph 2: Trade Balance by MDG regions 2010

(Bln US$)

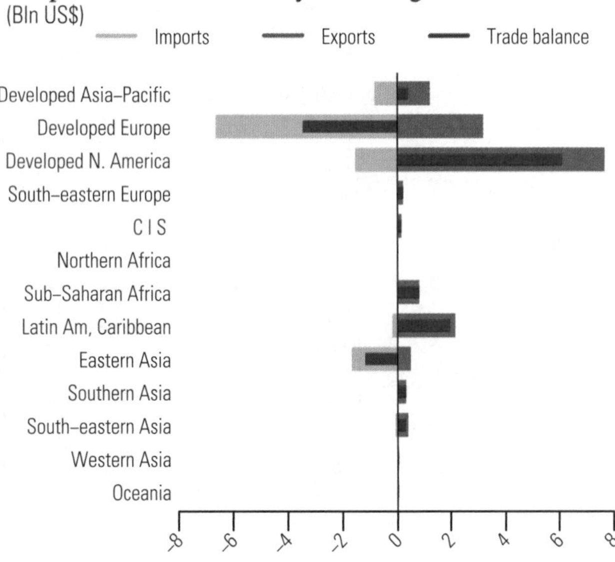

Table 3: Top importing countries or areas in 2010

Country or area	Value (million US$)	Avg. Growth (%) 06-10	Growth (%) 09-10	World share %	Cum.
World	11 005.3	11.1	32.2	100.0	
Germany	2 851.7	0.3	42.5	25.9	25.9
United Kingdom	1 956.3	12.9	42.1	17.8	43.7
Italy	1 100.8	59.6	46.8	10.0	53.7
USA	1 068.2	16.4	43.4	9.7	63.4
Japan	816.7	6.3	65.8	7.4	70.8
Rep. of Korea	794.2	137.3	19.3	7.2	78.0
China	609.9	98.1	107.6	5.5	83.6
Canada	482.2	16.1	-5.9	4.4	88.0
Switzerland	323.2	-2.2	42.0	2.9	90.9
China, Hong Kong SAR	169.1	21.9	51.0	1.5	92.4
Mexico	154.9	-11.0	37.5	1.4	93.8
Sweden	122.8	-0.5	-5.5	1.1	95.0
Other Asia, nes	105.2	99.9	124.9	1.0	95.9
Norway	82.0	18.9	96.8	0.7	96.7
Singapore	64.8	49.6	300.8	0.6	97.2

After several years of continuous growth marked by a peak of 7.3 bln US$ in 2008, the value (in current prices) of exports of crude animal materials, nes (SITC group 291) decreased in 2009 (by 10.8 percent) but bounced back in 2010 by 7.9 percent to amount to 7.1 bln US$ (see table 2). Imports showed a similar development with an increase of 9.7 percent to 7.2 bln US$ in 2010 (see table 3). Graph 1 shows that the increase in exports for 2010 in this product group was less than both the increase in world exports of inedible crude materials, except fuels (SITC section 2) of 40.2 percent and the increase in total world exports of 21.2 percent. Exports of crude animal materials, nes (SITC group 291) accounted for 1.0 percent of world exports of SITC section 2 and less than 0.1 percent of total world exports in 2010 (see table 1).

China, Germany and USA were the top exporting countries in 2010 (see table 2). They accounted respectively for 19.2, 10.5 and 10.5 percent of world exports. Germany and USA were also top destinations, together with Japan (see table 3). By MDG regions (see graph 2), Developed Europe was the origin and the destination of a large share of trade in crude animal materials, nes (SITC group 291). In 2010, its exports were valued at 2.8 bln US$ and imports at 3.4 bln US$, resulting in a trade deficit of 0.6 bln US$. Significant trade surpluses were recorded by Eastern Asia (+0.8 bln US$), and Latin America and the Caribbean (+0.2 bln US$).

Table 1: Imports (Imp.) and exports (Exp.), 1996-2010, in current prices

		1996	1997	1998	1999	2000	2001	2002	2003	2004	2005	2006	2007	2008	2009	2010
Values in Bln US$	Imp.	4.4	4.3	4.3	4.0	4.1	3.8	3.9	4.3	5.0	5.3	5.4	6.0	7.1	6.6	7.2
	Exp.	3.9	3.8	3.6	3.3	3.4	3.3	3.6	4.0	4.7	5.1	5.3	6.0	7.3	6.5	7.1
As a percentage of SITC section (%)	Imp.	1.7	1.7	1.8	1.7	1.7	1.6	1.6	1.5	1.3	1.3	1.1	1.0	0.9	1.2	1.0
	Exp.	1.7	1.7	1.7	1.7	1.6	1.6	1.7	1.5	1.5	1.4	1.2	1.1	1.1	1.3	1.0
As a percentage of world trade (%)	Imp.	0.1	0.1	0.1	0.1	0.1	0.1	0.1	0.1	0.1	0.0	0.0	0.0	0.0	0.1	0.0
	Exp.	0.1	0.1	0.1	0.1	0.1	0.1	0.1	0.1	0.1	0.0	0.0	0.0	0.0	0.1	0.0

Graph 1: Annual growth rates of exports, 1996–2010
(In percentage by year)

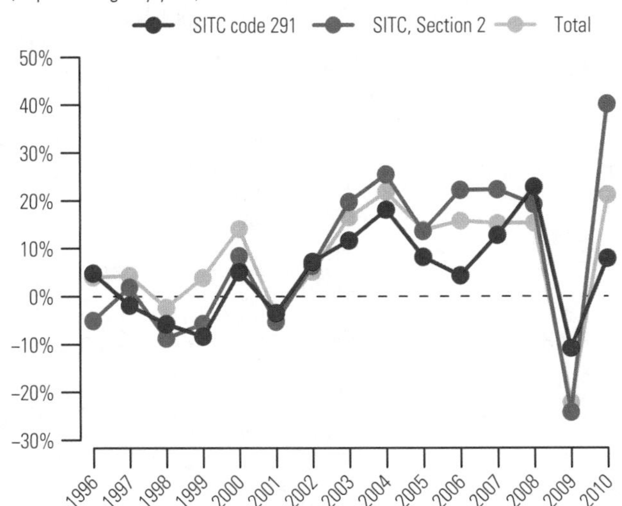

Table 2: Top exporting countries or areas in 2010

Country or area	Value (million US$)	Avg. Growth (%) 06-10	Growth (%) 09-10	World share %	Cum.
World	7066.2	7.5	7.9	100.0	
China	1357.3	8.3	11.5	19.2	19.2
Germany	742.2	8.0	6.0	10.5	29.7
USA	740.9	-0.1	-4.9	10.5	40.2
Netherlands	491.1	17.8	-4.6	6.9	47.1
Brazil	445.2	24.1	13.8	6.3	53.4
New Zealand	228.4	5.7	4.8	3.2	56.7
France	223.9	4.2	1.1	3.2	59.8
Canada	207.4	5.0	19.8	2.9	62.8
Spain	199.0	7.0	-6.7	2.8	65.6
Denmark	192.2	9.6	7.1	2.7	68.3
Poland	180.0	3.0	8.5	2.5	70.9
Other Asia, nes	178.6	1.2	42.8	2.5	73.4
Italy	137.7	13.4	24.7	1.9	75.3
United Kingdom	118.9	7.5	10.5	1.7	77.0
Belgium	112.8	5.6	-1.1	1.6	78.6

Graph 2: Trade Balance by MDG regions 2010
(Bln US$)

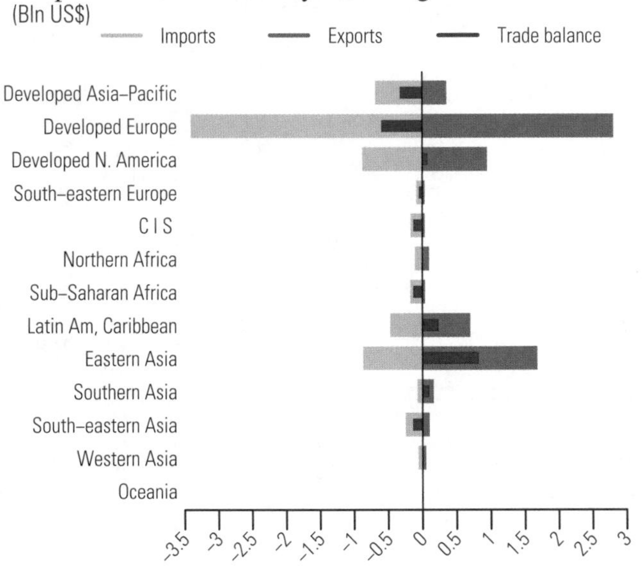

Table 3: Top importing countries or areas in 2010

Country or area	Value (million US$)	Avg. Growth (%) 06-10	Growth (%) 09-10	World share %	Cum.
World	7187.3	7.3	9.7	100.0	
Germany	797.6	6.5	2.2	11.1	11.1
USA	766.1	2.1	13.6	10.7	21.8
Japan	609.4	0.6	6.3	8.5	30.2
China	418.2	21.5	51.8	5.8	36.1
Netherlands	368.8	17.6	-5.7	5.1	41.2
France	362.0	4.6	-2.5	5.0	46.2
Italy	271.5	6.3	8.2	3.8	50.0
Poland	257.4	5.8	-7.2	3.6	53.6
Denmark	256.5	8.6	29.1	3.6	57.1
Spain	204.6	11.1	19.7	2.8	60.0
Mexico	183.3	5.4	8.2	2.6	62.5
Other Asia, nes	176.3	5.1	38.2	2.5	65.0
United Kingdom	165.0	4.3	11.4	2.3	67.3
Rep. of Korea	147.4	4.7	39.3	2.1	69.3
Brazil	139.0	17.5	-10.2	1.9	71.3

292 Crude vegetable materials, nes

After several years of continuous growth marked by a peak of 31.4 bln US$ in 2008, the value (in current prices) of exports of crude vegetable materials, nes (SITC group 292) dropped in 2009 (by 5.6 percent) but bounced back in 2010 by 6.4 percent to amount to 31.6 bln US$ (see table 2). Imports showed a similar development with an increase of 7.3 percent to 30.9 bln US$ in 2010 (see table 3). Graph 1 shows that the increase in exports for 2010 in this product group was less than both the increase in world exports of inedible crude materials, except fuels (SITC section 2) of 40.2 percent and the increase in total world exports of 21.2 percent. Exports of crude vegetable materials, nes (SITC group 292) accounted for 4.5 percent of world exports of SITC section 2 and 0.2 percent of total world exports in 2010 (see table 1).

Netherlands, the top exporting country in 2010, accounted for 30.8 percent of world exports (see table 2). Other major exporting countries were USA and Germany, respectively with 6.6 and 6.0 percent of world exports. Germany and USA were also the top destinations, together with France (see table 3). By MDG regions (see graph 2), a majority of trade in crude vegetable materials, nes (SITC group 292) occurred in Developed Europe. In 2010, its exports amounted to 17.8 bln US$ and imports were valued at 17.3 bln US$, resulting in a trade surplus of 0.5 bln US$. The largest trade surplus was recorded by Latin America and the Caribbean (+1.8 bln US$). Top trade deficits were recorded by Developed North America (-1.6 bln US$), Commonwealth of Independent States (-1.4 bln US$) and Developed Asia-Pacific (-1.2 bln US$).

Table 1: Imports (Imp.) and exports (Exp.), 1996-2010, in current prices

		1996	1997	1998	1999	2000	2001	2002	2003	2004	2005	2006	2007	2008	2009	2010
Values in Bln US$	Imp.	16.3	16.3	16.8	16.6	15.7	15.7	16.9	19.4	21.9	23.3	24.7	28.1	31.0	28.8	30.9
	Exp.	15.0	14.5	14.7	15.2	14.4	14.5	16.1	19.2	21.1	22.4	25.1	28.2	31.4	29.7	31.6
As a percentage of	Imp.	6.4	6.4	7.1	7.3	6.3	6.7	7.0	6.8	5.9	5.6	5.0	4.6	4.1	5.3	4.1
SITC section (%)	Exp.	6.7	6.4	7.1	7.8	6.8	7.2	7.5	7.5	6.5	6.1	5.6	5.1	4.8	6.0	4.5
As a percentage of	Imp.	0.3	0.3	0.3	0.3	0.2	0.3	0.3	0.3	0.2	0.2	0.2	0.2	0.2	0.2	0.2
world trade (%)	Exp.	0.3	0.3	0.3	0.3	0.2	0.2	0.3	0.3	0.2	0.2	0.2	0.2	0.2	0.2	0.2

Graph 1: Annual growth rates of exports, 1996–2010

(In percentage by year)

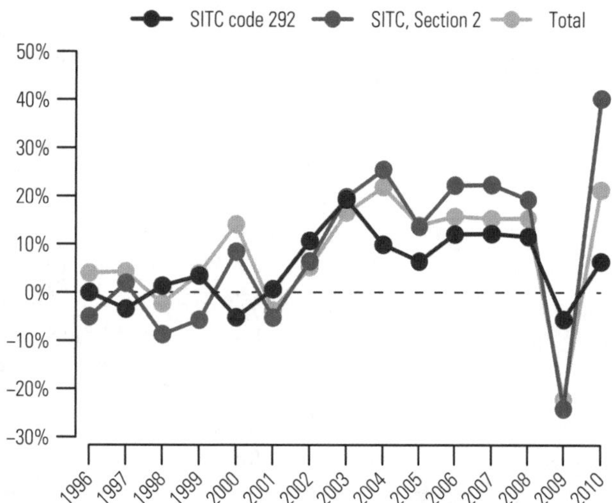

Table 2: Top exporting countries or areas in 2010

Country or area	Value (million US$)	Avg. Growth (%) 06-10	Growth (%) 09-10	World share %	Cum.
World	31 561.1	5.9	6.4	100.0	
Netherlands	9 722.9	4.4	0.2	30.8	30.8
USA	2 086.2	8.6	9.8	6.6	37.4
Germany	1 886.9	7.5	5.5	6.0	43.4
China	1 795.2	21.7	22.7	5.7	49.1
Colombia	1 263.1	6.5	18.6	4.0	53.1
Italy	1 199.7	4.9	4.5	3.8	56.9
Belgium	1 176.2	9.8	7.7	3.7	60.6
France	972.8	3.3	1.9	3.1	63.7
India	913.1	10.1	55.5	2.9	66.6
Denmark	880.8	-6.5	-12.2	2.8	69.4
Spain	621.8	4.0	5.5	2.0	71.3
Ecuador	615.2	8.7	11.6	1.9	73.3
Canada	556.3	-0.2	10.2	1.8	75.1
Kenya	525.1	8.2	-6.6	1.7	76.7
Israel	407.1	13.7	28.0	1.3	78.0

Graph 2: Trade Balance by MDG regions 2010

(Bln US$)

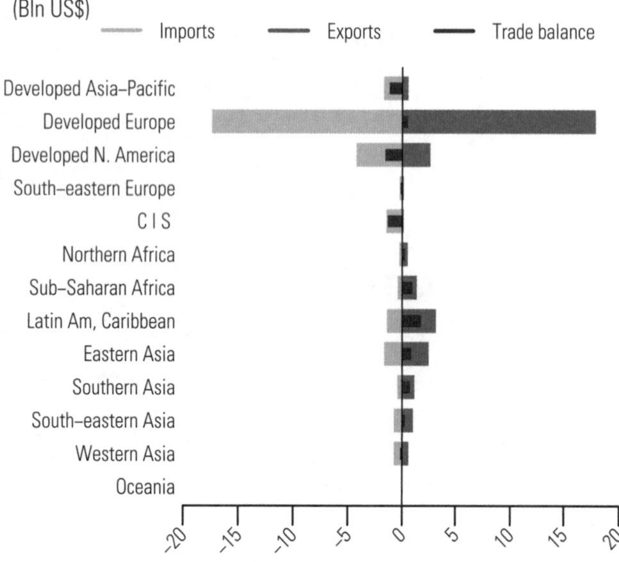

Table 3: Top importing countries or areas in 2010

Country or area	Value (million US$)	Avg. Growth (%) 06-10	Growth (%) 09-10	World share %	Cum.
World	30 905.3	5.7	7.3	100.0	
Germany	3 790.8	4.2	5.9	12.3	12.3
USA	3 509.0	2.5	10.9	11.4	23.6
France	2 250.6	4.7	1.2	7.3	30.9
Netherlands	2 099.5	4.8	-3.8	6.8	37.7
United Kingdom	2 090.4	0.3	11.6	6.8	44.5
Japan	1 446.8	3.8	11.7	4.7	49.1
Italy	1 149.3	4.2	9.6	3.7	52.9
Russian Federation	1 112.6	20.5	18.8	3.6	56.5
Belgium	953.0	7.6	-1.4	3.1	59.5
Switzerland	712.7	3.9	4.7	2.3	61.8
Canada	704.7	5.2	11.0	2.3	64.1
China	692.3	19.1	32.6	2.2	66.4
Spain	656.7	-0.2	-9.2	2.1	68.5
Austria	551.5	7.4	0.8	1.8	70.3
Poland	547.5	13.5	12.7	1.8	72.1

Mineral fuels, lubricants and related materials

(SITC Section 3)

321 Coal, whether or not pulverized, but not agglomerated

After several years of continuous growth marked by a peak of 94.4 bln US$ in 2008, the value (in current prices) of exports of coal, whether or not pulverized, but not agglomerated (SITC group 321) dropped in 2009 (by 14.4 percent) but bounced back in 2010 by 27.7 percent to amount to 103.3 bln US$ (see table 2). Imports showed a similar development with an increase of 17.4 percent to 113.3 bln US$ in 2010 (see table 3). Graph 1 shows that the increase in exports for 2010 in this product group was less than the increase in world exports of mineral fuels, lubricants and related materials (SITC section 3) of 28.1 percent, but greater than the increase in total world exports of 21.2 percent. Exports of coal, whether or not pulverized, but not agglomerated (SITC group 321) accounted for 4.6 percent of world exports of SITC section 3 and 0.7 percent of total world exports in 2010 (see table 1).

Exports of Australia, the top exporting country in 2010, increased by 24.7 percent and represented 37.3 percent of world exports (see table 2). Other major exporting countries were Indonesia and USA, respectively with 17.6 and 9.5 percent of world exports. Top destinations were Japan, China and Rep. of Korea (see table 3). By MDG regions (see graph 2), top trade surpluses were recorded by South-eastern Asia (+16.6 bln US$), Developed Asia-Pacific (+14.4 bln US$) and Developed North America (+13.1 bln US$). Top trade deficits were recorded by Eastern Asia (-33.9 bln US$), Developed Europe (-19.8 bln US$) and Southern Asia (-7.7 bln US$).

Table 1: Imports (Imp.) and exports (Exp.), 1996-2010, in current prices

		1996	1997	1998	1999	2000	2001	2002	2003	2004	2005	2006	2007	2008	2009	2010
Values in Bln US$	Imp.	24.2	24.8	22.7	19.9	21.0	25.0	25.4	28.0	43.7	58.3	60.5	70.1	123.5	96.5	113.3
	Exp.	20.0	20.3	18.6	15.9	16.6	20.7	20.4	21.9	31.6	46.1	49.7	52.4	94.4	80.9	103.3
As a percentage of SITC section (%)	Imp.	5.3	5.3	6.5	4.8	3.1	4.0	4.1	3.6	4.2	4.1	3.4	3.6	4.4	5.4	4.9
	Exp.	4.6	4.5	5.6	3.8	2.5	3.5	3.4	3.0	3.2	3.2	2.9	2.7	3.4	4.7	4.6
As a percentage of world trade (%)	Imp.	0.5	0.4	0.4	0.3	0.3	0.4	0.4	0.4	0.5	0.6	0.5	0.5	0.8	0.8	0.7
	Exp.	0.4	0.4	0.3	0.3	0.3	0.3	0.3	0.3	0.3	0.4	0.4	0.4	0.6	0.7	0.7

Graph 1: Annual growth rates of exports, 1996–2010
(In percentage by year)

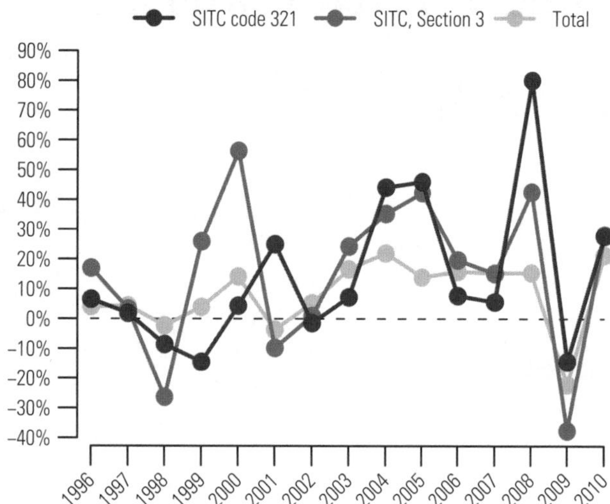

Table 2: Top exporting countries or areas in 2010

Country or area	Value (million US$)	Avg. Growth (%) 06-10	Growth (%) 09-10	World share %	Cum.
World	103304.5	20.1	27.7	100.0	
Australia	38571.8	21.7	24.7	37.3	37.3
Indonesia	18160.2	31.5	31.7	17.6	54.9
USA	9836.4	29.2	64.0	9.5	64.4
Russian Federation	9180.5	20.6	24.6	8.9	73.3
Canada	5815.8	19.7	33.6	5.6	79.0
Colombia	5520.8	18.4	5.0	5.3	84.3
South Africa	5436.4	14.8	29.3	5.3	89.6
China	2233.1	-11.7	-5.4	2.2	91.7
Viet Nam	*1654.1*	16.0	25.6	1.6	93.3
Poland	1193.0	-1.6	24.8	1.2	94.5
Czech Rep.	1021.1	13.2	21.4	1.0	95.5
Mongolia	*971.4*	115.5	731.7	0.9	96.4
Netherlands	813.9	2.4	35.4	0.8	97.2
Belgium	691.6	12.5	3.8	0.7	97.9
Ukraine	563.0	29.1	62.6	0.5	98.4

Graph 2: Trade Balance by MDG regions 2010
(Bln US$)

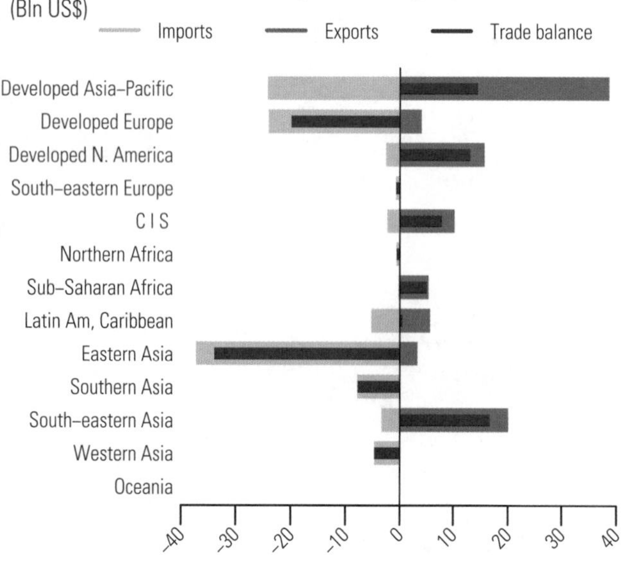

Table 3: Top importing countries or areas in 2010

Country or area	Value (million US$)	Avg. Growth (%) 06-10	Growth (%) 09-10	World share %	Cum.
World	113254.4	17.0	17.4	100.0	
Japan	24108.5	14.8	9.4	21.3	21.3
China	16918.4	79.8	60.0	14.9	36.2
Rep. of Korea	12847.6	25.1	29.9	11.3	47.6
India	7228.4	19.9	-4.8	6.4	54.0
Other Asia, nes	6676.8	16.5	14.1	5.9	59.8
Germany	4717.1	9.5	3.1	4.2	64.0
Turkey	3211.4	13.0	5.4	2.8	66.8
Italy	3061.6	8.3	22.3	2.7	69.6
Brazil	2926.5	18.5	41.6	2.6	72.1
United Kingdom	2860.8	-7.3	-31.0	2.5	74.7
France	2765.3	10.7	29.8	2.4	77.1
Netherlands	2013.7	5.9	5.6	1.8	78.9
Ukraine	1781.3	23.7	124.0	1.6	80.5
Poland	1720.7	49.9	62.3	1.5	82.0
Malaysia	1622.1	33.7	50.1	1.4	83.4

Since 2006, the value (in current prices) of exports of briquettes, lignite and peat (SITC group 322) increased on average by 34.7 percent each year and amounted to 3.4 bln US$ in 2010 (see table 2). During the same period, imports increased on average by 33.7 percent to 3.8 bln US$ (see table 3). Graph 1 shows that the increase of 24.3 percent in exports for 2010 in this product group was similar to the increase in world exports of mineral fuels, lubricants and related materials (SITC section 3) of 28.1 percent and the increase in total world exports of 21.2 percent. Exports of briquettes, lignite and peat (SITC group 322) accounted for 0.2 percent of world exports of mineral fuels, lubricants and related materials (SITC section 3) and less than 0.1 percent of total world exports in 2010 (see table 1).

In 2010, Uzbekistan, Indonesia and Germany were the top exporting countries (see table 2). They accounted respectively for 39.7, 10.4 and 10.3 percent of world exports. China, Afghanistan and USA were the top destinations (see table 3). By MDG regions (see graph 2), a large share of trade in briquettes, lignite and peat (SITC group 322) took place in Developed Europe. Its exports amounted to 1,023 mln US$ and imports were valued at 983 mln US$, resulting in a trade surplus of 40 mln US$. Commonwealth of Independent States also recorded a surplus of 1.5 bln US$. Significant deficits were recorded by Eastern Asia (-1.3 bln US$) and Southern Asia (-938 mln US$).

Table 1: Imports (Imp.) and exports (Exp.), 1996-2010, in current prices

		1996	1997	1998	1999	2000	2001	2002	2003	2004	2005	2006	2007	2008	2009	2010
Values in Bln US$	Imp.	1.0	0.9	0.8	0.8	0.7	0.7	0.8	0.9	1.0	1.1	1.2	1.4	1.8	2.5	3.8
	Exp.	0.9	0.8	0.7	0.7	0.7	0.7	0.7	0.8	0.8	0.9	1.0	1.2	1.5	2.7	3.4
As a percentage of SITC section (%)	Imp.	0.2	0.2	0.2	0.2	0.1	0.1	0.1	0.1	0.1	0.1	0.1	0.1	0.1	0.1	0.2
	Exp.	0.2	0.2	0.2	0.2	0.1	0.1	0.1	0.1	0.1	0.1	0.1	0.1	0.1	0.2	0.2
As a percentage of world trade (%)	Imp.	0.0	0.0	0.0	0.0	0.0	0.0	0.0	0.0	0.0	0.0	0.0	0.0	0.0	0.0	0.0
	Exp.	0.0	0.0	0.0	0.0	0.0	0.0	0.0	0.0	0.0	0.0	0.0	0.0	0.0	0.0	0.0

Graph 1: Annual growth rates of exports, 1996–2010
(In percentage by year)

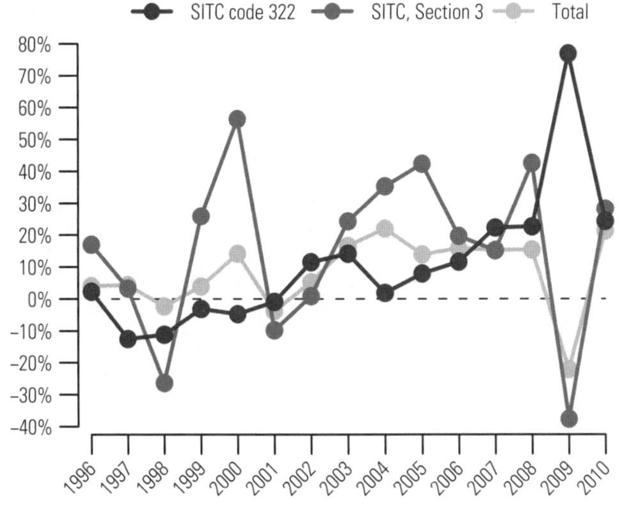

Graph 2: Trade Balance by MDG regions 2010
(Bln US$)

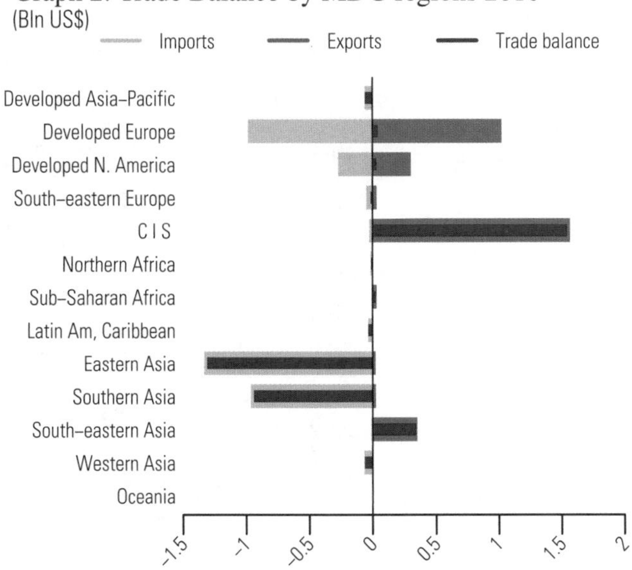

Table 2: Top exporting countries or areas in 2010

Country or area	Value (million US$)	Avg. Growth (%) 06-10	Growth (%) 09-10	World share %	Cum.
World	3364.1	34.7	24.3	100.0	
Uzbekistan	*1334.2*	1404.6	15.7	39.7	39.7
Indonesia	348.6	207.8	937.3	10.4	50.0
Germany	345.4	8.5	5.2	10.3	60.3
Canada	278.6	1.1	-2.6	8.3	68.6
Turkmenistan	*129.4*	...	53.1	3.8	72.4
Latvia	125.8	22.6	17.0	3.7	76.2
Netherlands	102.2	46.1	-3.9	3.0	79.2
Czech Rep.	88.8	3.1	-11.6	2.6	81.8
Ireland	75.6	2.9	4.8	2.2	84.1
Estonia	73.3	16.2	28.0	2.2	86.3
Belgium	59.9	13.3	14.3	1.8	88.0
Lithuania	46.4	9.4	4.4	1.4	89.4
Tajikistan	*37.2*	...	235.4	1.1	90.5
United Kingdom	35.4	36.9	11.8	1.1	91.6
South Africa	32.3	119.0	11496.1	1.0	92.5

Table 3: Top importing countries or areas in 2010

Country or area	Value (million US$)	Avg. Growth (%) 06-10	Growth (%) 09-10	World share %	Cum.
World	3814.5	33.7	50.7	100.0	
China	1280.2	267.3	280.4	33.6	33.6
Afghanistan	961.0	...	31.7	25.2	58.8
USA	262.3	0.9	-0.9	6.9	65.6
France	131.5	5.2	-5.3	3.4	69.1
Germany	113.1	11.3	57.6	3.0	72.0
Netherlands	111.2	9.7	-7.8	2.9	75.0
Italy	84.2	6.1	7.5	2.2	77.2
Belgium	74.9	7.9	8.7	2.0	79.1
Slovakia	60.6	9.7	-1.5	1.6	80.7
Slovenia	53.8	12.4	2.5	1.4	82.1
Japan	51.2	7.9	15.6	1.3	83.5
United Kingdom	47.1	2.2	10.1	1.2	84.7
Spain	39.0	0.1	0.2	1.0	85.7
Poland	35.1	45.6	54.7	0.9	86.6
Austria	33.8	-3.0	-1.9	0.9	87.5

 Source: UN Comtrade

325 Coke, semi-coke of coal, lignite or peat, agglomerated or not; retort carbon

After a sharp decline of 71.5 percent in 2009, the value (in current prices) of exports of coke, semi-coke of coal, lignite or peat, agglomerated or not; retort carbon (SITC group 325) rose significantly in 2010 by 108.8 percent to amount to 8.0 bln US$ (see table 2). Imports showed a similar development with an increase of 87.6 percent to 9.0 bln US$ in 2010 (see table 3). Graph 1 shows that the increase in exports for 2010 in this product group was more than triple the increase in world exports of mineral fuels, lubricants and related materials (SITC section 3) of 28.1 percent and the increase in total world exports of 21.2 percent. Exports of coke, semi-coke of coal, lignite or peat, agglomerated or not; retort carbon (SITC group 325) accounted for 0.4 percent of world exports of SITC section 3 and 0.1 percent of total world exports in 2010 (see table 1).

Exports of Poland, the top exporting country in 2010, rose significantly by 112.0 percent and accounted for 28.5 percent of world exports in 2010 (see table 2). Other major exporting countries were China and Russian Federation, respectively with 17.3 and 6.2 percent of world exports. Germany, Brazil and South Africa were the top destinations (see table 3). By MDG regions (see graph 2), Eastern Asia recorded a surplus of 862 mln US$. Top trade deficits were recorded by Southern Asia (-0.8 bln US$) and Sub-Saharan Africa (-0.5 bln US$).

Table 1: Imports (Imp.) and exports (Exp.), 1996-2010, in current prices

		1996	1997	1998	1999	2000	2001	2002	2003	2004	2005	2006	2007	2008	2009	2010
Values in Bln US$	Imp.	2.6	2.5	2.4	2.1	2.6	2.6	2.8	4.1	9.8	7.4	6.8	8.1	14.7	4.8	9.0
	Exp.	2.1	2.1	2.1	1.7	2.2	2.3	2.4	3.7	8.3	6.1	7.5	7.4	13.5	3.9	8.0
As a percentage of SITC section (%)	Imp.	0.6	0.5	0.7	0.5	0.4	0.4	0.5	0.5	0.9	0.5	0.4	0.4	0.5	0.3	0.4
	Exp.	0.5	0.5	0.6	0.4	0.3	0.4	0.4	0.5	0.8	0.4	0.4	0.4	0.5	0.2	0.4
As a percentage of world trade (%)	Imp.	0.0	0.0	0.0	0.0	0.0	0.0	0.0	0.1	0.1	0.1	0.1	0.1	0.1	0.0	0.1
	Exp.	0.0	0.0	0.0	0.0	0.0	0.0	0.0	0.0	0.1	0.1	0.1	0.1	0.1	0.0	0.1

Graph 1: Annual growth rates of exports, 1996–2010

(In percentage by year)

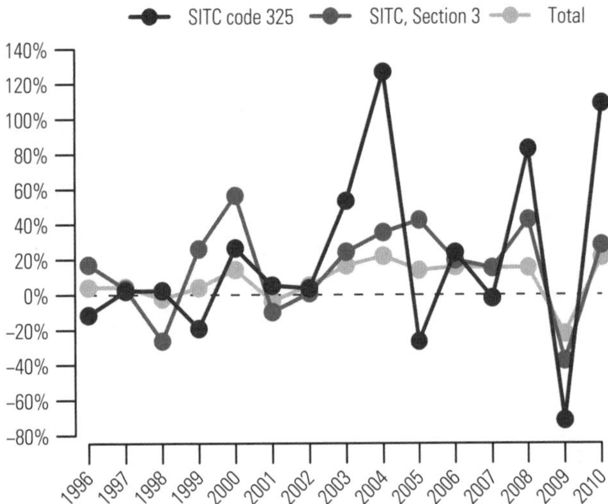

Table 2: Top exporting countries or areas in 2010

Country or area	Value (million US$)	Avg. Growth (%) 06-10	Growth (%) 09-10	World share %	Cum.
World	8044.0	1.7	108.8	100.0	
Poland	2290.2	19.6	112.0	28.5	28.5
China	1389.3	-8.9	580.2	17.3	45.7
Russian Federation	500.9	21.5	38.6	6.2	52.0
Colombia	494.4	47.0	210.2	6.1	58.1
Ukraine	444.5	64.6	166.9	5.5	63.6
Belgium	344.1	21.2	84.4	4.3	67.9
Czech Rep.	340.2	14.0	152.4	4.2	72.1
Japan	303.3	-2.0	45.1	3.8	75.9
USA	244.7	17.5	47.8	3.0	79.0
Bosnia Herzegovina	198.4	28.6	129.9	2.5	81.4
India	197.9	127.5	699.6	2.5	83.9
United Kingdom	182.8	67.5	423.0	2.3	86.2
Egypt	161.5	38.9	-15.6	2.0	88.2
Spain	150.7	-10.8	119.5	1.9	90.0
Australia	139.6	20.4	10.5	1.7	91.8

Graph 2: Trade Balance by MDG regions 2010

(Bln US$)

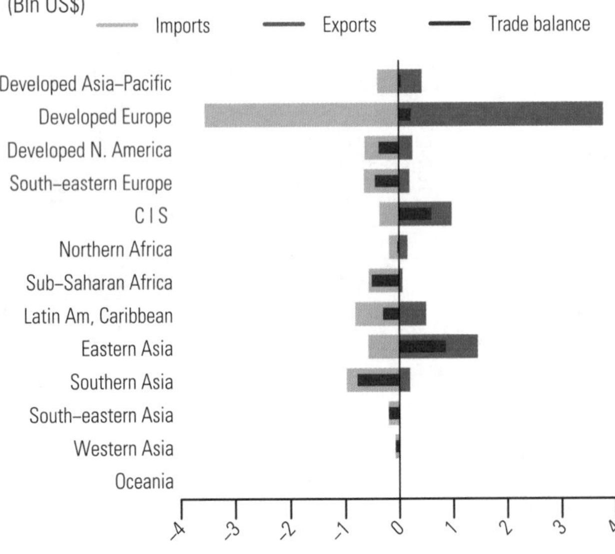

Table 3: Top importing countries or areas in 2010

Country or area	Value (million US$)	Avg. Growth (%) 06-10	Growth (%) 09-10	World share %	Cum.
World	9002.5	7.5	87.6	100.0	
Germany	1440.1	8.2	79.0	16.0	16.0
Brazil	648.4	25.8	235.2	7.2	23.2
South Africa	493.2	90.6	152.5	5.5	28.7
India	479.6	-11.4	-20.8	5.3	34.0
USA	433.5	-11.3	329.9	4.8	38.8
Austria	413.9	14.1	127.1	4.6	43.4
Iran	407.2	96.3	8.4	4.5	47.9
Japan	371.7	3.1	170.2	4.1	52.1
Romania	336.5	31.9	121.9	3.7	55.8
Other Asia, nes	308.0	53.4	1168.8	3.4	59.2
Slovakia	288.3	37.4	411.3	3.2	62.4
Serbia	285.0	11.8	47.1	3.2	65.6
Czech Rep.	260.8	20.4	176.2	2.9	68.5
Rep. of Korea	254.4	45.5	188.9	2.8	71.3
Belgium	249.3	29.1	18.1	2.8	74.1

After several years of continuous growth marked by a peak of 1,497.0 bln US$ in 2008, the value (in current prices) of exports of crude petroleum oils and oils obtained from bituminous minerals (SITC group 333) contracted sharply in 2009 (by 42.5 percent) but bounced back in 2010 by 27.8 percent to amount to 1,100.2 bln US$ (see table 2). Imports showed a similar development with an increase of 29.7 percent to 1,193.2 bln US$ in 2010 (see table 3). Graph 1 shows that the increase in exports for 2010 in this product group was slightly less than the increase in world exports of mineral fuels, lubricants and related materials (SITC section 3) of 28.1 percent, but higher than the increase in total world exports of 21.2 percent. Exports of crude petroleum oils and oils obtained from bituminous minerals (SITC group 333) accounted for 49.4 percent of world exports of SITC section 3 and 7.3 percent of total world exports in 2010 (see table 1).

The top exporting countries in 2010 were Saudi Arabia, Russian Federation and United Arab Emirates (see table 2). They accounted respectively for 17.2, 11.7 and 6.0 percent of world exports. USA, the top importing country, accounted for 22.3 percent of world imports (see table 3). Other major importing countries were China and Japan. By MDG regions (see graph 2), top trade surpluses were recorded by Western Asia (+342.0 bln US$), Commonwealth of Independent States (+171.9 bln US$) and Sub-Saharan Africa (+122.2 bln US$). Top trade deficits were recorded by Developed Europe (-248.3 bln US$), Developed North America (-237.5 bln US$) and Eastern Asia (-228.1 bln US$).

Table 1: Imports (Imp.) and exports (Exp.), 1996-2010, in current prices

		1996	1997	1998	1999	2000	2001	2002	2003	2004	2005	2006	2007	2008	2009	2010
Values in Bln US$	Imp.	249.7	256.4	177.3	224.6	389.9	340.4	339.9	427.5	576.3	799.2	991.0	1086.1	1565.9	919.9	1193.2
	Exp.	243.4	239.4	163.8	231.5	373.8	314.2	323.7	399.8	536.5	770.2	946.2	1072.9	1497.0	860.9	1100.2
As a percentage of SITC section (%)	Imp.	54.5	54.5	50.6	54.5	58.2	54.5	55.2	54.7	55.2	55.6	56.0	55.4	55.4	51.7	51.8
	Exp.	55.4	52.8	49.2	55.2	57.0	53.2	54.3	54.0	53.6	54.1	55.6	54.8	53.7	49.5	49.4
As a percentage of world trade (%)	Imp.	4.7	4.6	3.2	3.9	6.0	5.4	5.2	5.6	6.2	7.6	8.1	7.8	9.7	7.4	7.9
	Exp.	4.6	4.4	3.1	4.2	5.9	5.2	5.0	5.3	5.9	7.4	7.9	7.8	9.4	6.9	7.3

Graph 1: Annual growth rates of exports, 1996–2010
(In percentage by year)

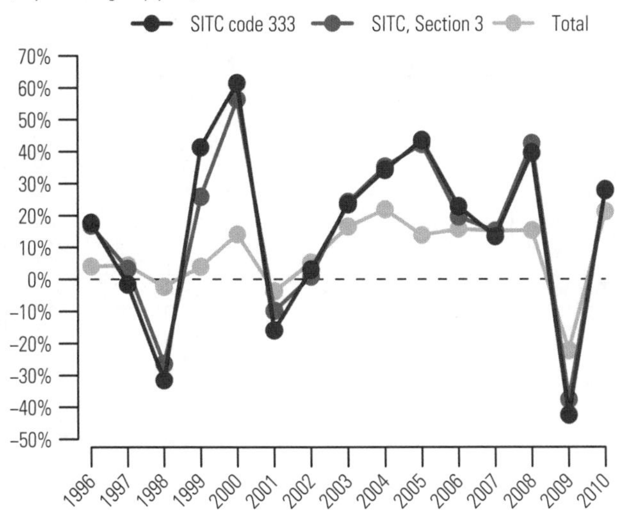

Table 2: Top exporting countries or areas in 2010

Country or area	Value (million US$)	Avg. Growth (%) 06-10	Growth (%) 09-10	World share %	Cum.
World	1100244.8	3.8	27.8	100.0	
Saudi Arabia	189433.6	4.0	33.2	17.2	17.2
Russian Federation	129126.3	7.5	38.0	11.7	29.0
United Arab Emirates	65482.1	5.0	50.4	6.0	34.9
Nigeria	60904.6	2.6	44.3	5.5	40.4
Canada	50458.8	10.8	34.1	4.6	45.0
Norway	46972.5	-2.0	17.6	4.3	49.3
Iran	46709.4	-1.8	6.3	4.2	53.5
Angola	*45034.0*	10.9	17.1	4.1	57.6
Venezuela	44156.6	-5.9	23.2	4.0	61.6
Kuwait	*37714.2*	0.7	27.2	3.4	65.1
Libya	*37273.1*	1.8	29.8	3.4	68.5
Kazakhstan	36982.3	11.9	41.1	3.4	71.8
Mexico	35907.4	0.9	39.8	3.3	75.1
Algeria	24779.4	-5.0	16.4	2.3	77.3
United Kingdom	24491.2	1.4	25.2	2.2	79.6

Graph 2: Trade Balance by MDG regions 2010
(Bln US$)

Imports — Exports — Trade balance

Developed Asia-Pacific
Developed Europe
Developed N. America
South-eastern Europe
C I S
Northern Africa
Sub-Saharan Africa
Latin Am, Caribbean
Eastern Asia
Southern Asia
South-eastern Asia
Western Asia
Oceania

-400 -300 -200 -100 0 100 200 300 400

Table 3: Top importing countries or areas in 2010

Country or area	Value (million US$)	Avg. Growth (%) 06-10	Growth (%) 09-10	World share %	Cum.
World	1193191.3	4.8	29.7	100.0	
USA	266638.3	3.4	32.9	22.3	22.3
China	135299.7	19.5	51.6	11.3	33.7
Japan	105814.3	1.7	32.3	8.9	42.6
Rep. of Korea	68669.4	5.3	35.3	5.8	48.3
India	65515.0	8.3	0.9	5.5	53.8
Germany	52596.8	0.2	21.3	4.4	58.2
Italy	46054.3	3.6	37.3	3.9	62.1
Netherlands	35933.1	5.8	38.8	3.0	65.1
France	35319.2	-3.0	11.1	3.0	68.0
United Kingdom	30142.7	3.3	33.1	2.5	70.6
Spain	30132.8	2.5	32.0	2.5	73.1
Other Asia, nes	25717.8	2.2	30.6	2.2	75.2
Singapore	24067.4	4.2	19.7	2.0	77.3
Thailand	23893.9	4.4	25.7	2.0	79.3
Canada	23169.7	3.0	24.1	1.9	81.2

334 Petroleum oils and oils obtained from bituminous minerals, (not crude)

After several years of continuous growth marked by a peak of 774.3 bln US$ in 2008, the value (in current prices) of exports of non-crude petroleum oils and oils obtained from bituminous minerals (SITC group 334) contracted sharply in 2009 (by 34.4 percent) but bounced back in 2010 by 32.8 percent to amount to 674.4 bln US$ (see table 2). Imports showed a similar development with an increase of 36.0 percent to 609.7 bln US$ in 2010 (see table 3). Graph 1 shows that the increase in exports for 2010 in this product group exceeded both the increase in world exports of mineral fuels, lubricants and related materials (SITC section 3) of 28.1 percent and the increase in total world exports of 21.2 percent. Exports of non-crude petroleum oils and oils obtained from bituminous minerals (SITC group 334) accounted for 30.3 percent of world exports of SITC section 3 and 4.5 percent of total world exports in 2010 (see table 1).

Russian Federation, Singapore and USA were the top exporting countries in 2010 with respectively 10.3, 8.2 and 8.0 percent of world exports (see table 2). USA and Singapore were among the top destinations (see table 3). By MDG regions (see graph 2), Developed Europe accounted for the majority of trade in non-crude petroleum oils and oils obtained from bituminous minerals (SITC group 334). In 2010, its exports and imports were valued at 188.1 bln US$ and 188.0 bln US$ respectively, resulting in a trade surplus of 0.1 bln US$. Top surpluses were recorded in Commonwealth of Independent States (+72.3 bln US$) and Western Asia (+38.1 bln US$). Top trade deficit was recorded by South-eastern Asia (-24.8 bln US$).

Table 1: Imports (Imp.) and exports (Exp.), 1996-2010, in current prices

		1996	1997	1998	1999	2000	2001	2002	2003	2004	2005	2006	2007	2008	2009	2010
Values in Bln US$	Imp.	108.8	109.4	82.5	97.8	155.8	141.7	136.6	171.3	237.4	342.6	426.3	499.2	704.2	448.3	609.7
	Exp.	106.4	114.3	84.2	101.8	161.0	146.6	147.5	177.7	259.8	378.7	465.9	538.0	774.3	507.9	674.4
As a percentage of SITC section (%)	Imp.	23.8	23.3	23.5	23.7	23.3	22.7	22.2	21.9	22.7	23.8	24.1	25.5	24.9	25.2	26.5
	Exp.	24.2	25.2	25.3	24.3	24.6	24.8	24.8	24.0	26.0	26.6	27.4	27.5	27.8	29.2	30.3
As a percentage of world trade (%)	Imp.	2.0	2.0	1.5	1.7	2.4	2.3	2.1	2.2	2.6	3.2	3.5	3.6	4.3	3.6	4.0
	Exp.	2.0	2.1	1.6	1.8	2.5	2.4	2.3	2.4	2.9	3.7	3.9	3.9	4.9	4.1	4.5

Graph 1: Annual growth rates of exports, 1996–2010

(In percentage by year)

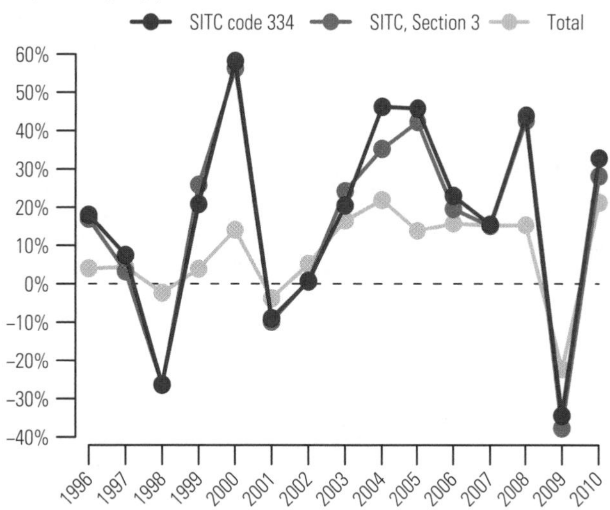

Table 2: Top exporting countries or areas in 2010

Country or area	Value (million US$)	Avg. Growth (%) 06-10	Growth (%) 09-10	World share %	Cum.
World	674414.1	9.7	32.8	100.0	
Russian Federation	69550.7	12.0	48.3	10.3	10.3
Singapore	55199.8	13.0	38.1	8.2	18.5
USA	53708.3	24.8	47.0	8.0	26.5
Netherlands	44928.0	9.2	40.3	6.7	33.1
India	36641.3	20.5	57.8	5.4	38.6
Rep. of Korea	30078.0	10.8	35.8	4.5	43.0
Belgium	23715.3	9.9	37.1	3.5	46.5
United Kingdom	20213.9	7.1	29.6	3.0	49.5
Kuwait	*19902.6*	8.0	27.2	3.0	52.5
Italy	18245.8	7.9	51.3	2.7	55.2
Venezuela	18160.4	205.3	-1.1	2.7	57.9
Saudi Arabia	17955.3	0.0	18.3	2.7	60.5
China	17028.0	24.7	35.7	2.5	63.1
Canada	14424.3	7.6	37.0	2.1	65.2
Other Asia, nes	13862.1	7.5	26.6	2.1	67.3

Graph 2: Trade Balance by MDG regions 2010

(Bln US$)

Imports — Exports — Trade balance

Developed Asia-Pacific
Developed Europe
Developed N. America
South-eastern Europe
CIS
Northern Africa
Sub-Saharan Africa
Latin Am, Caribbean
Eastern Asia
Southern Asia
South-eastern Asia
Western Asia
Oceania

-200 -150 -100 -50 0 50 100 150 200

Table 3: Top importing countries or areas in 2010

Country or area	Value (million US$)	Avg. Growth (%) 06-10	Growth (%) 09-10	World share %	Cum.
World	609685.1	9.4	36.0	100.0	
USA	69266.2	0.1	26.9	11.4	11.4
Singapore	56950.2	23.8	47.4	9.3	20.7
Netherlands	27859.2	15.4	42.5	4.6	25.3
Germany	25993.2	8.2	44.8	4.3	29.5
France	23518.0	6.0	33.1	3.9	33.4
China	22435.1	9.6	32.1	3.7	37.1
Japan	18761.2	4.5	47.4	3.1	40.1
Mexico	18269.7	17.9	55.8	3.0	43.1
United Kingdom	18241.1	1.8	29.0	3.0	46.1
Belgium	17841.9	5.8	18.5	2.9	49.1
Indonesia	17654.3	12.6	62.8	2.9	52.0
Rep. of Korea	17327.8	16.9	39.4	2.8	54.8
Spain	14522.3	5.4	31.2	2.4	57.2
China, Hong Kong SAR	12748.6	12.2	39.1	2.1	59.3
Other Asia, nes	11400.7	23.0	77.3	1.9	61.1

After several years of continuous growth marked by a peak of 39.0 bln US$ in 2008, the value (in current prices) of exports of residual petroleum products, nes, and related materials (SITC group 335) dropped in 2009 (by 31.3 percent) but bounced back in 2010 by 36.2 percent to amount to 36.5 bln US$ (see table 2). Imports showed a similar development with an increase of 35.4 percent to 38.1 bln US$ in 2010 (see table 3). Graph 1 shows that the increase in exports for 2010 in this product group exceeded both the increase in world exports of mineral fuels, lubricants and related materials (SITC section 3) of 28.1 percent and the increase in total world exports of 21.2 percent. Exports of residual petroleum products, nes, and related materials (SITC group 335) accounted for 1.6 percent of world exports of SITC section 3 and 0.2 percent of total world exports in 2010 (see table 1).

Exports of USA, the top exporting country in 2010, increased by 47.9 percent and represented 19.5 percent of world exports (see table 2). Other major exporting countries were Rep. of Korea and Germany, with respectively 6.1 and 5.5 percent of world exports. China, Netherlands and USA were the top destinations (see table 3). By MDG regions (see graph 2), Developed North America and South-eastern Asia recorded trade surpluses amounting respectively of 5.2 bln US$ and 2.6 bln US$. Top trade deficits were recorded by Eastern Asia (-4.9 bln US$), Latin America and the Caribbean (-3.2 bln US$) and Developed Asia-Pacific (-1.0 bln US$).

Table 1: Imports (Imp.) and exports (Exp.), 1996-2010, in current prices

		1996	1997	1998	1999	2000	2001	2002	2003	2004	2005	2006	2007	2008	2009	2010
Values in Bln US$	Imp.	7.5	8.6	7.3	7.6	9.6	9.9	10.4	13.0	18.6	21.2	27.0	37.2	39.0	28.2	38.1
	Exp.	6.4	8.5	7.1	7.7	8.3	8.5	9.0	11.6	15.1	17.6	22.4	27.7	39.0	26.8	36.5
As a percentage of SITC section (%)	Imp.	1.6	1.8	2.1	1.8	1.4	1.6	1.7	1.7	1.8	1.5	1.5	1.9	1.4	1.6	1.7
	Exp.	1.5	1.9	2.1	1.8	1.3	1.4	1.5	1.6	1.5	1.2	1.3	1.4	1.4	1.5	1.6
As a percentage of world trade (%)	Imp.	0.1	0.2	0.1	0.1	0.1	0.2	0.2	0.2	0.2	0.2	0.2	0.3	0.2	0.2	0.3
	Exp.	0.1	0.2	0.1	0.1	0.1	0.1	0.1	0.2	0.2	0.2	0.2	0.2	0.2	0.2	0.2

Graph 1: Annual growth rates of exports, 1996–2010

(In percentage by year)

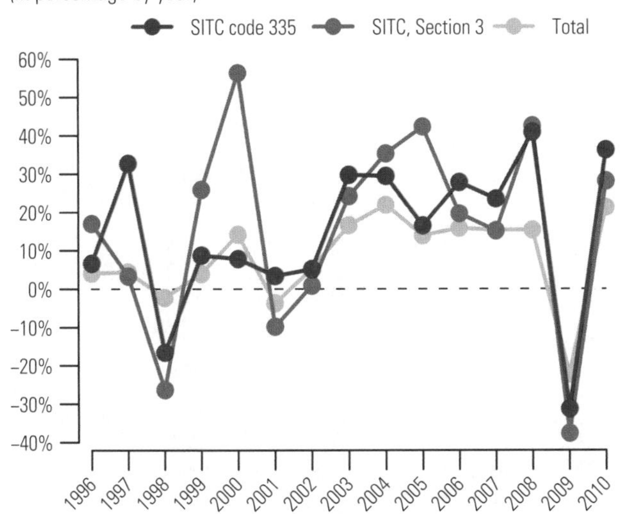

Table 2: Top exporting countries or areas in 2010

Country or area	Value (million US$)	Avg. Growth (%) 06-10	Growth (%) 09-10	World share %	Cum.
World	36489.2	12.9	36.2	100.0	
USA	7098.4	17.5	47.9	19.5	19.5
Rep. of Korea	2219.7	27.0	46.2	6.1	25.5
Germany	2018.2	-1.0	16.8	5.5	31.1
Indonesia	1992.7	54.3	33.0	5.5	36.5
Netherlands	1853.5	8.1	56.2	5.1	41.6
Belgium	1764.5	10.9	39.2	4.8	46.4
China	1697.0	8.4	56.2	4.7	51.1
Spain	1365.2	16.2	32.6	3.7	54.8
Singapore	1289.9	0.7	47.4	3.5	58.4
Canada	1251.9	9.9	31.4	3.4	61.8
France	1029.5	-0.7	40.1	2.8	64.6
Japan	975.8	4.4	11.9	2.7	67.3
Iran	958.1	12.9	6.3	2.6	69.9
India	897.1	32.5	55.6	2.5	72.4
Italy	894.6	21.5	18.3	2.5	74.8

Graph 2: Trade Balance by MDG regions 2010

(Bln US$)

Imports — Exports — Trade balance

Developed Asia-Pacific
Developed Europe
Developed N. America
South-eastern Europe
C I S
Northern Africa
Sub-Saharan Africa
Latin Am, Caribbean
Eastern Asia
Southern Asia
South-eastern Asia
Western Asia
Oceania

-14 -12 -10 -8 -6 -4 -2 0 2 4 6 8 10 12

Table 3: Top importing countries or areas in 2010

Country or area	Value (million US$)	Avg. Growth (%) 06-10	Growth (%) 09-10	World share %	Cum.
World	38122.9	9.1	35.4	100.0	
China	6365.7	31.9	104.6	16.7	16.7
Netherlands	3617.4	5.7	50.7	9.5	26.2
USA	2330.9	-5.0	21.1	6.1	32.3
Germany	1753.6	0.3	54.2	4.6	36.9
Rep. of Korea	1682.1	2.2	25.6	4.4	41.3
Japan	1467.7	-5.0	60.6	3.8	45.2
France	1139.4	-0.2	22.7	3.0	48.2
Brazil	1087.9	42.6	142.8	2.9	51.0
Ecuador	1016.9	15.8	32.3	2.7	53.7
Other Asia, nes	1005.7	74.6	43.3	2.6	56.3
Belgium	938.5	-3.4	18.3	2.5	58.8
Canada	860.7	4.9	25.6	2.3	61.0
India	806.7	5.7	-7.9	2.1	63.1
Thailand	806.5	17.3	35.5	2.1	65.3
Mexico	715.4	9.2	72.3	1.9	67.1

Source: UN Comtrade

342 Liquefied propane and butane

After several years of continuous growth marked by a peak of 42.3 bln US$ in 2008, the value (in current prices) of exports of liquefied propane and butane (SITC group 342) contracted sharply in 2009 (by 32.0 percent) but bounced back in 2010 by 35.3 percent to amount to 38.9 bln US$ (see table 2). Imports showed a similar development with an increase of 38.3 percent to 42.5 bln US$ in 2010 (see table 3). Graph 1 shows that the increase in exports for 2010 in this product group exceeded the increase in world exports of mineral fuels, lubricants and related materials (SITC section 3) of 28.1 percent and the increase in total world exports of 21.2 percent. Exports of liquefied propane and butane (SITC group 342) accounted for 1.7 percent of world exports of SITC section 3 and 0.3 percent of total world exports in 2010 (see table 1).

The top exporting countries in 2010 were Saudi Arabia, Algeria and Qatar (see table 2). They accounted respectively for 14.4, 13.0 and 10.7 percent of world exports. Top destinations were Japan, Rep. of Korea and USA (see table 3). By MDG regions (see graph 2), Western Asia recorded a surplus of 11.3 bln US$. Significant surpluses were also recorded by Northern Africa (+2.4 bln US$) and Sub-Saharan Africa (+2.0 bln US$). Top trade deficits were recorded by Developed Asia-Pacific (-8.3 bln US$), Eastern Asia (-6.8 bln US$) and South-eastern Asia (-2.5 bln US$).

Table 1: Imports (Imp.) and exports (Exp.), 1996-2010, in current prices

		1996	1997	1998	1999	2000	2001	2002	2003	2004	2005	2006	2007	2008	2009	2010
Values in Bln US$	Imp.	11.1	12.0	8.3	10.6	15.9	14.3	12.7	17.4	21.5	27.6	33.5	38.1	48.4	30.7	42.5
	Exp.	7.0	7.5	4.9	6.3	10.5	9.6	8.9	15.0	19.0	24.7	28.2	33.2	42.3	28.8	38.9
As a percentage of SITC section (%)	Imp.	2.4	2.5	2.4	2.6	2.4	2.3	2.1	2.2	2.1	1.9	1.9	1.9	1.7	1.7	1.8
	Exp.	1.6	1.7	1.5	1.5	1.6	1.6	1.5	2.0	1.9	1.7	1.7	1.7	1.5	1.7	1.7
As a percentage of world trade (%)	Imp.	0.2	0.2	0.2	0.2	0.2	0.2	0.2	0.2	0.2	0.3	0.3	0.3	0.3	0.2	0.3
	Exp.	0.1	0.1	0.1	0.1	0.2	0.2	0.1	0.2	0.2	0.2	0.2	0.2	0.3	0.2	0.3

Graph 1: Annual growth rates of exports, 1996–2010
(In percentage by year)

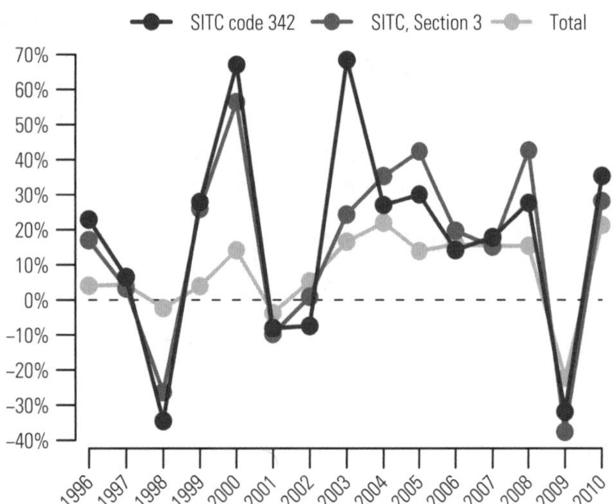

Graph 2: Trade Balance by MDG regions 2010
(Bln US$)

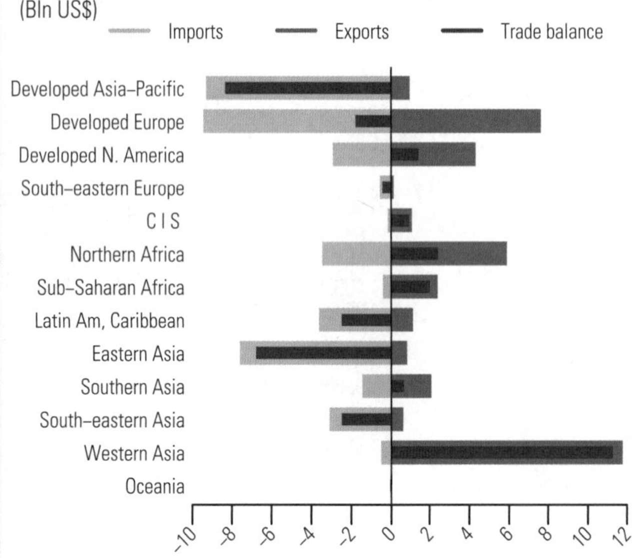

Table 2: Top exporting countries or areas in 2010

Country or area	Value (million US$)	Avg. Growth (%) 06-10	Growth (%) 09-10	World share %	Cum.
World	38925.2	8.4	35.3	100.0	
Saudi Arabia	5608.3	-3.3	32.7	14.4	14.4
Algeria	5071.1	5.8	52.3	13.0	27.4
Qatar	*4146.7*	37.6	24.3	10.7	38.1
Norway	2848.0	5.0	27.1	7.3	45.4
USA	2450.5	32.1	72.7	6.3	51.7
Iran	2098.0	19.4	6.3	5.4	57.1
Kuwait	*1998.7*	2.8	27.2	5.1	62.2
Canada	1868.2	-2.1	10.7	4.8	67.0
Nigeria	1671.6	...	223.0	4.3	71.3
United Kingdom	1551.7	12.4	37.3	4.0	75.3
Australia	957.5	4.8	21.7	2.5	77.8
Russian Federation	901.2	25.5	100.0	2.3	80.1
Belgium	703.2	25.4	53.9	1.8	81.9
France	676.6	-6.2	22.6	1.7	83.6
Netherlands	666.5	9.4	126.7	1.7	85.3

Table 3: Top importing countries or areas in 2010

Country or area	Value (million US$)	Avg. Growth (%) 06-10	Growth (%) 09-10	World share %	Cum.
World	42480.2	6.1	38.3	100.0	
Japan	8889.1	2.5	40.3	20.9	20.9
Rep. of Korea	4314.9	13.9	41.7	10.2	31.1
USA	2602.1	-13.3	14.6	6.1	37.2
China	2269.6	-5.9	11.2	5.3	42.6
Egypt	1806.2	14.8	40.3	4.3	46.8
France	1645.4	7.2	42.3	3.9	50.7
Italy	1508.1	10.1	61.6	3.6	54.2
India	1395.6	1.3	11.6	3.3	57.5
Morocco	1376.4	16.0	38.2	3.2	60.8
Thailand	1165.1	561.6	141.2	2.7	63.5
Brazil	1109.4	26.0	65.0	2.6	66.1
Poland	1056.0	19.9	91.1	2.5	68.6
Netherlands	892.6	-5.5	52.4	2.1	70.7
Spain	874.4	5.0	27.6	2.1	72.8
Indonesia	856.6	131.7	86.2	2.0	74.8

After a drop of 29.5 percent in 2009, the value (in current prices) of exports of natural gas, whether or not liquefied (SITC group 343) increased in 2010 by 16.8 percent to amount to 221.1 bln US$ (see table 2). Imports showed a similar increase of 16.7 percent to 248.8 bln US$ in 2010 (see table 3). Graph 1 shows that the increase in exports for 2010 in this product group was less than both the increase in world exports of mineral fuels, lubricants and related materials (SITC section 3) of 28.1 percent and the increase in total world exports of 21.2 percent. Exports of natural gas, whether or not liquefied (SITC group 343) accounted for 9.9 percent of world exports of SITC section 3 and 1.5 percent of total world exports in 2010 (see table 1).

Exports of Russian Federation, Norway and Qatar, the top exporting countries in 2010, accounted respectively for 21.0, 12.6 and 9.0 percent of world exports (see table 2). Japan, Germany and Italy were the major destinations (see table 3). By MDG regions (see graph 2), Developed Europe accounted for a large share of imports of natural gas, whether or not liquefied (SITC group 343): its imports amounted to 128.9 bln US$ compared to 46.7 bln US$ for exports, resulting in a trade deficit of 82.2 bln US$. Major deficits were also recorded by Developed Asia-Pacific (-32.6 bln US$) and Eastern Asia (-26.9 bln US$). Top surpluses were recorded by Commonwealth of Independent States (+36.1 bln US$), South-eastern Asia (+30.3 bln US$) and Western Asia (+25.7 bln US$).

Table 1: Imports (Imp.) and exports (Exp.), 1996-2010, in current prices

		1996	1997	1998	1999	2000	2001	2002	2003	2004	2005	2006	2007	2008	2009	2010
Values in Bln US$	Imp.	42.8	45.2	39.4	39.4	60.8	73.7	71.5	99.6	112.2	148.9	183.8	185.6	281.0	213.3	248.8
	Exp.	40.4	48.2	40.5	43.0	68.4	71.8	66.3	85.8	101.4	145.6	135.4	180.6	268.5	189.3	221.1
As a percentage of SITC section (%)	Imp.	9.3	9.6	11.2	9.5	9.1	11.8	11.6	12.7	10.7	10.3	10.4	9.5	9.9	12.0	10.8
	Exp.	9.2	10.6	12.1	10.2	10.4	12.2	11.1	11.6	10.1	10.2	8.0	9.2	9.6	10.9	9.9
As a percentage of world trade (%)	Imp.	0.8	0.8	0.7	0.7	0.9	1.2	1.1	1.3	1.2	1.4	1.5	1.3	1.7	1.7	1.6
	Exp.	0.8	0.9	0.8	0.8	1.1	1.2	1.0	1.1	1.1	1.4	1.1	1.3	1.7	1.5	1.5

Graph 1: Annual growth rates of exports, 1996–2010
(In percentage by year)

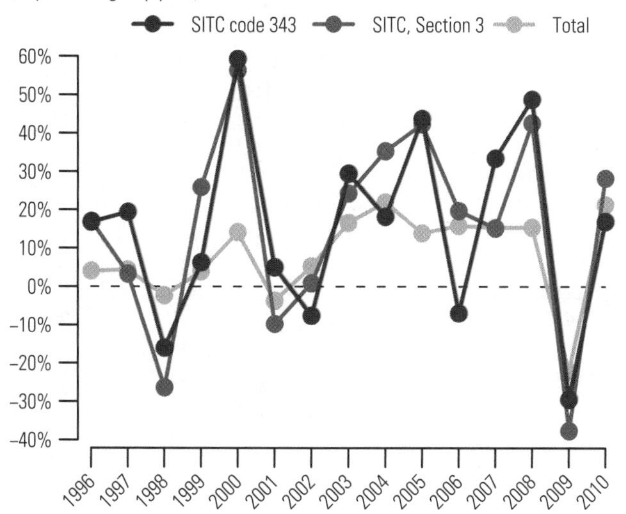

Table 2: Top exporting countries or areas in 2010

Country or area	Value (million US$)	Avg. Growth (%) 06-10	Growth (%) 09-10	World share %	Cum.
World	221084.6	13.0	16.8	100.0	
Russian Federation	46520.1	...	15.5	21.0	21.0
Norway	27936.4	5.1	14.6	12.6	33.7
Qatar	*19932.4*	13.9	24.3	9.0	42.7
Algeria	17390.8	3.5	19.7	7.9	50.6
Canada	15167.0	-11.3	8.2	6.9	57.4
Indonesia	13458.7	7.7	53.5	6.1	63.5
Malaysia	11845.2	16.9	33.7	5.4	68.9
Australia	8493.6	22.5	41.9	3.8	72.7
Belgium	6143.7	-5.2	38.5	2.8	75.5
Trinidad and Tobago	*4536.1*	0.9	22.2	2.1	77.5
Germany	4527.5	...	31.1	2.0	79.6
USA	4488.2	18.9	45.7	2.0	81.6
Brunei Darussalam	*4333.0*	18.3	14.8	2.0	83.6
Myanmar	*3647.8*	16.4	29.7	1.6	85.2
United Kingdom	3387.0	10.4	78.2	1.5	86.8

Graph 2: Trade Balance by MDG regions 2010
(Bln US$)

Imports — Exports — Trade balance

Developed Asia-Pacific
Developed Europe
Developed N. America
South-eastern Europe
C I S
Northern Africa
Sub-Saharan Africa
Latin Am, Caribbean
Eastern Asia
Southern Asia
South-eastern Asia
Western Asia
Oceania

-140 -120 -100 -80 -60 -40 -20 0 20 40 60

Table 3: Top importing countries or areas in 2010

Country or area	Value (million US$)	Avg. Growth (%) 06-10	Growth (%) 09-10	World share %	Cum.
World	248843.0	7.9	16.7	100.0	
Japan	39655.5	14.8	30.9	15.9	15.9
Germany	31207.0	0.4	-5.9	12.5	28.5
Italy	26152.6	...	7.5	10.5	39.0
Rep. of Korea	17010.0	9.3	22.6	6.8	45.8
France	16497.1	3.6	-0.1	6.6	52.5
USA	16275.2	-13.3	8.5	6.5	59.0
Belgium	10970.5	-4.2	37.8	4.4	63.4
United Kingdom	10593.3	23.0	42.3	4.3	67.7
Spain	10237.7	2.7	1.6	4.1	71.8
Ukraine	9392.9	18.5	17.7	3.8	75.5
Other Asia, nes	5793.6	11.5	42.5	2.3	77.9
Belarus	4046.0	42.2	55.5	1.6	79.5
China	4014.5	142.8	213.8	1.6	81.1
Czech Rep.	3984.2	16.6	28.0	1.6	82.7
Austria	3799.4	5.5	14.4	1.5	84.2

 Source: UN Comtrade

344 Petroleum gases and other gaseous hydrocarbons, nes

After a sharp decline of 71.8 percent in 2009, the value (in current prices) of exports of petroleum gases and other gaseous hydrocarbons, nes (SITC group 344) rose significantly in 2010 by 40.0 percent to amount to 8.2 bln US$ (see table 2). Imports showed a similar development with an increase of 44.4 percent to 11.3 bln US$ in 2010 (see table 3). Graph 1 shows that the increase in exports for 2010 in this product group exceeded both the increase in world exports of mineral fuels, lubricants and related materials (SITC section 3) of 28.1 percent and the increase in total world exports of 21.2 percent. Exports of petroleum gases and other gaseous hydrocarbons, nes (SITC group 344) accounted for 0.4 percent of world exports of SITC section 3 and 0.1 percent of total world exports in 2010 (see table 1).

Iran was the top exporting country in 2010: it accounted for 13.1 percent of world exports (see table 2). Other major exporting countries were Malaysia and Canada, respectively with 12.1 and 9.8 percent of world exports. Turkey, USA and Belgium were the major destinations (see table 3). By MDG regions (see graph 2), top surpluses were recorded by South-eastern Asia (+0.7 bln US$) and the Commonwealth of Independent States (+0.2 bln US$). Top trade deficits were recorded by Western Asia (-2.3 bln US$) and Latin America and the Caribbean (-1.3 bln US$).

Table 1: Imports (Imp.) and exports (Exp.), 1996-2010, in current prices

		1996	1997	1998	1999	2000	2001	2002	2003	2004	2005	2006	2007	2008	2009	2010
Values in Bln US$	Imp.	3.8	4.1	2.7	2.8	4.7	3.8	3.7	4.8	5.5	7.8	8.4	10.0	13.4	7.8	11.3
	Exp.	4.0	4.0	3.2	2.6	4.2	4.9	4.8	7.6	9.1	9.4	15.0	17.0	20.7	5.8	8.2
As a percentage of SITC section (%)	Imp.	0.8	0.9	0.8	0.7	0.7	0.6	0.6	0.6	0.5	0.5	0.5	0.5	0.5	0.4	0.5
	Exp.	0.9	0.9	1.0	0.6	0.6	0.8	0.8	1.0	0.9	0.7	0.9	0.9	0.7	0.3	0.4
As a percentage of world trade (%)	Imp.	0.1	0.1	0.0	0.0	0.1	0.1	0.1	0.1	0.1	0.1	0.1	0.1	0.1	0.1	0.1
	Exp.	0.1	0.1	0.1	0.0	0.1	0.1	0.1	0.1	0.1	0.1	0.1	0.1	0.1	0.0	0.1

Graph 1: Annual growth rates of exports, 1996–2010

(In percentage by year)

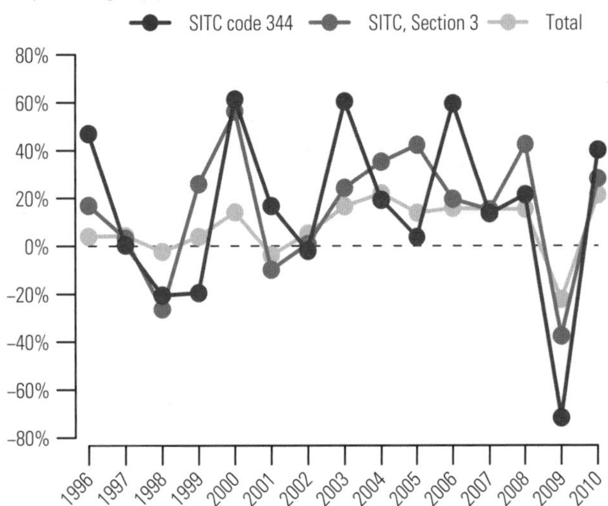

Graph 2: Trade Balance by MDG regions 2010

(Bln US$)

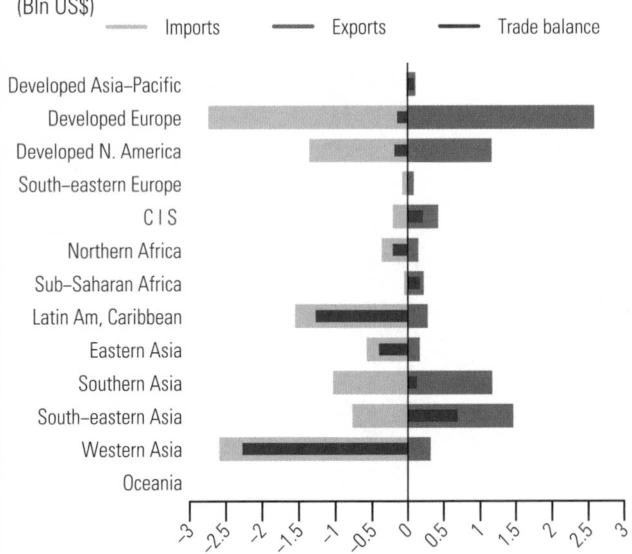

Table 2: Top exporting countries or areas in 2010

Country or area	Value (million US$)	Avg. Growth (%) 06-10	Growth (%) 09-10	World share %	Cum.
World	8150.1	-14.2	40.0	100.0	
Iran	1068.0	41.4	6.3	13.1	13.1
Malaysia	985.3	5.9	30.5	12.1	25.2
Canada	800.0	8.1	97.1	9.8	35.0
Netherlands	649.2	26.2	65.1	8.0	43.0
Norway	384.5	-0.2	64.6	4.7	47.7
Belgium	361.2	7.7	75.2	4.4	52.1
USA	360.0	0.3	18.1	4.4	56.5
Russian Federation	346.0	91.8	89.3	4.2	60.8
United Kingdom	276.9	-6.4	25.0	3.4	64.2
Argentina	222.6	9.0	59.2	2.7	66.9
Nigeria	213.7	...		2.6	69.5
Indonesia	210.6	23.4	79.2	2.6	72.1
Germany	185.0	-54.3	26.3	2.3	74.4
Turkey	153.1	-2.0	53.6	1.9	76.3
Qatar	*152.6*	-56.9	24.3	1.9	78.1

Table 3: Top importing countries or areas in 2010

Country or area	Value (million US$)	Avg. Growth (%) 06-10	Growth (%) 09-10	World share %	Cum.
World	11326.5	7.8	44.4	100.0	
Turkey	2273.4	9.9	44.2	20.1	20.1
USA	1217.7	4.2	89.4	10.8	30.8
Belgium	853.6	2.2	8.8	7.5	38.4
Mexico	790.4	-0.2	41.2	7.0	45.3
Germany	742.3	9.9	69.6	6.6	51.9
India	679.2	31.8	109.2	6.0	57.9
Ecuador	575.3	4.4	42.7	5.1	63.0
Rep. of Korea	469.9	21.6	108.3	4.1	67.1
Viet Nam	*375.6*	24.8	66.9	3.3	70.4
Tunisia	363.7	1.2	5.5	3.2	73.6
Sweden	290.6	11.4	135.1	2.6	76.2
Philippines	261.7	11.3	24.6	2.3	78.5
Poland	228.6	-22.8	-40.1	2.0	80.5
United Kingdom	166.6	39.1	114.9	1.5	82.0
Israel	154.6	34.6	46.8	1.4	83.4

After a drop of 20.6 percent in 2009, the value (in current prices) of exports of electric current (SITC group 351) increased in 2010 by 4.6 percent to amount to 32.2 bln US$ (see table 2). Imports showed a similar development with an increase of 12.0 percent to 32.1 bln US$ in 2010 (see table 3). Graph 1 shows that the increase in exports for 2010 in this product group was exceeded by both the increase in world exports of mineral fuels, lubricants and related materials (SITC section 3) of 28.1 percent and the increase in total world exports of 21.2 percent. Exports of electric current (SITC group 351) accounted for 1.4 percent of world exports of SITC section 3 and 0.2 percent of total world exports in 2010 (see table 1).

Switzerland, Germany and France were the major exporting countries in 2010 (see table 2). They accounted respectively for 15.1, 12.6 and 8.8 percent of world exports. Top destinations were Italy, Switzerland and Germany (see table 3). By MDG regions (see graph 2), Developed Europe accounted for a majority of trade in electric current (SITC group 351). In 2010, its exports amounted to 23.5 bln US$ and imports to 24.6 bln US$, resulting in a trade deficit of 1.1 bln US$. A surplus of 1.1 bln US$ was also recorded by Commonwealth of Independent States. Significant deficits were recorded by Latin America and the Caribbean (-0.3 bln US$) and South-eastern Asia (-0.2 bln US$).

Table 1: Imports (Imp.) and exports (Exp.), 1996-2010, in current prices

		1996	1997	1998	1999	2000	2001	2002	2003	2004	2005	2006	2007	2008	2009	2010
Values in Bln US$	Imp.	6.6	6.3	7.1	6.9	8.4	11.9	11.9	15.4	17.7	24.4	30.4	25.2	35.4	28.7	32.1
	Exp.	8.5	7.9	8.2	8.3	9.9	11.6	11.9	15.7	18.8	23.7	30.3	27.4	38.7	30.7	32.2
As a percentage of SITC section (%)	Imp.	1.4	1.3	2.0	1.7	1.3	1.9	1.9	2.0	1.7	1.7	1.7	1.3	1.3	1.6	1.4
	Exp.	1.9	1.7	2.4	2.0	1.5	2.0	2.0	2.1	1.9	1.7	1.8	1.4	1.4	1.8	1.4
As a percentage of world trade (%)	Imp.	0.1	0.1	0.1	0.1	0.1	0.2	0.2	0.2	0.2	0.2	0.2	0.2	0.2	0.2	0.2
	Exp.	0.2	0.1	0.2	0.2	0.2	0.2	0.2	0.2	0.2	0.2	0.3	0.2	0.2	0.2	0.2

Graph 1: Annual growth rates of exports, 1996–2010

(In percentage by year)

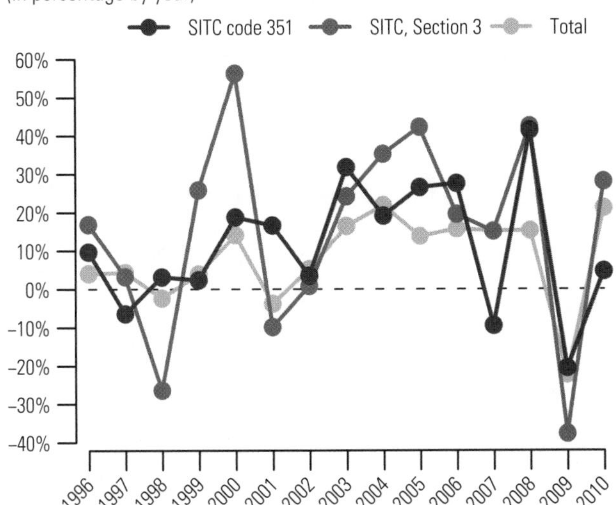

Table 2: Top exporting countries or areas in 2010

Country or area	Value (million US$)	Avg. Growth (%) 06-10	Growth (%) 09-10	World share %	Cum.
World	32154.7	1.5	4.6	100.0	
Switzerland	4863.7	11.4	16.3	15.1	15.1
Germany	4047.7	-2.7	-10.3	12.6	27.7
France	2821.8	-7.8	21.1	8.8	36.5
Canada	1964.6	-1.8	-6.2	6.1	42.6
Austria	1707.6	-24.1	14.0	5.3	47.9
Czech Rep.	1449.0	11.2	-20.1	4.5	52.4
Italy	1398.5	63.7	131.7	4.3	56.8
China	1173.2	12.9	8.7	3.6	60.4
Russian Federation	1028.3	11.4	55.5	3.2	63.6
Netherlands	824.6	...	2.3	2.6	66.2
Sweden	779.1	5.9	72.7	2.4	68.6
Denmark	744.5	-0.2	52.7	2.3	70.9
Belgium	708.1	1.9	14.7	2.2	73.1
USA	648.4	-11.4	12.7	2.0	75.1
Hungary	590.3	20.4	-23.6	1.8	77.0

Graph 2: Trade Balance by MDG regions 2010

(Bln US$)

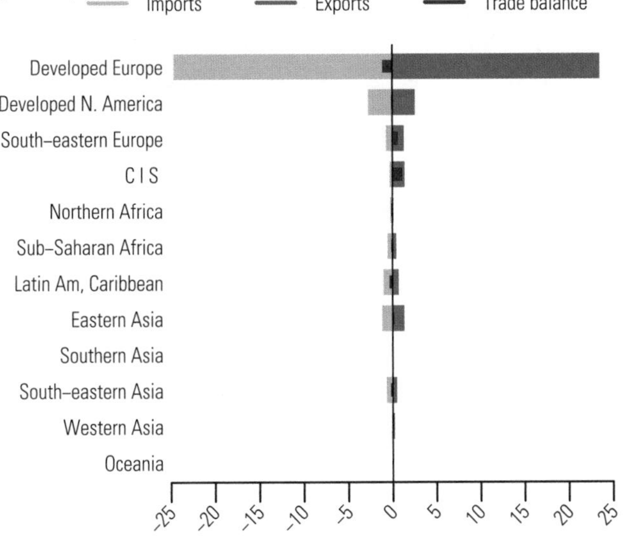

Table 3: Top importing countries or areas in 2010

Country or area	Value (million US$)	Avg. Growth (%) 06-10	Growth (%) 09-10	World share %	Cum.
World	32140.8	1.4	12.0	100.0	
Italy	5256.8	17.7	31.2	16.4	16.4
Switzerland	3590.6	11.5	28.2	11.2	27.5
Germany	2657.3	3.2	-17.0	8.3	35.8
USA	2071.5	-4.8	0.0	6.4	42.2
France	1432.2	20.3	2.4	4.5	46.7
Sweden	1277.5	3.2	74.6	4.0	50.7
Austria	1073.2	-33.1	-30.7	3.3	54.0
Czech Rep.	1070.7	32.0	0.6	3.3	57.3
Netherlands	1062.1	-11.4		3.3	60.6
Norway	1022.1	15.1	257.2	3.2	63.8
Finland	913.2	1.0	35.9	2.8	66.7
Hungary	906.2	7.0	-31.8	2.8	69.5
Belgium	776.1	-14.3	39.4	2.4	71.9
China, Hong Kong SAR	634.7	0.9	-2.0	2.0	73.9
Canada	631.2	-10.1	11.1	2.0	75.8

Animal and vegetable oils, fats and waxes

(SITC Section 4)

411 Animal oils and fats

After several years of continuous growth marked by a peak of 5.5 bln US$ in 2008, the value (in current prices) of exports of animal oils and fats (SITC group 411) dropped in 2009 (by 28.7 percent) but bounced back in 2010 by 20.2 percent to amount to 4.7 bln US$ (see table 2). Imports showed a similar development with an increase of 13.9 percent to 4.5 bln US$ in 2010 (see table 3). Graph 1 shows that the increase in exports for 2010 in this product group was exceeded by both the increase in world exports of animal and vegetable oils, fats and waxes (SITC section 4) of 40.2 percent and the increase in total world exports of 21.2 percent. Exports of animal oils and fats (SITC group 411) accounted for 0.7 percent of world exports of SITC section 4 and less than 0.1 percent of total world exports in 2010 (see table 1).

The top exporting countries in 2010 were USA, Germany and France (see table 2). They accounted respectively for 23.2, 7.5 and 6.9 percent of world exports. Major destinations were Mexico, Russian Federation and China (see table 3). By MDG regions (see graph 2), Developed Europe was the origin and the destination of a large share of trade in animal oils and fats (SITC group 411). In 2010, its exports amounted to 2.2 bln US$ compared to 1.8 bln US$ for imports, resulting in a trade surplus of 0.4 bln US$. Developed North America also recorded a surplus amounting to 1.0 bln US$. Significant deficits were recorded by Eastern Asia (-0.4 bln US$) and Commonwealth of Independent States (-0.4 bln US$).

Table 1: Imports (Imp.) and exports (Exp.), 1996-2010, in current prices

		1996	1997	1998	1999	2000	2001	2002	2003	2004	2005	2006	2007	2008	2009	2010
Values in Bln US$	Imp.	2.3	2.2	2.2	2.0	1.7	1.6	1.8	2.2	2.7	2.7	2.8	3.6	5.4	4.0	4.5
	Exp.	2.0	2.0	2.0	1.6	1.4	1.4	1.7	2.0	2.6	2.5	2.7	3.6	5.5	3.9	4.7
As a percentage of SITC section (%)	Imp.	0.9	0.9	0.9	0.9	0.7	0.7	0.7	0.8	0.7	0.6	0.6	0.6	0.7	0.7	0.6
	Exp.	0.9	0.9	0.9	0.8	0.7	0.7	0.8	0.8	0.8	0.7	0.6	0.7	0.8	0.8	0.7
As a percentage of world trade (%)	Imp.	0.0	0.0	0.0	0.0	0.0	0.0	0.0	0.0	0.0	0.0	0.0	0.0	0.0	0.0	0.0
	Exp.	0.0	0.0	0.0	0.0	0.0	0.0	0.0	0.0	0.0	0.0	0.0	0.0	0.0	0.0	0.0

Graph 1: Annual growth rates of exports, 1996–2010

(In percentage by year)

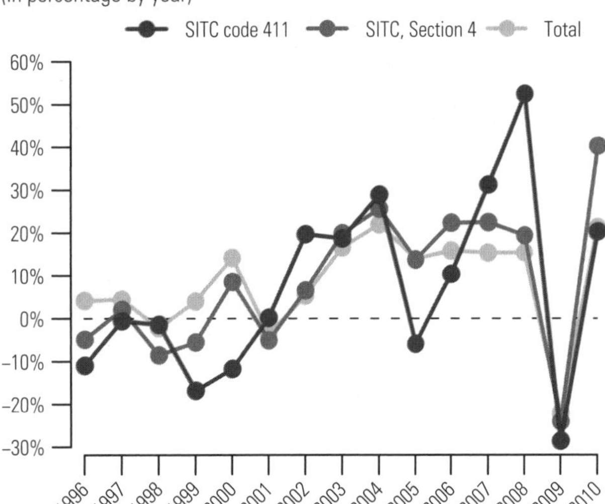

Graph 2: Trade Balance by MDG regions 2010

(Bln US$)

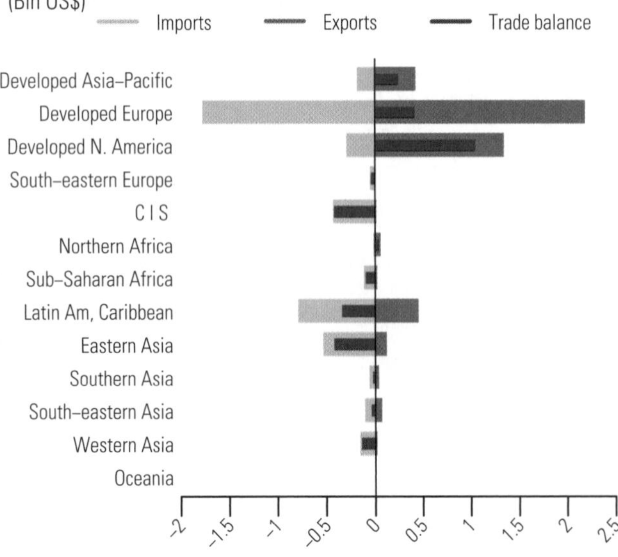

Table 2: Top exporting countries or areas in 2010

Country or area	Value (million US$)	Avg. Growth (%) 06-10	Growth (%) 09-10	World share %	Cum.
World	4691.6	14.4	20.2	100.0	
USA	1087.3	19.7	49.2	23.2	23.2
Germany	352.7	12.1	0.5	7.5	30.7
France	324.3	13.8	21.6	6.9	37.6
Denmark	278.8	11.6	31.3	5.9	43.5
Australia	276.8	15.3	29.8	5.9	49.4
Peru	274.3	8.7	6.4	5.8	55.3
Canada	245.1	8.5	28.2	5.2	60.5
Netherlands	202.8	13.6	7.5	4.3	64.8
Spain	169.2	12.8	-2.3	3.6	68.4
United Kingdom	157.4	17.0	44.0	3.4	71.8
Belgium	142.3	6.0	0.2	3.0	74.8
Norway	121.1	14.2	13.3	2.6	77.4
Italy	111.8	10.4	2.6	2.4	79.8
New Zealand	111.2	15.2	33.0	2.4	82.2
China	96.0	40.6	35.2	2.0	84.2

Table 3: Top importing countries or areas in 2010

Country or area	Value (million US$)	Avg. Growth (%) 06-10	Growth (%) 09-10	World share %	Cum.
World	4521.0	12.8	13.9	100.0	
Mexico	425.7	16.9	21.6	9.4	9.4
Russian Federation	360.2	19.6	-8.1	8.0	17.4
China	345.7	18.9	27.7	7.6	25.0
Norway	258.6	11.9	-0.8	5.7	30.8
Belgium	188.1	7.3	1.7	4.2	34.9
Netherlands	184.2	14.4	24.1	4.1	39.0
USA	178.4	14.4	20.9	3.9	42.9
Spain	170.8	10.9	22.2	3.8	46.7
Denmark	168.4	6.5	6.3	3.7	50.4
Germany	148.0	9.7	8.1	3.3	53.7
Japan	145.5	7.5	8.4	3.2	56.9
United Kingdom	143.3	6.4	-6.4	3.2	60.1
Turkey	136.9	13.0	28.7	3.0	63.1
Canada	113.9	16.4	27.4	2.5	65.6
France	112.5	8.4	19.2	2.5	68.1

After several years of continuous growth marked by a peak of 34.4 bln US$ in 2008, the value (in current prices) of exports of fixed vegetable fats and oils, 'soft', crude, refined or fractionated (SITC group 421) dropped in 2009 (by 28.4 percent) but bounced back in 2010 by 15.1 percent to amount to 28.3 bln US$ (see table 2). Imports showed a similar development with an increase of 4.1 percent to 27.0 bln US$ in 2010 (see table 3). Graph 1 shows that the increase in exports for 2010 in this product group was exceeded by both the increase in world exports of animal and vegetable oils, fats and waxes (SITC section 4) of 40.2 percent and the increase in total world exports of 21.2 percent. Exports of fixed vegetable fats and oils, 'soft', crude, refined or fractionated (SITC group 421) accounted for 4.1 percent of world exports of SITC section 4 and 0.2 percent of total world exports in 2010 (see table 1).

Argentina, Spain and USA were the top exporting countries with respectively 17.1, 10.5 and 8.5 percent of world exports in 2010 (see table 2). Major destinations were China, Italy and USA (see table 3). By MDG regions (see graph 2), Developed Europe was the origin and the destination of a large share of trade in fixed vegetable fats and oils, 'soft', crude, refined or fractionated (SITC group 421). In 2010, its exports and imports were valued at respectively 10.8 bln US$ and 10.3 bln US$, resulting in a trade surplus of 0.5 bln US$. Top trade surplus was recorded by Latin America and the Caribbean (+4.6 bln US$). Major deficits were recorded by Eastern Asia (-3.0 bln US$) and Southern Asia (-2.2 bln US$).

Table 1: Imports (Imp.) and exports (Exp.), 1996-2010, in current prices

		1996	1997	1998	1999	2000	2001	2002	2003	2004	2005	2006	2007	2008	2009	2010
Values in Bln US$	Imp.	11.7	12.3	13.1	11.2	8.9	9.0	10.9	13.8	16.3	17.0	20.0	24.9	35.1	25.9	27.0
	Exp.	11.2	12.5	13.4	11.0	8.3	8.6	10.6	13.3	15.6	16.6	19.8	24.7	34.4	24.6	28.3
As a percentage of SITC section (%)	Imp.	4.6	4.8	5.6	4.9	3.6	3.8	4.5	4.8	4.4	4.1	4.0	4.0	4.6	4.8	3.6
	Exp.	5.0	5.5	6.4	5.6	3.9	4.3	4.9	5.2	4.8	4.5	4.4	4.5	5.3	5.0	4.1
As a percentage of world trade (%)	Imp.	0.2	0.2	0.2	0.2	0.1	0.1	0.2	0.2	0.2	0.2	0.2	0.2	0.2	0.2	0.2
	Exp.	0.2	0.2	0.2	0.2	0.1	0.1	0.2	0.2	0.2	0.2	0.2	0.2	0.2	0.2	0.2

Graph 1: Annual growth rates of exports, 1996–2010

(In percentage by year)

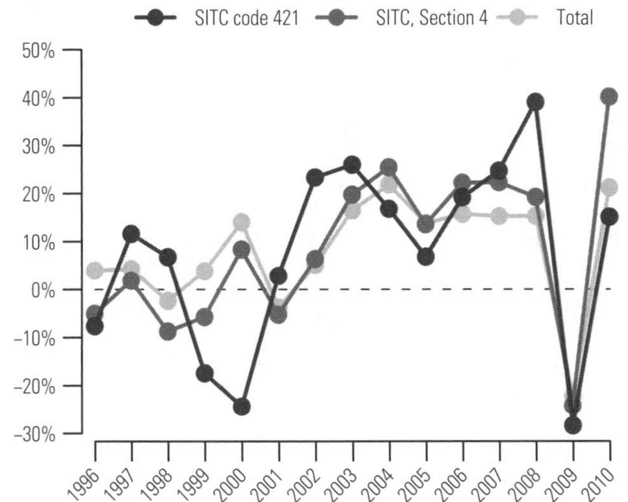

Table 2: Top exporting countries or areas in 2010

Country or area	Value (million US$)	Avg. Growth (%) 06-10	Growth (%) 09-10	World share %	Cum.
World	28346.1	9.3	15.1	100.0	
Argentina	4850.8	7.5	15.6	17.1	17.1
Spain	2966.2	5.4	16.0	10.5	27.6
USA	2417.7	26.6	34.9	8.5	36.1
Ukraine	2416.7	26.8	46.1	8.5	44.6
Canada	2193.4	29.2	55.4	7.7	52.4
Italy	1668.5	-1.5	10.0	5.9	58.3
Netherlands	1476.3	11.3	-11.7	5.2	63.5
Brazil	1409.5	2.5	8.0	5.0	68.4
Germany	913.1	8.6	6.9	3.2	71.7
France	871.7	5.4	-2.6	3.1	74.7
Russian Federation	615.1	10.0	-20.4	2.2	76.9
Belgium	609.2	1.3	-12.9	2.1	79.1
Tunisia	413.3	-14.3	-14.3	1.5	80.5
United Kingdom	344.8	8.5	8.0	1.2	81.7
Portugal	330.2	15.5	28.0	1.2	82.9

Graph 2: Trade Balance by MDG regions 2010

(Bln US$)

Imports — Exports — Trade balance

Developed Asia-Pacific
Developed Europe
Developed N. America
South-eastern Europe
CIS
Northern Africa
Sub-Saharan Africa
Latin Am, Caribbean
Eastern Asia
Southern Asia
South-eastern Asia
Western Asia
Oceania

-12 -10 -8 -6 -4 -2 0 2 4 6 8 10 12

Table 3: Top importing countries or areas in 2010

Country or area	Value (million US$)	Avg. Growth (%) 06-10	Growth (%) 09-10	World share %	Cum.
World	26983.9	7.7	4.1	100.0	
China	2440.2	29.2	0.2	9.0	9.0
Italy	2408.9	-0.7	13.4	8.9	18.0
USA	2206.4	7.4	6.4	8.2	26.1
India	1261.6	8.8	2.7	4.7	30.8
France	1199.2	2.8	-19.1	4.4	35.3
Germany	1036.0	-13.7	5.0	3.8	39.1
Belgium	910.2	11.1	-2.3	3.4	42.5
Netherlands	760.4	-2.0	3.9	2.8	45.3
United Kingdom	751.3	2.0	-6.4	2.8	48.1
Spain	578.9	-3.1	1.0	2.1	50.2
Iran	529.6	117.8	8.4	2.0	52.2
Algeria	524.2	22.7	18.0	1.9	54.1
Canada	495.2	11.2	10.2	1.8	56.0
Portugal	439.9	8.3	47.5	1.6	57.6
Rep. of Korea	428.6	13.0	17.5	1.6	59.2

422 Fixed vegetable fats and oils, crude, refined or fractionated, not 'soft'

After several years of continuous growth marked by a peak of 37.1 bln US$ in 2008, the value (in current prices) of exports of fixed vegetable fats and oils, crude, refined or fractionated, not 'soft' (SITC group 422) dropped in 2009 (by 25.0 percent) but bounced back in 2010 by 31.7 percent to amount to 36.6 bln US$ (see table 2). Imports showed a similar development with an increase of 19.3 percent to 35.4 bln US$ in 2010 (see table 3). Graph 1 shows that the increase in exports for 2010 in this product group was exceeded by the increase in world exports of animal and vegetable oils, fats and waxes (SITC section 4) of 40.2 percent, but was greater than the increase in total world exports of 21.2 percent. Exports of fixed vegetable fats and oils, crude, refined or fractionated, not 'soft' (SITC group 422) accounted for 5.3 percent of world exports of SITC section 4 and 0.2 percent of total world exports in 2010 (see table 1).

Indonesia and Malaysia were the top two exporting countries in 2010 (see table 2). They accounted respectively for 43.0 and 36.6 percent of world exports. China, India and Netherlands were the top destinations (see table 3). By MDG regions (see graph 2), South-eastern Asia accounted for a majority of exports of fixed vegetable fats and oils, crude, refined or fractionated, not 'soft' (SITC group 422). In 2010, its exports amounted to 30.9 bln US$ while imports were valued at 3.3 bln US$ resulting in a trade surplus of 27.6 bln US$. Top trade deficits were recorded by Eastern Asia (-6.3 bln US$), Developed Europe (-6.1 bln US$) and Southern Asia (-6.0 bln US$).

Table 1: Imports (Imp.) and exports (Exp.), 1996-2010, in current prices

		1996	1997	1998	1999	2000	2001	2002	2003	2004	2005	2006	2007	2008	2009	2010
Values in Bln US$	Imp.	8.1	8.2	9.3	8.4	7.0	6.6	8.8	11.9	14.9	15.2	16.9	23.5	36.4	29.7	35.4
	Exp.	7.8	8.8	8.6	8.0	6.4	5.8	8.3	10.7	13.0	13.4	15.4	24.2	37.1	27.8	36.6
As a percentage of SITC section (%)	Imp.	3.2	3.2	3.9	3.7	2.8	2.8	3.7	4.1	4.0	3.6	3.4	3.8	4.8	5.5	4.7
	Exp.	3.5	3.8	4.1	4.1	3.0	2.9	3.8	4.2	4.0	3.6	3.4	4.4	5.7	5.6	5.3
As a percentage of world trade (%)	Imp.	0.2	0.1	0.2	0.1	0.1	0.1	0.1	0.2	0.2	0.1	0.1	0.2	0.2	0.2	0.2
	Exp.	0.1	0.2	0.2	0.1	0.1	0.1	0.1	0.1	0.1	0.1	0.1	0.2	0.2	0.2	0.2

Graph 1: Annual growth rates of exports, 1996–2010

(In percentage by year)

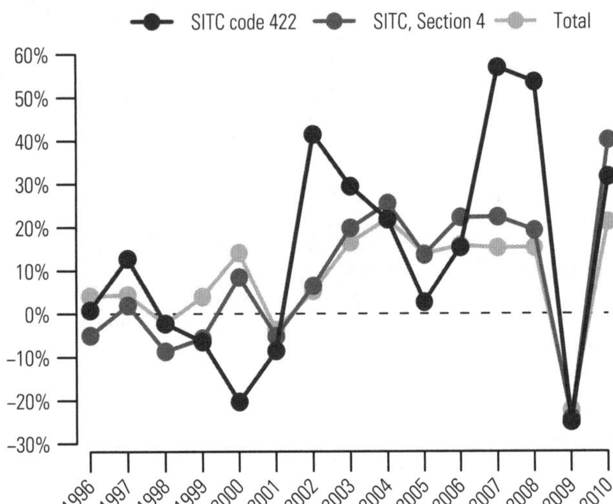

Graph 2: Trade Balance by MDG regions 2010

(Bln US$)

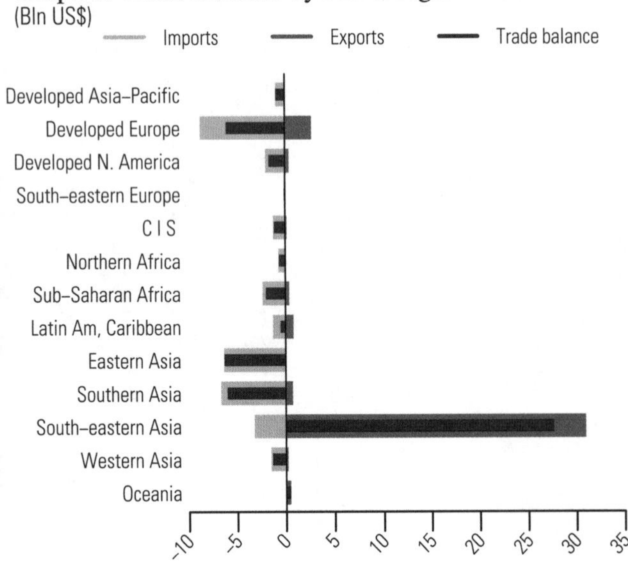

Table 2: Top exporting countries or areas in 2010

Country or area	Value (million US$)	Avg. Growth (%) 06-10	Growth (%) 09-10	World share %	Cum.
World	36629.8	24.2	31.7	100.0	
Indonesia	15768.5	28.9	33.1	43.0	43.0
Malaysia	13393.1	24.4	35.8	36.6	79.6
Netherlands	1544.1	14.7	6.9	4.2	83.8
Philippines	1269.8	21.7	113.5	3.5	87.3
India	626.4	30.0	34.1	1.7	89.0
Papua New Guinea	*410.5*	15.2	12.8	1.1	90.1
USA	346.7	4.1	10.0	0.9	91.1
Germany	324.4	11.3	19.0	0.9	92.0
Thailand	228.2	14.1	48.3	0.6	92.6
Singapore	218.2	14.6	1.5	0.6	93.2
Italy	178.7	7.7	2.1	0.5	93.7
Côte d'Ivoire	172.7	26.1	28.7	0.5	94.1
Belgium	158.3	5.4	-2.4	0.4	94.6
Ecuador	151.1	24.6	1.7	0.4	95.0
Guatemala	143.7	36.7	33.7	0.4	95.4

Table 3: Top importing countries or areas in 2010

Country or area	Value (million US$)	Avg. Growth (%) 06-10	Growth (%) 09-10	World share %	Cum.
World	35420.7	20.3	19.3	100.0	
China	5788.4	22.2	20.1	16.3	16.3
India	3519.4	29.1	-4.8	9.9	26.3
Netherlands	2032.4	15.9	14.3	5.7	32.0
Germany	2011.4	19.4	25.1	5.7	37.7
Malaysia	1918.9	37.7	69.5	5.4	43.1
USA	1892.3	19.0	26.6	5.3	48.5
Pakistan	1682.5	21.3	33.3	4.8	53.2
Italy	990.3	27.8	7.1	2.8	56.0
Russian Federation	841.8	21.4	32.5	2.4	58.4
Bangladesh	*795.5*	2.7	-26.8	2.2	60.6
Japan	767.2	18.2	23.5	2.2	62.8
Spain	677.8	30.3	19.1	1.9	64.7
France	583.7	13.1	11.0	1.6	66.4
Viet Nam	*583.0*	36.3	66.9	1.6	68.0
Egypt	572.6	12.9	18.1	1.6	69.6

After several years of continuous growth marked by a peak of 11.3 bln US$ in 2008, the value (in current prices) of exports of animal or vegetable fats and oils, processed; waxes of; inedible (SITC group 431) contracted sharply in 2009 (by 31.0 percent) but bounced back in 2010 by 26.7 percent to amount to 9.8 bln US$ (see table 2). Imports showed a similar development with an increase of 21.0 percent to 8.8 bln US$ in 2010 (see table 3). Graph 1 shows that the increase in exports for 2010 in this product group was less than the increase in world exports of animal and vegetable oils, fats and waxes (SITC section 4) of 40.2 percent but exceeded the increase in total world exports of 21.2 percent. Exports of animal or vegetable fats and oils, processed; waxes of; inedible (SITC group 431) accounted for 1.4 percent of world exports of SITC section 4 and 0.1 percent of total world exports in 2010 (see table 1).

Malaysia, Netherlands and Germany were the top exporting countries in 2010 (see table 2). They accounted respectively for 34.8, 9.2 and 8.7 percent of world exports. Top destinations were Germany, Netherlands and United Kingdom (see table 3). By MDG regions (see graph 2), a significant surplus was recorded by South-eastern Asia at 3.9 bln US$. Top trade deficits were recorded by Developed Europe (-1.1 bln US$), Eastern Asia (-0.6 bln US$) and Sub-Saharan Africa (-0.3 bln US$).

Table 1: Imports (Imp.) and exports (Exp.), 1996-2010, in current prices

		1996	1997	1998	1999	2000	2001	2002	2003	2004	2005	2006	2007	2008	2009	2010
Values in Bln US$	Imp.	3.4	3.3	3.4	3.3	3.0	2.9	3.3	4.0	4.7	5.0	5.7	7.3	10.2	7.3	8.8
	Exp.	3.8	3.5	3.9	3.5	3.0	3.0	3.8	4.5	5.6	5.6	6.2	8.1	11.3	7.8	9.8
As a percentage of	Imp.	1.3	1.3	1.4	1.5	1.2	1.3	1.4	1.4	1.3	1.2	1.2	1.2	1.3	1.3	1.2
SITC section (%)	Exp.	1.7	1.5	1.9	1.8	1.4	1.5	1.8	1.8	1.7	1.5	1.4	1.5	1.7	1.6	1.4
As a percentage of	Imp.	0.1	0.1	0.1	0.1	0.0	0.0	0.1	0.1	0.1	0.0	0.0	0.1	0.1	0.1	0.1
world trade (%)	Exp.	0.1	0.1	0.1	0.1	0.0	0.0	0.1	0.1	0.1	0.1	0.1	0.1	0.1	0.1	0.1

Graph 1: Annual growth rates of exports, 1996–2010
(In percentage by year)

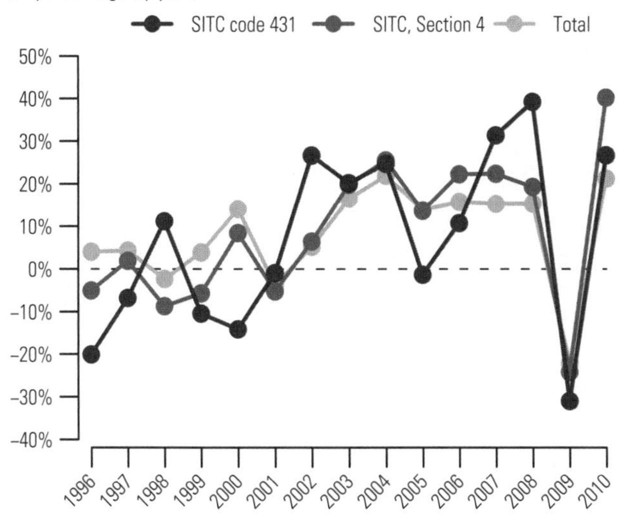

Table 2: Top exporting countries or areas in 2010

Country or area	Value (million US$)	Avg. Growth (%) 06-10	Growth (%) 09-10	World share %	Cum.
World	9839.0	12.4	26.7	100.0	
Malaysia	3425.6	18.4	46.5	34.8	34.8
Netherlands	909.1	10.3	1.8	9.2	44.1
Germany	852.7	8.7	19.0	8.7	52.7
Indonesia	836.5	15.2	76.4	8.5	61.2
USA	607.5	18.6	20.5	6.2	67.4
Belgium	317.5	8.2	-2.4	3.2	70.6
Brazil	179.0	17.3	58.4	1.8	72.4
Singapore	167.2	12.4	16.5	1.7	74.1
Italy	164.7	11.5	35.9	1.7	75.8
Argentina	150.3	16.0	31.1	1.5	77.3
Sweden	147.7	8.1	-0.5	1.5	78.8
India	129.7	16.5	25.0	1.3	80.2
China	124.1	26.5	46.1	1.3	81.4
France	118.5	6.9	24.3	1.2	82.6
Turkey	117.2	-2.6	-36.3	1.2	83.8

Graph 2: Trade Balance by MDG regions 2010
(Bln US$)

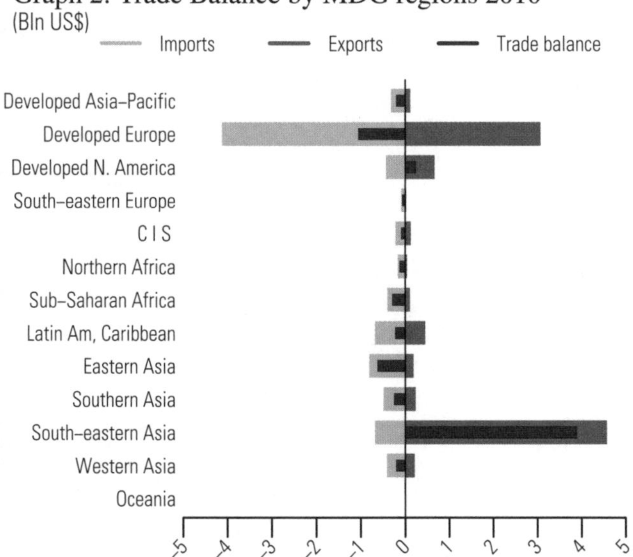

Table 3: Top importing countries or areas in 2010

Country or area	Value (million US$)	Avg. Growth (%) 06-10	Growth (%) 09-10	World share %	Cum.
World	8829.8	11.5	21.0	100.0	
Germany	785.1	13.7	19.1	8.9	8.9
Netherlands	583.0	17.2	35.7	6.6	15.5
United Kingdom	443.1	11.0	27.7	5.0	20.5
China	443.0	11.3	69.5	5.0	25.5
Italy	345.5	23.3	24.7	3.9	29.4
Spain	333.3	16.9	30.6	3.8	33.2
Belgium	292.8	7.2	1.6	3.3	36.5
USA	258.5	-1.3	33.9	2.9	39.5
Rep. of Korea	257.8	30.2	51.4	2.9	42.4
France	246.5	1.8	6.4	2.8	45.2
Japan	231.9	16.2	39.3	2.6	47.8
Sweden	221.3	11.9	2.7	2.5	50.3
Mexico	192.4	13.5	22.1	2.2	52.5
Denmark	183.2	11.2	22.4	2.1	54.6
Canada	170.6	13.8	-1.9	1.9	56.5

Chemicals and related products, n.e.s.
(SITC Section 5)

511 Hydrocarbons, nes, and their derivatives

After a drop of 26.4 percent in 2009, the value (in current prices) of exports of hydrocarbons, nes, and their derivatives (SITC group 511) increased in 2010 by 38.1 percent to amount to 71.6 bln US$ (see table 2). Imports showed a similar development with an increase of 38.2 percent to 75.0 bln US$ in 2010 (see table 3). Graph 1 shows that the increase in exports for 2010 in this product group exceeded both the increase in world exports of chemicals and related products, nes (SITC section 5) of 17.1 percent and the increase in total world exports of 21.2 percent. Exports of hydrocarbons, nes, and their derivatives (SITC group 511) accounted for 4.3 percent of world exports of SITC section 5 and 0.5 percent of total world exports in 2010 (see table 1).

Japan, Netherlands, and USA were the top exporting countries in 2010 (see table 2). They accounted respectively for 11.6, 11.5 and 11.1 percent of world exports. Major destinations were China, Belgium and USA (see table 3). Developed Europe accounted for a large share of trade in hydrocarbons, nes and their derivatives (SITC group 511). In 2010, its exports amounted to 22.8 bln US$, and its imports reached 25.6 bln US$, resulting in a trade deficit of 2.8 bln US$. Top trade deficits were also recorded by Eastern Asia (-11.7 bln US$) and Latin America and the Caribbean (-3.4 bln US$). Developed Asia-Pacific and Developed North America recorded trade surpluses amounting respectively to 7.0 bln US$ and 3.5 bln US$.

Table 1: Imports (Imp.) and exports (Exp.), 1996-2010, in current prices

		1996	1997	1998	1999	2000	2001	2002	2003	2004	2005	2006	2007	2008	2009	2010
Values in Bln US$	Imp.	18.7	20.4	16.7	18.2	26.4	21.9	23.4	31.5	46.3	53.4	61.3	72.8	77.4	54.3	75.0
	Exp.	20.2	18.1	14.9	16.6	23.2	19.7	21.9	29.4	43.6	48.3	56.8	68.4	70.4	51.9	71.6
As a percentage of SITC section (%)	Imp.	3.6	3.8	3.1	3.2	4.3	3.5	3.3	3.8	4.6	4.7	4.8	4.8	4.5	3.7	4.3
	Exp.	4.2	3.6	2.9	3.2	4.1	3.4	3.3	3.7	4.5	4.4	4.6	4.7	4.3	3.7	4.3
As a percentage of world trade (%)	Imp.	0.3	0.4	0.3	0.3	0.4	0.3	0.4	0.4	0.5	0.5	0.5	0.5	0.5	0.4	0.5
	Exp.	0.4	0.3	0.3	0.3	0.4	0.3	0.3	0.4	0.5	0.5	0.5	0.5	0.4	0.4	0.5

Graph 1: Annual growth rates of exports, 1996–2010
(In percentage by year)

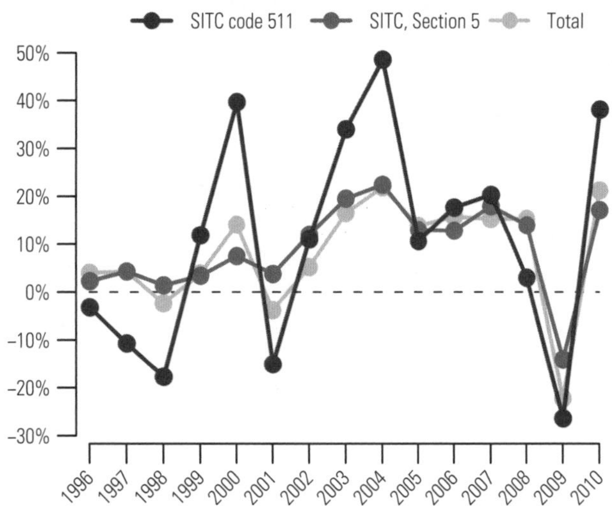

Graph 2: Trade Balance by MDG regions 2010
(Bln US$)

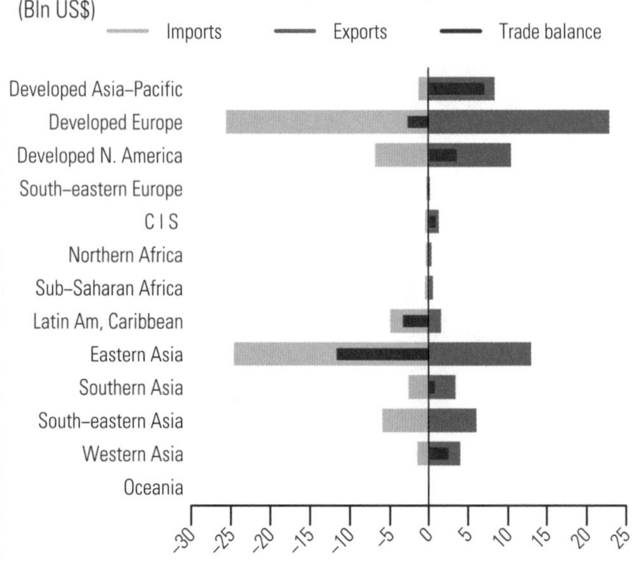

Table 2: Top exporting countries or areas in 2010

Country or area	Value (million US$)	Avg. Growth (%) 06-10	Growth (%) 09-10	World share %	Cum.
World	71621.5	5.9	38.1	100.0	
Japan	8287.2	4.9	16.5	11.6	11.6
Netherlands	8201.3	5.2	48.4	11.5	23.0
USA	7939.8	3.8	26.8	11.1	34.1
Rep. of Korea	7583.7	6.4	31.8	10.6	44.7
Germany	4255.5	2.9	33.6	5.9	50.6
Other Asia, nes	2838.2	42.3	29.8	4.0	54.6
Saudi Arabia	2571.5	14.8	51.4	3.6	58.2
China	2508.0	15.4	34.8	3.5	61.7
Singapore	2430.4	-0.4	48.5	3.4	65.1
Canada	2412.3	-0.6	54.2	3.4	68.5
United Kingdom	2381.5	-4.6	40.9	3.3	71.8
Belgium	2366.9	0.1	24.6	3.3	75.1
India	2006.7	4.2	42.7	2.8	77.9
Thailand	1489.9	13.1	41.9	2.1	80.0
Iran	1335.2	40.5	6.3	1.9	81.8

Table 3: Top importing countries or areas in 2010

Country or area	Value (million US$)	Avg. Growth (%) 06-10	Growth (%) 09-10	World share %	Cum.
World	74999.6	5.2	38.2	100.0	
China	14667.6	17.0	20.9	19.6	19.6
Belgium	7607.8	0.0	48.4	10.1	29.7
USA	5673.8	1.4	49.2	7.6	37.3
Other Asia, nes	5089.9	-0.3	51.8	6.8	44.1
Germany	4790.6	3.8	51.3	6.4	50.4
Rep. of Korea	4432.0	8.2	38.0	5.9	56.3
Netherlands	4114.0	3.7	47.9	5.5	61.8
Mexico	2894.6	9.4	35.3	3.9	65.7
France	2520.1	3.1	62.8	3.4	69.1
Indonesia	2303.1	8.4	28.2	3.1	72.1
India	1968.7	9.7	27.3	2.6	74.7
Malaysia	1248.3	10.8	49.9	1.7	76.4
Spain	1177.8	-3.0	22.9	1.6	78.0
Japan	1161.4	-0.7	29.1	1.5	79.5
Canada	1132.5	-2.2	23.3	1.5	81.0

After a sharp decline of 31.8 percent in 2009, the value (in current prices) of exports of alcohols, phenols, phenol-alcohols and their derivatives (SITC group 512) rose significantly in 2010 by 39.1 percent to amount to 42.6 bln US$ (see table 2). Imports showed a similar development with an increase of 42.0 percent to 50.8 bln US$ in 2010 (see table 3). Graph 1 shows that the increase in exports for 2010 in this product group exceeded both the increase in world exports of chemicals and related products, nes (SITC section 5) of 17.1 percent and the increase in total world exports of 21.2 percent. Exports of alcohols, phenols, phenol-alcohols and their derivatives (SITC group 512) accounted for 2.6 percent of world exports of SITC section 5 and 0.3 percent of total world exports in 2010 (see table 1).

USA, Saudi Arabia and Netherlands were the top exporting countries in 2010 (see table 2). They accounted respectively for 10.8, 8.4 and 7.5 percent of world exports. Top destinations were China, USA and Germany (see table 3). By MDG regions (see graph 2), Western Asia and South-eastern Asia recorded trade surpluses amounting respectively to 2.9 bln US$ and 1.2 bln US$. Top trade deficits were recorded by Eastern Asia (-11.3 bln US$) and Developed Europe (-2.4 bln US$).

Table 1: Imports (Imp.) and exports (Exp.), 1996-2010, in current prices

		1996	1997	1998	1999	2000	2001	2002	2003	2004	2005	2006	2007	2008	2009	2010
Values in Bln US$	Imp.	15.4	16.1	14.0	13.6	16.4	16.9	16.8	22.1	28.5	33.7	38.1	46.2	52.8	35.8	50.8
	Exp.	13.1	14.2	12.3	11.7	14.1	14.5	15.0	18.8	25.0	29.2	32.7	39.3	44.9	30.7	42.6
As a percentage of SITC section (%)	Imp.	3.0	3.0	2.6	2.4	2.7	2.7	2.4	2.6	2.8	2.9	3.0	3.1	3.1	2.4	2.9
	Exp.	2.7	2.8	2.4	2.2	2.5	2.5	2.3	2.4	2.6	2.7	2.7	2.7	2.7	2.2	2.6
As a percentage of world trade (%)	Imp.	0.3	0.3	0.3	0.2	0.3	0.3	0.3	0.3	0.3	0.3	0.3	0.3	0.3	0.3	0.3
	Exp.	0.2	0.3	0.2	0.2	0.2	0.2	0.2	0.3	0.3	0.3	0.3	0.3	0.3	0.2	0.3

Graph 1: Annual growth rates of exports, 1996–2010

(In percentage by year)

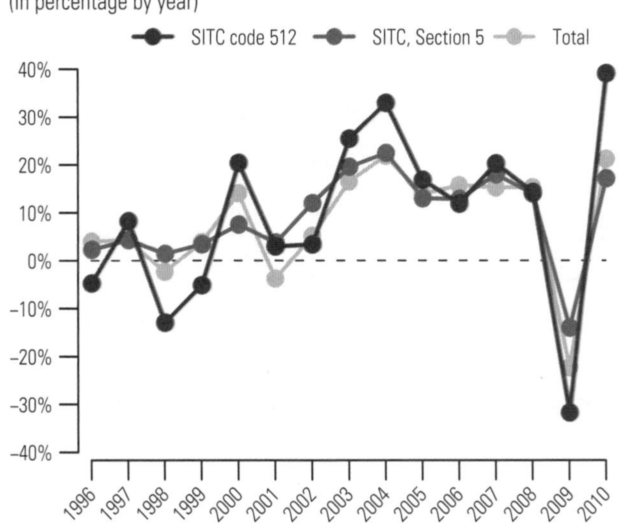

Graph 2: Trade Balance by MDG regions 2010

(Bln US$)

Imports — Exports — Trade balance

Developed Asia-Pacific
Developed Europe
Developed N. America
South-eastern Europe
CIS
Northern Africa
Sub-Saharan Africa
Latin Am, Caribbean
Eastern Asia
Southern Asia
South-eastern Asia
Western Asia
Oceania

-20 -15 -10 -5 0 5 10 15

Table 2: Top exporting countries or areas in 2010

Country or area	Value (million US$)	Avg. Growth (%) 06-10	Growth (%) 09-10	World share %	Cum.
World	42636.1	6.9	39.1	100.0	
USA	4599.0	7.2	60.4	10.8	10.8
Saudi Arabia	3595.2	11.4	42.8	8.4	19.2
Netherlands	3192.4	14.8	27.3	7.5	26.7
Germany	3114.0	-1.1	25.8	7.3	34.0
Belgium	2746.1	11.7	58.5	6.4	40.5
Other Asia, nes	2673.4	21.6	59.3	6.3	46.7
Singapore	2173.7	16.8	120.8	5.1	51.8
Japan	1926.6	5.6	29.5	4.5	56.3
Malaysia	1462.3	13.3	82.3	3.4	59.8
Rep. of Korea	1341.8	11.5	37.2	3.1	62.9
China	1328.1	2.0	46.1	3.1	66.0
Canada	1295.6	1.9	52.5	3.0	69.1
Brazil	1270.4	-8.3	-15.5	3.0	72.0
Iran	1220.4	62.3	6.3	2.9	74.9
France	1137.5	20.5	7.3	2.7	77.6

Table 3: Top importing countries or areas in 2010

Country or area	Value (million US$)	Avg. Growth (%) 06-10	Growth (%) 09-10	World share %	Cum.
World	50830.5	7.5	42.0	100.0	
China	13299.3	19.0	59.2	26.2	26.2
USA	4062.1	-4.6	38.0	8.0	34.2
Germany	3318.4	8.4	37.8	6.5	40.7
Netherlands	2602.2	5.1	4.1	5.1	45.8
Rep. of Korea	2134.3	4.5	50.3	4.2	50.0
Belgium	2019.6	9.6	37.4	4.0	54.0
Japan	1980.1	2.1	40.9	3.9	57.9
India	1502.8	17.2	6.0	3.0	60.8
Italy	1413.8	1.0	31.8	2.8	63.6
France	1248.1	2.2	22.9	2.5	66.1
Thailand	1238.9	2.5	71.2	2.4	68.5
Other Asia, nes	1221.6	-0.4	48.8	2.4	70.9
United Kingdom	1194.9	2.0	48.6	2.4	73.3
Singapore	1056.4	5.9	60.6	2.1	75.3
Canada	841.5	5.0	46.9	1.7	77.0

Source: UN Comtrade

513 Carboxylic acids, and their derivatives

After a drop of 19.6 percent in 2009, the value (in current prices) of exports of carboxylic acids and their derivatives (SITC group 513) increased in 2010 by 27.3 percent to amount to 42.2 bln US$ (see table 2). Imports showed a similar development with an increase of 27.1 percent to 46.8 bln US$ in 2010 (see table 3). Graph 1 shows that the increase in exports for 2010 in this product group exceeded both the increase in world exports of chemicals and related products, nes (SITC section 5) of 17.1 percent and the increase in total world exports of 21.2 percent. Exports of carboxylic acids and their derivatives (SITC group 513) accounted for 2.5 percent of world exports of SITC section 5 and 0.3 percent of total world exports in 2010 (see table 1).

Rep. of Korea, China and USA were the top exporting countries in 2010 (see table 2). They accounted respectively for 12.0, 11.1 and 10.8 percent of world exports. China accounted for 18.5 percent of world imports and was the top destination (see table 3). Other major destinations were USA and Germany, respectively at 7.2 and 6.8 percent of world imports. By MDG regions (see graph 2), top deficits were recorded by Developed Europe (-3.8 bln US$), Latin America and the Caribbean (-2.2 bln US$) and Western Asia (-1.7 bln US$). Top trade surpluses were recorded by Eastern Asia (+2.8 bln US$), South-eastern Asia (+1.7 bln US$) and Developed North America (+0.5 bln US$).

Table 1: Imports (Imp.) and exports (Exp.), 1996-2010, in current prices

		1996	1997	1998	1999	2000	2001	2002	2003	2004	2005	2006	2007	2008	2009	2010
Values in Bln US$	Imp.	19.1	18.7	17.6	17.6	20.0	20.5	22.0	25.7	32.3	36.7	40.2	43.8	45.5	36.8	46.8
	Exp.	15.3	15.8	14.8	14.6	16.6	16.4	17.9	22.2	28.3	32.7	37.2	40.2	41.3	33.2	42.2
As a percentage of SITC section (%)	Imp.	3.7	3.5	3.3	3.1	3.3	3.2	3.1	3.1	3.2	3.2	3.1	2.9	2.6	2.5	2.7
	Exp.	3.2	3.2	2.9	2.8	2.9	2.8	2.7	2.8	2.9	3.0	3.0	2.8	2.5	2.3	2.5
As a percentage of world trade (%)	Imp.	0.4	0.3	0.3	0.3	0.3	0.3	0.3	0.3	0.3	0.3	0.3	0.3	0.3	0.3	0.3
	Exp.	0.3	0.3	0.3	0.3	0.3	0.3	0.3	0.3	0.3	0.3	0.3	0.3	0.3	0.3	0.3

Graph 1: Annual growth rates of exports, 1996–2010

(In percentage by year)

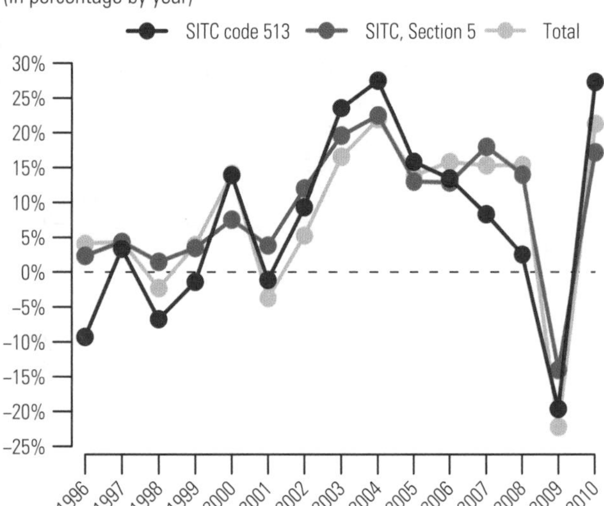

Table 2: Top exporting countries or areas in 2010

Country or area	Value (million US$)	Avg. Growth (%) 06-10	Growth (%) 09-10	World share %	Cum.
World	42218.2	3.2	27.3	100.0	
Rep. of Korea	5067.8	8.5	23.5	12.0	12.0
China	4695.8	19.6	53.0	11.1	23.1
USA	4573.7	1.7	23.0	10.8	34.0
Other Asia, nes	3821.6	8.6	34.9	9.1	43.0
Germany	3141.8	-2.0	27.1	7.4	50.5
Belgium	2975.7	-5.8	33.3	7.0	57.5
Netherlands	2067.6	1.5	17.8	4.9	62.4
Japan	1921.0	-1.0	21.6	4.6	66.9
Thailand	1579.7	7.2	21.5	3.7	70.7
Singapore	1516.9	9.2	53.5	3.6	74.3
Malaysia	1254.7	11.3	43.9	3.0	77.3
United Kingdom	996.9	-8.1	39.5	2.4	79.6
Mexico	942.1	7.3	8.8	2.2	81.8
Ireland	911.8	-4.3	-28.8	2.2	84.0
Italy	838.8	7.0	20.1	2.0	86.0

Graph 2: Trade Balance by MDG regions 2010

(Bln US$)

Imports — Exports — Trade balance

Developed Asia-Pacific
Developed Europe
Developed N. America
South-eastern Europe
CIS
Northern Africa
Sub-Saharan Africa
Latin Am, Caribbean
Eastern Asia
Southern Asia
South-eastern Asia
Western Asia
Oceania

-20 -15 -10 -5 0 5 10 15

Table 3: Top importing countries or areas in 2010

Country or area	Value (million US$)	Avg. Growth (%) 06-10	Growth (%) 09-10	World share %	Cum.
World	46781.7	3.9	27.1	100.0	
China	8648.6	-0.2	19.1	18.5	18.5
USA	3369.5	0.9	41.1	7.2	25.7
Germany	3194.8	1.9	21.4	6.8	32.5
Belgium	2784.0	-1.7	30.5	6.0	38.5
Italy	2093.3	1.9	31.8	4.5	42.9
India	1789.7	18.5	23.5	3.8	46.8
Netherlands	1617.1	5.6	38.3	3.5	50.2
France	1530.9	-0.8	26.6	3.3	53.5
Brazil	1358.1	21.6	29.5	2.9	56.4
Japan	1325.6	7.2	33.8	2.8	59.2
United Kingdom	1323.8	2.1	19.7	2.8	62.1
Other Asia, nes	1124.3	10.8	61.2	2.4	64.5
Spain	1057.9	0.2	29.6	2.3	66.7
Rep. of Korea	1055.1	6.7	33.5	2.3	69.0
Mexico	1016.8	4.6	12.5	2.2	71.2

After a drop of 14.7 percent in 2009, the value (in current prices) of exports of nitrogen-function compounds (SITC group 514) increased in 2010 by 19.5 percent to amount to 45.6 bln US$ (see table 2). Imports showed a similar development with an increase of 17.8 percent to 48.1 bln US$ in 2010 (see table 3). Graph 1 shows that the increase in exports for 2010 in this product group exceeded the increase in world exports of chemicals and related products, nes (SITC section 5) of 17.1 percent and was less than the increase in total world exports of 21.2 percent. Exports of nitrogen-function compounds (SITC group 514) accounted for 2.7 percent of world exports of SITC section 5 and 0.3 percent of total world exports in 2010 (see table 1).

USA, China and Belgium were the top exporting countries in 2010 (see table 2). They accounted respectively for 13.5, 11.1 and 9.6 percent of world exports. Germany, USA and China were the major destinations (see table 3). By MDG regions (see graph 2), Developed Europe accounted for a large share of trade in nitrogen-function compounds (SITC group 514). In 2010, its exports were valued at 21.9 bln US$ and its imports were valued at 22.5 bln US$, resulting a trade deficit of 0.6 bln US$. Top trade surpluses were recorded by South-eastern Asia (+1.8 bln US$) and Eastern Asia (+1.3 bln US$). Top trade deficits were recorded by Latin America and the Caribbean (-2.3 bln US$) and Southern Asia (-1.1 bln US$) among others.

Table 1: Imports (Imp.) and exports (Exp.), 1996-2010, in current prices

		1996	1997	1998	1999	2000	2001	2002	2003	2004	2005	2006	2007	2008	2009	2010
Values in Bln US$	Imp.	22.2	22.2	21.4	21.9	21.5	21.5	22.4	26.7	31.5	35.0	37.1	45.5	48.9	40.8	48.1
	Exp.	19.4	19.9	19.2	19.8	19.7	20.1	21.0	26.1	31.0	33.7	34.7	41.9	44.7	38.2	45.6
As a percentage of SITC section (%)	Imp.	4.3	4.2	4.0	3.9	3.5	3.4	3.2	3.2	3.1	3.0	2.9	3.0	2.8	2.8	2.8
	Exp.	4.0	4.0	3.8	3.8	3.5	3.4	3.2	3.3	3.2	3.1	2.8	2.9	2.7	2.7	2.7
As a percentage of world trade (%)	Imp.	0.4	0.4	0.4	0.4	0.3	0.3	0.3	0.3	0.3	0.3	0.3	0.3	0.3	0.3	0.3
	Exp.	0.4	0.4	0.4	0.4	0.3	0.3	0.3	0.3	0.3	0.3	0.3	0.3	0.3	0.3	0.3

Graph 1: Annual growth rates of exports, 1996–2010

(In percentage by year)

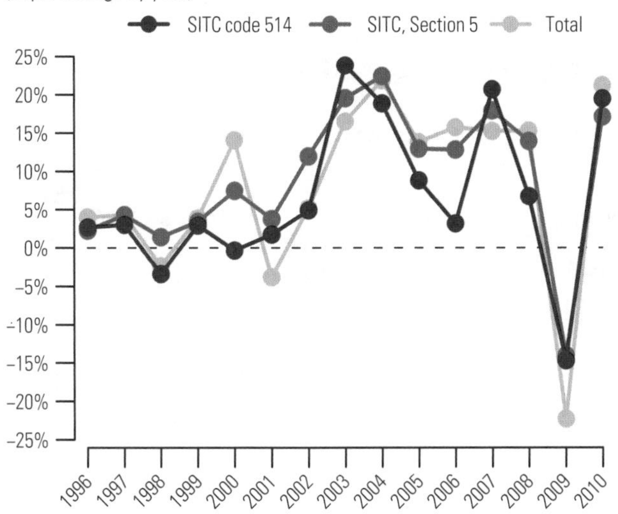

Table 2: Top exporting countries or areas in 2010

Country or area	Value (million US$)	Avg. Growth (%) 06-10	Growth (%) 09-10	World share %	Cum.
World	45577.8	7.0	19.5	100.0	
USA	6169.7	8.5	42.6	13.5	13.5
China	5054.6	16.0	22.7	11.1	24.6
Belgium	4362.0	11.5	11.7	9.6	34.2
Switzerland	3886.9	6.8	2.9	8.5	42.7
Germany	3771.2	1.1	17.7	8.3	51.0
Singapore	3752.9	13.2	35.5	8.2	59.2
Japan	2622.7	5.2	22.9	5.8	65.0
United Kingdom	1784.2	-0.2	2.5	3.9	68.9
Rep. of Korea	1720.2	4.3	27.4	3.8	72.7
Ireland	1709.7	5.7	33.4	3.8	76.4
Netherlands	1496.0	0.9	1.2	3.3	79.7
Italy	1043.2	0.1	1.7	2.3	82.0
France	759.9	-6.9	11.0	1.7	83.7
Brazil	737.6	17.5	29.2	1.6	85.3
India	714.2	10.5	15.4	1.6	86.9

Graph 2: Trade Balance by MDG regions 2010

(Bln US$)

Imports — Exports — Trade balance

Developed Asia-Pacific
Developed Europe
Developed N. America
South-eastern Europe
C I S
Northern Africa
Sub-Saharan Africa
Latin Am, Caribbean
Eastern Asia
Southern Asia
South-eastern Asia
Western Asia
Oceania

-25 -20 -15 -10 -5 0 5 10 15 20 25

Table 3: Top importing countries or areas in 2010

Country or area	Value (million US$)	Avg. Growth (%) 06-10	Growth (%) 09-10	World share %	Cum.
World	48083.5	6.7	17.8	100.0	
Germany	6182.2	11.4	15.9	12.9	12.9
USA	4548.1	6.1	3.6	9.5	22.3
China	3608.2	11.7	37.7	7.5	29.8
Belgium	3109.0	8.5	11.8	6.5	36.3
France	2347.9	1.9	9.2	4.9	41.2
United Kingdom	2258.5	-0.7	25.6	4.7	45.9
Japan	2177.7	6.0	9.4	4.5	50.4
Italy	1811.1	6.5	11.5	3.8	54.2
Netherlands	1791.3	10.6	29.4	3.7	57.9
Rep. of Korea	1287.3	9.7	24.4	2.7	60.6
Brazil	1272.4	13.3	37.0	2.6	63.2
India	1185.3	10.6	-0.2	2.5	65.7
Switzerland	1163.3	-1.6	-3.0	2.4	68.1
Spain	1132.4	-6.1	28.1	2.4	70.4
Other Asia, nes	856.5	3.0	48.4	1.8	72.2

515 Organo-inorganic and heterocyclic compounds, nucleic acids; salts

After a drop of 6.4 percent in 2009, the value (in current prices) of exports of organo-inorganic and heterocyclic compounds, nucleic acids; salts (SITC group 515) increased in 2010 by 5.8 percent to amount to 99.2 bln US$ (see table 2). Imports showed a similar development with an increase of 1.8 percent to 112.6 bln US$ in 2010 (see table 3). Graph 1 shows that the increase in exports for 2010 in this product group was far below both the increase in world exports of chemicals and related products, nes (SITC section 5) of 17.1 percent and the increase in total world exports of 21.2 percent. Exports of organo-inorganic and heterocyclic compounds, nucleic acids; salts (SITC group 515) accounted for 6.0 percent of world exports of SITC section 5 and 0.7 percent of total world exports in 2010 (see table 1).

Ireland, Belgium and USA were the top exporting countries in 2010 (see table 2). They accounted respectively for 22.7, 12.4 and 10.5 percent of world exports. USA accounted for 23.4 percent of world imports and was the top destination (see table 3). Other major destinations were Belgium and Japan. By MDG regions (see graph 2), Developed Europe was the origin and the destination of a majority of trade in organo-inorganic and heterocyclic compounds, nucleic acids; salts (SITC group 515). In 2010, its exports were valued at 65.6 bln US$ and imports at 51.7 bln US$ resulting in a trade surplus of 13.9 bln US$. Top trade deficits were recorded by Developed North America (-18.0 bln US$), Latin America and the Caribbean (-6.1 bln US$) and Developed Asia-Pacific (-3.8 bln US$).

Table 1: Imports (Imp.) and exports (Exp.), 1996-2010, in current prices

		1996	1997	1998	1999	2000	2001	2002	2003	2004	2005	2006	2007	2008	2009	2010
Values in Bln US$	Imp.	34.6	37.5	44.8	51.5	54.2	61.2	61.2	68.3	77.6	86.0	95.1	108.6	113.6	110.6	112.6
	Exp.	29.7	32.8	39.3	41.4	46.4	47.0	54.8	62.7	71.3	79.3	86.1	96.3	100.1	93.7	99.2
As a percentage of SITC section (%)	Imp.	6.7	7.0	8.3	9.1	8.9	9.7	8.7	8.2	7.7	7.5	7.4	7.2	6.6	7.5	6.5
	Exp.	6.2	6.5	7.7	7.9	8.2	8.0	8.3	8.0	7.4	7.3	7.0	6.7	6.1	6.6	6.0
As a percentage of world trade (%)	Imp.	0.6	0.7	0.8	0.9	0.8	1.0	0.9	0.9	0.8	0.8	0.8	0.8	0.7	0.9	0.7
	Exp.	0.6	0.6	0.7	0.7	0.7	0.8	0.9	0.8	0.8	0.8	0.7	0.7	0.6	0.8	0.7

Graph 1: Annual growth rates of exports, 1996–2010
(In percentage by year)

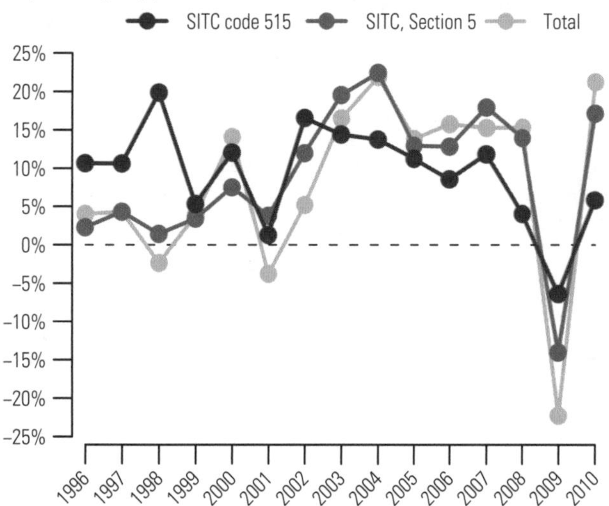

Graph 2: Trade Balance by MDG regions 2010
(Bln US$)

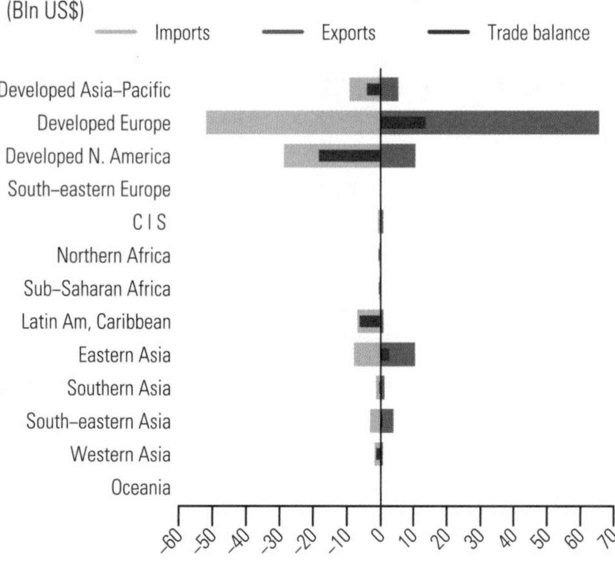

Table 2: Top exporting countries or areas in 2010

Country or area	Value (million US$)	Avg. Growth (%) 06-10	Growth (%) 09-10	World share %	Cum.
World	99191.1	3.6	5.8	100.0	
Ireland	22551.0	4.7	3.5	22.7	22.7
Belgium	12345.6	-0.6	-3.0	12.4	35.2
USA	10425.8	10.7	43.6	10.5	45.7
China	9376.6	24.3	25.5	9.5	55.1
Switzerland	7385.9	4.9	9.5	7.4	62.6
United Kingdom	6388.8	-1.0	-22.4	6.4	69.0
Germany	6198.0	-7.2	-13.9	6.2	75.3
Japan	5287.3	6.5	12.1	5.3	80.6
France	3721.2	-1.6	6.2	3.8	84.4
Singapore	3306.6	-11.6	-8.4	3.3	87.7
Netherlands	2225.0	9.8	12.2	2.2	89.9
Italy	1897.3	5.0	3.9	1.9	91.9
India	1020.7	24.3	33.5	1.0	92.9
Spain	931.7	2.2	6.3	0.9	93.8
Rep. of Korea	548.1	10.1	35.9	0.6	94.4

Table 3: Top importing countries or areas in 2010

Country or area	Value (million US$)	Avg. Growth (%) 06-10	Growth (%) 09-10	World share %	Cum.
World	112562.7	4.3	1.8	100.0	
USA	26358.2	2.6	-3.4	23.4	23.4
Belgium	10521.4	-1.4	-5.4	9.3	32.8
Japan	7337.1	9.3	1.1	6.5	39.3
United Kingdom	7220.0	0.5	-6.6	6.4	45.7
Germany	6914.7	-0.9	-14.6	6.1	51.8
Switzerland	5790.3	12.2	30.9	5.1	57.0
France	5009.2	0.1	-14.8	4.5	61.4
Italy	4950.1	-1.0	-2.9	4.4	65.8
China	4205.9	14.8	26.1	3.7	69.6
Spain	3417.5	2.0	3.6	3.0	72.6
Brazil	3411.1	17.7	5.5	3.0	75.6
Canada	2280.9	-2.3	5.8	2.0	77.7
Ireland	1804.2	8.3	36.5	1.6	79.3
Rep. of Korea	1756.5	9.6	19.3	1.6	80.8
Australia	1720.2	6.9	16.9	1.5	82.4

After a drop of 15.2 percent in 2009, the value (in current prices) of exports of other organic chemicals (SITC group 516) increased in 2010 by 23.0 percent to amount to 33.1 bln US$ (see table 2). Imports showed a similar development with an increase of 23.3 percent to 32.9 bln US$ in 2010 (see table 3). Graph 1 shows that the increase in exports for 2010 in this product group exceeded both the increase in world exports of chemicals and related products, nes (SITC section 5) of 17.1 percent and the increase in total world exports of 21.2 percent. Exports of other organic chemicals (SITC group 516) accounted for 2.0 percent of world exports of SITC section 5 and 0.2 percent of total world exports in 2010 (see table 1).

USA, Germany and Netherlands were the top exporting countries in 2010 (see table 2). They accounted respectively for 14.9, 12.3 and 10.7 percent of world exports. China, USA and Germany were top destinations (see table 3). By MDG regions (see graph 2), Developed Europe was the origin and the destination of a large share of trade in other organic chemicals (SITC group 516). In 2010, its exports amounted to 15.4 bln US$ while imports were valued at 14.2 bln US$, resulting in a trade surplus of 1.2 bln US$. Trade surpluses were also recorded by Developed North America (+2.1 bln US$) and Southern Asia (+1.3 bln US$). Top trade deficits were recorded by Latin America and the Caribbean (-1.6 bln US$) and Eastern Asia (-1.5 bln US$).

Table 1: Imports (Imp.) and exports (Exp.), 1996-2010, in current prices

		1996	1997	1998	1999	2000	2001	2002	2003	2004	2005	2006	2007	2008	2009	2010
Values in Bln US$	Imp.	12.5	13.0	12.4	12.8	14.4	14.0	14.3	16.5	20.1	24.7	26.6	29.8	32.8	26.7	32.9
	Exp.	11.3	12.2	12.0	12.2	13.7	13.5	14.3	16.7	19.6	23.6	26.1	29.3	31.8	26.9	33.1
As a percentage of SITC section (%)	Imp.	2.4	2.4	2.3	2.3	2.4	2.2	2.0	2.0	2.0	2.1	2.1	2.0	1.9	1.8	1.9
	Exp.	2.3	2.4	2.4	2.3	2.4	2.3	2.2	2.1	2.0	2.2	2.1	2.0	1.9	1.9	2.0
As a percentage of world trade (%)	Imp.	0.2	0.2	0.2	0.2	0.2	0.2	0.2	0.2	0.2	0.2	0.2	0.2	0.2	0.2	0.2
	Exp.	0.2	0.2	0.2	0.2	0.2	0.2	0.2	0.2	0.2	0.2	0.2	0.2	0.2	0.2	0.2

Graph 1: Annual growth rates of exports, 1996–2010

(In percentage by year)

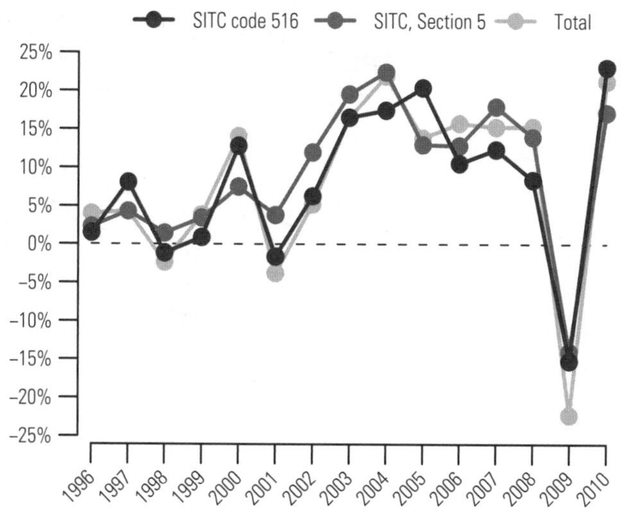

Table 2: Top exporting countries or areas in 2010

Country or area	Value (million US$)	Avg. Growth (%) 06-10	Growth (%) 09-10	World share %	Cum.
World	33 119.3	6.2	23.0	100.0	
USA	4 921.2	2.8	37.1	14.9	14.9
Germany	4 073.9	4.5	24.1	12.3	27.2
Netherlands	3 536.3	8.6	13.0	10.7	37.8
China	2 617.6	14.7	41.4	7.9	45.7
India	2 597.1	6.2	4.4	7.8	53.6
Belgium	2 143.1	5.3	28.8	6.5	60.1
Japan	1 595.9	3.1	12.7	4.8	64.9
France	1 424.6	0.0	8.3	4.3	69.2
Other Asia, nes	1 092.8	15.7	42.1	3.3	72.5
Denmark	1 075.6	16.1	7.4	3.2	75.7
Singapore	1 022.0	9.2	27.7	3.1	78.8
Saudi Arabia	929.4	-1.6	43.7	2.8	81.6
Finland	591.5	15.9	30.3	1.8	83.4
Spain	575.7	10.8	47.7	1.7	85.1
United Kingdom	545.3	1.0	25.4	1.6	86.8

Graph 2: Trade Balance by MDG regions 2010

(Bln US$)

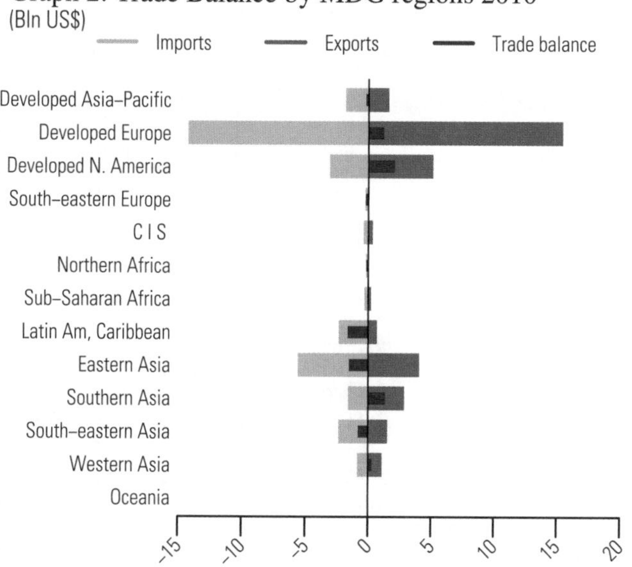

Table 3: Top importing countries or areas in 2010

Country or area	Value (million US$)	Avg. Growth (%) 06-10	Growth (%) 09-10	World share %	Cum.
World	32 892.7	5.4	23.3	100.0	
China	3 472.5	16.5	60.0	10.6	10.6
USA	2 633.8	1.9	28.0	8.0	18.6
Germany	2 191.5	-1.4	13.7	6.7	25.2
Netherlands	2 115.6	0.0	18.2	6.4	31.7
Belgium	1 836.6	2.9	29.8	5.6	37.2
Japan	1 661.0	17.0	96.5	5.0	42.3
Italy	1 451.7	1.2	17.2	4.4	46.7
France	1 360.7	5.9	-2.2	4.1	50.8
India	1 318.1	11.0	3.2	4.0	54.8
Rep. of Korea	1 279.0	15.3	48.9	3.9	58.7
United Kingdom	1 183.1	-3.9	62.8	3.6	62.3
Spain	1 176.7	10.0	52.3	3.6	65.9
Singapore	1 075.6	9.9	30.2	3.3	69.2
Mexico	886.3	9.2	9.9	2.7	71.9
Switzerland	879.7	3.4	10.0	2.7	74.6

Source: UN Comtrade

522 Inorganic chemical elements, oxides and halogen salts

After several years of continuous growth marked by a peak of 58.2 bln US$ in 2008, the value (in current prices) of exports of inorganic chemical elements, oxides and halogen salts (SITC group 522) contracted sharply in 2009 (by 39.8 percent) but bounced back in 2010 by 32.2 percent to amount to 46.3 bln US$ (see table 2). Imports showed a similar development with an increase of 27.8 percent to 53.1 bln US$ in 2010 (see table 3). Graph 1 shows that the increase in exports for 2010 in this product group exceeded both the increase in world exports of chemicals and related products, nes (SITC section 5) of 17.1 percent and the increase in total world exports of 21.2 percent. Exports of inorganic chemical elements, oxides and halogen salts (SITC group 522) accounted for 2.8 percent of world exports of SITC section 5 and 0.3 percent of total world exports in 2010 (see table 1).

USA, China and Germany were the top exporting countries in 2010 (see table 2). They accounted respectively for 13.8, 12.9 and 9.6 percent of world exports. USA and China were also the top destinations, together with Japan (see table 3). By MDG regions (see graph 2), large trade surpluses were recorded by Northern Africa (+2.2 bln US$) and Commonwealth of Independent States (+1.6 bln US$). Top trade deficits were recorded by Developed Europe (-4.0 bln US$), South-eastern Asia (-1.8 bln US$) and Southern Asia (-1.8 bln US$).

Table 1: Imports (Imp.) and exports (Exp.), 1996-2010, in current prices

		1996	1997	1998	1999	2000	2001	2002	2003	2004	2005	2006	2007	2008	2009	2010
Values in Bln US$	Imp.	18.3	18.7	18.7	17.4	18.7	19.0	18.3	21.9	27.0	32.6	37.2	44.3	66.1	41.5	53.1
	Exp.	16.2	16.7	15.9	15.2	16.3	16.7	16.2	18.8	24.0	28.6	32.3	39.1	58.2	35.0	46.3
As a percentage of SITC section (%)	Imp.	3.6	3.5	3.5	3.1	3.1	3.0	2.6	2.6	2.7	2.8	2.9	2.9	3.8	2.8	3.1
	Exp.	3.4	3.3	3.1	2.9	2.9	2.8	2.5	2.4	2.5	2.6	2.6	2.7	3.5	2.5	2.8
As a percentage of world trade (%)	Imp.	0.3	0.3	0.3	0.3	0.3	0.3	0.3	0.3	0.3	0.3	0.3	0.3	0.4	0.3	0.4
	Exp.	0.3	0.3	0.3	0.3	0.3	0.3	0.3	0.3	0.3	0.3	0.3	0.3	0.4	0.3	0.3

Graph 1: Annual growth rates of exports, 1996–2010

(In percentage by year)

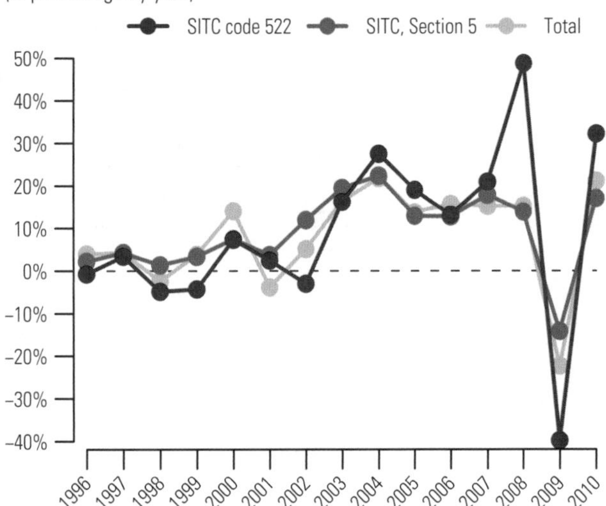

Graph 2: Trade Balance by MDG regions 2010

(Bln US$)

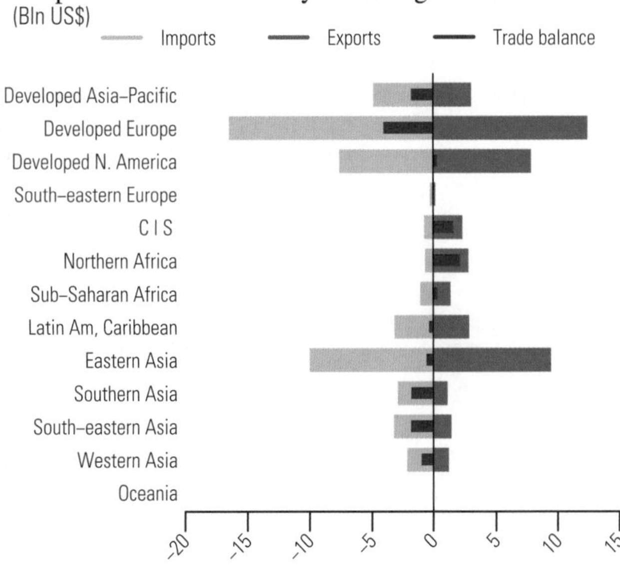

Table 2: Top exporting countries or areas in 2010

Country or area	Value (million US$)	Avg. Growth (%) 06-10	Growth (%) 09-10	World share %	Cum.
World	46288.3	9.4	32.2	100.0	
USA	6405.2	10.7	23.4	13.8	13.8
China	5979.0	12.4	65.6	12.9	26.8
Germany	4444.7	7.9	18.9	9.6	36.4
Japan	2607.5	5.8	17.3	5.6	42.0
Rep. of Korea	2320.6	38.8	44.8	5.0	47.0
Morocco	1662.2	12.9	62.9	3.6	50.6
Belgium	1592.3	12.6	20.9	3.4	54.0
Russian Federation	1551.1	2.5	24.7	3.4	57.4
Canada	1488.1	1.3	21.8	3.2	60.6
Netherlands	1457.5	8.1	19.2	3.1	63.7
Other Asia, nes	925.0	17.7	24.8	2.0	65.7
Brazil	737.3	13.7	39.2	1.6	67.3
South Africa	693.4	1.8	23.7	1.5	68.8
France	687.2	0.1	0.6	1.5	70.3
Chile	659.9	3.3	29.3	1.4	71.7

Table 3: Top importing countries or areas in 2010

Country or area	Value (million US$)	Avg. Growth (%) 06-10	Growth (%) 09-10	World share %	Cum.
World	53073.4	9.3	27.8	100.0	
USA	6658.1	3.8	41.9	12.5	12.5
China	4723.2	23.6	45.2	8.9	21.4
Japan	4136.3	9.2	34.3	7.8	29.2
Germany	3342.6	8.5	24.8	6.3	35.5
Rep. of Korea	2667.0	12.9	39.1	5.0	40.6
Other Asia, nes	2263.4	19.6	49.4	4.3	44.8
India	2107.2	1.3	-15.8	4.0	48.8
France	1925.4	3.3	20.5	3.6	52.4
Belgium	1766.5	6.3	17.5	3.3	55.8
United Kingdom	1295.9	8.4	26.3	2.4	58.2
Netherlands	1200.6	4.2	14.3	2.3	60.5
Italy	1034.1	2.9	18.9	1.9	62.4
Spain	1020.7	2.1	28.9	1.9	64.3
Turkey	1007.5	16.5	41.5	1.9	66.2
Brazil	942.7	9.3	11.4	1.8	68.0

After several years of continuous growth marked by a peak of 21.0 bln US$ in 2008, the value (in current prices) of exports of metal salts and peroxysalts, of inorganic acids (SITC group 523) contracted sharply in 2009 (by 27.2 percent) but bounced back in 2010 by 18.7 percent to amount to 18.1 bln US$ (see table 2). Imports showed a similar development with an increase of 12.8 percent to 21.7 bln US$ in 2010 (see table 3). Graph 1 shows that the increase in exports for 2010 in this product group was greater than the increase in world exports of chemicals and related products, nes (SITC section 5) of 17.1 percent but less than the increase in total world exports of 21.2 percent. Exports of metal salts and peroxysalts, of inorganic acids (SITC group 523) accounted for 1.1 percent of world exports of SITC section 5 and 0.1 percent of total world exports in 2010 (see table 1).

China, USA and Germany were the top exporting countries in 2010 (see table 2). They accounted respectively for 19.1, 14.4 and 8.6 percent of world exports. USA and Germany were also among the major destinations, together with Japan (see table 3). By MDG regions (see graph 2), Eastern Asia, Developed North America and South-eastern Europe recorded trade surpluses amounting respectively to 2.1 bln US$, 0.8 bln US$ and 0.1 bln US$. Top trade deficits were recorded by Latin America and the Caribbean (-1.4 bln US$), South-eastern Asia (-1.4 bln US$) and Developed Europe (-1.2 bln US$).

Table 1: Imports (Imp.) and exports (Exp.), 1996-2010, in current prices

		1996	1997	1998	1999	2000	2001	2002	2003	2004	2005	2006	2007	2008	2009	2010
Values in Bln US$	Imp.	9.9	10.1	9.7	9.4	9.5	9.6	10.0	10.7	12.4	14.1	15.7	18.6	24.3	19.3	21.7
	Exp.	7.7	8.1	7.7	7.5	7.5	8.1	8.2	9.0	10.5	12.1	13.9	16.4	21.0	15.3	18.1
As a percentage of SITC section (%)	Imp.	1.9	1.9	1.8	1.7	1.6	1.5	1.4	1.3	1.2	1.2	1.2	1.2	1.4	1.3	1.3
	Exp.	1.6	1.6	1.5	1.4	1.3	1.4	1.2	1.1	1.1	1.1	1.1	1.1	1.3	1.1	1.1
As a percentage of world trade (%)	Imp.	0.2	0.2	0.2	0.2	0.1	0.2	0.2	0.1	0.1	0.1	0.1	0.1	0.1	0.2	0.1
	Exp.	0.1	0.1	0.1	0.1	0.1	0.1	0.1	0.1	0.1	0.1	0.1	0.1	0.1	0.1	0.1

Graph 1: Annual growth rates of exports, 1996–2010
(In percentage by year)

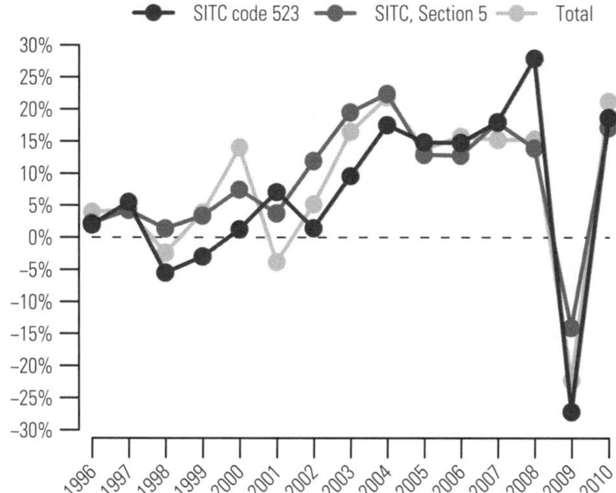

Table 2: Top exporting countries or areas in 2010

Country or area	Value (million US$)	Avg. Growth (%) 06-10	Growth (%) 09-10	World share %	Cum.
World	18128.0	6.9	18.7	100.0	
China	3466.2	8.8	9.2	19.1	19.1
USA	2602.0	6.3	17.3	14.4	33.5
Germany	1555.9	1.4	10.7	8.6	42.1
Belgium	892.5	16.6	30.2	4.9	47.0
Japan	575.3	9.7	31.3	3.2	50.2
Canada	550.8	6.9	-3.1	3.0	53.2
Chile	534.1	12.6	57.9	2.9	56.1
Netherlands	437.0	5.7	12.2	2.4	58.5
Finland	410.9	8.1	551.0	2.3	60.8
Spain	397.3	5.6	-3.3	2.2	63.0
Rep. of Korea	381.5	13.7	22.5	2.1	65.1
France	369.7	-2.6	4.4	2.0	67.2
Russian Federation	361.9	8.3	15.4	2.0	69.1
Mexico	346.1	5.1	32.4	1.9	71.1
India	341.8	17.7	30.6	1.9	72.9

Graph 2: Trade Balance by MDG regions 2010
(Bln US$)

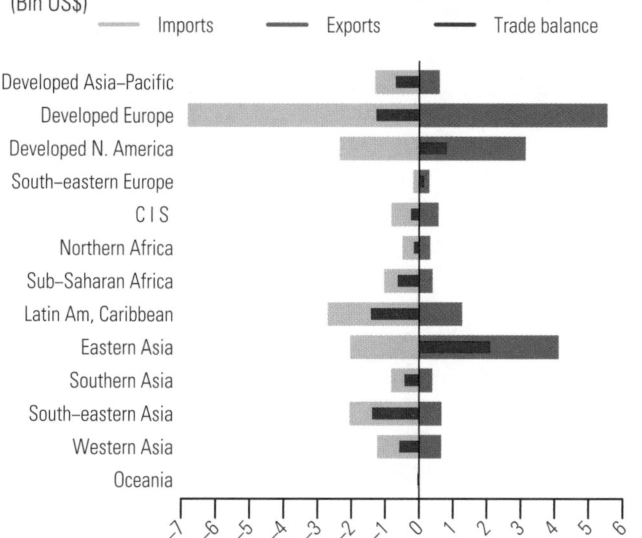

Table 3: Top importing countries or areas in 2010

Country or area	Value (million US$)	Avg. Growth (%) 06-10	Growth (%) 09-10	World share %	Cum.
World	21739.5	8.5	12.8	100.0	
USA	1765.7	5.1	14.0	8.1	8.1
Germany	1067.6	9.5	12.4	4.9	13.0
Japan	945.5	6.4	40.3	4.3	17.4
Rep. of Korea	836.3	14.4	35.7	3.8	21.2
China	748.8	10.4	33.8	3.4	24.7
France	742.7	4.0	0.6	3.4	28.1
Brazil	674.2	17.1	4.4	3.1	31.2
Belgium	638.5	3.3	15.2	2.9	34.1
Netherlands	621.8	5.1	7.8	2.9	37.0
Italy	601.0	3.8	14.7	2.8	39.8
Spain	582.9	12.6	15.1	2.7	42.4
Canada	569.6	3.3	21.3	2.6	45.1
Mexico	533.7	12.5	4.6	2.5	47.5
Indonesia	523.4	12.3	18.2	2.4	49.9
United Kingdom	508.2	5.5	10.3	2.3	52.3

Source: UN Comtrade

524 Other inorganic chemicals; organic, inorganic compounds precious metals

After a sharp decline of 38.7 percent in 2009, the value (in current prices) of exports of other inorganic chemicals; organic, inorganic compounds of precious metals (SITC group 524) rose significantly in 2010 by 59.3 percent to amount to 11.8 bln US$ (see table 2). Imports showed a similar development with an increase of 56.8 percent to 11.0 bln US$ in 2010 (see table 3). Graph 1 shows that the increase in exports for 2010 in this product group far exceeded both the increase in world exports of chemicals and related products, nes (SITC section 5) of 17.1 percent and the increase in total world exports of 21.2 percent. Exports of other inorganic chemicals; organic, inorganic compounds of precious metals (SITC group 524) accounted for 0.7 percent of world exports of SITC section 5 and 0.1 percent of total world exports in 2010 (see table 1).

The top exporting countries in 2010 were Germany, China and USA (see table 2). They accounted respectively for 13.5, 12.8 and 10.0 percent of world exports. Germany and Japan were also the top destinations, together with France (see table 3). By MDG regions (see graph 2), Developed Europe accounted for a large share of trade in other inorganic chemicals; organic, inorganic compounds of precious metals (SITC group 524). In 2010, its exports amounted to 5.2 bln US$ and its imports reached 5.1 bln US$, resulting in a trade surplus of 0.1 bln US$. Top trade deficits were recorded by South-eastern Asia (-0.6 bln US$) and Southern Asia (-0.2 bln US$) among others. Top trade surpluses were recorded by Commonwealth of Independent States (+1.0 bln US$) and Developed North America (+0.4 bln US$).

Table 1: Imports (Imp.) and exports (Exp.), 1996-2010, in current prices

		1996	1997	1998	1999	2000	2001	2002	2003	2004	2005	2006	2007	2008	2009	2010
Values in Bln US$	Imp.	3.7	3.7	3.8	3.9	5.0	4.8	3.9	4.1	5.5	6.7	7.9	9.7	10.8	7.0	11.0
	Exp.	3.2	3.3	3.3	3.4	4.6	4.5	3.6	3.9	5.3	6.7	8.1	10.3	12.1	7.4	11.8
As a percentage of SITC section (%)	Imp.	0.7	0.7	0.7	0.7	0.8	0.8	0.6	0.5	0.5	0.6	0.6	0.6	0.6	0.5	0.6
	Exp.	0.7	0.7	0.6	0.6	0.8	0.8	0.6	0.5	0.6	0.6	0.7	0.7	0.7	0.5	0.7
As a percentage of world trade (%)	Imp.	0.1	0.1	0.1	0.1	0.1	0.1	0.1	0.1	0.1	0.1	0.1	0.1	0.1	0.1	0.1
	Exp.	0.1	0.1	0.1	0.1	0.1	0.1	0.1	0.1	0.1	0.1	0.1	0.1	0.1	0.1	0.1

Graph 1: Annual growth rates of exports, 1996–2010

(In percentage by year)

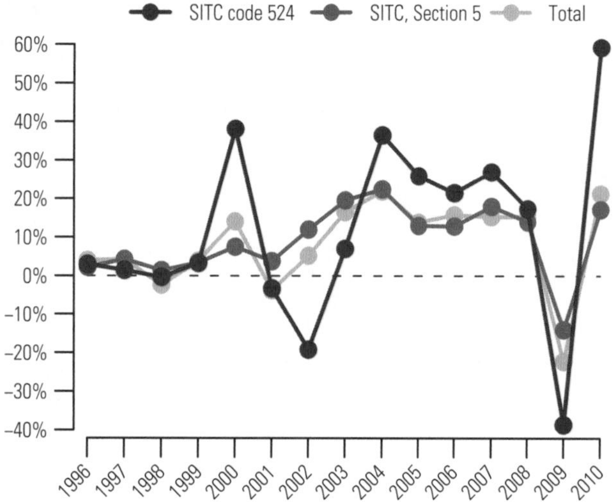

Graph 2: Trade Balance by MDG regions 2010

(Bln US$)

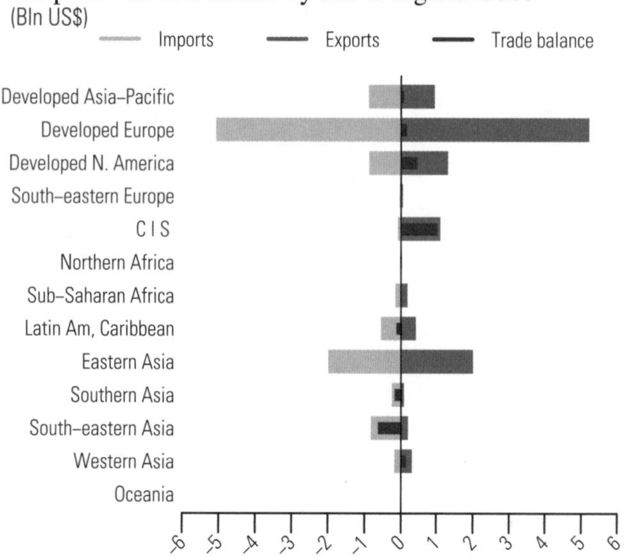

Table 2: Top exporting countries or areas in 2010

Country or area	Value (million US$)	Avg. Growth (%) 06-10	Growth (%) 09-10	World share %	Cum.
World	11 806.5	9.8	59.3	100.0	
Germany	1 597.3	4.1	65.9	13.5	13.5
China	1 506.7	9.4	99.7	12.8	26.3
USA	1 179.6	2.9	42.8	10.0	36.3
United Kingdom	1 103.3	8.6	76.1	9.3	45.6
Russian Federation	1 038.8	16.5	149.4	8.8	54.4
Japan	941.0	14.3	53.3	8.0	62.4
Italy	930.8	103.4	73.4	7.9	70.3
Switzerland	571.5	8.3	50.5	4.8	75.1
Israel	287.1	158.6	28.1	2.4	77.6
Netherlands	211.7	1.6	25.5	1.8	79.3
China, Hong Kong SAR	210.1	2.0	59.0	1.8	81.1
Brazil	208.0	15.0	10.5	1.8	82.9
Belgium	203.0	-2.9	-19.1	1.7	84.6
South Africa	176.4	-4.5	24.5	1.5	86.1
Rep. of Korea	165.0	12.8	76.2	1.4	87.5

Table 3: Top importing countries or areas in 2010

Country or area	Value (million US$)	Avg. Growth (%) 06-10	Growth (%) 09-10	World share %	Cum.
World	10 967.3	8.4	56.8	100.0	
Germany	1 467.9	21.3	52.5	13.4	13.4
Japan	825.0	8.1	110.1	7.5	20.9
France	750.5	8.2	35.4	6.8	27.8
USA	723.4	-1.8	53.2	6.6	34.3
Rep. of Korea	602.6	19.5	64.3	5.5	39.8
Italy	591.3	33.7	221.7	5.4	45.2
Switzerland	550.4	4.5	54.2	5.0	50.3
Other Asia, nes	492.7	14.6	67.8	4.5	54.7
Belgium	481.4	-0.1	52.1	4.4	59.1
China	471.5	0.4	31.9	4.3	63.4
China, Hong Kong SAR	415.5	10.9	52.7	3.8	67.2
Singapore	406.5	17.2	82.9	3.7	70.9
Mexico	243.3	-3.4	71.5	2.2	73.1
United Kingdom	226.7	-3.5	42.0	2.1	75.2
India	208.2	8.1	16.5	1.9	77.1

After a drop of 8.9 percent in 2009, the value (in current prices) of exports of radioactive and associated materials (SITC group 525) increased in 2010 by 11.6 percent to amount to 14.8 bln US$ (see table 2). Imports showed a similar development with an increase of 15.9 percent to 21.1 bln US$ in 2010 (see table 3). Graph 1 shows that the increase in exports for 2010 in this product group was exceeded by both the increase in world exports of chemicals and related products, nes (SITC section 5) of 17.1 percent and the increase in total world exports of 21.2 percent. Exports of radioactive and associated materials (SITC group 525) accounted for 0.9 percent of world exports of SITC section 5 and 0.1 percent of total world exports in 2010 (see table 1).

Exports of France, the top exporting country in 2010, decreased by 0.3 percent and accounted for 21.8 percent of world exports (see table 2). Other major exporting countries were Canada and Kazakhstan, respectively with 14.4 and 14.1 percent of world exports. USA and France were the two major destinations, together with China (see table 3). By MDG regions (see graph 2), Commonwealth of Independent States recorded a surplus amounting to 2.8 bln US$ and top deficits were recorded by Developed Europe (-2.8 bln US$), Eastern Asia (-2.5 bln US$) and Developed North America (-1.9 bln US$).

Table 1: Imports (Imp.) and exports (Exp.), 1996-2010, in current prices

		1996	1997	1998	1999	2000	2001	2002	2003	2004	2005	2006	2007	2008	2009	2010
Values in Bln US$	Imp.	5.9	6.0	6.1	6.3	6.9	6.9	7.4	9.3	10.1	11.2	13.6	17.8	18.5	18.2	21.1
	Exp.	4.9	5.1	4.4	4.3	5.0	4.5	5.0	5.8	6.3	7.4	9.4	14.8	14.6	13.3	14.8
As a percentage of SITC section (%)	Imp.	1.2	1.1	1.1	1.1	1.1	1.1	1.1	1.1	1.0	1.0	1.1	1.2	1.1	1.2	1.2
	Exp.	1.0	1.0	0.9	0.8	0.9	0.8	0.8	0.7	0.7	0.7	0.8	1.0	0.9	0.9	0.9
As a percentage of world trade (%)	Imp.	0.1	0.1	0.1	0.1	0.1	0.1	0.1	0.1	0.1	0.1	0.1	0.1	0.1	0.1	0.1
	Exp.	0.1	0.1	0.1	0.1	0.1	0.1	0.1	0.1	0.1	0.1	0.1	0.1	0.1	0.1	0.1

Graph 1: Annual growth rates of exports, 1996–2010

(In percentage by year)

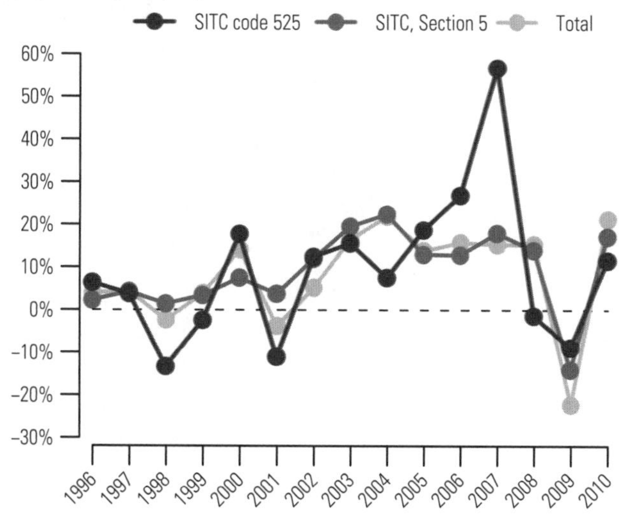

Graph 2: Trade Balance by MDG regions 2010

(Bln US$)

Imports — Exports — Trade balance

Developed Asia-Pacific
Developed Europe
Developed N. America
South-eastern Europe
C I S
Northern Africa
Sub-Saharan Africa
Latin Am, Caribbean
Eastern Asia
Southern Asia
South-eastern Asia
Western Asia
Oceania

-10 -8 -6 -4 -2 0 2 4 6 8

Table 2: Top exporting countries or areas in 2010

Country or area	Value (million US$)	Avg. Growth (%) 06-10	Growth (%) 09-10	World share %	Cum.
World	14830.4	12.0	11.6	100.0	
France	3239.5	16.8	-0.3	21.8	21.8
Canada	2134.7	2.5	39.0	14.4	36.2
Kazakhstan	2097.8	38.2	29.4	14.1	50.4
USA	1946.3	1.0	-15.3	13.1	63.5
Netherlands	1614.8	14.0	16.9	10.9	74.4
Uzbekistan	*1057.8*	45.4	55.0	7.1	81.5
Germany	865.0	4.0	-34.2	5.8	87.4
China	777.2	22.5	217.6	5.2	92.6
Japan	175.8	-10.4	58.6	1.2	93.8
Russian Federation	151.7	21.3	-36.2	1.0	94.8
South Africa	129.9	6.4	12.9	0.9	95.7
Belgium	128.7	0.9	-3.6	0.9	96.6
United Kingdom	91.2	-6.0	1.5	0.6	97.2
Austria	62.7	24.6	33.2	0.4	97.6
Ukraine	55.4	-3.8	22152.4	0.4	98.0

Table 3: Top importing countries or areas in 2010

Country or area	Value (million US$)	Avg. Growth (%) 06-10	Growth (%) 09-10	World share %	Cum.
World	21072.0	11.5	15.9	100.0	
USA	5216.7	6.7	14.0	24.8	24.8
France	2814.9	12.7	-10.7	13.4	38.1
China	2516.0	74.5	221.3	11.9	50.1
Germany	2006.4	9.7	0.9	9.5	59.6
Japan	1928.2	12.1	43.9	9.2	68.7
United Kingdom	1110.1	0.8	5.0	5.3	74.0
Sweden	852.5	25.4	29.0	4.0	78.0
Canada	760.4	17.2	30.8	3.6	81.6
Rep. of Korea	711.6	16.1	-8.3	3.4	85.0
Spain	672.4	21.0	13.9	3.2	88.2
Belgium	661.0	-6.8	-28.1	3.1	91.4
Netherlands	561.8	-4.3	-7.6	2.7	94.0
Russian Federation	447.2	15.4	11.2	2.1	96.1
Brazil	90.5	8.2	-17.8	0.4	96.6
Austria	68.4	25.0	107.0	0.3	96.9

531 Synthetic organic colouring matter and preparations based thereon

After a drop of 21.1 percent in 2009, the value (in current prices) of exports of synthetic organic coloring matter and preparations based thereon (SITC group 531) increased in 2010 by 24.0 percent to amount to 12.2 bln US$ (see table 2). Imports showed a similar development with an increase of 24.6 percent to 12.5 bln US$ in 2010 (see table 3). Graph 1 shows that the increase in exports for 2010 in this product group exceeded both the increase in world exports of chemicals and related products, nes (SITC section 5) of 17.1 percent and the increase in total world exports of 21.2 percent. Exports of synthetic organic coloring matter and preparations based thereon (SITC group 531) accounted for 0.7 percent of world exports of SITC section 5 and 0.1 percent of total world exports in 2010 (see table 1).

The top exporting countries in 2010 were China, Germany and India (see table 2). They accounted respectively for 19.3, 14.4 and 10.1 percent of world exports. Germany, USA and China were the top destinations (see table 3). By MDG regions (see graph 2), significant surpluses were recorded by Eastern Asia (+1.4 bln US$), Southern Asia (+0.6 bln US$) and Developed Europe (+0.5 bln US$). Top trade deficits were recorded by Latin America and the Caribbean (-0.8 bln US$), South-eastern Asia (-0.7 bln US$) and Western Asia (-0.6 bln US$).

Table 1: Imports (Imp.) and exports (Exp.), 1996-2010, in current prices

		1996	1997	1998	1999	2000	2001	2002	2003	2004	2005	2006	2007	2008	2009	2010
Values in Bln US$	Imp.	10.8	11.3	10.5	9.8	9.6	8.7	9.1	9.9	10.6	10.4	11.2	12.1	12.6	10.1	12.5
	Exp.	10.1	10.4	9.7	9.2	8.9	8.4	9.1	9.8	10.4	10.4	11.1	12.1	12.4	9.8	12.2
As a percentage of SITC section (%)	Imp.	2.1	2.1	1.9	1.7	1.6	1.4	1.3	1.2	1.0	0.9	0.9	0.8	0.7	0.7	0.7
	Exp.	2.1	2.1	1.9	1.7	1.6	1.4	1.4	1.2	1.1	1.0	0.9	0.8	0.8	0.7	0.7
As a percentage of world trade (%)	Imp.	0.2	0.2	0.2	0.2	0.1	0.1	0.1	0.1	0.1	0.1	0.1	0.1	0.1	0.1	0.1
	Exp.	0.2	0.2	0.2	0.2	0.1	0.1	0.1	0.1	0.1	0.1	0.1	0.1	0.1	0.1	0.1

Graph 1: Annual growth rates of exports, 1996–2010

(In percentage by year)

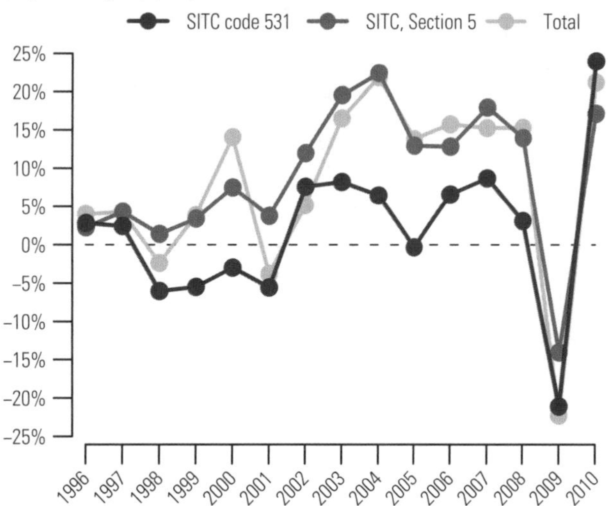

Graph 2: Trade Balance by MDG regions 2010

(Bln US$)

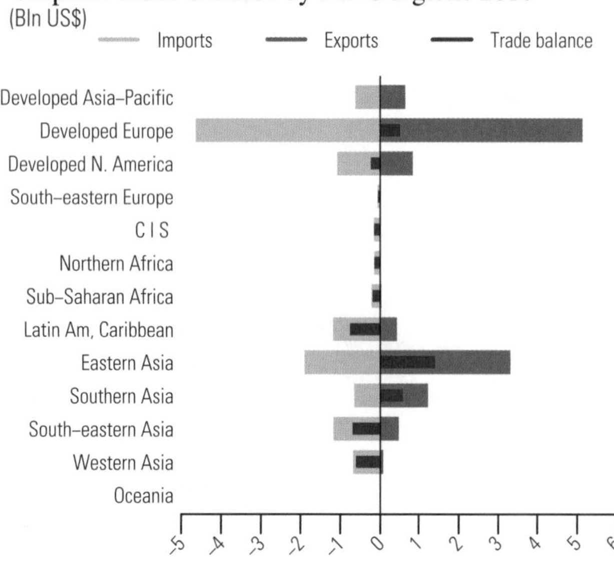

Table 2: Top exporting countries or areas in 2010

Country or area	Value (million US$)	Avg. Growth (%) 06-10	Growth (%) 09-10	World share %	Cum.
World	12157.5	2.3	24.0	100.0	
China	2341.6	11.8	34.2	19.3	19.3
Germany	1747.6	-3.3	14.8	14.4	33.6
India	1222.4	12.3	35.6	10.1	43.7
Switzerland	791.5	-8.1	14.9	6.5	50.2
USA	790.1	3.4	31.2	6.5	56.7
Japan	612.0	14.1	34.2	5.0	61.7
Belgium	467.2	-0.8	7.7	3.8	65.6
Rep. of Korea	400.2	7.7	33.3	3.3	68.9
United Kingdom	372.7	-6.3	23.2	3.1	71.9
France	354.9	-6.4	23.0	2.9	74.9
Other Asia, nes	302.9	3.5	18.6	2.5	77.3
Italy	291.5	5.1	10.2	2.4	79.7
Netherlands	284.6	-9.5	17.4	2.3	82.1
China, Hong Kong SAR	264.1	-5.4	13.6	2.2	84.3
Spain	260.5	0.2	20.6	2.1	86.4

Table 3: Top importing countries or areas in 2010

Country or area	Value (million US$)	Avg. Growth (%) 06-10	Growth (%) 09-10	World share %	Cum.
World	12519.3	2.9	24.6	100.0	
Germany	1119.9	3.4	33.3	8.9	8.9
USA	905.4	2.0	47.9	7.2	16.2
China	720.7	2.3	24.9	5.8	21.9
Rep. of Korea	604.4	13.4	31.2	4.8	26.8
Italy	554.8	-1.3	10.9	4.4	31.2
Japan	543.1	7.3	56.6	4.3	35.5
Turkey	430.2	2.4	16.9	3.4	39.0
Belgium	428.8	1.6	14.7	3.4	42.4
France	424.6	-6.1	21.2	3.4	45.8
Brazil	354.9	16.8	41.8	2.8	48.6
Switzerland	330.3	-4.8	50.5	2.6	51.3
Mexico	324.4	8.6	33.7	2.6	53.8
Other Asia, nes	309.9	3.8	36.0	2.5	56.3
Indonesia	306.7	10.5	25.2	2.4	58.8
United Kingdom	302.9	-4.6	25.1	2.4	61.2

After a drop of 6.9 percent in 2009, the value (in current prices) of exports of dyeing and tanning extracts, and synthetic tanning materials (SITC group 532) increased in 2010 by 28.9 percent to amount to 1.9 bln US$ (see table 2). Imports showed a similar development with an increase of 32.0 percent to 2.3 bln US$ in 2010 (see table 3). Graph 1 shows that the increase in exports for 2010 in this product group exceeded both the increase in world exports of chemicals and related products, nes (SITC section 5) of 17.1 percent and the increase in total world exports of 21.2 percent. Exports of dyeing and tanning extracts, and synthetic tanning materials (SITC group 532) accounted for 0.1 percent of world exports of SITC section 5 and less than 0.1 percent of total world exports in 2010 (see table 1).

The top exporting countries in 2010 were Italy, Germany and Spain (see table 2). They accounted respectively for 12.2, 10.4 and 6.9 percent of world exports. Top destinations were China, USA and Germany (see table 3). By MDG regions (see graph 2), Developed Europe accounted for a large share of trade in dyeing and tanning extracts, and synthetic tanning materials (SITC group 532). Its exports amounted to 1,069 mln US$ while imports were valued at 812 mln US$ resulting in a trade surplus of 257 mln US$. Significant deficits were recorded by Eastern Asia (-290 mln US$) and Developed Asia-Pacific (-126 mln US$).

Table 1: Imports (Imp.) and exports (Exp.), 1996-2010, in current prices

		1996	1997	1998	1999	2000	2001	2002	2003	2004	2005	2006	2007	2008	2009	2010
Values in Bln US$	Imp.	1.1	1.1	1.0	1.0	1.0	1.1	1.1	1.3	1.4	1.5	1.6	1.8	1.9	1.8	2.3
	Exp.	1.0	1.0	0.9	0.9	0.9	0.9	1.0	1.1	1.3	1.4	1.5	1.6	1.6	1.5	1.9
As a percentage of SITC section (%)	Imp.	0.2	0.2	0.2	0.2	0.2	0.2	0.2	0.2	0.1	0.1	0.1	0.1	0.1	0.1	0.1
	Exp.	0.2	0.2	0.2	0.2	0.2	0.2	0.1	0.1	0.1	0.1	0.1	0.1	0.1	0.1	0.1
As a percentage of world trade (%)	Imp.	0.0	0.0	0.0	0.0	0.0	0.0	0.0	0.0	0.0	0.0	0.0	0.0	0.0	0.0	0.0
	Exp.	0.0	0.0	0.0	0.0	0.0	0.0	0.0	0.0	0.0	0.0	0.0	0.0	0.0	0.0	0.0

Graph 1: Annual growth rates of exports, 1996–2010

(In percentage by year)

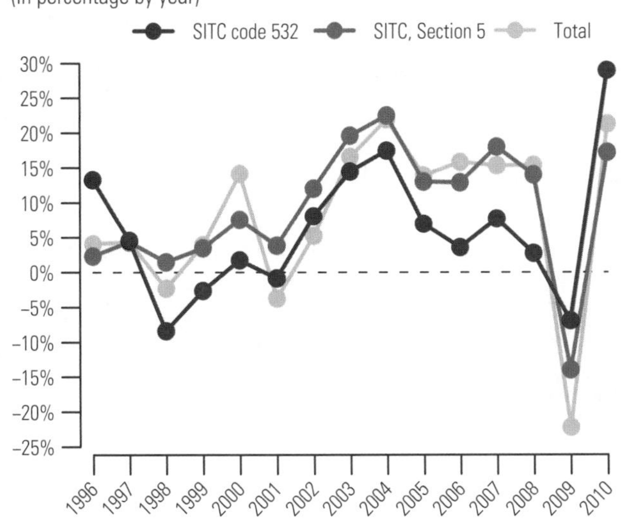

Table 2: Top exporting countries or areas in 2010

Country or area	Value (million US$)	Avg. Growth (%) 06-10	Growth (%) 09-10	World share %	Cum.
World	1 937.5	7.3	28.9	100.0	
Italy	236.5	8.0	33.4	12.2	12.2
Germany	201.6	6.1	27.7	10.4	22.6
Spain	132.8	8.0	17.4	6.9	29.5
France	125.9	5.7	26.0	6.5	36.0
Netherlands	120.5	22.4	15.1	6.2	42.2
USA	111.0	2.1	21.3	5.7	47.9
Peru	94.3	28.6	173.6	4.9	52.8
South Africa	92.3	7.6	48.1	4.8	57.5
Argentina	84.3	4.4	45.0	4.4	61.9
Denmark	79.3	17.0	60.1	4.1	66.0
Turkey	74.5	16.8	31.8	3.8	69.8
Brazil	65.3	10.3	27.6	3.4	73.2
India	52.6	9.3	24.4	2.7	75.9
Indonesia	52.0	33.1	30.9	2.7	78.6
United Kingdom	48.6	-6.3	25.4	2.5	81.1

Graph 2: Trade Balance by MDG regions 2010

(Bln US$)

Imports — Exports — Trade balance

Developed Asia-Pacific
Developed Europe
Developed N. America
South-eastern Europe
C I S
Northern Africa
Sub-Saharan Africa
Latin Am, Caribbean
Eastern Asia
Southern Asia
South-eastern Asia
Western Asia
Oceania

-1 -0.8 -0.6 -0.4 -0.2 0 0.2 0.4 0.6 0.8 1 1.2

Table 3: Top importing countries or areas in 2010

Country or area	Value (million US$)	Avg. Growth (%) 06-10	Growth (%) 09-10	World share %	Cum.
World	2 318.0	9.3	32.0	100.0	
China	251.4	8.0	43.8	10.8	10.8
USA	150.0	15.0	13.6	6.5	17.3
Germany	144.3	16.8	74.7	6.2	23.5
Japan	134.5	7.1	-1.8	5.8	29.3
Italy	130.1	3.4	43.5	5.6	35.0
Mexico	105.4	13.0	38.6	4.5	39.5
Spain	95.9	17.4	48.7	4.1	43.6
France	83.6	14.9	36.5	3.6	47.2
India	78.7	8.8	-7.3	3.4	50.6
United Kingdom	71.8	15.4	45.3	3.1	53.7
Brazil	63.6	16.3	82.5	2.7	56.5
Denmark	61.8	30.6	117.2	2.7	59.2
Rep. of Korea	53.5	2.9	11.5	2.3	61.5
China, Hong Kong SAR	47.9	-8.1	39.3	2.1	63.5
Turkey	47.6	5.4	33.1	2.1	65.6

533 Pigments, paints, varnishes and related materials

After a drop of 16.3 percent in 2009, the value (in current prices) of exports of pigments, paints, varnishes and related materials (SITC group 533) increased in 2010 by 17.6 percent to amount to 52.7 bln US$ (see table 2). Imports showed a similar development with an increase of 16.0 percent to 50.9 bln US$ in 2010 (see table 3). Graph 1 shows that the increase in exports for 2010 in this product group was greater than the increase in world exports of chemicals and related products, nes (SITC section 5) of 17.1 percent but less than the increase in total world exports of 21.2 percent. Exports of pigments, paints, varnishes and related materials (SITC group 533) accounted for 3.2 percent of world exports of SITC section 5 and 0.4 percent of total world exports in 2010 (see table 1).

Germany, USA and Japan were the three major exporting countries in 2010 (see table 2). They accounted respectively for 16.6, 12.7 and 7.7 percent of world exports. Top destinations were Germany, China and France (see table 3). By MDG regions (see graph 2), Developed Europe accounted for a large share of trade in pigments, paints, varnishes and related materials (SITC group 533). Its exports were valued at 29.7 bln US$ while imports amounted to 21.0 bln US$ resulting in a trade surplus of 8.7 bln US$. Top trade surpluses were also recorded by Developed North America (+3.5 bln US$) and Developed Asia-Pacific (+3.1 bln US$). Significant deficits were recorded by Latin America and the Caribbean (-2.7 bln US$), Commonwealth of Independent States (-2.2 bln US$) and Eastern Asia (-2.1 bln US$).

Table 1: Imports (Imp.) and exports (Exp.), 1996-2010, in current prices

		1996	1997	1998	1999	2000	2001	2002	2003	2004	2005	2006	2007	2008	2009	2010
Values in Bln US$	Imp.	20.4	21.4	22.0	23.0	24.5	24.2	26.0	30.0	35.0	38.1	42.4	47.9	51.8	43.9	50.9
	Exp.	20.4	21.7	22.5	23.3	24.8	24.3	26.2	30.5	35.9	39.0	43.7	49.5	53.5	44.8	52.7
As a percentage of SITC section (%)	Imp.	4.0	4.0	4.1	4.1	4.0	3.8	3.7	3.6	3.5	3.3	3.3	3.2	3.0	3.0	2.9
	Exp.	4.2	4.3	4.4	4.4	4.4	4.1	4.0	3.9	3.7	3.6	3.6	3.4	3.2	3.2	3.2
As a percentage of world trade (%)	Imp.	0.4	0.4	0.4	0.4	0.4	0.4	0.4	0.4	0.4	0.4	0.3	0.3	0.3	0.4	0.3
	Exp.	0.4	0.4	0.4	0.4	0.4	0.4	0.4	0.4	0.4	0.4	0.4	0.4	0.3	0.4	0.4

Graph 1: Annual growth rates of exports, 1996–2010

(In percentage by year)

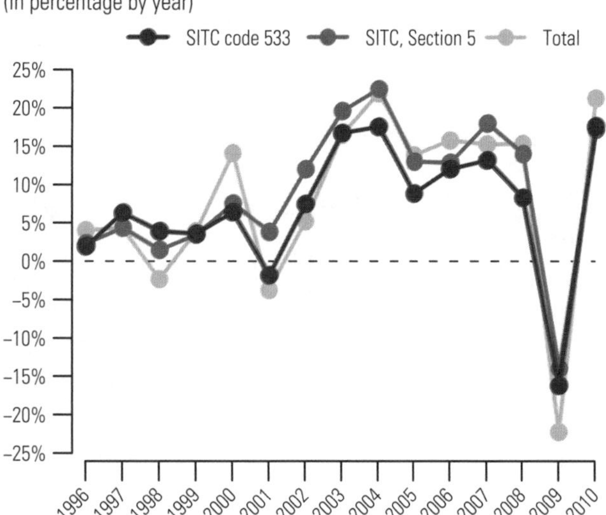

Table 2: Top exporting countries or areas in 2010

Country or area	Value (million US$)	Avg. Growth (%) 06-10	Growth (%) 09-10	World share %	Cum.
World	52723.4	4.8	17.6	100.0	
Germany	8744.9	2.9	11.8	16.6	16.6
USA	6677.2	9.4	33.4	12.7	29.3
Japan	4047.7	8.6	32.4	7.7	36.9
Belgium	3522.0	4.6	18.8	6.7	43.6
United Kingdom	2572.4	3.2	12.0	4.9	48.5
Italy	2377.0	4.6	13.9	4.5	53.0
Netherlands	2215.5	0.0	2.8	4.2	57.2
France	2063.4	-1.7	3.4	3.9	61.1
China	1863.1	8.0	49.6	3.5	64.6
Spain	1835.4	4.9	6.4	3.5	68.1
Switzerland	1354.7	3.0	10.0	2.6	70.7
Other Asia, nes	1209.8	8.9	30.0	2.3	73.0
Rep. of Korea	1143.2	8.1	30.0	2.2	75.2
Sweden	950.0	1.2	8.4	1.8	77.0
Singapore	920.6	7.5	11.5	1.7	78.7

Graph 2: Trade Balance by MDG regions 2010

(Bln US$)

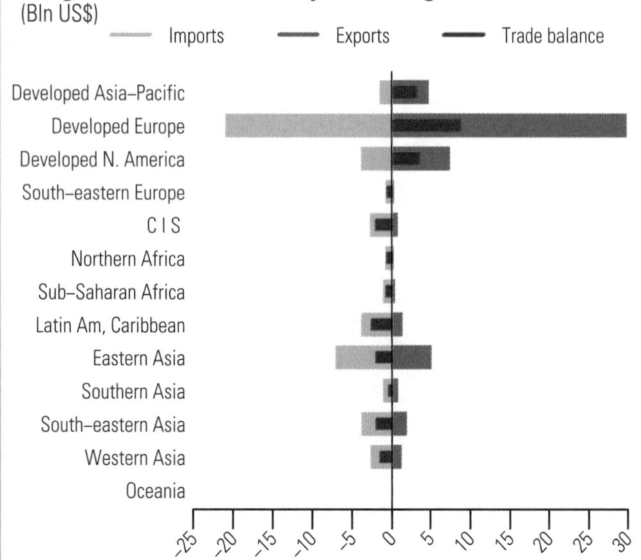

Table 3: Top importing countries or areas in 2010

Country or area	Value (million US$)	Avg. Growth (%) 06-10	Growth (%) 09-10	World share %	Cum.
World	50863.2	4.7	16.0	100.0	
Germany	3467.9	4.6	23.6	6.8	6.8
China	3431.5	6.4	21.2	6.7	13.6
France	2309.4	2.5	8.7	4.5	18.1
USA	2155.6	-1.1	22.5	4.2	22.3
Russian Federation	1840.7	11.3	24.1	3.6	26.0
Italy	1739.4	1.4	11.5	3.4	29.4
Canada	1722.1	2.4	19.2	3.4	32.8
United Kingdom	1596.4	-1.3	5.9	3.1	35.9
Belgium	1465.9	-5.2	-5.5	2.9	38.8
Rep. of Korea	1390.6	3.4	19.8	2.7	41.5
Poland	1321.9	4.0	7.1	2.6	44.1
Other Asia, nes	1293.5	10.5	44.0	2.5	46.7
Netherlands	1276.3	2.9	5.2	2.5	49.2
Spain	1269.1	-0.9	-6.1	2.5	51.7
Mexico	1162.1	2.3	22.6	2.3	54.0

Since 2006, the value (in current prices) of exports of medicinal and pharmaceutical products, other than medicaments of group 542 (SITC group 541) increased on average by 16.4 percent each year and amounted to 136.0 bln US$ in 2010 (see table 2). Imports showed a similar development with an average increase of 15.3 percent to 133.0 bln US$ in 2010 (see table 3). Graph 1 shows that the increase of 9.2 percent in exports for 2010 in this product group was exceeded by both the increase in world exports of chemicals and related products, nes (SITC section 5) of 17.1 percent and the increase in total world exports of 21.2 percent. Exports of medicinal and pharmaceutical products, other than medicaments of group 542 (SITC group 541) accounted for 8.2 percent of world exports of SITC section 5 and 0.9 percent of total world exports in 2010 (see table 1).

In 2010, Switzerland and Germany were the top two exporting countries. They represented 16.4 and 15.8 percent of world exports, respectively (see table 2). Another major exporting country was USA with 14.4 percent of world exports. Germany and USA were also among the top destinations, together with Belgium (see table 3). By MDG regions (see graph 2), Developed Europe accounted for a majority of trade in medicinal and pharmaceutical products (SITC group 541). Its exports were valued at 94.5 bln US$ while imports amounted to 76.9 bln US$, resulting in a trade surplus of 17.6 bln US$. Significant surpluses were also recorded by Eastern Asia (+5.6 bln US$) and Developed North America (+3.1 bln US$). Top trade deficits were recorded by Latin America and the Caribbean (-7.5 bln US$) and Developed Asia-Pacific (-5.3 bln US$).

Table 1: Imports (Imp.) and exports (Exp.), 1996-2010, in current prices

		1996	1997	1998	1999	2000	2001	2002	2003	2004	2005	2006	2007	2008	2009	2010
Values in Bln US$	Imp.	30.0	30.0	30.5	32.4	33.7	37.9	44.0	52.4	60.4	66.9	75.3	95.8	108.4	117.2	133.0
	Exp.	27.5	27.8	29.0	31.1	31.5	35.3	41.1	50.3	59.8	66.2	74.1	94.2	112.5	124.5	136.0
As a percentage of SITC section (%)	Imp.	5.8	5.6	5.6	5.7	5.5	6.0	6.3	6.3	6.0	5.8	5.9	6.3	6.3	7.9	7.7
	Exp.	5.7	5.5	5.7	5.9	5.6	6.0	6.3	6.4	6.2	6.1	6.0	6.5	6.8	8.8	8.2
As a percentage of world trade (%)	Imp.	0.6	0.5	0.6	0.6	0.5	0.6	0.7	0.7	0.6	0.6	0.6	0.7	0.7	0.9	0.9
	Exp.	0.5	0.5	0.5	0.6	0.5	0.6	0.6	0.7	0.7	0.6	0.6	0.7	0.7	1.0	0.9

Graph 1: Annual growth rates of exports, 1996–2010
(In percentage by year)

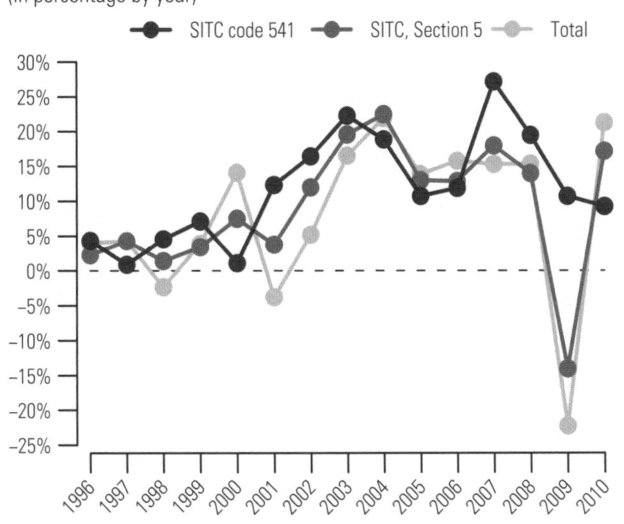

Table 2: Top exporting countries or areas in 2010

Country or area	Value (million US$)	Avg. Growth (%) 06-10	Growth (%) 09-10	World share %	Cum.
World	135998.6	16.4	9.2	100.0	
Switzerland	22244.9	18.1	13.9	16.4	16.4
Germany	21431.2	17.4	12.2	15.8	32.1
USA	19617.0	13.2	0.9	14.4	46.5
Belgium	14004.4	25.7	7.7	10.3	56.8
China	9192.8	23.9	23.9	6.8	63.6
Ireland	7856.0	28.5	7.4	5.8	69.4
France	6814.3	14.5	16.8	5.0	74.4
United Kingdom	5886.5	15.0	17.4	4.3	78.7
Italy	3228.8	8.3	0.0	2.4	81.1
Austria	3020.2	14.4	0.7	2.2	83.3
Denmark	2378.7	6.1	7.6	1.7	85.1
Netherlands	2044.4	-13.8	-12.1	1.5	86.6
Spain	1973.6	10.2	4.0	1.5	88.0
Panama	1824.0	102.4	-21.3	1.3	89.4
Canada	1783.4	22.0	21.8	1.3	90.7

Graph 2: Trade Balance by MDG regions 2010
(Bln US$)

Imports — Exports — Trade balance

Developed Asia-Pacific
Developed Europe
Developed N. America
South-eastern Europe
C I S
Northern Africa
Sub-Saharan Africa
Latin Am, Caribbean
Eastern Asia
Southern Asia
South-eastern Asia
Western Asia
Oceania

-80 -60 -40 -20 0 20 40 60 80 100

Table 3: Top importing countries or areas in 2010

Country or area	Value (million US$)	Avg. Growth (%) 06-10	Growth (%) 09-10	World share %	Cum.
World	132996.9	15.3	13.5	100.0	
Germany	18999.4	16.5	13.1	14.3	14.3
USA	14830.5	9.3	7.7	11.2	25.4
Belgium	11017.8	29.0	12.3	8.3	33.7
France	8973.2	16.8	21.1	6.7	40.5
Italy	7474.9	7.6	0.8	5.6	46.1
United Kingdom	6254.2	14.6	15.0	4.7	50.8
Switzerland	6129.0	12.3	26.5	4.6	55.4
Japan	5553.3	20.1	23.9	4.2	59.6
Austria	3868.0	16.1	19.2	2.9	62.5
Brazil	3595.6	30.6	48.5	2.7	65.2
Canada	3463.5	16.7	20.0	2.6	67.8
Spain	3408.6	13.2	-19.5	2.6	70.4
China	2257.8	36.0	32.8	1.7	72.1
Russian Federation	2087.6	19.5	28.9	1.6	73.6
Mexico	1899.5	14.8	13.6	1.4	75.0

542 Medicaments (including veterinary medicaments)

Since 2006, the value (in current prices) of exports of medicaments, including veterinary medicaments (SITC group 542) increased on average by 7.8 percent each year and amounted to 320.9 bln US$ in 2010 (see table 2). Imports for the same period also experienced an average increase of 8.1 percent and totaled 336.0 bln US$ in 2010 (see table 3). Graph 1 shows the increase of 3.5 percent in exports for 2010 in this product group was far below both the increase in world exports of chemicals and related products, nes (SITC section 5) of 17.1 percent and the increase in total world exports of 21.2 percent. Exports of medicaments, including veterinary medicaments (SITC group 542) accounted for 19.3 percent of world exports of SITC section 5 and 2.1 percent of total world exports in 2010 (see table 1).

In 2010, top exporting countries were Germany, Belgium and United Kingdom (see table 2). They accounted respectively for 13.8, 11.7 and 8.8 percent of world exports. Major destinations were USA, Belgium and Germany (see table 3). By MDG regions (see graph 2), Developed Europe accounted for a majority of trade in medicaments, including veterinary medicaments (SITC group 542). Its exports were valued at 254.2 bln US$ while imports amounted to 182.8 bln US$ resulting in a trade surplus of 71.4 bln US$. A significant surplus was also recorded by Southern Asia (+3.7 bln US$). Top trade deficits were recorded by Developed North America (-30.9 bln US$), Developed Asia-Pacific (-13.4 bln US$) and Commonwealth of Independent States (-13.0 bln US$).

Table 1: Imports (Imp.) and exports (Exp.), 1996-2010, in current prices

		1996	1997	1998	1999	2000	2001	2002	2003	2004	2005	2006	2007	2008	2009	2010
Values in Bln US$	Imp.	50.6	56.7	66.0	75.6	78.7	96.4	132.1	160.9	195.7	219.8	245.8	284.2	318.8	323.2	336.0
	Exp.	50.0	55.7	65.4	73.8	75.7	97.4	125.2	150.9	187.1	207.2	237.4	274.9	304.8	310.0	320.9
As a percentage of SITC section (%)	Imp.	9.8	10.6	12.2	13.4	12.9	15.2	18.8	19.3	19.3	19.2	19.1	18.8	18.5	21.8	19.4
	Exp.	10.4	11.1	12.8	14.0	13.4	16.6	19.0	19.2	19.4	19.1	19.4	19.0	18.5	21.9	19.3
As a percentage of world trade (%)	Imp.	0.9	1.0	1.2	1.3	1.2	1.5	2.0	2.1	2.1	2.1	2.0	2.0	2.0	2.6	2.2
	Exp.	1.0	1.0	1.2	1.3	1.2	1.6	2.0	2.0	2.1	2.0	2.0	2.0	1.9	2.5	2.1

Graph 1: Annual growth rates of exports, 1996–2010

(In percentage by year)

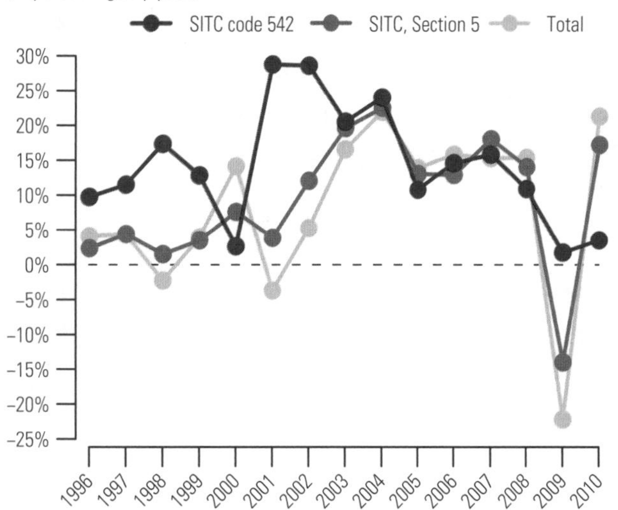

Graph 2: Trade Balance by MDG regions 2010

(Bln US$)

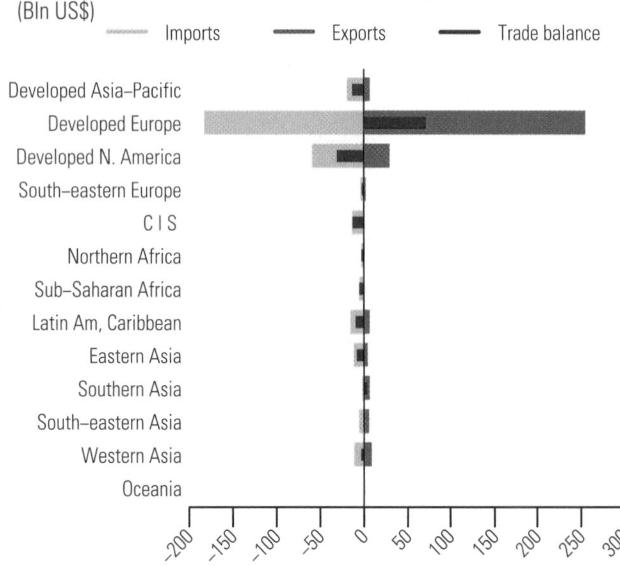

Table 2: Top exporting countries or areas in 2010

Country or area	Value (million US$)	Avg. Growth (%) 06-10	Growth (%) 09-10	World share %	Cum.
World	320 864.9	7.8	3.5	100.0	
Germany	44 402.6	7.1	-1.4	13.8	13.8
Belgium	37 436.2	3.4	-4.5	11.7	25.5
United Kingdom	28 082.5	6.5	6.1	8.8	34.3
Switzerland	27 820.4	8.9	7.2	8.7	42.9
France	27 538.2	7.5	-2.9	8.6	51.5
USA	24 779.8	9.6	0.6	7.7	59.2
Ireland	24 101.6	12.6	9.2	7.5	66.7
Italy	14 350.1	5.2	12.0	4.5	71.2
Netherlands	11 827.6	7.3	24.5	3.7	74.9
Spain	9 781.2	11.8	7.8	3.0	78.0
Sweden	7 659.6	-1.2	1.7	2.4	80.3
Israel	6 306.1	20.0	42.6	2.0	82.3
India	5 767.2	20.1	25.4	1.8	84.1
Austria	5 080.4	9.3	8.5	1.6	85.7
Singapore	4 445.2	3.8	12.5	1.4	87.1

Table 3: Top importing countries or areas in 2010

Country or area	Value (million US$)	Avg. Growth (%) 06-10	Growth (%) 09-10	World share %	Cum.
World	336 007.8	8.1	4.0	100.0	
USA	50 732.4	9.1	9.4	15.1	15.1
Belgium	31 328.3	-0.1	-7.1	9.3	24.4
Germany	28 300.9	3.9	-5.2	8.4	32.8
France	19 415.4	8.9	-1.8	5.8	38.6
United Kingdom	17 628.3	6.4	14.2	5.2	43.9
Italy	14 191.7	8.8	1.6	4.2	48.1
Switzerland	12 732.0	3.9	1.3	3.8	51.9
Japan	11 785.0	19.1	21.3	3.5	55.4
Spain	11 754.3	11.7	-7.8	3.5	58.9
Netherlands	10 467.8	3.7	0.1	3.1	62.0
Russian Federation	9 274.4	15.0	30.9	2.8	64.8
Canada	8 853.8	3.7	-3.4	2.6	67.4
Australia	7 122.8	11.7	17.5	2.1	69.5
China	5 772.6	29.5	15.5	1.7	71.2
Poland	4 922.6	11.7	16.6	1.5	72.7

After a drop of 7.8 percent in 2009, the value (in current prices) of exports of essential oils, perfume and flavor materials (SITC group 551) increased in 2010 by 9.9 percent to amount to 21.2 bln US$ (see table 2). Imports showed a similar development with an increase of 11.4 percent to 20.3 bln US$ in 2010 (see table 3). Graph 1 shows that the increase in exports for 2010 in this product group was exceeded by both the increase in world exports of chemicals and related products, nes (SITC section 5) of 17.1 percent and the increase in total world exports of 21.2 percent. Exports of essential oils, perfume and flavor materials (SITC group 551) accounted for 1.3 percent of world exports of SITC section 5 and 0.1 percent of total world exports in 2010 (see table 1).

Ireland, the top exporting country in 2010, accounted for almost a third (30.6 percent) of world exports (see table 2). Other major exporting countries were France and USA, respectively with 9.6 and 9.0 percent of world exports. Top destinations were USA, France and United Kingdom (see table 3). By MDG regions (see graph 2), Developed Europe was the origin and the destination of a majority of trade in essential oils, perfume and flavor materials (SITC group 551). Its exports were valued at 15.0 bln US$ while imports amounted to 9.1 bln US$, resulting in a trade surplus of 5.9 bln US$. Significant deficits were recorded by Developed North America (-1.0 bln US$), Latin America and the Caribbean (-1.0 bln US$) and Western Asia (-0.8 bln US$).

Table 1: Imports (Imp.) and exports (Exp.), 1996-2010, in current prices

		1996	1997	1998	1999	2000	2001	2002	2003	2004	2005	2006	2007	2008	2009	2010
Values in Bln US$	Imp.	6.3	6.9	6.9	7.1	7.7	8.2	9.2	11.7	13.8	14.9	15.7	17.6	19.3	18.3	20.3
	Exp.	6.5	7.1	7.4	8.0	7.8	8.6	10.0	12.9	14.8	15.6	16.6	18.7	20.9	19.3	21.2
As a percentage of SITC section (%)	Imp.	1.2	1.3	1.3	1.3	1.3	1.3	1.3	1.4	1.4	1.3	1.2	1.2	1.1	1.2	1.2
	Exp.	1.3	1.4	1.5	1.5	1.4	1.5	1.5	1.6	1.5	1.4	1.4	1.3	1.3	1.4	1.3
As a percentage of world trade (%)	Imp.	0.1	0.1	0.1	0.1	0.1	0.1	0.1	0.2	0.1	0.1	0.1	0.1	0.1	0.1	0.1
	Exp.	0.1	0.1	0.1	0.1	0.1	0.1	0.2	0.2	0.2	0.2	0.1	0.1	0.1	0.2	0.1

Graph 1: Annual growth rates of exports, 1996–2010

(In percentage by year)

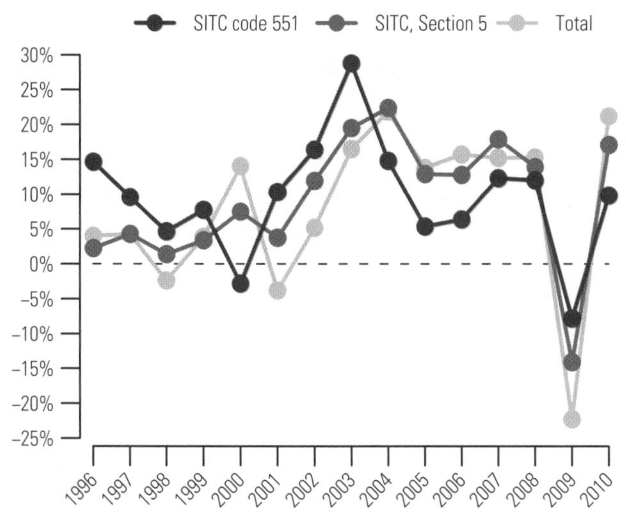

Graph 2: Trade Balance by MDG regions 2010

(Bln US$)

Imports — Exports — Trade balance

Developed Asia-Pacific; Developed Europe; Developed N. America; South-eastern Europe; C I S; Northern Africa; Sub-Saharan Africa; Latin Am, Caribbean; Eastern Asia; Southern Asia; South-eastern Asia; Western Asia; Oceania

-10 -8 -6 -4 -2 0 2 4 6 8 10 12 14 16

Table 2: Top exporting countries or areas in 2010

Country or area	Value (million US$)	Avg. Growth (%) 06-10	Growth (%) 09-10	World share %	Cum.
World	21 193.1	6.3	9.9	100.0	
Ireland	6 488.6	2.3	-1.7	30.6	30.6
France	2 033.6	6.1	13.3	9.6	40.2
USA	1 905.8	8.9	13.0	9.0	49.2
Germany	1 848.6	8.2	7.0	8.7	57.9
Switzerland	1 839.3	6.7	24.9	8.7	66.6
Singapore	1 071.4	22.3	49.7	5.1	71.7
United Kingdom	985.8	4.6	25.2	4.7	76.3
Netherlands	567.5	-0.5	-7.3	2.7	79.0
Spain	504.8	9.7	14.2	2.4	81.4
India	457.1	12.9	18.7	2.2	83.5
China	417.6	21.8	46.1	2.0	85.5
Japan	265.9	9.1	15.1	1.3	86.8
Swaziland	*234.9*	-9.9	-44.6	1.1	87.9
Italy	233.0	13.0	25.1	1.1	89.0
Brazil	218.6	7.5	29.6	1.0	90.0

Table 3: Top importing countries or areas in 2010

Country or area	Value (million US$)	Avg. Growth (%) 06-10	Growth (%) 09-10	World share %	Cum.
World	20 339.8	6.7	11.4	100.0	
USA	2 595.4	-0.1	6.4	12.8	12.8
France	2 512.0	9.2	15.1	12.4	25.1
United Kingdom	1 111.3	1.3	5.2	5.5	30.6
Germany	1 051.8	8.2	17.9	5.2	35.7
Mexico	811.7	6.5	13.4	4.0	39.7
Spain	775.1	2.9	-4.0	3.8	43.5
Italy	759.3	1.9	-2.0	3.7	47.3
Russian Federation	529.2	18.6	17.4	2.6	49.9
Japan	493.5	6.6	3.4	2.4	52.3
Netherlands	449.0	9.6	21.8	2.2	54.5
China	445.1	15.5	14.1	2.2	56.7
Canada	424.8	4.3	6.0	2.1	58.8
Poland	414.0	15.7	33.6	2.0	60.8
Turkey	394.8	12.9	13.5	1.9	62.8
Thailand	391.4	15.3	30.9	1.9	64.7

553 Perfumery, cosmetic or toilet preparations (excluding soaps)

After a drop of 9.1 percent in 2009, the value (in current prices) of exports of perfumery, cosmetic or toilet preparations, excluding soaps (SITC group 553) increased in 2010 by 12.9 percent to amount to 67.4 bln US$ (see table 2). Imports showed a similar development with an increase of 10.9 percent to 65.0 bln US$ in 2010 (see table 3). Graph 1 shows that the increase in exports for 2010 in this product group was exceeded by both the increase in world exports of chemicals and related products, nes (SITC section 5) of 17.1 percent and the increase in total world exports of 21.2 percent. Exports of perfumery, cosmetic or toilet preparations, excluding soaps (SITC group 553) accounted for 4.1 percent of world exports of SITC section 5 and 0.4 percent of total world exports in 2010 (see table 1).

The top exporting countries in 2010 were France, Germany and USA (see table 2). They accounted respectively for 18.4, 11.2 and 10.7 percent of world exports. Top destinations were USA, Germany and United Kingdom (see table 3). By MDG regions (see graph 2), Developed Europe accounted for a majority of exports and a large share of imports of perfumery, cosmetic or toilet preparations, excluding soaps (SITC group 553). In 2010, its exports were valued at 40.6 bln US$ and imports, at 27.6 bln US$, resulting in a trade surplus of 13.0 bln US$. Top trade deficits were recorded by Commonwealth of Independent States (-3.5 bln US$), Western Asia (-2.8 bln US$) and Developed Asia-Pacific (-1.9 bln US$).

Table 1: Imports (Imp.) and exports (Exp.), 1996-2010, in current prices

		1996	1997	1998	1999	2000	2001	2002	2003	2004	2005	2006	2007	2008	2009	2010
Values in Bln US$	Imp.	19.0	19.9	20.6	21.6	22.5	24.5	27.5	32.9	38.9	43.0	47.7	56.2	63.0	58.6	65.0
	Exp.	20.2	21.5	21.9	22.4	23.3	25.6	28.4	34.3	40.3	44.1	49.3	58.3	65.7	59.7	67.4
As a percentage of SITC section (%)	Imp.	3.7	3.7	3.8	3.8	3.7	3.9	3.9	3.9	3.8	3.7	3.7	3.7	3.7	4.0	3.7
	Exp.	4.2	4.3	4.3	4.3	4.1	4.4	4.3	4.4	4.2	4.1	4.0	4.0	4.0	4.2	4.1
As a percentage of world trade (%)	Imp.	0.4	0.4	0.4	0.4	0.3	0.4	0.4	0.4	0.4	0.4	0.4	0.4	0.4	0.5	0.4
	Exp.	0.4	0.4	0.4	0.4	0.4	0.4	0.4	0.5	0.4	0.4	0.4	0.4	0.4	0.5	0.4

Graph 1: Annual growth rates of exports, 1996–2010

(In percentage by year)

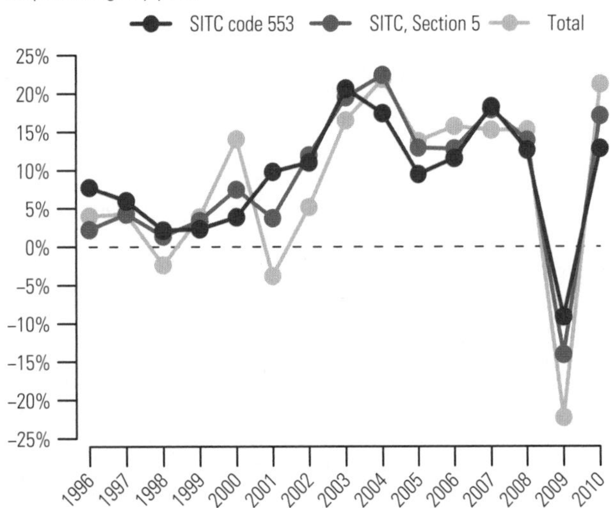

Graph 2: Trade Balance by MDG regions 2010

(Bln US$)

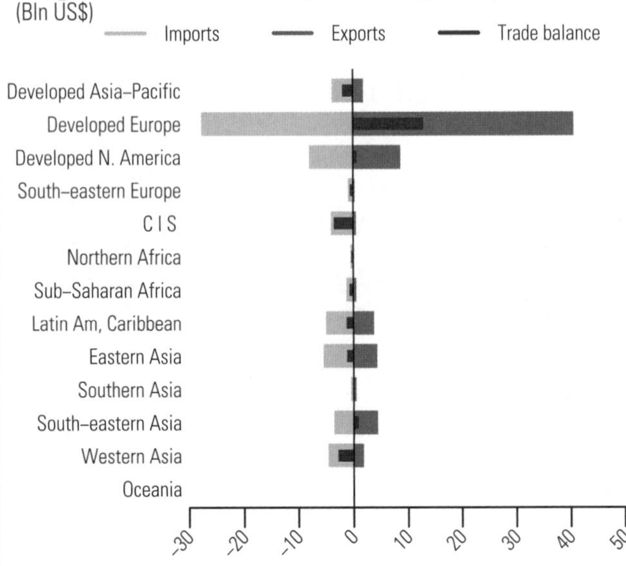

Table 2: Top exporting countries or areas in 2010

Country or area	Value (million US$)	Avg. Growth (%) 06-10	Growth (%) 09-10	World share %	Cum.
World	67369.9	8.1	12.9	100.0	
France	12418.3	3.5	4.7	18.4	18.4
Germany	7572.4	7.5	9.9	11.2	29.7
USA	7188.5	7.6	12.3	10.7	40.3
United Kingdom	3947.5	-0.6	2.5	5.9	46.2
Italy	3130.0	3.2	11.7	4.6	50.8
Spain	2773.9	10.2	19.5	4.1	55.0
Poland	2414.8	21.0	13.2	3.6	58.6
Belgium	2231.6	14.4	15.0	3.3	61.9
China	2076.4	12.9	25.8	3.1	64.9
Singapore	2068.7	14.8	45.6	3.1	68.0
Mexico	1571.4	19.7	-2.5	2.3	70.3
Thailand	1556.0	22.8	43.8	2.3	72.7
Japan	1505.3	15.8	24.9	2.2	74.9
Canada	1442.4	5.6	16.6	2.1	77.0
Netherlands	1381.9	1.5	-0.8	2.1	79.1

Table 3: Top importing countries or areas in 2010

Country or area	Value (million US$)	Avg. Growth (%) 06-10	Growth (%) 09-10	World share %	Cum.
World	64958.0	8.0	10.9	100.0	
USA	5648.8	5.5	17.9	8.7	8.7
Germany	4357.3	5.0	7.3	6.7	15.4
United Kingdom	4135.2	2.8	7.2	6.4	21.8
Russian Federation	2621.7	14.7	21.7	4.0	25.8
France	2421.1	3.1	3.9	3.7	29.5
Japan	2347.3	9.7	22.5	3.6	33.1
Canada	2287.5	6.7	12.2	3.5	36.7
Italy	2134.4	3.8	6.7	3.3	40.0
China, Hong Kong SAR	2073.3	15.0	27.2	3.2	43.1
Spain	2032.2	4.8	4.9	3.1	46.3
Netherlands	1743.8	4.1	-6.0	2.7	49.0
Belgium	1692.8	8.9	2.6	2.6	51.6
Singapore	1639.9	10.2	28.5	2.5	54.1
United Arab Emirates	1532.9	12.4	4.1	2.4	56.4
Poland	1385.9	18.9	15.0	2.1	58.6

After several years of continuous growth marked by a peak of 34.3 bln US$ in 2008, the value (in current prices) of exports of soap, cleansing and polishing preparations (SITC group 554) dropped in 2009 (by 8.7 percent) but bounced back in 2010 by 8.9 percent to amount to 34.1 bln US$ (see table 2). Imports showed a similar development with an increase of 9.6 percent to 33.8 bln US$ in 2010 (see table 3). Graph 1 shows that the increase in exports for 2010 in this product group was exceeded by both the increase in world exports of chemicals and related products, nes (SITC section 5) of 17.1 percent and the increase in total world exports of 21.2 percent. Exports of soap, cleansing and polishing preparations (SITC group 554) accounted for 2.1 percent of world exports of SITC section 5 and 0.2 percent of total world exports in 2010 (see table 1).

The top exporting countries in 2010 were Germany, USA and Belgium (see table 2), accounting respectively for 12.9, 11.9 and 5.9 percent of world exports. Germany is also the top destination, together with France and United Kingdom (see table 3). By MDG regions (see graph 2), Developed Europe accounted for a majority of trade in soap, cleansing and polishing preparations (SITC group 554). Its exports were valued at 18.4 bln US$ and imports, at 15.2 bln US$ resulting in a trade surplus of 3.2 bln US$. Top trade surpluses were also recorded by Developed North America (+1.3 bln US$) and South-eastern Asia (+0.6 bln US$). Top trade deficits were recorded by Commonwealth of Independent States (-1.3 bln US$), Latin America & the Caribbean (-0.9 bln US$) and Sub-Saharan Africa (-0.7 bln US$).

Table 1: Imports (Imp.) and exports (Exp.), 1996-2010, in current prices

		1996	1997	1998	1999	2000	2001	2002	2003	2004	2005	2006	2007	2008	2009	2010
Values in Bln US$	Imp.	11.5	11.6	11.9	12.6	12.7	13.4	15.1	17.9	20.3	22.1	24.8	28.4	33.2	30.8	33.8
	Exp.	12.1	12.2	12.5	13.0	13.0	13.6	15.4	18.3	20.8	22.3	25.0	29.0	34.3	31.4	34.1
As a percentage of SITC section (%)	Imp.	2.2	2.2	2.2	2.2	2.1	2.1	2.2	2.1	2.0	1.9	1.9	1.9	1.9	2.1	1.9
	Exp.	2.5	2.4	2.4	2.5	2.3	2.3	2.3	2.3	2.2	2.1	2.0	2.0	2.1	2.2	2.1
As a percentage of world trade (%)	Imp.	0.2	0.2	0.2	0.2	0.2	0.2	0.2	0.2	0.2	0.2	0.2	0.2	0.2	0.2	0.2
	Exp.	0.2	0.2	0.2	0.2	0.2	0.2	0.2	0.2	0.2	0.2	0.2	0.2	0.2	0.3	0.2

Graph 1: Annual growth rates of exports, 1996–2010

(In percentage by year)

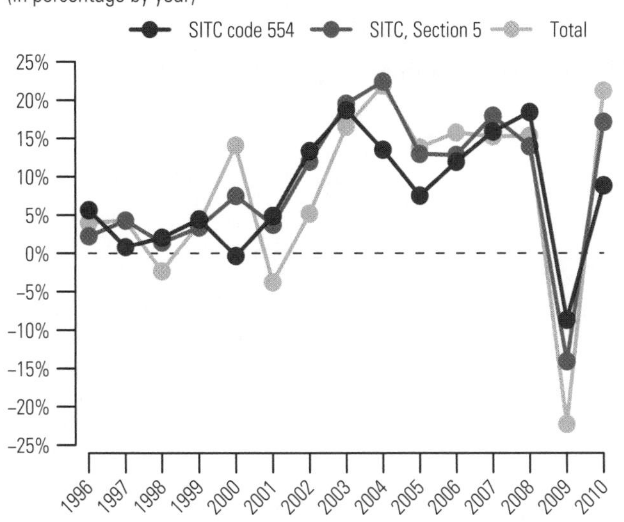

Graph 2: Trade Balance by MDG regions 2010

(Bln US$)

Imports — Exports — Trade balance

Developed Asia-Pacific
Developed Europe
Developed N. America
South-eastern Europe
C I S
Northern Africa
Sub-Saharan Africa
Latin Am, Caribbean
Eastern Asia
Southern Asia
South-eastern Asia
Western Asia
Oceania

-20 -15 -10 -5 0 5 10 15 20

Table 2: Top exporting countries or areas in 2010

Country or area	Value (million US$)	Avg. Growth (%) 06-10	Growth (%) 09-10	World share %	Cum.
World	34 138.1	8.1	8.9	100.0	
Germany	4 402.1	5.9	5.6	12.9	12.9
USA	4 078.9	10.1	13.5	11.9	24.8
Belgium	2 029.8	5.0	6.7	5.9	30.8
France	2 024.5	7.1	0.2	5.9	36.7
United Kingdom	1 687.3	2.8	-4.1	4.9	41.7
Italy	1 496.1	0.7	-1.4	4.4	46.0
Netherlands	1 434.3	4.6	22.5	4.2	50.2
China	1 297.7	32.3	33.8	3.8	54.0
Japan	1 060.0	9.7	31.6	3.1	57.2
Spain	973.5	0.7	1.3	2.9	60.0
Poland	887.1	15.7	3.5	2.6	62.6
Czech Rep.	751.4	8.1	-0.6	2.2	64.8
Turkey	644.0	8.3	5.2	1.9	66.7
Malaysia	637.4	13.2	14.7	1.9	68.6
Indonesia	589.6	13.4	10.7	1.7	70.3

Table 3: Top importing countries or areas in 2010

Country or area	Value (million US$)	Avg. Growth (%) 06-10	Growth (%) 09-10	World share %	Cum.
World	33 795.9	8.1	9.6	100.0	
Germany	2 346.7	5.6	8.1	6.9	6.9
France	1 930.2	2.0	-0.9	5.7	12.7
United Kingdom	1 693.8	3.0	1.5	5.0	17.7
Canada	1 662.9	8.0	8.0	4.9	22.6
USA	1 569.3	3.0	15.1	4.6	27.2
Belgium	1 338.6	4.7	7.2	4.0	31.2
China	1 294.5	13.5	24.4	3.8	35.0
Netherlands	997.5	6.8	7.3	3.0	38.0
Italy	917.6	3.6	3.2	2.7	40.7
Russian Federation	761.2	15.8	25.5	2.3	42.9
Spain	750.3	2.6	-4.7	2.2	45.2
Poland	705.5	11.7	17.6	2.1	47.2
Japan	685.4	5.8	7.7	2.0	49.3
Other Asia, nes	627.5	13.0	50.2	1.9	51.1
Austria	520.8	6.6	0.7	1.5	52.7

562 Fertilizers (other than those of group 272)

After several years of continuous growth marked by a peak of 71.6 bln US$ in 2008, the value (in current prices) of exports of fertilizers, other than those of group 272 (SITC group 562) contracted sharply in 2009 (by 44.7 percent) but bounced back in 2010 by 34.4 percent to amount to 53.2 bln US$ (see table 2). Imports showed a similar development with an increase of 28.7 percent to 57.7 bln US$ in 2010 (see table 3). Graph 1 shows that the increase in exports for 2010 in this product group exceeded both the increase in world exports of chemicals and related products, nes (SITC section 5) of 17.1 percent and the increase in total world exports of 21.2 percent. Exports of fertilizers, other than those of group 272 (SITC group 562) accounted for 3.2 percent of world exports of SITC section 5 and 0.4 percent of total world exports in 2010 (see table 1).

Exports of Russian Federation, the top exporting country in 2010, increased by 34.2 percent and accounted for 13.9 percent of world exports (see table 2). Other top exporting countries were Canada and China, respectively with 11.3 and 10.1 percent of world exports. Top destinations were USA, India and Brazil (see table 3). By MDG regions (see graph 2), Commonwealth of Independent States recorded a trade surplus of 10.4 bln US$. Top trade surpluses were also recorded by Western Asia (+4.9 bln US$) and Northern Africa (+3.3 bln US$). Major deficits were recorded by Latin America and the Caribbean (-8.8 bln US$) and Southern Asia (-7.4 bln US$) among others.

Table 1: Imports (Imp.) and exports (Exp.), 1996-2010, in current prices

		1996	1997	1998	1999	2000	2001	2002	2003	2004	2005	2006	2007	2008	2009	2010
Values in Bln US$	Imp.	21.0	19.1	18.3	17.4	17.6	17.4	17.7	21.5	27.7	32.6	33.3	46.0	86.8	44.9	57.7
	Exp.	17.9	16.4	15.8	15.0	12.4	12.2	12.4	15.4	19.2	23.7	24.4	36.0	71.6	39.6	53.2
As a percentage of SITC section (%)	Imp.	4.1	3.6	3.4	3.1	2.9	2.7	2.5	2.6	2.7	2.8	2.6	3.0	5.0	3.0	3.3
	Exp.	3.7	3.3	3.1	2.9	2.2	2.1	1.9	2.0	2.0	2.2	2.0	2.5	4.3	2.8	3.2
As a percentage of world trade (%)	Imp.	0.4	0.3	0.3	0.3	0.3	0.3	0.3	0.3	0.3	0.3	0.3	0.3	0.5	0.4	0.4
	Exp.	0.3	0.3	0.3	0.3	0.2	0.2	0.2	0.2	0.2	0.2	0.2	0.3	0.4	0.3	0.4

Graph 1: Annual growth rates of exports, 1996–2010

(In percentage by year)

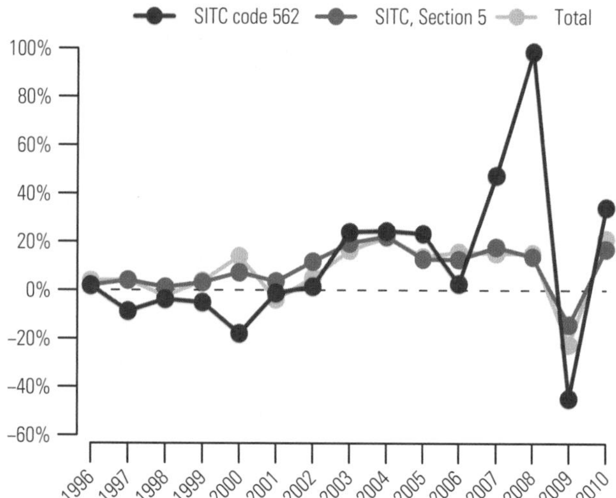

Graph 2: Trade Balance by MDG regions 2010

(Bln US$)

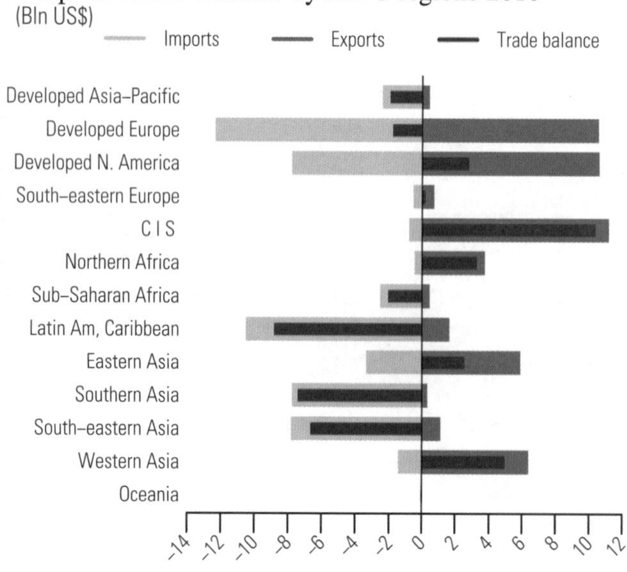

Table 2: Top exporting countries or areas in 2010

Country or area	Value (million US$)	Avg. Growth (%) 06-10	Growth (%) 09-10	World share %	Cum.
World	53221.4	21.5	34.4	100.0	
Russian Federation	7383.3	16.0	34.2	13.9	13.9
Canada	6019.6	18.9	44.2	11.3	25.2
China	5385.8	47.4	110.8	10.1	35.3
USA	4573.7	...	11.3	8.6	43.9
Belarus	2445.8	21.2	55.7	4.6	48.5
Germany	2235.5	5.7	4.6	4.2	52.7
Belgium	1939.2	11.8	32.0	3.6	56.3
Netherlands	1825.5	9.1	11.9	3.4	59.8
Israel	1794.5	27.4	61.0	3.4	63.1
Morocco	1561.9	32.0	123.3	2.9	66.1
Saudi Arabia	1249.8	16.9	17.0	2.3	68.4
Egypt	1151.8	96.2	1.0	2.2	70.6
Jordan	1083.4	50.1	37.6	2.0	72.6
Spain	981.4	31.3	80.0	1.8	74.5
Qatar	*976.8*	9.7	24.3	1.8	76.3

Table 3: Top importing countries or areas in 2010

Country or area	Value (million US$)	Avg. Growth (%) 06-10	Growth (%) 09-10	World share %	Cum.
World	57748.3	14.7	28.7	100.0	
USA	7008.7	17.1	61.4	12.1	12.1
India	5555.5	20.4	-8.2	9.6	21.8
Brazil	4929.2	20.3	26.7	8.5	30.3
China	2558.6	0.9	28.9	4.4	34.7
France	2372.6	12.2	48.4	4.1	38.8
Viet Nam	*2356.0*	36.3	66.9	4.1	42.9
Thailand	2000.8	21.0	50.2	3.5	46.4
Malaysia	1530.7	23.1	34.5	2.7	49.0
Indonesia	1370.2	25.0	64.7	2.4	51.4
Belgium	1343.7	14.4	24.7	2.3	53.7
Germany	1342.8	9.8	25.5	2.3	56.1
Australia	1188.1	19.2	59.3	2.1	58.1
United Kingdom	1130.8	14.6	49.0	2.0	60.1
Mexico	1078.7	6.5	31.7	1.9	61.9
Turkey	1011.3	6.7	-3.8	1.8	63.7

After a drop of 18.4 percent in 2009, the value (in current prices) of exports of polymers of ethylene, in primary forms (SITC group 571) increased in 2010 by 26.7 percent to amount to 62.4 bln US$ (see table 2). Imports showed a similar development with an increase of 29.5 percent to 62.4 bln US$ in 2010 (see table 3). Graph 1 shows that the increase in exports for 2010 in this product group exceeded both the increase in world exports of chemicals and related products, nes (SITC section 5) of 17.1 percent and the increase in total world exports of 21.2 percent. Exports of polymers of ethylene, in primary forms (SITC group 571) accounted for 3.8 percent of world exports of SITC section 5 and 0.4 percent of total world exports in 2010 (see table 1).

USA, Saudi Arabia and Belgium were the top exporting countries in 2010 (see table 2). They accounted respectively for 11.3, 10.0 and 9.9 percent of world exports. Top destinations were China, Germany and USA (see table 3). By MDG regions (see graph 2), Developed Europe accounted for a large share of trade in polymers of ethylene, in primary forms (SITC group 571). Its exports and imports were valued respectively at 22.0 bln US$ and 21.5 bln US$ resulting in a trade surplus of 0.5 bln US$. Top trade surpluses were recorded by Western Asia (+7.8 bln US$) and Developed North America (+6.0 bln US$). Significant deficits were recorded by Eastern Asia (-6.9 bln US$), Latin America and the Caribbean (-3.8 bln US$) and Sub-Saharan Africa (-1.7 bln US$).

Table 1: Imports (Imp.) and exports (Exp.), 1996-2010, in current prices

		1996	1997	1998	1999	2000	2001	2002	2003	2004	2005	2006	2007	2008	2009	2010
Values in Bln US$	Imp.	16.9	18.6	17.2	17.5	20.4	20.0	20.1	24.3	32.8	40.8	47.5	55.7	61.6	48.2	62.4
	Exp.	15.5	17.0	16.3	16.7	19.1	18.8	18.6	22.6	31.2	39.9	46.3	55.2	60.4	49.3	62.4
As a percentage of SITC section (%)	Imp.	3.3	3.5	3.2	3.1	3.3	3.2	2.9	2.9	3.2	3.6	3.7	3.7	3.6	3.3	3.6
	Exp.	3.2	3.4	3.2	3.2	3.4	3.2	2.8	2.9	3.2	3.7	3.8	3.8	3.7	3.5	3.8
As a percentage of world trade (%)	Imp.	0.3	0.3	0.3	0.3	0.3	0.3	0.3	0.3	0.4	0.4	0.4	0.4	0.4	0.4	0.4
	Exp.	0.3	0.3	0.3	0.3	0.3	0.3	0.3	0.3	0.3	0.4	0.4	0.4	0.4	0.4	0.4

Graph 1: Annual growth rates of exports, 1996–2010

(In percentage by year)

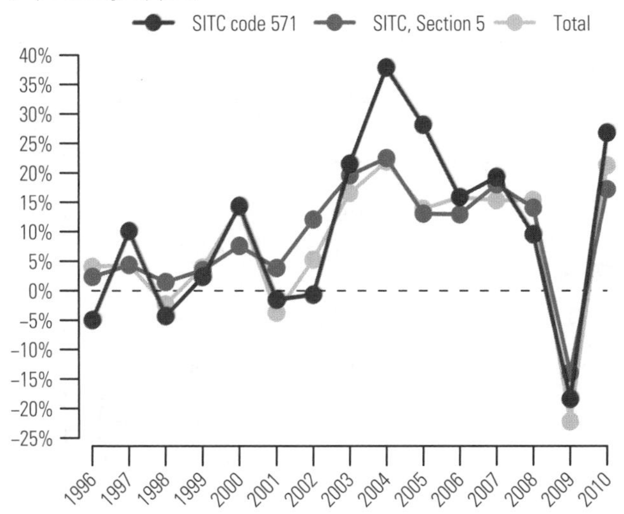

Table 2: Top exporting countries or areas in 2010

Country or area	Value (million US$)	Avg. Growth (%) 06-10	Growth (%) 09-10	World share %	Cum.
World	62429.3	7.8	26.7	100.0	
USA	7067.7	8.0	11.3	11.3	11.3
Saudi Arabia	6256.9	15.9	82.4	10.0	21.3
Belgium	6172.8	2.1	30.2	9.9	31.2
Canada	3566.1	-2.1	23.7	5.7	36.9
Germany	3507.8	2.7	21.1	5.6	42.6
Netherlands	3317.6	4.4	28.7	5.3	47.9
Rep. of Korea	3264.3	7.5	10.3	5.2	53.1
Singapore	2920.8	15.1	55.9	4.7	57.8
Kuwait	*2799.8*	34.8	27.2	4.5	62.3
France	2180.1	2.3	10.2	3.5	65.8
Thailand	1841.1	13.7	61.4	2.9	68.7
Iran	1814.4	99.0	6.3	2.9	71.6
Qatar	*1408.5*	6.1	24.3	2.3	73.9
Japan	1379.4	10.5	7.0	2.2	76.1
Other Asia, nes	1269.3	10.4	20.6	2.0	78.1

Graph 2: Trade Balance by MDG regions 2010

(Bln US$)

Imports — Exports — Trade balance

Developed Asia-Pacific
Developed Europe
Developed N. America
South-eastern Europe
C I S
Northern Africa
Sub-Saharan Africa
Latin Am, Caribbean
Eastern Asia
Southern Asia
South-eastern Asia
Western Asia
Oceania

-25 -20 -15 -10 -5 0 5 10 15 20 25

Table 3: Top importing countries or areas in 2010

Country or area	Value (million US$)	Avg. Growth (%) 06-10	Growth (%) 09-10	World share %	Cum.
World	62431.5	7.1	29.5	100.0	
China	11064.9	14.7	18.7	17.7	17.7
Germany	3934.3	3.6	34.0	6.3	24.0
USA	3452.0	-2.8	34.6	5.5	29.6
Belgium	3070.0	3.2	34.0	4.9	34.5
Italy	2694.5	-0.6	30.8	4.3	38.8
France	2160.1	1.4	20.3	3.5	42.2
United Kingdom	1886.8	2.7	28.1	3.0	45.3
Mexico	1677.2	-0.3	26.6	2.7	48.0
Turkey	1636.5	12.3	41.6	2.6	50.6
India	1614.4	31.9	27.5	2.6	53.2
Viet Nam	*1450.9*	22.1	66.9	2.3	55.5
Singapore	1419.9	79.1	134.9	2.3	57.8
Spain	1280.0	-5.5	15.2	2.1	59.8
Canada	1153.4	-2.4	33.8	1.8	61.7
Poland	1090.7	8.3	34.5	1.7	63.4

572 Polymers of styrene, in primary forms

After a sharp decline of 27.5 percent in 2009, the value (in current prices) of exports of polymers of styrene, in primary forms (SITC group 572) rose significantly in 2010 by 34.2 percent to amount to 23.6 bln US$ (see table 2). Imports showed a similar development with an increase of 31.6 percent to 24.3 bln US$ in 2010 (see table 3). Graph 1 shows that the increase in exports for 2010 in this product group exceeded both the increase in world exports of chemicals and related products, nes (SITC section 5) of 17.1 percent and the increase in total world exports of 21.2 percent. Exports of polymers of styrene, in primary forms (SITC group 572) accounted for 1.4 percent of world exports of SITC section 5 and 0.2 percent of total world exports in 2010 (see table 1).

Rep. of Korea was the top exporting country and accounted for 17.1 percent of world exports. China, the top destination, accounted for 27.4 percent of world imports (see table 3). By MDG regions (see graph 2), Eastern Asia accounted for a large share of trade in polymers of styrene, in primary forms (SITC group 572). Its exports amounted to 11.3 bln US$ and its imports, to 9.5 bln US$, resulting in a trade surplus of 1.8 bln US$. Trade surpluses were also recorded by Developed Asia-Pacific (+0.6 bln US$) and South-eastern Asia (+0.2 bln US$). Significant deficits were recorded by Western Asia (-0.8 bln US$), Latin America and the Caribbean (-0.7 bln US$) and Commonwealth of Independent States (-0.5 bln US$).

Table 1: Imports (Imp.) and exports (Exp.), 1996-2010, in current prices

		1996	1997	1998	1999	2000	2001	2002	2003	2004	2005	2006	2007	2008	2009	2010
Values in Bln US$	Imp.	10.5	10.2	10.0	9.9	12.3	10.8	11.7	13.3	16.7	18.7	20.4	23.7	24.1	18.5	24.3
	Exp.	9.9	9.8	9.3	9.4	12.1	10.2	11.3	13.0	16.9	19.1	21.0	24.5	24.2	17.6	23.6
As a percentage of SITC section (%)	Imp.	2.0	1.9	1.8	1.8	2.0	1.7	1.7	1.6	1.6	1.6	1.6	1.6	1.4	1.2	1.4
	Exp.	2.0	1.9	1.8	1.8	2.1	1.7	1.7	1.7	1.8	1.8	1.7	1.7	1.5	1.2	1.4
As a percentage of world trade (%)	Imp.	0.2	0.2	0.2	0.2	0.2	0.2	0.2	0.2	0.2	0.2	0.2	0.2	0.1	0.1	0.2
	Exp.	0.2	0.2	0.2	0.2	0.2	0.2	0.2	0.2	0.2	0.2	0.2	0.2	0.2	0.1	0.2

Graph 1: Annual growth rates of exports, 1996–2010

(In percentage by year)

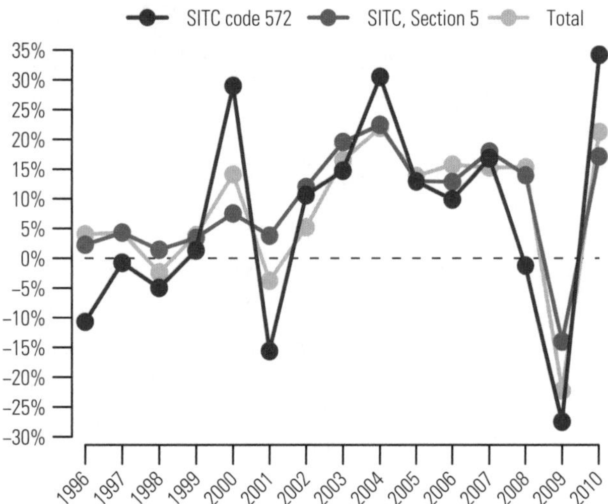

Graph 2: Trade Balance by MDG regions 2010

(Bln US$)

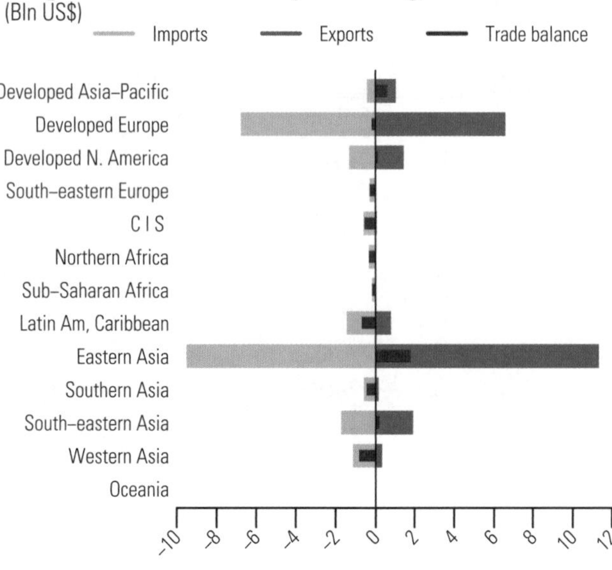

Table 2: Top exporting countries or areas in 2010

Country or area	Value (million US$)	Avg. Growth (%) 06-10	Growth (%) 09-10	World share %	Cum.
World	23566.6	2.9	34.2	100.0	
Rep. of Korea	4033.5	8.7	42.4	17.1	17.1
Other Asia, nes	3952.7	9.4	47.8	16.8	33.9
China, Hong Kong SAR	2650.7	-0.5	21.7	11.2	45.1
Belgium	2276.8	4.1	44.8	9.7	54.8
USA	1341.1	-0.2	30.1	5.7	60.5
Japan	1011.8	2.9	36.1	4.3	64.8
Germany	995.0	-9.2	34.3	4.2	69.0
France	781.2	-2.9	21.4	3.3	72.3
Netherlands	684.9	-10.4	-16.9	2.9	75.2
Malaysia	680.3	10.7	40.4	2.9	78.1
China	677.4	21.2	51.6	2.9	81.0
Singapore	610.5	7.4	33.2	2.6	83.6
Thailand	556.3	1.2	24.4	2.4	85.9
Mexico	508.1	6.0	43.6	2.2	88.1
Spain	361.0	0.4	28.2	1.5	89.6

Table 3: Top importing countries or areas in 2010

Country or area	Value (million US$)	Avg. Growth (%) 06-10	Growth (%) 09-10	World share %	Cum.
World	24332.8	4.5	31.6	100.0	
China	6678.9	8.6	23.5	27.4	27.4
China, Hong Kong SAR	2542.7	-2.4	29.8	10.4	37.9
Germany	1283.5	5.8	42.8	5.3	43.2
Italy	1090.1	-0.8	36.6	4.5	47.7
USA	904.8	-6.2	31.0	3.7	51.4
Turkey	779.7	5.3	57.8	3.2	54.6
Mexico	734.2	0.2	26.2	3.0	57.6
France	668.0	2.9	35.2	2.7	60.3
Poland	550.3	4.8	33.9	2.3	62.6
Viet Nam	*429.3*	24.5	66.9	1.8	64.4
Thailand	414.6	7.8	54.0	1.7	66.1
Malaysia	407.2	0.0	35.8	1.7	67.7
Canada	405.0	-3.9	27.7	1.7	69.4
United Kingdom	371.7	-1.7	28.2	1.5	70.9
Russian Federation	343.5	10.5	53.1	1.4	72.3

After a sharp decline of 24.7 percent in 2009, the value (in current prices) of exports of polymers of vinyl chloride or of other halogenated olefins (SITC group 573) rose significantly in 2010 by 31.4 percent to amount to 17.1 bln US$ (see table 2). Imports showed a similar development with an increase of 28.3 percent to 17.3 bln US$ in 2010 (see table 3). Graph 1 shows that the increase in exports for 2010 in this product group exceeded both the increase in world exports of chemicals and related products, nes (SITC section 5) of 17.1 percent and the increase in total world exports of 21.2 percent. Exports of polymers of vinyl chloride or of other halogenated olefins (SITC group 573) accounted for 1.0 percent of world exports of SITC section 5 and 0.1 percent of total world exports in 2010 (see table 1).

USA, Germany and Japan were the top exporting countries in 2010 (see table 2). They accounted respectively for 21.6, 11.9 and 7.6 percent of world exports. Top destinations were China, Germany and Italy (see table 3). By MDG regions (see graph 2), Developed Europe accounted for a large share of trade in polymers of vinyl chloride or of other halogenated olefins (SITC group 573). Its exports amounted to 7.2 bln US$ and imports, 5.8 bln US$ resulting in a trade surplus of 1.4 bln US$. Top trade surpluses were also recorded by Developed North America (+2.5 bln US$) and Developed Asia-Pacific (+1.0 bln US$). Significant deficits were recorded by Western Asia (-1.1 bln US$), Latin America and the Caribbean (-1.0 bln US$) and Southern Asia (-1.0 bln US$).

Table 1: Imports (Imp.) and exports (Exp.), 1996-2010, in current prices

		1996	1997	1998	1999	2000	2001	2002	2003	2004	2005	2006	2007	2008	2009	2010
Values in Bln US$	Imp.	7.5	8.2	8.0	7.7	9.1	8.0	8.2	9.2	11.6	12.6	13.8	16.0	17.7	13.5	17.3
	Exp.	6.7	7.7	7.6	7.3	8.6	7.9	7.9	8.9	11.6	12.3	13.5	16.1	17.2	13.0	17.1
As a percentage of SITC section (%)	Imp.	1.5	1.5	1.5	1.4	1.5	1.3	1.2	1.1	1.2	1.1	1.1	1.1	1.0	0.9	1.0
	Exp.	1.4	1.5	1.5	1.4	1.5	1.3	1.2	1.1	1.2	1.1	1.1	1.1	1.0	0.9	1.0
As a percentage of world trade (%)	Imp.	0.1	0.1	0.1	0.1	0.1	0.1	0.1	0.1	0.1	0.1	0.1	0.1	0.1	0.1	0.1
	Exp.	0.1	0.1	0.1	0.1	0.1	0.1	0.1	0.1	0.1	0.1	0.1	0.1	0.1	0.1	0.1

Graph 1: Annual growth rates of exports, 1996–2010
(In percentage by year)

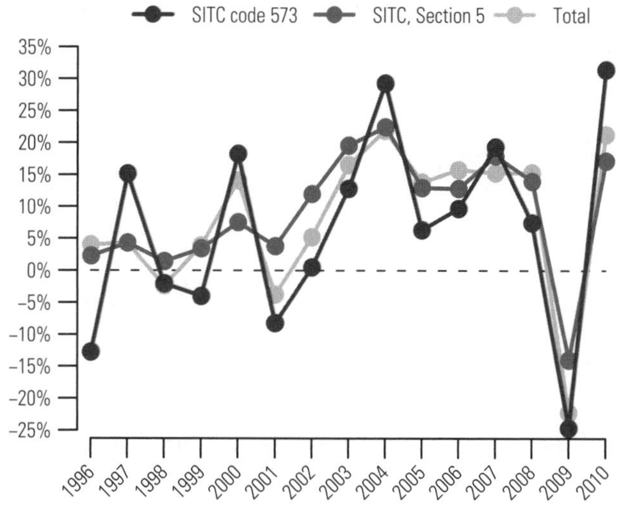

Graph 2: Trade Balance by MDG regions 2010
(Bln US$)

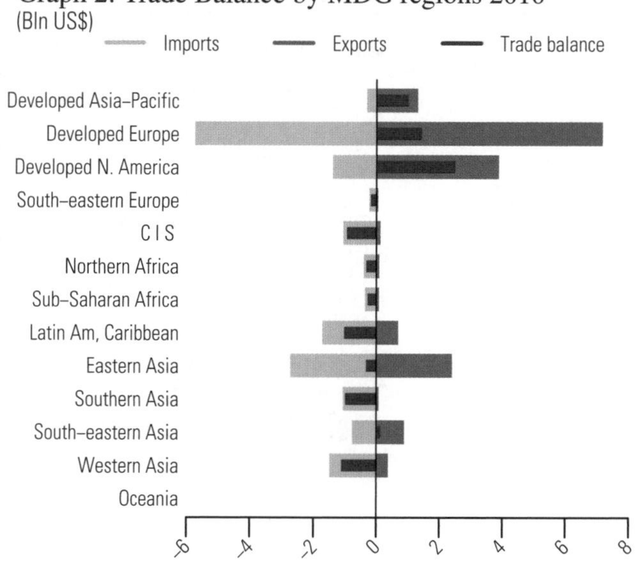

Table 2: Top exporting countries or areas in 2010

Country or area	Value (million US$)	Avg. Growth (%) 06-10	Growth (%) 09-10	World share %	Cum.
World	17063.1	6.1	31.4	100.0	
USA	3690.1	20.8	42.6	21.6	21.6
Germany	2032.5	2.6	27.8	11.9	33.5
Japan	1292.7	4.2	33.3	7.6	41.1
Netherlands	1041.4	4.9	27.7	6.1	47.2
Belgium	970.3	5.7	29.1	5.7	52.9
France	938.4	-3.9	19.6	5.5	58.4
Other Asia, nes	901.3	10.8	17.4	5.3	63.7
Rep. of Korea	713.3	10.6	19.1	4.2	67.9
China	544.8	3.9	42.9	3.2	71.1
Italy	471.8	0.4	33.2	2.8	73.8
Thailand	406.7	9.5	12.9	2.4	76.2
United Kingdom	320.0	-0.2	30.1	1.9	78.1
Saudi Arabia	314.4	32.0	177.3	1.8	79.9
Colombia	293.0	5.8	18.8	1.7	81.6
Sweden	268.6	5.4	28.4	1.6	83.2

Table 3: Top importing countries or areas in 2010

Country or area	Value (million US$)	Avg. Growth (%) 06-10	Growth (%) 09-10	World share %	Cum.
World	17294.1	5.9	28.3	100.0	
China	2061.0	7.9	8.9	11.9	11.9
Germany	1085.3	-1.5	25.4	6.3	18.2
Italy	1076.7	4.0	37.9	6.2	24.4
Turkey	859.9	7.0	42.3	5.0	29.4
USA	813.4	-4.5	59.4	4.7	34.1
India	742.9	32.6	13.9	4.3	38.4
Russian Federation	630.0	20.2	80.7	3.6	42.0
Belgium	627.6	8.6	24.7	3.6	45.7
Canada	584.5	-3.1	24.4	3.4	49.0
Brazil	539.2	33.9	60.1	3.1	52.2
France	508.6	-0.5	9.3	2.9	55.1
United Kingdom	464.1	-1.4	36.1	2.7	57.8
Mexico	462.4	11.9	25.3	2.7	60.5
Poland	447.2	4.2	36.0	2.6	63.0
Rep. of Korea	295.4	12.5	67.9	1.7	64.8

Source: UN Comtrade

574 Polyacetals, epoxide resins, etc, and other polyethers in primary forms

After a drop of 20.5 percent in 2009, the value (in current prices) of exports of polyacetals, epoxide resins, etc, and other polyethers in primary forms (SITC group 574) increased in 2010 by 29.3 percent to amount to 48.0 bln US$ (see table 2). Imports showed a similar development with an increase of 31.2 percent to 49.1 bln US$ in 2010 (see table 3). Graph 1 shows that the increase in exports for 2010 in this product group exceeded the increase in world exports of chemicals and related products, nes (SITC section 5) of 17.1 percent and the increase in total world exports of 21.2 percent. Exports of polyacetals, epoxide resins, etc, and other polyethers in primary forms (SITC group 574) accounted for 2.9 percent of world exports of SITC section 5 and 0.3 percent of total world exports in 2010 (see table 1).

The top exporting countries in 2010 were USA, Rep. of Korea and Germany (see table 2). They accounted respectively for 11.0, 8.9 and 8.3 percent of world exports. Top destinations were China, Germany and China, Hong Kong SAR (see table 3). By MDG regions (see graph 2), Developed Europe accounted for a large share of trade in polyacetals, epoxide resins, etc, and other polyethers in primary forms (SITC group 574). In 2010, its exports amounted to 18.2 bln US$ while imports were valued at 16.9 bln US$ resulting in a trade surplus of 1.3 bln US$. A large surplus was also recorded by Developed North America (+2.8 bln US$). Top trade deficits were recorded by Latin America and the Caribbean (-2.5 bln US$), Western Asia (-1.3 bln US$) and Commonwealth of Independent States (-1.2 bln US$).

Table 1: Imports (Imp.) and exports (Exp.), 1996-2010, in current prices

		1996	1997	1998	1999	2000	2001	2002	2003	2004	2005	2006	2007	2008	2009	2010
Values in Bln US$	Imp.	16.1	16.6	17.1	17.6	20.0	19.2	20.2	24.4	30.4	36.8	41.2	47.5	49.3	37.4	49.1
	Exp.	14.8	16.2	16.4	16.2	18.7	18.2	19.4	23.4	29.2	35.4	39.7	45.6	46.7	37.1	48.0
As a percentage of SITC section (%)	Imp.	3.1	3.1	3.2	3.1	3.3	3.0	2.9	2.9	3.0	3.2	3.2	3.1	2.9	2.5	2.8
	Exp.	3.1	3.2	3.2	3.1	3.3	3.1	2.9	3.0	3.0	3.3	3.2	3.2	2.8	2.6	2.9
As a percentage of world trade (%)	Imp.	0.3	0.3	0.3	0.3	0.3	0.3	0.3	0.3	0.3	0.3	0.3	0.3	0.3	0.3	0.3
	Exp.	0.3	0.3	0.3	0.3	0.3	0.3	0.3	0.3	0.3	0.3	0.3	0.3	0.3	0.3	0.3

Graph 1: Annual growth rates of exports, 1996–2010

(In percentage by year)

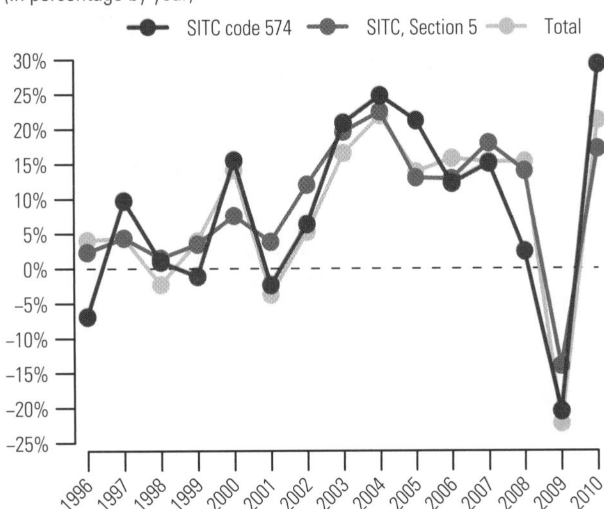

Graph 2: Trade Balance by MDG regions 2010

(Bln US$)

Imports | Exports | Trade balance

Developed Asia-Pacific
Developed Europe
Developed N. America
South-eastern Europe
C I S
Northern Africa
Sub-Saharan Africa
Latin Am, Caribbean
Eastern Asia
Southern Asia
South-eastern Asia
Western Asia
Oceania

-20 -15 -10 -5 0 5 10 15 20

Table 2: Top exporting countries or areas in 2010

Country or area	Value (million US$)	Avg. Growth (%) 06-10	Growth (%) 09-10	World share %	Cum.
World	47 999.3	4.9	29.3	100.0	
USA	5 301.2	2.6	37.9	11.0	11.0
Rep. of Korea	4 265.5	12.0	32.8	8.9	19.9
Germany	3 983.1	0.1	-0.2	8.3	28.2
Netherlands	3 885.4	4.2	22.0	8.1	36.3
Other Asia, nes	3 505.1	9.7	43.3	7.3	43.6
China	2 900.7	8.6	49.3	6.0	49.7
Japan	2 736.3	4.9	39.6	5.7	55.4
Belgium	2 265.7	3.1	22.5	4.7	60.1
China, Hong Kong SAR	2 012.1	6.1	40.2	4.2	64.3
Thailand	2 005.5	7.0	30.0	4.2	68.5
Spain	1 899.5	2.1	43.4	4.0	72.4
Italy	1 821.6	2.3	26.6	3.8	76.2
Singapore	1 688.5	-0.6	43.4	3.5	79.7
France	867.9	-2.4	18.1	1.8	81.5
Malaysia	790.5	11.5	39.7	1.6	83.2

Table 3: Top importing countries or areas in 2010

Country or area	Value (million US$)	Avg. Growth (%) 06-10	Growth (%) 09-10	World share %	Cum.
World	49 124.4	4.5	31.2	100.0	
China	8 553.4	10.8	39.4	17.4	17.4
Germany	3 259.9	2.6	31.3	6.6	24.0
China, Hong Kong SAR	2 371.9	3.4	46.4	4.8	28.9
Italy	2 033.8	-1.0	19.7	4.1	33.0
USA	1 995.5	-5.6	19.5	4.1	37.1
Japan	1 889.8	8.4	41.9	3.8	40.9
France	1 865.3	0.1	17.3	3.8	44.7
Belgium	1 668.2	2.1	25.1	3.4	48.1
Mexico	1 140.9	0.3	20.2	2.3	50.4
United Kingdom	1 081.9	0.4	25.5	2.2	52.6
Other Asia, nes	1 003.5	1.5	47.5	2.0	54.7
Turkey	982.0	9.4	41.8	2.0	56.7
Spain	924.5	-1.6	23.1	1.9	58.6
Netherlands	921.9	-0.6	17.2	1.9	60.4
Poland	879.7	10.4	26.9	1.8	62.2

After a drop of 23.4 percent in 2009, the value (in current prices) of exports of other plastics, in primary forms (SITC group 575) increased in 2010 by 30.6 percent to amount to 94.6 bln US$ (see table 2). Imports showed a similar development with an increase of 31.2 percent to 99.0 bln US$ in 2010 (see table 3). Graph 1 shows that the increase in exports for 2010 in this product group exceeded both the increase in world exports of chemicals and related products, nes (SITC section 5) of 17.1 percent and the increase in total world exports of 21.2 percent. Exports of other plastics, in primary forms (SITC group 575) accounted for 5.7 percent of world exports of SITC section 5 and 0.6 percent of total world exports in 2010 (see table 1).

USA, Germany and Belgium were the top exporting countries in 2010 (see table 2). They accounted respectively for 14.6, 10.8 and 10.2 percent of world exports. Top destinations were China, Germany and Italy (see table 3). By MDG regions (see graph 2), Developed Europe accounted for a majority of exports and a large share of imports of other plastics, in primary forms (SITC group 575). In 2010, its exports were valued at 43.5 bln US$, and imports, at 39.5 bln US$, resulting in a trade surplus of 4.0 bln US$. Top trade surpluses were also recorded by Developed North America (+8.0 bln US$) and Developed Asia-Pacific (+3.5 bln US$). Eastern Asia and Latin America and the Caribbean recorded trade deficits amounting respectively to 6.6 bln US$ and 5.1 bln US$.

Table 1: Imports (Imp.) and exports (Exp.), 1996-2010, in current prices

		1996	1997	1998	1999	2000	2001	2002	2003	2004	2005	2006	2007	2008	2009	2010
Values in Bln US$	Imp.	31.6	32.8	31.8	32.2	34.5	34.4	37.6	44.8	55.4	64.6	73.9	86.9	94.3	75.5	99.0
	Exp.	30.8	30.6	29.7	30.4	33.4	32.8	36.8	44.4	55.3	65.2	75.2	88.1	94.6	72.4	94.6
As a percentage of SITC section (%)	Imp.	6.1	6.2	5.9	5.7	5.7	5.4	5.4	5.4	5.5	5.6	5.8	5.8	5.5	5.1	5.7
	Exp.	6.4	6.1	5.8	5.8	5.9	5.6	5.6	5.6	5.8	6.0	6.1	6.1	5.7	5.1	5.7
As a percentage of world trade (%)	Imp.	0.6	0.6	0.6	0.6	0.5	0.5	0.6	0.6	0.6	0.6	0.6	0.6	0.6	0.6	0.7
	Exp.	0.6	0.6	0.6	0.5	0.5	0.5	0.6	0.6	0.6	0.6	0.6	0.6	0.6	0.6	0.6

Graph 1: Annual growth rates of exports, 1996–2010
(In percentage by year)

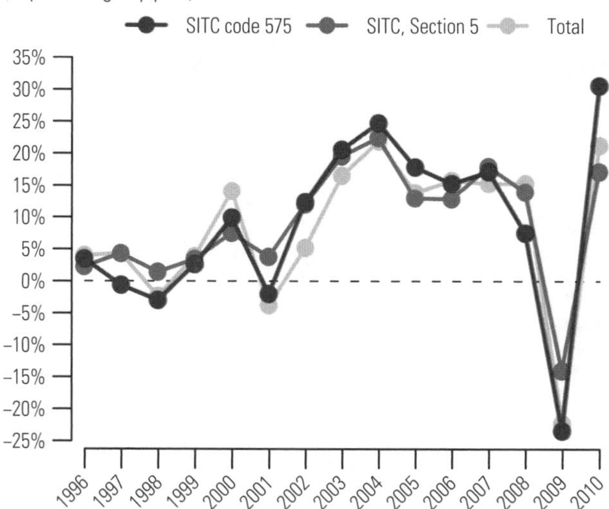

Graph 2: Trade Balance by MDG regions 2010
(Bln US$)

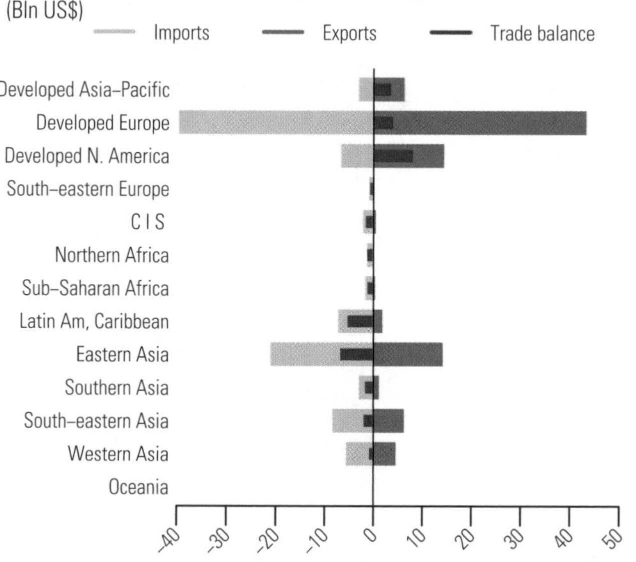

Table 2: Top exporting countries or areas in 2010

Country or area	Value (million US$)	Avg. Growth (%) 06-10	Growth (%) 09-10	World share %	Cum.
World	94591.1	5.9	30.6	100.0	
USA	13779.3	6.3	33.0	14.6	14.6
Germany	10256.2	-5.6	9.4	10.8	25.4
Belgium	9661.9	3.1	28.2	10.2	35.6
Japan	6242.0	8.7	34.8	6.6	42.2
Rep. of Korea	5485.8	16.3	31.5	5.8	48.0
Netherlands	4803.6	2.9	22.9	5.1	53.1
France	4369.2	3.5	20.6	4.6	57.7
Singapore	4118.5	18.9	77.6	4.4	62.1
Saudi Arabia	3542.6	40.7	97.8	3.7	65.8
Other Asia, nes	3480.0	8.8	28.4	3.7	69.5
China	2986.5	22.6	55.3	3.2	72.7
Italy	2781.0	2.3	24.0	2.9	75.6
United Kingdom	2621.0	-1.9	12.3	2.8	78.4
China, Hong Kong SAR	2364.6	2.8	21.1	2.5	80.9
Spain	1957.2	6.8	32.0	2.1	82.9

Table 3: Top importing countries or areas in 2010

Country or area	Value (million US$)	Avg. Growth (%) 06-10	Growth (%) 09-10	World share %	Cum.
World	99027.8	7.6	31.2	100.0	
China	15222.0	15.1	26.5	15.4	15.4
Germany	7243.8	2.2	31.2	7.3	22.7
Italy	5214.9	3.6	34.2	5.3	28.0
France	5018.4	5.3	27.4	5.1	33.0
Belgium	4432.2	3.1	28.3	4.5	37.5
USA	4016.4	2.9	38.4	4.1	41.6
Turkey	3378.8	9.4	43.7	3.4	45.0
Mexico	2847.6	5.7	39.3	2.9	47.8
United Kingdom	2813.5	3.6	27.0	2.8	50.7
China, Hong Kong SAR	2525.5	0.0	33.1	2.6	53.2
Canada	2520.9	2.1	35.5	2.5	55.8
Japan	2279.0	10.0	43.0	2.3	58.1
Netherlands	2274.8	3.9	18.9	2.3	60.4
Spain	2122.2	-0.3	23.1	2.1	62.5
Rep. of Korea	1910.3	6.5	34.5	1.9	64.4

Source: UN Comtrade

579 Waste, parings and scrap, of plastics

After a drop of 9.1 percent in 2009, the value (in current prices) of exports of waste, parings and scrap of plastics (SITC group 579) increased in 2010 by 20.8 percent to amount to 6.2 bln US$ (see table 2). Imports showed a similar development with an increase of 31.6 percent to 8.5 bln US$ in 2010 (see table 3). Graph 1 shows that the increase in exports for 2010 in this product group was greater than the increase in world exports of chemicals and related products, nes (SITC section 5) of 17.1 percent but less than the increase in total world exports of 21.2 percent. Exports of waste, parings and scrap of plastics (SITC group 579) accounted for 0.4 percent of world exports of SITC section 5 and less than 0.1 percent of total world exports in 2010 (see table 1).

The top exporting countries or areas in 2010 were China, Hong Kong SAR, USA and Japan (see table 2). They accounted respectively for 19.7, 15.3 and 13.2 percent of world exports. China was the destination of a majority of exports of waste, parings and scrap of plastics (SITC group 579). It accounted for 60.1 percent of world imports in 2010. Other major destinations were China, Hong Kong SAR and USA (see table 3). By MDG regions (see graph 2), Eastern Asia's exports were valued at 1.4 bln US$ while imports amounted to 6.9 bln US$ resulting in a trade deficit of 5.5 bln US$. Trade surpluses were recorded by Developed Europe (+1.1 bln US$), Developed Asia-Pacific (+0.9 bln US$) and Developed North America (+0.8 bln US$).

Table 1: Imports (Imp.) and exports (Exp.), 1996-2010, in current prices

		1996	1997	1998	1999	2000	2001	2002	2003	2004	2005	2006	2007	2008	2009	2010
Values in Bln US$	Imp.	1.1	1.0	1.2	1.2	1.6	1.6	1.6	2.0	3.1	4.4	5.6	6.4	7.9	6.4	8.5
	Exp.	1.0	0.9	1.1	1.1	1.4	1.4	1.5	1.8	2.6	3.6	4.4	5.3	5.7	5.1	6.2
As a percentage of SITC section (%)	Imp.	0.2	0.2	0.2	0.2	0.3	0.3	0.2	0.2	0.3	0.4	0.4	0.4	0.5	0.4	0.5
	Exp.	0.2	0.2	0.2	0.2	0.2	0.2	0.2	0.2	0.3	0.3	0.4	0.4	0.3	0.4	0.4
As a percentage of world trade (%)	Imp.	0.0	0.0	0.0	0.0	0.0	0.0	0.0	0.0	0.0	0.0	0.0	0.0	0.0	0.1	0.1
	Exp.	0.0	0.0	0.0	0.0	0.0	0.0	0.0	0.0	0.0	0.0	0.0	0.0	0.0	0.0	0.0

Graph 1: Annual growth rates of exports, 1996–2010
(In percentage by year)

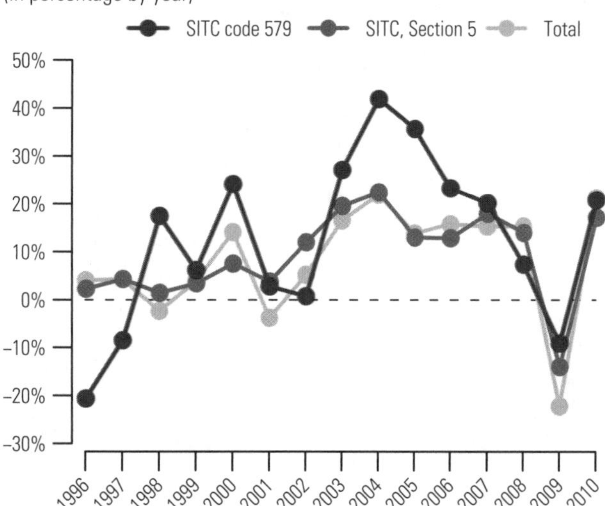

Table 2: Top exporting countries or areas in 2010

Country or area	Value (million US$)	Avg. Growth (%) 06-10	Growth (%) 09-10	World share %	Cum.
World	6217.2	9.1	20.8	100.0	
China, Hong Kong SAR	1222.5	5.1	7.8	19.7	19.7
USA	948.5	13.0	14.6	15.3	34.9
Japan	820.3	12.0	29.4	13.2	48.1
Germany	556.3	16.5	15.2	8.9	57.1
United Kingdom	265.4	11.1	26.7	4.3	61.3
France	245.2	7.5	39.0	3.9	65.3
Mexico	208.0	-4.3	11.0	3.3	68.6
Netherlands	172.1	-3.6	19.1	2.8	71.4
Belgium	172.0	1.2	4.0	2.8	74.2
Thailand	130.4	19.5	64.2	2.1	76.3
Canada	114.9	0.5	18.7	1.8	78.1
Italy	101.1	21.4	35.5	1.6	79.7
Spain	90.1	19.2	39.2	1.4	81.2
Malaysia	79.6	11.6	30.5	1.3	82.5
Indonesia	78.6	44.5	194.9	1.3	83.7

Graph 2: Trade Balance by MDG regions 2010
(Bln US$)

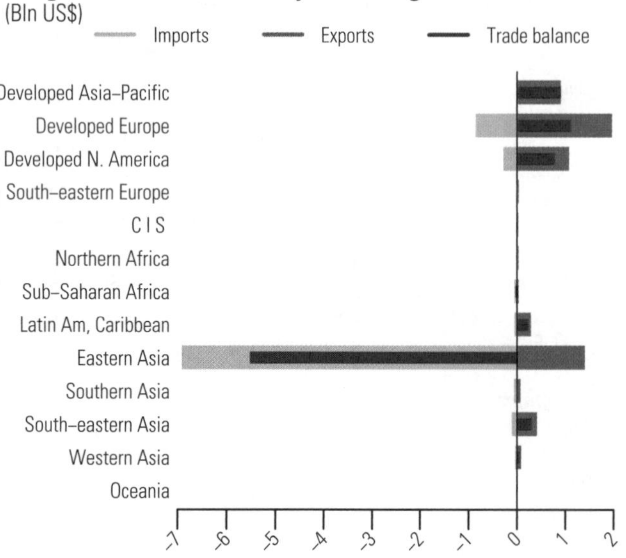

Table 3: Top importing countries or areas in 2010

Country or area	Value (million US$)	Avg. Growth (%) 06-10	Growth (%) 09-10	World share %	Cum.
World	8468.4	11.0	31.6	100.0	
China	5087.6	20.6	43.5	60.1	60.1
China, Hong Kong SAR	1735.5	0.8	12.8	20.5	80.6
USA	225.1	-14.7	9.0	2.7	83.2
Belgium	131.5	3.1	1.3	1.6	84.8
Netherlands	126.7	9.3	37.9	1.5	86.3
Germany	125.3	4.9	64.8	1.5	87.8
Italy	90.3	-6.4	59.4	1.1	88.8
Ireland	81.8	4.2	32.8	1.0	89.8
Canada	74.7	-11.2	16.0	0.9	90.7
Other Asia, nes	67.4	13.4	57.2	0.8	91.5
Viet Nam	*60.6*	35.4	66.9	0.7	92.2
Nigeria	52.2	129.9	-34.7	0.6	92.8
India	46.9	13.3	-44.6	0.6	93.4
Austria	42.6	11.7	76.1	0.5	93.9
France	40.2	11.0	114.1	0.5	94.3

After a drop of 17.4 percent in 2009, the value (in current prices) of exports of tubes, pipes and hoses, and fittings therefore of plastics (SITC group 581) increased in 2010 by 13.2 percent to amount to 17.9 bln US$ (see table 2). Imports showed a similar development with an increase of 11.7 percent to 17.4 bln US$ in 2010 (see table 3). Graph 1 shows that the increase in exports for 2010 in this product group was exceeded by both the increase in world exports of chemicals and related products, nes (SITC section 5) of 17.1 percent and the increase in total world exports of 21.2 percent. Exports of tubes, pipes and hoses, and fittings therefore of plastics (SITC group 581) accounted for 1.1 percent of world exports of SITC section 5 and 0.1 percent of total world exports in 2010 (see table 1).

The top exporting countries in 2010 were Germany, USA and Italy (see table 2). They accounted respectively for 18.6, 11.8 and 6.6 percent of world exports. Top destinations were Germany, USA and Mexico (see table 3). By MDG regions (see graph 2), Developed Europe accounted for a large share of trade in tubes, pipes and hoses, and fittings therefore of plastics (SITC group 581). In 2010, its exports amounted to 10.2 bln US$ while imports were valued at 7.7 bln US$, resulting in a trade surplus of 2.5 bln US$. Top trade deficits were recorded by Latin America and the Caribbean (-1.2 bln US$) and Commonwealth of Independent States (-0.9 bln US$).

Table 1: Imports (Imp.) and exports (Exp.), 1996-2010, in current prices

		1996	1997	1998	1999	2000	2001	2002	2003	2004	2005	2006	2007	2008	2009	2010
Values in Bln US$	Imp.	5.8	6.1	6.3	6.5	6.8	6.8	7.5	8.9	10.8	11.8	14.0	16.7	18.8	15.6	17.4
	Exp.	5.6	5.9	6.1	6.2	6.6	6.6	7.1	8.5	10.4	11.9	14.0	17.3	19.2	15.9	17.9
As a percentage of SITC section (%)	Imp.	1.1	1.1	1.2	1.1	1.1	1.1	1.1	1.1	1.1	1.0	1.1	1.1	1.1	1.1	1.0
	Exp.	1.2	1.2	1.2	1.2	1.2	1.1	1.1	1.1	1.1	1.1	1.1	1.2	1.2	1.1	1.1
As a percentage of world trade (%)	Imp.	0.1	0.1	0.1	0.1	0.1	0.1	0.1	0.1	0.1	0.1	0.1	0.1	0.1	0.1	0.1
	Exp.	0.1	0.1	0.1	0.1	0.1	0.1	0.1	0.1	0.1	0.1	0.1	0.1	0.1	0.1	0.1

Graph 1: Annual growth rates of exports, 1996–2010
(In percentage by year)

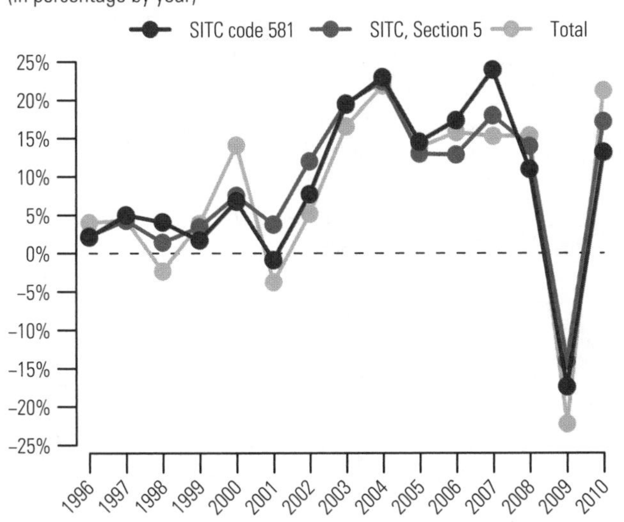

Graph 2: Trade Balance by MDG regions 2010
(Bln US$)

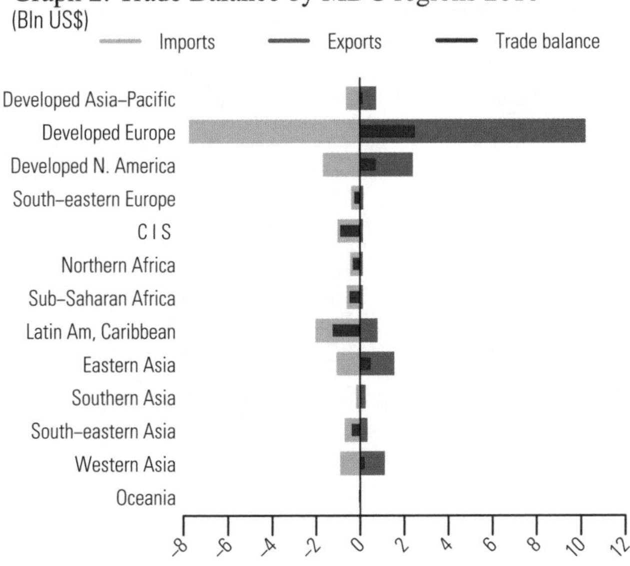

Table 2: Top exporting countries or areas in 2010

Country or area	Value (million US$)	Avg. Growth (%) 06-10	Growth (%) 09-10	World share %	Cum.
World	17943.6	6.5	13.2	100.0	
Germany	3330.7	6.3	14.9	18.6	18.6
USA	2109.6	7.0	19.5	11.8	30.3
Italy	1189.7	5.4	8.4	6.6	36.9
China	1165.5	19.2	34.2	6.5	43.4
United Kingdom	697.2	-2.3	4.6	3.9	47.3
Czech Rep.	667.2	9.2	4.7	3.7	51.0
Turkey	620.4	16.7	6.6	3.5	54.5
Japan	615.7	12.6	46.4	3.4	57.9
Poland	557.0	8.9	20.3	3.1	61.0
Switzerland	518.7	0.4	9.1	2.9	63.9
France	491.9	3.9	9.1	2.7	66.7
Spain	475.8	6.6	-0.7	2.7	69.3
Netherlands	464.8	3.2	3.4	2.6	71.9
Austria	393.7	2.8	2.9	2.2	74.1
Belgium	328.9	6.4	4.7	1.8	75.9

Table 3: Top importing countries or areas in 2010

Country or area	Value (million US$)	Avg. Growth (%) 06-10	Growth (%) 09-10	World share %	Cum.
World	17424.6	5.6	11.7	100.0	
Germany	1300.4	1.2	6.4	7.5	7.5
USA	1107.3	-1.0	17.1	6.4	13.8
Mexico	1014.4	1.6	18.0	5.8	19.6
France	891.4	3.4	7.8	5.1	24.8
China	659.3	13.9	35.9	3.8	28.5
Canada	566.8	4.0	27.0	3.3	31.8
Italy	532.1	2.1	11.5	3.1	34.8
Russian Federation	524.2	19.3	28.2	3.0	37.9
Czech Rep.	516.1	6.6	16.1	3.0	40.8
United Kingdom	482.4	0.9	10.5	2.8	43.6
Poland	479.3	9.8	19.4	2.8	46.3
Belgium	458.8	4.3	3.2	2.6	49.0
Switzerland	424.5	6.4	18.6	2.4	51.4
Austria	350.4	5.3	6.1	2.0	53.4
Netherlands	325.4	1.1	-9.7	1.9	55.3

582 Plates, sheets, film, foil and strip, of plastics

After a drop of 16.6 percent in 2009, the value (in current prices) of exports of plastic plates, sheets, film, foil and strip (SITC group 582) increased in 2010 by 24.0 percent to amount to 85.6 bln US$ (see table 2). Imports showed a similar development with an increase of 25.2 percent to 85.9 bln US$ in 2010 (see table 3). Graph 1 shows that the increase in exports for 2010 in this product group exceeded both the increase in world exports of chemicals and related products, nes (SITC section 5) of 17.1 percent and the increase in total world exports of 21.2 percent. Exports of plastic plates, sheets, film, foil and strip (SITC group 582) accounted for 5.2 percent of world exports of SITC section 5 and 0.6 percent of total world exports in 2010 (see table 1).

Japan, Germany and USA were the top exporting countries in 2010 (see table 2). They accounted respectively for 14.6, 12.8 and 9.9 percent of world exports. Top destinations were China, USA and Germany (see table 3). By MDG regions (see graph 2), Developed Europe accounted for a large share of trade in plastic plates, sheets, film, foil and strip (SITC group 582). In 2010, its exports amounted to 37.9 bln US$ while imports amounted to 33.2 bln US$, resulting in a trade surplus of 4.7 bln US$. Major surpluses were also recorded by Developed Asia-Pacific (+9.5 bln US$) and Developed North America (+2.3 bln US$). Top trade deficits were recorded by Eastern Asia (-6.4 bln US$), Latin America and the Caribbean (-4.1 bln US$) and Commonwealth of Independent States (-2.3 bln US$).

Table 1: Imports (Imp.) and exports (Exp.), 1996-2010, in current prices

		1996	1997	1998	1999	2000	2001	2002	2003	2004	2005	2006	2007	2008	2009	2010
Values in Bln US$	Imp.	29.2	30.2	30.7	31.5	33.1	32.3	35.5	42.0	50.5	57.2	64.3	73.8	80.3	68.6	85.9
	Exp.	29.2	30.4	30.2	31.0	33.3	32.4	35.5	42.0	50.8	57.4	65.9	76.2	82.8	69.0	85.6
As a percentage of SITC section (%)	Imp.	5.7	5.7	5.7	5.6	5.4	5.1	5.1	5.0	5.0	5.0	5.0	4.9	4.7	4.6	4.9
	Exp.	6.1	6.0	5.9	5.9	5.9	5.5	5.4	5.3	5.3	5.3	5.4	5.3	5.0	4.9	5.2
As a percentage of world trade (%)	Imp.	0.5	0.5	0.6	0.6	0.5	0.5	0.5	0.6	0.5	0.5	0.5	0.5	0.5	0.5	0.6
	Exp.	0.6	0.6	0.6	0.6	0.5	0.5	0.6	0.6	0.6	0.6	0.5	0.6	0.5	0.6	0.6

Graph 1: Annual growth rates of exports, 1996–2010

(In percentage by year)

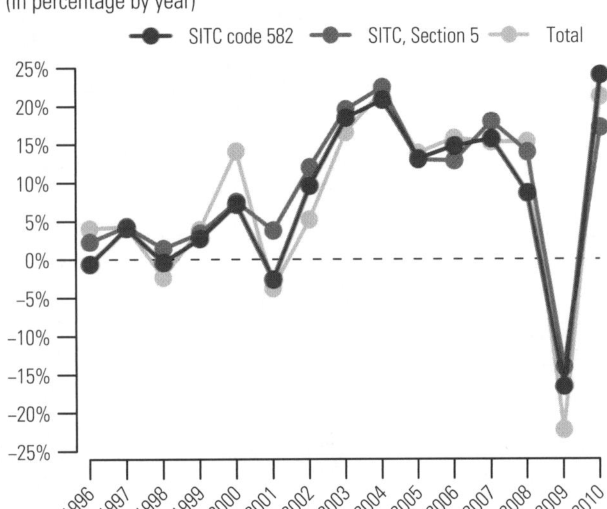

Table 2: Top exporting countries or areas in 2010

Country or area	Value (million US$)	Avg. Growth (%) 06-10	Growth (%) 09-10	World share %	Cum.
World	85589.2	6.8	24.0	100.0	
Japan	12503.4	15.9	38.1	14.6	14.6
Germany	10938.3	0.4	14.6	12.8	27.4
USA	8479.2	5.4	22.8	9.9	37.3
Italy	5247.2	0.9	10.9	6.1	43.4
China	5216.6	17.1	55.7	6.1	49.5
Rep. of Korea	3888.9	15.3	43.3	4.5	54.1
Other Asia, nes	3439.2	12.1	38.4	4.0	58.1
Belgium	3429.2	1.5	11.0	4.0	62.1
France	2580.8	0.9	9.1	3.0	65.1
United Kingdom	2380.8	1.4	17.1	2.8	67.9
Netherlands	2302.8	0.6	11.2	2.7	70.6
Canada	1868.6	-0.4	13.0	2.2	72.8
China, Hong Kong SAR	1784.9	8.1	44.6	2.1	74.8
Austria	1764.3	5.4	12.3	2.1	76.9
Spain	1561.7	4.5	16.0	1.8	78.7

Graph 2: Trade Balance by MDG regions 2010

(Bln US$)

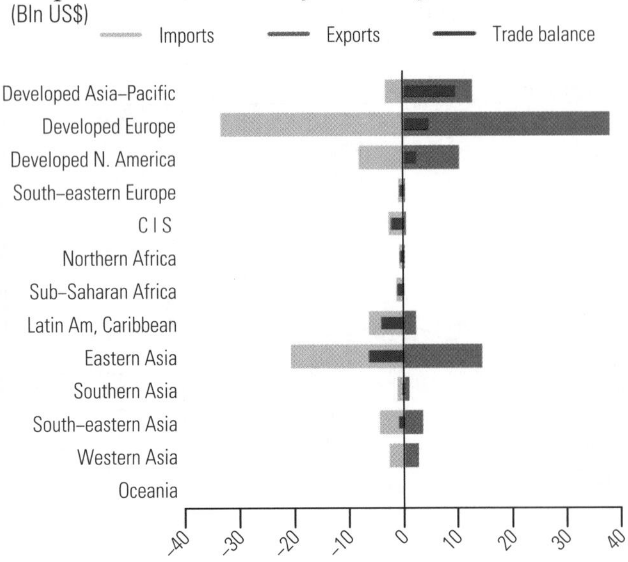

Table 3: Top importing countries or areas in 2010

Country or area	Value (million US$)	Avg. Growth (%) 06-10	Growth (%) 09-10	World share %	Cum.
World	85865.1	7.5	25.2	100.0	
China	10271.0	19.2	57.8	12.0	12.0
USA	5834.3	0.8	27.2	6.8	18.8
Germany	5489.5	4.6	19.9	6.4	25.1
Rep. of Korea	4776.0	21.6	41.6	5.6	30.7
France	4276.9	3.3	10.8	5.0	35.7
Other Asia, nes	3317.9	11.5	35.2	3.9	39.6
United Kingdom	3306.7	-0.4	14.2	3.9	43.4
Mexico	3101.1	4.2	32.2	3.6	47.0
Italy	2763.8	4.8	26.8	3.2	50.2
China, Hong Kong SAR	2341.2	8.3	42.0	2.7	53.0
Belgium	2326.2	2.6	9.3	2.7	55.7
Canada	2228.6	0.4	17.4	2.6	58.3
Poland	2058.8	9.5	24.6	2.4	60.7
Spain	1987.3	0.6	3.0	2.3	63.0
Japan	1962.9	7.8	35.0	2.3	65.3

After a drop of 18.3 percent in 2009, the value (in current prices) of exports of plastic monofilament of any cross-sectional dimension exceed 1 mm (SITC group 583) increased in 2010 by 10.1 percent to amount to 4.7 bln US$ (see table 2). Imports showed a similar development with an increase of 9.3 percent to 4.2 bln US$ in 2010 (see table 3). Graph 1 shows that the increase in exports for 2010 in this product group was exceeded by both the increase in world exports of chemicals and related products, nes (SITC section 5) of 17.1 percent and the increase in total world exports of 21.2 percent. Exports of plastic monofilament of any cross-sectional dimension exceed 1 mm (SITC group 583) accounted for 0.3 percent of world exports of SITC section 5 and less than 0.1 percent of total world exports in 2010 (see table 1).

Germany, the top exporting country in 2010, accounted for more than a third (38.9 percent) of world exports (see table 2). Other major exporting countries were Belgium and Turkey, respectively with 7.2 and 5.2 percent of world exports. Top destinations were France, Germany and USA (see table 3). By MDG regions (see graph 2), a majority of trade in plastic monofilament (SITC group 583) took place in Developed Europe. In 2010, its exports were valued at 3.5 bln US$ while imports reached 2.4 bln US$ resulting in a trade surplus of 1.1 bln US$. Significant deficits were recorded by Commonwealth of Independent States (-0.4 bln US$) and South-eastern Europe (-0.2 bln US$).

Table 1: Imports (Imp.) and exports (Exp.), 1996-2010, in current prices

		1996	1997	1998	1999	2000	2001	2002	2003	2004	2005	2006	2007	2008	2009	2010
Values in Bln US$	Imp.	1.6	1.7	1.8	1.8	1.9	2.0	2.2	2.7	3.2	3.5	4.2	4.8	5.3	3.9	4.2
	Exp.	1.5	1.6	1.8	1.8	1.9	1.9	2.2	2.7	3.3	3.7	4.3	4.8	5.3	4.3	4.7
As a percentage of SITC section (%)	Imp.	0.3	0.3	0.3	0.3	0.3	0.3	0.3	0.3	0.3	0.3	0.3	0.3	0.3	0.3	0.2
	Exp.	0.3	0.3	0.4	0.3	0.3	0.3	0.3	0.3	0.3	0.3	0.3	0.3	0.3	0.3	0.3
As a percentage of world trade (%)	Imp.	0.0	0.0	0.0	0.0	0.0	0.0	0.0	0.0	0.0	0.0	0.0	0.0	0.0	0.0	0.0
	Exp.	0.0	0.0	0.0	0.0	0.0	0.0	0.0	0.0	0.0	0.0	0.0	0.0	0.0	0.0	0.0

Graph 1: Annual growth rates of exports, 1996–2010

(In percentage by year)

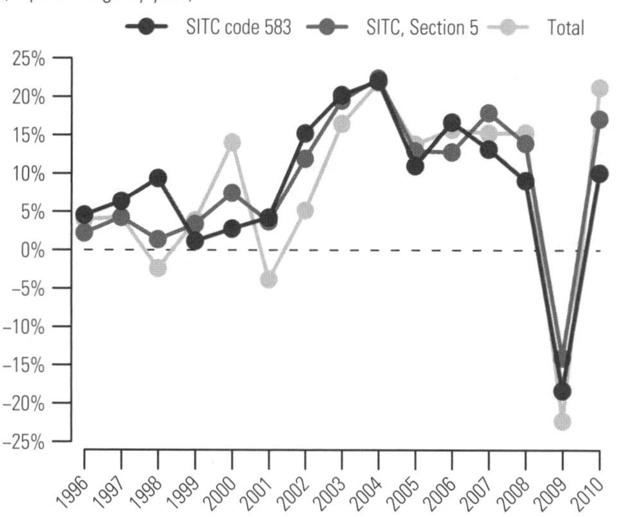

Table 2: Top exporting countries or areas in 2010

Country or area	Value (million US$)	Avg. Growth (%) 06-10	Growth (%) 09-10	World share %	Cum.
World	4744.5	2.7	10.1	100.0	
Germany	1845.5	3.0	3.3	38.9	38.9
Belgium	339.5	-2.0	9.2	7.2	46.1
Turkey	244.7	4.4	12.6	5.2	51.2
Poland	242.9	-1.0	6.0	5.1	56.3
USA	233.3	-2.9	30.6	4.9	61.2
China	207.7	22.0	39.9	4.4	65.6
Canada	170.2	-11.4	13.4	3.6	69.2
Austria	157.7	-2.3	4.1	3.3	72.5
Italy	154.2	3.2	6.1	3.2	75.8
United Kingdom	151.2	5.2	18.9	3.2	79.0
France	122.6	2.3	8.9	2.6	81.6
Netherlands	81.0	1.2	12.7	1.7	83.3
Denmark	59.5	10.4	16.2	1.3	84.5
Bulgaria	55.6	27.6	26.3	1.2	85.7
Malaysia	54.7	29.4	10.0	1.2	86.8

Graph 2: Trade Balance by MDG regions 2010

(Bln US$)

Imports — Exports — Trade balance

Developed Asia-Pacific
Developed Europe
Developed N. America
South-eastern Europe
C I S
Northern Africa
Sub-Saharan Africa
Latin Am, Caribbean
Eastern Asia
Southern Asia
South-eastern Asia
Western Asia
Oceania

-2.5 -2 -1.5 -1 -0.5 0 0.5 1 1.5 2 2.5 3 3.5

Table 3: Top importing countries or areas in 2010

Country or area	Value (million US$)	Avg. Growth (%) 06-10	Growth (%) 09-10	World share %	Cum.
World	4212.1	0.3	9.3	100.0	
France	347.2	4.8	1.5	8.2	8.2
Germany	317.4	7.1	21.9	7.5	15.8
USA	251.6	-8.8	17.1	6.0	21.8
Poland	211.1	-3.4	5.7	5.0	26.8
Czech Rep.	204.7	-5.1	-8.3	4.9	31.6
Italy	157.1	9.5	29.5	3.7	35.4
Belgium	156.0	5.4	-0.1	3.7	39.1
Russian Federation	149.8	-15.1	13.9	3.6	42.6
Ukraine	148.0	9.6	6.1	3.5	46.1
United Kingdom	143.0	-7.3	0.7	3.4	49.5
Romania	138.9	-2.4	-5.6	3.3	52.8
Austria	131.9	6.2	-0.8	3.1	55.9
Canada	114.5	7.3	19.9	2.7	58.7
Switzerland	112.7	5.9	5.9	2.7	61.3
Spain	91.5	-10.6	0.2	2.2	63.5

Source: UN Comtrade

591 Pesticides, disinfectant, put up in preparation, articles or packings for retail

After several years of continuous growth marked by a peak of 24.7 bln US$ in 2008, the value (in current prices) of exports of insecticides (SITC group 591) dropped in 2009 (by 13.0 percent) but bounced back in 2010 by 7.1 percent to amount to 23.0 bln US$ (see table 2). Imports showed a similar development with an increase of 6.1 percent to 24.9 bln US$ in 2010 (see table 3). Graph 1 shows that the increase in exports for 2010 in this product group was less than half of the increase in world exports of chemicals and related products, nes (SITC section 5) of 17.1 percent and the increase in total world exports of 21.2 percent. Exports of insecticides (SITC group 591) accounted for 1.4 percent of world exports of SITC section 5 and 0.2 percent of total world exports in 2010 (see table 1).

Exports of Germany, the top exporting country in 2010, decreased by 2.1 percent and represented 12.9 percent of world exports (see table 2). Other major exporting countries were France and USA, respectively with 11.9 and 11.5 percent of world exports. Top destinations were France, Brazil and Germany (see table 3). By MDG regions (see graph 2), Developed Europe and Eastern Asia recorded surpluses amounting respectively to 3.1 bln US$ and 1.3 bln US$. Top trade deficits were recorded by Latin America and the Caribbean (-3.1 bln US$), South-eastern Asia (-1.2 bln US$) and Sub-Saharan Africa (-1.1 bln US$).

Table 1: Imports (Imp.) and exports (Exp.), 1996-2010, in current prices

		1996	1997	1998	1999	2000	2001	2002	2003	2004	2005	2006	2007	2008	2009	2010
Values in Bln US$	Imp.	11.2	11.3	11.6	11.4	10.6	10.9	11.6	13.1	15.7	16.5	16.6	20.1	25.2	23.5	24.9
	Exp.	11.3	10.8	11.5	11.3	10.6	10.6	10.9	12.7	15.0	16.2	16.4	18.2	24.7	21.5	23.0
As a percentage of SITC section (%)	Imp.	2.2	2.1	2.1	2.0	1.7	1.7	1.7	1.6	1.6	1.4	1.3	1.3	1.5	1.6	1.4
	Exp.	2.4	2.2	2.3	2.1	1.9	1.8	1.7	1.6	1.6	1.5	1.3	1.3	1.5	1.5	1.4
As a percentage of world trade (%)	Imp.	0.2	0.2	0.2	0.2	0.2	0.2	0.2	0.2	0.2	0.2	0.1	0.1	0.2	0.2	0.2
	Exp.	0.2	0.2	0.2	0.2	0.2	0.2	0.2	0.2	0.2	0.2	0.1	0.1	0.2	0.2	0.2

Graph 1: Annual growth rates of exports, 1996–2010

(In percentage by year)

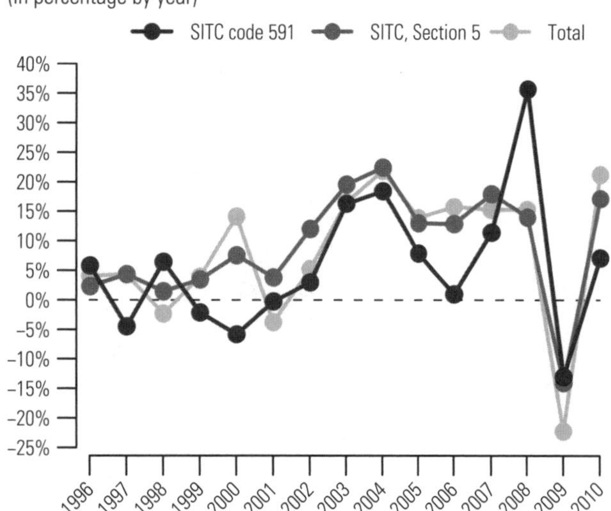

Graph 2: Trade Balance by MDG regions 2010

(Bln US$)

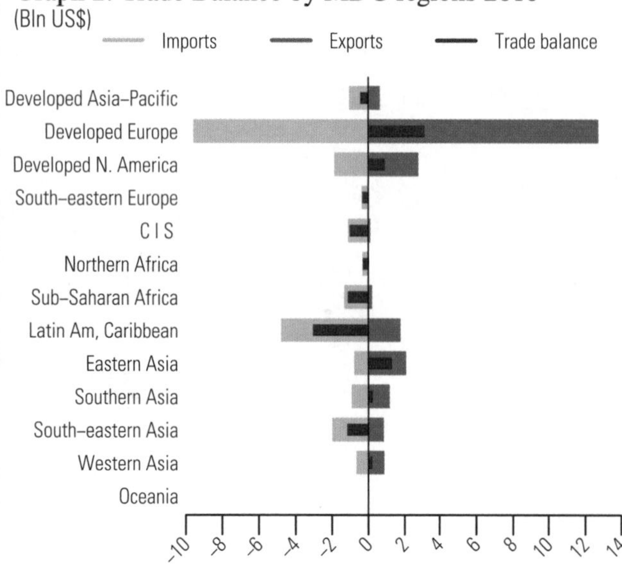

Table 2: Top exporting countries or areas in 2010

Country or area	Value (million US$)	Avg. Growth (%) 06-10	Growth (%) 09-10	World share %	Cum.
World	23 036.3	8.9	7.1	100.0	
Germany	2 983.0	6.9	-2.1	12.9	12.9
France	2 752.8	4.1	1.1	11.9	24.9
USA	2 654.6	8.6	10.3	11.5	36.4
China	1 769.7	14.2	25.0	7.7	44.1
Belgium	1 552.2	6.6	-13.3	6.7	50.8
United Kingdom	1 290.4	6.0	2.9	5.6	56.4
India	1 140.2	16.0	9.9	4.9	61.4
Switzerland	945.2	10.0	17.3	4.1	65.5
Spain	752.4	14.1	11.8	3.3	68.8
Netherlands	739.8	3.0	14.7	3.2	72.0
Israel	682.6	8.4	20.6	3.0	74.9
Italy	658.1	7.4	7.1	2.9	77.8
Japan	429.5	8.1	15.6	1.9	79.7
Brazil	422.9	14.9	27.5	1.8	81.5
Argentina	413.1	15.8	9.1	1.8	83.3

Table 3: Top importing countries or areas in 2010

Country or area	Value (million US$)	Avg. Growth (%) 06-10	Growth (%) 09-10	World share %	Cum.
World	24 893.3	10.6	6.1	100.0	
France	1 803.0	5.4	-14.5	7.2	7.2
Brazil	1 529.9	28.1	17.6	6.1	13.4
Germany	1 291.8	7.2	-11.0	5.2	18.6
Canada	1 104.9	6.4	-8.4	4.4	23.0
Viet Nam	*830.8*	27.0	66.9	3.3	26.4
United Kingdom	818.0	6.2	11.4	3.3	29.6
Italy	786.2	6.6	-3.9	3.2	32.8
USA	772.0	4.2	-0.4	3.1	35.9
Belgium	757.6	8.9	-14.2	3.0	38.9
Spain	681.0	10.9	-5.7	2.7	41.7
Poland	648.4	8.2	17.3	2.6	44.3
Netherlands	592.8	3.9	10.3	2.4	46.7
Argentina	530.9	24.3	78.4	2.1	48.8
Thailand	513.7	10.5	10.1	2.1	50.9
India	503.6	31.1	14.7	2.0	52.9

After a drop of 11.7 percent in 2009, the value (in current prices) of exports of starches, insulin and wheat gluten, albuminoidal substances, glues (SITC group 592) increased in 2010 by 15.7 percent to amount to 20.7 bln US$ (see table 2). Imports showed a similar development with an increase of 16.4 percent to 22.4 bln US$ in 2010 (see table 3). Graph 1 shows that the increase in exports for 2010 in this product group was below the increase in world exports of chemicals and related products, nes (SITC section 5) of 17.1 percent and the increase in total world exports of 21.2 percent. Exports of starches, insulin and wheat gluten, albuminoidal substances, glues (SITC group 592) accounted for 1.2 percent of world exports of SITC section 5 and 0.1 percent of total world exports in 2010 (see table 1).

The top exporting countries in 2010 were Germany, USA and China (see table 2). They accounted respectively for 14.5, 11.6 and 8.6 percent of world exports. China and USA were also the major destinations, together with Germany (see table 3). By MDG regions (see graph 2), Developed Europe accounted for a large share of trade in starches, insulin and wheat gluten, albuminoidal substances, glues (SITC group 592). In 2010, its exports were valued at 9.6 bln US$ while imports reached 8.2 bln US$ resulting in a trade surplus of 1.4 bln US$. Significant deficits were recorded by Eastern Asia (-1.1 bln US$), Latin America and the Caribbean (-0.8 bln US$) and Commonwealth of Independent States (-0.6 bln US$).

Table 1: Imports (Imp.) and exports (Exp.), 1996-2010, in current prices

		1996	1997	1998	1999	2000	2001	2002	2003	2004	2005	2006	2007	2008	2009	2010
Values in Bln US$	Imp.	9.3	9.1	9.1	9.0	9.4	9.8	10.2	11.8	13.9	15.1	16.4	19.4	22.4	19.3	22.4
	Exp.	8.2	8.5	8.5	8.4	8.8	9.3	9.7	11.0	12.7	13.8	14.9	17.8	20.3	17.9	20.7
As a percentage of SITC section (%)	Imp.	1.8	1.7	1.7	1.6	1.5	1.5	1.5	1.4	1.4	1.3	1.3	1.3	1.3	1.3	1.3
	Exp.	1.7	1.7	1.7	1.6	1.6	1.6	1.5	1.4	1.3	1.3	1.2	1.2	1.2	1.3	1.2
As a percentage of world trade (%)	Imp.	0.2	0.2	0.2	0.2	0.1	0.2	0.2	0.2	0.1	0.1	0.1	0.1	0.1	0.2	0.1
	Exp.	0.2	0.2	0.2	0.2	0.1	0.2	0.2	0.1	0.1	0.1	0.1	0.1	0.1	0.1	0.1

Graph 1: Annual growth rates of exports, 1996–2010
(In percentage by year)

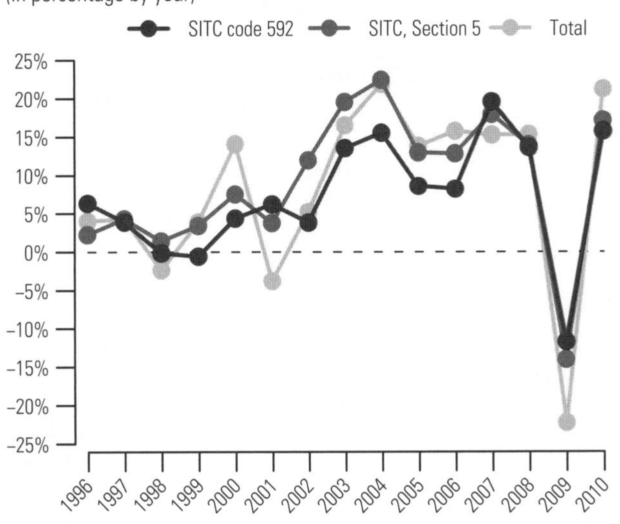

Graph 2: Trade Balance by MDG regions 2010
(Bln US$)

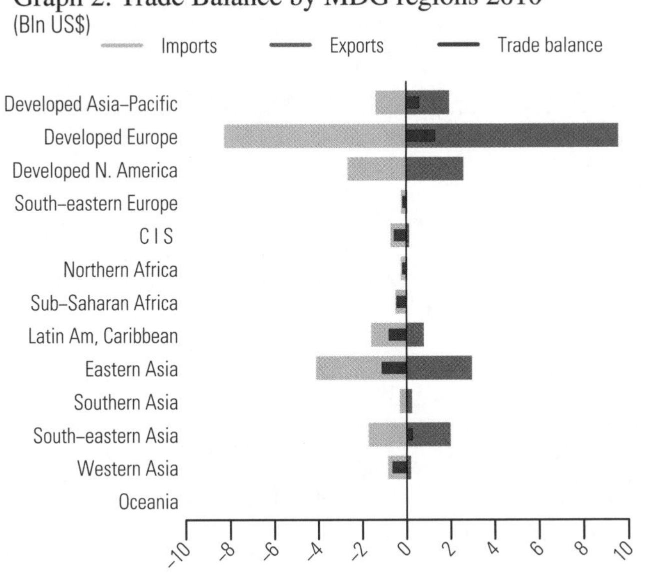

Table 2: Top exporting countries or areas in 2010

Country or area	Value (million US$)	Avg. Growth (%) 06-10	Growth (%) 09-10	World share %	Cum.
World	20697.4	8.5	15.7	100.0	
Germany	2997.1	8.1	11.6	14.5	14.5
USA	2410.2	7.8	20.6	11.6	26.1
China	1775.2	26.8	26.1	8.6	34.7
France	1442.0	2.8	4.0	7.0	41.7
Thailand	1339.4	17.2	45.2	6.5	48.1
Netherlands	1038.0	-2.7	-6.9	5.0	53.2
Japan	823.1	11.5	32.8	4.0	57.1
Belgium	696.1	5.9	0.6	3.4	60.5
Italy	682.9	5.4	10.3	3.3	63.8
New Zealand	649.6	1.8	-3.8	3.1	66.9
Other Asia, nes	522.2	11.0	47.3	2.5	69.5
Australia	493.6	16.5	18.8	2.4	71.8
Switzerland	434.2	14.0	12.6	2.1	73.9
Ireland	417.9	2.0	24.0	2.0	76.0
United Kingdom	367.6	-2.9	1.9	1.8	77.7

Table 3: Top importing countries or areas in 2010

Country or area	Value (million US$)	Avg. Growth (%) 06-10	Growth (%) 09-10	World share %	Cum.
World	22423.2	8.2	16.4	100.0	
China	2481.7	20.8	47.6	11.1	11.1
USA	1915.9	6.3	13.1	8.5	19.6
Germany	1704.7	4.1	7.5	7.6	27.2
Japan	1071.1	8.6	12.0	4.8	32.0
France	840.2	4.6	1.8	3.7	35.7
United Kingdom	805.9	3.9	5.5	3.6	39.3
Canada	722.7	3.7	12.3	3.2	42.6
Other Asia, nes	689.6	14.8	40.9	3.1	45.6
Netherlands	655.6	3.5	-1.8	2.9	48.6
Mexico	631.8	5.1	15.6	2.8	51.4
Indonesia	575.5	27.4	80.5	2.6	53.9
Poland	562.2	9.8	17.4	2.5	56.4
Italy	561.0	1.3	10.9	2.5	58.9
Belgium	556.5	-1.0	-4.0	2.5	61.4
Rep. of Korea	533.6	6.1	14.4	2.4	63.8

Source: UN Comtrade

593 Explosives and pyrotechnic products

After a drop of 4.0 percent in 2009, the value (in current prices) of exports of explosives and pyrotechnic products (SITC group 593) increased in 2010 by 17.9 percent to amount to 3.1 bln US$ (see table 2). Imports showed a similar development with an increase of 10.4 percent to 3.3 bln US$ in 2010 (see table 3). Graph 1 shows that the increase in exports for 2010 in this product group exceeded the increase in world exports of chemicals and related products, nes (SITC section 5) of 17.1 percent but was less than the increase in total world exports of 21.2 percent. Exports of explosives and pyrotechnic products (SITC group 593) accounted for 0.2 percent of world exports of SITC section 5 and less than 0.1 percent of total world exports in 2010 (see table 1).

USA and China were the top exporting countries in 2010 (see table 2). They accounted respectively for 24.6 and 20.1 percent of world exports. Germany was one of the top exporting countries and accounted for 7.0 percent of world exports. USA was also the top destination, together with Mexico and Germany (see table 3). By MDG regions (see graph 2), Eastern Asia recorded a trade surplus of 506 mln US$. Significant deficits were recorded by Latin America and the Caribbean (-257 mln US$) and South-eastern Asia (-183 mln US$) among others.

Table 1: Imports (Imp.) and exports (Exp.), 1996-2010, in current prices

		1996	1997	1998	1999	2000	2001	2002	2003	2004	2005	2006	2007	2008	2009	2010
Values in Bln US$	Imp.	1.3	1.4	1.3	1.4	1.4	1.3	1.5	1.8	2.1	2.2	2.6	3.0	3.2	3.0	3.3
	Exp.	1.3	1.3	1.2	1.2	1.2	1.1	1.2	1.5	1.8	1.9	2.3	2.5	2.8	2.6	3.1
As a percentage of SITC section (%)	Imp.	0.3	0.3	0.2	0.2	0.2	0.2	0.2	0.2	0.2	0.2	0.2	0.2	0.2	0.2	0.2
	Exp.	0.3	0.3	0.2	0.2	0.2	0.2	0.2	0.2	0.2	0.2	0.2	0.2	0.2	0.2	0.2
As a percentage of world trade (%)	Imp.	0.0	0.0	0.0	0.0	0.0	0.0	0.0	0.0	0.0	0.0	0.0	0.0	0.0	0.0	0.0
	Exp.	0.0	0.0	0.0	0.0	0.0	0.0	0.0	0.0	0.0	0.0	0.0	0.0	0.0	0.0	0.0

Graph 1: Annual growth rates of exports, 1996–2010

(In percentage by year)

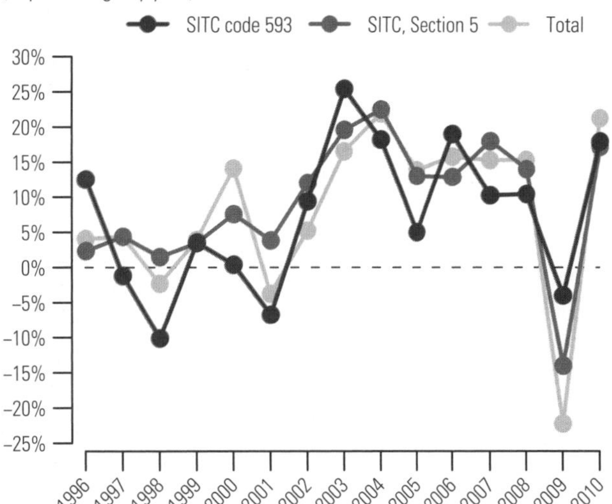

Graph 2: Trade Balance by MDG regions 2010

(Mln US$)

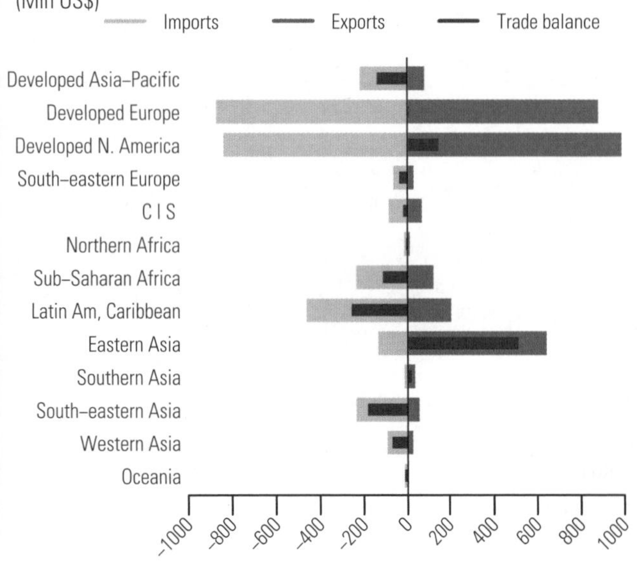

Table 2: Top exporting countries or areas in 2010

Country or area	Value (million US$)	Avg. Growth (%) 06-10	Growth (%) 09-10	World share %	Cum.
World	3116.0	8.3	17.9	100.0	
USA	766.5	9.2	28.9	24.6	24.6
China	627.6	5.6	-0.1	20.1	44.7
Germany	218.5	-0.5	4.3	7.0	51.8
Canada	218.0	13.0	36.0	7.0	58.7
Czech Rep.	187.9	20.1	31.7	6.0	64.8
France	167.3	9.5	73.8	5.4	70.1
Mexico	101.2	1.1	26.4	3.2	73.4
South Africa	98.0	14.7	24.0	3.1	76.5
Poland	60.4	40.0	42.2	1.9	78.5
Switzerland	58.4	1.6	17.0	1.9	80.4
Russian Federation	46.0	-10.4	-11.2	1.5	81.8
Belgium	41.9	27.6	38.6	1.3	83.2
Australia	38.6	13.0	31.8	1.2	84.4
Italy	32.7	7.9	2.6	1.0	85.5
Japan	32.5	37.0	72.3	1.0	86.5

Table 3: Top importing countries or areas in 2010

Country or area	Value (million US$)	Avg. Growth (%) 06-10	Growth (%) 09-10	World share %	Cum.
World	3288.8	6.4	10.4	100.0	
USA	633.3	2.9	16.5	19.3	19.3
Mexico	260.8	1.6	21.0	7.9	27.2
Germany	242.9	7.1	6.0	7.4	34.6
Canada	202.9	8.4	48.5	6.2	40.7
Japan	112.0	8.3	21.1	3.4	44.1
Australia	91.9	6.2	2.8	2.8	46.9
Indonesia	89.9	24.0	44.2	2.7	49.7
France	79.2	8.9	7.0	2.4	52.1
China	71.6	52.1	70.5	2.2	54.3
Italy	70.4	2.0	-5.4	2.1	56.4
Norway	68.7	11.8	28.7	2.1	58.5
Netherlands	53.0	11.1	-18.0	1.6	60.1
Romania	51.4	23.9	26.0	1.6	61.7
Switzerland	47.3	16.1	-7.0	1.4	63.1
Singapore	44.0	17.8	0.1	1.3	64.4

After several years of continuous growth marked by a peak of 18.3 bln US$ in 2008, the value (in current prices) of exports of prepared additives, de-icing and liquid for transmissions, lubricant (SITC group 597) dropped in 2009 (by 15.1 percent) but bounced back in 2010 by 22.1 percent to amount to 19.0 bln US$ (see table 2). Imports showed a similar development with an increase of 19.5 percent to 19.5 bln US$ in 2010 (see table 3). Graph 1 shows that the increase in exports for 2010 in this product group slightly exceeded both the increase in world exports of chemicals and related products, nes (SITC section 5) of 17.1 percent and the increase in total world exports of 21.2 percent. Exports of prepared additives, de-icing and liquid for transmissions, lubricant (SITC group 597) accounted for 1.1 percent of world exports of SITC section 5 and 0.1 percent of total world exports in 2010 (see table 1).

The top exporting countries in 2010 were USA, France and Germany (see table 2). They accounted respectively for 22.0, 14.7 and 12.8 percent of world exports. Top destinations were China, Germany and France (see table 3). By MDG regions (see graph 2), Developed Europe accounted for a majority of exports and a large share of imports. In 2010, its exports were valued at 10.5 bln US$ while imports amounted to 6.9 bln US$ resulting in a trade surplus of 3.6 bln US$. A large surplus was also recorded by Developed North America (+3.1 bln US$). Eastern Asia and Latin America and the Caribbean recorded trade deficits amounting respectively to 2.6 bln US$ and 1.3 bln US$.

Table 1: Imports (Imp.) and exports (Exp.), 1996-2010, in current prices

		1996	1997	1998	1999	2000	2001	2002	2003	2004	2005	2006	2007	2008	2009	2010
Values in Bln US$	Imp.	7.6	7.7	7.3	7.3	7.2	7.2	7.9	8.8	10.4	11.9	13.9	16.1	18.7	16.4	19.5
	Exp.	7.4	7.5	7.2	6.7	6.7	6.8	7.2	8.2	9.8	11.2	13.0	15.2	18.3	15.6	19.0
As a percentage of SITC section (%)	Imp.	1.5	1.4	1.4	1.3	1.2	1.1	1.1	1.1	1.0	1.0	1.1	1.1	1.1	1.1	1.1
	Exp.	1.5	1.5	1.4	1.3	1.2	1.2	1.1	1.0	1.0	1.0	1.1	1.1	1.1	1.1	1.1
As a percentage of world trade (%)	Imp.	0.1	0.1	0.1	0.1	0.1	0.1	0.1	0.1	0.1	0.1	0.1	0.1	0.1	0.1	0.1
	Exp.	0.1	0.1	0.1	0.1	0.1	0.1	0.1	0.1	0.1	0.1	0.1	0.1	0.1	0.1	0.1

Graph 1: Annual growth rates of exports, 1996–2010
(In percentage by year)

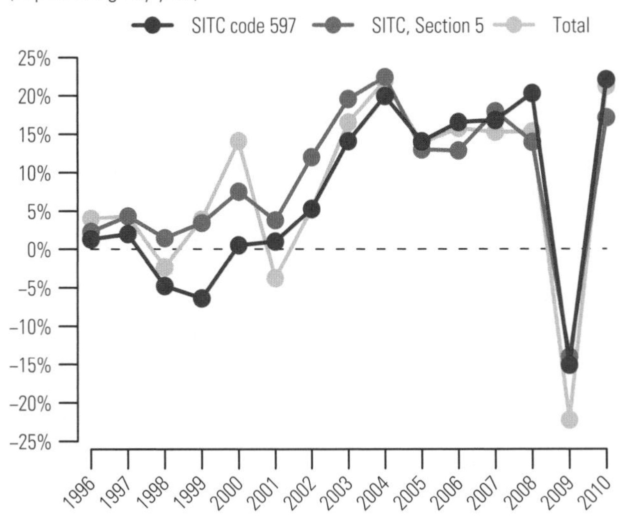

Graph 2: Trade Balance by MDG regions 2010
(Bln US$)

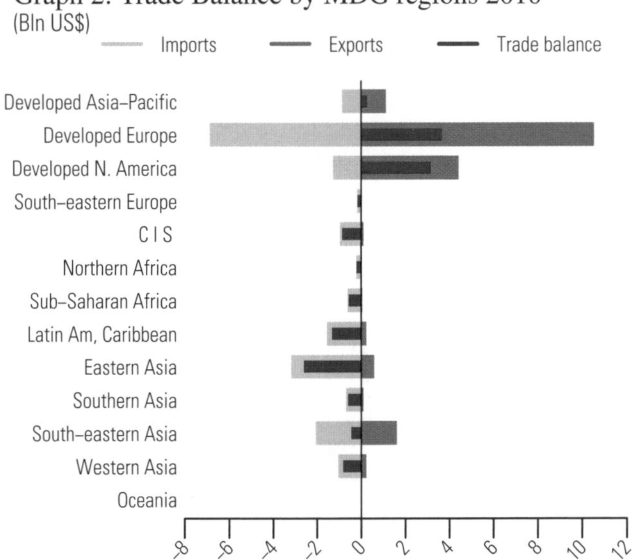

Table 2: Top exporting countries or areas in 2010

Country or area	Value (million US$)	Avg. Growth (%) 06-10	Growth (%) 09-10	World share %	Cum.
World	19003.9	9.9	22.1	100.0	
USA	4179.4	9.8	23.0	22.0	22.0
France	2794.9	8.1	15.6	14.7	36.7
Germany	2429.6	6.1	18.6	12.8	49.5
Singapore	1511.1	15.7	26.2	8.0	57.4
Belgium	1139.9	7.6	19.2	6.0	63.4
Netherlands	1137.7	15.4	45.2	6.0	69.4
Japan	1064.2	15.6	36.9	5.6	75.0
Italy	967.4	8.5	18.5	5.1	80.1
United Kingdom	656.4	2.4	11.7	3.5	83.6
Denmark	260.8	93.3	121.0	1.4	84.9
Canada	235.5	3.1	29.9	1.2	86.2
Spain	227.7	13.6	33.4	1.2	87.4
Switzerland	193.6	13.0	33.8	1.0	88.4
China	192.7	23.7	25.4	1.0	89.4
Sweden	186.6	9.0	23.4	1.0	90.4

Table 3: Top importing countries or areas in 2010

Country or area	Value (million US$)	Avg. Growth (%) 06-10	Growth (%) 09-10	World share %	Cum.
World	19539.0	8.9	19.5	100.0	
China	2087.6	18.0	40.3	10.7	10.7
Germany	1268.8	9.5	31.3	6.5	17.2
France	911.8	7.1	17.9	4.7	21.8
Belgium	814.5	2.7	4.4	4.2	26.0
Singapore	739.8	5.4	3.7	3.8	29.8
Russian Federation	688.0	19.2	29.2	3.5	33.3
USA	635.3	7.6	24.3	3.3	36.6
Canada	627.0	3.8	15.7	3.2	39.8
Italy	626.1	5.1	18.2	3.2	43.0
Netherlands	590.6	3.8	11.8	3.0	46.0
Japan	589.1	6.1	16.9	3.0	49.0
Rep. of Korea	584.4	12.6	26.9	3.0	52.0
Indonesia	447.9	16.5	38.6	2.3	54.3
Mexico	403.4	-3.3	30.0	2.1	56.4
United Kingdom	399.7	1.6	10.1	2.0	58.4

598 Miscellaneous chemical products, nes

After several years of continuous growth marked by a peak of 109.2 bln US$ in 2008, the value (in current prices) of exports of miscellaneous chemical products, nes (SITC group 598) dropped in 2009 (by 18.7 percent) but bounced back in 2010 by 21.4 percent to amount to 107.8 bln US$ (see table 2). Imports showed a similar development with an increase of 23.5 percent to 112.0 bln US$ in 2010 (see table 3). Graph 1 shows that the increase in exports for 2010 in this product group was greater than the increase in world exports of chemicals and related products, nes (SITC section 5) of 17.1 percent and the increase in total world exports of 21.2 percent. Exports of miscellaneous chemical products, nes (SITC group 598) accounted for 6.5 percent of world exports of SITC section 5 and 0.7 percent of total world exports in 2010 (see table 1).

The top exporting countries in 2010 were Germany and USA (see table 2). They represented 14.6 and 14.2 percent of world exports, respectively. Japan was also one of the top exporting countries: it accounted for 10.7 percent of world exports. Top destinations were China, Germany and USA (see table 3). By MDG regions (see graph 2), Developed Europe accounted for a large share of trade in miscellaneous chemical products, nes (SITC group 598). In 2010, its exports were valued at 51.9 bln US$ while imports amounted to 44.1 bln US$ resulting in a trade surplus of 7.8 bln US$. Major surpluses were also recorded by Developed North America (+6.8 bln US$) and Developed Asia-Pacific (+6.3 bln US$). Eastern Asia and Latin America and the Caribbean recorded trade deficits amounting respectively to 10.9 bln US$ and 4.0 bln US$.

Table 1: Imports (Imp.) and exports (Exp.), 1996-2010, in current prices

		1996	1997	1998	1999	2000	2001	2002	2003	2004	2005	2006	2007	2008	2009	2010
Values in Bln US$	Imp.	33.6	34.7	34.2	35.8	40.4	40.4	43.8	51.5	60.0	67.8	79.1	93.4	108.0	90.7	112.0
	Exp.	31.6	33.9	33.3	35.3	38.0	37.7	41.2	48.3	57.0	63.6	75.3	89.2	109.2	88.8	107.8
As a percentage of SITC section (%)	Imp.	6.5	6.5	6.3	6.4	6.6	6.4	6.3	6.2	5.9	5.9	6.2	6.2	6.3	6.1	6.5
	Exp.	6.6	6.7	6.5	6.7	6.7	6.4	6.3	6.1	5.9	5.9	6.1	6.2	6.6	6.3	6.5
As a percentage of world trade (%)	Imp.	0.6	0.6	0.6	0.6	0.6	0.6	0.7	0.7	0.6	0.6	0.6	0.7	0.7	0.7	0.7
	Exp.	0.6	0.6	0.6	0.6	0.6	0.6	0.6	0.6	0.6	0.6	0.6	0.6	0.7	0.7	0.7

Graph 1: Annual growth rates of exports, 1996–2010

(In percentage by year)

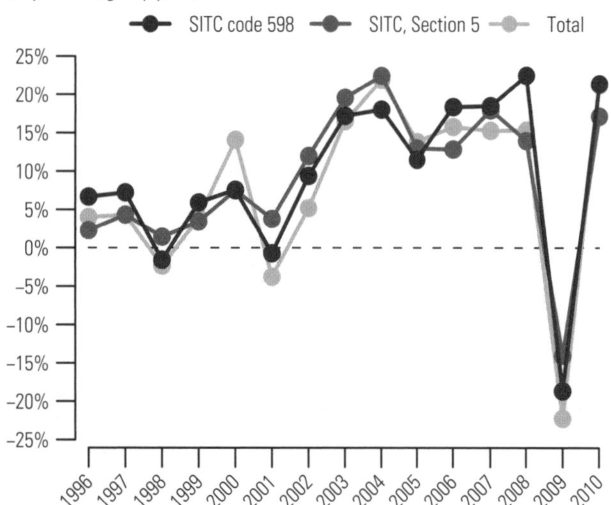

Table 2: Top exporting countries or areas in 2010

Country or area	Value (million US$)	Avg. Growth (%) 06-10	Growth (%) 09-10	World share %	Cum.
World	107 821.1	9.4	21.4	100.0	
Germany	15 722.1	7.2	20.9	14.6	14.6
USA	15 284.5	7.5	17.2	14.2	28.8
Japan	11 531.8	5.8	42.5	10.7	39.5
China	7 455.6	24.2	53.2	6.9	46.4
Netherlands	5 556.3	8.9	11.7	5.2	51.5
France	4 814.4	2.6	11.7	4.5	56.0
Belgium	4 787.6	8.3	5.3	4.4	60.4
United Kingdom	4 458.4	0.0	7.2	4.1	64.6
Ireland	3 066.5	4.1	-26.8	2.8	67.4
Italy	3 028.0	2.2	17.5	2.8	70.2
Other Asia, nes	3 020.2	11.4	55.7	2.8	73.0
Rep. of Korea	2 637.6	17.1	48.9	2.4	75.5
Israel	2 414.7	142.7	18.3	2.2	77.7
Singapore	1 989.1	8.5	15.5	1.8	79.5
Norway	1 939.8	36.4	24.7	1.8	81.3

Graph 2: Trade Balance by MDG regions 2010

(Bln US$)

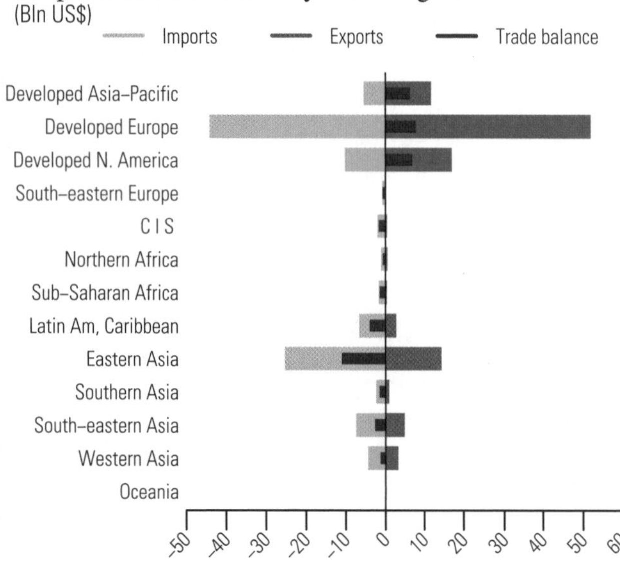

Table 3: Top importing countries or areas in 2010

Country or area	Value (million US$)	Avg. Growth (%) 06-10	Growth (%) 09-10	World share %	Cum.
World	111 962.3	9.1	23.5	100.0	
China	10 532.9	13.1	36.3	9.4	9.4
Germany	10 224.0	8.3	19.7	9.1	18.5
USA	7 848.0	4.1	22.9	7.0	25.5
Other Asia, nes	7 084.8	10.2	54.3	6.3	31.9
Rep. of Korea	6 139.6	9.0	31.7	5.5	37.4
France	4 525.1	2.9	10.4	4.0	41.4
Japan	4 496.6	5.0	35.2	4.0	45.4
Italy	4 475.4	9.0	20.7	4.0	49.4
United Kingdom	4 115.4	7.7	17.9	3.7	53.1
Netherlands	3 459.9	12.4	-3.3	3.1	56.2
Belgium	3 433.5	6.8	9.9	3.1	59.2
Spain	3 357.3	14.6	22.8	3.0	62.2
Singapore	2 599.2	10.1	52.8	2.3	64.6
Mexico	2 522.9	7.4	28.2	2.3	66.8
Canada	2 376.4	5.1	18.3	2.1	68.9

Manufactured goods classified chiefly by material

(SITC Section 6)

611 Leather

After a sharp decline of 28.2 percent in 2009, the value (in current prices) of exports of leather (SITC group 611) rose significantly in 2010 by 40.9 percent to amount to 23.4 bln US$ (see table 2). Imports showed a similar development with an increase of 31.8 percent to 19.9 bln US$ in 2010 (see table 3). Graph 1 shows that the increase in exports for 2010 in this product group was well above both the increase in world exports of manufactured goods classified chiefly by material (SITC section 6) of 24.5 percent and the increase in total world exports of 21.2 percent. Exports of leather (SITC group 611) accounted for 1.2 percent of world exports of SITC section 6 and 0.2 percent of total world exports in 2010 (see table 1).

The top exporting countries or areas in 2010 were Italy, Nigeria and China, Hong Kong SAR (see table 2). Their exports represented 18.7, 13.0 and 8.9 percent of world exports, respectively. Major destinations were China, China, Hong Kong SAR and Italy (see table 3). By MDG regions (see graph 2), Sub-Saharan Africa, Latin America and the Caribbean and Developed Europe recorded trade surpluses amounting respectively to 3.1 bln US$, 2.8 bln US$ and 1.1 bln US$. Top trade deficits were recorded by Eastern Asia (-3.2 bln US$), South-eastern Asia (-1.1 bln US$) and South-eastern Europe (-0.9 bln US$).

Table 1: Imports (Imp.) and exports (Exp.), 1996-2010, in current prices

		1996	1997	1998	1999	2000	2001	2002	2003	2004	2005	2006	2007	2008	2009	2010
Values in Bln US$	Imp.	14.9	15.1	13.9	13.2	15.2	16.4	16.2	18.0	19.8	19.9	21.7	23.2	21.6	15.1	19.9
	Exp.	16.1	16.2	14.8	14.1	16.4	17.3	16.8	18.5	20.5	20.6	22.9	25.0	23.1	16.6	23.4
As a percentage of SITC section (%)	Imp.	1.8	1.8	1.7	1.6	1.7	1.9	1.8	1.8	1.5	1.4	1.3	1.2	1.0	1.0	1.0
	Exp.	2.0	1.9	1.8	1.8	1.9	2.1	1.9	1.8	1.6	1.4	1.4	1.3	1.1	1.1	1.2
As a percentage of world trade (%)	Imp.	0.3	0.3	0.3	0.2	0.2	0.3	0.2	0.2	0.2	0.2	0.2	0.2	0.1	0.1	0.1
	Exp.	0.3	0.3	0.3	0.3	0.3	0.3	0.3	0.2	0.2	0.2	0.2	0.2	0.1	0.1	0.2

Graph 1: Annual growth rates of exports, 1996–2010

(In percentage by year)

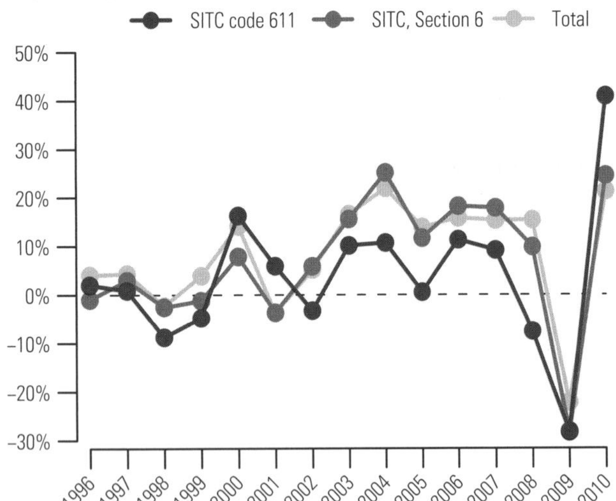

Graph 2: Trade Balance by MDG regions 2010

(Bln US$)

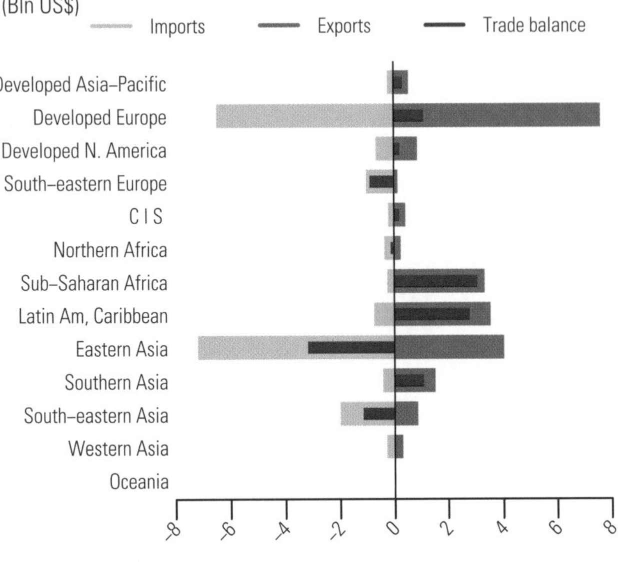

Table 2: Top exporting countries or areas in 2010

Country or area	Value (million US$)	Avg. Growth (%) 06-10	Growth (%) 09-10	World share %	Cum.
World	23360.6	0.5	40.9	100.0	
Italy	4368.0	-1.2	19.5	18.7	18.7
Nigeria	3036.8	149.6	492.5	13.0	31.7
China, Hong Kong SAR	2070.5	-8.8	29.5	8.9	40.6
Brazil	1732.0	-1.9	50.3	7.4	48.0
Argentina	990.5	2.9	52.1	4.2	52.2
USA	863.1	-4.5	53.8	3.7	55.9
Rep. of Korea	800.7	-0.8	18.6	3.4	59.3
India	784.9	2.7	44.3	3.4	62.7
Germany	744.8	-2.8	26.9	3.2	65.9
Other Asia, nes	731.1	-1.3	19.9	3.1	69.0
Spain	484.8	3.6	25.7	2.1	71.1
Austria	458.3	8.1	12.9	2.0	73.1
Thailand	434.5	6.8	32.8	1.9	74.9
Pakistan	413.5	6.8	53.1	1.8	76.7
China	406.7	-30.6	71.2	1.7	78.4

Table 3: Top importing countries or areas in 2010

Country or area	Value (million US$)	Avg. Growth (%) 06-10	Growth (%) 09-10	World share %	Cum.
World	19865.7	-2.2	31.8	100.0	
China	3906.1	-1.4	29.3	19.7	19.7
China, Hong Kong SAR	2660.0	-7.0	38.4	13.4	33.1
Italy	2284.9	-3.3	48.1	11.5	44.6
Viet Nam	*1044.0*	10.6	66.9	5.3	49.8
Germany	754.2	-1.6	18.6	3.8	53.6
Romania	613.9	-6.8	2.6	3.1	56.7
USA	562.1	-9.0	26.8	2.8	59.5
Spain	521.0	-2.1	27.9	2.6	62.1
Portugal	447.7	7.2	54.1	2.3	64.4
Poland	437.6	-5.0	29.1	2.2	66.6
France	433.6	3.1	20.6	2.2	68.8
Rep. of Korea	394.1	-4.4	33.1	2.0	70.8
Mexico	386.0	-13.4	28.1	1.9	72.7
Thailand	355.1	1.6	43.4	1.8	74.5
Indonesia	344.2	45.2	64.2	1.7	76.2

After a drop of 20.7 percent in 2009, the value (in current prices) of exports of manufactures of leather or of composition leather, nes (SITC group 612) increased in 2010 by 16.4 percent to amount to 3.1 bln US$ (see table 2). Imports showed a similar development with an increase of 22.4 percent to 2.7 bln US$ in 2010 (see table 3). Graph 1 shows that the increase in exports for 2010 in this product group was below both the increase in world exports of manufactured goods classified chiefly by material (SITC section 6) of 24.5 percent and the increase in total world exports of 21.2 percent. Exports of manufactures of leather or of composition leather, nes (SITC group 612) accounted for 0.2 percent of world exports of SITC section 6 and less than 0.1 percent of total world exports in 2010 (see table 1).

Exports of China, the top exporting country, increased by 24.6 percent in 2010 and represented 19.6 percent of world exports (see table 2). Other major exporting countries were France and Germany, respectively with 12.9 and 6.1 percent of world exports. Top destinations were USA, Mexico and Germany (see table 3). By MDG regions (see graph 2), Developed Europe accounted for a large share of trade in manufactures of leather or of composition leather, nes (SITC group 612). In 2010, its exports were valued at 1.5 bln US$ while imports amounted to 1.2 bln US$ resulting in a trade surplus of 0.3 bln US$. Surpluses were also recorded by Eastern Asia (+592 mln US$) and Southern Asia (+136 mln US$). Significant deficits were recorded by Developed North America (-411 mln US$) and Developed Asia-Pacific (-118 mln US$).

Table 1: Imports (Imp.) and exports (Exp.), 1996-2010, in current prices

		1996	1997	1998	1999	2000	2001	2002	2003	2004	2005	2006	2007	2008	2009	2010
Values in Bln US$	Imp.	1.0	1.0	1.1	1.1	1.3	1.4	1.5	1.9	2.4	2.4	2.5	2.7	2.8	2.2	2.7
	Exp.	1.0	1.2	1.3	1.5	1.7	1.7	2.0	2.3	2.9	3.1	3.4	3.5	3.4	2.7	3.1
As a percentage of SITC section (%)	Imp.	0.1	0.1	0.1	0.1	0.1	0.2	0.2	0.2	0.2	0.2	0.2	0.1	0.1	0.1	0.1
	Exp.	0.1	0.1	0.2	0.2	0.2	0.2	0.2	0.2	0.2	0.2	0.2	0.2	0.2	0.2	0.2
As a percentage of world trade (%)	Imp.	0.0	0.0	0.0	0.0	0.0	0.0	0.0	0.0	0.0	0.0	0.0	0.0	0.0	0.0	0.0
	Exp.	0.0	0.0	0.0	0.0	0.0	0.0	0.0	0.0	0.0	0.0	0.0	0.0	0.0	0.0	0.0

Graph 1: Annual growth rates of exports, 1996–2010

(In percentage by year)

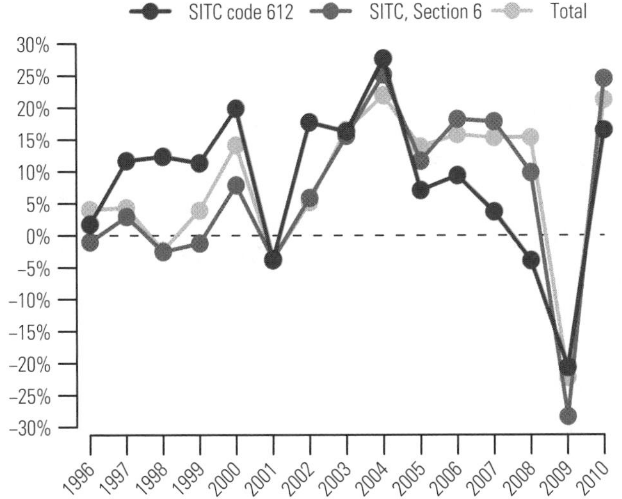

Graph 2: Trade Balance by MDG regions 2010

(Bln US$)

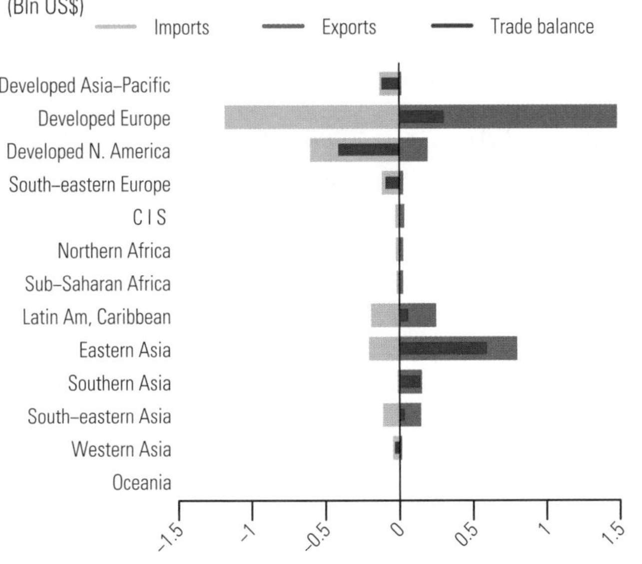

Table 2: Top exporting countries or areas in 2010

Country or area	Value (million US$)	Avg. Growth (%) 06-10	Growth (%) 09-10	World share %	Cum.
World	3140.2	-2.1	16.4	100.0	
China	615.0	-6.6	24.6	19.6	19.6
France	404.2	5.4	11.4	12.9	32.5
Germany	191.5	4.7	8.7	6.1	38.6
USA	169.9	-12.6	31.4	5.4	44.0
Italy	138.4	0.7	14.5	4.4	48.4
Hungary	132.7	2.3	21.5	4.2	52.6
India	130.4	-0.7	4.2	4.2	56.8
China, Hong Kong SAR	120.0	15.4	65.9	3.8	60.6
Mexico	113.1	-6.0	2.7	3.6	64.2
Croatia	94.3	18.8	45.0	3.0	67.2
Poland	84.6	-2.9	31.9	2.7	69.9
Austria	78.0	-4.4	8.7	2.5	72.4
Brazil	62.6	-10.8	-14.4	2.0	74.3
Slovakia	57.2	17.7	98.4	1.8	76.2
Thailand	51.9	-2.2	-16.6	1.7	77.8

Table 3: Top importing countries or areas in 2010

Country or area	Value (million US$)	Avg. Growth (%) 06-10	Growth (%) 09-10	World share %	Cum.
World	2678.4	1.8	22.4	100.0	
USA	514.4	1.2	25.3	19.2	19.2
Mexico	170.0	-11.4	64.5	6.3	25.6
Germany	160.0	5.7	12.5	6.0	31.5
France	140.1	9.9	11.7	5.2	36.8
United Kingdom	117.2	-2.7	0.0	4.4	41.1
China, Hong Kong SAR	102.2	22.4	51.8	3.8	44.9
Japan	88.9	-1.3	5.0	3.3	48.3
Czech Rep.	87.7	-4.5	5.0	3.3	51.5
Canada	87.5	-1.4	20.7	3.3	54.8
Italy	85.1	15.3	39.7	3.2	58.0
Romania	84.7	23.7	69.4	3.2	61.1
Singapore	78.3	10.6	26.7	2.9	64.1
China	68.3	-4.9	36.0	2.5	66.6
Spain	66.4	4.9	55.9	2.5	69.1
Poland	65.5	6.2	9.4	2.4	71.5

613 Furskins, tanned or dressed, other than those of heading 848.31

After a sharp decline of 25.2 percent in 2009, the value (in current prices) of exports of tanned or dressed furskins (SITC group 613) rose significantly in 2010 by 16.2 percent to amount to 1.6 bln US$ (see table 2). Imports showed a similar development with an increase of 30.0 percent to 2.0 bln US$ in 2010 (see table 3). Graph 1 shows that the increase in exports for 2010 in this product group was below both the increase in world exports of manufactured goods classified chiefly by material (SITC section 6) of 24.5 percent and the increase in total world exports of 21.2 percent. Exports of tanned or dressed furskins (SITC group 613) accounted for 0.1 percent of world exports of SITC section 6 and less than 0.1 percent of total world exports in 2010 (see table 1).

China, Hong Kong SAR, the top exporting area in 2010, accounted for 27.0 percent of world exports (see table 2). Other major exporting countries were China and Italy. They accounted respectively for 19.3 and 7.4 percent of world exports. China, Hong Kong SAR was also the top destination: it accounted for 51.0 percent of world imports. Other major destinations were China and Italy (see table 3). By MDG regions (see graph 2), Eastern Asia was the origin of a large share of imports and the destination of a majority of exports of tanned or dressed furskins (SITC group 613). In 2010, its exports amounted to 0.7 bln US$ while imports were valued at 1.3 bln US$ resulting in a trade deficit of 0.6 bln US$. Top trade surpluses were recorded by Developed Europe (+192 mln US$) and Latin America & the Caribbean (+68 mln US$).

Table 1: Imports (Imp.) and exports (Exp.), 1996-2010, in current prices

		1996	1997	1998	1999	2000	2001	2002	2003	2004	2005	2006	2007	2008	2009	2010
Values in Bln US$	Imp.	1.7	1.5	1.1	0.9	1.1	1.1	1.2	1.4	1.6	1.7	1.9	1.9	2.0	1.5	2.0
	Exp.	1.8	1.7	1.3	1.0	1.1	1.1	1.2	1.3	1.5	1.7	1.8	1.7	1.8	1.4	1.6
As a percentage of SITC section (%)	Imp.	0.2	0.2	0.1	0.1	0.1	0.1	0.1	0.1	0.1	0.1	0.1	0.1	0.1	0.1	0.1
	Exp.	0.2	0.2	0.2	0.1	0.1	0.1	0.1	0.1	0.1	0.1	0.1	0.1	0.1	0.1	0.1
As a percentage of world trade (%)	Imp.	0.0	0.0	0.0	0.0	0.0	0.0	0.0	0.0	0.0	0.0	0.0	0.0	0.0	0.0	0.0
	Exp.	0.0	0.0	0.0	0.0	0.0	0.0	0.0	0.0	0.0	0.0	0.0	0.0	0.0	0.0	0.0

Graph 1: Annual growth rates of exports, 1996–2010
(In percentage by year)

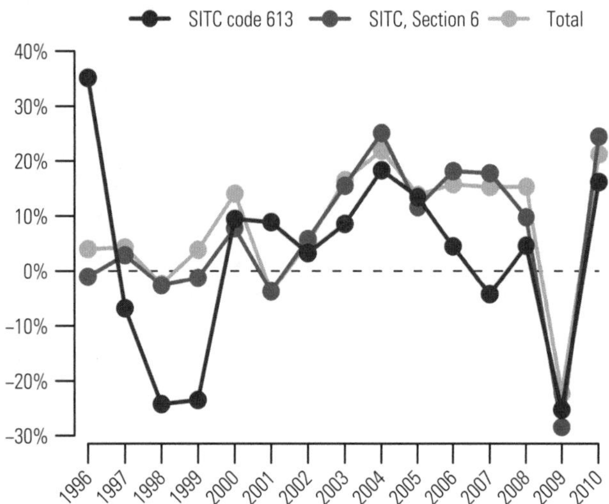

Graph 2: Trade Balance by MDG regions 2010
(Bln US$)

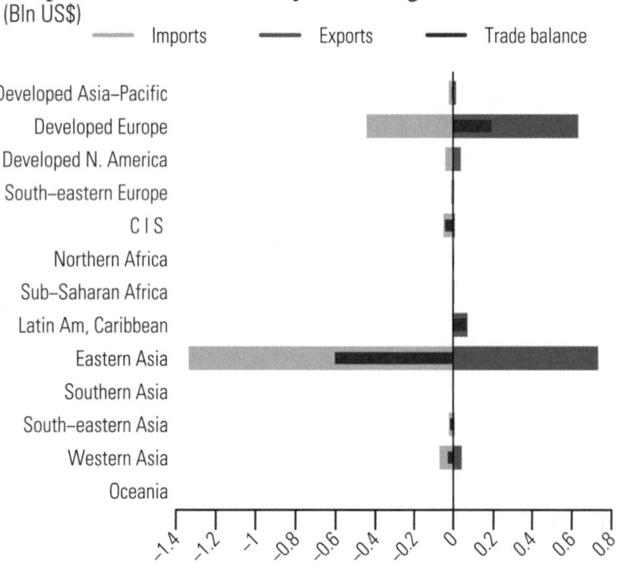

Table 2: Top exporting countries or areas in 2010

Country or area	Value (million US$)	Avg. Growth (%) 06-10	Growth (%) 09-10	World share %	Cum.
World	1 569.7	-3.4	16.2	100.0	
China, Hong Kong SAR	424.1	0.8	3.8	27.0	27.0
China	303.5	-1.5	1.5	19.3	46.4
Italy	116.3	-3.9	34.2	7.4	53.8
Spain	89.2	-12.3	-1.9	5.7	59.4
Poland	69.9	18.0	24.1	4.4	63.9
Netherlands	68.6	4.7	56.1	4.4	68.3
Germany	64.3	-8.8	28.9	4.1	72.4
Greece	48.4	-0.7	90.7	3.1	75.4
Turkey	39.3	-1.2	113.1	2.5	77.9
France	35.9	-12.3	48.0	2.3	80.2
Argentina	30.7	0.1	40.1	2.0	82.2
United Kingdom	29.6	-13.5	17.0	1.9	84.1
Brazil	26.5	1.5	28.4	1.7	85.8
Lithuania	22.5	21.2	98.5	1.4	87.2
USA	22.0	-10.7	41.8	1.4	88.6

Table 3: Top importing countries or areas in 2010

Country or area	Value (million US$)	Avg. Growth (%) 06-10	Growth (%) 09-10	World share %	Cum.
World	1 993.3	1.7	30.0	100.0	
China, Hong Kong SAR	1 016.4	10.1	27.7	51.0	51.0
China	236.1	9.0	23.1	11.8	62.8
Italy	101.9	-14.4	48.4	5.1	67.9
Greece	81.3	-16.2	22.5	4.1	72.0
Rep. of Korea	81.1	8.6	78.9	4.1	76.1
Turkey	68.0	-10.2	57.7	3.4	79.5
Germany	60.0	-5.8	7.7	3.0	82.5
Russian Federation	35.6	9.5	50.1	1.8	84.3
France	33.9	-4.8	47.4	1.7	86.0
Netherlands	25.7	-3.1	33.6	1.3	87.3
USA	25.0	-4.5	32.3	1.3	88.5
Denmark	23.5	-0.5	38.7	1.2	89.7
United Kingdom	21.9	-21.8	11.2	1.1	90.8
Viet Nam	*18.4*	27.3	66.9	0.9	91.7
Sweden	17.8	14.0	20.8	0.9	92.6

After a drop of 21.4 percent in 2009, the value (in current prices) of exports of materials of rubber (SITC group 621) increased in 2010 by 30.7 percent to amount to 20.2 bln US$ (see table 2). Imports showed a similar development with an increase of 33.5 percent to 21.0 bln US$ in 2010 (see table 3). Graph 1 shows that the increase in exports for 2010 in this product group exceeded both the increase in world exports of manufactured goods classified chiefly by material (SITC section 6) of 24.5 percent and the increase in total world exports of 21.2 percent. Exports of materials of rubber (SITC group 621) accounted for 1.0 percent of world exports of SITC section 6 and 0.1 percent of total world exports in 2010 (see table 1).

The top exporting countries in 2010 were Germany, Thailand and USA (see table 2). They accounted respectively for 15.4, 9.8 and 8.6 percent of world exports. Top destinations were China, USA and Germany (see table 3). By MDG regions (see graph 2), Developed Europe accounted for a large share of trade in materials of rubber (SITC group 621). In 2010, its exports and imports were valued respectively at 10.1 bln and 8.2 bln US$, resulting in a trade surplus of 1.9 bln US$. A significant trade surplus was also recorded by South-eastern Asia (+3.1 bln US$). Eastern Asia recorded a trade deficit of 3.6 bln US$.

Table 1: Imports (Imp.) and exports (Exp.), 1996-2010, in current prices

		1996	1997	1998	1999	2000	2001	2002	2003	2004	2005	2006	2007	2008	2009	2010
Values in Bln US$	Imp.	6.9	7.1	7.3	7.2	7.4	7.6	8.2	9.8	11.7	12.8	15.2	18.0	19.6	15.7	21.0
	Exp.	6.7	6.8	7.3	7.1	7.3	7.4	7.8	9.5	12.0	13.0	15.4	18.3	19.7	15.5	20.2
As a percentage of SITC section (%)	Imp.	0.8	0.8	0.9	0.9	0.8	0.9	0.9	1.0	0.9	0.9	0.9	0.9	0.9	1.0	1.1
	Exp.	0.8	0.8	0.9	0.9	0.9	0.9	0.9	0.9	0.9	0.9	0.9	0.9	0.9	1.0	1.0
As a percentage of world trade (%)	Imp.	0.1	0.1	0.1	0.1	0.1	0.1	0.1	0.1	0.1	0.1	0.1	0.1	0.1	0.1	0.1
	Exp.	0.1	0.1	0.1	0.1	0.1	0.1	0.1	0.1	0.1	0.1	0.1	0.1	0.1	0.1	0.1

Graph 1: Annual growth rates of exports, 1996–2010
(In percentage by year)

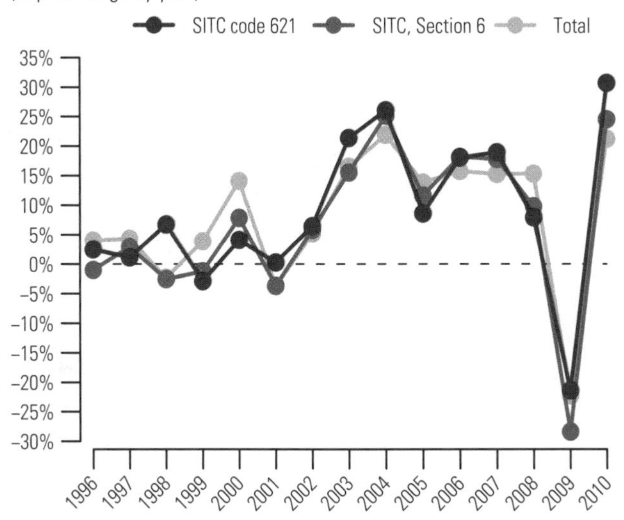

Table 2: Top exporting countries or areas in 2010

Country or area	Value (million US$)	Avg. Growth (%) 06-10	Growth (%) 09-10	World share %	Cum.
World	20 239.8	7.1	30.7	100.0	
Germany	3 110.0	2.0	31.0	15.4	15.4
Thailand	1 985.5	31.9	66.1	9.8	25.2
USA	1 732.8	4.3	29.6	8.6	33.7
Malaysia	1 581.4	23.1	48.0	7.8	41.6
Italy	1 325.8	0.9	19.5	6.6	48.1
Japan	1 063.4	10.5	45.8	5.3	53.4
France	1 006.7	-2.4	9.6	5.0	58.3
China	791.6	21.3	56.4	3.9	62.2
United Kingdom	728.7	-1.1	15.9	3.6	65.8
Belgium	655.5	1.9	14.9	3.2	69.1
Czech Rep.	589.5	10.4	39.5	2.9	72.0
Spain	556.0	1.1	2.8	2.7	74.7
Canada	430.2	-1.5	34.6	2.1	76.9
Netherlands	408.6	13.8	24.7	2.0	78.9
Poland	389.6	18.2	40.5	1.9	80.8

Graph 2: Trade Balance by MDG regions 2010
(Bln US$)

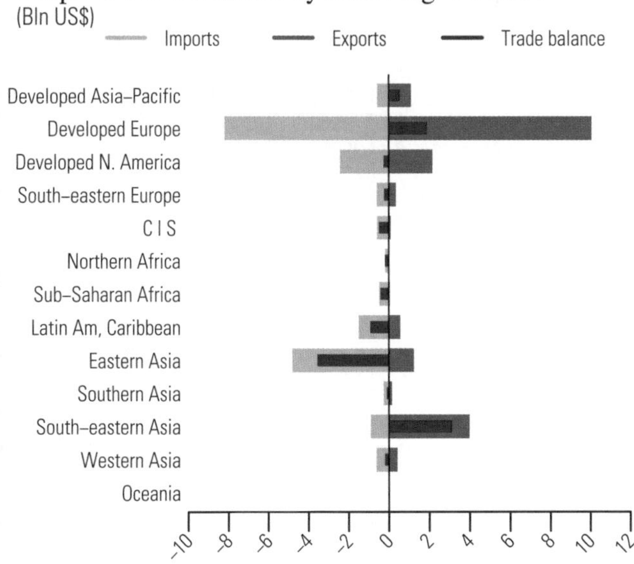

Table 3: Top importing countries or areas in 2010

Country or area	Value (million US$)	Avg. Growth (%) 06-10	Growth (%) 09-10	World share %	Cum.
World	21 021.4	8.4	33.5	100.0	
China	4 257.2	28.4	64.9	20.3	20.3
USA	1 665.9	2.9	40.6	7.9	28.2
Germany	1 617.2	2.0	19.4	7.7	35.9
France	973.1	0.8	26.8	4.6	40.5
United Kingdom	806.6	4.8	36.0	3.8	44.3
Canada	746.1	2.3	31.1	3.5	47.9
Spain	593.2	-2.9	6.6	2.8	50.7
Poland	582.5	9.3	23.3	2.8	53.5
Mexico	576.9	1.5	29.6	2.7	56.2
Belgium	537.8	3.4	21.1	2.6	58.8
Italy	525.0	0.4	29.9	2.5	61.3
Romania	489.1	14.1	38.1	2.3	63.6
Brazil	414.9	15.8	50.2	2.0	65.6
Netherlands	411.9	9.7	20.1	2.0	67.5
Russian Federation	350.6	15.4	59.5	1.7	69.2

625 Rubber tyres, interchangeable tyre treads, tyre flaps and inner tubes

After a drop of 14.4 percent in 2009, the value (in current prices) of exports of rubber tyres and tubes (SITC group 625) increased in 2010 by 23.6 percent to amount to 70.6 bln US$ (see table 2). Imports showed a similar development with an increase of 21.2 percent to 68.7 bln US$ in 2010 (see table 3). Graph 1 shows that the increase in exports for 2010 in this product group was similar to both the increase in world exports of manufactured goods classified chiefly by material (SITC section 6) of 24.5 percent and the increase in total world exports of 21.2 percent. Exports of rubber tyres and tubes (SITC group 625) accounted for 3.6 percent of world exports of SITC section 6 and 0.5 percent of total world exports in 2010 (see table 1).

China, Japan and Germany were the top exporting countries in 2010 (see table 2). They accounted respectively for 15.6, 10.0 and 7.9 percent of world exports. Top destinations were USA, Germany and France (see table 3). By MDG regions (see graph 2), Developed Europe accounted for a large share of trade in rubber tyres and tubes (SITC group 625). In 2010, its exports and imports were valued respectively at 26.7 bln and 29.0 bln US$ resulting in a trade deficit of 2.3 bln US$. Top trade deficits were also recorded by Developed North America (-7.7 bln US$) and Latin America and the Caribbean (-4.2 bln US$). Eastern Asia recorded a surplus amounting to 13.9 bln US$. Top trade surpluses were also recorded by Developed Asia-Pacific (+3.9 bln US$) and South-eastern Asia (+3.0 bln US$).

Table 1: Imports (Imp.) and exports (Exp.), 1996-2010, in current prices

		1996	1997	1998	1999	2000	2001	2002	2003	2004	2005	2006	2007	2008	2009	2010
Values in Bln US$	Imp.	24.4	24.2	25.3	25.5	25.5	24.8	26.9	31.7	38.4	44.1	50.0	60.4	66.5	56.7	68.7
	Exp.	24.6	25.1	25.8	25.7	24.8	24.0	26.0	30.9	37.9	43.6	49.9	60.0	66.7	57.1	70.6
As a percentage of SITC section (%)	Imp.	3.0	2.9	3.1	3.1	2.9	2.9	3.0	3.1	3.0	3.1	3.0	3.1	3.1	3.7	3.6
	Exp.	3.0	3.0	3.2	3.2	2.9	2.9	3.0	3.0	3.0	3.1	3.0	3.0	3.1	3.7	3.6
As a percentage of world trade (%)	Imp.	0.5	0.4	0.5	0.4	0.4	0.4	0.4	0.4	0.4	0.4	0.4	0.4	0.4	0.5	0.5
	Exp.	0.5	0.5	0.5	0.5	0.4	0.4	0.4	0.4	0.4	0.4	0.4	0.4	0.4	0.5	0.5

Graph 1: Annual growth rates of exports, 1996–2010
(In percentage by year)

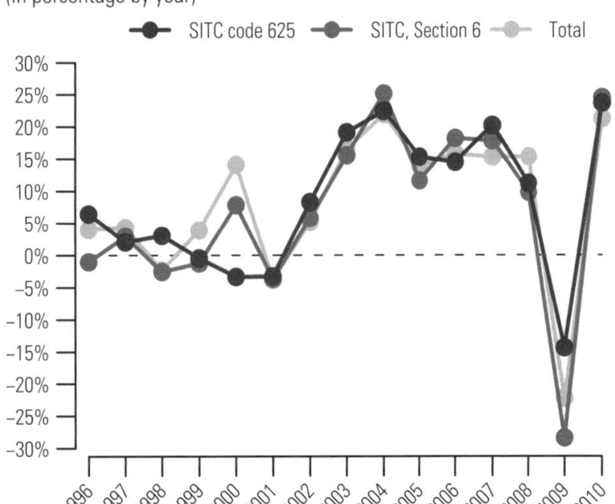

Table 2: Top exporting countries or areas in 2010

Country or area	Value (million US$)	Avg. Growth (%) 06-10	Growth (%) 09-10	World share %	Cum.
World	70557.3	9.0	23.6	100.0	
China	10978.3	19.2	34.7	15.6	15.6
Japan	7066.7	6.9	25.4	10.0	25.6
Germany	5585.5	6.1	22.8	7.9	33.5
USA	4555.7	8.1	15.2	6.5	39.9
France	3787.5	2.8	13.4	5.4	45.3
Rep. of Korea	3560.0	8.6	28.0	5.0	50.4
Thailand	2683.1	22.1	42.1	3.8	54.2
Spain	2408.3	0.4	8.7	3.4	57.6
Netherlands	2026.5	9.1	17.0	2.9	60.4
Canada	1977.1	3.0	22.7	2.8	63.3
Poland	1943.1	13.9	26.4	2.8	66.0
Czech Rep.	1942.3	10.4	17.5	2.8	68.8
Belgium	1602.3	8.0	8.7	2.3	71.0
Indonesia	1467.2	16.5	29.6	2.1	73.1
Brazil	1374.3	7.4	20.8	1.9	75.1

Graph 2: Trade Balance by MDG regions 2010
(Bln US$)

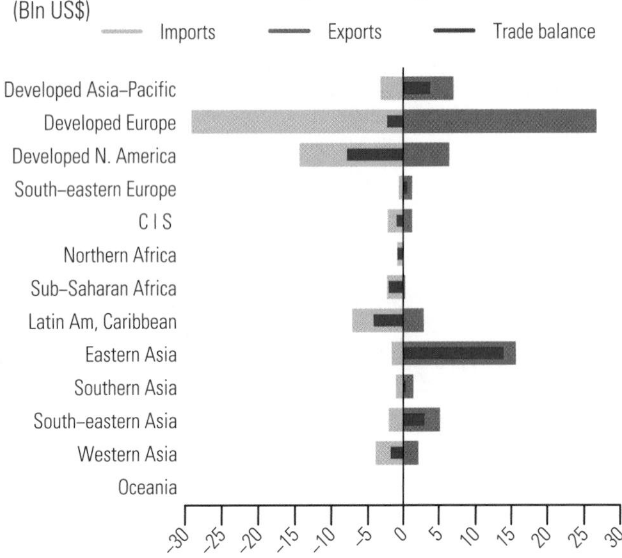

Table 3: Top importing countries or areas in 2010

Country or area	Value (million US$)	Avg. Growth (%) 06-10	Growth (%) 09-10	World share %	Cum.
World	68709.3	8.3	21.2	100.0	
USA	11335.7	5.2	31.9	16.5	16.5
Germany	6298.2	7.0	20.0	9.2	25.7
France	3607.2	10.6	11.8	5.3	30.9
Canada	2929.6	6.5	8.8	4.3	35.2
United Kingdom	2654.3	2.4	9.8	3.9	39.0
Italy	2383.8	4.9	5.9	3.5	42.5
Netherlands	2255.1	6.3	27.4	3.3	45.8
Mexico	2019.2	7.1	41.8	2.9	48.7
Belgium	1964.7	3.0	9.3	2.9	51.6
Australia	1952.2	11.7	28.9	2.8	54.4
Spain	1591.4	2.7	-1.9	2.3	56.7
Brazil	1333.7	30.4	87.9	1.9	58.7
Saudi Arabia	1309.7	16.7	15.7	1.9	60.6
Russian Federation	1228.1	15.2	44.7	1.8	62.4
Sweden	1001.4	-0.1	35.1	1.5	63.8

After a drop of 20.5 percent in 2009, the value (in current prices) of exports of rubber, nes (SITC group 629) increased in 2010 by 24.7 percent to amount to 25.6 bln US$ (see table 2). Imports showed a similar development with an increase of 28.5 percent to 28.8 bln US$ in 2010 (see table 3). Graph 1 shows that the increase in exports for 2010 in this product group was slightly above the increase in world exports of manufactured goods classified chiefly by material (SITC section 6) of 24.5 percent and the increase in total world exports of 21.2 percent. Exports of rubber, nes (SITC group 629) accounted for 1.3 percent of world exports of SITC section 6 and 0.2 percent of total world exports in 2010 (see table 1).

The top exporting countries in 2010 were Germany, Japan and USA (see table 2). They accounted respectively for 14.7, 9.1 and 8.9 percent of world exports. Top destinations were USA, Germany and China (see table 3). By MDG regions (see graph 2), Developed Europe accounted for a large share of trade in articles of rubber, nes (SITC group 629). In 2010, its exports and imports were valued respectively at 13.2 bln and 11.0 bln US$, resulting in a trade surplus of 2.2 bln US$. Top trade deficits were recorded by Latin America and the Caribbean (-2.0 bln US$) and Developed North America (-1.5 bln US$).

Table 1: Imports (Imp.) and exports (Exp.), 1996-2010, in current prices

		1996	1997	1998	1999	2000	2001	2002	2003	2004	2005	2006	2007	2008	2009	2010
Values in Bln US$	Imp.	10.3	10.9	11.5	11.9	12.5	12.6	13.6	15.8	18.5	20.0	22.0	25.8	28.0	22.4	28.8
	Exp.	9.6	10.1	10.5	10.7	11.3	11.3	12.2	14.5	17.0	18.3	20.5	24.1	25.8	20.5	25.6
As a percentage of SITC section (%)	Imp.	1.3	1.3	1.4	1.5	1.4	1.5	1.5	1.5	1.5	1.4	1.3	1.3	1.3	1.4	1.5
	Exp.	1.2	1.2	1.3	1.3	1.3	1.4	1.4	1.4	1.3	1.3	1.2	1.2	1.2	1.3	1.3
As a percentage of world trade (%)	Imp.	0.2	0.2	0.2	0.2	0.2	0.2	0.2	0.2	0.2	0.2	0.2	0.2	0.2	0.2	0.2
	Exp.	0.2	0.2	0.2	0.2	0.2	0.2	0.2	0.2	0.2	0.2	0.2	0.2	0.2	0.2	0.2

Graph 1: Annual growth rates of exports, 1996–2010
(In percentage by year)

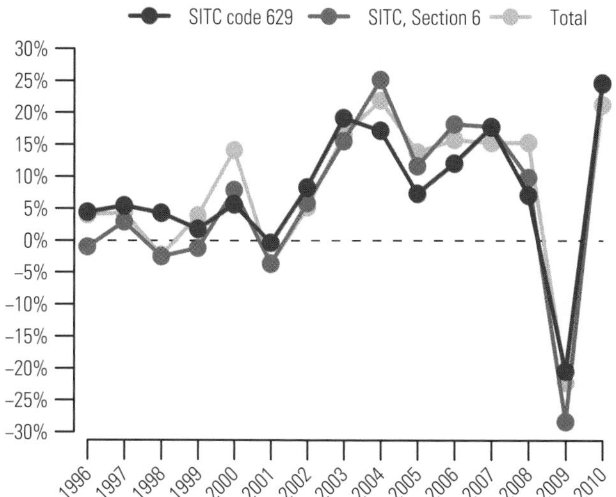

Graph 2: Trade Balance by MDG regions 2010
(Bln US$)

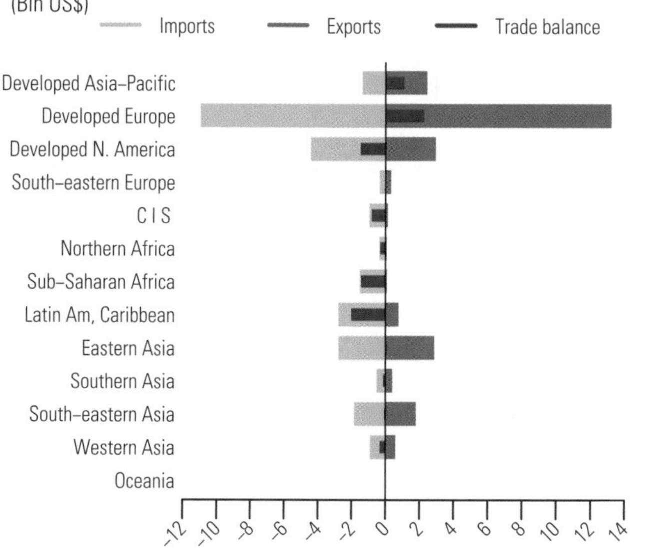

Table 2: Top exporting countries or areas in 2010

Country or area	Value (million US$)	Avg. Growth (%) 06-10	Growth (%) 09-10	World share %	Cum.
World	25585.6	5.7	24.7	100.0	
Germany	3754.5	4.9	18.5	14.7	14.7
Japan	2321.8	7.6	37.6	9.1	23.7
USA	2282.6	4.2	28.5	8.9	32.7
China	1970.7	14.1	40.2	7.7	40.4
France	1584.2	3.7	13.5	6.2	46.6
Italy	1327.9	3.8	31.8	5.2	51.8
Poland	1057.1	6.9	20.5	4.1	55.9
Belgium	884.3	8.8	13.2	3.5	59.3
Thailand	793.4	5.3	6.7	3.1	62.4
United Kingdom	727.2	0.9	20.6	2.8	65.3
Spain	700.8	1.2	32.1	2.7	68.0
Canada	666.8	-4.0	22.3	2.6	70.6
Sweden	565.0	6.3	24.4	2.2	72.8
Czech Rep.	508.6	7.5	20.7	2.0	74.8
Turkey	501.3	16.3	26.2	2.0	76.8

Table 3: Top importing countries or areas in 2010

Country or area	Value (million US$)	Avg. Growth (%) 06-10	Growth (%) 09-10	World share %	Cum.
World	28765.9	6.9	28.5	100.0	
USA	3465.9	2.2	33.9	12.0	12.0
Germany	2814.7	5.5	29.5	9.8	21.8
China	2024.4	15.1	37.8	7.0	28.9
France	1259.7	2.0	11.4	4.4	33.3
Mexico	1218.3	2.4	40.7	4.2	37.5
Canada	943.7	-0.8	18.3	3.3	40.8
Nigeria	908.1	144.6	472.8	3.2	43.9
United Kingdom	879.5	1.7	22.8	3.1	47.0
Japan	806.0	5.5	31.9	2.8	49.8
Italy	713.7	2.2	17.1	2.5	52.3
Belgium	661.7	2.3	11.3	2.3	54.6
Poland	661.4	7.0	15.3	2.3	56.9
Brazil	618.1	16.2	36.1	2.1	59.0
Czech Rep.	571.3	7.7	21.4	2.0	61.0
Spain	557.2	0.5	21.5	1.9	62.9

 Source: UN Comtrade

633 Cork manufacture

After a drop of 18.1 percent in 2009, the value (in current prices) of exports of cork manufactures (SITC group 633) increased in 2010 by 6.5 percent to amount to 1.4 bln US$ (see table 2). Imports showed a greater development with an increase of 11.7 percent to 1.5 bln US$ in 2010 (see table 3). Graph 1 shows that the increase in exports for 2010 in this product group was well below both the increase in world exports of manufactured goods classified chiefly by material (SITC section 6) of 24.5 percent and the increase in total world exports of 21.2 percent. Exports of cork manufactures (SITC group 633) accounted for 0.1 percent of world exports of SITC section 6 and less than 0.1 percent of total world exports in 2010 (see table 1).

Portugal, the top exporting country in 2010, accounted for nearly two-thirds (63.6 percent) of world exports (see table 2). Other major exporting countries were Spain and France, respectively with 11.9 and 4.4 percent of world exports. Major destinations were France, USA and Italy (see table 3). By MDG regions (see graph 2), Developed Europe accounted for a majority of exports and a large share of imports. In 2010 its exports and imports were valued respectively at 1.3 bln and 0.8 bln US$ resulting in a trade surplus of 0.5 bln US$. Top trade deficits were recorded by Developed North America (-205 mln US$) and Latin America and the Caribbean (-99 mln US$).

Table 1: Imports (Imp.) and exports (Exp.), 1996-2010, in current prices

		1996	1997	1998	1999	2000	2001	2002	2003	2004	2005	2006	2007	2008	2009	2010
Values in Bln US$	Imp.	1.0	1.0	1.1	1.2	1.2	1.2	1.2	1.4	1.5	1.5	1.5	1.7	1.6	1.3	1.5
	Exp.	1.0	1.1	1.2	1.2	1.2	1.2	1.3	1.5	1.6	1.5	1.6	1.7	1.7	1.4	1.4
As a percentage of SITC section (%)	Imp.	0.1	0.1	0.1	0.1	0.1	0.1	0.1	0.1	0.1	0.1	0.1	0.1	0.1	0.1	0.1
	Exp.	0.1	0.1	0.1	0.2	0.1	0.1	0.1	0.1	0.1	0.1	0.1	0.1	0.1	0.1	0.1
As a percentage of world trade (%)	Imp.	0.0	0.0	0.0	0.0	0.0	0.0	0.0	0.0	0.0	0.0	0.0	0.0	0.0	0.0	0.0
	Exp.	0.0	0.0	0.0	0.0	0.0	0.0	0.0	0.0	0.0	0.0	0.0	0.0	0.0	0.0	0.0

Graph 1: Annual growth rates of exports, 1996–2010

(In percentage by year)

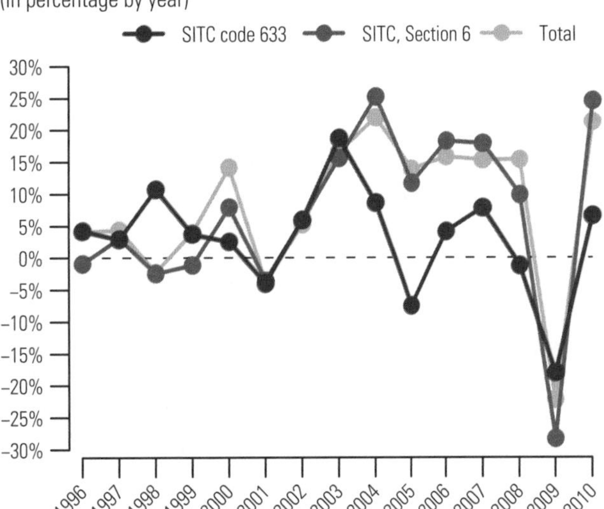

Graph 2: Trade Balance by MDG regions 2010

(Bln US$)

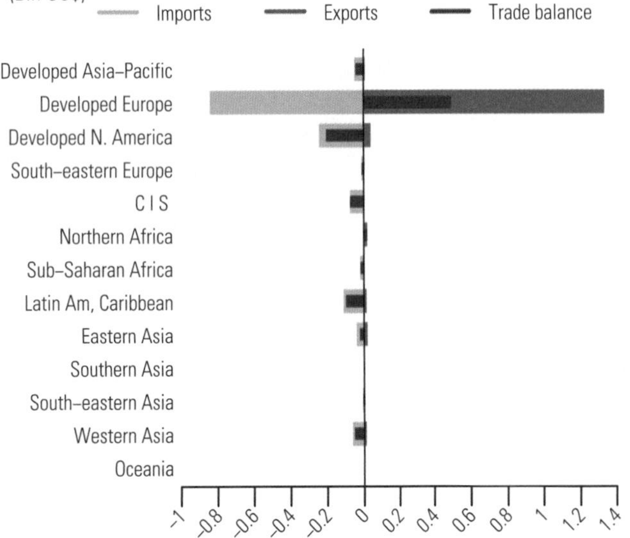

Table 2: Top exporting countries or areas in 2010

Country or area	Value (million US$)	Avg. Growth (%) 06-10	Growth (%) 09-10	World share %	Cum.
World	1440.5	-1.8	6.5	100.0	
Portugal	916.7	-0.4	7.6	63.6	63.6
Spain	170.8	-3.6	8.7	11.9	75.5
France	63.0	4.9	10.7	4.4	79.9
Italy	51.3	0.5	-3.9	3.6	83.4
Germany	36.0	-5.2	-5.3	2.5	85.9
USA	33.4	-15.6	-8.3	2.3	88.3
Switzerland	33.2	12.5	2.1	2.3	90.6
Belgium	19.4	-5.7	44.7	1.3	91.9
China	15.5	-7.2	11.7	1.1	93.0
Netherlands	12.4	15.2	69.0	0.9	93.8
Austria	11.4	-6.0	-16.3	0.8	94.6
United Arab Emirates	9.8	-16.6	10.9	0.7	95.3
Morocco	8.5	-1.2	-3.8	0.6	95.9
Chile	8.4	26.5	27.9	0.6	96.5
Tunisia	5.7	-2.0	-1.0	0.4	96.9

Table 3: Top importing countries or areas in 2010

Country or area	Value (million US$)	Avg. Growth (%) 06-10	Growth (%) 09-10	World share %	Cum.
World	1470.4	-1.2	11.7	100.0	
France	296.7	-0.4	7.1	20.2	20.2
USA	209.9	-2.3	1.2	14.3	34.4
Italy	129.4	-0.6	14.5	8.8	43.2
Germany	122.1	-3.0	17.6	8.3	51.6
Spain	95.3	-10.2	5.3	6.5	58.0
Russian Federation	51.2	35.4	78.0	3.5	61.5
Argentina	43.6	3.5	18.0	3.0	64.5
United Arab Emirates	40.2	-1.3	224.2	2.7	67.2
Chile	36.4	0.7	6.0	2.5	69.7
China	35.3	18.2	45.1	2.4	72.1
Switzerland	33.1	2.5	3.6	2.2	74.3
Canada	32.6	2.3	2.3	2.2	76.6
Portugal	31.1	-8.0	0.9	2.1	78.7
United Kingdom	26.4	3.0	36.2	1.8	80.5
Australia	24.4	-13.8	26.9	1.7	82.1

Source: UN Comtrade

The value (in current prices) of exports of veneers, plywood, particle board, and other wood, worked, nes (SITC group 634) increased by 16.1 percent and amounted to 30.3 bln US$ in 2010 (see table 2). Imports also increased by 17.3 percent to 29.2 bln US$ (see table 3). Graph 1 shows that the rise in exports for 2010 in this product group was exceeded by the increases in world exports of manufactured goods classified chiefly by material (SITC section 6) of 24.5 percent and in total world exports of 21.2 percent. Exports of veneers, plywood, particle board, and other wood, worked, nes (SITC group 634) accounted for 1.6 percent of world exports of SITC section 6 and 0.2 percent of total world exports (see table 1).

The top exporting countries in 2010 were China, Germany and Malaysia (see table 2). They accounted respectively for 15.8, 10.8 and 7.2 percent of world exports. Top destinations were USA, Japan and Germany (see table 3). By MDG regions (see graph 2), Developed Europe accounted for a large share of trade in veneers, plywood, etc (SITC group 634). In 2010, its exports amounted to 13.0 bln US$ while imports were valued at 11.9 bln US$ resulting in a trade surplus of 1.1 bln US$. Top surpluses were recorded by South-eastern Asia (+3.5 bln US$) and Eastern Asia (+3.0 bln US$). Top deficits were recorded by Developed Asia-Pacific (-2.1 bln US$) and Developed North America (-1.9 bln US$) among others.

Table 1: Imports (Imp.) and exports (Exp.), 1996-2010, in current prices

		1996	1997	1998	1999	2000	2001	2002	2003	2004	2005	2006	2007	2008	2009	2010
Values in Bln US$	Imp.	17.6	18.3	16.7	18.0	18.2	17.4	19.0	22.6	28.9	30.2	32.2	35.0	33.4	24.9	29.2
	Exp.	18.0	18.3	16.3	17.7	17.3	16.8	18.8	21.9	28.0	29.9	32.5	36.0	35.0	26.1	30.3
As a percentage of SITC section (%)	Imp.	2.2	2.2	2.0	2.2	2.0	2.1	2.1	2.2	2.3	2.1	1.9	1.8	1.6	1.6	1.5
	Exp.	2.2	2.2	2.0	2.2	2.0	2.0	2.1	2.2	2.2	2.1	1.9	1.8	1.6	1.7	1.6
As a percentage of world trade (%)	Imp.	0.3	0.3	0.3	0.3	0.3	0.3	0.3	0.3	0.3	0.3	0.3	0.3	0.2	0.2	0.2
	Exp.	0.3	0.3	0.3	0.3	0.3	0.3	0.3	0.3	0.3	0.3	0.3	0.3	0.2	0.2	0.2

Graph 1: Annual growth rates of exports, 1996–2010

(In percentage by year)

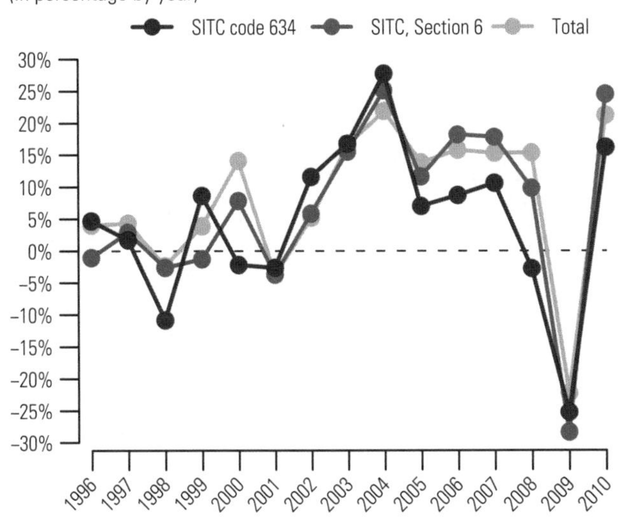

Table 2: Top exporting countries or areas in 2010

Country or area	Value (million US$)	Avg. Growth (%) 06-10	Growth (%) 09-10	World share %	Cum.
World	30328.5	-1.7	16.1	100.0	
China	4776.9	6.2	31.7	15.8	15.8
Germany	3287.6	-0.6	3.1	10.8	26.6
Malaysia	2177.9	-2.8	15.9	7.2	33.8
Indonesia	1719.3	-3.2	36.2	5.7	39.4
Canada	1493.4	-19.4	16.0	4.9	44.4
Austria	1397.4	1.4	2.1	4.6	49.0
Belgium	1255.8	-5.4	4.6	4.1	53.1
USA	1163.3	-2.1	25.9	3.8	56.9
France	965.1	-6.2	6.3	3.2	60.1
Russian Federation	941.0	5.8	25.6	3.1	63.2
Poland	828.6	-2.2	13.9	2.7	66.0
Spain	702.1	-2.8	2.6	2.3	68.3
Thailand	649.5	12.8	30.6	2.1	70.4
Chile	642.1	5.3	14.8	2.1	72.5
Italy	641.6	-0.8	21.6	2.1	74.7

Graph 2: Trade Balance by MDG regions 2010

(Bln US$)

Imports — Exports — Trade balance

Developed Asia-Pacific
Developed Europe
Developed N. America
South-eastern Europe
C I S
Northern Africa
Sub-Saharan Africa
Latin Am, Caribbean
Eastern Asia
Southern Asia
South-eastern Asia
Western Asia
Oceania

-12 -10 -8 -6 -4 -2 0 2 4 6 8 10 12 14

Table 3: Top importing countries or areas in 2010

Country or area	Value (million US$)	Avg. Growth (%) 06-10	Growth (%) 09-10	World share %	Cum.
World	29176.5	-2.4	17.3	100.0	
USA	3590.5	-16.0	16.8	12.3	12.3
Japan	2224.1	-6.2	24.1	7.6	19.9
Germany	1984.2	0.3	18.6	6.8	26.7
France	1266.1	4.1	8.4	4.3	31.1
United Kingdom	1253.9	-6.0	13.8	4.3	35.4
Italy	1054.2	-1.4	24.7	3.6	39.0
Canada	954.6	0.3	20.2	3.3	42.3
Rep. of Korea	814.3	-2.0	7.9	2.8	45.0
Netherlands	785.8	-2.1	-0.1	2.7	47.7
Belgium	725.2	-2.2	9.2	2.5	50.2
Poland	655.7	1.1	22.0	2.2	52.5
Mexico	555.7	-1.0	17.0	1.9	54.4
Turkey	542.5	8.2	77.1	1.9	56.2
Russian Federation	514.7	11.3	41.0	1.8	58.0
Other Asia, nes	489.9	0.4	52.9	1.7	59.7

635 Wood manufactures, nes

In 2010, the value (in current prices) of exports of wood manufactures, nes (SITC group 635) rose by 8.3 percent to 22.5 bln US$ (see table 2). Similarly, imports showed a 8.7 percent increase and amounted to 23.0 bln US$ (see table 3). Graph 1 shows that the rise in exports for 2010 in this product group was by far exceeded by increases in world exports of manufactured goods classified chiefly by material (SITC section 6) of 24.5 percent and in total world exports of 21.2 percent. Exports of wood manufactures, nes (SITC group 635) accounted for 1.2 percent of world exports of SITC section 6 and 0.1 percent of total world exports (see table 1).

China, Germany and Poland were the top exporting countries in 2010 (see table 2). They accounted respectively for 17.0, 8.3 and 7.7 percent of world exports. Top destinations were USA, Germany and Japan (see table 3). By MDG regions (see graph 2), Developed Europe accounted for a majority of trade in wood manufactures, nes (SITC group 635). In 2010, its exports and imports were valued respectively at 11.5 bln US$ and 12.6 bln US$ resulting in a trade deficit of 1.1 bln US$. Both Developed North America and Developed Asia-Pacific recorded trade deficits amounting to 2.3 bln US$ while top trade surpluses were recorded by Eastern Asia (+3.6 bln US$) and South-eastern Asia (+2.1 bln US$).

Table 1: Imports (Imp.) and exports (Exp.), 1996-2010, in current prices

		1996	1997	1998	1999	2000	2001	2002	2003	2004	2005	2006	2007	2008	2009	2010
Values in Bln US$	Imp.	11.0	12.0	12.2	13.3	13.8	13.6	14.6	16.8	19.6	20.8	23.1	26.3	26.5	21.1	23.0
	Exp.	11.8	12.6	12.3	13.9	14.3	13.9	14.7	16.8	20.0	21.0	24.0	26.1	26.0	20.8	22.5
As a percentage of SITC section (%)	Imp.	1.4	1.4	1.5	1.6	1.6	1.6	1.6	1.6	1.5	1.5	1.4	1.3	1.2	1.4	1.2
	Exp.	1.5	1.5	1.5	1.7	1.7	1.7	1.7	1.6	1.6	1.5	1.4	1.3	1.2	1.3	1.2
As a percentage of world trade (%)	Imp.	0.2	0.2	0.2	0.2	0.2	0.2	0.2	0.2	0.2	0.2	0.2	0.2	0.2	0.2	0.2
	Exp.	0.2	0.2	0.2	0.2	0.2	0.2	0.2	0.2	0.2	0.2	0.2	0.2	0.2	0.2	0.1

Graph 1: Annual growth rates of exports, 1996–2010

(In percentage by year)

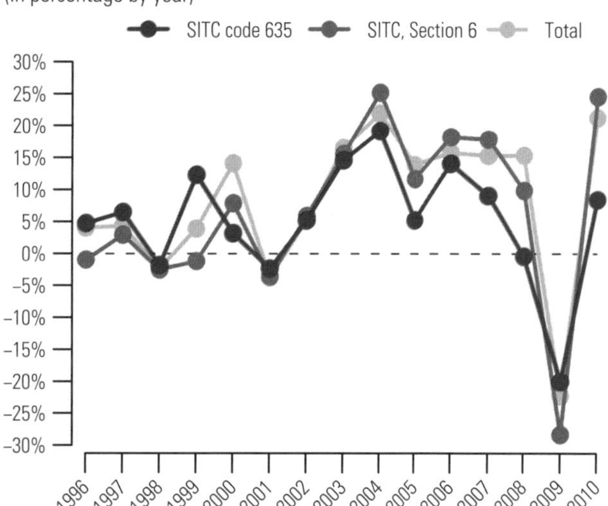

Table 2: Top exporting countries or areas in 2010

Country or area	Value (million US$)	Avg. Growth (%) 06-10	Growth (%) 09-10	World share %	Cum.
World	22 503.8	-1.6	8.3	100.0	
China	3 825.0	1.3	23.1	17.0	17.0
Germany	1 875.7	1.2	4.0	8.3	25.3
Poland	1 722.5	6.1	21.3	7.7	33.0
Austria	1 418.3	3.1	10.0	6.3	39.3
Canada	1 164.0	-17.3	6.0	5.2	44.5
USA	1 050.2	4.4	10.1	4.7	49.1
Philippines	1 028.7	12.1	25.4	4.6	53.7
France	765.0	-2.7	-7.4	3.4	57.1
Italy	750.5	0.2	3.2	3.3	60.4
Indonesia	570.3	-10.7	0.4	2.5	63.0
Sweden	569.6	-7.1	8.5	2.5	65.5
Denmark	527.9	-9.8	-14.8	2.3	67.8
Belgium	487.7	-0.2	8.1	2.2	70.0
Czech Rep.	413.7	-0.1	1.5	1.8	71.9
Malaysia	406.6	2.4	10.6	1.8	73.7

Graph 2: Trade Balance by MDG regions 2010

(Bln US$)

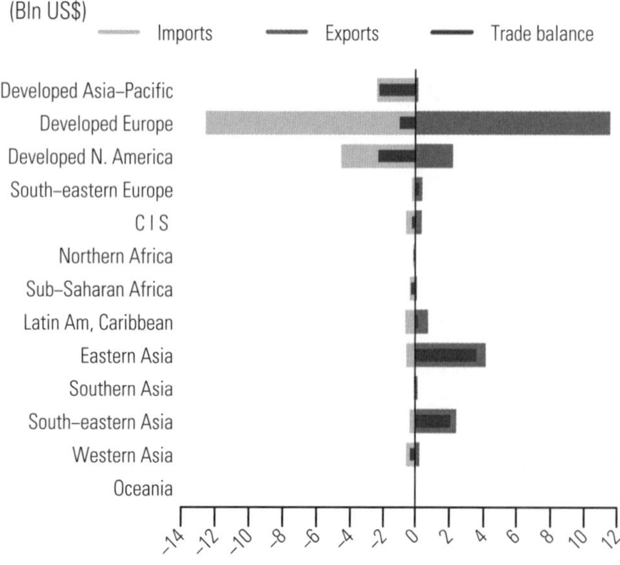

Table 3: Top importing countries or areas in 2010

Country or area	Value (million US$)	Avg. Growth (%) 06-10	Growth (%) 09-10	World share %	Cum.
World	22 973.1	-0.2	8.7	100.0	
USA	3 832.1	-10.6	7.4	16.7	16.7
Germany	2 248.0	1.6	8.9	9.8	26.5
Japan	1 998.1	1.6	16.6	8.7	35.2
France	1 462.5	5.2	2.7	6.4	41.5
United Kingdom	1 367.9	0.2	8.7	6.0	47.5
Italy	1 122.5	2.3	15.2	4.9	52.4
Switzerland	856.9	6.2	9.0	3.7	56.1
Belgium	721.3	3.7	6.0	3.1	59.2
Canada	683.8	2.4	17.0	3.0	62.2
Netherlands	637.2	2.5	3.3	2.8	65.0
Austria	569.9	3.2	-0.5	2.5	67.5
Norway	558.2	4.4	16.5	2.4	69.9
Denmark	522.0	-2.9	-5.7	2.3	72.2
Spain	511.4	-7.7	-0.2	2.2	74.4
Sweden	404.6	2.5	14.3	1.8	76.2

After a huge drop in 2009, the value (in current prices) of exports of paper and paperboard (SITC group 641) rose significantly by 12.0 percent to 110.5 bln US$ in 2010 (see table 2). Imports for the same year also increased by 11.1 percent to 112.4 bln US$ (see table 3). Graph 1 shows that the growth in exports for 2010 in this product group was exceeded by the increase in world exports of manufactured goods classified chiefly by material (SITC section 6) of 24.5 percent and the increase in total world exports of 21.2 percent. Exports of paper and paperboard (SITC group 641) accounted for 5.7 percent of world exports of SITC section 6 and 0.7 percent of total world exports (see table 1).

In 2010, Germany, USA and Finland were the top exporting countries (see table 2). They accounted for 14.1, 9.7 and 8.6 percent of world exports. USA, Germany and United Kingdom were the top destinations. By MDG regions, Developed Europe accounted for almost half of the trade in paper and paperboard (SITC group 641). In 2010, its exports amounted to 67.8 bln US$ and its imports to 52.6 bln US$ resulting in a trade surplus of 15.2 bln US$. A significant surplus was also recorded by Developed North America (+4.7 bln US$). Top trade deficits were recorded by Latin America and the Caribbean (-6.0 bln US$), Western Asia (-5.2 bln US$) and Southern Asia (-2.8 bln US$).

Table 1: Imports (Imp.) and exports (Exp.), 1996-2010, in current prices

		1996	1997	1998	1999	2000	2001	2002	2003	2004	2005	2006	2007	2008	2009	2010
Values in Bln US$	Imp.	69.1	67.4	69.3	68.9	71.7	69.5	75.9	85.3	95.8	99.7	106.1	115.8	122.7	101.2	112.4
	Exp.	66.7	65.6	67.2	66.5	70.5	67.6	73.8	83.0	93.1	95.8	103.2	112.9	119.5	98.7	110.5
As a percentage of SITC section (%)	Imp.	8.5	8.1	8.4	8.4	8.1	8.2	8.5	8.3	7.5	7.0	6.4	5.9	5.7	6.5	5.9
	Exp.	8.2	7.9	8.3	8.3	8.2	8.1	8.4	8.2	7.3	6.7	6.1	5.7	5.5	6.3	5.7
As a percentage of world trade (%)	Imp.	1.3	1.2	1.3	1.2	1.1	1.1	1.2	1.1	1.0	0.9	0.9	0.8	0.8	0.8	0.7
	Exp.	1.3	1.2	1.3	1.2	1.1	1.1	1.2	1.1	1.0	0.9	0.9	0.8	0.7	0.8	0.7

Graph 1: Annual growth rates of exports, 1996–2010

(In percentage by year)

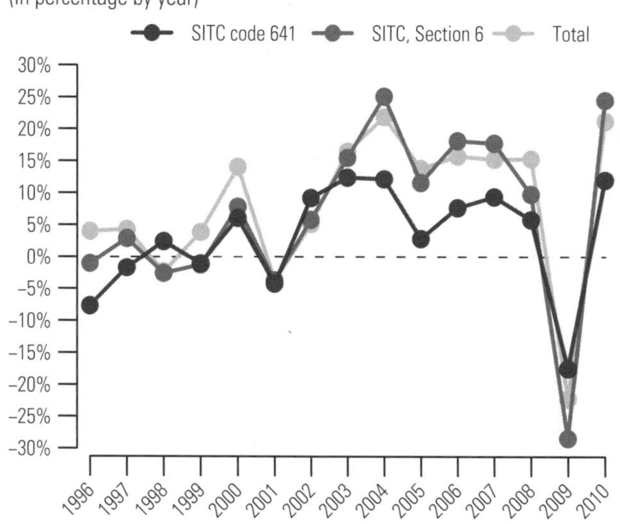

Table 2: Top exporting countries or areas in 2010

Country or area	Value (million US$)	Avg. Growth (%) 06-10	Growth (%) 09-10	World share %	Cum.
World	110499.5	1.7	12.0	100.0	
Germany	15604.5	1.2	12.6	14.1	14.1
USA	10698.9	4.7	17.6	9.7	23.8
Finland	9474.1	-1.9	10.5	8.6	32.4
Sweden	9467.1	1.7	7.1	8.6	40.9
Canada	7528.0	-8.2	0.7	6.8	47.8
France	5486.3	-0.4	5.2	5.0	52.7
Italy	4036.9	2.9	15.6	3.7	56.4
China	3790.8	9.6	20.9	3.4	59.8
Indonesia	3740.5	10.7	26.0	3.4	63.2
Austria	3479.9	0.3	4.5	3.1	66.3
Belgium	3267.4	0.8	11.3	3.0	69.3
Netherlands	2893.9	-3.2	6.5	2.6	71.9
Spain	2747.2	2.9	9.0	2.5	74.4
Japan	2554.9	4.7	34.7	2.3	76.7
Rep. of Korea	2247.5	4.6	20.1	2.0	78.7

Graph 2: Trade Balance by MDG regions 2010

(Bln US$)

Imports — Exports — Trade balance

Developed Asia-Pacific
Developed Europe
Developed N. America
South-eastern Europe
C I S
Northern Africa
Sub-Saharan Africa
Latin Am, Caribbean
Eastern Asia
Southern Asia
South-eastern Asia
Western Asia
Oceania

-60 -50 -40 -30 -20 -10 0 10 20 30 40 50 60 70

Table 3: Top importing countries or areas in 2010

Country or area	Value (million US$)	Avg. Growth (%) 06-10	Growth (%) 09-10	World share %	Cum.
World	112447.0	1.5	11.1	100.0	
USA	10379.6	-8.5	3.0	9.2	9.2
Germany	10216.7	-0.5	4.3	9.1	18.3
United Kingdom	6690.3	-1.6	6.8	5.9	24.3
France	6043.7	-0.6	-0.5	5.4	29.6
Italy	4979.0	1.7	14.3	4.4	34.1
China	3697.4	1.5	17.5	3.3	37.4
Belgium	3692.1	0.7	7.9	3.3	40.6
Spain	3111.3	-4.4	-0.2	2.8	43.4
Canada	3095.6	-2.0	7.2	2.8	46.2
Poland	3029.9	7.8	19.9	2.7	48.9
Netherlands	2918.3	-1.9	-3.6	2.6	51.4
Mexico	2774.4	1.3	24.9	2.5	53.9
Turkey	2493.0	8.3	29.5	2.2	56.1
Russian Federation	2406.6	12.6	22.8	2.1	58.3
Japan	2350.4	6.0	4.8	2.1	60.4

Source: UN Comtrade

642 Paper and paperboard, cut to size or shape; articles of paper or paperboard

During the recent five years, the value (in current prices) of exports of paper and paperboard, cut to size or shape and articles of paper or paperboard (SITC group 642) increased on average by 7.0 percent each year and amounted to 51.9 bln US$ in 2010 (see table 2). Similarly, imports for the 5-year period grew by 7.1 percent each year and in 2010 reached 52.5 bln US$ (see table 3). Graph 1 shows that the growth in exports for 2010 in this product group of 8.2 percent was by far exceeded by the increase in world exports of manufactured goods classified chiefly by material (SITC section 6) of 24.5 percent and by the increase in total world exports of 21.2 percent. Exports of paper and paperboard, cut to size or shape and articles of paper or paperboard (SITC group 642) accounted for 2.7 percent of world exports of SITC section 6 and 0.3 percent of total world exports (see table 1).

Germany, China and USA were the top exporting countries in 2010 (see table 2). They accounted respectively for 14.1, 10.2 and 8.8 percent of world exports. Top destinations were USA, France and Germany (see table 3). By MDG regions (see graph 2), a majority of trade in paper and paperboard, cut to size or shape and articles of paper or paperboard (SITC group 642) took place in Developed Europe. In 2010, its exports and imports were valued respectively at 28.0 bln US$ and 25.6 bln US$ resulting in a trade surplus of 2.4 bln US$ only. Eastern Asia recorded a large surplus amounting to 4.7 bln US$. Top trade deficit was recorded by Commonwealth of Independent States (-2.0 bln US$).

Table 1: Imports (Imp.) and exports (Exp.), 1996-2010, in current prices

		1996	1997	1998	1999	2000	2001	2002	2003	2004	2005	2006	2007	2008	2009	2010
Values in Bln US$	Imp.	26.0	26.0	26.7	27.9	29.2	30.1	27.0	31.0	34.8	37.1	39.9	48.3	53.8	48.8	52.5
	Exp.	26.4	25.7	26.5	27.6	28.8	29.8	26.9	30.7	34.2	36.3	39.5	47.3	52.0	48.0	51.9
As a percentage of SITC section (%)	Imp.	3.2	3.1	3.2	3.4	3.3	3.6	3.0	3.0	2.7	2.6	2.4	2.5	2.5	3.1	2.7
	Exp.	3.3	3.1	3.3	3.4	3.3	3.6	3.1	3.0	2.7	2.6	2.4	2.4	2.4	3.1	2.7
As a percentage of world trade (%)	Imp.	0.5	0.5	0.5	0.5	0.4	0.5	0.4	0.4	0.4	0.4	0.3	0.3	0.3	0.4	0.3
	Exp.	0.5	0.5	0.5	0.5	0.5	0.5	0.4	0.4	0.4	0.4	0.3	0.3	0.3	0.4	0.3

Graph 1: Annual growth rates of exports, 1996–2010

(In percentage by year)

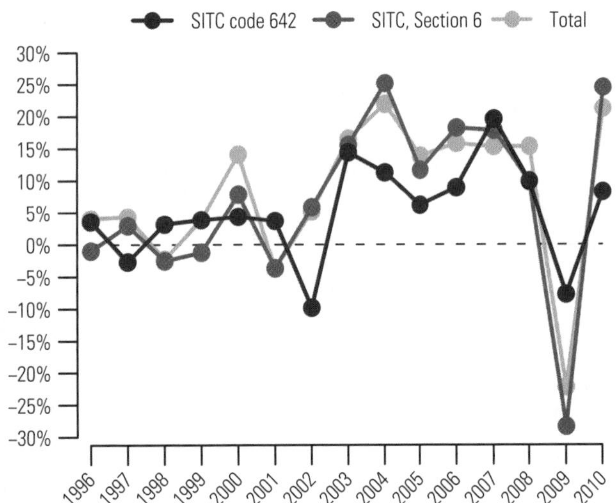

Graph 2: Trade Balance by MDG regions 2010

(Bln US$)

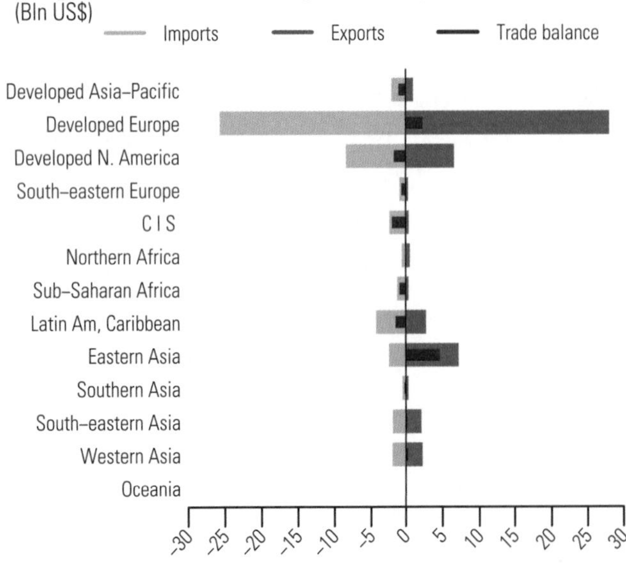

Table 2: Top exporting countries or areas in 2010

Country or area	Value (million US$)	Avg. Growth (%) 06-10	Growth (%) 09-10	World share %	Cum.
World	51 902.9	7.0	8.2	100.0	
Germany	7 302.1	4.9	2.0	14.1	14.1
China	5 308.4	20.1	30.6	10.2	24.3
USA	4 565.0	4.8	10.4	8.8	33.1
Italy	3 011.3	3.6	4.9	5.8	38.9
Netherlands	2 132.6	3.7	2.5	4.1	43.0
Canada	2 067.6	2.7	4.1	4.0	47.0
Poland	1 950.7	13.4	11.9	3.8	50.7
Belgium	1 920.5	1.7	-3.8	3.7	54.4
France	1 910.6	-1.8	-4.9	3.7	58.1
Spain	1 510.0	9.7	20.1	2.9	61.0
United Kingdom	1 395.9	-0.8	-2.2	2.7	63.7
Sweden	1 306.6	6.8	3.0	2.5	66.2
Mexico	1 077.1	2.0	11.2	2.1	68.3
Czech Rep.	1 006.3	10.2	2.4	1.9	70.3
Austria	978.7	4.2	-2.8	1.9	72.1

Table 3: Top importing countries or areas in 2010

Country or area	Value (million US$)	Avg. Growth (%) 06-10	Growth (%) 09-10	World share %	Cum.
World	52 461.7	7.1	7.6	100.0	
USA	5 847.1	4.7	12.4	11.1	11.1
France	3 632.9	4.9	0.6	6.9	18.1
Germany	3 593.3	2.9	4.6	6.8	24.9
United Kingdom	2 669.3	3.2	4.2	5.1	30.0
Canada	2 487.4	5.4	11.5	4.7	34.7
Belgium	1 739.3	3.4	-3.2	3.3	38.1
Netherlands	1 733.8	4.0	1.8	3.3	41.4
Mexico	1 680.4	1.7	9.1	3.2	44.6
Russian Federation	1 384.7	8.3	8.2	2.6	47.2
Spain	1 249.7	7.2	5.6	2.4	49.6
Switzerland	1 202.9	9.1	4.7	2.3	51.9
Japan	1 101.9	14.1	12.4	2.1	54.0
Italy	1 052.1	8.4	9.7	2.0	56.0
Poland	1 004.2	12.5	10.3	1.9	57.9
China, Hong Kong SAR	991.6	4.7	16.5	1.9	59.8

After a sharp decline in 2009, the value (in current prices) of exports of textile yarn (SITC group 651) went up by 31.1 percent to 49.8 bln US$ in 2010 (see table 2). Similarly, imports grew by 30.7 percent and totaled 47.4 bln US$ (see table 3). Graph 1 shows that the growth in exports for 2010 in this product group slightly exceeded the increases in world exports of manufactured goods classified chiefly by material (SITC section 6) of 24.5 percent and in total world exports of 21.2 percent. Exports of textile yarn (SITC group 651) accounted for 2.6 percent of world exports of SITC section 6 and 0.3 percent of total world exports (see table 1).

In 2010, China, India and China, Hong Kong SAR were the top exporting countries or areas (see table 2). They accounted respectively for 19.5, 8.8 and 6.6 percent of world exports. China, China, Hong Kong SAR and Italy were the top destinations (see table 3). By MDG regions (see graph 2), top trade surpluses were recorded by Eastern Asia (+4.5 bln US$), Southern Asia (+3.2 bln US$) and South-eastern Asia (+2.7 bln US$). Top trade deficits were recorded by Latin America and the Caribbean (-3.2 bln US$) and Developed Europe (-2.6 bln US$) among others.

Table 1: Imports (Imp.) and exports (Exp.), 1996-2010, in current prices

		1996	1997	1998	1999	2000	2001	2002	2003	2004	2005	2006	2007	2008	2009	2010
Values in Bln US$	Imp.	34.3	35.9	34.2	32.1	34.2	32.2	32.5	35.6	38.8	38.8	41.3	44.9	44.9	36.2	47.4
	Exp.	32.9	34.7	32.5	30.3	32.8	31.0	31.7	35.4	40.5	40.4	43.8	47.6	47.0	38.0	49.8
As a percentage of SITC section (%)	Imp.	4.2	4.3	4.1	3.9	3.8	3.8	3.7	3.5	3.0	2.7	2.5	2.3	2.1	2.3	2.5
	Exp.	4.1	4.2	4.0	3.8	3.8	3.7	3.6	3.5	3.2	2.8	2.6	2.4	2.2	2.4	2.6
As a percentage of world trade (%)	Imp.	0.6	0.6	0.6	0.6	0.5	0.5	0.5	0.5	0.4	0.4	0.3	0.3	0.3	0.3	0.3
	Exp.	0.6	0.6	0.6	0.5	0.5	0.5	0.5	0.5	0.4	0.4	0.4	0.3	0.3	0.3	0.3

Graph 1: Annual growth rates of exports, 1996–2010
(In percentage by year)

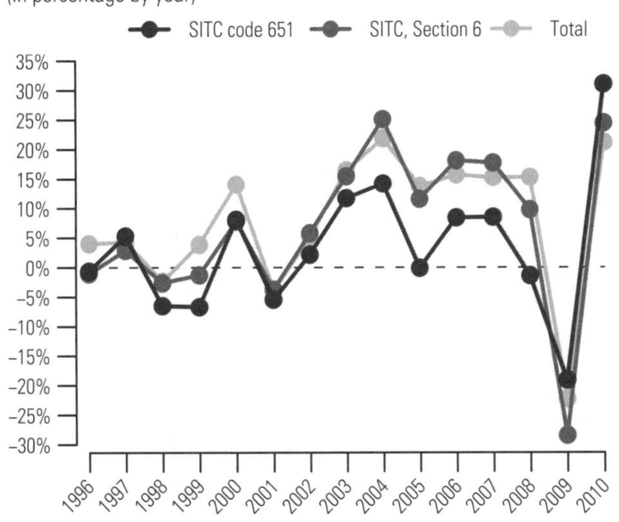

Graph 2: Trade Balance by MDG regions 2010
(Bln US$)

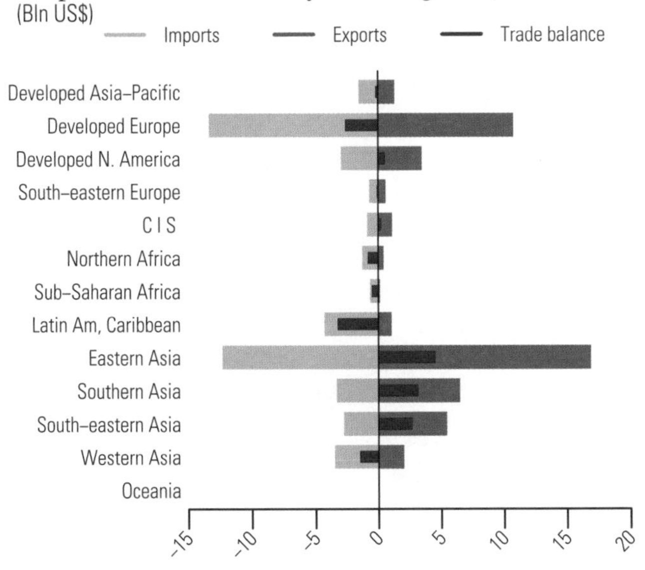

Table 2: Top exporting countries or areas in 2010

Country or area	Value (million US$)	Avg. Growth (%) 06-10	Growth (%) 09-10	World share %	Cum.
World	49829.5	3.2	31.1	100.0	
China	9722.0	10.1	38.1	19.5	19.5
India	4370.2	14.3	99.6	8.8	28.3
China, Hong Kong SAR	3280.3	-2.4	18.0	6.6	34.9
USA	2940.2	4.3	36.7	5.9	40.8
Italy	2625.1	-4.1	19.4	5.3	46.0
Other Asia, nes	2266.1	-0.8	26.8	4.5	50.6
Indonesia	2189.9	5.1	36.5	4.4	55.0
Germany	1787.1	-11.2	10.1	3.6	58.6
Pakistan	1697.7	3.1	27.7	3.4	62.0
Rep. of Korea	1600.2	3.6	36.1	3.2	65.2
Turkey	1299.8	2.9	23.7	2.6	67.8
Japan	1244.2	2.9	41.4	2.5	70.3
Thailand	1110.4	8.6	41.9	2.2	72.5
Viet Nam	*1030.9*	33.8	25.6	2.1	74.6
Belgium	923.7	-1.8	16.8	1.9	76.4

Table 3: Top importing countries or areas in 2010

Country or area	Value (million US$)	Avg. Growth (%) 06-10	Growth (%) 09-10	World share %	Cum.
World	47395.4	3.5	30.7	100.0	
China	5824.8	6.6	31.9	12.3	12.3
China, Hong Kong SAR	3617.1	-3.1	21.6	7.6	19.9
Italy	2797.2	-0.7	29.3	5.9	25.8
Turkey	2711.9	11.9	49.1	5.7	31.5
USA	2440.3	-2.4	33.0	5.1	36.7
Germany	2428.2	-0.3	30.1	5.1	41.8
Rep. of Korea	2321.1	8.1	48.9	4.9	46.7
Brazil	1574.4	19.7	35.1	3.3	50.0
Bangladesh	*1502.4*	32.7	151.7	3.2	53.2
Japan	1208.3	0.9	38.0	2.5	55.8
France	1154.0	-6.7	16.3	2.4	58.2
Belgium	979.3	-6.3	21.3	2.1	60.3
Viet Nam	*973.8*	22.4	66.9	2.1	62.3
United Kingdom	901.1	-3.6	26.6	1.9	64.2
Egypt	734.4	32.1	5.8	1.5	65.8

Source: UN Comtrade

652 Cotton fabrics, woven (not including narrow or special fabrics)

The value (in current prices) of exports of woven cotton fabrics (SITC group 652) increased by 17.9 percent and amounted to 28.4 bln US$ in 2010 (see table 2). For the same period, imports also increased by 22.9 percent to 24.3 bln US$ (see table 3). Graph 1 shows that the growth in exports for 2010 in this product group was exceeded by increases in world exports of manufactured goods classified chiefly by material (SITC section 6) of 24.5 percent and in total world exports of 21.2 percent. Exports of woven cotton fabrics (SITC group 652) accounted for 1.5 percent of world exports of SITC section 6 and 0.2 percent of total world exports (see table 1).

China, the top exporting country in 2010, accounted for 40.0 percent of world exports (see table 2). Other major exporting countries or areas were Pakistan and China, Hong Kong SAR, with 7.3 and 7.2 percent respectively (see table 3). By MDG regions (see graph 2), Eastern Asia recorded a trade surplus amounting to 10.0 bln US$. Top trade surpluses were also recorded by Developed Europe (+1.1 bln US$) and Southern Asia (+0.6 bln US$). Top trade deficits were recorded by South-eastern Asia (-2.5 bln US$), Northern Africa (-1.5 bln US$) and Latin America and the Caribbean (-1.4 bln US$).

Table 1: Imports (Imp.) and exports (Exp.), 1996-2010, in current prices

		1996	1997	1998	1999	2000	2001	2002	2003	2004	2005	2006	2007	2008	2009	2010
Values in Bln US$	Imp.	20.7	20.7	20.6	19.5	19.7	19.5	21.1	22.6	24.9	25.0	23.8	24.7	25.8	19.8	24.3
	Exp.	22.5	23.0	22.0	21.1	22.0	22.2	24.5	26.5	28.8	28.9	30.0	29.8	30.6	24.0	28.4
As a percentage of SITC section (%)	Imp.	2.5	2.5	2.5	2.4	2.2	2.3	2.4	2.2	2.0	1.7	1.4	1.3	1.2	1.3	1.3
	Exp.	2.8	2.8	2.7	2.6	2.5	2.7	2.8	2.6	2.3	2.0	1.8	1.5	1.4	1.5	1.5
As a percentage of world trade (%)	Imp.	0.4	0.4	0.4	0.3	0.3	0.3	0.3	0.3	0.3	0.2	0.2	0.2	0.2	0.2	0.2
	Exp.	0.4	0.4	0.4	0.4	0.3	0.4	0.4	0.4	0.3	0.3	0.3	0.2	0.2	0.2	0.2

Graph 1: Annual growth rates of exports, 1996–2010

(In percentage by year)

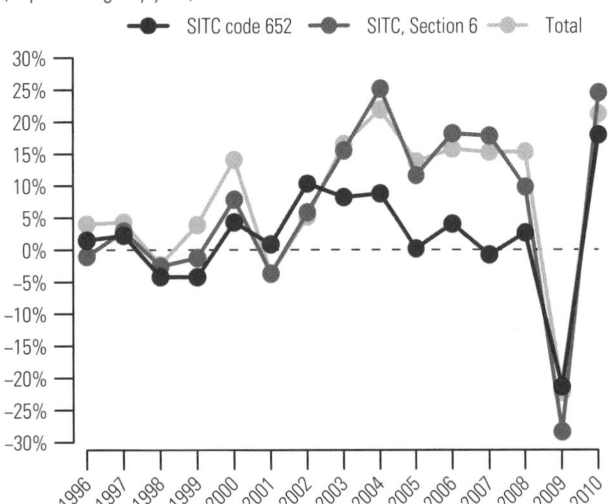

Graph 2: Trade Balance by MDG regions 2010

(Bln US$)

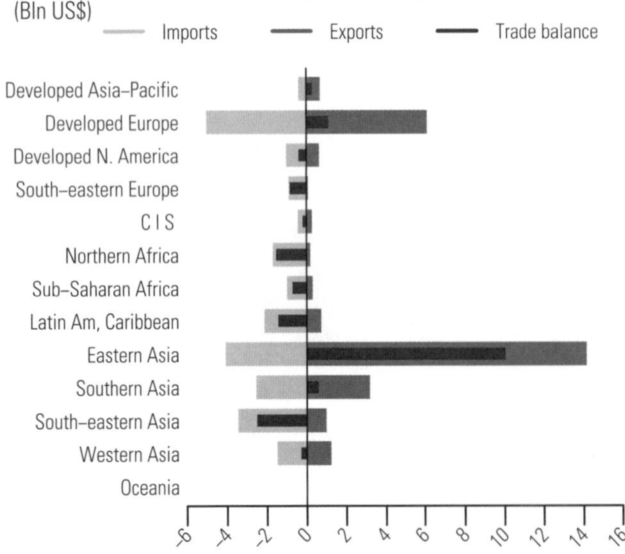

Table 2: Top exporting countries or areas in 2010

Country or area	Value (million US$)	Avg. Growth (%) 06-10	Growth (%) 09-10	World share %	Cum.
World	28364.3	-1.4	17.9	100.0	
China	11342.0	9.4	34.0	40.0	40.0
Pakistan	2081.8	0.3	23.6	7.3	47.3
China, Hong Kong SAR	2034.2	-10.7	3.2	7.2	54.5
Italy	1918.1	-9.3	7.4	6.8	61.3
India	1049.7	4.1	19.9	3.7	65.0
Germany	1029.9	-6.6	6.1	3.6	68.6
Turkey	1013.7	3.2	9.9	3.6	72.2
Japan	654.4	-10.2	-0.1	2.3	74.5
Spain	631.8	-3.1	12.6	2.2	76.7
USA	616.0	-13.1	7.8	2.2	78.9
France	512.4	-11.9	-4.7	1.8	80.7
Thailand	496.5	6.5	32.7	1.8	82.4
Rep. of Korea	454.0	-8.1	17.1	1.6	84.0
Belgium	386.0	-9.6	3.6	1.4	85.4
Netherlands	323.9	3.2	3.7	1.1	86.5

Table 3: Top importing countries or areas in 2010

Country or area	Value (million US$)	Avg. Growth (%) 06-10	Growth (%) 09-10	World share %	Cum.
World	24315.7	0.6	22.9	100.0	
Bangladesh	*1850.4*	69.9	360.0	7.6	7.6
China, Hong Kong SAR	1840.6	-10.0	3.1	7.6	15.2
China	1724.5	-6.5	1.1	7.1	22.3
Viet Nam	*1707.0*	33.2	66.9	7.0	29.3
Turkey	1126.7	4.7	36.6	4.6	33.9
Italy	1090.6	-1.1	24.2	4.5	38.4
Indonesia	1012.7	71.5	57.4	4.2	42.6
USA	905.6	-7.9	27.0	3.7	46.3
Tunisia	844.7	2.5	1.9	3.5	49.8
Germany	731.4	-6.2	13.0	3.0	52.8
Mexico	583.6	-9.1	17.2	2.4	55.2
Morocco	503.0	-4.6	6.1	2.1	57.2
Romania	487.5	-11.9	1.0	2.0	59.3
Spain	472.1	-3.3	21.3	1.9	61.2
France	472.1	-8.0	3.4	1.9	63.1

After a 15.8 percent decrease in 2009, the value (in current prices) of exports of woven fabrics of man-made textile materials (SITC group 653) increased by 14.5 percent and totaled 36.2 bln US$ (see table 2). Imports for the same year also grew by 17.3 percent to 29.7 bln US$ (see table 3). Graph 1 shows that the growth in exports in 2010 for this product group was exceeded by increases in world exports of manufactured goods classified chiefly by material (SITC section 6) of 24.5 percent and in total world exports of 21.2 percent. Exports of woven fabrics of man-made textile materials (SITC group 653) accounted for 1.9 percent of world exports of SITC section 6 and 0.2 percent of total world exports (see table 1).

China, the top exporting country in 2010, accounted for 34.4 percent of world exports (see table 2). China was also the top destination, together with Viet Nam and United Arab Emirates (see table 3). By MDG regions (see graph 2), Eastern Asia recorded a trade surplus amounting to 13.3 bln US$. Trade surpluses were also recorded by Southern Asia (+1.4 bln US$) and Developed Asia-Pacific (+1.1 bln US$). Top trade deficits were recorded by Latin America and the Caribbean (-2.5 bln US$), South-eastern Asia (-2.5 bln US$) and Northern Africa (-1.3 bln US$).

Table 1: Imports (Imp.) and exports (Exp.), 1996-2010, in current prices

		1996	1997	1998	1999	2000	2001	2002	2003	2004	2005	2006	2007	2008	2009	2010
Values in Bln US$	Imp.	31.4	31.0	30.5	28.8	29.2	26.6	25.9	26.8	28.7	28.2	28.7	30.3	30.9	25.3	29.7
	Exp.	34.3	34.8	32.1	30.3	31.6	28.3	27.7	29.8	32.6	32.3	33.5	36.3	37.6	31.6	36.2
As a percentage of SITC section (%)	Imp.	3.9	3.7	3.7	3.5	3.3	3.1	2.9	2.6	2.2	2.0	1.7	1.5	1.4	1.6	1.6
	Exp.	4.2	4.2	4.0	3.8	3.7	3.4	3.1	2.9	2.6	2.3	2.0	1.8	1.7	2.0	1.9
As a percentage of world trade (%)	Imp.	0.6	0.6	0.6	0.5	0.4	0.4	0.4	0.4	0.3	0.3	0.2	0.2	0.2	0.2	0.2
	Exp.	0.7	0.6	0.6	0.5	0.5	0.5	0.4	0.4	0.4	0.3	0.3	0.3	0.2	0.3	0.2

Graph 1: Annual growth rates of exports, 1996–2010

(In percentage by year)

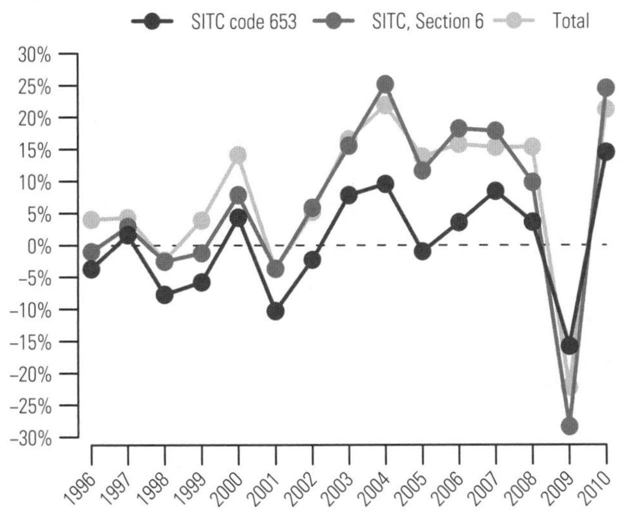

Table 2: Top exporting countries or areas in 2010

Country or area	Value (million US$)	Avg. Growth (%) 06-10	Growth (%) 09-10	World share %	Cum.
World	36220.1	2.0	14.5	100.0	
China	12468.7	8.3	26.3	34.4	34.4
Rep. of Korea	2246.4	1.8	19.9	6.2	40.6
Other Asia, nes	2121.7	-0.6	19.3	5.9	46.5
India	1986.7	18.6	4.1	5.5	52.0
Japan	1664.2	-1.2	6.8	4.6	56.6
Italy	1618.9	-4.8	5.1	4.5	61.0
Germany	1443.5	-5.4	2.8	4.0	65.0
Turkey	1353.9	2.6	7.6	3.7	68.8
United Arab Emirates	1144.0	6.0	6.1	3.2	71.9
Indonesia	1020.9	5.7	23.4	2.8	74.7
China, Hong Kong SAR	943.6	-8.7	13.8	2.6	77.3
USA	888.2	-7.2	19.0	2.5	79.8
Belgium	757.3	-6.8	0.3	2.1	81.9
France	738.0	-7.4	-5.0	2.0	83.9
Thailand	655.0	5.5	15.3	1.8	85.7

Graph 2: Trade Balance by MDG regions 2010

(Bln US$)

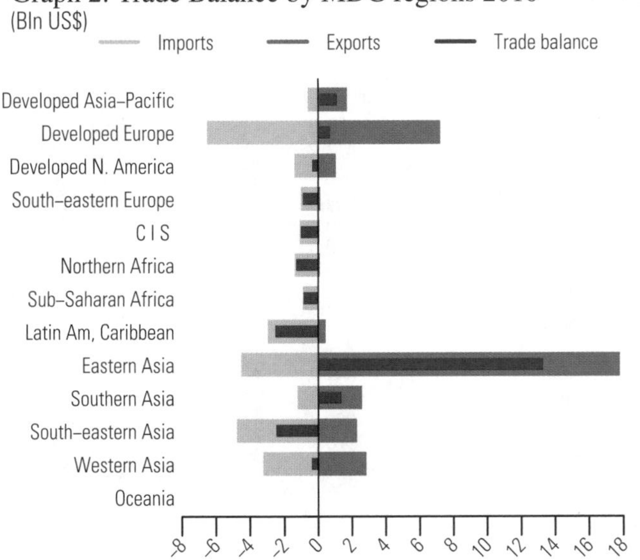

Table 3: Top importing countries or areas in 2010

Country or area	Value (million US$)	Avg. Growth (%) 06-10	Growth (%) 09-10	World share %	Cum.
World	29691.1	0.8	17.3	100.0	
China	2861.8	-1.9	10.1	9.6	9.6
Viet Nam	*2599.0*	15.0	66.9	8.8	18.4
United Arab Emirates	1152.8	0.2	-2.7	3.9	22.3
China, Hong Kong SAR	1114.0	-9.1	13.5	3.8	26.0
USA	1106.9	-4.7	21.7	3.7	29.8
Germany	1043.3	-4.5	7.3	3.5	33.3
Turkey	913.1	8.3	34.5	3.1	36.3
Indonesia	804.0	82.6	64.7	2.7	39.1
Italy	766.8	0.4	18.9	2.6	41.6
Mexico	729.1	-9.3	20.0	2.5	44.1
Poland	669.1	-3.3	7.6	2.3	46.3
United Kingdom	660.5	-7.4	6.4	2.2	48.6
Bangladesh	*660.3*	-2.7	136.5	2.2	50.8
France	638.7	-2.9	4.3	2.2	52.9
Romania	595.8	-7.7	5.6	2.0	55.0

Source: UN Comtrade

654 Other textile fabrics, woven

The value (in current prices) of exports of other textile fabrics, woven (SITC group 654) rose by 11.2 percent and amounted to 9.9 bln US$ in 2010 (see table 2). Imports, displaying a similar development, also increased by 9.7 percent and totaled 8.8 bln US$ (see table 3). Graph 1 shows that the increase in exports for 2010 in this product group was by far exceeded by increases in world exports of manufactured goods classified chiefly by material (SITC section 6) of 24.5 percent and in total world exports of 21.2 percent. Exports of other textile fabrics, woven (SITC group 654) accounted for 0.5 percent of world exports of SITC section 6 and 0.1 percent of total world exports (see table 1).

China and Italy, the top exporting countries for 2010, accounted respectively for 24.5 and 20.1 percent of world exports. Germany, another top exporting country accounted for 6.0 percent. Top destinations were China, Germany and China, Hong Kong SAR (see table 3). By MDG regions (see graph 2), Developed Europe accounted for a majority of exports and a large share of imports. In 2010, its exports were valued at 4.6 bln US$ while imports reached 3.2 bln US$, resulting in a trade surplus of 1.4 bln US$. The same surplus amount was recorded by Eastern Asia. Top trade deficits were recorded by South-eastern Asia (0.4 bln US$), Developed North America (0.4 bln US$) and South-eastern Europe (0.3 bln US$).

Table 1: Imports (Imp.) and exports (Exp.), 1996-2010, in current prices

		1996	1997	1998	1999	2000	2001	2002	2003	2004	2005	2006	2007	2008	2009	2010
Values in Bln US$	Imp.	9.3	9.4	8.9	8.3	8.6	8.1	7.9	8.5	10.1	10.4	10.6	11.1	11.1	8.0	8.8
	Exp.	10.2	10.8	9.9	9.3	9.9	9.1	8.6	9.3	11.1	11.1	11.4	11.9	11.9	8.9	9.9
As a percentage of SITC section (%)	Imp.	1.1	1.1	1.1	1.0	1.0	1.0	0.9	0.8	0.8	0.7	0.6	0.6	0.5	0.5	0.5
	Exp.	1.3	1.3	1.2	1.2	1.1	1.1	1.0	0.9	0.9	0.8	0.7	0.6	0.6	0.6	0.5
As a percentage of world trade (%)	Imp.	0.2	0.2	0.2	0.1	0.1	0.1	0.1	0.1	0.1	0.1	0.1	0.1	0.1	0.1	0.1
	Exp.	0.2	0.2	0.2	0.2	0.2	0.1	0.1	0.1	0.1	0.1	0.1	0.1	0.1	0.1	0.1

Graph 1: Annual growth rates of exports, 1996–2010

(In percentage by year)

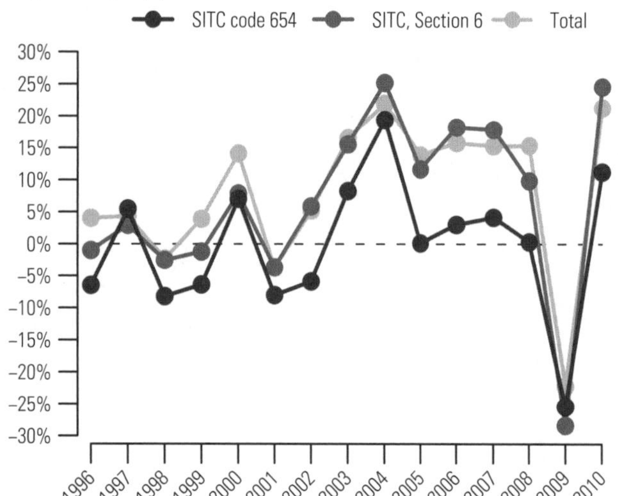

Table 2: Top exporting countries or areas in 2010

Country or area	Value (million US$)	Avg. Growth (%) 06-10	Growth (%) 09-10	World share %	Cum.
World	9906.7	-3.5	11.2	100.0	
China	2431.8	2.4	25.4	24.5	24.5
Italy	1991.2	-6.9	5.4	20.1	44.6
Germany	597.1	-6.6	1.7	6.0	50.7
India	517.9	2.1	30.7	5.2	55.9
Japan	500.4	-2.4	10.2	5.1	61.0
China, Hong Kong SAR	430.6	-5.8	9.0	4.3	65.3
United Kingdom	391.2	-7.9	3.0	3.9	69.2
France	355.9	-5.9	-5.5	3.6	72.8
Other Asia, nes	316.8	6.1	82.2	3.2	76.0
USA	257.4	-2.3	6.8	2.6	78.6
Czech Rep.	210.4	-4.1	8.6	2.1	80.8
Rep. of Korea	189.6	-6.1	9.2	1.9	82.7
Belgium	187.1	-5.4	11.1	1.9	84.6
Spain	175.6	-8.4	-1.8	1.8	86.3
Turkey	142.9	-1.0	6.6	1.4	87.8

Graph 2: Trade Balance by MDG regions 2010

(Bln US$)

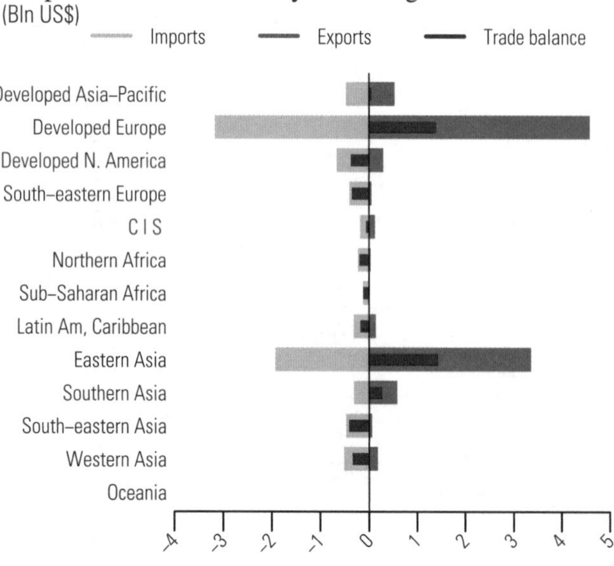

Table 3: Top importing countries or areas in 2010

Country or area	Value (million US$)	Avg. Growth (%) 06-10	Growth (%) 09-10	World share %	Cum.
World	8769.9	-4.5	9.7	100.0	
China	1014.6	-1.5	22.3	11.6	11.6
Germany	590.0	-5.6	12.1	6.7	18.3
China, Hong Kong SAR	554.5	-5.7	12.2	6.3	24.6
USA	515.0	-10.5	16.7	5.9	30.5
Italy	509.9	-4.5	14.3	5.8	36.3
Japan	392.4	-4.5	22.1	4.5	40.8
France	388.9	-2.8	2.0	4.4	45.2
Rep. of Korea	291.1	-6.9	25.9	3.3	48.5
Turkey	272.2	-4.1	16.4	3.1	51.6
Spain	228.5	-9.6	-7.9	2.6	54.2
United Kingdom	228.2	-6.3	7.7	2.6	56.8
Romania	220.9	-9.3	-5.5	2.5	59.4
Viet Nam	*202.8*	4.4	66.9	2.3	61.7
Poland	172.6	-8.4	6.1	2.0	63.6
India	171.7	-6.8	-23.6	2.0	65.6

In 2010, the value (in current prices) of exports of knitted or crocheted fabrics, nes, (SITC group 655) increased by 20.1 percent and amounted to 26.2 bln US$ (see table 2). Similarly, imports also increased by 20.8 percent to 20.3 bln US$ (see table 3). Graph 1 shows that the rise in exports for 2010 in this product group was slightly exceeded by the increase in world exports of manufactured goods classified chiefly by material (SITC section 6) of 24.5 percent and the increase in total world exports of 21.2 percent. Exports of knitted or crocheted fabrics, nes, (SITC group 655) accounted for 1.4 percent of world exports of SITC section 6 and 0.2 percent of total world exports (see table 1).

The top exporting country for 2010 was China, accounting for 33.0 percent of world exports. Rep. of Korea and China, Hong Kong SAR, the two other major exporting countries or areas, accounted respectively for 14.1 and 9.6 percent of world exports. China and China, Hong Kong SAR were also among the top destinations, together with Viet Nam (see table 3). By MDG regions (see graph 2), Eastern Asia and Developed Europe recorded trade surpluses amounting respectively to 12.3 bln US$ and 1.0 bln US$ in 2010. Top trade deficits were recorded by South-eastern Asia (-3.8 bln US$) and Latin America and the Caribbean (-2.0 bln US$).

Table 1: Imports (Imp.) and exports (Exp.), 1996-2010, in current prices

		1996	1997	1998	1999	2000	2001	2002	2003	2004	2005	2006	2007	2008	2009	2010
Values in Bln US$	Imp.	10.6	11.7	12.3	12.6	13.7	12.6	12.9	14.2	15.5	16.6	17.4	19.5	19.7	16.8	20.3
	Exp.	12.8	14.3	14.4	14.5	15.8	14.8	16.0	17.7	19.4	19.8	21.8	24.2	24.9	21.8	26.2
As a percentage of SITC section (%)	Imp.	1.3	1.4	1.5	1.5	1.5	1.5	1.4	1.4	1.2	1.2	1.0	1.0	0.9	1.1	1.1
	Exp.	1.6	1.7	1.8	1.8	1.8	1.8	1.8	1.7	1.5	1.4	1.3	1.2	1.1	1.4	1.4
As a percentage of world trade (%)	Imp.	0.2	0.2	0.2	0.2	0.2	0.2	0.2	0.2	0.2	0.2	0.1	0.1	0.1	0.1	0.1
	Exp.	0.2	0.3	0.3	0.3	0.2	0.2	0.2	0.2	0.2	0.2	0.2	0.2	0.2	0.2	0.2

Graph 1: Annual growth rates of exports, 1996–2010
(In percentage by year)

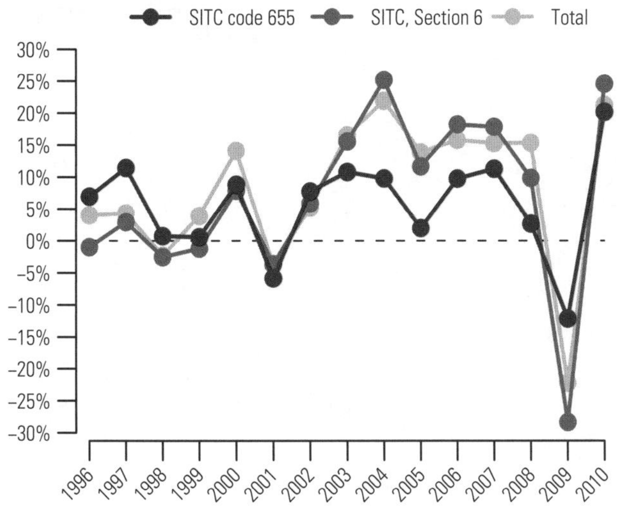

Graph 2: Trade Balance by MDG regions 2010
(Bln US$)

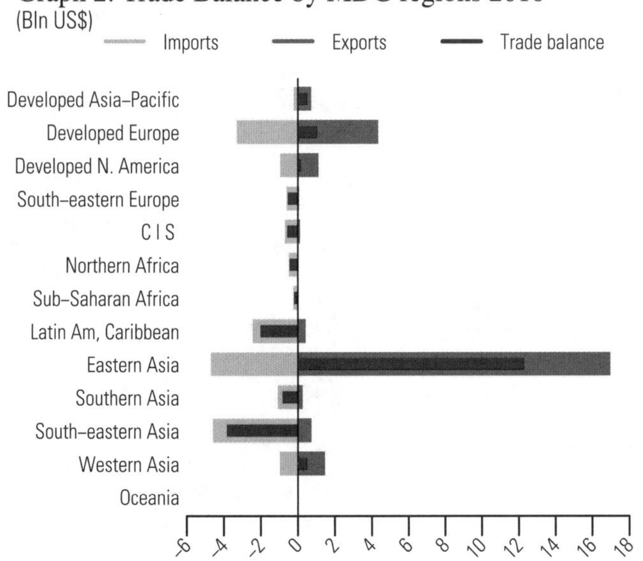

Table 2: Top exporting countries or areas in 2010

Country or area	Value (million US$)	Avg. Growth (%) 06-10	Growth (%) 09-10	World share %	Cum.
World	26234.9	4.8	20.1	100.0	
China	8666.5	16.9	34.9	33.0	33.0
Rep. of Korea	3703.8	6.3	17.3	14.1	47.2
China, Hong Kong SAR	2522.3	-4.9	11.0	9.6	56.8
Other Asia, nes	2060.1	1.1	22.7	7.9	64.6
Turkey	1267.1	13.9	29.4	4.8	69.4
Italy	1168.1	-1.0	7.5	4.5	73.9
USA	1062.2	-10.3	16.6	4.0	78.0
Germany	977.5	-2.4	10.9	3.7	81.7
Japan	688.7	2.2	12.0	2.6	84.3
France	502.4	-2.6	2.8	1.9	86.2
Spain	270.0	-3.2	8.0	1.0	87.2
Thailand	260.8	13.1	40.4	1.0	88.2
Belgium	191.1	0.0	2.7	0.7	89.0
United Kingdom	177.4	-3.9	8.0	0.7	89.6
Austria	170.4	-1.3	8.2	0.6	90.3

Table 3: Top importing countries or areas in 2010

Country or area	Value (million US$)	Avg. Growth (%) 06-10	Growth (%) 09-10	World share %	Cum.
World	20327.4	4.0	20.8	100.0	
China	2345.4	2.2	9.7	11.5	11.5
China, Hong Kong SAR	2183.6	-6.4	5.1	10.7	22.3
Viet Nam	*1688.3*	42.0	66.9	8.3	30.6
Cambodia	1001.4	14.7	35.8	4.9	35.5
Indonesia	948.1	90.8	50.8	4.7	40.2
Mexico	798.4	-4.6	22.7	3.9	44.1
USA	780.0	-6.7	12.1	3.8	47.9
Italy	665.4	10.3	25.0	3.3	51.2
Brazil	522.3	65.3	54.3	2.6	53.8
Sri Lanka	479.7	3.9	15.4	2.4	56.1
Germany	454.0	-2.2	12.5	2.2	58.4
France	401.3	-1.1	-1.4	2.0	60.4
Thailand	399.9	1.4	27.4	2.0	62.3
Bangladesh	*393.0*	91.5	815.4	1.9	64.3
El Salvador	391.7	-4.7	30.8	1.9	66.2

656 Tulles, lace, embroidery, ribbons, trimmings and other smallwares

After a huge drop in 2009, the value (in current prices) of exports of tulles, lace, embroidery, ribbons, trimmings and other small wares (SITC group 656) rose by 16.0 percent to 8.7 bln US$ in 2010 (see table 2). Imports for the same year also increased by 20.2 percent and totaled 7.4 bln US$ (see table 3). Graph 1 shows that the increase in exports in 2010 for this product group was exceeded by the increase in world exports of manufactured goods classified chiefly by material (SITC section 6) of 24.5 percent and the increase in total world exports of 21.2 percent. Exports of tulles, lace, embroidery, ribbons, trimmings and other small wares (SITC group 656) accounted for 0.4 percent of world exports of SITC section 6 and 0.1 percent of total world exports (see table 1).

China was the top exporting country in 2010 and accounted for 28.8 percent of world exports. Viet Nam and China were among the top destinations, together with China, Hong Kong SAR (see table 3). By MDG regions (see graph 2), Eastern Asia recorded a trade surplus amounting to 3.2 bln US$ in 2010. Developed Europe recorded a trade surplus of 0.4 bln US$ while South-eastern Asia and Latin America and the Caribbean recorded trade deficits amounting respectively to 0.8 bln and 0.4 bln US$.

Table 1: Imports (Imp.) and exports (Exp.), 1996-2010, in current prices

		1996	1997	1998	1999	2000	2001	2002	2003	2004	2005	2006	2007	2008	2009	2010
Values in Bln US$	Imp.	4.6	4.7	4.8	4.9	5.3	5.0	5.4	5.9	6.6	7.1	7.4	7.5	7.5	6.1	7.4
	Exp.	4.8	5.1	5.1	5.3	5.9	5.7	6.2	6.8	7.6	8.2	9.0	9.5	9.5	7.5	8.7
As a percentage of SITC section (%)	Imp.	0.6	0.6	0.6	0.6	0.6	0.6	0.6	0.6	0.5	0.5	0.4	0.4	0.3	0.4	0.4
	Exp.	0.6	0.6	0.6	0.7	0.7	0.7	0.7	0.7	0.6	0.6	0.5	0.5	0.4	0.5	0.4
As a percentage of world trade (%)	Imp.	0.1	0.1	0.1	0.1	0.1	0.1	0.1	0.1	0.1	0.1	0.1	0.1	0.0	0.0	0.0
	Exp.	0.1	0.1	0.1	0.1	0.1	0.1	0.1	0.1	0.1	0.1	0.1	0.1	0.1	0.1	0.1

Graph 1: Annual growth rates of exports, 1996–2010

(In percentage by year)

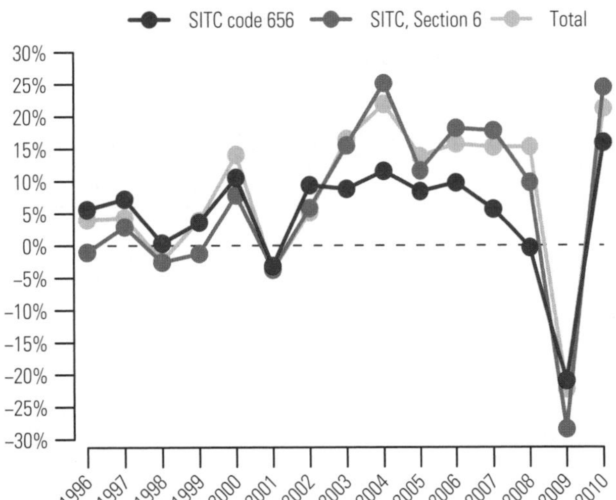

Table 2: Top exporting countries or areas in 2010

Country or area	Value (million US$)	Avg. Growth (%) 06-10	Growth (%) 09-10	World share %	Cum.
World	8679.2	-0.9	16.0	100.0	
China	2503.1	5.2	21.9	28.8	28.8
China, Hong Kong SAR	789.8	-1.3	21.0	9.1	37.9
Other Asia, nes	593.9	-0.5	21.7	6.8	44.8
USA	481.3	-3.7	16.0	5.5	50.3
Rep. of Korea	478.4	-6.3	14.8	5.5	55.8
France	430.0	-8.6	-0.5	5.0	60.8
Germany	401.3	-2.1	8.2	4.6	65.4
Italy	382.2	-5.1	11.3	4.4	69.8
Turkey	268.1	-7.4	7.7	3.1	72.9
India	208.9	11.4	25.6	2.4	75.3
Japan	200.2	-2.3	8.7	2.3	77.6
Thailand	191.9	2.7	18.6	2.2	79.8
Austria	140.3	-7.4	0.7	1.6	81.5
Spain	137.1	1.9	15.7	1.6	83.0
Switzerland	123.9	-6.1	6.9	1.4	84.5

Graph 2: Trade Balance by MDG regions 2010

(Bln US$)

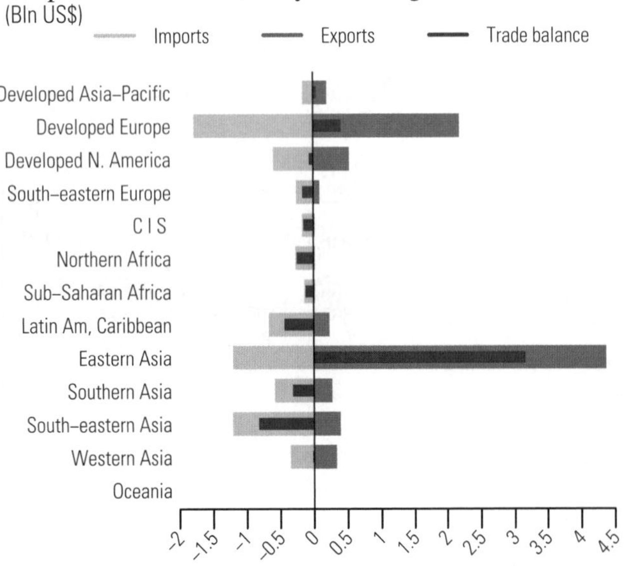

Table 3: Top importing countries or areas in 2010

Country or area	Value (million US$)	Avg. Growth (%) 06-10	Growth (%) 09-10	World share %	Cum.
World	7360.5	0.0	20.2	100.0	
Viet Nam	*594.2*	17.4	66.9	8.1	8.1
China	581.7	-2.6	12.1	7.9	16.0
China, Hong Kong SAR	537.5	-0.3	20.3	7.3	23.3
USA	504.6	-4.7	22.5	6.9	30.1
Mexico	336.8	-4.3	27.8	4.6	34.7
Germany	276.2	1.3	9.7	3.8	38.5
Italy	252.1	-3.6	18.9	3.4	41.9
Indonesia	227.5	78.8	41.8	3.1	45.0
France	207.3	-7.6	5.5	2.8	47.8
Sri Lanka	151.7	6.3	22.4	2.1	49.9
Bangladesh	*150.7*	94.7	1002.9	2.0	51.9
Romania	150.7	-7.0	9.5	2.0	54.0
United Kingdom	137.4	-8.2	7.3	1.9	55.8
Poland	137.0	-3.9	16.1	1.9	57.7
Turkey	136.7	3.9	34.9	1.9	59.5

After a 13.9 percent drop in 2009, the exports of special yarns, special textile fabrics and related products (SITC group 657) bounced back by 20.6 percent and amounted to 41.3 bln US$ in 2010 (see table 2). Similarly, imports also increased by 20.4 percent to 36.8 bln US$ (see table 3). Graph 1 shows that the rise in exports for 2010 in this product group was exceeded by increases in world exports of manufactured goods classified chiefly by material (SITC section 6) of 24.5 percent and in total world exports of 21.2 percent. Exports of special yarns, special textile fabrics and related products (SITC group 657) accounted for 2.1 percent of world exports of SITC section 6 and 0.3 percent of total world exports (see table 1).

China, Germany and USA were the top exporting countries in 2010 and accounted for 19.8, 11.1 and 9.2 percent of world exports respectively (see table 2). USA, China and Germany were also the top destinations (see table 3). By MDG regions (see graph 2), Eastern Asia and Developed Europe recorded trade surpluses amounting respectively to 7.8 bln US$ and 4.0 bln US$ in 2010. Top trade deficits were recorded by Latin America and the Caribbean (-2.0 bln US$) and South-eastern Asia (-1.6 bln US$).

Table 1: Imports (Imp.) and exports (Exp.), 1996-2010, in current prices

		1996	1997	1998	1999	2000	2001	2002	2003	2004	2005	2006	2007	2008	2009	2010
Values in Bln US$	Imp.	18.0	18.4	18.4	18.5	19.1	18.8	20.0	22.6	25.5	27.6	29.8	34.1	36.2	30.5	36.8
	Exp.	21.7	22.4	21.3	21.5	22.1	21.2	22.3	25.4	27.8	29.7	32.3	36.1	39.8	34.2	41.3
As a percentage of SITC section (%)	Imp.	2.2	2.2	2.2	2.3	2.2	2.2	2.2	2.2	2.0	1.9	1.8	1.7	1.7	2.0	1.9
	Exp.	2.7	2.7	2.6	2.7	2.6	2.5	2.5	2.5	2.2	2.1	1.9	1.8	1.8	2.2	2.1
As a percentage of world trade (%)	Imp.	0.3	0.3	0.3	0.3	0.3	0.3	0.3	0.3	0.3	0.3	0.2	0.2	0.2	0.2	0.2
	Exp.	0.4	0.4	0.4	0.4	0.3	0.3	0.3	0.3	0.3	0.3	0.3	0.3	0.2	0.3	0.3

Graph 1: Annual growth rates of exports, 1996–2010
(In percentage by year)

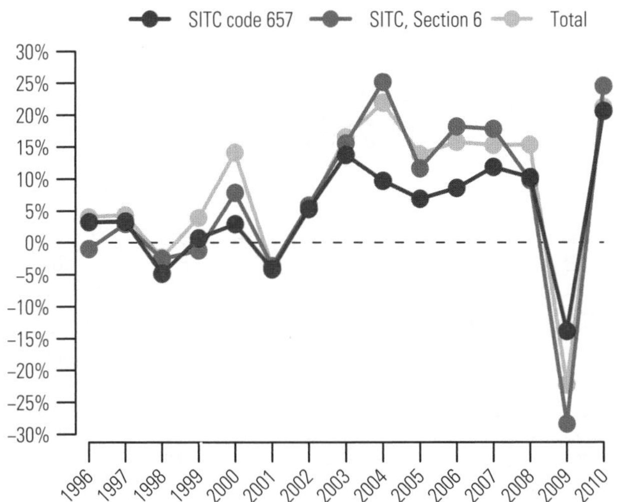

Table 2: Top exporting countries or areas in 2010

Country or area	Value (million US$)	Avg. Growth (%) 06-10	Growth (%) 09-10	World share %	Cum.
World	41 296.2	6.4	20.6	100.0	
China	8 180.0	26.8	40.1	19.8	19.8
Germany	4 586.7	2.8	14.8	11.1	30.9
USA	3 803.4	2.5	26.8	9.2	40.1
Italy	2 455.7	1.7	12.1	5.9	46.1
Japan	1 934.7	5.9	24.4	4.7	50.8
Rep. of Korea	1 931.6	1.4	24.2	4.7	55.4
Other Asia, nes	1 828.8	1.4	22.4	4.4	59.9
France	1 339.3	-0.9	7.2	3.2	63.1
Belgium	1 029.3	-0.9	11.6	2.5	65.6
United Kingdom	957.6	-4.1	8.7	2.3	67.9
Netherlands	954.6	3.0	7.5	2.3	70.2
China, Hong Kong SAR	940.7	3.0	28.5	2.3	72.5
Spain	783.8	3.9	10.6	1.9	74.4
Canada	705.7	0.3	17.6	1.7	76.1
Czech Rep.	648.0	6.3	15.1	1.6	77.7

Graph 2: Trade Balance by MDG regions 2010
(Bln US$)

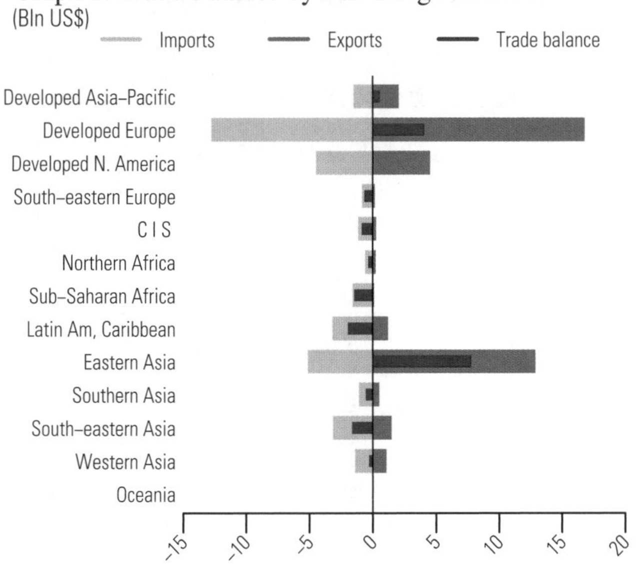

Table 3: Top importing countries or areas in 2010

Country or area	Value (million US$)	Avg. Growth (%) 06-10	Growth (%) 09-10	World share %	Cum.
World	36 793.9	5.4	20.4	100.0	
USA	3 523.8	4.3	25.1	9.6	9.6
China	2 981.2	5.3	23.5	8.1	17.7
Germany	2 311.5	-1.8	-2.1	6.3	24.0
Mexico	1 347.9	-0.4	28.6	3.7	27.6
France	1 338.0	0.0	7.3	3.6	31.3
Viet Nam	*1 279.2*	20.4	66.9	3.5	34.7
United Kingdom	1 223.2	2.2	15.6	3.3	38.1
Japan	1 096.6	7.6	20.6	3.0	41.0
Italy	1 045.9	2.9	18.0	2.8	43.9
Nigeria	1 016.0	159.3	403.2	2.8	46.6
China, Hong Kong SAR	1 010.5	2.8	25.9	2.7	49.4
Poland	996.4	4.3	13.4	2.7	52.1
Canada	930.6	0.2	17.3	2.5	54.6
Rep. of Korea	784.0	11.3	25.5	2.1	56.8
Netherlands	718.6	3.7	16.2	2.0	58.7

658 Made-up articles, wholly or chiefly of textile materials, nes

The value (in current prices) of exports of made-up articles, wholly or chiefly of textiles materials, nes (SITC group 658) grew by 13.8 percent and totaled 44.2 bln US$ in 2010 (see table 2). Imports also rose by 12.4 percent to 41.1 bln US$ (see table 3). Graph 1 shows that the growth in exports for 2010 in this product group was exceeded by increases in world exports of manufactured goods classified chiefly by material (SITC section 6) of 24.5 percent and in total world exports of 21.2 percent. Exports of made-up articles, wholly or chiefly of textiles materials, nes (SITC group 658) accounted for 2.3 percent of world exports of SITC section 6 and 0.3 percent of total world exports (see table 1).

Exports of China, the top exporting country, accounted for 44.3 percent of world exports in 2010 (see table 2). Other major exporting countries were Pakistan and India, respectively with 7.4 and 6.4 percent of world exports. USA accounted for 28.5 percent of imports and was the top destination. Other major destinations were Germany and Japan (see table 3). By MDG regions (see graph 2), Eastern Asia and Southern Asia recorded trade surpluses amounting respectively to 19.3 bln US$ and 6.5 bln US$ in 2010. Developed North America, Developed Europe and Developed Asia-Pacific recorded trade deficits of respectively 11.5 bln US$, 7.7 bln US$ and 3.8 bln US$.

Table 1: Imports (Imp.) and exports (Exp.), 1996-2010, in current prices

		1996	1997	1998	1999	2000	2001	2002	2003	2004	2005	2006	2007	2008	2009	2010
Values in Bln US$	Imp.	13.8	14.2	15.0	16.0	17.1	17.5	19.1	23.0	27.0	29.9	33.2	37.1	39.6	36.5	41.1
	Exp.	13.9	14.8	15.3	16.2	17.2	17.5	19.3	23.5	27.3	31.6	34.2	37.6	41.5	38.8	44.2
As a percentage of SITC section (%)	Imp.	1.7	1.7	1.8	2.0	1.9	2.1	2.1	2.2	2.1	2.1	2.0	1.9	1.8	2.4	2.2
	Exp.	1.7	1.8	1.9	2.0	2.0	2.1	2.2	2.3	2.1	2.2	2.0	1.9	1.9	2.5	2.3
As a percentage of world trade (%)	Imp.	0.3	0.3	0.3	0.3	0.3	0.3	0.3	0.3	0.3	0.3	0.3	0.3	0.2	0.3	0.3
	Exp.	0.3	0.3	0.3	0.3	0.3	0.3	0.3	0.3	0.3	0.3	0.3	0.3	0.3	0.3	0.3

Graph 1: Annual growth rates of exports, 1996–2010

(In percentage by year)

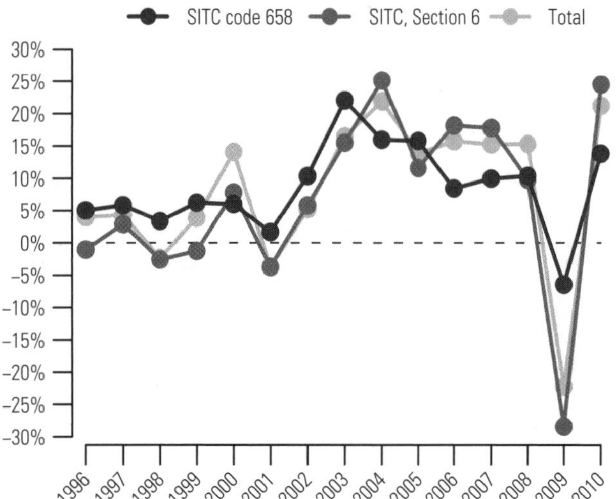

Graph 2: Trade Balance by MDG regions 2010

(Bln US$)

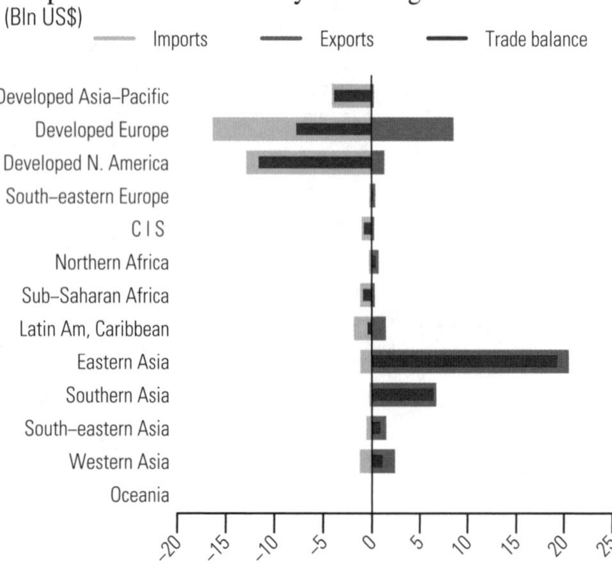

Table 2: Top exporting countries or areas in 2010

Country or area	Value (million US$)	Avg. Growth (%) 06-10	Growth (%) 09-10	World share %	Cum.
World	44 188.4	6.6	13.8	100.0	
China	19 576.8	13.1	17.4	44.3	44.3
Pakistan	3 263.6	0.3	12.5	7.4	51.7
India	2 845.5	5.0	27.2	6.4	58.1
Turkey	1 831.5	-1.0	11.7	4.1	62.3
Germany	1 769.3	5.8	8.2	4.0	66.3
USA	1 093.8	3.5	7.9	2.5	68.8
Belgium	892.5	2.2	5.7	2.0	70.8
Mexico	696.5	-3.6	9.1	1.6	72.3
France	689.1	1.0	0.4	1.6	73.9
Viet Nam	*673.4*	16.0	25.6	1.5	75.4
Poland	659.4	3.4	12.2	1.5	76.9
Portugal	656.2	-2.6	15.2	1.5	78.4
Netherlands	608.0	11.7	7.8	1.4	79.8
Italy	587.2	-2.8	6.9	1.3	81.1
Bangladesh	*522.5*	12.4	38.6	1.2	82.3

Table 3: Top importing countries or areas in 2010

Country or area	Value (million US$)	Avg. Growth (%) 06-10	Growth (%) 09-10	World share %	Cum.
World	41 063.1	5.5	12.4	100.0	
USA	11 702.2	2.8	19.7	28.5	28.5
Germany	3 401.7	6.1	14.2	8.3	36.8
Japan	2 974.7	6.6	-11.4	7.2	44.0
France	2 310.3	5.2	7.4	5.6	49.7
United Kingdom	2 060.1	0.6	9.6	5.0	54.7
Canada	1 108.9	4.9	16.2	2.7	57.4
Italy	1 084.1	5.0	13.7	2.6	60.0
Spain	1 060.6	4.2	8.3	2.6	62.6
Netherlands	1 020.5	8.6	12.8	2.5	65.1
Belgium	994.5	3.8	6.4	2.4	67.5
Australia	882.4	9.9	23.2	2.1	69.6
Russian Federation	589.8	14.5	29.9	1.4	71.1
Switzerland	579.5	5.7	6.5	1.4	72.5
Austria	512.6	5.0	5.1	1.2	73.7
Poland	509.3	13.3	8.9	1.2	75.0

After several years of continuous growth marked by a peak of 15.1 bln US$ in 2008, the value (in current prices) of exports of floor coverings, etc (SITC group 659) dropped in 2009 but bounced back in 2010 by 12.3 percent and amounted to 14.1 bln US$ (see table 2). Imports for the same year also grew by 10.9 percent to 12.3 bln US$ (see table 3). Graph 1 shows that the increase in exports for 2010 in this product group was far exceeded by increases in world exports of manufactured goods classified chiefly by material (SITC section 6) of 24.5 percent and in total world exports of 21.2 percent. Exports of floor coverings, etc (SITC group 659) accounted for 0.7 percent of world exports of SITC section 6 and 0.1 percent of total world exports (see table 1).

The top exporting countries in 2010 were Belgium, China and India (see table 2). They accounted respectively for 14.7, 14.0 and 9.4 percent of world exports. Top destinations were USA, Germany and United Kingdom (see table 3). By MDG regions (see graph 2), trade surpluses were recorded by Southern Asia (+2.4 bln US$) and Eastern Asia (+1.7 bln US$). Top deficits were recorded by Developed North America (-1.6 bln US$) and Developed Asia-Pacific (-0.8 bln US$).

Table 1: Imports (Imp.) and exports (Exp.), 1996-2010, in current prices

		1996	1997	1998	1999	2000	2001	2002	2003	2004	2005	2006	2007	2008	2009	2010
Values in Bln US$	Imp.	8.9	9.4	8.5	8.3	8.2	8.0	8.2	9.1	10.4	11.1	12.0	13.2	13.4	11.1	12.3
	Exp.	9.8	10.8	9.1	9.1	8.8	8.2	8.4	9.5	10.7	11.5	12.8	14.5	15.1	12.6	14.1
As a percentage of SITC section (%)	Imp.	1.1	1.1	1.0	1.0	0.9	0.9	0.9	0.9	0.8	0.8	0.7	0.7	0.6	0.7	0.6
	Exp.	1.2	1.3	1.1	1.1	1.0	1.0	1.0	0.9	0.8	0.8	0.8	0.7	0.7	0.8	0.7
As a percentage of world trade (%)	Imp.	0.2	0.2	0.2	0.1	0.1	0.1	0.1	0.1	0.1	0.1	0.1	0.1	0.1	0.1	0.1
	Exp.	0.2	0.2	0.2	0.2	0.1	0.1	0.1	0.1	0.1	0.1	0.1	0.1	0.1	0.1	0.1

Graph 1: Annual growth rates of exports, 1996–2010

(In percentage by year)

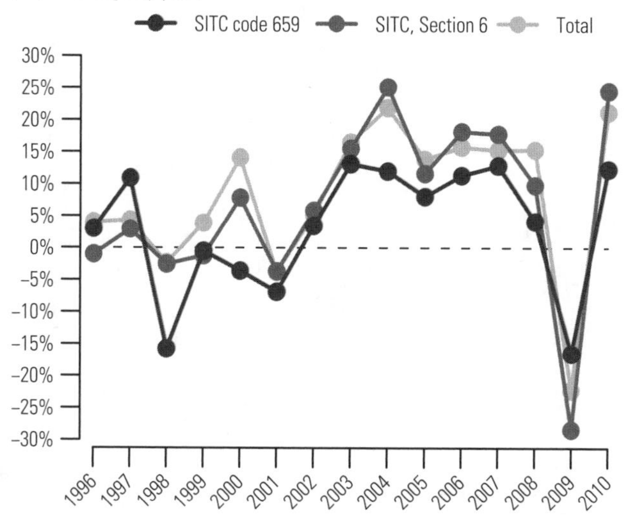

Graph 2: Trade Balance by MDG regions 2010

(Bln US$)

Imports — Exports — Trade balance

Developed Asia-Pacific
Developed Europe
Developed N. America
South-eastern Europe
C I S
Northern Africa
Sub-Saharan Africa
Latin Am, Caribbean
Eastern Asia
Southern Asia
South-eastern Asia
Western Asia
Oceania

-6 -5 -4 -3 -2 -1 0 1 2 3 4 5 6

Table 2: Top exporting countries or areas in 2010

Country or area	Value (million US$)	Avg. Growth (%) 06-10	Growth (%) 09-10	World share %	Cum.
World	14121.4	2.4	12.3	100.0	
Belgium	2078.6	-5.3	1.0	14.7	14.7
China	1980.6	16.7	29.9	14.0	28.7
India	1330.4	2.1	36.0	9.4	38.2
Turkey	1269.1	14.3	17.8	9.0	47.2
Netherlands	1014.5	-1.3	1.1	7.2	54.3
USA	1014.0	-0.1	17.0	7.2	61.5
Iran	877.0	10.1	6.3	6.2	67.7
Germany	652.3	-0.7	4.7	4.6	72.3
Egypt	359.1	261.0	18.9	2.5	74.9
United Kingdom	354.7	-5.0	0.2	2.5	77.4
France	283.1	-4.1	3.5	2.0	79.4
Italy	197.4	-0.3	-3.7	1.4	80.8
Poland	190.7	13.1	39.8	1.4	82.2
Thailand	181.6	9.4	27.7	1.3	83.4
Saudi Arabia	179.3	-2.9	20.8	1.3	84.7

Table 3: Top importing countries or areas in 2010

Country or area	Value (million US$)	Avg. Growth (%) 06-10	Growth (%) 09-10	World share %	Cum.
World	12300.2	0.6	10.9	100.0	
USA	1897.1	-4.6	17.7	15.4	15.4
Germany	1294.8	0.4	4.5	10.5	25.9
United Kingdom	1104.8	-7.5	-1.0	9.0	34.9
Canada	805.7	0.4	14.1	6.6	41.5
Japan	607.4	3.8	20.6	4.9	46.4
France	563.3	4.3	6.5	4.6	51.0
Netherlands	362.2	-4.4	-1.8	2.9	53.9
Australia	330.6	10.4	23.6	2.7	56.6
Italy	276.0	-0.9	13.9	2.2	58.9
Belgium	260.8	-0.8	15.3	2.1	61.0
Poland	246.9	7.9	13.2	2.0	63.0
Switzerland	226.2	3.4	9.7	1.8	64.8
Sweden	211.5	5.5	16.8	1.7	66.6
Austria	201.5	6.5	0.0	1.6	68.2
Spain	186.6	-2.6	-11.8	1.5	69.7

661 Lime, cement, and fabricated construction materials (except glass and clay)

The value (in current prices) of exports of lime, cement, and fabricated construction materials, except glass and clay (SITC group 661) rose by 4.5 percent to 25.5 bln US$ in 2010 (see table 2). Imports also increased by 4.3 percent and amounted to 26.3 bln US$ (see table 3). Graph 1 shows that the growth in exports in 2010 for this product group was significantly exceeded by increases in world exports of manufactured goods classified chiefly by material (SITC section 6) of 24.5 percent and in total world exports of 21.2 percent. Exports of lime, cement, and fabricated construction materials, except glass and clay (SITC group 661) accounted for 1.3 percent of world exports of SITC section 6 and 0.2 percent of total world exports (see table 1).

China, Italy and Turkey were the top exporting countries in 2010 (see table 2). They accounted respectively for 19.4, 8.4 and 7.9 percent of world exports. USA, France and Germany were the three major destinations (see table 3). By MDG regions (see graph 2), Eastern Asia recorded a trade surplus of 4.0 bln US$ in 2010. Major deficits were recorded by Developed North America (-2.6 bln US$) and Sub-Saharan Africa (-2.5 bln US$).

Table 1: Imports (Imp.) and exports (Exp.), 1996-2010, in current prices

		1996	1997	1998	1999	2000	2001	2002	2003	2004	2005	2006	2007	2008	2009	2010
Values in Bln US$	Imp.	12.1	12.3	11.6	11.9	12.1	12.7	13.1	15.1	18.0	22.1	25.2	29.3	31.6	25.2	26.3
	Exp.	12.0	11.9	10.9	10.9	10.9	11.1	12.2	13.3	15.7	19.0	22.7	26.0	30.4	24.4	25.5
As a percentage of SITC section (%)	Imp.	1.5	1.5	1.4	1.5	1.4	1.5	1.5	1.5	1.4	1.5	1.5	1.5	1.5	1.6	1.4
	Exp.	1.5	1.4	1.3	1.4	1.3	1.3	1.4	1.3	1.2	1.3	1.4	1.3	1.4	1.6	1.3
As a percentage of world trade (%)	Imp.	0.2	0.2	0.2	0.2	0.2	0.2	0.2	0.2	0.2	0.2	0.2	0.2	0.2	0.2	0.2
	Exp.	0.2	0.2	0.2	0.2	0.2	0.2	0.2	0.2	0.2	0.2	0.2	0.2	0.2	0.2	0.2

Graph 1: Annual growth rates of exports, 1996–2010

(In percentage by year)

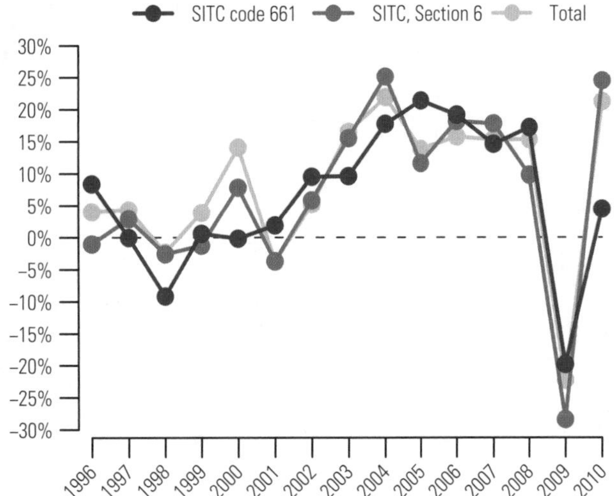

Table 2: Top exporting countries or areas in 2010

Country or area	Value (million US$)	Avg. Growth (%) 06-10	Growth (%) 09-10	World share %	Cum.
World	25494.4	3.0	4.5	100.0	
China	4946.5	5.6	13.4	19.4	19.4
Italy	2147.3	-4.0	0.8	8.4	27.8
Turkey	2001.5	13.2	0.6	7.9	35.7
Germany	1106.5	3.5	-6.7	4.3	40.0
Spain	1100.0	1.8	5.7	4.3	44.3
India	1016.8	1.2	16.5	4.0	48.3
Belgium	781.0	-1.2	-3.5	3.1	51.4
Brazil	769.5	-3.7	23.5	3.0	54.4
USA	742.1	8.5	29.2	2.9	57.3
Thailand	731.5	7.3	9.0	2.9	60.2
Iran	654.1	48.0	6.3	2.6	62.7
Canada	635.6	1.0	5.3	2.5	65.2
Pakistan	471.7	40.3	-12.6	1.9	67.1
France	449.1	-1.9	8.6	1.8	68.9
Portugal	428.2	4.5	16.4	1.7	70.5

Graph 2: Trade Balance by MDG regions 2010

(Bln US$)

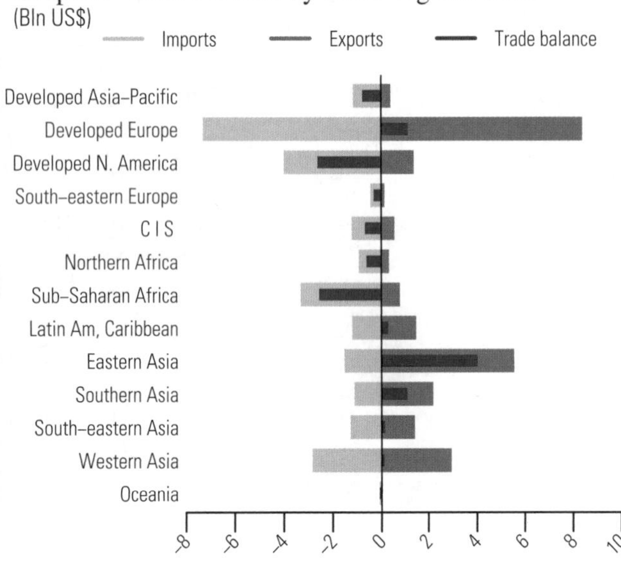

Table 3: Top importing countries or areas in 2010

Country or area	Value (million US$)	Avg. Growth (%) 06-10	Growth (%) 09-10	World share %	Cum.
World	26261.0	1.1	4.3	100.0	
USA	3142.6	-16.8	7.8	12.0	12.0
France	1142.8	4.0	4.8	4.4	16.3
Germany	950.6	-1.0	7.1	3.6	19.9
Rep. of Korea	913.7	5.5	3.3	3.5	23.4
Japan	840.8	-2.1	-0.8	3.2	26.6
Canada	806.8	13.1	28.4	3.1	29.7
Belgium	621.5	7.0	10.0	2.4	32.1
United Kingdom	608.4	-1.9	2.8	2.3	34.4
Netherlands	547.5	-1.5	-5.4	2.1	36.5
Nigeria	544.2	15.5	27.0	2.1	38.5
United Arab Emirates	489.3	-4.9	-38.5	1.9	40.4
Italy	436.1	-6.1	-12.0	1.7	42.1
Russian Federation	407.3	12.7	23.8	1.6	43.6
Qatar	387.1	12.8	-16.7	1.5	45.1
Switzerland	346.7	3.3	1.4	1.3	46.4

In 2010, the value (in current prices) of exports of clay construction materials and refractory construction materials (SITC group 662) increased by 9.8 percent amounting to 22.1 bln US$ (see table 2). Imports for the same year also rose by 10.7 percent to 21.4 bln US$ (see table 3). Graph 1 shows that the increase in exports for 2010 in this product group was greatly exceeded by increases in world exports of manufactured goods classified chiefly by material (SITC section 6) of 24.5 percent and in total world exports of 21.2 percent. Exports of clay construction materials and refractory construction materials (SITC group 662) accounted for 1.1 percent of world exports of SITC section 6 and 0.1 percent of total world exports (see table 1).

The top exporting countries in 2010 were China, Italy and Spain (see table 2). They accounted respectively for 24.6, 19.3 and 11.5 percent of world exports. Top destinations were USA, France and Germany (see table 3). By MDG regions (see graph 2), Developed Europe accounted for the majority of exports and imports. In 2010, its exports and imports were valued respectively at 11.7 bln and 7.3 bln US$ resulting in a trade surplus of 4.4 bln US$. Eastern Asia also recorded a trade surplus of 4.4 bln US$. Top trade deficits were recorded by Sub-Saharan Africa (-1.5 bln US$), Developed North America (-1.5 bln US$) and Western Asia (-1.3 bln US$).

Table 1: Imports (Imp.) and exports (Exp.), 1996-2010, in current prices

		1996	1997	1998	1999	2000	2001	2002	2003	2004	2005	2006	2007	2008	2009	2010
Values in Bln US$	Imp.	10.6	10.6	10.7	10.5	10.4	10.3	11.1	13.2	15.5	17.0	19.2	22.2	24.1	19.3	21.4
	Exp.	10.9	10.5	10.4	10.4	10.1	10.3	11.2	13.3	16.0	16.8	19.3	22.2	24.7	20.1	22.1
As a percentage of SITC section (%)	Imp.	1.3	1.3	1.3	1.3	1.2	1.2	1.2	1.3	1.2	1.2	1.2	1.1	1.1	1.2	1.1
	Exp.	1.3	1.3	1.3	1.3	1.2	1.2	1.3	1.3	1.3	1.2	1.1	1.1	1.1	1.3	1.1
As a percentage of world trade (%)	Imp.	0.2	0.2	0.2	0.2	0.2	0.2	0.2	0.2	0.2	0.2	0.2	0.2	0.1	0.2	0.1
	Exp.	0.2	0.2	0.2	0.2	0.2	0.2	0.2	0.2	0.2	0.2	0.2	0.2	0.2	0.2	0.1

Graph 1: Annual growth rates of exports, 1996–2010
(In percentage by year)

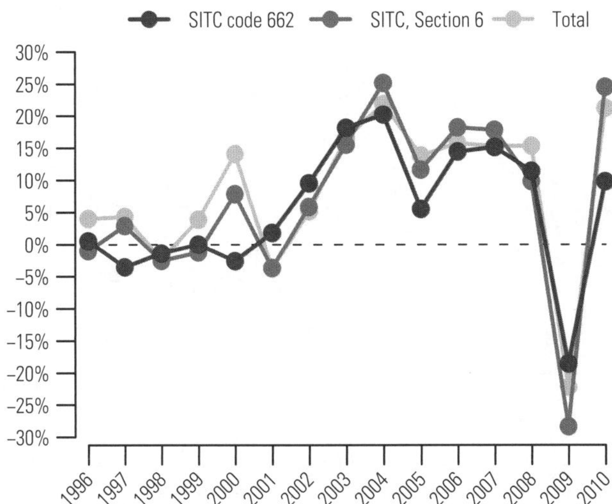

Graph 2: Trade Balance by MDG regions 2010
(Bln US$)

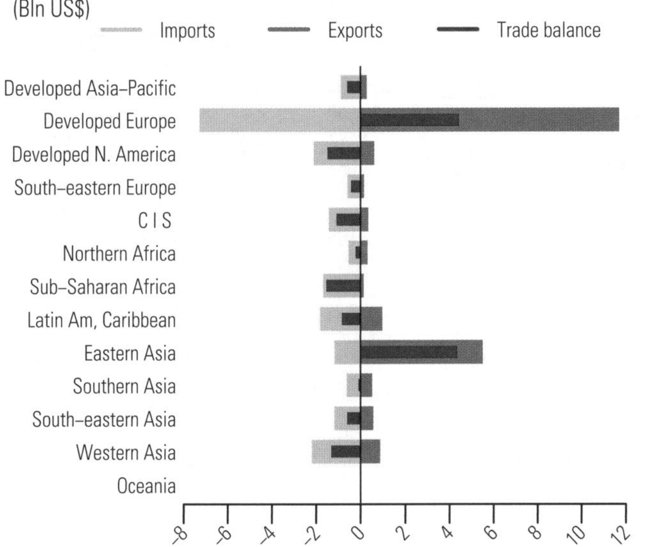

Table 2: Top exporting countries or areas in 2010

Country or area	Value (million US$)	Avg. Growth (%) 06-10	Growth (%) 09-10	World share %	Cum.
World	22086.0	3.5	9.8	100.0	
China	5436.7	19.4	30.2	24.6	24.6
Italy	4259.9	-3.4	1.3	19.3	43.9
Spain	2533.1	-3.7	-1.5	11.5	55.4
Germany	1833.2	1.0	1.1	8.3	63.7
Turkey	580.6	5.7	16.9	2.6	66.3
USA	552.8	5.1	10.8	2.5	68.8
France	532.1	-3.6	-6.1	2.4	71.2
Austria	465.4	14.7	18.9	2.1	73.3
Mexico	363.2	-2.5	9.5	1.6	75.0
Poland	353.0	8.4	14.7	1.6	76.6
Portugal	344.9	3.5	0.2	1.6	78.1
Brazil	334.7	-9.0	5.0	1.5	79.6
Iran	297.0	31.9	6.3	1.3	81.0
Egypt	268.8	58.2	-14.8	1.2	82.2
Japan	265.3	12.6	40.6	1.2	83.4

Table 3: Top importing countries or areas in 2010

Country or area	Value (million US$)	Avg. Growth (%) 06-10	Growth (%) 09-10	World share %	Cum.
World	21409.4	2.8	10.7	100.0	
USA	1579.3	-13.2	10.7	7.4	7.4
France	1535.4	2.2	0.2	7.2	14.5
Germany	946.4	-2.8	2.2	4.4	19.0
Nigeria	677.5	45.0	87.3	3.2	22.1
Russian Federation	615.3	12.0	34.9	2.9	25.0
United Kingdom	601.7	-7.9	-6.7	2.8	27.8
Saudi Arabia	586.6	7.9	1.9	2.7	30.6
Belgium	515.3	0.2	-3.7	2.4	33.0
Canada	508.2	6.0	28.6	2.4	35.3
Japan	501.4	5.0	9.2	2.3	37.7
Rep. of Korea	496.8	6.1	1.9	2.3	40.0
Italy	394.5	2.4	17.0	1.8	41.8
Poland	384.9	13.3	9.6	1.8	43.6
India	366.0	11.0	10.2	1.7	45.4
Ukraine	330.2	6.3	57.9	1.5	46.9

663 Mineral manufactures, nes

After a significant decline in 2009, the value (in current prices) of exports of mineral manufactures, nes (SITC group 663) bounced back by 21.8 percent to 29.5 bln US$ in 2010 (see table 2). Imports also increased by 21.0 percent and totaled 28.7 bln US$ (see table 3). Graph 1 shows that the growth in exports for 2010 in this product group was exceeded by the increase in world exports of manufactured goods classified chiefly by material (SITC section 6) of 24.5 percent but was higher than the increase in total world exports of 21.2 percent. Exports of mineral manufactures, nes (SITC group 663) accounted for 1.5 percent of world exports of SITC section 6 and 0.2 percent of total world exports (see table 1).

Germany, Japan and USA were the top exporting countries in 2010 (see table 2). They accounted respectively for 16.0, 11.3 and 10.8 percent of world exports. Top destinations were USA, Germany and France (see table 3). By MDG regions (see graph 2), Developed Europe and Developed Asia-Pacific recorded trade surpluses amounting respectively to 2.8 bln US$ and 2.1 bln US$ in 2010. Top trade deficits were recorded by Latin America and the Caribbean (-861 mln US$), Developed North America (-773 mln US$) and Commonwealth of Independent States (-751 mln US$).

Table 1: Imports (Imp.) and exports (Exp.), 1996-2010, in current prices

		1996	1997	1998	1999	2000	2001	2002	2003	2004	2005	2006	2007	2008	2009	2010
Values in Bln US$	Imp.	12.1	12.7	12.8	13.1	13.5	13.4	13.9	15.8	18.9	21.1	24.3	28.7	30.8	23.7	28.7
	Exp.	13.4	13.5	13.5	13.6	13.8	13.4	13.6	15.7	19.2	21.4	24.9	29.5	31.7	24.2	29.5
As a percentage of	Imp.	1.5	1.5	1.5	1.6	1.5	1.6	1.6	1.5	1.5	1.5	1.5	1.5	1.4	1.5	1.5
SITC section (%)	Exp.	1.7	1.6	1.7	1.7	1.6	1.6	1.5	1.5	1.5	1.5	1.5	1.5	1.5	1.6	1.5
As a percentage of	Imp.	0.2	0.2	0.2	0.2	0.2	0.2	0.2	0.2	0.2	0.2	0.2	0.2	0.2	0.2	0.2
world trade (%)	Exp.	0.3	0.2	0.3	0.2	0.2	0.2	0.2	0.2	0.2	0.2	0.2	0.2	0.2	0.2	0.2

Graph 1: Annual growth rates of exports, 1996–2010
(In percentage by year)

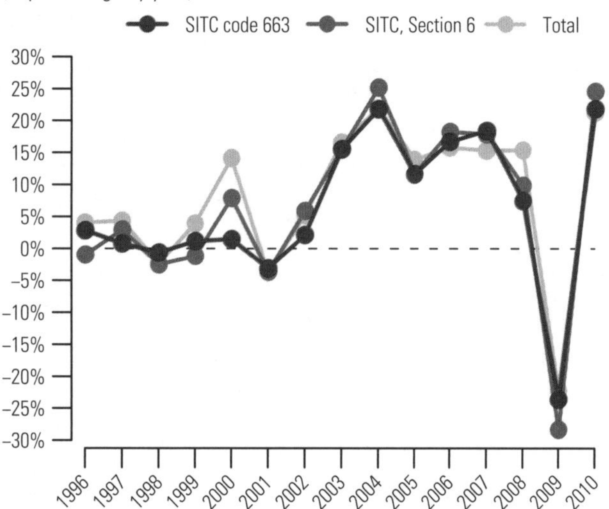

Graph 2: Trade Balance by MDG regions 2010
(Bln US$)

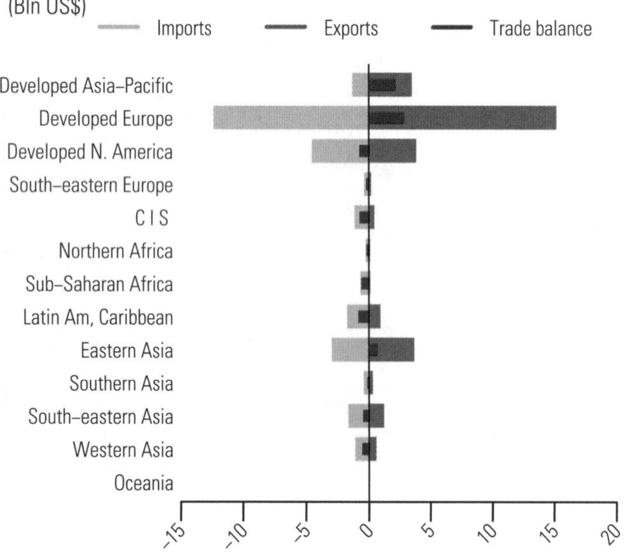

Table 2: Top exporting countries or areas in 2010

Country or area	Value (million US$)	Avg. Growth (%) 06-10	Growth (%) 09-10	World share %	Cum.
World	29466.0	4.3	21.8	100.0	
Germany	4710.5	3.5	14.1	16.0	16.0
Japan	3328.4	5.9	40.9	11.3	27.3
USA	3187.6	5.3	39.3	10.8	38.1
China	2720.9	23.1	59.4	9.2	47.3
United Kingdom	1111.5	-6.0	9.8	3.8	51.1
Italy	1106.9	-0.9	13.2	3.8	54.9
France	1060.6	1.3	16.7	3.6	58.5
Poland	1036.2	7.9	17.8	3.5	62.0
Belgium	1017.9	3.0	-0.7	3.5	65.4
Austria	779.3	2.1	12.5	2.6	68.1
Spain	757.1	3.1	4.4	2.6	70.6
Canada	586.4	-7.3	2.8	2.0	72.6
Netherlands	574.4	3.0	-0.1	1.9	74.6
Rep. of Korea	519.6	4.5	33.0	1.8	76.4
Hungary	479.8	20.4	6.8	1.6	78.0

Table 3: Top importing countries or areas in 2010

Country or area	Value (million US$)	Avg. Growth (%) 06-10	Growth (%) 09-10	World share %	Cum.
World	28698.3	4.3	21.0	100.0	
USA	3614.5	-1.0	30.1	12.6	12.6
Germany	2487.1	4.8	20.3	8.7	21.3
France	1385.5	2.1	9.4	4.8	26.1
China	1320.6	14.6	48.1	4.6	30.7
United Kingdom	1183.2	1.0	17.4	4.1	34.8
Italy	1001.9	1.5	12.5	3.5	38.3
Canada	918.5	5.2	18.9	3.2	41.5
Japan	838.7	5.5	36.2	2.9	44.4
Rep. of Korea	821.5	7.8	32.5	2.9	47.3
Netherlands	764.9	3.6	1.5	2.7	50.0
Belgium	702.5	7.2	11.3	2.4	52.4
Mexico	629.8	3.2	38.8	2.2	54.6
Switzerland	587.1	4.7	9.0	2.0	56.6
Russian Federation	579.2	7.1	53.5	2.0	58.7
Austria	571.5	5.9	12.7	2.0	60.7

From 2006 to 2010, the value (in current prices) of exports of glass (SITC group 664) increased on average by 5.0 percent and amounted to 34.0 bln US$ in 2010 (see table 2). For the same period, imports had a similar development with an average increase of 5.3 percent and amounted to 36.2 bln US$ in 2010 (see table 3). Graph 1 shows that the rise in exports for 2010 in this product group was surpassed by increases in both world exports of manufactured goods classified chiefly by material (SITC section 6) of 24.5 percent and total world exports of 21.2 percent. Exports of glass (SITC group 664) accounted for 1.8 percent of world exports of SITC section 6 and 0.2 percent of total world exports (see table 1).

The top exporting countries in 2010 were Japan, China and USA (see table 2). They accounted respectively for 14.4, 13.5 and 10.2 percent of world exports. Germany was a top destination, together with USA and Rep. of Korea (see table 3). By MDG regions (see graph 2), a large part of trade in glass (SITC group 664) took place in Developed Europe. In 2010, its exports and imports were valued at 14.1 bln US$ and 14.0 bln US$ respectively. Developed Asia-Pacific recorded a surplus of 3.2 bln US$. Significant trade deficits were recorded by Eastern Asia (-1.6 bln US$), Latin America and the Caribbean (-904 mln US$) and Sub-Saharan Africa (-680 mln US$).

Table 1: Imports (Imp.) and exports (Exp.), 1996-2010, in current prices

		1996	1997	1998	1999	2000	2001	2002	2003	2004	2005	2006	2007	2008	2009	2010
Values in Bln US$	Imp.	14.5	14.6	14.9	15.7	17.0	17.0	18.3	21.0	24.6	26.6	29.5	33.5	36.0	29.7	36.2
	Exp.	14.1	14.4	14.5	15.3	16.8	16.7	18.0	20.5	24.1	25.2	28.0	32.3	36.5	29.6	34.0
As a percentage of SITC section (%)	Imp.	1.8	1.8	1.8	1.9	1.9	2.0	2.0	2.0	1.9	1.9	1.8	1.7	1.7	1.9	1.9
	Exp.	1.7	1.7	1.8	1.9	1.9	2.0	2.0	2.0	1.9	1.8	1.7	1.6	1.7	1.9	1.8
As a percentage of world trade (%)	Imp.	0.3	0.3	0.3	0.3	0.3	0.3	0.3	0.3	0.3	0.3	0.2	0.2	0.2	0.2	0.2
	Exp.	0.3	0.3	0.3	0.3	0.3	0.3	0.3	0.3	0.3	0.2	0.2	0.2	0.2	0.2	0.2

Graph 1: Annual growth rates of exports, 1996–2010
(In percentage by year)

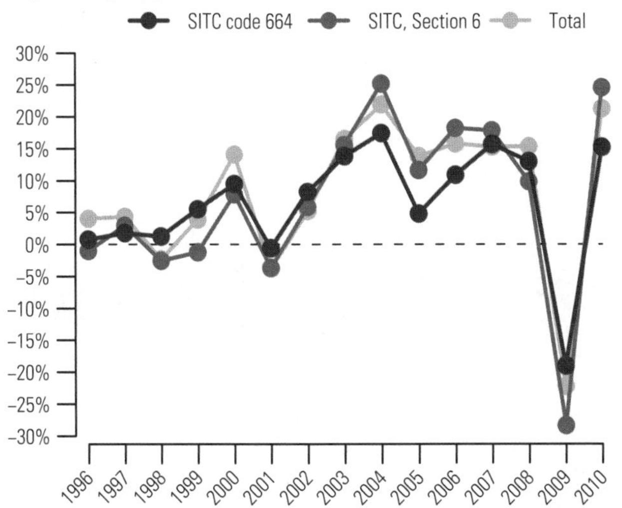

Table 2: Top exporting countries or areas in 2010

Country or area	Value (million US$)	Avg. Growth (%) 06-10	Growth (%) 09-10	World share %	Cum.
World	34047.4	5.0	15.2	100.0	
Japan	4919.4	28.4	41.2	14.4	14.4
China	4592.5	15.2	33.4	13.5	27.9
USA	3459.8	2.7	19.6	10.2	38.1
Germany	3325.4	-1.4	5.5	9.8	47.9
Belgium	1872.1	-2.2	-1.3	5.5	53.4
France	1317.5	-1.7	4.3	3.9	57.2
Italy	1171.6	-1.3	5.5	3.4	60.7
Other Asia, nes	912.9	14.9	35.6	2.7	63.4
Poland	847.9	6.7	17.6	2.5	65.8
Czech Rep.	789.4	1.6	-0.4	2.3	68.2
United Kingdom	741.4	1.5	11.5	2.2	70.3
Spain	730.1	1.1	1.7	2.1	72.5
Mexico	687.1	-2.9	18.0	2.0	74.5
Netherlands	521.7	1.2	4.1	1.5	76.0
Rep. of Korea	519.1	5.9	17.0	1.5	77.6

Graph 2: Trade Balance by MDG regions 2010
(Bln US$)

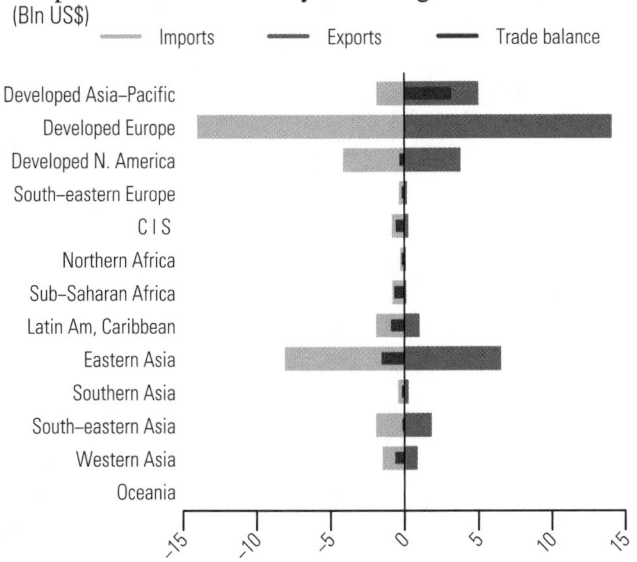

Table 3: Top importing countries or areas in 2010

Country or area	Value (million US$)	Avg. Growth (%) 06-10	Growth (%) 09-10	World share %	Cum.
World	36174.5	5.3	21.7	100.0	
Germany	2745.4	2.9	9.5	7.6	7.6
USA	2737.1	-3.3	23.2	7.6	15.2
Rep. of Korea	2655.5	12.0	34.7	7.3	22.5
China	2585.9	16.5	67.5	7.1	29.6
Other Asia, nes	2241.3	13.7	56.5	6.2	35.8
France	1689.1	-0.6	1.8	4.7	40.5
Japan	1455.8	2.5	16.5	4.0	44.5
Canada	1370.7	1.9	17.5	3.8	48.3
United Kingdom	1231.7	2.9	24.0	3.4	51.7
Belgium	1110.6	1.2	11.9	3.1	54.8
Italy	933.6	2.8	14.2	2.6	57.4
Poland	760.9	5.6	18.2	2.1	59.5
Mexico	734.6	-6.2	45.8	2.0	61.5
Spain	727.6	0.7	1.4	2.0	63.5
Netherlands	660.9	3.7	-1.9	1.8	65.4

665 Glassware

After a 13.5 percent drop in 2009, the value (in current prices) of exports of glassware (SITC group 665) bounced back by 17.8 percent to 22.9 bln US$ in 2010 (see table 2). Imports for the same year increased by 15.3 percent to 22.2 bln US$ (see table 3). Graph 1 shows that the rise in exports for 2010 in this product group was exceeded by increases in world exports of manufactured goods classified chiefly by material (SITC section 6) of 24.5 percent and in total world exports of 21.2 percent. Exports of glassware (SITC group 665) accounted for 1.2 percent of world exports of SITC section 6 and 0.2 percent of total world exports (see table 1).

Exports of China, the top exporting country, grew by 37.1 percent and accounted for 21.0 percent of world exports in 2010 (see table 2). Other major exporting countries were Germany and France, respectively with 9.6 and 8.0 percent of world exports. Top destinations were USA, China and France (see table 3). By MDG regions (see graph 2), Developed Europe accounted for a large share of exports and imports of glassware (SITC group 665). In 2010, its exports and imports were valued respectively at 10.3 bln US$ and 8.8 bln US$, resulting in a trade surplus of 1.5 bln US$. Eastern Asia recorded a trade surplus of 2.3 bln US$ while Developed North America recorded a deficit of 2.0 bln US$.

Table 1: Imports (Imp.) and exports (Exp.), 1996-2010, in current prices

		1996	1997	1998	1999	2000	2001	2002	2003	2004	2005	2006	2007	2008	2009	2010
Values in Bln US$	Imp.	10.2	10.2	10.1	10.3	10.8	10.7	11.4	13.2	15.6	16.7	18.1	21.4	23.0	19.2	22.2
	Exp.	10.3	10.6	10.3	10.3	10.8	11.0	11.7	13.6	16.1	17.2	19.6	21.9	22.5	19.4	22.9
As a percentage of SITC section (%)	Imp.	1.3	1.2	1.2	1.3	1.2	1.3	1.3	1.3	1.2	1.2	1.1	1.1	1.1	1.2	1.2
	Exp.	1.3	1.3	1.3	1.3	1.3	1.3	1.3	1.3	1.3	1.2	1.2	1.1	1.0	1.3	1.2
As a percentage of world trade (%)	Imp.	0.2	0.2	0.2	0.2	0.2	0.2	0.2	0.2	0.2	0.2	0.1	0.2	0.1	0.2	0.1
	Exp.	0.2	0.2	0.2	0.2	0.2	0.2	0.2	0.2	0.2	0.2	0.2	0.2	0.1	0.2	0.2

Graph 1: Annual growth rates of exports, 1996–2010
(In percentage by year)

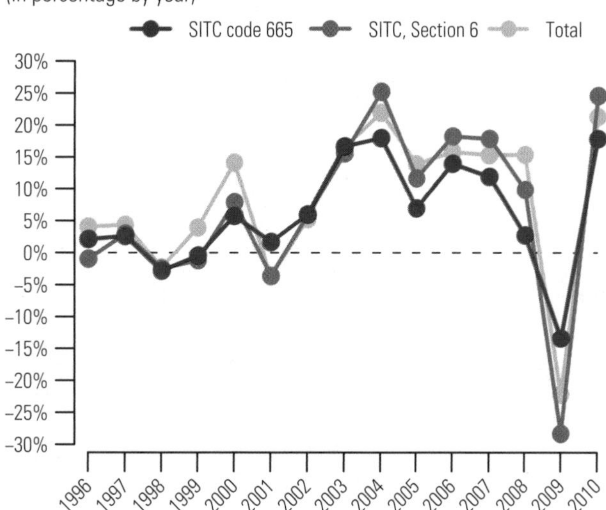

Graph 2: Trade Balance by MDG regions 2010
(Bln US$)

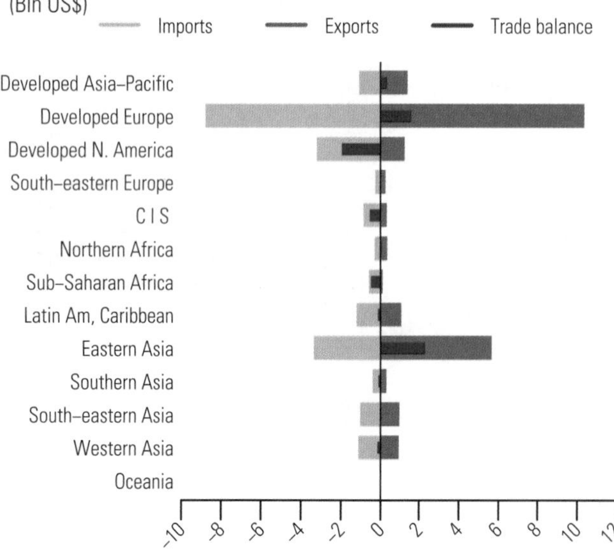

Table 2: Top exporting countries or areas in 2010

Country or area	Value (million US$)	Avg. Growth (%) 06-10	Growth (%) 09-10	World share %	Cum.
World	22 906.6	4.0	17.8	100.0	
China	4 814.6	20.4	37.1	21.0	21.0
Germany	2 192.7	2.6	3.2	9.6	30.6
France	1 824.6	-1.6	7.4	8.0	38.6
Italy	1 356.5	2.2	6.7	5.9	44.5
Japan	1 330.4	-8.3	57.1	5.8	50.3
USA	1 115.5	3.8	18.2	4.9	55.2
Czech Rep.	681.8	-7.6	11.8	3.0	58.1
Mexico	637.3	12.2	42.0	2.8	60.9
Austria	526.9	-15.0	2.8	2.3	63.2
Portugal	486.9	11.3	4.2	2.1	65.3
Spain	483.9	3.3	14.0	2.1	67.5
Turkey	482.3	7.9	1.2	2.1	69.6
Netherlands	464.1	12.5	14.2	2.0	71.6
Poland	447.3	-0.3	17.9	2.0	73.5
Belgium	384.1	0.2	-0.6	1.7	75.2

Table 3: Top importing countries or areas in 2010

Country or area	Value (million US$)	Avg. Growth (%) 06-10	Growth (%) 09-10	World share %	Cum.
World	22 194.9	5.2	15.3	100.0	
USA	2 522.6	-0.5	19.0	11.4	11.4
China	1 720.8	11.8	51.3	7.8	19.1
France	1 522.2	9.6	10.8	6.9	26.0
Germany	1 196.5	4.9	16.1	5.4	31.4
Italy	881.0	2.8	11.3	4.0	35.3
China, Hong Kong SAR	859.1	-4.9	11.7	3.9	39.2
United Kingdom	787.2	2.0	8.6	3.5	42.8
Spain	701.2	1.3	1.4	3.2	45.9
Japan	676.2	-2.0	29.6	3.0	49.0
Canada	668.7	6.5	8.3	3.0	52.0
Belgium	558.8	0.7	-3.0	2.5	54.5
Switzerland	478.7	4.7	4.4	2.2	56.6
Rep. of Korea	432.6	6.9	24.2	1.9	58.6
Russian Federation	404.4	10.3	52.4	1.8	60.4
Netherlands	369.8	1.3	-0.3	1.7	62.1

The value (in current prices) of exports of pottery (SITC group 666) increased by 21.4 percent to 7.6 bln US$ in 2010 (see table 2). Similarly, imports increased by 18.5 percent and totaled 7.9 bln US$ (see table 3). Graph 1 shows that the rise in exports for 2010 in this product group was exceeded by increases in world exports of manufactured goods classified chiefly by material (SITC section 6) of 24.5 percent but was slightly higher than increases in total world exports of 21.2 percent. Exports of pottery (SITC group 666) accounted for 0.4 percent of world exports of SITC section 6 and 0.1 percent of total world exports (see table 1).

China, the top exporting country in 2010, accounted for more than half (51.7 percent) of world exports (see table 2). Other major exporting countries were Germany and United Kingdom, respectively with 7.2 and 3.1 percent of world exports. Top destinations were USA, Germany and France (see table 3). By MDG regions (see graph 2), Eastern Asia recorded a trade surplus of 3.8 bln US$ in 2010 while Developed North America and Developed Europe recorded trade deficits amounting respectively to 1.7 bln US$ and 1.1 bln US$.

Table 1: Imports (Imp.) and exports (Exp.), 1996-2010, in current prices

		1996	1997	1998	1999	2000	2001	2002	2003	2004	2005	2006	2007	2008	2009	2010
Values in Bln US$	Imp.	5.9	6.1	5.9	5.9	6.1	5.7	5.7	6.4	6.9	7.2	7.4	8.2	8.3	6.7	7.9
	Exp.	5.6	5.9	5.6	5.4	5.5	4.9	5.1	5.7	6.2	6.4	6.6	6.8	6.8	6.3	7.6
As a percentage of SITC section (%)	Imp.	0.7	0.7	0.7	0.7	0.7	0.7	0.6	0.6	0.5	0.5	0.4	0.4	0.4	0.4	0.4
	Exp.	0.7	0.7	0.7	0.7	0.6	0.6	0.6	0.6	0.5	0.4	0.4	0.3	0.3	0.4	0.4
As a percentage of world trade (%)	Imp.	0.1	0.1	0.1	0.1	0.1	0.1	0.1	0.1	0.1	0.1	0.1	0.1	0.1	0.1	0.1
	Exp.	0.1	0.1	0.1	0.1	0.1	0.1	0.1	0.1	0.1	0.1	0.1	0.0	0.0	0.1	0.1

Graph 1: Annual growth rates of exports, 1996–2010
(In percentage by year)

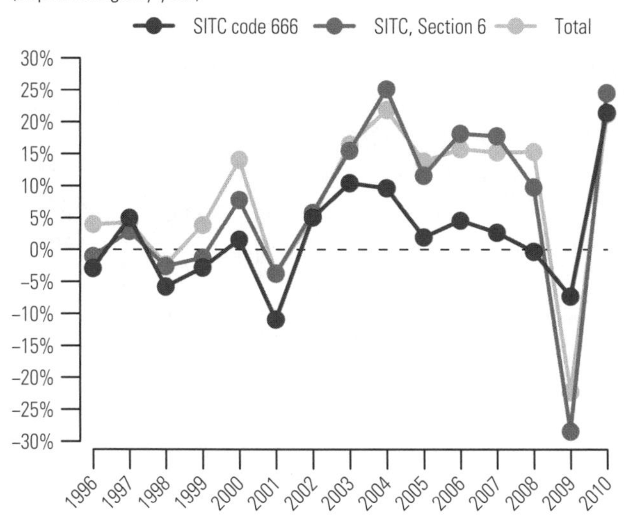

Graph 2: Trade Balance by MDG regions 2010
(Bln US$)

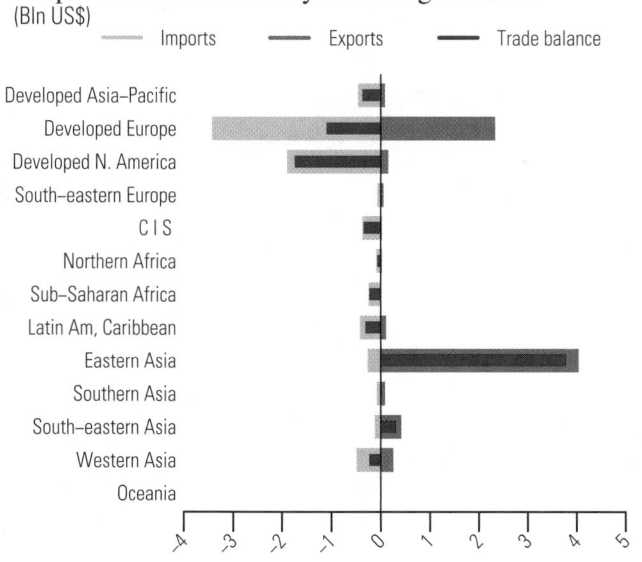

Table 2: Top exporting countries or areas in 2010

Country or area	Value (million US$)	Avg. Growth (%) 06-10	Growth (%) 09-10	World share %	Cum.
World	7649.9	3.6	21.4	100.0	
China	3955.5	9.9	37.7	51.7	51.7
Germany	553.3	0.0	-3.5	7.2	58.9
United Kingdom	240.3	-9.9	6.9	3.1	62.1
France	229.4	-1.7	1.3	3.0	65.1
Portugal	214.4	-2.1	17.9	2.8	67.9
Thailand	191.6	-2.2	17.0	2.5	70.4
Belgium	164.4	7.0	1.2	2.1	72.5
Italy	163.8	-7.3	8.4	2.1	74.7
Netherlands	156.9	5.3	9.2	2.1	76.7
United Arab Emirates	154.8	-0.8	27.0	2.0	78.7
USA	143.1	0.9	4.3	1.9	80.6
Spain	120.1	-4.1	0.7	1.6	82.2
Indonesia	119.7	8.0	34.8	1.6	83.8
Czech Rep.	108.2	-4.5	-15.3	1.4	85.2
Poland	91.6	-3.6	8.3	1.2	86.4

Table 3: Top importing countries or areas in 2010

Country or area	Value (million US$)	Avg. Growth (%) 06-10	Growth (%) 09-10	World share %	Cum.
World	7900.2	1.7	18.5	100.0	
USA	1659.5	-4.4	27.2	21.0	21.0
Germany	579.1	5.1	11.7	7.3	28.3
France	458.6	3.4	8.9	5.8	34.1
United Kingdom	436.6	0.1	13.5	5.5	39.7
Italy	367.5	1.0	2.5	4.7	44.3
Japan	298.2	-1.9	12.7	3.8	48.1
Canada	234.5	-1.9	17.8	3.0	51.1
Russian Federation	234.0	16.8	86.0	3.0	54.0
Netherlands	216.2	5.2	13.6	2.7	56.8
Belgium	198.7	3.4	8.2	2.5	59.3
Spain	186.1	-4.2	8.7	2.4	61.6
Turkey	172.0	6.4	39.7	2.2	63.8
Switzerland	140.2	4.5	13.6	1.8	65.6
Austria	130.4	3.4	-0.1	1.7	67.2
Australia	127.9	2.9	11.1	1.6	68.9

667 Pearls and precious or semiprecious stones, unworked or worked

After several years of continuous growth marked by a peak of 114.9 bln US$ in 2008, the value (in current prices) of exports of pearls and precious or semiprecious stones (SITC group 667) declined by 22.5 percent in 2009 but bounced back by 43.1 percent to 127.5 bln US$ in 2010 (see table 2). Similarly, imports showed a 43.7 percent increase to 117.4 bln US$ for the year (see table 3). Graph 1 shows that the substantial increase in exports for 2010 in this product group far exceeded the increases in world exports of manufactured goods classified chiefly by material (SITC section 6) of 24.5 percent and in total world exports of 21.2 percent. Exports of pearls and precious or semiprecious stones (SITC group 667) accounted for 6.6 percent of world exports of SITC section 6 and 0.8 percent of total world exports (see table 1).

In 2010, India, Belgium and Israel were the top exporting countries (see table 2). They accounted respectively for 17.7, 13.0 and 12.9 percent of world exports. Top destinations were India, USA and China, Hong Kong SAR (see table 3). By MDG regions (see graph 2), Western Asia, Sub-Saharan Africa and Commonwealth of Independent States recorded trade surpluses respectively of 10.0 bln US$, 5.2 bln US$ and 2.6 bln US$ in 2010. Top trade deficits were recorded by Eastern Asia (-5.7 bln US$), Developed North America (-2.7 bln US$) and Developed Asia-Pacific (-1.0 bln US$).

Table 1: Imports (Imp.) and exports (Exp.), 1996-2010, in current prices

		1996	1997	1998	1999	2000	2001	2002	2003	2004	2005	2006	2007	2008	2009	2010
Values in Bln US$	Imp.	45.7	46.4	43.2	52.6	60.5	47.0	59.7	62.5	76.0	89.6	84.7	95.6	105.8	81.7	117.4
	Exp.	42.5	43.0	38.9	45.9	54.8	47.5	58.7	63.2	75.9	92.4	89.4	104.4	114.9	89.1	127.5
As a percentage of SITC section (%)	Imp.	5.6	5.6	5.2	6.4	6.8	5.5	6.7	6.1	5.9	6.3	5.1	4.9	4.9	5.3	6.1
	Exp.	5.2	5.2	4.8	5.7	6.3	5.7	6.7	6.2	6.0	6.5	5.3	5.3	5.3	5.7	6.6
As a percentage of world trade (%)	Imp.	0.9	0.8	0.8	0.9	0.9	0.7	0.9	0.8	0.8	0.8	0.7	0.7	0.7	0.7	0.8
	Exp.	0.8	0.8	0.7	0.8	0.9	0.8	0.9	0.8	0.8	0.9	0.7	0.8	0.7	0.7	0.8

Graph 1: Annual growth rates of exports, 1996–2010
(In percentage by year)

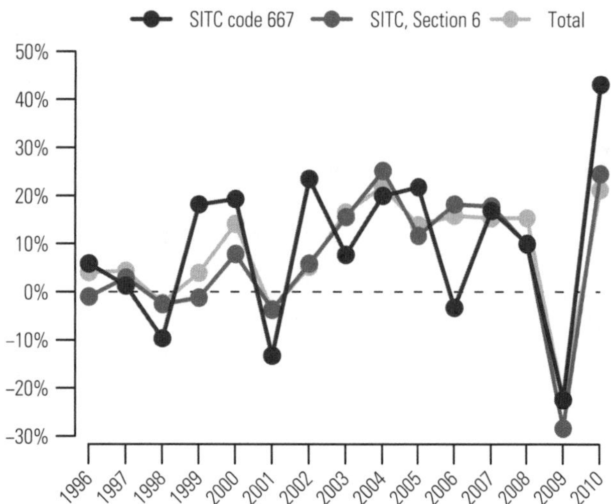

Table 2: Top exporting countries or areas in 2010

Country or area	Value (million US$)	Avg. Growth (%) 06-10	Growth (%) 09-10	World share %	Cum.
World	127 526.4	9.3	43.1	100.0	
India	22 589.0	20.6	33.1	17.7	17.7
Belgium	16 529.4	1.4	49.1	13.0	30.7
Israel	16 437.8	0.4	41.1	12.9	43.6
United Arab Emirates	15 219.2	70.0	96.2	11.9	55.5
USA	14 916.1	10.4	41.6	11.7	67.2
China, Hong Kong SAR	12 331.8	18.9	36.2	9.7	76.9
United Kingdom	7 779.5	-2.5	37.3	6.1	83.0
Botswana	3 192.5	-0.5	47.6	2.5	85.5
Russian Federation	2 630.2	11.2	126.3	2.1	87.5
Canada	2 624.3	13.2	51.6	2.1	89.6
China	2 341.6	4.6	30.9	1.8	91.4
South Africa	1 955.5	-5.6	49.6	1.5	93.0
Switzerland	1 865.8	1.1	2.8	1.5	94.4
Thailand	1 666.6	8.8	30.0	1.3	95.7
Namibia	*676.1*	-6.9	21.2	0.5	96.3

Graph 2: Trade Balance by MDG regions 2010
(Bln US$)

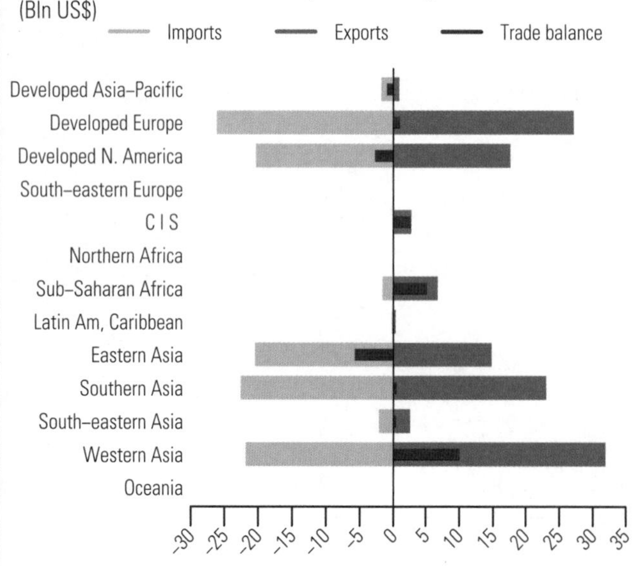

Table 3: Top importing countries or areas in 2010

Country or area	Value (million US$)	Avg. Growth (%) 06-10	Growth (%) 09-10	World share %	Cum.
World	117 352.1	8.5	43.7	100.0	
India	22 309.5	30.9	44.5	19.0	19.0
USA	19 755.5	1.7	44.9	16.8	35.8
China, Hong Kong SAR	15 519.9	13.1	36.0	13.2	49.1
Belgium	14 305.9	0.6	42.3	12.2	61.3
United Arab Emirates	13 144.7	49.4	80.8	11.2	72.5
Israel	8 399.1	-1.9	57.4	7.2	79.6
United Kingdom	7 665.0	-4.6	34.6	6.5	86.2
China	4 541.5	14.8	58.6	3.9	90.0
Switzerland	2 191.0	-0.9	3.7	1.9	91.9
Japan	1 230.0	-6.4	13.7	1.0	92.9
Thailand	1 128.4	-7.1	6.0	1.0	93.9
France	683.8	2.3	14.4	0.6	94.5
Botswana	659.1	106.3	79.2	0.6	95.0
Singapore	625.4	1.3	-12.0	0.5	95.6
South Africa	622.6	-9.7	39.4	0.5	96.1

The value (in current prices) of exports of pig iron, spiegeleisen, sponge iron, iron or steel granules and powders (SITC group 671) in 2010 rose by 55.9 percent and totaled 34.5 bln US$ (see table 2). Similarly, imports showed a 51.8 percent growth and amounted to 40.1 bln US$ (see table 3). Graph 1 shows that the rise in exports for 2010 in this product group far exceeded the increases in world exports of manufactured goods classified chiefly by material (SITC section 6) of 24.5 percent and in total world exports of 21.2 percent. Exports of pig iron, spiegeleisen, sponge iron, iron or steel granules and powders (SITC group 671) accounted for 1.8 percent of world exports of SITC section 6 and 0.2 percent of total world exports (see table 1).

South Africa, Russian Federation and Brazil were the three major exporting countries in 2010 (see table 2). They accounted respectively for 14.4, 10.1 and 8.8 percent of world exports. Top destinations were USA, China and Germany (see table 3). By MDG regions (see graph 2), trade surpluses were recorded by Commonwealth of Independent States (+6.4 bln US$), Sub-Saharan Africa (+4.8 bln US$) and Latin America and the Caribbean (+4.5 bln US$). Developed Europe, Eastern Asia and Developed North America recorded trade deficits amounting respectively to 8.1 bln US$, 6.0 bln US$ and 4.8 bln US$.

Table 1: Imports (Imp.) and exports (Exp.), 1996-2010, in current prices

		1996	1997	1998	1999	2000	2001	2002	2003	2004	2005	2006	2007	2008	2009	2010
Values in Bln US$	Imp.	12.5	12.4	11.4	9.8	11.6	10.0	10.9	14.1	26.1	30.7	31.2	43.5	58.9	26.4	40.1
	Exp.	9.9	8.8	7.9	7.7	8.8	8.0	8.8	11.8	21.3	25.9	25.9	36.2	47.9	22.1	34.5
As a percentage of SITC section (%)	Imp.	1.5	1.5	1.4	1.2	1.3	1.2	1.2	1.4	2.0	2.1	1.9	2.2	2.7	1.7	2.1
	Exp.	1.2	1.1	1.0	1.0	1.0	1.0	1.0	1.2	1.7	1.8	1.5	1.8	2.2	1.4	1.8
As a percentage of world trade (%)	Imp.	0.2	0.2	0.2	0.2	0.2	0.2	0.2	0.2	0.3	0.3	0.3	0.3	0.4	0.2	0.3
	Exp.	0.2	0.2	0.1	0.1	0.1	0.1	0.1	0.2	0.2	0.2	0.2	0.3	0.3	0.2	0.2

Graph 1: Annual growth rates of exports, 1996–2010
(In percentage by year)

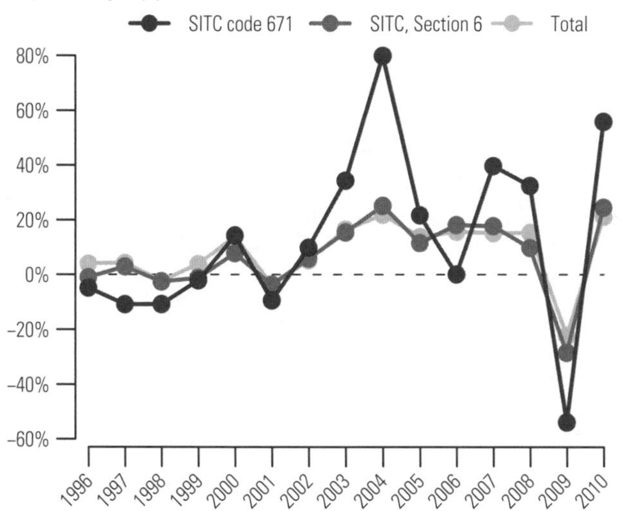

Graph 2: Trade Balance by MDG regions 2010
(Bln US$)

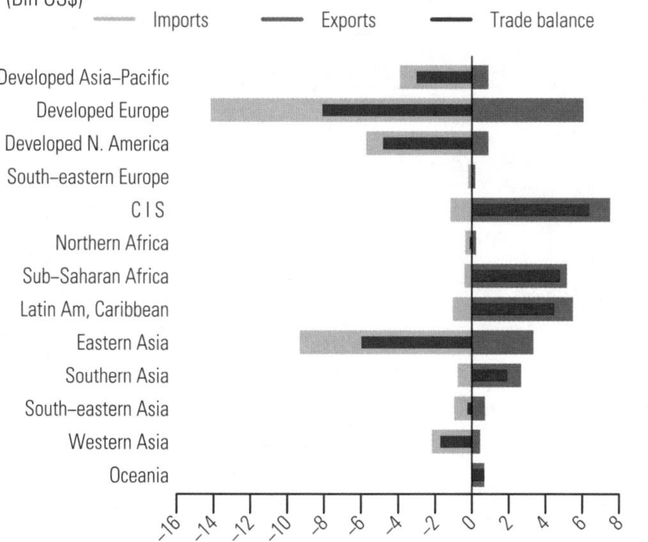

Table 2: Top exporting countries or areas in 2010

Country or area	Value (million US$)	Avg. Growth (%) 06-10	Growth (%) 09-10	World share %	Cum.
World	34452.6	7.4	55.9	100.0	
South Africa	4976.8	18.6	70.9	14.4	14.4
Russian Federation	3495.6	6.4	21.7	10.1	24.6
Brazil	3027.8	5.1	19.7	8.8	33.4
China	2661.1	-1.8	95.0	7.7	41.1
India	2436.8	45.8	145.0	7.1	48.2
Kazakhstan	1825.7	17.7	53.6	5.3	53.5
Ukraine	1812.1	12.1	66.1	5.3	58.7
Netherlands	1248.4	11.4	55.7	3.6	62.4
Belgium	989.0	-5.4	62.5	2.9	65.2
Colombia	967.9	-3.3	33.3	2.8	68.0
Japan	893.8	7.0	20.1	2.6	70.6
Venezuela	826.4	-3.0	95.5	2.4	73.0
Germany	818.9	4.2	67.7	2.4	75.4
Norway	694.3	13.9	56.0	2.0	77.4
New Caledonia	684.1	0.9	24.8	2.0	79.4

Table 3: Top importing countries or areas in 2010

Country or area	Value (million US$)	Avg. Growth (%) 06-10	Growth (%) 09-10	World share %	Cum.
World	40092.3	6.4	51.8	100.0	
USA	5188.5	3.1	107.4	12.9	12.9
China	4326.9	38.1	-11.1	10.8	23.7
Germany	3852.5	5.3	75.0	9.6	33.3
Japan	3743.0	7.6	81.7	9.3	42.7
Rep. of Korea	2962.0	11.5	64.4	7.4	50.1
Italy	2543.9	-0.3	70.3	6.3	56.4
Other Asia, nes	1958.8	4.9	59.8	4.9	61.3
Belgium	1306.8	-3.1	57.8	3.3	64.6
Netherlands	1290.2	2.2	40.4	3.2	67.8
Spain	1232.8	-4.3	65.3	3.1	70.8
Turkey	1020.5	19.1	46.8	2.5	73.4
France	799.8	-2.7	42.7	2.0	75.4
Saudi Arabia	659.7	57.1	108.7	1.6	77.0
Sweden	601.5	0.5	81.4	1.5	78.5
Canada	524.5	4.8	97.9	1.3	79.8

672 Ingots and other primary forms, of iron or steel; semi-finished products

From 2006 to 2010, the value (in current prices) of exports of ingots and other primary forms, of iron or steel; semi-finished products (SITC group 672) increased on average by 3.0 percent and amounted to 34.8 bln US$ in 2010 (see table 2). Similarly, imports went up on average by 3.3 percent and totaled 37.5 bln US$ (see table 3). Graph 1 shows that the increase in exports for 2010 in this product group exceeded the increases in world exports of manufactured goods classified chiefly by material (SITC section 6) of 24.5 percent and in total world exports of 21.2 percent. Exports of ingots and other primary forms, of iron or steel; semi-finished products (SITC group 672) accounted for 1.8 percent of world exports of SITC section 6 and 0.2 percent of total world exports (see table 1).

The top exporting countries in 2010 were Russian Federation, Ukraine and Japan (see table 2). Their exports increased respectively by 45.9, 37.1 and 17.5 percent to represent 20.6, 15.6 and 8.0 percent of world exports. Rep. of Korea, USA and Iran were the three major destinations (see table 3). By MDG regions (see graph 2), Commonwealth of Independent States recorded a trade surplus of 13.0 bln US$. Major surpluses were also recorded by Latin America and the Caribbean (+2.7 bln US$) and Developed Asia-Pacific (+2.6 bln US$). Top trade deficits were recorded by Eastern Asia (-5.7 bln US$), South-eastern Asia (-5.2 bln US$) and Southern Asia (-2.9 bln US$).

Table 1: Imports (Imp.) and exports (Exp.), 1996-2010, in current prices

		1996	1997	1998	1999	2000	2001	2002	2003	2004	2005	2006	2007	2008	2009	2010
Values in Bln US$	Imp.	13.2	13.5	11.6	11.1	13.7	12.2	13.9	17.5	28.9	31.7	32.9	40.7	57.1	28.9	37.5
	Exp.	11.9	12.6	10.0	9.6	11.5	10.6	12.2	15.3	26.0	28.5	30.9	39.2	54.2	24.4	34.8
As a percentage of SITC section (%)	Imp.	1.6	1.6	1.4	1.4	1.5	1.4	1.6	1.7	2.3	2.2	2.0	2.1	2.7	1.9	2.0
	Exp.	1.5	1.5	1.2	1.2	1.3	1.3	1.4	1.5	2.0	2.0	1.8	2.0	2.5	1.6	1.8
As a percentage of world trade (%)	Imp.	0.2	0.2	0.2	0.2	0.2	0.2	0.2	0.2	0.3	0.3	0.3	0.3	0.4	0.2	0.2
	Exp.	0.2	0.2	0.2	0.2	0.2	0.2	0.2	0.2	0.3	0.3	0.3	0.3	0.3	0.2	0.2

Graph 1: Annual growth rates of exports, 1996–2010

(In percentage by year)

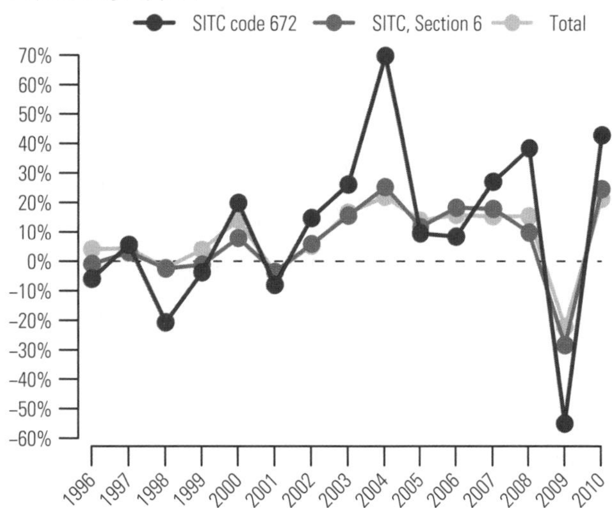

Graph 2: Trade Balance by MDG regions 2010

(Bln US$)

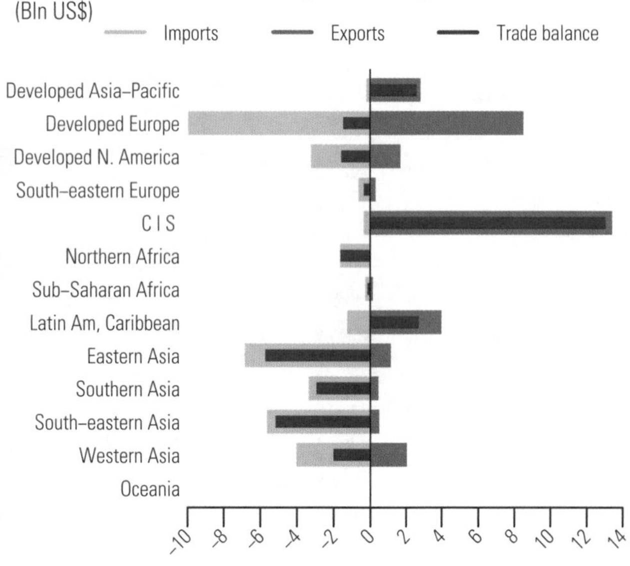

Table 2: Top exporting countries or areas in 2010

Country or area	Value (million US$)	Avg. Growth (%) 06-10	Growth (%) 09-10	World share %	Cum.
World	34787.1	3.0	42.8	100.0	
Russian Federation	7171.7	7.2	45.9	20.6	20.6
Ukraine	5437.6	5.7	37.1	15.6	36.2
Japan	2777.1	14.2	17.5	8.0	44.2
Brazil	2592.8	3.3	49.5	7.5	51.7
Turkey	1978.6	30.1	98.0	5.7	57.4
Germany	1469.6	0.2	35.7	4.2	61.6
France	1378.5	-5.7	24.5	4.0	65.6
United Kingdom	1264.6	-8.4	-13.5	3.6	69.2
Canada	1025.4	52.6	167.5	2.9	72.1
Mexico	939.3	-6.6	115.0	2.7	74.8
Italy	869.6	2.5	77.1	2.5	77.3
Rep. of Korea	672.0	39.6	332.9	1.9	79.3
USA	625.0	22.2	2.7	1.8	81.1
Netherlands	584.5	28.1	245.6	1.7	82.7
Sweden	456.7	7.5	95.8	1.3	84.1

Table 3: Top importing countries or areas in 2010

Country or area	Value (million US$)	Avg. Growth (%) 06-10	Growth (%) 09-10	World share %	Cum.
World	37476.2	3.3	29.6	100.0	
Rep. of Korea	3656.8	12.6	42.0	9.8	9.8
USA	2994.9	-9.6	166.3	8.0	17.7
Iran	2488.5	121.1	8.4	6.6	24.4
Other Asia, nes	2444.3	-2.0	35.5	6.5	30.9
Italy	2183.5	-6.7	53.2	5.8	36.7
Thailand	2165.5	9.2	33.0	5.8	42.5
Viet Nam	*1765.2*	22.6	66.9	4.7	47.2
Indonesia	1416.5	15.1	51.8	3.8	51.0
Belgium	1362.6	1.8	37.9	3.6	54.6
France	1311.3	1.3	38.5	3.5	58.1
Turkey	1280.1	0.9	-13.4	3.4	61.6
Germany	1235.4	-9.4	28.3	3.3	64.9
Egypt	868.3	14.5	4.7	2.3	67.2
Syria	*811.2*	46.6	-15.7	2.2	69.3
Saudi Arabia	689.4	-2.0	243.1	1.8	71.2

From 2006 to 2010, the value (in current prices) of exports of flat-rolled iron, etc (SITC group 673) increased on average by 2.4 percent to 79.4 bln US$ in 2010 (see table 2). In the same period, imports experienced an average growth of 3.1 percent and amounted to 83.9 bln US$ in 2010 (see table 3). Graph 1 shows that the increase in exports for 2010 in this product group exceeded the increases in world exports of manufactured goods classified chiefly by material (SITC section 6) of 24.5 percent and in total world exports of 21.2 percent. Exports of flat-rolled iron, etc (SITC group 673) accounted for 4.1 percent of world exports of SITC section 6 and 0.5 percent of total world exports (see table 1).

Japan, China and Rep. of Korea were the top exporting countries in 2010 (see table 2). They accounted respectively for 15.5, 10.3 and 10.1 percent of world exports. Top destinations were Rep. of Korea, China and Germany (see table 3). By MDG regions (see graph 2), Developed Europe accounted for a large share of trade in flat-rolled iron, etc (SITC group 673). In 2010, its exports and imports were valued respectively at 25.0 bln US$ and 26.3 bln US$, resulting in a trade deficit of 1.3 bln US$. Major deficits were also recorded by South-eastern Asia (-10.1 bln US$) and Western Asia (-5.2 bln US$) among others. Developed Asia-Pacific and Commonwealth of Independent States recorded trade surpluses amounting respectively to 11.1 bln US$ and 6.9 bln US$.

Table 1: Imports (Imp.) and exports (Exp.), 1996-2010, in current prices

		1996	1997	1998	1999	2000	2001	2002	2003	2004	2005	2006	2007	2008	2009	2010
Values in Bln US$	Imp.	33.8	34.2	33.7	27.5	32.6	28.1	29.5	40.0	58.1	69.6	74.2	91.4	118.4	65.4	83.9
	Exp.	30.7	32.2	30.4	25.1	29.5	24.6	27.7	36.9	55.4	65.7	72.1	89.1	112.7	59.4	79.4
As a percentage of SITC section (%)	Imp.	4.2	4.1	4.1	3.4	3.7	3.3	3.3	3.9	4.5	4.9	4.5	4.7	5.5	4.2	4.4
	Exp.	3.8	3.9	3.7	3.1	3.4	3.0	3.1	3.6	4.3	4.6	4.3	4.5	5.2	3.8	4.1
As a percentage of world trade (%)	Imp.	0.6	0.6	0.6	0.5	0.5	0.4	0.5	0.5	0.6	0.7	0.6	0.7	0.7	0.5	0.6
	Exp.	0.6	0.6	0.6	0.5	0.5	0.4	0.4	0.5	0.6	0.6	0.6	0.6	0.7	0.5	0.5

Graph 1: Annual growth rates of exports, 1996–2010
(In percentage by year)

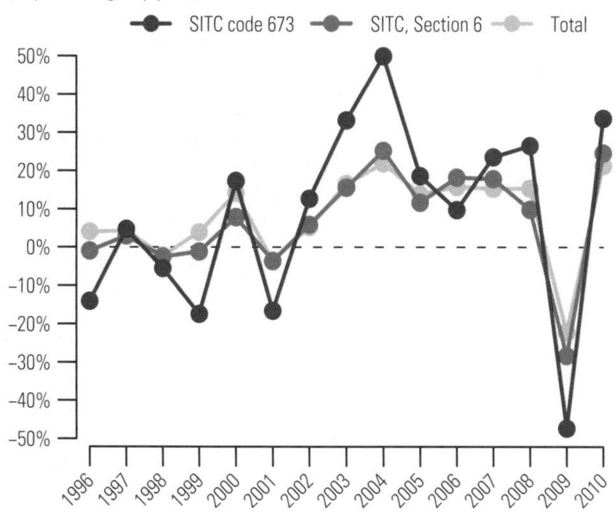

Table 2: Top exporting countries or areas in 2010

Country or area	Value (million US$)	Avg. Growth (%) 06-10	Growth (%) 09-10	World share %	Cum.
World	79356.6	2.4	33.6	100.0	
Japan	12336.7	13.1	37.4	15.5	15.5
China	8167.5	1.9	100.1	10.3	25.8
Rep. of Korea	7982.2	16.3	34.3	10.1	35.9
Belgium	4476.7	-5.9	13.1	5.6	41.5
Germany	4390.4	-4.3	9.8	5.5	47.1
Russian Federation	4309.5	1.8	11.9	5.4	52.5
Ukraine	3545.0	-0.1	44.9	4.5	57.0
Italy	2913.3	3.1	39.1	3.7	60.6
Other Asia, nes	2785.8	3.2	16.3	3.5	64.1
USA	2717.3	6.2	40.2	3.4	67.6
Netherlands	2322.6	-2.3	25.1	2.9	70.5
France	1833.8	-5.2	20.2	2.3	72.8
Austria	1615.4	2.3	11.9	2.0	74.8
Slovakia	1439.5	-1.2	40.5	1.8	76.7
India	1360.1	4.6	57.9	1.7	78.4

Graph 2: Trade Balance by MDG regions 2010
(Bln US$)

Imports — Exports — Trade balance

Developed Asia-Pacific
Developed Europe
Developed N. America
South-eastern Europe
C I S
Northern Africa
Sub-Saharan Africa
Latin Am, Caribbean
Eastern Asia
Southern Asia
South-eastern Asia
Western Asia
Oceania

-30 -25 -20 -15 -10 -5 0 5 10 15 20 25

Table 3: Top importing countries or areas in 2010

Country or area	Value (million US$)	Avg. Growth (%) 06-10	Growth (%) 09-10	World share %	Cum.
World	83934.0	3.1	28.3	100.0	
Rep. of Korea	8187.9	8.7	12.9	9.8	9.8
China	5364.1	6.9	-9.4	6.4	16.1
Germany	4834.4	-0.1	28.7	5.8	21.9
Viet Nam	*4448.3*	34.4	66.9	5.3	27.2
Italy	3514.7	-6.6	34.1	4.2	31.4
France	3242.4	-2.9	25.6	3.9	35.3
Turkey	3176.2	-1.8	27.9	3.8	39.0
USA	2905.5	-16.4	41.6	3.5	42.5
India	2790.4	9.0	-7.2	3.3	45.8
Iran	2457.3	64.7	8.4	2.9	48.8
Thailand	2382.3	9.5	63.0	2.8	51.6
Belgium	2100.7	-10.0	18.4	2.5	54.1
Japan	1997.7	9.1	57.6	2.4	56.5
Spain	1905.4	-8.4	52.8	2.3	58.7
Canada	1827.9	-4.8	59.8	2.2	60.9

 Source: UN Comtrade

674 Flat-rolled products of iron or non-alloy steel, clad, plated or coated

After a 35.8 percent drop in 2009, the value (in current prices) of exports of flat-rolled products of iron or non-alloy steel, clad, plated or coated (SITC group 674) bounced back by 36.4 percent amounting to 49.2 bln US$ in 2010 (see table 2). Imports in the same year also grew by 33.4 percent to 51.3 bln US$ (see table 3). Graph 1 shows that the rise in exports for 2010 in this product group exceeded the increases in world exports of manufactured goods classified chiefly by material (SITC section 6) of 24.5 percent and in total world exports of 21.2 percent. Exports of flat-rolled products of iron or non-alloy steel, clad, plated or coated (SITC group 674) accounted for 2.5 percent of world exports of SITC section 6 and 0.3 percent of total world exports (see table 1).

China's exports increased by 137.5 percent representing 13.6 percent of world exports in 2010 (see table 2). Other major exporting countries were Japan and Rep. of Korea, respectively with 11.0 and 10.5 percent of world exports. China, Germany and France were the top destinations (see table 3). By MDG regions (see graph 2), Developed Europe accounted for a large share of trade in flat-rolled products of iron or non-alloy steel, clad, plated or coated (SITC group 674) in 2010, with exports and imports valued respectively at 20.8 bln US$ and 21.0 bln US$ resulting in a trade deficit of 174 mln US$. Major deficits were also recorded by South-eastern Asia (-4.2 bln US$) and Latin America and the Caribbean (-3.6 bln US$). Top trade surpluses were recorded by Eastern Asia (+8.2 bln US$) and Developed Asia-Pacific (+4.4 bln US$).

Table 1: Imports (Imp.) and exports (Exp.), 1996-2010, in current prices

		1996	1997	1998	1999	2000	2001	2002	2003	2004	2005	2006	2007	2008	2009	2010
Values in Bln US$	Imp.	17.6	17.9	18.9	17.9	19.7	18.1	19.7	24.9	32.7	36.2	41.4	50.6	56.8	38.4	51.3
	Exp.	17.1	17.6	18.8	17.3	19.0	17.0	18.7	23.4	30.9	34.2	40.3	48.3	56.1	36.1	49.2
As a percentage of SITC section (%)	Imp.	2.2	2.2	2.3	2.2	2.2	2.1	2.2	2.4	2.6	2.5	2.5	2.6	2.6	2.5	2.7
	Exp.	2.1	2.1	2.3	2.2	2.2	2.0	2.1	2.3	2.4	2.4	2.4	2.4	2.6	2.3	2.5
As a percentage of world trade (%)	Imp.	0.3	0.3	0.3	0.3	0.3	0.3	0.3	0.3	0.4	0.3	0.3	0.4	0.4	0.3	0.3
	Exp.	0.3	0.3	0.4	0.3	0.3	0.3	0.3	0.3	0.3	0.3	0.3	0.3	0.4	0.3	0.3

Graph 1: Annual growth rates of exports, 1996–2010
(In percentage by year)

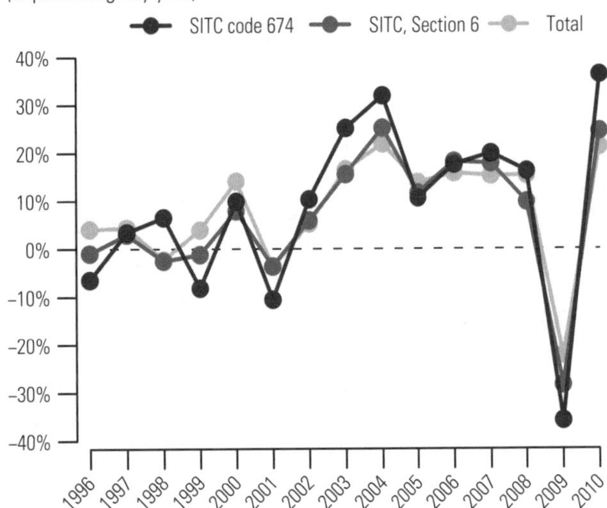

Table 2: Top exporting countries or areas in 2010

Country or area	Value (million US$)	Avg. Growth (%) 06-10	Growth (%) 09-10	World share %	Cum.
World	49181.7	5.1	36.4	100.0	
China	6712.0	26.6	137.5	13.6	13.6
Japan	5392.7	8.4	52.0	11.0	24.6
Rep. of Korea	5185.0	11.4	45.1	10.5	35.2
Belgium	4456.3	1.4	10.0	9.1	44.2
Germany	4371.4	-0.8	9.8	8.9	53.1
France	2131.0	-2.6	11.6	4.3	57.4
Netherlands	2120.8	4.9	23.7	4.3	61.7
Other Asia, nes	2007.9	1.9	39.7	4.1	65.8
USA	1784.9	9.9	34.7	3.6	69.5
Italy	1493.1	2.7	77.5	3.0	72.5
India	1464.7	-3.5	16.8	3.0	75.5
Austria	1248.1	-1.3	18.2	2.5	78.0
Slovakia	1122.6	15.1	16.2	2.3	80.3
Canada	781.3	2.5	17.5	1.6	81.9
United Kingdom	740.9	-2.7	15.8	1.5	83.4

Graph 2: Trade Balance by MDG regions 2010
(Bln US$)

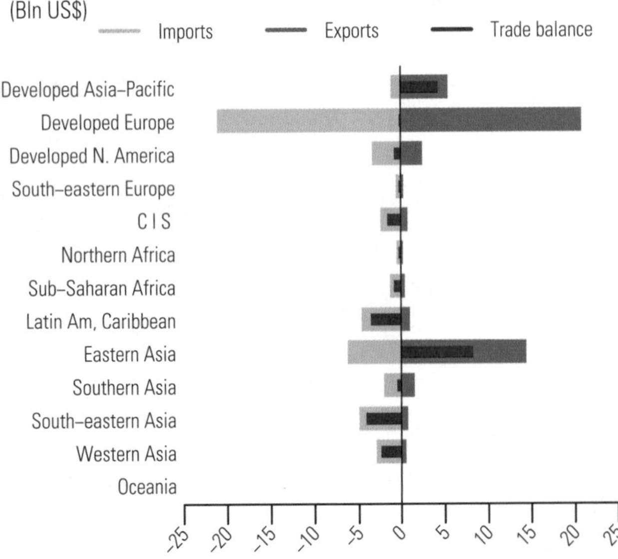

Table 3: Top importing countries or areas in 2010

Country or area	Value (million US$)	Avg. Growth (%) 06-10	Growth (%) 09-10	World share %	Cum.
World	51252.8	5.5	33.4	100.0	
China	4336.5	3.6	38.2	8.5	8.5
Germany	3852.9	4.7	19.9	7.5	16.0
France	2436.4	2.5	12.6	4.8	20.7
Thailand	2254.3	16.8	88.9	4.4	25.1
USA	2231.6	-12.2	35.9	4.4	29.5
Italy	1953.7	-1.5	17.9	3.8	33.3
Poland	1793.0	9.6	22.8	3.5	36.8
Spain	1648.4	-0.5	41.4	3.2	40.0
Mexico	1632.8	5.9	33.2	3.2	43.2
Belgium	1595.9	-1.7	11.8	3.1	46.3
Russian Federation	1343.6	15.5	69.0	2.6	48.9
United Kingdom	1319.8	-3.7	25.5	2.6	51.5
Czech Rep.	1127.6	4.7	20.1	2.2	53.7
Brazil	1110.3	73.9	172.5	2.2	55.9
Canada	1110.3	6.0	43.0	2.2	58.0

The value (in current prices) of exports of flat-rolled products of alloy steel (SITC group 675) increased by 38.2 percent and amounted to 59.3 bln US$ in 2010 (see table 2). Similarly, imports showed a 34.0 percent growth and totaled 55.2 bln US$ (see table 3). Graph 1 shows that the rise in exports for 2010 in this product group exceeded the increases in world exports of manufactured goods classified chiefly by material (SITC section 6) of 24.5 percent and in total world exports of 21.2 percent. Exports of flat-rolled products of alloy steel (SITC group 675) accounted for 3.1 percent of world exports of SITC section 6 and 0.4 percent of total world exports (see table 1).

In 2010, top exporting countries were Japan, Germany and France (see table 2). They accounted respectively for 15.0, 9.6 and 8.5 percent of world exports. China, Germany and Italy were the three main destinations (see table 3). By MDG regions (see graph 2), Developed Europe accounted for a majority of trade in flat-rolled products of alloy steel (SITC group 675). In 2010, its exports and imports were valued respectively at 30.9 bln US$ and 24.9 bln US$, resulting in a trade surplus of 6.0 bln US$. Developed Asia-Pacific recorded a trade surplus of 7.9 bln US$. Top trade deficits were recorded by South-eastern Asia (-3.7 bln US$), Latin America and the Caribbean (-3.0 bln US$) and Southern Asia (-2.1 bln US$).

Table 1: Imports (Imp.) and exports (Exp.), 1996-2010, in current prices

		1996	1997	1998	1999	2000	2001	2002	2003	2004	2005	2006	2007	2008	2009	2010
Values in Bln US$	Imp.	18.4	17.9	18.0	16.7	20.0	18.2	20.4	26.4	37.7	43.4	54.1	70.1	68.9	41.2	55.2
	Exp.	18.4	18.7	18.5	17.5	21.1	18.5	21.3	28.0	39.5	44.3	56.8	72.3	73.1	42.9	59.3
As a percentage of SITC section (%)	Imp.	2.3	2.1	2.2	2.0	2.2	2.1	2.3	2.6	2.9	3.0	3.3	3.6	3.2	2.7	2.9
	Exp.	2.3	2.2	2.3	2.2	2.4	2.2	2.4	2.8	3.1	3.1	3.4	3.7	3.4	2.8	3.1
As a percentage of world trade (%)	Imp.	0.3	0.3	0.3	0.3	0.3	0.3	0.3	0.3	0.4	0.4	0.4	0.5	0.4	0.3	0.4
	Exp.	0.3	0.3	0.3	0.3	0.3	0.3	0.3	0.4	0.4	0.4	0.5	0.5	0.5	0.3	0.4

Graph 1: Annual growth rates of exports, 1996–2010
(In percentage by year)

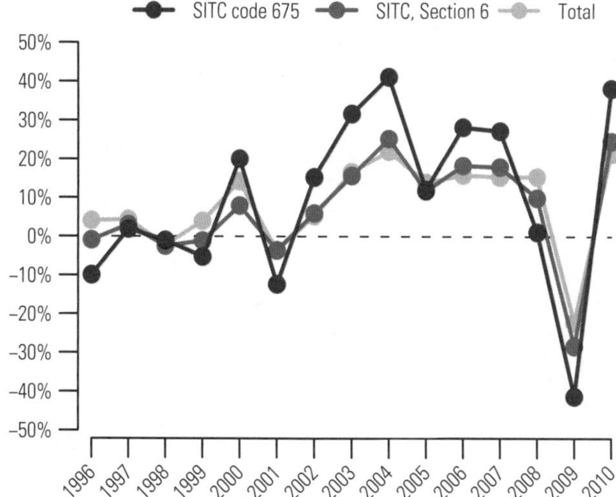

Graph 2: Trade Balance by MDG regions 2010
(Bln US$)

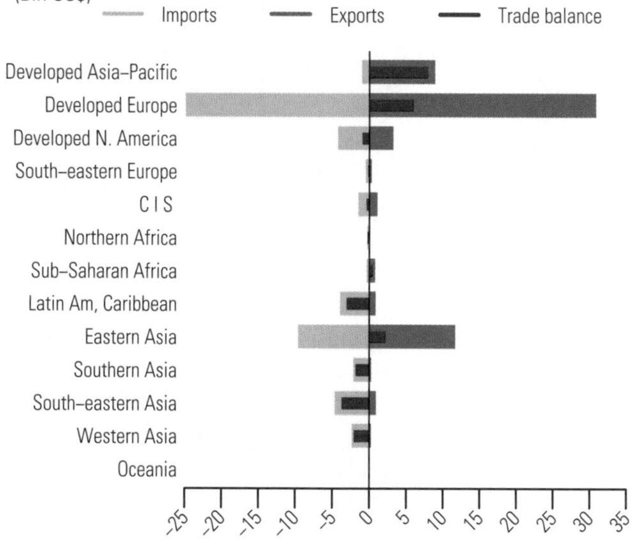

Table 2: Top exporting countries or areas in 2010

Country or area	Value (million US$)	Avg. Growth (%) 06-10	Growth (%) 09-10	World share %	Cum.
World	59341.8	1.1	38.2	100.0	
Japan	8918.1	9.3	41.8	15.0	15.0
Germany	5698.1	-1.1	19.3	9.6	24.6
France	5032.2	1.6	10.5	8.5	33.1
Belgium	4643.2	-3.2	31.6	7.8	40.9
China	4489.7	24.0	164.4	7.6	48.5
Rep. of Korea	3444.8	1.3	35.6	5.8	54.3
Sweden	3216.5	-3.3	39.4	5.4	59.7
Other Asia, nes	3085.8	0.2	41.6	5.2	64.9
Finland	3000.4	-4.3	62.1	5.1	70.0
USA	2766.8	8.1	38.4	4.7	74.6
Netherlands	2406.8	-0.9	63.6	4.1	78.7
Italy	2246.4	-2.5	29.1	3.8	82.5
Spain	1428.1	-6.0	41.0	2.4	84.9
Austria	1284.4	17.2	21.6	2.2	87.1
Russian Federation	857.3	-10.1	75.8	1.4	88.5

Table 3: Top importing countries or areas in 2010

Country or area	Value (million US$)	Avg. Growth (%) 06-10	Growth (%) 09-10	World share %	Cum.
World	55210.3	0.5	34.0	100.0	
China	5152.5	-6.7	5.3	9.3	9.3
Germany	4410.0	-3.2	39.3	8.0	17.3
Italy	4273.0	-4.2	49.5	7.7	25.1
USA	2921.4	-4.2	63.7	5.3	30.4
France	2548.7	-6.8	30.4	4.6	35.0
Netherlands	2317.0	1.6	46.1	4.2	39.2
Mexico	2171.3	6.9	53.5	3.9	43.1
Rep. of Korea	1922.9	6.1	20.7	3.5	46.6
Belgium	1797.2	8.5	15.3	3.3	49.8
Turkey	1668.7	12.1	46.5	3.0	52.9
Other Asia, nes	1624.5	10.3	82.3	2.9	55.8
Spain	1559.8	1.0	28.4	2.8	58.6
India	1524.9	15.1	2.2	2.8	61.4
Thailand	1460.8	10.3	74.0	2.6	64.0
Canada	1289.7	-2.1	40.7	2.3	66.4

Source: UN Comtrade

676 Iron and steel bars, rods, angles, shapes and sections

After several years of continuous growth marked by a peak of 112.6 bln US$ in 2008, the value (in current prices) of exports of iron and steel bars, rods, angles, shapes and sections (SITC group 676) dramatically fell by 54.6 percent in 2009 but bounced back by 34.5 percent to 68.7 bln US$ in 2010 (see table 2). In the same year, imports also increased by 29.8 percent and totaled 68.6 bln US$ (see table 3). Graph 1 shows that the increase in exports for 2010 in this product group exceeded the increases in world exports of manufactured goods classified chiefly by material (SITC section 6) of 24.5 percent and in total world exports of 21.2 percent. Exports of iron and steel bars, rods, angles, shapes and sections (SITC group 676) accounted for 3.6 percent of world exports of SITC section 6 and 0.5 percent of total world exports (see table 1).

The top exporting countries in 2010 were Germany, Turkey and China (see table 2). They accounted respectively for 9.1, 7.5 and 7.5 percent of world exports. Germany, USA and Rep. of Korea were the three main destinations (see table 3). By MDG regions (see graph 2), Developed Europe accounted for a large share of trade in iron and steel bars, rods, angles, shapes and sections (SITC group 676). In 2010, its exports and imports were valued respectively at 32.6 bln US$ and 25.6 bln US$, resulting in a trade surplus of 7.0 bln US$. Large surpluses were also recorded by Developed Asia-Pacific (+3.5 bln US$) and Commonwealth of Independent States (+2.9 bln US$). Top trade deficits were recorded by South-eastern Asia (-4.6 bln US$), Northern Africa (-2.3 bln US$) and Latin America and the Caribbean (-2.2 bln US$).

Table 1: Imports (Imp.) and exports (Exp.), 1996-2010, in current prices

		1996	1997	1998	1999	2000	2001	2002	2003	2004	2005	2006	2007	2008	2009	2010
Values in Bln US$	Imp.	26.1	25.3	25.9	22.5	24.2	23.3	24.0	29.8	46.5	52.6	63.7	85.2	108.7	52.9	68.6
	Exp.	25.5	25.5	24.8	21.4	23.1	22.8	23.3	29.6	46.5	51.9	64.1	88.2	112.6	51.1	68.7
As a percentage of SITC section (%)	Imp.	3.2	3.0	3.1	2.7	2.7	2.7	2.7	2.9	3.6	3.7	3.8	4.3	5.0	3.4	3.6
	Exp.	3.1	3.1	3.1	2.7	2.7	2.7	2.7	2.9	3.7	3.7	3.8	4.5	5.2	3.3	3.6
As a percentage of world trade (%)	Imp.	0.5	0.5	0.5	0.4	0.4	0.4	0.4	0.4	0.5	0.5	0.5	0.6	0.7	0.4	0.5
	Exp.	0.5	0.5	0.5	0.4	0.4	0.4	0.4	0.4	0.5	0.5	0.5	0.6	0.7	0.4	0.5

Graph 1: Annual growth rates of exports, 1996–2010

(In percentage by year)

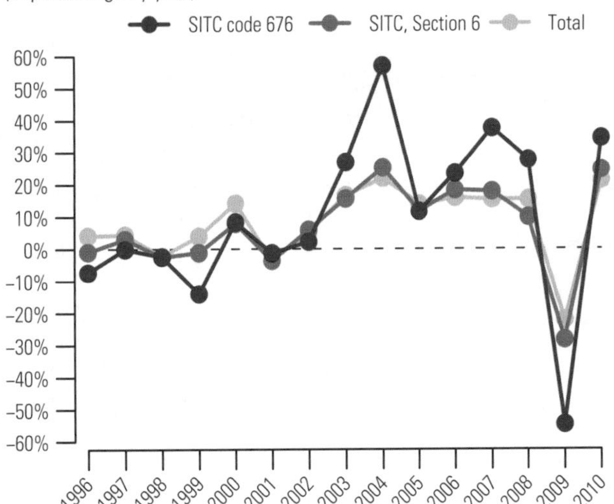

Graph 2: Trade Balance by MDG regions 2010

(Bln US$)

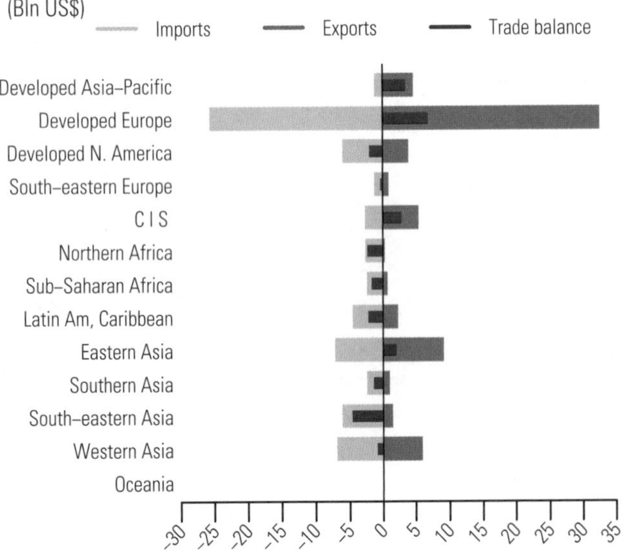

Table 2: Top exporting countries or areas in 2010

Country or area	Value (million US$)	Avg. Growth (%) 06-10	Growth (%) 09-10	World share %	Cum.
World	68694.7	1.8	34.5	100.0	
Germany	6225.6	-0.6	32.2	9.1	9.1
Turkey	5167.5	4.0	-4.5	7.5	16.6
China	5147.1	-3.8	108.7	7.5	24.1
Japan	4554.5	12.1	62.9	6.6	30.7
Spain	4429.1	9.9	30.2	6.4	37.2
Italy	4118.2	-3.6	26.8	6.0	43.2
Ukraine	3217.9	1.1	55.0	4.7	47.8
USA	2792.8	7.2	49.2	4.1	51.9
Rep. of Korea	2465.8	9.0	20.8	3.6	55.5
France	2446.5	-2.9	44.8	3.6	59.1
Luxembourg	2113.8	-0.8	21.9	3.1	62.1
United Kingdom	1926.2	-1.5	44.1	2.8	64.9
Russian Federation	1730.3	-0.9	6.6	2.5	67.5
Poland	1645.9	9.4	39.3	2.4	69.8
Czech Rep.	1519.9	2.0	36.3	2.2	72.1

Table 3: Top importing countries or areas in 2010

Country or area	Value (million US$)	Avg. Growth (%) 06-10	Growth (%) 09-10	World share %	Cum.
World	68621.7	1.9	29.8	100.0	
Germany	5705.0	-0.6	44.7	8.3	8.3
USA	3991.2	-10.4	57.9	5.8	14.1
Rep. of Korea	3205.0	6.9	58.5	4.7	18.8
France	2770.9	-2.2	25.0	4.0	22.8
Italy	2675.0	-3.7	55.4	3.9	26.7
China	2052.6	11.5	41.8	3.0	29.7
Canada	1928.1	-1.6	52.2	2.8	32.5
Netherlands	1754.7	-0.4	16.3	2.6	35.1
United Arab Emirates	1683.9	-4.7	5.6	2.5	37.5
Thailand	1613.3	15.6	84.3	2.4	39.9
Algeria	1492.5	9.1	-23.8	2.2	42.1
United Kingdom	1481.1	-5.5	46.1	2.2	44.2
Iran	1404.0	118.8	8.4	2.0	46.3
Saudi Arabia	1389.0	19.4	113.8	2.0	48.3
Belgium	1338.6	-5.1	14.7	2.0	50.3

In 2010, the value (in current prices) of exports of rails or railway track construction material, of iron or steel (SITC group 677) rose by 1.5 percent to 3.8 bln US$ (see table 2). Imports declined by 3.5 percent and amounted to 4.2 bln US$ (see table 3). Graph 1 shows that the rise in exports for 2010 in this product group was significantly less than the increases in world exports of manufactured goods classified chiefly by material (SITC section 6) of 24.5 percent and in total world exports of 21.2 percent. Exports of rails or railway track construction material, of iron or steel (SITC group 677) accounted for 0.2 percent of world exports of SITC section 6 and less than 0.1 percent of total world exports (see table 1).

Japan, Austria and Germany were the top exporting countries in 2010 (see table 2). They accounted respectively for 14.4, 13.4 and 10.7 percent of world exports. Top destinations were Brazil, Germany and USA (see table 3). By MDG regions (see graph 2), Developed Europe and Developed Asia-Pacific recorded trade surpluses amounting respectively to 675 mln US$ and 495 mln US$. Major deficits were recorded by Latin America and the Caribbean (-620 mln US$) and Western Asia (-301 mln US$).

Table 1: Imports (Imp.) and exports (Exp.), 1996-2010, in current prices

		1996	1997	1998	1999	2000	2001	2002	2003	2004	2005	2006	2007	2008	2009	2010
Values in Bln US$	Imp.	1.3	1.4	1.7	1.3	1.1	1.4	1.5	1.8	2.1	2.6	2.9	3.8	5.3	4.4	4.2
	Exp.	1.2	1.4	1.4	1.2	1.0	1.2	1.3	1.6	1.9	2.2	2.5	3.3	4.3	3.8	3.8
As a percentage of SITC section (%)	Imp.	0.2	0.2	0.2	0.2	0.1	0.2	0.2	0.2	0.2	0.2	0.2	0.2	0.2	0.3	0.2
	Exp.	0.2	0.2	0.2	0.1	0.1	0.1	0.2	0.2	0.2	0.2	0.1	0.2	0.2	0.2	0.2
As a percentage of world trade (%)	Imp.	0.0	0.0	0.0	0.0	0.0	0.0	0.0	0.0	0.0	0.0	0.0	0.0	0.0	0.0	0.0
	Exp.	0.0	0.0	0.0	0.0	0.0	0.0	0.0	0.0	0.0	0.0	0.0	0.0	0.0	0.0	0.0

Graph 1: Annual growth rates of exports, 1996–2010
(In percentage by year)

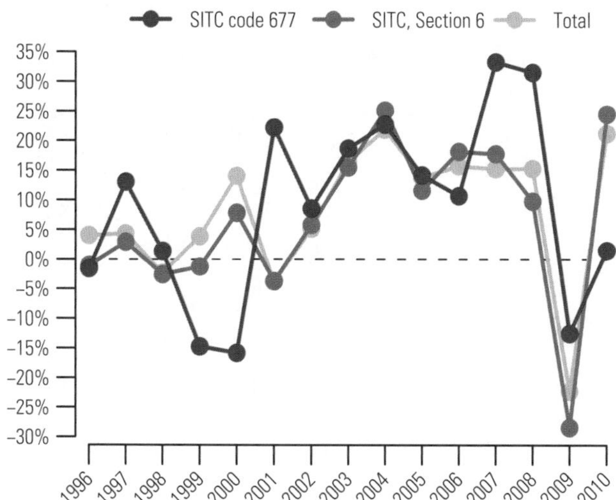

Graph 2: Trade Balance by MDG regions 2010
(Bln US$)

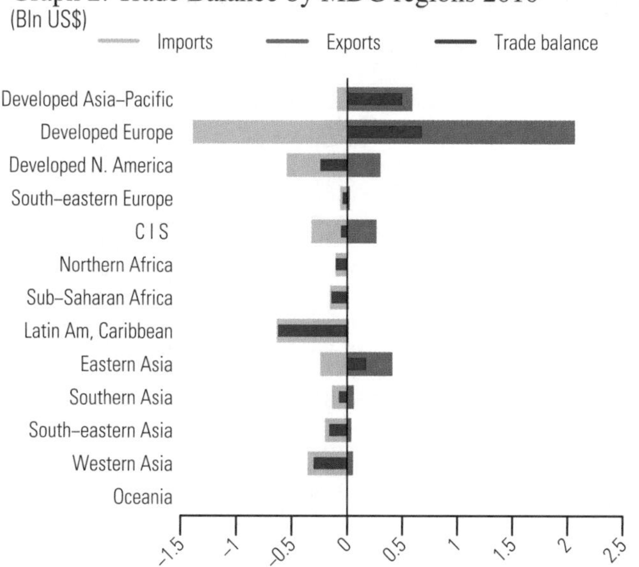

Table 2: Top exporting countries or areas in 2010

Country or area	Value (million US$)	Avg. Growth (%) 06-10	Growth (%) 09-10	World share %	Cum.
World	3832.4	11.7	1.5	100.0	
Japan	551.8	23.1	46.2	14.4	14.4
Austria	512.5	17.2	5.6	13.4	27.8
Germany	411.2	8.1	8.5	10.7	38.5
China	377.7	29.1	-27.4	9.9	48.4
USA	216.1	5.4	-1.1	5.6	54.0
Italy	215.6	21.1	32.2	5.6	59.6
Czech Rep.	208.0	3.8	-6.8	5.4	65.0
Russian Federation	181.5	3.5	34.7	4.7	69.8
Spain	147.1	12.7	-24.2	3.8	73.6
Poland	144.4	10.1	-9.6	3.8	77.4
Belgium	99.7	12.8	-37.3	2.6	80.0
United Kingdom	90.1	1.6	-12.9	2.4	82.3
Canada	84.8	0.5	29.6	2.2	84.6
Luxembourg	82.2	-3.0	-22.2	2.1	86.7
Ukraine	73.4	13.9	39.3	1.9	88.6

Table 3: Top importing countries or areas in 2010

Country or area	Value (million US$)	Avg. Growth (%) 06-10	Growth (%) 09-10	World share %	Cum.
World	4244.9	9.7	-3.5	100.0	
Brazil	438.8	54.4	141.6	10.3	10.3
Germany	367.2	8.9	43.8	8.7	19.0
USA	353.8	-3.4	4.2	8.3	27.3
Canada	192.6	0.8	18.4	4.5	31.9
Saudi Arabia	128.5	47.2	-47.6	3.0	34.9
Belgium	119.6	5.6	-29.1	2.8	37.7
Turkey	112.7	42.3	33.4	2.7	40.4
France	105.8	13.7	2.9	2.5	42.9
China	104.0	15.4	-16.6	2.4	45.3
Russian Federation	103.9	70.3	1049.5	2.4	47.8
Sweden	91.2	17.5	0.4	2.1	49.9
Kazakhstan	86.2	-5.8	16.1	2.0	51.9
Switzerland	83.1	-0.5	-13.7	2.0	53.9
Netherlands	77.9	10.6	43.1	1.8	55.7
Australia	70.9	22.4	-33.9	1.7	57.4

678 Wire of iron or steel

After a sharp decline in 2009, the value (in current prices) of exports of wire of iron or steel (SITC group 678) bounced back by 38.2 percent and totaled 10.8 bln US$ in 2010 (see table 2). Imports for the same year also increased by 35.0 percent to 10.6 bln US$ (see table 3). Graph 1 shows that the growth in exports for 2010 in this product group exceeded the increases in world exports of manufactured goods classified chiefly by material (SITC section 6) of 24.5 percent and in total world exports of 21.2 percent. Exports of wire of iron or steel (SITC group 678) accounted for 0.6 percent of world exports of SITC section 6 and 0.1 percent of total world exports (see table 1).

Exports of China, the top exporting country, increased by 48.3 percent and accounted for 15.1 percent of world exports in 2010 (see table 2). Other major exporting countries were Rep. of Korea and Japan, respectively with 8.7 and 8.2 percent of world exports. Germany, USA and China were the three major destinations (see table 3). By MDG regions (see graph 2), Developed Europe accounted for a large share of trade in wire of iron or steel (SITC group 678). In 2010, its exports and imports were valued at 4.4 bln US$ and 4.3 bln US$ respectively and resulted in a small trade surplus of 57 mln US$. Developed North America recorded a trade deficit of 516 mln US$ and Eastern Asia recorded a trade surplus of 1.7 bln US$.

Table 1: Imports (Imp.) and exports (Exp.), 1996-2010, in current prices

		1996	1997	1998	1999	2000	2001	2002	2003	2004	2005	2006	2007	2008	2009	2010
Values in Bln US$	Imp.	4.1	4.1	4.3	4.0	4.3	4.1	4.2	5.0	7.0	7.9	8.6	10.8	12.7	7.9	10.6
	Exp.	3.8	3.9	3.9	3.6	3.8	3.6	3.8	4.5	6.6	7.1	8.2	10.3	12.6	7.8	10.8
As a percentage of SITC section (%)	Imp.	0.5	0.5	0.5	0.5	0.5	0.5	0.5	0.5	0.6	0.6	0.5	0.6	0.6	0.5	0.6
	Exp.	0.5	0.5	0.5	0.4	0.4	0.4	0.4	0.4	0.5	0.5	0.5	0.5	0.6	0.5	0.6
As a percentage of world trade (%)	Imp.	0.1	0.1	0.1	0.1	0.1	0.1	0.1	0.1	0.1	0.1	0.1	0.1	0.1	0.1	0.1
	Exp.	0.1	0.1	0.1	0.1	0.1	0.1	0.1	0.1	0.1	0.1	0.1	0.1	0.1	0.1	0.1

Graph 1: Annual growth rates of exports, 1996–2010

(In percentage by year)

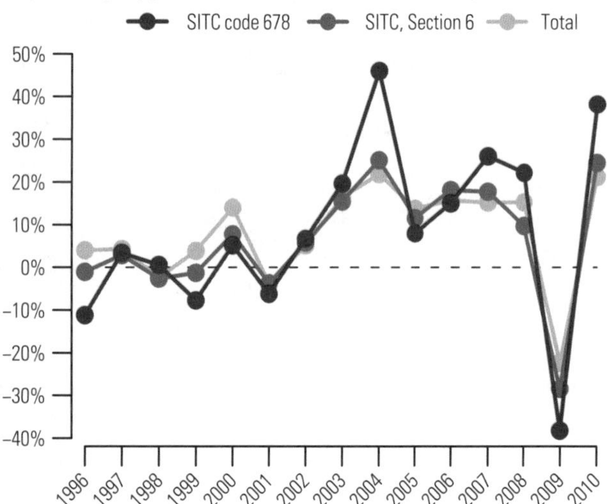

Graph 2: Trade Balance by MDG regions 2010

(Bln US$)

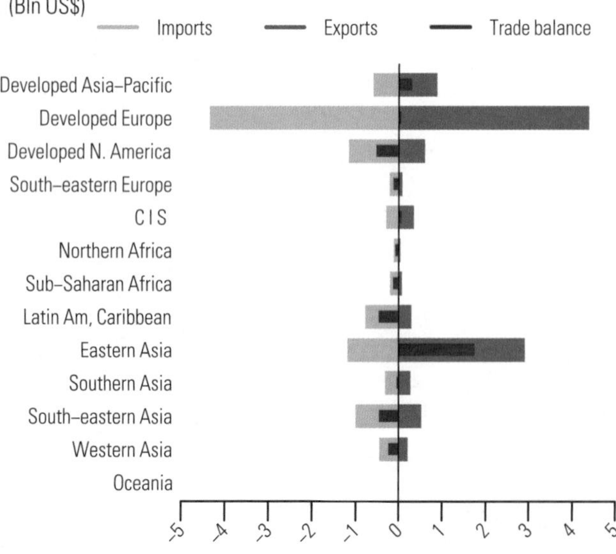

Table 2: Top exporting countries or areas in 2010

Country or area	Value (million US$)	Avg. Growth (%) 06-10	Growth (%) 09-10	World share %	Cum.
World	10772.7	7.0	38.2	100.0	
China	1623.4	19.8	48.3	15.1	15.1
Rep. of Korea	938.2	11.4	47.8	8.7	23.8
Japan	880.3	18.1	71.6	8.2	31.9
Germany	848.6	0.1	28.3	7.9	39.8
Italy	534.1	-0.5	31.7	5.0	44.8
France	431.0	0.2	35.1	4.0	48.8
Czech Rep.	404.9	3.8	19.9	3.8	52.5
USA	394.4	6.0	39.2	3.7	56.2
Spain	323.2	7.5	25.6	3.0	59.2
Sweden	308.9	0.1	45.8	2.9	62.1
Slovakia	281.0	27.8	21.6	2.6	64.7
Other Asia, nes	274.4	4.6	42.5	2.5	67.2
India	263.4	7.7	94.4	2.4	69.7
Belgium	259.7	18.0	41.3	2.4	72.1
Malaysia	238.6	24.3	28.8	2.2	74.3

Table 3: Top importing countries or areas in 2010

Country or area	Value (million US$)	Avg. Growth (%) 06-10	Growth (%) 09-10	World share %	Cum.
World	10647.6	5.4	35.0	100.0	
Germany	1086.5	3.9	36.2	10.2	10.2
USA	930.2	-3.6	41.6	8.7	18.9
China	620.6	8.8	42.3	5.8	24.8
France	490.9	-2.2	15.8	4.6	29.4
Japan	455.2	10.4	42.4	4.3	33.7
Italy	301.9	-3.4	32.1	2.8	36.5
Poland	298.4	10.2	29.3	2.8	39.3
Brazil	285.6	31.7	73.1	2.7	42.0
Rep. of Korea	266.4	18.3	58.7	2.5	44.5
Thailand	247.1	18.0	32.5	2.3	46.8
United Kingdom	240.2	3.4	38.5	2.3	49.1
Indonesia	238.2	31.2	68.7	2.2	51.3
Viet Nam	*228.5*	21.1	66.9	2.1	53.4
Spain	218.1	-5.1	30.3	2.0	55.5
Switzerland	212.4	4.4	37.6	2.0	57.5

After several years of continuous growth marked by a peak of 106.4 bln US$ in 2008, the value (in current prices) of exports of tubes, pipes and hollow profiles, and tube or pipe fittings of iron or steel (SITC group 679) declined by 33.5 percent in 2009 but increased slightly in 2010 to 5.8 percent to 75.0 bln US$ (see table 2). Imports for the same year declined by 3.8 percent to 75.8 bln US$ (see table 3). Graph 1 shows the increase in exports for 2010 in this product group was far less than the increases in world exports of manufactured goods classified chiefly by material (SITC section 6) of 24.5 percent and in total world exports of 21.2 percent. Exports of tubes, pipes and hollow profiles, and tube or pipe fittings of iron or steel (SITC group 679) accounted for 3.9 percent of world exports of SITC section 6 and 0.5 percent of total world exports (see table 1).

China's exports increased by 7.4 percent and represented 13.7 percent of world exports in 2010 (see table 2). Other major exporting countries were Germany and Italy, respectively with 10.0 and 9.1 percent of world exports. USA, Germany and Canada were the top destinations (see table 3). By MDG regions (see graph 2), Developed Europe accounted for a large share of trade in tubes, pipes and hollow profiles, and tube or pipe fittings of iron or steel (SITC group 679) in 2010, with exports and imports valued at respectively 30.1 bln US$ and 21.6 bln US$, resulting in a trade surplus of 8.5 bln US$. A large surplus was also recorded by Eastern Asia (+10.0 bln US$). Developed North America and Western Asia recorded trade deficits amounting respectively to 5.8 bln US$ and 5.0 bln US$.

Table 1: Imports (Imp.) and exports (Exp.), 1996-2010, in current prices

		1996	1997	1998	1999	2000	2001	2002	2003	2004	2005	2006	2007	2008	2009	2010
Values in Bln US$	Imp.	26.0	26.6	27.6	22.0	23.1	26.4	27.4	30.2	41.3	54.2	69.8	87.5	106.8	78.9	75.8
	Exp.	25.5	26.6	26.9	21.3	22.2	25.0	26.5	29.5	41.3	54.1	69.6	86.2	106.4	70.8	75.0
As a percentage of SITC section (%)	Imp.	3.2	3.2	3.3	2.7	2.6	3.1	3.1	2.9	3.2	3.8	4.2	4.5	5.0	5.1	4.0
	Exp.	3.1	3.2	3.3	2.7	2.6	3.0	3.0	2.9	3.2	3.8	4.1	4.4	4.9	4.6	3.9
As a percentage of world trade (%)	Imp.	0.5	0.5	0.5	0.4	0.4	0.4	0.4	0.4	0.4	0.5	0.6	0.6	0.7	0.6	0.5
	Exp.	0.5	0.5	0.5	0.4	0.4	0.4	0.4	0.4	0.5	0.5	0.6	0.6	0.7	0.6	0.5

Graph 1: Annual growth rates of exports, 1996–2010
(In percentage by year)

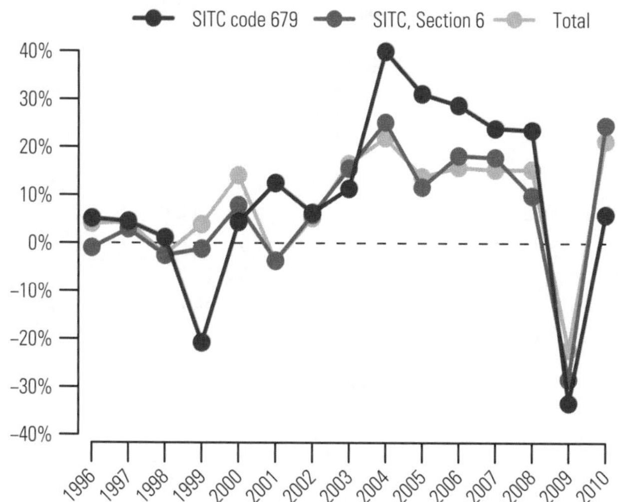

Table 2: Top exporting countries or areas in 2010

Country or area	Value (million US$)	Avg. Growth (%) 06-10	Growth (%) 09-10	World share %	Cum.
World	74964.4	1.9	5.8	100.0	
China	10299.5	9.4	7.4	13.7	13.7
Germany	7497.4	-2.8	-7.1	10.0	23.7
Italy	6842.2	-1.1	1.6	9.1	32.9
Japan	5669.0	-2.8	2.5	7.6	40.4
USA	5400.0	6.8	17.0	7.2	47.6
India	3559.6	26.8	72.1	4.7	52.4
Rep. of Korea	3346.4	12.5	54.4	4.5	56.8
France	2501.6	-4.3	-7.8	3.3	60.2
United Kingdom	1704.1	-4.7	-17.0	2.3	62.5
Canada	1629.0	-2.4	25.1	2.2	64.6
Turkey	1591.6	9.5	4.4	2.1	66.8
Austria	1432.4	-4.5	4.3	1.9	68.7
Spain	1412.7	-0.7	1.5	1.9	70.5
Netherlands	1383.5	1.6	-12.2	1.8	72.4
Ukraine	1380.7	-7.7	-2.6	1.8	74.2

Graph 2: Trade Balance by MDG regions 2010
(Bln US$)

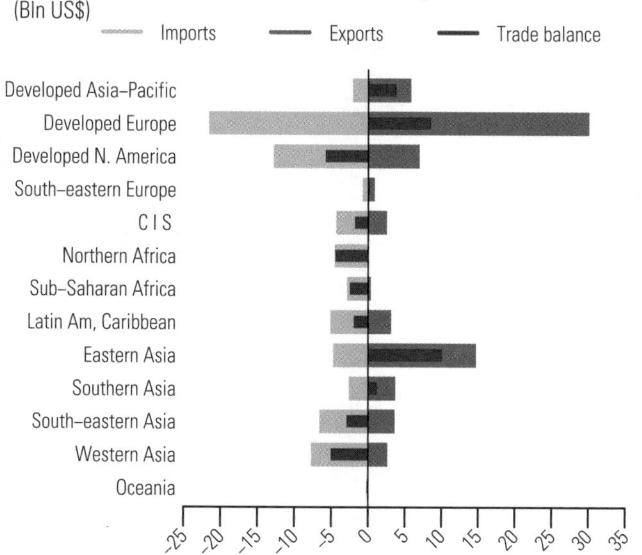

Table 3: Top importing countries or areas in 2010

Country or area	Value (million US$)	Avg. Growth (%) 06-10	Growth (%) 09-10	World share %	Cum.
World	75842.3	2.1	-3.8	100.0	
USA	9418.9	-0.7	4.4	12.4	12.4
Germany	3931.2	0.8	14.8	5.2	17.6
Canada	3388.8	2.1	29.7	4.5	22.1
Algeria	3207.4	21.7	-7.1	4.2	26.3
China	2475.9	-7.2	-29.7	3.3	29.6
Russian Federation	2314.7	5.9	107.3	3.1	32.6
France	2251.9	0.4	17.5	3.0	35.6
Saudi Arabia	1979.0	-6.0	-2.2	2.6	38.2
United Kingdom	1916.9	-1.3	6.8	2.5	40.7
United Arab Emirates	1845.4	6.2	-22.1	2.4	43.2
Singapore	1676.0	-1.0	-10.9	2.2	45.4
Indonesia	1594.5	24.5	19.6	2.1	47.5
Rep. of Korea	1578.6	8.3	3.7	2.1	49.5
Italy	1511.1	-5.8	-9.3	2.0	51.5
Netherlands	1435.7	-1.5	-2.5	1.9	53.4

681 Silver, platinum and other metals of the platinum group

In 2010, the value (in current prices) of exports of silver, platinum and other metals of the platinum group (SITC group 681) increased by 39.4 percent to 47.7 bln US$ (see table 2). In the same year, imports also rose by 32.2 percent to 50.2 bln US$ (see table 3). Graph 1 shows that the increase in exports for 2010 in this product group far surpassed the growth in world exports of manufactured goods classified chiefly by material (SITC section 6) of 24.5 percent and in total world exports of 21.2 percent. Exports of silver, platinum and other metals of the platinum group (SITC group 681) accounted for 2.5 percent of world exports of SITC section 6 and 0.3 percent of total world exports (see table 1).

South Africa, Switzerland and USA were the three major exporting countries in 2010 (see table 2). They accounted respectively for 19.7, 10.0 and 9.7 percent of world exports. Top destinations were USA, Japan and United Kingdom (see table 3). By MDG regions (see graph 2), top surpluses were recorded by Sub-Saharan Africa (+9.4 bln US$) and Latin America and the Caribbean (+2.9 bln US$). Top trade deficits were recorded by Eastern Asia (-5.0 bln US$), Developed Asia-Pacific (-4.1 bln US$) and Developed North America (-3.6 bln US$) .

Table 1: Imports (Imp.) and exports (Exp.), 1996-2010, in current prices

		1996	1997	1998	1999	2000	2001	2002	2003	2004	2005	2006	2007	2008	2009	2010
Values in Bln US$	Imp.	9.0	10.8	13.4	14.0	21.6	20.2	14.7	15.2	19.3	23.0	36.5	44.9	55.2	37.9	50.2
	Exp.	6.3	7.4	10.5	10.7	12.1	14.3	10.5	13.3	18.1	21.7	37.1	45.6	50.9	34.2	47.7
As a percentage of SITC section (%)	Imp.	1.1	1.3	1.6	1.7	2.4	2.4	1.7	1.5	1.5	1.6	2.2	2.3	2.6	2.4	2.6
	Exp.	0.8	0.9	1.3	1.3	1.4	1.7	1.2	1.3	1.4	1.5	2.2	2.3	2.3	2.2	2.5
As a percentage of world trade (%)	Imp.	0.2	0.2	0.2	0.2	0.3	0.3	0.2	0.2	0.2	0.2	0.3	0.3	0.3	0.3	0.3
	Exp.	0.1	0.1	0.2	0.2	0.2	0.2	0.2	0.2	0.2	0.2	0.3	0.3	0.3	0.3	0.3

Graph 1: Annual growth rates of exports, 1996–2010
(In percentage by year)

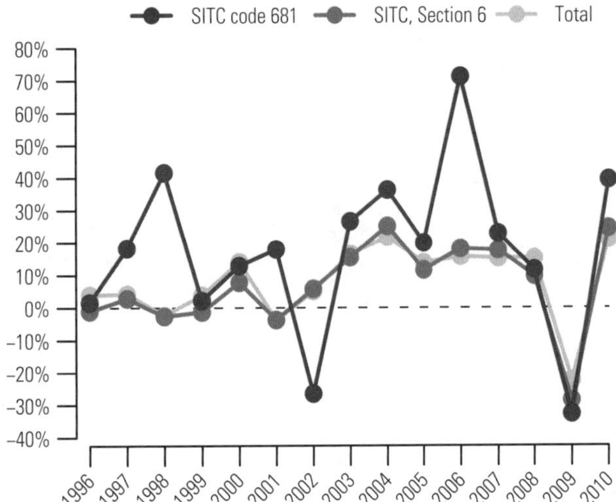

Graph 2: Trade Balance by MDG regions 2010
(Bln US$)

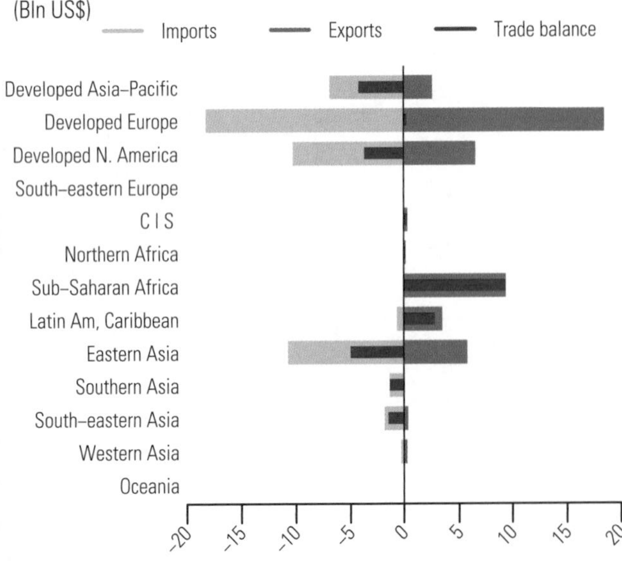

Table 2: Top exporting countries or areas in 2010

Country or area	Value (million US$)	Avg. Growth (%) 06-10	Growth (%) 09-10	World share %	Cum.
World	47735.9	6.5	39.4	100.0	
South Africa	9394.9	4.0	38.8	19.7	19.7
Switzerland	4785.4	15.5	69.3	10.0	29.7
USA	4616.1	-2.3	72.7	9.7	39.4
Germany	4292.4	4.0	42.9	9.0	48.4
United Kingdom	4197.6	8.1	49.3	8.8	57.2
China, Hong Kong SAR	2754.9	19.4	33.7	5.8	62.9
Mexico	2543.8	20.0	80.3	5.3	68.3
Japan	2322.6	22.4	33.4	4.9	73.1
Canada	1946.2	30.0	169.1	4.1	77.2
Belgium	1905.8	8.4	43.1	4.0	81.2
Rep. of Korea	1018.5	22.5	34.2	2.1	83.3
China	1011.3	-11.5	-41.7	2.1	85.4
Other Asia, nes	984.6	60.3	39.3	2.1	87.5
Italy	922.3	10.5	68.9	1.9	89.4
Poland	798.7	14.6	41.9	1.7	91.1

Table 3: Top importing countries or areas in 2010

Country or area	Value (million US$)	Avg. Growth (%) 06-10	Growth (%) 09-10	World share %	Cum.
World	50170.8	8.3	32.2	100.0	
USA	8539.7	2.5	66.2	17.0	17.0
Japan	6592.4	5.4	56.0	13.1	30.2
United Kingdom	6504.7	18.1	44.2	13.0	43.1
China	5500.3	35.2	77.4	11.0	54.1
Germany	4695.4	6.9	51.6	9.4	63.4
Switzerland	3237.3	-5.4	-15.8	6.5	69.9
China, Hong Kong SAR	2694.0	-0.9	-25.2	5.4	75.3
Canada	1661.4	45.3	113.1	3.3	78.6
Other Asia, nes	1580.3	24.6	60.1	3.1	81.7
Italy	1429.4	-1.5	30.5	2.8	84.6
India	1284.0	64.1	-59.6	2.6	87.1
Rep. of Korea	949.2	-5.2	72.1	1.9	89.0
Thailand	799.0	19.2	46.7	1.6	90.6
France	637.6	13.7	110.9	1.3	91.9
Singapore	520.1	4.9	31.1	1.0	92.9

After a huge drop in 2009, the value (in current prices) of exports of copper (SITC group 682) increased by 48.7 percent and amounted to 129.5 bln US$ in 2010 (see table 2). Similarly, imports showed a 47.3 percent rise and totaled 123.1 bln US$ (see table 3). Graph 1 shows that the increase in exports for 2010 in this product group far exceeded the increases in world exports of manufactured goods classified chiefly by material (SITC section 6) of 24.5 percent and in total world exports of 21.2 percent. Exports of copper (SITC group 682) accounted for 6.7 percent of world exports of SITC section 6 and 0.9 percent of total world exports (see table 1).

Chile, the top exporting country in 2010, accounted for 20.9 percent of world exports (see table 2). Other major exporting countries were Germany and Japan, respectively with 7.8 and 6.1 percent of world exports. Major destinations were China, Germany and USA (see table 3). By MDG regions (see graph 2), Latin America and the Caribbean recorded a trade surplus amounting to 26.2 bln US$. A significant surplus was also recorded by Developed Asia-Pacific (+8.3 bln US$). Top trade deficits were recorded by Eastern Asia (-31.8 bln US$), Western Asia (-6.8 bln US$) and Developed Europe (-3.2 bln US$).

Table 1: Imports (Imp.) and exports (Exp.), 1996-2010, in current prices

		1996	1997	1998	1999	2000	2001	2002	2003	2004	2005	2006	2007	2008	2009	2010
Values in Bln US$	Imp.	31.7	32.7	28.6	27.4	33.0	29.7	29.3	33.3	50.7	62.3	107.1	121.3	121.5	83.5	123.1
	Exp.	31.9	33.4	28.8	28.0	32.1	29.8	28.9	32.8	51.1	63.3	111.4	123.6	122.4	87.1	129.5
As a percentage of SITC section (%)	Imp.	3.9	3.9	3.5	3.3	3.7	3.5	3.3	3.3	4.0	4.4	6.5	6.2	5.6	5.4	6.4
	Exp.	3.9	4.0	3.5	3.5	3.7	3.6	3.3	3.2	4.0	4.5	6.6	6.2	5.6	5.6	6.7
As a percentage of world trade (%)	Imp.	0.6	0.6	0.5	0.5	0.5	0.5	0.4	0.4	0.5	0.6	0.9	0.9	0.8	0.7	0.8
	Exp.	0.6	0.6	0.5	0.5	0.5	0.5	0.5	0.4	0.6	0.6	0.9	0.9	0.8	0.7	0.9

Graph 1: Annual growth rates of exports, 1996–2010
(In percentage by year)

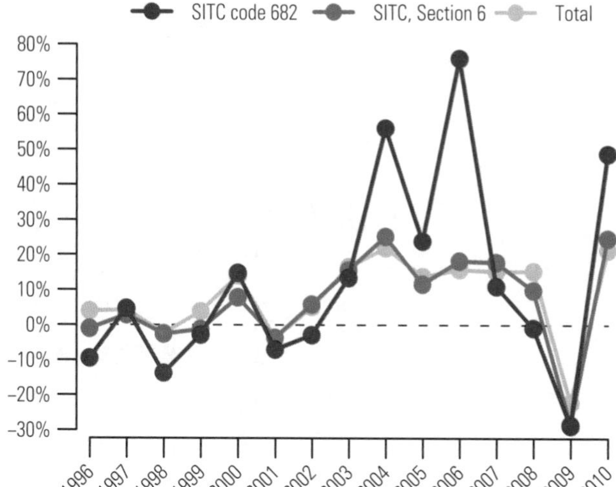

Graph 2: Trade Balance by MDG regions 2010
(Bln US$)

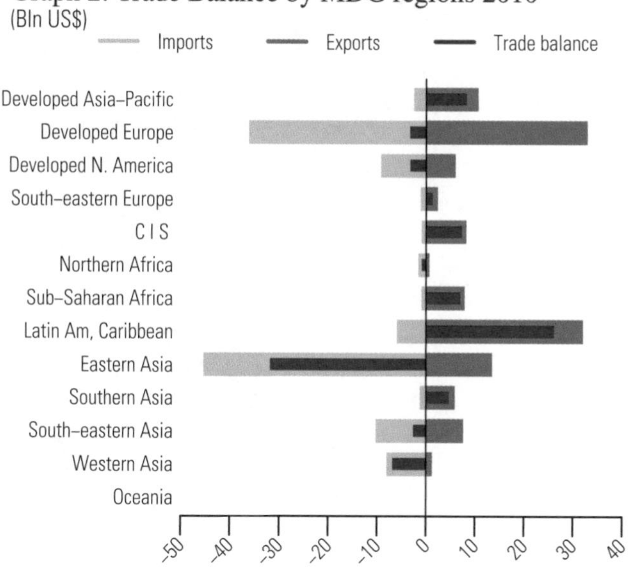

Table 2: Top exporting countries or areas in 2010

Country or area	Value (million US$)	Avg. Growth (%) 06-10	Growth (%) 09-10	World share %	Cum.
World	129 497.2	3.8	48.7	100.0	
Chile	27 099.4	6.7	45.3	20.9	20.9
Germany	10 058.7	0.5	42.8	7.8	28.7
Japan	7 929.8	9.4	43.8	6.1	34.8
Zambia	5 412.8	20.0	87.4	4.2	39.0
India	5 233.3	19.7	283.6	4.0	43.0
Russian Federation	4 873.0	2.5	37.9	3.8	46.8
China	4 182.3	-5.3	32.4	3.2	50.0
Rep. of Korea	3 988.4	3.0	51.4	3.1	53.1
Poland	3 885.7	6.9	51.6	3.0	56.1
Belgium	3 848.8	4.6	50.6	3.0	59.1
USA	3 496.2	0.7	43.7	2.7	61.8
Other Asia, nes	3 112.3	0.1	48.4	2.4	64.2
Indonesia	3 104.9	15.7	37.4	2.4	66.6
Peru	3 068.4	-3.5	40.0	2.4	69.0
Italy	2 803.5	-0.9	32.8	2.2	71.1

Table 3: Top importing countries or areas in 2010

Country or area	Value (million US$)	Avg. Growth (%) 06-10	Growth (%) 09-10	World share %	Cum.
World	123 095.4	3.6	47.3	100.0	
China	32 850.8	27.5	45.2	26.7	26.7
Germany	8 470.4	-3.0	53.0	6.9	33.6
USA	7 901.7	-11.7	39.2	6.4	40.0
Italy	7 231.7	-2.6	66.4	5.9	45.9
Other Asia, nes	5 435.0	0.6	61.0	4.4	50.3
Rep. of Korea	4 617.1	1.2	24.7	3.8	54.0
France	4 117.6	-7.8	46.1	3.3	57.4
Thailand	3 385.1	5.0	72.1	2.7	60.1
Turkey	3 233.1	7.5	65.2	2.6	62.8
Malaysia	2 974.8	4.8	64.3	2.4	65.2
Belgium	2 707.7	-0.4	30.4	2.2	67.4
China, Hong Kong SAR	2 430.7	-1.9	27.4	2.0	69.3
Brazil	2 417.4	10.9	87.7	2.0	71.3
Mexico	2 264.4	-1.8	60.2	1.8	73.1
United Kingdom	2 219.4	-5.8	48.0	1.8	74.9

 Source: UN Comtrade

683 Nickel

In 2010, the value (in current prices) of exports of nickel (SITC group 683) increased by 44.3 percent and reached 19.2 bln US$ (see table 2). Imports increased by 47.3 percent to reach 20.2 bln US$ in 2010 (see table 3). Graph 1 shows that the growth in exports for 2010 in this product group far exceeded the increases in world exports of manufactured goods classified chiefly by material (SITC section 6) of 24.5 percent and in total world exports of 21.2 percent. Exports of nickel (SITC group 683) accounted for 1.0 percent of world exports of SITC section 6 and 0.1 percent of total world exports (see table 1).

The top exporting countries in 2010 were Russian Federation, Canada and Norway (see table 2). Their exports grew respectively by 47.9, 30.0 and 56.7 percent and represented 28.0, 11.1 and 10.2 percent of world exports. China, USA and Germany were the main destinations (see table 3). By MDG regions (see graph 2), a major surplus was recorded by Commonwealth of Independent States (+5.2 bln US$). Top trade deficits were recorded by Eastern Asia (-4.7 bln US$) and Developed Europe (-1.0 bln US$).

Table 1: Imports (Imp.) and exports (Exp.), 1996-2010, in current prices

		1996	1997	1998	1999	2000	2001	2002	2003	2004	2005	2006	2007	2008	2009	2010
Values in Bln US$	Imp.	5.4	5.8	5.0	5.4	8.2	6.2	6.7	9.0	12.9	14.6	21.8	32.7	22.4	13.7	20.2
	Exp.	5.3	5.8	4.8	5.2	7.4	6.2	7.1	8.0	12.2	13.3	20.9	31.6	20.9	13.3	19.2
As a percentage of SITC section (%)	Imp.	0.7	0.7	0.6	0.7	0.9	0.7	0.8	0.9	1.0	1.0	1.3	1.7	1.0	0.9	1.1
	Exp.	0.7	0.7	0.6	0.7	0.9	0.7	0.8	0.8	1.0	0.9	1.2	1.6	1.0	0.9	1.0
As a percentage of world trade (%)	Imp.	0.1	0.1	0.1	0.1	0.1	0.1	0.1	0.1	0.1	0.1	0.2	0.2	0.1	0.1	0.1
	Exp.	0.1	0.1	0.1	0.1	0.1	0.1	0.1	0.1	0.1	0.1	0.2	0.2	0.1	0.1	0.1

Graph 1: Annual growth rates of exports, 1996–2010

(In percentage by year)

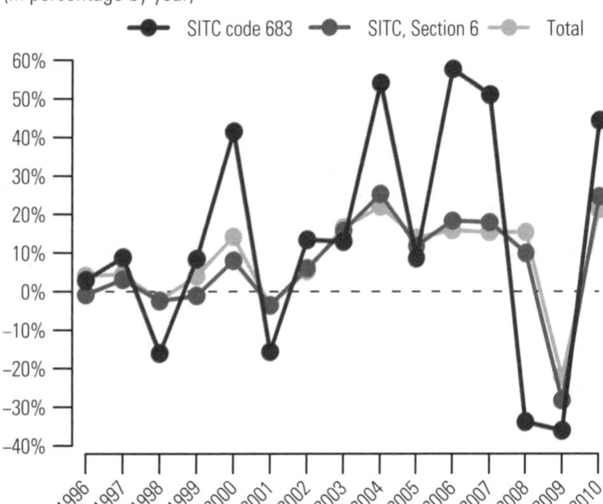

Table 2: Top exporting countries or areas in 2010

Country or area	Value (million US$)	Avg. Growth (%) 06-10	Growth (%) 09-10	World share %	Cum.
World	19190.0	-2.2	44.3	100.0	
Russian Federation	5381.4	-4.1	47.9	28.0	28.0
Canada	2135.6	-9.5	30.0	11.1	39.2
Norway	1966.2	1.3	56.7	10.2	49.4
China	1246.4	29.4	97.6	6.5	55.9
USA	1231.6	3.3	21.4	6.4	62.3
United Kingdom	1105.0	-2.3	65.7	5.8	68.1
Germany	841.7	-10.9	16.7	4.4	72.5
Japan	693.8	12.6	44.1	3.6	76.1
Finland	691.6	-7.0	36.5	3.6	79.7
Singapore	638.2	26.1	166.2	3.3	83.0
France	590.6	-3.1	20.2	3.1	86.1
Australia	575.4	-6.3	15.4	3.0	89.1
Belgium	321.1	-10.6	9.7	1.7	90.8
South Africa	317.5	1.6	125.1	1.7	92.4
Rep. of Korea	236.7	-5.2	60.0	1.2	93.7

Graph 2: Trade Balance by MDG regions 2010

(Bln US$)

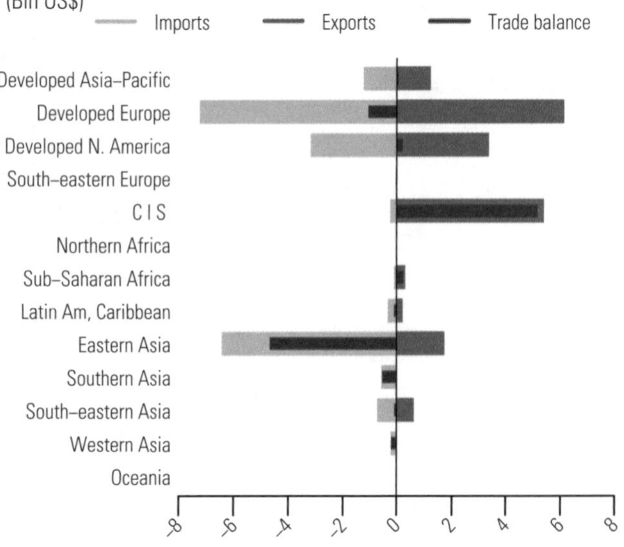

Table 3: Top importing countries or areas in 2010

Country or area	Value (million US$)	Avg. Growth (%) 06-10	Growth (%) 09-10	World share %	Cum.
World	20246.9	-1.8	47.3	100.0	
China	4364.4	13.7	8.6	21.6	21.6
USA	2991.0	-2.9	78.3	14.8	36.3
Germany	2025.0	-3.7	103.2	10.0	46.3
Japan	1184.1	-3.3	113.5	5.8	52.2
Italy	1017.8	-6.9	64.3	5.0	57.2
Rep. of Korea	891.3	-1.4	44.6	4.4	61.6
France	858.7	-2.8	61.7	4.2	65.8
Other Asia, nes	853.7	-10.7	44.2	4.2	70.1
United Kingdom	662.1	-6.9	48.2	3.3	73.3
Sweden	605.9	-4.7	109.3	3.0	76.3
India	531.9	6.1	45.0	2.6	79.0
Singapore	512.1	24.3	9.6	2.5	81.5
Belgium	510.8	-16.9	55.6	2.5	84.0
Spain	433.0	-13.3	59.3	2.1	86.1
Finland	343.8	-13.3	146.8	1.7	87.8

After several years of continuous growth marked by a peak of 116.0 bln US$ in 2008, the value (in current prices) of exports of aluminium (SITC group 684) declined by 35.2 percent in 2009 but bounced back by 34.1 percent reaching 100.8 bln US$ in 2010 (see table 2). Similarly, imports showed a 31.4 percent increase in the same year and amounted to 100.0 bln US$ (see table 3). Graph 1 shows that the increase in exports for 2010 in this product group surpassed the increases in world exports of manufactured goods classified chiefly by material (SITC section 6) of 24.5 percent and in total world exports of 21.2 percent. Exports of aluminium (SITC group 684) accounted for 5.2 percent of world exports of SITC section 6 and 0.7 percent of total world exports (see table 1).

In 2010, Germany, China and Canada were the top exporting countries (see table 2). They accounted respectively for 9.6, 9.0 and 7.5 percent of world exports. Top destinations were Germany, USA and Japan (see table 3). By MDG regions (see graph 2), Developed Europe accounted for a large share of trade in aluminium (SITC group 684). In 2010, its exports amounted to 42.4 bln US$ while imports were valued at 45.5 bln US$, resulting in a trade deficit of 3.1 bln US$. Top trade surpluses were recorded by Commonwealth of Independent States (+7.5 bln US$) and Sub-Saharan Africa (+2.6 bln US$). In addition to Developed Europe, top deficits were also recorded by South-eastern Asia (-4.6 bln US$) and Latin America & the Caribbean (-1.6 bln US$).

Table 1: Imports (Imp.) and exports (Exp.), 1996-2010, in current prices

		1996	1997	1998	1999	2000	2001	2002	2003	2004	2005	2006	2007	2008	2009	2010
Values in Bln US$	Imp.	42.1	45.6	44.4	44.0	50.4	48.0	49.7	56.6	69.8	77.8	103.6	117.0	115.5	76.1	100.0
	Exp.	42.6	44.4	43.5	43.3	48.9	47.5	48.4	55.2	67.4	76.2	99.9	113.5	116.0	75.1	100.8
As a percentage of SITC section (%)	Imp.	5.2	5.5	5.4	5.4	5.7	5.7	5.6	5.5	5.5	5.4	6.2	6.0	5.4	4.9	5.2
	Exp.	5.3	5.3	5.4	5.4	5.7	5.7	5.5	5.4	5.3	5.4	6.0	5.7	5.3	4.8	5.2
As a percentage of world trade (%)	Imp.	0.8	0.8	0.8	0.8	0.8	0.8	0.8	0.7	0.8	0.7	0.9	0.8	0.7	0.6	0.7
	Exp.	0.8	0.8	0.8	0.8	0.8	0.8	0.8	0.7	0.7	0.7	0.8	0.8	0.7	0.6	0.7

Graph 1: Annual growth rates of exports, 1996–2010

(In percentage by year)

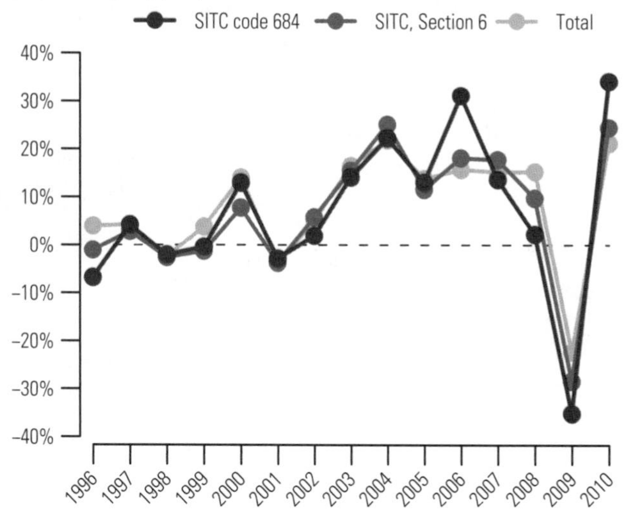

Table 2: Top exporting countries or areas in 2010

Country or area	Value (million US$)	Avg. Growth (%) 06-10	Growth (%) 09-10	World share %	Cum.
World	100 757.0	0.2	34.1	100.0	
Germany	9 682.4	-0.6	24.9	9.6	9.6
China	9 078.3	7.9	77.9	9.0	18.6
Canada	7 530.0	-4.6	37.3	7.5	26.1
Russian Federation	6 764.5	-0.7	18.7	6.7	32.8
USA	5 530.7	-1.2	22.9	5.5	38.3
Norway	4 392.2	-3.7	26.1	4.4	42.7
Australia	3 971.4	-2.9	24.1	3.9	46.6
Italy	3 152.6	3.3	34.9	3.1	49.7
France	2 997.9	-2.5	19.5	3.0	52.7
Netherlands	2 773.2	-2.2	27.4	2.8	55.5
Japan	2 448.3	6.5	39.1	2.4	57.9
Belgium	2 426.5	-3.4	39.8	2.4	60.3
Austria	2 317.1	3.9	27.2	2.3	62.6
Spain	2 064.8	2.0	26.8	2.0	64.6
United Kingdom	2 034.8	-7.2	37.3	2.0	66.7

Graph 2: Trade Balance by MDG regions 2010

(Bln US$)

Imports Exports Trade balance

Developed Asia-Pacific
Developed Europe
Developed N. America
South-eastern Europe
C I S
Northern Africa
Sub-Saharan Africa
Latin Am, Caribbean
Eastern Asia
Southern Asia
South-eastern Asia
Western Asia
Oceania

-50 -40 -30 -20 -10 0 10 20 30 40 50

Table 3: Top importing countries or areas in 2010

Country or area	Value (million US$)	Avg. Growth (%) 06-10	Growth (%) 09-10	World share %	Cum.
World	99 956.8	-0.9	31.4	100.0	
Germany	11 317.1	-0.2	43.2	11.3	11.3
USA	11 034.6	-7.7	24.1	11.0	22.4
Japan	6 669.8	-4.8	77.2	6.7	29.0
Italy	4 257.7	-3.1	56.2	4.3	33.3
France	4 158.6	-2.7	23.0	4.2	37.5
China	3 926.7	0.9	-26.5	3.9	41.4
Rep. of Korea	3 893.8	-0.2	49.1	3.9	45.3
Mexico	3 151.5	2.7	42.9	3.2	48.4
Netherlands	2 920.3	-4.3	34.0	2.9	51.4
United Kingdom	2 846.2	-2.3	8.9	2.8	54.2
Belgium	2 787.3	-2.7	50.6	2.8	57.0
Turkey	2 290.8	8.0	57.1	2.3	59.3
Canada	2 138.1	-6.8	36.5	2.1	61.4
Poland	2 112.7	3.3	36.8	2.1	63.5
Thailand	2 035.2	4.5	53.7	2.0	65.6

Source: UN Comtrade

685 Lead

The value (in current prices) of exports of lead (SITC group 685) grew by 23.8 percent and totaled 5.6 bln US$ in 2010 (see table 2). For the same year, imports increased by 25.9 percent to 5.7 bln US$ (see table 3). Graph 1 shows that the rise in exports for 2010 in this product group was slightly less than the increases in world exports of manufactured goods classified chiefly by material (SITC section 6) of 24.5 percent, but higher than total world exports of 21.2 percent. Exports of lead (SITC group 685) accounted for 0.3 percent of world exports of SITC section 6 and less than 0.1 percent of total world exports (see table 1).

Australia, Canada and Germany were the three major exporting countries in 2010 (see table 2). They accounted respectively for 12.7, 10.3 and 10.1 percent of world exports. Top importing countries were USA, United Kingdom and Rep. of Korea (see table 3). By MDG regions (see graph 2), Developed Asia-Pacific recorded a trade surplus of 791 mln US$. Trade surpluses were also recorded by Commonwealth of Independent States (+312 mln US$) and South-eastern Europe (+173 mln US$) among others. Major deficits were recorded by South-eastern Asia (-782 mln US$), Southern Asia (-253 mln US$) and Western Asia (-219 mln US$).

Table 1: Imports (Imp.) and exports (Exp.), 1996-2010, in current prices

		1996	1997	1998	1999	2000	2001	2002	2003	2004	2005	2006	2007	2008	2009	2010
Values in Bln US$	Imp.	2.0	1.9	1.5	1.6	1.5	1.5	1.5	1.5	2.6	3.0	3.9	6.4	6.2	4.6	5.7
	Exp.	1.8	1.7	1.5	1.5	1.4	1.4	1.4	1.5	2.3	2.8	3.8	6.2	5.8	4.5	5.6
As a percentage of SITC section (%)	Imp.	0.2	0.2	0.2	0.2	0.2	0.2	0.2	0.2	0.2	0.2	0.2	0.3	0.3	0.3	0.3
	Exp.	0.2	0.2	0.2	0.2	0.2	0.2	0.2	0.1	0.2	0.2	0.2	0.3	0.3	0.3	0.3
As a percentage of world trade (%)	Imp.	0.0	0.0	0.0	0.0	0.0	0.0	0.0	0.0	0.0	0.0	0.0	0.0	0.0	0.0	0.0
	Exp.	0.0	0.0	0.0	0.0	0.0	0.0	0.0	0.0	0.0	0.0	0.0	0.0	0.0	0.0	0.0

Graph 1: Annual growth rates of exports, 1996–2010

(In percentage by year)

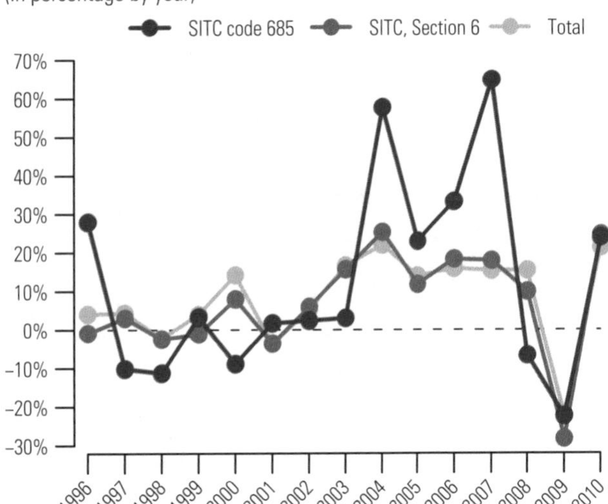

Graph 2: Trade Balance by MDG regions 2010

(Bln US$)

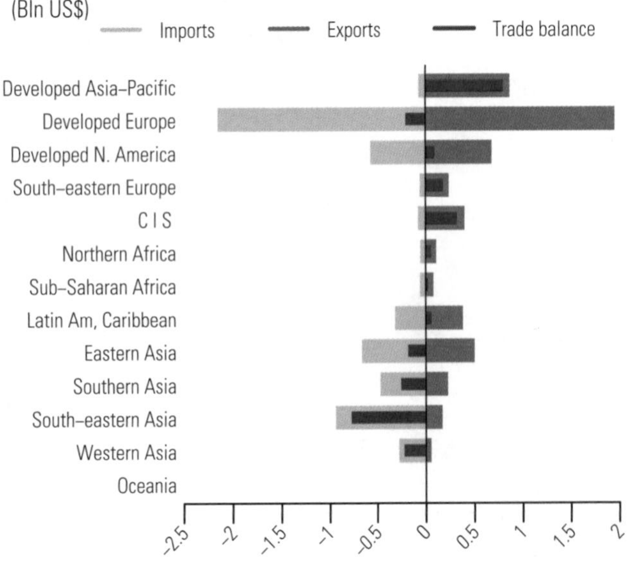

Table 2: Top exporting countries or areas in 2010

Country or area	Value (million US$)	Avg. Growth (%) 06-10	Growth (%) 09-10	World share %	Cum.
World	5588.4	10.2	23.8	100.0	
Australia	708.3	10.6	6.5	12.7	12.7
Canada	576.9	17.6	37.5	10.3	23.0
Germany	562.1	17.7	21.4	10.1	33.1
United Kingdom	425.3	16.7	16.6	7.6	40.7
Belgium	294.9	8.9	42.3	5.3	45.9
Rep. of Korea	240.9	44.4	10.0	4.3	50.3
Mexico	228.2	63.5	-14.8	4.1	54.3
Russian Federation	182.6	35.8	28.6	3.3	57.6
Kazakhstan	177.5	13.1	51.9	3.2	60.8
Bulgaria	174.5	18.9	30.3	3.1	63.9
China	164.6	-30.9	41.6	2.9	66.8
Japan	135.0	59.0	4.6	2.4	69.3
France	126.7	22.8	215.3	2.3	71.5
Sweden	121.4	2.0	40.7	2.2	73.7
India	120.8	65.2	65.8	2.2	75.9

Table 3: Top importing countries or areas in 2010

Country or area	Value (million US$)	Avg. Growth (%) 06-10	Growth (%) 09-10	World share %	Cum.
World	5735.0	9.9	25.9	100.0	
USA	571.5	6.7	35.7	10.0	10.0
United Kingdom	533.8	11.7	45.8	9.3	19.3
Rep. of Korea	374.3	22.0	9.4	6.5	25.8
India	371.6	18.3	7.1	6.5	32.3
Germany	352.7	9.2	84.2	6.1	38.4
Viet Nam	*273.3*	47.6	66.9	4.8	43.2
Italy	255.8	10.8	56.1	4.5	47.7
Spain	254.6	3.5	10.0	4.4	52.1
Thailand	211.6	14.7	44.9	3.7	55.8
Indonesia	200.3	24.4	46.0	3.5	59.3
Brazil	193.0	18.1	44.0	3.4	62.6
Czech Rep.	190.5	13.0	34.2	3.3	66.0
Other Asia, nes	181.4	3.4	-14.9	3.2	69.1
Turkey	173.6	12.3	21.9	3.0	72.2
Singapore	129.4	-8.0	188.2	2.3	74.4

In 2010, the value (in current prices) of exports of zinc (SITC group 686) increased by 45.1 percent and amounted to 11.7 bln US$ (see table 2). Imports also rose by 36.8 percent to 11.7 bln US$ (see table 3). Graph 1 shows that the increase in exports for 2010 in this product group was higher than the increases in world exports of manufactured goods classified chiefly by material (SITC section 6) of 24.5 percent and in total world exports of 21.2 percent. Exports of zinc (SITC group 686) accounted for 0.6 percent of world exports of SITC section 6 and 0.1 percent of total world exports (see table 1).

The top exporting countries in 2010 were Canada, Spain and Belgium (see table 2). They accounted respectively for 11.0, 7.7 and 7.6 percent of world exports. Top destinations were USA, Germany and China (see table 3). By MDG regions (see graph 2), Eastern Asia recorded a deficit amounting to 866 mln US$ in 2010. Major deficits were also recorded by South-eastern Asia (-740 mln US$) and Western Asia (-705 mln US$). Developed Asia-Pacific and Commonwealth of Independent States recorded trade surpluses amounting respectively to 999 mln US$ and 774 mln US$.

Table 1: Imports (Imp.) and exports (Exp.), 1996-2010, in current prices

		1996	1997	1998	1999	2000	2001	2002	2003	2004	2005	2006	2007	2008	2009	2010
Values in Bln US$	Imp.	4.6	6.1	5.3	5.4	6.0	5.1	4.7	5.0	6.4	7.6	15.8	18.9	11.4	8.5	11.7
	Exp.	4.4	5.4	4.8	4.9	5.3	4.6	4.3	4.8	5.9	6.8	15.7	18.0	10.9	8.0	11.7
As a percentage of SITC section (%)	Imp.	0.6	0.7	0.6	0.7	0.7	0.6	0.5	0.5	0.5	0.5	1.0	1.0	0.5	0.5	0.6
	Exp.	0.5	0.7	0.6	0.6	0.6	0.6	0.5	0.5	0.5	0.5	0.9	0.9	0.5	0.5	0.6
As a percentage of world trade (%)	Imp.	0.1	0.1	0.1	0.1	0.1	0.1	0.1	0.1	0.1	0.1	0.1	0.1	0.1	0.1	0.1
	Exp.	0.1	0.1	0.1	0.1	0.1	0.1	0.1	0.1	0.1	0.1	0.1	0.1	0.1	0.1	0.1

Graph 1: Annual growth rates of exports, 1996–2010

(In percentage by year)

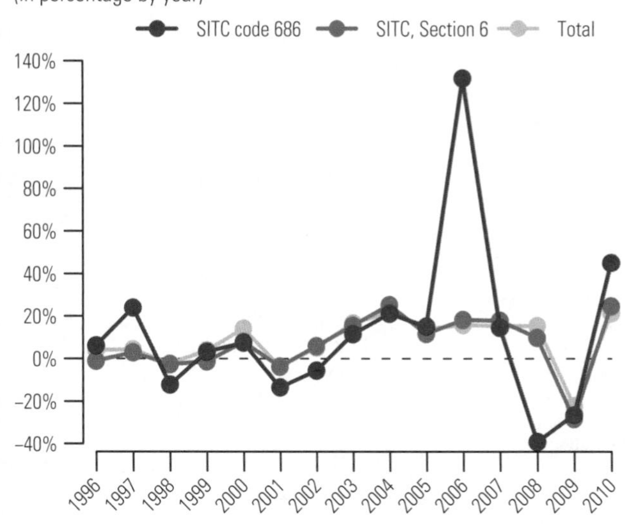

Table 2: Top exporting countries or areas in 2010

Country or area	Value (million US$)	Avg. Growth (%) 06-10	Growth (%) 09-10	World share %	Cum.
World	11 666.0	-7.1	45.1	100.0	
Canada	1 278.1	-5.7	30.7	11.0	11.0
Spain	899.0	-5.1	93.1	7.7	18.7
Belgium	884.2	33.8	441.1	7.6	26.2
Rep. of Korea	870.5	-2.5	34.6	7.5	33.7
Australia	839.5	-6.1	20.2	7.2	40.9
India	664.7	6.7	95.8	5.7	46.6
Finland	626.7	-6.2	31.0	5.4	52.0
Kazakhstan	554.7	-8.9	38.6	4.8	56.7
Netherlands	518.6	-18.5	35.9	4.4	61.2
Mexico	462.1	-4.5	22.3	4.0	65.1
Peru	388.8	-3.2	82.4	3.3	68.5
Norway	334.2	-9.9	39.8	2.9	71.3
China, Hong Kong SAR	289.1	-12.5	46.2	2.5	73.8
Japan	281.8	-1.6	-3.0	2.4	76.2
Poland	251.0	1.2	56.3	2.2	78.4

Graph 2: Trade Balance by MDG regions 2010

(Bln US$)

Imports — Exports — Trade balance

Developed Asia-Pacific
Developed Europe
Developed N. America
South-eastern Europe
C I S
Northern Africa
Sub-Saharan Africa
Latin Am, Caribbean
Eastern Asia
Southern Asia
South-eastern Asia
Western Asia
Oceania

-5 -4 -3 -2 -1 0 1 2 3 4 5

Table 3: Top importing countries or areas in 2010

Country or area	Value (million US$)	Avg. Growth (%) 06-10	Growth (%) 09-10	World share %	Cum.
World	11 658.3	-7.4	36.8	100.0	
USA	1 519.8	-7.7	30.6	13.0	13.0
Germany	1 160.8	-6.3	62.0	10.0	23.0
China	1 135.5	-6.1	-14.2	9.7	32.7
Italy	667.8	-7.6	142.0	5.7	38.5
Netherlands	605.3	-3.2	103.3	5.2	43.7
Other Asia, nes	576.2	-11.6	62.9	4.9	48.6
Belgium	539.1	7.8	8.2	4.6	53.2
France	502.6	-11.8	37.4	4.3	57.5
Turkey	428.3	-2.6	72.9	3.7	61.2
China, Hong Kong SAR	325.0	-14.9	37.5	2.8	64.0
Malaysia	320.8	9.9	34.7	2.8	66.7
Indonesia	269.4	0.4	48.4	2.3	69.1
United Kingdom	261.1	-14.1	47.0	2.2	71.3
Austria	190.0	-14.4	27.6	1.6	72.9
Viet Nam	*175.5*	5.2	66.9	1.5	74.4

687 Tin

During the recent five years, the value (in current prices) of exports of tin (SITC group 687) increased on the average by 12.6 percent and reached 5.5 bln US$ in 2010 (see table 2). Imports for the same period also experienced an average increase of 14.6 percent and, in 2010, totaled 6.3 bln US$ (see table 3). Graph 1 shows that the growth in exports for 2010 in this product group was significantly higher than the increases in world exports of manufactured goods classified chiefly by material (SITC section 6) of 24.5 percent and in total world exports of 21.2 percent. Exports of tin (SITC group 687) accounted for 0.3 percent of world exports of SITC section 6 and less than 0.1 percent of total world exports (see table 1).

Exports of Indonesia, the top exporting country, rose by 36.9 percent and accounted for 31.6 percent of world exports (see table 2). Other major exporting countries were Malaysia and Singapore, respectively with 13.4 and 12.1 percent of world exports. USA, Japan and Singapore were the top destinations (see table 3). By MDG regions (see graph 2), South-eastern Asia accounted for the majority of trade. In 2010, its exports were valued at 3.6 bln US$ and imports at 1.5 bln US$, resulting in a trade surplus of 2.1 bln US$. Latin America and the Caribbean also recorded a surplus of 0.4 bln US$. Major deficits were recorded by Eastern Asia and Developed Europe, both at 0.8 bln US$.

Table 1: Imports (Imp.) and exports (Exp.), 1996-2010, in current prices

		1996	1997	1998	1999	2000	2001	2002	2003	2004	2005	2006	2007	2008	2009	2010
Values in Bln US$	Imp.	1.5	1.4	1.4	1.4	1.5	1.3	1.2	1.6	3.3	3.4	3.7	5.0	6.2	4.3	6.3
	Exp.	1.6	1.6	1.6	1.6	1.7	1.3	1.3	1.6	3.0	3.1	3.4	4.7	6.1	3.8	5.5
As a percentage of SITC section (%)	Imp.	0.2	0.2	0.2	0.2	0.2	0.2	0.1	0.2	0.3	0.2	0.2	0.3	0.3	0.3	0.3
	Exp.	0.2	0.2	0.2	0.2	0.2	0.2	0.1	0.2	0.2	0.2	0.2	0.2	0.3	0.2	0.3
As a percentage of world trade (%)	Imp.	0.0	0.0	0.0	0.0	0.0	0.0	0.0	0.0	0.0	0.0	0.0	0.0	0.0	0.0	0.0
	Exp.	0.0	0.0	0.0	0.0	0.0	0.0	0.0	0.0	0.0	0.0	0.0	0.0	0.0	0.0	0.0

Graph 1: Annual growth rates of exports, 1996–2010

(In percentage by year)

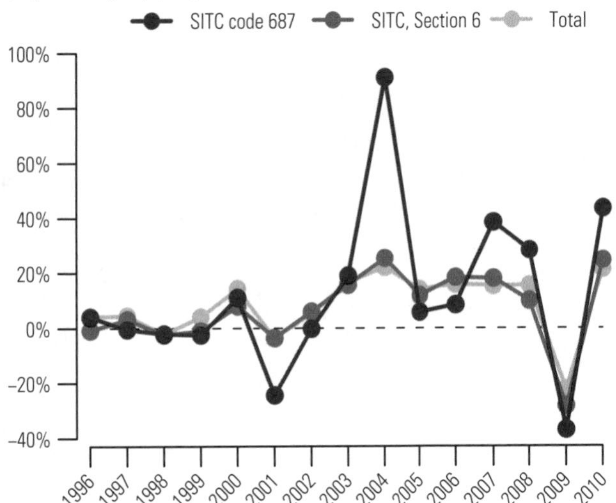

Graph 2: Trade Balance by MDG regions 2010

(Bln US$)

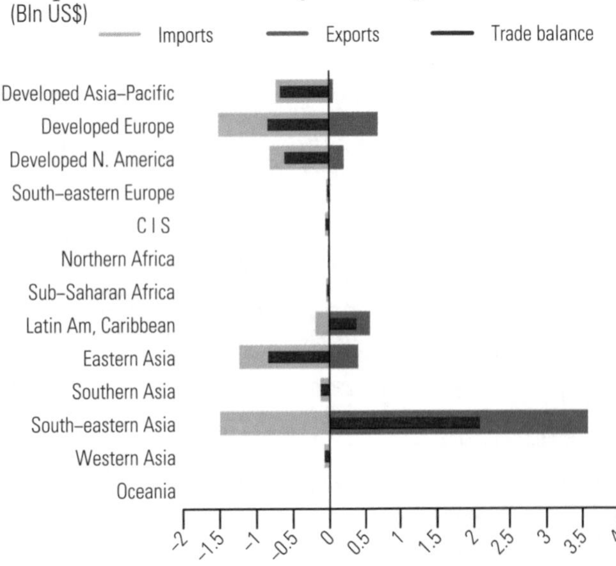

Table 2: Top exporting countries or areas in 2010

Country or area	Value (million US$)	Avg. Growth (%) 06-10	Growth (%) 09-10	World share %	Cum.
World	5489.9	12.6	43.5	100.0	
Indonesia	1733.0	17.0	36.9	31.6	31.6
Malaysia	735.3	38.1	96.1	13.4	45.0
Singapore	666.9	7.4	11.3	12.1	57.1
Thailand	411.7	20.6	78.0	7.5	64.6
Bolivia	294.4	25.9	42.1	5.4	70.0
Belgium	230.2	29.7	69.4	4.2	74.2
Peru	199.1	-7.2	-23.7	3.6	77.8
China, Hong Kong SAR	166.0	20.3	67.9	3.0	80.8
USA	165.4	13.9	96.7	3.0	83.8
Other Asia, nes	155.6	9.9	42.0	2.8	86.7
Netherlands	145.8	19.7	156.2	2.7	89.3
Germany	90.9	9.7	41.4	1.7	91.0
Japan	52.9	-9.5	72.8	1.0	91.9
United Kingdom	51.6	-21.9	154.5	0.9	92.9
China	42.2	-32.7	93.7	0.8	93.6

Table 3: Top importing countries or areas in 2010

Country or area	Value (million US$)	Avg. Growth (%) 06-10	Growth (%) 09-10	World share %	Cum.
World	6317.3	14.6	48.4	100.0	
USA	736.5	13.9	59.7	11.7	11.7
Japan	707.4	20.2	122.2	11.2	22.9
Singapore	503.6	-0.6	-31.2	8.0	30.8
China	503.0	8.9	16.2	8.0	38.8
Malaysia	484.1	34.5	34.0	7.7	46.5
Thailand	448.1	24.9	216.5	7.1	53.5
Germany	401.6	17.2	92.2	6.4	59.9
Rep. of Korea	355.9	22.3	58.1	5.6	65.5
Netherlands	293.3	16.6	96.7	4.6	70.2
Other Asia, nes	258.6	11.8	62.9	4.1	74.3
Spain	131.9	17.1	63.0	2.1	76.4
France	130.1	8.7	43.5	2.1	78.4
United Kingdom	125.9	20.1	42.1	2.0	80.4
Mexico	119.3	23.1	94.9	1.9	82.3
China, Hong Kong SAR	113.1	1.7	6.8	1.8	84.1

After a sharp decline in 2009, the value (in current prices) of exports of miscellaneous non-ferrous base metals employed in metallurgy and cermets (SITC group 689) bounced back by 57.0 percent to a value of 8.5 bln US$ in 2010 (see table 2). Similarly, imports showed a 63.0 percent increase and reached 9.8 bln US$ (see table 3). Graph 1 shows that the rise in exports for 2010 in this product group far exceeded the increases in world exports of manufactured goods classified chiefly by material (SITC section 6) of 24.5 percent and in total world exports of 21.2 percent. Exports of miscellaneous non-ferrous base metals employed in metallurgy and cermets (SITC group 689) accounted for 0.4 percent of world exports of SITC section 6 and 0.1 percent of total world exports (see table 1).

China, the top exporting country in 2010, accounted for 24.6 percent of world exports (see table 2). Other major exporting countries were USA, Dem.Rep. of the Congo and Germany, respectively with 7.4, 6.2 and 6.2 percent of world exports. Top destinations were USA, Japan and China (see table 3). By MDG regions (see graph 2), Eastern Asia recorded a trade surplus of 732 mln US$. Other trade surpluses were also recorded by Sub-Saharan Africa and the Commonwealth of Independent States (+626 mln US$ and +484 mln US$ respectively). Major deficits were recorded by Developed Europe (-1.0 bln US$), Developed North America (-0.9 bln US$) and Developed Asia-Pacific (-0.8 bln US$).

Table 1: Imports (Imp.) and exports (Exp.), 1996-2010, in current prices

		1996	1997	1998	1999	2000	2001	2002	2003	2004	2005	2006	2007	2008	2009	2010
Values in Bln US$	Imp.	4.0	4.3	4.2	3.7	4.1	4.0	3.4	3.9	6.6	8.0	8.6	10.3	13.0	6.0	9.8
	Exp.	3.4	4.0	3.6	3.4	3.8	3.8	3.1	3.9	6.3	7.2	8.5	9.9	12.0	5.4	8.5
As a percentage of SITC section (%)	Imp.	0.5	0.5	0.5	0.4	0.5	0.5	0.4	0.4	0.5	0.6	0.5	0.5	0.6	0.4	0.5
	Exp.	0.4	0.5	0.4	0.4	0.4	0.5	0.4	0.4	0.5	0.5	0.5	0.5	0.6	0.4	0.4
As a percentage of world trade (%)	Imp.	0.1	0.1	0.1	0.1	0.1	0.1	0.1	0.1	0.1	0.1	0.1	0.1	0.1	0.0	0.1
	Exp.	0.1	0.1	0.1	0.1	0.1	0.1	0.0	0.1	0.1	0.1	0.1	0.1	0.1	0.0	0.1

Graph 1: Annual growth rates of exports, 1996–2010
(In percentage by year)

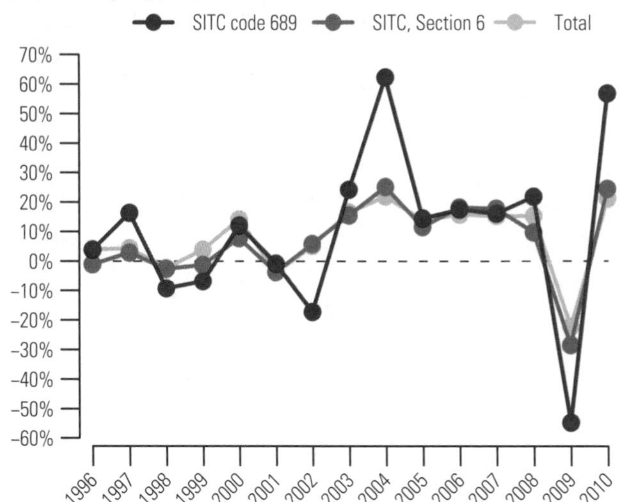

Graph 2: Trade Balance by MDG regions 2010
(Bln US$)

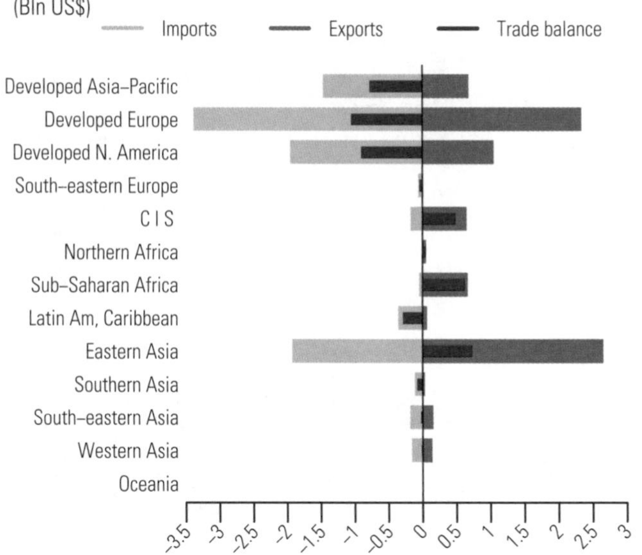

Table 2: Top exporting countries or areas in 2010

Country or area	Value (million US$)	Avg. Growth (%) 06-10	Growth (%) 09-10	World share %	Cum.
World	8539.9	0.2	57.0	100.0	
China	2101.4	0.3	67.9	24.6	24.6
USA	633.0	-14.8	23.7	7.4	32.0
Dem.Rep. of the Congo	*531.3*	27.4	46.2	6.2	38.2
Germany	527.4	-9.2	52.7	6.2	44.4
Japan	500.7	-7.4	50.8	5.9	50.3
Canada	419.9	-2.0	19.2	4.9	55.2
Russian Federation	406.8	2.2	53.8	4.8	60.0
United Kingdom	378.5	6.5	63.7	4.4	64.4
Netherlands	326.4	21.4	139.3	3.8	68.2
Finland	281.8	6.6	3932.0	3.3	71.5
China, Hong Kong SAR	255.7	19.5	230.9	3.0	74.5
France	187.8	2.9	66.2	2.2	76.7
Australia	183.9	11.5	36.2	2.2	78.9
Rep. of Korea	179.7	5.5	45.8	2.1	81.0
Austria	171.3	19.9	51.9	2.0	83.0

Table 3: Top importing countries or areas in 2010

Country or area	Value (million US$)	Avg. Growth (%) 06-10	Growth (%) 09-10	World share %	Cum.
World	9801.4	3.4	63.0	100.0	
USA	1734.8	0.1	52.3	17.7	17.7
Japan	1419.8	-0.1	78.4	14.5	32.2
China	927.3	20.0	62.3	9.5	41.6
Germany	878.2	-2.4	63.8	9.0	50.6
Rep. of Korea	618.8	11.8	72.3	6.3	56.9
United Kingdom	534.7	-5.3	51.5	5.5	62.4
Netherlands	356.4	9.2	80.7	3.6	66.0
France	325.0	4.1	60.3	3.3	69.3
Other Asia, nes	218.3	-0.6	49.3	2.2	71.6
Canada	215.2	4.3	74.2	2.2	73.8
Belgium	196.2	2.0	99.1	2.0	75.8
Finland	180.1	14.7	53.4	1.8	77.6
Austria	177.7	9.1	64.0	1.8	79.4
China, Hong Kong SAR	158.0	-3.6	129.4	1.6	81.0
Mexico	148.6	23.5	65.9	1.5	82.5

691 Structures and parts of structures, nes, of iron, steel or aluminium

In 2010, the value (in current prices) of exports of structures and parts of structures, nes, of iron, steel or aluminium (SITC group 691) diminished by 8.0 percent and amounted to 44.4 bln US$ (see table 2). In the same year, imports decreased by 2.6 percent to 41.5 bln US$ (see table 3). Graph 1 shows that the decline in exports for 2010 in this product group, compared with increases in world exports of manufactured goods classified chiefly by material (SITC section 6) of 24.5 percent and in total world exports of 21.2 percent. Exports of structures and parts of structures, nes, of iron, steel or aluminium (SITC group 691) accounted for 2.3 percent of world exports of SITC section 6 and 0.3 percent of total world exports (see table 1).

The top exporting countries were China, Germany and Italy. Respectively, they accounted for 20.7, 12.5 and 4.1 percent of world exports. Top destinations were USA, Germany and France (see table 3). By MDG regions (see graph 2), Developed Europe accounted for the majority of exports and imports. In 2010, its exports amounted to 22.8 bln US$ while imports were valued at 16.6 bln US$, resulting in a trade surplus of 6.2 bln US$. Eastern Asia recorded a surplus of 7.5 bln US$. Top trade deficits were recorded by Developed Asia-Pacific (-2.2 bln US$), Sub-Saharan Africa (-2.2 bln US$), and the Commonwealth of Independent States (-1.5 bln US$).

Table 1: Imports (Imp.) and exports (Exp.), 1996-2010, in current prices

		1996	1997	1998	1999	2000	2001	2002	2003	2004	2005	2006	2007	2008	2009	2010
Values in Bln US$	Imp.	12.0	12.5	13.2	13.3	12.3	13.0	14.2	16.3	20.2	24.0	31.0	40.8	51.3	42.6	41.5
	Exp.	13.2	14.1	13.4	13.7	13.4	14.0	15.5	17.8	22.4	27.1	34.5	45.6	57.4	48.3	44.4
As a percentage of SITC section (%)	Imp.	1.5	1.5	1.6	1.6	1.4	1.5	1.6	1.6	1.6	1.7	1.9	2.1	2.4	2.7	2.2
	Exp.	1.6	1.7	1.7	1.7	1.6	1.7	1.8	1.7	1.8	1.9	2.1	2.3	2.6	3.1	2.3
As a percentage of world trade (%)	Imp.	0.2	0.2	0.2	0.2	0.2	0.2	0.2	0.2	0.2	0.2	0.3	0.3	0.3	0.3	0.3
	Exp.	0.3	0.3	0.3	0.2	0.2	0.2	0.2	0.2	0.2	0.3	0.3	0.3	0.4	0.4	0.3

Graph 1: Annual growth rates of exports, 1996–2010

(In percentage by year)

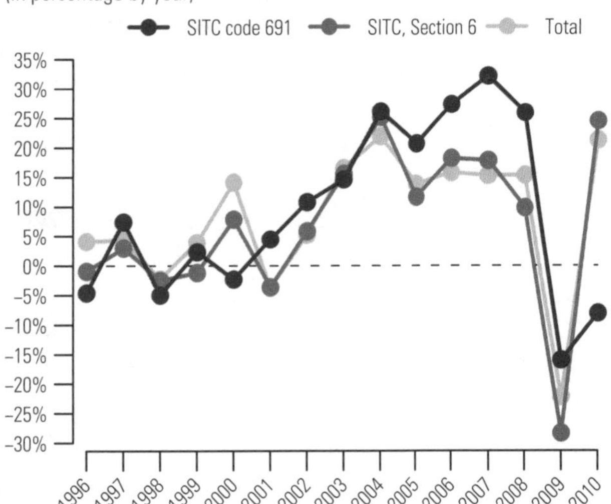

Table 2: Top exporting countries or areas in 2010

Country or area	Value (million US$)	Avg. Growth (%) 06-10	Growth (%) 09-10	World share %	Cum.
World	44374.6	6.5	-8.0	100.0	
China	9205.4	18.0	1.9	20.7	20.7
Germany	5557.2	1.6	0.1	12.5	33.3
Italy	1831.5	2.2	-18.8	4.1	37.4
USA	1716.0	6.3	9.2	3.9	41.3
Poland	1690.3	1.6	-4.9	3.8	45.1
Netherlands	1660.4	9.7	25.3	3.7	48.8
Belgium	1375.9	1.7	-9.8	3.1	51.9
Austria	1339.9	1.9	12.5	3.0	54.9
Spain	1292.7	23.2	28.2	2.9	57.8
Rep. of Korea	1194.6	-2.3	-54.2	2.7	60.5
Turkey	1134.8	12.1	-4.1	2.6	63.1
Denmark	1125.0	13.1	-26.0	2.5	65.6
Czech Rep.	1061.1	3.8	-4.4	2.4	68.0
France	1049.8	4.3	3.9	2.4	70.4
Canada	1046.2	-9.0	-9.5	2.4	72.7

Graph 2: Trade Balance by MDG regions 2010

(Bln US$)

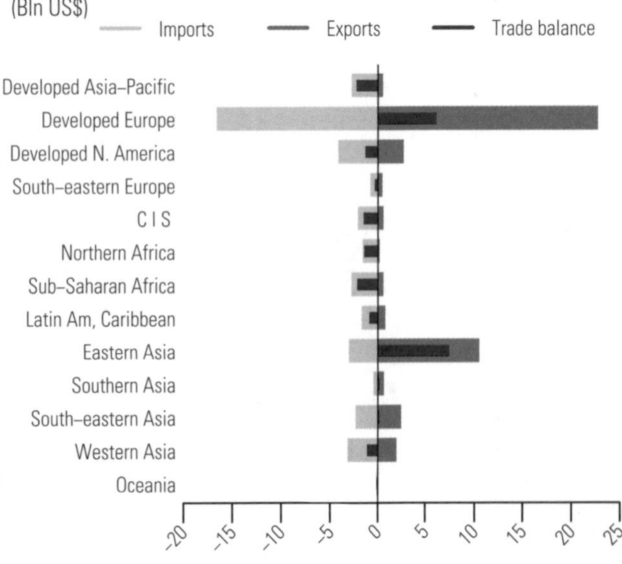

Table 3: Top importing countries or areas in 2010

Country or area	Value (million US$)	Avg. Growth (%) 06-10	Growth (%) 09-10	World share %	Cum.
World	41545.1	7.6	-2.6	100.0	
USA	2992.1	-3.0	-13.9	7.2	7.2
Germany	2826.5	4.8	-0.4	6.8	14.0
France	2109.8	5.5	11.1	5.1	19.1
Rep. of Korea	2050.6	46.2	14.1	4.9	24.0
Japan	1989.7	2.9	-8.6	4.8	28.8
United Kingdom	1377.5	4.7	1.6	3.3	32.1
Switzerland	1132.5	6.6	9.5	2.7	34.9
Canada	1042.3	7.3	35.1	2.5	37.4
Algeria	995.0	35.9	13.5	2.4	39.8
Belgium	986.0	9.0	5.7	2.4	42.1
Austria	965.8	0.7	-0.8	2.3	44.5
Netherlands	952.4	6.5	-21.6	2.3	46.7
Saudi Arabia	935.0	12.0	-24.2	2.3	49.0
Norway	916.9	1.5	-0.5	2.2	51.2
Russian Federation	865.8	11.0	11.7	2.1	53.3

The value (in current prices) of exports of metal containers for storage or transport (SITC group 692) increased by 5.1 percent totaling to 17.2 bln US$ in 2010 (see table 2). Imports decreased by 2.1 percent to 16.0 bln US$ (see table 3). Graph 1 shows that the increase in exports for 2010 in this product group was way below the increases in world exports of manufactured goods classified chiefly by material (SITC section 6) of 24.5 percent and in total world exports of 21.2 percent. Exports of metal containers for storage or transport (SITC group 692) accounted for 0.9 percent of world exports of SITC section 6 and 0.1 percent of total world exports (see table 1).

In 2009, Germany, USA and Italy were the top exporting countries (see table 2). They accounted respectively for 11.3, 8.9 and 7.6 percent of world exports. USA and Germany were the top destinations, together with France (see table 3). By MDG regions (see graph 2), Developed Europe accounted for a majority of both imports and exports of metal containers (SITC group 692). In 2010, its exports were valued at 9.2 bln US$ while imports amounted to 6.6 bln US$, resulting in a trade surplus of 2.6 bln US$. A major trade surplus was also recorded by Eastern Asia (+1.3 bln US$). Top trade deficits were recorded by Sub-Saharan Africa (-550 mln US$), Latin America & the Caribbean (-487 mln US$) and Northern Africa (-437 mln US$).

Table 1: Imports (Imp.) and exports (Exp.), 1996-2010, in current prices

		1996	1997	1998	1999	2000	2001	2002	2003	2004	2005	2006	2007	2008	2009	2010
Values in Bln US$	Imp.	6.9	6.7	6.7	6.6	6.4	6.7	7.2	8.1	9.4	10.5	12.2	15.3	17.6	16.4	16.0
	Exp.	7.6	7.3	7.3	7.0	6.8	6.8	7.2	8.5	9.8	11.3	13.6	17.0	19.5	16.3	17.2
As a percentage of SITC section (%)	Imp.	0.8	0.8	0.8	0.8	0.7	0.8	0.8	0.8	0.7	0.7	0.7	0.8	0.8	1.1	0.8
	Exp.	0.9	0.9	0.9	0.9	0.8	0.8	0.8	0.8	0.8	0.8	0.8	0.9	0.9	1.1	0.9
As a percentage of world trade (%)	Imp.	0.1	0.1	0.1	0.1	0.1	0.1	0.1	0.1	0.1	0.1	0.1	0.1	0.1	0.1	0.1
	Exp.	0.1	0.1	0.1	0.1	0.1	0.1	0.1	0.1	0.1	0.1	0.1	0.1	0.1	0.1	0.1

Graph 1: Annual growth rates of exports, 1996–2010
(In percentage by year)

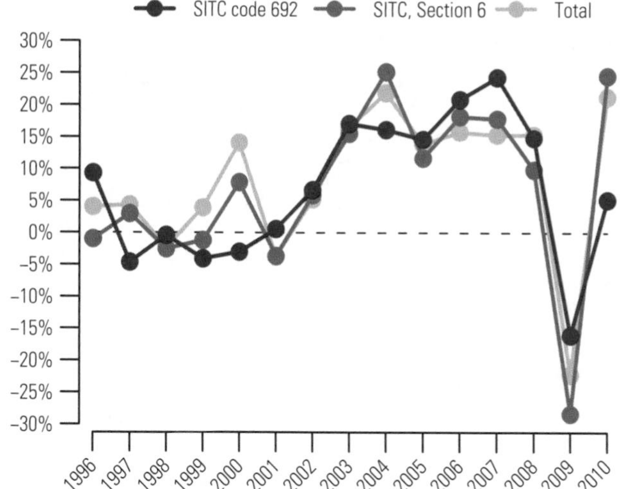

Graph 2: Trade Balance by MDG regions 2010
(Bln US$)

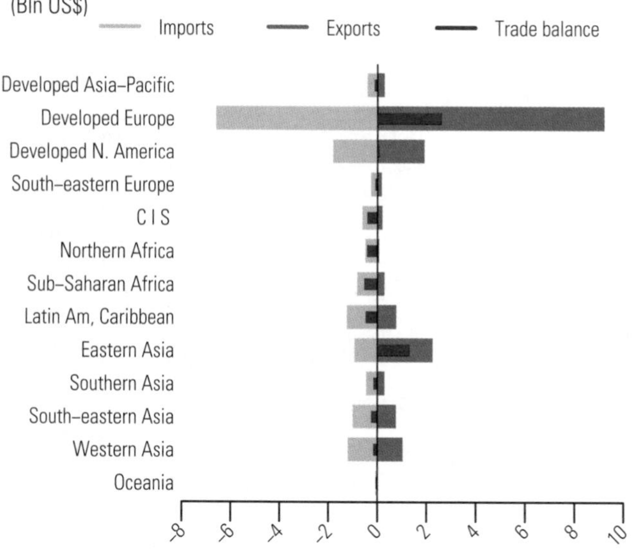

Table 2: Top exporting countries or areas in 2010

Country or area	Value (million US$)	Avg. Growth (%) 06-10	Growth (%) 09-10	World share %	Cum.
World	17177.6	5.9	5.1	100.0	
Germany	1949.1	2.6	-3.9	11.3	11.3
USA	1522.3	7.7	10.5	8.9	20.2
Italy	1304.8	8.5	2.2	7.6	27.8
China	1214.7	12.7	26.3	7.1	34.9
France	817.1	0.4	-7.1	4.8	39.6
Rep. of Korea	771.7	-0.2	-16.2	4.5	44.1
Spain	756.2	4.5	8.4	4.4	48.5
United Kingdom	596.5	1.7	0.4	3.5	52.0
Poland	501.0	4.6	9.0	2.9	54.9
Netherlands	497.9	4.0	-4.6	2.9	57.8
Czech Rep.	496.1	4.9	0.8	2.9	60.7
Canada	369.4	-1.4	6.3	2.2	62.9
Austria	367.1	2.1	-2.1	2.1	65.0
Mexico	364.5	9.5	37.6	2.1	67.1
Belgium	357.1	-2.1	-12.6	2.1	69.2

Table 3: Top importing countries or areas in 2010

Country or area	Value (million US$)	Avg. Growth (%) 06-10	Growth (%) 09-10	World share %	Cum.
World	16024.0	7.0	-2.1	100.0	
USA	1085.5	3.7	-18.2	6.8	6.8
Germany	970.2	4.1	2.5	6.1	12.8
France	912.5	5.5	1.3	5.7	18.5
Canada	733.2	9.4	13.5	4.6	23.1
Belgium	623.9	-1.8	-6.4	3.9	27.0
Netherlands	541.5	0.2	-13.2	3.4	30.4
United Kingdom	512.4	-3.2	8.1	3.2	33.6
Rep. of Korea	436.0	13.6	-20.0	2.7	36.3
Spain	365.9	-9.6	-20.4	2.3	38.6
Switzerland	354.1	10.4	-8.1	2.2	40.8
Poland	346.9	13.2	-1.0	2.2	42.9
United Arab Emirates	336.0	28.7	13.2	2.1	45.0
China	334.3	21.2	19.8	2.1	47.1
Russian Federation	296.2	16.3	29.9	1.8	49.0
Thailand	281.7	27.1	-6.4	1.8	50.7

Source: UN Comtrade

693 Wire products (excluding insulated electrical wiring) and fencing grills

The value (in current prices) of exports of wire products and fencing grills (SITC group 693) showed an average annual increase of 4.7 percent over the last five years, and amounted to 12.8 bln US$ in 2010 (see table 2). Similarly, imports for the same period also showed an average annual increase of 4.7 percent to 12.7 bln US$ in 2010 (see table 3). Graph 1 shows that the rise in exports for 2010 in this product group was lower than the increases in world exports of manufactured goods classified chiefly by material (SITC section 6) of 24.5 percent and in total world exports of 21.2 percent. Exports of wire products and fencing grills in 2010 (SITC group 693) accounted for 0.7 percent of world exports of SITC section 6 and 0.1 percent of total world exports (see table 1).

Exports of China, the top exporting country increased by 22.4 percent and represented 16.4 percent of world exports in 2010 (see table 2). Other major exporting countries were Germany and Italy accounting respectively for 11.5 and 6.5 percent of world exports. USA, Germany and France were the top destinations (see table 3). By MDG regions (see graph 2), Developed Europe accounted for a large share of trade in wire products and fencing grills (SITC group 693). In 2010, its exports and imports were valued at 5.8 bln and 5.4 bln US$, respectively, resulting in a surplus of 0.4 bln US$. Eastern Asia recorded a surplus amounting to 2.0 bln US$ and Developed North America, a deficit of 0.7 bln US$.

Table 1: Imports (Imp.) and exports (Exp.), 1996-2010, in current prices

		1996	1997	1998	1999	2000	2001	2002	2003	2004	2005	2006	2007	2008	2009	2010
Values in Bln US$	Imp.	4.9	4.8	4.7	4.6	4.6	4.7	4.8	5.7	7.6	8.8	10.5	12.8	15.4	10.9	12.7
	Exp.	4.8	4.8	4.7	4.8	4.8	4.8	4.9	5.7	7.9	9.0	10.7	13.0	15.7	10.7	12.8
As a percentage of SITC section (%)	Imp.	0.6	0.6	0.6	0.6	0.5	0.6	0.5	0.6	0.6	0.6	0.6	0.7	0.7	0.7	0.7
	Exp.	0.6	0.6	0.6	0.6	0.6	0.6	0.6	0.6	0.6	0.6	0.6	0.7	0.7	0.7	0.7
As a percentage of world trade (%)	Imp.	0.1	0.1	0.1	0.1	0.1	0.1	0.1	0.1	0.1	0.1	0.1	0.1	0.1	0.1	0.1
	Exp.	0.1	0.1	0.1	0.1	0.1	0.1	0.1	0.1	0.1	0.1	0.1	0.1	0.1	0.1	0.1

Graph 1: Annual growth rates of exports, 1996–2010
(In percentage by year)

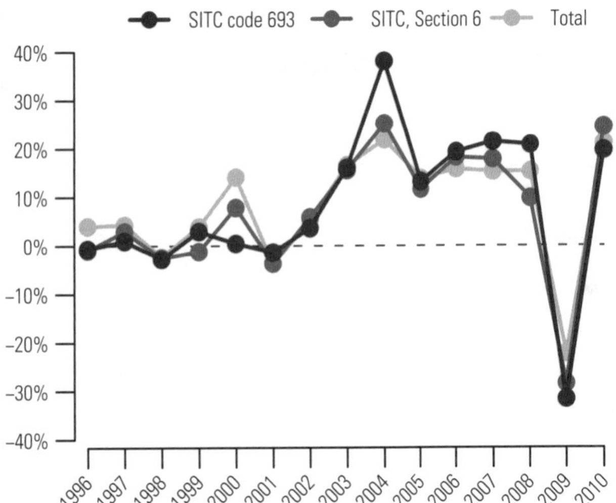

Graph 2: Trade Balance by MDG regions 2010
(Bln US$)

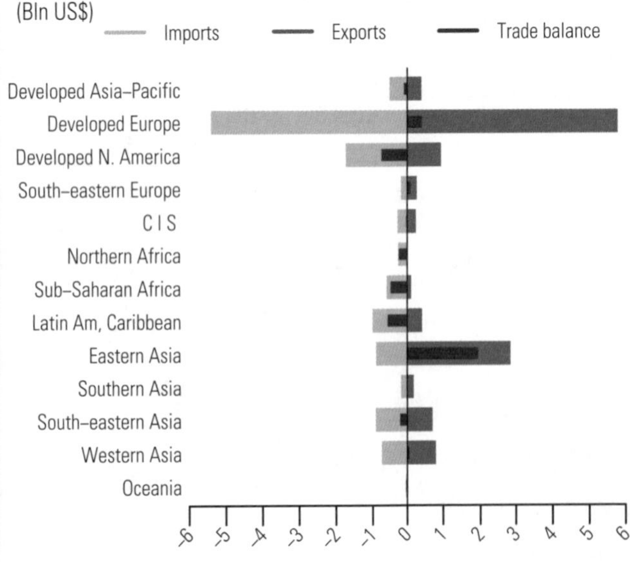

Table 2: Top exporting countries or areas in 2010

Country or area	Value (million US$)	Avg. Growth (%) 06-10	Growth (%) 09-10	World share %	Cum.
World	12 848.8	4.7	19.7	100.0	
China	2 101.3	11.0	22.4	16.4	16.4
Germany	1 475.9	0.9	18.1	11.5	27.8
Italy	833.0	1.3	32.5	6.5	34.3
USA	795.0	4.4	26.0	6.2	40.5
Rep. of Korea	646.9	5.0	15.5	5.0	45.5
Turkey	536.4	10.7	56.8	4.2	49.7
Spain	466.7	7.3	18.5	3.6	53.4
Netherlands	417.2	4.6	27.7	3.2	56.6
France	388.7	-3.8	7.0	3.0	59.6
Belgium	366.9	-0.8	-2.1	2.9	62.5
Japan	366.4	6.9	21.0	2.9	65.3
United Kingdom	294.1	-5.5	-4.5	2.3	67.6
Poland	261.6	7.9	67.8	2.0	69.7
Malaysia	236.8	11.6	21.5	1.8	71.5
Romania	194.6	18.2	36.7	1.5	73.0

Table 3: Top importing countries or areas in 2010

Country or area	Value (million US$)	Avg. Growth (%) 06-10	Growth (%) 09-10	World share %	Cum.
World	12 667.4	4.7	16.4	100.0	
USA	1 288.9	-3.8	13.0	10.2	10.2
Germany	825.9	2.2	13.9	6.5	16.7
France	796.3	1.4	26.1	6.3	23.0
China	457.6	7.2	2.9	3.6	26.6
Canada	406.1	7.2	34.7	3.2	29.8
Belgium	361.9	3.2	13.7	2.9	32.7
Italy	361.4	0.7	26.9	2.9	35.5
United Kingdom	337.4	-2.2	11.9	2.7	38.2
Spain	311.0	-7.3	8.9	2.5	40.6
Mexico	304.4	8.6	28.6	2.4	43.0
Netherlands	289.7	6.2	4.3	2.3	45.3
Japan	260.0	7.3	22.2	2.1	47.4
Singapore	246.5	13.1	9.5	1.9	49.3
Rep. of Korea	244.2	17.6	27.2	1.9	51.2
Poland	237.9	11.6	40.8	1.9	53.1

After a sharp decline in 2009, the value (in current prices) of exports of nails, screws, nuts, bolts, and the like of iron, steel, copper, aluminum (SITC group 694) grew by 31.8 percent in 2010 to reach 30.7 bln US$ (see table 2). In the same year, imports also increased by 27.1 percent to 35.1 bln US$ (see table 3). Graph 1 shows that the rise in exports for 2010 in this product group was higher than the increases in world exports of manufactured goods classified chiefly by material (SITC section 6) of 24.5 percent and in total world exports of 21.2 percent. Exports of nails, screws, nuts, bolts, and the like of iron, steel, copper, aluminum (SITC group 694) accounted for 1.6 percent of world exports of SITC section 6 and 0.2 percent of total world exports (see table 1).

In 2010, the top exporting countries were Germany and China (see table 2). They accounted respectively for 15.4 and 14.8 percent of world exports. Top destinations were USA, Germany and China (see table 3). By MDG regions (see graph 2), Developed Europe accounted for a large share of trade in nails screws, nuts, etc. (SITC group 694). In 2010, its exports were valued at 13.0 bln US$ and imports at 13.5 bln US$, resulting in a trade deficit of 0.5 bln US$. Larger trade deficits were recorded by Latin America and the Caribbean (-3.2 bln US$) and Developed North America (-2.6 bln US$). Eastern Asia recorded a trade surplus amounting to 4.7 bln US$.

Table 1: Imports (Imp.) and exports (Exp.), 1996-2010, in current prices

		1996	1997	1998	1999	2000	2001	2002	2003	2004	2005	2006	2007	2008	2009	2010
Values in Bln US$	Imp.	12.1	12.7	13.3	13.6	14.8	14.2	14.8	17.3	22.0	24.9	28.1	33.8	38.0	27.6	35.1
	Exp.	10.9	11.0	11.6	11.5	12.5	11.6	12.5	14.8	18.8	21.3	24.4	29.2	33.2	23.3	30.7
As a percentage of	Imp.	1.5	1.5	1.6	1.7	1.7	1.7	1.7	1.7	1.7	1.7	1.7	1.7	1.8	1.8	1.8
SITC section (%)	Exp.	1.3	1.3	1.4	1.4	1.4	1.4	1.4	1.5	1.5	1.5	1.5	1.5	1.5	1.5	1.6
As a percentage of	Imp.	0.2	0.2	0.2	0.2	0.2	0.2	0.2	0.2	0.2	0.2	0.2	0.2	0.2	0.2	0.2
world trade (%)	Exp.	0.2	0.2	0.2	0.2	0.2	0.2	0.2	0.2	0.2	0.2	0.2	0.2	0.2	0.2	0.2

Graph 1: Annual growth rates of exports, 1996–2010

(In percentage by year)

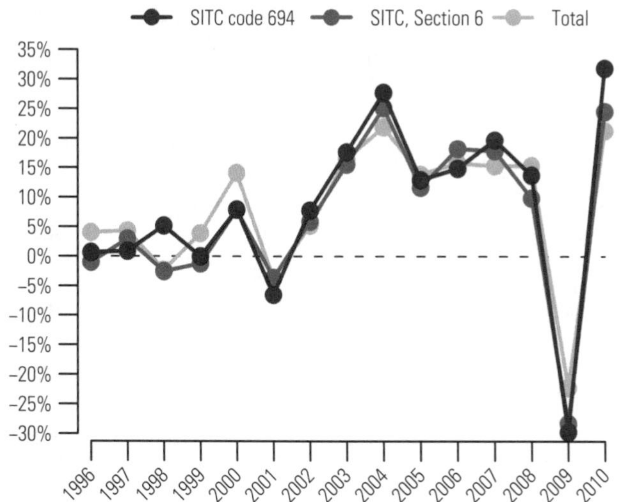

Graph 2: Trade Balance by MDG regions 2010

(Bln US$)

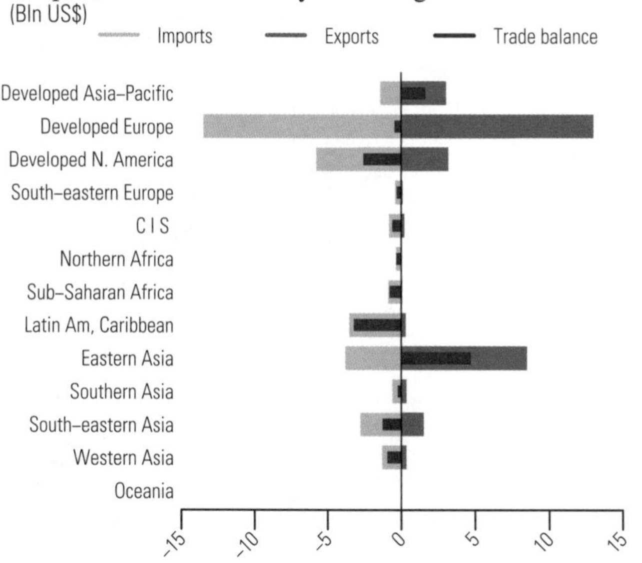

Table 2: Top exporting countries or areas in 2010

Country or area	Value (million US$)	Avg. Growth (%) 06-10	Growth (%) 09-10	World share %	Cum.
World	30740.2	5.9	31.8	100.0	
Germany	4720.4	5.5	28.0	15.4	15.4
China	4555.1	8.3	39.2	14.8	30.2
Other Asia, nes	3208.8	5.7	55.7	10.4	40.6
Japan	2960.8	11.2	41.9	9.6	50.2
USA	2795.1	2.5	25.2	9.1	59.3
Italy	1644.5	2.6	26.9	5.3	64.7
France	1347.9	5.7	13.7	4.4	69.1
Switzerland	987.7	1.4	29.1	3.2	72.3
United Kingdom	630.3	1.2	11.9	2.1	74.3
Malaysia	553.2	14.7	49.4	1.8	76.1
Netherlands	537.0	6.3	22.2	1.7	77.9
Spain	493.4	5.6	33.0	1.6	79.5
Belgium	490.0	5.4	8.5	1.6	81.1
Canada	398.2	-6.5	26.3	1.3	82.4
Thailand	390.3	12.0	53.4	1.3	83.6

Table 3: Top importing countries or areas in 2010

Country or area	Value (million US$)	Avg. Growth (%) 06-10	Growth (%) 09-10	World share %	Cum.
World	35110.7	5.7	27.1	100.0	
USA	4357.9	-3.1	36.3	12.4	12.4
Germany	3129.7	5.8	31.8	8.9	21.3
China	2911.9	14.9	26.3	8.3	29.6
Mexico	1898.7	2.3	42.7	5.4	35.0
France	1542.9	2.2	17.0	4.4	39.4
Canada	1387.6	0.5	31.4	4.0	43.4
United Kingdom	1134.3	0.6	21.4	3.2	46.6
Thailand	940.3	14.2	37.9	2.7	49.3
Japan	863.8	4.1	24.6	2.5	51.7
Brazil	772.3	17.4	38.3	2.2	53.9
Italy	760.7	6.1	35.1	2.2	56.1
Poland	710.9	8.6	26.9	2.0	58.1
Spain	707.1	-3.1	-3.5	2.0	60.1
Netherlands	691.1	3.0	24.0	2.0	62.1
Czech Rep.	677.9	4.0	20.3	1.9	64.0

 Source: UN Comtrade

695 Tools for use in the hand or in machines

From 2006 to 2010, the value (in current prices) of exports of tools for use in the hand or in machines (SITC group 695) increased on average by 4.2 percent annually and in 2010 amounted to 40.6 bln US$ (see table 2). Similarly, imports showed an average annual increase of 4.2 percent to a total of 40.6 bln US$ in 2010 (see table 3). Graph 1 shows that the increase in exports for 2010 in this product group was comparable to the increase in world exports of manufactured goods classified chiefly by material (SITC section 6) of 24.5 percent and was slightly higher than the that of total world exports of 21.2 percent. Exports of tools for use in the hand or in machines (SITC group 695) accounted for 2.1 percent of world exports of SITC section 6 and 0.3 percent of total world exports (see table 1).

Germany, China and USA were the top exporting countries in 2010 (see table 2). They accounted respectively for 15.3, 13.9 and 10.2 percent of world exports. USA, Germany and China were also the top destinations (see table 3). By MDG regions (see graph 2), Developed Europe accounted for nearly half of the trade in tools for use in the hand or in machines (SITC group 695). In 2010, its exports and imports were valued respectively at 18.3 and 16.4 bln US$, resulting in a trade surplus of 1.9 bln US$. Eastern Asia and Developed Asia-Pacific recorded trade surpluses amounting respectively to 5.2 and 1.7 bln US$. Top trade deficits of 2.1 and 2.0 bln US$ were recorded by Developed North America and Latin America and the Caribbean, respectively.

Table 1: Imports (Imp.) and exports (Exp.), 1996-2010, in current prices

		1996	1997	1998	1999	2000	2001	2002	2003	2004	2005	2006	2007	2008	2009	2010
Values in Bln US$	Imp.	18.1	19.0	19.4	19.3	20.2	20.2	20.5	23.4	28.3	30.9	34.4	39.8	44.8	32.8	40.6
	Exp.	17.7	18.9	18.8	19.7	20.8	20.8	21.1	23.4	27.8	30.3	34.3	39.2	44.4	32.6	40.5
As a percentage of SITC section (%)	Imp.	2.2	2.3	2.3	2.4	2.3	2.4	2.3	2.3	2.2	2.2	2.1	2.0	2.1	2.1	2.1
	Exp.	2.2	2.3	2.3	2.5	2.4	2.5	2.4	2.3	2.2	2.1	2.0	2.0	2.0	2.1	2.1
As a percentage of world trade (%)	Imp.	0.3	0.3	0.4	0.3	0.3	0.3	0.3	0.3	0.3	0.3	0.3	0.3	0.3	0.3	0.3
	Exp.	0.3	0.3	0.4	0.4	0.3	0.3	0.3	0.3	0.3	0.3	0.3	0.3	0.3	0.3	0.3

Graph 1: Annual growth rates of exports, 1996–2010

(In percentage by year)

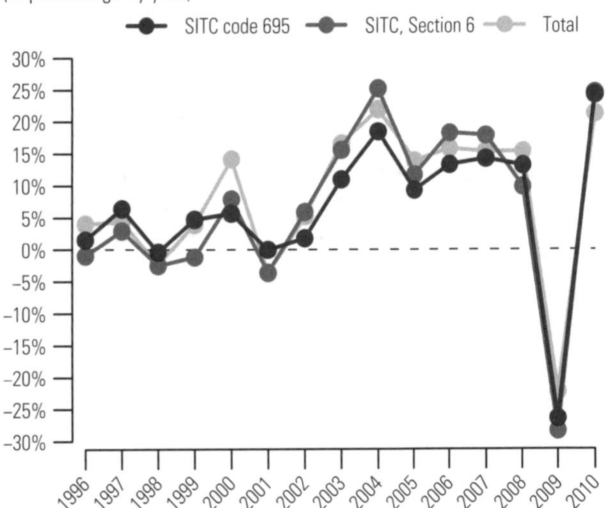

Graph 2: Trade Balance by MDG regions 2010

(Bln US$)

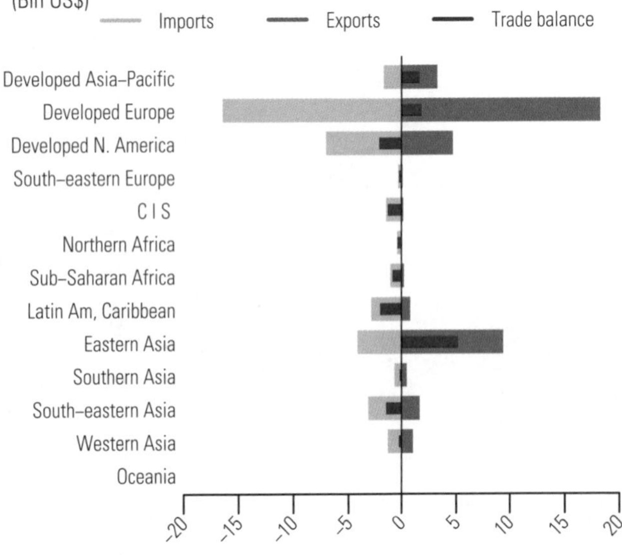

Table 2: Top exporting countries or areas in 2010

Country or area	Value (million US$)	Avg. Growth (%) 06-10	Growth (%) 09-10	World share %	Cum.
World	40548.0	4.2	24.2	100.0	
Germany	6219.0	1.2	14.4	15.3	15.3
China	5651.0	11.8	39.6	13.9	29.3
USA	4132.0	5.5	29.0	10.2	39.5
Japan	3200.0	2.6	37.3	7.9	47.4
Other Asia, nes	2071.9	2.7	35.9	5.1	52.5
Netherlands	1806.8	44.0	30.2	4.5	56.9
Italy	1344.0	-2.5	15.3	3.3	60.2
Switzerland	1325.4	2.0	16.3	3.3	63.5
Rep. of Korea	1275.9	6.1	20.3	3.1	66.7
Belgium	1201.3	1.2	20.9	3.0	69.6
Sweden	1190.7	2.5	43.1	2.9	72.6
Singapore	1171.0	6.2	26.5	2.9	75.4
United Kingdom	1040.2	-5.4	5.3	2.6	78.0
France	978.4	-1.8	5.3	2.4	80.4
Austria	836.0	-1.2	10.2	2.1	82.5

Table 3: Top importing countries or areas in 2010

Country or area	Value (million US$)	Avg. Growth (%) 06-10	Growth (%) 09-10	World share %	Cum.
World	40580.9	4.2	23.9	100.0	
USA	5254.9	0.0	31.8	12.9	12.9
Germany	3539.9	2.7	20.0	8.7	21.7
China	2581.1	10.1	31.4	6.4	28.0
Netherlands	1857.2	27.7	37.3	4.6	32.6
Canada	1668.2	-0.4	28.0	4.1	36.7
France	1540.4	0.7	9.4	3.8	40.5
United Kingdom	1323.4	-2.8	20.2	3.3	43.8
Singapore	1263.9	10.9	56.8	3.1	46.9
Italy	1178.5	-3.5	17.5	2.9	49.8
Belgium	1136.1	0.8	9.9	2.8	52.6
Mexico	1110.8	1.6	27.1	2.7	55.3
Russian Federation	1027.7	28.9	99.7	2.5	57.9
Japan	969.0	1.2	37.4	2.4	60.3
Thailand	908.4	10.3	56.2	2.2	62.5
Switzerland	743.3	1.1	8.3	1.8	64.3

The value (in current prices) of exports of cutlery (SITC group 696) rose by 24.9 percent and amounted to 9.6 bln US$ in 2010 (see table 2). During the same year, imports also increased by 19.2 percent to 9.8 bln US$ (see table 3). Graph 1 shows that the rise in exports for 2010 in this product group was comparable to the increase in world exports of manufactured goods classified chiefly by material (SITC section 6) of 24.5 percent and was higher than that for total world exports of 21.2 percent. Exports of cutlery (SITC group 696) accounted for 0.5 percent of world exports of SITC section 6 and 0.1 percent of total world exports (see table 1).

China was the top exporting country in 2010. It accounted for 32.3 percent of world exports (see table 2). Other major exporting countries were Germany and Poland, accounting respectively for 9.6 and 9.3 percent of world exports. USA, Germany and United Kingdom were the top destinations (see table 3). By MDG regions (see graph 2), Eastern Asia recorded a trade surplus of 3.0 bln US$ in 2010. Top trade deficits were recorded by Developed North America (-1.5 bln US$), Commonwealth of Independent States (-0.4 bln US$) and Western Asia (-0.4 bln US$).

Table 1: Imports (Imp.) and exports (Exp.), 1996-2010, in current prices

		1996	1997	1998	1999	2000	2001	2002	2003	2004	2005	2006	2007	2008	2009	2010
Values in Bln US$	Imp.	4.6	4.8	4.9	5.3	5.3	5.4	5.7	6.2	7.0	7.5	7.9	9.0	9.5	8.2	9.8
	Exp.	4.2	4.4	4.4	4.8	5.0	5.2	5.5	6.1	6.7	7.2	7.9	8.4	9.1	7.7	9.6
As a percentage of SITC section (%)	Imp.	0.6	0.6	0.6	0.6	0.6	0.6	0.6	0.6	0.5	0.5	0.5	0.5	0.4	0.5	0.5
	Exp.	0.5	0.5	0.5	0.6	0.6	0.6	0.6	0.6	0.5	0.5	0.5	0.4	0.4	0.5	0.5
As a percentage of world trade (%)	Imp.	0.1	0.1	0.1	0.1	0.1	0.1	0.1	0.1	0.1	0.1	0.1	0.1	0.1	0.1	0.1
	Exp.	0.1	0.1	0.1	0.1	0.1	0.1	0.1	0.1	0.1	0.1	0.1	0.1	0.1	0.1	0.1

Graph 1: Annual growth rates of exports, 1996–2010

(In percentage by year)

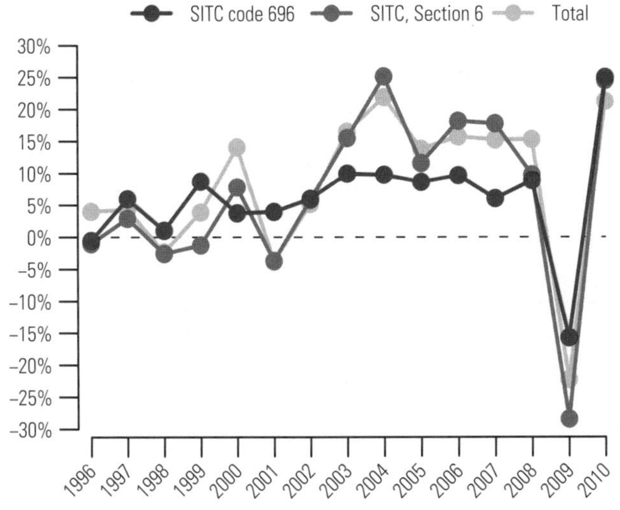

Table 2: Top exporting countries or areas in 2010

Country or area	Value (million US$)	Avg. Growth (%) 06-10	Growth (%) 09-10	World share %	Cum.
World	9622.9	5.0	24.9	100.0	
China	3105.5	7.3	33.7	32.3	32.3
Germany	920.9	-1.4	9.8	9.6	41.8
Poland	897.4	27.5	30.1	9.3	51.2
USA	540.2	1.4	13.5	5.6	56.8
Mexico	407.6	18.1	100.7	4.2	61.0
China, Hong Kong SAR	358.4	-1.5	18.7	3.7	64.7
Belgium	337.5	17.4	2.1	3.5	68.2
Czech Rep.	246.0	56.9	74.4	2.6	70.8
United Kingdom	241.9	-26.5	59.1	2.5	73.3
France	219.4	0.9	3.8	2.3	75.6
Japan	203.4	7.0	26.6	2.1	77.7
Netherlands	179.4	16.7	-12.3	1.9	79.6
Brazil	174.7	4.3	23.9	1.8	81.4
Switzerland	163.2	4.7	9.1	1.7	83.1
Italy	149.5	-0.3	13.4	1.6	84.6

Graph 2: Trade Balance by MDG regions 2010

(Bln US$)

Imports — Exports — Trade balance

Developed Asia-Pacific
Developed Europe
Developed N. America
South-eastern Europe
C I S
Northern Africa
Sub-Saharan Africa
Latin Am, Caribbean
Eastern Asia
Southern Asia
South-eastern Asia
Western Asia
Oceania

-4 -3 -2 -1 0 1 2 3 4

Table 3: Top importing countries or areas in 2010

Country or area	Value (million US$)	Avg. Growth (%) 06-10	Growth (%) 09-10	World share %	Cum.
World	9796.4	5.4	19.2	100.0	
USA	1707.9	1.4	21.9	17.4	17.4
Germany	708.1	11.4	6.2	7.2	24.7
United Kingdom	469.1	-6.8	10.6	4.8	29.5
France	400.8	4.3	1.5	4.1	33.5
Poland	393.8	16.8	215.4	4.0	37.6
Canada	317.8	0.5	16.0	3.2	40.8
China, Hong Kong SAR	310.8	0.3	24.6	3.2	44.0
Japan	296.0	8.7	16.7	3.0	47.0
Mexico	283.7	19.3	89.2	2.9	49.9
Russian Federation	283.6	19.6	32.2	2.9	52.8
Belgium	269.3	1.9	-8.3	2.7	55.5
Italy	246.6	3.6	5.8	2.5	58.1
Spain	220.2	-0.8	12.2	2.2	60.3
Netherlands	211.0	3.2	4.3	2.2	62.5
China	181.9	12.9	23.5	1.9	64.3

697 Household equipment of base metal, nes

In 2010, the value (in current prices) of exports of household equipment of base metal, nes (SITC group 697) increased by 16.2 percent and totaled 25.3 bln US$ (see table 2). Similarly, imports showed an increase of 13.8 percent amounting to 26.2 bln US$ (see table 3). Graph 1 shows that the rise in exports for 2010 in this product group was lower than increases in world exports of manufactured goods classified chiefly by material (SITC section 6) of 24.5 percent and in total world exports of 21.2 percent. Exports of household equipment of base metal, nes (SITC group 697) accounted for 1.3 percent of world exports of SITC section 6 and 0.2 percent of total world exports (see table 1).

Exports of China, the top exporting country, accounted for more than a third (38.3 percent) of world exports (see table 2). Other major exporting countries were Italy and Germany, respectively accounting for 8.5 and 5.6 percent of world exports. Top destinations were USA, Germany and France (see table 3). By MDG regions (see graph 2), Developed Europe accounted for a large share of trade in household equipment of base metal, nes (SITC group 697). In 2010, its exports and imports were valued respectively at 8.4 and 10.2 bln US$, resulting in a trade deficit of 1.8 bln US$. A larger trade deficit was recorded by Developed North America (-6.0 bln US$). Eastern Asia recorded a trade surplus amounting to 10.0 bln US$.

Table 1: Imports (Imp.) and exports (Exp.), 1996-2010, in current prices

		1996	1997	1998	1999	2000	2001	2002	2003	2004	2005	2006	2007	2008	2009	2010
Values in Bln US$	Imp.	10.4	10.8	10.9	11.5	12.4	12.4	13.7	15.9	18.6	20.1	22.3	25.3	26.8	23.0	26.2
	Exp.	10.5	10.8	10.7	10.9	12.0	11.9	12.9	14.9	17.4	18.7	21.2	23.7	25.2	21.8	25.3
As a percentage of SITC section (%)	Imp.	1.3	1.3	1.3	1.4	1.4	1.5	1.5	1.6	1.5	1.4	1.3	1.3	1.2	1.5	1.4
	Exp.	1.3	1.3	1.3	1.4	1.4	1.4	1.5	1.5	1.4	1.3	1.3	1.2	1.2	1.4	1.3
As a percentage of world trade (%)	Imp.	0.2	0.2	0.2	0.2	0.2	0.2	0.2	0.2	0.2	0.2	0.2	0.2	0.2	0.2	0.2
	Exp.	0.2	0.2	0.2	0.2	0.2	0.2	0.2	0.2	0.2	0.2	0.2	0.2	0.2	0.2	0.2

Graph 1: Annual growth rates of exports, 1996–2010

(In percentage by year)

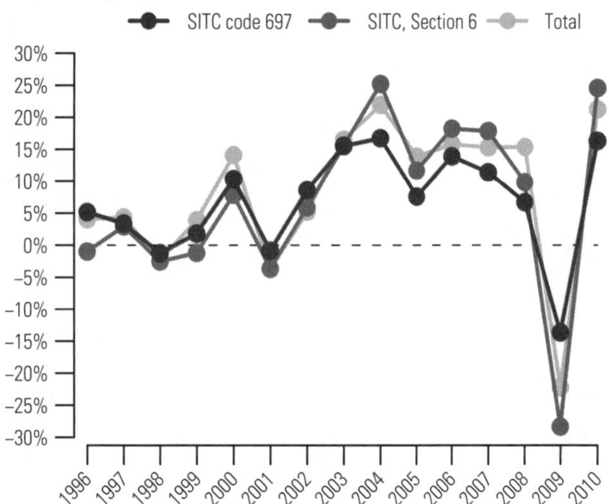

Table 2: Top exporting countries or areas in 2010

Country or area	Value (million US$)	Avg. Growth (%) 06-10	Growth (%) 09-10	World share %	Cum.
World	25292.2	4.5	16.2	100.0	
China	9698.2	11.4	32.3	38.3	38.3
Italy	2160.2	-1.0	8.1	8.5	46.9
Germany	1417.8	0.5	-0.6	5.6	52.5
USA	901.5	4.6	14.2	3.6	56.1
France	841.6	-0.1	7.0	3.3	59.4
India	655.3	4.5	20.4	2.6	62.0
Turkey	637.6	7.4	10.2	2.5	64.5
Other Asia, nes	581.0	-4.7	12.3	2.3	66.8
China, Hong Kong SAR	510.5	-8.5	10.8	2.0	68.8
Netherlands	501.7	9.4	8.7	2.0	70.8
Mexico	473.9	16.5	12.2	1.9	72.7
Belgium	473.0	0.1	0.5	1.9	74.5
Spain	466.5	-1.4	5.3	1.8	76.4
Thailand	394.5	1.0	30.9	1.6	77.9
Poland	381.5	3.0	8.6	1.5	79.5

Graph 2: Trade Balance by MDG regions 2010

(Bln US$)

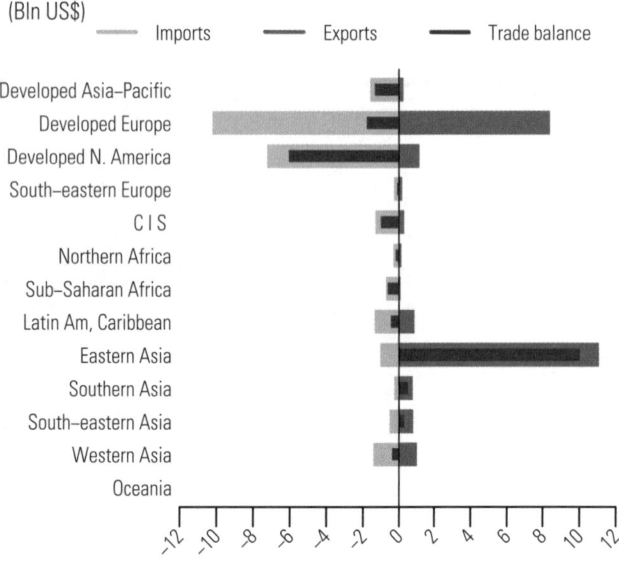

Table 3: Top importing countries or areas in 2010

Country or area	Value (million US$)	Avg. Growth (%) 06-10	Growth (%) 09-10	World share %	Cum.
World	26172.6	4.1	13.8	100.0	
USA	6179.1	-1.4	18.1	23.6	23.6
Germany	1835.6	3.9	7.4	7.0	30.6
France	1365.4	6.9	8.3	5.2	35.8
United Kingdom	1295.6	1.4	10.7	5.0	40.8
Canada	999.7	5.6	13.9	3.8	44.6
Russian Federation	973.6	26.0	39.8	3.7	48.3
Japan	905.0	4.2	6.8	3.5	51.8
Italy	695.2	5.2	17.4	2.7	54.4
Netherlands	652.9	7.7	7.8	2.5	56.9
Spain	582.5	1.9	11.6	2.2	59.2
Australia	576.5	8.8	15.5	2.2	61.4
Belgium	570.2	3.9	-1.7	2.2	63.5
China, Hong Kong SAR	469.9	-7.0	11.0	1.8	65.3
Switzerland	419.7	3.1	-0.6	1.6	66.9
Austria	386.2	2.3	-0.7	1.5	68.4

After several years of continuous growth marked by a peak of 141.3 bln US$ in 2008, the value (in current prices) of exports of manufactures of base metal, nes (SITC group 699) declined by 26.5 percent in 2009 but bounced back 16.5 percent in 2010 to a total of 121.0 bln US$ (see table 2). Imports also increased by 17.2 percent to 123.3 bln US$ for the same year (see table 3). Graph 1 shows that the growth in exports for 2010 in this product group was less than the increases in world exports of manufactured goods classified chiefly by material (SITC section 6) of 24.5 percent and in total world exports of 21.2 percent. Exports of manufactures of base metal, nes (SITC group 699) accounted for 6.3 percent of world exports of SITC section 6 and 0.8 percent of total world exports (see table 1).

China, Germany and USA were the top exporting countries in 2010 (see table 2). They accounted respectively for 14.6, 13.3 and 8.7 percent of world exports. Top destinations were USA, Germany and France (see table 3). By MDG regions (see graph 2), Developed Europe accounted for a majority of exports and imports. In 2010, its exports amounted to 59.4 bln US$ while imports were valued at 51.0 bln US$, resulting in a trade surplus of 8.4 bln US$. A larger trade surplus was recorded by Eastern Asia (+14.8 bln US$). Major deficits were recorded by Developed North America (-5.8 bln US$), Latin America and the Caribbean (-4.6 bln US$) and South-eastern Asia (-4.0 bln US$) among others.

Table 1: Imports (Imp.) and exports (Exp.), 1996-2010, in current prices

		1996	1997	1998	1999	2000	2001	2002	2003	2004	2005	2006	2007	2008	2009	2010
Values in Bln US$	Imp.	43.5	46.1	49.4	51.6	54.2	52.9	56.1	64.4	77.6	89.2	103.5	123.4	138.5	105.2	123.3
	Exp.	44.5	46.5	49.3	50.0	53.1	52.3	55.7	64.3	78.9	90.7	107.0	127.9	141.3	103.8	120.9
As a percentage of SITC section (%)	Imp.	5.4	5.5	6.0	6.3	6.1	6.2	6.3	6.3	6.1	6.2	6.2	6.3	6.4	6.8	6.5
	Exp.	5.5	5.6	6.1	6.2	6.1	6.3	6.3	6.3	6.2	6.4	6.4	6.5	6.5	6.7	6.3
As a percentage of world trade (%)	Imp.	0.8	0.8	0.9	0.9	0.8	0.8	0.9	0.8	0.8	0.8	0.9	0.9	0.9	0.8	0.8
	Exp.	0.8	0.8	0.9	0.9	0.8	0.9	0.9	0.9	0.9	0.9	0.9	0.9	0.9	0.8	0.8

Graph 1: Annual growth rates of exports, 1996–2010
(In percentage by year)

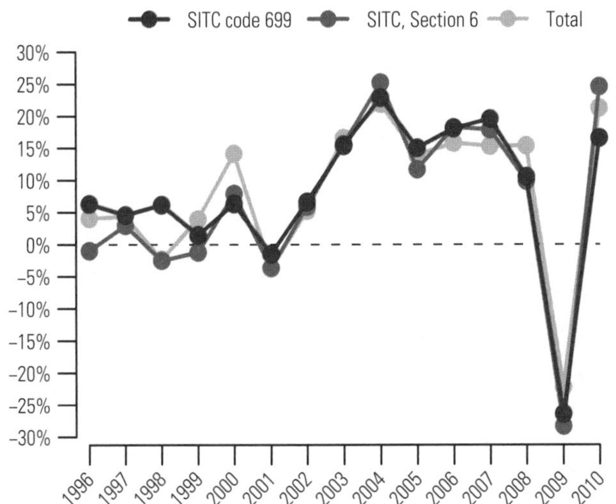

Table 2: Top exporting countries or areas in 2010

Country or area	Value (million US$)	Avg. Growth (%) 06-10	Growth (%) 09-10	World share %	Cum.
World	120912.6	3.1	16.5	100.0	
China	17614.1	7.7	29.4	14.6	14.6
Germany	16136.3	1.6	13.3	13.3	27.9
USA	10558.0	1.3	17.3	8.7	36.6
Italy	9009.7	-1.3	2.2	7.5	44.1
France	5218.8	0.3	8.0	4.3	48.4
Japan	4173.2	3.9	26.9	3.5	51.9
Other Asia, nes	3668.4	0.9	31.0	3.0	54.9
Austria	3624.8	4.7	15.5	3.0	57.9
Czech Rep.	3375.5	3.5	19.5	2.8	60.7
Mexico	3125.8	-5.2	11.5	2.6	63.3
Spain	3082.5	3.3	13.7	2.5	65.8
United Kingdom	3012.2	-2.1	6.6	2.5	68.3
Poland	2735.3	2.1	19.6	2.3	70.6
Rep. of Korea	2731.7	10.8	18.1	2.3	72.8
Netherlands	2219.7	1.9	7.7	1.8	74.7

Graph 2: Trade Balance by MDG regions 2010
(Bln US$)

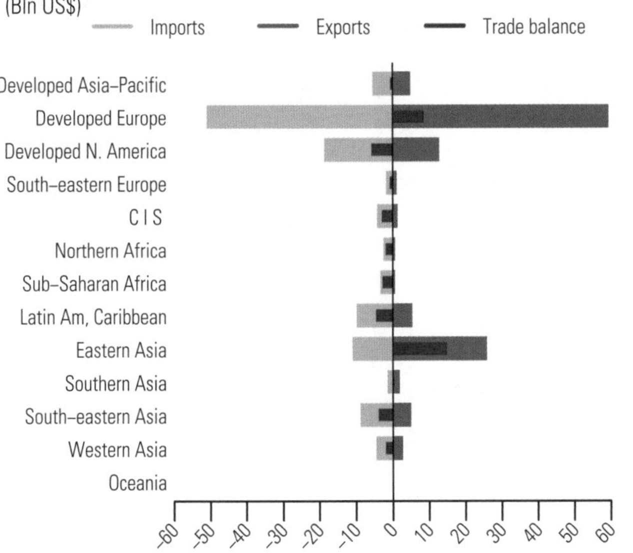

Table 3: Top importing countries or areas in 2010

Country or area	Value (million US$)	Avg. Growth (%) 06-10	Growth (%) 09-10	World share %	Cum.
World	123336.1	4.5	17.2	100.0	
USA	14568.9	-2.0	24.2	11.8	11.8
Germany	10350.5	2.3	14.8	8.4	20.2
France	6486.8	3.4	8.0	5.3	25.5
China	5480.5	11.1	30.1	4.4	29.9
Mexico	5337.9	-1.4	23.6	4.3	34.2
United Kingdom	4483.4	0.4	15.9	3.6	37.9
Canada	4013.6	0.1	13.4	3.3	41.1
Italy	3570.4	3.7	16.6	2.9	44.0
Japan	3526.2	2.1	18.1	2.9	46.9
Thailand	3373.9	12.6	36.1	2.7	49.6
Poland	2943.3	3.9	15.5	2.4	52.0
Rep. of Korea	2889.1	10.7	14.4	2.3	54.3
Spain	2754.8	-1.4	-4.7	2.2	56.6
Russian Federation	2634.8	20.8	43.1	2.1	58.7
Austria	2602.9	3.6	13.9	2.1	60.8

Machinery and transport equipment

(SITC Section 7)

711 Steam boilers, superheated water boiler; auxiliary plants; parts thereof

After a slight decline of 0.1 percent in 2009, the value (in current prices) of exports of steam boilers, superheated water boiler; auxiliary plants; parts thereof (SITC group 711) dropped further by 10.8 percent to reach 8.1 bln US$ in 2010 (see table 2). Imports also declined but at a higher rate of 25.4 percent and amounted to 6.6 bln US$ (see table 3). Graph 1 shows the contrast between the fall in exports for 2010 in this product group and the increases in world exports of machinery and transport equipment (SITC section 7) of 22.1 percent and in total world exports of 21.2 percent. Exports of steam boilers, superheated water boiler; auxiliary plants; parts thereof (SITC group 711) accounted for 0.2 percent of world exports of SITC section 7 and 0.1 percent of total world exports (see table 1).

In 2010, exports of China, the top exporting country, decreased by 9.4 percent and represented 32.5 percent of world exports (see table 2). Other major exporting countries were Rep. of Korea and Japan, respectively with 12.7 and 8.6 percent of world exports. Top destinations were Indonesia, USA and Saudi Arabia (see table 3). By MDG regions (see graph 2), Eastern Asia and Developed Europe recorded trade surpluses amounting respectively to 3.3 bln US$ and 0.9 bln US$ in 2010. Significant trade deficits were recorded by Western Asia (-0.8 bln US$), South-eastern Asia (-0.7 bln US$) and Latin America and the Caribbean (-0.4 bln US$).

Table 1: Imports (Imp.) and exports (Exp.), 1996-2010, in current prices

		1996	1997	1998	1999	2000	2001	2002	2003	2004	2005	2006	2007	2008	2009	2010
Values in Bln US$	Imp.	3.8	3.3	3.9	3.1	2.8	3.1	2.9	2.6	2.9	3.6	3.5	5.4	7.9	8.8	6.6
	Exp.	3.4	3.5	3.6	2.7	2.5	2.8	2.5	2.7	3.1	3.9	4.1	5.7	9.1	9.1	8.1
As a percentage of SITC section (%)	Imp.	0.2	0.2	0.2	0.1	0.1	0.1	0.1	0.1	0.1	0.1	0.1	0.1	0.1	0.2	0.1
	Exp.	0.2	0.2	0.2	0.1	0.1	0.1	0.1	0.1	0.1	0.1	0.1	0.1	0.2	0.2	0.2
As a percentage of world trade (%)	Imp.	0.1	0.1	0.1	0.1	0.0	0.0	0.0	0.0	0.0	0.0	0.0	0.0	0.0	0.1	0.0
	Exp.	0.1	0.1	0.1	0.0	0.0	0.0	0.0	0.0	0.0	0.0	0.0	0.0	0.1	0.1	0.1

Graph 1: Annual growth rates of exports, 1996–2010

(In percentage by year)

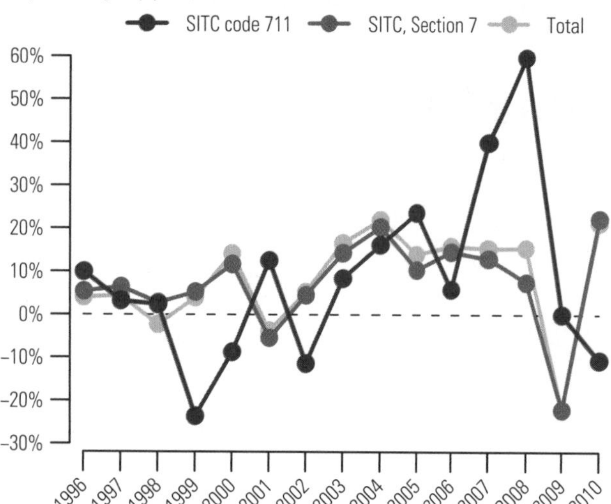

Graph 2: Trade Balance by MDG regions 2010

(Bln US$)

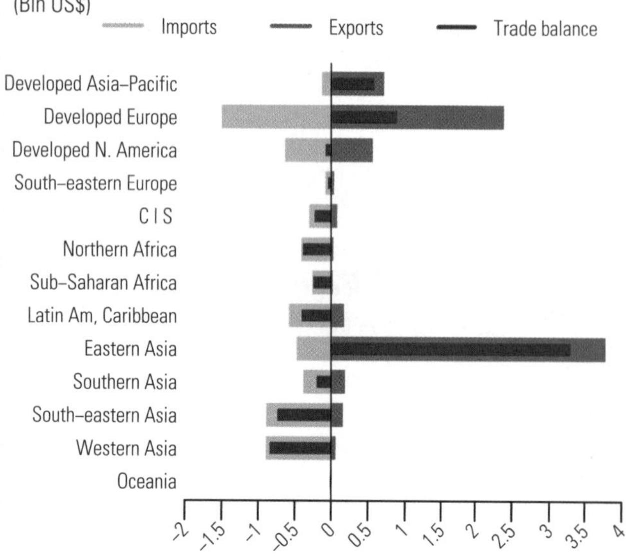

Table 2: Top exporting countries or areas in 2010

Country or area	Value (million US$)	Avg. Growth (%) 06-10	Growth (%) 09-10	World share %	Cum.
World	8128.6	18.8	-10.8	100.0	
China	2643.5	57.4	-9.4	32.5	32.5
Rep. of Korea	1033.5	32.7	-10.2	12.7	45.2
Japan	699.8	11.7	15.4	8.6	53.8
Italy	521.3	22.6	14.4	6.4	60.3
USA	452.6	5.3	-10.8	5.6	65.8
Germany	373.6	5.6	-8.2	4.6	70.4
Poland	234.7	13.1	-13.8	2.9	73.3
Finland	186.8	-1.6	4.7	2.3	75.6
India	167.5	24.9	15.8	2.1	77.7
Denmark	141.1	8.7	-22.4	1.7	79.4
Czech Rep.	106.8	21.9	37.8	1.3	80.7
Canada	104.3	-4.9	-45.6	1.3	82.0
Austria	99.7	14.8	-9.0	1.2	83.2
Mexico	95.6	33.7	-40.1	1.2	84.4
United Kingdom	93.7	1.7	-12.5	1.2	85.6

Table 3: Top importing countries or areas in 2010

Country or area	Value (million US$)	Avg. Growth (%) 06-10	Growth (%) 09-10	World share %	Cum.
World	6589.2	16.8	-25.4	100.0	
Indonesia	637.8	65.1	-6.6	9.7	9.7
USA	548.5	10.2	-38.8	8.3	18.0
Saudi Arabia	437.0	19.6	37.1	6.6	24.6
Algeria	256.4	88.3	-29.7	3.9	28.5
India	231.2	51.9	-52.8	3.5	32.0
Turkey	227.9	31.0	-38.4	3.5	35.5
United Kingdom	221.4	34.7	9.6	3.4	38.9
Netherlands	216.7	61.6	72.9	3.3	42.1
Germany	213.3	30.2	6.9	3.2	45.4
Rep. of Korea	189.6	-4.8	-22.5	2.9	48.3
Chile	179.1	57.5	-65.2	2.7	51.0
China	178.8	-7.7	-29.2	2.7	53.7
Russian Federation	154.7	27.4	6.8	2.3	56.0
Spain	148.1	9.4	-25.6	2.2	58.3
France	132.2	20.9	-6.7	2.0	60.3

The value (in current prices) of exports of steam turbines and other vapour turbines and parts thereof, nes (SITC group 712) decreased by 1.2 percent to 8.2 bln US$ in 2010 (see table 2). Imports had a decrease of 3.4 percent and totaled 7.7 bln US$ (see table 3). Graph 1 contrasts the decrease in exports for 2010 in this product group to the increases in world exports of machinery and transport equipment (SITC section 7) of 22.1 percent and in total world exports of 21.2 percent. Exports of steam turbines and other vapour turbines and parts thereof, nes (SITC group 712) accounted for 0.2 percent of world exports of SITC section 7 and 0.1 percent of total world exports (see table 1).

Japan, China and Germany were the top exporting countries in 2010 (see table 2). They accounted respectively for 22.3, 16.4 and 13.5 percent of world exports. Top destinations were South Africa, China and USA (see table 3). By MDG regions (see graph 2), Developed Europe accounted for a large share of exports of steam turbines and other vapour turbines and parts thereof, nes (SITC group 712). In 2010, its exports amounted to 3.3 bln US$ while imports amounted to 1.7 bln US$ resulting in a trade surplus of 1.6 bln US$. A large surplus was also recorded by Developed Asia-Pacific (+1.5 bln US$). Major deficits were recorded by South-eastern Asia (-0.9 bln US$), Sub-Saharan Africa (-0.8 bln US$) and Southern Asia (-0.6 bln US$).

Table 1: Imports (Imp.) and exports (Exp.), 1996-2010, in current prices

		1996	1997	1998	1999	2000	2001	2002	2003	2004	2005	2006	2007	2008	2009	2010
Values in Bln US$	Imp.	3.2	2.9	3.4	2.8	3.0	3.3	3.3	2.7	3.3	4.5	4.6	5.0	6.1	7.9	7.7
	Exp.	3.0	2.6	3.1	2.4	2.5	3.0	3.1	2.7	3.2	4.1	4.3	5.1	6.8	8.3	8.2
As a percentage of SITC section (%)	Imp.	0.2	0.1	0.2	0.1	0.1	0.1	0.1	0.1	0.1	0.1	0.1	0.1	0.1	0.2	0.1
	Exp.	0.1	0.1	0.1	0.1	0.1	0.1	0.1	0.1	0.1	0.1	0.1	0.1	0.1	0.2	0.2
As a percentage of world trade (%)	Imp.	0.1	0.1	0.1	0.0	0.0	0.1	0.1	0.0	0.0	0.0	0.0	0.0	0.0	0.1	0.1
	Exp.	0.1	0.0	0.1	0.0	0.0	0.0	0.0	0.0	0.0	0.0	0.0	0.0	0.0	0.1	0.1

Graph 1: Annual growth rates of exports, 1996–2010
(In percentage by year)

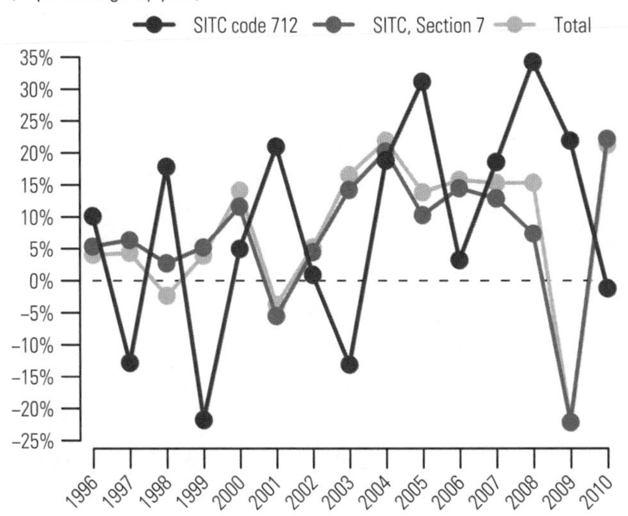

Graph 2: Trade Balance by MDG regions 2010
(Bln US$)

Imports — Exports — Trade balance

Developed Asia-Pacific
Developed Europe
Developed N. America
South-eastern Europe
C I S
Northern Africa
Sub-Saharan Africa
Latin Am, Caribbean
Eastern Asia
Southern Asia
South-eastern Asia
Western Asia
Oceania

-2 -1.5 -1 -0.5 0 0.5 1 1.5 2 2.5 3 3.5

Table 2: Top exporting countries or areas in 2010

Country or area	Value (million US$)	Avg. Growth (%) 06-10	Growth (%) 09-10	World share %	Cum.
World	8 175.8	17.6	-1.2	100.0	
Japan	1 824.3	10.0	16.6	22.3	22.3
China	1 343.5	66.8	9.1	16.4	38.7
Germany	1 102.8	10.1	-11.2	13.5	52.2
USA	705.5	13.3	-20.7	8.6	60.9
Italy	547.8	30.2	7.1	6.7	67.6
France	363.9	27.0	14.4	4.5	72.0
Sweden	292.8	59.2	-10.6	3.6	75.6
Poland	249.0	25.7	0.9	3.0	78.6
Rep. of Korea	171.4	22.1	11.7	2.1	80.7
Czech Rep.	157.5	4.6	-40.2	1.9	82.7
Mexico	140.6	22.3	14.7	1.7	84.4
United Kingdom	139.4	-6.8	-43.6	1.7	86.1
Russian Federation	127.7	19.7	6.2	1.6	87.7
Austria	126.4	0.5	-26.2	1.5	89.2
Singapore	85.7	2.7	62.4	1.0	90.2

Table 3: Top importing countries or areas in 2010

Country or area	Value (million US$)	Avg. Growth (%) 06-10	Growth (%) 09-10	World share %	Cum.
World	7 673.7	13.8	-3.4	100.0	
South Africa	783.2	123.3	121.4	10.2	10.2
China	624.5	-3.2	7.8	8.1	18.3
USA	588.5	15.2	1.6	7.7	26.0
Indonesia	505.2	39.9	29.2	6.6	32.6
Germany	438.7	13.8	-13.6	5.7	38.3
India	364.0	35.1	-22.0	4.7	43.1
Iran	231.7	72.0	8.4	3.0	46.1
Rep. of Korea	223.2	-2.3	-25.4	2.9	49.0
Japan	190.5	4.2	3.0	2.5	51.5
United Kingdom	186.1	21.8	8.9	2.4	53.9
Switzerland	168.3	16.4	-22.5	2.2	56.1
Romania	161.9	95.8	517.5	2.1	58.2
Algeria	155.1	111.7	121.9	2.0	60.2
Saudi Arabia	143.1	5.7	184.9	1.9	62.1
Chile	142.7	67.2	7.9	1.9	63.9

713 Internal combustion piston engines and parts thereof, nes

After several years of continuous growth marked by a peak of 150.7 bln US$ in 2008, the value (in current prices) of exports of internal combustion piston engines and parts thereof, nes (SITC group 713) dropped by 30.1 percent in 2009 but bounced back by a 29.9 percent rise in 2010 to 137.0 bln US$ (see table 2). Similarly, imports showed a 30.4 percent growth and totaled 138.3 bln US$ in 2010 (see table 3). Graph 1 shows that the increase in exports for 2010 in this product group was above the increases in world exports of machinery and transport equipment (SITC section 7) of 22.1 percent and in total world exports of 21.2 percent. Exports of internal combustion piston engines and parts thereof, nes (SITC group 713) accounted for 2.7 percent of world exports of SITC section 7 and 0.9 percent of total world exports (see table 1).

In 2010, top exporting countries were Germany, Japan and USA (see table 2). They accounted respectively for 16.0, 13.8 and 11.1 percent of world exports. USA, Germany and China were the top destinations (see table 3). By MDG regions (see graph 2), Developed Europe accounted for a majority of exports and imports of internal combustion piston engines and parts thereof, nes (SITC group 713). In 2010, its exports were valued at 69.3 bln US$ while imports amounted to 56.1 bln US$, resulting in a trade surplus of 13.2 bln US$. Developed Asia-Pacific also recorded a trade surplus of similar size (+15.4 bln US$). Top trade deficits were recorded by Developed North America (-6.7 bln US$), Eastern Asia (-5.1 bln US$) and Latin America & the Caribbean (-3.8 bln US$).

Table 1: Imports (Imp.) and exports (Exp.), 1996-2010, in current prices

		1996	1997	1998	1999	2000	2001	2002	2003	2004	2005	2006	2007	2008	2009	2010
Values in Bln US$	Imp.	56.7	58.9	63.9	67.6	70.8	68.2	75.0	85.4	102.3	113.3	122.4	144.0	151.4	106.1	138.3
	Exp.	57.7	59.4	62.3	66.1	69.2	66.2	71.9	83.7	101.0	113.2	124.3	144.9	150.7	105.4	137.0
As a percentage of SITC section (%)	Imp.	2.8	2.8	2.9	2.9	2.7	2.8	2.9	2.9	2.9	2.9	2.8	2.9	2.8	2.5	2.7
	Exp.	2.8	2.7	2.8	2.8	2.6	2.7	2.8	2.8	2.9	2.9	2.8	2.9	2.8	2.5	2.7
As a percentage of world trade (%)	Imp.	1.1	1.1	1.2	1.2	1.1	1.1	1.1	1.1	1.1	1.1	1.0	1.0	0.9	0.8	0.9
	Exp.	1.1	1.1	1.2	1.2	1.1	1.1	1.1	1.1	1.1	1.1	1.0	1.0	0.9	0.9	0.9

Graph 1: Annual growth rates of exports, 1996–2010
(In percentage by year)

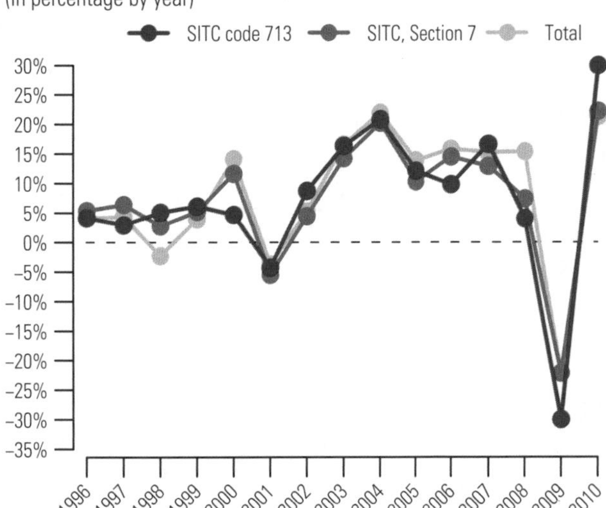

Graph 2: Trade Balance by MDG regions 2010
(Bln US$)

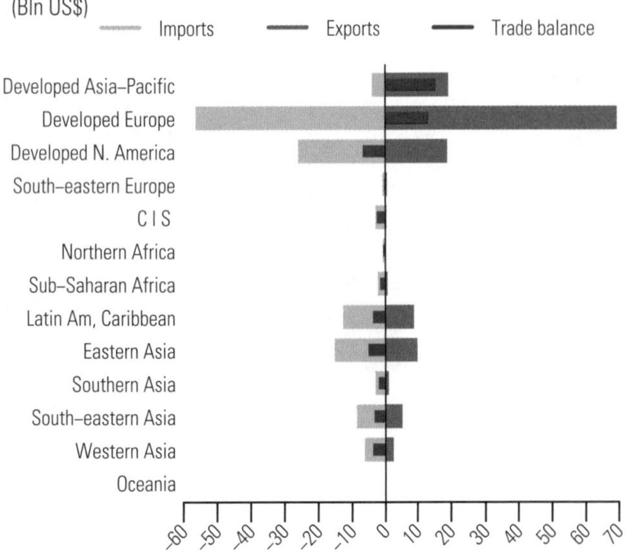

Table 2: Top exporting countries or areas in 2010

Country or area	Value (million US$)	Avg. Growth (%) 06-10	Growth (%) 09-10	World share %	Cum.
World	136 968.9	2.5	29.9	100.0	
Germany	21 906.2	-0.6	26.3	16.0	16.0
Japan	18 920.7	6.5	47.6	13.8	29.8
USA	15 210.9	-0.7	41.2	11.1	40.9
France	7 327.6	-0.4	20.4	5.3	46.3
United Kingdom	6 838.7	1.0	22.6	5.0	51.3
Mexico	5 977.1	5.0	75.9	4.4	55.6
Hungary	5 900.3	-3.6	11.1	4.3	59.9
Austria	5 820.6	7.0	22.0	4.2	64.2
China	5 128.2	19.8	39.2	3.7	67.9
Italy	4 936.6	1.2	17.1	3.6	71.5
Rep. of Korea	4 206.7	29.6	14.1	3.1	74.6
Poland	3 991.0	-2.1	14.2	2.9	77.5
Canada	3 848.0	-3.0	43.4	2.8	80.3
Brazil	2 529.0	-4.0	61.4	1.8	82.2
Thailand	2 508.7	12.2	59.4	1.8	84.0

Table 3: Top importing countries or areas in 2010

Country or area	Value (million US$)	Avg. Growth (%) 06-10	Growth (%) 09-10	World share %	Cum.
World	138 320.1	3.1	30.4	100.0	
USA	18 397.0	-2.8	50.3	13.3	13.3
Germany	15 452.7	1.4	19.9	11.2	24.5
China	11 186.9	25.1	40.4	8.1	32.6
Canada	7 340.4	-5.9	37.7	5.3	37.9
Mexico	6 948.6	8.3	65.5	5.0	42.9
United Kingdom	6 101.6	1.5	41.8	4.4	47.3
France	5 751.5	-1.3	15.9	4.2	51.5
Spain	4 151.0	-1.9	10.4	3.0	54.5
Italy	3 697.4	-1.9	15.3	2.7	57.1
Belgium	3 635.0	-3.2	20.5	2.6	59.8
Turkey	3 176.1	1.7	28.0	2.3	62.1
Poland	2 728.5	2.1	9.5	2.0	64.0
Rep. of Korea	2 644.8	10.1	24.8	1.9	65.9
Thailand	2 632.5	16.2	77.2	1.9	67.8
Austria	2 625.2	-1.3	20.7	1.9	69.7

Engines and motors, non-electric; parts, nes (not those of 712, 713 and 718) 714

In 2010, the value (in current prices) of exports of engines and motors, non-electric; parts, nes (SITC group 714) increased by 3.0 percent to 76.2 bln US$ (see table 2). For the same year, imports went up by 1.1 percent to 88.8 bln US$ (see table 3). Graph 1 shows that the rise in exports for 2010 in this product group was way below the increases in world exports of machinery and transport equipment (SITC section 7) of 22.1 percent and in total world exports of 21.2 percent. Exports of engines and motors, non-electric; parts, nes (SITC group 714) accounted for 1.5 percent of world exports of SITC section 7 and 0.5 percent of total world exports (see table 1).

United Kingdom, the top exporting country in 2010, accounted for 20.5 percent of world exports (see table 2). Other major exporting countries were France and USA, respectively with 12.9 and 12.1 percent of world exports. USA, United Kingdom and Germany were the top destinations (see table 3). By MDG regions (see graph 2), Developed Europe accounted for a majority of trade in engines and motors, non-electric; parts, nes (SITC group 714). In 2010, its exports and imports were valued respectively at 47.3 bln US$ and 35.1 bln US$, resulting in a trade surplus of 12.2 bln US$. Major deficits were recorded by Developed North America (-5.3 bln US$), Western Asia (-4.3 bln US$) and South-eastern Asia (-4.3 bln US$).

Table 1: Imports (Imp.) and exports (Exp.), 1996-2010, in current prices

		1996	1997	1998	1999	2000	2001	2002	2003	2004	2005	2006	2007	2008	2009	2010
Values in Bln US$	Imp.	28.6	35.1	40.6	42.6	45.5	50.2	48.0	47.6	53.9	59.9	68.2	75.3	87.2	87.8	88.8
	Exp.	28.8	34.8	42.0	44.8	47.6	55.3	52.4	53.7	61.5	68.0	78.0	83.0	94.8	74.0	76.2
As a percentage of SITC section (%)	Imp.	1.4	1.6	1.8	1.8	1.7	2.0	1.9	1.6	1.5	1.5	1.5	1.5	1.6	2.1	1.7
	Exp.	1.4	1.6	1.9	1.9	1.8	2.2	2.0	1.8	1.7	1.7	1.7	1.6	1.8	1.8	1.5
As a percentage of world trade (%)	Imp.	0.5	0.6	0.7	0.7	0.7	0.8	0.7	0.6	0.6	0.6	0.6	0.5	0.5	0.7	0.6
	Exp.	0.5	0.6	0.8	0.8	0.8	0.9	0.8	0.7	0.7	0.7	0.7	0.6	0.6	0.6	0.5

Graph 1: Annual growth rates of exports, 1996–2010

(In percentage by year)

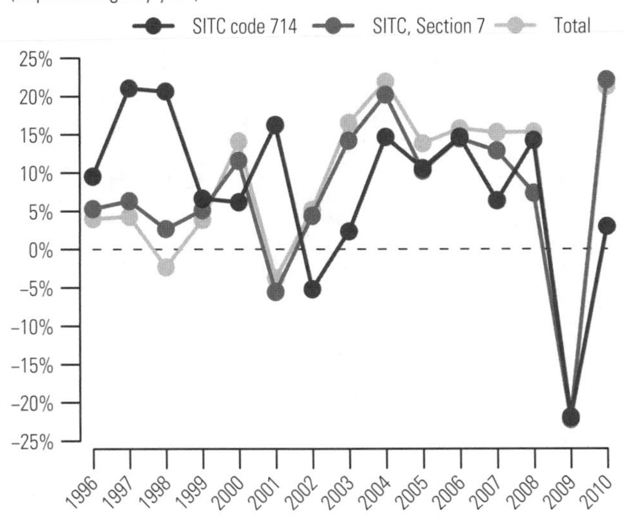

Table 2: Top exporting countries or areas in 2010

Country or area	Value (million US$)	Avg. Growth (%) 06-10	Growth (%) 09-10	World share %	Cum.
World	76 225.0	-0.6	3.0	100.0	
United Kingdom	15 632.7	0.3	4.6	20.5	20.5
France	9 838.3	10.5	5.6	12.9	33.4
USA	9 219.5	-20.2	-6.2	12.1	45.5
Germany	8 439.6	-2.3	6.0	11.1	56.6
Canada	3 982.2	5.8	1.1	5.2	61.8
Italy	3 471.9	8.4	-9.2	4.6	66.4
Japan	3 441.2	7.3	-8.9	4.5	70.9
Netherlands	2 339.7	7.2	-1.1	3.1	73.9
China, Hong Kong SAR	2 332.9	17.6	-8.6	3.1	77.0
Switzerland	1 814.2	5.2	-19.3	2.4	79.4
Singapore	1 738.1	8.1	5.7	2.3	81.7
China	1 535.6	22.0	30.8	2.0	83.7
Mexico	1 498.5	7.7	25.7	2.0	85.6
Sweden	1 344.0	8.5	59.5	1.8	87.4
Russian Federation	1 302.6	5.9	23.0	1.7	89.1

Graph 2: Trade Balance by MDG regions 2010

(Bln US$)

Imports
Exports
Trade balance

Developed Asia-Pacific
Developed Europe
Developed N. America
South-eastern Europe
C I S
Northern Africa
Sub-Saharan Africa
Latin Am, Caribbean
Eastern Asia
Southern Asia
South-eastern Asia
Western Asia
Oceania

-40 -30 -20 -10 0 10 20 30 40 50

Table 3: Top importing countries or areas in 2010

Country or area	Value (million US$)	Avg. Growth (%) 06-10	Growth (%) 09-10	World share %	Cum.
World	88 801.6	6.8	1.1	100.0	
USA	14 703.4	4.1	2.7	16.6	16.6
United Kingdom	11 843.5	11.1	7.8	13.3	29.9
Germany	7 204.5	-5.1	4.5	8.1	38.0
France	6 833.5	7.1	-8.0	7.7	45.7
Singapore	4 586.2	15.4	28.6	5.2	50.9
Japan	3 869.6	-2.0	-13.5	4.4	55.2
Canada	3 783.8	6.4	-5.0	4.3	59.5
China, Hong Kong SAR	3 522.3	13.4	-13.4	4.0	63.5
China	2 841.5	15.2	26.6	3.2	66.7
United Arab Emirates	2 208.2	16.9	-0.9	2.5	69.1
Netherlands	1 971.8	8.3	-20.6	2.2	71.4
Brazil	1 768.8	8.7	-14.0	2.0	73.4
Italy	1 555.7	3.5	-9.0	1.8	75.1
Mexico	1 264.2	11.6	27.9	1.4	76.5
Rep. of Korea	1 241.6	13.0	10.9	1.4	77.9

716 Rotating electric plant and parts thereof, nes

From 2006 to 2010, the value (in current prices) of exports of rotating electric plant and parts thereof, nes (SITC group 716) increased on average by 7.2 percent and reached 80.5 bln US$ in 2010 (see table 2). During the same period, imports increased at an annual average rate of 7.5 percent and amounted to 83.3 bln US$ in 2010 (see table 3). Graph 1 shows that the growth in exports for 2010 in this product group was below the increases in world exports of machinery and transport equipment (SITC section 7) of 22.1 percent and in total world exports of 21.2 percent. Exports of rotating electric plant and parts thereof, nes (SITC group 716) accounted for 1.6 percent of world exports of SITC section 7 and 0.5 percent of total world exports (see table 1).

China, Germany and USA were the top exporting countries in 2010 (see table 2). They accounted respectively for 15.6, 14.5 and 9.9 percent of world exports. USA, China and Germany were also the top destinations (see table 3). By MDG regions (see graph 2), Developed Europe accounted for a majority of exports and imports of rotating electric plant and parts thereof, nes (SITC group 716). In 2010, its exports were valued at 37.6 bln US$ while imports amounted to 25.1 bln US$, resulting in a trade surplus of 12.5 bln US$. Trade surpluses were also recorded by Eastern Asia (+6.0 bln US$) and Developed Asia-Pacific (+2.1 bln US$). Top trade deficits were recorded by Latin America & the Caribbean (-4.2 bln US$), Developed North America (-4.1 bln US$) and Western Asia (-3.9 bln US$).

Table 1: Imports (Imp.) and exports (Exp.), 1996-2010, in current prices

		1996	1997	1998	1999	2000	2001	2002	2003	2004	2005	2006	2007	2008	2009	2010
Values in Bln US$	Imp.	27.1	28.6	30.1	31.1	32.5	34.7	36.6	39.8	45.2	52.8	62.4	76.0	89.6	77.3	83.3
	Exp.	26.3	26.8	27.8	29.0	30.8	32.5	33.0	37.6	44.6	51.5	61.0	72.9	87.2	72.0	80.5
As a percentage of SITC section (%)	Imp.	1.3	1.3	1.4	1.3	1.2	1.4	1.4	1.4	1.3	1.3	1.4	1.5	1.7	1.8	1.6
	Exp.	1.3	1.2	1.2	1.2	1.2	1.3	1.3	1.3	1.3	1.3	1.4	1.4	1.6	1.7	1.6
As a percentage of world trade (%)	Imp.	0.5	0.5	0.6	0.5	0.5	0.6	0.6	0.5	0.5	0.5	0.5	0.5	0.6	0.6	0.6
	Exp.	0.5	0.5	0.5	0.5	0.5	0.5	0.5	0.5	0.5	0.5	0.5	0.5	0.5	0.6	0.5

Graph 1: Annual growth rates of exports, 1996–2010
(In percentage by year)

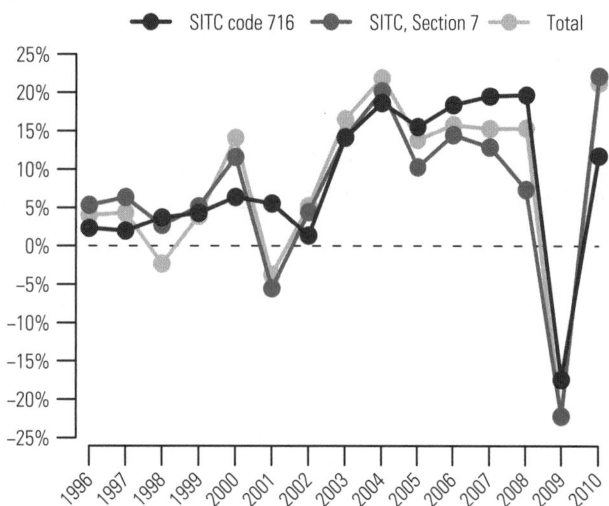

Graph 2: Trade Balance by MDG regions 2010
(Bln US$)

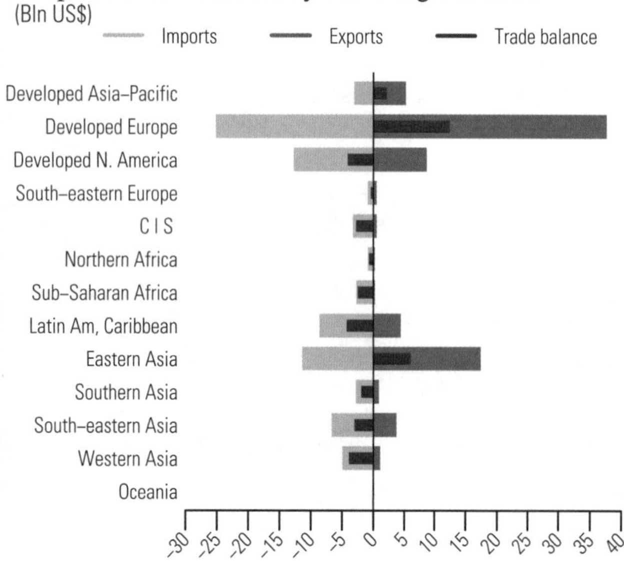

Table 2: Top exporting countries or areas in 2010

Country or area	Value (million US$)	Avg. Growth (%) 06-10	Growth (%) 09-10	World share %	Cum.
World	80470.4	7.2	11.7	100.0	
China	12590.2	17.8	34.2	15.6	15.6
Germany	11635.7	9.6	16.1	14.5	30.1
USA	7977.3	7.3	16.6	9.9	40.0
Japan	5038.9	5.0	3.2	6.3	46.3
Italy	3153.6	4.1	-2.4	3.9	50.2
Mexico	3003.4	2.1	32.9	3.7	53.9
France	2951.0	0.9	3.5	3.7	57.6
Spain	2787.0	17.9	-11.3	3.5	61.1
United Kingdom	2713.1	-0.6	3.5	3.4	64.4
China, Hong Kong SAR	2581.4	0.5	40.9	3.2	67.6
Denmark	2508.0	-3.9	-17.9	3.1	70.8
Czech Rep.	1672.0	7.0	14.1	2.1	72.8
Finland	1648.4	7.4	-14.8	2.0	74.9
Rep. of Korea	1495.2	14.8	21.8	1.9	76.7
Austria	1458.9	6.5	-4.5	1.8	78.6

Table 3: Top importing countries or areas in 2010

Country or area	Value (million US$)	Avg. Growth (%) 06-10	Growth (%) 09-10	World share %	Cum.
World	83271.1	7.5	7.7	100.0	
USA	9770.8	-0.2	0.1	11.7	11.7
China	5943.0	6.1	3.8	7.1	18.9
Germany	5921.3	1.8	10.4	7.1	26.0
Canada	2958.5	5.5	35.8	3.6	29.5
China, Hong Kong SAR	2716.8	3.2	39.2	3.3	32.8
United Kingdom	2684.4	12.5	27.0	3.2	36.0
Italy	2664.7	7.1	5.1	3.2	39.2
France	2636.8	3.9	12.0	3.2	42.4
Russian Federation	2522.0	33.1	-3.9	3.0	45.4
Mexico	2422.2	3.1	35.3	2.9	48.3
Japan	2065.1	-0.6	18.9	2.5	50.8
Rep. of Korea	2013.1	7.1	13.6	2.4	53.2
Turkey	1955.2	33.2	21.8	2.3	55.6
Brazil	1727.2	34.5	57.4	2.1	57.6
Venezuela	1519.4	76.7	257.7	1.8	59.5

The value (in current prices) of exports of power generating machinery and parts thereof, nes (SITC group 718) increased by 21.0 percent and amounted to 20.6 bln US$ in 2010 (see table 2). Imports for the same year grew by 19.0 percent to 22.3 bln US$ (see table 3). Graph 1 shows that the rise in exports for 2010 in this product group was slightly less than the increase in world exports of machinery and transport equipment (SITC section 7) of 22.1 percent and that of total world exports of 21.2 percent. Exports of power generating machinery and parts thereof, nes (SITC group 718) accounted for 0.4 percent of world exports of SITC section 7 and 0.1 percent of total world exports (see table 1).

The top exporting countries in 2010 were Germany, USA and Japan (see table 2). They accounted respectively for 17.6, 11.7 and 8.2 percent of world exports. USA, China and Germany were the top destinations (see table 3). By MDG regions (see graph 2), Developed Europe accounted for a majority of exports and imports. In 2010, its exports and imports were valued respectively at 11.1 bln US$ and 8.9 bln US$, resulting in a trade surplus of 2.2 bln US$. Top trade deficits were recorded by Eastern Asia (-1.8 bln US$) and South-eastern Asia (-0.9 bln US$).

Table 1: Imports (Imp.) and exports (Exp.), 1996-2010, in current prices

		1996	1997	1998	1999	2000	2001	2002	2003	2004	2005	2006	2007	2008	2009	2010
Values in Bln US$	Imp.	6.4	6.6	6.3	6.9	7.3	7.1	7.5	9.2	10.6	11.8	13.2	17.0	21.8	18.7	22.3
	Exp.	5.2	5.4	5.2	6.3	6.1	6.1	6.7	8.1	9.7	11.4	13.1	16.2	20.7	17.0	20.6
As a percentage of SITC section (%)	Imp.	0.3	0.3	0.3	0.3	0.3	0.3	0.3	0.3	0.3	0.3	0.3	0.3	0.4	0.4	0.4
	Exp.	0.3	0.2	0.2	0.3	0.2	0.2	0.3	0.3	0.3	0.3	0.3	0.3	0.4	0.4	0.4
As a percentage of world trade (%)	Imp.	0.1	0.1	0.1	0.1	0.1	0.1	0.1	0.1	0.1	0.1	0.1	0.1	0.1	0.1	0.1
	Exp.	0.1	0.1	0.1	0.1	0.1	0.1	0.1	0.1	0.1	0.1	0.1	0.1	0.1	0.1	0.1

Graph 1: Annual growth rates of exports, 1996–2010

(In percentage by year)

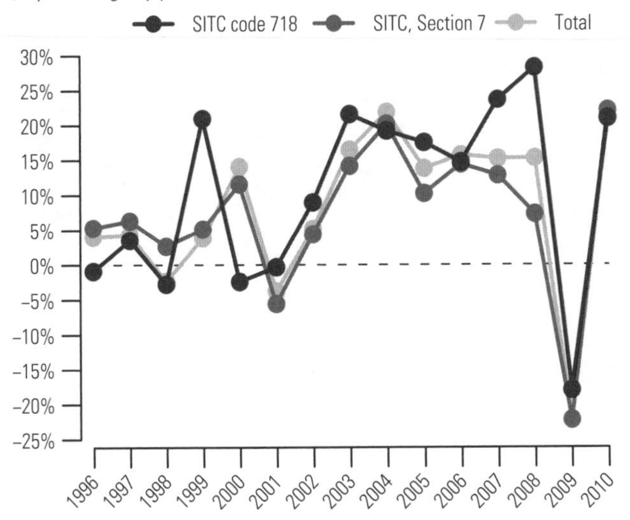

Table 2: Top exporting countries or areas in 2010

Country or area	Value (million US$)	Avg. Growth (%) 06-10	Growth (%) 09-10	World share %	Cum.
World	20580.8	12.0	21.0	100.0	
Germany	3615.1	7.5	7.8	17.6	17.6
USA	2406.0	13.4	43.8	11.7	29.3
Japan	1696.2	17.0	77.8	8.2	37.5
Russian Federation	1464.1	14.8	19.3	7.1	44.6
China	1427.1	39.7	37.0	6.9	51.5
Sweden	1057.5	3.3	-3.0	5.1	56.7
France	902.1	16.9	35.5	4.4	61.1
Belgium	867.9	-3.2	-1.1	4.2	65.3
Denmark	742.5	28.2	44.8	3.6	68.9
Spain	699.6	24.8	1.8	3.4	72.3
Canada	595.3	4.7	-8.0	2.9	75.2
United Kingdom	488.1	2.5	13.5	2.4	77.6
Italy	488.0	5.2	-5.0	2.4	79.9
Netherlands	449.2	14.9	11.6	2.2	82.1
Austria	332.6	6.9	3.0	1.6	83.7

Graph 2: Trade Balance by MDG regions 2010

(Bln US$)

Imports — Exports — Trade balance

Developed Asia-Pacific
Developed Europe
Developed N. America
South-eastern Europe
C I S
Northern Africa
Sub-Saharan Africa
Latin Am, Caribbean
Eastern Asia
Southern Asia
South-eastern Asia
Western Asia
Oceania

-10 -8 -6 -4 -2 0 2 4 6 8 10 12

Table 3: Top importing countries or areas in 2010

Country or area	Value (million US$)	Avg. Growth (%) 06-10	Growth (%) 09-10	World share %	Cum.
World	22277.4	13.9	19.0	100.0	
USA	2806.1	11.5	9.0	12.6	12.6
China	2662.9	23.3	23.3	12.0	24.5
Germany	2658.3	10.8	29.1	11.9	36.5
France	1670.7	13.7	-2.0	7.5	44.0
Japan	746.3	23.5	-11.1	3.3	47.3
Canada	724.0	11.0	27.9	3.2	50.6
Ukraine	656.9	13.3	24.5	2.9	53.5
United Kingdom	618.3	3.7	65.8	2.8	56.3
Sweden	502.5	4.8	28.5	2.3	58.6
Other Asia, nes	450.6	16.8	117.0	2.0	60.6
Viet Nam	*412.6*	46.8	66.9	1.9	62.4
Rep. of Korea	401.6	21.3	2.4	1.8	64.2
Australia	385.6	27.3	85.4	1.7	66.0
Brazil	375.4	21.9	63.9	1.7	67.7
Italy	349.2	1.9	34.7	1.6	69.2

Source: UN Comtrade

721 Agricultural machinery (excluding tractors) and parts thereof

After a significant decline in 2009, the value (in current prices) of exports of agricultural machinery (excluding tractors) and parts thereof (SITC group 721) rose by 9.1 percent amounting to 28.9 bln US$ in 2010 (see table 2). Imports also grew by 8.5 percent and totaled 28.1 bln US$ (see table 3). Graph 1 shows that the rise in exports for 2010 in this product group was way below the increases in world exports of machinery and transport equipment (SITC section 7) of 22.1 percent and in total world exports of 21.2 percent. Exports of agricultural machinery (excluding tractors) and parts thereof (SITC group 721) accounted for 0.6 percent of world exports of SITC section 7 and 0.2 percent of total world exports (see table 1).

Germany, USA and Italy were the top exporting countries in 2010 (see table 2). They accounted respectively for 16.9, 15.7 and 8.5 percent of world exports. USA, France and Germany were the top destinations (see table 3). By MDG regions (see graph 2), Developed Europe accounted for a majority of trade in agricultural machinery (excluding tractors) and parts thereof (SITC group 721). In 2010, its exports and imports were valued respectively at 17.6 bln US$ and 13.0 bln US$, resulting in a trade surplus of 4.6 bln US$. Trade surpluses were also recorded by Eastern Asia (+1.4 bln US$) and Developed North America (+1.0 bln US$). Top deficits were recorded by Commonwealth of Independent States (-2.0 bln US$) and Latin America and the Caribbean (-1.3 bln US$).

Table 1: Imports (Imp.) and exports (Exp.), 1996-2010, in current prices

		1996	1997	1998	1999	2000	2001	2002	2003	2004	2005	2006	2007	2008	2009	2010
Values in Bln US$	Imp.	12.0	12.3	12.3	11.4	10.7	11.0	12.5	14.9	17.6	19.9	22.2	27.0	34.4	25.9	28.1
	Exp.	11.6	12.0	12.3	11.1	10.8	11.0	12.5	14.9	17.9	20.5	22.6	27.8	35.9	26.5	28.9
As a percentage of SITC section (%)	Imp.	0.6	0.6	0.6	0.5	0.4	0.4	0.5	0.5	0.5	0.5	0.5	0.5	0.6	0.6	0.5
	Exp.	0.6	0.6	0.6	0.5	0.4	0.4	0.5	0.5	0.5	0.5	0.5	0.6	0.7	0.6	0.6
As a percentage of world trade (%)	Imp.	0.2	0.2	0.2	0.2	0.2	0.2	0.2	0.2	0.2	0.2	0.2	0.2	0.2	0.2	0.2
	Exp.	0.2	0.2	0.2	0.2	0.2	0.2	0.2	0.2	0.2	0.2	0.2	0.2	0.2	0.2	0.2

Graph 1: Annual growth rates of exports, 1996–2010
(In percentage by year)

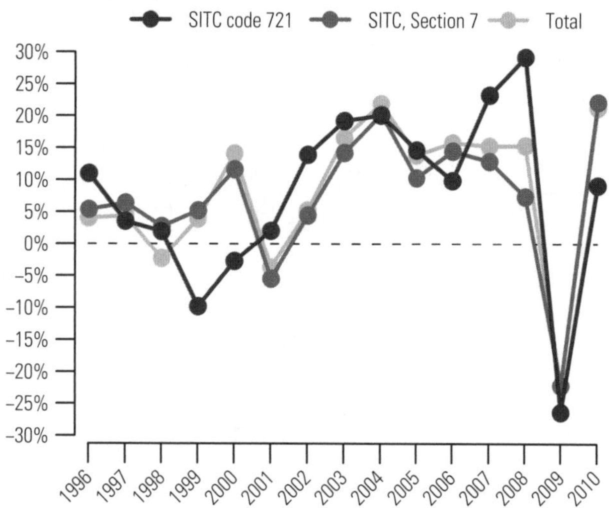

Table 2: Top exporting countries or areas in 2010

Country or area	Value (million US$)	Avg. Growth (%) 06-10	Growth (%) 09-10	World share %	Cum.
World	28872.6	6.4	9.1	100.0	
Germany	4881.7	2.3	5.5	16.9	16.9
USA	4531.9	7.4	13.8	15.7	32.6
Italy	2442.5	1.7	8.1	8.5	41.1
China	1943.6	34.1	25.6	6.7	47.8
Netherlands	1779.3	7.0	7.4	6.2	54.0
France	1594.0	2.6	1.7	5.5	59.5
Belgium	1288.1	1.2	-13.8	4.5	63.9
Canada	1153.7	4.4	-1.3	4.0	67.9
Denmark	745.7	2.7	-3.0	2.6	70.5
Brazil	697.5	14.6	70.9	2.4	72.9
United Kingdom	697.5	5.8	13.7	2.4	75.3
Austria	637.1	7.7	-2.8	2.2	77.6
Poland	576.6	8.5	12.5	2.0	79.6
Sweden	503.7	4.2	26.6	1.7	81.3
Japan	483.8	7.9	7.1	1.7	83.0

Graph 2: Trade Balance by MDG regions 2010
(Bln US$)

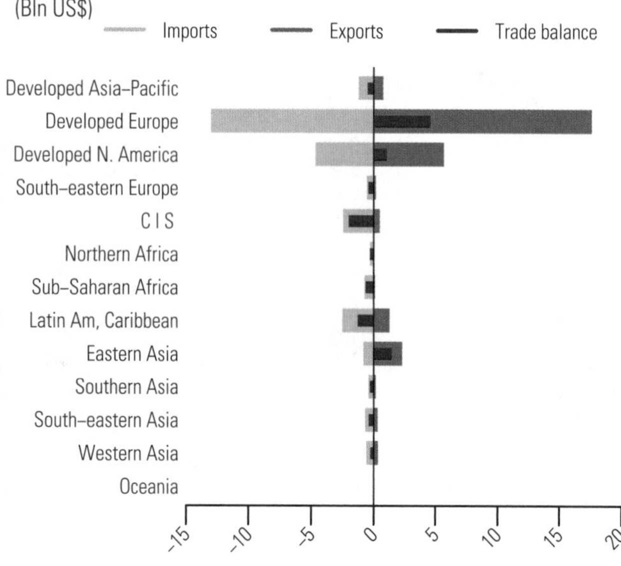

Table 3: Top importing countries or areas in 2010

Country or area	Value (million US$)	Avg. Growth (%) 06-10	Growth (%) 09-10	World share %	Cum.
World	28076.6	6.1	8.5	100.0	
USA	2664.6	5.9	9.8	9.5	9.5
France	2175.7	3.7	-6.4	7.7	17.2
Germany	2072.0	1.3	1.9	7.4	24.6
Canada	2005.7	10.3	15.3	7.1	31.8
Russian Federation	1297.3	2.6	45.6	4.6	36.4
United Kingdom	1227.0	2.1	-5.1	4.4	40.8
Netherlands	806.8	7.3	-0.2	2.9	43.6
Belgium	778.3	-1.3	-16.7	2.8	46.4
Australia	699.0	7.8	-6.0	2.5	48.9
Poland	685.0	16.6	24.5	2.4	51.3
Venezuela	660.2	47.4	77.1	2.4	53.7
Sweden	642.3	12.1	32.3	2.3	56.0
Italy	634.9	9.1	21.5	2.3	58.2
Austria	593.5	10.5	-1.6	2.1	60.3
China	497.0	20.0	22.8	1.8	62.1

In 2010, the value (in current prices) of exports of tractors (SITC group 722) increased by 5.9 percent and amounted to 17.1 bln US$ (see table 2). For the same year, imports increased by 6.8 percent to 16.6 bln US$ (see table 3). Graph 1 shows that the increase in exports for 2010 in this product group was well below the increases in world exports of machinery and transport equipment (SITC section 7) of 22.1 percent and in total world exports of 21.2 percent. Exports of tractors (SITC group 722) accounted for 0.3 percent of world exports of SITC section 7 and 0.1 percent of total world exports (see table 1).

Germany, USA and Japan were the top exporting countries in 2010 (see table 2). They accounted respectively for 17.2, 15.9 and 10.2 percent of world exports. Top destinations were USA, Canada and France (see table 3). By MDG regions (see graph 2), Developed Europe accounted for a majority of trade in tractors (SITC group 722). In 2010, its exports and imports amounted respectively to 9.1 bln US$ and 7.6 bln US$, resulting in a trade surplus of 1.5 bln US$. Developed Asia-Pacific also recorded a trade surplus amounting to 1.1 bln US$. Top trade deficits were recorded by Developed North America (-0.6 bln US$) and Sub-Saharan Africa (-0.5 bln US$).

Table 1: Imports (Imp.) and exports (Exp.), 1996-2010, in current prices

		1996	1997	1998	1999	2000	2001	2002	2003	2004	2005	2006	2007	2008	2009	2010
Values in Bln US$	Imp.	9.4	9.6	9.4	7.7	7.6	7.4	8.6	10.4	13.1	14.7	16.0	17.9	22.4	15.6	16.6
	Exp.	9.3	10.0	9.6	8.2	7.8	7.4	8.7	10.2	12.7	14.2	15.6	18.9	24.0	16.2	17.1
As a percentage of SITC section (%)	Imp.	0.5	0.5	0.4	0.3	0.3	0.3	0.3	0.4	0.4	0.4	0.4	0.4	0.4	0.4	0.3
	Exp.	0.5	0.5	0.4	0.3	0.3	0.3	0.3	0.3	0.4	0.4	0.4	0.4	0.4	0.4	0.3
As a percentage of world trade (%)	Imp.	0.2	0.2	0.2	0.1	0.1	0.1	0.1	0.1	0.1	0.1	0.1	0.1	0.1	0.1	0.1
	Exp.	0.2	0.2	0.2	0.1	0.1	0.1	0.1	0.1	0.1	0.1	0.1	0.1	0.2	0.1	0.1

Graph 1: Annual growth rates of exports, 1996–2010

(In percentage by year)

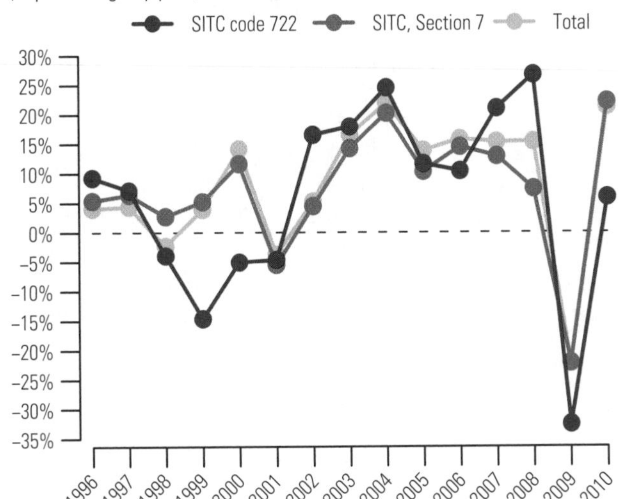

Graph 2: Trade Balance by MDG regions 2010

(Bln US$)

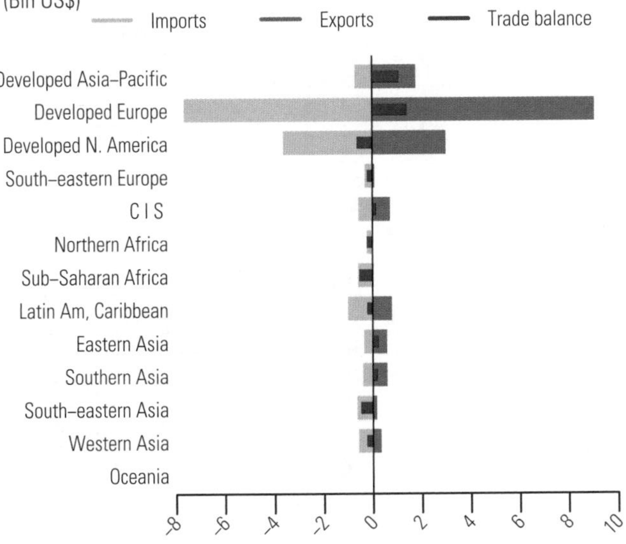

Table 2: Top exporting countries or areas in 2010

Country or area	Value (million US$)	Avg. Growth (%) 06-10	Growth (%) 09-10	World share %	Cum.
World	17122.0	2.3	5.9	100.0	
Germany	2949.1	0.3	-7.6	17.2	17.2
USA	2730.7	2.9	1.8	15.9	33.2
Japan	1749.9	-1.1	33.8	10.2	43.4
Italy	1685.2	1.0	-1.8	9.8	53.2
United Kingdom	1234.2	-4.4	1.9	7.2	60.4
France	1075.0	0.5	2.3	6.3	66.7
Belarus	664.2	3.2	17.6	3.9	70.6
Austria	578.9	9.3	-13.2	3.4	74.0
Brazil	530.3	3.9	18.3	3.1	77.1
India	524.8	23.4	97.5	3.1	80.1
Finland	424.3	-1.2	2.6	2.5	82.6
China	328.7	11.7	19.1	1.9	84.5
Canada	255.8	4.1	0.5	1.5	86.0
Belgium	255.6	6.3	-20.6	1.5	87.5
Rep. of Korea	252.8	5.6	12.8	1.5	89.0

Table 3: Top importing countries or areas in 2010

Country or area	Value (million US$)	Avg. Growth (%) 06-10	Growth (%) 09-10	World share %	Cum.
World	16635.2	1.0	6.8	100.0	
USA	2414.7	-6.7	21.0	14.5	14.5
Canada	1208.4	7.1	14.2	7.3	21.8
France	1196.0	2.3	-17.4	7.2	29.0
Germany	979.0	4.0	-1.8	5.9	34.9
United Kingdom	831.3	5.3	-7.3	5.0	39.9
Poland	613.8	15.6	45.1	3.7	43.5
Spain	488.5	-3.2	18.3	2.9	46.5
Italy	474.0	5.4	0.1	2.8	49.3
Australia	455.3	3.1	-23.2	2.7	52.1
Belgium	409.7	-1.8	-15.9	2.5	54.5
Austria	362.5	10.8	15.9	2.2	56.7
Thailand	357.3	9.5	3.6	2.1	58.9
Netherlands	345.7	5.8	12.9	2.1	60.9
Sweden	313.1	8.5	34.9	1.9	62.8
Norway	274.4	1.1	56.5	1.6	64.5

 Source: UN Comtrade

723 Civil engineering and contractors' plant and equipment; parts thereof

After several years of continuous growth marked by a peak of 125.1 bln US$ in 2008, the value (in current prices) of exports of civil engineering and contractors' plant and equipment; parts thereof (SITC group 723) declined by 38.5 percent in 2009 but bounced back in 2010 by 24.2 percent to reach 95.6 bln US$ (see table 2). Imports also increased by 21.8 percent to 89.4 bln US$ in 2010 (see table 3). Graph 1 shows that the increase in exports for 2010 in this product group was larger than the increases in world exports of machinery and transport equipment (SITC section 7) of 22.1 percent and in total world exports of 21.2 percent. Exports of civil engineering and contractors' plant and equipment; parts thereof (SITC group 723) accounted for 1.9 percent of world exports of SITC section 7 and 0.6 percent of total world exports (see table 1).

The top exporting countries in 2010 were USA, Japan and Germany (see table 2). They accounted respectively for 18.8, 12.8 and 8.5 percent of world exports. China, USA and Singapore were the top importing countries (see table 3). By MDG regions (see graph 2), top trade surpluses were recorded by Developed Europe (+13.4 bln US$), Developed Asia-Pacific (+9.2 bln US$) and Developed North America (+8.3 bln US$). Top trade deficits were recorded by South-eastern Asia (-5.5 bln US$), Western Asia (-5.3 bln US$) and Latin America & the Caribbean (-5.3 bln US$).

Table 1: Imports (Imp.) and exports (Exp.), 1996-2010, in current prices

		1996	1997	1998	1999	2000	2001	2002	2003	2004	2005	2006	2007	2008	2009	2010
Values in Bln US$	Imp.	29.7	30.8	31.5	29.0	29.4	30.8	33.7	40.3	52.0	65.4	81.0	103.3	118.1	73.4	89.4
	Exp.	30.6	33.3	35.1	31.0	32.5	34.0	36.3	43.6	56.0	69.5	84.3	108.3	125.1	77.0	95.6
As a percentage of SITC section (%)	Imp.	1.5	1.4	1.4	1.2	1.1	1.2	1.3	1.4	1.5	1.7	1.8	2.1	2.2	1.7	1.7
	Exp.	1.5	1.5	1.6	1.3	1.2	1.4	1.4	1.5	1.6	1.8	1.9	2.1	2.3	1.8	1.9
As a percentage of world trade (%)	Imp.	0.6	0.6	0.6	0.5	0.5	0.5	0.5	0.5	0.6	0.6	0.7	0.7	0.7	0.6	0.6
	Exp.	0.6	0.6	0.7	0.6	0.5	0.6	0.6	0.6	0.6	0.7	0.7	0.8	0.8	0.6	0.6

Graph 1: Annual growth rates of exports, 1996–2010
(In percentage by year)

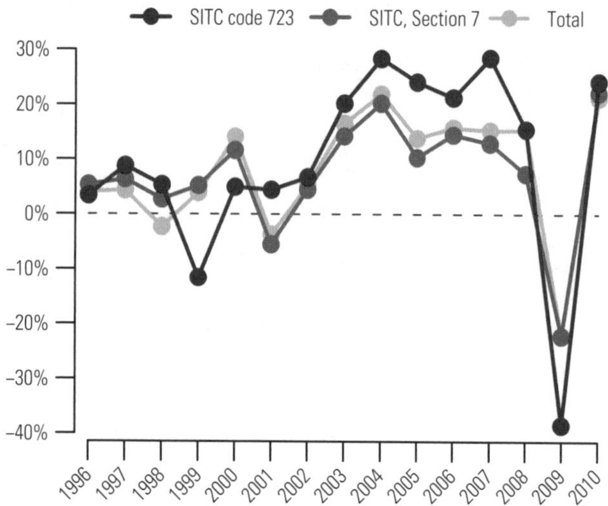

Graph 2: Trade Balance by MDG regions 2010
(Bln US$)

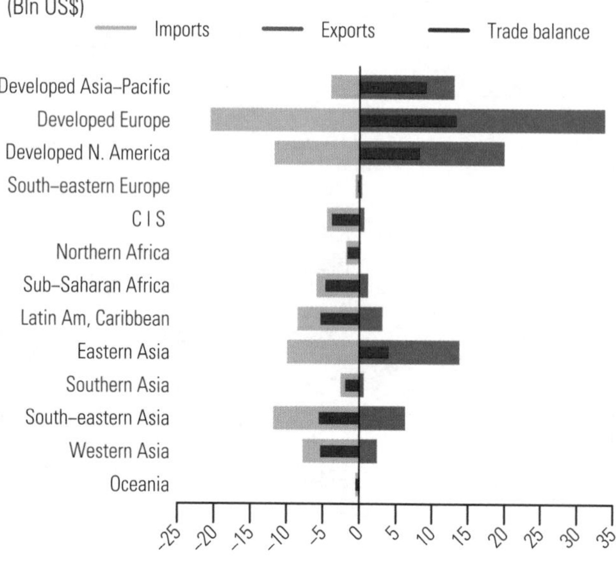

Table 2: Top exporting countries or areas in 2010

Country or area	Value (million US$)	Avg. Growth (%) 06-10	Growth (%) 09-10	World share %	Cum.
World	95603.4	3.2	24.2	100.0	
USA	17980.5	2.1	10.1	18.8	18.8
Japan	12234.4	2.9	86.7	12.8	31.6
Germany	8150.7	-0.2	18.7	8.5	40.1
China	7346.6	16.4	28.0	7.7	47.8
Rep. of Korea	5619.0	11.8	93.2	5.9	53.7
Singapore	4466.1	5.4	-15.8	4.7	58.4
United Kingdom	4032.8	-5.9	23.8	4.2	62.6
France	3258.0	-5.5	18.7	3.4	66.0
Netherlands	3141.2	4.2	15.0	3.3	69.3
Belgium	3103.2	-3.5	30.3	3.2	72.5
Italy	2912.9	-6.0	4.0	3.0	75.6
Canada	1951.7	1.3	3.1	2.0	77.6
Sweden	1653.6	4.2	29.1	1.7	79.3
Austria	1527.2	-3.7	9.9	1.6	80.9
Brazil	1502.8	-2.4	108.5	1.6	82.5

Table 3: Top importing countries or areas in 2010

Country or area	Value (million US$)	Avg. Growth (%) 06-10	Growth (%) 09-10	World share %	Cum.
World	89418.9	2.5	21.8	100.0	
China	7171.5	25.9	69.2	8.0	8.0
USA	6929.6	-12.5	40.8	7.7	15.8
Singapore	5728.6	16.2	10.9	6.4	22.2
Canada	4708.8	-0.1	34.1	5.3	27.4
Germany	3109.9	-3.9	22.2	3.5	30.9
Australia	2739.8	6.3	34.5	3.1	34.0
Russian Federation	2666.2	4.0	47.9	3.0	37.0
France	2464.7	-6.6	29.9	2.8	39.7
Indonesia	2361.3	27.7	53.2	2.6	42.4
Netherlands	2036.5	-3.0	42.1	2.3	44.6
Belgium	2011.0	-2.0	32.7	2.2	46.9
United Arab Emirates	1990.6	4.3	-3.3	2.2	49.1
United Kingdom	1982.7	-11.9	27.6	2.2	51.3
Saudi Arabia	1945.6	9.8	24.9	2.2	53.5
Brazil	1662.4	25.0	60.8	1.9	55.4

The value (in current prices) of exports of textile and leather machinery, and parts thereof, nes (SITC group 724) rose by 38.1 percent to 27.0 bln US$ in 2010 (see table 2). Imports for the same year grew by 30.9 percent and totaled 27.7 bln US$ (see table 3). Graph 1 shows that the increase in exports for 2010 in this product group significantly exceeded the increases in world exports of machinery and transport equipment (SITC section 7) of 22.1 percent and in total world exports of 21.2 percent. Exports of textile and leather machinery, and parts thereof, nes (SITC group 724) accounted for 0.5 percent of world exports of SITC section 7 and 0.2 percent of total world exports (see table 1).

Exports of Germany, the top exporting country in 2010, increased by 33.6 percent and represented 16.2 percent of world exports (see table 2). Other major exporting countries were China and Japan, respectively with 13.6 and 12.0 percent of world exports. Imports of China, the top destination, soared by 66.9 percent and represented 17.2 percent of world imports. Other major destinations were USA and India (see table 3). By MDG regions (see graph 2), Developed Europe accounted for a large share of exports of textile and leather machinery, and parts thereof, nes (SITC group 724). In 2010, its exports and imports were valued respectively at 11.6 bln US$ and 4.4 bln US$, resulting in a trade surplus of 7.2 bln US$. Top trade surpluses were also recorded by Developed Asia-Pacific (+2.4 bln US$) and Eastern Asia (+1.6 bln US$). Top trade deficits were recorded by Southern Asia (-2.8 bln US$), Developed North America (-2.8 bln US$) and Latin America and the Caribbean (-1.9 bln US$).

Table 1: Imports (Imp.) and exports (Exp.), 1996-2010, in current prices

		1996	1997	1998	1999	2000	2001	2002	2003	2004	2005	2006	2007	2008	2009	2010
Values in Bln US$	Imp.	24.9	24.2	21.9	18.2	20.3	18.9	21.0	23.6	25.2	25.9	27.1	30.7	29.5	21.1	27.7
	Exp.	24.4	23.9	20.9	18.2	20.1	18.9	20.2	23.5	25.1	25.3	27.4	30.4	27.8	19.5	27.0
As a percentage of SITC section (%)	Imp.	1.2	1.1	1.0	0.8	0.8	0.8	0.8	0.8	0.7	0.7	0.6	0.6	0.5	0.5	0.5
	Exp.	1.2	1.1	0.9	0.8	0.8	0.8	0.8	0.8	0.7	0.6	0.6	0.6	0.5	0.5	0.5
As a percentage of world trade (%)	Imp.	0.5	0.4	0.4	0.3	0.3	0.3	0.3	0.3	0.3	0.2	0.2	0.2	0.2	0.2	0.2
	Exp.	0.5	0.4	0.4	0.3	0.3	0.3	0.3	0.3	0.3	0.2	0.2	0.2	0.2	0.2	0.2

Graph 1: Annual growth rates of exports, 1996–2010
(In percentage by year)

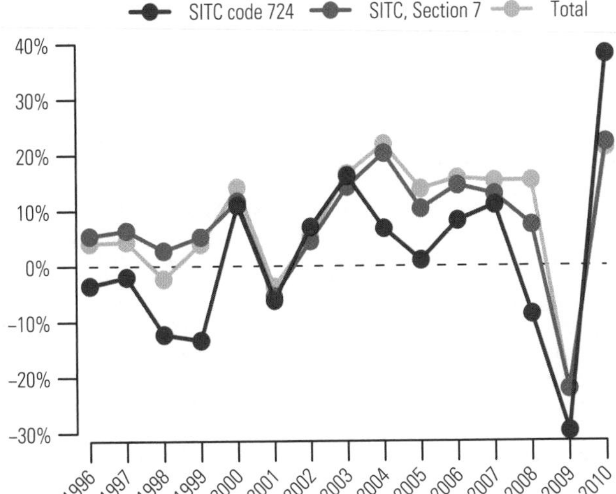

Table 2: Top exporting countries or areas in 2010

Country or area	Value (million US$)	Avg. Growth (%) 06-10	Growth (%) 09-10	World share %	Cum.
World	26 951.8	-0.4	38.1	100.0	
Germany	4 363.8	-6.1	33.6	16.2	16.2
China	3 676.0	9.5	51.7	13.6	29.8
Japan	3 237.8	0.8	102.0	12.0	41.8
Italy	2 762.0	-4.0	31.8	10.2	52.1
Rep. of Korea	2 586.4	11.1	35.4	9.6	61.7
USA	1 440.9	0.0	17.3	5.3	67.0
Switzerland	1 318.5	-6.8	51.6	4.9	71.9
Other Asia, nes	1 081.9	-1.8	54.0	4.0	75.9
China, Hong Kong SAR	766.4	-5.6	7.1	2.8	78.8
France	715.7	-8.2	42.0	2.7	81.4
Mexico	502.0	45.0	35.4	1.9	83.3
Belgium	486.8	5.0	32.3	1.8	85.1
Singapore	464.2	-2.4	46.3	1.7	86.8
Czech Rep.	461.8	-5.1	40.7	1.7	88.5
Thailand	377.5	19.5	11.1	1.4	89.9

Graph 2: Trade Balance by MDG regions 2010
(Bln US$)

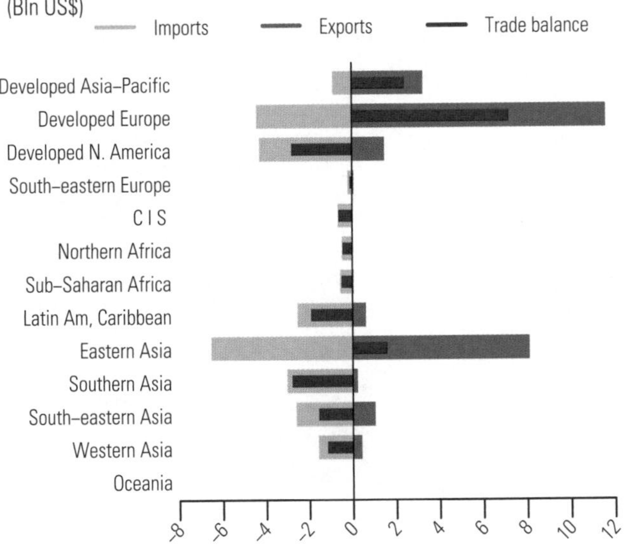

Table 3: Top importing countries or areas in 2010

Country or area	Value (million US$)	Avg. Growth (%) 06-10	Growth (%) 09-10	World share %	Cum.
World	27 680.9	0.6	30.9	100.0	
China	4 768.0	0.9	66.9	17.2	17.2
USA	3 569.0	16.4	27.0	12.9	30.1
India	1 383.8	-11.8	6.8	5.0	35.1
Turkey	1 164.6	-4.3	130.5	4.2	39.3
China, Hong Kong SAR	898.3	-6.0	24.4	3.2	42.6
Viet Nam	*839.3*	11.4	66.9	3.0	45.6
Germany	820.6	-7.5	14.7	3.0	48.6
Brazil	753.3	12.3	33.2	2.7	51.3
Japan	713.8	1.8	34.7	2.6	53.9
Canada	701.2	13.8	8.9	2.5	56.4
Bangladesh	*691.5*	-2.0	-21.0	2.5	58.9
Italy	688.2	-7.0	34.7	2.5	61.4
Mexico	672.9	1.6	42.2	2.4	63.8
Indonesia	641.1	23.2	88.6	2.3	66.1
Pakistan	455.2	-11.3	109.7	1.6	67.8

725 Paper and paper manufacture machinery, and parts thereof

In 2010, the value (in current prices) of exports of paper and paper manufacture machinery, and parts thereof (SITC group 725) increased by 9.3 percent to 10.1 bln US$ (see table 2). For the same year, imports had a small increase of 3.4 percent and totaled 9.5 bln US$ (see table 3). Graph 1 shows that the increase in exports for 2010 in this product group was far less than the increases in world exports of machinery and transport equipment (SITC section 7) of 22.1 percent and in total world exports of 21.2 percent. Exports of paper and paper manufacture machinery, and parts thereof (SITC group 725) accounted for 0.2 percent of world exports of SITC section 7 and 0.1 percent of total world exports (see table 1).

Germany, Italy and Finland were the top exporting countries in 2010 (see table 2). They accounted respectively for 21.6, 12.1 and 10.1 percent of world exports. Imports of China, the top destination, increased by 13.1 percent and represented 14.2 percent of world imports (see table 3). Other major importing countries were USA and Germany. By MDG regions (see graph 2), Developed Europe accounted for a majority of exports and imports of paper and paper manufacture machinery, and parts thereof (SITC group 725). In 2010, its exports were valued at 7.5 bln US$ compared to 3.2 bln US$ for imports, resulting in a trade surplus of 4.3 bln US$. Top trade deficits were recorded by South-eastern Asia (-937 mln US$), Eastern Asia (-731 mln US$) and Latin America & the Caribbean (-650 mln US$).

Table 1: Imports (Imp.) and exports (Exp.), 1996-2010, in current prices

		1996	1997	1998	1999	2000	2001	2002	2003	2004	2005	2006	2007	2008	2009	2010
Values in Bln US$	Imp.	8.9	8.0	7.8	6.6	6.5	6.6	6.1	7.6	8.3	9.1	9.1	11.4	12.3	9.2	9.5
	Exp.	8.7	8.1	7.6	6.6	6.9	6.7	6.6	7.7	8.7	9.3	10.0	11.8	12.0	9.2	10.1
As a percentage of SITC section (%)	Imp.	0.4	0.4	0.4	0.3	0.2	0.3	0.2	0.3	0.2	0.2	0.2	0.2	0.2	0.2	0.2
	Exp.	0.4	0.4	0.3	0.3	0.3	0.3	0.3	0.3	0.2	0.2	0.2	0.2	0.2	0.2	0.2
As a percentage of world trade (%)	Imp.	0.2	0.1	0.1	0.1	0.1	0.1	0.1	0.1	0.1	0.1	0.1	0.1	0.1	0.1	0.1
	Exp.	0.2	0.1	0.1	0.1	0.1	0.1	0.1	0.1	0.1	0.1	0.1	0.1	0.1	0.1	0.1

Graph 1: Annual growth rates of exports, 1996–2010

(In percentage by year)

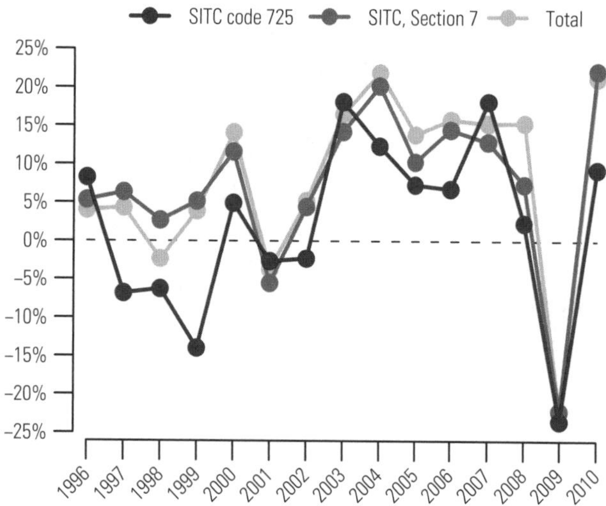

Graph 2: Trade Balance by MDG regions 2010

(Bln US$)

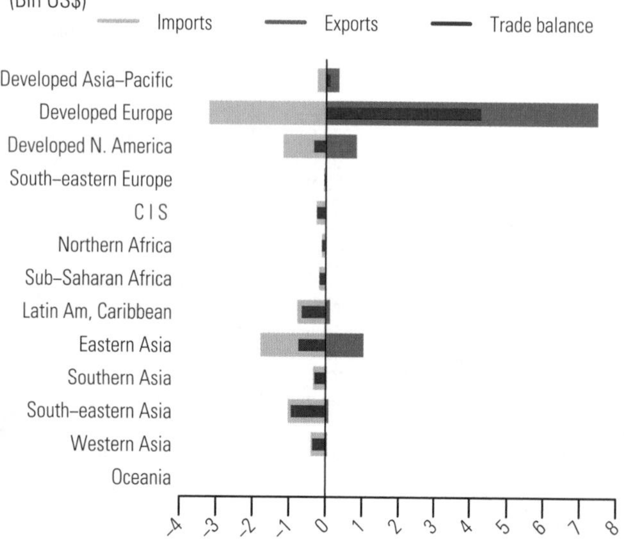

Table 2: Top exporting countries or areas in 2010

Country or area	Value (million US$)	Avg. Growth (%) 06-10	Growth (%) 09-10	World share %	Cum.
World	10071.2	0.3	9.3	100.0	
Germany	2176.7	-1.9	-5.4	21.6	21.6
Italy	1216.4	1.6	1.9	12.1	33.7
Finland	1022.0	2.1	6.5	10.1	43.8
USA	621.7	-1.1	8.9	6.2	50.0
China	605.2	22.1	36.4	6.0	56.0
Switzerland	560.4	-1.2	19.3	5.6	61.6
France	505.2	-2.4	9.2	5.0	66.6
Sweden	489.1	-6.4	20.7	4.9	71.5
Austria	452.5	-4.7	-0.8	4.5	76.0
Japan	336.3	11.4	51.9	3.3	79.3
Other Asia, nes	297.0	7.0	59.9	2.9	82.2
United Kingdom	229.0	-8.0	15.4	2.3	84.5
Canada	221.9	2.3	35.3	2.2	86.7
Spain	214.0	-1.4	0.3	2.1	88.8
Netherlands	152.6	1.0	2.6	1.5	90.4

Table 3: Top importing countries or areas in 2010

Country or area	Value (million US$)	Avg. Growth (%) 06-10	Growth (%) 09-10	World share %	Cum.
World	9508.8	1.1	3.4	100.0	
China	1353.5	11.6	13.1	14.2	14.2
USA	928.3	-1.7	16.5	9.8	24.0
Germany	616.3	-6.0	-13.8	6.5	30.5
Viet Nam	*403.1*	66.7	66.9	4.2	34.7
France	381.7	0.6	7.1	4.0	38.7
Switzerland	377.0	30.4	219.5	4.0	42.7
Indonesia	340.0	-1.3	30.9	3.6	46.3
Rep. of Korea	320.5	29.2	442.1	3.4	49.6
Mexico	292.3	12.8	86.7	3.1	52.7
Italy	284.5	-3.3	0.3	3.0	55.7
Canada	238.8	-4.1	10.6	2.5	58.2
United Kingdom	190.9	-11.8	-5.6	2.0	60.2
Spain	181.1	-14.5	15.9	1.9	62.1
Brazil	160.5	7.5	-42.2	1.7	63.8
Poland	158.2	-1.9	5.1	1.7	65.5

Source: UN Comtrade

After a sizeable decline in 2009, the value (in current prices) of exports of printing and bookbinding machinery and parts thereof (SITC group 726) bounced back by 11.9 percent to 14.8 bln US$ in 2010 (see table 2). Imports also increased by 11.6 percent to 15.3 bln US$ (see table 3). Graph 1 shows that the increase in exports for 2010 in this product group was less than the increases in world exports of machinery and transport equipment (SITC section 7) of 22.1 percent and in total world exports of 21.2 percent. Exports of printing and bookbinding machinery and parts thereof (SITC group 726) accounted for 0.3 percent of world exports of SITC section 7 and 0.1 percent of total world exports (see table 1).

Germany, Japan and USA were the top exporting countries in 2010 (see table 2). They accounted respectively for 31.0, 8.7 and 7.9 percent of world exports. Top destinations were China, Germany and USA (see table 3). By MDG regions (see graph 2), Developed Europe accounted for a majority of exports and imports of printing and bookbinding machinery and parts thereof (SITC group 726). In 2010, its exports amounted to 9.7 bln US$ while imports were valued at 4.9 bln US$, resulting in a trade surplus exceeding 4.8 bln US$. Developed Asia-Pacific recorded a trade surplus amounting to 0.8 bln US$. Top deficits were recorded by Eastern Asia (-1.6 bln US$) and Latin America and the Caribbean (-1.4 bln US$).

Table 1: Imports (Imp.) and exports (Exp.), 1996-2010, in current prices

		1996	1997	1998	1999	2000	2001	2002	2003	2004	2005	2006	2007	2008	2009	2010
Values in Bln US$	Imp.	14.3	14.1	13.9	13.8	13.7	13.8	12.9	14.0	16.2	18.0	20.0	19.7	19.0	13.7	15.3
	Exp.	14.4	14.3	14.6	14.3	14.2	14.4	13.2	14.0	16.4	18.5	20.4	19.4	19.9	13.2	14.8
As a percentage of SITC section (%)	Imp.	0.7	0.7	0.6	0.6	0.5	0.6	0.5	0.5	0.5	0.5	0.5	0.4	0.4	0.3	0.3
	Exp.	0.7	0.7	0.7	0.6	0.5	0.6	0.5	0.5	0.5	0.5	0.5	0.4	0.4	0.3	0.3
As a percentage of world trade (%)	Imp.	0.3	0.3	0.3	0.2	0.2	0.2	0.2	0.2	0.2	0.2	0.2	0.1	0.1	0.1	0.1
	Exp.	0.3	0.3	0.3	0.3	0.2	0.2	0.2	0.2	0.2	0.2	0.2	0.1	0.1	0.1	0.1

Graph 1: Annual growth rates of exports, 1996–2010
(In percentage by year)

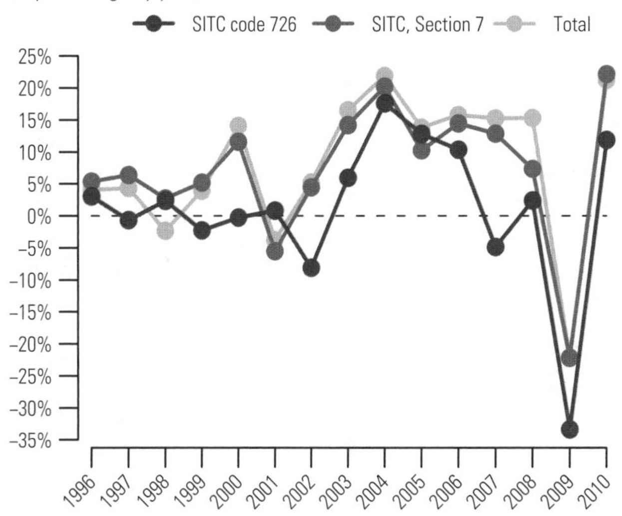

Table 2: Top exporting countries or areas in 2010

Country or area	Value (million US$)	Avg. Growth (%) 06-10	Growth (%) 09-10	World share %	Cum.
World	14814.5	-7.7	11.9	100.0	
Germany	4593.5	-10.9	8.8	31.0	31.0
Japan	1281.6	-10.0	31.8	8.7	39.7
USA	1174.7	-3.1	11.5	7.9	47.6
Switzerland	903.6	-13.4	15.5	6.1	53.7
Italy	757.8	-3.9	25.3	5.1	58.8
United Kingdom	659.7	-11.9	19.9	4.5	63.3
Belgium	649.3	18.7	8.4	4.4	67.6
France	476.9	-13.9	-8.7	3.2	70.9
China	452.5	5.4	31.2	3.1	73.9
China, Hong Kong SAR	395.4	-0.1	44.6	2.7	76.6
Netherlands	357.8	-20.0	-33.4	2.4	79.0
Israel	340.0	3.9	33.2	2.3	81.3
Austria	339.2	-6.0	1.9	2.3	83.6
Other Asia, nes	289.4	-1.3	54.3	2.0	85.5
Malaysia	235.6	-0.6	18.1	1.6	87.1

Graph 2: Trade Balance by MDG regions 2010
(Bln US$)

Imports — Exports — Trade balance

Developed Asia-Pacific
Developed Europe
Developed N. America
South-eastern Europe
C I S
Northern Africa
Sub-Saharan Africa
Latin Am, Caribbean
Eastern Asia
Southern Asia
South-eastern Asia
Western Asia
Oceania

-6 -4 -2 0 2 4 6 8 10

Table 3: Top importing countries or areas in 2010

Country or area	Value (million US$)	Avg. Growth (%) 06-10	Growth (%) 09-10	World share %	Cum.
World	15328.7	-6.4	11.6	100.0	
China	1654.8	2.4	49.3	10.8	10.8
Germany	989.0	-10.3	8.8	6.5	17.2
USA	887.0	-21.4	-11.5	5.8	23.0
Indonesia	789.3	62.9	46.5	5.1	28.2
China, Hong Kong SAR	697.2	5.6	53.6	4.5	32.7
Brazil	661.4	20.4	47.4	4.3	37.0
France	562.6	-12.1	4.4	3.7	40.7
Belgium	561.1	3.0	-9.8	3.7	44.4
United Arab Emirates	448.5	35.5	21.6	2.9	47.3
Italy	445.5	-14.4	0.0	2.9	50.2
United Kingdom	391.0	-21.1	-4.4	2.6	52.8
Malaysia	306.7	8.2	39.3	2.0	54.8
Switzerland	295.7	-9.0	1.1	1.9	56.7
Canada	288.7	-15.4	9.4	1.9	58.6
Mexico	271.8	-5.9	14.1	1.8	60.3

727 Food- processing machines (excluding domestic); parts thereof

The value (in current prices) of exports of food-processing machines (excluding domestic) and parts thereof (SITC group 727) increased by 7.4 percent to 12.0 bln US$ in 2010 (see table 2). Imports for the same year also rose by 8.3 percent and totaled 11.6 bln US$ (see table 3). Graph 1 shows that the rise in exports for 2010 in this product group was exceeded by both the increases in world exports of machinery and transport equipment (SITC section 7) of 22.1 percent and in total world exports of 21.2 percent. Exports of food-processing machines (excluding domestic) and parts thereof (SITC group 727) accounted for 0.2 percent of world exports of SITC section 7 and 0.1 percent of total world exports (see table 1).

Germany, Italy and Netherlands were the top exporting countries in 2010 (see table 2). They accounted respectively for 18.8, 14.3 and 10.8 percent of world exports (see table 3). USA, Russian Federation and Germany were the top destinations. By MDG regions (see graph 2), Developed Europe accounted for a majority of exports of food-processing machines (excluding domestic) and parts thereof (SITC group 727). In 2010, its exports reached 8.7 bln US$ while imports were valued at 3.9 bln US$, resulting in a trade surplus of 4.8 bln US$. Top trade deficits were recorded by Latin America and the Caribbean (-925 mln US$), Sub-Saharan Africa (-895 mln US$) and Commonwealth of Independent States (-813 mln US$).

Table 1: Imports (Imp.) and exports (Exp.), 1996-2010, in current prices

		1996	1997	1998	1999	2000	2001	2002	2003	2004	2005	2006	2007	2008	2009	2010
Values in Bln US$	Imp.	7.4	6.6	6.5	5.8	5.4	5.6	5.9	6.9	8.1	8.7	9.7	11.6	12.6	10.7	11.6
	Exp.	7.1	6.6	6.5	5.8	5.6	5.6	6.2	7.3	8.6	9.3	10.5	12.7	14.2	11.2	12.0
As a percentage of SITC section (%)	Imp.	0.4	0.3	0.3	0.2	0.2	0.2	0.2	0.2	0.2	0.2	0.2	0.2	0.2	0.2	0.2
	Exp.	0.3	0.3	0.3	0.2	0.2	0.2	0.2	0.2	0.2	0.2	0.2	0.3	0.3	0.3	0.2
As a percentage of world trade (%)	Imp.	0.1	0.1	0.1	0.1	0.1	0.1	0.1	0.1	0.1	0.1	0.1	0.1	0.1	0.1	0.1
	Exp.	0.1	0.1	0.1	0.1	0.1	0.1	0.1	0.1	0.1	0.1	0.1	0.1	0.1	0.1	0.1

Graph 1: Annual growth rates of exports, 1996–2010
(In percentage by year)

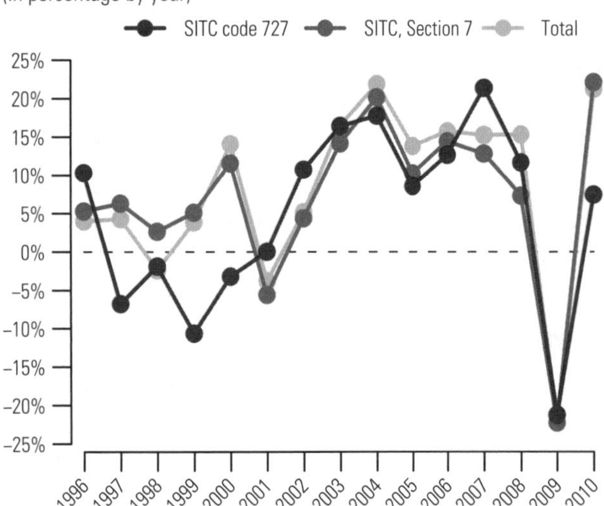

Graph 2: Trade Balance by MDG regions 2010
(Bln US$)

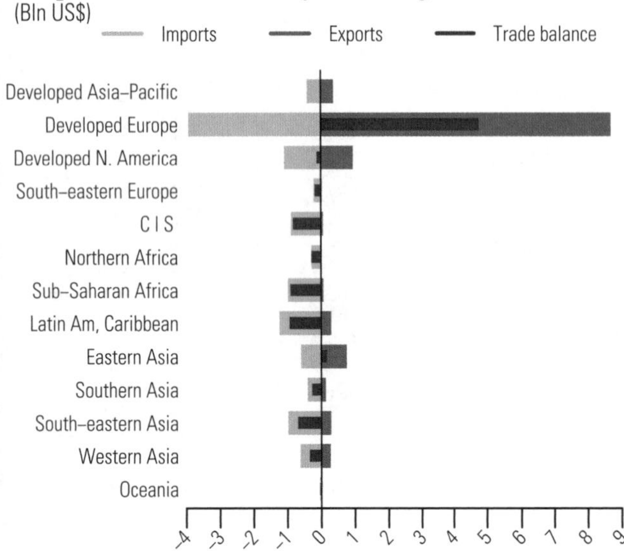

Table 2: Top exporting countries or areas in 2010

Country or area	Value (million US$)	Avg. Growth (%) 06-10	Growth (%) 09-10	World share %	Cum.
World	11 990.2	3.5	7.4	100.0	
Germany	2 250.9	1.5	3.6	18.8	18.8
Italy	1 709.8	3.5	5.4	14.3	33.0
Netherlands	1 296.1	0.3	7.5	10.8	43.8
USA	863.3	9.0	12.3	7.2	51.0
Switzerland	601.5	2.4	-1.3	5.0	56.1
China	594.8	22.4	23.7	5.0	61.0
France	556.1	-2.1	-1.6	4.6	65.7
Denmark	545.4	0.8	15.6	4.5	70.2
Japan	301.3	15.2	62.5	2.5	72.7
Spain	300.7	3.6	12.6	2.5	75.2
Austria	291.8	-2.4	11.4	2.4	77.7
United Kingdom	255.9	-5.9	-0.3	2.1	79.8
Turkey	234.8	18.5	12.9	2.0	81.8
Belgium	232.7	1.5	-21.6	1.9	83.7
Poland	121.0	-6.0	23.6	1.0	84.7

Table 3: Top importing countries or areas in 2010

Country or area	Value (million US$)	Avg. Growth (%) 06-10	Growth (%) 09-10	World share %	Cum.
World	11 567.9	4.4	8.3	100.0	
USA	790.6	-0.8	10.1	6.8	6.8
Russian Federation	548.8	-0.8	29.0	4.7	11.6
Germany	478.6	3.7	7.6	4.1	15.7
United Kingdom	452.6	5.9	43.0	3.9	19.6
France	418.0	1.7	-0.3	3.6	23.2
China	361.9	9.0	42.9	3.1	26.4
Spain	298.6	-10.1	-7.7	2.6	29.0
Indonesia	284.6	18.2	53.5	2.5	31.4
Canada	279.3	-4.2	-11.6	2.4	33.8
Viet Nam	*277.6*	25.1	66.9	2.4	36.2
Belgium	250.1	3.9	-13.3	2.2	38.4
Venezuela	247.3	45.5	-6.8	2.1	40.5
Italy	245.5	4.8	-3.7	2.1	42.6
Netherlands	239.5	5.1	8.9	2.1	44.7
Austria	212.3	9.1	28.6	1.8	46.6

After several years of continuous growth marked by a peak of 160.6 bln US$ in 2008, the value (in current prices) of exports of other machinery, equipment for specialized industries, and parts nes (SITC group 728) declined by 29.4 percent in 2009 but had a significant increase of 40.8 percent to reach 159.7 bln US$ in 2010 (see table 2). For the same period, imports also increased by 36.9 percent to 158.6 bln US$ (see table 3). Graph 1 shows that the increase in exports for 2010 in this product group far exceeded the increases in world exports of machinery and transport equipment (SITC section 7) of 22.1 percent and in total world exports of 21.2 percent. Exports of other machinery, equipment for specialized industries, and parts nes (SITC group 728) accounted for 3.1 percent of world exports of SITC section 7 and 1.1 percent of total world exports (see table 1).

In 2010, Japan, Germany and USA were the top exporting countries (see table 2). They accounted respectively for 20.2, 14.1 and 13.6 percent of world exports. China was the top destination representing 16.8 percent of world exports (see table 3). By MDG regions (see graph 2), Developed Europe accounted for a majority of exports of other machinery, equipment for specialized industries, and parts nes (SITC group 728). In 2010, its exports were valued at 68.3 bln US$ while imports at 31.2 bln US$. This resulted in a trade surplus of 37.1 bln US$. Top trade surpluses were also recorded by Developed Asia-Pacific (+26.9 bln US$) and Developed North America (+7.8 bln US$). Top trade deficits were recorded by Eastern Asia (-40.1 bln US$), South-eastern Asia (-6.9 bln US$) and Latin America and the Caribbean (-6.5 bln US$).

Table 1: Imports (Imp.) and exports (Exp.), 1996-2010, in current prices

		1996	1997	1998	1999	2000	2001	2002	2003	2004	2005	2006	2007	2008	2009	2010
Values in Bln US$	Imp.	68.3	65.8	60.1	62.0	72.2	63.1	62.1	73.0	95.2	99.4	110.1	142.1	153.8	115.9	158.6
	Exp.	63.4	63.7	57.9	61.8	74.3	63.0	61.5	73.4	94.2	97.9	110.5	148.1	160.6	113.4	159.7
As a percentage of SITC section (%)	Imp.	3.4	3.1	2.7	2.7	2.8	2.5	2.4	2.5	2.7	2.5	2.5	2.8	2.9	2.7	3.1
	Exp.	3.1	2.9	2.6	2.6	2.8	2.6	2.4	2.5	2.7	2.5	2.5	2.9	3.0	2.7	3.1
As a percentage of world trade (%)	Imp.	1.3	1.2	1.1	1.1	1.1	1.0	0.9	1.0	1.0	0.9	0.9	1.0	0.9	0.9	1.0
	Exp.	1.2	1.2	1.1	1.1	1.2	1.0	1.0	1.0	1.0	0.9	0.9	1.1	1.0	0.9	1.1

Graph 1: Annual growth rates of exports, 1996–2010
(In percentage by year)

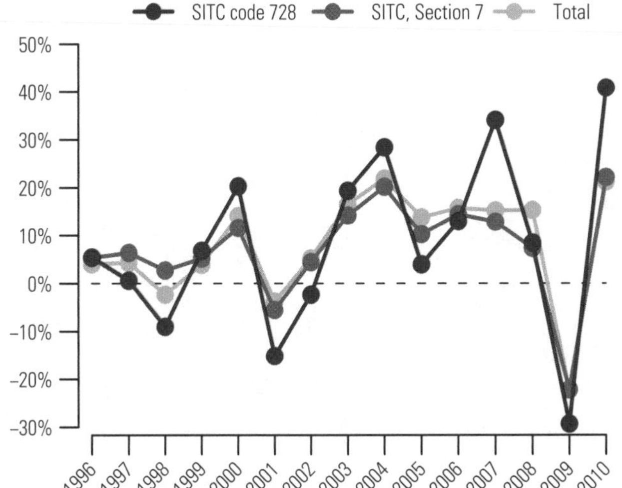

Graph 2: Trade Balance by MDG regions 2010
(Bln US$)

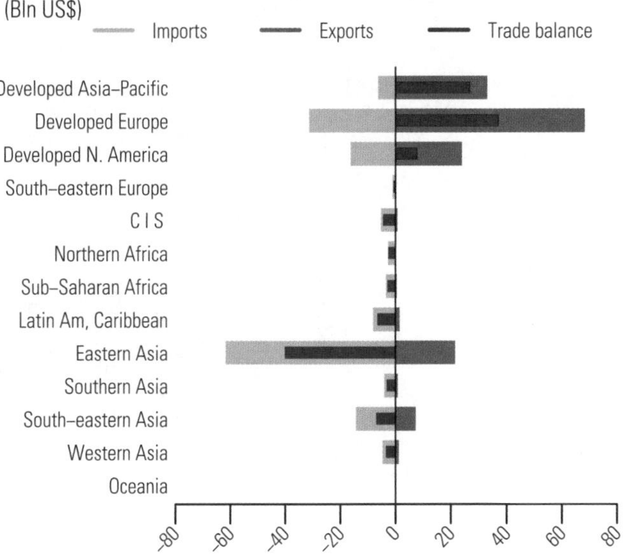

Table 2: Top exporting countries or areas in 2010

Country or area	Value (million US$)	Avg. Growth (%) 06-10	Growth (%) 09-10	World share %	Cum.
World	159671.9	9.6	40.8	100.0	
Japan	32265.0	13.8	100.4	20.2	20.2
Germany	22464.4	2.7	14.7	14.1	34.3
USA	21672.5	12.3	61.2	13.6	47.8
Italy	11286.1	0.5	8.8	7.1	54.9
Netherlands	8748.8	47.8	96.9	5.5	60.4
China	8228.3	24.4	40.1	5.2	65.6
Rep. of Korea	7007.0	15.5	66.4	4.4	69.9
Singapore	5507.5	33.0	125.7	3.4	73.4
Switzerland	4594.8	10.4	35.3	2.9	76.3
Other Asia, nes	4232.5	8.0	51.5	2.7	78.9
Austria	3493.2	1.6	15.6	2.2	81.1
United Kingdom	3324.3	2.2	14.7	2.1	83.2
France	2920.0	-1.9	1.7	1.8	85.0
Canada	2327.5	0.1	-3.4	1.5	86.5
China, Hong Kong SAR	2152.8	6.4	92.9	1.3	87.8

Table 3: Top importing countries or areas in 2010

Country or area	Value (million US$)	Avg. Growth (%) 06-10	Growth (%) 09-10	World share %	Cum.
World	158565.8	9.6	36.9	100.0	
China	26675.7	16.4	80.9	16.8	16.8
Other Asia, nes	16621.8	21.6	108.2	10.5	27.3
Rep. of Korea	15756.1	24.1	92.2	9.9	37.2
USA	13584.7	5.9	32.9	8.6	45.8
Germany	7120.1	4.0	23.3	4.5	50.3
Singapore	5344.6	13.2	75.4	3.4	53.7
Japan	4357.7	5.7	42.5	2.7	56.4
Russian Federation	3626.7	9.8	10.4	2.3	58.7
France	3490.8	5.0	9.3	2.2	60.9
Mexico	2800.4	-2.7	10.1	1.8	62.7
Malaysia	2664.8	9.2	46.3	1.7	64.4
Canada	2590.6	-1.2	18.9	1.6	66.0
China, Hong Kong SAR	2522.4	10.1	104.1	1.6	67.6
Netherlands	2363.0	17.2	43.1	1.5	69.1
United Kingdom	2309.5	-0.9	27.8	1.5	70.5

731 Machine tools working by removing metal or other material

The value (in current prices) of exports of machine tools working by removing metal or other material (SITC group 731) increased by 25.7 percent and amounted to 26.9 bln US$ in 2010 (see table 2). Imports showed a similar increase of 23.3 percent to 26.1 bln US$ (see table 3). Graph 1 shows the increase in exports for 2010 in this product group exceeded both the increases in world exports of machinery and transport equipment (SITC section 7) of 22.1 percent and in total world exports of 21.2 percent. Exports of machine tools working by removing metal or other material (SITC group 731) accounted for 0.5 percent of world exports of SITC section 7 and 0.2 percent of total world exports (see table 1).

The top exporting countries in 2010 were Japan and Germany (see table 2). They accounted respectively for 25.8 and 18.6 percent of world exports. China, USA and Germany were the top destinations (see table 3). By MDG regions (see graph 2), Developed Europe accounted for a majority of exports of machine tools working by removing metal or other material (SITC group 731). In 2010, its exports were valued at 11.6 bln US$ while imports amounted to 5.9 bln US$, resulting in a trade surplus of 5.7 bln US$. Developed Asia-Pacific recorded a trade surplus amounting to 6.4 bln US$. Top trade deficits were recorded by Eastern Asia (-4.5 bln US$), South-eastern Asia (-1.6 bln US$) and Latin America and the Caribbean (-1.3 bln US$).

Table 1: Imports (Imp.) and exports (Exp.), 1996-2010, in current prices

		1996	1997	1998	1999	2000	2001	2002	2003	2004	2005	2006	2007	2008	2009	2010
Values in Bln US$	Imp.	18.1	17.4	17.6	16.9	18.9	18.1	16.0	18.1	24.0	27.3	32.0	33.5	36.9	21.2	26.1
	Exp.	18.1	17.4	17.6	16.7	18.6	17.6	15.9	18.1	23.7	27.3	32.1	32.7	36.9	21.4	26.9
As a percentage of SITC section (%)	Imp.	0.9	0.8	0.8	0.7	0.7	0.7	0.6	0.6	0.7	0.7	0.7	0.7	0.7	0.5	0.5
	Exp.	0.9	0.8	0.8	0.7	0.7	0.7	0.6	0.6	0.7	0.7	0.7	0.6	0.7	0.5	0.5
As a percentage of world trade (%)	Imp.	0.3	0.3	0.3	0.3	0.3	0.3	0.2	0.2	0.3	0.3	0.3	0.2	0.2	0.2	0.2
	Exp.	0.3	0.3	0.3	0.3	0.3	0.3	0.2	0.2	0.3	0.3	0.3	0.2	0.2	0.2	0.2

Graph 1: Annual growth rates of exports, 1996–2010

(In percentage by year)

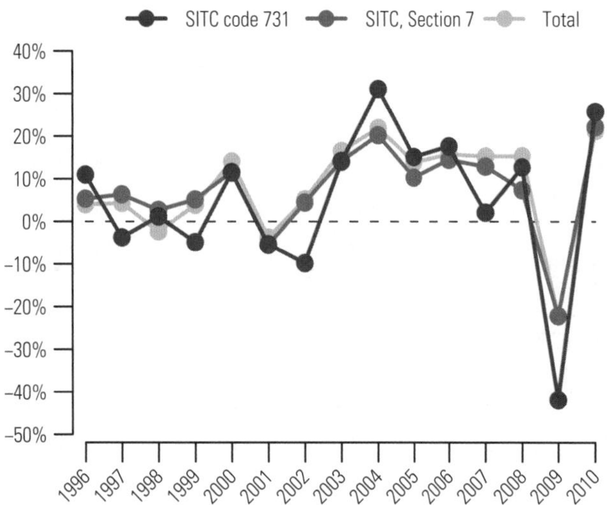

Graph 2: Trade Balance by MDG regions 2010

(Bln US$)

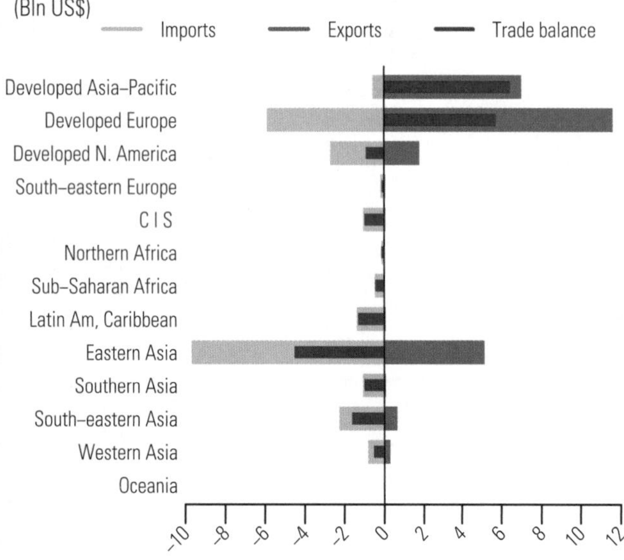

Table 2: Top exporting countries or areas in 2010

Country or area	Value (million US$)	Avg. Growth (%) 06-10	Growth (%) 09-10	World share %	Cum.
World	26899.2	-4.3	25.7	100.0	
Japan	6950.3	-3.2	101.7	25.8	25.8
Germany	5013.2	-4.1	-5.7	18.6	44.5
Other Asia, nes	2319.5	-0.3	75.2	8.6	53.1
Italy	1818.2	0.7	-3.9	6.8	59.9
Switzerland	1727.1	-6.3	16.7	6.4	66.3
USA	1652.7	-21.6	23.7	6.1	72.4
China	1284.2	8.8	34.6	4.8	77.2
Rep. of Korea	1180.9	-0.8	36.8	4.4	81.6
Czech Rep.	500.2	3.6	-6.0	1.9	83.4
Belgium	424.9	-7.9	-0.6	1.6	85.0
United Kingdom	411.0	-12.1	0.5	1.5	86.6
Spain	394.4	-3.2	-27.0	1.5	88.0
Austria	390.7	6.1	-1.8	1.5	89.5
China, Hong Kong SAR	388.2	-1.2	105.1	1.4	90.9
Singapore	356.7	-2.0	67.6	1.3	92.2

Table 3: Top importing countries or areas in 2010

Country or area	Value (million US$)	Avg. Growth (%) 06-10	Growth (%) 09-10	World share %	Cum.
World	26109.2	-4.9	23.3	100.0	
China	7526.3	8.3	65.1	28.8	28.8
USA	2248.3	-14.0	16.7	8.6	37.4
Germany	1530.1	-10.3	-17.6	5.9	43.3
Rep. of Korea	1145.6	-16.3	41.7	4.4	47.7
India	836.3	3.1	21.6	3.2	50.9
Thailand	822.5	1.4	88.1	3.2	54.0
Russian Federation	704.9	19.5	2.8	2.7	56.7
Italy	675.7	-12.9	-4.8	2.6	59.3
Other Asia, nes	572.2	-26.2	111.5	2.2	61.5
Brazil	566.8	13.8	18.9	2.2	63.7
Mexico	541.6	-4.8	2.2	2.1	65.8
France	529.0	-10.0	-13.3	2.0	67.8
Turkey	485.4	-5.7	59.2	1.9	69.6
United Kingdom	448.6	-10.2	18.2	1.7	71.4
Canada	436.3	-10.9	14.7	1.7	73.0

After a sizeable decline in 2009, the value (in current prices) of exports of machine tools for working metal, sintered metal carbides or cermets (SITC group 733) increased by 8.2 percent totaling 9.8 bln US$ in 2010 (see table 2). In the same year, imports also increased by 5.4 percent to 10.0 bln US$ (see table 3). Graph 1 shows that the growth in exports for 2010 in this product group was well below the increases in world exports of machinery and transport equipment (SITC section 7) of 22.1 percent and in total world exports of 21.2 percent. Exports of machine tools for working metal, sintered metal carbides or cermets (SITC group 733) accounted for 0.2 percent of world exports of SITC section 7 and 0.1 percent of total world exports (see table 1).

Germany, Italy and Japan were the top exporting countries in 2010 (see table 2). They accounted respectively for 16.3, 14.7 and 11.6 percent of world exports. China, USA and Thailand were the top destinations (see table 3). By MDG regions (see graph 2), Developed Europe accounted for a majority of exports of machine tools for working metal, sintered metal carbides or cermets (SITC group 733). In 2010, its exports were valued at 5.1 bln US$ and imports amounted to 2.0 bln US$. This resulted in a trade surplus of 3.1 bln US$. Developed Asia-Pacific recorded a trade surplus amounting to 1.0 bln US$. Top trade deficits were recorded by South-eastern Asia (-1.2 bln US$), Latin America and the Caribbean (-950 mln US$) and Eastern Asia (-596 mln US$).

Table 1: Imports (Imp.) and exports (Exp.), 1996-2010, in current prices

		1996	1997	1998	1999	2000	2001	2002	2003	2004	2005	2006	2007	2008	2009	2010
Values in Bln US$	Imp.	7.6	7.1	6.9	6.3	6.6	6.3	5.9	6.8	8.3	9.7	10.8	12.4	13.7	9.5	10.0
	Exp.	7.6	7.0	6.7	6.2	6.5	6.1	5.7	6.6	7.9	9.0	10.2	12.3	13.4	9.1	9.8
As a percentage of SITC section (%)	Imp.	0.4	0.3	0.3	0.3	0.3	0.3	0.2	0.2	0.2	0.2	0.2	0.2	0.3	0.2	0.2
	Exp.	0.4	0.3	0.3	0.3	0.2	0.2	0.2	0.2	0.2	0.2	0.2	0.2	0.2	0.2	0.2
As a percentage of world trade (%)	Imp.	0.1	0.1	0.1	0.1	0.1	0.1	0.1	0.1	0.1	0.1	0.1	0.1	0.1	0.1	0.1
	Exp.	0.1	0.1	0.1	0.1	0.1	0.1	0.1	0.1	0.1	0.1	0.1	0.1	0.1	0.1	0.1

Graph 1: Annual growth rates of exports, 1996–2010
(In percentage by year)

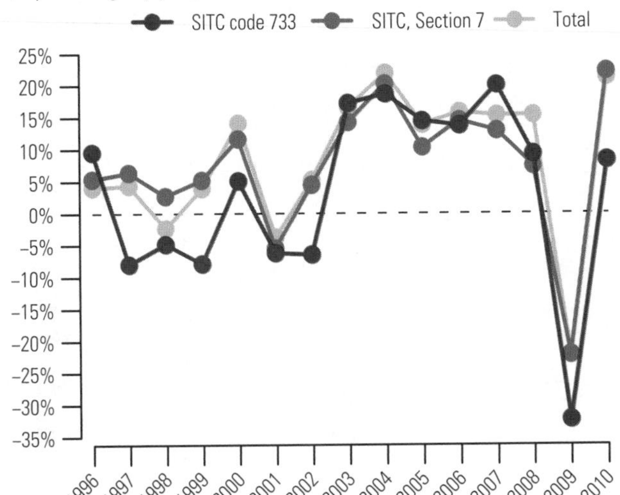

Graph 2: Trade Balance by MDG regions 2010
(Bln US$)

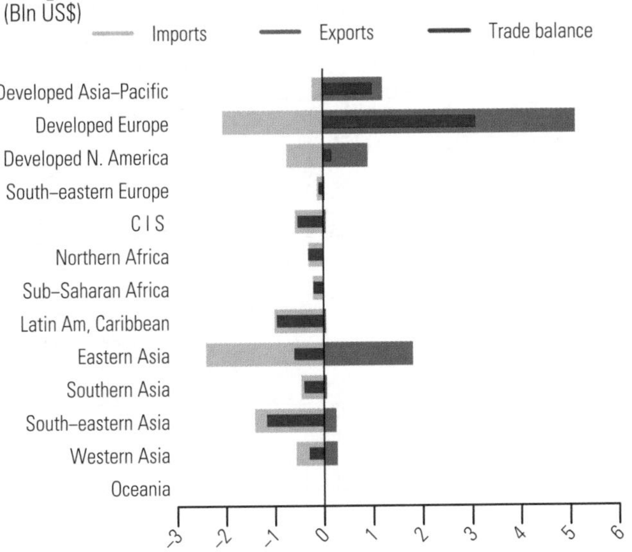

Table 2: Top exporting countries or areas in 2010

Country or area	Value (million US$)	Avg. Growth (%) 06-10	Growth (%) 09-10	World share %	Cum.
World	9804.4	-1.0	8.2	100.0	
Germany	1593.4	-3.9	-12.6	16.3	16.3
Italy	1444.4	-3.4	-3.2	14.7	31.0
Japan	1142.1	-3.1	25.0	11.6	42.6
USA	809.6	3.0	25.4	8.3	50.9
Other Asia, nes	628.1	-1.7	49.6	6.4	57.3
China	571.5	21.8	24.9	5.8	63.1
Rep. of Korea	500.9	7.1	43.3	5.1	68.2
Austria	342.5	10.4	37.6	3.5	71.7
Switzerland	336.1	-1.3	-4.9	3.4	75.2
Spain	247.4	-1.8	-4.2	2.5	77.7
Turkey	241.7	1.6	7.1	2.5	80.1
Belgium	221.9	-1.5	-14.1	2.3	82.4
United Kingdom	215.3	1.9	42.6	2.2	84.6
France	213.3	-9.2	-7.0	2.2	86.8
Netherlands	108.8	-4.5	12.6	1.1	87.9

Table 3: Top importing countries or areas in 2010

Country or area	Value (million US$)	Avg. Growth (%) 06-10	Growth (%) 09-10	World share %	Cum.
World	10037.2	-1.8	5.4	100.0	
China	1892.1	1.7	41.4	18.9	18.9
USA	561.9	-14.0	-0.6	5.6	24.4
Thailand	433.9	-0.3	51.5	4.3	28.8
Russian Federation	414.1	1.4	7.0	4.1	32.9
Mexico	394.8	-5.5	2.2	3.9	36.8
Germany	374.9	-6.5	3.7	3.7	40.6
Brazil	374.7	21.9	-10.9	3.7	44.3
Viet Nam	*340.0*	17.9	66.9	3.4	47.7
India	333.9	3.1	-34.5	3.3	51.0
Malaysia	329.1	8.3	78.3	3.3	54.3
Rep. of Korea	290.6	4.3	-10.5	2.9	57.2
Italy	247.6	-2.2	24.7	2.5	59.7
Turkey	205.5	-9.4	7.0	2.0	61.7
Indonesia	183.9	15.2	30.7	1.8	63.5
Belgium	175.9	9.5	25.9	1.8	65.3

Source: UN Comtrade

735 Parts, nes, accessories suitable for use with machines falling within 731&733

In 2010, the value (in current prices) of exports of parts, nes, accessories suitable for use with machines falling within SITC groups 731 and 733 (SITC group 735) increased by 24.7 percent and totaled 13.0 bln US$ (see table 2). Imports also rose by 25.5 percent to 12.2 bln US$ (see table 3). Graph 1 shows that the increase in exports for 2010 in this product group was slightly above the increases in world exports of machinery and transport equipment (SITC section 7) of 22.1 percent and in total world exports of 21.2 percent. Exports of parts, nes, accessories suitable for use with machines falling within SITC groups 731 and 733 (SITC group 735) accounted for 0.3 percent of world exports of SITC section 7 and 0.1 percent of total world exports (see table 1).

Exports of Japan, one of the top exporting countries in 2010, grew by 69.6 percent (see table 2). Other major exporters were Germany and USA which accounted respectively for 18.1 and 12.2 percent of world exports. USA and Germany were also among the top destinations, together with China (see table 3). By MDG regions (see graph 2), Developed Europe's exports and imports amounted respectively to 7.1 bln US$ and 5.0 bln US$, resulting in a trade surplus of 2.1 bln US$. Developed Asia-Pacific recorded a trade surplus of 778 mln US$. Top trade deficits were recorded by South-eastern Asia (-558 mln US$), Eastern Asia (-540 mln US$) and Latin America and the Caribbean (-538 mln US$).

Table 1: Imports (Imp.) and exports (Exp.), 1996-2010, in current prices

		1996	1997	1998	1999	2000	2001	2002	2003	2004	2005	2006	2007	2008	2009	2010
Values in Bln US$	Imp.	6.7	6.9	7.4	7.0	7.6	7.3	6.7	8.0	10.0	11.0	12.4	13.4	15.6	9.7	12.2
	Exp.	7.1	7.4	7.6	7.5	8.3	7.5	7.4	8.6	10.6	11.8	13.2	13.7	16.3	10.4	13.0
As a percentage of SITC section (%)	Imp.	0.3	0.3	0.3	0.3	0.3	0.3	0.3	0.3	0.3	0.3	0.3	0.3	0.3	0.2	0.2
	Exp.	0.3	0.3	0.3	0.3	0.3	0.3	0.3	0.3	0.3	0.3	0.3	0.3	0.3	0.2	0.3
As a percentage of world trade (%)	Imp.	0.1	0.1	0.1	0.1	0.1	0.1	0.1	0.1	0.1	0.1	0.1	0.1	0.1	0.1	0.1
	Exp.	0.1	0.1	0.1	0.1	0.1	0.1	0.1	0.1	0.1	0.1	0.1	0.1	0.1	0.1	0.1

Graph 1: Annual growth rates of exports, 1996–2010

(In percentage by year)

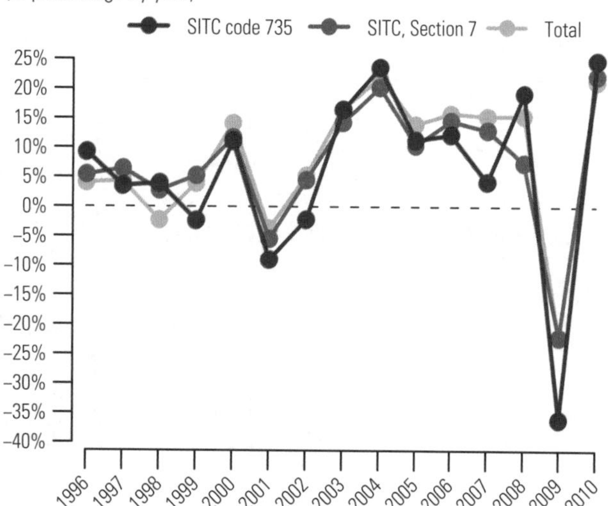

Graph 2: Trade Balance by MDG regions 2010

(Bln US$)

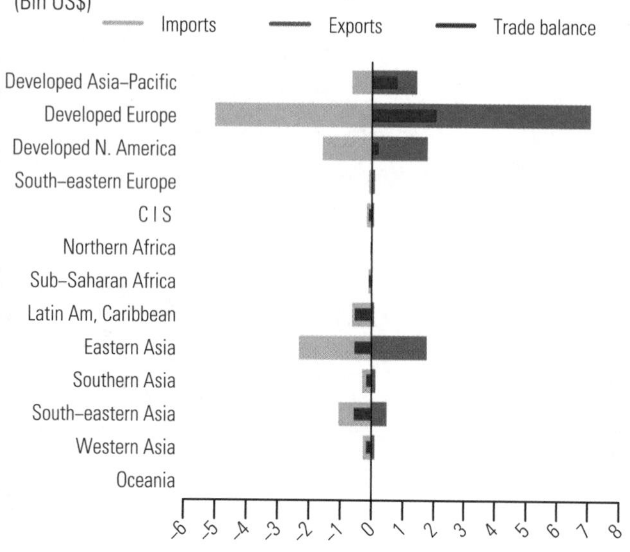

Table 2: Top exporting countries or areas in 2010

Country or area	Value (million US$)	Avg. Growth (%) 06-10	Growth (%) 09-10	World share %	Cum.
World	12 999.9	-0.3	24.7	100.0	
Germany	2 349.9	-1.5	17.3	18.1	18.1
USA	1 590.3	-4.3	26.9	12.2	30.3
Japan	1 408.0	-4.3	69.6	10.8	41.1
Switzerland	948.8	1.7	32.6	7.3	48.4
Italy	798.2	-0.6	6.3	6.1	54.6
Other Asia, nes	655.5	10.3	98.2	5.0	59.6
China	591.6	8.1	31.0	4.6	64.2
France	484.4	-3.8	-9.4	3.7	67.9
Netherlands	448.9	34.6	42.3	3.5	71.4
Rep. of Korea	358.9	8.7	47.4	2.8	74.1
Sweden	346.4	4.7	43.4	2.7	76.8
United Kingdom	301.1	-12.4	6.1	2.3	79.1
Austria	287.9	8.4	9.8	2.2	81.3
Belgium	275.4	-0.5	9.7	2.1	83.4
Singapore	261.7	-8.4	15.7	2.0	85.4

Table 3: Top importing countries or areas in 2010

Country or area	Value (million US$)	Avg. Growth (%) 06-10	Growth (%) 09-10	World share %	Cum.
World	12 150.6	-0.5	25.5	100.0	
China	1 591.0	17.5	66.5	13.1	13.1
USA	1 301.8	-6.2	28.8	10.7	23.8
Germany	1 096.1	-3.9	8.5	9.0	32.8
Japan	540.5	-5.4	51.6	4.4	37.3
France	508.5	-6.0	7.6	4.2	41.5
Switzerland	492.7	-1.5	22.9	4.1	45.5
Netherlands	433.1	25.4	50.9	3.6	49.1
United Kingdom	432.5	-4.9	25.3	3.6	52.6
Singapore	416.9	6.6	69.1	3.4	56.1
Italy	403.7	-1.9	4.6	3.3	59.4
Mexico	365.2	-0.1	27.6	3.0	62.4
Rep. of Korea	324.0	-7.3	31.3	2.7	65.1
Belgium	286.4	-4.4	16.2	2.4	67.4
Canada	278.6	-6.5	7.8	2.3	69.7
India	263.3	4.7	7.3	2.2	71.9

Source: UN Comtrade

From 2006 to 2010, the value (in current prices) of exports of metalworking machinery and parts thereof, nes (SITC group 737) increased on average by 0.9 percent to reach 19.7 bln US$ in 2010 (see table 2). During the same period, imports rose on average by 1.4 percent to 19.6 bln US$ (see table 3). Graph 1 shows that the increase in exports for 2010 in this product group was well below the increases in world exports of machinery and transport equipment (SITC section 7) of 22.1 percent and in total world exports of 21.2 percent. Exports of metalworking machinery and parts thereof, nes (SITC group 737) accounted for 0.4 percent of world exports of SITC section 7 and 0.1 percent of total world exports (see table 1).

The top exporting countries in 2010 were Germany, Italy and China (see table 2). They accounted respectively for 15.9, 12.2 and 12.1 percent of world exports. Top destinations were China, USA and Russian Federation (see table 3). By MDG regions (see graph 2), exports and imports of Developed Europe were valued respectively at 9.8 bln US$ and 4.4 bln US$, resulting in a trade surplus of 5.4 bln US$. Developed Asia-Pacific recorded a trade surplus amounting to 1.7 bln US$. Top trade deficits were recorded by Commonwealth of Independent States (-1.5 bln US$), Latin America & the Caribbean (-1.4 bln US$) and South-eastern Asia (-1.2 bln US$).

Table 1: Imports (Imp.) and exports (Exp.), 1996-2010, in current prices

		1996	1997	1998	1999	2000	2001	2002	2003	2004	2005	2006	2007	2008	2009	2010
Values in Bln US$	Imp.	11.3	12.1	11.1	10.2	10.1	9.0	9.3	11.0	13.9	15.7	18.5	20.3	23.3	19.5	19.6
	Exp.	10.6	10.8	10.2	9.4	9.8	9.0	9.0	10.8	14.0	15.9	19.0	20.8	24.4	18.7	19.7
As a percentage of SITC section (%)	Imp.	0.6	0.6	0.5	0.4	0.4	0.4	0.4	0.4	0.4	0.4	0.4	0.4	0.4	0.5	0.4
	Exp.	0.5	0.5	0.5	0.4	0.4	0.4	0.3	0.4	0.4	0.4	0.4	0.4	0.5	0.4	0.4
As a percentage of world trade (%)	Imp.	0.2	0.2	0.2	0.2	0.2	0.1	0.1	0.1	0.1	0.1	0.2	0.1	0.1	0.2	0.1
	Exp.	0.2	0.2	0.2	0.2	0.2	0.1	0.1	0.1	0.2	0.2	0.2	0.2	0.2	0.2	0.1

Graph 1: Annual growth rates of exports, 1996–2010

(In percentage by year)

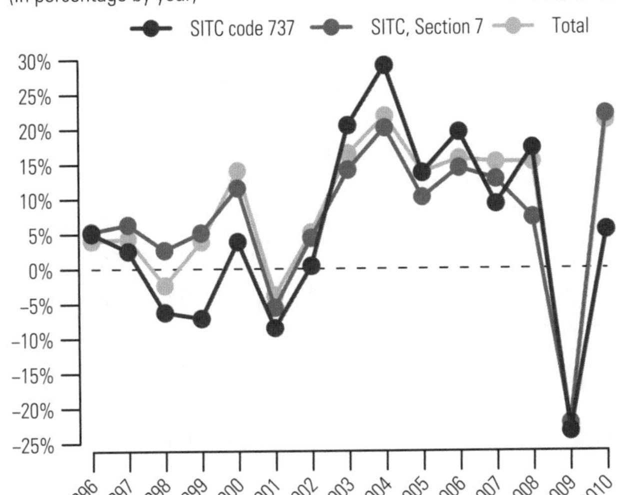

Graph 2: Trade Balance by MDG regions 2010

(Bln US$)

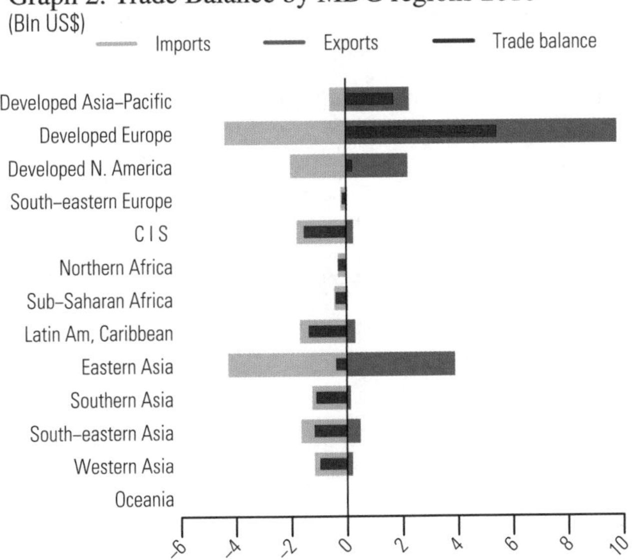

Table 2: Top exporting countries or areas in 2010

Country or area	Value (million US$)	Avg. Growth (%) 06-10	Growth (%) 09-10	World share %	Cum.
World	19706.9	0.9	5.5	100.0	
Germany	3140.0	-0.5	-7.4	15.9	15.9
Italy	2414.0	-0.4	-10.0	12.2	28.2
China	2381.9	18.9	-4.6	12.1	40.3
Japan	2237.8	-0.5	26.3	11.4	51.6
USA	1892.6	-0.2	21.6	9.6	61.2
China, Hong Kong SAR	848.4	10.8	112.3	4.3	65.5
Switzerland	659.4	-2.0	17.0	3.3	68.9
Austria	608.4	-5.0	9.0	3.1	72.0
France	509.9	-3.0	-12.0	2.6	74.6
Rep. of Korea	458.0	5.8	9.9	2.3	76.9
United Kingdom	455.5	-2.7	0.6	2.3	79.2
Sweden	445.9	-6.0	4.0	2.3	81.5
Canada	330.7	-6.8	41.4	1.7	83.1
Netherlands	260.6	-0.7	5.1	1.3	84.5
Singapore	247.3	-19.6	31.2	1.3	85.7

Table 3: Top importing countries or areas in 2010

Country or area	Value (million US$)	Avg. Growth (%) 06-10	Growth (%) 09-10	World share %	Cum.
World	19609.4	1.4	0.5	100.0	
China	2662.9	-3.1	6.9	13.6	13.6
USA	1630.5	-6.3	1.8	8.3	21.9
Russian Federation	1483.0	29.4	16.9	7.6	29.5
Germany	768.2	-4.4	-4.6	3.9	33.4
Rep. of Korea	702.6	-0.3	-18.6	3.6	37.0
Mexico	700.8	6.2	55.1	3.6	40.5
India	681.0	3.0	-33.6	3.5	44.0
Brazil	593.5	32.3	104.2	3.0	47.0
China, Hong Kong SAR	477.1	-1.3	50.0	2.4	49.5
Iran	461.2	86.8	8.4	2.4	51.8
Other Asia, nes	431.5	3.7	-32.5	2.2	54.0
United Arab Emirates	425.7	28.6	-6.5	2.2	56.2
Malaysia	424.5	13.0	60.8	2.2	58.4
Italy	404.1	-3.6	-18.1	2.1	60.4
Viet Nam	*400.4*	30.6	66.9	2.0	62.5

Source: UN Comtrade

741 Heating and cooling equipment and parts thereof, nes

After a 21.5 percent drop in 2009, the value (in current prices) of exports of heating and cooling equipment and parts thereof, nes (SITC group 741) grew by 7.4 percent and amounted to 94.7 bln US$ in 2010 (see table 2). For the same period, imports also increased by 6.7 percent to 96.4 bln US$ (see table 3). Graph 1 shows that the growth in exports for 2010 in this product group was below the increases in world exports of machinery and transport equipment (SITC section 7) of 22.1 percent and in total world exports of 21.2 percent. Exports of heating and cooling equipment and parts thereof, nes (SITC group 741) accounted for 1.8 percent of world exports of SITC section 7 and 0.6 percent of total world exports (see table 1).

China, Germany and USA were the top exporting countries in 2010 (see table 2). They accounted respectively for 16.7, 11.0 and 9.5 percent of world exports. USA, China and Germany were also the top destinations (see table 3). By MDG regions (see graph 2), Developed Europe accounted for a majority of exports and a large share of imports. In 2010, its exports and imports were respectively valued at 42.4 bln US$ and 30.1 bln US$, resulting in a trade surplus of 12.3 bln US$. Eastern Asia recorded a trade surplus amounting to 9.3 bln US$. Top trade deficits were recorded by Western Asia (-5.0 bln US$), Commonwealth of Independent States (-4.4 bln US$) and Latin America and the Caribbean (-3.9 bln US$).

Table 1: Imports (Imp.) and exports (Exp.), 1996-2010, in current prices

		1996	1997	1998	1999	2000	2001	2002	2003	2004	2005	2006	2007	2008	2009	2010
Values in Bln US$	Imp.	43.1	42.7	41.9	41.7	42.3	42.1	43.0	51.1	63.8	70.8	80.2	98.0	111.5	90.4	96.4
	Exp.	41.3	40.0	39.9	39.2	41.2	41.2	42.8	50.5	63.0	68.5	80.1	98.9	112.4	88.2	94.7
As a percentage of SITC section (%)	Imp.	2.1	2.0	1.9	1.8	1.6	1.7	1.7	1.7	1.8	1.8	1.8	2.0	2.1	2.1	1.9
	Exp.	2.0	1.8	1.8	1.7	1.6	1.7	1.7	1.7	1.8	1.8	1.8	2.0	2.1	2.1	1.8
As a percentage of world trade (%)	Imp.	0.8	0.8	0.8	0.7	0.6	0.7	0.7	0.7	0.7	0.7	0.7	0.7	0.7	0.7	0.6
	Exp.	0.8	0.7	0.7	0.7	0.7	0.7	0.7	0.7	0.7	0.7	0.7	0.7	0.7	0.7	0.6

Graph 1: Annual growth rates of exports, 1996–2010
(In percentage by year)

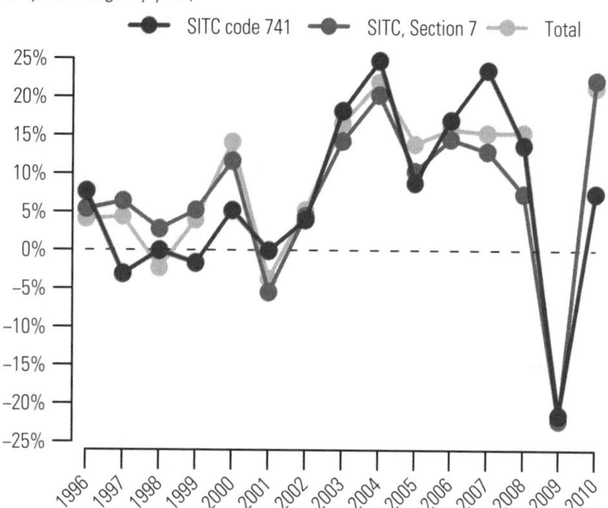

Table 2: Top exporting countries or areas in 2010

Country or area	Value (million US$)	Avg. Growth (%) 06-10	Growth (%) 09-10	World share %	Cum.
World	94711.5	4.3	7.4	100.0	
China	15794.6	16.3	29.8	16.7	16.7
Germany	10411.4	1.8	-6.4	11.0	27.7
USA	8975.3	1.6	15.0	9.5	37.1
Italy	8378.4	2.1	-5.7	8.8	46.0
Japan	5513.7	-1.0	12.0	5.8	51.8
Thailand	4018.6	10.6	36.1	4.2	56.1
France	3538.6	-3.0	-8.9	3.7	59.8
Rep. of Korea	3451.8	6.8	3.8	3.6	63.4
Mexico	3214.5	5.3	25.6	3.4	66.8
Czech Rep.	2437.6	5.3	15.9	2.6	69.4
Belgium	2141.3	0.0	-13.6	2.3	71.7
Sweden	2013.9	3.1	0.9	2.1	73.8
United Kingdom	1753.2	-1.5	-7.0	1.9	75.6
Netherlands	1708.4	-1.3	0.7	1.8	77.4
Austria	1661.0	1.1	-14.0	1.8	79.2

Graph 2: Trade Balance by MDG regions 2010
(Bln US$)

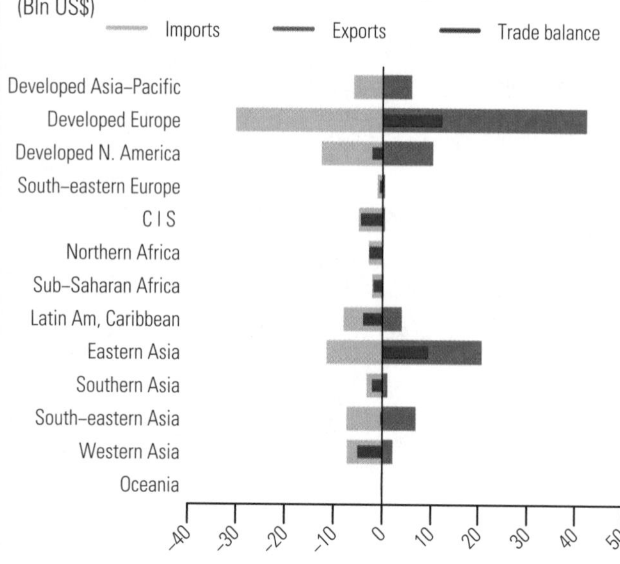

Table 3: Top importing countries or areas in 2010

Country or area	Value (million US$)	Avg. Growth (%) 06-10	Growth (%) 09-10	World share %	Cum.
World	96430.9	4.7	6.7	100.0	
USA	9500.9	1.8	5.9	9.9	9.9
China	6397.4	5.1	7.9	6.6	16.5
Germany	5435.8	-0.2	3.3	5.6	22.1
Japan	3672.1	2.7	12.9	3.8	25.9
France	3560.8	1.7	-2.0	3.7	29.6
Russian Federation	3339.1	10.5	20.5	3.5	33.1
Canada	3006.0	0.2	13.1	3.1	36.2
Italy	2946.8	3.8	20.7	3.1	39.3
Spain	2495.4	-3.3	8.1	2.6	41.8
United Kingdom	2471.4	-2.5	9.0	2.6	44.4
Mexico	2190.2	-0.8	16.0	2.3	46.7
Brazil	2134.0	34.6	63.8	2.2	48.9
Australia	2018.9	6.7	18.4	2.1	51.0
Other Asia, nes	1968.0	-8.8	35.1	2.0	53.0
Viet Nam	*1837.1*	31.0	66.9	1.9	54.9

Source: UN Comtrade

Pumps for liquids; liquid elevators; parts for such pumps and liquid elevators 742

After a 20.1 percent drop in 2009, the value (in current prices) of exports of pumps for liquids, liquid elevators, parts for such pumps and liquid elevators (SITC group 742) bounced back in 2010 by 18.0 percent to 51.1 bln US$ (see table 2). Imports showed a similar development with an increase of 19.5 percent and amounted to 53.6 bln US$ (see table 3). Graph 1 shows that the increase in exports for 2010 in this product group was slightly exceeded by increases in world exports of machinery and transport equipment (SITC section 7) of 22.1 percent and in total world exports of 21.2 percent. Exports of pumps for liquids, liquid elevators, parts for such pumps and liquid elevators (SITC group 742) accounted for 1.0 percent of world exports of SITC section 7 and 0.3 percent of total world exports in 2010 (see table 1).

Germany, USA and Japan were the top exporting countries in 2010 (see table 2). They accounted respectively for 18.7, 13.5 and 9.0 percent of world exports. USA, China and Germany were the top destinations (see table 3). By MDG regions (see graph 2), Developed Europe accounted for a majority of trade in pumps for liquids, liquid elevators, parts for such pumps and liquid elevators (SITC group 742). In 2010, its exports were valued at 27.7 bln US$ while imports amounted to 18.5 bln US$. This resulted in a trade surplus of 9.2 bln US$. Developed Asia-Pacific recorded a trade surplus amounting to 3.0 bln US$. Top trade deficits were recorded by Western Asia (-2.6 bln US$), Latin America and the Caribbean (-2.3 bln US$) and South-eastern Asia (-1.8 bln US$).

Table 1: Imports (Imp.) and exports (Exp.), 1996-2010, in current prices

		1996	1997	1998	1999	2000	2001	2002	2003	2004	2005	2006	2007	2008	2009	2010
Values in Bln US$	Imp.	19.5	19.8	19.9	19.9	20.1	20.4	21.8	26.1	30.7	34.1	38.3	48.1	55.2	44.8	53.6
	Exp.	18.5	18.9	19.1	19.1	19.5	19.7	21.1	25.6	31.2	33.8	38.0	47.0	54.2	43.3	51.1
As a percentage of SITC section (%)	Imp.	1.0	0.9	0.9	0.8	0.8	0.8	0.9	0.9	0.9	0.9	0.9	1.0	1.0	1.0	1.0
	Exp.	0.9	0.9	0.9	0.8	0.7	0.8	0.8	0.9	0.9	0.9	0.9	0.9	1.0	1.0	1.0
As a percentage of world trade (%)	Imp.	0.4	0.4	0.4	0.3	0.3	0.3	0.3	0.3	0.3	0.3	0.3	0.3	0.3	0.4	0.4
	Exp.	0.4	0.3	0.4	0.3	0.3	0.3	0.3	0.3	0.3	0.3	0.3	0.3	0.3	0.3	0.3

Graph 1: Annual growth rates of exports, 1996–2010

(In percentage by year)

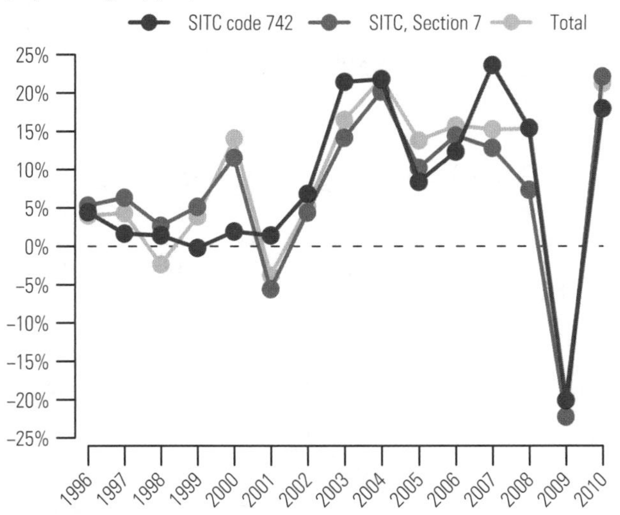

Graph 2: Trade Balance by MDG regions 2010

(Bln US$)

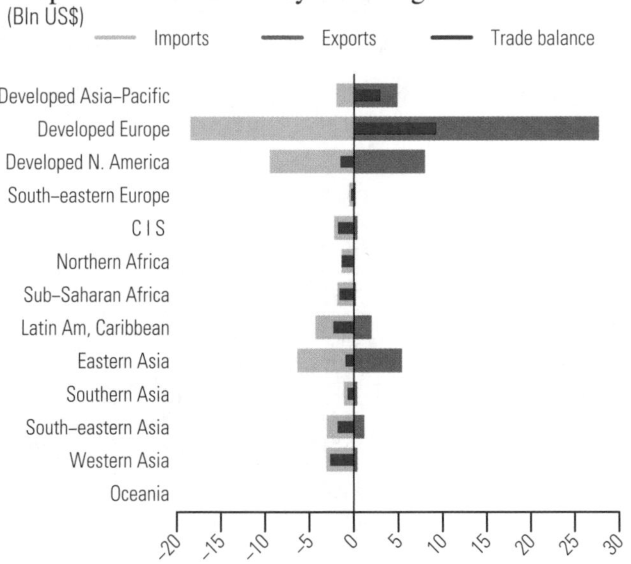

Table 2: Top exporting countries or areas in 2010

Country or area	Value (million US$)	Avg. Growth (%) 06-10	Growth (%) 09-10	World share %	Cum.
World	51 133.1	7.7	18.0	100.0	
Germany	9 560.5	3.3	15.0	18.7	18.7
USA	6 909.8	10.0	25.5	13.5	32.2
Japan	4 582.9	12.4	31.5	9.0	41.2
China	3 920.5	20.3	35.2	7.7	48.8
Italy	3 872.1	3.5	8.3	7.6	56.4
France	2 420.5	2.1	0.0	4.7	61.1
United Kingdom	1 803.3	5.0	10.4	3.5	64.7
Netherlands	1 413.3	13.7	0.8	2.8	67.4
Czech Rep.	1 382.8	4.0	37.9	2.7	70.1
Mexico	1 242.1	14.9	34.5	2.4	72.6
Canada	1 087.0	2.0	16.1	2.1	74.7
Denmark	1 059.0	4.9	9.9	2.1	76.8
Rep. of Korea	903.5	16.8	22.9	1.8	78.5
Sweden	848.6	3.6	7.7	1.7	80.2
Spain	810.4	11.7	13.9	1.6	81.8

Table 3: Top importing countries or areas in 2010

Country or area	Value (million US$)	Avg. Growth (%) 06-10	Growth (%) 09-10	World share %	Cum.
World	53 579.7	8.8	19.5	100.0	
USA	7 124.1	6.1	35.4	13.3	13.3
China	4 101.7	20.4	27.6	7.7	21.0
Germany	3 853.7	7.0	21.8	7.2	28.1
Canada	2 338.1	4.1	28.2	4.4	32.5
France	2 264.1	0.6	7.2	4.2	36.7
United Kingdom	2 050.3	5.4	19.9	3.8	40.6
Rep. of Korea	1 548.5	11.1	0.3	2.9	43.5
Italy	1 471.2	0.0	9.5	2.7	46.2
Mexico	1 413.1	8.5	28.5	2.6	48.8
Russian Federation	1 378.6	20.1	38.8	2.6	51.4
Japan	1 096.2	5.2	20.3	2.0	53.5
Belgium	989.7	2.8	7.1	1.8	55.3
Brazil	931.5	21.2	51.8	1.7	57.0
Poland	907.0	8.2	20.0	1.7	58.7
Spain	865.3	1.8	11.3	1.6	60.3

743 Pumps (other than liquid), air or other gas compressors and fans, etc; parts

After several years of continuous growth marked by a peak of 107.1 bln US$ in 2008, the value (in current prices) of exports of pumps, air or other gas compressors and fans, etc; parts (SITC group 743) declined by 17.1 percent in 2009 but bounced back in 2010 by 18.7 percent to reach 105.4 bln US$ (see table 2). Imports showed a similar development with an increase of 15.8 percent to 107.1 bln US$ in 2010 (see table 3). Graph 1 shows that the increase in exports for 2010 in this product group was slightly exceeded by the increase in world exports of machinery and transport equipment (SITC section 7) of 22.1 percent and the increase in total world exports of 21.2 percent. Exports of pumps, air or other gas compressors and fans, etc; parts (SITC group 743) accounted for 2.1 percent of world exports of SITC section 7 and 0.7 percent of total world exports in 2010 (see table 1).

In 2010, Germany, USA and China were the top exporting countries (see table 2). They accounted respectively for 16.4, 12.3 and 10.4 percent of world exports. USA, China and Germany were also the top destinations (see table 3). By MDG regions (see graph 2), Developed Europe accounted for a very large share of exports of pumps, air or other gas compressors and fans, etc (SITC group 743). In 2010, its exports were valued at 51.3 bln US$ while imports amounted to 36.4 bln US$, resulting in a trade surplus of 14.9 bln US$. Top trade deficits were recorded by Latin America and the Caribbean (-4.9 bln US$) and Western Asia (-4.6 bln US$).

Table 1: Imports (Imp.) and exports (Exp.), 1996-2010, in current prices

		1996	1997	1998	1999	2000	2001	2002	2003	2004	2005	2006	2007	2008	2009	2010
Values in Bln US$	Imp.	38.5	38.3	39.0	40.1	42.7	45.3	47.0	54.1	65.9	72.2	82.3	98.0	109.3	92.5	107.1
	Exp.	36.8	37.1	37.2	38.4	41.4	42.9	44.5	53.0	65.2	69.6	79.8	96.4	107.1	88.8	105.4
As a percentage of SITC section (%)	Imp.	1.9	1.8	1.8	1.7	1.6	1.8	1.8	1.8	1.9	1.8	1.9	2.0	2.0	2.2	2.1
	Exp.	1.8	1.7	1.7	1.6	1.6	1.7	1.7	1.8	1.8	1.8	1.8	1.9	2.0	2.1	2.1
As a percentage of world trade (%)	Imp.	0.7	0.7	0.7	0.7	0.7	0.7	0.7	0.7	0.7	0.7	0.7	0.7	0.7	0.7	0.7
	Exp.	0.7	0.7	0.7	0.7	0.7	0.7	0.7	0.7	0.7	0.7	0.7	0.7	0.7	0.7	0.7

Graph 1: Annual growth rates of exports, 1996–2010
(In percentage by year)

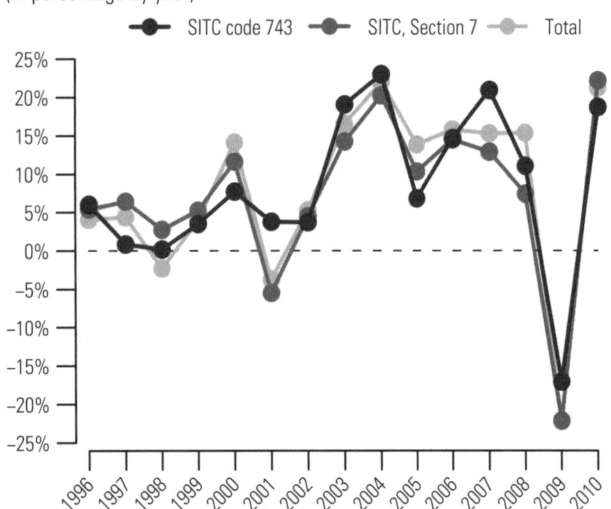

Table 2: Top exporting countries or areas in 2010

Country or area	Value (million US$)	Avg. Growth (%) 06-10	Growth (%) 09-10	World share %	Cum.
World	105 402.3	7.2	18.7	100.0	
Germany	17 297.3	5.6	11.2	16.4	16.4
USA	12 923.4	5.9	12.5	12.3	28.7
China	10 966.1	18.6	34.9	10.4	39.1
Japan	8 680.8	8.7	33.8	8.2	47.3
Italy	6 216.5	2.1	-1.9	5.9	53.2
France	4 969.9	1.6	8.2	4.7	57.9
Belgium	3 962.6	14.8	46.8	3.8	61.7
United Kingdom	3 629.5	2.5	24.3	3.4	65.1
Mexico	2 970.7	8.0	36.6	2.8	67.9
Rep. of Korea	2 425.1	16.1	49.9	2.3	70.2
Netherlands	2 369.2	7.0	14.5	2.2	72.5
South Africa	2 246.2	-2.1	33.4	2.1	74.6
Thailand	2 164.3	19.1	55.3	2.1	76.7
Switzerland	2 002.7	8.6	11.7	1.9	78.6
Canada	1 629.2	-3.5	-9.2	1.5	80.1

Graph 2: Trade Balance by MDG regions 2010
(Bln US$)

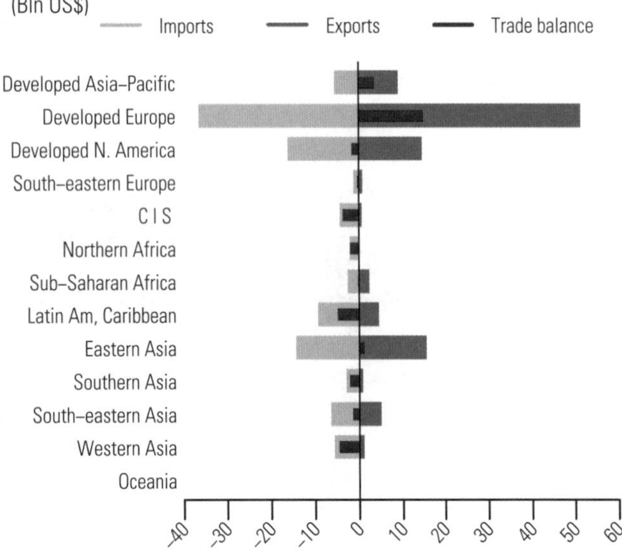

Table 3: Top importing countries or areas in 2010

Country or area	Value (million US$)	Avg. Growth (%) 06-10	Growth (%) 09-10	World share %	Cum.
World	107 129.0	6.8	15.8	100.0	
USA	12 939.3	1.6	24.2	12.1	12.1
China	8 905.2	9.9	23.3	8.3	20.4
Germany	7 603.6	4.2	19.8	7.1	27.5
France	4 246.3	2.6	16.8	4.0	31.5
Mexico	3 689.9	6.3	28.4	3.4	34.9
Italy	3 282.0	3.2	18.2	3.1	38.0
Japan	3 277.3	8.7	23.1	3.1	41.0
Canada	3 199.4	-0.3	9.0	3.0	44.0
United Kingdom	3 055.8	2.4	20.7	2.9	46.9
Russian Federation	2 977.0	12.8	41.4	2.8	49.6
Rep. of Korea	2 962.2	9.1	18.9	2.8	52.4
Belgium	2 542.4	5.6	10.3	2.4	54.8
Spain	2 291.1	-0.6	9.9	2.1	56.9
Brazil	2 169.2	29.7	56.1	2.0	58.9
Australia	1 994.2	12.7	-31.1	1.9	60.8

From 2006 to 2010, the value (in current prices) of exports of mechanical handling equipment and parts thereof, nes (SITC group 744) increased on average by 1.2 percent each year and amounted to 65.1 bln US$ (see table 2). Similarly, imports went up on average by 0.9 percent each year to 63.0 bln US$ (see table 3). Graph 1 shows that the increase in exports for 2010 of 3.7 percent in this product group was by far exceeded by the increases in world exports of machinery and transport equipment (SITC section 7) of 22.1 percent and in total world exports of 21.2 percent. Exports of mechanical handling equipment and parts thereof, nes (SITC group 744) accounted for 1.3 percent of world exports of SITC section 7 and 0.4 percent of total world exports in 2010 (see table 1).

The top exporting countries in 2010 were Germany, China and USA (see table 2). They accounted respectively for 16.5, 12.8 and 10.3 percent of world exports (see table 2). USA, China and Germany were also the top destinations (see table 3). By MDG regions (see graph 2), Developed Europe accounted for a majority of trade in mechanical handling equipment and parts thereof, nes (SITC group 744). In 2010, its exports were valued at 36.2 bln US$ while imports at 21.9 bln US$, resulting in a trade surplus of 14.3 bln US$. Top trade surpluses were also recorded by Eastern Asia (+4.2 bln US$) and Developed Asia-Pacific (+2.2 bln US$). Top trade deficits were recorded by Latin America and the Caribbean (-4.2 bln US$), Western Asia (-3.9 bln US$) and South-eastern Asia (-3.3 bln US$).

Table 1: Imports (Imp.) and exports (Exp.), 1996-2010, in current prices

		1996	1997	1998	1999	2000	2001	2002	2003	2004	2005	2006	2007	2008	2009	2010
Values in Bln US$	Imp.	29.5	29.7	29.7	28.4	28.9	28.8	28.7	33.5	42.0	51.3	60.7	74.3	87.1	60.2	63.0
	Exp.	30.1	29.9	29.5	28.9	29.5	29.8	30.1	34.9	44.1	52.1	62.0	77.4	91.9	62.7	65.1
As a percentage of SITC section (%)	Imp.	1.5	1.4	1.4	1.2	1.1	1.2	1.1	1.1	1.2	1.3	1.4	1.5	1.6	1.4	1.2
	Exp.	1.5	1.4	1.3	1.2	1.1	1.2	1.2	1.2	1.2	1.3	1.4	1.5	1.7	1.5	1.3
As a percentage of world trade (%)	Imp.	0.6	0.5	0.5	0.5	0.4	0.5	0.4	0.4	0.5	0.5	0.5	0.5	0.5	0.5	0.4
	Exp.	0.6	0.5	0.6	0.5	0.5	0.5	0.5	0.5	0.5	0.5	0.5	0.6	0.6	0.5	0.4

Graph 1: Annual growth rates of exports, 1996–2010

(In percentage by year)

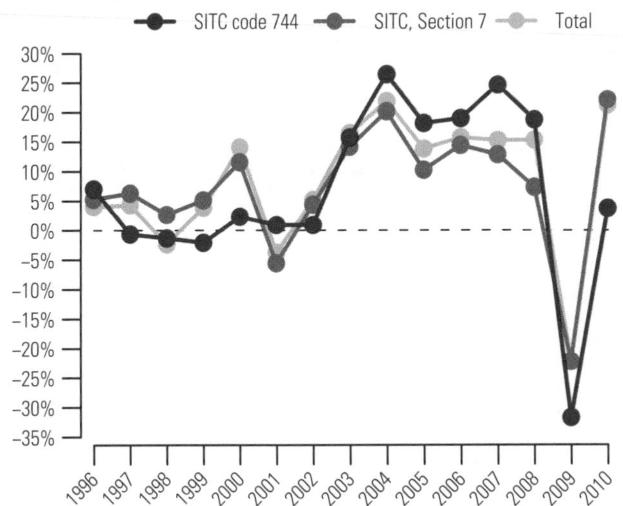

Table 2: Top exporting countries or areas in 2010

Country or area	Value (million US$)	Avg. Growth (%) 06-10	Growth (%) 09-10	World share %	Cum.
World	65094.8	1.2	3.7	100.0	
Germany	10744.0	1.0	2.6	16.5	16.5
China	8355.1	16.0	1.7	12.8	29.3
USA	6702.8	0.6	3.8	10.3	39.6
Italy	4490.2	-0.9	6.5	6.9	46.5
Japan	4310.5	-3.5	13.0	6.6	53.2
France	2994.3	-7.2	-5.8	4.6	57.8
Netherlands	2382.9	-0.6	7.3	3.7	61.4
Sweden	2302.1	-1.8	10.9	3.5	65.0
United Kingdom	2088.1	-10.0	1.2	3.2	68.2
Austria	1928.2	-0.3	3.1	3.0	71.1
Canada	1707.3	-8.2	-2.9	2.6	73.7
Spain	1705.9	5.3	2.5	2.6	76.4
Rep. of Korea	1583.8	6.2	9.3	2.4	78.8
Singapore	1257.0	9.4	16.0	1.9	80.7
Belgium	1238.3	-5.3	-10.0	1.9	82.6

Graph 2: Trade Balance by MDG regions 2010

(Bln US$)

Imports — Exports — Trade balance

Developed Asia-Pacific
Developed Europe
Developed N. America
South-eastern Europe
C I S
Northern Africa
Sub-Saharan Africa
Latin Am, Caribbean
Eastern Asia
Southern Asia
South-eastern Asia
Western Asia
Oceania

-25 -20 -15 -10 -5 0 5 10 15 20 25 30 35 40

Table 3: Top importing countries or areas in 2010

Country or area	Value (million US$)	Avg. Growth (%) 06-10	Growth (%) 09-10	World share %	Cum.
World	63001.4	0.9	4.7	100.0	
USA	6249.4	-9.2	3.9	9.9	9.9
China	3726.0	7.3	17.1	5.9	15.8
Germany	3276.6	-1.6	0.8	5.2	21.0
France	3007.7	-1.7	2.8	4.8	25.8
United Kingdom	2147.0	-8.3	3.4	3.4	29.2
Canada	2132.5	-2.2	21.9	3.4	32.6
Russian Federation	1989.3	7.2	11.8	3.2	35.8
Italy	1768.6	-1.2	8.5	2.8	38.6
Netherlands	1591.1	-3.8	-2.2	2.5	41.1
Rep. of Korea	1577.1	6.4	-14.0	2.5	43.6
Belgium	1544.5	-4.3	-3.4	2.5	46.0
Australia	1493.9	4.2	11.6	2.4	48.4
Brazil	1490.8	36.9	49.7	2.4	50.8
Singapore	1440.5	5.1	-4.1	2.3	53.1
Spain	1357.5	-14.2	-5.8	2.2	55.2

Source: UN Comtrade

745 Non-electrical machinery, tools and mechanical apparatus, parts thereof, nes

After a 23.5 percent drop in 2009, the value (in current prices) of exports of non-electrical machinery, tools and mechanical apparatus, parts thereof, nes (SITC group 745) bounced back in 2010 by 13.1 percent to 48.3 bln US$ (see table 2). Imports showed a similar development with an increase of 13.6 percent and amounted to 47.3 bln US$ in 2010 (see table 3). Graph 1 shows that the increase in exports for 2010 in this product group was exceeded by the increases in world exports of machinery and transport equipment (SITC section 7) of 22.1 percent and in total world exports of 21.2 percent. Exports of non-electrical machinery, tools and mechanical apparatus, parts thereof, nes (SITC group 745) accounted for 0.9 percent of world exports of SITC section 7 and 0.3 percent of total world exports in 2010 (see table 1).

Germany, Italy and USA were the top exporting countries in 2010 (see table 2). They accounted respectively for 20.4, 15.2 and 10.9 percent of world exports. USA and Germany were also among top destinations, together with China (see table 3). By MDG regions (see graph 2), Developed Europe accounted for a majority of trade in non-electrical machinery, tools and mechanical apparatus, parts thereof, nes (SITC group 745). In 2010, its exports reached 28.5 bln US$ while imports amounted to 17.4 bln US$, resulting in a trade surplus of 11.1 bln US$. Eastern Asia recorded a trade surplus of 2.1 bln US$. Top trade deficits were recorded by Latin America and the Caribbean (-3.0 bln US$), Commonwealth of Independent States (-2.1 bln US$) and Developed North America (-1.7 bln US$).

Table 1: Imports (Imp.) and exports (Exp.), 1996-2010, in current prices

		1996	1997	1998	1999	2000	2001	2002	2003	2004	2005	2006	2007	2008	2009	2010
Values in Bln US$	Imp.	23.3	23.3	23.5	22.6	22.7	22.9	24.9	29.4	34.8	37.9	42.3	47.4	52.2	41.6	47.3
	Exp.	23.6	23.3	24.0	23.0	23.1	23.4	25.9	30.0	36.9	39.5	44.0	50.6	55.9	42.7	48.3
As a percentage of	Imp.	1.2	1.1	1.1	1.0	0.9	0.9	1.0	1.0	1.0	1.0	1.0	0.9	1.0	1.0	0.9
SITC section (%)	Exp.	1.2	1.1	1.1	1.0	0.9	0.9	1.0	1.0	1.0	1.0	1.0	1.0	1.0	1.0	0.9
As a percentage of	Imp.	0.4	0.4	0.4	0.4	0.3	0.4	0.4	0.4	0.4	0.4	0.3	0.3	0.3	0.3	0.3
world trade (%)	Exp.	0.4	0.4	0.4	0.4	0.4	0.4	0.4	0.4	0.4	0.4	0.4	0.4	0.4	0.3	0.3

Graph 1: Annual growth rates of exports, 1996–2010
(In percentage by year)

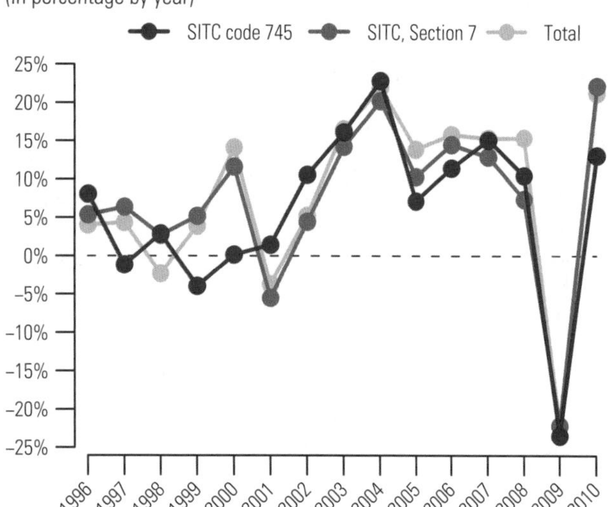

Graph 2: Trade Balance by MDG regions 2010
(Bln US$)

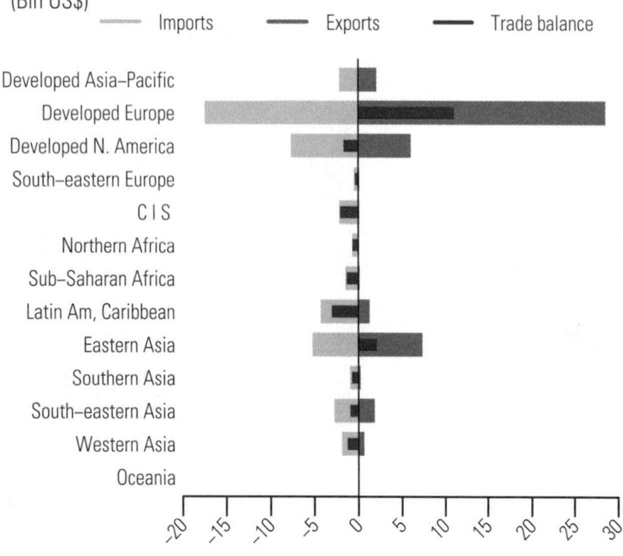

Table 2: Top exporting countries or areas in 2010

Country or area	Value (million US$)	Avg. Growth (%) 06-10	Growth (%) 09-10	World share %	Cum.
World	48316.7	2.4	13.1	100.0	
Germany	9876.5	-2.6	1.0	20.4	20.4
Italy	7342.9	2.1	9.5	15.2	35.6
USA	5253.5	0.1	15.3	10.9	46.5
China	5249.0	17.6	31.7	10.9	57.4
Japan	1889.2	-0.5	33.4	3.9	61.3
Switzerland	1374.8	3.0	13.6	2.8	64.1
Netherlands	1365.8	5.6	13.2	2.8	67.0
France	1311.2	2.1	7.2	2.7	69.7
Sweden	1228.7	-1.2	15.6	2.5	72.2
United Kingdom	1187.1	-4.4	10.7	2.5	74.7
Other Asia, nes	1025.2	0.1	37.8	2.1	76.8
Indonesia	962.5	106.2	4.6	2.0	78.8
Belgium	922.6	-1.6	10.8	1.9	80.7
Spain	887.6	3.2	10.6	1.8	82.5
Canada	745.9	-5.2	15.1	1.5	84.1

Table 3: Top importing countries or areas in 2010

Country or area	Value (million US$)	Avg. Growth (%) 06-10	Growth (%) 09-10	World share %	Cum.
World	47292.8	2.8	13.6	100.0	
USA	6112.1	-1.6	18.1	12.9	12.9
China	3714.5	17.1	63.0	7.9	20.8
Germany	2708.7	-0.2	6.7	5.7	26.5
France	2411.3	1.8	2.5	5.1	31.6
United Kingdom	1664.7	-2.3	14.8	3.5	35.1
Canada	1539.3	1.0	10.4	3.3	38.4
Russian Federation	1532.1	10.8	20.6	3.2	41.6
Italy	1399.0	1.2	14.3	3.0	44.6
Mexico	1321.3	-1.6	10.7	2.8	47.4
Belgium	1188.6	-1.4	4.9	2.5	49.9
Japan	1064.3	3.3	26.3	2.3	52.1
Spain	1051.7	-6.0	-5.5	2.2	54.4
Brazil	943.0	22.3	28.0	2.0	56.4
Australia	927.5	3.7	11.0	2.0	58.3
Switzerland	911.2	1.4	5.0	1.9	60.2

After a 28.9 percent decrease in 2009, the value (in current prices) of exports of ball or roller bearings (SITC group 746) rose by 33.6 percent in 2010 and amounted to 29.4 bln US$ (see table 2). Imports also increased by 27.8 percent to 30.2 bln US$ (see table 3). Graph 1 shows that the increase in exports for 2010 in this product group exceeded the increases in world exports of machinery and transport equipment (SITC section 7) of 22.1 percent and in total world exports of 21.2 percent. Exports of ball or roller bearings (SITC group 746) accounted for 0.6 percent of world exports of SITC section 7 and 0.2 percent of total world exports in 2010 (see table 1).

Germany, Japan and China were the top exporting countries in 2010 (see table 2). They accounted respectively for 16.7, 15.8 and 10.9 percent of world exports. China and Germany were also among top destinations, together with USA (see table 3). By MDG regions (see graph 2), Developed Europe accounted for a large share of trade in ball or roller bearings (SITC group 746). In 2010, its exports and imports were valued respectively at 13.7 bln US$ and 11.4 bln US$, resulting in a trade surplus of 2.3 bln US$. A larger trade surplus was recorded by Developed Asia-Pacific (+3.8 bln US$). Top trade deficits were recorded by Latin America and the Caribbean (-1.8 bln US$), Eastern Asia (-1.5 bln US$) and South-eastern Asia (-0.9 bln US$).

Table 1: Imports (Imp.) and exports (Exp.), 1996-2010, in current prices

		1996	1997	1998	1999	2000	2001	2002	2003	2004	2005	2006	2007	2008	2009	2010
Values in Bln US$	Imp.	13.2	12.8	12.4	12.2	13.1	12.6	13.0	15.4	18.5	20.7	22.9	26.8	31.6	23.6	30.2
	Exp.	12.5	12.0	11.7	11.5	12.5	12.0	12.5	14.8	17.7	19.7	21.9	26.0	30.9	22.0	29.4
As a percentage of SITC section (%)	Imp.	0.7	0.6	0.6	0.5	0.5	0.5	0.5	0.5	0.5	0.5	0.5	0.5	0.6	0.6	0.6
	Exp.	0.6	0.6	0.5	0.5	0.5	0.5	0.5	0.5	0.5	0.5	0.5	0.5	0.6	0.5	0.6
As a percentage of world trade (%)	Imp.	0.2	0.2	0.2	0.2	0.2	0.2	0.2	0.2	0.2	0.2	0.2	0.2	0.2	0.2	0.2
	Exp.	0.2	0.2	0.2	0.2	0.2	0.2	0.2	0.2	0.2	0.2	0.2	0.2	0.2	0.2	0.2

Graph 1: Annual growth rates of exports, 1996–2010

(In percentage by year)

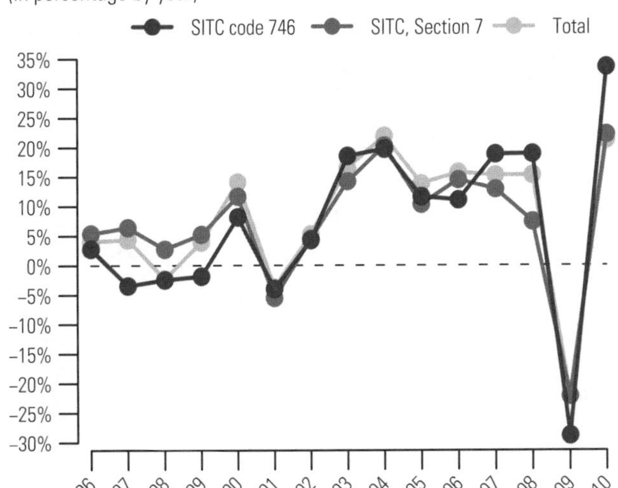

Graph 2: Trade Balance by MDG regions 2010

(Bln US$)

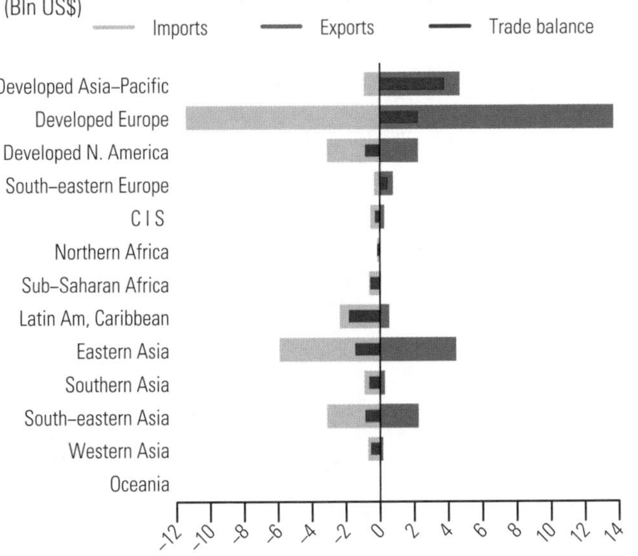

Table 2: Top exporting countries or areas in 2010

Country or area	Value (million US$)	Avg. Growth (%) 06-10	Growth (%) 09-10	World share %	Cum.
World	29368.0	7.6	33.6	100.0	
Germany	4914.7	7.8	23.7	16.7	16.7
Japan	4647.5	11.4	61.6	15.8	32.6
China	3194.8	19.2	64.9	10.9	43.4
France	1891.3	2.3	10.7	6.4	49.9
USA	1876.0	3.7	27.7	6.4	56.3
Singapore	1525.8	7.3	28.0	5.2	61.5
Italy	1386.4	3.7	25.2	4.7	66.2
Sweden	800.7	-0.9	9.2	2.7	68.9
Belgium	748.2	4.0	22.3	2.5	71.5
Netherlands	695.2	1.8	26.2	2.4	73.8
Slovakia	667.0	6.2	41.7	2.3	76.1
Romania	642.2	22.9	23.7	2.2	78.3
Austria	634.0	6.1	35.2	2.2	80.4
China, Hong Kong SAR	605.1	11.1	11.1	2.1	82.5
United Kingdom	578.6	0.3	16.6	2.0	84.5

Table 3: Top importing countries or areas in 2010

Country or area	Value (million US$)	Avg. Growth (%) 06-10	Growth (%) 09-10	World share %	Cum.
World	30163.1	7.2	27.8	100.0	
China	3712.9	22.1	33.0	12.3	12.3
Germany	3518.1	3.9	24.7	11.7	24.0
USA	2267.3	2.8	44.1	7.5	31.5
Singapore	1433.6	8.5	42.5	4.8	36.2
France	1325.7	2.5	11.4	4.4	40.6
Italy	1177.5	0.7	24.5	3.9	44.5
Rep. of Korea	1006.6	10.4	45.7	3.3	47.9
Belgium	956.2	3.7	16.1	3.2	51.0
Canada	823.1	-0.9	25.4	2.7	53.8
China, Hong Kong SAR	810.9	8.7	2.0	2.7	56.5
Mexico	800.2	7.8	47.7	2.7	59.1
Brazil	799.0	15.6	43.8	2.6	61.8
India	669.2	14.1	18.2	2.2	64.0
Netherlands	652.0	4.2	29.5	2.2	66.1
Thailand	635.0	10.9	52.8	2.1	68.3

747 Taps, cocks, valves, etc; pressure-reducing, thermostatically control valves

After a 19.5 percent drop in 2009, the value (in current prices) of exports of taps, cocks, valves, etc; pressure-reducing, thermostatically control valves (SITC group 747) bounced back by 14.6 percent in 2010 to reach 65.2 bln US$ (see table 2). Imports, after a 17.4 percent drop in 2009, increased by 14.2 percent in 2010 and totaled 68.4 bln US$ (see table 3). Graph 1 shows that the increase in exports for 2010 in this product group was exceeded by both the increases in world exports of machinery of and transport equipment (SITC section 7) of 22.1 percent and in total world exports of 21.2 percent. Exports of taps, cocks, valves, etc; pressure-reducing, thermostatically control valves (SITC group 747) accounted for 1.3 percent of world exports of SITC section 7 and 0.4 percent of total world exports in 2010 (see table 1).

The top exporting countries in 2010 were China, Germany and USA (see table 2). They accounted respectively for 15.1, 15.0 and 12.0 percent of world exports. USA, China and Germany were also the top destinations (see table 3). By MDG regions (see graph 2), Developed Europe accounted for a majority of exports of taps, cocks, valves, etc; pressure-reducing, thermostatically control valves (SITC group 747). In 2010, its exports were valued at 32.8 bln US$ while imports amounted to 23.2 bln US$. This resulted in a trade surplus of 9.6 bln US$. Eastern Asia also recorded a trade surplus of 3.3 bln US$. Top trade deficits were recorded by Developed North America (-3.7 bln US$), Western Asia (-3.2 bln US$) and Latin America and the Caribbean (-2.6 bln US$).

Table 1: Imports (Imp.) and exports (Exp.), 1996-2010, in current prices

		1996	1997	1998	1999	2000	2001	2002	2003	2004	2005	2006	2007	2008	2009	2010
Values in Bln US$	Imp.	22.3	23.5	24.3	24.0	25.0	25.4	27.8	32.8	40.2	45.3	52.4	63.9	72.5	59.9	68.4
	Exp.	20.7	21.5	22.2	22.2	22.9	23.4	25.4	29.8	36.4	40.8	50.0	61.8	70.7	56.9	65.2
As a percentage of SITC section (%)	Imp.	1.1	1.1	1.1	1.0	1.0	1.0	1.1	1.1	1.1	1.2	1.2	1.3	1.4	1.4	1.3
	Exp.	1.0	1.0	1.0	0.9	0.9	0.9	1.0	1.0	1.0	1.0	1.1	1.2	1.3	1.4	1.3
As a percentage of world trade (%)	Imp.	0.4	0.4	0.4	0.4	0.4	0.4	0.4	0.4	0.4	0.4	0.4	0.5	0.4	0.5	0.5
	Exp.	0.4	0.4	0.4	0.4	0.4	0.4	0.4	0.4	0.4	0.4	0.4	0.4	0.4	0.5	0.4

Graph 1: Annual growth rates of exports, 1996–2010

(In percentage by year)

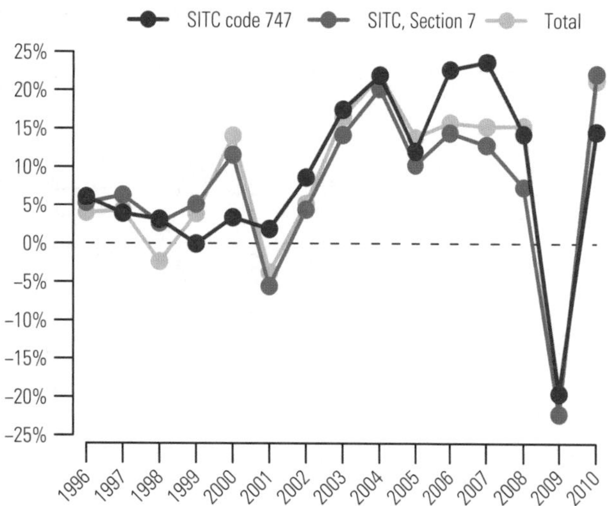

Table 2: Top exporting countries or areas in 2010

Country or area	Value (million US$)	Avg. Growth (%) 06-10	Growth (%) 09-10	World share %	Cum.
World	65164.4	6.8	14.6	100.0	
China	9819.3	14.5	30.0	15.1	15.1
Germany	9767.9	5.4	11.8	15.0	30.1
USA	7797.3	9.3	19.6	12.0	42.0
Italy	6805.7	2.0	-5.5	10.4	52.5
Japan	4491.0	10.7	52.3	6.9	59.4
United Kingdom	2753.8	6.9	16.8	4.2	63.6
France	2619.9	2.5	3.2	4.0	67.6
Mexico	1681.6	-0.4	21.5	2.6	70.2
Switzerland	1376.7	6.0	30.6	2.1	72.3
Denmark	1235.4	4.2	28.9	1.9	74.2
Spain	1196.3	1.5	-3.9	1.8	76.0
Rep. of Korea	1146.1	8.0	3.1	1.8	77.8
Canada	1119.8	-0.2	8.3	1.7	79.5
Netherlands	952.7	2.8	-16.3	1.5	81.0
Other Asia, nes	922.0	1.5	37.6	1.4	82.4

Graph 2: Trade Balance by MDG regions 2010

(Bln US$)

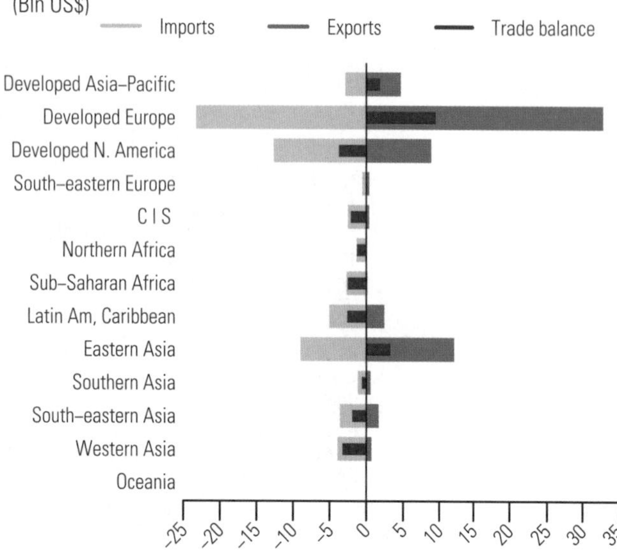

Table 3: Top importing countries or areas in 2010

Country or area	Value (million US$)	Avg. Growth (%) 06-10	Growth (%) 09-10	World share %	Cum.
World	68411.2	6.9	14.2	100.0	
USA	10006.1	2.1	28.2	14.6	14.6
China	6130.1	15.7	20.8	9.0	23.6
Germany	4730.7	2.8	12.7	6.9	30.5
United Kingdom	2772.9	2.5	13.6	4.1	34.6
France	2763.4	3.7	8.7	4.0	38.6
Canada	2616.2	1.4	13.5	3.8	42.4
Mexico	2172.7	5.4	32.9	3.2	45.6
Italy	1805.1	1.9	9.3	2.6	48.2
Rep. of Korea	1744.2	8.5	16.9	2.5	50.8
Japan	1723.7	3.5	25.3	2.5	53.3
Russian Federation	1606.7	30.6	46.2	2.3	55.7
Spain	1363.3	0.0	10.2	2.0	57.6
Belgium	1149.6	6.9	9.4	1.7	59.3
Netherlands	1087.8	3.0	-1.0	1.6	60.9
Singapore	1067.9	11.7	-6.1	1.6	62.5

Source: UN Comtrade

After several years of continuous growth marked by a peak of 48.3 bln US$ in 2008, the value (in current prices) of exports of transmission shafts and cranks, and parts thereof (SITC group 748) dropped by 23.9 percent in 2009, but bounced back by 20.8 percent to 44.4 bln US$ in 2010 (see table 2). Similarly, imports dropped by 24.4 percent in 2009 but rose by 20.9 percent to 46.8 bln US$ in 2010 (see table 3). Graph 1 shows that the increase in exports for 2010 in this product group was slightly lower than the increases in world exports of machinery and transport equipment (SITC section 7) of 22.1 percent and in total world exports of 21.2 percent. Exports of transmission shafts and cranks, and parts thereof (SITC group 748) accounted for 0.9 percent of world exports of SITC section 7 and 0.3 percent of total world exports in 2010 (see table 1).

The top exporting countries in 2010 were Germany, Japan and USA (see table 2), accounting respectively for 23.7, 13.2 and 9.3 percent of world exports. Top destinations were USA, China and Germany (see table 3). By MDG regions (see graph 2), Developed Europe accounted for a large share of exports of transmission shafts and cranks, and parts thereof (SITC group 748). In 2010, its exports were valued at 23.7 bln US$ while imports amounted to 17.0 bln US$, resulting in a trade surplus of 6.7 bln US$. Developed Asia-Pacific recorded a trade surplus amounting to 3.8 bln US$. Top trade deficits were recorded by Latin America and the Caribbean (-3.1 bln US$), Developed North America (-2.9 bln US$) and South-eastern Asia (-2.1 bln US$).

Table 1: Imports (Imp.) and exports (Exp.), 1996-2010, in current prices

		1996	1997	1998	1999	2000	2001	2002	2003	2004	2005	2006	2007	2008	2009	2010
Values in Bln US$	Imp.	15.9	16.0	16.6	17.0	17.5	17.7	19.0	22.2	27.3	31.0	34.9	42.8	51.2	38.7	46.8
	Exp.	15.0	15.1	15.5	15.4	16.1	16.3	17.6	20.7	25.4	29.6	33.5	40.4	48.3	36.8	44.4
As a percentage of SITC section (%)	Imp.	0.8	0.8	0.8	0.7	0.7	0.7	0.7	0.8	0.8	0.8	0.8	0.9	1.0	0.9	0.9
	Exp.	0.7	0.7	0.7	0.7	0.6	0.7	0.7	0.7	0.7	0.8	0.8	0.8	0.9	0.9	0.9
As a percentage of world trade (%)	Imp.	0.3	0.3	0.3	0.3	0.3	0.3	0.3	0.3	0.3	0.3	0.3	0.3	0.3	0.3	0.3
	Exp.	0.3	0.3	0.3	0.3	0.3	0.3	0.3	0.3	0.3	0.3	0.3	0.3	0.3	0.3	0.3

Graph 1: Annual growth rates of exports, 1996–2010

(In percentage by year)

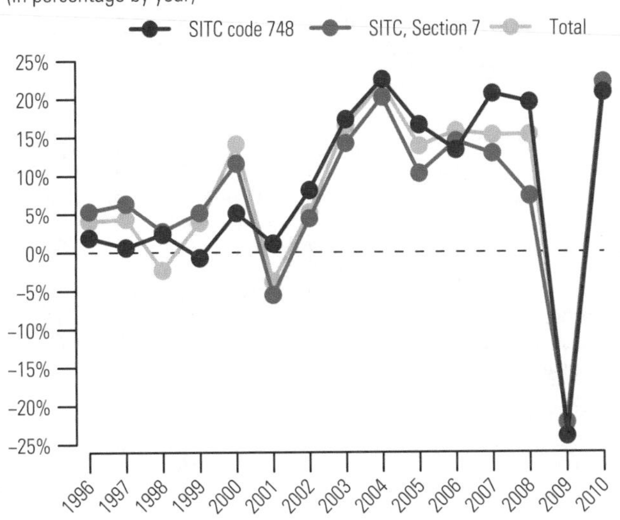

Table 2: Top exporting countries or areas in 2010

Country or area	Value (million US$)	Avg. Growth (%) 06-10	Growth (%) 09-10	World share %	Cum.
World	44 393.0	7.3	20.8	100.0	
Germany	10 521.2	4.4	9.0	23.7	23.7
Japan	5 874.8	7.8	40.7	13.2	36.9
USA	4 132.8	9.0	31.4	9.3	46.2
China	3 980.5	24.0	47.2	9.0	55.2
Italy	2 901.5	3.0	18.8	6.5	61.7
France	1 858.8	5.7	11.1	4.2	65.9
Belgium	1 534.5	3.7	-9.1	3.5	69.4
Canada	945.3	0.1	18.5	2.1	71.5
United Kingdom	913.5	1.6	12.9	2.1	73.6
Rep. of Korea	894.4	21.7	37.3	2.0	75.6
Spain	816.9	9.8	11.8	1.8	77.4
Slovakia	767.6	18.6	59.8	1.7	79.2
Other Asia, nes	751.3	15.9	78.2	1.7	80.9
Mexico	698.5	-0.3	35.4	1.6	82.4
Austria	664.6	3.5	2.7	1.5	83.9

Graph 2: Trade Balance by MDG regions 2010

(Bln US$)

Imports — Exports — Trade balance

Developed Asia-Pacific
Developed Europe
Developed N. America
South-eastern Europe
C I S
Northern Africa
Sub-Saharan Africa
Latin Am, Caribbean
Eastern Asia
Southern Asia
South-eastern Asia
Western Asia
Oceania

-20 -15 -10 -5 0 5 10 15 20 25

Table 3: Top importing countries or areas in 2010

Country or area	Value (million US$)	Avg. Growth (%) 06-10	Growth (%) 09-10	World share %	Cum.
World	46 840.2	7.6	20.9	100.0	
USA	6 167.4	1.8	28.3	13.2	13.2
China	5 489.4	23.7	38.7	11.7	24.9
Germany	3 778.6	5.5	17.3	8.1	33.0
Canada	1 843.4	4.6	20.8	3.9	36.9
Mexico	1 828.4	4.9	48.9	3.9	40.8
France	1 726.7	1.1	17.3	3.7	44.5
Japan	1 445.9	5.2	27.2	3.1	47.6
United Kingdom	1 412.4	5.2	27.8	3.0	50.6
Brazil	1 383.8	15.2	39.6	3.0	53.5
Italy	1 310.2	4.0	7.8	2.8	56.3
Rep. of Korea	1 309.6	9.8	21.0	2.8	59.1
Indonesia	1 090.9	26.9	51.0	2.3	61.5
Belgium	1 015.3	3.7	5.0	2.2	63.6
Austria	951.3	4.1	25.1	2.0	65.7
Hungary	875.1	0.5	15.9	1.9	67.5

Source: UN Comtrade

749 Non-electric parts and accessories of machinery, nes

In 2010, the value (in current prices) of exports of non-electric parts and accessories of machinery, nes (SITC group 749) rose by 10.9 percent to 25.4 bln US$ (see table 2). Similarly, imports showed a 8.0 percent increase and amounted to 24.7 bln US$ (see table 3). Graph 1 shows that the rise in exports for 2010 in this product group was by far exceeded by the increases in world exports of machinery and transport equipment (SITC section 7) of 22.1 percent and in total world exports of 21.2 percent. Exports of non-electric parts and accessories of machinery, nes (SITC group 749) accounted for 0.5 percent of world exports of SITC section 7 and 0.2 percent of total world exports (see table 1).

Germany, China and Japan were the top exporting countries in 2010 (see table 2). They accounted respectively for 13.8, 12.4 and 11.4 percent of world exports. Top destinations were China, USA and Mexico (see table 3). By MDG regions (see graph 2), Developed Europe's exports and imports amounted respectively to 10.7 bln US$ and 7.0 bln US$, resulting in a trade surplus of 3.7 bln US$. Top trade surpluses were also recorded by Developed Asia-Pacific (+1.8 bln US$) and Eastern Asia (+1.1 bln US$). Top trade deficits were recorded by Latin America and the Caribbean (-2.0 bln US$), South-eastern Asia (-1.1 bln US$) and Western Asia (-0.9 bln US$).

Table 1: Imports (Imp.) and exports (Exp.), 1996-2010, in current prices

		1996	1997	1998	1999	2000	2001	2002	2003	2004	2005	2006	2007	2008	2009	2010
Values in Bln US$	Imp.	12.7	12.8	13.3	13.5	13.8	13.7	14.3	16.1	18.9	20.5	22.2	23.9	26.6	22.8	24.7
	Exp.	13.8	14.0	14.5	14.9	15.6	15.3	16.0	18.2	21.1	21.8	24.3	25.8	28.5	22.9	25.4
As a percentage of SITC section (%)	Imp.	0.6	0.6	0.6	0.6	0.5	0.6	0.6	0.5	0.5	0.5	0.5	0.5	0.5	0.5	0.5
	Exp.	0.7	0.6	0.7	0.6	0.6	0.6	0.6	0.6	0.6	0.6	0.5	0.5	0.5	0.5	0.5
As a percentage of world trade (%)	Imp.	0.2	0.2	0.2	0.2	0.2	0.2	0.2	0.2	0.2	0.2	0.2	0.2	0.2	0.2	0.2
	Exp.	0.3	0.3	0.3	0.3	0.2	0.3	0.2	0.2	0.2	0.2	0.2	0.2	0.2	0.2	0.2

Graph 1: Annual growth rates of exports, 1996–2010
(In percentage by year)

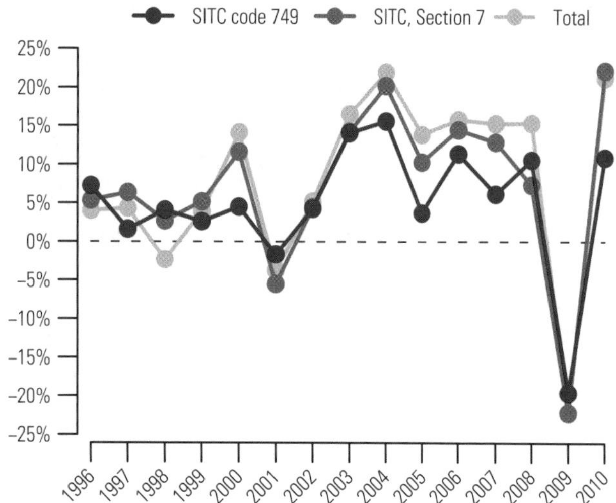

Table 2: Top exporting countries or areas in 2010

Country or area	Value (million US$)	Avg. Growth (%) 06-10	Growth (%) 09-10	World share %	Cum.
World	25 437.1	1.1	10.9	100.0	
Germany	3 522.4	-3.8	10.5	13.8	13.8
China	3 144.4	23.2	11.6	12.4	26.2
Japan	2 910.4	1.1	19.8	11.4	37.7
USA	1 949.7	0.6	8.2	7.7	45.3
Italy	1 499.9	-3.1	-3.5	5.9	51.2
Rep. of Korea	1 432.4	7.6	34.0	5.6	56.8
Singapore	1 249.5	4.0	52.4	4.9	61.8
France	826.3	-8.4	-6.4	3.2	65.0
Other Asia, nes	814.7	-1.1	23.7	3.2	68.2
Canada	723.3	-8.2	6.5	2.8	71.1
United Kingdom	589.1	-11.6	-5.5	2.3	73.4
Austria	568.0	3.1	14.3	2.2	75.6
China, Hong Kong SAR	564.8	1.4	16.3	2.2	77.8
Switzerland	471.7	0.9	7.0	1.9	79.7
Portugal	460.2	1.2	-7.3	1.8	81.5

Graph 2: Trade Balance by MDG regions 2010
(Bln US$)

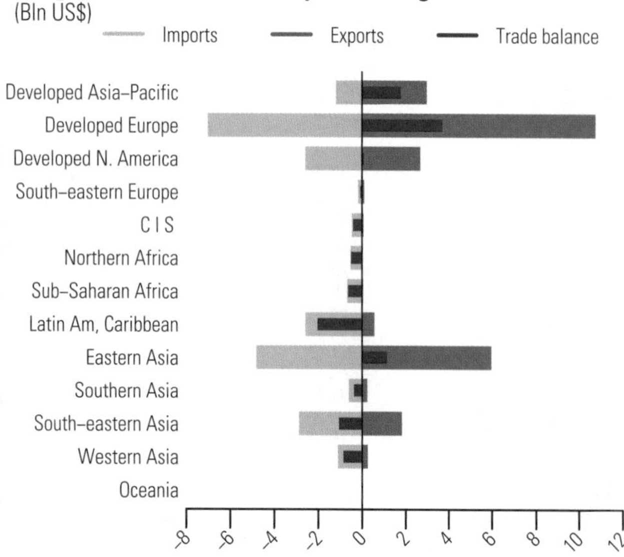

Table 3: Top importing countries or areas in 2010

Country or area	Value (million US$)	Avg. Growth (%) 06-10	Growth (%) 09-10	World share %	Cum.
World	24 662.3	2.7	8.0	100.0	
China	2 785.9	10.1	12.2	11.3	11.3
USA	1 978.6	-5.0	18.2	8.0	19.3
Mexico	1 474.9	1.6	5.6	6.0	25.3
Germany	1 449.6	-3.5	5.9	5.9	31.2
Rep. of Korea	1 132.8	33.7	33.3	4.6	35.8
Japan	941.9	0.8	15.6	3.8	39.6
France	770.8	-0.8	3.3	3.1	42.7
Thailand	731.3	2.7	42.2	3.0	45.7
Singapore	715.0	-1.8	-13.3	2.9	48.6
Italy	695.8	2.0	10.0	2.8	51.4
China, Hong Kong SAR	652.3	6.1	26.6	2.6	54.0
Canada	607.3	-1.8	17.7	2.5	56.5
United Kingdom	592.8	-7.7	7.2	2.4	58.9
Malaysia	533.8	1.6	19.1	2.2	61.1
Viet Nam	*441.1*	26.9	66.9	1.8	62.9

After a 15.0 percent drop in 2009, the value (in current prices) of office machines (SITC group 751) bounced back in 2010 by 16.4 percent to 48.9 bln US$ (see table 2). Imports showed a similar development with an increase of 15.4 percent and amounted to 49.3 bln US$ in 2010 (see table 3). Graph 1 shows that the increase in exports for 2010 in this product group was exceeded by the increases in world exports of machinery and transport equipment (SITC section 7) of 22.1 percent and in total world exports of 21.2 percent. Exports of office machines (SITC group 751) accounted for 1.0 percent of world exports of SITC section 7 and 0.3 percent of total world exports in 2010 (see table 1).

China, Netherlands and Germany were the top exporting countries in 2010 (see table 2). They accounted respectively for 37.6, 10.0 and 7.8 percent of world exports. Top destinations were USA, Germany and Netherlands (see table 3). By MDG regions (see graph 2), Eastern Asia and South-eastern Asia recorded trade surpluses amounting respectively to 16.2 bln US$ and 3.2 bln US$. Top trade deficits were recorded by Developed North America (-7.7 bln US$), Developed Europe (-5.1 bln US$) and Developed Asia-Pacific (-1.7 bln US$).

Table 1: Imports (Imp.) and exports (Exp.), 1996-2010, in current prices

		1996	1997	1998	1999	2000	2001	2002	2003	2004	2005	2006	2007	2008	2009	2010
Values in Bln US$	Imp.	16.7	16.7	15.5	14.3	13.8	12.9	12.2	14.0	16.1	17.1	19.4	48.9	52.2	42.7	49.3
	Exp.	15.3	16.0	14.8	14.2	14.4	13.6	11.6	11.7	12.8	15.2	18.3	44.9	49.4	42.0	48.9
As a percentage of SITC section (%)	Imp.	0.8	0.8	0.7	0.6	0.5	0.5	0.5	0.5	0.5	0.4	0.4	1.0	1.0	1.0	1.0
	Exp.	0.7	0.7	0.7	0.6	0.6	0.6	0.4	0.4	0.4	0.4	0.4	0.9	0.9	1.0	1.0
As a percentage of world trade (%)	Imp.	0.3	0.3	0.3	0.3	0.2	0.2	0.2	0.2	0.2	0.2	0.2	0.3	0.3	0.3	0.3
	Exp.	0.3	0.3	0.3	0.3	0.2	0.2	0.2	0.2	0.1	0.1	0.2	0.3	0.3	0.3	0.3

Graph 1: Annual growth rates of exports, 1996–2010

(In percentage by year)

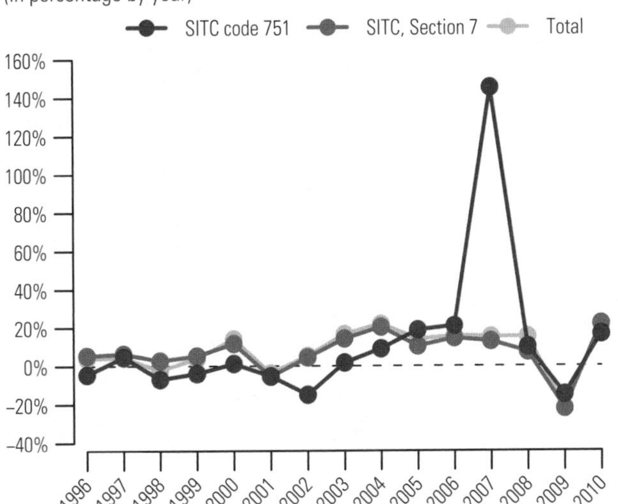

Table 2: Top exporting countries or areas in 2010

Country or area	Value (million US$)	Avg. Growth (%) 06-10	Growth (%) 09-10	World share %	Cum.
World	48 897.2	27.8	16.4	100.0	
China	18 369.6	28.2	37.2	37.6	37.6
Netherlands	4 899.3	27.5	-7.6	10.0	47.6
Germany	3 802.3	20.0	19.0	7.8	55.4
USA	2 817.6	22.7	9.0	5.8	61.1
Japan	2 258.5	41.6	11.9	4.6	65.7
China, Hong Kong SAR	2 235.3	39.0	42.8	4.6	70.3
Singapore	1 831.2	71.8	12.7	3.7	74.1
Viet Nam	*1 519.3*	811.4	25.6	3.1	77.2
Thailand	1 513.2	232.5	40.4	3.1	80.3
Rep. of Korea	1 066.7	31.0	29.1	2.2	82.4
France	1 025.7	8.9	-21.2	2.1	84.5
Malaysia	1 024.4	44.2	-36.0	2.1	86.6
Mexico	1 021.5	73.5	1.1	2.1	88.7
Belgium	929.1	46.9	-2.9	1.9	90.6
United Kingdom	799.7	-5.1	5.2	1.6	92.3

Graph 2: Trade Balance by MDG regions 2010

(Bln US$)

Imports — Exports — Trade balance

Developed Asia-Pacific
Developed Europe
Developed N. America
South-eastern Europe
C I S
Northern Africa
Sub-Saharan Africa
Latin Am, Caribbean
Eastern Asia
Southern Asia
South-eastern Asia
Western Asia
Oceania

-20 -15 -10 -5 0 5 10 15 20 25

Table 3: Top importing countries or areas in 2010

Country or area	Value (million US$)	Avg. Growth (%) 06-10	Growth (%) 09-10	World share %	Cum.
World	49 331.9	26.2	15.4	100.0	
USA	9 667.8	21.1	8.8	19.6	19.6
Germany	4 917.8	30.0	36.4	10.0	29.6
Netherlands	3 842.4	28.8	4.2	7.8	37.4
Japan	3 012.9	61.1	20.2	6.1	43.5
China	2 634.7	50.9	41.4	5.3	48.8
China, Hong Kong SAR	2 163.6	41.8	40.2	4.4	53.2
France	1 929.7	13.5	-11.1	3.9	57.1
United Kingdom	1 792.2	12.0	0.6	3.6	60.7
Singapore	1 478.6	63.1	30.5	3.0	63.7
Italy	1 267.1	17.9	3.1	2.6	66.3
Canada	1 139.4	18.4	24.7	2.3	68.6
Russian Federation	1 058.1	39.0	49.3	2.1	70.8
Australia	919.7	17.7	19.3	1.9	72.6
Mexico	877.6	39.2	9.1	1.8	74.4
Spain	762.1	13.3	-4.2	1.5	75.9

Source: UN Comtrade

752 Automatic data processing machines and units thereof

After a 14.1 percent drop in 2009, the value (in current prices) of exports of automatic data processing machines and units thereof (SITC group 752) bounced back in 2010 by 23.8 percent to 323.9 bln US$ (see table 2). Imports showed a similar development with an increase of 23.8 percent and amounted to 319.1 bln US$ (see table 3). Graph 1 shows that the increase in exports for 2010 in this product group exceeded the increases in world exports of machinery and transport equipment (SITC section 7) of 22.1 percent and in total world exports of 21.2 percent. Exports of automatic data processing machines and units thereof (SITC group 752) accounted for 6.3 percent of world exports of SITC section 7 and 2.2 percent of total world exports in 2010 (see table 1).

In 2010, China, the top exporting country, accounted for 45.9 percent of world exports (see table 2). Other major exporting countries were USA and Netherlands, respectively with 7.8 and 5.5 percent of world exports. USA and China were also among the top destinations, together with Germany (see table 3). By MDG regions (see graph 2), Eastern Asia accounted for a large share of exports of automatic data processing machines and units thereof (SITC group 752). In 2010, its exports were valued at 170.4 bln US$ while imports amounted to 50.7 bln US$, resulting in a trade surplus of 119.7 bln US$. South-eastern Asia also recorded a trade surplus amounting to 27.4 bln US$. Top trade deficits were recorded by Developed North America (-58.0 bln US$), Developed Europe (-43.0 bln US$) and Developed Asia-Pacific (-18.7 bln US$).

Table 1: Imports (Imp.) and exports (Exp.), 1996-2010, in current prices

		1996	1997	1998	1999	2000	2001	2002	2003	2004	2005	2006	2007	2008	2009	2010
Values in Bln US$	Imp.	157.4	172.8	179.2	197.9	219.6	200.0	201.0	224.6	263.1	286.1	305.9	292.7	300.5	257.7	319.1
	Exp.	151.0	171.5	168.8	180.2	198.5	184.1	182.0	209.2	249.1	271.8	298.6	302.2	304.4	261.5	323.9
As a percentage of SITC section (%)	Imp.	7.8	8.1	8.1	8.5	8.4	8.1	7.8	7.7	7.4	7.3	6.9	5.9	5.6	6.0	6.1
	Exp.	7.4	7.9	7.6	7.7	7.6	7.5	7.1	7.1	7.0	7.0	6.7	6.0	5.6	6.2	6.3
As a percentage of world trade (%)	Imp.	2.9	3.1	3.3	3.5	3.4	3.2	3.1	2.9	2.8	2.7	2.5	2.1	1.9	2.1	2.1
	Exp.	2.9	3.1	3.2	3.2	3.1	3.0	2.8	2.8	2.7	2.6	2.5	2.2	1.9	2.1	2.2

Graph 1: Annual growth rates of exports, 1996–2010
(In percentage by year)

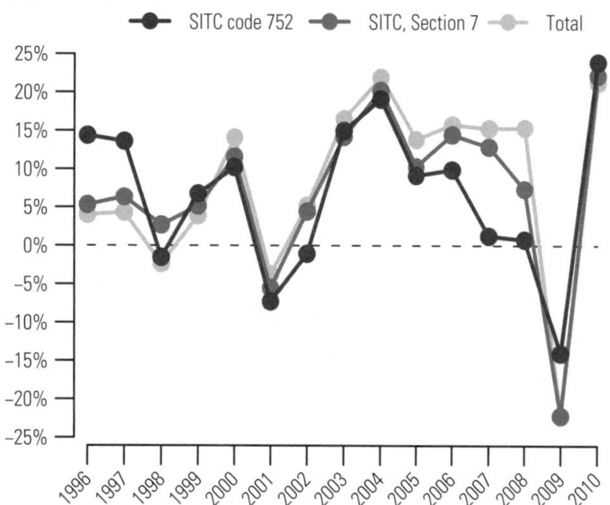

Table 2: Top exporting countries or areas in 2010

Country or area	Value (million US$)	Avg. Growth (%) 06-10	Growth (%) 09-10	World share %	Cum.
World	323871.9	2.1	23.8	100.0	
China	148802.6	12.5	33.0	45.9	45.9
USA	25211.0	-1.3	19.4	7.8	53.7
Netherlands	17710.7	-5.0	20.4	5.5	59.2
Mexico	13731.1	9.6	64.2	4.2	63.4
China, Hong Kong SAR	13619.6	5.1	33.1	4.2	67.6
Thailand	13025.8	4.7	15.5	4.0	71.7
Germany	12296.0	-8.8	4.0	3.8	75.5
Malaysia	11407.2	-8.6	12.3	3.5	79.0
Singapore	9288.0	-8.0	18.9	2.9	81.9
Czech Rep.	8570.0	10.5	33.3	2.6	84.5
Philippines	8207.0	15.2	42.7	2.5	87.0
Rep. of Korea	4975.8	-12.6	9.2	1.5	88.6
United Kingdom	3953.2	-22.7	-6.5	1.2	89.8
Poland	3495.2	111.2	17.4	1.1	90.9
Japan	3427.0	-16.5	8.1	1.1	91.9

Graph 2: Trade Balance by MDG regions 2010
(Bln US$)

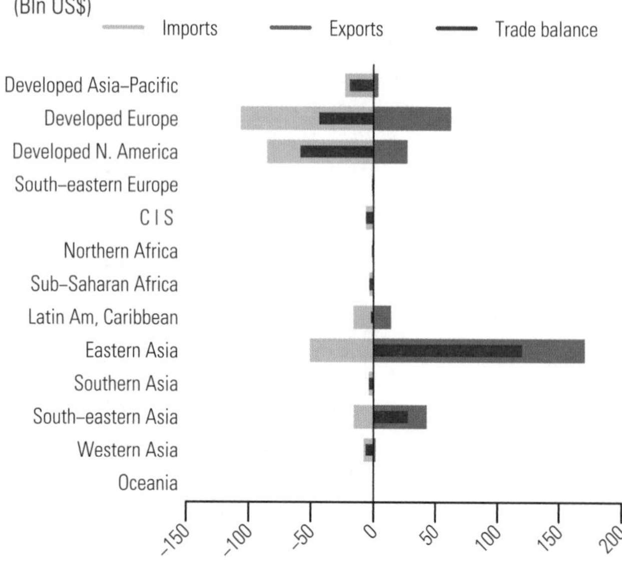

Table 3: Top importing countries or areas in 2010

Country or area	Value (million US$)	Avg. Growth (%) 06-10	Growth (%) 09-10	World share %	Cum.
World	319056.5	1.1	23.8	100.0	
USA	76351.2	2.7	30.5	23.9	23.9
China	27632.7	8.5	21.5	8.7	32.6
Germany	20891.5	-4.4	19.5	6.5	39.1
Netherlands	18672.3	-5.8	35.0	5.9	45.0
Japan	15347.3	-4.0	27.1	4.8	49.8
China, Hong Kong SAR	14489.9	9.2	28.6	4.5	54.3
United Kingdom	13635.1	-6.0	13.0	4.3	58.6
France	10044.5	-5.0	7.6	3.1	61.8
Canada	8649.8	-1.6	22.9	2.7	64.5
Mexico	7089.7	2.1	23.9	2.2	66.7
Australia	6308.7	6.9	30.7	2.0	68.7
Singapore	6042.5	-2.7	30.0	1.9	70.6
Czech Rep.	5973.3	19.4	52.8	1.9	72.4
Italy	5965.4	-2.1	14.0	1.9	74.3
Rep. of Korea	5365.8	4.6	37.0	1.7	76.0

After a 17.4 percent drop in 2009, the value (in current prices) of exports of parts and accessories for machines of 751-752 (office machines) (SITC group 759) increased by 15.9 percent in 2010 to reach 203.5 bln US$ (see table 2). For the same period, imports also increased by 17.4 percent to 212.4 bln US$ (see table 3). Graph 1 shows that the increase in exports for 2010 in this product group was exceeded by both the increases in world exports of exports of machinery and transport equipment (SITC section 7) of 22.1 percent and in total world exports of 21.2 percent. Exports of parts and accessories for machines of 751-752 (office machines) (SITC group 759) accounted for 4.0 percent of world exports of SITC section 7 and 1.4 percent of total world exports in 2010 (see table 1).

China, China, Hong Kong SAR and Singapore were the top exporting countries or areas in 2010 (see table 2). They accounted respectively for 19.1, 13.7 and 9.1 percent of world exports. Top destinations were USA, China and China, Hong Kong SAR (see table 3). By MDG regions (see graph 2), Eastern Asia recorded a trade surplus amounting to 25.2 bln US$ in 2010. Top trade surpluses were also recorded by South-eastern Asia (+10.2 bln US$) and Developed Asia-Pacific (+6.9 bln US$). Top trade deficits were recorded by Developed North America (-18.5 bln US$), Developed Europe (-16.8 bln US$) and Latin America and the Caribbean (-9.4 bln US$).

Table 1: Imports (Imp.) and exports (Exp.), 1996-2010, in current prices

		1996	1997	1998	1999	2000	2001	2002	2003	2004	2005	2006	2007	2008	2009	2010
Values in Bln US$	Imp.	100.2	113.3	120.4	135.1	153.7	140.2	138.9	155.5	180.8	199.0	220.4	221.4	217.2	180.8	212.4
	Exp.	104.1	116.3	120.9	136.7	165.8	148.8	149.2	162.1	182.9	201.5	222.0	217.7	212.6	175.6	203.5
As a percentage of SITC section (%)	Imp.	5.0	5.3	5.5	5.8	5.9	5.7	5.4	5.3	5.1	5.1	5.0	4.4	4.1	4.2	4.1
	Exp.	5.1	5.4	5.4	5.8	6.3	6.0	5.8	5.5	5.2	5.2	5.0	4.3	3.9	4.2	4.0
As a percentage of world trade (%)	Imp.	1.9	2.0	2.2	2.4	2.4	2.2	2.1	2.0	1.9	1.9	1.8	1.6	1.3	1.4	1.4
	Exp.	2.0	2.1	2.3	2.5	2.6	2.4	2.3	2.2	2.0	1.9	1.9	1.6	1.3	1.4	1.4

Graph 1: Annual growth rates of exports, 1996–2010
(In percentage by year)

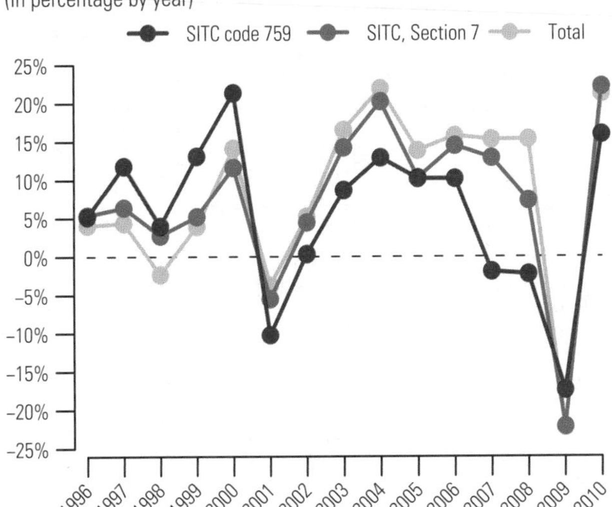

Table 2: Top exporting countries or areas in 2010

Country or area	Value (million US$)	Avg. Growth (%) 06-10	Growth (%) 09-10	World share %	Cum.
World	203475.9	-2.2	15.9	100.0	
China	38818.9	2.9	21.2	19.1	19.1
China, Hong Kong SAR	27869.2	-0.8	31.9	13.7	32.8
Singapore	18578.7	-0.5	20.8	9.1	41.9
USA	17797.7	-4.4	11.7	8.7	50.7
Japan	15041.0	-2.3	14.1	7.4	58.0
Netherlands	14922.7	-3.1	3.1	7.3	65.4
Malaysia	11271.4	-0.3	17.2	5.5	70.9
Germany	10986.9	-2.0	-0.1	5.4	76.3
Rep. of Korea	8841.4	-0.5	52.7	4.3	80.7
Other Asia, nes	7828.1	-6.9	28.7	3.8	84.5
United Kingdom	4179.2	-17.1	0.8	2.1	86.6
Thailand	3840.4	0.3	18.3	1.9	88.5
Ireland	2635.6	-15.9	-17.5	1.3	89.7
Belgium	2337.7	3.7	-5.1	1.1	90.9
Czech Rep.	2251.5	9.6	28.1	1.1	92.0

Graph 2: Trade Balance by MDG regions 2010
(Bln US$)

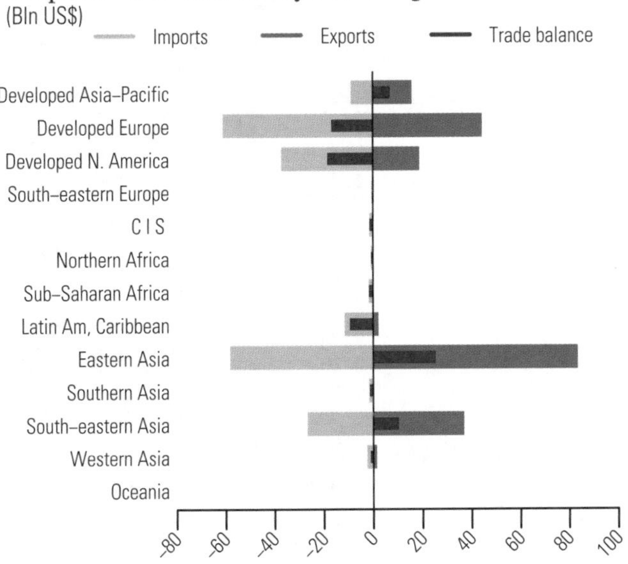

Table 3: Top importing countries or areas in 2010

Country or area	Value (million US$)	Avg. Growth (%) 06-10	Growth (%) 09-10	World share %	Cum.
World	212353.2	-0.9	17.4	100.0	
USA	34391.9	-0.6	16.5	16.2	16.2
China	26554.1	7.0	43.8	12.5	28.7
China, Hong Kong SAR	25855.6	-0.1	30.5	12.2	40.9
Netherlands	14687.5	-2.5	12.2	6.9	47.8
Germany	13878.7	-3.1	16.4	6.5	54.3
Singapore	10251.9	-4.8	14.6	4.8	59.2
Mexico	6972.3	9.6	49.6	3.3	62.4
Japan	6764.2	-3.7	23.9	3.2	65.6
United Kingdom	6096.1	-12.9	0.6	2.9	68.5
Malaysia	5763.1	-5.6	-12.0	2.7	71.2
Thailand	4627.0	1.7	4.2	2.2	73.4
Czech Rep.	4402.5	10.7	26.1	2.1	75.5
France	4271.5	-4.9	3.5	2.0	77.5
Philippines	4094.3	3.3	11.8	1.9	79.4
Rep. of Korea	3667.7	2.6	33.5	1.7	81.1

Source: UN Comtrade

761 Television receivers

From 2006 to 2010, the value (in current prices) of exports of television receivers (SITC group 761) increased on average by 6.4 percent each year and amounted to 99.7 bln US$ (see table 2). Similarly, imports went up on average by 6.6 percent each year to 100.6 bln US$ (see table 3). Graph 1 shows that the increase in exports for 2010 of 16.7 percent in this product group was exceeded by the increases in world exports of machinery and transport equipment (SITC section 7) of 22.1 percent and in total world exports of 21.2 percent. Exports of television receivers (SITC group 761) accounted for 1.9 percent of world exports of SITC section 7 and 0.7 percent of total world exports in 2010 (see table 1).

China, Mexico and Slovakia were the top exporting countries in 2010 (see table 2). They accounted respectively for 22.2, 20.4 and 7.5 percent of world exports. USA accounted for about a third of world imports (30.6 percent) and was the top destination (see table 3). Other major destinations were Germany and Japan. By MDG regions (see graph 2), top trade surpluses were recorded by Eastern Asia (+23.9 US$), Latin America and the Caribbean (+15.4 bln US$) and South-eastern Asia (+5.5 bln US$). Top deficits were recorded by Developed North America (-29.6 bln US$), Developed Asia-Pacific (-7.3 bln US$) and Developed Europe (-4.6 bln US$) .

Table 1: Imports (Imp.) and exports (Exp.), 1996-2010, in current prices

		1996	1997	1998	1999	2000	2001	2002	2003	2004	2005	2006	2007	2008	2009	2010
Values in Bln US$	Imp.	20.6	19.8	22.2	22.1	25.9	27.6	31.3	35.7	48.6	58.9	78.0	92.3	100.8	88.8	100.6
	Exp.	24.5	23.6	24.0	23.4	29.1	28.8	32.5	37.6	48.9	57.5	77.7	89.8	96.9	85.4	99.7
As a percentage of SITC section (%)	Imp.	1.0	0.9	1.0	0.9	1.0	1.1	1.2	1.2	1.4	1.5	1.8	1.8	1.9	2.1	1.9
	Exp.	1.2	1.1	1.1	1.0	1.1	1.2	1.3	1.3	1.4	1.5	1.7	1.8	1.8	2.0	1.9
As a percentage of world trade (%)	Imp.	0.4	0.4	0.4	0.4	0.4	0.4	0.5	0.5	0.5	0.6	0.6	0.7	0.6	0.7	0.7
	Exp.	0.5	0.4	0.4	0.4	0.5	0.5	0.5	0.5	0.5	0.6	0.6	0.6	0.6	0.7	0.7

Graph 1: Annual growth rates of exports, 1996–2010
(In percentage by year)

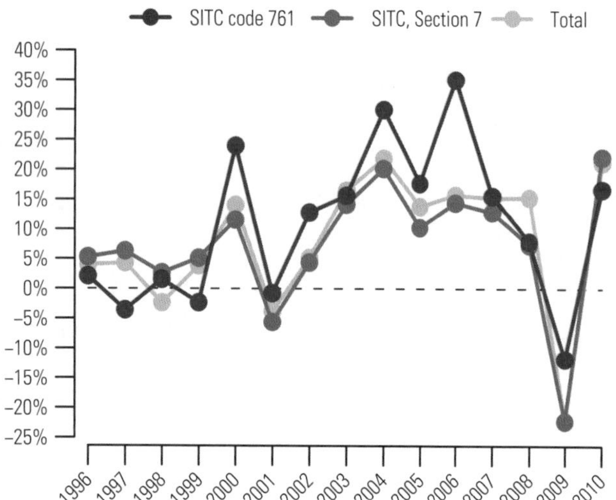

Table 2: Top exporting countries or areas in 2010

Country or area	Value (million US$)	Avg. Growth (%) 06-10	Growth (%) 09-10	World share %	Cum.
World	99685.2	6.4	16.7	100.0	
China	22149.0	14.3	35.4	22.2	22.2
Mexico	20298.4	5.1	13.2	20.4	42.6
Slovakia	7504.5	25.1	-3.5	7.5	50.1
Poland	7294.5	21.1	10.0	7.3	57.4
Hungary	5861.2	20.1	11.5	5.9	63.3
Malaysia	4895.2	39.6	102.9	4.9	68.2
USA	3833.1	11.6	36.9	3.8	72.1
Netherlands	3433.6	1.9	-8.2	3.4	75.5
Czech Rep.	3097.3	12.1	17.2	3.1	78.6
Germany	2196.0	-3.9	2.3	2.2	80.8
Rep. of Korea	1945.0	-3.9	13.2	2.0	82.8
Turkey	1747.7	-11.7	0.4	1.8	84.5
Thailand	1311.1	-9.9	0.9	1.3	85.8
Spain	1199.9	-19.2	4.2	1.2	87.0
Other Asia, nes	1105.6	-19.8	16.5	1.1	88.1

Graph 2: Trade Balance by MDG regions 2010
(Bln US$)

Imports — Exports — Trade balance

Developed Asia-Pacific
Developed Europe
Developed N. America
South-eastern Europe
CIS
Northern Africa
Sub-Saharan Africa
Latin Am, Caribbean
Eastern Asia
Southern Asia
South-eastern Asia
Western Asia
Oceania

-50 -40 -30 -20 -10 0 10 20 30 40

Table 3: Top importing countries or areas in 2010

Country or area	Value (million US$)	Avg. Growth (%) 06-10	Growth (%) 09-10	World share %	Cum.
World	100605.2	6.6	13.3	100.0	
USA	30829.1	2.5	5.0	30.6	30.6
Germany	7274.7	7.6	3.3	7.2	37.9
Japan	6044.5	48.9	145.3	6.0	43.9
United Kingdom	4862.0	-4.3	-3.8	4.8	48.7
France	4852.9	8.6	6.3	4.8	53.5
Netherlands	4305.5	3.0	6.5	4.3	57.8
Italy	3394.9	7.9	1.3	3.4	61.2
Spain	3116.2	4.3	25.9	3.1	64.3
Canada	2988.7	6.0	17.4	3.0	67.3
Australia	2105.0	8.9	-3.4	2.1	69.4
Mexico	1682.3	16.0	26.2	1.7	71.0
Sweden	1648.9	2.1	7.6	1.6	72.7
Slovakia	1461.7	40.2	17.2	1.5	74.1
China, Hong Kong SAR	1204.3	-6.2	16.6	1.2	75.3
Russian Federation	1089.5	9.1	21.0	1.1	76.4

After a 27.1 percent drop in 2009, the value (in current prices) of exports of radio-broadcast receivers (SITC group 762) bounced back by 21.8 percent in 2010 to reach 16.0 bln US$ (see table 2). Imports, after a 24.1 percent drop in 2009, increased by 22.9 percent in 2010 and totaled 17.5 bln US$ (see table 3). Graph 1 shows that the increase in exports for 2010 in this product group is similar to the increase in world exports of machinery and transport equipment (SITC section 7) of 22.1 percent and slightly exceeded total world exports of 21.2 percent. Exports of radio-broadcast receivers (SITC group 762) accounted for 0.3 percent of world exports of SITC section 7 and 0.1 percent of total world exports in 2010 (see table 1).

China, Malaysia and China, Hong Kong SAR were the top exporting countries or areas in 2010 (see table 2). They accounted respectively for 23.8, 10.9 and 7.0 percent of world exports. USA, Germany and Japan were the top destinations (see table 3). By MDG regions (see graph 2), Eastern Asia and South-eastern Asia recorded trade surpluses amounting respectively to 3.7 bln US$ and 3.0 bln US$. Top trade deficits were recorded by Developed North America (-4.4 bln US$), Developed Asia-Pacific (-1.3 bln US$) and Developed Europe (-0.9 bln US$).

Table 1: Imports (Imp.) and exports (Exp.), 1996-2010, in current prices

		1996	1997	1998	1999	2000	2001	2002	2003	2004	2005	2006	2007	2008	2009	2010
Values in Bln US$	Imp.	20.9	20.5	20.3	20.2	22.2	20.3	20.8	20.0	21.0	21.2	21.2	21.4	18.8	14.3	17.5
	Exp.	19.9	18.8	17.7	17.3	19.4	16.9	16.9	16.7	17.8	18.6	18.9	19.4	18.1	13.2	16.0
As a percentage of SITC section (%)	Imp.	1.0	1.0	0.9	0.9	0.8	0.8	0.8	0.7	0.6	0.5	0.5	0.4	0.4	0.3	0.3
	Exp.	1.0	0.9	0.8	0.7	0.7	0.7	0.7	0.6	0.5	0.5	0.4	0.4	0.3	0.3	0.3
As a percentage of world trade (%)	Imp.	0.4	0.4	0.4	0.4	0.3	0.3	0.3	0.3	0.2	0.2	0.2	0.2	0.1	0.1	0.1
	Exp.	0.4	0.3	0.3	0.3	0.3	0.3	0.3	0.2	0.2	0.2	0.2	0.1	0.1	0.1	0.1

Graph 1: Annual growth rates of exports, 1996–2010

(In percentage by year)

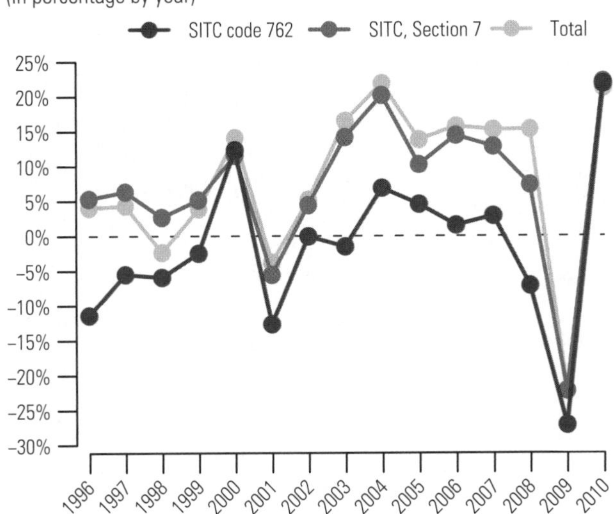

Table 2: Top exporting countries or areas in 2010

Country or area	Value (million US$)	Avg. Growth (%) 06-10	Growth (%) 09-10	World share %	Cum.
World	16032.4	-4.0	21.8	100.0	
China	3811.5	-3.5	24.8	23.8	23.8
Malaysia	1740.0	-1.2	16.3	10.9	34.6
China, Hong Kong SAR	1126.0	-14.1	18.8	7.0	41.7
Thailand	1090.9	8.0	88.6	6.8	48.5
Portugal	1090.6	0.8	20.0	6.8	55.3
USA	1038.1	0.1	31.0	6.5	61.7
Mexico	981.4	-12.7	39.9	6.1	67.9
Germany	707.9	-2.3	27.0	4.4	72.3
Czech Rep.	581.8	8.4	23.8	3.6	75.9
Belgium	495.4	-7.7	14.6	3.1	79.0
Israel	397.5	13.6	16.3	2.5	81.5
Hungary	363.6	4.5	22.7	2.3	83.7
Indonesia	360.7	1.9	4.1	2.2	86.0
Netherlands	271.5	-3.8	-9.6	1.7	87.7
France	234.4	-8.7	5.9	1.5	89.1

Graph 2: Trade Balance by MDG regions 2010

(Bln US$)

Imports — Exports — Trade balance

Developed Asia-Pacific
Developed Europe
Developed N. America
South-eastern Europe
CIS
Northern Africa
Sub-Saharan Africa
Latin Am, Caribbean
Eastern Asia
Southern Asia
South-eastern Asia
Western Asia
Oceania

-6 -5 -4 -3 -2 -1 0 1 2 3 4 5 6

Table 3: Top importing countries or areas in 2010

Country or area	Value (million US$)	Avg. Growth (%) 06-10	Growth (%) 09-10	World share %	Cum.
World	17511.9	-4.7	22.9	100.0	
USA	4587.4	-6.7	42.3	26.2	26.2
Germany	1330.3	-3.8	16.1	7.6	33.8
Japan	1072.9	-1.7	20.9	6.1	39.9
Canada	975.4	0.7	47.7	5.6	45.5
China, Hong Kong SAR	846.6	-9.8	23.9	4.8	50.3
United Kingdom	669.6	-5.0	0.6	3.8	54.1
France	591.4	-7.5	-2.5	3.4	57.5
Belgium	502.1	-9.3	7.0	2.9	60.4
Mexico	498.1	-3.7	69.2	2.8	63.2
Russian Federation	436.0	4.7	46.1	2.5	65.7
Netherlands	362.9	-3.9	-13.5	2.1	67.8
Australia	354.3	0.7	7.9	2.0	69.8
Spain	332.4	-15.9	0.8	1.9	71.7
Italy	266.0	-14.3	6.3	1.5	73.2
China	265.1	-13.9	47.9	1.5	74.8

Source: UN Comtrade

763 Sound recorders or reproducers; television image and sound recorders

In 2010, the value (in current prices) of exports of sound recorders or reproducers, television image and sound recorders (SITC group 763) rose by 6.3 percent to 63.3 bln US$ (see table 2). Similarly, imports showed a 11.7 percent increase and amounted to 66.4 bln US$ (see table 3). Graph 1 shows that the rise in exports for 2010 in this product group was far exceeded by increases in world exports of machinery and transport equipment (SITC section 7) of 22.1 percent and in total world exports of 21.2 percent. Exports of sound recorders or reproducers, television image and sound recorders (SITC group 763) accounted for 1.2 percent of world exports of SITC section 7 and 0.4 percent of total world exports (see table 1).

China, the top exporting country in 2010, accounted for 33.2 percent of world exports (see table 2). Other major exporting countries or areas were Japan and China, Hong Kong SAR, respectively with 15.2 and 9.4 percent of world exports. USA, China, Hong Kong SAR and China were the top destinations (see table 3). By MDG regions (see graph 2), Eastern Asia recorded a trade surplus amounting to 15.8 bln US$ in 2010. Major surpluses were also recorded by South-eastern Asia (+4.1 bln US$) and Developed Asia-Pacific (+3.8 bln US$). Top trade deficits were recorded by Developed North America (-10.8 bln US$), Developed Europe (-9.7 bln US$) and Latin America and the Caribbean (-2.6 bln US$).

Table 1: Imports (Imp.) and exports (Exp.), 1996-2010, in current prices

		1996	1997	1998	1999	2000	2001	2002	2003	2004	2005	2006	2007	2008	2009	2010
Values in Bln US$	Imp.	23.8	21.9	21.5	24.2	29.3	29.6	35.8	45.9	60.3	66.7	66.3	70.8	69.1	59.4	66.4
	Exp.	20.9	20.1	20.3	23.2	27.6	27.1	32.7	42.9	56.5	62.4	62.2	64.9	67.1	59.6	63.3
As a percentage of SITC section (%)	Imp.	1.2	1.0	1.0	1.0	1.1	1.2	1.4	1.6	1.7	1.7	1.5	1.4	1.3	1.4	1.3
	Exp.	1.0	0.9	0.9	1.0	1.1	1.1	1.3	1.5	1.6	1.6	1.4	1.3	1.2	1.4	1.2
As a percentage of world trade (%)	Imp.	0.4	0.4	0.4	0.4	0.4	0.5	0.5	0.6	0.6	0.6	0.5	0.5	0.4	0.5	0.4
	Exp.	0.4	0.4	0.4	0.4	0.4	0.4	0.5	0.6	0.6	0.6	0.5	0.5	0.4	0.5	0.4

Graph 1: Annual growth rates of exports, 1996–2010

(In percentage by year)

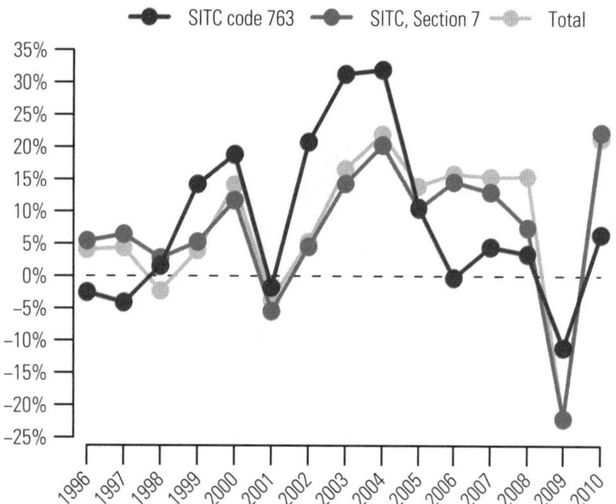

Graph 2: Trade Balance by MDG regions 2010

(Bln US$)

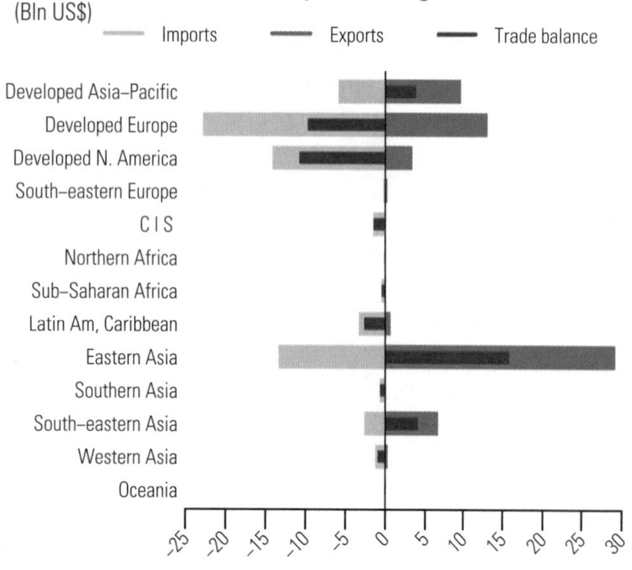

Table 2: Top exporting countries or areas in 2010

Country or area	Value (million US$)	Avg. Growth (%) 06-10	Growth (%) 09-10	World share %	Cum.
World	63318.0	0.4	6.3	100.0	
China	21028.4	-0.3	-2.3	33.2	33.2
Japan	9651.8	-3.5	4.4	15.2	48.5
China, Hong Kong SAR	5934.1	-7.7	1.3	9.4	57.8
Netherlands	3684.2	7.3	38.9	5.8	63.6
USA	2914.0	6.7	17.8	4.6	68.2
Germany	2387.0	1.1	3.6	3.8	72.0
Indonesia	1871.8	16.5	-2.6	3.0	75.0
Thailand	1771.4	18.7	40.1	2.8	77.8
Malaysia	1496.1	-8.0	5.8	2.4	80.1
United Kingdom	1414.2	-6.8	16.2	2.2	82.4
Slovakia	1181.8	31.3	12.3	1.9	84.2
Other Asia, nes	1116.3	39.8	86.7	1.8	86.0
Singapore	1101.1	2.7	23.0	1.7	87.7
Rep. of Korea	1086.4	2.4	10.5	1.7	89.5
Belgium	712.7	-3.5	-4.1	1.1	90.6

Table 3: Top importing countries or areas in 2010

Country or area	Value (million US$)	Avg. Growth (%) 06-10	Growth (%) 09-10	World share %	Cum.
World	66369.5	0.0	11.7	100.0	
USA	12178.9	-7.8	3.7	18.4	18.4
China, Hong Kong SAR	6841.1	-3.1	8.5	10.3	28.7
China	4676.0	19.5	35.3	7.0	35.7
Japan	4469.5	8.1	40.5	6.7	42.4
Germany	4091.7	-2.7	-3.2	6.2	48.6
United Kingdom	3863.5	1.6	7.7	5.8	54.4
Netherlands	3462.7	1.5	24.2	5.2	59.6
France	2185.4	-5.1	2.8	3.3	62.9
Canada	1938.7	1.2	14.4	2.9	65.9
Russian Federation	1354.3	25.6	41.1	2.0	67.9
Singapore	1344.0	0.4	7.6	2.0	69.9
Italy	1331.7	-3.7	0.4	2.0	71.9
Australia	1280.8	2.2	0.8	1.9	73.9
Mexico	1089.6	-3.8	10.5	1.6	75.5
Spain	1032.1	-10.8	-7.4	1.6	77.1

After several years of continuous growth marked by a peak of 451.4 bln US$ in 2008, the value (in current prices) of exports of telecommunications equipment, nes, and parts and accessories, nes (SITC group 764) decreased by 14.9 percent in 2009 but increased again by 16.1 percent in 2010 and amounted to 446.1 bln US$ (see table 2). Imports, with a similar development, increased by 20.2 percent in 2010 to reach 490.9 bln US$ (see table 3). Graph 1 shows that the increase in exports for 2010 in this product group was exceeded by the increases in world exports of machinery and transport equipment (SITC section 7) of 22.1 percent and in total world exports of 21.2 percent. Exports of telecommunications equipment, nes, and parts and accessories, nes (SITC group 764) accounted for 8.7 percent of world exports of SITC section 7 and 3.0 percent of total world exports in 2010 (see table 1).

China, China, Hong Kong SAR and Rep. of Korea were the top exporting countries or areas in 2010 (see table 2). They accounted respectively for 29.9, 12.8 and 7.9 percent of world exports. USA, China, Hong Kong SAR and China were the top destinations (see table 3). By MDG regions (see graph 2), Eastern Asia accounted for a large share of exports of telecommunications equipment, nes, and parts and accessories, nes (SITC group 764). In 2010, its exports amounted to 238.3 bln US$ while imports were valued at 95.9 bln US$. This resulted in a trade surplus of 142.4 bln US$. Top trade deficits were recorded by Developed North America (-58.5 bln US$) and Developed Europe (-38.1 bln US$).

Table 1: Imports (Imp.) and exports (Exp.), 1996-2010, in current prices

		1996	1997	1998	1999	2000	2001	2002	2003	2004	2005	2006	2007	2008	2009	2010
Values in Bln US$	Imp.	123.4	139.0	146.1	169.0	221.7	204.4	192.5	218.5	286.5	344.4	406.4	431.8	471.4	408.5	490.9
	Exp.	128.5	145.7	151.6	171.8	224.0	207.0	207.5	230.2	296.1	355.2	424.7	420.2	451.4	384.3	446.1
As a percentage of SITC section (%)	Imp.	6.1	6.5	6.6	7.2	8.5	8.3	7.5	7.5	8.1	8.8	9.2	8.6	8.8	9.5	9.5
	Exp.	6.3	6.7	6.8	7.3	8.6	8.4	8.0	7.8	8.4	9.1	9.5	8.3	8.3	9.1	8.7
As a percentage of world trade (%)	Imp.	2.3	2.5	2.7	3.0	3.4	3.3	2.9	2.9	3.1	3.3	3.3	3.1	2.9	3.3	3.2
	Exp.	2.4	2.7	2.8	3.1	3.5	3.4	3.2	3.1	3.3	3.4	3.5	3.0	2.8	3.1	3.0

Graph 1: Annual growth rates of exports, 1996–2010
(In percentage by year)

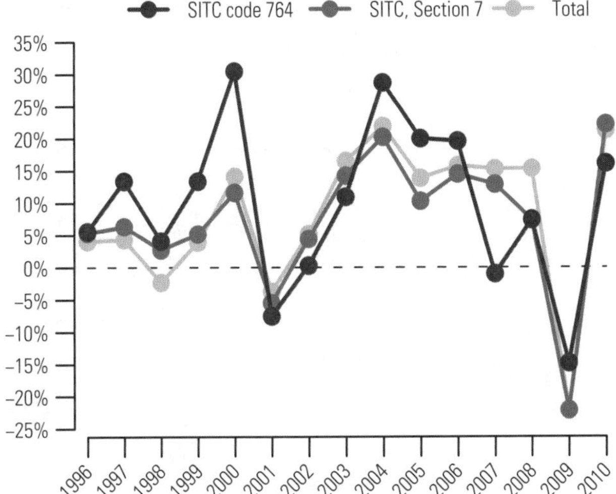

Graph 2: Trade Balance by MDG regions 2010
(Bln US$)

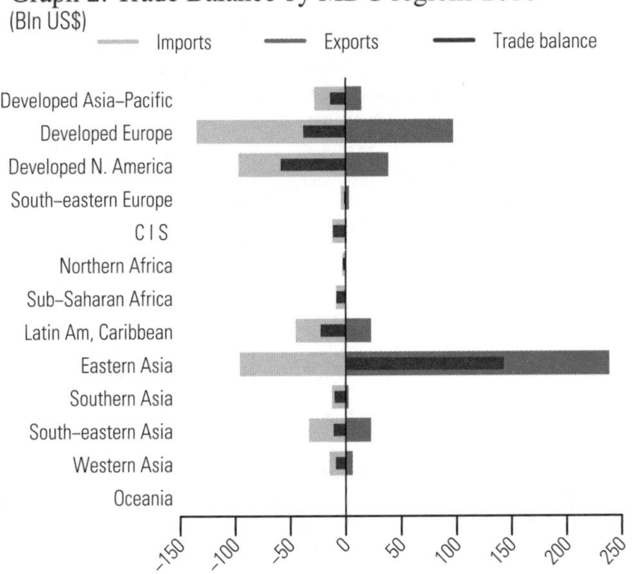

Table 2: Top exporting countries or areas in 2010

Country or area	Value (million US$)	Avg. Growth (%) 06-10	Growth (%) 09-10	World share %	Cum.
World	446062.6	1.2	16.1	100.0	
China	133436.9	11.9	23.7	29.9	29.9
China, Hong Kong SAR	56911.9	13.3	25.9	12.8	42.7
Rep. of Korea	35273.0	1.0	-2.8	7.9	50.6
USA	33406.2	3.8	14.2	7.5	58.1
Mexico	20734.4	11.4	14.4	4.6	62.7
Germany	16210.7	-11.2	22.9	3.6	66.4
Netherlands	15532.5	16.8	17.3	3.5	69.8
Japan	13548.7	-7.8	0.7	3.0	72.9
Other Asia, nes	12688.4	9.4	60.7	2.8	75.7
Hungary	12656.8	11.8	15.6	2.8	78.6
Sweden	10047.7	-2.2	43.3	2.3	80.8
Singapore	8996.4	-13.2	9.4	2.0	82.8
United Kingdom	8409.6	-36.3	5.2	1.9	84.7
France	6689.2	-13.9	5.9	1.5	86.2
Malaysia	4933.9	-14.4	15.0	1.1	87.3

Table 3: Top importing countries or areas in 2010

Country or area	Value (million US$)	Avg. Growth (%) 06-10	Growth (%) 09-10	World share %	Cum.
World	490895.6	4.8	20.2	100.0	
USA	86537.0	6.9	19.6	17.6	17.6
China, Hong Kong SAR	48990.3	10.8	26.4	10.0	27.6
China	35098.6	1.9	16.2	7.1	34.8
Mexico	25768.0	12.5	21.5	5.2	40.0
Japan	21306.8	15.6	30.3	4.3	44.3
Germany	20412.9	-4.9	16.2	4.2	48.5
United Kingdom	17709.5	-13.6	20.1	3.6	52.1
Netherlands	16709.2	16.2	20.0	3.4	55.5
France	12281.4	-3.4	12.7	2.5	58.0
Singapore	10508.5	-6.6	18.7	2.1	60.2
Canada	10289.3	8.0	26.8	2.1	62.3
India	9940.4	9.2	-5.8	2.0	64.3
Russian Federation	9391.4	7.8	67.9	1.9	66.2
Hungary	9329.1	14.4	18.7	1.9	68.1
Rep. of Korea	7756.1	5.6	19.5	1.6	69.7

771 Electric power machinery, and parts thereof

After a 14.4 percent drop in 2009, the value (in current prices) of exports of electric power machinery and parts thereof (SITC group 771) bounced back by 25.7 percent in 2010 to reach 85.6 bln US$ (see table 2). Imports, after a 13.8 percent drop in 2009, increased by 26.5 percent in 2010 and totaled 87.2 bln US$ (see table 3). Graph 1 shows that the increase in exports for 2010 in this product group exceeded the increases in world exports of machinery and transport equipment (SITC section 7) of 22.1 percent and total world exports of 21.2 percent. Exports of electric power machinery and parts thereof (SITC group 771) accounted for 1.7 percent of world exports of SITC section 7 and 0.6 percent of total world exports in 2010 (see table 1).

The top exporting countries or areas in 2010 were China, China, Hong Kong SAR and Germany (see table 2). They accounted respectively for 23.6, 11.5 and 10.8 percent of world exports. China, USA and China, Hong Kong SAR were also the top destinations (see table 3). By MDG regions (see graph 2), Eastern Asia recorded a trade surplus amounting to 10.5 bln US$. Top trade surpluses were also recorded by Developed Europe (+4.5 bln US$) and South-eastern Asia (+0.7 bln US$). Top trade deficits were recorded by Developed North America (-7.4 bln US$), Latin America and the Caribbean (-2.6 bln US$) and Sub-Saharan Africa (-2.4 bln US$).

Table 1: Imports (Imp.) and exports (Exp.), 1996-2010, in current prices

		1996	1997	1998	1999	2000	2001	2002	2003	2004	2005	2006	2007	2008	2009	2010
Values in Bln US$	Imp.	27.2	31.4	31.7	33.7	39.6	35.7	34.3	38.0	44.9	49.7	58.3	70.8	79.9	68.9	87.2
	Exp.	26.2	30.2	29.4	31.3	37.0	33.9	31.8	35.5	41.8	45.6	55.7	68.9	79.6	68.1	85.6
As a percentage of SITC section (%)	Imp.	1.3	1.5	1.4	1.4	1.5	1.4	1.3	1.3	1.3	1.3	1.3	1.4	1.5	1.6	1.7
	Exp.	1.3	1.4	1.3	1.3	1.4	1.4	1.2	1.2	1.2	1.2	1.2	1.4	1.5	1.6	1.7
As a percentage of world trade (%)	Imp.	0.5	0.6	0.6	0.6	0.6	0.6	0.5	0.5	0.5	0.5	0.5	0.5	0.5	0.6	0.6
	Exp.	0.5	0.6	0.6	0.6	0.6	0.6	0.5	0.5	0.5	0.4	0.5	0.5	0.5	0.5	0.6

Graph 1: Annual growth rates of exports, 1996–2010

(In percentage by year)

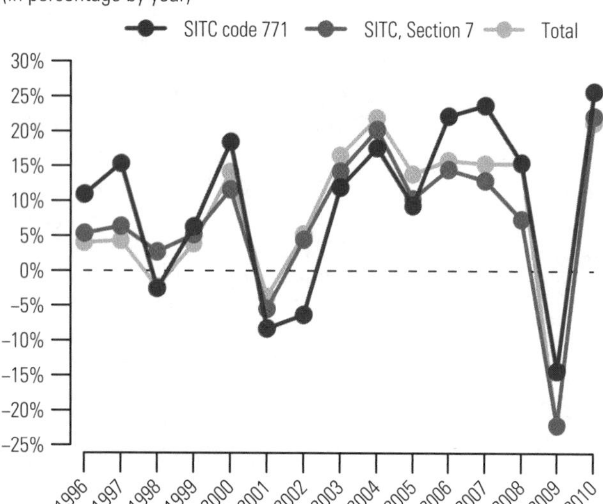

Table 2: Top exporting countries or areas in 2010

Country or area	Value (million US$)	Avg. Growth (%) 06-10	Growth (%) 09-10	World share %	Cum.
World	85580.3	11.3	25.7	100.0	
China	20193.8	16.4	37.6	23.6	23.6
China, Hong Kong SAR	9881.6	7.8	44.9	11.5	35.1
Germany	9272.4	15.2	32.8	10.8	46.0
USA	5023.8	5.9	23.0	5.9	51.8
Japan	3646.0	9.0	27.8	4.3	56.1
Rep. of Korea	2938.5	18.5	18.8	3.4	59.5
Italy	2569.0	11.4	15.0	3.0	62.5
Mexico	2169.1	-0.6	7.8	2.5	65.1
Austria	1957.4	11.9	15.6	2.3	67.4
Netherlands	1948.8	16.2	36.1	2.3	69.6
France	1808.2	4.4	0.0	2.1	71.8
Other Asia, nes	1697.6	4.6	40.4	2.0	73.7
Singapore	1479.6	3.4	9.7	1.7	75.5
Switzerland	1438.8	16.5	16.3	1.7	77.1
Thailand	1277.2	10.7	47.5	1.5	78.6

Graph 2: Trade Balance by MDG regions 2010

(Bln US$)

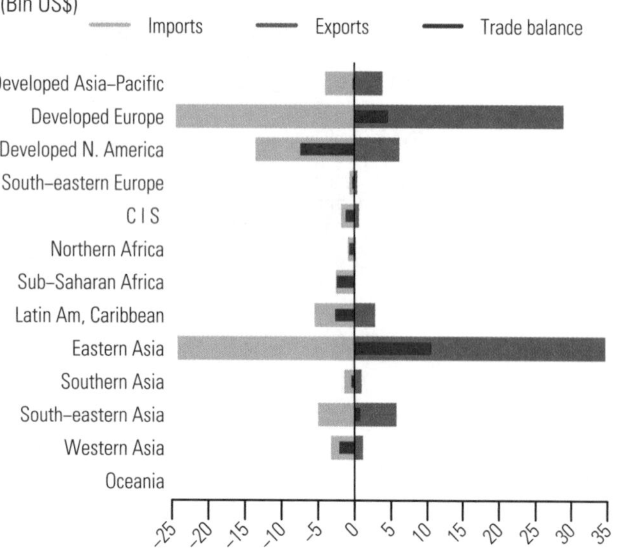

Table 3: Top importing countries or areas in 2010

Country or area	Value (million US$)	Avg. Growth (%) 06-10	Growth (%) 09-10	World share %	Cum.
World	87242.2	10.6	26.5	100.0	
China	11830.4	15.7	36.8	13.6	13.6
USA	11772.2	5.1	19.7	13.5	27.1
China, Hong Kong SAR	8832.5	12.6	51.0	10.1	37.2
Germany	6057.8	10.9	35.1	6.9	44.1
Japan	2911.5	2.2	24.5	3.3	47.5
Mexico	2763.1	4.8	27.2	3.2	50.6
France	2387.1	11.1	36.6	2.7	53.4
Italy	2373.0	17.3	74.2	2.7	56.1
Rep. of Korea	2204.8	3.3	21.4	2.5	58.6
Canada	1743.8	9.0	12.8	2.0	60.6
United Kingdom	1736.9	6.0	18.5	2.0	62.6
Netherlands	1646.1	5.7	33.3	1.9	64.5
Singapore	1526.3	3.0	19.8	1.7	66.2
Other Asia, nes	1290.1	1.3	42.5	1.5	67.7
Russian Federation	1253.8	23.2	29.8	1.4	69.2

After several years of continuous growth marked by a peak of 200.0 bln US$ in 2008, the value (in current prices) of exports of electrical apparatus for switching, protecting or connecting electrical circuits (SITC group 772) decreased by 19.1 percent in 2009 but increased again by 26.5 percent in 2010 and amounted to 204.6 bln US$ (see table 2). Similarly, imports increased by 25.9 percent in 2010 to reach 208.1 bln US$ (see table 3). Graph 1 shows that the increase in exports for 2010 in this product group exceeded both the increase in world exports of machinery and transport equipment (SITC section 7) of 22.1 percent and the increase in total world exports of 21.2 percent. Exports of electrical apparatus for switching, protecting or connecting electrical circuits (SITC group 772) accounted for 4.0 percent of world exports of SITC section 7 and 1.4 percent of total world exports in 2010 (see table 1).

In 2010, Germany, China and Japan were the top exporting countries (see table 2). They accounted respectively for 13.5, 13.3 and 9.8 percent of world exports. Top destinations were China, USA and China, Hong Kong SAR (see table 3). By MDG regions (see graph 2), Developed Europe and Developed Asia-Pacific recorded trade surpluses amounting respectively to 17.0 bln US$ and 13.0 bln US$. Top trade deficits were recorded by Latin America and the Caribbean (-8.4 bln US$), Western Asia and Developed North America (both -4.7 bln US$).

Table 1: Imports (Imp.) and exports (Exp.), 1996-2010, in current prices

		1996	1997	1998	1999	2000	2001	2002	2003	2004	2005	2006	2007	2008	2009	2010
Values in Bln US$	Imp.	68.0	73.6	76.9	80.9	95.5	88.5	88.7	103.1	127.2	142.1	165.0	189.0	203.1	165.3	208.1
	Exp.	69.1	74.2	77.4	81.8	96.2	86.9	89.2	104.3	128.2	142.4	164.2	185.9	200.0	161.7	204.6
As a percentage of SITC section (%)	Imp.	3.4	3.4	3.5	3.5	3.7	3.6	3.5	3.5	3.6	3.6	3.7	3.8	3.8	3.9	4.0
	Exp.	3.4	3.4	3.5	3.5	3.7	3.5	3.5	3.5	3.6	3.7	3.7	3.7	3.7	3.8	4.0
As a percentage of world trade (%)	Imp.	1.3	1.3	1.4	1.4	1.5	1.4	1.4	1.4	1.4	1.3	1.4	1.4	1.3	1.3	1.4
	Exp.	1.3	1.4	1.4	1.5	1.5	1.4	1.4	1.4	1.4	1.4	1.4	1.3	1.3	1.3	1.4

Graph 1: Annual growth rates of exports, 1996–2010
(In percentage by year)

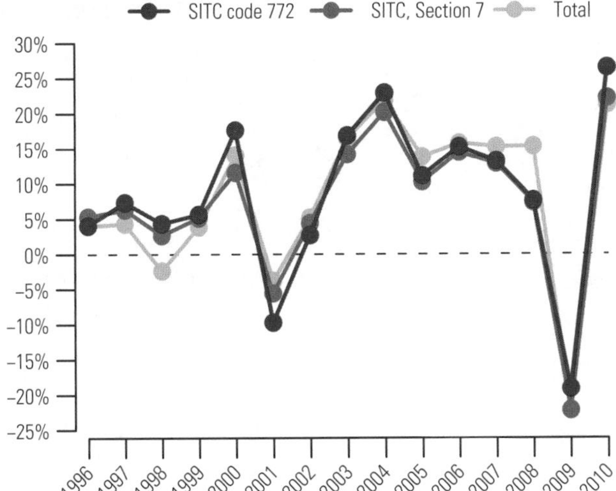

Table 2: Top exporting countries or areas in 2010

Country or area	Value (million US$)	Avg. Growth (%) 06-10	Growth (%) 09-10	World share %	Cum.
World	204 566.2	5.7	26.5	100.0	
Germany	27 543.5	4.4	19.5	13.5	13.5
China	27 159.0	14.6	36.5	13.3	26.7
Japan	19 994.3	5.0	41.0	9.8	36.5
China, Hong Kong SAR	18 274.9	9.4	36.4	8.9	45.4
USA	17 232.2	1.2	21.2	8.4	53.9
France	9 062.6	2.5	9.9	4.4	58.3
Other Asia, nes	8 181.3	0.4	33.0	4.0	62.3
Mexico	6 350.6	1.0	29.4	3.1	65.4
Rep. of Korea	6 280.9	15.1	32.2	3.1	68.5
Singapore	5 610.2	-0.9	23.6	2.7	71.2
Italy	5 127.5	4.7	12.6	2.5	73.7
Malaysia	4 985.4	3.8	52.1	2.4	76.2
Switzerland	4 122.2	5.8	11.0	2.0	78.2
United Kingdom	3 737.7	-1.7	14.1	1.8	80.0
Czech Rep.	3 480.7	8.9	22.7	1.7	81.7

Graph 2: Trade Balance by MDG regions 2010
(Bln US$)

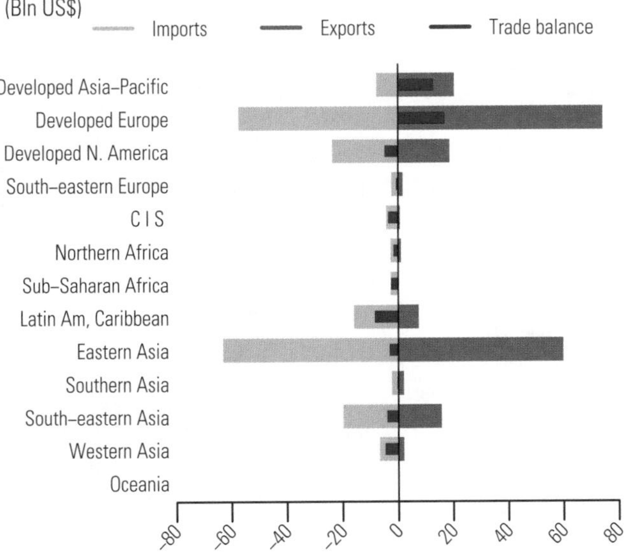

Table 3: Top importing countries or areas in 2010

Country or area	Value (million US$)	Avg. Growth (%) 06-10	Growth (%) 09-10	World share %	Cum.
World	208 077.6	6.0	25.9	100.0	
China	34 512.1	10.2	28.7	16.6	16.6
USA	19 517.2	1.9	34.3	9.4	26.0
China, Hong Kong SAR	17 143.3	8.3	39.0	8.2	34.2
Germany	13 664.3	4.3	30.2	6.6	40.8
Mexico	9 839.9	0.4	36.8	4.7	45.5
Rep. of Korea	7 501.3	10.8	32.5	3.6	49.1
France	6 070.2	3.5	19.7	2.9	52.0
Japan	5 895.6	2.2	31.4	2.8	54.9
Malaysia	5 078.5	1.3	28.8	2.4	57.3
Singapore	4 974.2	0.2	31.1	2.4	59.7
Thailand	4 933.5	11.3	37.9	2.4	62.1
United Kingdom	4 361.5	-0.4	12.6	2.1	64.2
Italy	4 273.2	2.7	24.4	2.1	66.2
Canada	3 954.8	0.3	17.4	1.9	68.1
Other Asia, nes	3 777.3	2.4	55.1	1.8	69.9

Source: UN Comtrade

773 Equipment for distributing electricity, nes

After a 27.7 percent drop in 2009, the value (in current prices) of exports of equipment for distributing electricity, nes (SITC group 773) bounced back by 26.4 percent in 2010 to reach 92.8 bln US$ (see table 2). Imports, after a 26.2 percent drop in 2009, increased by 26.5 percent in 2010 and totaled 93.8 bln US$ (see table 3). Graph 1 shows that the increase in exports for 2010 in this product group exceeded the increases in world exports of machinery and transport equipment (SITC section 7) of 22.1 percent and in total world exports of 21.2 percent. Exports of equipment for distributing electricity, nes (SITC group 773) accounted for 1.8 percent of world exports of SITC section 7 and 0.6 percent of total world exports in 2010 (see table 1).

China, USA and Germany were the top exporting countries in 2010 (see table 2). They accounted respectively for 14.7, 8.8 and 8.2 percent of world exports. Top destinations were USA, Germany and Japan (see table 3). By MDG regions (see graph 2), top trade surpluses were recorded by Eastern Asia (+9.9 bln US$), Northern Africa (+1.6 bln US$) and South-eastern Europe (+1.4 bln US$). Top deficits were recorded by Developed North America (-7.2 bln US$), Developed Asia-Pacific (-3.1 bln US$) and Sub-Saharan Africa (-1.7 bln US$).

Table 1: Imports (Imp.) and exports (Exp.), 1996-2010, in current prices

		1996	1997	1998	1999	2000	2001	2002	2003	2004	2005	2006	2007	2008	2009	2010
Values in Bln US$	Imp.	34.3	37.4	38.4	39.9	43.7	43.6	42.6	47.1	55.4	62.4	77.7	92.5	100.6	74.2	93.8
	Exp.	33.4	35.5	36.1	37.9	43.1	41.5	39.9	44.7	54.0	61.3	77.3	91.7	101.6	73.5	92.8
As a percentage of SITC section (%)	Imp.	1.7	1.8	1.7	1.7	1.7	1.8	1.7	1.6	1.6	1.6	1.8	1.9	1.9	1.7	1.8
	Exp.	1.6	1.6	1.6	1.6	1.6	1.7	1.5	1.5	1.5	1.6	1.7	1.8	1.9	1.7	1.8
As a percentage of world trade (%)	Imp.	0.6	0.7	0.7	0.7	0.7	0.7	0.6	0.6	0.6	0.6	0.6	0.7	0.6	0.6	0.6
	Exp.	0.6	0.6	0.7	0.7	0.7	0.7	0.6	0.6	0.6	0.6	0.6	0.7	0.6	0.6	0.6

Graph 1: Annual growth rates of exports, 1996–2010

(In percentage by year)

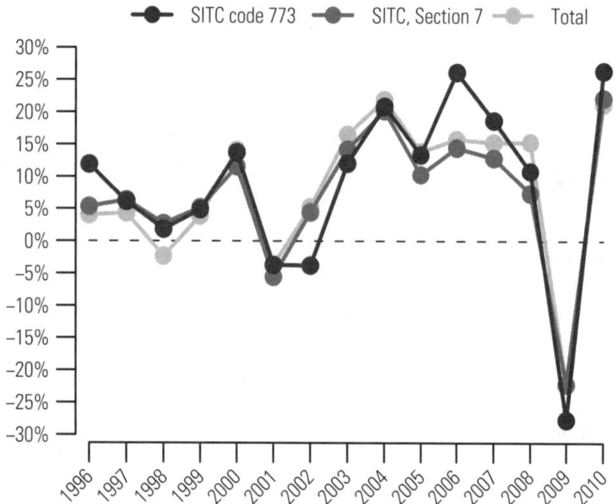

Table 2: Top exporting countries or areas in 2010

Country or area	Value (million US$)	Avg. Growth (%) 06-10	Growth (%) 09-10	World share %	Cum.
World	92 847.3	4.7	26.4	100.0	
China	13 634.7	15.6	39.1	14.7	14.7
USA	8 146.0	4.2	31.0	8.8	23.5
Germany	7 629.1	2.5	22.0	8.2	31.7
Mexico	6 835.0	-4.0	34.3	7.4	39.0
Italy	3 234.4	2.4	25.7	3.5	42.5
Japan	3 184.0	4.0	10.8	3.4	45.9
Rep. of Korea	3 178.5	10.4	24.1	3.4	49.4
China, Hong Kong SAR	2 803.2	5.8	45.2	3.0	52.4
Romania	2 627.5	7.8	15.8	2.8	55.2
Poland	2 579.3	-0.7	30.7	2.8	58.0
France	2 474.2	0.9	5.7	2.7	60.7
Czech Rep.	2 383.2	2.4	35.2	2.6	63.2
Hungary	1 995.4	0.0	22.2	2.1	65.4
Spain	1 845.8	1.6	23.8	2.0	67.4
Turkey	1 839.6	12.2	28.3	2.0	69.4

Graph 2: Trade Balance by MDG regions 2010

(Bln US$)

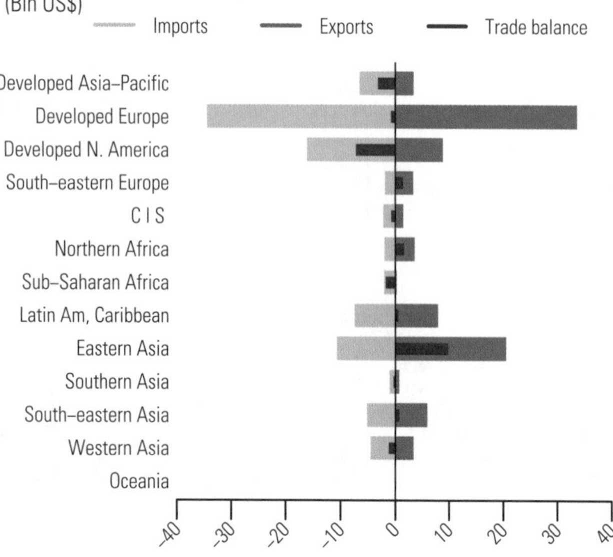

Table 3: Top importing countries or areas in 2010

Country or area	Value (million US$)	Avg. Growth (%) 06-10	Growth (%) 09-10	World share %	Cum.
World	93 847.4	4.8	26.5	100.0	
USA	12 933.2	-0.2	39.8	13.8	13.8
Germany	8 930.3	6.4	25.8	9.5	23.3
Japan	5 495.5	4.8	38.0	5.9	29.2
China	5 473.1	8.5	24.6	5.8	35.0
Mexico	4 365.9	1.9	34.9	4.7	39.6
France	3 638.5	2.1	24.0	3.9	43.5
United Kingdom	3 232.2	0.6	35.1	3.4	47.0
Canada	3 097.9	3.7	33.7	3.3	50.3
China, Hong Kong SAR	2 521.9	3.4	37.8	2.7	52.9
Spain	2 155.6	0.8	17.4	2.3	55.2
Rep. of Korea	2 037.1	9.1	33.7	2.2	57.4
Czech Rep.	1 836.6	5.4	52.8	2.0	59.4
Hungary	1 708.7	5.0	10.1	1.8	61.2
Italy	1 566.2	1.4	20.6	1.7	62.9
Romania	1 384.1	7.7	24.3	1.5	64.3

In 2010, the value (in current prices) of exports of electro-medical and radiological equipment (SITC group 774) rose by 10.8 percent to 37.9 bln US$ (see table 2). Similarly, imports showed a 11.2 percent increase and amounted to 36.9 bln US$ (see table 3). Graph 1 shows that the rise in exports for 2010 in this product group was by far exceeded by increases in world exports of machinery and transport equipment (SITC section 7) of 22.1 percent and in total world exports of 21.2 percent. Exports of electro-medical and radiological equipment (SITC group 774) accounted for 0.7 percent of world exports of SITC section 7 and 0.3 percent of total world exports (see table 1).

The top exporting countries in 2010 were USA, Germany and Netherlands (see table 2). They accounted respectively for 24.9, 20.7 and 9.9 percent of world exports. USA, China and Germany were the top destinations (see table 3). By MDG regions (see graph 2), Developed Europe accounted for a large share of exports of electro-medical and radiological equipment (SITC group 774). In 2010, its exports amounted to 18.5 bln US$ and imports, to 11.9 bln US$. This resulted in a trade surplus of 6.6 bln US$. Top trade surpluses were also recorded by Developed North America (+1.7 bln US$) and Developed Asia-Pacific (+0.6 bln US$). Top trade deficits were recorded by Eastern Asia (-1.9 bln US$) and Commonwealth of Independent States (-1.8 bln US$).

Table 1: Imports (Imp.) and exports (Exp.), 1996-2010, in current prices

		1996	1997	1998	1999	2000	2001	2002	2003	2004	2005	2006	2007	2008	2009	2010
Values in Bln US$	Imp.	12.2	12.0	12.7	13.1	13.8	15.6	17.0	19.2	22.0	25.1	28.8	32.3	35.4	33.2	36.9
	Exp.	13.2	13.2	14.0	14.1	14.7	15.7	17.2	20.2	23.1	25.9	29.4	33.6	36.9	34.2	37.9
As a percentage of SITC section (%)	Imp.	0.6	0.6	0.6	0.6	0.5	0.6	0.7	0.7	0.6	0.6	0.7	0.6	0.7	0.8	0.7
	Exp.	0.6	0.6	0.6	0.6	0.6	0.6	0.7	0.7	0.7	0.7	0.7	0.7	0.7	0.8	0.7
As a percentage of world trade (%)	Imp.	0.2	0.2	0.2	0.2	0.2	0.2	0.3	0.3	0.2	0.2	0.2	0.2	0.2	0.3	0.2
	Exp.	0.3	0.2	0.3	0.3	0.2	0.3	0.3	0.3	0.3	0.2	0.2	0.2	0.2	0.3	0.3

Graph 1: Annual growth rates of exports, 1996–2010

(In percentage by year)

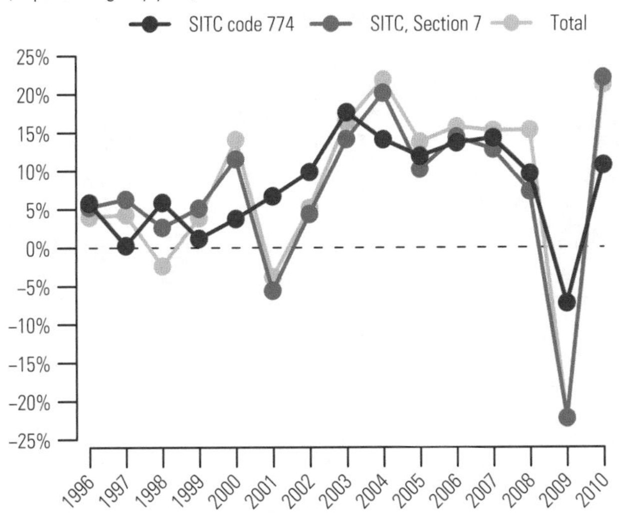

Graph 2: Trade Balance by MDG regions 2010

(Bln US$)

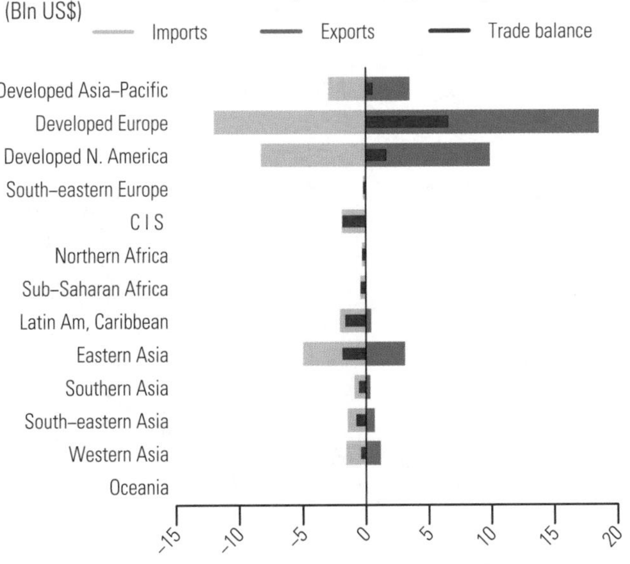

Table 2: Top exporting countries or areas in 2010

Country or area	Value (million US$)	Avg. Growth (%) 06-10	Growth (%) 09-10	World share %	Cum.
World	37879.1	6.5	10.8	100.0	
USA	9426.0	5.7	10.3	24.9	24.9
Germany	7830.7	6.1	8.7	20.7	45.6
Netherlands	3758.2	6.7	8.4	9.9	55.5
Japan	3404.2	2.7	12.5	9.0	64.5
France	1980.8	7.0	11.3	5.2	69.7
China	1946.7	21.4	29.2	5.1	74.8
United Kingdom	1460.1	7.7	5.0	3.9	78.7
Israel	920.3	5.8	11.5	2.4	81.1
Rep. of Korea	757.6	12.9	31.6	2.0	83.1
Italy	581.3	0.8	4.2	1.5	84.7
Finland	499.8	-0.9	12.4	1.3	86.0
Switzerland	489.8	7.2	6.5	1.3	87.3
Canada	481.3	-1.3	19.1	1.3	88.5
Austria	428.9	10.9	12.7	1.1	89.7
China, Hong Kong SAR	383.8	17.5	13.5	1.0	90.7

Table 3: Top importing countries or areas in 2010

Country or area	Value (million US$)	Avg. Growth (%) 06-10	Growth (%) 09-10	World share %	Cum.
World	36920.1	6.4	11.2	100.0	
USA	7382.3	2.0	15.1	20.0	20.0
China	3462.3	18.5	29.9	9.4	29.4
Germany	2658.5	3.3	0.7	7.2	36.6
Japan	2315.0	7.6	25.4	6.3	42.8
Netherlands	2240.9	5.0	1.5	6.1	48.9
France	1531.3	2.0	4.0	4.1	53.1
Russian Federation	1306.6	8.3	-5.0	3.5	56.6
United Kingdom	1107.1	3.4	3.2	3.0	59.6
Canada	862.9	5.1	7.0	2.3	61.9
Italy	814.4	2.0	-11.3	2.2	64.1
Rep. of Korea	796.5	5.4	36.1	2.2	66.3
Brazil	745.9	20.2	38.7	2.0	68.3
Singapore	592.4	23.1	13.4	1.6	69.9
Spain	572.1	-3.1	-0.6	1.5	71.5
Australia	569.5	7.2	14.5	1.5	73.0

Source: UN Comtrade

775 Household-type electrical and non-electrical equipment, nes

From 2006 to 2010, the value (in current prices) of exports of household-type electrical and non-electrical equipment, nes (SITC group 775) increased on average by 4.6 percent each year and amounted to 84.9 bln US$ (see table 2). Similarly, imports went up on average by 5.2 percent each year to 87.3 bln US$ (see table 3). Graph 1 shows that the increase in exports for 2010 of 14.6 percent in this product group was exceeded by the increases in world exports of machinery and transport equipment (SITC section 7) of 22.1 percent and in total world exports of 21.2 percent. Exports of household-type electrical and non-electrical equipment, nes (SITC group 775) accounted for 1.7 percent of world exports of SITC section 7 and 0.6 percent of total world exports in 2010 (see table 1).

China, the top exporting country in 2010, accounted for 30.7 percent of world exports (see table 2). Other major exporting countries were Germany and Italy, respectively with 10.4 and 6.1 percent of world exports. USA, Germany and France were the top destinations (see table 3). By MDG regions (see graph 2), Eastern Asia recorded a trade surplus amounting to 27.8 bln US$ in 2010. A significant trade surplus was also recorded by South-eastern Asia (+2.9 bln US$). Top trade deficits were recorded by Developed North America (-14.2 bln US$), Developed Europe (-6.9 bln US$) and Developed Asia-Pacific (-5.9 bln US$).

Table 1: Imports (Imp.) and exports (Exp.), 1996-2010, in current prices

		1996	1997	1998	1999	2000	2001	2002	2003	2004	2005	2006	2007	2008	2009	2010
Values in Bln US$	Imp.	32.6	33.1	33.3	34.4	36.5	37.9	41.8	49.0	57.2	63.9	71.2	82.1	87.4	76.4	87.3
	Exp.	33.5	34.8	34.1	35.0	36.3	37.4	41.6	48.8	58.2	63.7	71.0	81.1	86.0	74.0	84.9
As a percentage of SITC section (%)	Imp.	1.6	1.6	1.5	1.5	1.4	1.5	1.6	1.7	1.6	1.6	1.6	1.6	1.6	1.8	1.7
	Exp.	1.6	1.6	1.5	1.5	1.4	1.5	1.6	1.7	1.6	1.6	1.6	1.6	1.6	1.8	1.7
As a percentage of world trade (%)	Imp.	0.6	0.6	0.6	0.6	0.6	0.6	0.6	0.6	0.6	0.6	0.6	0.6	0.5	0.6	0.6
	Exp.	0.6	0.6	0.6	0.6	0.6	0.6	0.6	0.7	0.6	0.6	0.6	0.6	0.5	0.6	0.6

Graph 1: Annual growth rates of exports, 1996–2010

(In percentage by year)

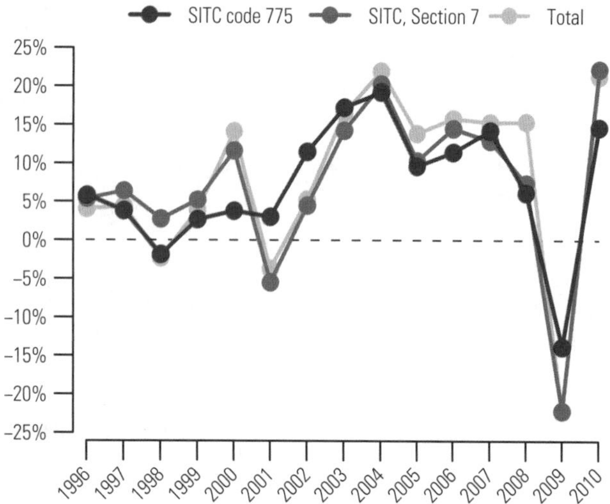

Graph 2: Trade Balance by MDG regions 2010

(Bln US$)

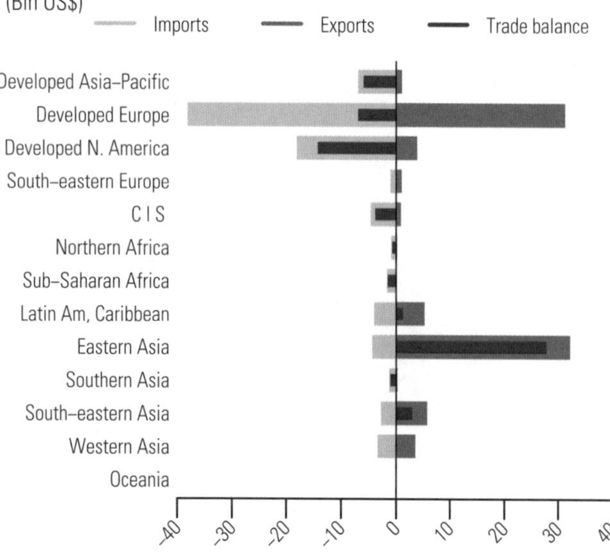

Table 2: Top exporting countries or areas in 2010

Country or area	Value (million US$)	Avg. Growth (%) 06-10	Growth (%) 09-10	World share %	Cum.
World	84 854.2	4.6	14.6	100.0	
China	26 071.4	12.6	26.3	30.7	30.7
Germany	8 819.0	-0.3	1.8	10.4	41.1
Italy	5 140.8	-6.9	-3.6	6.1	47.2
Mexico	4 479.2	13.5	15.3	5.3	52.5
Poland	3 588.1	11.5	14.8	4.2	56.7
Rep. of Korea	3 477.1	1.5	20.1	4.1	60.8
USA	3 232.6	-1.8	10.4	3.8	64.6
Turkey	2 969.5	8.8	10.5	3.5	68.1
Thailand	2 875.7	9.0	21.7	3.4	71.5
China, Hong Kong SAR	2 428.0	-0.1	20.0	2.9	74.3
France	1 947.8	-1.6	-1.6	2.3	76.6
Hungary	1 399.5	8.8	12.2	1.6	78.3
Sweden	1 328.3	1.7	10.9	1.6	79.9
Slovenia	1 168.4	1.5	8.0	1.4	81.2
Netherlands	1 152.3	1.5	9.3	1.4	82.6

Table 3: Top importing countries or areas in 2010

Country or area	Value (million US$)	Avg. Growth (%) 06-10	Growth (%) 09-10	World share %	Cum.
World	87 266.5	5.2	14.3	100.0	
USA	15 115.1	1.8	20.3	17.3	17.3
Germany	7 066.2	5.3	12.8	8.1	25.4
France	5 317.4	6.3	4.7	6.1	31.5
Japan	4 766.1	9.9	13.9	5.5	37.0
United Kingdom	4 519.3	-0.2	5.2	5.2	42.2
Russian Federation	3 317.9	10.8	47.9	3.8	46.0
Italy	3 001.3	6.6	11.5	3.4	49.4
Canada	2 939.2	4.2	20.0	3.4	52.8
Spain	2 364.4	-0.5	11.0	2.7	55.5
China, Hong Kong SAR	2 186.5	3.2	21.3	2.5	58.0
Netherlands	2 042.6	1.7	-1.0	2.3	60.3
Australia	1 845.3	9.0	12.0	2.1	62.4
Belgium	1 832.1	5.0	1.5	2.1	64.5
Sweden	1 653.0	6.0	4.1	1.9	66.4
Poland	1 412.5	4.8	7.1	1.6	68.0

After a 10.2 percent drop in 2009, the value (in current prices) of exports of thermionic, microcircuits, transistors, valves, cathodes, diodes, etc (SITC group 776) bounced back by 34.7 percent in 2010 to reach 543.5 bln US$ (see table 2). Imports, after an 11.6 percent drop in 2009, increased by 35.2 percent in 2010 and totaled 632.8 bln US$ (see table 3). Graph 1 shows that the rise in exports for 2010 in this product group exceeded the increases in world exports of machinery and transport equipment (SITC section 7) of 22.1 percent and in total world exports of 21.2 percent. Exports of thermionic, microcircuits, transistors, valves, cathodes, diodes, etc (SITC group 776) accounted for 10.6 percent of world exports of SITC section 7 and 3.6 percent of total world exports (see table 1).

In 2010, Singapore, China, Hong Kong SAR and China were the top exporting countries or areas (see table 2). They accounted respectively for 15.9, 11.8 and 11.6 percent of world exports. Top destinations were China, China, Hong Kong SAR and Singapore (see table 3). By MDG regions (see graph 2), Eastern Asia accounted for a majority of trade in thermionic, microcircuits, transistors, valves, cathodes, diodes, etc (SITC group 776). In 2010, its exports and imports were valued respectively at 231.3 bln US$ and 327.7 bln US$, resulting in a trade deficit of 96.4 bln US$. Major trade deficits were also recorded by Developed Europe (-33.5 bln US$) and Latin America and the Caribbean (-16.6 bln US$). Top trade surpluses were recorded by South-eastern Asia (+25.7 bln US$), Developed Asia-Pacific (+21.4 bln US$) and Developed North America (+14.7 bln US$).

Table 1: Imports (Imp.) and exports (Exp.), 1996-2010, in current prices

		1996	1997	1998	1999	2000	2001	2002	2003	2004	2005	2006	2007	2008	2009	2010
Values in Bln US$	Imp.	203.9	216.3	208.9	242.4	326.4	261.8	278.1	321.3	397.7	429.4	489.9	526.1	529.5	468.2	632.8
	Exp.	194.5	210.4	204.4	241.2	309.7	238.6	253.3	291.2	347.3	365.7	424.2	456.7	449.4	403.4	543.5
As a percentage of SITC section (%)	Imp.	10.1	10.1	9.5	10.4	12.5	10.6	10.8	11.0	11.2	11.0	11.1	10.5	9.9	10.9	12.2
	Exp.	9.5	9.7	9.2	10.3	11.8	9.7	9.8	9.9	9.8	9.4	9.5	9.1	8.3	9.6	10.6
As a percentage of world trade (%)	Imp.	3.8	3.9	3.8	4.3	5.0	4.2	4.2	4.2	4.3	4.1	4.0	3.8	3.3	3.7	4.2
	Exp.	3.7	3.8	3.8	4.3	4.9	3.9	3.9	3.9	3.8	3.5	3.5	3.3	2.8	3.3	3.6

Graph 1: Annual growth rates of exports, 1996–2010

(In percentage by year)

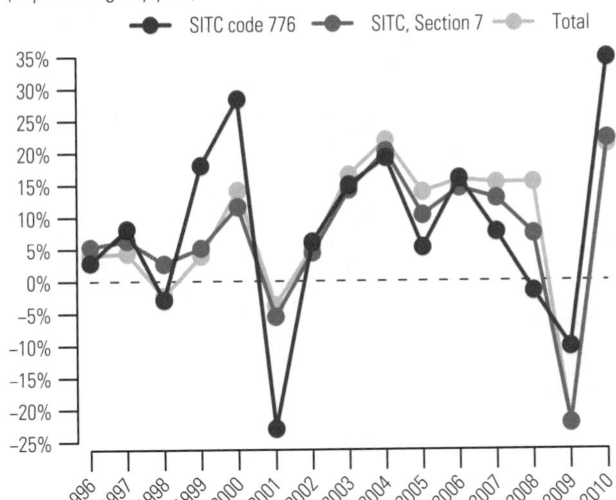

Graph 2: Trade Balance by MDG regions 2010

(Bln US$)

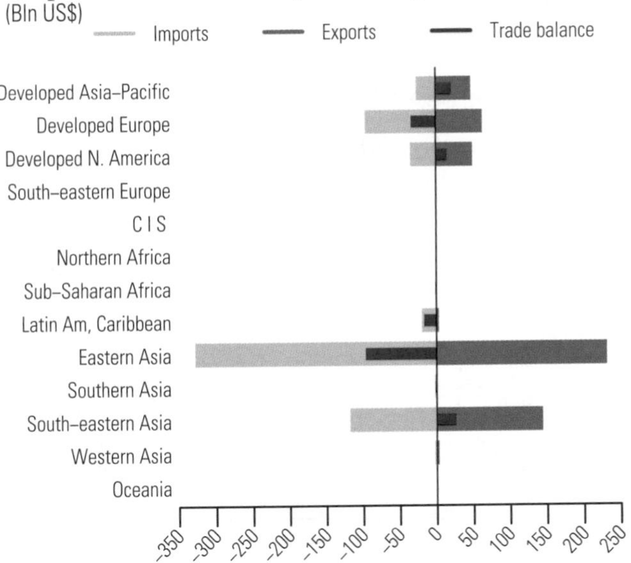

Table 2: Top exporting countries or areas in 2010

Country or area	Value (million US$)	Avg. Growth (%) 06-10	Growth (%) 09-10	World share %	Cum.
World	543521.8	6.4	34.7	100.0	
Singapore	86391.7	6.2	39.7	15.9	15.9
China, Hong Kong SAR	64155.7	14.1	23.6	11.8	27.7
China	62923.5	21.1	56.0	11.6	39.3
Other Asia, nes	60799.0	8.0	39.4	11.2	50.5
USA	47578.0	-2.7	25.3	8.8	59.2
Japan	47429.6	3.3	29.4	8.7	67.9
Rep. of Korea	43383.2	11.1	60.7	8.0	75.9
Malaysia	30473.7	4.5	15.2	5.6	81.5
Germany	21097.6	5.5	39.5	3.9	85.4
Philippines	16546.2	-0.6	49.5	3.0	88.5
France	9488.8	2.3	46.2	1.7	90.2
Thailand	9383.8	3.1	27.1	1.7	91.9
Netherlands	6742.2	-3.2	28.9	1.2	93.2
United Kingdom	4394.8	-11.9	12.6	0.8	94.0
Ireland	2582.3	-12.2	-16.9	0.5	94.5

Table 3: Top importing countries or areas in 2010

Country or area	Value (million US$)	Avg. Growth (%) 06-10	Growth (%) 09-10	World share %	Cum.
World	632781.4	6.6	35.2	100.0	
China	180994.6	10.4	32.2	28.6	28.6
China, Hong Kong SAR	81338.5	13.1	29.7	12.9	41.5
Singapore	57629.7	3.8	37.5	9.1	50.6
Other Asia, nes	36412.7	3.3	35.6	5.8	56.3
Malaysia	31852.6	0.4	42.7	5.0	61.4
Germany	31216.2	11.0	54.5	4.9	66.3
USA	30169.8	1.8	37.8	4.8	71.1
Rep. of Korea	28927.3	4.0	14.2	4.6	75.6
Japan	24397.9	-0.3	29.5	3.9	79.5
Italy	14258.8	39.1	192.4	2.3	81.7
Mexico	12971.4	2.1	36.4	2.0	83.8
Philippines	12703.2	-8.4	28.3	2.0	85.8
Thailand	12056.4	4.4	33.8	1.9	87.7
France	9444.3	8.4	62.4	1.5	89.2
Czech Rep.	5467.0	25.6	56.2	0.9	90.1

Source: UN Comtrade

778 Electrical machinery and apparatus, nes

After a sharp decline in 2009, the value (in current prices) of exports of electrical machinery and apparatus, nes (SITC group 778) went up by 25.9 percent to 199.2 bln US$ in 2010 (see table 2). Similarly, imports grew by 23.4 percent and totaled 196.2 bln US$ (see table 3). Graph 1 shows that the growth in exports for 2010 in this product group slightly exceeded the increases in world exports of machinery and transport equipment (SITC section 7) of 22.1 percent and in total world exports of 21.2 percent. Exports of electrical machinery and apparatus, nes (SITC group 778) accounted for 3.9 percent of world exports of SITC section 7 and 1.3 percent of total world exports (see table 1).

In 2010, China, Japan and Germany were the top exporting countries (see table 2). They accounted respectively for 19.1, 11.0 and 8.9 percent of world exports. Top destinations were USA, China and Germany (see table 3). By MDG regions (see graph 2), Developed Europe's exports and imports were valued respectively at 60.6 bln US$ and 60.7 bln US$, resulting in a trade deficit of 0.1 bln US$. Top trade deficits were recorded by Developed North America (-14.2 bln US$), Latin America and the Caribbean (-5.2 bln US$) and Western Asia (-4.9 bln US$). Top trade surpluses were recorded by Eastern Asia (+21.7 bln US$) and Developed Asia-Pacific (+14.0 bln US$).

Table 1: Imports (Imp.) and exports (Exp.), 1996-2010, in current prices

		1996	1997	1998	1999	2000	2001	2002	2003	2004	2005	2006	2007	2008	2009	2010
Values in Bln US$	Imp.	76.9	82.6	82.4	88.1	105.7	94.2	96.4	113.2	139.9	148.8	162.8	177.4	192.7	159.0	196.2
	Exp.	78.8	82.8	81.0	87.6	103.2	90.0	94.4	109.1	135.6	148.0	167.1	180.5	195.1	158.2	199.2
As a percentage of SITC section (%)	Imp.	3.8	3.9	3.7	3.8	4.1	3.8	3.8	3.9	3.9	3.8	3.7	3.5	3.6	3.7	3.8
	Exp.	3.9	3.8	3.6	3.7	3.9	3.6	3.7	3.7	3.8	3.8	3.7	3.6	3.6	3.8	3.9
As a percentage of world trade (%)	Imp.	1.4	1.5	1.5	1.5	1.6	1.5	1.5	1.5	1.5	1.4	1.3	1.3	1.2	1.3	1.3
	Exp.	1.5	1.5	1.5	1.6	1.6	1.5	1.5	1.5	1.5	1.4	1.4	1.3	1.2	1.3	1.3

Graph 1: Annual growth rates of exports, 1996–2010
(In percentage by year)

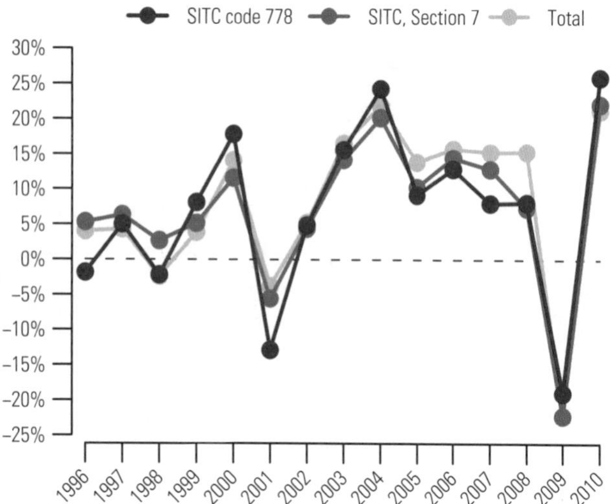

Graph 2: Trade Balance by MDG regions 2010
(Bln US$)

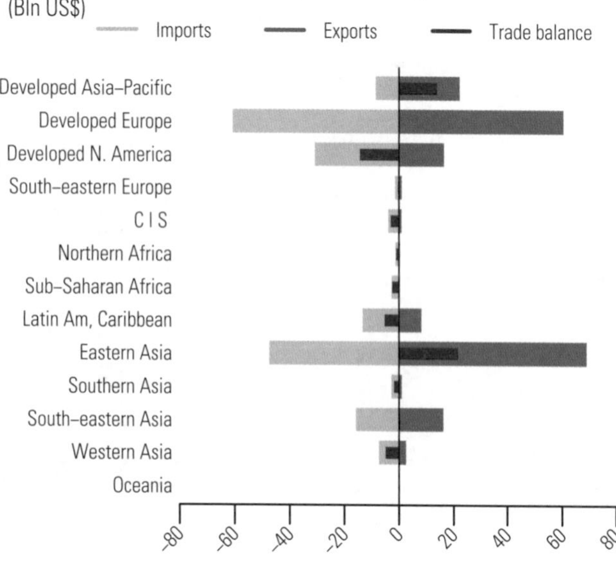

Table 2: Top exporting countries or areas in 2010

Country or area	Value (million US$)	Avg. Growth (%) 06-10	Growth (%) 09-10	World share %	Cum.
World	199184.4	4.5	25.9	100.0	
China	38075.2	16.0	36.9	19.1	19.1
Japan	21936.1	2.1	30.4	11.0	30.1
Germany	17820.3	0.7	18.0	8.9	39.1
USA	14672.4	-1.2	23.8	7.4	46.4
China, Hong Kong SAR	10787.5	6.0	39.0	5.4	51.9
Rep. of Korea	10421.6	3.4	43.0	5.2	57.1
Other Asia, nes	9890.5	0.5	11.5	5.0	62.1
Mexico	6670.6	-2.8	20.8	3.3	65.4
Singapore	6229.5	4.1	43.7	3.1	68.5
France	5981.3	3.9	7.7	3.0	71.5
United Kingdom	4485.3	-4.7	16.5	2.3	73.8
Netherlands	4300.6	6.6	24.3	2.2	75.9
Belgium	4195.3	-2.5	8.3	2.1	78.1
Italy	3587.4	1.2	6.5	1.8	79.9
Thailand	3444.8	10.9	38.5	1.7	81.6

Table 3: Top importing countries or areas in 2010

Country or area	Value (million US$)	Avg. Growth (%) 06-10	Growth (%) 09-10	World share %	Cum.
World	196159.3	4.8	23.4	100.0	
USA	26029.2	3.6	32.7	13.3	13.3
China	25212.2	10.9	34.0	12.9	26.1
Germany	14401.9	2.4	20.1	7.3	33.5
China, Hong Kong SAR	10979.9	5.5	31.2	5.6	39.1
Rep. of Korea	7043.2	-1.6	8.1	3.6	42.7
France	6945.1	3.9	13.2	3.5	46.2
Mexico	6592.3	3.7	27.9	3.4	49.6
Japan	5983.5	-0.6	22.6	3.1	52.6
United Kingdom	5906.7	-1.2	24.6	3.0	55.6
Canada	4679.4	3.6	23.9	2.4	58.0
Singapore	4665.0	-0.6	36.5	2.4	60.4
Italy	4304.9	3.3	16.0	2.2	62.6
Other Asia, nes	4164.7	-2.3	33.4	2.1	64.7
Thailand	3879.0	10.1	42.3	2.0	66.7
Netherlands	3847.0	4.6	17.8	2.0	68.6

Cars, other motor vehicles principally designed for the transports of persons 781

After several years of continuous growth marked by a peak of 636.3 bln US$ in 2008, the value (in current prices) of exports of cars, other motor vehicles principally designed for the transports of persons (SITC group 781) dropped by 31.1 percent in 2009 but increased by 27.5 percent in 2010 to 559.0 bln US$ (see table 2). Similarly, imports increased by 23.2 percent in 2010 totaling 544.8 bln US$ (see table 3). Graph 1 shows that the increase in exports for 2010 in this product group exceeded the increases in world exports of machinery and transport equipment (SITC section 7) of 22.1 percent and in total world exports of 21.2 percent. Exports of cars, other motor vehicles principally designed for the transports of persons (SITC group 781) accounted for 10.9 percent of world exports of SITC section 7 and 3.7 percent of total world exports in 2010 (see table 1).

In 2010, Germany, Japan and USA were the top exporting countries (see table 2). They accounted respectively for 23.0, 16.2 and 7.0 percent of world exports. USA, Germany and United Kingdom were among the top destinations (see table 3). By MDG regions (see graph 2), Developed Europe accounted for a large share of trade in cars, other motor vehicles principally designed for the transports of persons (SITC group 781). In 2010, its exports amounted to 288.7 bln US$ while imports were valued at 229.2 bln US$, resulting in a trade surplus of 59.5 bln US$. Developed Asia-Pacific recorded a trade surplus of 69.3 bln US$. Top trade deficits were recorded by Developed North America (-63.0 bln US$) and Western Asia (-26.3 bln US$).

Table 1: Imports (Imp.) and exports (Exp.), 1996-2010, in current prices

		1996	1997	1998	1999	2000	2001	2002	2003	2004	2005	2006	2007	2008	2009	2010
Values in Bln US$	Imp.	245.2	256.7	273.6	295.1	307.0	313.4	341.9	388.8	453.0	478.1	532.1	615.6	625.3	442.1	544.8
	Exp.	247.2	261.1	278.6	293.7	303.7	308.9	343.9	393.7	455.7	486.8	536.3	621.9	636.3	438.6	559.0
As a percentage of SITC section (%)	Imp.	12.1	12.0	12.4	12.6	11.8	12.6	13.3	13.3	12.8	12.2	12.0	12.3	11.7	10.3	10.5
	Exp.	12.1	12.0	12.5	12.5	11.6	12.5	13.3	13.4	12.9	12.5	12.0	12.3	11.8	10.4	10.9
As a percentage of world trade (%)	Imp.	4.6	4.6	5.0	5.2	4.7	5.0	5.2	5.1	4.9	4.5	4.4	4.4	3.9	3.5	3.6
	Exp.	4.7	4.8	5.2	5.3	4.8	5.1	5.4	5.3	5.0	4.7	4.5	4.5	4.0	3.5	3.7

Graph 1: Annual growth rates of exports, 1996–2010

(In percentage by year)

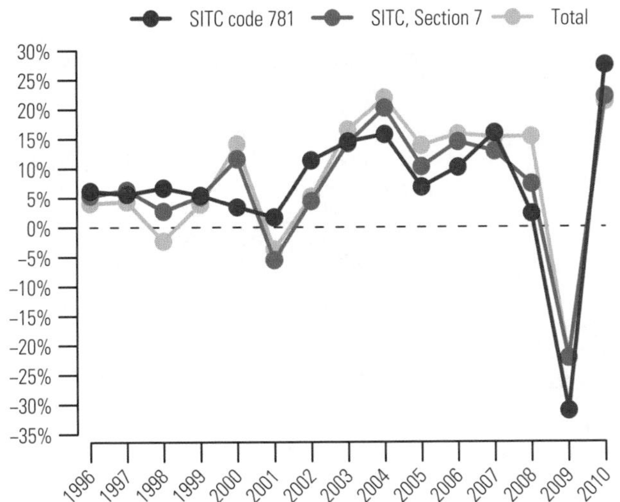

Table 2: Top exporting countries or areas in 2010

Country or area	Value (million US$)	Avg. Growth (%) 06-10	Growth (%) 09-10	World share %	Cum.
World	558 965.9	1.0	27.5	100.0	
Germany	128 670.9	2.6	25.6	23.0	23.0
Japan	90 372.8	-1.1	45.1	16.2	39.2
USA	39 297.8	2.6	38.6	7.0	46.2
Canada	36 901.0	-0.6	58.1	6.6	52.8
Rep. of Korea	31 774.1	0.9	41.9	5.7	58.5
United Kingdom	26 499.2	3.1	43.3	4.7	63.2
Spain	26 011.2	1.6	-0.3	4.7	67.9
Belgium	23 487.9	-6.0	-2.1	4.2	72.1
Mexico	23 091.1	7.3	52.9	4.1	76.2
France	21 089.0	-9.0	6.0	3.8	80.0
Czech Rep.	12 490.0	10.3	17.9	2.2	82.2
Slovakia	9 210.9	9.9	20.9	1.6	83.9
Poland	8 812.6	5.9	-8.9	1.6	85.5
Italy	8 539.8	-2.9	7.5	1.5	87.0
Thailand	7 027.6	24.5	71.8	1.3	88.2

Graph 2: Trade Balance by MDG regions 2010

(Bln US$)

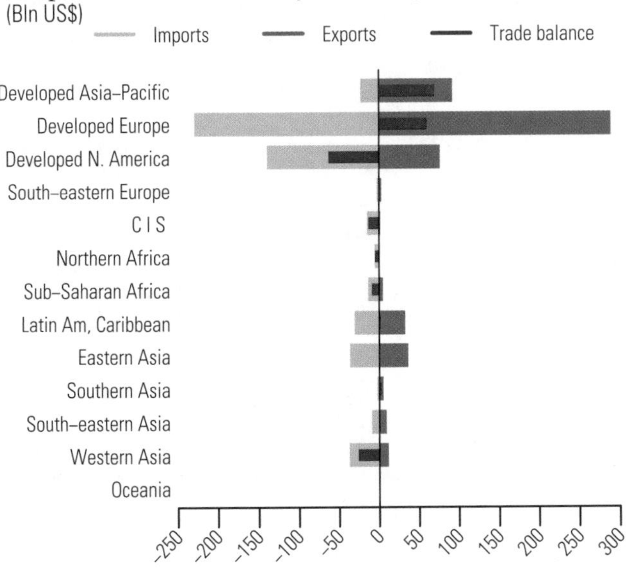

Table 3: Top importing countries or areas in 2010

Country or area	Value (million US$)	Avg. Growth (%) 06-10	Growth (%) 09-10	World share %	Cum.
World	544 826.6	0.6	23.2	100.0	
USA	116 768.0	-4.0	42.0	21.4	21.4
Germany	35 208.9	-4.3	-9.7	6.5	27.9
United Kingdom	31 320.2	-3.5	21.2	5.7	33.6
France	31 166.6	2.4	2.2	5.7	39.4
China	28 921.3	42.8	101.3	5.3	44.7
Italy	28 048.5	-3.1	-5.5	5.1	49.8
Belgium	24 619.6	3.4	8.6	4.5	54.3
Canada	22 359.6	-0.7	31.0	4.1	58.4
Australia	14 300.1	10.8	54.5	2.6	61.1
Spain	11 608.9	-16.8	-10.2	2.1	63.2
Russian Federation	11 391.6	-2.7	33.8	2.1	65.3
Saudi Arabia	10 639.9	9.3	28.8	2.0	67.2
Netherlands	9 762.6	2.0	15.4	1.8	69.0
Switzerland	8 965.3	9.0	24.9	1.6	70.7
Brazil	8 305.0	44.3	51.9	1.5	72.2

Source: UN Comtrade

782 Motor vehicles for the transport of goods; special-purpose motor vehicles

After a sharp decline in 2009 of 40.6 percent, the value (in current prices) of motor vehicles for the transport of goods, special-purpose motor vehicles (SITC group 782) bounced back by 30.2 percent in 2010 to reach 103.9 bln US$ (see table 2). Imports, after a 39.1 percent drop in 2009, increased by 29.8 percent in 2010 and totaled 109.5 bln US$ (see table 3). Graph 1 shows that the rise in exports for 2010 in this product group exceeded the increases in world exports of machinery and transport equipment (SITC section 7) of 22.1 percent and in total world exports of 21.2 percent. Exports of motor vehicles for the transport of goods, special-purpose motor vehicles (SITC group 782) accounted for 2.0 percent of world exports of SITC section 7 and 0.7 percent of total world exports (see table 1).

The top exporting countries in 2010 were USA, Germany and Japan (see table 2). They accounted respectively for 14.9, 11.9 and 10.2 percent of world exports. USA, Canada and Germany were the top destinations (see table 3). By MDG regions (see graph 2), Developed Europe accounted for a large share of exports of motor vehicles for the transport of goods, special-purpose motor vehicles (SITC group 782). In 2010, its exports were valued at 40.1 bln US$ while imports amounted to 34.9 bln US$. This resulted in a trade surplus of 5.2 bln US$. Major trade surpluses were also recorded by Developed Asia-Pacific (+4.6 bln US$) and Eastern Asia (+3.3 bln US$). Top trade deficits were recorded by Developed North America (-7.7 bln US$), Sub-Saharan Africa (-6.5 bln US$) and Northern Africa (-3.2 bln US$).

Table 1: Imports (Imp.) and exports (Exp.), 1996-2010, in current prices

		1996	1997	1998	1999	2000	2001	2002	2003	2004	2005	2006	2007	2008	2009	2010
Values in Bln US$	Imp.	48.7	53.3	53.9	56.3	58.8	58.8	63.6	71.1	83.3	93.7	106.3	132.6	138.6	84.3	109.5
	Exp.	49.1	55.0	54.2	53.4	57.0	56.3	60.1	68.2	80.4	89.8	103.0	127.6	134.5	79.8	103.9
As a percentage of SITC section (%)	Imp.	2.4	2.5	2.5	2.4	2.3	2.4	2.5	2.4	2.4	2.4	2.4	2.7	2.6	2.0	2.1
	Exp.	2.4	2.5	2.4	2.3	2.2	2.3	2.3	2.3	2.3	2.3	2.3	2.5	2.5	1.9	2.0
As a percentage of world trade (%)	Imp.	0.9	1.0	1.0	1.0	0.9	0.9	1.0	0.9	0.9	0.9	0.9	0.9	0.9	0.7	0.7
	Exp.	0.9	1.0	1.0	1.0	0.9	0.9	0.9	0.9	0.9	0.9	0.9	0.9	0.8	0.6	0.7

Graph 1: Annual growth rates of exports, 1996–2010
(In percentage by year)

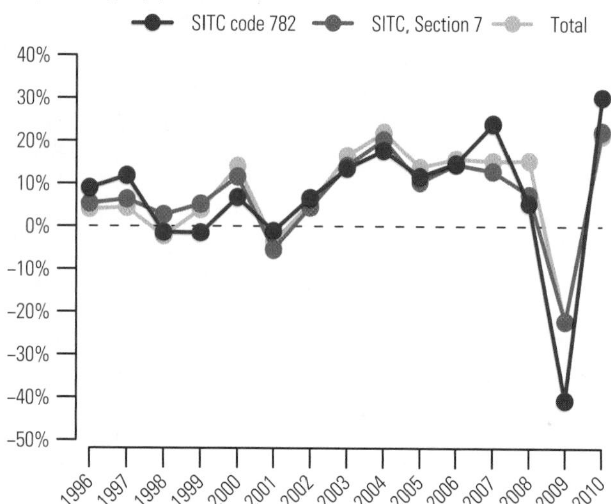

Table 2: Top exporting countries or areas in 2010

Country or area	Value (million US$)	Avg. Growth (%) 06-10	Growth (%) 09-10	World share %	Cum.
World	103917.9	0.2	30.2	100.0	
USA	15460.9	5.3	31.8	14.9	14.9
Germany	12403.9	-2.8	19.5	11.9	26.8
Japan	10567.7	5.3	55.1	10.2	37.0
Mexico	10514.0	5.3	60.8	10.1	47.1
Thailand	5859.0	12.3	64.8	5.6	52.7
Spain	5086.8	-6.2	32.4	4.9	57.6
Italy	5044.9	-1.5	25.9	4.9	62.5
France	3948.5	-6.6	8.3	3.8	66.3
Turkey	3429.1	2.8	40.6	3.3	69.6
China	3297.5	21.4	12.2	3.2	72.8
Argentina	2493.7	15.2	68.8	2.4	75.2
United Kingdom	2455.7	-3.8	34.8	2.4	77.5
Belgium	2393.7	5.1	25.3	2.3	79.8
Rep. of Korea	2328.8	10.9	19.5	2.2	82.1
Netherlands	2199.1	-5.4	10.2	2.1	84.2

Graph 2: Trade Balance by MDG regions 2010
(Bln US$)

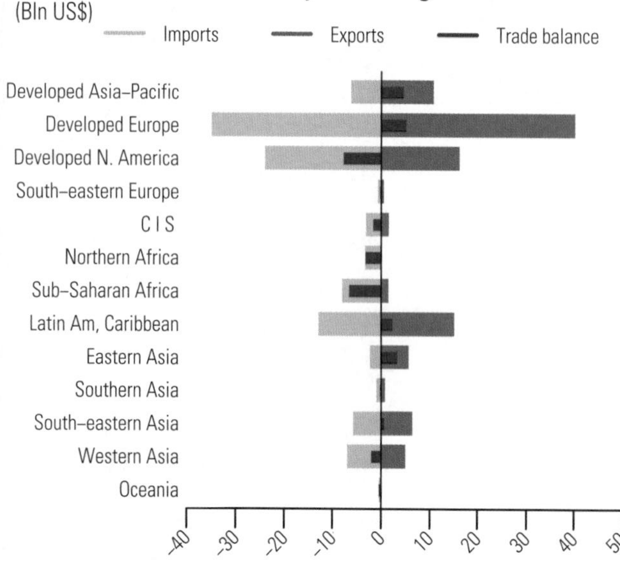

Table 3: Top importing countries or areas in 2010

Country or area	Value (million US$)	Avg. Growth (%) 06-10	Growth (%) 09-10	World share %	Cum.
World	109458.4	0.7	29.8	100.0	
USA	12119.9	-11.3	42.0	11.1	11.1
Canada	11819.8	5.7	46.2	10.8	21.9
Germany	5488.5	2.3	29.3	5.0	26.9
France	5430.0	-5.2	21.6	5.0	31.8
Australia	5407.9	11.5	56.3	4.9	36.8
United Kingdom	4858.8	-3.8	62.5	4.4	41.2
Belgium	3075.8	5.5	10.4	2.8	44.0
Italy	2904.1	-5.2	-0.2	2.7	46.7
Saudi Arabia	2604.5	15.5	1.7	2.4	49.1
Indonesia	2543.9	47.5	100.4	2.3	51.4
Brazil	2290.3	28.0	43.2	2.1	53.5
Mexico	2271.3	-4.8	9.9	2.1	55.6
Chile	2262.4	18.1	107.0	2.1	57.6
Nigeria	2103.8	73.0	78.2	1.9	59.5
Netherlands	2090.5	-1.3	16.8	1.9	61.5

In 2010, the value (in current prices) of exports of road motor vehicles, nes (SITC group 783) rose by 30.8 percent to 32.8 bln US$ (see table 2). Similarly, imports showed a 19.7 percent increase and amounted to 30.2 bln US$ (see table 3). Graph 1 shows that the rise in exports for 2010 in this product group exceeded the increases in world exports of machinery and transport equipment (SITC section 7) of 22.1 percent and in total world exports of 21.2 percent. Exports of road motor vehicles, nes (SITC group 783) accounted for 0.6 percent of world exports of SITC section 7 and 0.2 percent of total world exports (see table 1).

The top exporting countries in 2010 were Germany, Mexico and Netherlands (see table 2). They accounted respectively for 15.0, 10.4 and 9.9 percent of world exports. Top destinations were USA, Canada and France (see table 3). By MDG regions (see graph 2), Developed Europe accounted for a large share of trade in road motor vehicles, nes (SITC group 783). In 2010, its exports were valued at 17.2 bln US$ while imports amounted to 10.5 bln US$. This resulted in a trade surplus of 6.7 bln US$. Major trade surpluses were also recorded by Developed Asia-Pacific (+2.7 bln US$) and Eastern Asia (+2.0 bln US$). Top trade deficits were recorded by Sub-Saharan Africa (-2.7 bln US$), Developed North America (-2.6 bln US$) and South-eastern Asia (-1.5 bln US$).

Table 1: Imports (Imp.) and exports (Exp.), 1996-2010, in current prices

		1996	1997	1998	1999	2000	2001	2002	2003	2004	2005	2006	2007	2008	2009	2010
Values in Bln US$	Imp.	14.7	14.6	16.2	16.5	15.2	13.6	14.8	17.6	23.4	26.0	30.9	39.1	45.0	25.3	30.2
	Exp.	16.1	15.9	17.9	17.8	16.3	14.8	16.6	20.9	27.7	30.2	34.3	41.4	49.9	25.1	32.8
As a percentage of SITC section (%)	Imp.	0.7	0.7	0.7	0.7	0.6	0.6	0.6	0.6	0.7	0.7	0.7	0.8	0.8	0.6	0.6
	Exp.	0.8	0.7	0.8	0.8	0.6	0.6	0.6	0.7	0.8	0.8	0.8	0.8	0.9	0.6	0.6
As a percentage of world trade (%)	Imp.	0.3	0.3	0.3	0.3	0.2	0.2	0.2	0.2	0.3	0.2	0.3	0.3	0.3	0.2	0.2
	Exp.	0.3	0.3	0.3	0.3	0.3	0.2	0.3	0.3	0.3	0.3	0.3	0.3	0.3	0.2	0.2

Graph 1: Annual growth rates of exports, 1996–2010
(In percentage by year)

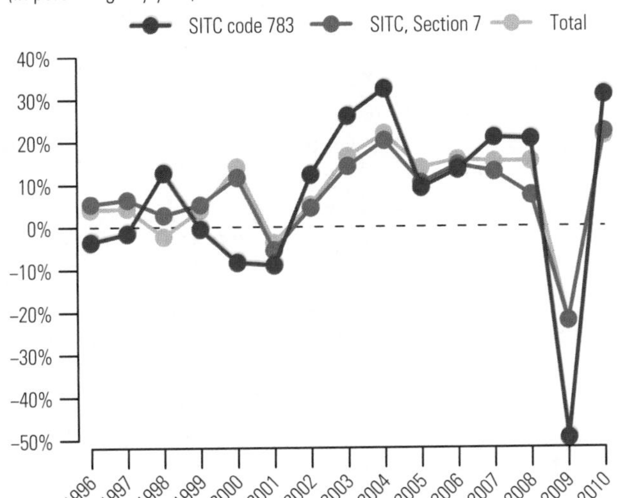

Table 2: Top exporting countries or areas in 2010

Country or area	Value (million US$)	Avg. Growth (%) 06-10	Growth (%) 09-10	World share %	Cum.
World	32790.7	-1.1	30.8	100.0	
Germany	4926.1	-7.5	28.0	15.0	15.0
Mexico	3425.0	27.8	49.4	10.4	25.5
Netherlands	3238.5	-6.4	58.6	9.9	35.3
Japan	2974.9	8.1	38.4	9.1	44.4
USA	2466.0	-3.7	48.9	7.5	51.9
Belgium	1925.6	-6.2	42.9	5.9	57.8
France	1891.8	-5.9	47.8	5.8	63.6
China	1738.8	29.1	67.2	5.3	68.9
Sweden	1422.8	2.9	85.2	4.3	73.2
Poland	1412.2	17.4	-6.8	4.3	77.5
Rep. of Korea	1025.1	16.4	28.1	3.1	80.7
Turkey	923.4	-0.6	-16.9	2.8	83.5
Brazil	810.8	-4.7	97.5	2.5	85.9
Czech Rep.	506.7	6.4	-18.2	1.5	87.5
Spain	400.2	-5.9	8.8	1.2	88.7

Graph 2: Trade Balance by MDG regions 2010
(Bln US$)

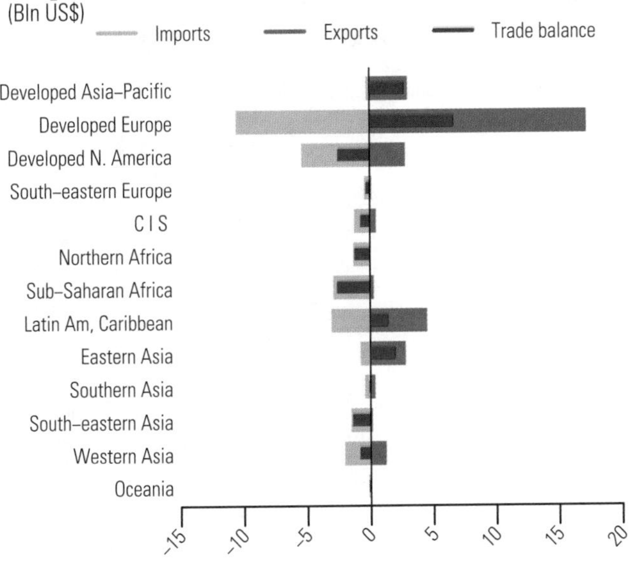

Table 3: Top importing countries or areas in 2010

Country or area	Value (million US$)	Avg. Growth (%) 06-10	Growth (%) 09-10	World share %	Cum.
World	30233.4	-0.6	19.7	100.0	
USA	3398.8	-4.0	14.3	11.2	11.2
Canada	1962.1	-4.9	56.0	6.5	17.7
France	1758.4	4.4	-0.6	5.8	23.5
Germany	1446.5	-2.4	32.6	4.8	28.3
Nigeria	1131.1	148.5	-11.8	3.7	32.1
Italy	1018.0	-8.6	33.2	3.4	35.4
Russian Federation	814.7	-8.6	135.9	2.7	38.1
Chile	793.0	16.4	106.2	2.6	40.8
Poland	757.7	-7.5	83.9	2.5	43.3
Turkey	687.4	-2.9	116.0	2.3	45.5
Algeria	622.6	12.3	-9.7	2.1	47.6
Belgium	606.9	-8.4	-8.4	2.0	49.6
United Kingdom	584.8	-9.1	29.7	1.9	51.5
Spain	487.1	-22.4	102.9	1.6	53.1
Thailand	483.7	20.8	64.8	1.6	54.7

Source: UN Comtrade

784 Parts and accessories of the motor vehicles of 722, 781, 782 and 783

After a sharp decline of 26.2 percent in 2009, the value (in current prices) of exports of parts and accessories of motor vehicles (SITC group 784) bounced back in 2010 by 31.8 percent to amount to 301.2 bln US$ (see table 2). Imports showed a similar development with an increase of 29.8 percent to 290.3 bln US$ (see table 3). Graph 1 shows that the increase in exports for 2010 in this product group exceeded the increases in world exports of machinery and transport equipment (SITC section 7) of 22.1 percent and in total world exports of 21.2 percent. Exports of exports of parts and accessories of motor vehicles (SITC group 784) accounted for 5.9 percent of world exports of SITC section 7 and 2.0 percent of total world exports in 2010 (see table 1).

Germany, Japan and USA were the top exporting countries in 2010 (see table 2). They accounted respectively for 14.7, 12.0 and 11.0 percent of world exports. USA and Germany were also among the top importing countries, together with China (see table 3). By MDG regions (see graph 2), Developed Europe was the origin and the destination of a majority of trade in parts and accessories for motor vehicles (SITC group 784). In 2010, its exports and imports were valued respectively at 141.7 bln US$ and 126.4 bln US$, resulting in a trade surplus of 15.3 bln US$. A larger trade surplus was recorded by Developed Asia-Pacific (+28.6 bln US$). Top trade deficits were recorded by Developed North America (-19.9 bln US$), Commonwealth of Independent States (-9.1 bln US$) and Latin America and the Caribbean (-6.2 bln US$).

Table 1: Imports (Imp.) and exports (Exp.), 1996-2010, in current prices

		1996	1997	1998	1999	2000	2001	2002	2003	2004	2005	2006	2007	2008	2009	2010
Values in Bln US$	Imp.	120.4	123.5	128.9	138.4	144.5	140.5	155.9	182.0	215.0	231.1	254.2	294.0	304.8	223.6	290.3
	Exp.	118.1	123.6	127.1	134.1	142.5	137.5	152.8	179.4	214.2	234.3	258.1	296.2	309.7	228.5	301.2
As a percentage of SITC section (%)	Imp.	6.0	5.8	5.9	5.9	5.5	5.7	6.1	6.2	6.1	5.9	5.7	5.9	5.7	5.2	5.6
	Exp.	5.8	5.7	5.7	5.7	5.4	5.6	5.9	6.1	6.1	6.0	5.8	5.9	5.7	5.4	5.9
As a percentage of world trade (%)	Imp.	2.3	2.2	2.4	2.4	2.2	2.2	2.4	2.4	2.3	2.2	2.1	2.1	1.9	1.8	1.9
	Exp.	2.2	2.3	2.4	2.4	2.2	2.3	2.4	2.4	2.4	2.3	2.2	2.1	1.9	1.8	2.0

Graph 1: Annual growth rates of exports, 1996–2010

(In percentage by year)

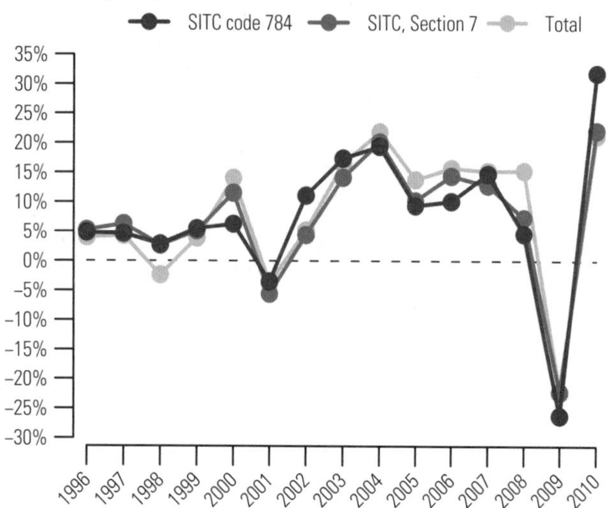

Graph 2: Trade Balance by MDG regions 2010

(Bln US$)

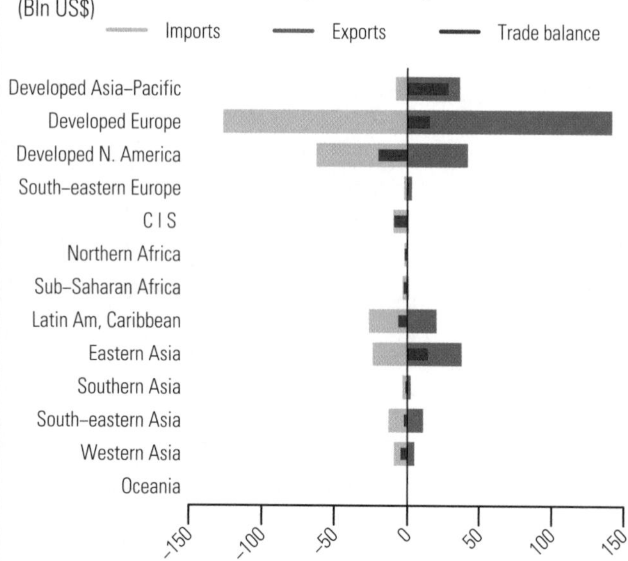

Table 2: Top exporting countries or areas in 2010

Country or area	Value (million US$)	Avg. Growth (%) 06-10	Growth (%) 09-10	World share %	Cum.
World	301 226.1	3.9	31.8	100.0	
Germany	44 373.9	3.7	31.1	14.7	14.7
Japan	36 067.0	8.1	42.7	12.0	26.7
USA	33 016.5	-0.7	37.3	11.0	37.7
Rep. of Korea	17 995.8	17.3	63.6	6.0	43.6
France	17 618.8	0.4	15.8	5.8	49.5
China	16 822.5	17.1	43.8	5.6	55.1
Mexico	13 920.8	4.7	49.7	4.6	59.7
Italy	13 117.0	-0.7	24.0	4.4	64.0
Spain	10 471.4	-2.4	12.5	3.5	67.5
Canada	9 144.5	-9.4	40.1	3.0	70.6
Czech Rep.	8 840.0	8.0	15.4	2.9	73.5
Poland	8 110.2	13.5	19.1	2.7	76.2
Belgium	6 759.3	-2.3	15.9	2.2	78.4
Sweden	5 679.9	-1.9	47.1	1.9	80.3
United Kingdom	5 637.1	-7.9	12.4	1.9	82.2

Table 3: Top importing countries or areas in 2010

Country or area	Value (million US$)	Avg. Growth (%) 06-10	Growth (%) 09-10	World share %	Cum.
World	290 286.3	3.4	29.8	100.0	
USA	44 092.3	-0.8	44.5	15.2	15.2
Germany	27 979.1	4.4	21.0	9.6	24.8
China	18 078.7	18.9	45.1	6.2	31.1
Canada	17 936.7	-3.5	35.5	6.2	37.2
Spain	14 994.2	-2.7	9.8	5.2	42.4
Mexico	14 936.9	5.8	36.5	5.1	47.5
United Kingdom	13 516.2	-5.1	34.6	4.7	52.2
France	12 789.7	-2.0	12.8	4.4	56.6
Belgium	9 311.0	-2.7	14.6	3.2	59.8
Russian Federation	7 756.0	31.9	108.4	2.7	62.5
Italy	6 418.2	-1.2	10.1	2.2	64.7
Czech Rep.	5 701.2	9.4	16.8	2.0	66.7
Poland	5 640.8	8.8	21.9	1.9	68.6
Japan	5 572.6	5.4	40.7	1.9	70.5
Thailand	5 480.0	17.8	75.9	1.9	72.4

In 2010, the value (in current prices) of exports of motorcycles and cycles motorized and non-motorized, invalid carriages (SITC group 785) rose by 12.9 percent to 39.7 bln US$ (see table 2). Similarly, imports showed a 8.5 percent increase and amounted to 37.8 bln US$ (see table 3). Graph 1 shows that the rise in exports for 2010 in this product group was exceeded by increases of 22.1 percent in world exports of machinery and transport equipment (SITC section 7) and of 21.2 percent in total world exports. Exports of motorcycles and cycles motorized and non-motorized, invalid carriages (SITC group 785) accounted for 0.8 percent of world exports of SITC section 7 and 0.3 percent of total world exports (see table 1).

The top exporting countries in 2010 were China and Japan (see table 2). They accounted respectively for 27.4 and 12.1 percent of world exports. Top destinations were USA, Germany and France (see table 3). By MDG regions (see graph 2), Eastern Asia and Developed Asia-Pacific recorded trade surpluses amounting respectively to 13.2 bln US$ and 2.1 bln US$. Top trade deficits were recorded by Developed Europe (-5.7 bln US$), Developed North America (-2.7 bln US$) and Latin America and the Caribbean (-2.4 bln US$).

Table 1: Imports (Imp.) and exports (Exp.), 1996-2010, in current prices

		1996	1997	1998	1999	2000	2001	2002	2003	2004	2005	2006	2007	2008	2009	2010
Values in Bln US$	Imp.	17.5	17.9	18.1	18.9	20.5	19.8	20.7	24.3	28.8	32.1	34.3	40.6	45.1	34.8	37.8
	Exp.	18.4	18.6	18.7	19.4	21.3	19.9	21.1	24.9	29.7	32.5	35.5	40.6	46.6	35.2	39.7
As a percentage of SITC section (%)	Imp.	0.9	0.8	0.8	0.8	0.8	0.8	0.8	0.8	0.8	0.8	0.8	0.8	0.8	0.8	0.7
	Exp.	0.9	0.9	0.8	0.8	0.8	0.8	0.8	0.8	0.8	0.8	0.8	0.8	0.9	0.8	0.8
As a percentage of world trade (%)	Imp.	0.3	0.3	0.3	0.3	0.3	0.3	0.3	0.3	0.3	0.3	0.3	0.3	0.3	0.3	0.2
	Exp.	0.3	0.3	0.3	0.3	0.3	0.3	0.3	0.3	0.3	0.3	0.3	0.3	0.3	0.3	0.3

Graph 1: Annual growth rates of exports, 1996–2010

(In percentage by year)

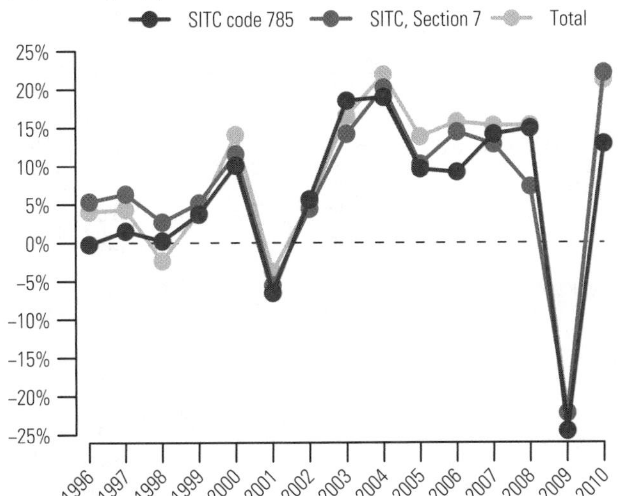

Graph 2: Trade Balance by MDG regions 2010

(Bln US$)

Imports
Exports
Trade balance

Developed Asia-Pacific
Developed Europe
Developed N. America
South-eastern Europe
C I S
Northern Africa
Sub-Saharan Africa
Latin Am, Caribbean
Eastern Asia
Southern Asia
South-eastern Asia
Western Asia
Oceania

-20 -15 -10 -5 0 5 10 15 20

Table 2: Top exporting countries or areas in 2010

Country or area	Value (million US$)	Avg. Growth (%) 06-10	Growth (%) 09-10	World share %	Cum.
World	39702.2	2.8	12.9	100.0	
China	10894.7	10.8	32.4	27.4	27.4
Japan	4788.1	-11.8	2.3	12.1	39.5
Other Asia, nes	3975.5	7.5	16.8	10.0	49.5
Italy	2929.8	0.4	2.9	7.4	56.9
Germany	2156.0	5.1	4.7	5.4	62.3
USA	1998.0	2.6	4.8	5.0	67.4
Thailand	1384.8	11.7	12.7	3.5	70.8
Netherlands	1337.8	10.3	-5.5	3.4	74.2
Belgium	1128.7	-2.9	-13.1	2.8	77.1
India	1058.8	17.3	37.4	2.7	79.7
Spain	795.9	-5.5	-3.9	2.0	81.7
France	790.6	-5.6	-9.3	2.0	83.7
Singapore	776.2	11.4	35.9	2.0	85.7
Austria	710.7	1.7	6.4	1.8	87.5
United Kingdom	573.7	2.1	10.1	1.4	88.9

Table 3: Top importing countries or areas in 2010

Country or area	Value (million US$)	Avg. Growth (%) 06-10	Growth (%) 09-10	World share %	Cum.
World	37772.2	2.5	8.5	100.0	
USA	4131.9	-10.6	-5.4	10.9	10.9
Germany	3123.5	3.6	0.5	8.3	19.2
France	2508.3	2.2	-4.4	6.6	25.8
Italy	2121.2	-1.7	3.6	5.6	31.5
Japan	1768.9	5.4	0.4	4.7	36.1
United Kingdom	1741.8	5.3	17.5	4.6	40.8
Netherlands	1739.1	12.2	0.9	4.6	45.4
Spain	1386.0	-7.6	10.9	3.7	49.0
Belgium	1109.1	-6.2	-3.2	2.9	52.0
Other Asia, nes	990.2	14.3	18.9	2.6	54.6
Australia	900.0	4.0	6.1	2.4	57.0
Canada	889.4	-2.6	-7.2	2.4	59.3
Indonesia	678.2	12.8	32.8	1.8	61.1
Switzerland	666.7	10.1	5.6	1.8	62.9
Nigeria	646.4	65.1	40.5	1.7	64.6

786 Trailers, semi-trailers; other vehicles, not mechanically propelled

After a sharp decline of 53.2 percent in 2009, the value (in current prices) of exports of trailers, semi-trailers, other vehicles, not mechanically propelled (SITC group 786) bounced back in 2010 by 47.4 percent to amount to 25.5 bln US$ (see table 2). Similarly, imports increased by 19.3 percent to 18.5 bln US$ (see table 3). Graph 1 shows that the increase in exports for 2010 in this product group by far exceeded the increases in world exports of machinery and transport equipment (SITC section 7) of 22.1 percent and in total world exports of 21.2 percent. Exports of trailers, semi-trailers, other vehicles, not mechanically propelled (SITC group 786) accounted for 0.5 percent of world exports of SITC section 7 and 0.2 percent of total world exports in 2010 (see table 1).

China, the top exporting country in 2010, accounted for 36.6 percent of world exports (see table 2). Other major exporting countries were Germany and USA, respectively with 15.8 and 10.9 percent of world exports. Canada, USA and Germany were the top destinations (see table 3). By MDG regions (see graph 2), Developed Europe accounted for a majority of exports and imports of trailers, semi-trailers, other vehicles, not mechanically propelled (SITC group 786). In 2010, its exports and imports were valued respectively at 10.6 bln US$ and 8.9 bln US$, resulting in a trade surplus of 1.7 bln US$. A larger trade surplus was recorded by Eastern Asia (+9.2 bln US$). Top trade deficits were recorded by Developed North America (-0.9 bln US$) and Commonwealth of Independent States (-0.8 bln US$).

Table 1: Imports (Imp.) and exports (Exp.), 1996-2010, in current prices

		1996	1997	1998	1999	2000	2001	2002	2003	2004	2005	2006	2007	2008	2009	2010
Values in Bln US$	Imp.	6.8	7.2	8.1	8.3	9.3	8.3	8.9	11.0	14.3	16.9	20.5	26.6	28.2	15.5	18.5
	Exp.	9.5	9.5	10.9	10.3	11.1	10.4	11.1	14.9	20.0	23.2	26.7	34.9	37.0	17.3	25.5
As a percentage of SITC section (%)	Imp.	0.3	0.3	0.4	0.4	0.4	0.3	0.3	0.4	0.4	0.4	0.5	0.5	0.5	0.4	0.4
	Exp.	0.5	0.4	0.5	0.4	0.4	0.4	0.4	0.5	0.6	0.6	0.6	0.7	0.7	0.4	0.5
As a percentage of world trade (%)	Imp.	0.1	0.1	0.1	0.1	0.1	0.1	0.1	0.1	0.2	0.2	0.2	0.2	0.2	0.1	0.1
	Exp.	0.2	0.2	0.2	0.2	0.2	0.2	0.2	0.2	0.2	0.2	0.2	0.3	0.2	0.1	0.2

Graph 1: Annual growth rates of exports, 1996–2010

(In percentage by year)

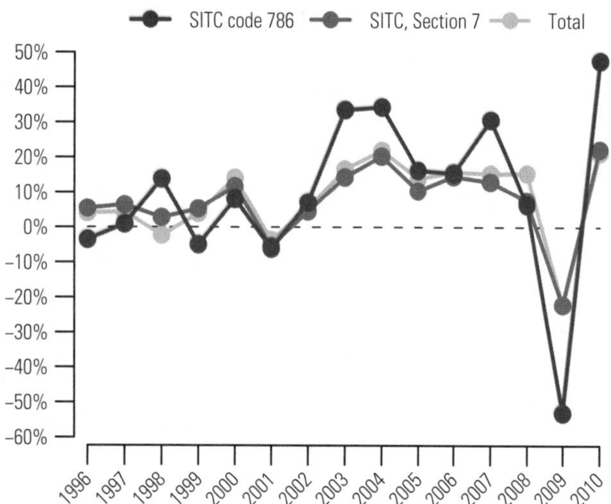

Graph 2: Trade Balance by MDG regions 2010

(Bln US$)

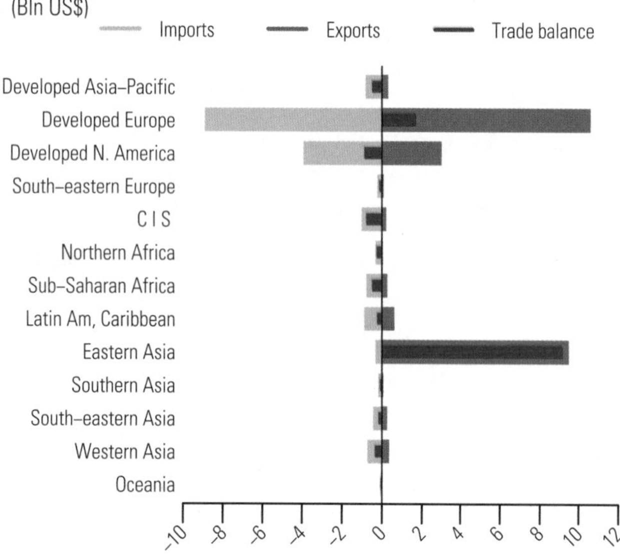

Table 2: Top exporting countries or areas in 2010

Country or area	Value (million US$)	Avg. Growth (%) 06-10	Growth (%) 09-10	World share %	Cum.
World	25545.8	-1.1	47.4	100.0	
China	9356.2	5.3	168.9	36.6	36.6
Germany	4045.7	-7.6	25.3	15.8	52.5
USA	2787.7	0.3	37.3	10.9	63.4
Netherlands	794.8	-1.0	4.4	3.1	66.5
France	758.6	-7.3	-4.4	3.0	69.5
Belgium	580.1	-4.5	-8.8	2.3	71.7
Poland	569.6	-1.8	22.9	2.2	74.0
United Kingdom	555.4	-4.2	14.8	2.2	76.1
Italy	536.7	-2.9	10.3	2.1	78.2
Mexico	392.7	-6.3	75.0	1.5	79.8
Hungary	386.9	-5.4	51.3	1.5	81.3
Austria	363.3	-6.8	10.7	1.4	82.7
Denmark	277.6	-12.8	-6.9	1.1	83.8
Canada	257.0	-18.5	7.3	1.0	84.8
Sweden	243.2	-1.7	11.6	1.0	85.7

Table 3: Top importing countries or areas in 2010

Country or area	Value (million US$)	Avg. Growth (%) 06-10	Growth (%) 09-10	World share %	Cum.
World	18475.7	-2.6	19.3	100.0	
Canada	2191.8	0.2	49.4	11.9	11.9
USA	1716.8	-6.5	36.7	9.3	21.2
Germany	1639.1	-5.5	21.4	8.9	30.0
France	1076.4	-2.5	6.7	5.8	35.9
United Kingdom	748.6	-3.4	27.8	4.1	39.9
Russian Federation	703.3	7.6	83.0	3.8	43.7
Netherlands	627.4	-6.4	14.2	3.4	47.1
Belgium	609.5	-3.8	-1.7	3.3	50.4
Australia	488.9	14.7	40.2	2.6	53.1
Italy	450.6	-2.1	20.2	2.4	55.5
Austria	404.3	-3.9	8.2	2.2	57.7
Poland	397.2	-7.2	64.6	2.1	59.8
Norway	373.7	-3.9	7.8	2.0	61.9
Sweden	372.2	-5.5	9.2	2.0	63.9
Switzerland	348.5	6.6	2.1	1.9	65.8

After several years of continuous growth marked by a peak of 26.2 bln US$ in 2008, the value (in current prices) of exports of railway vehicles and associated equipment (SITC group 791) decreased by 16.7 percent in 2009 but increased again by 12.7 percent in 2010 and amounted to 24.6 bln US$ (see table 2). Similarly, imports increased by 8.5 percent in 2010 to reach 23.2 bln US$ (see table 3). Graph 1 shows that the increase in exports for 2010 in this product group was exceeded by the increases of 22.1 percent in world exports of machinery and transport equipment (SITC section 7) and in 21.2 percent in total world exports. Exports of railway vehicles and associated equipment (SITC group 791) accounted for 0.5 percent of world exports of SITC section 7 and 0.2 percent of total world exports in 2010 (see table 1).

Germany, Ukraine and USA were the top exporting countries in 2010 (see table 2). They accounted respectively for 20.8, 9.7 and 9.5 percent of world exports. Russian Federation, Germany and China were the top destinations (see table 3). By MDG regions (see graph 2), Developed Europe accounted for a majority of trade in railway vehicles and associated equipment (SITC group 791). In 2010, its exports amounted to 14.3 bln US$ while imports to 9.6 bln US$. This resulted in a trade surplus of 4.7 bln US$. Trade surpluses were also recorded by Developed North America (+0.8 bln US$). Top trade deficits were recorded by Western Asia (-0.9 bln US$), Latin America and the Caribbean (-0.8 bln US$) and Northern Africa (-0.6 bln US$).

Table 1: Imports (Imp.) and exports (Exp.), 1996-2010, in current prices

		1996	1997	1998	1999	2000	2001	2002	2003	2004	2005	2006	2007	2008	2009	2010
Values in Bln US$	Imp.	6.8	7.3	8.9	9.0	8.0	8.7	8.4	11.4	14.3	15.6	16.0	19.1	24.5	21.4	23.2
	Exp.	7.2	7.8	9.7	8.9	8.3	8.8	9.2	12.4	15.8	16.3	18.3	21.6	26.2	21.8	24.6
As a percentage of SITC section (%)	Imp.	0.3	0.3	0.4	0.4	0.3	0.4	0.3	0.4	0.4	0.4	0.4	0.4	0.5	0.5	0.4
	Exp.	0.4	0.4	0.4	0.4	0.3	0.4	0.4	0.4	0.4	0.4	0.4	0.4	0.5	0.5	0.5
As a percentage of world trade (%)	Imp.	0.1	0.1	0.2	0.2	0.1	0.1	0.1	0.1	0.2	0.1	0.1	0.1	0.2	0.2	0.2
	Exp.	0.1	0.1	0.2	0.2	0.1	0.1	0.1	0.2	0.2	0.2	0.2	0.2	0.2	0.2	0.2

Graph 1: Annual growth rates of exports, 1996–2010

(In percentage by year)

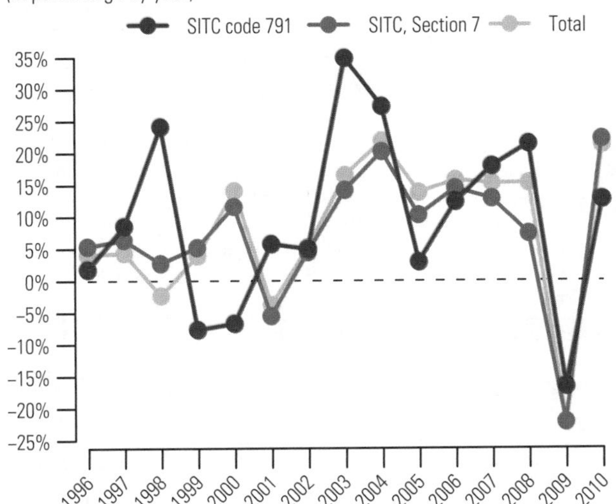

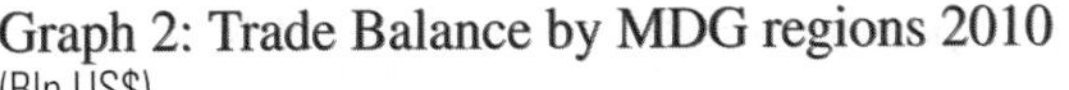

Table 2: Top exporting countries or areas in 2010

Country or area	Value (million US$)	Avg. Growth (%) 06-10	Growth (%) 09-10	World share %	Cum.
World	24584.2	7.7	12.7	100.0	
Germany	5123.8	8.0	11.9	20.8	20.8
Ukraine	2393.2	22.7	209.9	9.7	30.6
USA	2338.8	-2.4	11.8	9.5	40.1
Austria	2004.3	12.0	3.0	8.2	48.2
China	1683.5	26.0	80.6	6.8	55.1
Italy	1182.3	17.6	-2.2	4.8	59.9
France	1171.0	2.3	4.4	4.8	64.7
Spain	863.6	12.1	-19.3	3.5	68.2
Czech Rep.	765.4	5.3	-9.7	3.1	71.3
Japan	668.0	-5.4	-33.8	2.7	74.0
Rep. of Korea	646.3	31.7	112.4	2.6	76.6
Poland	637.5	21.5	28.9	2.6	79.2
Switzerland	614.7	7.7	-37.8	2.5	81.7
Brazil	559.6	23.1	202.2	2.3	84.0
Russian Federation	510.4	-3.5	19.0	2.1	86.1

Graph 2: Trade Balance by MDG regions 2010

(Bln US$)

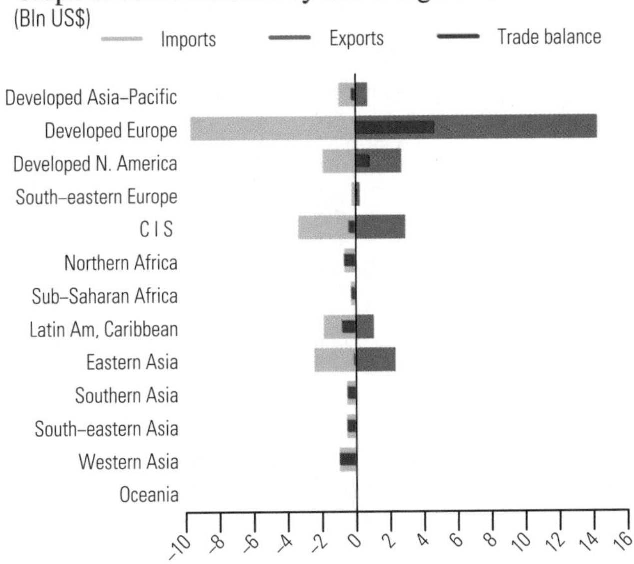

Table 3: Top importing countries or areas in 2010

Country or area	Value (million US$)	Avg. Growth (%) 06-10	Growth (%) 09-10	World share %	Cum.
World	23160.5	9.6	8.5	100.0	
Russian Federation	2062.8	25.3	117.6	8.9	8.9
Germany	2017.7	5.8	11.9	8.7	17.6
China	2011.2	13.8	28.1	8.7	26.3
Netherlands	1104.9	29.2	77.4	4.8	31.1
Brazil	1104.4	42.1	344.7	4.8	35.8
USA	1087.3	-7.9	3.3	4.7	40.5
Austria	976.8	13.2	9.6	4.2	44.8
Canada	799.4	-8.1	9.2	3.5	48.2
Australia	765.0	49.4	12.0	3.3	51.5
Kazakhstan	655.7	10.7	24.8	2.8	54.3
Switzerland	613.2	-0.1	-33.6	2.6	57.0
Italy	606.1	3.9	-11.2	2.6	59.6
Turkey	518.6	47.1	-29.9	2.2	61.8
France	503.3	2.1	-17.4	2.2	64.0
Belgium	483.3	34.7	55.3	2.1	66.1

Source: UN Comtrade

792 Aircraft and associated equipment; spacecraft and their launch vehicles; parts

After a 35.4 percent drop in 2009, the value (in current prices) of exports of aircraft and associated equipment, spacecraft and their launch vehicles, parts (SITC group 792) increased by 8.0 percent in 2010 to reach 137.6 bln US$ (see table 2). Imports, after a 12.2 percent drop in 2009, rose by 3.7 percent in 2010 and totaled 155.1 bln US$ (see table 3). Graph 1 shows that the increase in exports for 2010 in this product group was exceeded by increases in world exports of machinery and transport equipment (SITC section 7) of 22.1 percent and in total world exports of 21.2 percent. Exports of aircraft and associated equipment, spacecraft and their launch vehicles, parts (SITC group 792) accounted for 2.7 percent of world exports of SITC section 7 and 0.9 percent of total world exports in 2010 (see table 1).

France, the top exporting country, accounted for 33.7 percent of world exports in 2010 (see table 2). Other major exporting countries were Germany and Canada, respectively with 22.0 and 7.0 percent of world exports. Germany, France and USA were the top importing countries (see table 3). By MDG regions (see graph 2), Developed Europe recorded a trade surplus amounting to 24.0 bln US$. Top trade deficits were recorded by Eastern Asia (-13.9 bln US$), Western Asia (-7.7 bln US$) and Developed North America (-7.5 bln US$).

Table 1: Imports (Imp.) and exports (Exp.), 1996-2010, in current prices

		1996	1997	1998	1999	2000	2001	2002	2003	2004	2005	2006	2007	2008	2009	2010
Values in Bln US$	Imp.	63.0	74.5	88.5	90.9	83.0	88.9	83.9	87.7	104.4	110.1	131.0	143.6	170.5	149.6	155.1
	Exp.	77.5	91.6	112.2	110.5	100.6	108.5	109.6	108.3	120.7	128.7	161.5	182.8	197.5	127.5	137.6
As a percentage of SITC section (%)	Imp.	3.1	3.5	4.0	3.9	3.2	3.6	3.3	3.0	2.9	2.8	3.0	2.9	3.2	3.5	3.0
	Exp.	3.8	4.2	5.0	4.7	3.8	4.4	4.3	3.7	3.4	3.3	3.6	3.6	3.7	3.0	2.7
As a percentage of world trade (%)	Imp.	1.2	1.3	1.6	1.6	1.3	1.4	1.3	1.2	1.1	1.0	1.1	1.0	1.1	1.2	1.0
	Exp.	1.5	1.7	2.1	2.0	1.6	1.8	1.7	1.4	1.3	1.2	1.3	1.3	1.2	1.0	0.9

Graph 1: Annual growth rates of exports, 1996–2010
(In percentage by year)

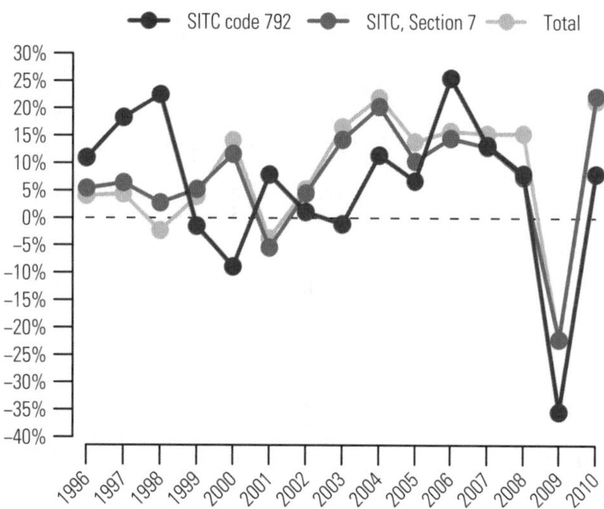

Table 2: Top exporting countries or areas in 2010

Country or area	Value (million US$)	Avg. Growth (%) 06-10	Growth (%) 09-10	World share %	Cum.
World	137647.7	-3.9	8.0	100.0	
France	46389.6	12.5	34.3	33.7	33.7
Germany	30293.9	4.8	-5.4	22.0	55.7
Canada	9627.4	2.2	0.9	7.0	62.7
USA	7363.4	-42.4	-9.9	5.3	68.1
Italy	4874.2	11.6	4.2	3.5	71.6
Singapore	4624.0	18.9	15.1	3.4	75.0
Brazil	4361.6	6.1	4.0	3.2	78.1
Spain	3470.8	8.8	2.5	2.5	80.6
Japan	2619.1	6.6	3.4	1.9	82.5
United Arab Emirates	1806.5	75.7	39.8	1.3	83.9
Israel	1692.5	15.1	-3.7	1.2	85.1
India	1534.6	126.8	41.0	1.1	86.2
Switzerland	1317.3	-6.7	-40.7	1.0	87.2
Netherlands	1312.1	3.9	12.2	1.0	88.1
China	1260.4	-0.6	34.4	0.9	89.0

Graph 2: Trade Balance by MDG regions 2010
(Bln US$)

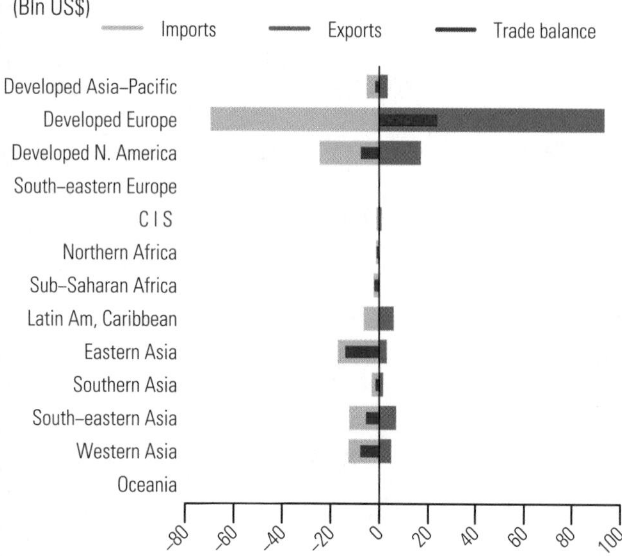

Table 3: Top importing countries or areas in 2010

Country or area	Value (million US$)	Avg. Growth (%) 06-10	Growth (%) 09-10	World share %	Cum.
World	155136.4	4.3	3.7	100.0	
Germany	25964.9	0.4	3.6	16.7	16.7
France	24428.8	17.2	51.0	15.7	32.5
USA	19058.6	1.9	3.3	12.3	44.8
China	12390.8	3.2	17.7	8.0	52.8
Singapore	5498.5	-1.5	-29.6	3.5	56.3
Canada	5407.8	0.9	-0.1	3.5	59.8
United Arab Emirates	5063.7	29.7	-2.2	3.3	63.0
Japan	4282.5	-4.1	-11.9	2.8	65.8
Indonesia	3523.0	38.0	8.7	2.3	68.1
Ireland	3317.4	18.3	-36.8	2.1	70.2
Turkey	3155.0	20.7	200.7	2.0	72.3
Rep. of Korea	2816.3	2.0	91.4	1.8	74.1
Spain	2723.2	-3.9	8.4	1.8	75.8
India	2671.7	-15.3	-48.6	1.7	77.5
Switzerland	2417.2	2.0	15.9	1.6	79.1

From 2006 to 2010, the value (in current prices) of exports of ships, boats and floating structures (SITC group 793) increased on average by 18.5 percent each year and amounted to 168.8 bln US$ (see table 2). Similarly, imports went up on average by 9.4 percent each year to 71.9 bln US$ (see table 3). Graph 1 shows that the increase of 18.8 percent in exports for 2010 in this product group was exceeded by the increases in world exports of machinery and transport equipment (SITC section 7) of 22.1 percent and in total world exports of 21.2 percent. Exports of ships, boats and floating structures (SITC group 793) accounted for 3.3 percent of world exports of SITC section 7 and 1.1 percent of total world exports in 2010 (see table 1).

The top exporting countries in 2010 were Rep. of Korea, China and Japan (see table 2). They accounted respectively for 28.0, 23.9 and 15.4 percent of world exports. Top destinations were Germany, Italy and Greece (see table 3). By MDG regions (see graph 2), Eastern Asia recorded a trade surplus amounting to 83.0 bln US$ in 2010. Major trade surpluses were also recorded by Developed Asia-Pacific (+24.9 bln US$) and Western Asia (+1.3 bln US$). Top trade deficits were recorded by Developed Europe (-11.2 bln US$), South-eastern Asia (-1.2 bln US$) and Sub-Saharan Africa (-1.0 bln US$).

Table 1: Imports (Imp.) and exports (Exp.), 1996-2010, in current prices

		1996	1997	1998	1999	2000	2001	2002	2003	2004	2005	2006	2007	2008	2009	2010
Values in Bln US$	Imp.	18.6	19.5	18.2	18.9	19.2	19.6	21.5	30.0	36.2	42.3	50.3	48.8	69.3	58.3	71.9
	Exp.	37.6	37.3	42.0	40.2	39.9	43.9	46.4	52.9	62.9	68.7	85.7	104.6	141.3	142.1	168.8
As a percentage of SITC section (%)	Imp.	0.9	0.9	0.8	0.8	0.7	0.8	0.8	1.0	1.0	1.1	1.1	1.0	1.3	1.4	1.4
	Exp.	1.8	1.7	1.9	1.7	1.5	1.8	1.8	1.8	1.8	1.8	1.9	2.1	2.6	3.4	3.3
As a percentage of world trade (%)	Imp.	0.3	0.4	0.3	0.3	0.3	0.3	0.3	0.4	0.4	0.4	0.4	0.3	0.4	0.5	0.5
	Exp.	0.7	0.7	0.8	0.7	0.6	0.7	0.7	0.7	0.7	0.7	0.7	0.8	0.9	1.1	1.1

Graph 1: Annual growth rates of exports, 1996–2010

(In percentage by year)

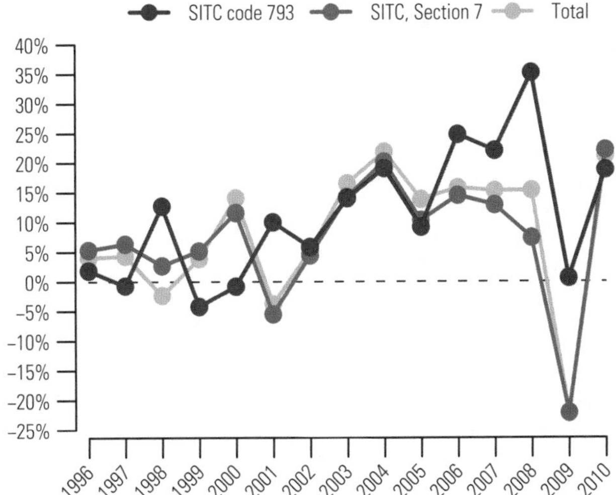

Table 2: Top exporting countries or areas in 2010

Country or area	Value (million US$)	Avg. Growth (%) 06-10	Growth (%) 09-10	World share %	Cum.
World	168761.7	18.5	18.8	100.0	
Rep. of Korea	47189.7	21.7	11.1	28.0	28.0
China	40296.4	49.3	42.1	23.9	51.8
Japan	26036.9	16.7	17.3	15.4	67.3
Germany	6600.5	15.4	113.9	3.9	71.2
Italy	5394.7	8.4	-3.9	3.2	74.4
India	4223.3	52.4	12.2	2.5	76.9
Poland	3219.7	0.4	-6.1	1.9	78.8
France	2775.7	4.4	31.1	1.6	80.4
USA	2617.8	-0.8	28.2	1.6	82.0
Singapore	2312.4	28.4	-2.0	1.4	83.4
United Kingdom	2239.6	17.0	65.0	1.3	84.7
Netherlands	2103.8	14.8	-11.2	1.2	85.9
Spain	1972.0	-20.9	13.6	1.2	87.1
United Arab Emirates	1807.5	76.0	239.0	1.1	88.2
Finland	1587.9	-0.4	-25.2	0.9	89.1

Graph 2: Trade Balance by MDG regions 2010

(Bln US$)

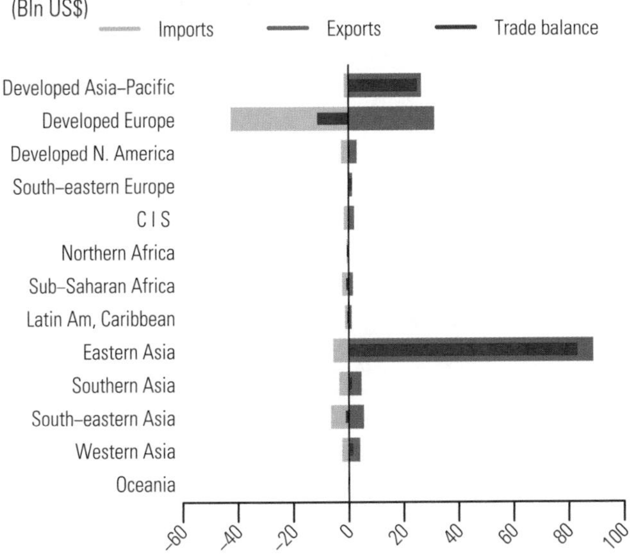

Table 3: Top importing countries or areas in 2010

Country or area	Value (million US$)	Avg. Growth (%) 06-10	Growth (%) 09-10	World share %	Cum.
World	71918.5	9.4	23.5	100.0	
Germany	14496.9	13.3	120.0	20.2	20.2
Italy	4117.6	21.9	72.9	5.7	25.9
Greece	3919.5	3.6	-25.1	5.4	31.3
Norway	3858.0	13.5	18.5	5.4	36.7
Rep. of Korea	3358.7	34.4	19.0	4.7	41.4
Poland	2889.5	15.3	25.3	4.0	45.4
United Kingdom	2887.0	51.2	414.0	4.0	49.4
India	2620.1	-5.2	-13.3	3.6	53.0
Spain	2365.1	-15.1	443.7	3.3	56.3
Denmark	1982.6	25.3	-37.2	2.8	59.1
Indonesia	1959.5	6.9	-27.5	2.7	61.8
China	1678.2	33.3	-32.3	2.3	64.1
USA	1636.3	0.7	26.6	2.3	66.4
Portugal	1419.2	127.7	497.8	2.0	68.4
France	1367.8	-8.3	-16.2	1.9	70.3

Source: UN Comtrade

Miscellaneous manufactured articles
(SITC Section 8)

811 Prefabricated buildings

After a sharp decline in 2009 of 30.5 percent, the value (in current prices) of prefabricated buildings (SITC group 811) bounced back by 11.0 percent in 2010 to reach 7.3 bln US$ (see table 2). Imports, after a 27.0 percent drop in 2009, increased by 6.2 percent in 2010 and totaled 6.0 bln US$ (see table 3). Graph 1 shows that the rise in exports for 2010 in this product group was exceeded by the increases in world exports of miscellaneous manufactured articles (SITC section 8) of 15.0 percent and in total world exports of 21.2 percent. Exports of prefabricated buildings (SITC group 811) accounted for 0.4 percent of world exports of SITC section 8 and less than 0.1 percent of total world exports (see table 1).

In 2010, China, USA and Italy were the top exporting countries (see table 2). They accounted respectively for 16.7, 12.2 and 6.3 percent of world exports. Top destinations were Canada, Germany and Kazakhstan (see table 3). By MDG regions (see graph 2), Developed Europe accounted for a large share of trade in prefabricated buildings (SITC group 811). In 2010, its exports amounted to 3.6 bln US$ while imports reached 2.2 bln US$. This resulted in a trade surplus of 1.4 bln US$. Eastern Asia recorded a trade surplus amounting to 1.1 bln US$. Top trade deficits were recorded by Commonwealth of Independent States (-521 mln US$), Sub-Saharan Africa (-507 mln US$) and Latin America and the Caribbean (-342 mln US$).

Table 1: Imports (Imp.) and exports (Exp.), 1996-2010, in current prices

		1996	1997	1998	1999	2000	2001	2002	2003	2004	2005	2006	2007	2008	2009	2010
Values in Bln US$	Imp.	2.5	2.6	2.5	2.6	2.5	2.7	2.7	3.2	4.0	4.5	5.4	6.7	7.8	5.7	6.0
	Exp.	3.0	3.0	3.0	3.0	2.8	2.8	3.1	3.8	4.7	5.3	6.3	8.0	9.4	6.5	7.3
As a percentage of SITC section (%)	Imp.	0.4	0.4	0.4	0.3	0.3	0.3	0.3	0.3	0.4	0.4	0.4	0.4	0.5	0.4	0.4
	Exp.	0.4	0.4	0.4	0.4	0.4	0.4	0.4	0.4	0.4	0.5	0.5	0.5	0.6	0.5	0.4
As a percentage of world trade (%)	Imp.	0.0	0.0	0.0	0.0	0.0	0.0	0.0	0.0	0.0	0.0	0.0	0.0	0.0	0.0	0.0
	Exp.	0.1	0.1	0.1	0.1	0.0	0.0	0.0	0.1	0.1	0.1	0.1	0.1	0.1	0.1	0.0

Graph 1: Annual growth rates of exports, 1996–2010

(In percentage by year)

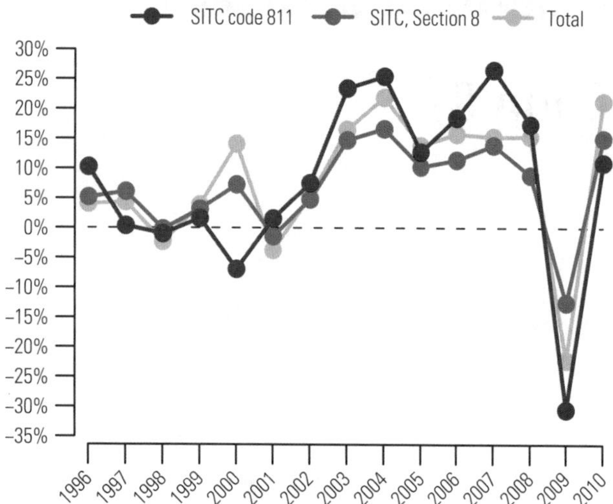

Graph 2: Trade Balance by MDG regions 2010

(Bln US$)

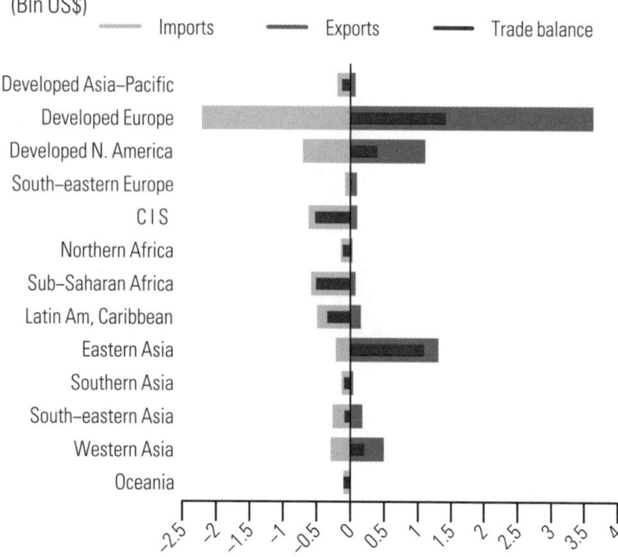

Table 2: Top exporting countries or areas in 2010

Country or area	Value (million US$)	Avg. Growth (%) 06-10	Growth (%) 09-10	World share %	Cum.
World	7259.5	3.4	11.0	100.0	
China	1215.0	17.5	13.7	16.7	16.7
USA	884.5	16.4	39.1	12.2	28.9
Italy	454.4	18.5	24.2	6.3	35.2
Germany	434.7	2.8	8.1	6.0	41.2
Netherlands	300.6	-1.4	26.3	4.1	45.3
Czech Rep.	274.6	-4.9	1.8	3.8	49.1
Belgium	269.0	-3.6	-20.5	3.7	52.8
France	230.5	4.4	20.9	3.2	56.0
Canada	218.8	-15.7	5.1	3.0	59.0
Finland	204.6	-7.8	-2.3	2.8	61.8
Spain	200.6	-4.1	-2.6	2.8	64.6
Sweden	197.2	-14.5	-5.3	2.7	67.3
Estonia	188.9	6.2	43.3	2.6	69.9
Turkey	163.8	3.5	-16.7	2.3	72.1
Slovenia	126.1	-0.8	-2.8	1.7	73.9

Table 3: Top importing countries or areas in 2010

Country or area	Value (million US$)	Avg. Growth (%) 06-10	Growth (%) 09-10	World share %	Cum.
World	6027.2	2.6	6.2	100.0	
Canada	449.6	19.4	34.5	7.5	7.5
Germany	389.3	-2.3	9.1	6.5	13.9
Kazakhstan	352.7	43.8	137.7	5.9	19.8
France	327.3	-0.1	-0.3	5.4	25.2
Norway	263.3	0.0	12.2	4.4	29.6
USA	249.0	-13.3	10.5	4.1	33.7
Switzerland	224.1	6.4	0.1	3.7	37.4
Mexico	200.1	-15.1	38.2	3.3	40.7
United Kingdom	170.0	-8.3	-23.2	2.8	43.6
China	162.3	77.9	355.4	2.7	46.3
Sudan	*145.6*	8.9	16.0	2.4	48.7
Russian Federation	141.0	5.3	-14.2	2.3	51.0
Austria	107.1	3.1	10.7	1.8	52.8
Australia	104.6	44.8	38.0	1.7	54.5
Angola	*94.9*	28.4	-47.3	1.6	56.1

After a 20.1 percent drop in 2009, the value (in current prices) of exports of sanitary, plumbing and heating fixtures and fittings, nes (SITC group 812) bounced back in 2010 by 4.0 percent to 13.6 bln US$ (see table 2). Imports showed a similar development with an increase of 5.8 percent and amounted to 14.1 bln US$ (see table 3). Graph 1 shows that the increase in exports for 2010 in this product group was by far exceeded by increases in world exports of miscellaneous manufactured articles (SITC section 8) of 15.0 percent and in total world exports of 21.2 percent. Exports of sanitary, plumbing and heating fixtures and fittings, nes (SITC group 812) accounted for 0.8 percent of world exports of SITC section 8 and 0.1 percent of total world exports in 2010 (see table 1).

Germany, Italy and China were the top exporting countries in 2010 (see table 2). They accounted respectively for 17.7, 12.2 and 7.3 percent of world exports. Top destinations were Germany, United Kingdom and USA (see table 3). By MDG regions (see graph 2), Developed Europe accounted for a majority of exports and imports of sanitary, plumbing and heating fixtures and fittings, nes (SITC group 812). In 2010, its exports and imports were valued respectively at 9.4 bln US$ and 8.8 bln US$, resulting in a trade surplus of 0.6 bln US$. Major trade surpluses were also recorded by Eastern Asia (+0.8 bln US$) and Western Asia (+0.4 bln US$). Top trade deficits were recorded by Developed North America (-1.2 bln US$), Commonwealth of Independent States (-0.7 bln US$) and Sub-Saharan Africa (-0.3 bln US$).

Table 1: Imports (Imp.) and exports (Exp.), 1996-2010, in current prices

		1996	1997	1998	1999	2000	2001	2002	2003	2004	2005	2006	2007	2008	2009	2010
Values in Bln US$	Imp.	5.6	5.6	5.7	5.9	5.6	5.7	6.5	8.4	10.1	11.3	13.3	14.8	16.2	13.3	14.1
	Exp.	5.8	5.8	5.9	6.0	6.2	5.8	6.6	8.5	10.2	11.3	13.5	15.0	16.4	13.1	13.6
As a percentage of SITC section (%)	Imp.	0.8	0.8	0.8	0.8	0.7	0.7	0.8	0.9	0.9	0.9	1.0	1.0	1.0	0.9	0.9
	Exp.	0.9	0.8	0.8	0.8	0.8	0.8	0.8	0.9	1.0	1.0	1.0	1.0	1.0	0.9	0.8
As a percentage of world trade (%)	Imp.	0.1	0.1	0.1	0.1	0.1	0.1	0.1	0.1	0.1	0.1	0.1	0.1	0.1	0.1	0.1
	Exp.	0.1	0.1	0.1	0.1	0.1	0.1	0.1	0.1	0.1	0.1	0.1	0.1	0.1	0.1	0.1

Graph 1: Annual growth rates of exports, 1996–2010

(In percentage by year)

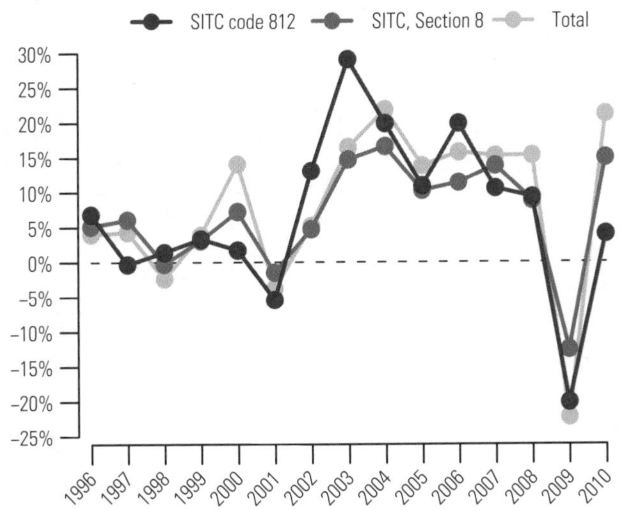

Graph 2: Trade Balance by MDG regions 2010

(Bln US$)

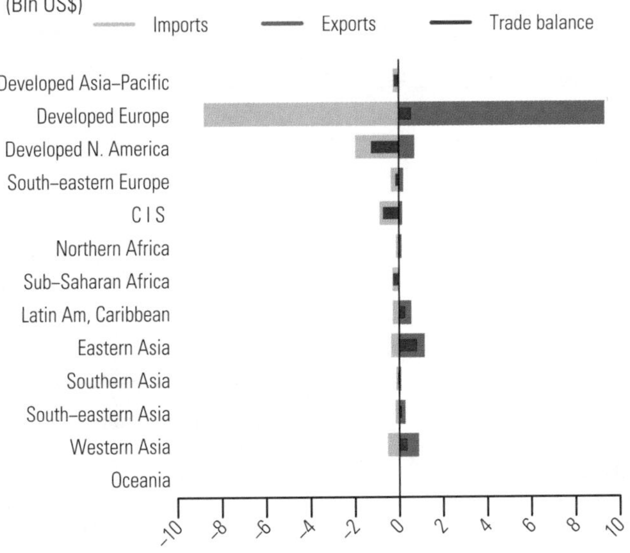

Table 2: Top exporting countries or areas in 2010

Country or area	Value (million US$)	Avg. Growth (%) 06-10	Growth (%) 09-10	World share %	Cum.
World	13603.0	0.1	4.0	100.0	
Germany	2413.0	0.9	4.5	17.7	17.7
Italy	1665.1	-3.9	3.6	12.2	30.0
China	987.2	7.1	18.6	7.3	37.2
Turkey	806.7	3.6	9.4	5.9	43.2
France	707.4	-2.4	-1.1	5.2	48.4
Netherlands	658.4	2.2	1.5	4.8	53.2
Poland	602.5	7.4	13.4	4.4	57.6
Slovakia	538.4	10.5	-1.7	4.0	61.6
USA	532.4	1.3	-3.7	3.9	65.5
Austria	475.8	-1.2	-15.0	3.5	69.0
Belgium	433.4	-1.9	-7.2	3.2	72.2
Mexico	425.4	0.9	12.4	3.1	75.3
Czech Rep.	377.2	-2.5	5.2	2.8	78.1
United Kingdom	207.6	-7.7	1.8	1.5	79.6
Spain	203.9	-2.3	0.4	1.5	81.1

Table 3: Top importing countries or areas in 2010

Country or area	Value (million US$)	Avg. Growth (%) 06-10	Growth (%) 09-10	World share %	Cum.
World	14086.6	1.5	5.8	100.0	
Germany	1505.3	0.4	3.7	10.7	10.7
United Kingdom	1426.9	-2.3	0.6	10.1	20.8
USA	1345.2	-0.5	13.9	9.5	30.4
France	1087.7	2.4	1.3	7.7	38.1
Italy	693.0	1.9	5.1	4.9	43.0
Canada	605.0	5.4	6.0	4.3	47.3
Belgium	594.0	7.2	3.5	4.2	51.5
Spain	587.8	-5.0	4.3	4.2	55.7
Netherlands	539.4	7.3	-0.6	3.8	59.5
Russian Federation	532.9	12.4	44.4	3.8	63.3
Poland	355.0	1.9	6.1	2.5	65.8
Austria	319.0	0.8	-3.0	2.3	68.1
Switzerland	256.1	4.2	2.9	1.8	69.9
Romania	245.9	-3.0	12.0	1.7	71.7
Turkey	207.4	-10.3	15.7	1.5	73.1

813 Lighting fixtures and fittings, nes

After several years of continuous growth marked by a peak of 28.5 bln US$ in 2008, the value (in current prices) of exports of lighting fixtures and fittings, nes (SITC group 813) decreased by 17.4 percent in 2009 but increased again by 18.0 percent in 2010 and amounted to 27.8 bln US$ (see table 2). Similarly, imports increased by 19.9 percent in 2010 to reach 29.7 bln US$ (see table 3). Graph 1 shows that the increase in exports for 2010 in this product group was above the increase of 15.0 percent in world exports of miscellaneous manufactured articles (SITC section 8) but below the increase of 21.2 percent in total world exports. Exports of lighting fixtures and fittings, nes (SITC group 813) accounted for 1.7 percent of world exports of SITC section 8 and 0.2 percent of total world exports in 2010 (see table 1).

China, the top exporting country in 2010, accounted for more than a third (40.4 percent) of world exports (see table 2). Other major exporting countries were Germany and Italy, respectively with 9.7 and 6.3 percent of world exports. Top destinations were USA, Germany and France (see table 3). By MDG regions (see graph 2), Eastern Asia recorded a trade surplus amounting to 10.3 bln US$. Top trade deficits were recorded by Developed North America (-5.7 bln US$), Developed Europe (-1.9 bln US$) and Western Asia (-1.2 bln US$).

Table 1: Imports (Imp.) and exports (Exp.), 1996-2010, in current prices

		1996	1997	1998	1999	2000	2001	2002	2003	2004	2005	2006	2007	2008	2009	2010
Values in Bln US$	Imp.	11.2	11.7	12.4	13.9	14.8	14.4	15.4	17.6	20.3	22.2	24.3	27.9	29.5	24.8	29.7
	Exp.	10.5	10.9	11.3	11.9	12.4	12.5	13.4	15.2	17.2	19.1	21.1	24.9	28.5	23.6	27.8
As a percentage of SITC section (%)	Imp.	1.6	1.6	1.7	1.8	1.8	1.8	1.8	1.8	1.8	1.8	1.8	1.8	1.8	1.7	1.8
	Exp.	1.6	1.6	1.6	1.6	1.6	1.6	1.7	1.7	1.6	1.6	1.6	1.7	1.7	1.7	1.7
As a percentage of world trade (%)	Imp.	0.2	0.2	0.2	0.2	0.2	0.2	0.2	0.2	0.2	0.2	0.2	0.2	0.2	0.2	0.2
	Exp.	0.2	0.2	0.2	0.2	0.2	0.2	0.2	0.2	0.2	0.2	0.2	0.2	0.2	0.2	0.2

Graph 1: Annual growth rates of exports, 1996–2010
(In percentage by year)

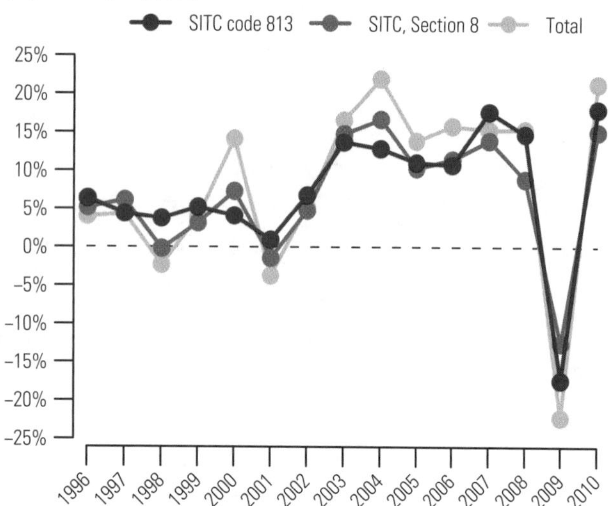

Graph 2: Trade Balance by MDG regions 2010
(Bln US$)

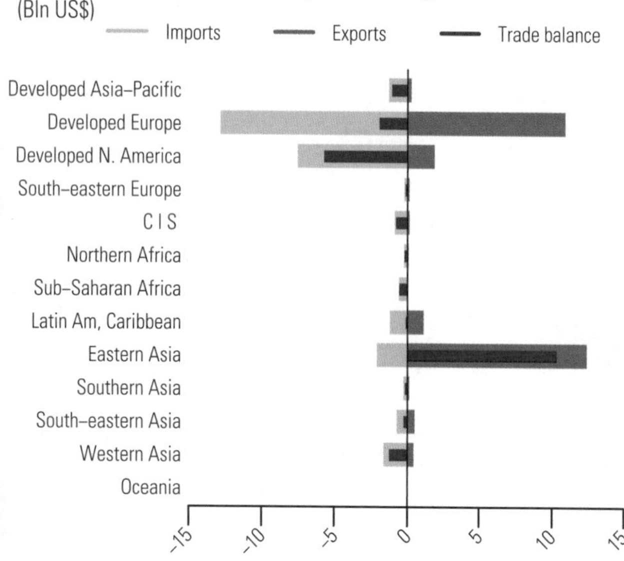

Table 2: Top exporting countries or areas in 2010

Country or area	Value (million US$)	Avg. Growth (%) 06-10	Growth (%) 09-10	World share %	Cum.
World	27 807.6	7.1	18.0	100.0	
China	11 221.3	16.0	35.9	40.4	40.4
Germany	2 708.4	6.3	7.9	9.7	50.1
Italy	1 753.5	-0.9	0.5	6.3	56.4
USA	1 438.3	6.3	17.9	5.2	61.6
Mexico	957.5	-4.0	10.6	3.4	65.0
France	843.4	2.7	5.0	3.0	68.0
Belgium	793.2	2.9	2.1	2.9	70.9
China, Hong Kong SAR	744.0	-9.0	10.2	2.7	73.6
Austria	742.7	5.2	4.3	2.7	76.2
Netherlands	571.9	12.7	10.7	2.1	78.3
United Kingdom	553.4	0.1	-1.0	2.0	80.3
Spain	488.8	-0.9	-6.6	1.8	82.1
Canada	393.7	-1.8	9.5	1.4	83.5
Sweden	363.0	2.1	5.4	1.3	84.8
Poland	333.8	4.8	5.1	1.2	86.0

Table 3: Top importing countries or areas in 2010

Country or area	Value (million US$)	Avg. Growth (%) 06-10	Growth (%) 09-10	World share %	Cum.
World	29 718.4	5.1	19.9	100.0	
USA	6 294.6	-2.8	24.0	21.2	21.2
Germany	2 334.6	6.4	15.4	7.9	29.0
France	1 630.1	9.2	14.2	5.5	34.5
United Kingdom	1 408.1	3.1	19.4	4.7	39.3
Canada	1 227.9	4.7	21.5	4.1	43.4
China	1 183.4	74.3	125.5	4.0	47.4
Netherlands	764.5	6.5	11.8	2.6	49.9
Italy	762.6	7.2	15.1	2.6	52.5
Belgium	762.3	3.6	2.9	2.6	55.1
Spain	702.5	-0.9	7.6	2.4	57.4
Japan	662.9	1.4	17.9	2.2	59.7
Austria	648.9	5.0	3.5	2.2	61.9
Russian Federation	595.5	26.1	100.7	2.0	63.9
Switzerland	562.4	6.8	9.7	1.9	65.8
Australia	553.6	12.5	24.0	1.9	67.6

Source: UN Comtrade

From 2006 to 2010, the value (in current prices) of exports of furniture and parts thereof, stuffed furnishings (SITC group 821) increased on average by 4.5 percent each year and amounted to 129.1 bln US$ (see table 2). Similarly, imports went up on average by 2.6 percent each year to 130.1 bln US$ (see table 3). Graph 1 shows that the increase of 14.9 percent in exports for 2010 in this product group was slightly exceeded by the increases in world exports of miscellaneous manufactured articles (SITC section 8) of 15.0 percent and in total world exports of 21.2 percent. Exports of furniture and parts thereof, stuffed furnishings (SITC group 821) accounted for 7.9 percent of world exports of SITC section 8 and 0.9 percent of total world exports in 2010 (see table 1).

China was the top exporting country in 2010 (see table 2). It accounted for 30.1 percent of world exports. Other major exporting countries were Germany and Italy, respectively with 8.3 and 8.1 percent of world exports. USA, Germany and France were the top destinations (see table 3). By MDG regions (see graph 2), Developed Europe's exports and imports amounted respectively to 55.0 bln US$ and 58.5 bln US$, resulting in a trade deficit of 3.5 bln US$. Top trade deficits were recorded by Developed North America (-30.7 bln US$) and Developed Asia-Pacific (-6.6 bln US$). Top trade surpluses were recorded by Eastern Asia (+36.7 bln US$), South-eastern Asia (+6.8 bln US$), and South-eastern Europe (+1.5 bln US$).

Table 1: Imports (Imp.) and exports (Exp.), 1996-2010, in current prices

		1996	1997	1998	1999	2000	2001	2002	2003	2004	2005	2006	2007	2008	2009	2010
Values in Bln US$	Imp.	46.1	48.5	52.7	58.6	63.2	63.6	70.0	82.4	97.0	106.9	117.5	135.3	140.1	113.0	130.1
	Exp.	48.9	50.7	53.3	57.1	61.3	60.8	65.4	76.0	89.8	97.5	108.2	126.9	136.3	112.4	129.1
As a percentage of SITC section (%)	Imp.	6.8	6.8	7.3	7.8	7.8	7.9	8.3	8.5	8.6	8.7	8.7	8.8	8.5	7.9	8.0
	Exp.	7.4	7.2	7.6	7.9	7.9	8.0	8.2	8.3	8.4	8.3	8.2	8.5	8.4	7.9	7.9
As a percentage of world trade (%)	Imp.	0.9	0.9	1.0	1.0	1.0	1.0	1.1	1.1	1.0	1.0	1.0	1.0	0.9	0.9	0.9
	Exp.	0.9	0.9	1.0	1.0	1.0	1.0	1.0	1.0	1.0	0.9	0.9	0.9	0.9	0.9	0.9

Graph 1: Annual growth rates of exports, 1996–2010

(In percentage by year)

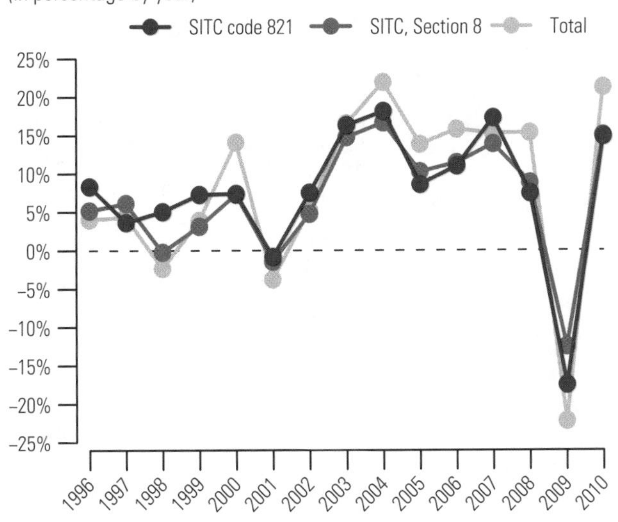

Table 2: Top exporting countries or areas in 2010

Country or area	Value (million US$)	Avg. Growth (%) 06-10	Growth (%) 09-10	World share %	Cum.
World	129148.8	4.5	14.9	100.0	
China	38921.5	16.8	29.6	30.1	30.1
Germany	10773.8	3.4	3.8	8.3	38.5
Italy	10515.3	-2.1	0.8	8.1	46.6
Poland	7970.7	6.5	12.9	6.2	52.8
USA	5877.0	0.7	22.4	4.6	57.3
Mexico	4353.5	-1.9	37.7	3.4	60.7
Canada	3476.6	-11.6	20.8	2.7	63.4
Viet Nam	*3046.0*	14.3	25.6	2.4	65.8
France	2751.5	-3.7	-13.1	2.1	67.9
Malaysia	2548.1	3.1	14.5	2.0	69.9
Czech Rep.	2260.6	4.5	14.9	1.8	71.6
Sweden	2229.6	2.3	7.1	1.7	73.3
Belgium	2084.7	-0.9	-4.7	1.6	75.0
Denmark	2032.0	-6.7	-5.1	1.6	76.5
Indonesia	1954.1	1.0	18.0	1.5	78.0

Graph 2: Trade Balance by MDG regions 2010

(Bln US$)

Imports — Exports — Trade balance

Developed Asia-Pacific
Developed Europe
Developed N. America
South-eastern Europe
C I S
Northern Africa
Sub-Saharan Africa
Latin Am, Caribbean
Eastern Asia
Southern Asia
South-eastern Asia
Western Asia
Oceania

-60 -50 -40 -30 -20 -10 0 10 20 30 40 50 60

Table 3: Top importing countries or areas in 2010

Country or area	Value (million US$)	Avg. Growth (%) 06-10	Growth (%) 09-10	World share %	Cum.
World	130132.5	2.6	15.2	100.0	
USA	34166.2	-1.5	27.9	26.3	26.3
Germany	12374.1	3.9	9.0	9.5	35.8
France	8358.6	4.7	9.0	6.4	42.2
United Kingdom	7430.7	-1.3	10.8	5.7	47.9
Canada	5836.8	2.4	22.1	4.5	52.4
Japan	5501.8	2.1	12.4	4.2	56.6
Spain	3338.1	3.1	14.3	2.6	59.2
Netherlands	3224.7	3.7	5.0	2.5	61.7
Belgium	3114.4	-0.4	-3.0	2.4	64.0
Switzerland	2974.9	4.9	5.5	2.3	66.3
Italy	2597.8	3.6	9.4	2.0	68.3
Australia	2362.2	8.7	13.3	1.8	70.1
Austria	2343.5	4.7	-3.2	1.8	71.9
Russian Federation	2021.7	21.8	35.6	1.6	73.5
Sweden	2011.8	1.5	14.3	1.5	75.0

831 Travel goods, handbags, etc, of leather, plastics, textile, others

After a 12.0 percent drop in 2009, the value (in current prices) of exports of travel goods, handbags, etc (SITC group 831) bounced back in 2010 by 23.1 percent to 40.8 bln US$ (see table 2). Imports showed a similar development with an increase of 17.9 percent and amounted to 43.4 bln US$ (see table 3). Graph 1 shows that the increase in exports for 2010 in this product group exceeded the increases in world exports of miscellaneous manufactured articles (SITC section 8) of 15.0 percent and in total world exports of 21.2 percent. Exports of travel goods, handbags, etc (SITC group 831) accounted for 2.5 percent of world exports of SITC section 8 and 0.3 percent of total world exports in 2010 (see table 1).

Exports of China, the top exporting country in 2010, increased by 40.6 percent and represented more than a third (44.5 percent) of world exports (see table 2). Other major exporting countries or areas were China, Hong Kong SAR and France, respectively with 13.2 and 10.0 percent of world exports. USA, Japan and China, Hong Kong SAR were the top destinations (see table 3). By MDG regions (see graph 2), Eastern Asia accounted for a majority of exports of travel goods, handbags, etc (SITC group 831). In 2010, its exports amounted to 23.7 bln US$ while imports amounted to 7.3 bln US$, resulting in a trade surplus of 16.4 bln US$. Top deficits were recorded by Developed North America (-8.5 bln US$), Developed Asia-Pacific (-5.3 bln US$) and Developed Europe (-2.3 bln US$).

Table 1: Imports (Imp.) and exports (Exp.), 1996-2010, in current prices

		1996	1997	1998	1999	2000	2001	2002	2003	2004	2005	2006	2007	2008	2009	2010
Values in Bln US$	Imp.	18.0	17.9	17.3	18.5	19.6	19.6	19.8	22.0	26.1	29.2	32.6	38.5	42.8	36.9	43.4
	Exp.	15.3	15.6	14.7	15.3	16.5	16.3	16.0	17.8	21.3	23.8	27.0	32.3	37.7	33.1	40.8
As a percentage of SITC section (%)	Imp.	2.6	2.5	2.4	2.5	2.4	2.4	2.3	2.3	2.3	2.4	2.4	2.5	2.6	2.6	2.7
	Exp.	2.3	2.2	2.1	2.1	2.1	2.1	2.0	1.9	2.0	2.0	2.1	2.2	2.3	2.3	2.5
As a percentage of world trade (%)	Imp.	0.3	0.3	0.3	0.3	0.3	0.3	0.3	0.3	0.3	0.3	0.3	0.3	0.3	0.3	0.3
	Exp.	0.3	0.3	0.3	0.3	0.3	0.3	0.3	0.2	0.2	0.2	0.2	0.2	0.2	0.3	0.3

Graph 1: Annual growth rates of exports, 1996–2010

(In percentage by year)

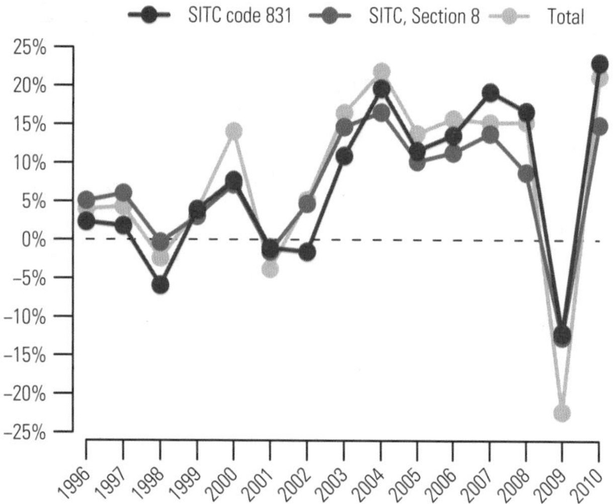

Graph 2: Trade Balance by MDG regions 2010

(Bln US$)

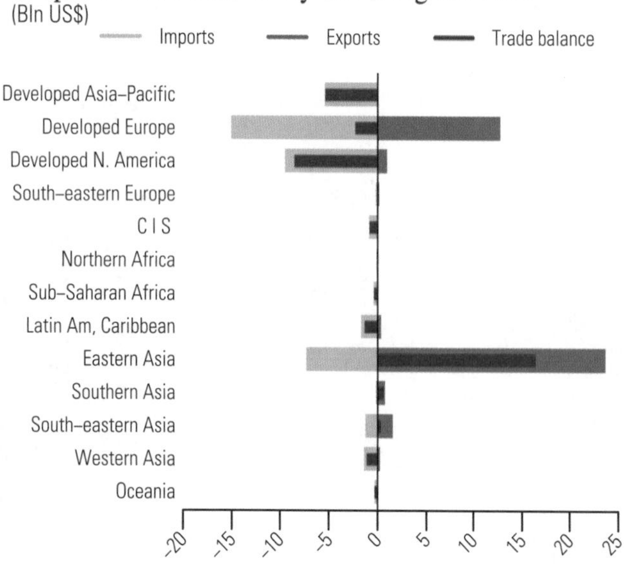

Table 2: Top exporting countries or areas in 2010

Country or area	Value (million US$)	Avg. Growth (%) 06-10	Growth (%) 09-10	World share %	Cum.
World	40766.3	10.8	23.1	100.0	
China	18135.5	19.9	40.6	44.5	44.5
China, Hong Kong SAR	5369.9	1.2	9.1	13.2	57.7
France	4079.7	7.8	13.7	10.0	67.7
Italy	3854.8	6.0	16.3	9.5	77.1
Germany	1062.4	7.0	6.0	2.6	79.7
Belgium	1001.8	1.3	-0.5	2.5	82.2
USA	844.6	6.8	7.3	2.1	84.3
Viet Nam	*747.6*	22.7	25.6	1.8	86.1
India	722.8	6.2	7.9	1.8	87.9
United Kingdom	575.8	6.4	25.2	1.4	89.3
Spain	515.9	6.8	0.2	1.3	90.5
Netherlands	501.4	9.6	12.4	1.2	91.8
Switzerland	354.9	5.8	21.3	0.9	92.6
Singapore	344.0	13.4	10.5	0.8	93.5
Thailand	231.3	2.9	24.1	0.6	94.1

Table 3: Top importing countries or areas in 2010

Country or area	Value (million US$)	Avg. Growth (%) 06-10	Growth (%) 09-10	World share %	Cum.
World	43438.5	7.4	17.9	100.0	
USA	8519.0	3.2	25.4	19.6	19.6
Japan	4617.2	3.2	7.2	10.6	30.2
China, Hong Kong SAR	4493.6	3.8	16.3	10.3	40.6
France	2487.0	8.1	11.9	5.7	46.3
United Kingdom	2261.4	5.5	14.2	5.2	51.5
Italy	2247.2	7.1	13.0	5.2	56.7
Germany	2245.1	7.4	11.8	5.2	61.9
Spain	1191.4	6.3	12.9	2.7	64.6
Rep. of Korea	1182.4	21.3	40.8	2.7	67.3
Canada	941.2	10.0	19.6	2.2	69.5
China	915.5	40.4	60.4	2.1	71.6
Belgium	773.1	1.6	2.4	1.8	73.4
Australia	683.6	10.9	10.5	1.6	75.0
Singapore	679.1	17.8	30.9	1.6	76.5
Russian Federation	673.7	41.3	50.3	1.6	78.1

In 2010, the value (in current prices) of exports of men's or boys' outerwear, of textile fabrics, not knitted or crocheted (SITC group 841) rose by 7.1 percent to 58.5 bln US$ (see table 2). Similarly, imports showed a 7.6 percent increase and amounted to 58.0 bln US$ (see table 3). Graph 1 shows that the rise in exports for 2010 in this product group was by far exceeded by increases of 15.0 percent in world exports of miscellaneous manufactured articles (SITC section 8) and of 21.2 percent in total world exports. Exports of men's or boys' outerwear, of textile fabrics, not knitted or crocheted (SITC group 841) accounted for 3.6 percent of world exports of SITC section 8 and 0.4 percent of total world exports (see table 1).

China, the top exporting country in 2010, accounted for 30.0 percent of world exports (see table 2). Other major exporting countries were Italy and Germany. Top destinations were USA, Germany and Japan (see table 3). By MDG regions (see graph 2), Developed Europe accounted for a large share of trade in men's or boys' outerwear, of textile fabrics, not knitted or crocheted (SITC group 841). In 2010, it's exports amounted to 16.3 bln US$ and imports to 27.8 bln US$, resulting in a deficit of 11.5 bln US$. Higher trade deficit was recorded by Developed North America (-13.5 bln US$). Top trade surpluses were recorded by Eastern Asia (+16.6 bln US$), Southern Asia (+6.0 bln US$) and South-eastern Asia (+5.1 bln US$).

Table 1: Imports (Imp.) and exports (Exp.), 1996-2010, in current prices

		1996	1997	1998	1999	2000	2001	2002	2003	2004	2005	2006	2007	2008	2009	2010
Values in Bln US$	Imp.	38.5	39.3	39.9	39.6	41.1	39.9	39.3	43.6	47.8	50.9	54.0	58.8	62.7	53.9	58.0
	Exp.	38.3	40.0	40.7	39.9	41.8	39.5	40.5	45.4	49.4	53.3	56.3	60.4	63.9	54.6	58.5
As a percentage of SITC section (%)	Imp.	5.6	5.5	5.5	5.2	5.1	4.9	4.6	4.5	4.3	4.1	4.0	3.8	3.8	3.8	3.6
	Exp.	5.8	5.7	5.8	5.5	5.4	5.2	5.1	4.9	4.6	4.5	4.3	4.0	3.9	3.8	3.6
As a percentage of world trade (%)	Imp.	0.7	0.7	0.7	0.7	0.6	0.6	0.6	0.6	0.5	0.5	0.4	0.4	0.4	0.4	0.4
	Exp.	0.7	0.7	0.8	0.7	0.7	0.6	0.6	0.6	0.5	0.5	0.5	0.4	0.4	0.4	0.4

Graph 1: Annual growth rates of exports, 1996–2010

(In percentage by year)

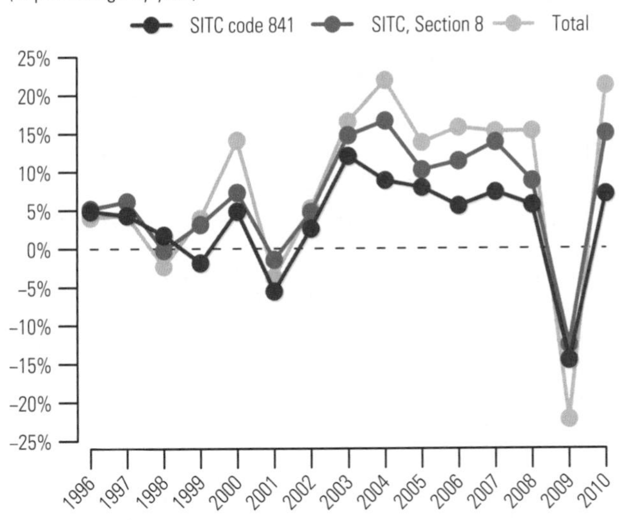

Table 2: Top exporting countries or areas in 2010

Country or area	Value (million US$)	Avg. Growth (%) 06-10	Growth (%) 09-10	World share %	Cum.
World	58 463.9	0.9	7.1	100.0	
China	17 555.1	5.0	14.3	30.0	30.0
Italy	3 516.3	-1.6	-6.3	6.0	36.0
Germany	3 462.4	3.9	0.0	5.9	42.0
Bangladesh	*3 094.2*	2.1	5.2	5.3	47.3
China, Hong Kong SAR	2 771.4	-3.6	6.9	4.7	52.0
Viet Nam	*2 379.6*	8.7	25.6	4.1	56.1
Turkey	1 875.2	2.1	8.8	3.2	59.3
Mexico	1 751.5	-5.6	5.4	3.0	62.3
India	1 542.1	0.2	-2.6	2.6	64.9
Indonesia	1 427.3	0.3	20.4	2.4	67.3
Netherlands	1 306.9	9.5	5.6	2.2	69.6
Belgium	1 161.4	-2.7	-15.1	2.0	71.6
Spain	992.4	6.5	2.6	1.7	73.3
France	936.9	0.6	-9.9	1.6	74.9
Pakistan	931.2	4.0	18.6	1.6	76.5

Graph 2: Trade Balance by MDG regions 2010

(Bln US$)

Imports — Exports — Trade balance

Developed Asia-Pacific
Developed Europe
Developed N. America
South-eastern Europe
C I S
Northern Africa
Sub-Saharan Africa
Latin Am, Caribbean
Eastern Asia
Southern Asia
South-eastern Asia
Western Asia
Oceania

-30 -25 -20 -15 -10 -5 0 5 10 15 20 25

Table 3: Top importing countries or areas in 2010

Country or area	Value (million US$)	Avg. Growth (%) 06-10	Growth (%) 09-10	World share %	Cum.
World	58 022.2	1.8	7.6	100.0	
USA	12 915.3	-2.4	13.3	22.3	22.3
Germany	6 104.3	3.2	5.9	10.5	32.8
Japan	4 145.8	-0.1	1.3	7.1	39.9
United Kingdom	3 468.7	-0.6	2.8	6.0	45.9
France	3 259.4	2.0	-1.9	5.6	51.5
Italy	3 164.1	0.6	5.2	5.5	57.0
Spain	2 260.6	2.9	11.1	3.9	60.9
China, Hong Kong SAR	2 013.3	0.6	11.1	3.5	64.3
Netherlands	1 653.2	4.8	2.4	2.8	67.2
Belgium	1 290.0	-2.4	-13.1	2.2	69.4
Canada	1 265.4	4.7	10.5	2.2	71.6
Switzerland	1 004.7	0.4	-1.2	1.7	73.3
Rep. of Korea	973.5	3.1	32.9	1.7	75.0
Russian Federation	916.8	30.9	39.5	1.6	76.6
Austria	875.0	4.9	4.2	1.5	78.1

842 Women's or girls' outerwear, of textile fabrics, not knitted or crocheted

After several years of continuous growth marked by a peak of 78.4 bln US$ in 2008, the value (in current prices) of exports of women's or girls' outerwear of textile fabrics, not knitted or crocheted (SITC group 842) decreased by 13.7 percent in 2009 but increased again by 6.9 percent in 2010 and amounted to 72.3 bln US$ (see table 2). Similarly, imports increased by 5.5 percent in 2010 to reach 74.6 bln US$ (see table 3). Graph 1 shows that the increase in exports for 2010 in this product group was well below the increase in world exports of miscellaneous manufactured articles (SITC section 8) of 15.0 percent and the increase in total world exports of 21.2 percent. Exports of women's or girls' outerwear of textile fabrics, not knitted or crocheted (SITC group 842) accounted for 4.4 percent of world exports of SITC section 8 and 0.5 percent of total world exports in 2010 (see table 1).

China was the top exporting country in 2010 with 32.7 percent of world exports (see table 2). Other major exporting countries or areas were China, Hong Kong SAR and Italy, respectively with 7.2 and 6.6 percent of world exports. Top destinations were USA, Germany and Japan (see table 3). By MDG regions (see graph 2), Eastern Asia recorded a trade surplus amounting to 23.6 bln US$. Major trade surpluses were also recorded by Southern Asia (+6.1 bln US$) and South-eastern Asia (+4.6 bln US$). Top trade deficits were recorded by Developed North America (-16.6 bln US$), Developed Europe (-14.4 bln US$) and Developed Asia-Pacific (-7.0 bln US$).

Table 1: Imports (Imp.) and exports (Exp.), 1996-2010, in current prices

		1996	1997	1998	1999	2000	2001	2002	2003	2004	2005	2006	2007	2008	2009	2010
Values in Bln US$	Imp.	41.5	42.3	43.3	43.2	45.7	46.9	49.7	56.3	62.9	68.5	73.2	78.4	81.0	70.7	74.6
	Exp.	37.9	39.6	41.0	40.3	43.1	43.1	47.0	52.6	59.4	65.0	69.7	75.4	78.4	67.6	72.3
As a percentage of SITC section (%)	Imp.	6.1	5.9	6.0	5.7	5.6	5.8	5.9	5.8	5.6	5.6	5.4	5.1	4.9	4.9	4.6
	Exp.	5.7	5.6	5.8	5.6	5.5	5.6	5.9	5.7	5.5	5.5	5.3	5.0	4.8	4.7	4.4
As a percentage of world trade (%)	Imp.	0.8	0.8	0.8	0.8	0.7	0.7	0.8	0.7	0.7	0.6	0.6	0.6	0.5	0.6	0.5
	Exp.	0.7	0.7	0.8	0.7	0.7	0.7	0.7	0.7	0.7	0.6	0.6	0.5	0.5	0.5	0.5

Graph 1: Annual growth rates of exports, 1996–2010

(In percentage by year)

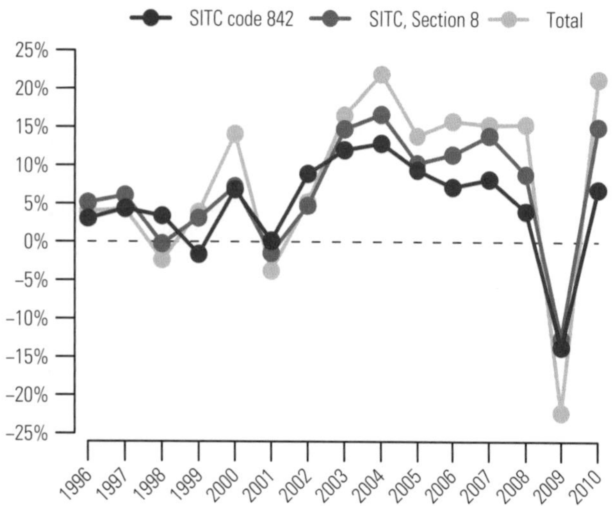

Table 2: Top exporting countries or areas in 2010

Country or area	Value (million US$)	Avg. Growth (%) 06-10	Growth (%) 09-10	World share %	Cum.
World	72282.1	0.9	6.9	100.0	
China	23653.7	6.0	15.1	32.7	32.7
China, Hong Kong SAR	5196.8	-8.4	-0.3	7.2	39.9
Italy	4756.7	-0.3	1.0	6.6	46.5
Germany	3755.7	0.2	-4.7	5.2	51.7
India	3458.9	1.4	0.0	4.8	56.5
Turkey	2542.4	-2.3	7.7	3.5	60.0
Viet Nam	*2482.4*	17.2	25.6	3.4	63.4
Spain	2439.1	8.8	11.7	3.4	66.8
France	2021.3	2.3	-7.0	2.8	69.6
Indonesia	1608.9	2.3	13.2	2.2	71.8
Bangladesh	*1546.7*	6.9	25.3	2.1	74.0
United Kingdom	1400.5	5.6	7.0	1.9	75.9
Belgium	1300.4	-2.4	-15.1	1.8	77.7
Morocco	1236.1	0.5	-2.2	1.7	79.4
Netherlands	1091.3	3.5	3.6	1.5	80.9

Graph 2: Trade Balance by MDG regions 2010

(Bln US$)

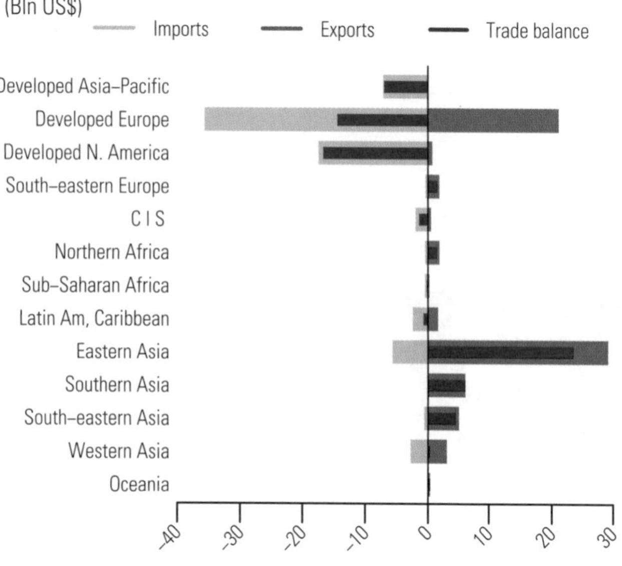

Table 3: Top importing countries or areas in 2010

Country or area	Value (million US$)	Avg. Growth (%) 06-10	Growth (%) 09-10	World share %	Cum.
World	74622.5	0.5	5.5	100.0	
USA	15747.6	-4.8	6.9	21.1	21.1
Germany	6780.3	0.9	1.0	9.1	30.2
Japan	5793.0	0.7	6.5	7.8	38.0
United Kingdom	5441.7	-1.5	2.8	7.3	45.2
France	4703.9	1.8	-1.9	6.3	51.5
Spain	3643.9	6.3	13.4	4.9	56.4
China, Hong Kong SAR	3483.1	-6.6	2.7	4.7	61.1
Italy	3011.7	1.8	1.6	4.0	65.1
Netherlands	1837.4	2.4	0.9	2.5	67.6
Russian Federation	1663.9	39.3	42.2	2.2	69.8
Canada	1601.3	1.7	4.5	2.1	72.0
Belgium	1553.6	-5.3	-19.4	2.1	74.1
Rep. of Korea	1263.4	1.9	29.5	1.7	75.7
Switzerland	1182.8	0.5	-4.2	1.6	77.3
Austria	1118.6	0.4	-0.1	1.5	78.8

From 2006 to 2010, the value (in current prices) of exports of men's or boys' outerwear of textile fabrics, knitted or crocheted (SITC group 843) increased on average by 7.2 percent each year and amounted to 24.0 bln US$ (see table 2). Similarly, imports went up on average by 6.1 percent each year to 18.4 bln US$ (see table 3). Graph 1 shows that the increase of 14.8 percent in exports for 2010 in this product group was slightly exceeded by the increases of 15.0 percent in world exports of miscellaneous manufactured articles (SITC section 8) and 21.2 percent in total world exports. Exports of men's or boys' outerwear of textile fabrics, knitted or crocheted (SITC group 843) accounted for 1.5 percent of world exports of SITC section 8 and 0.2 percent of total world exports in 2010 (see table 1).

Exports of China, the top exporting country in 2010, went up by 23.1 percent and represented 44.6 percent of world exports (see table 2). Other major exporting countries or areas were China, Hong Kong SAR and India. USA, the top destination, accounted for 29.0 percent of world imports (see table 3). Other major importing countries were Japan and United Kingdom. By MDG regions (see graph 2), top trade surpluses were recorded by Eastern Asia (+10.6 bln US$), Southern Asia (+2.8 bln US$) and South-eastern Asia (+2.5 bln US$). Top trade deficits were recorded by Developed North America (-5.6 bln US$), Developed Europe (-3.7 bln US$) and Developed Asia-Pacific (-1.5 bln US$).

Table 1: Imports (Imp.) and exports (Exp.), 1996-2010, in current prices

		1996	1997	1998	1999	2000	2001	2002	2003	2004	2005	2006	2007	2008	2009	2010
Values in Bln US$	Imp.	8.8	10.4	10.1	9.9	10.0	9.7	9.9	10.9	11.9	12.9	14.5	16.6	17.9	16.1	18.4
	Exp.	8.6	11.7	10.6	10.2	10.5	10.3	11.0	12.8	14.1	15.1	18.2	24.0	24.2	20.9	24.0
As a percentage of SITC section (%)	Imp.	1.3	1.5	1.4	1.3	1.2	1.2	1.2	1.1	1.1	1.1	1.1	1.1	1.1	1.1	1.1
	Exp.	1.3	1.7	1.5	1.4	1.3	1.3	1.4	1.4	1.3	1.3	1.4	1.6	1.5	1.5	1.5
As a percentage of world trade (%)	Imp.	0.2	0.2	0.2	0.2	0.2	0.2	0.2	0.1	0.1	0.1	0.1	0.1	0.1	0.1	0.1
	Exp.	0.2	0.2	0.2	0.2	0.2	0.2	0.2	0.2	0.2	0.1	0.2	0.2	0.2	0.2	0.2

Graph 1: Annual growth rates of exports, 1996–2010

(In percentage by year)

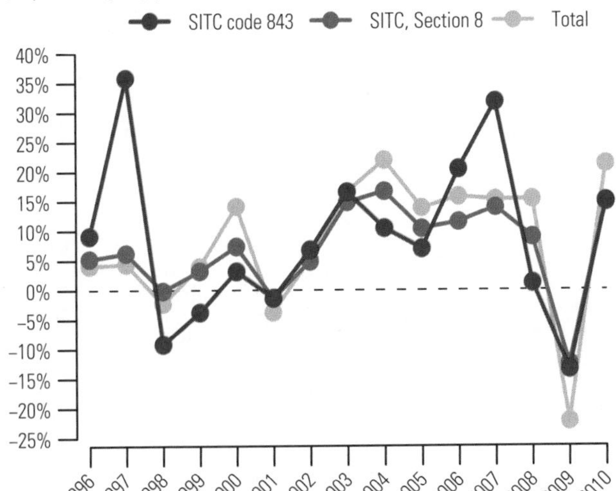

Table 2: Top exporting countries or areas in 2010

Country or area	Value (million US$)	Avg. Growth (%) 06-10	Growth (%) 09-10	World share %	Cum.
World	24028.9	7.2	14.8	100.0	
China	10719.3	13.6	23.1	44.6	44.6
China, Hong Kong SAR	1217.9	3.7	13.1	5.1	49.7
India	995.6	8.3	0.0	4.1	53.8
Pakistan	906.7	0.1	22.0	3.8	57.6
Viet Nam	*813.2*	18.1	25.6	3.4	61.0
Bangladesh	*725.4*	6.2	19.3	3.0	64.0
Cambodia	669.8	4.2	19.7	2.8	66.8
Italy	590.8	8.7	12.6	2.5	69.2
Germany	504.9	8.9	12.4	2.1	71.3
Turkey	491.0	5.2	-7.0	2.0	73.4
Thailand	476.1	-4.2	8.6	2.0	75.4
Indonesia	436.5	-1.0	15.0	1.8	77.2
Belgium	423.5	10.1	-5.0	1.8	78.9
Netherlands	378.4	16.5	20.1	1.6	80.5
France	351.5	3.5	1.2	1.5	82.0

Graph 2: Trade Balance by MDG regions 2010

(Bln US$)

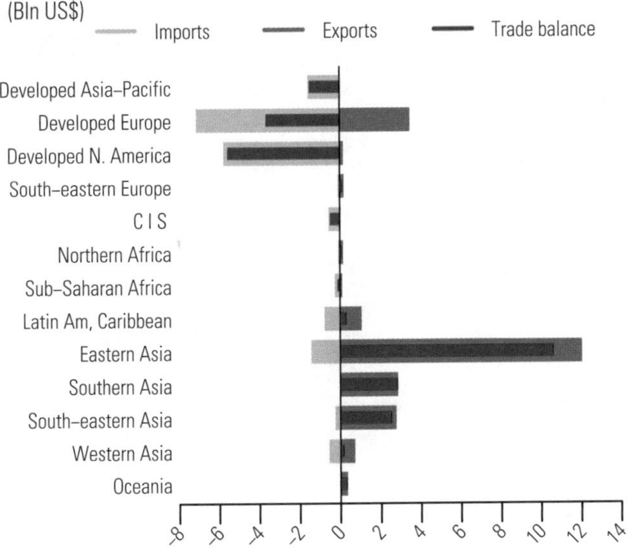

Table 3: Top importing countries or areas in 2010

Country or area	Value (million US$)	Avg. Growth (%) 06-10	Growth (%) 09-10	World share %	Cum.
World	18411.9	6.1	14.5	100.0	
USA	5342.8	1.7	16.7	29.0	29.0
Japan	1261.2	8.3	8.1	6.8	35.9
United Kingdom	1223.3	1.6	15.1	6.6	42.5
Germany	1121.0	6.1	9.1	6.1	48.6
China, Hong Kong SAR	949.0	3.8	13.4	5.2	53.8
Italy	908.7	8.0	8.1	4.9	58.7
France	851.0	9.7	1.3	4.6	63.3
Spain	580.7	4.5	-7.3	3.2	66.5
Netherlands	474.2	11.3	13.6	2.6	69.0
Canada	424.4	6.6	13.5	2.3	71.3
Belgium	373.9	5.3	-1.7	2.0	73.4
Tajikistan	*282.3*	109.4	144.8	1.5	74.9
Australia	240.9	9.0	22.0	1.3	76.2
Austria	199.5	6.5	5.9	1.1	77.3
Russian Federation	178.4	33.8	57.5	1.0	78.3

Source: UN Comtrade

844 Women's or girls' outerwear, of textile fabrics, knitted or crocheted

In 2010, the value (in current prices) of exports of women's or girls' outerwear, of textile fabrics, knitted or crocheted (SITC group 844) rose by 18.4 percent to 45.4 bln US$ (see table 2). Similarly, imports showed a 14.0 percent increase and amounted to 36.8 bln US$ (see table 3). Graph 1 shows that the rise in exports for 2010 in this product group was above the increase of 15.0 percent in world exports of miscellaneous manufactured articles (SITC section 8) but below the increase of 21.2 percent in total world exports. Exports of women's or girls' outerwear, of textile fabrics, knitted or crocheted (SITC group 844) accounted for 2.8 percent of world exports of SITC section 8 and 0.3 percent of total world exports (see table 1).

In 2010, exports of China, the top exporting country accounted for 43.6 percent of world exports (see table 2). Other major exporting countries or areas were China, Hong Kong SAR and Turkey, respectively with 6.0 and 4.3 percent of world exports. USA, Germany and Japan were the top destinations (see table 3). By MDG regions (see graph 2), Eastern Asia's exports amounted to 22.8 bln US$ and imports to 2.5 bln US$, resulting in a trade surplus of 20.3 bln US$. Major trade surpluses were also recorded by South-eastern Asia (+4.2 bln US$) and Southern Asia (+2.9 bln US$). Top trade deficits were recorded by Developed North America (-9.4 bln US$), Developed Europe (-7.9 bln US$) and Developed Asia-Pacific (-3.7 bln US$).

Table 1: Imports (Imp.) and exports (Exp.), 1996-2010, in current prices

		1996	1997	1998	1999	2000	2001	2002	2003	2004	2005	2006	2007	2008	2009	2010
Values in Bln US$	Imp.	14.1	16.3	16.5	16.8	16.9	16.8	17.9	20.5	22.6	23.9	26.8	32.1	34.5	32.2	36.8
	Exp.	14.1	19.3	17.7	17.6	17.6	17.0	19.1	23.1	25.8	26.5	32.1	41.7	41.7	38.3	45.4
As a percentage of SITC section (%)	Imp.	2.1	2.3	2.3	2.2	2.1	2.1	2.1	2.1	2.0	1.9	2.0	2.1	2.1	2.3	2.3
	Exp.	2.1	2.7	2.5	2.4	2.3	2.2	2.4	2.5	2.4	2.2	2.4	2.8	2.6	2.7	2.8
As a percentage of world trade (%)	Imp.	0.3	0.3	0.3	0.3	0.3	0.3	0.3	0.3	0.2	0.2	0.2	0.2	0.2	0.3	0.2
	Exp.	0.3	0.4	0.3	0.3	0.3	0.3	0.3	0.3	0.3	0.3	0.3	0.3	0.3	0.3	0.3

Graph 1: Annual growth rates of exports, 1996–2010

(In percentage by year)

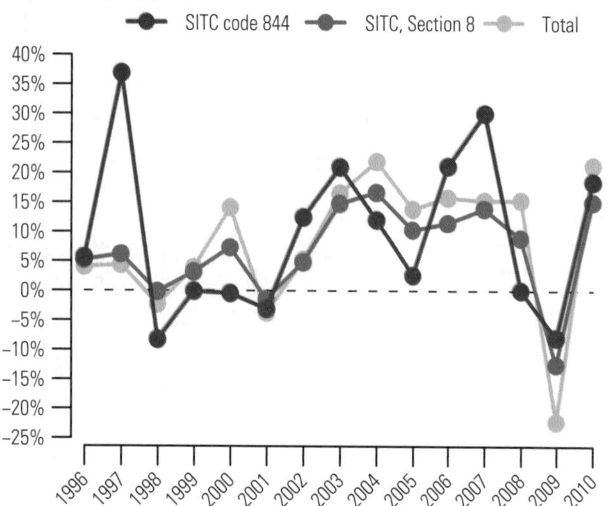

Graph 2: Trade Balance by MDG regions 2010

(Bln US$)

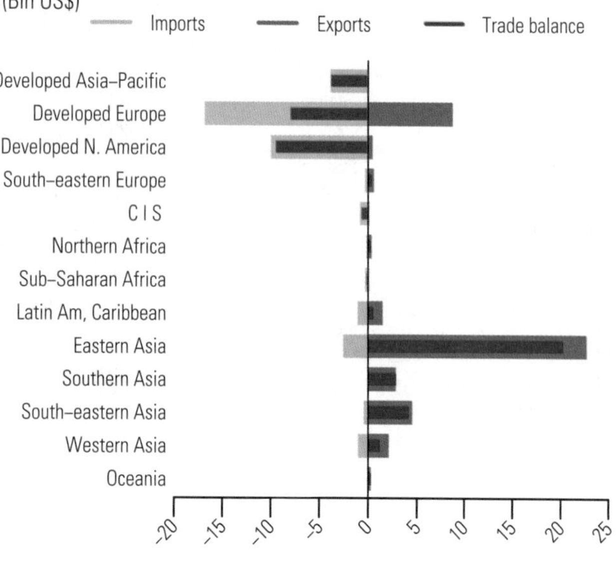

Table 2: Top exporting countries or areas in 2010

Country or area	Value (million US$)	Avg. Growth (%) 06-10	Growth (%) 09-10	World share %	Cum.
World	45398.7	9.1	18.4	100.0	
China	19812.8	15.9	35.3	43.6	43.6
China, Hong Kong SAR	2746.5	-1.8	8.4	6.0	49.7
Turkey	1972.3	7.6	16.5	4.3	54.0
Germany	1729.7	16.2	13.1	3.8	57.8
Viet Nam	*1366.5*	21.1	25.6	3.0	60.9
Cambodia	1159.0	5.4	29.6	2.6	63.4
Italy	1088.3	9.0	13.8	2.4	65.8
India	1052.4	7.5	-23.5	2.3	68.1
Bangladesh	*917.3*	26.4	47.9	2.0	70.1
France	896.5	8.4	5.3	2.0	72.1
Indonesia	781.8	5.2	0.0	1.7	73.8
Spain	737.8	19.7	-20.4	1.6	75.5
Sri Lanka	676.8	6.2	6.9	1.5	77.0
Belgium	651.9	8.6	-5.9	1.4	78.4
Guatemala	589.4	161.3	9.9	1.3	79.7

Table 3: Top importing countries or areas in 2010

Country or area	Value (million US$)	Avg. Growth (%) 06-10	Growth (%) 09-10	World share %	Cum.
World	36770.6	8.3	14.0	100.0	
USA	8991.0	4.1	17.0	24.5	24.5
Germany	3484.8	11.8	13.7	9.5	33.9
Japan	3221.4	7.2	8.8	8.8	42.7
United Kingdom	2503.8	7.6	20.0	6.8	49.5
France	2151.9	9.8	10.3	5.9	55.4
China, Hong Kong SAR	1914.1	-1.0	7.7	5.2	60.6
Italy	1321.0	10.4	7.7	3.6	64.1
Spain	1299.3	15.0	3.5	3.5	67.7
Netherlands	973.0	16.4	21.3	2.6	70.3
Canada	907.5	11.3	17.2	2.5	72.8
Belgium	722.8	7.4	-4.8	2.0	74.8
Russian Federation	588.5	47.1	68.1	1.6	76.4
Austria	576.3	8.2	11.8	1.6	77.9
Switzerland	498.5	12.7	9.0	1.4	79.3
Denmark	477.0	6.7	7.0	1.3	80.6

After a decline of 12.7 percent in 2009, the value (in current prices) of exports of articles of apparel, of textile fabrics, whether or not knitted or crocheted, nes (SITC group 845) bounced back by 11.0 percent in 2010 to reach 120.7 bln US$ (see table 2). Imports, after a 9.4 percent drop in 2009, increased by 7.8 percent in 2010 and totaled 121.3 bln US$ (see table 3). Graph 1 shows that the rise in exports for 2010 in this product group was exceeded by the increases in world exports of miscellaneous manufactured articles (SITC section 8) of 15.0 percent and in total world exports of 21.2 percent. Exports of articles of apparel, of textile fabrics, whether or not knitted or crocheted, nes (SITC group 845) accounted for 7.4 percent of world exports of SITC section 8 and 0.8 percent of total world exports (see table 1).

China, the top exporting country in 2010, accounted for nearly a third (33.0 percent) of world exports (see table 2). Other major exporting countries or areas were China, Hong Kong SAR and Italy, respectively with 8.7 and 4.9 percent of world exports. USA, Germany and Japan were the top destinations (see table 3). By MDG regions (see graph 2), Eastern Asia recorded a trade surplus of 41.7 bln US$ in 2010. Major trade surpluses were also recorded by Southern Asia (+9.4 bln US$) and South-eastern Asia (+8.1 bln US$). Top trade deficits were recorded by Developed North America (-29.6 bln US$), Developed Europe (-24.5 bln US$) and Developed Asia-Pacific (-10.6 bln US$).

Table 1: Imports (Imp.) and exports (Exp.), 1996-2010, in current prices

		1996	1997	1998	1999	2000	2001	2002	2003	2004	2005	2006	2007	2008	2009	2010
Values in Bln US$	Imp.	52.4	56.5	59.5	64.0	69.6	71.3	72.9	81.7	92.1	98.4	106.8	116.0	124.1	112.5	121.3
	Exp.	48.2	54.0	54.3	57.0	62.5	62.4	65.2	74.6	84.5	93.0	107.8	119.7	124.5	108.7	120.7
As a percentage of SITC section (%)	Imp.	7.7	7.9	8.3	8.5	8.6	8.8	8.6	8.5	8.2	8.0	7.9	7.5	7.5	7.9	7.4
	Exp.	7.3	7.7	7.7	7.9	8.1	8.2	8.1	8.1	7.9	7.9	8.2	8.0	7.6	7.6	7.4
As a percentage of world trade (%)	Imp.	1.0	1.0	1.1	1.1	1.1	1.1	1.1	1.1	1.0	0.9	0.9	0.8	0.8	0.9	0.8
	Exp.	0.9	1.0	1.0	1.0	1.0	1.0	1.0	1.0	0.9	0.9	0.9	0.9	0.8	0.9	0.8

Graph 1: Annual growth rates of exports, 1996–2010

(In percentage by year)

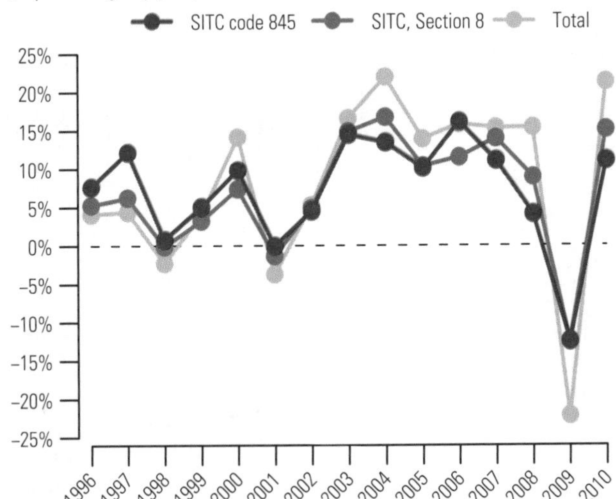

Table 2: Top exporting countries or areas in 2010

Country or area	Value (million US$)	Avg. Growth (%) 06-10	Growth (%) 09-10	World share %	Cum.
World	120 685.0	2.9	11.0	100.0	
China	39 814.7	5.0	19.1	33.0	33.0
China, Hong Kong SAR	10 449.1	-2.0	5.3	8.7	41.6
Italy	5 917.4	-0.4	1.0	4.9	46.6
Germany	5 354.5	6.3	5.2	4.4	51.0
Bangladesh	*5 244.3*	12.5	53.9	4.3	55.3
Turkey	4 461.0	0.0	12.8	3.7	59.0
France	4 296.8	0.1	1.1	3.6	62.6
Viet Nam	*3 270.4*	26.9	25.6	2.7	65.3
Belgium	3 239.7	2.6	-2.7	2.7	68.0
Spain	2 786.7	11.9	0.1	2.3	70.3
India	2 784.5	5.2	-9.8	2.3	72.6
Netherlands	2 213.6	7.4	2.1	1.8	74.4
Indonesia	2 073.1	9.7	18.9	1.7	76.2
United Kingdom	1 777.4	-0.1	5.3	1.5	77.6
Tunisia	1 708.9	3.8	6.4	1.4	79.0

Graph 2: Trade Balance by MDG regions 2010

(Bln US$)

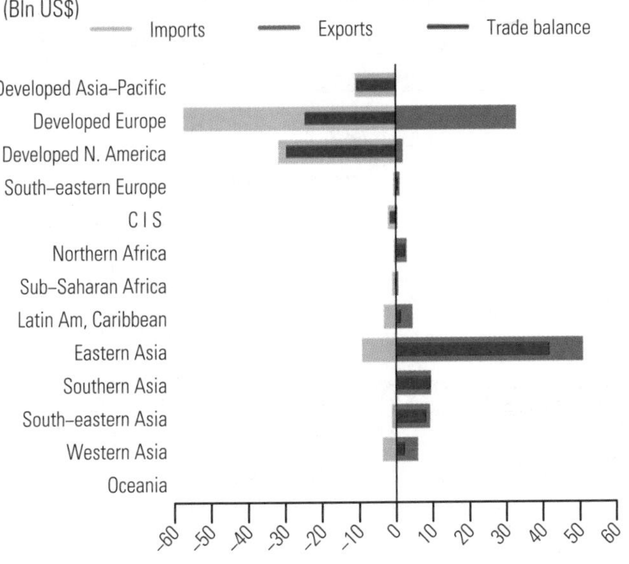

Table 3: Top importing countries or areas in 2010

Country or area	Value (million US$)	Avg. Growth (%) 06-10	Growth (%) 09-10	World share %	Cum.
World	121 273.7	3.2	7.8	100.0	
USA	28 711.8	0.9	14.1	23.7	23.7
Germany	11 014.6	4.4	5.1	9.1	32.8
Japan	8 908.0	3.6	3.2	7.3	40.1
United Kingdom	8 063.8	1.2	4.3	6.6	46.8
France	7 971.1	3.2	5.1	6.6	53.3
China, Hong Kong SAR	6 896.2	-2.0	6.3	5.7	59.0
Italy	5 801.3	3.6	1.7	4.8	63.8
Spain	4 869.1	5.4	-0.1	4.0	67.8
Belgium	3 109.9	0.2	-7.5	2.6	70.4
Netherlands	3 059.3	6.2	7.3	2.5	72.9
Canada	2 807.3	5.0	9.3	2.3	75.2
Austria	1 809.0	4.2	3.2	1.5	76.7
Switzerland	1 698.1	4.0	2.0	1.4	78.1
Australia	1 592.5	11.2	18.8	1.3	79.4
Russian Federation	1 571.6	37.6	51.9	1.3	80.7

 Source: UN Comtrade

846 Clothing accessories, of textile fabrics, whether or not knitted or crocheted

In 2010, the value (in current prices) of exports of clothing accessories, of textile fabrics, whether or not knitted or crocheted (SITC group 846) rose by 15.0 percent to 24.5 bln US$ (see table 2). Similarly, imports showed a 15.7 percent increase and amounted to 22.7 bln US$ (see table 3). Graph 1 shows that the rise in exports for 2010 in this product group equaled the increase in world exports of miscellaneous manufactured articles (SITC section 8) of 15.0 percent but was below the increase in total world exports of 21.2 percent. Exports of clothing accessories, of textile fabrics, whether or not knitted or crocheted (SITC group 846) accounted for 1.5 percent of world exports of SITC section 8 and 0.2 percent of total world exports (see table 1).

Exports of China, the top exporting country in 2010, went up by 22.1 percent and accounted for more than a third (38.8 percent) of world exports (see table 2). Other major exporting countries were Italy and Germany, respectively with 10.0 and 4.6 percent of world exports. Top destinations were USA, Germany and Japan (see table 3). By MDG regions (see graph 2), top trade surpluses were recorded by Eastern Asia (+10.0 bln US$) and Southern Asia (+1.3 bln US$). Top trade deficits were recorded by Developed North America (-3.7 bln US$), Developed Europe (-2.6 bln US$) and Developed Asia-Pacific (-2.2 bln US$).

Table 1: Imports (Imp.) and exports (Exp.), 1996-2010, in current prices

		1996	1997	1998	1999	2000	2001	2002	2003	2004	2005	2006	2007	2008	2009	2010
Values in Bln US$	Imp.	11.2	12.0	12.6	12.2	12.5	12.2	12.6	14.1	16.1	16.9	17.5	19.2	21.6	19.7	22.7
	Exp.	11.4	12.7	13.0	12.3	12.9	12.5	12.9	14.5	16.3	17.5	18.6	20.2	23.7	21.3	24.5
As a percentage of SITC section (%)	Imp.	1.6	1.7	1.7	1.6	1.5	1.5	1.5	1.5	1.4	1.4	1.3	1.2	1.3	1.4	1.4
	Exp.	1.7	1.8	1.9	1.7	1.7	1.6	1.6	1.6	1.5	1.5	1.4	1.3	1.5	1.5	1.5
As a percentage of world trade (%)	Imp.	0.2	0.2	0.2	0.2	0.2	0.2	0.2	0.2	0.2	0.2	0.1	0.1	0.1	0.2	0.2
	Exp.	0.2	0.2	0.2	0.2	0.2	0.2	0.2	0.2	0.2	0.2	0.2	0.1	0.1	0.2	0.2

Graph 1: Annual growth rates of exports, 1996–2010

(In percentage by year)

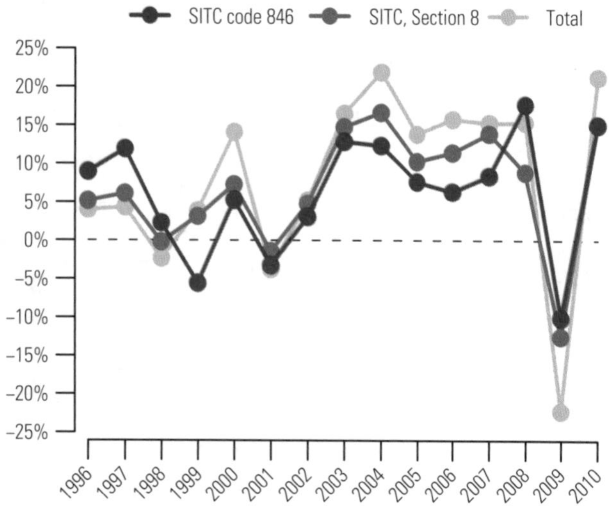

Graph 2: Trade Balance by MDG regions 2010

(Bln US$)

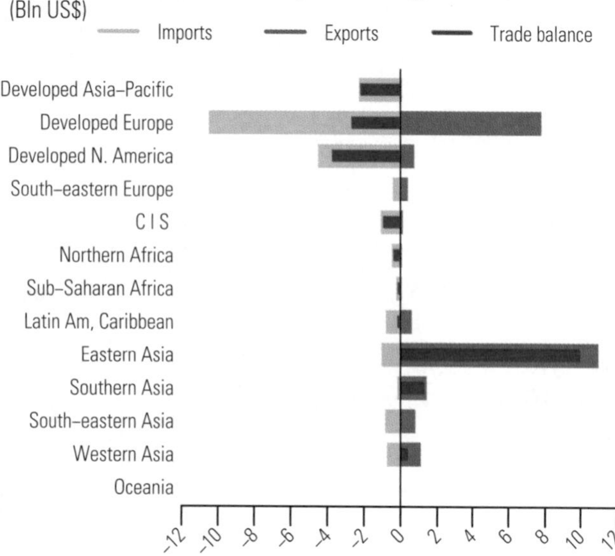

Table 2: Top exporting countries or areas in 2010

Country or area	Value (million US$)	Avg. Growth (%) 06-10	Growth (%) 09-10	World share %	Cum.
World	24517.2	7.1	15.0	100.0	
China	9516.8	16.4	22.1	38.8	38.8
Italy	2462.8	-1.9	2.9	10.0	48.9
Germany	1136.3	7.1	9.4	4.6	53.5
Turkey	1039.8	6.7	8.0	4.2	57.7
India	770.5	15.2	-5.0	3.1	60.9
France	717.7	6.3	9.7	2.9	63.8
Rep. of Korea	707.8	-2.0	27.8	2.9	66.7
USA	679.7	-6.0	13.2	2.8	69.5
Belgium	553.3	2.9	1.2	2.3	71.7
China, Hong Kong SAR	501.8	-10.4	9.5	2.0	73.8
Netherlands	422.3	7.3	6.2	1.7	75.5
United Kingdom	416.4	-4.3	1.2	1.7	77.2
Pakistan	404.3	4.6	13.1	1.6	78.8
Spain	310.2	9.3	10.9	1.3	80.1
Other Asia, nes	277.0	-3.1	18.3	1.1	81.2

Table 3: Top importing countries or areas in 2010

Country or area	Value (million US$)	Avg. Growth (%) 06-10	Growth (%) 09-10	World share %	Cum.
World	22748.2	6.8	15.7	100.0	
USA	3938.4	5.8	21.7	17.3	17.3
Germany	2074.0	9.6	19.3	9.1	26.4
Japan	1939.8	5.8	9.3	8.5	35.0
France	1416.7	7.1	9.5	6.2	41.2
United Kingdom	1340.4	3.3	10.2	5.9	47.1
Italy	997.9	8.7	13.0	4.4	51.5
Spain	649.0	5.7	5.8	2.9	54.3
Russian Federation	631.8	49.9	80.9	2.8	57.1
Canada	537.5	9.5	15.2	2.4	59.5
Netherlands	534.4	5.9	5.7	2.3	61.8
Belgium	480.7	1.4	2.9	2.1	63.9
China, Hong Kong SAR	453.6	-15.4	12.0	2.0	65.9
Switzerland	350.4	6.4	9.2	1.5	67.5
Austria	343.5	6.3	12.3	1.5	69.0
Tunisia	303.3	4.8	3.6	1.3	70.3

After a decline in 2009 of 10.5 percent, the value (in current prices) of exports of articles of apparel, and clothing accessories not textile fabrics; headgear (SITC group 848) bounced back by 18.8 percent in 2010 to reach 24.7 bln US$ (see table 2). Imports, after a 11.5 percent drop in 2009, increased by 15.6 percent in 2010 and totaled 25.0 bln US$ (see table 3). Graph 1 shows that the rise in exports for 2010 in this product group exceeded the increase in world exports of miscellaneous manufactured articles (SITC section 8) of 15.0 percent but was below the increase in total world exports of 21.2 percent. Exports of articles of apparel, and clothing accessories not textile fabrics; headgear (SITC group 848) accounted for 1.5 percent of world exports of SITC section 8 and 0.2 percent of total world exports (see table 1).

The top exporting countries in 2010 were China, Malaysia and Italy. They accounted respectively for 35.4, 11.5 and 6.6 percent of world exports (see table 2). USA, Germany and Japan were the top destinations (see table 3). By MDG regions (see graph 2), top trade surpluses were recorded by Eastern Asia (+8.6 bln US$), South-eastern Asia (+3.9 bln US$) and Southern Asia (+1.3 bln US$). Top trade deficits were recorded by Developed North America (-6.2 bln US$), Developed Europe (-3.8 bln US$) and Developed Asia-Pacific (-1.9 bln US$).

Table 1: Imports (Imp.) and exports (Exp.), 1996-2010, in current prices

		1996	1997	1998	1999	2000	2001	2002	2003	2004	2005	2006	2007	2008	2009	2010
Values in Bln US$	Imp.	13.5	13.5	12.8	12.6	14.7	15.4	15.3	16.3	17.8	19.3	20.8	22.1	24.5	21.6	25.0
	Exp.	13.0	13.1	12.4	11.8	13.7	14.2	14.5	16.9	19.0	21.1	20.6	21.5	23.3	20.8	24.7
As a percentage of SITC section (%)	Imp.	2.0	1.9	1.8	1.7	1.8	1.9	1.8	1.7	1.6	1.6	1.5	1.4	1.5	1.5	1.5
	Exp.	2.0	1.9	1.8	1.6	1.8	1.9	1.8	1.8	1.8	1.8	1.6	1.4	1.4	1.5	1.5
As a percentage of world trade (%)	Imp.	0.3	0.2	0.2	0.2	0.2	0.2	0.2	0.2	0.2	0.2	0.2	0.2	0.2	0.2	0.2
	Exp.	0.2	0.2	0.2	0.2	0.2	0.2	0.2	0.2	0.2	0.2	0.2	0.2	0.1	0.2	0.2

Graph 1: Annual growth rates of exports, 1996–2010

(In percentage by year)

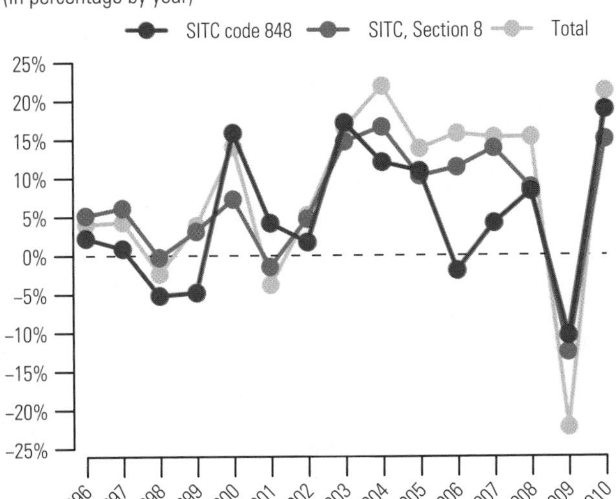

Table 2: Top exporting countries or areas in 2010

Country or area	Value (million US$)	Avg. Growth (%) 06-10	Growth (%) 09-10	World share %	Cum.
World	24734.9	4.6	18.8	100.0	
China	8747.9	6.6	28.9	35.4	35.4
Malaysia	2850.0	16.8	35.8	11.5	46.9
Italy	1630.1	0.3	14.5	6.6	53.5
China, Hong Kong SAR	1165.4	-8.4	13.2	4.7	58.2
Thailand	1064.4	13.3	43.7	4.3	62.5
Germany	1027.2	4.7	4.4	4.2	66.6
France	775.4	6.3	6.9	3.1	69.8
USA	701.1	2.7	3.0	2.8	72.6
India	625.3	3.3	-9.8	2.5	75.1
Belgium	560.5	8.9	27.7	2.3	77.4
Pakistan	486.1	-7.2	3.4	2.0	79.4
Netherlands	383.8	7.9	8.0	1.6	80.9
Turkey	378.6	-1.5	13.7	1.5	82.5
United Kingdom	361.7	-1.9	7.0	1.5	83.9
Indonesia	319.0	8.9	25.5	1.3	85.2

Graph 2: Trade Balance by MDG regions 2010

(Bln US$)

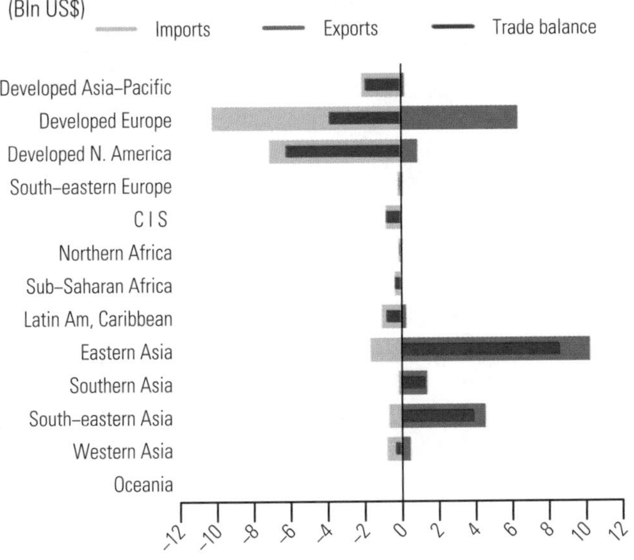

Table 3: Top importing countries or areas in 2010

Country or area	Value (million US$)	Avg. Growth (%) 06-10	Growth (%) 09-10	World share %	Cum.
World	25026.1	4.8	15.6	100.0	
USA	6295.6	0.8	19.5	25.2	25.2
Germany	2042.9	7.9	15.6	8.2	33.3
Japan	1604.7	2.7	8.3	6.4	39.7
France	1440.7	6.9	12.3	5.8	45.5
United Kingdom	1190.0	3.9	8.7	4.8	50.2
Italy	1052.3	3.6	15.5	4.2	54.4
China, Hong Kong SAR	935.4	-4.5	16.7	3.7	58.2
Canada	771.8	3.6	10.1	3.1	61.3
Spain	680.5	0.0	4.4	2.7	64.0
Russian Federation	677.4	32.4	69.0	2.7	66.7
Belgium	548.1	4.6	3.7	2.2	68.9
Netherlands	547.0	6.7	7.2	2.2	71.1
Australia	392.3	9.0	14.1	1.6	72.6
Switzerland	380.0	2.1	-0.6	1.5	74.2
Austria	366.7	6.9	5.6	1.5	75.6

Source: UN Comtrade

851 Footwear

After several years of continuous growth marked by a peak of 91.6 bln US$ in 2008, the value (in current prices) of exports of footwear (SITC group 851) decreased by 11.0 percent in 2009 but increased again by 17.7 percent in 2010 and amounted to 96.0 bln US$ (see table 2). Similarly, imports increased by 16.4 percent in 2010 to reach 100.3 bln US$ (see table 3). Graph 1 shows that the increase in exports for 2010 in this product group exceeded the increase of 15.0 percent in world exports of miscellaneous manufactured articles (SITC section 8) but was below the increase in total world exports of 21.2 percent. Exports of footwear (SITC group 851) accounted for 5.9 percent of world exports of SITC section 8 and 0.6 percent of total world exports in 2010 (see table 1).

Exports of China, the top exporting country in 2010, increased by 27.2 percent and represented more than a third (37.1 percent) of world exports (see table 2). Other major exporting countries or areas were Italy and China, Hong Kong SAR, respectively with 10.2 and 5.8 percent of world exports. USA, Germany and France were the top destinations (see table 3). By MDG regions (see graph 2), Eastern Asia recorded a trade surplus amounting to 34.1 bln US$ in 2010. Major trade surpluses were also recorded by South-eastern Asia (+7.6 bln US$) and Southern Asia (+1.7 bln US$). Top trade deficits were recorded by Developed North America (-22.5 bln US$), Developed Europe (-11.3 bln US$) and Developed Asia-Pacific (-6.1 bln US$).

Table 1: Imports (Imp.) and exports (Exp.), 1996-2010, in current prices

		1996	1997	1998	1999	2000	2001	2002	2003	2004	2005	2006	2007	2008	2009	2010
Values in Bln US$	Imp.	51.6	53.6	49.8	50.0	51.2	52.8	54.8	60.0	66.3	73.3	80.2	88.1	96.3	86.2	100.3
	Exp.	49.3	49.6	45.9	45.4	46.6	47.2	48.6	54.0	60.1	66.4	73.4	82.4	91.6	81.5	96.0
As a percentage of SITC section (%)	Imp.	7.6	7.5	6.9	6.6	6.3	6.5	6.5	6.2	5.9	6.0	5.9	5.7	5.8	6.0	6.2
	Exp.	7.4	7.0	6.5	6.3	6.0	6.2	6.1	5.9	5.6	5.6	5.6	5.5	5.6	5.7	5.9
As a percentage of world trade (%)	Imp.	1.0	1.0	0.9	0.9	0.8	0.8	0.8	0.8	0.7	0.7	0.7	0.6	0.6	0.7	0.7
	Exp.	0.9	0.9	0.9	0.8	0.7	0.8	0.8	0.7	0.7	0.6	0.6	0.6	0.6	0.7	0.6

Graph 1: Annual growth rates of exports, 1996–2010
(In percentage by year)

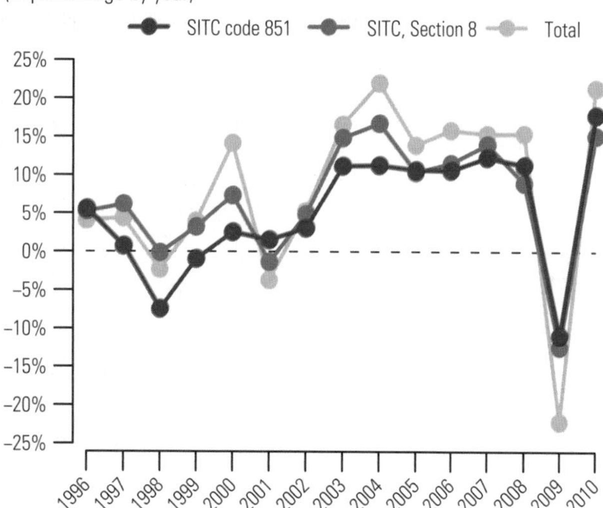

Table 2: Top exporting countries or areas in 2010

Country or area	Value (million US$)	Avg. Growth (%) 06-10	Growth (%) 09-10	World share %	Cum.
World	95952.9	6.9	17.7	100.0	
China	35633.9	13.1	27.2	37.1	37.1
Italy	9754.5	0.3	7.7	10.2	47.3
China, Hong Kong SAR	5576.9	-1.9	17.2	5.8	53.1
Viet Nam	*5216.4*	9.3	25.6	5.4	58.6
Belgium	3742.2	5.9	7.3	3.9	62.5
Germany	3738.7	7.0	8.3	3.9	66.3
Spain	2593.0	2.9	-0.7	2.7	69.1
Indonesia	2501.8	11.8	44.1	2.6	71.7
Netherlands	2443.1	11.0	7.8	2.5	74.2
France	2081.7	5.5	9.2	2.2	76.4
Portugal	1780.2	3.9	10.8	1.9	78.2
India	1642.9	8.4	10.9	1.7	79.9
Brazil	1631.5	-4.6	10.5	1.7	81.6
Romania	1475.8	-3.5	8.5	1.5	83.2
United Kingdom	1309.5	8.5	18.3	1.4	84.5

Graph 2: Trade Balance by MDG regions 2010
(Bln US$)

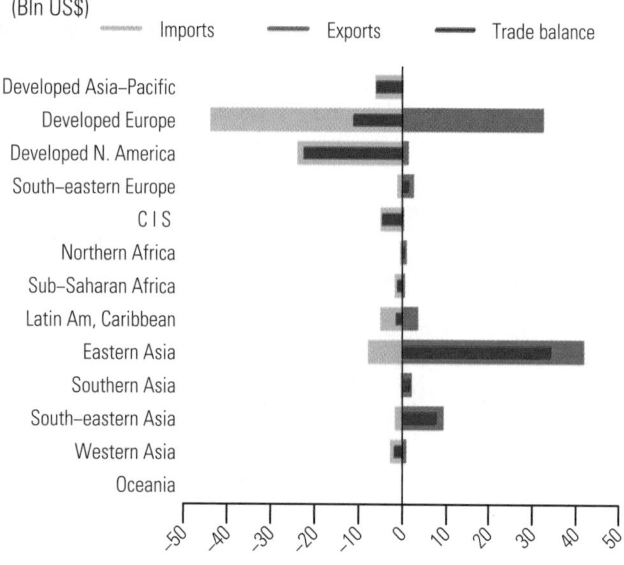

Table 3: Top importing countries or areas in 2010

Country or area	Value (million US$)	Avg. Growth (%) 06-10	Growth (%) 09-10	World share %	Cum.
World	100311.2	5.8	16.4	100.0	
USA	21932.3	2.1	20.2	21.9	21.9
Germany	7324.9	5.3	13.3	7.3	29.2
France	5998.7	4.6	7.8	6.0	35.1
Italy	5787.6	3.5	11.5	5.8	40.9
United Kingdom	5645.1	2.9	16.1	5.6	46.5
China, Hong Kong SAR	4976.8	-1.3	18.7	5.0	51.5
Japan	4787.3	5.8	9.1	4.8	56.3
Russian Federation	3950.7	35.6	74.3	3.9	60.2
Spain	2931.0	7.8	14.3	2.9	63.1
Netherlands	2800.8	8.5	10.7	2.8	65.9
Belgium	2585.2	5.6	-0.7	2.6	68.5
Canada	1928.1	5.6	13.6	1.9	70.4
Austria	1414.2	4.1	6.4	1.4	71.8
Rep. of Korea	1260.0	10.8	36.5	1.3	73.1
Switzerland	1221.6	6.6	6.7	1.2	74.3

In 2010, the value (in current prices) of exports of optical instruments and apparatus, nes (SITC group 871) rose by 34.7 percent to 97.4 bln US$ (see table 2). Similarly, imports showed a 29.3 percent increase and amounted to 80.1 bln US$ (see table 3). Graph 1 shows that the rise in exports for 2010 in this product group exceeded the increases in world exports of miscellaneous manufactured articles (SITC section 8) of 15.0 percent and in total world exports of 21.2 percent. Exports of optical instruments and apparatus, nes (SITC group 871) accounted for 5.9 percent of world exports of SITC section 8 and 0.6 percent of total world exports (see table 1).

Rep. of Korea and China were the top exporting countries in 2010 (see table 2). They accounted respectively for 30.9 and 29.1 percent of world exports. China was also the top destination (see table 3), accounting for 64.9 percent of world imports. Other major importing countries or areas were China, Hong Kong SAR and Rep. of Korea. By MDG regions (see graph 2), Eastern Asia accounted for a majority of exports and imports of optical instruments and apparatus, nes (SITC group 871). In 2010, its exports and imports amounted respectively to 79.3 bln US$ and 60.7 bln US$, resulting in a trade surplus of 18.6 bln US$. Top trade deficits were recorded by Latin America and the Caribbean (-4.2 bln US$), Developed Europe (-1.3 bln US$) and Southern Asia (-0.6 bln US$).

Table 1: Imports (Imp.) and exports (Exp.), 1996-2010, in current prices

		1996	1997	1998	1999	2000	2001	2002	2003	2004	2005	2006	2007	2008	2009	2010
Values in Bln US$	Imp.	6.9	7.9	7.3	9.9	13.5	12.2	13.8	25.3	39.9	49.8	63.1	75.8	80.6	62.0	80.1
	Exp.	6.1	8.3	9.2	12.6	14.5	12.3	12.5	20.2	32.6	44.7	57.3	71.8	81.5	72.3	97.4
As a percentage of SITC section (%)	Imp.	1.0	1.1	1.0	1.3	1.7	1.5	1.6	2.6	3.6	4.0	4.6	4.9	4.9	4.3	4.9
	Exp.	0.9	1.2	1.3	1.7	1.9	1.6	1.6	2.2	3.0	3.8	4.4	4.8	5.0	5.1	5.9
As a percentage of world trade (%)	Imp.	0.1	0.1	0.1	0.2	0.2	0.2	0.2	0.3	0.4	0.5	0.5	0.5	0.5	0.5	0.5
	Exp.	0.1	0.2	0.2	0.2	0.2	0.2	0.2	0.3	0.4	0.4	0.5	0.5	0.5	0.6	0.6

Graph 1: Annual growth rates of exports, 1996–2010

(In percentage by year)

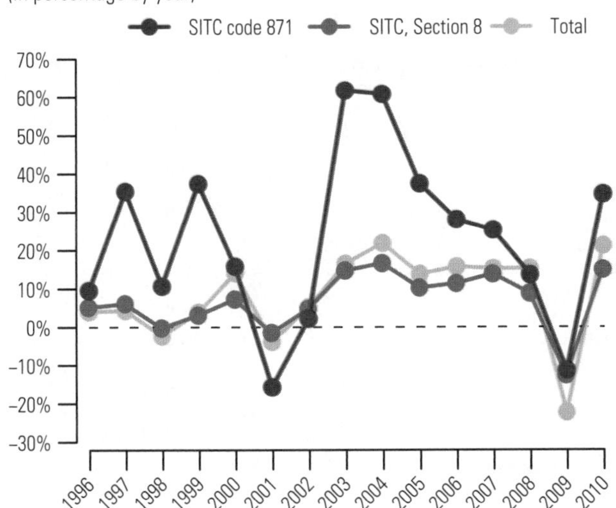

Table 2: Top exporting countries or areas in 2010

Country or area	Value (million US$)	Avg. Growth (%) 06-10	Growth (%) 09-10	World share %	Cum.
World	97 385.1	14.2	34.7	100.0	
Rep. of Korea	30 140.1	20.0	28.6	30.9	30.9
China	28 291.1	18.9	36.8	29.1	60.0
Other Asia, nes	17 936.2	5.2	49.6	18.4	78.4
Japan	7 473.7	17.0	66.4	7.7	86.1
USA	3 123.8	5.5	9.3	3.2	89.3
China, Hong Kong SAR	2 934.1	11.0	13.8	3.0	92.3
Germany	2 707.8	6.2	29.0	2.8	95.1
United Kingdom	637.9	11.0	32.6	0.7	95.7
Canada	568.1	26.2	24.7	0.6	96.3
Singapore	469.9	2.0	17.7	0.5	96.8
Netherlands	426.3	1.6	13.7	0.4	97.3
France	330.4	2.9	-3.0	0.3	97.6
Switzerland	267.0	2.9	33.0	0.3	97.9
Israel	266.7	19.8	14.0	0.3	98.1
Thailand	241.6	12.5	32.5	0.2	98.4

Graph 2: Trade Balance by MDG regions 2010

(Bln US$)

Imports — Exports — Trade balance

Developed Asia-Pacific
Developed Europe
Developed N. America
South-eastern Europe
CIS
Northern Africa
Sub-Saharan Africa
Latin Am, Caribbean
Eastern Asia
Southern Asia
South-eastern Asia
Western Asia
Oceania

-80 -60 -40 -20 0 20 40 60 80

Table 3: Top importing countries or areas in 2010

Country or area	Value (million US$)	Avg. Growth (%) 06-10	Growth (%) 09-10	World share %	Cum.
World	80 090.9	6.2	29.3	100.0	
China	51 987.3	9.5	34.5	64.9	64.9
China, Hong Kong SAR	3 856.6	4.4	5.6	4.8	69.7
Rep. of Korea	3 252.8	18.5	78.2	4.1	73.8
Mexico	3 121.3	-2.9	27.7	3.9	77.7
USA	2 828.8	7.7	9.3	3.5	81.2
Japan	1 908.0	-20.0	11.9	2.4	83.6
Poland	1 691.1	139.7	14.3	2.1	85.7
Other Asia, nes	1 634.0	-7.9	32.3	2.0	87.8
Germany	1 248.0	6.1	36.3	1.6	89.3
Brazil	1 039.4	5.8	6.7	1.3	90.6
Slovakia	731.8	-21.5	7.1	0.9	91.5
Malaysia	725.0	35.0	92.1	0.9	92.4
United Kingdom	513.9	2.1	-10.5	0.6	93.1
Canada	513.0	8.4	2.4	0.6	93.7
Netherlands	511.5	15.9	93.3	0.6	94.3

872 Instruments and appliances, nes, for medical and veterinary sciences

After several years of continuous growth marked by a peak of 74.9 bln US$ in 2008, the value (in current prices) of exports of instruments and appliances, nes, for medical and veterinary sciences (SITC group 872) decreased by 3.3 percent in 2009 but increased again by 8.7 percent in 2010 and amounted to 78.7 bln US$ (see table 2). Similarly, imports increased by 8.6 percent in 2010 to reach 79.6 bln US$ (see table 3). Graph 1 shows that the increase in exports for 2010 in this product group was exceeded by the increases of 15.0 percent in world exports of miscellaneous manufactured articles (SITC section 8) and 21.2 percent in total world exports. Exports of instruments and appliances, nes, for medical and veterinary sciences (SITC group 872) accounted for 4.8 percent of world exports of SITC section 8 and 0.5 percent of total world exports in 2010 (see table 1).

USA, Germany and Netherlands were the top exporting countries in 2010 (see table 2). They accounted respectively for 23.6, 12.4 and 6.5 percent of world exports. USA, Germany and Japan were the top destinations (see table 3). By MDG regions (see graph 2), top trade surpluses were recorded by Developed Europe (+2.9 bln US$), Developed North America (+2.8 bln US$) and Latin America & the Caribbean (+1.4 bln US$). Top trade deficits were recorded by Developed Asia-Pacific (-3.4 bln US$), Commonwealth of Independent States (-2.2 bln US$) and Western Asia (-1.5 bln US$).

Table 1: Imports (Imp.) and exports (Exp.), 1996-2010, in current prices

		1996	1997	1998	1999	2000	2001	2002	2003	2004	2005	2006	2007	2008	2009	2010
Values in Bln US$	Imp.	21.9	22.7	23.7	26.0	27.4	30.1	32.9	39.3	47.3	54.5	59.7	66.8	76.5	73.3	79.6
	Exp.	21.0	22.6	23.6	25.5	26.6	29.7	32.5	39.9	46.5	53.2	56.6	63.9	74.9	72.4	78.7
As a percentage of	Imp.	3.2	3.2	3.3	3.4	3.4	3.7	3.9	4.1	4.2	4.4	4.4	4.3	4.6	5.1	4.9
SITC section (%)	Exp.	3.2	3.2	3.4	3.5	3.4	3.9	4.1	4.3	4.3	4.5	4.3	4.3	4.6	5.1	4.8
As a percentage of	Imp.	0.4	0.4	0.4	0.5	0.4	0.5	0.5	0.5	0.5	0.5	0.5	0.5	0.5	0.6	0.5
world trade (%)	Exp.	0.4	0.4	0.4	0.5	0.4	0.5	0.5	0.5	0.5	0.5	0.5	0.5	0.5	0.6	0.5

Graph 1: Annual growth rates of exports, 1996–2010

(In percentage by year)

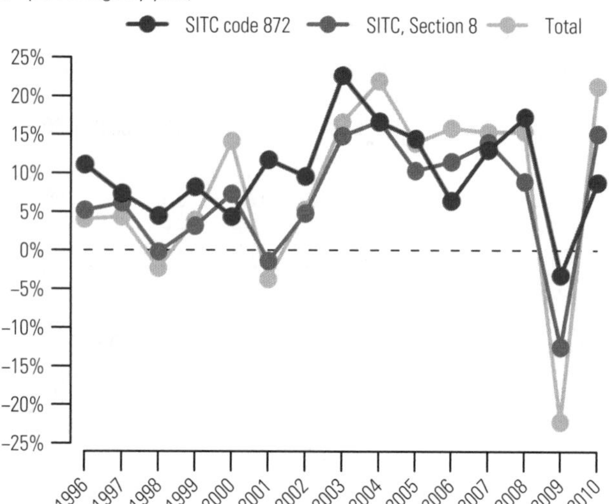

Graph 2: Trade Balance by MDG regions 2010

(Bln US$)

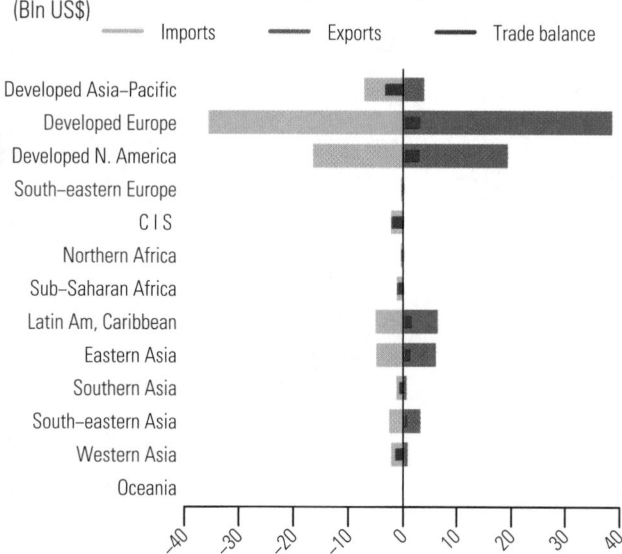

Table 2: Top exporting countries or areas in 2010

Country or area	Value (million US$)	Avg. Growth (%) 06-10	Growth (%) 09-10	World share %	Cum.
World	78715.1	8.6	8.7	100.0	
USA	18613.3	9.4	9.7	23.6	23.6
Germany	9761.1	7.4	5.0	12.4	36.0
Netherlands	5080.0	6.4	10.4	6.5	42.5
Mexico	4687.9	10.3	16.5	6.0	48.5
Belgium	4623.6	16.0	7.9	5.9	54.3
China	4165.0	18.5	17.0	5.3	59.6
Ireland	3431.2	13.0	2.1	4.4	64.0
France	3113.0	5.6	-1.7	4.0	67.9
Japan	2595.5	6.1	15.5	3.3	71.2
Switzerland	2414.2	9.4	13.3	3.1	74.3
United Kingdom	2189.9	-3.1	7.2	2.8	77.1
Italy	1961.2	4.1	3.5	2.5	79.6
Singapore	1829.6	8.4	23.9	2.3	81.9
Sweden	1064.5	3.2	1.7	1.4	83.2
Denmark	977.4	1.4	-0.5	1.2	84.5

Table 3: Top importing countries or areas in 2010

Country or area	Value (million US$)	Avg. Growth (%) 06-10	Growth (%) 09-10	World share %	Cum.
World	79622.3	7.4	8.6	100.0	
USA	14047.2	4.8	11.1	17.6	17.6
Germany	6273.0	8.7	6.3	7.9	25.5
Japan	5202.2	8.6	25.0	6.5	32.1
Belgium	4293.3	14.4	-2.2	5.4	37.4
Netherlands	4271.5	1.0	1.2	5.4	42.8
France	4113.6	8.4	5.5	5.2	48.0
United Kingdom	3433.3	-2.9	-8.0	4.3	52.3
Italy	2948.5	5.1	1.9	3.7	56.0
Canada	2363.9	6.4	7.2	3.0	59.0
China	2146.0	24.7	25.3	2.7	61.7
Spain	1942.9	5.9	-0.2	2.4	64.1
Mexico	1765.3	7.0	10.7	2.2	66.3
Russian Federation	1687.2	18.9	35.4	2.1	68.4
Australia	1655.9	11.4	14.0	2.1	70.5
Switzerland	1419.4	10.6	8.7	1.8	72.3

After several years of continuous growth marked by a peak of 9.7 bln US$ in 2008, the value (in current prices) of exports of meters and counters, nes (SITC group 873) decreased by 13.9 percent in 2009 but went up again by 21.4 percent in 2010 and amounted to 10.1 bln US$ (see table 2). Similarly, imports increased by 19.2 percent in 2010 to reach 10.0 bln US$ (see table 3). Graph 1 shows that the increase in exports for 2010 in this product group exceeded the increase in world exports of miscellaneous manufactured articles (SITC section 8) of 15.0 percent and the increase in total world exports of 21.2 percent. Exports of meters and counters, nes (SITC group 873) accounted for 0.6 percent of world exports of SITC section 8 and 0.1 percent of total world exports in 2010 (see table 1).

In 2010, the top exporting countries were Germany, China and Mexico (see table 2). They accounted respectively for 13.8, 11.5 and 10.8 percent of world exports. USA, Germany and France were the top destinations (see table 3). By MDG regions (see graph 2), Developed Europe accounted for a majority of exports of meters and counters, nes (SITC group 873). In 2010, its exports were valued at 4.6 bln US$, compared to 3.8 bln US$ for imports. This resulted in a trade surplus of 0.8 bln US$. A significant trade surplus was also recorded by Eastern Asia (+0.9 bln US$). Developed North America recorded a trade deficit amounting to 1.3 bln US$. Major trade deficits were also recorded by South-eastern Asia and Western Asia, both at 0.2 bln US$.

Table 1: Imports (Imp.) and exports (Exp.), 1996-2010, in current prices

		1996	1997	1998	1999	2000	2001	2002	2003	2004	2005	2006	2007	2008	2009	2010
Values in Bln US$	Imp.	4.2	4.2	4.3	4.4	4.6	4.6	5.0	6.0	6.8	7.1	7.7	9.1	9.8	8.4	10.0
	Exp.	3.6	3.8	3.8	3.9	4.1	4.2	4.7	5.4	6.2	6.6	7.1	8.6	9.7	8.3	10.1
As a percentage of SITC section (%)	Imp.	0.6	0.6	0.6	0.6	0.6	0.6	0.6	0.6	0.6	0.6	0.6	0.6	0.6	0.6	0.6
	Exp.	0.5	0.5	0.5	0.5	0.5	0.6	0.6	0.6	0.6	0.6	0.5	0.6	0.6	0.6	0.6
As a percentage of world trade (%)	Imp.	0.1	0.1	0.1	0.1	0.1	0.1	0.1	0.1	0.1	0.1	0.1	0.1	0.1	0.1	0.1
	Exp.	0.1	0.1	0.1	0.1	0.1	0.1	0.1	0.1	0.1	0.1	0.1	0.1	0.1	0.1	0.1

Graph 1: Annual growth rates of exports, 1996–2010

(In percentage by year)

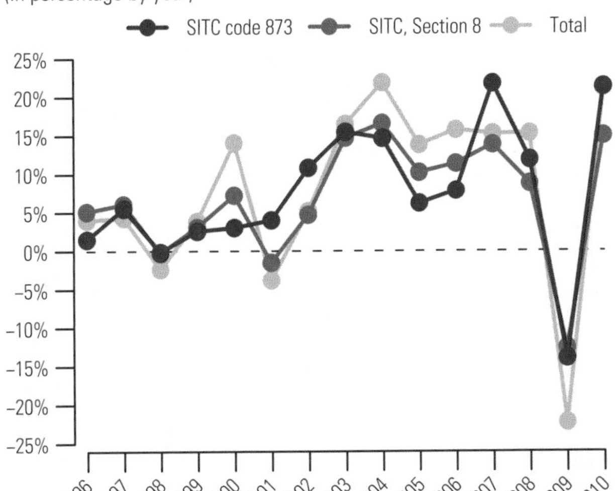

Table 2: Top exporting countries or areas in 2010

Country or area	Value (million US$)	Avg. Growth (%) 06-10	Growth (%) 09-10	World share %	Cum.
World	10097.6	9.2	21.4	100.0	
Germany	1394.6	-1.3	14.1	13.8	13.8
China	1163.6	19.0	25.6	11.5	25.3
Mexico	1085.9	23.0	29.2	10.8	36.1
USA	969.3	5.0	27.5	9.6	45.7
Japan	526.7	4.1	44.2	5.2	50.9
France	499.5	5.6	5.3	4.9	55.9
Hungary	442.6	41.3	13.9	4.4	60.2
China, Hong Kong SAR	379.1	30.7	58.5	3.8	64.0
United Kingdom	338.5	4.4	32.7	3.4	67.3
Italy	325.1	14.9	14.6	3.2	70.6
Spain	201.1	2.8	34.0	2.0	72.6
Slovakia	198.4	17.3	10.4	2.0	74.5
Switzerland	175.6	2.0	18.2	1.7	76.3
Czech Rep.	167.4	2.1	13.2	1.7	77.9
Thailand	164.3	19.7	37.7	1.6	79.5

Graph 2: Trade Balance by MDG regions 2010

(Bln US$)

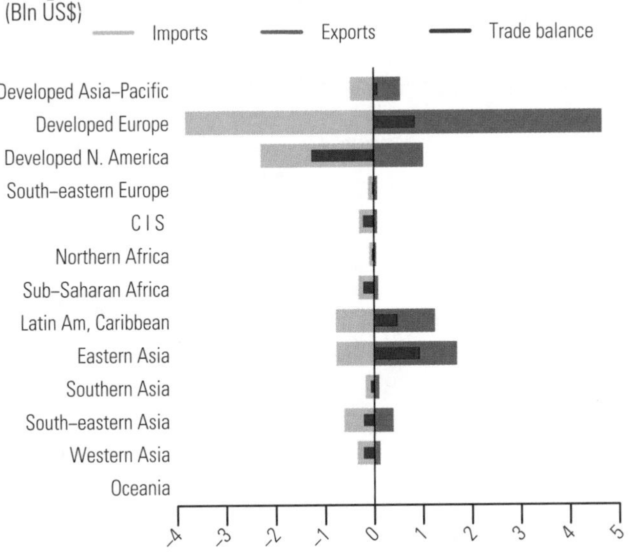

Table 3: Top importing countries or areas in 2010

Country or area	Value (million US$)	Avg. Growth (%) 06-10	Growth (%) 09-10	World share %	Cum.
World	10036.0	7.0	19.2	100.0	
USA	1796.6	6.2	18.2	17.9	17.9
Germany	871.5	3.4	17.2	8.7	26.6
France	513.3	4.7	11.6	5.1	31.7
Canada	486.8	4.4	22.5	4.9	36.6
United Kingdom	434.3	9.5	44.9	4.3	40.9
China	376.6	14.5	39.2	3.8	44.6
Mexico	374.8	10.4	39.6	3.7	48.4
Japan	307.9	13.9	19.6	3.1	51.4
Belgium	247.1	-1.0	12.0	2.5	53.9
Italy	237.5	-3.1	0.1	2.4	56.3
China, Hong Kong SAR	225.4	23.6	32.8	2.2	58.5
Spain	223.4	1.9	3.3	2.2	60.7
Indonesia	222.8	38.9	110.5	2.2	63.0
Slovakia	160.4	20.8	54.2	1.6	64.6
Netherlands	144.4	-1.5	-0.5	1.4	66.0

874 Measuring, checking, analyzing and controlling instruments, apparatus nes

From 2006 to 2010, the value (in current prices) of exports of measuring, checking, analyzing and controlling instruments, apparatus nes (SITC group 874) increased on average by 5.1 percent each year and amounted to 153.2 bln US$ (see table 2). Similarly, imports went up on average by 4.9 percent each year to 154.4 bln US$ (see table 3). Graph 1 shows that the increase in exports for 2010 of 23.7 percent in this product group exceeded the increases in world exports of miscellaneous manufactured articles (SITC section 8) of 15.0 percent and in total world exports of 21.2 percent. Exports of measuring, checking, analyzing and controlling instruments, apparatus nes (SITC group 874) accounted for 9.3 percent of world exports of SITC section 8 and 1.0 percent of total world exports in 2010 (see table 1).

In 2010, USA, Germany and Japan were the top exporting countries (see table 2). They accounted respectively for 19.0, 17.0 and 10.6 percent of world exports. Top destinations were China, USA and Germany (see table 3). By MDG regions (see graph 2), top trade surpluses were recorded by Developed Europe (+20.2 bln US$), Developed Asia-Pacific (+8.0 bln US$) and Developed North America (+7.4 bln US$). Top trade deficits were recorded by Eastern Asia (-19.5 bln US$), Latin America and the Caribbean (-5.1 bln US$) and Western Asia (-2.5 bln US$).

Table 1: Imports (Imp.) and exports (Exp.), 1996-2010, in current prices

		1996	1997	1998	1999	2000	2001	2002	2003	2004	2005	2006	2007	2008	2009	2010
Values in Bln US$	Imp.	59.9	63.9	63.8	66.3	77.0	74.9	74.8	86.0	106.1	112.4	127.2	142.6	152.1	125.3	154.4
	Exp.	55.7	60.2	60.7	63.7	73.0	72.1	72.8	83.2	103.5	110.9	125.7	140.3	149.4	123.8	153.2
As a percentage of SITC section (%)	Imp.	8.8	8.9	8.8	8.8	9.5	9.3	8.8	8.9	9.5	9.1	9.4	9.3	9.2	8.8	9.5
	Exp.	8.4	8.6	8.6	8.8	9.4	9.4	9.1	9.1	9.7	9.4	9.6	9.4	9.2	8.7	9.3
As a percentage of world trade (%)	Imp.	1.1	1.2	1.2	1.2	1.2	1.2	1.1	1.1	1.1	1.1	1.0	1.0	0.9	1.0	1.0
	Exp.	1.1	1.1	1.1	1.1	1.2	1.2	1.1	1.1	1.1	1.1	1.0	1.0	0.9	1.0	1.0

Graph 1: Annual growth rates of exports, 1996–2010

(In percentage by year)

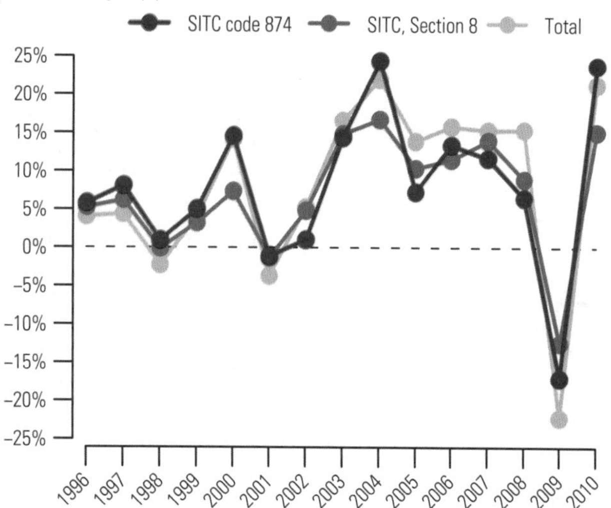

Graph 2: Trade Balance by MDG regions 2010

(Bln US$)

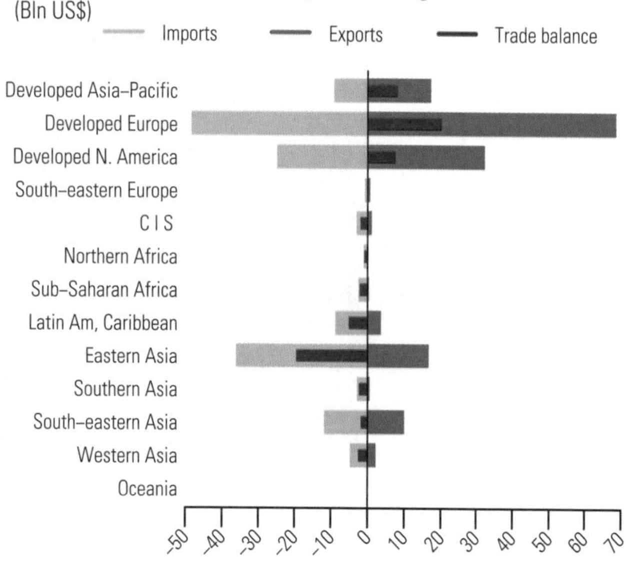

Table 2: Top exporting countries or areas in 2010

Country or area	Value (million US$)	Avg. Growth (%) 06-10	Growth (%) 09-10	World share %	Cum.
World	153 202.6	5.1	23.7	100.0	
USA	29 071.8	1.4	19.9	19.0	19.0
Germany	26 052.6	3.6	21.1	17.0	36.0
Japan	16 277.8	5.2	48.9	10.6	46.6
China	8 535.7	20.6	36.0	5.6	52.2
United Kingdom	8 309.0	1.9	11.9	5.4	57.6
France	6 487.9	0.2	10.8	4.2	61.8
Singapore	5 091.4	17.6	39.2	3.3	65.2
Switzerland	4 561.7	7.3	16.2	3.0	68.1
China, Hong Kong SAR	4 168.9	11.1	30.7	2.7	70.9
Malaysia	3 864.2	12.3	83.3	2.5	73.4
Netherlands	3 521.0	3.4	3.4	2.3	75.7
Italy	3 467.9	0.7	9.0	2.3	77.9
Canada	3 220.9	0.2	6.2	2.1	80.0
Mexico	3 061.1	-4.9	27.2	2.0	82.0
Rep. of Korea	2 153.4	14.3	49.0	1.4	83.4

Table 3: Top importing countries or areas in 2010

Country or area	Value (million US$)	Avg. Growth (%) 06-10	Growth (%) 09-10	World share %	Cum.
World	154 350.7	4.9	23.2	100.0	
China	20 627.5	16.3	41.2	13.4	13.4
USA	19 775.3	2.7	25.7	12.8	26.2
Germany	12 042.4	3.0	12.9	7.8	34.0
Japan	6 557.3	-2.5	27.2	4.2	38.2
Rep. of Korea	6 535.7	2.7	45.4	4.2	42.5
United Kingdom	6 130.7	-0.6	12.6	4.0	46.4
France	5 665.8	0.1	14.3	3.7	50.1
Other Asia, nes	5 215.8	2.9	75.5	3.4	53.5
Canada	5 057.0	0.9	19.5	3.3	56.8
Singapore	4 664.9	5.5	34.5	3.0	59.8
Italy	3 902.0	2.3	15.8	2.5	62.3
China, Hong Kong SAR	3 730.6	11.3	31.5	2.4	64.7
Mexico	3 583.6	1.2	15.3	2.3	67.0
Netherlands	3 222.7	4.9	12.8	2.1	69.1
Malaysia	2 595.2	0.2	31.8	1.7	70.8

After a decline in 2009 of 20.8 percent, the value (in current prices) of exports of photographic apparatus and equipments, nes (SITC group 881) bounced back by 12.9 percent in 2010 to reach 7.2 bln US$ (see table 2). Imports, after a 41.7 percent drop in 2009, increased by 17.0 percent in 2010 and totaled 6.0 bln US$ (see table 3). Graph 1 shows that the rise in exports for 2010 in this product group was exceeded by the 15.0 percent increase in world exports of miscellaneous manufactured articles (SITC section 8) and the increase in total world exports of 21.2 percent. Exports of photographic apparatus and equipments, nes (SITC group 881) accounted for 0.4 percent of world exports of SITC section 8 and less than 0.1 percent of total world exports (see table 1).

The top exporting countries or areas in 2010 were USA, Philippines and China, Hong Kong SAR (see table 2). They accounted respectively for 12.1, 11.5 and 9.3 percent of world exports. Top destinations were USA, China and China, Hong Kong SAR (see table 3). By MDG regions (see graph 2), top trade surpluses were recorded by South-eastern Asia (+1.4 bln US$), Developed North America (+0.2 bln US$) and Developed Asia-Pacific (+0.1 bln US$). Major trade deficits were recorded by Sub-Saharan Africa (-0.2 bln US$) and Western Asia (-0.1 bln US$).

Table 1: Imports (Imp.) and exports (Exp.), 1996-2010, in current prices

		1996	1997	1998	1999	2000	2001	2002	2003	2004	2005	2006	2007	2008	2009	2010
Values in Bln US$	Imp.	13.8	14.0	13.8	15.1	18.0	15.5	14.7	15.3	17.8	16.1	16.0	10.1	8.8	5.1	6.0
	Exp.	14.0	14.7	13.9	15.1	18.9	16.1	15.5	15.8	18.6	16.9	17.4	8.5	8.0	6.4	7.2
As a percentage of SITC section (%)	Imp.	2.0	2.0	1.9	2.0	2.2	1.9	1.7	1.6	1.6	1.3	1.2	0.7	0.5	0.4	0.4
	Exp.	2.1	2.1	2.0	2.1	2.4	2.1	1.9	1.7	1.7	1.4	1.3	0.6	0.5	0.4	0.4
As a percentage of world trade (%)	Imp.	0.3	0.3	0.3	0.3	0.3	0.2	0.2	0.2	0.2	0.2	0.1	0.1	0.1	0.0	0.0
	Exp.	0.3	0.3	0.3	0.3	0.3	0.3	0.2	0.2	0.2	0.2	0.1	0.1	0.1	0.1	0.0

Graph 1: Annual growth rates of exports, 1996–2010

(In percentage by year)

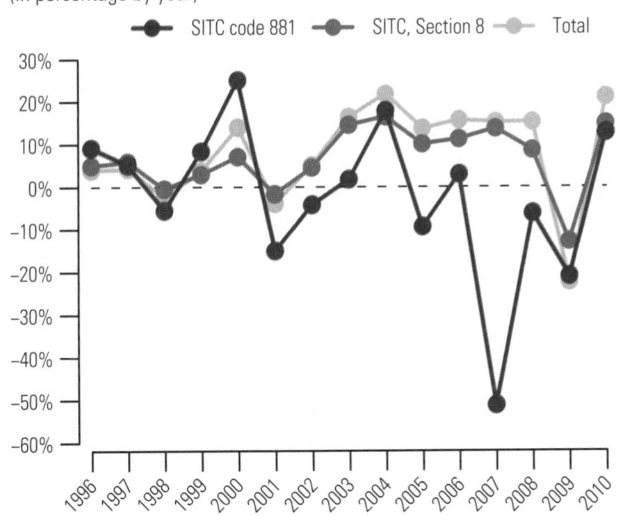

Graph 2: Trade Balance by MDG regions 2010

(Bln US$)

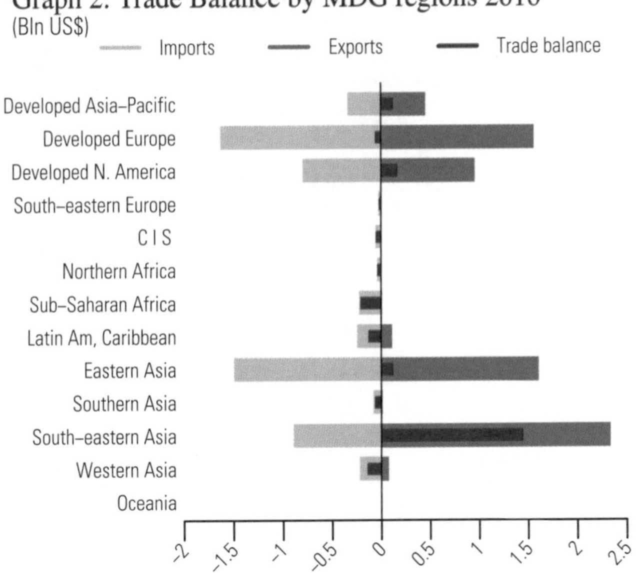

Table 2: Top exporting countries or areas in 2010

Country or area	Value (million US$)	Avg. Growth (%) 06-10	Growth (%) 09-10	World share %	Cum.
World	7170.3	-19.9	12.9	100.0	
USA	865.6	-5.2	8.7	12.1	12.1
Philippines	822.6	12.6	17.6	11.5	23.5
China, Hong Kong SAR	663.5	-13.1	18.9	9.3	32.8
China	658.6	3.5	14.5	9.2	42.0
Viet Nam	*512.2*	84.4	25.6	7.1	49.1
Japan	413.8	-44.2	1.0	5.8	54.9
Singapore	409.7	0.9	20.2	5.7	60.6
Malaysia	405.4	0.7	34.0	5.7	66.3
Germany	386.6	-17.1	-3.7	5.4	71.7
Other Asia, nes	214.1	-6.1	7.4	3.0	74.6
United Kingdom	191.8	-11.5	17.7	2.7	77.3
Italy	177.1	-8.5	2.1	2.5	79.8
Netherlands	168.8	-57.5	16.0	2.4	82.1
Thailand	157.1	0.7	22.2	2.2	84.3
France	140.9	-14.0	-2.5	2.0	86.3

Table 3: Top importing countries or areas in 2010

Country or area	Value (million US$)	Avg. Growth (%) 06-10	Growth (%) 09-10	World share %	Cum.
World	6013.8	-21.7	17.0	100.0	
USA	659.3	-30.0	13.5	11.0	11.0
China	546.1	-20.3	47.9	9.1	20.0
China, Hong Kong SAR	523.5	-11.6	20.4	8.7	28.7
Germany	315.2	-19.5	24.5	5.2	34.0
Singapore	312.4	-8.2	41.9	5.2	39.2
Japan	233.4	-25.3	7.0	3.9	43.1
Other Asia, nes	222.3	-43.9	49.5	3.7	46.8
Rep. of Korea	188.3	-45.7	88.6	3.1	49.9
France	176.2	-11.2	-30.8	2.9	52.8
United Kingdom	176.2	-20.2	21.0	2.9	55.8
Netherlands	172.1	-29.1	6.9	2.9	58.6
Spain	153.2	-0.2	40.4	2.5	61.2
Malaysia	148.1	-7.0	-21.2	2.5	63.6
Viet Nam	*146.7*	29.6	66.9	2.4	66.1
Canada	132.4	-5.3	12.4	2.2	68.3

Source: UN Comtrade

882 Photographic and cinematographic supplies

In 2010, the value (in current prices) of exports of photographic and cinematographic supplies (SITC group 882) rose by 7.1 percent to 17.2 bln US$ (see table 2). Similarly, imports showed a 4.0 percent increase and amounted to 17.0 bln US$ (see table 3). Graph 1 shows that the rise in exports for 2010 in this product group was exceeded by the increases in world exports of miscellaneous manufactured articles (SITC section 8) of 15.0 percent and in total world exports of 21.2 percent. Exports of photographic and cinematographic supplies (SITC group 882) accounted for 1.0 percent of world exports of SITC section 8 and 0.1 percent of total world exports (see table 1).

Japan, the top exporting country in 2010, accounted for 27.3 percent of world exports (see table 2). Other major exporting countries were USA and Belgium, respectively with 16.4 and 9.0 percent of world exports. China was the top destination (see table 3). By MDG regions (see graph 2), Developed Asia-Pacific recorded a trade surplus amounting to 4.0 bln US$. Significant trade surpluses were also recorded by Developed North America and Developed Europe, both at 1.0 bln US$. Top trade deficits were recorded by Eastern Asia (-2.8 bln US$), Latin America and the Caribbean (-0.9 bln US$) and South-eastern Asia (-0.7 bln US$).

Table 1: Imports (Imp.) and exports (Exp.), 1996-2010, in current prices

		1996	1997	1998	1999	2000	2001	2002	2003	2004	2005	2006	2007	2008	2009	2010
Values in Bln US$	Imp.	18.7	18.6	17.3	18.0	18.6	16.5	17.1	18.1	19.5	19.4	19.3	19.5	19.1	16.3	17.0
	Exp.	18.0	19.2	17.4	17.3	18.5	16.3	16.9	18.8	19.8	19.2	19.1	18.6	18.4	16.0	17.2
As a percentage of SITC section (%)	Imp.	2.7	2.6	2.4	2.4	2.3	2.0	2.0	1.9	1.7	1.6	1.4	1.3	1.2	1.1	1.0
	Exp.	2.7	2.7	2.5	2.4	2.4	2.1	2.1	2.0	1.8	1.6	1.4	1.2	1.1	1.1	1.0
As a percentage of world trade (%)	Imp.	0.3	0.3	0.3	0.3	0.3	0.3	0.3	0.2	0.2	0.2	0.2	0.1	0.1	0.1	0.1
	Exp.	0.3	0.4	0.3	0.3	0.3	0.3	0.3	0.3	0.2	0.2	0.2	0.1	0.1	0.1	0.1

Graph 1: Annual growth rates of exports, 1996–2010

(In percentage by year)

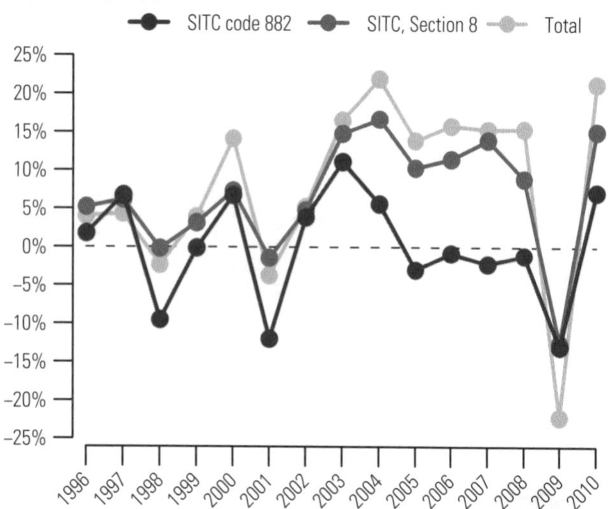

Graph 2: Trade Balance by MDG regions 2010

(Bln US$)

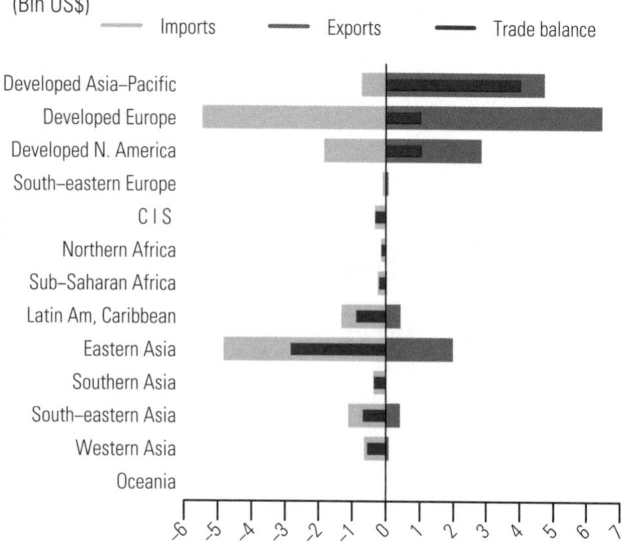

Table 2: Top exporting countries or areas in 2010

Country or area	Value (million US$)	Avg. Growth (%) 06-10	Growth (%) 09-10	World share %	Cum.
World	17152.0	-2.6	7.1	100.0	
Japan	4686.6	-0.1	20.5	27.3	27.3
USA	2806.6	-1.6	2.7	16.4	43.7
Belgium	1551.9	-6.6	3.7	9.0	52.7
Germany	1388.6	-6.5	-5.2	8.1	60.8
Netherlands	1300.8	23.2	9.0	7.6	68.4
China	1072.8	8.5	33.2	6.3	74.7
United Kingdom	813.1	-6.0	-0.6	4.7	79.4
France	715.5	-14.7	-13.6	4.2	83.6
Other Asia, nes	347.2	6.6	23.3	2.0	85.6
Rep. of Korea	323.5	8.4	27.8	1.9	87.5
Singapore	279.0	-22.2	-12.6	1.6	89.1
Mexico	255.4	-15.0	-2.4	1.5	90.6
China, Hong Kong SAR	252.6	-8.4	-19.8	1.5	92.1
Italy	202.6	-7.5	9.1	1.2	93.3
Spain	159.9	-10.1	-30.0	0.9	94.2

Table 3: Top importing countries or areas in 2010

Country or area	Value (million US$)	Avg. Growth (%) 06-10	Growth (%) 09-10	World share %	Cum.
World	16990.6	-3.1	4.0	100.0	
China	1902.1	16.1	26.8	11.2	11.2
Other Asia, nes	1480.1	3.1	32.4	8.7	19.9
USA	1441.8	-6.0	16.8	8.5	28.4
Rep. of Korea	1040.5	5.3	24.8	6.1	34.5
Germany	934.3	-10.4	-2.6	5.5	40.0
United Kingdom	737.0	-2.2	-2.0	4.3	44.4
France	729.6	-12.5	-17.1	4.3	48.6
Belgium	604.4	-10.5	-7.9	3.6	52.2
Singapore	566.5	-3.9	8.2	3.3	55.5
Netherlands	544.1	-1.8	7.8	3.2	58.7
Italy	527.5	-11.7	-19.8	3.1	61.8
Mexico	518.7	-9.5	5.6	3.1	64.9
China, Hong Kong SAR	391.3	-5.6	-7.4	2.3	67.2
Canada	383.8	-10.8	-11.3	2.3	69.5
Japan	370.3	1.5	4.1	2.2	71.6

The value (in current prices) of exports of cinematographic film, exposed and developed (SITC group 883) continued to decline by 13.2 percent in 2010 to 639 mln US$ (see table 2). Similarly, imports showed a 14.1 percent decrease and amounted to 612 mln US$ (see table 3). Graph 1 shows the drop in exports for 2010 in this product group, compared with the increase in world exports of miscellaneous manufactured articles (SITC section 8) of 15.0 percent and the increase in total world exports of 21.2 percent. Exports of cinematographic film, exposed and developed (SITC group 883) accounted for less than 0.1 percent of both world exports of SITC section 8 and total world exports (see table 1).

Canada was the top exporting country in 2010. It accounted for 45.5 percent of world exports (see table 2). Other major exporting countries were Italy and Thailand, respectively with 17.9 and 6.3 percent of world exports. USA, the top destination, accounted for 49.0 percent of world imports (see table 3). Other major importing countries were Rep. of Korea and China. By MDG regions (see graph 2), Developed North America's exports and imports amounted to 322 mln US$ and 306 mln US$, resulting in a trade surplus of 16 mln US$. A larger trade surplus was recorded by Developed Europe (+98 mln US$). Eastern Asia recorded a trade deficit of 88 mln US$.

Table 1: Imports (Imp.) and exports (Exp.), 1996-2010, in current prices

		1996	1997	1998	1999	2000	2001	2002	2003	2004	2005	2006	2007	2008	2009	2010
Values in Mln US$	Imp.	368.7	329.1	308.5	343.7	361.1	447.3	428.3	535.4	605.3	658.8	701.0	709.6	705.6	712.7	612.5
	Exp.	381.0	381.8	391.5	431.3	369.3	371.4	472.5	569.3	666.0	667.6	738.1	815.9	793.1	736.2	638.9
As a percentage of SITC section (%)	Imp.	0.1	0.0	0.0	0.0	0.0	0.1	0.1	0.1	0.1	0.1	0.1	0.0	0.0	0.0	0.0
	Exp.	0.1	0.1	0.1	0.1	0.0	0.0	0.1	0.1	0.1	0.1	0.1	0.1	0.0	0.1	0.0
As a percentage of world trade (%)	Imp.	0.0	0.0	0.0	0.0	0.0	0.0	0.0	0.0	0.0	0.0	0.0	0.0	0.0	0.0	0.0
	Exp.	0.0	0.0	0.0	0.0	0.0	0.0	0.0	0.0	0.0	0.0	0.0	0.0	0.0	0.0	0.0

Graph 1: Annual growth rates of exports, 1996–2010

(In percentage by year)

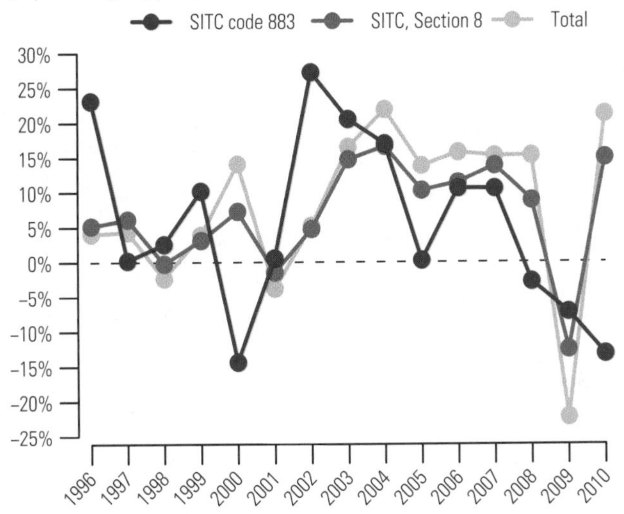

Table 2: Top exporting countries or areas in 2010

Country or area	Value (million US$)	Avg. Growth (%) 06-10	Growth (%) 09-10	World share %	Cum.
World	638.9	-3.5	-13.2	100.0	
Canada	290.6	-2.7	-13.3	45.5	45.5
Italy	114.3	-15.2	-28.6	17.9	63.4
Thailand	40.2	41.5	71.1	6.3	69.7
USA	31.6	-0.9	-29.9	4.9	74.6
India	28.9	12.1	67.5	4.5	79.1
Bulgaria	21.2	17.6	53.1	3.3	82.4
United Kingdom	20.1	-8.7	-49.1	3.1	85.6
Mexico	14.8	9.9	8.1	2.3	87.9
France	13.5	-11.6	12.9	2.1	90.0
Germany	9.5	5.6	-18.8	1.5	91.5
Spain	9.1	20.4	-45.8	1.4	92.9
Australia	8.4	-2.0	-21.3	1.3	94.2
China, Hong Kong SAR	6.7	29.3	31.7	1.0	95.3
Argentina	6.3	2.1	-3.6	1.0	96.3
Russian Federation	4.2	22.0	33.5	0.7	96.9

Graph 2: Trade Balance by MDG regions 2010

(Mln US$)

Imports — Exports — Trade balance

Developed Asia-Pacific
Developed Europe
Developed N. America
South-eastern Europe
C I S
Northern Africa
Sub-Saharan Africa
Latin Am, Caribbean
Eastern Asia
Southern Asia
South-eastern Asia
Western Asia
Oceania

-350 -300 -250 -200 -150 -100 -50 0 50 100 150 200 250 300 350

Table 3: Top importing countries or areas in 2010

Country or area	Value (million US$)	Avg. Growth (%) 06-10	Growth (%) 09-10	World share %	Cum.
World	612.5	-3.3	-14.1	100.0	
USA	300.2	-5.0	-12.4	49.0	49.0
Rep. of Korea	60.9	-1.0	-0.8	9.9	59.0
China	27.4	16.0	-17.4	4.5	63.4
France	25.8	-10.2	-37.2	4.2	67.6
Japan	22.6	10.6	58.4	3.7	71.3
United Kingdom	10.6	-21.7	-39.9	1.7	73.1
Ukraine	10.1	25.5	6.1	1.7	74.7
United Arab Emirates	9.9	13.4	4.1	1.6	76.3
Australia	9.0	2.7	-15.0	1.5	77.8
Switzerland	8.8	4.9	-16.9	1.4	79.2
Mexico	6.9	10.3	-14.5	1.1	80.4
Thailand	6.7	4.4	-10.6	1.1	81.5
Singapore	6.7	38.4	26.9	1.1	82.5
Germany	6.1	-23.6	-21.3	1.0	83.5
Other Asia, nes	5.6	6.3	-2.2	0.9	84.5

Source: UN Comtrade

884 Optical goods, nes

After an 8.1 percent drop in 2009, the value (in current prices) of exports of optical goods, nes (SITC group 884) bounced back in 2010 by 25.9 percent to 50.3 bln US$ (see table 2). Imports showed a similar development with an increase of 25.0 percent and amounted to 50.1 bln US$ (see table 3). Graph 1 shows that the increase in exports for 2010 in this product group by far exceeded the increases in world exports of miscellaneous manufactured articles (SITC section 8) of 15.0 percent and in total world exports of 21.2 percent. Exports of optical goods, nes (SITC group 884) accounted for 3.1 percent of world exports of SITC section 8 and 0.3 percent of total world exports in 2010 (see table 1).

In 2010, Japan, China and China, Hong Kong SAR were the top exporting countries or areas (see table 2). They accounted respectively for 17.6, 14.1 and 8.3 percent of world exports. China, USA and China, Hong Kong SAR were the top destinations (see table 3). By MDG regions (see graph 2), Developed Asia-Pacific recorded a trade surplus amounting to 4.8 bln US$ in 2010. A trade surplus was also recorded by South-eastern Asia (+0.8 bln US$). Top trade deficits were recorded by Developed North America (-2.4 bln US$), Latin America and the Caribbean (-0.9 bln US$) and Western Asia (-0.7 bln US$).

Table 1: Imports (Imp.) and exports (Exp.), 1996-2010, in current prices

		1996	1997	1998	1999	2000	2001	2002	2003	2004	2005	2006	2007	2008	2009	2010
Values in Bln US$	Imp.	11.0	12.3	12.2	14.2	17.9	18.2	16.5	20.0	25.0	28.9	34.1	39.5	44.2	40.1	50.1
	Exp.	11.4	13.2	13.2	14.7	19.4	19.5	17.8	21.0	26.7	30.7	35.2	40.4	43.5	39.9	50.3
As a percentage of SITC section (%)	Imp.	1.6	1.7	1.7	1.9	2.2	2.2	1.9	2.1	2.2	2.3	2.5	2.6	2.7	2.8	3.1
	Exp.	1.7	1.9	1.9	2.0	2.5	2.6	2.2	2.3	2.5	2.6	2.7	2.7	2.7	2.8	3.1
As a percentage of world trade (%)	Imp.	0.2	0.2	0.2	0.2	0.3	0.3	0.3	0.3	0.3	0.3	0.3	0.3	0.3	0.3	0.3
	Exp.	0.2	0.2	0.2	0.3	0.3	0.3	0.3	0.3	0.3	0.3	0.3	0.3	0.3	0.3	0.3

Graph 1: Annual growth rates of exports, 1996–2010
(In percentage by year)

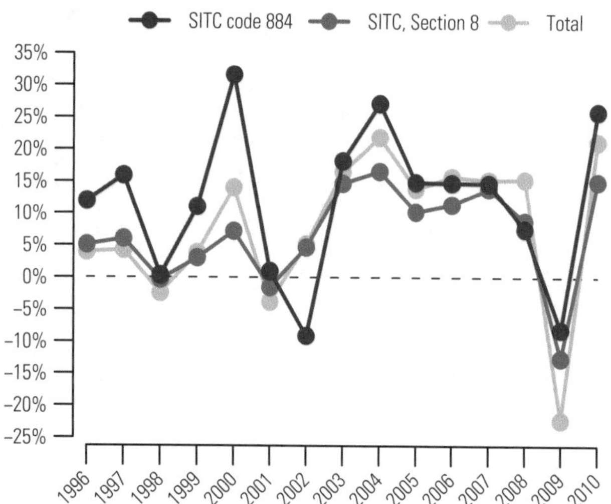

Table 2: Top exporting countries or areas in 2010

Country or area	Value (million US$)	Avg. Growth (%) 06-10	Growth (%) 09-10	World share %	Cum.
World	50 269.4	9.3	25.9	100.0	
Japan	8 845.0	3.6	24.6	17.6	17.6
China	7 099.1	16.9	37.3	14.1	31.7
China, Hong Kong SAR	4 173.6	8.2	34.1	8.3	40.0
Germany	4 091.0	5.7	47.0	8.1	48.2
Rep. of Korea	3 941.4	31.9	28.2	7.8	56.0
USA	3 926.8	2.4	17.2	7.8	63.8
Italy	3 041.6	3.0	11.8	6.1	69.9
Other Asia, nes	2 856.9	21.9	49.3	5.7	75.5
Thailand	1 825.5	15.8	30.8	3.6	79.2
Ireland	1 439.6	8.1	15.3	2.9	82.0
United Kingdom	1 342.7	4.7	12.2	2.7	84.7
Netherlands	1 210.4	16.5	38.1	2.4	87.1
France	922.5	1.3	5.4	1.8	89.0
Singapore	886.7	8.0	22.0	1.8	90.7
Czech Rep.	435.0	17.1	-0.6	0.9	91.6

Graph 2: Trade Balance by MDG regions 2010
(Bln US$)

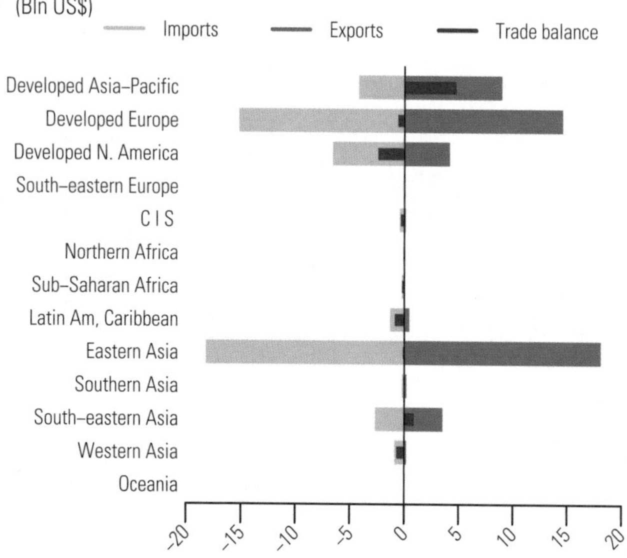

Table 3: Top importing countries or areas in 2010

Country or area	Value (million US$)	Avg. Growth (%) 06-10	Growth (%) 09-10	World share %	Cum.
World	50 109.3	10.1	25.0	100.0	
China	9 726.4	15.5	22.6	19.4	19.4
USA	5 634.6	5.9	22.0	11.2	30.7
China, Hong Kong SAR	3 682.2	13.9	44.3	7.3	38.0
Japan	3 529.8	4.0	28.0	7.0	45.0
Netherlands	2 790.7	14.2	114.0	5.6	50.6
Rep. of Korea	2 670.4	4.4	28.1	5.3	55.9
Germany	2 556.2	8.2	15.5	5.1	61.0
Other Asia, nes	2 092.4	4.3	31.9	4.2	65.2
France	1 748.0	9.3	12.1	3.5	68.7
United Kingdom	1 565.6	4.3	17.0	3.1	71.8
Italy	1 342.8	5.9	13.3	2.7	74.5
Canada	933.9	9.1	17.9	1.9	76.4
Singapore	853.3	7.4	11.4	1.7	78.1
Spain	719.0	4.3	5.5	1.4	79.5
Thailand	657.9	28.3	39.0	1.3	80.8

After several years of continuous growth marked by a peak of 35.9 bln US$ in 2008, the value (in current prices) of exports of watches and clocks (SITC group 885) went down by 18.7 percent in 2009 but went up again by 26.4 percent in 2010 and amounted to 36.8 bln US$ (see table 2). Similarly, imports increased by 24.9 percent in 2010 to reach 35.9 bln US$ (see table 3). Graph 1 shows that the increase in exports for 2010 in this product group exceeded the increases of 15.0 percent in world exports of miscellaneous manufactured articles (SITC section 8) and 21.2 percent in total world exports. Exports of watches and clocks (SITC group 885) accounted for 2.2 percent of world exports of SITC section 8 and 0.2 percent of total world exports in 2010 (see table 1).

Switzerland, the top exporting country in 2010, accounted for 42.2 percent of world exports (see table 2). Other major exporting countries or areas were China, Hong Kong SAR and China, respectively with 20.1 and 8.3 percent of world exports. Top destinations were China, Hong Kong SAR, USA and Switzerland (see table 3). By MDG regions (see graph 2), Developed Europe accounted for a majority of exports of watches and clocks (SITC group 885). In 2010, its exports were valued at 21.2 bln US$, while imports amounted to 11.7 bln US$. This resulted in a trade surplus of 9.5 bln US$. Top trade deficits were recorded by Developed North America (-3.2 bln US$), Western Asia (-1.5 bln US$) and Developed Asia-Pacific (-1.4 bln US$).

Table 1: Imports (Imp.) and exports (Exp.), 1996-2010, in current prices

		1996	1997	1998	1999	2000	2001	2002	2003	2004	2005	2006	2007	2008	2009	2010
Values in Bln US$	Imp.	21.4	20.8	19.9	19.5	19.8	18.8	19.6	21.5	24.3	25.4	27.0	31.4	35.4	28.7	35.9
	Exp.	22.1	21.5	20.4	19.6	19.9	18.8	19.4	21.3	24.3	25.3	27.3	31.4	35.9	29.2	36.8
As a percentage of SITC section (%)	Imp.	3.1	2.9	2.8	2.6	2.4	2.3	2.3	2.2	2.2	2.1	2.0	2.0	2.1	2.0	2.2
	Exp.	3.3	3.1	2.9	2.7	2.6	2.5	2.4	2.3	2.3	2.1	2.1	2.1	2.2	2.0	2.2
As a percentage of world trade (%)	Imp.	0.4	0.4	0.4	0.3	0.3	0.3	0.3	0.3	0.3	0.2	0.2	0.2	0.2	0.2	0.2
	Exp.	0.4	0.4	0.4	0.4	0.3	0.3	0.3	0.3	0.3	0.2	0.2	0.2	0.2	0.2	0.2

Graph 1: Annual growth rates of exports, 1996–2010

(In percentage by year)

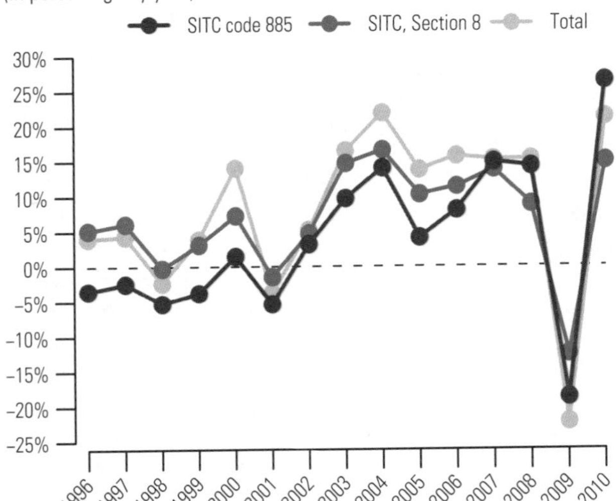

Table 2: Top exporting countries or areas in 2010

Country or area	Value (million US$)	Avg. Growth (%) 06-10	Growth (%) 09-10	World share %	Cum.
World	36848.9	7.8	26.4	100.0	
Switzerland	15541.2	9.1	27.5	42.2	42.2
China, Hong Kong SAR	7415.0	5.2	31.4	20.1	62.3
China	3049.0	11.2	24.3	8.3	70.6
Germany	1568.0	5.9	23.9	4.3	74.8
France	1473.9	8.8	14.7	4.0	78.8
Singapore	1410.3	20.3	36.3	3.8	82.7
Japan	1078.3	3.3	44.2	2.9	85.6
Italy	990.8	5.7	18.4	2.7	88.3
USA	918.4	8.1	17.7	2.5	90.8
Thailand	480.4	5.3	31.7	1.3	92.1
United Kingdom	382.1	5.1	10.2	1.0	93.1
Spain	321.1	5.6	14.7	0.9	94.0
Austria	263.4	5.0	9.9	0.7	94.7
Malaysia	216.6	12.8	63.9	0.6	95.3
Netherlands	158.7	16.0	5.4	0.4	95.7

Graph 2: Trade Balance by MDG regions 2010

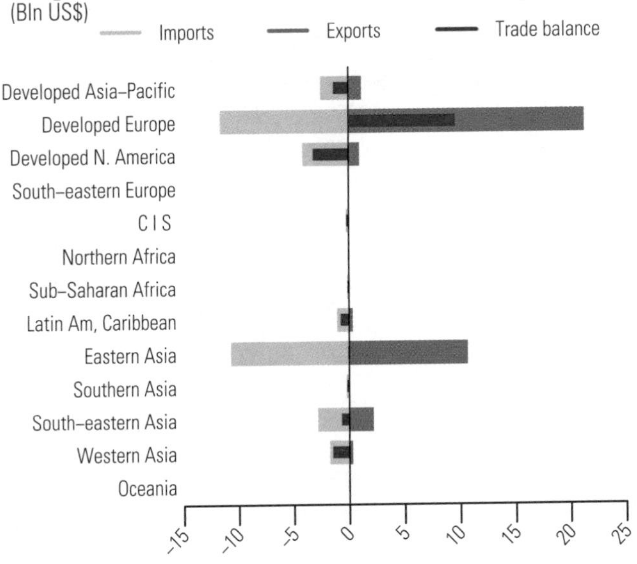

Table 3: Top importing countries or areas in 2010

Country or area	Value (million US$)	Avg. Growth (%) 06-10	Growth (%) 09-10	World share %	Cum.
World	35881.2	7.4	24.9	100.0	
China, Hong Kong SAR	7428.3	14.2	46.8	20.7	20.7
USA	3833.6	-2.1	21.6	10.7	31.4
Switzerland	2540.3	9.1	24.0	7.1	38.5
China	2187.6	18.6	39.2	6.1	44.6
Japan	2144.0	-1.9	14.8	6.0	50.5
France	1988.1	10.3	12.8	5.5	56.1
Germany	1803.8	6.1	20.4	5.0	61.1
Singapore	1529.6	11.4	29.7	4.3	65.4
Italy	1362.9	1.1	5.0	3.8	69.2
United Kingdom	1218.0	3.7	13.2	3.4	72.6
Spain	757.8	-2.5	10.6	2.1	74.7
Malaysia	687.6	22.5	58.9	1.9	76.6
United Arab Emirates	655.8	12.6	28.8	1.8	78.4
Thailand	466.9	7.0	23.0	1.3	79.7
Rep. of Korea	403.4	15.6	38.8	1.1	80.8

Source: UN Comtrade

891 Arms and ammunition

In 2010, the value (in current prices) of exports of arms and ammunition (SITC group 891) rose by 3.9 percent to 11.8 bln US$ (see table 2). However, imports showed a 3.1 percent decrease and amounted to 10.9 bln US$ (see table 3). Graph 1 shows that the rise in exports for 2010 in this product group was exceeded by the increases in world exports of miscellaneous manufactured articles (SITC section 8) of 15.0 percent and in total world exports of 21.2 percent. Exports of arms and ammunition (SITC group 891) accounted for 0.7 percent of world exports of SITC section 8 and 0.1 percent of total world exports (see table 1).

Exports of USA, the top exporting country in 2010, increased by 13.2 percent and represented 42.7 percent of world exports (see table 2). Other major exporting countries were Canada and Italy, respectively with 8.2 and 6.0 percent of world exports. USA accounted for 37.3 percent of world imports and was the top destination (see table 3). Other major destinations were Canada and Rep. of Korea. By MDG regions (see graph 2), top trade surpluses were recorded by Developed North America and Developed Europe, both at 1.2 bln US$. Top trade deficits were recorded by Developed Asia-Pacific (-0.7 bln US$), South-eastern Asia and Northern Africa, both at 0.4 bln US$.

Table 1: Imports (Imp.) and exports (Exp.), 1996-2010, in current prices

		1996	1997	1998	1999	2000	2001	2002	2003	2004	2005	2006	2007	2008	2009	2010
Values in Bln US$	Imp.	5.0	5.0	4.9	4.5	3.9	3.9	4.9	6.1	7.1	6.6	8.1	9.1	10.8	11.2	10.9
	Exp.	8.6	6.9	7.0	6.3	5.3	4.9	5.9	6.3	7.6	7.4	8.3	9.7	10.7	11.4	11.8
As a percentage of SITC section (%)	Imp.	0.7	0.7	0.7	0.6	0.5	0.5	0.6	0.6	0.6	0.5	0.6	0.6	0.7	0.8	0.7
	Exp.	1.3	1.0	1.0	0.9	0.7	0.6	0.7	0.7	0.7	0.6	0.6	0.6	0.7	0.8	0.7
As a percentage of world trade (%)	Imp.	0.1	0.1	0.1	0.1	0.1	0.1	0.1	0.1	0.1	0.1	0.1	0.1	0.1	0.1	0.1
	Exp.	0.2	0.1	0.1	0.1	0.1	0.1	0.1	0.1	0.1	0.1	0.1	0.1	0.1	0.1	0.1

Graph 1: Annual growth rates of exports, 1996–2010
(In percentage by year)

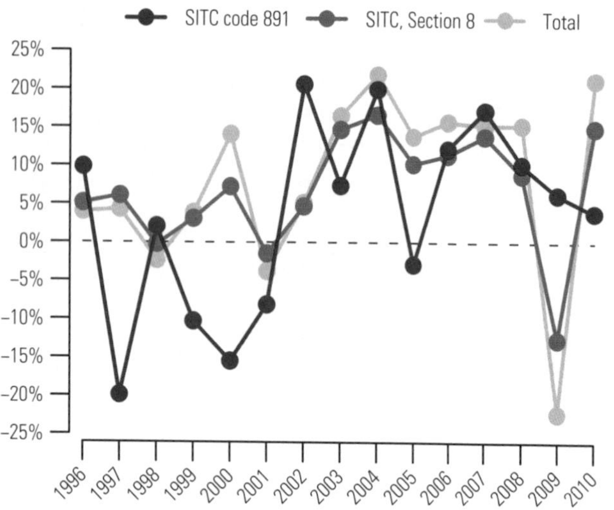

Graph 2: Trade Balance by MDG regions 2010
(Bln US$)

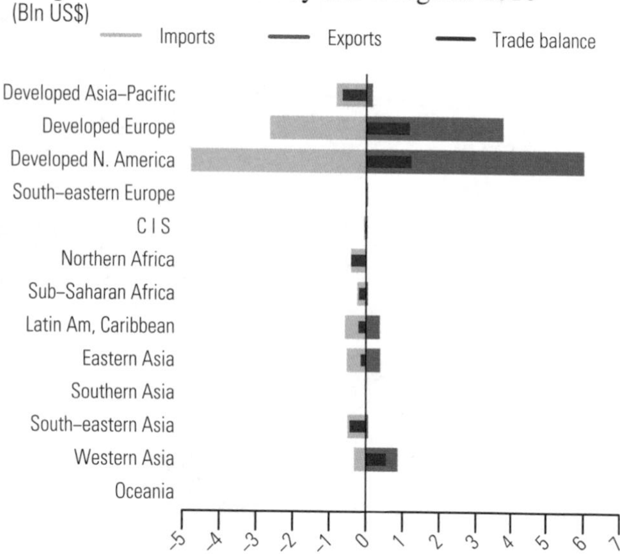

Table 2: Top exporting countries or areas in 2010

Country or area	Value (million US$)	Avg. Growth (%) 06-10	Growth (%) 09-10	World share %	Cum.
World	11809.1	9.3	3.9	100.0	
USA	5039.4	7.4	13.2	42.7	42.7
Canada	968.8	15.4	3.0	8.2	50.9
Italy	709.9	8.8	12.1	6.0	56.9
Germany	505.5	7.5	-0.7	4.3	61.2
Switzerland	499.0	19.4	-5.5	4.2	65.4
Norway	434.5	11.1	-12.4	3.7	69.1
France	358.5	-2.5	-5.8	3.0	72.1
Lebanon	333.3	349.8	560.2	2.8	74.9
Israel	331.9	271.6	-19.2	2.8	77.7
Brazil	312.2	23.9	-6.8	2.6	80.4
Rep. of Korea	247.3	18.5	3.6	2.1	82.5
Spain	229.3	12.7	-5.0	1.9	84.4
Czech Rep.	217.6	17.9	13.1	1.8	86.3
United Kingdom	144.9	-1.4	18.8	1.2	87.5
Turkey	124.0	9.0	6.1	1.0	88.5

Table 3: Top importing countries or areas in 2010

Country or area	Value (million US$)	Avg. Growth (%) 06-10	Growth (%) 09-10	World share %	Cum.
World	10890.8	7.8	-3.1	100.0	
USA	4065.9	15.4	-2.2	37.3	37.3
Canada	708.7	8.8	-0.1	6.5	43.8
Rep. of Korea	507.2	13.1	74.9	4.7	48.5
Australia	445.2	4.1	4.7	4.1	52.6
Morocco	401.5	211.1	481.1	3.7	56.3
Japan	293.8	15.0	35.1	2.7	59.0
Colombia	254.1	24.0	67.6	2.3	61.3
Netherlands	252.8	131.6	1898.7	2.3	63.6
Switzerland	252.2	-0.7	-9.3	2.3	65.9
Norway	246.4	13.7	-19.0	2.3	68.2
Spain	223.5	4.0	3.8	2.1	70.3
Indonesia	218.9	117.3	151.6	2.0	72.3
United Kingdom	204.4	5.7	-27.4	1.9	74.1
France	199.0	8.3	13.1	1.8	76.0
Thailand	195.0	58.3	-12.2	1.8	77.8

After several years of continuous growth marked by a peak of 52.8 bln US$ in 2008, the value (in current prices) of exports of printed matter (SITC group 892) decreased by 9.9 percent in 2009 but increased again by 4.8 percent in 2010 and amounted to 49.8 bln US$ (see table 2). Similarly, imports increased by 4.6 percent in 2010 to reach 46.5 bln US$ (see table 3). Graph 1 shows that the increase in exports for 2010 in this product group was exceeded by the increases of 15.0 percent in world exports of miscellaneous manufactured articles (SITC section 8) and 21.2 percent in total world exports. Exports of printed matter (SITC group 892) accounted for 3.0 percent of world exports of SITC section 8 and 0.3 percent of total world exports in 2010 (see table 1).

USA, Germany and United Kingdom were the top exporting countries in 2010 (see table 2). They accounted respectively for 12.6, 11.9 and 7.9 percent of world exports. Top destinations were USA, Canada and United Kingdom (see table 3). By MDG regions (see graph 2), Developed Europe accounted for a majority of exports and imports of printed matter (SITC group 892). In 2010, its exports were valued at 24.1 bln US$ while imports amounted to 20.3 bln US$, resulting in a trade surplus of 3.8 bln US$. Major trade surpluses were also recorded by South-eastern Asia (+3.7 bln US$) and Eastern Asia (+2.5 bln US$). Top trade deficits were recorded by Latin America and the Caribbean (-1.4 bln US$), Developed Asia-Pacific (-1.0 bln US$) and Developed North America (-0.9 bln US$).

Table 1: Imports (Imp.) and exports (Exp.), 1996-2010, in current prices

		1996	1997	1998	1999	2000	2001	2002	2003	2004	2005	2006	2007	2008	2009	2010
Values in Bln US$	Imp.	26.7	26.9	27.2	27.4	27.5	27.8	29.0	32.9	36.7	39.6	42.0	47.9	50.8	44.4	46.5
	Exp.	26.0	25.8	26.8	26.7	27.0	27.5	28.6	32.5	36.7	39.6	42.0	48.5	52.8	47.5	49.8
As a percentage of SITC section (%)	Imp.	3.9	3.8	3.8	3.6	3.4	3.4	3.4	3.4	3.3	3.2	3.1	3.1	3.1	3.1	2.9
	Exp.	3.9	3.7	3.8	3.7	3.5	3.6	3.6	3.5	3.4	3.4	3.2	3.2	3.2	3.3	3.0
As a percentage of world trade (%)	Imp.	0.5	0.5	0.5	0.5	0.4	0.4	0.4	0.4	0.4	0.4	0.3	0.3	0.3	0.4	0.3
	Exp.	0.5	0.5	0.5	0.5	0.4	0.5	0.4	0.4	0.4	0.4	0.4	0.4	0.3	0.4	0.3

Graph 1: Annual growth rates of exports, 1996–2010

(In percentage by year)

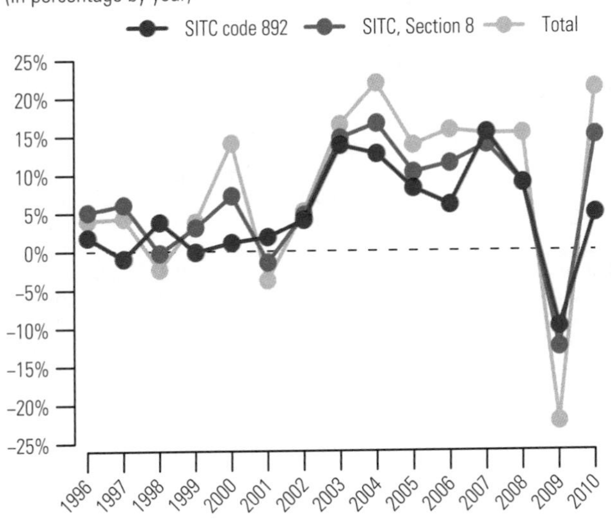

Table 2: Top exporting countries or areas in 2010

Country or area	Value (million US$)	Avg. Growth (%) 06-10	Growth (%) 09-10	World share %	Cum.
World	49805.8	4.3	4.8	100.0	
USA	6264.0	1.0	6.0	12.6	12.6
Germany	5941.9	-0.3	-3.9	11.9	24.5
United Kingdom	3927.6	-1.4	-1.5	7.9	32.4
China	3166.4	17.7	16.1	6.4	38.8
China, Hong Kong SAR	2385.4	1.5	11.7	4.8	43.5
France	2260.2	1.3	-2.1	4.5	48.1
Thailand	2117.6	104.2	33.7	4.3	52.3
Italy	1981.2	0.2	5.4	4.0	56.3
Cambodia	1777.0	28.5	-11.2	3.6	59.9
Netherlands	1587.4	6.0	6.4	3.2	63.1
Belgium	1544.1	0.7	-0.9	3.1	66.2
Singapore	1409.8	8.0	37.3	2.8	69.0
Canada	1193.8	-9.2	5.0	2.4	71.4
Czech Rep.	1124.7	6.9	-6.3	2.3	73.6
Spain	1029.3	-5.3	-4.2	2.1	75.7

Graph 2: Trade Balance by MDG regions 2010

(Bln US$)

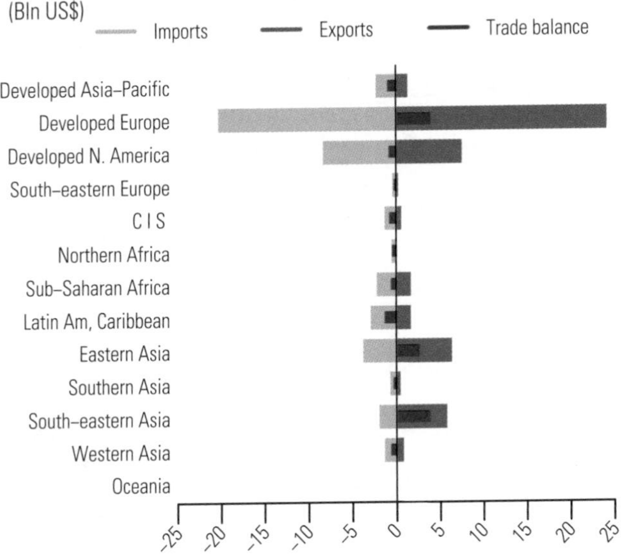

Table 3: Top importing countries or areas in 2010

Country or area	Value (million US$)	Avg. Growth (%) 06-10	Growth (%) 09-10	World share %	Cum.
World	46496.9	2.6	4.6	100.0	
USA	4810.3	-2.8	8.9	10.3	10.3
Canada	3423.6	1.3	8.9	7.4	17.7
United Kingdom	2739.8	-2.6	0.9	5.9	23.6
France	2727.2	2.3	-5.4	5.9	29.5
Germany	2500.3	1.3	-8.2	5.4	34.8
Switzerland	1863.9	0.9	0.2	4.0	38.9
China, Hong Kong SAR	1611.1	5.4	13.6	3.5	42.3
China	1584.7	17.6	18.8	3.4	45.7
Belgium	1419.0	0.7	1.2	3.1	48.8
Austria	1227.5	4.2	-1.4	2.6	51.4
Netherlands	1149.9	2.8	-0.9	2.5	53.9
Japan	1036.0	5.3	2.6	2.2	56.1
Mexico	991.2	-3.1	10.1	2.1	58.3
Australia	927.9	4.0	8.8	2.0	60.2
Italy	859.9	0.8	0.7	1.8	62.1

Source: UN Comtrade

893 Articles, nes, of plastics

After several years of continuous growth marked by a peak of 116.3 bln US$ in 2008, the value (in current prices) of exports of articles, nes, of plastics (SITC group 893) decreased by 14.6 percent in 2009 but increased again by 15.8 percent in 2010 and amounted to 114.9 bln US$ (see table 2). Similarly, imports increased by 15.9 percent in 2010 to reach 119.2 bln US$ (see table 3). Graph 1 shows that the increase in exports for 2010 in this product group exceeded the increase of 15.0 percent in world exports of miscellaneous manufactured articles (SITC section 8), but was below the 21.2 percent increase in total world exports. Exports of articles, nes, of plastics (SITC group 893) accounted for 7.0 percent of world exports of SITC section 8 and 0.8 percent of total world exports in 2010 (see table 1).

In 2010, China, Germany and USA were the top exporting countries (see table 2). They accounted respectively for 16.2, 12.4 and 9.2 percent of world exports. USA and Germany were also the top destinations for imports, together with France (see table 3). By MDG regions (see graph 2), Developed Europe accounted for a majority of exports and imports of articles, nes, of plastics (SITC group 893). In 2010, its exports and imports were valued respectively at 53.7 bln US$ and 52.4 bln US$, resulting in a trade surplus of 1.3 bln US$. A larger trade surplus was recorded by Eastern Asia (+18.0 bln US$). Top trade deficits were recorded by Developed North America (-7.9 bln US$), Latin America and the Caribbean (-6.5 bln US$) and Developed Asia-Pacific (-4.0 bln US$).

Table 1: Imports (Imp.) and exports (Exp.), 1996-2010, in current prices

		1996	1997	1998	1999	2000	2001	2002	2003	2004	2005	2006	2007	2008	2009	2010
Values in Bln US$	Imp.	43.5	45.8	47.6	50.7	54.0	54.3	59.4	68.3	78.8	87.6	97.5	110.4	120.5	102.9	119.2
	Exp.	43.5	45.9	47.2	49.7	53.8	53.9	57.5	66.1	77.0	85.5	95.2	107.7	116.3	99.2	114.9
As a percentage of SITC section (%)	Imp.	6.4	6.4	6.6	6.7	6.7	6.7	7.0	7.1	7.0	7.1	7.2	7.2	7.3	7.2	7.3
	Exp.	6.6	6.5	6.7	6.9	6.9	7.0	7.2	7.2	7.2	7.2	7.2	7.2	7.1	7.0	7.0
As a percentage of world trade (%)	Imp.	0.8	0.8	0.9	0.9	0.8	0.9	0.9	0.9	0.8	0.8	0.8	0.8	0.7	0.8	0.8
	Exp.	0.8	0.8	0.9	0.9	0.8	0.9	0.9	0.9	0.8	0.8	0.8	0.8	0.7	0.8	0.8

Graph 1: Annual growth rates of exports, 1996–2010

(In percentage by year)

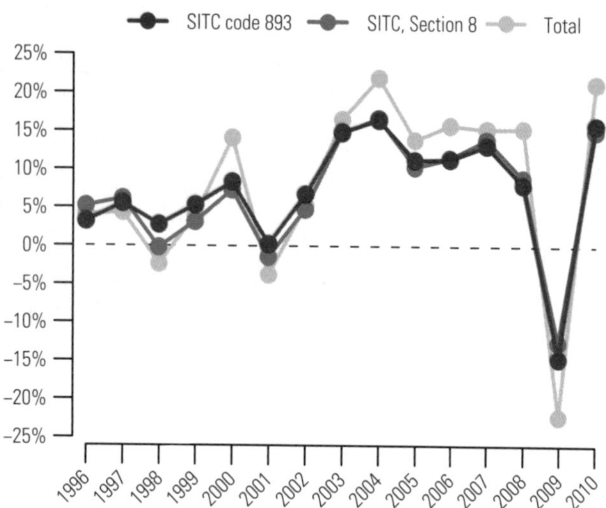

Table 2: Top exporting countries or areas in 2010

Country or area	Value (million US$)	Avg. Growth (%) 06-10	Growth (%) 09-10	World share %	Cum.
World	114929.8	4.8	15.8	100.0	
China	18673.7	8.9	29.5	16.2	16.2
Germany	14267.3	4.9	9.4	12.4	28.7
USA	10624.0	3.0	18.4	9.2	37.9
France	5388.8	1.5	4.6	4.7	42.6
Italy	5254.0	2.5	10.0	4.6	47.2
Belgium	3757.3	1.5	-0.8	3.3	50.4
Canada	3252.9	-4.7	10.3	2.8	53.3
Poland	3133.1	13.5	25.6	2.7	56.0
United Kingdom	2997.4	-0.8	11.8	2.6	58.6
Netherlands	2856.0	3.4	-0.2	2.5	61.1
China, Hong Kong SAR	2845.2	-1.7	19.0	2.5	63.6
Other Asia, nes	2773.0	3.7	21.6	2.4	66.0
Japan	2641.4	5.7	32.6	2.3	68.3
Mexico	2424.1	-0.8	18.2	2.1	70.4
Rep. of Korea	2030.3	9.9	29.0	1.8	72.1

Graph 2: Trade Balance by MDG regions 2010

(Bln US$)

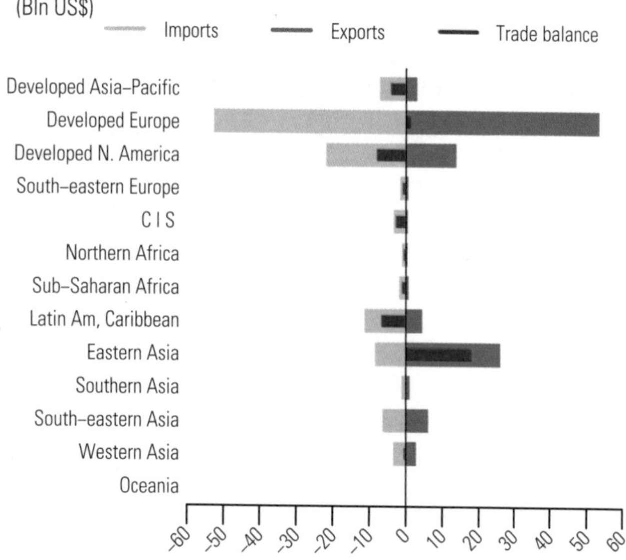

Table 3: Top importing countries or areas in 2010

Country or area	Value (million US$)	Avg. Growth (%) 06-10	Growth (%) 09-10	World share %	Cum.
World	119176.9	5.2	15.9	100.0	
USA	17234.1	2.1	17.5	14.5	14.5
Germany	8986.6	5.5	11.3	7.5	22.0
France	7178.7	5.1	9.0	6.0	28.0
Mexico	6321.8	0.8	52.5	5.3	33.3
United Kingdom	5474.5	1.7	13.0	4.6	37.9
Japan	5003.5	6.4	16.7	4.2	42.1
Canada	4459.5	5.8	15.4	3.7	45.9
China	4000.6	9.2	28.6	3.4	49.2
Belgium	3579.1	2.4	-1.2	3.0	52.2
Netherlands	3218.1	6.0	4.3	2.7	54.9
Italy	2910.2	5.0	13.3	2.4	57.4
Spain	2708.5	1.5	-1.1	2.3	59.6
Poland	2388.2	8.5	15.5	2.0	61.6
China, Hong Kong SAR	2220.9	-0.6	17.6	1.9	63.5
Switzerland	2074.4	7.0	8.3	1.7	65.2

Source: UN Comtrade

After a decline in 2009 of 16.1 percent, the value (in current prices) of exports of baby carriages, toys, games and sporting goods (SITC group 894) bounced back by 2.8 percent in 2010 to reach 87.2 bln US$ (see table 2). Imports, after a 14.3 percent drop in 2009, increased by 3.0 percent in 2010 and totaled 111.9 bln US$ (see table 3). Graph 1 shows that the rise in exports for 2010 in this product group was exceeded by the increases in world exports of miscellaneous manufactured articles (SITC section 8) of 15.0 percent and in total world exports of 21.2 percent. Exports of baby carriages, toys, games and sporting goods (SITC group 894) accounted for 5.3 percent of world exports of SITC section 8 and less than 0.6 percent of total world exports (see table 1).

China, the top exporting country in 2010, accounted for more than a third (36.0 percent) of world exports (see table 2). Other major exporting countries or areas were China, Hong Kong SAR and USA, respectively with 13.0 and 8.0 percent of world exports. USA, the top destination, accounted for 28.6 percent of world imports (see table 3). Other major importing countries or areas were China, Hong Kong SAR and Germany. By MDG regions (see graph 2), Eastern Asia accounted for a majority of exports of baby carriages, toys, games and sporting goods (SITC group 894). In 2010, its exports were valued at 45.1 bln US$ while imports amounted to 12.8 bln US$. This resulted in a trade surplus of 32.3 bln US$. Major trade deficits were recorded by Developed North America (-28.5 bln US$) and Developed Europe (-15.4 bln US$).

Table 1: Imports (Imp.) and exports (Exp.), 1996-2010, in current prices

		1996	1997	1998	1999	2000	2001	2002	2003	2004	2005	2006	2007	2008	2009	2010
Values in Bln US$	Imp.	49.4	54.2	54.2	55.8	59.8	58.5	62.1	66.9	73.4	83.0	90.9	112.7	126.7	108.6	111.9
	Exp.	43.1	46.0	44.6	46.2	48.1	45.4	49.0	52.1	56.9	64.4	71.3	86.6	101.1	84.8	87.2
As a percentage of SITC section (%)	Imp.	7.2	7.6	7.5	7.4	7.4	7.3	7.3	6.9	6.5	6.7	6.7	7.3	7.7	7.6	6.9
	Exp.	6.5	6.5	6.4	6.4	6.2	5.9	6.1	5.7	5.3	5.5	5.4	5.8	6.2	6.0	5.3
As a percentage of world trade (%)	Imp.	0.9	1.0	1.0	1.0	0.9	0.9	0.9	0.9	0.8	0.8	0.7	0.8	0.8	0.9	0.7
	Exp.	0.8	0.8	0.8	0.8	0.8	0.7	0.8	0.7	0.6	0.6	0.6	0.6	0.6	0.7	0.6

Graph 1: Annual growth rates of exports, 1996–2010

(In percentage by year)

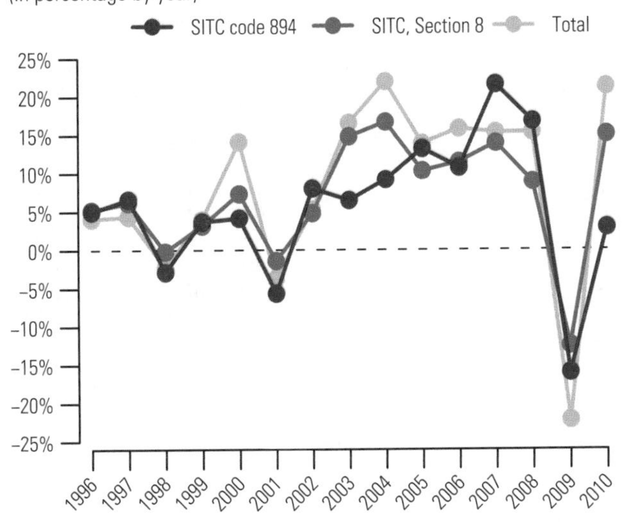

Table 2: Top exporting countries or areas in 2010

Country or area	Value (million US$)	Avg. Growth (%) 06-10	Growth (%) 09-10	World share %	Cum.
World	87 247.7	5.2	2.8	100.0	
China	31 393.7	6.6	11.5	36.0	36.0
China, Hong Kong SAR	11 382.9	-0.7	-15.9	13.0	49.0
USA	6 977.4	5.9	-0.3	8.0	57.0
Germany	6 488.3	6.9	-13.5	7.4	64.5
Netherlands	3 141.1	17.3	-8.1	3.6	68.1
Japan	2 270.0	-5.2	-5.9	2.6	70.7
Czech Rep.	2 174.3	21.1	39.3	2.5	73.2
Other Asia, nes	1 922.2	1.3	24.2	2.2	75.4
United Kingdom	1 884.0	4.3	8.2	2.2	77.5
Italy	1 794.1	0.7	11.1	2.1	79.6
Belgium	1 612.8	4.3	-2.5	1.8	81.4
France	1 608.4	-0.4	0.4	1.8	83.3
Austria	1 490.5	1.0	10.5	1.7	85.0
Mexico	1 292.1	13.0	-22.8	1.5	86.5
Canada	1 223.2	4.1	13.8	1.4	87.9

Graph 2: Trade Balance by MDG regions 2010

(Bln US$)

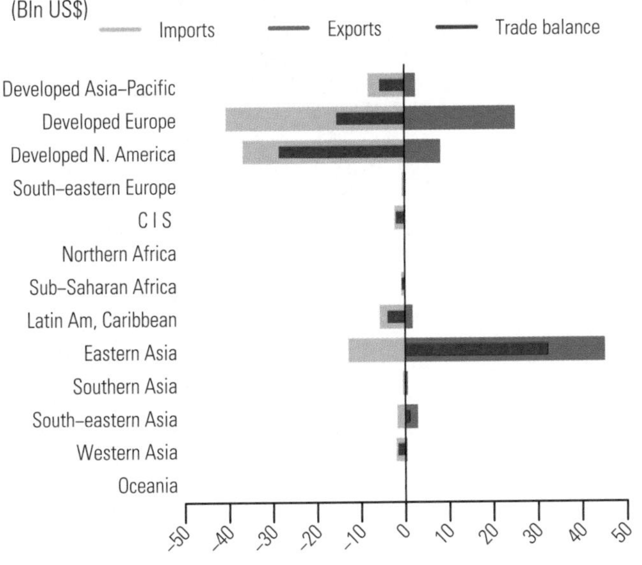

Table 3: Top importing countries or areas in 2010

Country or area	Value (million US$)	Avg. Growth (%) 06-10	Growth (%) 09-10	World share %	Cum.
World	111 934.3	5.3	3.0	100.0	
USA	32 066.2	3.2	10.7	28.6	28.6
China, Hong Kong SAR	9 885.3	-0.7	-16.7	8.8	37.5
Germany	7 119.7	8.6	-18.9	6.4	43.8
United Kingdom	6 518.9	3.0	0.5	5.8	49.7
Japan	5 552.6	-1.1	-8.7	5.0	54.6
France	4 850.7	6.0	3.4	4.3	59.0
Canada	4 590.0	5.8	9.7	4.1	63.1
Netherlands	3 760.9	18.3	-4.0	3.4	66.4
Italy	3 124.2	10.0	9.5	2.8	69.2
Spain	2 592.9	4.9	10.4	2.3	71.5
Australia	2 304.6	10.2	3.0	2.1	73.6
Mexico	2 113.2	6.6	-9.3	1.9	75.5
Belgium	1 971.4	4.1	0.7	1.8	77.2
Russian Federation	1 773.6	25.9	73.2	1.6	78.8
Austria	1 506.5	6.5	17.8	1.3	80.2

Source: UN Comtrade

895 Office and stationery supplies, nes

In 2010, the value (in current prices) of exports of office and stationery supplies, nes (SITC group 895) rose by 20.3 percent to 14.1 bln US$ (see table 2). Similarly, imports showed a 17.9 percent increase and amounted to 15.6 bln US$ (see table 3). Graph 1 shows that the rise in exports for 2010 in this product group exceeded the increase in world exports of miscellaneous manufactured articles (SITC section 8) of 15.0 percent but was below the increase in total world exports of 21.2 percent. Exports of office and stationery supplies, nes (SITC group 895) accounted for 0.9 percent of world exports of SITC section 8 and 0.1 percent of total world exports (see table 1).

In 2010, the top exporting countries were China, Germany and Japan (see table 2). They accounted respectively for 20.2, 11.7 and 9.3 percent of world exports. Top destinations were USA, France and Germany (see table 3). By MDG regions (see graph 2), Eastern Asia recorded a trade surplus amounting to 2.4 bln US$. A significant trade surplus was also recorded by Developed Asia-Pacific (+0.8 bln US$). Top trade deficits were recorded by Developed Europe and Developed North America, both at 1.4 bln US$, as well as Western Asia (-0.7 bln US$).

Table 1: Imports (Imp.) and exports (Exp.), 1996-2010, in current prices

		1996	1997	1998	1999	2000	2001	2002	2003	2004	2005	2006	2007	2008	2009	2010
Values in Bln US$	Imp.	7.5	8.2	8.2	8.5	9.1	8.7	9.1	9.7	11.2	11.7	12.6	14.1	14.8	13.2	15.6
	Exp.	7.1	7.6	7.5	8.0	8.3	7.5	7.9	8.9	9.9	10.5	11.6	12.9	13.6	11.7	14.1
As a percentage of SITC section (%)	Imp.	1.1	1.1	1.1	1.1	1.1	1.1	1.1	1.0	1.0	1.0	0.9	0.9	0.9	0.9	1.0
	Exp.	1.1	1.1	1.1	1.1	1.1	1.0	1.0	1.0	0.9	0.9	0.9	0.9	0.8	0.8	0.9
As a percentage of world trade (%)	Imp.	0.1	0.1	0.1	0.1	0.1	0.1	0.1	0.1	0.1	0.1	0.1	0.1	0.1	0.1	0.1
	Exp.	0.1	0.1	0.1	0.1	0.1	0.1	0.1	0.1	0.1	0.1	0.1	0.1	0.1	0.1	0.1

Graph 1: Annual growth rates of exports, 1996–2010

(In percentage by year)

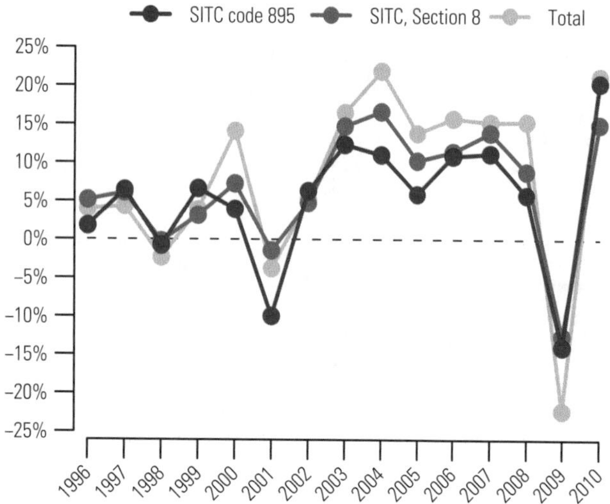

Graph 2: Trade Balance by MDG regions 2010

(Bln US$)

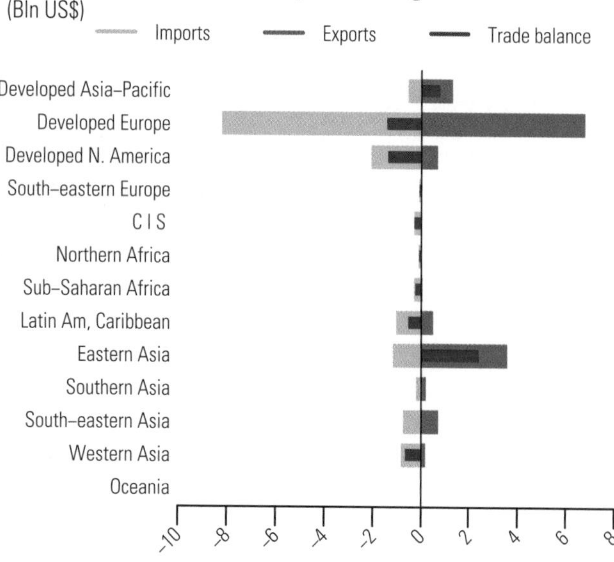

Table 2: Top exporting countries or areas in 2010

Country or area	Value (million US$)	Avg. Growth (%) 06-10	Growth (%) 09-10	World share %	Cum.
World	14118.3	5.0	20.3	100.0	
China	2851.7	12.7	25.1	20.2	20.2
Germany	1653.9	7.7	21.6	11.7	31.9
Japan	1320.0	2.2	15.4	9.3	41.3
Netherlands	1203.6	22.2	16.3	8.5	49.8
France	871.3	5.1	20.8	6.2	56.0
United Kingdom	702.9	-4.6	2.3	5.0	60.9
USA	661.6	-4.6	7.8	4.7	65.6
Czech Rep.	387.8	26.5	146.9	2.7	68.4
Mexico	327.7	-3.8	21.6	2.3	70.7
China, Hong Kong SAR	319.6	-4.5	20.8	2.3	73.0
Spain	305.0	0.6	29.6	2.2	75.1
Italy	284.5	-3.5	9.0	2.0	77.1
Singapore	263.5	-9.7	12.9	1.9	79.0
Malaysia	239.9	11.6	11.6	1.7	80.7
Ireland	227.9	48.8	197.0	1.6	82.3

Table 3: Top importing countries or areas in 2010

Country or area	Value (million US$)	Avg. Growth (%) 06-10	Growth (%) 09-10	World share %	Cum.
World	15570.6	5.5	17.9	100.0	
USA	1786.5	-2.2	18.3	11.5	11.5
France	1586.1	7.2	9.4	10.2	21.7
Germany	1435.1	16.3	37.1	9.2	30.9
Netherlands	967.3	16.1	11.4	6.2	37.1
United Kingdom	873.5	0.2	5.7	5.6	42.7
Spain	702.1	3.6	25.9	4.5	47.2
Italy	582.0	1.7	18.8	3.7	50.9
China	454.1	13.3	33.3	2.9	53.9
Mexico	417.0	1.9	27.6	2.7	56.5
China, Hong Kong SAR	349.7	-1.2	13.1	2.2	58.8
Japan	341.3	3.9	19.0	2.2	61.0
Belgium	290.8	1.9	8.9	1.9	62.8
Canada	280.0	-3.4	7.3	1.8	64.6
Czech Rep.	254.5	23.6	99.0	1.6	66.3
Saudi Arabia	251.0	28.6	48.5	1.6	67.9

After a decline of 28.2 percent in 2009, the value (in current prices) of exports of works of art, collectors' pieces and antiques (SITC group 896) bounced back by 15.6 percent in 2010 to reach 17.6 bln US$ (see table 2). Imports, after a 36.1 percent drop in 2009, increased by 27.0 percent in 2010 and totaled 16.7 bln US$ (see table 3). Graph 1 shows that the rise in exports for 2010 in this product group exceeded the increase in world exports of miscellaneous manufactured articles (SITC section 8) of 15.0 percent but was below the increase in total world exports of 21.2 percent. Exports of works of art, collectors' pieces and antiques (SITC group 896) accounted for 1.1 percent of world exports of SITC section 8 and 0.1 percent of total world exports (see table 1).

In 2010, USA, United Kingdom and Switzerland were the top exporting countries in 2010, respectively with 37.0, 29.8 and 7.4 percent of world exports (see table 2). USA, United Kingdom and Switzerland were also the top destinations (see table 3). By MDG regions (see graph 2), top trade surpluses were recorded by Developed Europe (+1.1 bln US$), Developed North America (+0.4 bln US$) and Southern Asia (+0.2 bln US$). Top trade deficits were recorded by Eastern Asia (-0.4 bln US$) and Developed Asia-Pacific (-0.2 bln US$).

Table 1: Imports (Imp.) and exports (Exp.), 1996-2010, in current prices

		1996	1997	1998	1999	2000	2001	2002	2003	2004	2005	2006	2007	2008	2009	2010
Values in Bln US$	Imp.	6.8	8.5	9.4	10.1	11.5	11.5	11.2	10.2	12.6	14.0	16.3	22.6	20.5	13.1	16.7
	Exp.	6.2	7.4	7.9	7.8	10.1	10.2	9.5	10.2	12.7	14.7	17.1	20.7	21.2	15.2	17.6
As a percentage of SITC section (%)	Imp.	1.0	1.2	1.3	1.3	1.4	1.4	1.3	1.1	1.1	1.1	1.2	1.5	1.2	0.9	1.0
	Exp.	0.9	1.1	1.1	1.1	1.3	1.3	1.2	1.1	1.2	1.2	1.3	1.4	1.3	1.1	1.1
As a percentage of world trade (%)	Imp.	0.1	0.2	0.2	0.2	0.2	0.2	0.2	0.1	0.1	0.1	0.1	0.2	0.1	0.1	0.1
	Exp.	0.1	0.1	0.1	0.1	0.2	0.2	0.1	0.1	0.1	0.1	0.1	0.1	0.1	0.1	0.1

Graph 1: Annual growth rates of exports, 1996–2010

(In percentage by year)

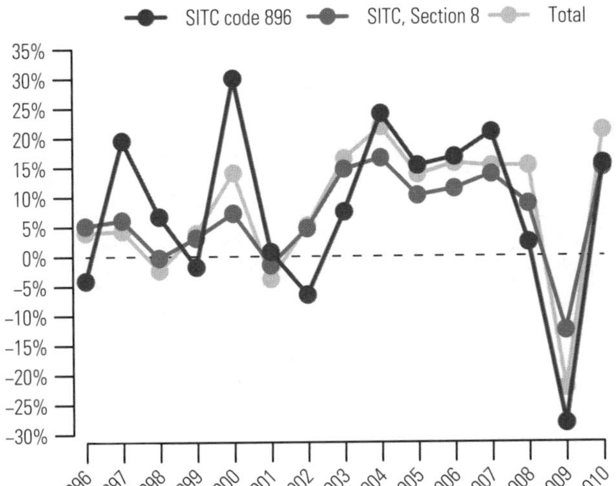

Graph 2: Trade Balance by MDG regions 2010

(Bln US$)

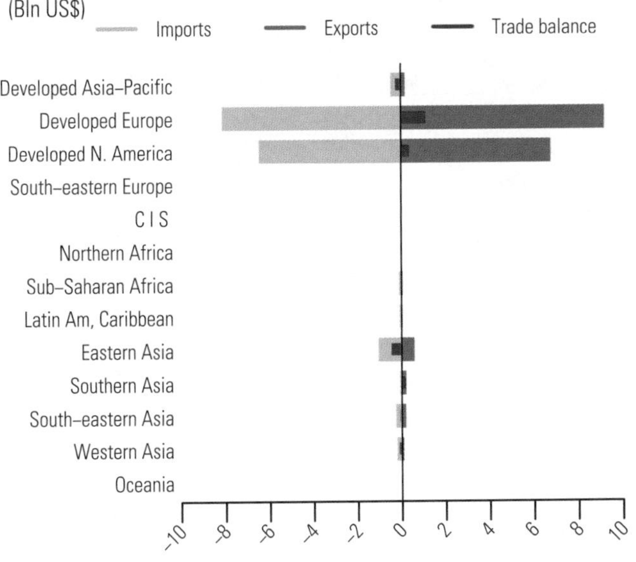

Table 2: Top exporting countries or areas in 2010

Country or area	Value (million US$)	Avg. Growth (%) 06-10	Growth (%) 09-10	World share %	Cum.
World	17564.5	0.7	15.6	100.0	
USA	6496.9	3.9	0.0	37.0	37.0
United Kingdom	5226.7	0.3	57.3	29.8	66.7
Switzerland	1304.1	0.6	23.2	7.4	74.2
France	969.8	-4.0	-18.2	5.5	79.7
Germany	877.7	10.6	34.6	5.0	84.7
Canada	310.8	-9.0	8.1	1.8	86.5
China, Hong Kong SAR	291.3	6.1	28.3	1.7	88.1
Italy	285.1	15.7	108.3	1.6	89.7
India	219.6	-16.0	7.3	1.3	91.0
Singapore	160.8	-4.1	48.5	0.9	91.9
China	160.5	25.3	217.9	0.9	92.8
Japan	137.2	12.4	22.2	0.8	93.6
Rep. of Korea	136.2	-20.9	-53.1	0.8	94.4
Austria	128.2	-24.8	-3.2	0.7	95.1
Netherlands	92.1	-2.1	43.2	0.5	95.6

Table 3: Top importing countries or areas in 2010

Country or area	Value (million US$)	Avg. Growth (%) 06-10	Growth (%) 09-10	World share %	Cum.
World	16650.8	0.5	27.0	100.0	
USA	6264.3	-1.6	23.7	37.6	37.6
United Kingdom	4237.6	-0.7	47.9	25.4	63.1
Switzerland	1662.8	7.6	29.9	10.0	73.1
China, Hong Kong SAR	782.6	19.8	44.2	4.7	77.8
France	569.2	6.5	3.3	3.4	81.2
Germany	406.8	0.9	5.9	2.4	83.6
Netherlands	292.3	9.5	39.2	1.8	85.4
Japan	270.8	-4.5	-3.1	1.6	87.0
Austria	196.3	13.9	34.8	1.2	88.2
Singapore	191.9	14.5	70.2	1.2	89.3
Rep. of Korea	186.5	-5.9	-12.8	1.1	90.5
Canada	171.4	-0.7	-1.5	1.0	91.5
Greece	164.9	93.7	86.4	1.0	92.5
Italy	131.8	8.0	33.5	0.8	93.3
Belgium	128.5	8.7	-9.7	0.8	94.0

Source: UN Comtrade

897 Gold, silverware, jewellery and articles of precious materials, nes

From 2006 to 2010, the value (in current prices) of exports of gold, silverware, jewellery and articles of precious materials, nes (SITC group 897) increased on average by 12.3 percent each year and amounted to 77.5 bln US$ (see table 2). Similarly, imports went up on average by 10.0 percent each year to 61.5 bln US$ (see table 3). Graph 1 shows that the increase of 17.5 percent in exports for 2010 in this product group exceeded the increase of 15.0 percent in world exports of miscellaneous manufactured articles (SITC section 8) but was below the 21.2 percent increase in total world exports. Exports of gold, silverware, jewellery and articles of precious materials, nes (SITC group 897) accounted for 4.7 percent of world exports of SITC section 8 and 0.5 percent of total world exports in 2010 (see table 1).

India, China and USA were the top exporting countries in 2010 (see table 2). They accounted respectively for 11.8, 11.6 and 9.1 percent of world exports. Top destinations were USA, Switzerland and China, Honk Kong SAR (see table 3). By MDG regions (see graph 2), top trade surpluses were recorded by Southern Asia (+9.6 bln US$), Eastern Asia (+6.4 bln US$) and South-eastern Asia (+6.0 bln US$). Top trade deficits were recorded by Developed North America (-4.1 bln US$), Western Asia (-2.2 bln US$) and Developed Asia-Pacific (-0.4 bln US$).

Table 1: Imports (Imp.) and exports (Exp.), 1996-2010, in current prices

		1996	1997	1998	1999	2000	2001	2002	2003	2004	2005	2006	2007	2008	2009	2010
Values in Bln US$	Imp.	16.6	17.6	17.6	17.7	19.8	20.0	23.2	26.3	31.4	36.4	42.0	48.9	53.0	48.1	61.5
	Exp.	19.7	20.9	22.0	21.2	22.4	23.3	25.8	28.8	35.9	41.0	48.7	57.8	65.0	65.9	77.5
As a percentage of SITC section (%)	Imp.	2.4	2.5	2.4	2.3	2.4	2.5	2.7	2.7	2.8	3.0	3.1	3.2	3.2	3.4	3.8
	Exp.	3.0	3.0	3.1	2.9	2.9	3.0	3.2	3.1	3.4	3.5	3.7	3.9	4.0	4.6	4.7
As a percentage of world trade (%)	Imp.	0.3	0.3	0.3	0.3	0.3	0.3	0.4	0.3	0.3	0.3	0.3	0.3	0.3	0.4	0.4
	Exp.	0.4	0.4	0.4	0.4	0.4	0.4	0.4	0.4	0.4	0.4	0.4	0.4	0.4	0.5	0.5

Graph 1: Annual growth rates of exports, 1996–2010
(In percentage by year)

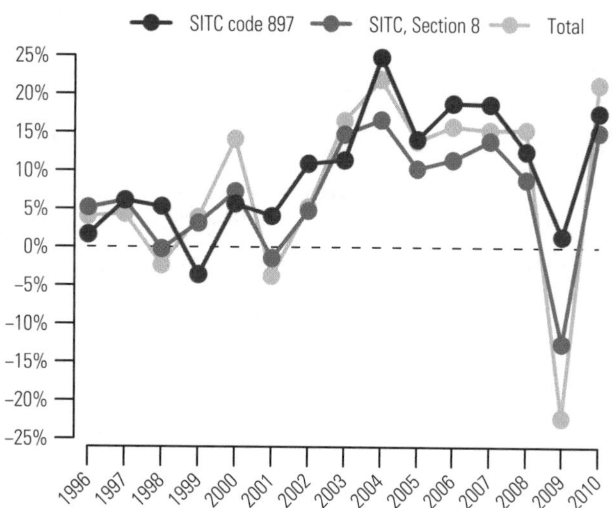

Graph 2: Trade Balance by MDG regions 2010
(Bln US$)

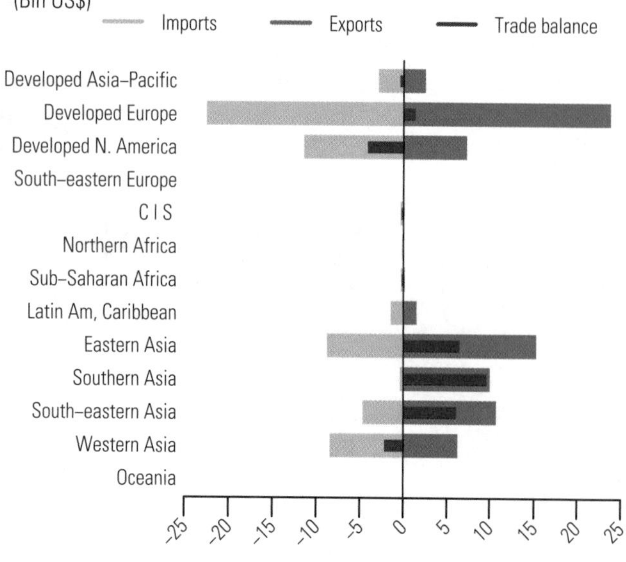

Table 2: Top exporting countries or areas in 2010

Country or area	Value (million US$)	Avg. Growth (%) 06-10	Growth (%) 09-10	World share %	Cum.
World	77465.3	12.3	17.5	100.0	
India	9149.9	16.5	-32.9	11.8	11.8
China	8971.2	29.3	131.0	11.6	23.4
USA	7075.2	5.7	12.3	9.1	32.5
Switzerland	6161.6	13.6	25.2	8.0	40.5
Italy	5772.8	0.3	20.9	7.5	47.9
China, Hong Kong SAR	5630.2	4.1	21.3	7.3	55.2
United Kingdom	4458.1	5.6	18.2	5.8	61.0
United Arab Emirates	3720.1	47.5	21.4	4.8	65.8
Thailand	3437.1	16.0	25.4	4.4	70.2
Singapore	2559.5	41.0	52.9	3.3	73.5
France	2483.1	8.6	26.3	3.2	76.7
Viet Nam	*2355.5*	110.1	25.6	3.0	79.7
Japan	2128.7	32.7	75.8	2.7	82.5
Malaysia	2014.3	17.5	27.7	2.6	85.1
Germany	1892.9	-0.6	23.2	2.4	87.5

Table 3: Top importing countries or areas in 2010

Country or area	Value (million US$)	Avg. Growth (%) 06-10	Growth (%) 09-10	World share %	Cum.
World	61476.1	10.0	27.7	100.0	
USA	10306.7	-2.4	16.4	16.8	16.8
Switzerland	8844.6	30.0	45.9	14.4	31.2
China, Hong Kong SAR	6758.1	21.3	52.3	11.0	42.1
United Arab Emirates	6349.2	16.5	17.7	10.3	52.5
United Kingdom	3806.2	-4.1	10.9	6.2	58.7
Singapore	2892.2	27.6	53.7	4.7	63.4
France	2501.8	9.7	24.3	4.1	67.4
Japan	1847.5	-2.4	20.7	3.0	70.4
Germany	1787.1	7.5	16.0	2.9	73.4
Italy	1472.3	9.8	40.9	2.4	75.7
Canada	1118.0	8.6	28.1	1.8	77.6
Malaysia	1030.7	86.5	196.4	1.7	79.2
Australia	923.3	14.4	14.5	1.5	80.7
China	776.8	22.3	36.7	1.3	82.0
Spain	662.4	0.5	20.7	1.1	83.1

After a decline of 13.4 percent in 2009, the value (in current prices) of exports of musical instruments, parts/accessories; records, tapes and similar recordings (SITC group 898) bounced back by 5.8 percent in 2010 to reach 57.5 bln US$ (see table 2). Imports, after an 11.1 percent drop in 2009, increased by 4.9 percent in 2010 and totaled 60.9 bln US$ (see table 3). Graph 1 shows that the rise in exports for 2010 in this product group was exceeded by the increases in world exports of miscellaneous manufactured articles (SITC section 8) of 15.0 percent and in total world exports of 21.2 percent. Exports of musical instruments, parts/accessories; records, tapes and similar recordings (SITC group 898) accounted for 3.5 percent of world exports of SITC section 8 and 0.4 percent of total world exports (see table 1).

The top exporting countries in 2010 were China and Germany (see table 2). They accounted respectively for 12.5 and 11.5 percent of world exports. China, USA and Germany were the top destinations (see table 3). By MDG regions (see graph 2), top trade surpluses were recorded by South-eastern Asia and Eastern Asia, both at 3.0 bln US$. Top trade deficits were recorded by Latin America & the Caribbean (-2.2 bln US$), Developed Europe (-1.8 bln US$) and Developed North America (-1.5 bln US$).

Table 1: Imports (Imp.) and exports (Exp.), 1996-2010, in current prices

		1996	1997	1998	1999	2000	2001	2002	2003	2004	2005	2006	2007	2008	2009	2010
Values in Bln US$	Imp.	31.9	31.6	31.8	33.9	33.9	32.9	34.2	39.0	45.4	51.8	54.6	63.6	65.3	58.1	60.9
	Exp.	32.4	32.7	32.1	34.4	34.2	33.1	33.7	39.1	44.3	50.8	52.8	61.6	62.8	54.3	57.5
As a percentage of SITC section (%)	Imp.	4.7	4.4	4.4	4.5	4.2	4.1	4.1	4.0	4.0	4.2	4.0	4.1	3.9	4.1	3.7
	Exp.	4.9	4.6	4.6	4.8	4.4	4.3	4.2	4.3	4.1	4.3	4.0	4.1	3.8	3.8	3.5
As a percentage of world trade (%)	Imp.	0.6	0.6	0.6	0.6	0.5	0.5	0.5	0.5	0.5	0.5	0.4	0.5	0.4	0.5	0.4
	Exp.	0.6	0.6	0.6	0.6	0.5	0.5	0.5	0.5	0.5	0.5	0.4	0.4	0.4	0.4	0.4

Graph 1: Annual growth rates of exports, 1996–2010
(In percentage by year)

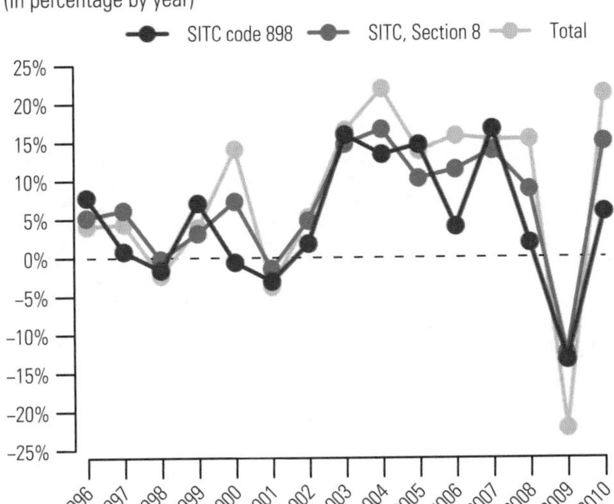

Table 2: Top exporting countries or areas in 2010

Country or area	Value (million US$)	Avg. Growth (%) 06-10	Growth (%) 09-10	World share %	Cum.
World	57525.1	2.2	5.8	100.0	
China	7197.4	22.7	4.0	12.5	12.5
Germany	6614.6	0.6	-0.5	11.5	24.0
Other Asia, nes	5628.4	2.3	35.8	9.8	33.8
USA	5308.4	-3.3	1.8	9.2	43.0
Singapore	4749.0	6.0	22.6	8.3	51.3
Japan	3953.8	-7.3	-0.2	6.9	58.2
China, Hong Kong SAR	3235.3	35.9	10.8	5.6	63.8
Netherlands	2404.6	-3.2	2.3	4.2	68.0
United Kingdom	2304.1	-10.0	2.3	4.0	72.0
Rep. of Korea	1831.1	7.4	30.8	3.2	75.1
Austria	1673.0	2.9	11.4	2.9	78.1
Malaysia	1579.5	7.9	10.0	2.7	80.8
Ireland	1485.1	-8.7	-8.1	2.6	83.4
France	1485.0	-0.4	10.2	2.6	86.0
Czech Rep.	1054.0	16.3	-20.8	1.8	87.8

Graph 2: Trade Balance by MDG regions 2010
(Bln US$)

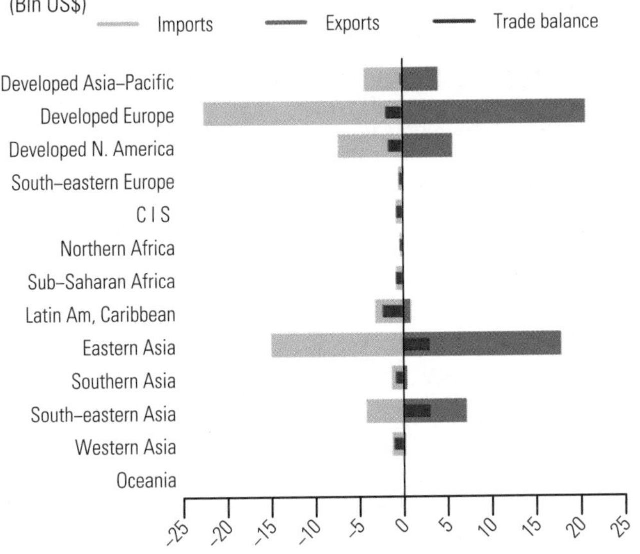

Table 3: Top importing countries or areas in 2010

Country or area	Value (million US$)	Avg. Growth (%) 06-10	Growth (%) 09-10	World share %	Cum.
World	60899.4	2.8	4.9	100.0	
China	6060.3	11.4	21.0	10.0	10.0
USA	5118.8	-8.4	3.4	8.4	18.4
Germany	4313.8	-2.6	-1.8	7.1	25.4
China, Hong Kong SAR	4301.9	50.6	7.7	7.1	32.5
Japan	3064.8	5.7	19.0	5.0	37.5
United Kingdom	3007.6	-3.8	-4.0	4.9	42.5
Rep. of Korea	2414.7	4.1	42.8	4.0	46.4
France	2356.0	-1.1	-1.3	3.9	50.3
Thailand	2299.0	4.6	18.0	3.8	54.1
Netherlands	2176.5	3.7	13.5	3.6	57.7
Other Asia, nes	2144.1	19.1	58.6	3.5	61.2
Canada	2130.0	3.6	6.5	3.5	64.7
Italy	1403.6	-7.5	-12.0	2.3	67.0
Mexico	1235.8	6.9	12.5	2.0	69.0
Singapore	1141.5	-4.0	21.7	1.9	70.9

Source: UN Comtrade

899 Miscellaneous manufactured articles , nes

After several years of continuous growth marked by a peak of 65.9 bln US$ in 2008, the value (in current prices) of exports of miscellaneous manufactured articles, nes (SITC group 899) decreased by 3.1 percent in 2009 but went up again by 14.0 percent in 2010 and amounted to 72.8 bln US$ (see table 2). Similarly, imports increased by 12.0 percent in 2010 to reach 71.7 bln US$ (see table 3). Graph 1 shows that the increase in exports for 2010 in this product group was exceeded by the increases in world exports of miscellaneous manufactured articles (SITC section 8) of 15.0 percent and in total world exports of 21.2 percent. Exports of miscellaneous manufactured articles, nes (SITC group 899) accounted for 4.4 percent of world exports of SITC section 8 and 0.5 percent of total world exports in 2010 (see table 1).

In 2010, China, USA and Switzerland were the top exporting countries (see table 2). They accounted respectively for 19.8, 13.3 and 8.3 percent of world exports. Top destinations were USA, France and Germany (see table 3). By MDG regions (see graph 2), Developed Europe accounted for a majority of exports and imports of miscellaneous manufactured articles, nes (SITC group 899). In 2010, its exports and imports were valued respectively at 37.4 bln US$ and 33.4 bln US$, resulting in a trade surplus of 4.0 bln US$. A larger trade surplus was recorded by Eastern Asia (+12.7 bln US$). Top trade deficits were recorded by Developed North America (-5.4 bln US$), Developed Asia-Pacific (-4.4 bln US$) and Latin America and the Caribbean (-1.5 bln US$).

Table 1: Imports (Imp.) and exports (Exp.), 1996-2010, in current prices

		1996	1997	1998	1999	2000	2001	2002	2003	2004	2005	2006	2007	2008	2009	2010
Values in Bln US$	Imp.	21.5	22.1	22.6	24.9	26.0	27.6	30.5	37.0	42.8	46.8	51.1	58.1	66.5	64.0	71.7
	Exp.	20.5	21.3	21.0	22.9	24.2	25.1	27.2	33.4	40.0	44.4	49.6	56.4	65.9	63.8	72.8
As a percentage of SITC section (%)	Imp.	3.2	3.1	3.1	3.3	3.2	3.4	3.6	3.8	3.8	3.8	3.8	3.8	4.0	4.5	4.4
	Exp.	3.1	3.0	3.0	3.2	3.1	3.3	3.4	3.6	3.7	3.8	3.8	3.8	4.0	4.5	4.4
As a percentage of world trade (%)	Imp.	0.4	0.4	0.4	0.4	0.4	0.4	0.5	0.5	0.5	0.4	0.4	0.4	0.4	0.5	0.5
	Exp.	0.4	0.4	0.4	0.4	0.4	0.4	0.4	0.4	0.4	0.4	0.4	0.4	0.4	0.5	0.5

Graph 1: Annual growth rates of exports, 1996–2010

(In percentage by year)

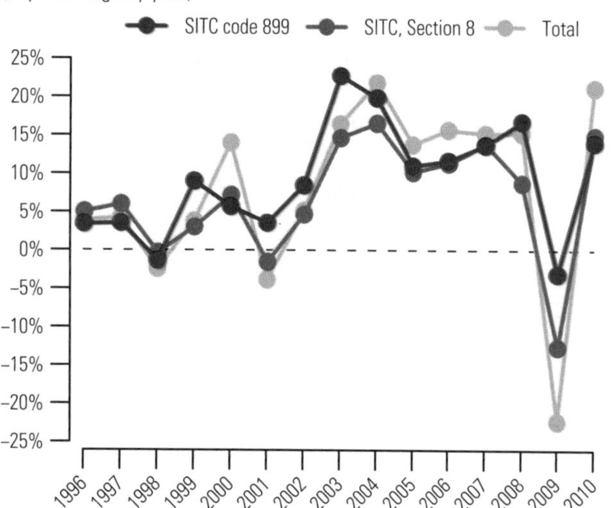

Table 2: Top exporting countries or areas in 2010

Country or area	Value (million US$)	Avg. Growth (%) 06-10	Growth (%) 09-10	World share %	Cum.
World	72812.0	10.1	14.0	100.0	
China	14381.6	15.9	23.2	19.8	19.8
USA	9662.1	9.6	5.5	13.3	33.0
Switzerland	6064.4	7.9	1.6	8.3	41.4
Germany	5271.1	8.7	6.7	7.2	48.6
Netherlands	4924.0	15.6	39.9	6.8	55.4
France	4801.4	9.3	5.9	6.6	61.9
Ireland	4630.8	11.7	10.1	6.4	68.3
Belgium	3048.5	20.7	29.7	4.2	72.5
China, Hong Kong SAR	2192.9	-1.5	12.7	3.0	75.5
United Kingdom	1849.8	-6.0	0.7	2.5	78.0
Italy	1628.4	5.2	14.5	2.2	80.3
Sweden	1320.2	14.5	11.0	1.8	82.1
Denmark	1301.9	6.8	9.5	1.8	83.9
Singapore	999.5	8.2	41.4	1.4	85.3
Mexico	908.6	7.8	1.0	1.2	86.5

Graph 2: Trade Balance by MDG regions 2010

(Bln US$)

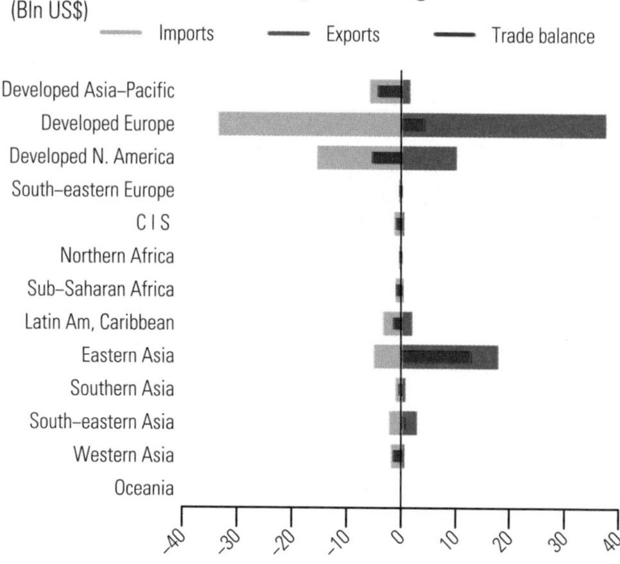

Table 3: Top importing countries or areas in 2010

Country or area	Value (million US$)	Avg. Growth (%) 06-10	Growth (%) 09-10	World share %	Cum.
World	71721.4	8.8	12.0	100.0	
USA	13691.3	9.5	15.8	19.1	19.1
France	5608.0	10.3	10.7	7.8	26.9
Germany	5451.0	7.3	10.0	7.6	34.5
Japan	4183.6	8.9	11.5	5.8	40.3
Netherlands	3872.5	7.1	4.3	5.4	45.7
United Kingdom	2911.8	3.7	8.3	4.1	49.8
Italy	2686.6	5.0	7.7	3.7	53.5
Belgium	2302.9	16.1	4.1	3.2	56.8
China	2063.5	14.4	25.8	2.9	59.6
Switzerland	1993.6	10.8	5.1	2.8	62.4
Canada	1755.8	6.9	8.8	2.4	64.9
Spain	1683.7	6.2	6.6	2.3	67.2
China, Hong Kong SAR	1617.5	1.5	18.6	2.3	69.5
Australia	1426.9	10.3	14.9	2.0	71.5
Sweden	1289.8	11.4	12.8	1.8	73.3

Commodities and transactions not classified elsewhere in the SITC (SITC Section 9)

931 Special transactions and commodities not classified according to kind

After several years of continuous growth marked by a peak of 586.9 bln US$ in 2008, the value (in current prices) of exports of special transactions and commodities not classified according to kind (SITC group 931) decreased by 4.1 percent in 2009 but rose again by 8.1 percent in 2010 and amounted to 608.4 bln US$ (see table 2). Imports increased by 16.2 percent in 2010 to reach 504.7 bln US$ (see table 3). Graph 1 shows that the increase in exports for 2010 in this product group was exceeded by the increases in world exports of commodities and transactions not classified elsewhere in SITC (SITC section 9) of 11.4 percent and in total world exports of 21.2 percent. Exports of special transactions and commodities not classified according to kind (SITC group 931) accounted for 79.5 percent of world exports of SITC section 9 and 4.0 percent of total world exports in 2010 (see table 1).

USA, Germany, and Netherlands were the top exporting countries in 2010 (see table 2). They accounted respectively for 18.7, 13.9 and 11.7 percent of world exports. Germany, India and USA were the top destinations (see table 3). By MDG regions (see graph 2), Developed Europe accounted for a majority of exports and imports of special transactions and commodities not classified according to kind (SITC group 931). In 2010, its exports and imports were valued respectively at 263.8 bln US$ and 210.7 bln US$, resulting in a trade surplus of 53.1 bln US$. A larger trade surplus was recorded by Developed North America (+63.2 bln US$). Top trade deficit was recorded by Southern Asia (-66.2 bln US$).

Table 1: Imports (Imp.) and exports (Exp.), 1996-2010, in current prices

		1996	1997	1998	1999	2000	2001	2002	2003	2004	2005	2006	2007	2008	2009	2010
Values in Bln US$	Imp.	131.2	141.0	129.8	140.1	240.6	211.0	218.9	246.4	304.4	304.1	426.3	501.7	632.3	434.2	504.7
	Exp.	129.1	133.3	117.8	127.6	238.5	227.9	239.6	289.2	346.8	343.0	431.6	490.2	586.9	562.7	608.4
As a percentage of SITC section (%)	Imp.	81.5	80.3	79.6	84.1	90.7	89.0	89.4	88.5	87.2	86.1	87.5	87.4	86.3	81.8	79.6
	Exp.	82.3	83.3	79.7	85.7	91.6	91.5	91.3	89.7	90.0	90.1	87.6	87.2	84.6	81.9	79.5
As a percentage of world trade (%)	Imp.	2.5	2.5	2.4	2.5	3.7	3.4	3.3	3.2	3.3	2.9	3.5	3.6	3.9	3.5	3.3
	Exp.	2.5	2.4	2.2	2.3	3.8	3.7	3.7	3.9	3.8	3.3	3.6	3.5	3.7	4.5	4.0

Graph 1: Annual growth rates of exports, 1996–2010

(In percentage by year)

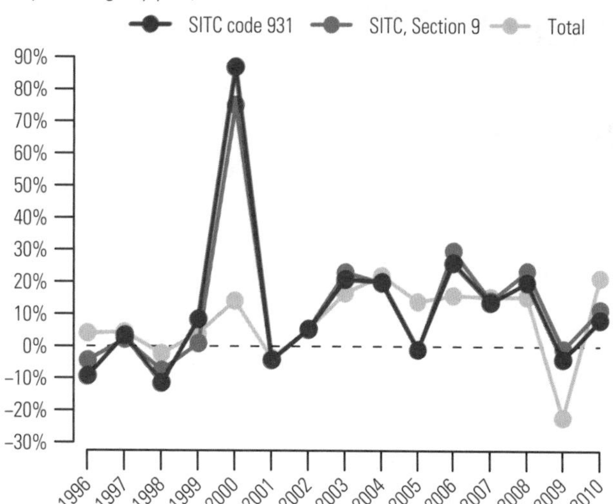

Graph 2: Trade Balance by MDG regions 2010

(Bln US$)

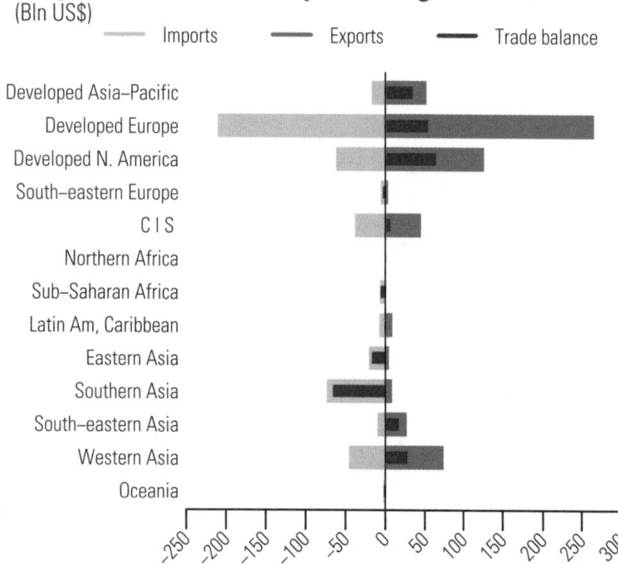

Table 2: Top exporting countries or areas in 2010

Country or area	Value (million US$)	Avg. Growth (%) 06-10	Growth (%) 09-10	World share %	Cum.
World	608 432.3	9.0	8.1	100.0	
USA	113 746.5	36.8	7.8	18.7	18.7
Germany	84 782.9	17.1	1.0	13.9	32.6
Netherlands	71 249.4	6.3	2.9	11.7	44.3
United Arab Emirates	51 994.9	9.3	-2.2	8.5	52.9
Russian Federation	42 345.4	-11.0	57.6	7.0	59.8
Japan	40 038.7	7.2	16.9	6.6	66.4
United Kingdom	25 714.7	5.8	14.9	4.2	70.7
Singapore	24 935.5	21.2	36.3	4.1	74.8
Qatar	13 032.1	134.3	24.3	2.1	76.9
France	12 592.7	6.8	9.2	2.1	79.0
Canada	11 934.4	-7.5	-8.3	2.0	80.9
Australia	9 996.0	3.7	33.6	1.6	82.6
Belgium	9 400.8	1.6	11.1	1.5	84.1
Italy	9 103.8	-4.0	-19.2	1.5	85.6
Sweden	9 052.8	2.3	34.7	1.5	87.1

Table 3: Top importing countries or areas in 2010

Country or area	Value (million US$)	Avg. Growth (%) 06-10	Growth (%) 09-10	World share %	Cum.
World	504 666.2	4.3	16.2	100.0	
Germany	77 162.2	15.6	-5.9	15.3	15.3
India	67 401.7	134.1	1135.1	13.4	28.6
USA	56 013.6	-1.3	1.3	11.1	39.7
Netherlands	55 275.5	15.1	1.4	11.0	50.7
Russian Federation	35 802.0	41.5	161.8	7.1	57.8
United Kingdom	31 455.1	-19.2	17.8	6.2	64.0
Iraq	20 163.0	15.6	8.1	4.0	68.0
China	18 433.3	73.6	457.8	3.7	71.7
Turkey	12 672.8	8.1	17.4	2.5	74.2
Japan	11 961.6	7.8	16.8	2.4	76.6
Singapore	8 454.1	15.7	16.9	1.7	78.2
Hungary	7 473.6	-1.2	-21.5	1.5	79.7
Oman	6 400.7	112.4	1161.7	1.3	81.0
Italy	6 389.5	-33.4	-22.2	1.3	82.2
Canada	6 222.3	3.7	17.7	1.2	83.5

In 2010, the value (in current prices) of exports of coin (other than gold coin), not being legal tender (SITC group 961) increased by 31.4 percent to 580 mln US$ (see table 2). Similarly, imports rose by 23.9 percent and amounted to 561 mln US$ (see table 3). Graph 1 shows the increase in exports for 2010 in this product group exceeded the increases in world exports of commodities and transactions not classified elsewhere in SITC (SITC section 9) of 11.4 percent and in total world exports of 21.2 percent. Exports of coin (other than gold coin), not being legal tender (SITC group 961) accounted for 0.1 percent of world exports of SITC section 9 and less than 0.1 percent of total world exports (see table 1).

The top exporting countries in 2010 were India, USA and United Kingdom (see table 2). They accounted respectively for 40.9, 12.0 and 10.7 percent of world exports. Top destinations were Germany, Netherlands and USA (see table 3). By MDG regions (see graph 2), Developed Europe accounted for a majority of exports of coin (other than gold coin), not being legal tender (SITC group 961). In 2010, its exports amounted to 200 mln US$, and imports of 403 mln US$, resulting in a trade deficit of 203 mln US$. Trade surpluses were recorded by Southern Asia (+222 mln US$) and Developed North America (+70 mln US$).

Table 1: Imports (Imp.) and exports (Exp.), 1996-2010, in current prices

		1996	1997	1998	1999	2000	2001	2002	2003	2004	2005	2006	2007	2008	2009	2010
Values in Mln US$	Imp.	103.3	103.9	99.0	81.8	709.5	100.5	93.7	118.9	107.6	106.3	106.4	146.4	183.7	452.7	560.9
	Exp.	127.9	132.4	66.2	68.3	718.1	89.6	105.8	155.6	217.5	186.5	233.8	326.2	360.0	441.3	579.9
As a percentage of SITC section (%)	Imp.	0.1	0.1	0.1	0.0	0.3	0.0	0.0	0.0	0.0	0.0	0.0	0.0	0.0	0.1	0.1
	Exp.	0.1	0.1	0.0	0.0	0.3	0.0	0.0	0.0	0.1	0.0	0.0	0.1	0.1	0.1	0.1
As a percentage of world trade (%)	Imp.	0.0	0.0	0.0	0.0	0.0	0.0	0.0	0.0	0.0	0.0	0.0	0.0	0.0	0.0	0.0
	Exp.	0.0	0.0	0.0	0.0	0.0	0.0	0.0	0.0	0.0	0.0	0.0	0.0	0.0	0.0	0.0

Graph 1: Annual growth rates of exports, 1996–2010
(In percentage by year)

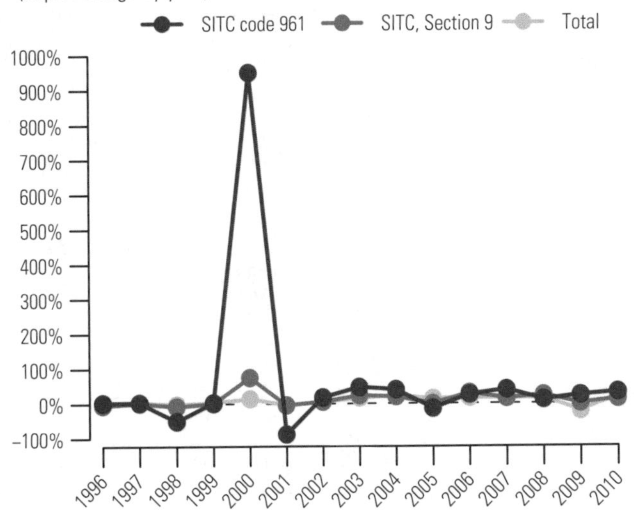

Graph 2: Trade Balance by MDG regions 2010
(Mln US$)

Imports — Exports — Trade balance

Developed Asia-Pacific
Developed Europe
Developed N. America
South-eastern Europe
C I S
Northern Africa
Sub-Saharan Africa
Latin Am, Caribbean
Eastern Asia
Southern Asia
South-eastern Asia
Western Asia
Oceania

-500 -400 -300 -200 -100 0 100 200 300

Table 2: Top exporting countries or areas in 2010

Country or area	Value (million US$)	Avg. Growth (%) 06-10	Growth (%) 09-10	World share %	Cum.
World	579.9	25.5	31.4	100.0	
India	237.0	161.0	418.2	40.9	40.9
USA	69.5	43.8	164.4	12.0	52.9
United Kingdom	62.3	4.3	-48.1	10.7	63.6
Canada	32.5	21.9	-41.3	5.6	69.2
Germany	31.6	18.1	47.9	5.5	74.6
Finland	28.9	-7.6	-17.9	5.0	79.6
France	17.4	-12.2	-31.0	3.0	82.6
Mexico	16.7	34.1	35.2	2.9	85.5
Slovakia	15.3	23.4	-36.0	2.6	88.1
Netherlands	9.9	28.8	60.7	1.7	89.8
Poland	8.8	24.8	-10.1	1.5	91.4
Chile	6.2	12.2	-62.8	1.1	92.4
Luxembourg	6.0	25.5	21.3	1.0	93.5
Singapore	5.4	43.2	30.8	0.9	94.4
Austria	4.7	-19.3	53.5	0.8	95.2

Table 3: Top importing countries or areas in 2010

Country or area	Value (million US$)	Avg. Growth (%) 06-10	Growth (%) 09-10	World share %	Cum.
World	560.9	51.5	23.9	100.0	
Germany	318.8	118.6	88.2	56.8	56.8
Netherlands	49.7	356.5	-18.3	8.9	65.7
USA	29.4	5.7	-49.6	5.2	70.9
Indonesia	21.9	343.3	5492.4	3.9	74.8
Argentina	18.1	427.1	-39.4	3.2	78.1
Bangladesh	*9.2*	...		1.6	79.7
Singapore	7.4	93.7	38.2	1.3	81.0
South Africa	7.3	158.7	1697.2	1.3	82.3
Panama	7.2	470.7	78.0	1.3	83.6
Qatar	6.3	1077.1	18008.8	1.1	84.7
Costa Rica	6.3	11.6	-9.0	1.1	85.8
United Kingdom	5.7	-1.3	26.8	1.0	86.9
Luxembourg	5.5	28.4	-34.0	1.0	87.8
New Zealand	4.7	58.5	406.4	0.8	88.7
Japan	4.3	116.0	49.9	0.8	89.5

Source: UN Comtrade

971 Gold, non-monetary (excluding gold ores and concentrates)

In 2010, the value (in current prices) of exports of gold, non-monetary (excluding gold ores and concentrates) (SITC group 971) increased by 25.9 percent to 156.0 bln US$ (see table 2). Similarly, imports rose by 33.6 percent and amounted to 128.7 bln US$ (see table 3). Graph 1 shows that the increase in exports for 2010 in this product group exceeded the increases in world exports of commodities and transactions not classified elsewhere in SITC (SITC section 9) of 11.4 percent and in total world exports of 21.2 percent. Exports of gold, non-monetary (excluding gold ores and concentrates) (SITC group 971) accounted for 20.4 percent of world exports of SITC section 9 and 1.0 percent of total world exports (see table 1).

USA, Canada and Australia were the top exporting countries in 2010 (see table 2). They accounted respectively for 11.4, 8.8 and 8.3 percent of world exports. India, United Arab Emirates and USA were the top destinations (see table 3). By MDG regions (see graph 2), top trade surpluses were recorded by Latin America & the Caribbean (+21.3 bln US$), Developed Asia-Pacific (+12.4 bln US$) and Sub-Saharan Africa (+10.3 bln US$). Trade deficits were recorded by Southern Asia (-29.4 bln US$), Western Asia (-6.8 bln US$) and South-eastern Asia (-1.5 bln US$).

Table 1: Imports (Imp.) and exports (Exp.), 1996-2010, in current prices

		1996	1997	1998	1999	2000	2001	2002	2003	2004	2005	2006	2007	2008	2009	2010
Values in Bln US$	Imp.	29.6	34.5	33.2	26.3	24.0	26.0	25.9	31.8	44.6	48.9	60.6	72.0	100.4	96.3	128.7
	Exp.	27.6	26.6	29.9	21.2	21.2	21.2	22.7	33.1	38.5	37.4	61.0	71.9	106.1	123.9	156.0
As a percentage of SITC section (%)	Imp.	18.4	19.6	20.3	15.8	9.0	10.9	10.6	11.4	12.8	13.8	12.4	12.5	13.7	18.1	20.3
	Exp.	17.6	16.6	20.2	14.2	8.1	8.5	8.7	10.3	10.0	9.8	12.4	12.8	15.3	18.0	20.4
As a percentage of world trade (%)	Imp.	0.6	0.6	0.6	0.5	0.4	0.4	0.4	0.4	0.5	0.5	0.5	0.5	0.6	0.8	0.9
	Exp.	0.5	0.5	0.6	0.4	0.3	0.3	0.4	0.4	0.4	0.4	0.5	0.5	0.7	1.0	1.0

Graph 1: Annual growth rates of exports, 1996–2010

(In percentage by year)

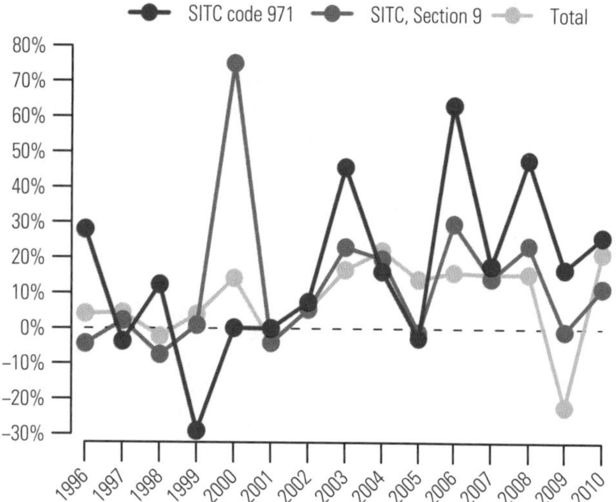

Graph 2: Trade Balance by MDG regions 2010

(Bln US$)

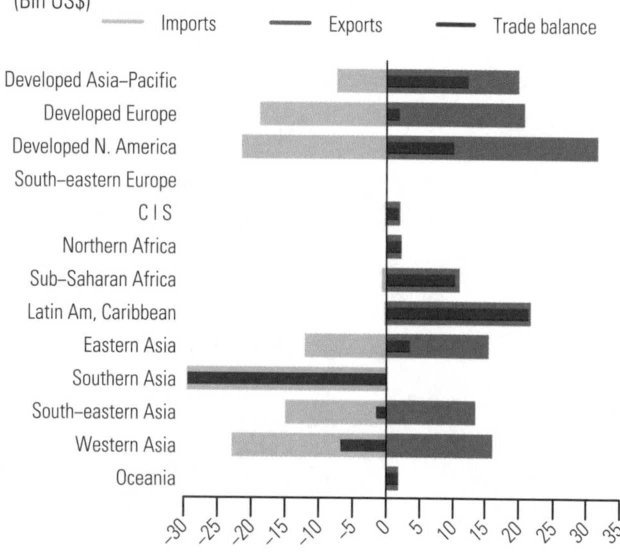

Table 2: Top exporting countries or areas in 2010

Country or area	Value (million US$)	Avg. Growth (%) 06-10	Growth (%) 09-10	World share %	Cum.
World	156015.1	26.4	25.9	100.0	
USA	17809.4	19.3	27.4	11.4	11.4
Canada	13806.6	28.0	80.4	8.8	20.3
Australia	12970.8	17.1	9.9	8.3	28.6
United Arab Emirates	12669.5	27.0	10.5	8.1	36.7
China, Hong Kong SAR	10557.4	15.9	-3.2	6.8	43.5
Peru	7715.4	17.8	14.3	4.9	48.4
Germany	7076.2	53.3	136.9	4.5	52.9
Thailand	6511.8	85.6	14.6	4.2	57.1
Japan	6417.7	20.9	43.1	4.1	61.2
Mexico	5852.4	52.5	44.1	3.8	65.0
Italy	4024.0	46.9	34.3	2.6	67.6
Singapore	3952.0	23.9	39.6	2.5	70.1
Ghana	3367.9	31.4	14.4	2.2	72.3
Rep. of Korea	2991.9	37.7	5.6	1.9	74.2
Colombia	2122.6	26.5	36.1	1.4	75.5

Table 3: Top importing countries or areas in 2010

Country or area	Value (million US$)	Avg. Growth (%) 06-10	Growth (%) 09-10	World share %	Cum.
World	128679.9	20.7	33.6	100.0	
India	28339.2	20.8	21.3	22.0	22.0
United Arab Emirates	18214.1	24.9	23.1	14.2	36.2
USA	12526.7	22.2	43.5	9.7	45.9
Canada	8968.7	28.5	51.2	7.0	52.9
China, Hong Kong SAR	8267.2	67.1	68.1	6.4	59.3
Thailand	7849.3	42.7	107.4	6.1	65.4
Australia	6330.6	9.7	-13.1	4.9	70.3
Germany	6049.0	38.9	36.9	4.7	75.0
Italy	4622.9	5.9	28.8	3.6	78.6
Singapore	3821.2	21.9	35.8	3.0	81.6
Turkey	2523.5	-10.9	54.6	2.0	83.6
Austria	2350.7	87.5	-15.8	1.8	85.4
Other Asia, nes	2260.9	15.2	34.7	1.8	87.1
Malaysia	1994.7	5.3	6.5	1.6	88.7
Switzerland	1643.6	4.4	231.8	1.3	90.0